The Dictionary of the Book

The Dictionary of the Book

A Glossary for Book Collectors, Booksellers, Librarians, and Others

Second Edition

Sidney E. Berger

ROWMAN & LITTLEFIELD
Lanham • Boulder • New York • London

Published by Rowman & Littlefield
An imprint of The Rowman & Littlefield Publishing Group, Inc.
4501 Forbes Boulevard, Suite 200, Lanham, Maryland 20706
www.rowman.com

86–90 Paul Street, London EC2A 4NE

British Library Cataloguing in Publication Information Available

Library of Congress Cataloging-in-Publication Data

Names: Berger, Sidney E., author.
Title: The dictionary of the book : a glossary for book collectors, booksellers, librarians, and others / Sidney E. Berger.
Description: 2nd edition. | Lanham : Rowman & Littlefield, [2022] | Includes bibliographical references and index.
Identifiers: LCCN 2022019212 (print) | LCCN 2022019213 (ebook) | ISBN 9781538151327 (cloth) | ISBN 9781538151334 (epub)
Subjects: LCSH: Bibliography—Dictionaries. | Book industries and trade—Dictionaries. | Book collecting—Dictionaries. | Library science—Dictionaries.
Classification: LCC Z1006 .B42 2022 (print) | LCC Z1006 (ebook) | DDC 002.03—dc23/eng/20220419
LC record available at https://lccn.loc.gov/2022019212
LC ebook record available at https://lccn.loc.gov/2022019213

To the memory of extraordinary Rafe,
to the equally extraordinary and amazing Aaron,
to Joe and Frances, Dan and Fred, for their sweetness and love,
and to the incomparable and perfect Michèle—
all of whom contributed to this book in their own wondrous ways.

Contents

Foreword to the First Edition by Nicholas Basbanes ix

Foreword to the Second Edition by Joel Silver xi

Introduction to the First Edition 1

Introduction to the Second Edition 5

The Dictionary 11

Appendix A: Paper and Paper-Related Terminology in the Present Volume 509

Appendix B: Typeface Terminology 511

Appendix C: Paper Sizes 517

Appendix D: Binding Terminology in the Present Volume 521

Appendix E: Book Collectors' Clubs and Societies 525

Bibliography 531

About the Author 561

Foreword to the First Edition

All the talk in recent years about the shape and structure information-delivery devices we know as *books* will be taking in the decades to come has occasioned, in a curious sort of way, a renewed appreciation for material culture, with social scientists in particular paying close attention to the relationship between people and things and probing the various ways that objects become integral to the molding and interpretation of human events.

This freshly considered focus on materiality has gone well beyond the writing of professional articles and monographs to enter the realm of general discourse. A 100-part radio series and exhibition mounted jointly by the BBC and the British Museum in 2010, *A History of the World in 100 Objects*, was a critical success that drew enormous crowds, and led to the publication of a highly successful book (Viking, 2010) edited by the museum's director, Neil MacGregor. Especially noteworthy was the scholarly approach MacGregor took to integrate artifacts and analysis in a sweeping continuum that spanned two million years, from the introduction of the stone hand ax at the dawn of humanity to the development of solar-powered lamps and chargers in these early decades of the third millennium.

Not to be outdone by their London counterparts, the Smithsonian Institution in Washington, DC, followed three years later with *A History of America in 101 Objects*, curated by the noted cultural anthropologist Richard Kurin, whose day job is Under Secretary for History, Art, and Culture at the Smithsonian. In his introduction to the exhibit catalog (Penguin, 2013), Kurin noted that while there is no way that a museum can re-create such pivotal historical events as the Civil War, "a hand-drawn battle map of the time, a bullet or gunnery shelf, a uniform bearing evidence of wounds, and broken metal shackles are all objects that, having been present at the event depicted, can speak to the larger story. The parts stand for the whole."

Among the items he and his team of advisors chose to tell America's story was the Model A7L Apollo spacesuit worn by Neil Armstrong when the pioneering astronaut first set foot on the Moon's surface in 1969—a blend of "cutting-edge technology and Old World craftsmanship," according to one former NASA scientist—with Julia Child's kitchen, Sitting Bull's ledger, Louis Armstrong's trumpet, Dorothy's red ruby slippers, Cesar Chavez's union jacket, and the World War II bomber *Enola Gay*, which ushered in the Nuclear Age, comprising some of the others.

And the concept has been extended in other, more localized ways. *A History of New York in 101 Objects* (Simon & Schuster, 2013) showcased items chosen by Sam Roberts, urban affairs correspondent of the *New York Times*, that illumine the special character of the Big Apple; a work devoted specifically to the War Between the States, *The Civil War in 50 Objects* (Penguin, 2013), featured artifacts drawn from the collections of the New York Historical Society, with text by Harold Holzer, and issued to coincide with the 150th anniversary of the Battle of Gettysburg.

Especially pertinent to the subject at hand is *A History of the Book in 100 Books* (British Library, 2015), with an explicit emphasis on the *physical* book, in all its accumulated glory. The authors, Roderick Cave and Sara Ayad, explained in their foreword the premise they followed in making their selections: "We are by no means persuaded that the future form of the book will be entirely electronic; what is certain is that, over the past 10,000 plus years of history, humankind has developed ways of preserving and transmitting information which are deeply embedded in our subconsciousness."

A word that has been around for a while, according to the *Oxford English Dictionary*, but which is fairly new to my experience, especially as it is being used in this context—*realia*—defines materials from everyday life that are used as teaching aids, and include such items as specimens, samples, relics, artifacts, souvenirs, even models and dioramas. At Rare Book School, an independent institute located on the campus of the University of Virginia at Charlottesville to study the history, care, and use of written, printed, and digital materials, some 20 tons of bookmaking tools and printing paraphernalia of every description—be they woodcuts, copperplate engravings, lithographic prints, hand-tooled bindings, blind-stamped cloth boards, marbled endsheets, or hand-made and machine-made papers—create a unique bibliographical laboratory for instructing bibliophiles of every description in the myriad nuances of this endlessly fascinating world.

A central goal of the program is for students to hone a kind of interpretive power, what director Michael F. Suarez, S.J., coeditor in 2010 of the *Oxford Companion to the Book*, a monumental two-volume reference work of one million words on every conceivable aspect of book history, calls a "360-degree perspective" that will help them appreciate the factors and materials that have gone into the making, marketing, and reception of books over the centuries. "We want to understand the book *in* history, and oftentimes we even want to understand the book as an agent *of* history, and the only way to do that is to take the materiality seriously, and to look not only at the language, but to look at the material embodiments," he told me for a profile I wrote of him in 2014 for *Humanities* magazine.

For these reasons, and for so many more, people who wish to be fluent in this very specialized world have to know the language, and for more than seven decades, John Carter's *ABC for Book Collectors* has been the go-to guide for clarification of such staple bibliographical essentials as *condition*, *rarity*, *printings*, *editions*, *blank versos*, *points*, dozens upon dozens of terms, all of them comprising the *lingua franca* of this endlessly fascinating world.

But trends have changed dramatically since Carter first appeared in 1952, practices have changed as well, tastes have changed, and the need for a more contemporary reference has been very urgently in need. Into this void has stepped Sidney Berger, a multitalented individual with an impressive résumé of accomplishments embracing librarianship, scholarship, teaching, collecting, papermaking, printing, binding, indeed every aspect of bookmaking, with an impeccably researched, impressively augmented, and gracefully explained compendium that will become, of this I have no doubt, a reference of first resort. I can think of no one more qualified or better equipped, both professionally and temperamentally, to take on the formidable task of bringing John Carter's indispensable reference into the 21st century, and recommend it highly to anyone who shares an abiding passion for books.

—Nicholas Basbanes

Foreword to the Second Edition

Every profession and avocation develops its own terminology, and many of the words that collectors, antiquarian booksellers, and special collections librarians use to describe the history, forms, and uses of books have evolved over many centuries. The language of any field can easily seem off-putting and exclusionary to outsiders, and until relatively recently, many of those in the world of antiquarian books haven't gone out of their way to make the uninitiated feel any more welcome. With the availability of the Internet, however, it's much easier to find definitions of words than it used to be, and to anyone who grew up before the existence of online resources, the range of what's freely available online is astonishing. Even the eighth edition of Carter's *ABC for Book Collectors* is available for free download, and there may be more people who have consulted the book in electronic form than would ever have considered purchasing a physical copy.

One of the strengths of Carter's *ABC*, even in its later revisions published after Carter's death in 1975, is the clearly expressed viewpoint of the author, which was based on Carter's background and experience in the world of collecting and the antiquarian book trade. Though the book world that Carter knew has been irrevocably transformed, his definitions stand as elucidations and explanations of how collectors of his day wrote about and described books and their pursuit. Just as Carter's *ABC* reflects what its author learned as a collector, writer, antiquarian bookseller, bibliographer, and auction house consultant, so does Sidney E. Berger's newly revised *The Dictionary of the Book* reflect Berger's multifaceted experience with books in all of their aspects. As Nicholas Basbanes wrote in his foreword to the first edition of the *Dictionary*, Berger's accomplishments include "librarianship, scholarship, teaching, collecting, papermaking, printing, binding—indeed every aspect of bookmaking," and it's this hands-on experience, gained over many decades, that gives Berger's work its foundation and authority. Berger's definitions are accurate, interesting, and readable, and they're also detailed enough that they tell us what we want and need to know, and then lead us to the places—both online and in print—where we can learn even more if we wish to.

As Basbanes noted, Berger was and is a teacher, and this spirit of making available to others what he has learned is evident throughout the *Dictionary*. The choice of entries reflects Berger's judgment about what information his readers are most likely to be seeking, and he knows what can easily be found elsewhere, as well as how some of the other frequently consulted resources might mislead or fail to provide a sufficient explanation of a less common term. This can be especially true of some of the definitions concerning aspects of the technical processes of the creation of books and their physical components, and Berger's many years of direct involvement with papermaking, printing, and bookbinding are evident in the clarity with which he explains what a term means, and how it relates to other words or concepts.

Just as Carter's *ABC* can be used with profit by those new to the world of antiquarian books, but is also still useful to readers who have spent years in the field, so can Berger's *Dictionary* be consulted and read by a very wide range of researchers, collectors, booksellers, and librarians. With his assembly and organization of so much up-to-date information, Berger has produced a work that will benefit anyone who wants to learn more about books of any period, and how these books have been created, used, collected, valued, bought, and sold.

One of the joys of working with Carter's *ABC* is that it's possible to open the book anywhere, and to let the entries and their references guide your journey through its pages. Readers will discover that this is also, happily, the case with Berger's *Dictionary*, and with the nearly 2,000 entries in this enlarged and revised second edition, those who dip into it are very likely to encounter terms and details they hadn't met before. In the bibliography appended to the second edition of *A History of Illuminated Manuscripts* (Phaidon Press, 1994), Christopher de Hamel described Neil R. Ker's *Medieval Libraries of Great Britain* as "a fascinating book of the kind in which one cannot look up one reference only; 20 minutes later one is still absorbed, pages from where one started." I'm looking forward to many such journeys with this greatly expanded edition of *The Dictionary of the Book.*

—Joel Silver

Introduction to the First Edition

Sixty-four years ago, John Carter published what has turned out to be a classic: *ABC for Book Collectors* (Rupert Hart-Davis, 1952), a glossary of terms that aimed to educate collectors on how to use the vocabulary of the book trade. Carter's preface begins: "Every specialised profession or pursuit develops its own jargon, much of which is unintelligible to the layman. . . . Book-collecting is no exception" (p. 7). He then says,

> [A]lthough a good many of its specialised terms are defined in such broader works as *The Bookman's Glossary* (New York, Bowker, 3rd edition, 1951), while others are explained in the more elementary manuals for collectors, no attempt, so far as I know, has been made to deal comprehensively with the terminology of this particular subject and no other between one pair of covers.
>
> My objective, then has been to set down, and to define, and sometimes comment upon, such words and phrases, commonly used in book-collecting, as would be likely to puzzle an educated reader faced for the first time by a bookseller's or an auctioneer's catalogue. (p. 7)

He mentions the host of technical terms with which this pursuit (book collecting) has become "heavily encrusted." He makes it clear that his audience is collectors, and by extension those who feed the passions of these collectors—booksellers. And he implies that the glossary he is compiling will be helpful, too, for his colleagues in the book trade. Certainly there is a need for all in one profession to be speaking the same language.

(I must add parenthetically that librarians are "in the book trade"—especially since some of them acquire books, some curate books, some do research using them, some guide patrons to information in them, and so forth. So the book Carter created has been a great help to librarians over the decades.)

This may be the most-published and most-sold volume in the world of books about books. It has reached its eighth edition (with the help of Nicolas Barker), and its sales remain strong. I have used this volume myself over the years, for my own edification and enjoyment (for it is amusingly written), and as a textbook in the many classes I have taught in book history, rare book librarianship, and other book-related courses. My only complaint with the *ABC* was that it didn't have enough terms. I often used terms in class or in a conversation with colleagues, and when they said, "What does that mean?" I said, look it up in Carter, only to find that it was not in Carter. Carter was writing for an audience of collectors, and the approximately 450 terms he defined were sufficient for his audience. Today there is a more learned and sophisticated audience—including collectors, booksellers, scholars in many fields, librarians, archivists, historians, and others, and the number of terms they use (or should be aware of in dealing with books) is greater than the number that Carter thought was appropriate for his audience.

Additionally, Carter was writing for a particular readership at a particular time. Some of the terms that may have been current then are not so today, and I have left out of this dictionary a host of Carter's terms that would be met with a blank stare by current booksellers, bibliophiles, collectors, scholars, and others. One might never encounter "honest copy," "chronological obsession," or "bundles," or many other such locutions.

I have added to the Carter glossary a host of terms that are fairly common in the book trade. That is, anyone collecting or buying or selling or talking about books might use many of the words that Carter did not think were needed in his own list. Perhaps he thought some words did not need to be defined. Also, as I said above, Carter was working in a particular time. Some of the terms he used have gone out of fashion and are not used anymore, some have evolved in their meaning, and new words and concepts have come into the book world which Carter could not have anticipated. Too bad that he did not put an entry into his *ABC* about the Internet. I would love to see what he would say about it as a term in the book world.

I have also added numerous terms that are not necessarily in the vocabulary of those dealing with books—but terms that explain a great deal about how books are made and how they got into our hands. And I have added a number of terms from the world of manuscripts that augment what Carter has about books from the era of print. Some of the specialized terminology of the world of printing and papermaking, for instance, is useful for describing books and manuscripts, and even if readers are not likely to use a term listed here, knowing it may add to their knowledge of bookmaking and collecting, and so should add to their appreciation of the artifacts that we cherish, collect, and read.

Since completing my text, I have learned that a ninth edition of the Carter *ABC* is in production and will soon be in print. I have based my own text on the most recent one available to me, the eighth edition (Oak Knoll Press, 2004), but I am happy to see that this venerable text is being revised.

This dictionary is aimed at anyone who wants to speak intelligently about books—to use the right terms in the right contexts . . . and with the right meanings. Even schooled and experienced booksellers do not always use "edition" or "issue" correctly. I have seen some of them talk about "papyrus paper" or "rice paper," neither of which exists.

As just noted, I have also included in this volume some technical terms from the world of book creation—papermaking, typefaces, binding, printing, and so forth. People in the book world will discuss such things as the chain lines and wire lines in paper, and how these were produced, and how they figure into a discussion about the format and ages of books. I think it important that one's vocabulary, in discussing books, should be precise about such matters as shadowmarks, pulling the bar of a press, the use of registration gauges and registration pins (the latter of which can leave visible marks on books that might need to be explained), the use of the Washington press as opposed to using a Vandercook, and so on. Hence, many words that a collector might not need are included here since a bookseller, librarian, or scholar might use them, and then the collector will need to know what the words mean.

Drawer-handle tool; Esteemed; et infra; Even working; Longitudinal labels, Paste action. These are a few of the terms in Carter that I have left out of the present volume. Carter was writing for his time and for his particular audience: collectors and their suppliers, the booksellers. Many of the terms he used, current in his day, are no longer the standard parlance of these or any other audiences of today. Further, as with language in general, the meanings of words evolve, and terms that were used one way for Carter are now used differently for us (see his entries for Binder's cloth, Boards, Early printing, and Encapsulation, for instance).

I have tried to offer "further readings" for most of the entries here, leading readers to more extensive treatments than could be given in the short definitions below. Carter was remiss in this, but I suppose he thought that the users of his *ABC* would be checking it for basic meanings and not needing more. This dictionary is aimed at people curious about what they collect and read, and that curiosity may lead them to wanting more information than is available here, hence the extensive bibliography at the end of this book.

A good many of my own publications are cited in the bibliography. I hope the reader sees this as stemming from my long experience in the field that prepared me to compile this dictionary and not from any egotistical tendencies. I have used the latest (the eighth) edition of Carter liberally here, along with many other authoritative sources. Citations that read only "Berger" refer to my book *Rare Books and Special Collections*. All others by me have "Berger" plus a title. All of my sources are listed in the bibliography at the end of this volume, which also includes references to further reading for many of the entries. In some instances, I have given the full citation in the definition (not in the bibliography)—especially when the item cited does not have wider significance than for the single entry in which it was used.

For many of the bookbinding-related definitions in this glossary, I have liberally dipped into the superb volume by Matt T. Roberts and Don Etherington: *Bookbinding and the Conservation of Books: A Dictionary of Descriptive Terms* (Library of Congress, 1982). Despite this volume's age, it is an excellent, thorough, learned, and beautifully written text, and while I could have put many of their definitions in my own words, I would not have improved their write-ups by doing so. In some cases, their definitions were out of date (as with, for example, "Lamination"), and my own commentary brings the information about these entries up to date.

Another volume of value has been the tremendously informative *American Dictionary of Printing and Bookmaking* (Howard Lockwood & Co., 1894; reprint, Burt Franklin, 1970). As with Carter, some of the terms defined here had meanings for its own audience that have evolved for ours. But many of the definitions were written by experts actually practicing the things they were writing about; and they wrote when the things they define were fresher and more part of the active world of books and bookmaking, so the definitions have a level of authority and a sense of immediate freshness that they might lack had they been written a hundred years later. A single case in point is the entry for "Lithography" (pp. 341–46—printed in small type, 86 lines per page, in two columns!). (This volume is cited throughout the text as *American Dictionary of Printing*.)

One volume that I have dipped into but have not used to any great extent is *Glaister's Glossary of the Book* (see the bibliography). It is a large volume (at 550 pages), but its definitions are not always as good as those in other sources, and some of them are simply not right. For instance, for "Punch" Glaister gives: "a piece of steel on which is engraved a type character. It is then hardened and used as a die to strike the matrices from which type is cast." I needn't explain the several inaccuracies of this definition (the words "engraved" and "a type character" are enough to make his definition suspect). Similarly, his explanation of "Typecasting" is not crystal clear. He even offers a picture of a "hand-cast" piece of type (on p. 490), and it is clear that it was one made by a machine. (*See* my own definitions in this dictonary, based on my own experience of having cut my own punch, made and justified my own matrix, and hand-cast my own type.) The volume is a great source of much information, but I have used it sparingly in this dictionary.

Other useful volumes will be cited throughout the definitions below, and they will all be given full bibliographic citations in the bibliography at the end of this book. A good definition that needs no rewriting deserves to be offered; I did not need to reinvent any wheels in the compilation of this book.

This dictionary contains a great number of technical terms. As noted above, I believe that those working with books—especially with rare books (like booksellers and librarians)—or people who are book collectors should understand a good deal about the physical makeup of the objects of their interest. The large vocabulary of the book is amply represented in published bibliographies and learned dealers' catalogs (not to mention in rare book cataloging), so I have presented here a range of words and phrases larger than Carter's. Further, within many definitions I have used words that are defined elsewhere in this book, so I have usually given cross-references (using "q.v." or "See" references) when I thought it was useful. Additionally, when I drew information from online sources, I have given the date I accessed that information, knowing that websites get updated and modified; the information I quote was the way I used it *on the date I took the information from the web.*

One special note: I have been working on this dictionary for more than a decade. In 2010, Oxford University Press published its monumental *Oxford Companion to the Book* (*OCB*; see the full citation in the bibliography). This amazing reference tool is in two large and heavy volumes. I wanted my own text to be in a single volume for convenience and portability. Further, I have added many terms that *OCB* does not have; and I have omitted a great number of references that *OCB* has that I thought not appropriate *for my audience.* Many people and organizations, libraries and collectors, societies and presses simply did not fit into my scheme—which was to appeal to an audience for whom the terms I have selected might be useful. I cannot see my readers coming to my text for Sunitikumar Chattopadhyay (*OCB*, I, 605; the Indian linguist), Hye-bong Chŏn (*OCB*, I, 609; bibliographer and university professor), or Hafiz Osman (*OCB*, II, 776; Ottoman calligrapher). Nor do I think that people wanting general and specific technical terminology of the book would need to know about Chitalishta (*OCB*, I, 609, "Eastern European associations of educated, well-to-do citizens"), Polar Libraries (*OCB* II, 1039), or *Wisden Cricketers' Almanack* (*OCB*, II, 1262; a sporting almanac focusing on cricket). Information on these and hundreds of other entries in *OCB* can be gotten from *OCB* itself, or from the Wikipedia or other online sources.

Finally, Carter's volume had no illustrations. That made sense at the time, because of the kinds of terms he was listing and the added cost that illustrations would have engendered. A great number of the terms I have added, however, required pictures, and I have supplied them where I thought they were needed.

I wish to thank Charles Harmon of Rowman & Littlefield for his steady encouragement and great insight in bringing this book to fruition, and for his willingness to allow me to shape it the way I have done. He is more a partner here than an editor, and I cherish his friendship.

I am deeply grateful to Joel Silver and Valerie Hotchkiss for their prudent counsel, their careful reading, and their kindness. Joel's additions to this book are many; and Valerie's advice and the images she supplied from the Rare Book and Manuscript Library at the University of Illinois at Urbana-Champaign have improved this text remarkably.

Also instrumental in getting this book into print are Rachel Cohen, Anna Dorste, and Esme Rabin, whose tireless assistance with the images and charts, permissions, and correspondence allowed us to use innumerable pictures for the text.

And finally, there are no words to describe the wonderful contributions that Michèle Cloonan has made to this book—with her proofreading, insight, guidance, and tenderness.

As I have noted above, the entries are arranged alphabetically, letter for letter. In the entries themselves I have used "(q.v.)" (that is, *quod vide*—"which see") references for any cross-reference that I thought would be useful. Additionally, I have "See" and "See also" references, mostly for bibliographical references, which are cited in the text by authors' names, followed by key words in the titles, and with page numbers where appropriate. The bibliography at the end lists texts cited throughout along with further readings.

There are also appendices that give information and additional terminology that I did not wish to put into the main dictionary—specialized vocabulary on types and papers and such.

As with any reference tool, especially one like the present with its highly specialized vocabulary, the selection of what to include—and, of course, what to omit—is idiosyncratic. I chose what I thought would be useful and edifying and in some cases amusing. I am sure critics will say, "This volume should have included ______," and that blank could be filled in with innumerable possibilities, including people and libraries, technical terms and aesthetic movements that appear in typography, scholars who have written about books, and titles of books that would have been valuable to have appeared in the bibliography. And perhaps many of these potential inclusions will be actual entries when the eighth edition of this dictionary comes out.

For the present, however, I just hope that my readers get as much use and pleasure out of this book as I have had fun in compiling it.

Introduction to the Second Edition

When the first edition of this dictionary came out in 2016, I began hearing from people in the book world saying they sure wished I had included the term ______, and that blank could be filled in with lots of words and phrases. My own research in the field exposed me to more and more literature that had terms that could fill in that blank. In fact, with the proliferation of texts on the web—original scholarship as well as digitized texts from the past, sometimes the distant past—I saw increasingly the vocabulary of the trade that had been hidden away in older sources. It became clear that with this proliferation of available materials, old and new, there was a growth in the number of words and ideas that needed to be defined or commented on.

So I immediately opened two files, one a folder in my desk, the other on my computer, into which I began saving information. Along with my own scholarship, I have scoured the pages of hundreds of booksellers' catalogs, published bibliographies, and scholarly books and articles. And I have worked with booksellers, collectors, scholars, librarians, archivists, conservators, bookbinders, students, and others whose suggestions and advice have been of immeasurable value. What has emerged from this immersion is that in the world of books, an enormous vocabulary exists of terms that, for the most part, are still in use; or if they are no longer in use, they are being exposed with digital texts that are becoming more and more available. The first edition of this dictionary was pretty much in response to the work of John Carter. This second edition is not, though Carter does figure into the impetus of the present text.

Another realization has shaped my work on this second edition: one of the things I observed in the Carter volume was his inclusion of terms that were obsolete and that were not only never used today but were beyond the current parlance of those working in the field. But in all of my preparations for working on this new edition, in immersing myself in the literature of the field, as I have just indicated, I encountered hundreds of terms and abbreviations pertaining to books that others may also encounter in *their* work. That is, the obsolescence of a word or abbreviation was not a reason to keep it out of the present volume. In fact, those obscure words needed a modern repository to assist a modern audience. With this in mind, I have added well over 550 new terms to this text, including a few that were in Carter that I chose to ignore in my earlier edition.

Hence, certain issues have influenced what is in the present volume:

1. Older publications that my readers may consult use many of the older terms that I chose to leave out of the first edition. These terms need a modern presentation to enlighten a modern audience.
2. Carter needed to have a new edition done. Nicolas Barker did a remarkable job with the editions that he came up with (the 6th through 8th), and most of his additions and edits were spot on. But many of Carter's old entries needed more work than he gave to them. And the latest edition, the ninth, was done by someone who clearly chose not to emend where emendation was in order. Simran Thadani had an opportunity to revise Carter's obsolete definitions; fix his mistakes; expand his entries where they needed expansion; and add new terms to reflect a new world of scholarship and to fill in gaps that Carter left. She did not do what she could (and should) have done to fix Carter's older entries, though she did add many terms, but not enough; and when she did, she did not always get them right. Some of her additions are too short, misconceived, or in error. As I said, she did not fix Carter's entries when they needed to be fixed. She just let them stand as he had them. Some examples:

- In the entry for "Decorated paper and type," the method called "paste marbling" is described as follows: "a pattern worked with a stylus or brush in dyed paste is transferred to paper" (pp. 92–93). I do not know what "paste marbling" is; it certainly is not marbling, nor does it mean "paste paper." And the method described is strange, to say the least, and impossible. On what does one create the pattern? How is a stylus or brush used? How is a pattern then "transferred to paper"? What about decorated papers that do not have any controlled patterns? It looks as if the writer has never made paste papers or done marbling.

- In the same entry there is a mention of "gilt or bronze paper." These designations are equally strange since there are formal terms for them (*see*, in the dictionary below, the entry for Dutch gilt paper). If the idea of the glossary is to help readers understand what they may encounter in the book world, these terms ("gilt or bronze paper") tell them nothing. We do not get a picture of what they are, how they are made, when, or by whom. Nor do we know what they look like or how they were used. And the terminology is strange; there are proper terms for decorated papers that this definition does not seem to recognize.
- Under the entry for "Bearer type," it is clear that the person who wrote this definition does not understand what bearers are in printing on a handpress. My own entry clears it up.
- There is an entry for "Colours of cloth and leather," but it does not mention the equally important colors of paper.
- Carter has an entry for "Book Auction Records," but it says nothing about the limited use of these volumes for appraisal and book identification.
- "China paper" was not necessarily made in China.
- The Carter volume[1] speaks of "wood letter" (p. 261). Does this mean "wood type"? No one familiar with the world of books speaks of "wood letter."
- In Carter's list of abbreviations we see one for "Folio" and we are told that it is "a size of book." The problem is that in strict bibliographical terms, size is not an issue. See my definition. Also, the word is defined here in terms of size, but that is not mentioned in the definition at the entry on p. 122. Also, on p. 22 there is a section called "SIZES OF BOOKS" in which are listed "Folio," "Quarto," "Octavo," and so on. But these are not designations of sizes. If the audience for Carter is book collectors, they deserve a more scholarly and responsible definition. Is it okay for a collector to be told that a quarto is to be defined by its size, without showing the bibliographical definition of that word? Booksellers tend to be learned enough to know what a quarto really is—how it is made and put together. John Carter's own definition was insufficient, with its mere three short sentence fragments. And under the word "format," Carter still relates the terms designating formats to size—something that later editors should have corrected or clarified.
- In bringing the *ABC* up to date, Thadani tried her best, but as I said, she was not quite up to the task. For "RDA" she says that AACR was succeeded by "Resource Description and Access." This is not really accurate. RDA is another cataloging scheme/system, and some libraries, but by no means all, have adopted RDA over LC (the Library of Congress system), but Thadani's entry makes it sound as if LC is dead since it was succeeded by RDA. And RDA has seen a shake-up in the cataloging world.
- Carter's entry for "Antique," definition 2, says that it is "A kind of paper, with a rough uncalendered finish, either wove or laid." Absolutely not! Antique refers to one kind of laid paper—the kind with shadows around the chain lines. Whether the paper is calendered or not is not the point. See my text, with illustrations.
- For "Point holes" (hyphenated in Carter) the writer says, "Pins were mounted on a transverse shank [and] fastened to the sides of the tympan"; this reveals the writer's ignorance of printing practices, as my definition of it makes clear. Perhaps Carter, Barker, and Thadani did not have the experience that I have had as a handpress printer.

This listing could go on for pages. To be sure, many of these issues stem from Carter's own text, for there are scores of such weaknesses in the Carter volume in the editions before Nicolas Barker came on board—problems that the latest editor had the opportunity to fix, but she missed the boat. Carter's ninth edition has many errors in, or inadequately thought-out, definitions; it has practically no bibliographical references; and it has some weaknesses in prose (grammar, word choice, punctuation), not to mention a few typographical errors. And if the book was aimed at book collectors, it needed to include several hundred more terms than it has—terms that collectors will encounter and will need definitions of. If the idea of doing a new edition is to bring it up to date, to fix mistakes, and to add valuable information where it belongs, the new editor has not done her job.

3. The added terms in the present volume reflect a new vocabulary that Carter did not have access to, and access to a host of older sources now available online that

Carter did not look at (or chose not to draw from) but that were available in analog form.

4. Carter's book, as its title through all nine editions says, is for book collectors. Book collectors collect all kind of books, and much more. One of the genres of things they gather is manuscripts, and to have created a text, as he did, only about the printed word was to cut out of his audience a significant portion of potential readership. That is why I chose to include a host of terms pertaining to manuscripts, calligraphy, ephemera, and other areas of the book world not serviced by the *ABC*. This is one of the things that accounts for the number of entries in the present volume that far outstrips the number in Carter.
5. And since booksellers sell—and collectors collect—much more than books, and since these parties are the primary audiences for the present volume, I have included here some of the tools of bookmaking that they should know about, along with the kinds of things they are likely see, and collect, in a visit to a book fair. Hence the inclusion of such terms as "Blook" and "Zograscope."

I mentioned above the expanding access to older texts since the first edition of *The Dictionary* was published. In the last five years, access to a great number of online publications germane to the book world has increased—as has the availability of an enormous number of items that are paper based but that are now accessible online, free or for some use fee. For example, one realm of publications is serials of all kinds that have been digitized and mounted on the web. The contents of full runs of important magazines and scholarly journals are now accessible. This has added to my own work in culling terms that appear in early publications—terms that needed to be added to this dictionary since their availability has exposed them to all scholars and other researchers in the book world. And the vocabulary of these older scholarly texts—and other texts in the bookselling and book-collecting world—may befuddle many a modern reader, even some deeply immersed in the field. A single entry from my list of abbreviations will demonstrate this.

> *Cae.* (or, more commonly, *Cæ.*), *Cael.*—*Cælavit*, engraved by

In describing a book or print, a bookseller might come across *Cae.* on the item or in a 19th-century auction catalog or scholarly bibliography. Where must a collector (or the bookseller herself) go to find out what that abbreviation means? Not to Carter. It's not there. This is one of the many abbreviations I encountered when I perused 18th- and 19th-century booksellers' and auction catalogs—many of which are now available on the web in full text, and for free. The list of abbreviations given in the dictionary is extensive, covering many shortcuts that have appeared in print for centuries. It is not comprehensive, but it covers terms and concepts that collectors and booksellers and librarians are likely to encounter.

Since it is the predilection of many, in their research, to turn first to the web, and to look for easy-to-find, at-one's-fingertips resources rather than having to locate a book on their shelves or at their libraries, I have shifted from paper-based to online sources when they are convenient. The Roberts and Etherington book, for example, is cited and quoted many times here, in most cases with URLs leading to their entries. And with the proliferation of websites filled with information, much of it only on the web, there are many citations to these sources as well. And I have brought the URLs of the first edition up to date. It is remarkable how much "link-rot" there has been, and old URLs by the hundreds have died and needed to be renewed. This was not possible in a number of cases, and in those instances I have left in the old links when the information at them was valuable and current, but no longer accessible (except possibly on the Wayback Machine of the INTERNET ARCHIVE). And I have rewritten many entries when new information at these sites needed to be brought up to date.

Because the Carter book has long-standing cachet, and since many readers of the present volume will probably have a copy of the latest edition, I have cited all of my Carter references from that ninth edition, except where reference to earlier editions requires my use of the pagination or text of those editions.

In this edition of *The Dictionary*, I have added a number of terms that are related to book sales and book collecting (and also to librarianship), but that are somewhat peripheral to them. These are terms that one might not expect to see if one is expecting vocabulary of only the *book* world. For instance, there is an entry for "cels," those little film-composed items from which cartoons are generated. Booksellers of course sell books, but any visit to an antiquarian book fair will reveal to a visitor a host of things at booksellers' booths that are definitely not books. Cels are among them. So are old flags and pennants, bookends, jewelry composed of miniature books, decks of cards, and other ephemera that booksellers have on hand that they think visitors to the book fairs might be interested in. The ephemera are covered in an entry on that topic, but most other pieces of ephemera are not singled out unless they are the kinds of things one sees often at book fairs, like cels. The fact that my computer's Smell Check does not recognize the word *cel* does not change the fact that cels are common objects that booksellers purvey. Swell Check often gets things wrong. (I tell my students, whose spelling can be abominable, that they should definitely not rely on Shell Check. It won't help them.) So the present volume, aimed at book collectors, booksellers, librarians, and others, will have terminology that these parties are likely to use in their active lives, and that includes words for other book-related objects.

As I said in the first edition, critics, seeing the breadth of coverage that this volume aims to treat, will say, "If ______ is here, then ______ should also be here"; or "This volume needed an entry for ______." And, of course, such comments would be correct from these commentators' perspectives. What these kinds of comments reveal is that the world of the book—and its vocabulary—is tremendously extensive, and no single volume can encompass it all. I have strived to come up with the more common terms, salted here and there with others that are less common, but ones that I have actually seen used in the many sources I have consulted. These are terms that, if I have encountered them, my readers may well come across.

The main users of this dictionary will be collectors, booksellers, and librarians, all of whom are scholars in their own way and for their own ends. They will be seeking information about the materials in their possession, or items they may wish to add to their holdings, or text they encounter. With the amazing world of technology at their fingertips, they will be able to learn a great deal from their online searches, and they will have access to reference materials beyond anything available to scholars even as recently as 10 years ago, with an increasing number of texts available to them every day. As I have pointed out, this means that earlier scholarship—from the 18th and 19th centuries, for instance—that was hidden away will no longer be invisible. And they must come to terms with words from the world of books that were common in the days when those books were produced, but that have today fallen out of vogue.

To test this premise, I have looked extensively into early booksellers' and auction catalogs, where there is a great deal of excellent scholarship, and a vocabulary used that the original readers of these catalogs were familiar with. The 1888 Bernard Quaritch catalog mentioned in the entry for "Sina nota" is a well of information about the printing and publishing of books, about typefaces and publishers, about authorship and readers. The extensive prose entry in his catalog at "Woodcut/Wood engraving" shows this. And whether Quaritch's research is still current or not, modern readers, collectors, and scholars should be well informed of what his catalogers and customers knew, to help us know today what he was writing about, and also what the state of scholarship was in his time. Modern scholars stand on the shoulders of scholars of the past. If you use his catalogs to their best advantage, you need to be up on his vocabulary.

In the introduction to the first edition of this dictionary I mentioned that many of the terms that Carter had that were no longer in use probably had no place in the present text. They were no longer used and they hardly appeared in reference books or booksellers' catalogs or library records. Clearly, I have changed my stance on this. With access to these obsolete terms made easy through online searches, readers are now discovering these words in ways that Carter could not have predicted. I hope that current readers will find these older terms useful in their own work.

This fascinating world of books is so multifarious that it has spawned innumerable societies, sodalities, organizations, clubs, sororities and fraternities, groups, and institutions. Several entries in the dictionary and Appendix E in the present volume give only a small glimpse into this world. There is no space for the dozens of other groups that could have been included. Glaister lists, for instance, a host of groups beyond the interests of the present volume; for example: Associated Booksellers of Great Britain & Ireland; of American Publishers; of Little Presses; of Publishers' Educational Representatives; and Association Typographique Internationale; Société de la Reliure Originale; Société des Bibliophiles et Iconophiles de Belgique; Société des Gens de Lettres; Society of Italic Handwriting; Antiquarian Booksellers' Employees; of Bookmen; of Calligraphers; of Indexers; of Printers; of Scribes and Illuminators; of Typographic Designers; of Women Employed in Bookbinding; and of Young Publishers (see Glaister, *Glaister's Glossary*, pp. 21, 449–51). There may also somewhere be the Society of Endleaf Worshipers, Collectors of ACEPHALOUS Books, and the Association of Collectors of Atlases Lacking their Maps. (By the way, there *is* a new Facebook group called "We Love Endpapers"! I love this group. You can read about them at https://www.facebook.com/groups/WeLoveEndpapers/ [accessed 15 May 2021].) There simply was no room for all of these important groups in the present volume, but they can be researched with a judicial use of the web.

Likewise, there are scores of important fine (and commercial) presses and publishers who may have deserved to be mentioned, along with untold numbers of people who have made serious contributions to the book world. I have tried to select the ones most likely to be looked at by collectors and booksellers. As I have said, I am sure critics will decry my not including ______ and ______ and ______, *ad infinitum*. My only response is: *mea culpa*: tell me about it.

In the first edition of this dictionary, there were about 1,300 terms. For the present volume I have added more than 550 new ones. As noted, all URLs have been brought up to date, where the original texts or images still exist on the web. Cross-references are now indicated with SMALL CAPS rather than the old-fashioned "q.v." When a cross-reference is indicated but the key word does not appear where that reference might be, the cross-reference is indicated in parentheses.

A host of readers have shown their appreciation for the citations to pertinent sources and the bibliography, which has been substantially expanded here, with hundreds of new entries. In many of the entries there is a reference to "Berger" or "Berger, *Rare Books*." This is to the frequently cited volume *Rare Books and Special Collections* (see the bibliography). All other references to this author will be designated by their titles.

The work on this second edition began the moment I sent the copy of the first edition to the publisher. In the last five years I have been assisted by so many people that there is no way for me to thank them all, let alone remember all of them. A few deserve top billing. John Crichton of Brick Row Books has added substantially to the present volume with his ongoing suggestions and discoveries, and his sage advice. John Windle, whose advice for the first edition was invaluable, has also contributed to this second edition with further assistance and encouragement. Valerie Hotchkiss, former head of the Rare Book Library at the University of Illinois, Urbana-Champaign, helped me in too many ways to recount, especially with her assistance in selecting images for this book. Elizabeth Nosari brilliantly improved this volume with her intrepid and insightful research, especially with respect to the availability of sources. Richard Murian and Linda Smith of Alcuin Books contributed terms, images, conversation, and support. And many booksellers over the years, printers, collectors, and scholars contributed in a variety of ways to this text. A few of them are Edwin Bloemsat; Claire and David Bolton; Rodolphe Chamonal; Justin Croft; Muir and Glen Dawson; Diane DeBlois; Stanley Dempsey; Luc Devroye; Ted Dunn; Florisatus Fine Books, Manuscripts & Musicalia; Christelle Gonzalo Sr.; Shar Grant; Michelle Koth; Martin Majoor; P. J. M. Marks; Claude Mediavilla; John Mustain; Antiquariat F. Neidhardt; Max Neidhardt; Philip J. Pirages; Michael Quinion; Larry Rakow, John and Rosalind Randall; Rob Rulon-Miller; Alan Runfeldt; Susanne Schulz-Falster; Kenneth Soehner; Jessica Spring, David Szewczyk and Cynthia Buffington; Hubert van Hecke.

A special paragraph to honor and thank Charles Harmon and his excellent staff at Rowman & Littlefield, whose encouragement and sage advice through the work on both editions of this dictionary were invaluable. A singular thank you to Naomi Minkoff, whose editorship on this volume has been Herculean and superb.

It is clear from these acknowledgements that there could have been many more people to thank; we in the book world are indebted to all of us in the book world. This is a large and congenial sorority and fraternity, and we all lean on one another for sustenance of all kinds. For me, my parents got the ball rolling by having scads of well-read books in the house and encouraging my brothers and me to read them all, taking us as soon as we could walk to the public library and getting us our own library cards, and making us proud to have them and use them aplenty. The wonderful, patient, friendly booksellers in my neighborhood in Los Angeles nurtured this incipient bibliophilia, and some of the booksellers, like the Dawsons, fanned the flames. There is no way to thank everyone who has contributed to the present volume—there are too many of you out there.

But one person stands above all the rest: my wife Michèle Cloonan, who is a partner in all of our collecting, scholarship, teaching, scouting, book-fairing, publishing, and all other pursuits of the mind that contribute to this book in a host of ways. Her truly magnificent proofreading of the present text, and the extensive suggestions she has made, improved it immeasurably, and her enduring love and support have gotten me through all the "bad times," so that, with her by my side, they have all been good times.

NOTE

1. In my text when I speak of "Carter" or "the Carter volume," I am speaking generically of all the editions—primarily the last one, the ninth, edited by Thadani.

THE DICTIONARY

AACR, AACR2, AACR2R. *See* Anglo-American Cataloguing Rules.

AAT. *See* Art and Architecture Thesaurus.

ABA. The Antiquarian Booksellers' Association, the British organization of high-end booksellers. *See* ABAA. (Berger, pp. 320 ff.; http://www.aba.org.uk [accessed 31 May 2021].)

ABAA. The Antiquarian Booksellers' Association of America, the U.S. organization of high-end booksellers. This and the preceding organization (the ABA) are the premiere bookselling entities in the English-speaking world. (There are also the Antiquarian Booksellers' Association of Canada [ABAC], the Australian and New Zealand Association of Antiquarian Booksellers [ANZAAB], the Southern African Bookdealers Association, and the International League of Antiquarian Booksellers [ILAB].) These organizations are made up of members who have a longstanding track record of usually high-end book sales and equally high-end inventory. Membership purportedly guarantees that the dealer is upstanding, ethical, and experienced, though the levels of these traits may vary considerably from one party to the next. This somewhat cynical statement emanates from decades of observation, and while the great majority of booksellers are honest, knowledgeable, and eminently qualified, there is always the possibility of a damaged apple in the barrel. Almost all of these professionals usually provide superior service, and they are the main movers of fine library materials through the world of scholarship and collecting. They are often the librarians' and collectors' best friends. (Berger, pp. 320 ff.; http://www.abaa.org [accessed 1 June 2021]; http://www.abac.org [accessed 1 June 2021]; https://ilab.org/association/the-australian-and-new-zealand-association-of-antiquarian-booksellers [accessed 1 June 2021]; https://www.ilab.org [accessed 1 June 2021].)

ABAC. (Antiquarian Booksellers' Association of Canada; Association de la Librairie Ancienne du Canada). *See* ABAA.

ABANDONWARE. *See* Orphan Works.

ABBREVIATIONS. In the world of books and other materials that booksellers sell and that collectors collect, purveyors, collectors, bibliographers, editors, and librarians, among others, have created their own vocabulary, some of which is presented in shorthand in dealers' catalogs or published bibliographies. Also, human beings are prone to using shorthand locutions, so in the world of books—as is the case of many other "worlds" with their own organizations and jargon—abbreviations trip off the tongue that most members of that world understand. ("I saw Smith at SNEAB and ABAA last year" would not need glossing by a certain group of listeners.)

That is, abbreviations save space for all concerned, and while one might expect a consistency in the use of abbreviations across the world of books, there is nonetheless a great diversity in the use of these shorthand tools. Below is a listing of some of the more common (and not so common) abbreviations that one might find in published bibliographies or in booksellers' catalogs, or in the literature or speech of the field. There are variations in styling of these, but many of them are self-explanatory. The listing here for the most part uses lowercase letters, but these abbreviations often are styled with capitals; the use of periods may also vary from one user to the next, as may the use of italics. Some of these abbreviations are so seldom seen that they barely made it to the listing below. For instance, few booksellers would use "y.e." for "yellow edges" since such an abbreviation is so uncommon that a reader of the catalog might not understand what those letters refer to. Other abbreviations may never appear in a dealer's catalog, but may appear in the margin of a 17th-century illustration. Common, for instance, is "*sculps.*"; for this reason, such abbreviations, useful to book collectors and booksellers alike, are listed here.

This listing does not encourage modern catalogers (booksellers in particular) to use many of the abbreviations here; it is here to enlighten readers who encounter these short forms. (Taken, with some emendations, from Berger, pp. 498–500; from Carter, *ABC*; and from a host of other sources.) As the note at the entry for *Ibid.* says, many of the Latin abbreviations that one might encounter in citations of sources are obsolete, and many publishers discourage (or forbid) their use. They are listed here since scholars, collectors, booksellers, and others are likely to encounter them. (Abbreviations followed by an asterisk [*] have entries in the present volume.) The more bookseller catalogs I perused, the longer this list became. For the most part, the abbreviations here are those *actually used* in the profession. As noted above, many of these abbreviations are not user friendly: one cannot figure them out on their own. (How many readers would know that "fon" means "former owner's name"? or that "*Af*" means "engraved by"?) It behooves booksellers to have a table at the beginning of their catalogs of "Abbreviations Used Herein"—or something like this. For individual items listed in online services, such obscure abbreviations should probably be avoided.

I have included a number of abbreviations for booksellers' associations. In certain parts of the country or among certain speakers, these short forms would be immediately understood. This listing contains only those abbreviations that I have actually seen. I am sure there are many others out there that could have been added. (These will be added in the next edition.)

AA—author's alteration s
AABA—Arkansas Antiquarian Booksellers Association
AACR—Anglo-American Cataloguing Rules*
AAT—Art & Architecture Thesaurus*
*AB—AB/Bookman's Weekly**
ABA—Antiquarian Booksellers' Association*
ABAA—Antiquarian Booksellers' Association of America*
ABAC—Antiquarian Booksellers Association of Canada
ABAJ—Antiquarian Booksellers Association of Japan
*ABPC—American Book Prices Current**
abbr.—abbreviation, of course
ab init.—ab initio, from the beginning
abr.—abbreviated, abridged, abridgment
act.—active
a.d.—autographed document
ad init.—ad initium, at the beginning
ad int.—ad interim, in the meantime, in the intervening time
ad loc.—ad locum (at the place [in a text] cited)
a.d.s.—autograph document signed
ads., advts., adverts.—advertisements*
a.e.g.—all edges gilt*
a.e.m.—all edges marbled
a.e.s.—all edges stained
A.f., aq., aqua., aquaf.—Aqua forti, engraved by
a.l.—autograph letter
a.l.s.—autograph letter signed
a.m.s.—autograph manuscript signed
a.n.s.—autograph note signed
anony.—anonymous*
ANZAAB—Australian & New Zealand Association of Antiquarian Booksellers
APDR, APR.—Avec privilège du roi, with the PRIVILEGE of the king
ARC—advance reader's copy (*see* Advance copy)
ASE—Armed Services Editions*
assoc. cop.—association copy*
b.—born
b&w—black and white (as adjectival, hyphenated)
*BAL—Bibliography of American Literature**
*BAR—Book Auction Records**
B.A.T.—Bon à tirer, "good to pull"; that is, fit to print*
bce—book club edition*
bd.—bound (or, in a German text, *Band*, volume)
bdg.—binding
bds.—boards*
bk.—book
bkpl.—bookplate*
bkstrp—backstrip (i.e., the spine of the book) (*see under* Back*)
bl.—blind (as in bl. st. = blind stamped*)
BL—British Library*
BLC—British Library Catalogue*
BM—British Museum
BMC—British Museum Catalogue (could refer to *British Museum Catalogue of Books Printed in the Fifteenth Century*)*
BMSTC—British Museum Short Title Catalogue
BN—Bibliothèque Nationale*
bndg.—binding*
BOMC—Book of the Month Club
*BPI—Bookman's Price Index**
bw, b/w—black and white (as in photographs) (as adjectival, hyphenated)
c., ca.—circa (about)

c.—copyright (as in "c. 1955"; possibly confusing because "c." could also mean "circa")*
c & p—collated and perfect*
C&P—Chandler and Price (a CLAMSHELL printing press)
CABS—Colorado Antiquarian Book Seminar*
Cae. (or, more commonly, *Cæ.*), *Cael.—Cælavit*, engraved by
CBA—Cascade Booksellers Association
*CBEL—Cambridge Bibliography of English Literature**
cf.—calf*
ch., chap., chp., chpt., chptr—chapter
cl.—cloth*
col.—colored (*see* Colors*)
coll.—collected; collection (*see* Collected edition*)
comp.—compiled (by); compiler
cond.—condition (as in "exc. cond.")*
C1S/C2S—(said of paper) Coated one side / Coated two sides*
cont.—contemporary (as in "cont. bndg.")* (*also* continued)
corr.—corrected
CPSCM—*Cum privilegio Sacrae Caesaris Maiestatis**
cr.—crown (size of paper) (hence, for example, cr. 8vo = crown octavo)
cvr(s)—cover(s)*
cwo—[send] check (or cash) with order
d.—died
DAB—Dictionary of American Biography
dec.—decorated (as in "dec. bds.")
Del., delin.—Delineavit, drawn by
Deping., Depingeb.—Depingebat, depicted (painted) by
Desig.—Designavit, designed by
disb.—disbound*
diss.—dissertation
div.—division; divorced
d.j.—dust jacket*
DNB—Dictionary of National Biography
do.—ditto
doc.—document
ds—document signed
d.w.—dust wrapper (same as "d.j.")
duodec.—duodecimo (= 12mo.; book format)*
ed.—edited, edition, editor
e.d.l.—edition de luxe (*see* Deluxe edition)
edn.—edition*
e.f.—extremely fine
Effig.—Effigiavit, drawn by
e.g.—exempli gratia, for example
ency. or encyc.—encyclopedia
endpg.—endpage ("endpaper" is better) (*see* Endleaves)
endp(s).—endpaper(s) (*see* Endleaves)*
engr(s).—engraved, engraving(s)*
enl., enlg.—enlarged*
e.p.—endpaper(s) (*see* Endleaves)*
*ESTC—English Short-Title Catalogue**
et al.—et alii (or *et alia*), and the others (usually used for people)
et inf.—et infra, and below*
et seq.—et sequentes, and the following (and others that follow this)
Ex., exc., exct., excud.—Excudit, published by; printed by
ex.lib. (sometimes "exlib" or "ex-lib")—former library copy*
ex(c).—excellent (condition) ("ex. cond.")
exp.—expanded
extrms., extrems.—extremities (the outer edges of a book, especially the corners and edges of the binding; the catalog this was in said "Sl. wear to extrems.")*
f.—fine
F., fec., fect.—Fecit, made by
f, F, f°, F°, fol.—folio (the format of a book; a leaf in a book)*
FABA—Florida Antiquarian Booksellers Association
Fac.—*faciebat* (made by; a seldom-seen abbr.)
facs.—facsimile*
f&g's—folded and gathered sheets (with respect to unbound books)*
fasc.—fascicle*
fcp.—foolscap (size of paper)*
fep.—front end paper (*see* Endleaves)
ff.—folios (said of leaves in a book; *see* Leaf); and following (e.g., "pp. 55 ff.")
ff.—leaves (i.e., folios; see "ll."); and following as in "pp. 55 ff." (*see* Folio)
ffep.—front free end paper
Fig.—figurabit (drawn by; a seldom-seen abbr.); figure (as in an illustration in a book: "See Fig. 5.")
fl(s)—flyleaf (flyleaves)*
fldg.—folding (as in "fldg. map")
fly—flyleaf (a blank leaf at the front or back)*
fr. fly—front flyleaf
fo., fol.—folio*
foi—former owner's initials
fon—former owner's name
fos—former owner's signature
fp, frontis.—frontispiece*
fr.—front (or "fair" as in "this bk. is in fr. cond.")
frag.—fragment
frnt.—front (but why abbreviate this?)
f.v.—*folio verso* (that is, on the back of the leaf)
fxd., fxng.—foxed, foxing*

GABA—Georgia Antiquarian Booksellers Association (other states have their own organizations, and locally they may be listed with an abbreviation)
g., gd.—good (condition)
g., gt.—gilt*
g.e.—gilt edges*
Gedr. (zu).—Gedruckt (zu), printed (at)
Gez.—Gezeichnet, drawn by
*GKW, GW—Gesamtkatalog der Wiegendrucke**
Gt—gilt top
hc—hard cover
H.C.—*Hors de commerce*, not for sale
hf.—half (as in "hf-bnd" [half bound]; "hf t" [half title])
ht.—height; half title
IAMA—International Antiquarian Mapsellers Association
ibid.—ibidem (in the same place; same as above [i.e., the immediately preceding entry])*
IBOOKNET—Independent Booksellers' Network (UK)
id.—idem, the same
i.e.—id est, that is
IGI—*Indice Generale degli Incunaboli*, General Index of the Incunabula of Italian Libraries (published in 6 volumes by the Rome State Library, 1943–1981)
ILAB/LILA—International League of Antiquarian Booksellers*/Ligue Internationale de la Librairie Ancienne
ill., illus.—illustrated, illustration(s)
IMO—International Money Order
imp.—imperial (size of paper)
Imp.—*Imprimit*, printed by
impft—imperfect*
Inc., indic.—*Incidit* or *incidebat*, engraved by
Index—Index Librorum Prohibitorum*
inf.—infra, below
in pr.—in principio, in the beginning
inscrb. (or some variation of this)—inscribed (someone's signature)*
inscrpt.—inscription (someone's handwritten note) (*see* Inscribed)*
intro(d).—introduction
IOBA—Independent Online Booksellers Association*
ISBN—International Standard Book Number*
ISSN—International Standard Serial Number*
ISTC—Incunabula Short-Title Catalogue*
ital., itals.—italic (type), italics*
l., ll.—line, lines
LC—Library of Congress* (sometimes LoC)
LEC—Limited Editions Club*
Lev—levant morocco (leather used in binding)*
lg., lge.—large
lg. pap. copy (also LP)—large paper copy (often noted in the item description in boldface type)*
lib., libr.—library*
Lith., litho., lithog.—lithograph; lithographed by (*see under* Lithography)*
ll.—leaves (as distinguished from pp. [pages]); also lines (as in poetry) (*see* Leaf)*
LoC (*see* LC)
loc. cit.—loco citato (in the place cited)
loq.—loquitur, he or she speaks
LP (*see* lg. pap. copy)
l.s.—letter (not in holograph), signed
lt.—light (e.g., "lt. bkstrp. fading")
ltd.—limited
lt(d). ed.—limited edition*
m—mint (condition)*
MABA—Maine Antiquarian Booksellers Association; Midwest Antiquarian Booksellers Association
MARIAB—Massachusetts and Rhode Island Antiquarian Booksellers (superseded by SNEAB)
m.e.—marbled edges
med.—medium (size of paper)
m.m.—*mutatis mutandis*, necessary changes being made
mmp, mmpb—mass-market paperback*
mod.—moderately (somewhere between "sl." and "v.")
mor.—morocco (leather)*
ms, mss—manuscript(s)*
n.—*natus*, born (usually followed by a place or date)
n.b.—*nota bene*, note well (that is, observe carefully)
*NCBEL—New Cambridge Bibliography of English Literature**
n.d.—no date (of publication)*
n.f.—near fine
NHABA—New Hampshire Antiquarian Bookseller Association
no., nos.—number, numbers
N.p.—no place (of publication)*
n.p.—no publisher*
nr.—near (as in nr.f. = near fine)
n.s. (or, often, NS)—new series
NS—New Style (said of dates) (*see entry at* Old Style and New Style)*
NUC—National Union Catalog (usually refers to the 754-volume pre-1956 volumes)*
n.y.—no year
ob.—obiit, died
ob., obl.—oblong (usually denoting landscape format)*
obs.—obsolete
OCLC—Online Computer Library Center* (originally Ohio College Library Center, rarely spelled out)
oct—octavo*
OED—Oxford English Dictionary
o.p.—out of print*

op. cit.—*opus citatum* or *opere citato* (in the work[s] cited) (*see entry* for *Ibid.*)
or., Orig.—original
or.cl.—original cloth
o.s.—old series; out of series*
OS—Old Style (said of dates)*
o/w, o.w.—otherwise (as in "spine removed, joints split, o.w. fine+")
Oxon.—*Oxoniensis* (i.e., Oxford)
p., pg(s), pp.—page(s)*
par., para.—paragraph
pass.—Latin for "passim": here and there or in various places (through the text)
pb (or ppb)—paperback*
PBFA—Provincial Booksellers Fairs Association
pbo—paperback original (i.e., a first edition of a title that was issued first in paper cover)
p.c.—price clipped (as in "p.c. d.j.") (*see* Clipped*)
PDF—Portable Document Format*
perf.—perfect
phots.—photographs
Ph. sc.—Photo sculpsit (photographed by)
pict.—pictorial (as in "pict. cvr.")
Pinx., ping., pinxt.—*Pinxit* or *pingebat*, painted by
pl(s).—plate(s)*
PMM—*Printing and the Mind of Man**
p.o.d.—print on demand*
pol.—polished (as in pol. cf. ["polished calf"])*
por—price on request (said of an unpriced item in a dealer's catalog)*
port.—portrait (usually refers to portrait format, as opposed to landscape format)*
posth.—posthumous(ly)
p.p.—privately printed*
ppd—postage paid; post paid
pres.—presentation (as in "presentation copy")*
prlms., prelims.—preliminary leaves/pages*
PRO—Public Records Office*
prof.—profusely (as in "prof. ill.")
prox.—*proximo*, next month
pseud.—pseudonym; pseudonymous*
pt(s).—part(s)*
ptd.—printed
ptg.—printing*
pub.—publication, published, publisher*
pvt.—private(ly) (as in "pvt. ptd.")*
qto., Q°—quarto*
qtr.—quarter (as in "qtr. bnd.")*
q.v.—*quo vide* (which see; an abbreviation keyed to a cross-reference)
r.—recto, the page on the right (e.g., "B3r": the front of the third leaf in SIGNATURE B)*
R.—*rex*, King; *regina*, Queen
RBS—(Royal Bank of Scotland), but for this volume, Rare Book School*
RDA—Resource Description and Access (*see under* MARC records)
r.e.—red edges*
repr., rpt.—reprint(ed)*
rev.—revised*
rfep—rear free end paper (*see* Endpapers)
r. fly—rear flyleaf
RLIN—Research Libraries Information Network*
RMABA—Rocky Mountain Antiquarian Booksellers Association
rom.—roman (type; numeral)*
roy.—royal (size of paper)
rpts.—reprints*
rubd.—rubbed*
s.a.—*sine anno* (without a date)
sc., sculp., sculps., sculpt.—*Sculpsit*, engraved by
scr., scrip.—*Scripsit*, engraved text by
sgd.—signed*
sig.—signature*
sigd.—signed*
s.l.—*sine loco* (no place [of publication]; an archaic abbreviation; better is "N.p."—no place)
sl.—slight(ly) (as in "sl. fxd.")
slc—slipcase*
sm.—small
SMR—sheet music REMOVED (this abbreviation from a bookseller whose lists contained many pieces of sheet music)
S.n.—*Sina* [or *Sine*] nota (also S.n. & l.) (no publisher or place of publication given)*
s.n.—*sine nomine* (without a name; archaic; better is "anony.")
SNEAB—Southern New England Antiquarian Booksellers
SOED—*Shorter Oxford English Dictionary*
sp.—spine (as in "sp. sl. torn off")*
spr.—sprinkled*
sq.—square
STC—Short-Title Catalogue*
sub anno—under the year
TABA—Tennessee Antiquarian Booksellers Association
tba—to be announced
TBA—Texas Booksellers Association
t.e.g.—top edge gilt
thk—thick
t.l.s.—typed letter signed
TLS—*Times Literary Supplement*

TOC—table of contents
t.p., t-p—title page*
t.s.—typescript*
trans.—translated (by), translator
UDC—Universal Decimal Classification (a cataloging system)
UK—United Kingdom
ult.—ultimatus, ultimate, last; *ultimo*, last month
unb., unbd.—unbound*
U.P., UP—university press; UNCORRECTED proof
usu.—usual(ly)
ut sup.—ut supra, as above
v.—very (e.g., "vg")
v.—verso (e.g., "B3v": the back of the third leaf of signature B)*
VABA—Vermont Antiquarian Booksellers Association; Virginia Antiquarian Booksellers Association
v.d.—various dates (of course; what else did you think this could be?)*
v.f.—very fine (copy)
v.g., vg—very good (condition)
vig(s).—vignette(s) (*see under* Headpiece)*
vol(s).—volume(s)*
v.p.—various places
v.y.—various years (of publication)
w.—width (used along with "ht.")
w., w/—with
w.a.f.—with all faults (sold "as is," indicating that the item is defective)*
Wing—Wing's *Short-Title Catalogue of English Books, 1641–1700**
wo., w/o—without
wr., wraps, wrps.—wrappers (paper covers)*
y.e.—yellow edges
2^0, fo., f^o, fol.—folio*
4to, 4^0—quarto*
8vo, 8^0—octavo*
12mo, 12°—duodecimo (also called "twelvemo")*
16mo, 16^0—sextodecimo (also called "sixteenmo")*
32mo, 32^0—trigesimo-secundo (also called "thirty-twomo")

AB/BW (*Antiquarian Bookman/Bookman's Weekly*). One of the most important publications for booksellers, collectors, librarians, and others in the book world. Sol M. Malkin started it as an R. R. Bowker title. From the 1950s to the 1990s, it was the premiere source for used and out-of-print books in America. Jacob L. (Jake) Chernofsky bought the magazine in 1972, when it had over 10,000 subscribers. (See Fox, "Mary Ann Malkin, Journal Editor and Rare-Book Collector, Dies at 92.") By the 1990s, ONLINE BOOK SALES had already reared its head, but Jake thought he could keep the paper-based publication going. At the end of 1999, the magazine closed its doors.

This magazine is the amalgamation of these two earlier publications: *Antiquarian Bookman* and *Bookman's Weekly*. It was a powerful force in the acquisition and dissemination of books in the world. It contained educated articles written by those in the trade and other scholars, and each weekly issue listed thousands of books wanted and books for sale. It also listed "Books Received" and sometimes book reviews, and it had a section on bookish activities throughout the United States (book sales, exhibitions, lectures, and so on). When the occasion called for it, it had obituaries of important people in the book world. And it listed stolen books when they were reported to its editor. It attempted to set a standard for terminology related to book CONDITION (for dealers' catalog descriptions), but that effort never caught on: booksellers were happy with their own idiosyncratic methods and terms for describing condition. Before online bookselling databases, this publication was the most important source of information for the availability of books and was also the number one book-search tool in the world. It had a large circulation to booksellers, librarians, and collectors who pored over its pages the moment it was delivered into their hands—not wanting to miss an opportunity to acquire a long-sought-after item. This "essential" tool of the book trade was buried in an unmarked grave once online bookselling sites hit the e-waves. (See Berger, *Rare Books*, pp. 307–09; Holzenberg, "Second-Hand and Antiquarian Books on the Internet.")

ABCDERIUM. (Plural is "Abcderia.") (Spelled with varying numbers of the opening letters capitalized.) (Sometimes called an "Abecedary" or an "Alphabet book.") An alphabet book, and one of the most popular genres of bookmaking, appealing to people of all ages. Though showing the alphabet (presumably to teach it) to the reader, the volume also often shows other characters, like punctuation, ASTERISKS, AMPERSANDS, and the like. These can be MANUSCRIPT or printed, often showing the 26 LETTERS of the English alphabet using that many different FONTS. Alphabet books can also show various pieces of punctuation, and there can be a single image that usually accompanies each character, no images at all, or several. They can also display a text at each character (in prose, verse, or both, or a single word naming something on the page, like an elephant to show the letter *E*), and—if these volumes are aimed at children, which most of them are—they may show UPPER- and LOWERCASE letters. While the standard term is "alphabet book," the word "ABCDerium" is preferred since not all such "texts" are in book form; they may be BROADSIDES as well. Early ABCderia were in the form of HORN BOOKS or BATTLEDORES.

ABEBOOKS (originally Advanced Book Exchange). One of a host of ONLINE BOOKSELLING sites, listing many millions of items. The ABE site says, "AbeBooks is an online marketplace for books. Millions of brand new books, used books, rare books, and OUT-OF-PRINT books are offered for sale through the AbeBooks websites from thousands of booksellers around the world. Readers can find BESTSELLERS, collectors can find rare books, students can find new and used textbooks, and treasure hunters can find long-lost books. / AbeBooks Inc. is a subsidiary of Amazon.com, Inc. AbeBooks, an online bookselling pioneer, was acquired in December 2008 and remains a stand-alone operation with headquarters in Victoria, British Columbia, Canada, and a European office in Munich, Germany. / Our mission is to help people find and buy any book from any bookseller and our business stretches around the world with six international sites—AbeBooks.com, AbeBooks.co.uk, AbeBooks.de, AbeBooks.fr, AbeBooks.it, IberLibro.com, and ZVAB.com, a worldwide marketplace for German rare books. / Founded in 1995 by two couples from Victoria, AbeBooks.com went live in 1996 and immediately began to transform the world's used book business by making hard-to-find books easy to locate and purchase. In 2002, *The New York Times* described the company as 'an actual Internet success story.' By 2003, the United Nations acclaimed AbeBooks as one of the world's leading ecommerce companies at its World Summit. / The unique inventory of books for sale from booksellers includes the world's finest antiquarian books dating back to the 15th century, countless out-of-print gems, millions of signed books, millions of used copies, a vast selection of college textbooks and new books too" (https://www.abebooks.com/books/CompanyInformation [accessed 5 June 2021]). (*See* viaLibri.) While there are other excellent search services on the web, ABE is a favorite of many collectors and booksellers because of its Advanced Search capabilities and the speed of its responses. Other sites do not allow the extent of Boolean searches that ABE offers. (Beware! It is very easy to buy books on this site. And the selection is wide and tempting.)

ABHB (*Annual Bibliography of the History of the Printed Book and Libraries*). Since this dictionary is about books, the reader should be familiar with one of the important reference tools regarding the world of books and libraries. "ABHB is the current international bibliography in the field of book and library history. It records all publications of scholarly value, written from an historical point of view. This may include monographs, articles and reviews, dealing with the history of the printed book, its arts, crafts, techniques and equipment, its economic, social and cultural environment involved in its production, distribution preservation and description. More specifically, ABHB contains information on the history of printing and publishing, papermaking, bookbinding, book illustration, type design and typefounding, bibliophily and book collecting, libraries and scholars. . . . / ABHB has been issued each year from 1970 on. It contains a main section in which the titles are arranged by subject, an author index and an index of geographical and personal names. In 1987 a cumulative index of geographical and personal names on volumes 1–17 (1970–1986) appeared. Since 1992, starting with the titles for volume 21, publications of 1990, the titles are entered in a cumulative database." Scholars from 30 countries contribute to the database ("ABHB," http://www.springer.com/series/5559 [accessed 1 June 2021]).

ABRIDGED EDITION. (Sometimes called a "concise edition.") As the term says, this refers to any text that is a shorter VERSION of the full text, made shorter by having material left out. The word "EDITION" here suggests that the abridged version is printed from the same setting of TYPE as the full version but one that has simply had words and phrases removed. But publishers can use the phrase in any way they like, so it is possible that the "abridged edition" is actually a new edition altogether, with the text it contains printed from a new setting of type. (*See* Edition, Impression [Printing], Issue, and State; Points; Unabridged.) Similar to an abridged edition is a condensation (a condensed edition), which implies abridgement, but not really rewriting; the text has merely been reduced in length by the removal of words and paragraphs, sections or chapters. As with an "abridged edition," the word "edition" may not be accurate if the original text has been shortened and set into type anew.

ACANTHUS LEAVES. Too often I have seen in booksellers' catalogs the phrase "acanthus leaf pattern" or something akin to that, and the catalog does not give a picture of this pattern. In fact, I have also seen many pictures of "acanthus leaves," and the images do not align with one another. The phrase has come to mean something generic that indicates an old pattern that one might find in a manuscript or early printed book. The *Encyclopaedia Britannica* online says, "Acanthus, in architecture and decorative arts, a stylized ornamental motif based on a characteristic Mediterranean plant with jagged leaves, *Acanthus spinosus*. It was first used by the Greeks in the 5th century BC on temple roof ornaments, on wall friezes, and on the capital of the Corinthian column" (*Encyclopaedia Britannica*, "Acanthus," https://www.britannica.com/art/acanthus-ornamental-motif [accessed 24 May

Drawings of acanthus leaves.
Courtesy of Ad Meskins.

2021]). To encourage accuracy, the present text offers an image of acanthus designs.

ACCIDENTALS/ACCIDENTAL VARIANTS. In the world of BIBLIOGRAPHY, accidentals are variations in text, from one version to another, that are not SUBSTANTIVE in nature—usually such things as spelling, punctuation, or emphasis. Hence, one copy of the text might read, "I was here; you were there"; another copy might read, "I was here—you were there." Or one version might spell "steamboat" as a single word, while another might hyphenate it as a compound word. These are accidentals in which meaning is not affected. However, many an accidental can have the weight of a substantive. "Let's eat, Grandma," without its comma, has a distinctly different meaning from the version with a comma. Likewise, "I like your hat" varies in meaning from "I like your *hat*," the first signifying that the speaker likes someone else's hat, the second signifying that the speaker likes the other person's hat but does not like the rest of the wearer's outfit. (*See* Bibliography; Emendations; Substantives.)

ACCORDION FOLD. *See* Concertina fold.

ACE DOUBLES. A popular series of books published by Ace Books beginning in 1952 (and ending in 1978), almost all of which were science fiction, westerns, and mysteries. Each volume contained two texts in the TÊTE-BÊCHE binding LAYOUT. They were printed on cheap, acidic paper and were PERFECT BOUND, so their survival rate was seriously compromised. The tête-bêche format was what made them doubles since each volume contained two texts. (There is a Wikipedia site titled "List of Ace Double Titles" at https://en.wikipedia.org/wiki/List_of_Ace_double_titles#Referencesarticle [accessed 6 June 2021].)

ACEPHALOUS. Headless. Said of a volume missing its TITLE PAGE (and possibly other front LEAVES). Usually such volumes have lost much of their value, for the title page tells us a great deal of information. But sometimes the acephalousness of a volume might not be a serious defect. The Phillips Library at the Peabody Essex Museum has an acephalous religious text; the volume itself is not worth much, even in perfect condition. But it is signed on its front pastedown by its first owner, William Bradford, first governor of Massachusetts, and by its next owner, Cotton Mather. It is also signed on its rear pastedown by a subsequent owner, John Hancock, in his immediately distinguishable hand.

ACETATE. A clear plastic sheet that is often used for DUST JACKETS, and it can also be used inside volumes with prints as protection for the prints and for the pages facing them. It predates MYLAR, which is more likely to be archival, and many an acetate jacket has become opaque, yellowed, or brittle, or it could shrink. Such deterioration threatens to damage the volume it touches (the one it is on, and the ones it touches on a shelf). If a book is issued with an acetate dust jacket, but that jacket is damaging the volume, does the collector or bookseller jettison it to protect the book, or keep it so that the book can be had AS ISSUED? One solution is to place an archival piece of paper, in the shape of the dust jacket, between the acetate and the book's binding. But ACID MIGRATION could eventually damage the volume. Collectors would want the jacket, but not the damage.

ACID MIGRATION. "The transfer of acid from a material containing it to one with less or no acid" (Greenfield, *ABC of Bookbinding*). Common forms of acid migration are in volumes that had newspaper clippings interleaved, with their typical brownish stain on the two leaves the clippings touched and possible neighboring leaves since the migration keeps migrating. The acid can also come from leather or adhesives like rubber cement. This kind of staining also appears on ENDLEAVES when acidic adhesives on TURN-INS or BOOKPLATES leave their marks. And it is common to see acid migration on TURN-INS where the leather is acidic.

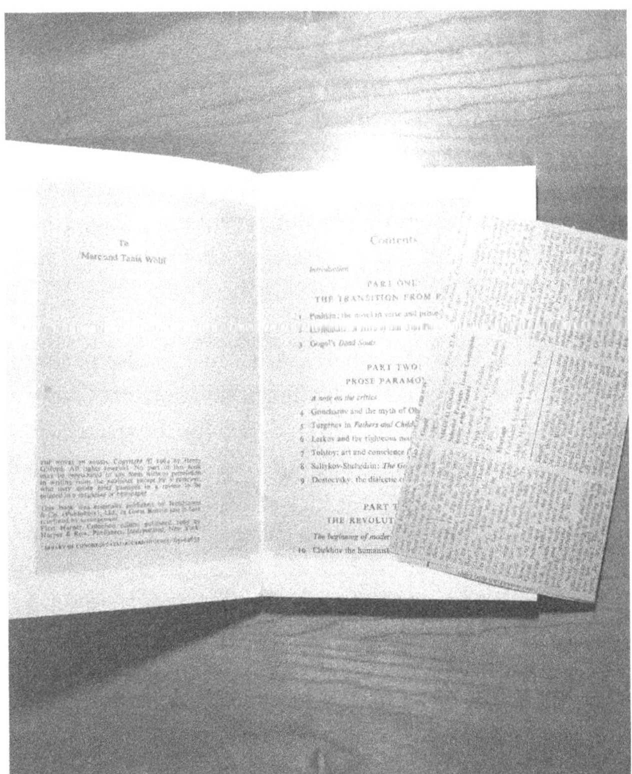

Acid migration from a newspaper clipping left in an inexpensive paperback book (Gifford, *The Novel in Russia from Pushkin to Pasternak*). Acid is nasty: it has migrated not only onto the leaves shown (the title page and table of contents leaf), but also onto the half title (in front) and the leaf following the table of contents. The image also shows the newspaper clipping that caused the damage.

Collection of the author.

ACKNOWLEDGMENTS (or Acknowledgements). The part of the book (usually at the beginning, hence part of the PRELIMS) in which an author thanks all those who have had something to do with the production of the text, the volume, or his own life. These can be brief ("Thanks to my editor for bringing this to publication") or many pages, in which the author thanks everyone from his delivery room nurses to his undertaker. They are sometimes saccharine and can be filled with floral prose aimed at greasing the philanthropy of a patron or sponsor. But sometimes the historical or biographical information revealed in the acknowledgments can be useful to a scholar. (*See* Foreword.)

ADAMS. The abbreviated form of the two-volume work by H. M. Adams, *Catalogue of Books Printed in the Continent of Europe, 1501–1600, In Cambridge Libraries.* Cited by scholars as "Adams," but now superseded by vast online resources.

ADDED ENDLEAVES. *See* Inserted endleaves.

ADDENDUM/ADDENDA. Any text or illustration added to a volume after it is too late to incorporate it into the main part of the text where it would naturally have been placed. Sometimes it is LAID IN, but as often it is printed and bound in at the end of the volume. (*See* Corrigendum/Corrigenda; Erratum/Errata.)

ADDRESS TO THE READER. A statement in the front matter (*see* Prelims) of a volume aimed at the book's reader(s) that explains "the acquisition or creation of the text, changes made to it during the printing process, and its ability to meet readers' needs. Borrowing language and in some cases epistolary formatting from dedications to named patrons, these texts addressed groups of anonymous potential readers, anticipating criticism and attempting to guide reader response. Unlike many manufactured objects, books provide an opportunity for their creators to describe what they are, how they came to be, and why their audience should buy them" (Meaghan J. Brown, "Addresses to the Reader," p. 83). These addresses can be found in INCUNABULA. WILLIAM CAXTON's *Recueil des histoires de Troyes* (Bruges: 1473[?]) has such an address, "an autobiographical explanation of his choices as . . . translator and printer" (Brown, p. 83). Most of these addresses, in the form of letters, are fairly short—a page or less. But some can run on for several pages. "The majority of direct addresses to readers come from the author, translator, printer, or others who had a direct hand in creating the work" (Brown, p. 84).

ADHESIVE BINDING (or Adhesive Structure Binding). *See* Perfect binding.

ADJUSTABLE MOLD. *See* Mold (type casting).

ADVANCE. (Also called "author's advance.") An adjective indicating the priority of something, as with ADVANCE COPY. The term as a noun indicates the money paid to an author or editor before the volume he or she is responsible for is issued. The publisher gives the author the advance usually at the signing of the contract (since such an advance would be written into the contract) or sometime before the MANUSCRIPT is completed, and it could be returnable if the volume does not reach enough sales to cover the amount the author would have earned in ROYALTIES. A prominent and successful author, however, may have the "advance" clause in the contract say that the advance is not returnable under any circumstances. The advance may help the author with the expenses incurred in the composition of the text; or it may simply be the publisher's incentive to the author to finish the work.

ADVANCE COPY. (Sometimes called "advanced copy," though this is strictly an error.) A copy of a volume sent out by a publisher to a reader for a variety of purposes: to have a reader vet the work for quality; to secure a review from a critic—a statement that may wind up as a BLURB on the DUST JACKET; to interest members of a book club and to get them to adopt the book; to get someone in the press to write a review for a newspaper, television, or radio; to entice a bookseller to carry it in her stock. An advance copy could be the final version that will be released to the public, or it may be an early version of the text, before final editing, printed on inferior paper, with no (or with black-and-white) illustrations when the commercial one will have them in color, and with a binding (and/or dust jacket) that is identical to or differing from the one that will be used on the commercial version. They are often marked "Advanced Copy," "Advanced Reader's Copy," "Advance Reading Copy," or in some other way that distinguishes them from the regular commercial version, and they can be called "Reader's Edition," though the word "edition" is inaccurate since the text in them is printed from the same type as is used for the regular published version, so they would be the same edition (*see* Edition, Impression [Printing], Issue, and State; Points). To COMPLETIST collectors, the advance copy is an essential since it is a variant manifestation of what they collect. "Because they are produced in relatively short numbers, they do not constitute a true 'edition' of their own (or a different 'issue' of the edition they are a part of)" (Berger, p. 262). But as Carter points out, because they are "advanced," they represent an early state of printing in the PRESSRUN, so the text might have readings that could have been changed for later-printed copy (see Carter, pp. 23–24). For this reason they may have bibliographical or textual interest. Carter also points out that while these advance copies could represent an early version of the text, they do not usurp the designation "first edition" for the rest of the pressrun—the volumes released generally to the public on the day of publication. Many private presses in the 20th century issued small numbers of advance copies—in wrappers, often on proof paper, sometimes with a paper band around (or a pasted-on label on) the covers. The small number of these copies makes them yield high prices on the collectors' market. (*See* Review copy.) Carter says that an advance copy could be one that the binder sends to the publisher as a proposed model, for the publisher's approval or one that the binder sends to the author; the former is strictly a binder's copy or BINDER'S DUMMY, not a true advance copy, though it, of course, exists in advance of the final published version. The word "advance" yields several possible interpretations, and they have not been used consistently in the book world. (*See* Author's copies.)

ADVANCE SHEETS. The unbound sheets of a book, often early in the book's production, as with GALLEY PROOFS, sent out before the book is published. They could be sent to an author or editor as PROOFS, or to a reviewer. Such sheets can have a text in its earliest in-print form, and could be bibliographically significant to a TEXTUAL BIBLIOGRAPHER. However, the VARIANTS they contain could be purely compositorial (*see* Compositor), not AUTHORIAL. Either way, advance sheets can tell a researcher about the publishing house's printing and publishing practices.

ADVERTISEMENTS. Different kinds of advertisements exist in printed books, laid or bound in in various ways, sometimes on paper different from that used for the text, and not always included in all of the copies of the volume by that book's publisher. Much can be learned from these ads. For example, Carter points out that in the 19th century, some publishers dated their catalogs, which could inform us of the priority of the dates of two EXEMPLARS of a title (see Carter, pp. 24–25). He warns, however, that such evidence must be taken cautiously since the dating of the advertising catalogs that are inserted in published books may not coincide perfectly with the dating of the issue of the book itself. And to say that a copy of the volume without the inserted catalog is earlier than copies with that insertion is also suspect (Carter, pp. 24–25). Complications arise as well in interpreting the importance of ads for books issued IN PARTS, those issued with state variants in a single edition, runs of volumes with variant issue dates, and MADE-UP SETS. An additional difficulty could be introduced into the world of bibliography if an advertising pamphlet bound into the back of a book lists "Forthcoming Publications," one or some of which never came forth, in which case we would have a GHOST BOOK: a bibliographical reference to a volume that never was. One feature of the advertisements that many a collector (and bookseller) might be interested in is the original selling price of the items listed. Also, the ads may have binding descriptions that could be useful to bibliographers. (*See* Priority.)

AEG. *See* All edges gilt.

A4 PAPER. Using the "standard" size of business stationery, called in Great Britain (and elsewhere) "A4 paper," this is composed of sheets measuring 8¼ × 11¾ in. (210 × 297 mm). Standard size in the United States, of course, is 8½ × 11 in. Inasmuch as readers of this volume will be dealing with sellers from countries other than the United States, they are likely to encounter this designation (e.g., "ALS on A4 paper"). There is also the standard European size called A3 paper, twice the dimensions of A4 (that is, 16½ × 11¾ in.; 297 × 420 mm).

AGATE. A size of type (5½ point; see Appendix C). Also, a stone used to burnish paper, leather, gold leaf, and other materials. Also, in the 19th and early 20th centuries, marblers polished their sheets with agates.

AHEARN PRICE GUIDES. Allen and Patricia Ahearn, proprietors of Quill & Brush booksellers, compiled a series of volumes and pamphlets giving prices for thousands of books, mostly first editions of English and American authors. For example, their *Collected Books: The Guide to Identification and Values*, in its fourth edition, has been a valuable guide to book prices since its publication. The Ahearns also published a series of author price guides, issued in simple stapled pamphlets, for dozens of authors. They were available as individual FASCICLES, and they were gathered into bound volumes, each containing the guides for dozens of authors' works (*Author Price Guides*; the 700-page volume [vol. 2] of the guides contained listings for 51 authors). Although the problems with such guides are that they are dated, that authors' popularity as collectable rises and falls, and that the specific volumes they were looking at when they came up with the prices could differ in a variety of ways from the volumes a user might be looking at, they are still decent indications of prices at a particular moment in history.

AI (*American Imprints*). This is the massive bibliography compiled by Ralph R. Shaw and Richard H. Shoemaker and others, covering items printed in what is now the United States from 1801 to the middle of the 19th century. It is referred to by its initials since it is immediately recognizable by those who use it and because it is the most comprehensive such reference tool in the field. It is, unfortunately, not "complete"—that is, it was clearly impossible for the compilers to have located every imprint in any given year, and often booksellers and collectors find items not listed in this important tool—items that ought to be there. (*See* Shaw and Shoemaker.)

AIGA (American Institute of Graphic Arts). "[T]he professional association for design. . . ." Its mission statement says, "AIGA advances design as a professional craft, strategic advantage, and vital cultural force" (aiga.org [accessed 7 June 2021]). For about 90 years, the AIGA has been giving awards for design, many (for books) in its "Fifty Books of the Year" competition. "Beginning in 1923, the Fifty Books of the Year competition was a yearly mainstay of AIGA. As dust jackets became more common, covers were added to the competition" (https://www.aiga.org/professional-development/competitions-campaigns/50-books-50-covers [accessed 7 June 2021]). A host of private presses whose books often wind up in special collections and rare book departments have won this award. (Despite its focus on design, it currently has one of the worst, cluttered, and off-putting home pages on the web one can imagine.) The organization sees itself as a collective of "web design professionals. An organization that supports the efforts of both traditional and digital designers is the American Institute of Graphic Arts or AIGA as the group prefers to be called. AIGA was founded in 1914 to help build awareness of the benefits that design practitioners bring to industry and society at large. Recently, the profession has received a boost as technology has enabled designers to innovate more quickly and share their creations with larger audiences. Also, there is an increased expectation for more engaging and interactive web page designs by most internet users" (Graphic Design Degree Hub, "What Is AIGA?"; https://www.graphicdesigndegreehub.com/faq/what-is-aiga/ [accessed 24 May 2021]).

ALA. *See* American Library Association.

À LA GRECQUE/ALLA GRECA. *See* Greek style.

À LA POUPÉE. (French for "with the doll.") A method of color printing in which a small bundle of fabric is dipped into a colored pigment and dabbed onto a printing plate; other such bundles with different colors are then added to the plate, and the sheet laid over the colored surface and printed in a ROLLING PRESS, as it would be done for all INTAGLIO printing. (The little bundles look like dolls; hence the name of the process.) The method produces a colored intaglio image with a single pull of the press, rather than having to use a different plate for each color. For a single copy of an image, this method is excellent. For many copies, the inking must be done with some precision to have all of the resulting prints look the same—though of course, since this is a hand process, there will always be some variation from one image to the next. While a hand process, it uses machinery for the actual printing. And the final results have the look of hand coloring (that is, something printed in one color and then fully colored by hand), so many a person describing a print created à la poupée will think he is looking at a hand-colored piece.

ALBION PRESS. A 19th-century iron HANDPRESS (invented in England about 1820 by Richard Whittaker Cope) employing a toggle mechanism, quite popular in the fine-press movement. Cope is thought to have assisted GEORGE CLYMER, maker of the Columbian press. The Albion shows little of Clymer's influence. Cope eliminated decoration, used a toggle instead of a beam for leverage, and employed a spring instead of a counterweight to raise the platen. For 10 years, I printed on two small Albions, and it was really fun—easy to use, with a feel of solidity and sureness.

"Cope died in 1828, only eight years after the introduction of his press. J. & J. Barrett were Cope's executors and carried on his business under the direction of John Hopkinson, Cope's foreman" (https://www.rit.edu/news/cary-collection-purchases-1890s-hand-press [accessed 7 June 2021]). The Kelmscott Albion press is now at the Rochester Institute of Technology. Cope also made tabletop models of this press, for small FORMES. The Albion is a high-performing press for many FINE-PRESS printers on its floor model and the ones designed for a tabletop (see Moran, pp. 74, 88–99).

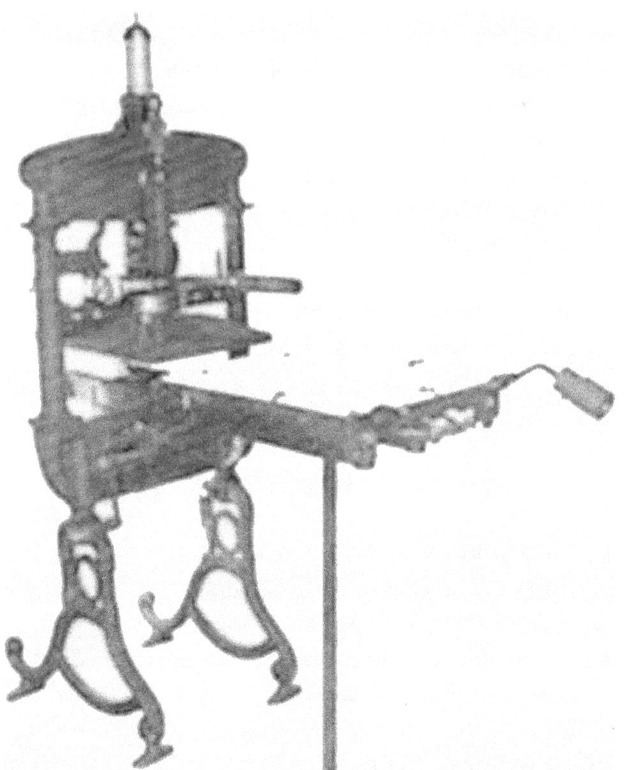

Albion press.
Courtesy of International Printing Museum, Carson, CA.

ALBUM. A book with blank leaves designed for receiving autographs or TIPPED-IN photographs, clippings, or all kinds of ephemera. Some albums, especially those in the 19th century, were elaborately bound (often of poor-quality materials) and, though glitzy when they were issued, did not hold up well over time. These volumes sometimes contain the wretched verse of sentimentality and sometimes the signatures of long-forgotten and fairly unknown people and the witticisms of their times, usually lost on (or groaned at) by people today. The albums could also contain clippings from newspapers that no longer exist, but the sources of the clippings may not be identified. There are also letters (sometimes of great historical interest), artwork that could be done by accomplished artists, and bits of historical information that could be important to scholars. (*See* Album amicorum.) Albums were often bound with extra STUBS to allow for the insertion of all the things that got TIPPED IN. When the volume was empty (i.e., before any tip-ins were added), the stubs made the covers close more closely at the FORE-EDGE than at the spine. But with the pages laden with their treasures, the front and back covers would lie parallel to one another (unless the pages were overloaded with inclusions, in which case the covers would splay apart). At least the stubs gave the album half a chance, but the acid paper did not.

ALBUM AMICORUM (also called "liber amicorum"). This is a "friendship album," similar to a modern-day autograph album, containing INSCRIPTIONS from friends—often accompanied by art of various kinds and also movable parts like VOLVELLES or TIP-INS that can be manipulated. They were first created in the 16th century, and they were popular in the 18th century and later, and were often small, landscape-oriented (*see* Landscape format) volumes. Until the 19th century, the term meant a gathering of short texts from a variety of sources, usually with inscriptions to friends and relatives and often accompanied by watercolor illustrations, tip-ins, calligraphic texts and flourishes, and other artistic embellishments, offered up by the "signers" and usually requested by the albums' owners. The contents could be original or copied verse, rebuses, family escutcheons, still-lifes or landscapes, architectural pictures, music, witty sayings, and pithy quotations from classical and other literature. They also sometimes had autographs of well-known people. In most cases, the artwork in them was of excellent quality.

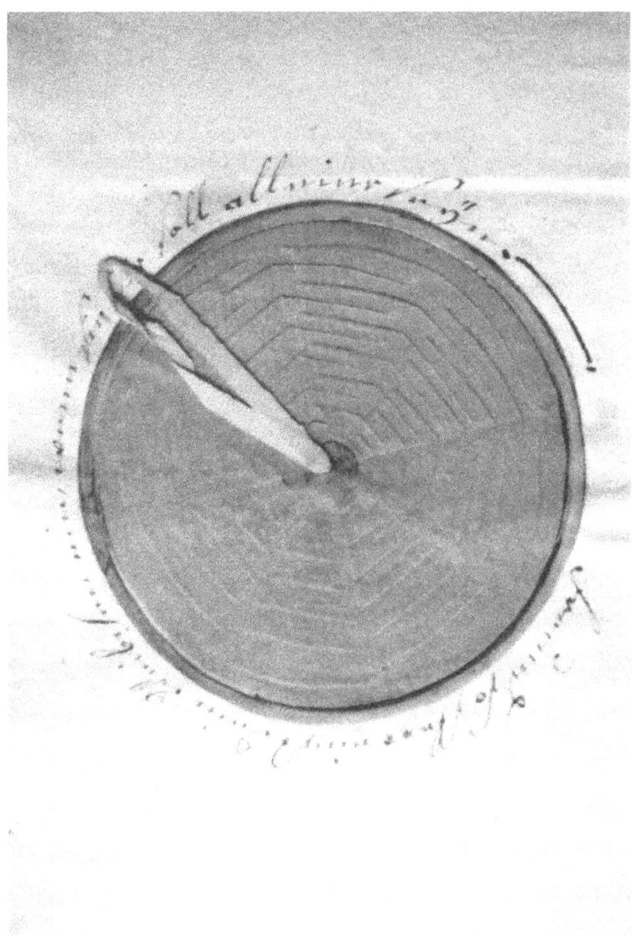

Page from an album amicorum with a cobweb picture—cobweb closed.

Courtesy of Elizabeth Baird.

Page from an album amicorum with a cobweb picture—cobweb open.

Courtesy of Elizabeth Baird.

Typical album amicorum two-page spread, with calligraphy and fine painting. *Dendermonde, private collection.*

The album inscription is dated June 18, 1639. This album was offered in June 2006 by the Brussels auction house The Romantic Agony and is shown in catalog no. 30 (cover and p. 131).

(One of the many that I have seen, done in the 18th century, had a page with a circular disk on it, the disk with an attractive drawing on it. The paper of the disk was cut into perhaps 10 or 15 parallel circular slits, leaving the entire disk in a single piece. It had a small string affixed to the center of the disk, which was attached to the page beneath only on the circular strip around the outside of the disk. When one pulled the string upward, the entire disk lifted off the sheet [except where it was glued down to the page], revealing a sometimes erotic watercolor drawing beneath. This was called a "COBWEB page.") (*See also* Commonplace book.)

ALDINE BINDING. "A style of bookbinding originated by Aldus Manutius but not restricted to the books printed by Aldus or his family. Aldine bindings, which were produced during the late 15th and early 16th centuries, were characterized by the use of brown or red morocco; by solid-faced ornaments with no shading (which were similar to those used in printing the text); and by title or author in simple panels in the center of the upper cover, which could be read while the book lay on a shelf or table. Early examples of the Aldine style were tooled in blind with an outer frame and a center ornament. Possibly because of the Greek binders Aldus employed, as well as the fact that gold tooling (probably) originated in the Near East, Aldine tools display definite signs of Eastern origin" (Roberts and Etherington, "Aldine style [*Italian style*]"; https://cool.culturalheritage.org/don/dt/dt0075.html [accessed 5 April 2021]).

ALDINES. *See* Aldus Manutius.

ALDUS MANUTIUS/ALDINE. (Italian version of his name = Aldo Manuzio). Perhaps, after Gutenberg, Aldus was the most important printer in the world in the 15th century. The printer is referred to by those in the know as "Aldus" and by those out of the know as "Manutius," and the books from his press (and that of his son) are referred to as "Aldines." (His birth and death dates are not certain; Carter gives 1452–1515 [Carter, p. 27]; the *Encyclopaedia Britannica* says 1449–1515 [https://www.britannica.com/biography/Aldus-Manutius; accessed 1 June 2021]). Aldus's books were beautifully designed, and the editions he printed were based on his sound scholarship, often emanating from his textual comparisons of manuscripts of a single work. Aldus is credited with having invented italic type (for his edition of Virgil), using commas and semicolons in the way we use them today, and—perhaps most important for us—popularizing the "pocket book," the small-format volume that slips into pockets and feels comfortable in our hands. After his death, the Aldine press was headed by members of his family: his wife; Aldus the Elder; his third son and final child, Paulus; and his namesake grandson, Paulus's only son, Aldus the Younger, until 1597. (See H. Fletcher, *In Praise of Aldus Manutius*, p. 23. See also Barker, *Aldus Manutius and the Development of Greek Script*, and Barker, *Aldus Manutius: Mercantile Empire*; and the entry in the bibliography for *Gazette of the Grolier Club*, New Series, Number 70.)

ALIA (Australian Library and Information Association). "The Australian Library and Information Association (ALIA) has been proudly representing the Australian library and information sector as the peak body for professionals, staff, institutions, vendors, educators and other stakeholders since 1937. Membership of ALIA is open to professionals, non-professionals, individuals and organisations. We welcome anyone with an interest in libraries and information management. Our 4,200 personal members (individuals) and 800 institutional members (libraries and other organisations) are drawn from the library and information sector-related fields. We advocate on behalf of some 12 million library users" ("Australian Library and Information Association," https://www.alia.org.au/sites/default/files/documents/ALIA-Fact-Sheet%20September%202014.pdf [accessed 1 June 2021]). The organization has many committees aimed at health and public libraries, higher education, schools, special libraries, and other constituents. Their activities have to do with awards and outreach, research and publication, and professional support in dealing with legal issues, such as copyright. (*See* American Library Association; Canadian Library Association; Chartered Institute of Library and Information Professionals.)

ALIBRIS. One of a number of online companies selling books—and, for this site, also movies and music. Conceived of by Richard Weatherford in the early 1980s as Interloc, the company's original aim was to be a search service for booksellers. By the end of the 1990s, when the Internet was growing, the real power of online sales was being realized, and Weatherford was joined by Marty Manley to launch Alibris. "Today, Alibris is a vibrant marketplace operating in the three fastest-growing areas of the worldwide media business: online sales, textbook rentals, and used/OUT-OF-PRINT books, music, and movies. Alibris helps independent sellers find buyers through marketplace solutions and partnerships with scores of leading global media retailers, including Chapters/Indigo (Canada), and Waterstone's (UK)" (see Alibris in the bibliography). (*See* Online book sales.)

ALIGNING FIGURE. *See* Lining figure.

ALL ALONG. (Also called "all across" or "all on.") "A method of sewing a book, usually by hand and generally on cords or tapes. The thread goes 'all along,' inside the fold of the section—that is, from kettle stitch to kettle stitch of each successive section, one complete length of thread for each section. 'All along' is traditionally associated with the best method of sewing a book by hand, although books were sewn two on and even three on when the sections were very thin or when an economical method was required. The term is also used, somewhat incorrectly, to describe machine book sewing when each section is sewn with the full number of threads. Also called 'one on' and 'one sheet on'" (Roberts and Etherington, "all along"; https://cool.culturalheritage.org/don/dt/dt0082.html [accessed 27 January 2021]). Normally I would not include this in the *Dictionary*, but I just got a catalog from a bookseller in which the term was used (Bruce McKitterick, forthcoming catalog).

ALL EDGES GILT. A self-explanatory term, though I will explain it: A description of the three exposed edges of the TEXT BLOCK of a volume (HEAD, FORE-EDGE, and TAIL) usually smoothly cut and then covered in gold. (Some books have gilded rough edges; *see* Gilt; Rough gilt). Traditionally abbreviated in dealers' catalogs as "AEG," as differentiated from "TEG" (TOP EDGE GILT). There is also All edges marbled (AEM) and All edges stained (AES).

ALL PUBLISHED. Twenty years ago, I bought a volume on Mexico that contained scores of photographs. It was marked "Volume 1." I subsequently learned that a Volume 2 was never produced. In a bibliography, I could have listed Volume 1 with the note "All published." The same designation can be used for any publication that ostensibly has more volumes than were actually produced, as with a serial that lacks a volume or seems to contain a long run of issues but does not. For example, the marbling periodical *Ink & Gall* appeared in issues 1 to 4 and 6 to 9. A bibliographical record showing this could add "All published." (*See* Complete; Odd volumes.)

ALL RIGHTS RESERVED. A term that appears on many copyright pages indicating that the contents of the volume are protected by copyright. Anyone wanting to quote from the text must secure PERMISSION from the copyright holder.

ALMANAC. (Sometimes spelled with a "k" or an "h" following the "c.") "An annual publication including calendars with weather forecasts, astronomical information, tide tables, and other related tabular information" (*American Heritage Dictionary*, p. 49). Of course, this definition does not account for the centuries of such volumes with varying content, nor does it indicate anything about the physical format they have been produced in. Almanacs could contain information on sunrise and sunset times, dates of eclipses, religious festivals, and even husbandry information, along with household remedies, cookery information, and agricultural advice, among much other data. The nature of the texts of these volumes—with predictions about the weather and such—even led some producers of almanacs to include divination of fortune. The annual nature of the text led to their becoming ANNUALS, and since the information they contained became obsolete at the end of each year, they may also be seen as pieces of EPHEMERA. Hence, as ephemera, they often got fairly inexpensive bindings; most of them are in WRAPPERS, or, if in hard covers, inexpensive ones with simple or decorated paper covers. In the 18th century, for example, almanacs were issued in inexpensive but quite beautiful block-printed papers, sometimes over boards, but more often with the decorated paper the only cover. For their texts, but also merely for their bindings, they have become COLLECTIBLE. According to the *Encyclopedia of Ephemera*, "the first printed almanac was published in Vienna in 1457 and the first American almanac, *Almanack Calculated for New England*, was published in 1639 by William Pierce in Cambridge, Massachusetts" (New York State Library, *Guide to Almanac Collection*). These "reference tools" were frequently consulted, so some of them were issued with a string loop bound at the HEAD of the volume so they could be hung in a convenient place.

Collecting these publications can be a challenge. As the American Antiquarian Society website explains, "An almanac from the same (or substantially the same) setting of type frequently was issued simultaneously in multiple locations with different publishers credited on the wrappers. AAS collects these 'duplicates' because the wrappers contain local advertisements and business information not available elsewhere. Sometimes the text, advertisements, or even illustrations have been changed in the main body of the almanac. Also numerous almanacs were published anonymously or pseudonymously, but many of their calculators have been identified through close comparison with other almanacs for the same year and region" (American Antiquarian Society, *Almanacs*). Inasmuch as many people swore by their almanacs, they used them assiduously and discarded them when the next year's almanac was issued. Hence, these revered volumes could be considered ephemera.

ALPHABET BOOK. *See* ABCderium.

ALPHABET WHEEL. A teaching device, freestanding or in a volume, that is composed of a wheel that contains an alphabet attached beneath a sheet with a cut-out hole that reveals the individual letter when the wheel is turned. Or it could be made of a sheet containing an alphabet (uppercase) printed in a circle, with a wheel containing another alphabet (lowercase) attached on top of the other alphabet.

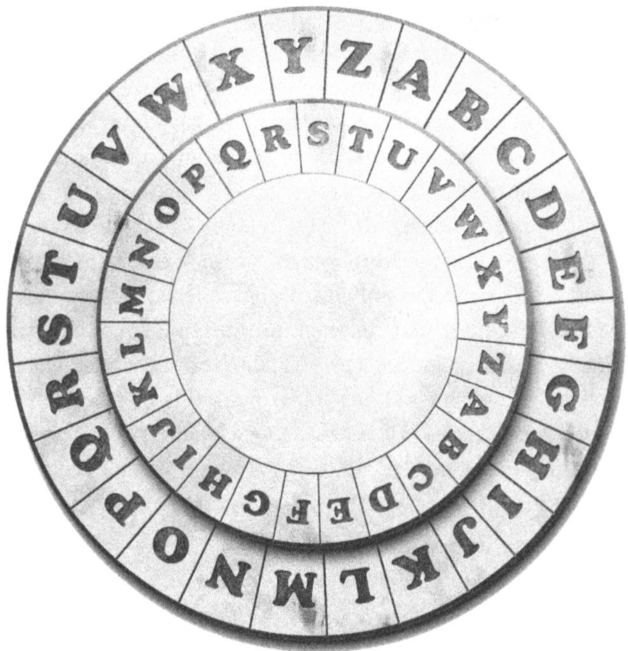

Alphabet wheel.
Getty Images, iStock.

A third kind, used to create codes or ciphers, has an alphabet in a circle, with an attached disk containing numbers. When the disk is turned to particular letters, corresponding numbers can be strung out to write a coded text.

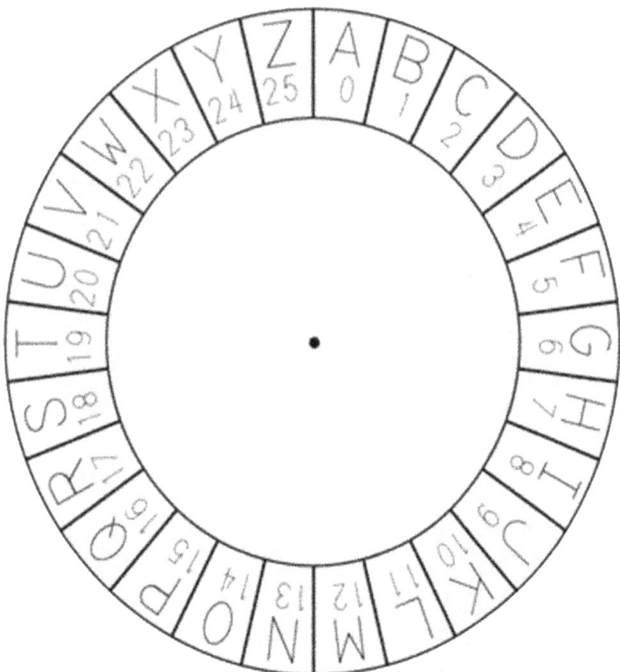

Alphabet wheel.
Abhay Kumar Prajapat, "Alphabet Wheel: Making a Paper Cipher Wheel"; Kodlogs; https://kodlogs.com/blog/618/alphabet-wheel (accessed 17 February 2021).

ALS (Autograph Letter Signed). Self-explanatory: this is a letter in the handwriting of its author, signed by said author. Certainly, such a letter is worth more than a TLS (typed letter signed), especially since a full page of an author's handwriting may be useful in authenticating the signature below the text, while the signature on a TLS needs another autograph text for verification of the signature. In either case, whether the handwriting is that of the original author still may need to be verified.

ALTERATION. A change made in a text. The term crops up often in textual editing when an editor spots a VARIANT. (*See* Bibliography.) The alteration could be AUTHORIAL, compositorial (*see* Compositor), or editorial. The alteration could be a point in an edition. (*See* Edition, Impression [Printing], Issue, and State; Points.)

ALTERED BOOK. "A book is considered *altered* where a straightforward binding or TEXT BLOCK has been altered with additions or subtractions of material. Although altered books are usually associated with modern book art, examples exist from the nineteenth century and earlier" (Julia Miller, *Books Will Speak Plain*, p. 413). What Miller refers to as "modern book art" is a whole world of artists who take books (old, new, in perfect or terrible condition, illustrated or not) and transform them into works of "art" in a variety of ways. Sometimes leaves are folded so that the book looks like a cathedral about to take flight, sometimes the text block is carved away in architectural or human or animal forms, sometimes the text is altered with markers or highlighters to change the text (a book on censorship might have 99 percent of its printed text blacked out), and all kinds of other alterations can be done, with TIP-INS and scissors and sharp blades and glue, metal brads, clips, zippers, drills, rubber stamps, bolts, saws, hammers, flames, glue, paints, strings, and anything else the artist uses or does to change the original volume into something no one ever thought it would become. A final "altered book" could be an amalgam of more than one volume or a fraction of the original.

The final product is a work of art (or of "art"—not all of them are artistic), and many of them command luxury prices. One hopes that the original volume is not the last exemplar of its title. Some books are so transformed that they become sculptures and lose the status of "book," and while such BIBLIOCLASM is abhorred by purists, the practice will continue as long as there is a market for the altered volumes, as long as artists (or "artists") can make a profit from them, and as long as artists view a book as a medium. (*See* Book safe.)

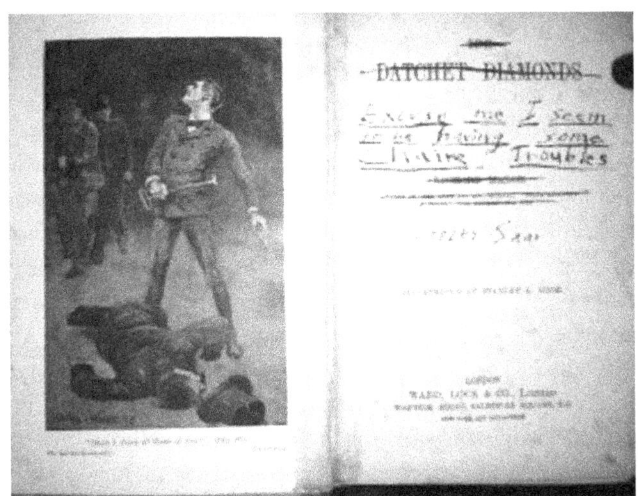

Altered book. Original text: Richard Marsh (Richard Bernard Heldmann), *The Datchet Diamonds* (London: Ward, Lock & Co., 1899); new text: Lezley Saar, *Excuse Me I Seem to Be Having Some Chair Troubles* (N.p.: n.p., 1984).

Courtesy of artist Lezley Saar. Collection of the author.

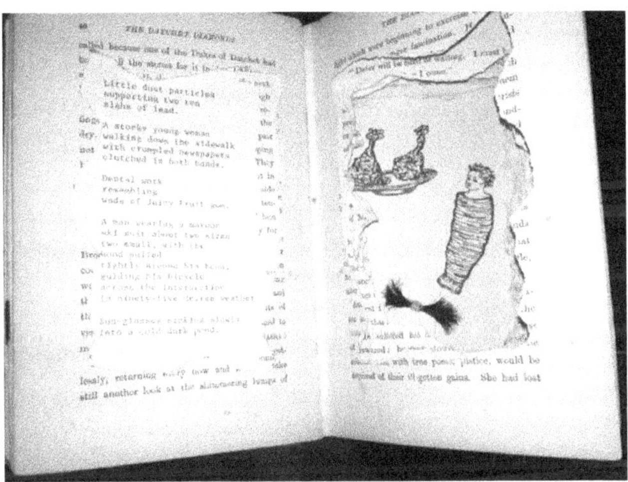

Altered book (*see* previous figure).

Courtesy of Lezley Saar.

ALUM ROSIN SIZE. "A type of . . . size for paper containing a rosin-alum mixture. Starting in the 1820s, aluminum sulfate, or papermakers alum, was added to rosin size causing it to flocculate to the cellulosic fibers in the pulp solution. However, residual alum in the paper produces an acidic environment that accelerates the degradation of paper" ("Alum rosin size," at Museum of Fine Arts, Boston; http://cameo.mfa.org/wiki/Alum_rosin_size [accessed 1 June 2021]). Alum in small amounts was not a problem, as one can see with MARBLED PAPER, on which alum is used as a mordant. Although most paper in the first half of the 19th century was made from rags, themselves with no INHERENT VICE (except for bleach), the alum rosin SIZING introduced acid into the papermaking process and could be the cause of the deterioration of some papers made in an era from which one would not have expected paper to deteriorate. (To flocculate is "to cause [individual particles of clay] to aggregate into clotlike masses or precipitate into small lumps"; *American Heritage Dictionary of the English Language*, p. 673.)

Roberts and Etherington explain, "The papermaker's alum in use today is not true alum, but either aluminum sulfate ($Al_2 (SO_4)_3 \cdot 14H_2O$), ($Al_2(SO_4)_3 \cdot 18H_2O$), or a mixture of these hydrates, and is manufactured by treating pulverized bauxite with sulfuric acid. It is soluble in water, and, while slightly alkaline in the dry form, it is decidedly acidic when dissolved in water. Alum has two major functions in papermaking: 1) to control pH; and 2) because of its floculating [*sic*] ability, to retain other additives in the paper, notably the sizing agent. / Rosin is a basic material used in sizing paper today. As a sizing agent it imparts water (ink) resistance to paper; however, in order for the rosin to be able to impart water resistance it must be rendered insoluble, which is the function of alum. / Although the excessive use of alum is considered detrimental to the permanence of paper, the papermaker tends to overdose with alum rather than underdose, so as to avoid soft-sizing. In addition, alum is considered by some papermakers to be a panacea for other troubles, such as frothing, sticking of the paper web to the wet presses of the papermaking machine, etc. Overdosing with alum leads to excessive acidity and, under certain circumstances, may lead to severe deterioration of the paper. While alum is not a particularly strong acid, in the presence of certain other substances it can assume a greater strength. Chlorides, which may be present in the paper as a result of bleaching processes, or natural to the water itself, can be particularly harmful" (p. 9).

In the history of papermaking, we often hear of the effects of alum rosin size, which solves some problems and introduces others, the primary one of which is acidity, which has led to deterioration of many 19th- and 20th-century books and papers.

ALUM TAWING. *See* Tawing.

AMATE/AMATL (both spellings are acceptable, the former the preferred one). Mexican bark paper, made from the pounded inner bark of a ficus tree. Since the fibers are not macerated—they are simply pounded into the shape of a leaf—the final product is not strictly paper despite its being called "bark paper." It is used for leaves of books and sometimes for bindings. Aztec and Maya codices were made from amate. Today amate is produced in Mexico for the tourist trade. It is made the same way it was made centuries ago, before Columbus came and brought "civilization" to the Aztecs—hence wiping them out as well as he could, taking their gold, and burning thousands of their books. (See Amith, *La Tradición del Amate*; Cristensen and Marti, *Brujerías*; Lenz, *Mexican Indian Paper*; Sandstrom and Sandstrom, *Traditional Papermaking and Paper Cult Figures of Mexico*; and von Hagen, *The Aztec and Maya Papermakers*.)

AMAZON. Well, who does not know about Amazon? Perhaps the largest "bookstore" in the universe. Started by Jeff Bezos in 1994 as a purveyor of books, the company has become a marketplace for untold numbers of products and services. Today, Amazon sells books by the millions—for all publishers and those self-published, and as an agent for bookstores and other purveyors of new and used books. The controversies they have engendered with respect to their pricing policies and competition with brick-and-mortar stores seem constant. But one thing is for sure: they are making books available by the millions at competitive prices and with efficient delivery services. Their competitive pricing has purportedly caused the closure of many independent booksellers. While a fat book could be written about Amazon and books, it suffices to mention them here since they are deeply embedded in the world of the book—the commodity that got the company started in the first place. (*See* Online book sales.)

AMERICANA. Printed, manuscript, or illustrative materials pertaining to or created in America—strictly the United States but more generally any of the Americas. Also, such materials pertaining to Americans. Carter says that items can fall under the rubric "Americana" for various reasons. He says that the Columbus Letter is about the discovery of what is now known as America, so it fits under the rubric "Americana." The first book printed in the colonies, the *Bay Psalm Book*, is likewise "Americana," as is Thomas Paine's *Common Sense* because of the influence it had on the American Revolution. Literary works (like poems and novels) written in the United States, however, that are not specifically about America are not pieces of Americana. And works like *Huckleberry Finn* or Thoreau's *Walden* could border on being Americana since they describe American topography and inhabitants (see Carter, pp. 29–30). Carter also considers Latin Americana and works for Canada, Mexico, and Central and South America. The suffix "-ana" (*see* Ana) means a compilation of items, and in its generic use it could be any kind of items. Hence, trade cards and product labels, business cards, and other kinds of advertising pieces from American companies may well be termed "Americana," and considerable collections of these exist in research libraries.

William S. Reese distinguishes between two types of Americana: "Americana easily divides into two major classes: European accounts, and issues of the press in the New World. The latter class also rightfully includes works by American authors, wherever printed. These two divisions could be labeled 'exterior' and 'interior' Americana. The European accounts, especially the earliest voyages, are descriptive and comparative, and deal directly with America. Interior accounts are Americana by virtue of where they came into being" (Reese, *Winnowers of the Past*, pp. 7–8). He adds, "The productions of the New World press and the writings of New World authors contain a sense of the American spirit of place, as D. H. Lawrence called it, which the exterior narratives could not completely capture" (p. 8). Joel Silver observes, "Some sources, such as SABIN, include both types, but others, such as European Americana, only include exterior Americana" (personal communication, 13 October 2015). (For Sabin, see Joseph Sabin in the bibliography. For *European Americana*, see Alden and Landis, eds., in the bibliography.)

AMERICAN ANTIQUARIAN SOCIETY. A research library in Worcester, Massachusetts, founded in 1812 by Isaiah Thomas, a printer who moved his press away from Boston to protect himself from the invading British. It is noted for having the world's greatest collection of American imprints from the earliest days of printing in the colonies through its cutoff date of 1876 (the date arbitrarily chosen because it was the centennial of the country).

AMERICAN BOOKBINDERS MUSEUM. A museum in San Francisco, California, whose aim is to preserve and promote "the art and history of bookbinding." Its mission is to "tell the story of the book, presenting the art of western bookbinding as a hand process through early mechanization, promoting a deeper understanding of the impact of book production on the American experience" (American Bookbinders Museum; https://bookbindersmuseum.org/about-us/ [accessed 28 May 2022]).

***AMERICAN BOOK PRICES CURRENT* AND *BOOK AUCTION RECORDS*.** Before computers, for AUCTION prices, *American Book Prices Current* (*ABPC*) and *Book Auction Records* (*BAR*) for auctions in the United States and Great Britain, respectively, were essential tools. They listed all items that sold at auction for the preceding year at the major (and some of the lesser) auction houses. The information was published in a large, thick volume once a year, and libraries had shelves of these important pricing tools. These were mentioned in chapter 2 (Berger) in the discussion of books to keep in the rare book department despite the fact that many people from the general public wanted to have access to the volumes whenever the library was open. Today, these tools are published digitally. The website for *ABPC* says,

> American Book Prices Current is an annual record of books, manuscripts, autographs, maps and broadsides sold at auction. Regions covered include North America and the UK, with sales from such other countries as Switzerland, Germany, Monaco, the Netherlands, Australia and France. ABPC is not just a transcribed record of titles and prices, copied unquestioningly from the season's auction catalogues. ABPC is the standard tool used by dealers, appraisers, auction houses, scholars and tax authorities. It is, moreover, the only work in English in which each listing of printed material has been checked as to title, format, date of publication, edition, and limitation. Sales of autographs and manuscripts are reported in a separate database. For these reasons, ABPC is an essential tool for buying, selling and evaluating books, serials, autographs, manuscripts, broadsides, maps and documents, based on actual figures realized at auction. (http://www.bookpricescurrent.com/?AspxAutoDetectCookieSupport=1; no italics used in this passage [accessed 1 June 2021])

Another paragraph from this website explains other "shortcomings" of *ABPC*: "In keeping with previous editorial policy, auction lots consisting of groupings of miscellaneous volumes are not listed, for the prices realized by such lots can give no accurate indication of the value of individual items. Similarly, listings of badly broken runs or seriously incomplete sets of printed books do not appear. Listings of books in non-Western languages realizing less than $100 have been selectively excluded, as have peripheral works such as panoramas. Items which are sold by auction houses as 'a collection of plates' or which are deemed to be bound prints rather than books, are excluded from these pages. *Listings of books after 1900 frequently appear without format or binding information* [emphasis added]. In such instances it may be assumed that these books are octavo or duodecimo and bound in cloth or boards." Since a great number of 20th-century books are listed, a good portion of this database is fairly light on information. The editors themselves recognize their imperfections: "As to effort and diligence, we try like mad to get it all correct, but as we are human beings and imperfect, we do not accept legal responsibility for the information in our databases. Having said that for the benefit of our lawyers, let us reiterate that we want to do as excellent a job as we possibly can."

The database is available on DVD, on a thumb drive, and online. It is loaded with information, as this blurb indicates. (*See also Book Auction Records.*)

On September 30, 2022, Abigail Leab Martin of *ABPC* sent out an email announcing that as of December 2022 they were ceasing all operations. It looks as if ONLINE BOOK SALES, with its hundreds of millions of items for sale, have become the main guide for pricing and reduced *ABPC*'s customer base.

AMERICAN BOOKSELLERS ASSOCIATION. Not to be confused with the ABAA (the Antiquarian Booksellers' Association of America), this organization deals primarily with the distribution of new books through independent bookstores. Their website says, "Founded in 1900, the American Booksellers Association is a national not-for-profit trade organization that works to help independently owned bookstores grow and succeed. ABA's core members are key participants in their communities' local economy and culture, and to assist them ABA provides education, information dissemination, business products, and services; creates relevant programs; and engages in public policy, industry, and local first advocacy. A volunteer board of 13 booksellers governs the Association. Member booksellers also serve on the ABA Diversity, Equity & Inclusion Committee (DEIC) in support of ABA's commitment to anti-white supremacy, antiracism, representation, equity, and dignity for all Peoples. ABA is headquartered in White Plains, NY. / Certain programs and benefits available to ABA members are managed and administered by Booksellers Order Services, Inc. (BOS), a for-profit holding company owned by the American Booksellers Association. BOS operates two subsidiary companies: Book Sense, Inc. and LIBRIS Indemnity Company, which manages a portfolio of business insurance policies for bookstores. Book Sense, Inc. administers the IndieCommerce program; efforts regarding publisher-sponsored promotions for independent bookstores; the Indie Next List program; and the Advance Access program" (American Booksellers Association; "Who We Are," https://www.bookweb.org/about-aba [accessed 28 August 2022]).

AMERICAN IMPRINTS (*AI*). *See* Charles Evans.

AMERICAN INCUNABULA. *See* Incunabula.

AMERICAN LIBRARY ASSOCIATION. In the United States, the professional organization for librarians and anyone else who joins (students, booksellers, or private parties). Its own statement says, "The American Library Association (ALA) is the oldest and largest library association in the world, providing association information, news, events, and advocacy resources for members, librarians, and library users. / Founded on October 6, 1876 during the Centennial Exposition in Philadelphia, the mission of ALA is to provide leadership for the development, promotion, and improvement of library and information services and the profession of librarianship in order to enhance learning and ensure access to information for all" (http://www.ala.org/aboutala [accessed 1 June 2021]). Despite the not-perfectly grammatical prose, this statement describes the ALA succinctly. (*See* Australian Library and Information Association; Canadian Federation of Library Associations; Canadian Library Association; Chartered Institute of Library and Information Professionals.)

AMERICAN TYPE FOUNDERS (ATF). A company formed with the merger of 23 type foundries in 1892. It was the premier supplier of printing types to those in the industry and to fine and hobby printers in the United States. The origin of the merger was much influenced by the emergence of Linotype as well as the problems engendered by competition among the major foundries, with prices being driven down by this competition. Under the leadership of Robert Wickham Nelson (beginning in 1894 when Nelson took over the helm), ATF began to prosper, and with new ties to the advertising industry, standardization in the production of types, new typefaces being offered to their customers, and the introduction of a new product, the Kelly Press (a "fast automatic flatbed cylinder press" named after its inventor, William M. Kelley), the founders expanded their business (information taken from David Pankow, "The Rise and Fall of ATF").

The company excelled in the 1920s, "[w]ith sales branches in twenty-seven different American cities and one in Vancouver, B.C." (Pankow, p. 8). It produced 60,000 copies of its magnificent 1923 catalog (*Specimen Book and Catalogue, 1923* [Jersey City, NJ: American Type Founders, 1923]; this was a huge affair at 1,148 pages and is one of the most recognizable and sought-after type specimen books—a tour de force of printing; *see* Type specimen book), and it added a wide range of printer's supplies and equipment to its product lines, producing strong sales (though they may have overextended themselves). The rest of the story of the rise and fall of ATF is detailed in the Pankow article referenced above.

The company was in competition with the Lanston Monotype Corporation and the Mergenthaler Linotype company, but their products, foundry type, were of extremely high quality (harder than the metals used by their competitors) and are still sought after by fine-press printers today. The company lasted long enough to be part of a revolution in printing in which photocomposition and digital composition were part of their operations. The company went bankrupt in 1993 when its bankruptcy led to an auction (on 23 August 1993) that completely eviscerated the firm. Almost all of its hundreds of thousands of irreplaceable matrices and great quantities of machines went to scrap.

I followed the demise of ATF, right down to the auction, which caused many a grown man to cry. Thousands of matrices were lost forever, their metal being melted down for other purposes. Pankow says of the sale, "The forced sale value of the American Type Founders Company was estimated at approximately $149,000. The gross receipts from the bankruptcy auction totaled about $78,000. Subtracting all expenses, the total net proceeds amounted to $26,000, a far cry from the $20,000,000 value once placed on the matrix collection alone, and an ignoble finale for the company" (p. 14). An organization also called ATF (American Typecasting Fellowship) emerged from the tears, a group of dedicated type people carrying on some of the old traditions. They are commemorated in the Henry Morris Bird & Bull book *So Long, Hot-Metal Men* (see bibliography under Henricus de Nova Villa) and in the volume edited by Richard L. Hopkins, *The Private Typecasters* (see bibliography). (Note that the Pankow article appears in *Printing History* 43/44 [22, nos. 1 and 2], the issue devoted entirely to the ATF.)

AMIGOS LIBRARY SERVICES, INC. *See* Regional Alliance for Preservation.

AMPERSAND. From the Latin "and per se and" (i.e., "and" by itself, meaning "and"). The figure "&"—designed with many shapes—often looks like the Latin word *et* (meaning "and"), with a capital "E" and a small "t" hooked onto the lower swash stroke of the "E," presumably where the figure came from.

Ampersands.

Courtesy of Dennis Howlett, Diginomica; http://diginomica.com/2015/05/14/citrix-synergy-selling-the-ampersand-not-the-silos/#.VeJotJeYE20 (accessed 11 July 2021).

ANA. In one of its early senses, "ana" denotes a gathering of sayings, tales, chat, table talk, narratives, and so on. But in its more common sense today, "-ana" (almost always tacked on as a suffix) means items on a single subject. Hence, all you need to do is take a subject and tack on the suffix "-ana," and you have a designation of a genre of materials related to whatever that subject is. As above, "Americana" is material related to America. "Twainiana" is material related to Mark Twain (Samuel Langhorne Clemens). The term designates various materials relating to a single (though possibly broad) subject area; that is, any kind of research items in any genre that fall under one topic; for example, Shakespeariana, Maritimeana, and so on. Some words that designate topics of a collecting area do not lend themselves comfortably to the suffix. Carter shows this with words like "Shaviana" (for works related to or by George Bernard Shaw), and "Hardyana" (for Thomas Hardy), the latter of which Carter calls "repugnant to Latinity" (p. 30). Scholars and booksellers often tack this word onto others as a suffix: "Catalog of Shoeana." It may be barbaric or awkward, but it is a shorthand that has become a recognizable and understandable staple in the book person's vocabulary.

ANALECTS. A collection of written passages by a single author or by various authors. Similar to a COMMONPLACE BOOK.

ANAMORPHOSCOPE. A printed, drawn, or painted image that looks distorted unless it is observed from a special device. In the book world, the device is often a circular tube with a mirror on its outer surface. The distorted image lies flat on a surface, and a circular mirror is placed vertically beside it. The image is "perfect-reading" in the mirror. The Merriam-Webster online dictionary says that an anamorphoscope is "an optical device consisting usually of a cylindrical mirror or lens that restores to its normal proportions an image distorted by anamorphosis" (Merriam-Webster online dictionary, "Anamorphoscope"; https://www.merriam-webster.com/dictionary/anamorphoscope [accessed 3

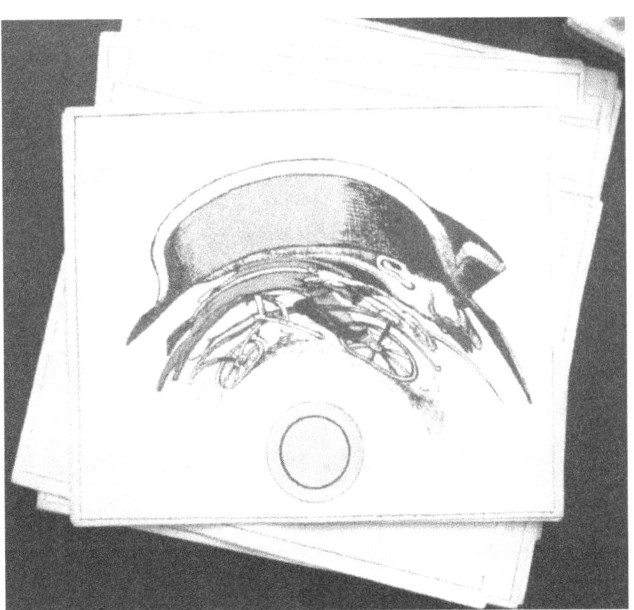

An anamorphic plate from Henri Télory (ill.), *Les Anamorphoses*, [Paris?]: Jullien editeur, c. 1868, with the circle printed on it to indicate where the mirror is to be placed.

Courtesy of Christelle Gonzalo, Librairie sur le fil de Paris—Livres et documents anciens.

Leaf from the anamorphoscope; see caption for previous figure.

Courtesy of Christelle Gonzalo.

March 2021]). At an online book fair (3 March 2021), the bookseller Sur le fil de Paris (Christelle Gonzalo) offered the following: Henri Télory (ill.), *Les Anamorphoses*, ([Paris?]: Jullien editeur, c. 1868 [the Getty catalog gives {185–?}]), with 24 CHROMOLITHOGRAPHED plates, all distorted such that they needed the tubular mirror to be seen correctly.

In 2007, Foolscap Press published Ursula Le Guin's story *Direction of the Road* (see her entry in the bibliography) with a woodcut by Aaron Johnson that is an anamorphoscopic image. (See Schuyt and Elffers, *Anamorphoses: Games of Perception and Illusion in Art.*)

ANATOMICAL ATLAS. A volume showing human anatomy (or the anatomy of other living creatures). A web search also reveals that the term can be used for charts (like BROADSIDES) that serve the same function. These have been produced for centuries. "The History of Medicine Division of the National Library of Medicine has a rich collection of illustrated anatomical atlases dating from the 15th to the 20th century" (National Library of Medicine, "Historical Anatomies on the Web"). Many of them are FLAP BOOKS, and they are generally illustrated with WOODCUTS.

ANGLE-BRACKET QUOTATION MARKS. *See* Guillemets.

ANGLO-AMERICAN CATALOGUING RULES. (Abbreviated AACR, AACR2 [the second edition]; and AACR2R [the second edition revised].) The longstanding international set of rules for cataloging library materials, "used for descriptive cataloging of various types of information resources by libraries in the United States, Great Britain, Canada, and Australia as well as in many other countries. It was first developed in

1967 and updated regularly until 2005" (see bibliography under Librarianship Studies & Information Technology, *Anglo-American Cataloguing Rules [AACR, AACR2, AACR2R]*). These general rules were designed to be used by all libraries, regardless of size, and they could be adapted to the most general public library collections as well as the needs of the most sophisticated and extensive rare book collections. "The rules cover the standard description of areas like, the title, publisher, edition, series, etc., as well as the provision of choice and form of access points (headings) for all materials which a library may hold or to which it may have access, including books, serials, cartographic materials, electronic resources, etc. AACR also provides rules for the formulation of standard forms of names and titles to provide access to and grouping of those descriptions. AACR2 standardized cataloging and ensured consistency within the catalog and between the catalogs of libraries using the same code in describing the physical attributes of library materials identically. AACR marked a shift from the previous cataloging rules, which were criticized for being too detailed, complex, and mere compilations of rules to handle specific bibliographic cases. Anglo-American Cataloguing Rules are considered as the most important advances in English-language codes for descriptive cataloging during the twentieth century." Because this cataloging code tried to cover a huge range of information, and because it took a good deal of training to use, it was seen as too unwieldy for most libraries and for those charged with creating MARC RECORDS using the rules.

In recent years this system of cataloging has begun being replaced in many libraries with RDA (*see under* MARC records). In consulting with one of the world's foremost professors on library cataloging, Daniel Joudrey, I have recently received this message: "AACR2 was replaced by RDA in 2013. Although not everyone switched over immediately, it has not been updated since 2010 and I would guess that very few libraries are still using it. Figures on usage, however, are nonexistent as far as I know. / Now, RDA, which was based on FRBR [Functional Requirements for Bibliographic Records], is being replaced. In 2020, 'new RDA' was released. It is based on a new conceptual model—IFLA's LRM (Library Reference Model)—which is a harmonization of the three FR models: FRBR, FRAD [Functional Requirements for Authority Data], and FRSAD [Functional Requirements for Subject Authority Data]. The new RDA is not being used yet, so most folks are continuing to use what's now unhelpfully being called 'Original RDA.' New RDA, when it goes into effect, will no longer contain rules, only suggestions. Every choice will be a right answer. This is where things stand right now" (Daniel Joudrey, private communication, 13 July 2021).

As the note at the end of the entry for "MARC records" indicates, this kind of information will, in one way or another, impact the lives of all in the book world who seek bibliographic information.

ANIME. The Japanese term "anime" denotes any kind of animation from anywhere in the world. In English-speaking countries, it refers to a particular kind of animation that originates in Japan. (See Lesley Aeschliman, "What Is Anime?"; http://www.bellaonline.com/articles/art4260.asp [accessed 22 March 2015]). Although the term comes from the word "animation," it has spawned a large field of published books and COMIC BOOKS with characters drawn from the original animated works (the closely related genre that is clearly print oriented: MANGA). Many of the characters have large eyes and exaggerated facial expressions, or else they are characters that are non-human or part human, part other animal. Hence, the characters are spirits, robots, various kinds of animals, or demons. (*See* Aeschliman).

The popularity of this genre has led to a large collecting craze of materials in digital form, especially among young people, but also with adults, and collections of these "films" and "videos" are now in academic library special collections as part of cultural heritage and popular culture holdings. This genre may be seen as a subgenre of GRAPHIC NOVELS; the roots of anime are in animation, and those of graphic novels are not.

ANNONAY PAPER. (Also called by its French name, Papier d'Annonay.) A speckled paper (*see* Scratting) commonly

Notebook covered in Annonay paper.
Photo by the author.

used over notebooks and ledgers. In fact, millions of such notebooks have graced the desks and backpacks of school students for centuries. The pattern is splattered over the sheet and let dry. "It is named after a town in France, which is famed for it's [*sic*] paper manufacture. These papers were a popular and decent substitute for the more expensive marbled papers for bookbindings & other uses. Indeed, so popular are these papers, that they are still used today. However, unlike the originals, which were made by speckling paper with paint, these examples tend to be printed." (*See* Decorated Paper in bibliography.) In describing bindings, booksellers need a specific term for this tremendously common decorated paper. Now they have it. (Another term sometimes used is "German marble" paper, something of a misnomer since, strictly speaking, this is not MARBLING since the pattern is not created on a bath and picked up by a sheet of paper; it is formed directly onto the sheet. See Miura, *The Art of Marbled Paper*, p. 134.)

ANNUALS. (Also called "gift books" or "keepsakes.") Any series of works (usually printed) that are issued once each year. If a title comes out, say, in 1850 and then again in 1851 (with the same title and from the same publisher), but not again, one would be hard-pressed to call it an annual. How many issues does one need—that is, over how many years—for them to be considered annuals? There is no set number, but two or three, or even four, years would probably not qualify.

Carter distinguishes two types: 1) literary anthologies, containing essays, short fiction, and poetry, and sometimes longer works. They were often illustrated, sometimes extensively, like those that were issued in the 19th century under such titles as *The Keepsake*, *The Talisman*, *Magnolia*, *Friendship's Offering*, or *The Literary Souvenir* (to these one might add *The Opal*, *The Gift*, *The Liberty Bell* [published by abolitionists], *National Temperance Offering*, and several others). And they were given fancy, if not extravagant, bindings, sometimes in full (but cheap) leather, gold stamped, and with gilt edges, and later in attractive publisher's cloth. They were often intended to be gifts; hence the alternate designation "gift books." And since they were year-end gifts, they were often published in the fall. 2) Christmas annuals, with much the same kind of content as type 1, but usually with a holiday emphasis. Rudolph Ackermann, in England, published perhaps the first of these, in 1822: *Forget-Me-Not: A Christmas and New Years Present for 1823*. Other titles include *The Mistletoe Bough*, *The Garland, or Token of Friendship*, *The Token: A Christmas and New Years Present*, and *Beeton's Christmas Annual*. As perfect presents for the youth of their day (though also meant for other family members and lovers), they were usually educational and morally uplifting. Their popularity waned by the last quarter of the 19th century, and scholars think of the golden age of these as from 1822 to about 1850 or slightly later.

As some of these titles indicate, while most were created by commercial publishers, some came from religious, philanthropic, or social organizations. Some published the work of important authors, and those volumes could be seriously collectible. *The Keepsake for 1829* (London: Hurst, Chance, & Co., 1828) contained the first printing of two stories by Mary Shelley ("The Sisters of Albano" and "Fernando Eboli"). Most showcased sentimental verse, or prose of second- or third-tier writers, and they are collectible today mostly for their bindings. As Simon Cooke notes, "the books' most striking characteristic was their elaborate bindings. Described by Edmund King in his encyclopaedic *Victorian Decorated Trade Bindings* (2003), these outer casings are emblematic products of mid-Victorian culture. Typified by coloured cloth, embossed surfaces and elaborate gilt and polychromatic paper overlays, the bindings are fascinating examples of the intersection between bourgeois taste, the visual encoding of the values of Christmas, and industrial production." Unfortunately, as noted above, the items at their issue were far more beautiful than well made, and to find ones in good condition today is difficult.

The term "annual" could also be applied as a simple adjective ("an annual publication") or a noun ("they published an annual") to any publication that comes out once a year. In the book world, among many others, a few sterling examples stand out: *The* PENROSE ANNUAL, GUTENBERG JAHRBUCH, and *MATRIX*. (*See* Almanacs.) (See Ball, *Victorian Publishers' Bindings*, Cooke, "Book Bindings of the 1860s: The Christmas Gift Book"; and Mulder, "A Token of My Affection.")

ANONYMOUS. As Carter points out, there are two kinds of anonymity for authors of books and other texts: books whose authors are known though their names do not appear on their publications and books with no known author. There are also books published under pseudonyms, like those of Lewis Carroll (real name Charles Lutwidge Dodgson), the books of George Sand (pseudonym for Amantine-Lucile-Aurore Dupin), Currer Bell (Charlotte Brontë), Mark Twain (Samuel Langhorne Clemens), and Artemis Ward (born Charles Farrar Browne). Sometimes, rather than using a name, the title pages might say "by A Gentlewoman" or "by A Lady." Actors, politicians, sports figures, and many others have taken on pseudonyms, and untold numbers of books and pamphlets and other publications exist with no known author.

A good place to look for the names of authors of anonymous works is Halkett and Laing (*see* the entry for these writers, who published under their own names). Of course, the Internet is another excellent place a researcher should go to to learn the names of the authors of most anonymous works, though Halkett and Laing is still a superb resource.

In a related legal issue in the United States, books with no known copyright holder are called "ORPHAN WORKS."

ANOPISTHOGRAPHIC. *See* Block book.

ANTHROPODERMIC BIBLIOPEGY. Bookbinding using human skin. In recent days there have been several occurrences of publications mentioning this most unusual kind of binding. Writers love to show their brilliance by using this sesquipedalian phrase to talk—almost as a euphemism—about this titillating topic. Many a library has a cataloged example of such books, but as one website has pointed out, many such attributions are suspect at best, outright wrong at worst. At the Anthropodermic Book Project site, researchers point out that many of the books claimed to have been bound in human skin were not. (See the Anthropodermic Book Project in the bibliography; Rosenbloom, *Dark Archives*.)

ANTHROPOMORPHIC BORDERS. *See* Borders.

ANTHROPOMORPHIC INITIAL. An initial containing an image of a human being—often stylized and not necessarily showing a full person. Michelle Brown says, "Anthropomorphic motifs occur in [many] decorative contexts" (*Understanding Illuminated Manuscripts*, p. 11).

ANTIPHONAL LEAF. This item deserves an entry of its own since these objects seem to appear regularly in book fairs. Antiphonals, or antiphonies, are bound volumes containing the responsive musical part of the divine office, taking their words from the psalms, and usually sung by a choir or by the religious figures of the monastery or nunnery. The J. Paul Getty Museum website explains: "Antiphonals contain all of the chants sung by choirs of monks or nuns during the divine office (the cycle of prayers said at specific hours throughout the day). In the most luxurious examples, each chant in an antiphonal begins with a large decorative letter that acts as a bookmark for the singers" (J. Paul Getty Museum, "Three Leaves from an Antiphonal"; http://www.getty.edu/art/collection/objects/225494/circle-of-the-master-of-the-golden-bull-three-leaves-from-an-antiphonal-bohemian-about-1405/ [accessed 23 April 2021]). Since the ILLUMINATED majuscules of many of these manuscripts are quite beautiful, they were often sliced out of their volumes and sold individually, usually framed. These volumes had to be large enough for those reading them to see them from afar, so the leaves of the books were usually quite large. Their manuscript nature made them unique, and the large pages left much room for decoration, within the text, at the MAJUSCULES, and in the MARGINS. The decoration, along with the shaped notes and calligraphic texts, and the exoticism of having a text on vellum, made them ripe for being seen as art, not as part of devotional texts. This prompted BREAKERS to sell off individual leaves and parts of leaves, and thousands of them are floating around the rare book world matted and framed or not, and at fairly hefty prices, depending on how attractive they are and the condition they are in. Even those from the world of printing can command hefty prices because they are often printed in red and black, adding to their allure.

ANTIQUARIAN BOOKMAN/BOOKMAN'S WEEKLY. *See AB/BW* (the way it was generally referred to in the profession).

ANTIQUARIAN BOOKS / ANTIQUARIAN BOOKSELLER. A loose term used to designate old (and, by implication, valuable) books. One old definition of "antique" was 100 years old or older, but a search through an antiquarian bookshop will yield great numbers of books younger than that. As Carter says, "The lines of demarcation between 'rare books,' 'old books' and 'second-hand books' have never been, and can never be, clearly defined" (p. 31). He points out that an antiquarian bookseller can deal with books old and new and in any collecting area. At what point does a BOOK SCOUT become a "used-book dealer"? and a used-book dealer become an "antiquarian bookseller"? Is it determined by the quality of her stock, the average age of the items on her shelves, the prices she charges, the professional organizations she belongs to, her parents from whom she inherited the business, or a combination of these? or something else? Despite the lack of specificity in the definition of the term, the word itself seems to carry a bit of magic, and when a bookseller describes a volume as "antiquarian," one can assume its price will be higher than that of the same book described by another bookseller as "old" or "used." Similarly, books in "antiquarian bookshops" tend to be more "valuable" than those in "used-book stores." And one can be reasonably sure that when one hears "antiquarian bookseller," the adjective refers to the books.

ANTIQUARIAN BOOKSELLERS' ASSOCIATION. *See* ABA; ABAA.

ANTIQUARIAN BOOKSELLERS' ASSOCIATION OF AMERICA. *See* ABAA.

ANTIQUE. A word used to describe bindings. Carter says that this word for bookbindings has a specific meaning but a meaning that can be misrepresentative; that is, books that have been rebound fairly recently but in the style of a period more contemporary to the book's original publication.

He recommends as more accurate, "old-style calf" or "half calf, period style" (p. 32). While this term was much more in use in Carter's day than it is today, it does on rare occasion appear in today's booksellers' catalogs. Booksellers who use it, however, may be impressed by how old a binding is (or looks) and may use the word "antique" to justify an enhanced valuation. Most of their customers will be more impressed by the *notion* of "antique" than by the term's original use. (*See* Antiquarian.)

ANTIQUE LAID PAPER. Paper made on a hand mold that has a single layer of wires drawn across it, the wires sewn to the supports under them by chain stitches. During COUCHING onto a felt (couching is the transfer of the sheet from the mold to the felt), the pressure exerted by the supports under the chain stitches compacts the fibers in the sheet more than the fibers are compacted between the supports, making the paper a bit more dense where the chain stitches are. It is possible, also, that more fibers will have gathered at the point of the supports than between them, so the paper would have more fibers there to give it a small amount of extra thickness, adding to the shadow look when the sheet is held up to the light. This density and thickness reduces light's ability to shine through the sheet as brightly as where the fibers in the sheet are not so compressed, yielding what looks like a shadow around the chain lines. Laid paper has "LAID LINES"—composed of WIRE LINES and CHAIN LINES; with antique laid paper, there is a shadow surrounding the chain lines, and the sheet is designated "antique laid paper." (For images of antique laid paper, *see* Laid paper; Vatman's tear; *see also* Chain lines; Dandy roll; Fourdrinier; Laid lines; Modern laid paper; Wire lines.)

ANTI-SETOFF PAPERS. *See* Offset sheets.

ANZAAB (Australian and New Zealand Association of Antiquarian Booksellers). *See* ABAA.

APA STYLE. In the world of publishing—especially in the realms of science and the social sciences—the American Psychological Association has published one of the most used STYLE MANUALS: *Publication Manual of the American Psychological Association*, now in its seventh edition. The APA website says about this manual: "it is the style manual of choice for writers, researchers, editors, students, and educators in the social and behavioral sciences, natural sciences, nursing, communications, education, business, engineering, and other fields" (https://apastyle.apa.org/products/publication-manual-7th-edition [accessed 1 February 2021]).

Scholars in the sciences are particularly interested in up-to-date information, so the bibliographical entries in this style give a date immediately after the author's name. But it also does some things that scholars in the humanities may find irritating or illogical. In bibliographies it makes sense to have last names first in alphabetical lists, but the APA style puts last name first in FOOTNOTES. Further, APA style requires authors to be identified by their last names and the initials of their first names. No first names are given in notes or references. Where is the logic in that? And the use of the *Chicago Manual* is best suited to the bookselling world where the first name of authors is crucial.

APOCRYPHAL. A term used for any work which is of doubtful authorship. The Hitler Diaries were called apocryphal since there was no way to authenticate their authorship. (See McGrane, "Diary of the Hitler Diary Hoax.")

APPARATUS. *See* Critical apparatus.

APPENDIX. (Plural is appendixes or appendices.) A section or a table in the ENDMATTER of a volume that contains supplemental information that would not fit comfortably into the main text but is germane to the text in a variety of ways. R. M. Ritter says that it could consist of "chronologies, genealogical tables, survey questionnaires, or texts of documents, laws, or correspondence discussed in the text" (Ritter, *The Oxford Guide to Style*, p. 20). A volume could have no appendices or several. The present volume has five.

APPLIED COVERS. "Decorative plaques, generally of metalwork or ivory, which are set into or onto the boards of a binding. They are encountered from the early Christian period on" (Michelle P. Brown, *Understanding Illuminated Manuscripts*, p. 13).

APPRAISAL (of books; in archives). Appraisal of books is their evaluation, generally for their monetary worth. It may be said that if a collection is being weeded (*see* Weeding), the holdings are being appraised for their intellectual value or for their likelihood of being used (or possibly, for damaged items, for what they would cost to conserve to make usable) (see Berger, pp. 323–31).

Appraisal in archives is the evaluation of a collection that will determine what items will be kept and what will be discarded (see Berger, pp. 70–71). According to the Society of American Archivists, appraisal has three meanings: "1. The process of identifying materials offered to an archives that have sufficient value to be accessioned.–2. The process of determining the length of time records should be retained, based on legal requirements and on their current and potential usefulness.–3. The process of determining the market value of an item; monetary appraisal" ("Glossary," Society of American Archivists, http://www2.archivists.org/glossary/terms/a/appraisal [accessed 13 July 2021]).

People wishing to get appraisals of their books and manuscripts should remember that booksellers are in the *business* of books and usually wish to be compensated for appraisals. Collectors should not put the bookseller on the spot by asking, off the cuff, for an appraisal (presumably for free). Appraisals of collections are another matter: they entail a formal relationship between the appraiser and his or her client, and a contract should be drawn up between them to spell out the terms of the work, the costs, the shape of the final appraisal document, the reason for the appraisal (tax purposes, replacement value, sale, estate purposes, etc.), and the method(s) and schedule of payment.

Booksellers price their books based on many criteria: supply and demand, and condition (the two top features), along with subject matter (and how popular the subject is at the time of the pricing), author and his or her popularity, illustrations (kind, number, hand colored or not, etc.), binding (by whom; condition; materials; complete with DUST JACKET, etc.), how much it cost them to acquire (including actual price paid plus transportation to get it), years of experience they have in the trade that made it possible for them to understand where the value lies in the item, their overhead to run their business, and much more.

Collectors and librarians must appraise books and other collectibles for various purposes, the chief of which is this: "Is the price asked for this item reasonable" and "Is it affordable?—Is there enough in the coffers for this to be a reasonable purchase?" Both parties must consider what the fudge factor is: How much is the bookseller willing to come down, and how much of a discount is the potential buyer going to ask for? (*See* Consignment.) Also, books that are potential gifts must be appraised by the donor for tax purposes.

Many tools are available to help these parties decide what books should sell for; most of the tools are online bookselling sites. (*See* Online book sales.) (See Van Wingen, *Your Old Books*. See also the Ahearn guides, listed in the bibliography; *Mandeville's Used Book Price Guide*; and McGrath, ed., *Bookman's Price Index: A Guide to the Values of Rare and Other Out-of-Print Books*. And *see* "Old but not rare" in this dictionary.)

APPROVAL COPY. A copy of a book—usually a textbook—sent to an instructor by a publisher with the hopes that the instructor will adopt the text for her classes. Such approval guarantees a number of sales. At one time these were created with no indication that they were sent for approval, and they are just the regular issue that went on sale to the general public. But to discourage instructors from ordering these copies and then selling them to intermediaries who then sold them to students, the publishers began making such copies different from the ones headed for the students. The copies may have "Instructor's Copy" and/or "Not For Resale" printed on the cover; they may be bound in paper while the ones intended for the students would be in boards, or vice versa; they may contain much material geared only for the instructors (study questions, CDs, quiz questions, and other teaching materials). As textbooks, they would have little collectability; and as approval copies, they would have little additional value.

AQUA FORTI. (Abbreviated *A.f.*, *Aq.*, *Aqua.*, or *Aquaf.*) An archaic term for nitric acid, the acid used in ETCHING of copper plates. Hence, the phrase (or its abbreviation) means "etched." As is explained under B.A.T., English texts seldom use this term, but a researcher may encounter it in a foreign-language catalog or bibliography or on a plate in an old book. Such terms, then, have a place in the present volume. Others are mentioned in the list of abbreviations.

AQUATINT. "[A] variety of ETCHING widely used by printmakers to achieve a broad range of tonal values. The process is called aquatint because finished prints often resemble watercolour drawings or wash drawings. The technique consists of exposing a copperplate to acid through a layer of melted granulated resin. The acid bites away the plate only in the interstices between the resin grains, leaving an evenly pitted surface that yields broad areas of tone when the grains are removed and the plate is printed. An infinite number of tones can be achieved by exposing various parts of the plate to acid baths of different strengths for different periods of time. Tones can also be altered by scraping and burnishing. Etched or engraved lines are often used with aquatint to achieve greater definition of form" ("Aquatint," *Encyclopaedia Britannica*, http://www.britannica.com/topic/aquatint [accessed 13 July 2021]). The popularity of this medium was great since the final product could look exactly like a watercolor painting, with a wide range of colors and exceptionally accurate reproduction of originals (see Morrow, *The Art of Aquatint*). (*See also* Etching.)

ARABIC NUMERALS. The standard figures used to denote page numbers and all other numbers in texts, composed of the nine numbers plus zero: 1, 2, 3, and so forth. These pose no problems for anyone in the Western world. The problems arise with the use of ROMAN NUMERALS, frequently seen in dates, as the entry for these characters shows.

ARCHETYPE. *See* Stemma/stemmatics.

ARCHIVAL. A term that suggests that whatever is being described will be around for a long time. That is, for instance, "archival paper" purports to have no INHERENT VICE and will be available perhaps for centuries. Accelerated aging tests and acid-testing pens, among other things, may be used to assess whether an item is truly archival. There are many products on the market for those in the book world—adhesives, sleeves for holding papers and pamphlets, book jackets, and such—that call themselves "archival." Only time will tell.

ARCHIVE/ARCHIVES. Strictly speaking, the records of an organization, including all kinds of materials generated over time by that entity and also including many sorts of business records; personnel papers; items having to do with hiring, firing, payroll, acquisitions, and correspondence (incoming and outgoing); and anything else that reveals the life history of the entity.

The SOCIETY OF AMERICAN ARCHIVISTS has a superb online dictionary in which the term is extensively commented on. Here is one part of that entry: "1. an institution's or individual's entire preserved body of interrelated and interdependent records; 2. a selection of digital records or digital surrogates of records made available as a curated online collection; 3. a collection of manuscript collections managed as a thematic unit and representing a collecting specialization of an archival repository; 4. an organization that collects the records of individuals, families, or other organizations; a collecting archives; 5. (usually construed as sing., earlier treated as pl.) the division within an organization responsible for acquiring and maintaining the organization's records of continuing value; institutional archives; 6. (capitalized and usually preceded by the) the official repository of a nation, state, territory, or institution's records of continuing value; 7. the building, buildings, or portion thereof housing records of continuing value; 8. the professional discipline, practice, and study of administering such collections and organizations" ("Archives," SAA [Society of American Archives], *A Dictionary of Archives Terminology*, https://dictionary.archivists.org/entry/archives.html [accessed 7 June 2021]). (The page leading into this dictionary is at https://dictionary.archivists.org/ [accessed 7 June 2021].) (See Berger, chapter 3, "Archives," pp. 61–75.)

AREOPAGITICA. John Milton's 1644 tract written "to protest an order issued by Parliament the previous year requiring government approval and licensing of all published books. . . . Milton argues that to mandate licensing is to follow the example of the detested papacy. He defends the free circulation of ideas as essential to moral and intellectual development. Furthermore, he asserts, to attempt to preclude falsehood is to underestimate the power of truth. While the immediate objective of the Areopagitica—repeal of licensing—was not obtained for another 50 years, the tract has earned a permanent place in the literature of human rights" (*Britannica*, "Areopagitica"). Perhaps one of the most important texts in book history in its influence on freedom of the press.

ARION PRESS. The commercial and fine press of Andrew Hoyem, who took over the operation of the Grabhorn Press in 1965. The Arion Press prints LIMITED EDITIONS of classic works, using the best materials and letterpress printing techniques. (See https://www.arionpress.com/arion-about [accessed 7 June 2021].) The Grabhorn brothers at their GRABHORN PRESS in San Francisco ceded their operations to Hoyem, who in 1974 renamed the company Arion Press after the legendary Greek poet who was saved from the sea by a dolphin. The press's website says that in 1974 it "launched a series of limited-edition books, printed by letterpress and bound by hand. Many of them were illustrated by prominent artists; some were accompanied by separate editions of original prints. To this day, the list of Arion publications is characterized by its diversity, with titles that range from ancient literature to modern classics. The Press has also developed new material for publication, and resurrected 'lost' texts. The Arion Press edition of Herman Melville's *Moby-Dick*, handset and printed in a folio edition on handmade paper, with 100 wood engravings by Barry Moser, has been hailed as 'a modern masterpiece of bookmaking' (University of California Press)" (https://www.arionpress.com/arion-about [accessed 7 June 2021]).

In the 1980s, the press began in earnest publishing ARTISTS' BOOKS with original prints by artists like Jim Dine, Jasper Johns, and Robert Motherwell. It also purchased (in 1989) the type manufactory of Mackenzie & Harris; so it sets the type for its own books and offers typefounding services to others. Hoyem retired from the press in 2018; Rolph Blythe is now its director.

ARMED SERVICES EDITIONS. (Often designated ASE in booksellers' catalogs.) Small, landscape-oriented PAPERBACK volumes (3½ × 5 in.) sent out by the thousands to members of the U.S. military during World War II. They were "a series produced by the Council on Books in Wartime, from 1943 to 1947. It's estimated that over 122 million copies of 1,322 titles were distributed to service members during the second world war" (Weisenburg, "Books are weapons in the war of ideas"). The Council on Books in Wartime (often referred to as simply CBW) published them to entertain and inform troops overseas. They were often fiction, but many were nonfiction texts on issues related to the military, history, or politics. They were small enough to fit into soldiers' pockets, and for that reason most of these little volumes perished as a biblio-related victim of war. Many of those that survive are in wretched condition. Though collectible and of some historical interest, they are often inexpensive. The authors represented in these volumes included: Mark Twain, W. Somerset Maugham, Bram Stoker, John Steinbeck, H. G. Welles, James Thurber, Edgar Allan Poe, C. S. Forester, Erle Stanley Gardner, William Faulkner, F. Scott Fitzgerald, and hundreds of writers whose names my readers would probably not recognize. (See Manning and Anderson, *The Best-Read Army in the World.*) (*See* Books for Sammies.)

ARMORIAL BINDINGS. "Leather or cloth bindings embossed with armorial seals or plaques, frequently in a panel, or embroidered bindings in which the arms were raised in relief and worked in thread" (Roberts and Etherington, p. 12). Armorial imagery is often used on bookplates. Also, an armorial is a book of heraldry that contains families' or individuals' coats of arms. The arrangement of these in the volume is often by rank, from dukes to barons.

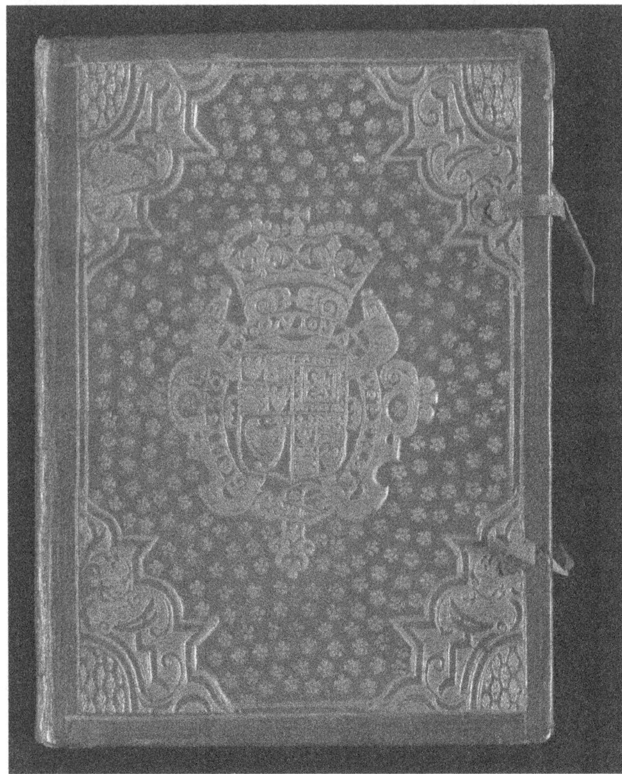

Armorial binding. William Gouge, *The Whole-armor of God: or A Christians Spiritual Furniture, to Keepe Him Safe from all the Assaults of Satan* (London: Printed by John Beale, 1619), with the crest of King James I on the cover.

Courtesy of the Rare Books & Manuscript Library of the University of Illinois at Urbana–Champaign.

ARSENIC. Since this is a volume for BIBLIOPHILES, it is in their best interest to know about the dangers of some books. In the 19th century, textiles were often dyed a bright green, a color achieved with the use of copper acetoarsenite, also called "emerald green." For collectors', booksellers', and librarians' protection (as well as the safety of anyone else coming into contact with green publishers' bindings of the 19th and early 20th centuries), it is important to handle these volumes carefully, housing them in protective coverings of various kinds, and keeping pets and children away from them. The Poison Book Project at Winterthur has a website (http://wiki.winterthur.org/wiki/Poison_Book_Project [accessed 13 January 2021]) on which we read: "Nearly 40% of the nineteenth-century cloth-case bindings analyzed for this project, to date, contain lead in the bookcloth colorant. Analysis of a range of bookcloth colors has also identified barium, chromium, copper, iron, and mercury. / No matter which pigments or dyes may be present, it is best practice to avoid ingesting anything or touching the face while handling nineteenth-century, cloth-bound books. It is also best practice to wash hands after handling books, especially before eating, drinking, or smoking." [And to protect yourself further, don't smoke.] (See Pogcar, "Arsenic and Old Books"; Tedone, "Poison Book Project.")

ARS MORIENDI. The "art of dying," a theme in countless volumes printed to prepare people to die. The religious texts taught people which prayers to say, how to act in a spiritually clean manner, and what obeisances need to be made to their church. Simon Thomas writes, "In the Bodleian Library's incunable collection are several editions, copies, and versions of a popular fifteenth-century work called *Ars moriendi* (or *The Art of Dying*). This tract was intended to bring Christian comfort and practical instruction to the dying man and his family, and all later versions relate to two Latin texts dating from 1415 (the 'long version') and c.1450 (the 'short version'). The popularity of these works was no doubt in part due to the wide spread of fatal diseases throughout the period. . . . Copies in manuscript were incredibly popular, and many printed editions were published throughout Europe after the advent of the printing press; there were nearly 100 editions of the long version before 1500. . . . [WILLIAM] CAXTON interrupted his translation of *The Book of Eneydos* to translate a French abridgement of the *Ars moriendi*, which he completed on 15 June 1490 under the title *The Art and craft to know well to die*" (Simon Thomas, "Ars moriendi—The Art of Dying"; Bodleian Library, http://bav.bodleian.ox.ac.uk/news/ars-moriendi-the-art-of-dying [accessed 24 May 2021]). Texts exist in several European languages. The readers were given hope and told to avoid temptations and to emulate Christ. Many of these tracts are INCUNABULA and are particularly collectible. (See Berger, *The Book of Death.*)

ART AND ARCHITECTURE THESAURUS. A structured vocabulary of terminology for describing works of visual art and architecture. It was created by the Getty Research Institute. It "can be used to improve access to information for art, architecture, and other material culture" (Getty Research Institute, https://www.getty.edu/research/tools/vocabularies/aat/about.html [accessed 20 February 2021]). The thesaurus contains a tremendous amount of information usable for describing books, and is worth dipping into. It is available free online at the URL provided here: https://www.getty.edu/research/tools/vocabularies/aat/ (accessed 28 May 2022).

ARTIFACTUAL VALUE. The value inherent in an item regardless of its text—that is, its value as a physical object. Value may indeed lie in the information the item has, but as an artifact, the item may also be valuable because it was signed by an important (collectible) person, it may be in a fine binding, or it may have valuable tip-ins, as with a LEAF BOOK. Many a volume that would otherwise be valueless might have artifactual value if something in its physical makeup or its PROVENANCE can be shown to be especially desirable to a collector or library.

ARTIFICIAL. *See* Faux.

ARTISTS' BOOKS. Works of art, often in the shape of books, but not necessarily. They are created by artists or book artists, usually in unique copies or in small editions of a few copies, though some can be in larger editions of perhaps a hundred or more. By implication, artists' books are produced with a good deal of hand work (drawing, painting, sketching, folding, sewing, letterpress printing, binding, tipping-in, and so on), but many artists are using Xeroxing, ink-jet printing, and other mechanical methods of composition. They are often the work of individuals, though they could be done by or for publishers. Some are exquisite; some are shoddy and carelessly and cheaply produced. There has been a fairly strong collecting market in these productions, though in recent years word of mouth indicates that the market for them at academic institutions is drying up a bit, partly because many of them have little or no scholarly use, they are difficult to store, and they are often quite expensive. The French term *LIVRES D'ARTISTES* is often used incorrectly to make an artist's book seem deluxe and exotic. But in fact, a livre d'artiste is a different thing altogether. (See Klima, *Artists Books: A Critical Survey of the Literature.*)

ARTIST'S PROOF. An impression of a work of art done while the artist is creating the image—allowing her to look at the work while it is being created, usually before the final image is arrived at. The proof is in a state that permits the artist to continue working on it until she is satisfied that the final image has been created. These early stages of the image may be jettisoned by the artist, but they often survive, and can be used by scholars to examine the incremental growth of the final work. Since they are usually in short supply, possibly unique from one proof to the next, never sold on the market (certainly not by the artist herself, though if they fall into the hands of a bookseller or print dealer they may make it to the market), and since they are usually kept by the artist herself, they are quite rare and can therefore command prices far beyond what the final proof (that may exist in an edition of dozens or hundreds of exemplars) would sell for. They may also be signed by an artist, but not numbered, as would be the exemplars of the final edition. The scholar must be wary of such "proofs," since they may not be proofs at all, just unsigned or unnumbered pieces. For the David Milne illustration in *Colophon*, Volume 5, there are several states of that engraving, necessitated by the large number of copies that the artist had to make. These are not proofs at all, just retouchings and re-engravings of the plate.

ASCENDERS. Portions of characters that ascend above the X-HEIGHT of letters. Letters such as the lowercase *b*, *d*, and *h* have ascenders. (*See also* Descenders.)

AS ISSUED. A bookseller's term indicating that an item being described may have some kind of peculiarity or phenomenon that might reduce its value, except for the fact that the piece is the way it was issued by the publisher. For example, the Windhover Press volume *Kenney's: Twenty Poems for a Lost Tavern* contains a leaf with a hole cut out of it where a paragraph has been excised. The bookseller's description might say, "With a paragraph excised from final text leaf, as issued." As noted, this is a way to explain what might otherwise look like a defect that could affect the item's intellectual or monetary value. Quite common, especially for private-press books, is this: "With no dust jacket, as issued." (I have noted in my career this last "as issued" is sometimes stated incorrectly—where a DUST JACKET was indeed created for the book but is lacking in almost all copies and thus has become a GHOST for many booksellers. That is, a bookseller might say, "In 45 years of bookselling I have never seen a jacket on this book." Another dealer extrapolates, "With no dust jacket, as usual," and this is picked up by another bookseller as, "With no dust jacket, as issued." *Caveat emptor.*)

AS NEW. A bookseller's term meaning that while the volume is "used," it looks and feels and smells and tastes as if it is almost PRISTINE. The message is that it is not a new book; it is "secondhand" or "preowned."

ASS (or Asp) (in papermaking). A little rack or projection on a papermaker's vat designed to allow the VATMAN to prop the paper MOLD up for a few seconds to allow water to drain from a recently dipped sheet. The proper term is *ass*, but in the name of propriety, someone decided to call it an *asp*, and that word appears now and then. After the vatman has formed a sheet on the mold, he sends that mold to the LAYMAN. The layman couches (*see* Couch/Coucher/Couching) the sheet and returns the mold to the vatman (who, in the meantime, has been forming another sheet on the twin mold). The layman must place a felt over the recently couched sheet; while he does this, he sets the mold with a newly formed sheet against the ass to allow water to continue to drain from the sheet. Once the new felt is in place, he can couch the new sheet. The ass is part of the operation.

ASSOCIATION COPY. A copy of a book, manuscript, or other kind of material that can be shown to have been in the hands of someone noteworthy. A copy of a manuscript that bears a signature of a former owner, such as a well-known duke or playwright, a sports personality or criminal, or a library or academic institution, is said to be an association copy—associated with the person, library, or institution. A copy of the same item bearing the signature of a person of no repute is more likely said to be defaced. While this latter is something of an exaggeration, the point is that association copies can be worth more than others because of their association, while copies bearing the ownership or handling of someone obscure will probably be worth less. A problem in the book world, of course, is that association based on SIGNATURES, BOOKPLATES, LAID-IN or TIPPED-IN items, rubber stamps, or other features can be faked. As with "AS ISSUED," *caveat emptor*. (See *Other People's Books: Association Copies and the Stories They Tell*. In this volume, see especially Tanselle, *Introduction*, pp. 7–19.)

Carter says that the term "association copy" refers to a copy the author owned or wrote in, one that someone else owned but who was affiliated with the author in some way, or one that was owned by someone else who, him- or herself, was noteworthy. He adds that the association copy may also be linked to a person who is in some way connected to the *contents* of the volume (see Carter, p. 33). He then adds that the term has also been used to mean any volume that was in the possession of any well-known person, but that that "possession" may be difficult or impossible to prove. He also points out, as I have indicated, that any book can have something laid into it from a well-known party, making it look as if that party is somehow associated with the copy of the book, whereas that link is, as he says, "thoroughly bogus" (p. 35). And he relates the term to "PRESENTATION COPY" and "INSCRIBED COPY."

Additionally, association copies can be associated not with people, but with noted events, as with an item that survived the Chicago fire, one that was on a particular space mission, or one that made it through the Florence flood. (See Williams, *The Elements of Book-Collecting*, pp. 140–53, and Winterich and Randall, *A Primer of Book Collecting*, chapter 2, "Association Books," pp. 58–73.)

ASSOCIATION INTERNATIONALE DE BIBLIOPHILE (International Association of Bibliophiles). As the name indicates, this is a group of book lovers, mostly French, founded on 10 October 1963, with the aims to "Encourage love of books; stimulate an appreciation for rare books and the diffusion of knowledge about them" (https://uia.org/s/or/en/1100027027 [accessed 5 January 2021]). They hold a congress every two years, and a shorter meeting in the intervening years, and publish the periodical *Bulletin du bibliophile*, along with many other kinds of publications: "Catalogs, Conference papers and proceedings, Exhibition catalogs, Biographies, Bibliographies, History, [and] Directories" (this comes from WorldCat: http://worldcat.org/identities/lccn-n82056604/ [accessed 5 January 2021]. See this website for a list of their more prominent publications).

ASTERISK. *See* Footnote. (But before you go to "Footnote," please remember how to pronounce this word. Here is a verse to help you: "Little Mary donned her skates / Upon thin ice to frisk; / Wasn't she a silly girl / Her little * !")

ASTERISM. A configuration of three asterisks in a triangle, showing minor breaks in a text, emphasizing a particular passage, or separating sub-chapters in a book.

This is the Times New Roman asterism, one of its regular glyphs in its typeface family.
From Times New Roman.

AS USUAL. As with "AS ISSUED," this term suggests that the item being described has some peculiarity or defect that may affect its price but that the person describing the item says the copy is like all (or most) others. Typical is this: "With foxing on the edges and endpapers, as usual," or "With brown stains on the cover label from its adhesive, as usual." It is a way for a bookseller to minimize the impact of the condition by saying essentially, "This is the condition of pretty much all copies. I have taken this into account in my appraisal of the item." Another bookseller might say, "Without the usual staining on the cover label." Certain defacing features on otherwise desirable books get to be known in the trade, and the word "usual" signals the expertise and experience of the one writing the description.

A3 PAPER. *See* A4 paper.

AT PRESS. *See* Forthcoming.

AUCTION CATALOGS. Volumes (in print or online) that announce upcoming (or, eventually, past) auction sales, listing each lot (*see* Auctions), usually, these days, with pictures of most or all LOTS and with estimated prices (generally given in ranges: "$1,200 to $1,500"). The estimates are educated guesses made by the experts in the auction house, based on their often extensive experience. These experts can be specialists in various kinds of books, books of different centuries, works by particular authors, or other categories of items. And the estimates give a range of likely HAMMER PRICES. The estimates could be spot on, or they could be off by a great amount, depending on the dynamics of the auction or the fact that the person creating the range of possible bids missed something in the lot that two or more keen-eyed bidders saw. Also, given the nature of collectors, a volume that, under normal circumstances, would sell for, say, $500 might go for five times that if two determined collectors are bidding against one another. Hence, the estimates could be right in the range they suggest, but far off in the final bidding.

The catalog will also contain all kinds of information about the location and conditions of the sale (buyer's premium, shipping options, insurance, reserves, and so on). These are produced, sometimes in large numbers, to be distributed to any potential buyer, private, corporate, or institutional; or they are online for all to access. The auction house employees who create these volumes are usually experts in their fields, so the work they do to produce the write-ups for each lot yields descriptions with good, reliable information, sometimes accompanied by statements of PROVENANCE and bibliographical references. These catalogs are collected by many institutions and private collectors since they are great reference tools. Some catalogs achieve legendary status (the Thomas Winthrop Streeter Sale, the Robert Hoe Sale, the Garden Sale, the Estelle Doheney Sale, the Jerome Kern Sale, the H. Bradley Martin Sale, and scores of others) and have become collectibles in themselves. (The Streeter catalog is so well known that there is an entry for it in the bibliography under "Streeter.")

The potential bidder, however, must remember that the catalog is a cross between a reference tool and a promotional/advertising piece and must weigh the superlatives and selling points against the realities of the world. Is this "the finest copy to come on the market in the last 2,000 years"? Is this really "the most desirable title on this subject ever created" and is it really "exceptionally rare in this immaculate condition"? (In fact, is the condition as described really as PRISTINE as the catalog says it is?) Can we believe the compiler who says, "Lightly foxed, as typical"? How lightly is "lightly"? Is it really typical of other copies? How many other copies has the cataloger seen? One? Then 100 percent of the other copies he has seen are foxed. Does this constitute "typical"?

One of the drawbacks of these catalogs is necessarily that they do not list what the hammer prices of the lots were. Since these are produced before the sales, they obviously cannot supply this information. But since auctions are public affairs, the information on "prices realized" is also public (though some lots are bought in [*see* Auctions] and thus have no realized price), so the auction houses will publish (on paper or online) the actual hammer prices. Collectors of these catalogs will want to get this information and keep it interleaved in the catalogs.

Catalogs are usually sent to potential buyers on the auction house's list of clients at no charge. But if collectors are eager to have particular catalogs (as with, for example, sales of books in spectacular bindings—and there is a large market for bookbinding books), the auction house might retain copies for some time (even years) for sale. The auction houses are also known to dispose of large numbers of these catalogs (to clear their shelves), and some vendors buy them for resale at whatever price they think they can get for them. Hence, there is a strong secondary market for auction catalogs. For some people, drawbacks are that there are too many of them and that, being printed on coated stock, they are heavy. Of course, auction houses also post their catalogs online, so not all of them are paper-based.

One source of research that is often overlooked—especially when it comes to determining hammer prices—is the "priced catalog," a copy of the auction catalog with the prices written in the margins. This volume presumably was in the hands of someone attending the actual auction. (*See* Auction rings.) (See Munby and Coral, *British Book Sale Catalogues*, and McKay, *American Book Auction Catalogues*.)

AUCTION PRICING GUIDES. *See American Book Prices Current; Book Auction Records.*

AUCTION RINGS. An arrangement among potential bidders at an auction (usually, in the book world, a collection of booksellers) not to bid against one another, the aim being to keep bids exceptionally low at the auction. Once the sale is over, the group—the ring—meets at another venue and holds another auction among themselves. (For a thorough treatment of this, see Freeman and Freeman, *Anatomy of an Auction*. Thanks to the survival of a set of priced catalogs [*see* Auction catalogs], the Freemans were able to get a great deal of information about the rings at the Ruxley Lodge sale.) Once the main auction is over, the participants in the ring meet at what is called a "knockout" or a "settlement," the second auction among themselves. At that knockout, the participants have another auction among themselves as they "redistribute the purchases and share the incremental money as 'dividends'" (Freeman and Freeman, *Anatomy*, p. 29). The Freemans continue, "The private auction is also called a 'settlement,' and this name is given as well to the handing-over of cash after the secondary transactions. 'Ring' is the name for the society of participants in the original agreement; a sale is said to be 'ringed' if substantially affected by such a group; LOTS that have changed hands after the public sale at new prices are said to have been 'settled'" (p. 29). "[I]n January 1928, with the passage of Lord Darling's Auctions (bidding Agreements) Act, ring and settlement were formally outlawed in Great Britain" (p. 39). But that does not mean that they no longer exist.

AUCTIONS. The fact that Carter devotes nearly five full pages to this term indicates its complexity and breadth (pp. 35–40). The term itself need not be defined here since I assume my readers know what an auction is. Here are some of the very basic elements of an auction. (1) The *consignor*—the person who is selling the book(s) or other materials through the auction house. The consignor can be a private party or a bookseller who, for any reason, decides she can do better selling the item at auction than she can through the regular bookselling channels (from a shop, through quotes to potential buyers, or in a catalog). The consignor can also be a library parting with its duplicates or an estate dispersing the holdings of a deceased or incapacitated collector. (2) The *auction house*—the company that takes items from consignors and sells them to the highest bidders. The auction house will have its experts who appraise and catalog the contents of each lot. (3) The *auctioneer*—the employee at the auction house who conducts the auction, guiding the bidding and determining who has made each bid and who makes the winning bid. (4) The *bidders*—those who offer to buy items at the auction. (5) The *bids*—the incremental amounts offered by bidders who wish to purchase the items for sale. Bids can be made in person, by phone, or online. They can even be mailed in—on paper, though this method is near extinction. (6) The *lots*—a lot is a single item or many (bid on in a single bidding operation) that will go to the highest bidder. A lot could consist of 100 or more items (books, pamphlets, photographs, periodicals, manuscripts, or anything else, or any combination of these) that the auction house determined would make a reasonable lot. (7) *Estimates*—the prices, predicted by an expert at the auction house, that the individual lots will go for at the auction. The auction house employs experts in the various categories of their sales. The appraisals are generally revealed in the auction catalog as a range, from low to high estimates. These estimates are based on a wide range of information and phenomena, but in the end, the final bids are often dependent on the dynamics of the auction itself. Two insistent and well-heeled bidders can drive the final bid to heights not imagined by the expert(s) who determined the estimates. Or, after a lunch break in the auction, bidders can be somnolent and let a lot go for far under the predicted low value. Also, even the best experts can misjudge the market value of an item. *Caveat venditor* (let the seller beware). At one time, potential buyers may have assumed that the low estimates shown in the auction catalog were the reserves (*see below*), but this was not necessarily so. (8) *Increments in bids*—at lower valuations, the increments in the bids are fairly low; at higher valuations, the increments in bids can be in the tens of thousands of dollars. (9) The *hammer price*—the final bidder will have called out the last bid at the highest price bid. The auctioneer says something like, "Going, going, sold to ——." He or she then hits an anvil with a gavel, like striking with a hammer. This signals the hammer price: the last (and thus the highest) price bid. The auction house will then publish a list of *prices realized* sometime after the auction is complete (and presumably after all the buyers have paid for their lots). (10) The *buyer's premium*—the winning bidder pays the hammer price plus a premium (anywhere from 10 to 25 percent, possibly more), the premium being the amount the auction house charges the buyer for its services. When an auction house lists the selling price of the item, that listing today generally includes the buyer's premium, though this was not always the case. (11) The *seller's premium*—the amount the consignor pays the auction house for selling the lot; so the consignor eventually gets the hammer price *less* whatever premium the consignor and the auction house have set between them (anywhere from 10 to 25 percent, more or less). (12) The *reserve*—the lowest bid the consignor is willing to take on a lot. That is, if a consignor puts a book into an auction and insists that it fetch at least $5,000, he or she can make that the reserve; hence, if the bidding ends below that price, the book will not be sold but will be "*bought in*" (removed from the sale without going to the highest bidder). The reserves are not usually made public. Some auction houses may proclaim that a particular auction has no reserves, suggesting that bargains can be had. (13) The *underbidder*—the person who has the next-to-last bid. (As Carter says, the underbidder is important since he is the one whose bid leads to the final bid, so the underbidder in a way influences the hammer price, and a wise auctioneer will remember who the underbidder is in case the final bidder decides for one reason or another not to take the lot; then the auction house can contact the underbidder for the sale [see Carter, p. 252].) (14) *Knocked down*—means "sold," the action taken by the auctioneer who proclaims at the moment of sale who the final bidder is; the knocking down is the striking of the gavel onto the anvil or tabletop to signal that the final bid has been issued and that the sale has been made. The "hammer price" is determined at the moment of the knockdown. (As the entry for PREMIUMS explains, one auction house has raised its seller's premium to 26% as of January 2021.)

Auction houses send out calls to all their clients and anyone else on their snail-mail or online mailing list announcing that they plan to hold an auction in a given subject area or in a group of (usually) related subject areas, and asking for contributions to that sale. Consignors can offer items, and the auction house determines which one(s) they think are appropriate for that sale, often determined by the value of the item. Some auction houses, like Christie's and Sotheby's, will accept only items that will fetch a certain amount of money. A single party with a major collection may offer the entire collection to the house, and it will be sold as The Collection of _____, and the bigger the name in the collecting world, the more prestigious the sale will be. Some of the major collectors (or collecting institutions) have had sales that brought a great deal of splash to the auction house and to the book world. (*See* Auction catalogs.) It happens, also, that the auction house does not have enough lots from such a single-collection sale to fill a full auction; or it has been offered a number of items from consignors other than the one whose auction it is featuring. So it may add these "stray" lots into the main auction. The association of these other volumes with those of the primary collector whose auction is the advertised one could enhance the value of these other volumes. This practice is called "salting," and the salted auction may have a catalog that says something like, "The Extraordinary Library of Bradley Lewis, and Other Valuable Properties."

Bidding can be done in the auction house itself by the person wishing to buy the lot, by phone, by proxy, or by bids that have been sent in in advance. Thus, a potential buyer may contact the auction house a month before the auction and lodge bids that are then executed by an employee of the auction house on behalf of the buyer in the latter's absence. Also, bidding can be done by a bookseller (or someone else) on behalf of a client who has engaged the dealer (or other party) to do the bidding. The dealer is said to be bidding ON COMMISSION. (For a more extensive discussion, see Carter, and Berger, pp. 312–19.) (*See also* Other properties.)

In the July/August 2015 issue of *The Art Newspaper* (vol. 24, no. 270, pp. 1, 4), the article "Sale Reveals Complex System of Guarantees" explains that auction houses, in strong competition with one another, are offering consignors guarantees for the hammer prices of items they have consigned to the house. This arrangement is generally done only for items of high value. To convince owners of items ripe for auction to choose their house over that of their competitors, the houses are using "a complicated system of financing in which third-party money is used by Christie's to offset risk but not in the form of a traditional 'guarantee.' At least five works in the auction were backed in some way by external investors without this information being made public in the sale catalogue. The auctioneer announced at the start of the sale that 'a party with a financial interest' may be bidding on the works, but if this 'party' had chosen not to bid, the auction house would not have disclosed its involvement" (p. 1). The article adds, "In the catalogue, Christie's described these five works . . . as lots in which only the auction house 'has a direct financial interest,' qualified as possibly including a guaranteed minimum price or an advance on a work (marked in the catalogue with a small black circle and generally referred to as an 'in-house guarantee')" (pp. 1, 4).

To obfuscate matters further, the reporters asked Christie's to explain this arcane arrangement, and the auction house said that it uses "third-party guarantors" and "third-party partners," the difference between them being somewhat murky. "The distinction between the two is difficult to discern, although one difference is that third-party guarantors are counted as live bidders, whereas third-party partners are not. However, third-party partners can still bid on the works they have a stake in, provided Christie's discloses this before the sale, If 'partners' do not intend to bid, their involvement is not revealed, despite the fact that they would end up co-owning the work they have a stake in with the auction house should it fail to sell" (p. 4). The article explains the extensive legal implications of this arrangement in Great Britain and the United States.

The complications of the auction world could leave the bidder in a fog, but auctions certainly are constructed to improve the bottom line for the consignor (and usually for the auction house, which reaps its premiums from sellers and buyers but not necessarily on these "guarantee" arrangements). Those in the book world may wish to know of this kind of guarantee, especially if they are contemplating putting items up for auction and wish to create a guarantee greater and more solid than that created by establishing reserves. With a reserve, an item can be bought in, and the consignor gets nothing. With these new guarantees, it looks as if the item consigned will automatically be sold—and at a level that should satisfy the consignor—even if the auction house does not make as much profit as it had hoped to. (*See also* Bundles; Sealed-bid auctions.)

Bidders must rely on the honesty and propriety of the auction house. Sotheby's was caught faking over-the-phone bids, conjured up in the sales room by their employees to drive up the bidding by clients in the room. One auction house took more than a dozen bids from a client (call him Bidder A) who had sent in his bids long in advance of the auction. Normally, such bids would either be successful (at some price beneath the actual amount bid) or would be unsuccessful, the lot going for more than the bidder was willing to pay. So, for instance, a lot comes up that Bidder A sent in an advance bid of $500; if the lot sold for more than that, Bidder A didn't get it. But if the bidding went to $450, that would be what Bidder A would have to pay (plus the buyer's premium). The chances that the lot went for exactly what the Bidder A said was *the highest amount he was willing to pay* are slim, though it could happen. At that auction, Bidder A got about 10 of the lots he wanted *at exactly his highest bid*. The chances that this would happen are mighty slim. The auction house clearly let the bidding stop where it did, then charged Bidder A whatever his highest bid was. This was probably illegal, but there was no way for Bidder A to question it since he was not in the auction house to do the bidding.

An important addition to all of this discussion of classical auctions is that with the coming of the web, we also have seen the coming of online auctions. And the granddaddy of the online-auction realm is EBAY. (*See also* Online book sales.)

AUDIOBOOKS. As the term indicates, these are audio versions of books, sometimes in the voice of the original author, but more often that of a professional reader. The texts could be complete or abridged, and they could be of any kind of written material. When I was in high school about 150 years ago, I purchased a set of vinyl records that were the plays of Shakespeare. These would qualify as audiobooks, though the term has taken on a more specific meaning today: the oral version of a text that may have appeared in analog form. One thinks of novels or poetry readings, how-to books, and texts on economics or history, biography or even newspaper articles. These are created for the blind as well as the sighted. They have been around in various forms for perhaps 100 years, with wax cylinders, wire recorders, and vinyl, which was replaced by cassette tapes, then 8-track tapes, compact discs, DVDs, and thumb drives—any medium that can record sound. Large libraries of these have been amassed, but with modern technology, one can pull up an audiobook on a smart phone or other handheld device.

AUSTRALIAN LIBRARY AND INFORMATION ASSOCIATION (ALIA). The professional organization of librarians in Australia, founded as the Australian Institute of Librarians in 1937. It became the Library Association of Australia in 1949, and became the ALIA in 1989 (ALIA, "History of the Association"; http://www.alia.org.au/about-alia/history-association [accessed 8 June 2021]). The organization hosts conferences and has a professional publication, *The Journal of the Australian Library and Information Association*. (*See* American Library Association; Canadian Federation of Library Associations; Canadian Library Association; Chartered Institute of Library and Information Professionals.)

AUTHORIAL (as in authorial text, authorial corrections). In the realm of BIBLIOGRAPHY, this term signifies that a text or the corrections in it have the sanction of the author, presumably because they were made by him or because they have been vetted by the author and approved of. (*See* Authoritative edition.)

AUTHORITATIVE EDITION. In the realm of bibliography, an edition of a text that has been carefully edited in such a way as to create a version that the author would have sanctioned. It could be authoritative because the author him- or herself created it or because it was done by an editor who used standard, well-codified editorial principles and used as a COPY-TEXT versions of the texts that the author him- or herself created or fully sanctioned. "Authoritative," then, means something like "sanctioned by the author" or—especially if the author is dead—"a version that the author *is likely* to have sanctioned." (*See* Authorial; Authorized edition; Bibliography.)

AUTHORIZED EDITION. This term has two distinct meanings. At the end of the 19th century and the beginning of the 20th, publishers like Harper's issued large sets of authors' works, labeling them "Authorized edition" (or sometimes "Author's edition"). The term in this context does not signify what it does in BIBLIOGRAPHY. The publishers issued multivolume sets comprised of whatever editions they could get their hands on and then paid the author a fee for using his or her works. The sets were "authorized" by such authors insofar as they said, "Yes, go ahead with this publication. You have paid me, so I authorize you to publish these volumes."

These "authorized editions" were not authoritative in the bibliographic sense. They were merely versions of the text that the publishers could get at as good a price as they could find. (*See* Authorial; Authoritative edition.)

A second meaning is revealed in Carter's entry for "Authorised Edition" (pp. 33–34), in which he points out that from the 16th to the 18th centuries, many texts were published without the author's approval (sometimes, and often, without the author's knowledge). The publisher of these may have used reliable or corrupt texts—either printed or manuscript versions, so the unauthorized versions could be quite good or quite inaccurate textually (see Carter, p. 41). He also points out that if a work was serialized over many months, it was possible for a publisher to print the first edition in book form from the serialized version before the original publisher could get its own copy out. (*See* Edition, Impression [Printing], Issue, and State; Points.) He concludes that in France, when the term *édition originale* is employed to refer to a native author, it does not mean "first edition but the first authorised edition printed in France" (Carter, p. 41). In England and the United States, booksellers and their customers generally think that an edition that is unauthorized, even if it is the first in the country of its origin, must be worth more than any other, and "the products of foreign enterprise, whether translated or (more rarely) in the original, have a special fascination for the keen author-collector" (p. 41). (*See* Pirate; Unauthorized edition.)

AUTHOR'S ADVANCE. *See* Advance.

AUTHOR'S BINDING. Carter says that authors sometimes had special bindings put onto their own texts, the volumes to be presented to public figures or acquaintances as gifts. He says that such bindings that did not look like those of the regular edition released to the public were not always recognizable as one of their making. Thus, without some clear indication that the variant binding (which is usually of better quality than the publisher's binding) was actually done by the author, it should be viewed with suspicion, especially when a leather volume is described by anyone as "in an author's binding." He also says that such a volume may be called a "dedication volume" simply because of its more sumptuous binding, but that claim is also suspect (see Carter, p. 40). Carter also says that if a book that normally is bound in one publisher's cloth binding appears in a different one, the assumption could be made that the variant was at the behest of the author so that she could give the variant to a relative or friend, but he warns that unless there is proof that such a change in binding was created by the author, the variant must be assumed to be the work of the publisher, not the author. It is not at all uncommon for publishers to issue books in their standard cloth versions (some copies in one cloth, some in another) and some copies with a leather spine or in full leather as "deluxe" versions. As the entry at SALESMAN'S DUMMY/SALESMAN'S SAMPLE BOOK indicates, publishers often offered their books sold by canvassers in a choice of bindings. So five books of the same edition could have that many different kinds of covers (e.g., red, blue, green, or brown cloth along with a leather version). The first edition of Mark Twain's *Pudd'nhead Wilson* was issued by the American Publishing Company in a full binding of terracotta cloth or with a leather spine.

Though in a different realm, today's authors sometimes have a say in selecting the decoration and text on the covers of their books. Publishers' artists who are designing the binding may send the author samples of designs from which the author chooses the one she thinks best. Authors may also weigh in on the text, the typography, and the placement of the elements on the covers—even to the extent of tweaking an illustration or choosing a different one from those offered. These decisions do not constitute an "author's binding," but they do show that authors may have a say in the binding of their books.

AUTHOR'S COPIES. Copies of a volume given to the author by the publisher. These are often ADVANCE COPIES, so they may have differences in text or binding from the ones released to the public; or they may be exactly like the regularly published ones, in which case they may be indistinguishable from those of the rest of the edition. Correspondence or some other slip LAID INTO the copies may indicate that they are those sent to the author. If they can be authenticated as author's copies, they are ASSOCIATION copies and may have special value. Publishers' contracts will spell out how many copies the author will get—usually only a few for most commercially published books, and perhaps one or two for FINE-PRESS books.

AUTHOR'S CORRECTIONS. Once a book is set into type but before it is published, a common practice is that the author is sent first GALLEY PROOFS and then PAGE PROOFS. At each of these stages, the author may make changes. Presumably, if the COMPOSITORS have done their job carefully, the author will have only minor changes to make, correcting TYPOGRAPHICAL ERRORS. But authors could continue to work on the text at any point at which they could make changes, and at both of these opportunities, they might emend the text. The word "corrections," then, might be a misnomer, for the text might be "correct" at the point at which the authors decide to change it.

The changes could be ACCIDENTALS or SUBSTANTIVES, and they could be made when the book is well into production, not necessarily at the proofing stages. These changes could create copies of the final text with state variants (*see* Edition, Impression [Printing], Issue, and State; Points, the section "States"; *see also* State variants), or they could occasion printers to make STOP-PRESS CORRECTIONS or to CANCEL parts of the text. As Carter points out, such variants yield multiple "versions" of a text, to the delight of collectors. (*See also* Points.)

AUTHOR'S FINAL INTENTIONS. A term from textual editing (*see* Bibliography), referencing the text closest to what the author wrote *and sanctioned* before the text went to press. Determining what those intentions were can be difficult or impossible, but an assiduous editor may be able to glean what the author wanted his text to say (and the way it was to be said) from a HOLOGRAPH manuscript, from correspondence to and from the author, from GALLEY PROOFS or PAGE PROOFS that the author worked on, from the author's notes or comments recorded by others, or from some other source. These "final intentions" should weigh heavily in the publisher's version of the text and in the work textual editors do to establish a reliable text. (*See* Chronological obsession.)

AUTHOR'S PORTRAIT. An image, printed LETTERPRESS or INTAGLIO, or in photography, often facing the title page (as with a FRONTISPIECE) showing the author. The image could also be on the TITLE PAGE, and it normally shows a bust of the author. In the 20th century the picture, if there is one, will often be on the rear FLAP of the DUST JACKET, above a biographical statement about the author (or, for a PAPERBACK, on the rear cover). Luisa Calè says about such portraits from the HANDPRESS PERIOD, "As separate plates, representations of the author could be sourced from existing portraits engraved from a range of media, including coins, busts, and paintings produced for other purposes, sometimes engraved as part of independent series, then repurposed as frontispieces TIPPED INTO the book" (Calè, "Frontispieces," p. 29).

AUTHOR'S PROOFS. *See* Proofs.

AUTOGRAPH. An autograph is a signature. It can be that of an author or former owner of an item, an illustrator, or a publisher. But in the world of bibliography, as Carter points out, the word should be used as an adjective, as in an "autograph document" or an "autograph manuscript," meaning in the hand (handwriting) of the author. Sometimes this can be shown if the author has signed the item or if the handwriting of a written text is that of a particular person. The adjective also refers to other writing, as in MARGINALIA, annotations, or notes of various kinds. In the list of ABBREVIATIONS above, "ALS" means "Autograph letter signed," indicating that the letter in question is in the hand of a particular author. Carter says that when the word "autograph" is used as a noun, it usually means an author's signature. In some autograph albums, these signatures can be viciously excised from their original documents (like letters). And he concludes, "Albums of such objects now induce melancholy contemplation of the fate of the letters and documents from which they were barbarously shorn" (Carter, p. 42; Carter then cites Munby's *The Cult of the Autograph Letter in England*). Furthermore, many a document with an "original" signature, made with a pen, was actually signed by an autopen, a device holding a pencil or pen, the machine running the tip of the writing implement over the writing surface to create the signature. These have been in use for centuries; even Thomas Jefferson had one at his disposal. Andrea Seabruck says, "The first autopen was patented in 1803 by a man named John Isaac Hawkins. The Polygraph, as it was called, was immediately pounced on by America's original early adopter of cutting-edge technology, President Thomas Jefferson." (See Seabruck, "Obama Wields His . . . Autopen?") Hence, an actual autograph, discernible by the groove left in the sheet by the pen, may not be directly from the hand of the signer. Genuine autographs can add considerably to the value of a piece, but they may need to be authenticated—especially with comparison to known actual autographs.

AUTOGRAPH ALBUM (or autograph book). A (usually small) volume used for obtaining the signatures (and other words) of targeted people: friends, actors, politicians, or anyone else the owner of the album thinks worth commemorating in one's memory. As with GUEST BOOKS, such albums can be worthless or valuable, depending on the contents—that is, the people who have signed the volume and the things they said or drew in it. An autograph album with a witticism from Mark Twain or a drawing by Pablo Picasso could have extraordinary value. The typical album of a primary or secondary school student may contain an early signature of someone who has gone on to achieve great fame. (*See* Slam book.)

AUTONYM. "[A] book published under the real name of the author" (Dictionary.com, "Autonym").

AUTOPEN. *See* Autograph.

AWARDS. *See* Book awards.

B

BABEWYNES (in medieval manuscripts). Bizarre creatures appearing in the margins of medieval manuscripts, usually composed of various parts of different animals. "The most common species to appear in medieval margins has no established pedigree, either from mythology or literary sources, but is made up from parts of different beings, animal and human, as well as plants and things of uncertain origin. 'Hybrid' is one very general name given to these creatures. Some modern scholars have called them 'nondescripts,' a term borrowed from the science of natural history for forms not easily named. In a fourteenth-century English sermon, they were referred to as *babewynes* and equated with hypocrites" (Nishimura, *Images in the Margins*, p. 46; see also Camille, *Image on the Edge*, and Wood, "On the Edge"). (*See* Bestiary.) One particular kind of babewyne is a GROTESQUE. If the figure is purely humorous, it may be called a drollery.

BACK (in binding) (sometimes called the "backbone"). The SPINE of a book. Carter says that the original backs were glued to the back of the SIGNATURES, creating flexible backs. In the 18th century, improved tooling and the desire to save money led to the HOLLOW back (see Carter, p. 42). The term "backstrip" usually denotes the paper strip that covers the spine of a volume, and the word "back" in this context is not to be used for the back cover of the volume. Carter warns that it should never be used in such a way as to indicate the back (or lower) cover of a book (Carter, p. 42).

BACKED. If a leaf in a book or a single sheet of, for example, a print or a map is covered on its VERSO with some material (e.g., paper or silk), it is said to be "backed." The word can also be used in such adjectival phrases as "cloth-backed" or "vellum-backed," indicating that the SPINE of a book is made of cloth or vellum. The backing in many cases is done to strengthen the element that is backed. An engraving, for instance, on a thin piece of paper may be backed to allow it to be turned as a leaf in a book or to keep it from being wrinkled in the handling of the volume. (*See* Rebacked.)

BACKING. *See* Rounding and backing.

BACK ISSUE. Any issue of a periodical that predates the current one. Publishers of serials usually publish more copies of their periodical than they need to satisfy immediate demand, and they keep the back issues for later sales. Sometimes one issue is of particular interest to a wide audience and it goes OUT OF PRINT, making it available only on the secondary market, and often driving its price up.

BACK MATTER. The opposite of the PRELIMS: "The elements of a book that follow the main text and that may include a glossary, appendices, endnotes, bibliography, index, colophon, or similar copy. Back matter usually begins on a RECTO" (Eckersley et al., *Glossary of Typesetting Terms*, p. 8).

BACKSTRIP. *See* Back.

BACK-TO-BACK BINDING. *See* Dos-à-dos binding.

BACKUP. When a sheet is PERFECTED, it is printed on both sides. If the text is in lines of type, the lines should back up from one side of the leaf to the other such that no SHOW-THROUGH is visible. That is, lines of type should superimpose on those on the opposite side of the leaf. This is called "backup." Poor backup yields annoying show-through. (For a detailed explanation of this phenomenon, *see* Point-holes.) "Backup" is sometimes called "REGISTRATION." Additionally, if there is an illustration printed on one side of the leaf, text on the other, the printer usually tries to achieve good backup so that whatever is on the RECTO does not show through to the VERSO, if that is possible. That is, backup is not necessarily only for verbal matter.

BAEDEKERS. As a genre, the term refers to travel guides. But more precisely, they are the guides published by the German publisher Verlag Karl Baedeker, started by Karl Baedeker (1801–1859) in 1827. The company was carried on—publishing these immediately recognizable books—by his offspring, and then by other publishers who bought the Baedeker rights, until today. These handy (large) pocket-sized volumes, usually bound in a flexible red cloth cover (so they would fit into the pockets of travelers), were filled with information written by expert travelers. Each one, generally focusing on a country or region, had advice on routes, places to go, tourist attractions, lodgings, prices, food, buildings, museums, and much more; and each had fold-out maps. They went into second and third and later editions, many with several impressions. (*See* Edition, Impression [Printing], Issue, and State; Points.) These have become COLLECTIBLE, though many of them are not terribly costly. Some can command hefty prices. (At a recent book fair I saw one for *Russia: With Teheran, Port Arthur, and Peking* [Leipzig: Baedeker, 1914] for $1250!) Originally they were published in German, but many were eventually translated into other languages. An impressive website lists hundreds of editions of these (see BDKR.com, "Baedeker Checklist"; http://bdkr.com/chklist.php [accessed 7 April 2021]). They set the standards for the genre, and many publishers now issue their own baedekers (though use of that word as a generic for "travel guide" has never caught on completely in a world where "travel guide" is more common). Trying to assemble a full collection of these, for all countries, cities, and geographical areas, and in all editions and impressions, is a fool's task.

BAL. *See* Blanck, Jacob.

BALBOA ART CONSERVATION CENTER. *See* Regional Alliance for Preservation.

BALLS. *See* Inkballs.

BAMBAM (Bookline Alert: Missing Book and Manuscripts). Originally a paper-based, and then an online, database notifying its users (primarily booksellers) of stolen books and manuscripts. The information was eventually published into a volume (*BAMBAM: Bookline Alert: Missing Books and Manuscripts* [New York: American Book Prices Current, 1982], edited by Katharine Kyes Leab). The word "missing" in the term almost always indicated that the reporting library suspected the missing item had been stolen, so people sometimes assumed that a book in the listing had actually been pilfered. Libraries, discovering a gap on the shelves where a relatively valuable book should have been, were encouraged to do as thorough and expeditious a search as possible and then, if the item did not turn up, to contact the keepers of BAMBAM quickly. The sooner that the item was listed in the database, the more likely it would be recovered.

BANCROFT LIBRARY. The rare book and special collections library of the University of California, Berkeley. The library was originally the repository of the holdings of Hubert Howe Bancroft whose collection on California and the West was exemplary. In 1950, "the original scope of the library was enlarged to include a number of other unique and special collections, including the Rare Books Collection. . . . The Bancroft Library now includes the Center for the Tebtunis Papyri, the History of Science and Technology Collection, Mark Twain Papers & Project, the Oral History Center, the Pictorial Collection, the University of California Archives, and many other distinctive collections in addition to the original core collections of Western and Latin Americana. . . . It has become one of the largest—and busiest—special collections libraries in the United States" (https://www.lib.berkeley.edu/libraries/bancroft-library/history [accessed 1 June 2021).

BANDE DESSINÉE. *See* Graphic novels.

BANDS. *See* Endbands.

BANKS, PAUL N. (1934–2000). One of America's most important conservators of library materials and teacher of many others in the field. Ellen McCrady says, "From 1964 to 1981 he served as Conservator and Head of the Conservation Department at the Newberry Library, where he improved the binding and repair practices then in use, and began training apprentices and staff in conservation. . . . Paul published one or more articles every year on bookbinding, book and paper conservation, and problems related to conservation from 1965 onward. Every time he saw a problem that was not being addressed, he would publish one of his calm, overwhelmingly thorough and rational analyses and advocate a solution" (McCrady, "In Memoriam: Paul N. Banks, 1934–2000"). Banks created the curriculum that was eventually adopted at Columbia University for library conservators and preservation administrators. The classes began on August 1, 1981, in Columbia's library school. The program, now closed, was transferred to the University of Texas at Austin in 1992. The impact he had on the world of conservation was immense.

Ellen Cunningham-Kruppa says of Banks, his "career is a window to the world of people, ideas, institutions, and mindsets that are central to an understanding of the professionalization of the field of library and archives conservation" (*Mooring a Field*, p. 10). She says that Banks, in the field of conservation, "became the field's primary educational architect" (dust jacket blurb).

BANNED BOOKS. Whole books have been written about this topic, and other entries in this dictionary touch on such items. (*See*, for instance, Bisquing; Censorship; Expurgated; *Index Librorum Expurgatorum*; *Index Librorum Prohibitorum*.) Books can be banned from libraries once they have been published and issued, or before they are issued if someone finds out what their content is and challenges it on some grounds. (*See* Edition, Impression [Printing], Issue, and State; Points.) And the grounds could be legal, moral, political, or idiotic. The banning is often local (a single public library) or regional (a county or state, or a department of education), though it could be much more widely enforced—banned by governments. Many libraries banned Salman Rushdie's *Satanic Verses*, while others "banned" it by hiding it behind a circulation desk and making it available, in a sort of hushed fashion, to patrons who sort of surreptitiously asked for it. Some of the great books have been banned, like Mark Twain's *The Adventures of Huckleberry Finn*, J. D. Salinger's *Catcher in the Rye*, Harper Lee's *To Kill a Mockingbird*, Alice Walker's *The Color Purple*, John Steinbeck's *Of Mice and Men* and *The Grapes of Wrath*, and even the Bible—along with thousands of others. The banning could come from outraged parents (who have not read the book they want their child's school library to ban), or from religious authorities, or from a group of angry people who are outraged more by the title or a single, slightly suggestive illustration than by the text. So the banning could be for textual or illustrative matter, or both. Often such action spurs the curiosity of the public and accelerates the sale of the volume. Such acceleration could drive up the price of the item—at least for a while. The Salman Rushdie book can now be had for a few dollars, though it sold for a premium immediately after it was issued.

BAR. *See Book Auction Records.*

BAR. The long handle on a platen press that is pulled to make the PLATEN descend, pressing the platen down onto the sheet of paper waiting to be printed. It is sometimes called "the Devil's tail," and the act of making an impression in the press is called "pulling the Devil's tail."

BARCHAM GREEN PAPER MILL. One of the premiere handmade-paper mills in England, supplier of paper for artists and printers and for other paper mills. Simon Barcham Green says, "Hayle Mill was built in 1808 and operated by the Green family from 1813 to 1987 when production of handmade paper ended" (see http://papermoulds.typepad.com [accessed 2 June 2021]; see also Green, *Papermaking at Hayle Mill 1808–1987*). For additional research in the field, the company's archives are particularly rich. Green says, "The Hayle Mill Archives are regarded as unique in British papermaking history in terms of their scope and completeness. This is unusual as most companies disposed of their records by intent or accident and very few paper companies survive that existed in anything like their present form prior to 1900. Hayle Mill collection mainly dates from the 1830s to 2005 and is particularly complete from 1850. In addition the archive collection is complemented by the unrivalled collection of paper samples and the finest collection of paper making moulds in Europe" (https://sites.google.com/site/simonbarchamgreen [accessed 2 June 2021]). (*See* Wookey Hole Paper Mill.)

BARGAIN BOOK. When one enters a brick-and-mortar chain bookstore (or even a local mom-and-pop one), she might see a sign for "Bargain Books." These could be REMAINDERS or just CHEAP COPIES, sold to the public as great deals. But often they are not. (*See* Remainders; Book sales; Closeouts.)

BARGAINING FOR BOOKS WITH BOOKSELLERS. *See* Consignment.

BARKER, NICOLAS. (Born John Nicolas Barker; 1932–) One of the leading bibliographers and book historians of the 20th (and now into the 21st) century. For more than 50 years he edited the eminent journal *THE BOOK COLLECTOR*, exposing him to some of the great writers about books, printing, book arts, and the rest of the wide range of topics in the book world. He worked in the publishing industry at Rupert-HartDavis, Macmillan, and Oxford University Press. At the British Library he was Head of Conservation from 1976 to 1992, and, as author or editor, he has published important studies on several bibliographical subjects. See, for example, *Two East Anglian Picture Books: A Facsimile of the Helmingham Herbal and Bestiary and Bodleian MS. Ashmole 1504*, and his studies on Aldus Manutius and Stanley Morison (listed in the bibliography of the present volume). His volumes *The Oxford University Press and the Spread of Learning, 1468–1978* and *The Butterfly Books* are other monuments of his scholarship.

BARRIER SHEET. *See* Offset sheets.

BASE TEXT. *See* Copy-text.

BASE WEIGHT (or "basis weight"). *See* Weight (of paper).

BASIL. "A vegetable-tanned, sheep- or lamb-skin, producing a soft, smooth leather but with only moderately good wearing qualities. Its smooth surface lends itself well to graining in imitation of other skins, such as goat" (Roberts and Etherington, p. 19). (*See* Roan.)

BASKERVILLE, JOHN (1706–1775). English printer and type designer also known for his japanning and PAPIER-MÂCHÉ. One of England's premier printers of the 18th century. He worked with JAMES WHATMAN to develop WOVE PAPER (ca. 1756–1757). (See Benton, *John Baskerville*, and Gaskell, *John Baskerville*.) As a type designer, Baskerville created a typeface that had SERIFS so fine that they were not printing well on LAID PAPER. When the serif landed on the sheet where a laid line was (i.e., where the paper was a bit thinner than the sheet around it), it was not printing sharply. He consulted with James Whatman, one of England's premier papermakers of the day, and they came up with paper made from a woven screen or a cloth-covered mold that had no laid lines. At the time, Baskerville was printing his edition of Virgil (*Bucolica, Georgica et Aeneis*), and one part of the book was printed on laid paper, the rest on wove paper. Since the book (the first to use wove paper) was dated 1757, we can fairly accurately date the invention of wove paper. No one knows who is responsible for the actual invention of wove paper—Baskerville or Whatman. Besides the paper, Baskerville also created several type fonts, some of which have transitioned happily to digital versions. (For a discussion, *see* Whatman, James.) (See also Bennett, *John Baskerville the Birmingham Printer*, and Pardoe, *John Baskerville of Birmingham*.) See the entry for James Whatman for a citation of Cathleen A. Baker's article on Whatman's creation of wove paper.

But Baskerville's contributions went far beyond paper. As Alan Bartram says, Baskerville "produced a distinguished and original type . . . which was generously proportioned, readable, well-fitting, masculine: very different from the chilly *romain du roi* [a late 17th-century typeface]. Sticking closer to the Aldine model than that French design, curved forms were nonetheless given a vertical stress; but stronger contrast between thicks and thins did not here result in a feeling of compression because the gradation was gentler. . . . Like much, perhaps most, good text type design, it was based on the living pen forms of its time, and not some theoretical construct. . . . Baskerville printed it well leaded [*see* Leading], on his own high-quality hot-pressed [*see* Calendered] Whatman paper, with inks he developed himself, on his own improved presses, and with generous margins. And he used it with no decoration of any kind. The whole course of subsequent typography, both in the UK and in continental Europe, was changed by this wealthy manufacturer turned 'amateur' printer" (Alan Bartram, *Five Hundred Years of Book Design*, p. 17).

BASKIN, LEONARD (1922–2000). (Gehenna Press). American sculptor, printmaker, book illustrator for children's and adult books, author, teacher, and proprietor of the Gehenna Press for more than 50 years. Best known as a sculptor (his 30-foot-long casting of Franklin Delano Roosevelt's funeral cortege is the centerpiece of the FDR Memorial in Washington, DC, and his sculptures are in museums worldwide), Baskin was also a fine-press printer, having been strongly influenced by William Blake, whose original work he early admired. Blake oversaw the creation of texts and images, paired in harmony, and Baskin excelled at this. While it was the standard position for an author to create a text and the artist to illustrate it—and Baskin did work that way with many poets and prose writers—he excelled in COPPERPLATE ENGRAVINGS and WOODCUTS and in his later years created many works of art on paper to which poets (most notably Ted Hughes) wrote verse.

Baskin began printing under the imprint of the Gehenna Press in 1942 and had several books in progress when he died 58 years later. The Gehenna Press was one of the longest-lived and most successful FINE PRESSES in the United States in the 20th century. One signature characteristic of his books is his extensive use of illustration. Another is his insistence on using the highest-quality materials available. And a third is his ability to identify and collaborate with excellent printers, papermakers, printmakers, and bookbinders. (See Baskin et al., *The Gehenna Press*; Berger, "Leonard Baskin and the Art of Printing"; Bright, "Fine Press Auguries," in *No Longer Innocent*, pp. 56–58; and Franklin, Baskin, and Baskin, *The Gehenna Press: The Work of Fifty Years, 1942–1992*.)

BASTARD TITLE. *See* Half title.

B.A.T. French abbbreviation for *Bon à tirer*, literally "good to pull," but meaning "fit to go to press, ready for the press." It is almost certainly a reference to the physical action of pulling the Devil's tail (*see under* Bar). While this term and its abbreviation are almost never used in the English-speaking world, a bookseller or collector, librarian, cataloger, or scholar may encounter it in a French bibliography or catalog.

BATCHELOR, JOSEPH (papermaker). Papermaker who supplied WILLIAM MORRIS for his Kelmscott Press. (See Peterson, *A Bibliography of the Kelmscott Press*, esp. pp. 95 ff.; and Ward, "William Morris and His Papermaker Joseph Batchelor.")

BATHYMETRIC MAP. A topographic map that shows "the depth and features of the sea floor, including coastal zones (bays and estuaries), or of some other large body of water, usually by means of contour lines called isobaths" (Reitz, *Online Dictionary for Library and Information Science*).

BATTERED. Said of PRINTING TYPE that is well used and shows it. (Hence, one may hear the phrase "broken type," though "broken" is not quite accurate since the type itself—the SORTS which constitute the "type"—are not really broken, just abused and worn.) Battered type will have broken SERIFS, missing diacritics, nicks in its characters, and so on, and it could indicate that the text printed with such type came late in the printing of the PRESSRUN, or was old and damaged before the pressrun began—and also that the type was carelessly handled. Some FINE-PRESS printers meticulously look for battered type in their PROOFREADING and jettison any sort that exhibits damage of any kind, consigning the offending sort to the hell box (*see* Black art). The printer would usually "bow" (that is, break in half) the piece of type before dropping it into the hell box, so that it could never be reused. (Of course, the metal can be recast into new type.) Also, metal plates can show signs of being battered, but the term is almost exclusively used for printing type.

BATTLEDORE. "[A] child's primer usually made of two or three pages of stiff cardboard on which were printed or impressed the alphabet, numerals, and other rudimentary material and used especially in the 17th and 18th centuries" (Merriam-Webster online dictionary, "Battledore") (*See* ABCderium.)

BAXTER PRINT. (Or Baxter-process print.) "A color PRINT produced from INTAGLIO PLATES (or sometimes from LITHOGRAPHIC stones or plates) to which oil ink is applied, using up to twenty wood or metal BLOCKS, one for each color, in a process patented by George Baxter (1804–1867) in 1835. In wide use up to the 1870s, the process produced fine quality images, intended to give the appearance of oil painting" (Reitz, *Online Dictionary for Library and Information Science*).

BEARERS (in printing). When the CHASE of the press is on the press's BED, and if the type in the chase will be inked with a ROLLER (and not with INKBALLS), printers sometimes used bearers—TYPE-HIGH strips (usually made of metal or wood) that ran parallel to two opposite sides of the FORME—to level the roller so that it would be perfectly at a right angle to the face of the type. All of the printed sorts would thus be inked smoothly and evenly. The bearers would, of course, receive ink from the roller, but they would be beyond the edges of the sheet to be printed so that the ink on the bearers would not print on the sheet.

This is something of a simplification. The bearers could have been composed of strips of wood or metal that were not as high as type height but could have thin LEADS hinged on top of them to make type-high bearers. The roller would roll over the bearers, inking the type and the bearers; the leads would then be flipped back so that they were no longer type high, and the sheet would be printed—even with the bearers within the sheet's edges—with no ink imparted to it where the bearers were.

There is another kind of bearer. With a PLATEN press, the printer could put four small type-high bearers in the four corners of the bed, beneath the platen, so that the platen would be borne up in its four corners when the printer is pulling the BAR, ensuring that the platen's surface is perfectly parallel to the surface of the face of the type. This allows the leveled-off platen to press the sheet to be printed perfectly smoothly over the type's face.

When the platen descended over a full forme of type, all of the type held the platen level. But if part of the forme were empty, the platen could be unevenly pressed over the type. Sometimes, especially in early printing (through the 17th century), a printer might fill the blank area in the chase with type or a BLOCK from another part of the book (or from another text altogether), not cutting a hole in the FRISKET. Since the frisket was closed at this point, the inked type or block would not print on the sheet that was being printed, and the inked type on the other side of the frisket would act as a bearer, keeping the platen level. Although no ink was printed onto the sheet where the frisket was closed, sometimes a BLIND-STAMPED (i.e., uninked) impression was made on the sheet showing where the type or block under the frisket was. And it was possible, as well, for a printer to use uninked type as a bearer to keep the platen's face parallel to the face of the type; in which case, a blind-stamped image of the text in that type could be made. (Carter is wrong to claim that the text of type used as a bearer, but separated from the printed sheet by the frisket, would be legible. It may not have been.)

BEATTY, CHESTER (collector; library). Collector of books, manuscripts, and other artifacts and founder of the Chester Beatty Library in Dublin, Ireland. (See Berger, "Chester Beatty." See also http://www.cbl.ie/Collections/Introduction.aspx [accessed 2 June 2021].)

BED (of the press). The surface in a press on which the FORME sits. Sometimes called the "coffin." (*See* Printing.) It was made of wood, stone, or metal. In a traditional handpress, the bed would be rolled under the PLATEN for printing. (*See also* Black art; Rounce.)

BEEHIVE. *See* Cobweb.

BEINECKE RARE BOOK & MANUSCRIPT LIBRARY. The main rare book library at Yale University in New Haven, Connecticut. The library's website says that it is "one of the world's largest libraries devoted entirely to rare books and manuscripts and is Yale's principal repository for literary archives, early manuscripts, and rare books" ("Beinecke Rare Book & Manuscript Library," Yale University Library, http://beinecke.library.yale.edu [accessed 2 June 2021]).

The library "contains the principal rare books and literary manuscripts of Yale University. . . . / One of the largest buildings in the world devoted entirely to rare books and manuscripts, the library has room in the central tower for 180,000 volumes and in the underground book stacks for more than a million volumes" (same source as above). The architecture of the building is remarkable. "The building, of Vermont marble and granite, bronze and glass, was designed by Gordon Bunshaft, of the firm of Skidmore, Owings and Merrill; the George A. Fuller Construction Company was the general contractor. Work began on the building in 1960 and was completed in 1963. The white, gray-veined marble panes of the exterior are one and one-quarter inches thick and are framed by shaped light gray Vermont Woodbury granite. These marble panels filter light so that rare materials can be displayed without damage" (same source as above).

The Beinecke family endowed the university with the resources to form the library; thus, it is not governed by Yale but is a corporation of its own. It outgrew the Sterling Library on the campus, so in 1963 a separate building was opened for the collection, which houses, among much more, the collections of American literature, western Americana, and German literature, joined by extensive holdings in other fields and in many genres. (See Taylor, *The Yale University Library 1701–1978*, and Parks, ed., *The Beinecke Library of Yale University*.)

BELLMAN'S VERSE. *See* Carriers' addresses.

BELLY BAND. *See* Wraparound band.

BENDAY SCREEN. *See* Halftone illustration.

BENEDICTIONAL. "[A] book containing a collection of benedictions or blessings in use in the Roman Catholic Church, essentially collected from those in sacramentary. The Anglo-Saxon Benedictional of St. Æthelwold is the most famous of the relatively infrequent illuminated manuscript examples, which are mostly Early Medieval" (See the Definitions.net website, "Benedictional").

BESPOKE BINDING. A binding done specifically for a customer of the bindery, presumably a one-off, thus unique, and presumably of high quality and fancy design. Booksellers are likely to call attention to this feature of an expensive volume, and to use the word "bespoke" to emphasize the rarity (i.e., the uniqueness) of the item.

BEST EDITION. Carter has an entry for this term in which he says that the edition in question was not necessarily the most AUTHORITATIVE or reliable text (*see* the entry on Bibliography, especially the section "Textual Bibliography"), but the one the particular bookseller who used the term preferred. When the bookseller is inveigled by the beauty of the volume rather than by the quality of the text—and a good text is one that scholars can rely on to be as free from errors as the editor could make it and that the author would almost certainly approve of—the seller could claim that the edition (that is to say, the physical volume) is the best one available. Scholars and discerning readers, however, would prefer a text that has gone through a rigorous editing process and that is reliable to one that looks great on one's shelves. Today's booksellers are canny enough to know the difference, and can generally be relied on to use the term properly. (*See* Favorite edition.)

BESTIARY. A book of beasts. This medieval genre "consists of descriptions and tales of animals, birds, fantastic creatures, and stones, real and imaginary, which are imbued with Christian symbolism or moral lessons. The rising of the phoenix from the pyre, for example, is related to Christ's Resurrection. / The bestiary, in all its varied manifestations, enjoyed great popularity during the twelfth and thirteenth centuries, especially in England. Among the most beloved of picture books, a favorite of the literate laity, it functioned as a library and school book and as homiletic source material. The text was frequently illustrated, in styles catering to a variety of purses, and motifs drawn from it are widely encountered in other decorative contexts, including bas-de-page scenes, heraldry, and encyclopedic world maps" (Michelle P. Brown, *Understanding Illuminated Manuscripts*, p. 17). "Bas-de-page scenes" are, literally, those at the "bottom of the page"—the BABEWYNES and bizarre creatures one finds in illuminated manuscripts. (See Camille, *Image on the Edge*, and Strickland, *The Mark of the Beast*.) Of course, modern examples abound, especially in the realm of children's picture books, but only those with fantastic creatures can rightly be called bestiaries.

BEST SELLER. (Sometimes spelled hyphenated or as a single word.) A term that has practically lost its meaning since the word "best" is a superlative, meaning that there can be only one, while the market is littered with so many of them that one cannot count how many best sellers there are. Best sellers are listed in prominent publications (e.g., in the *New York Times* or other major U.S. newspapers in their Books sections, in magazines, from the large brick-and-mortar bookstores, and—more recently—from online sales from sites such as Barnes & Noble or Amazon), based on the number of volumes sold (as reported by the publishers), the frequency of their being borrowed from libraries, or other figures. The best-seller lists are often broken down by categories: fiction, nonfiction, PAPERBACK, hardback (*see under* Boards), children's, self-help, cookbooks, and so on. Some lists are broken down into classifications and specialties (number one best-selling new novel, nonfiction book, cookbook, etc.).

The problems are the following: (1) One of the measures of "best-selling" for some of the reporting sites is "frequently borrowed," but this does not mean "frequently sold." A borrowed book could be read dozens of times. Does this add to the sales? Not really, for it represents the sale of only one copy. (2) Such information about best sellers may not be verifiable. The information about what is currently "best-selling" comes from various sources, some of which (e.g., the *New York Times*) do not divulge their own sources. (3) Large numbers of books sold to retailers may bulk up the best-seller image, but the actual number sold *by the retailer* is not always determinable. (4) Lists are sometimes created from book orders, not necessarily book sales. (See Powell, "The Bestseller Book That Didn't Exist.")

A religious text might be published, and a church may buy half a million copies to give away to its parishioners and others. The sales number is large and could make the text wind up on a best-seller list.

Also, just because a book is a best seller does not mean that it will automatically be valuable. It was certainly printed in a great many copies (that is one of the things that makes it a *best seller*), so with the law of supply and demand, there will likely be many copies, reducing the value. And the fad of the moment that gets the volume to the best-seller list might not be great reading and the volume might lose its popularity, condemning it to the list of innumerable books that have no readership within a few years. (Look at the list of Pulitzer Prizes since 1917 and see how many titles you recognize.) Thus, the fact that a title becomes a best seller does not necessarily mean that it will become COLLECTIBLE. Nor does it mean that the text is of any literary merit. Publishers may decide that a title they produced is a best seller, and will put that designation on the volume's cover—"Look, everyone! this is a bestseller. Everyone is buying it. If you don't, you are not keeping up with all those in the know. Don't be left behind." Don't be fooled by the term. Even the fact that one's local brick-and-mortar store has a whole section of them should tell you that "best" does not designate one or two.

BETTER LITTLE BOOKS. *See* Big Little Books.

BETTER WORLD BOOKS. While it is not the aim of this volume to promote any commercial enterprise, this one entry makes an exception, since though Better World Books is a .com (they are a for-profit company), they have an impact on the world in a philanthropic way.

Their website explains: "Better World Books is a for-profit social enterprise that collects and sells books online to fund literacy initiatives worldwide. With more than eight million new and used titles in stock, Better World Books is a self-sustaining company that balances the social, economic and environmental values of its stakeholders. Since its founding in 2003, the company has raised millions for its nonprofit literacy and library partners; diverted hundreds of thousand tons [*sic*] of books from landfills; achieved tons of carbon offsets through carbon-neutral shipping and created hundreds of full-time jobs with meaningful benefits in multiple locations around the world. / Better World Books diverts books from landfills by collecting material from libraries, bookstores, college campuses through the community and in other areas where surplus materials exist. It then sells those used books and contributes a portion of the revenue on each sale to support literacy, libraries and education. Books that cannot be sold are frequently donated to at risk communities in the U.S. . . . / Two billion pounds of books each year are sent to landfills. Our Drop Box program addresses the environmental impact while also building advocacy around education and book donations. The free program helps raise funds for libraries and education, supports literacy efforts locally and globally. One parking spot can help change the world. To date we have over 800 Drop Box locations and counting" (Better World Books, "About Better World Books"; https://press.betterworldbooks.com/about/ [accessed 29 July 2021]).

The company does not buy any of the books it sells; all come in from donations from the sources they mention (*see above*). Their prices, then, are fairly low for almost everything they sell, and they are seriously competitive on the USED-BOOK market. Since many of their items come from libraries, they are EX-LIB copies. But they also have untold numbers that are not from libraries and are in the really "COLLECTIBLE" category.

BEVELED EDGES. Said of the BOARDS of a binding when the board's edges have been obliquely pared down, making "beveled boards." Roberts and Etherington say, "The boards of a book, and especially the large, thick boards of heavy books, which have been cut or sanded on the outside or inside edge along the HEAD, TAIL, and FORE-EDGE. The purpose of beveling is to remove the clumsy effect of thick boards and create a pleasing, tactile quality" (p. 21).

BIBELOT. A very small (usually decorated) book. (*See* Miniature.) THOMAS BIRD MOSHER published an annual periodical called *Bibelot.*

BIBLE PAPER. *See* China paper.

BIBLIA PAUPERUM. The so-called Bible of the Poor. A BLOCK BOOK that was "one of the most popular works of the Middle Ages. Copies of this work . . .[were] illustrated with miniatures or woodcuts" (Soltész, *Biblia Pauperum*, p. III). Paul Needham explains that this genre "is a famous one, very popular late-medieval picture-text to which considerable mystery still adheres, despite the extensive body of commentary, from Heinecken (1768) onward, that has tried to eradicate it. It presents a series of scenes of the life of Christ (architypes [*sic*]), each linked to two Old Testament scenes of prefigurations (types) and accompanied by three levels of surrounding explanatory text. . . . / Dozens of manuscripts of the Biblia pauperum survive, from the early fourteenth to the end of the fifteenth century" (Needham, "Late-medieval Mysteries"), and—beyond the manuscripts—the block books that are reproduced in a few facsimiles. (The Soltész volume is one FACSIMILE. The one reviewed by Needham is another; *see* Henry, *Biblia Pauperum*, in the bibliography.) It was once thought that the block-book structure, with images and text carved into the blocks, was transitional between MANUSCRIPTS and INCUNABULA. But more recent scholarship indicates that printed volumes of the *Biblia pauperum* postdate the work of GUTENBERG.

BIBLIO.COM. *See* Online book sales.

BIBLIOCLASM. The destruction of books (also called "libricide"). This can take many forms, including book burning and mutilation. The use of "libricide" is more political, premeditated, wholesale, and of greater magnitude than is "biblioclasm" since the former is often politically inspired and state sponsored. (See Knuth, *Libricide.*) "In natural disasters, human agency is, at most, a secondary force at play, and damage to cultural materials does not raise questions about the basic order of society. The case is entirely different when books and libraries are systematically looted, bombed, and burned, for then a deliberate and calculated attack on the culture of a group is launched, and the world responds from a sense that the whole of human culture has come under attack" (Knuth, *Libricide*, p. vii; *see also* Book of hours.) The person responsible for biblioclasm is called a "biblioclast."

BIBLIOGNOST. A person who knows a great deal about books and bibliography. But for me, those who call themselves bibliognosts should be relegated to the same cell into which ANTHROPOMORPHIC BIBLIOPEGISTS are detained.

BIBLIOGRAPHICAL DESCRIPTION. The account done by a bibliographer to show what a book looks like: how it is printed and the component parts assembled, among many other things. This description allows scholars to compare copies that are not side by side. A bibliographical description consists of the following parts:

1. Typical publication information (author, title, place of publication, city of publication, and date) and possibly other things, such as size, number of pages, limitation (number of copies printed), and so on.
2. Statement of FORMAT—folio, folio in 8s, quarto, octavo, octavo in ½ sheets, duodecimo, and so on.
3. COLLATIONAL FORMULA—a list of all the SIGNATURES in the book, usually designated by letters and numbers and possibly other symbols—for example,

   π2 a-c8 A-I8 K6 (*4) (±G3)

   Since one common practice was to sign PRELIMS with lowercase letters and the main text with uppercase letters, this collational formula presumably shows a folio in 8s or an octavo with a two-leaf unsigned signature (bibliographic practice has unsigned signatures delineated with the Greek letter pi) and three eight-leaf signatures (a–c) for the prelims, followed by nine eight-leaf signatures (A–I), followed by a six-leaf signature (K). Prelims were almost always printed last—after the main text, the primary reason being that if a table of contents were present, the printer needed to have the main text in print so that she could put correct page numbers in for the contents. The K signature, in this example, would most likely have been printed with the pi (unsigned) signature since the press was set up for an octavo (in which 8 pages are printed at a time) and the first two leaves of the book and the six leaves of the last signature would allow for eight pages of printed matter in a single PRESSRUN. Note also that there is no J in the collational formula since that letter was originally a SWASH "I" and was not part of the normal alphabet. (Also lacking in the HANDPRESS PERIOD were the U or V [printers used one or the other] and the W.) Note that this is a greatly simplified collational formula. (For a thorough discussion, see Bowers, *Principles of Bibliographical Description*.) (For fuller discussion, *see* Collational formula.)

4. Notes—a section of the bibliographical description that gives information about the copy that is being described. The notes section may include copy-specific information about printing peculiarities (TYPOGRAPHICAL ERRORS, errors in CATCHWORDS, RUNNING HEADS, PAGINATION), the physical condition of the copy under scrutiny, the binding, presence of BOOKPLATES or binders' and other TICKETS, signatures of former owners, library marks, and so on. (See Berger, "The $A^8B^8C^8$s of Bibliographical Description.")

In doing the bibliographical description, the scholar wants to show what the copy she is describing looks like, but in so doing, she is also creating a description of an IDEAL COPY.

BIBLIOGRAPHICAL SOCIETY OF AMERICA. "The Bibliographical Society of America (BSA) is the oldest scholarly society in North America dedicated to the study of books and manuscripts as physical objects. It was organized in 1904 and incorporated in 1927 with the principal objectives of promoting bibliographical research and issuing bibliographical publications. These objectives have been and continue to be accomplished through a broad array of activities, including meetings, lectures, and fellowship programs, as well as the publishing of books and the *Papers of the Bibliographical Society of America* (*PBSA*), North America's leading bibliographical journal, published since 1904. The Society is open to all those interested in bibliographical problems and projects, and its membership includes bibliographers, librarians, professors, students, booksellers, and collectors worldwide" (http://bibsocamer.org/about-us/the-society [accessed 2 June 2021]).

BIBLIOGRAPHIC CONTROL. *See* Universal bibliographic control.

BIBLIOGRAPHY (the discipline: enumerative, analytical, descriptive, historical, textual). In its simplest terms, the word means "writing about books," but the word has taken on a tremendously broad range of meanings since, as an academic discipline, "bibliography" covers at least four main realms of inquiry, referred to as (1) enumerative (or distributive), (2) analytical (or descriptive), (3) historical, and (4) textual.

1. Enumerative bibliography—the most commonly understood—is the one with the greatest impact on readers of this dictionary. Traditionally, a bibliography is a listing of source materials. Thus, in this branch of bibliography, people looking for information are assisted by those who have compiled that information and made it available through references to texts that carry the materials that scholars and others are looking for. In enumerative bibliography, researchers are given citations to the scholarly sources that hold the information they seek. That is, the discipline does not offer up the actual information that people want but rather gives them the information on how to get that material by showing them where it is stored. The listing could be at the end of an article or a chapter in a book, or it could constitute the complete contents of a whole book in itself. And increasingly, bibliographical information is available on the Internet. Hence, we may hear, "The article [or chapter] has a bibliography" or "This volume is a bibliography." (One magnificent source for bibliographies is Besterman, *A World Bibliography of Bibliographies and of Bibliographical Catalogues, Calendars, Abstracts, Digests, Indexes, and the Like*. See also Silver, "Bibliographies, Checklists, and Catalogs"; and *Standard Citation Forms for Published Bibliographies and Catalogs*.)
2. Analytical bibliography (also called "critical bibliography" and closely related to descriptive bibliography) is the branch of the discipline that examines how books are put together—looking at books as physical objects. Hence, the analytical bibliographer understands and can explain the materials used (paper, vellum, and leather; boards of various kinds; metal [as in CLASPS and BOSSES]; and cloth), sewing structures, and other things having to do with binding, printing practices, tools and equipment, inks, illustration techniques, FORMAT, PAGINATION, FOLIATION, and much more. The descriptive bibliography sub-branch is the arm that shows one how to record all this information using standardized notation and templates that have been in the field for more than half a century.
3. In descriptive bibliography, the scholar, using traditional nomenclature, abbreviations, and conventions, describes a volume in such a way that someone far away with no view of that volume will know what an IDEAL COPY will look like as well as what the particular copy under scrutiny looks like, how it was put together, and how that copy differs from all others. (For a description of the standard method of creating this "picture," *see* Bibliographical description.)
4. Historical bibliography is the broadest of the branches of bibliography. "Books are historic objects, influencing all kinds of people, movements, ideas, and creations, and, themselves, influenced by and related to the vast

world around them. Bibliography, as the word's etymology suggests, is writing about books. And historical bibliography is writing about books in history and emanating from all the things which influenced their creation, reading, manufacture, movement, buying and selling, collecting, theft, censorship, illustration, and anything else that aids in the understanding of the Book. / Clearly, this branch of bibliography is exceptionally broad, for there are practically no areas of scholarly inquiry that are outside its purview. That is, there is a practically infinite number of questions to be asked about books in general and about specific ones and an equally infinite universe of information 'out there' to help researchers answer those questions. Roy Stokes says, 'In its broadest sense [historical bibliography] comprises the whole history of the book from its beginnings to the present day. . . . No detailed examination of a book can be done without regard to the social, cultural, economic, artistic background against which it was produced. Each book was produced by a particular society to serve clearly defined purposes[,] and methods at every stage of production depended upon these circumstances. Historical bibliography, therefore, includes the history of printing, illustration methods, binding, paper making, typography, authorship, bookselling, publishing, reading tastes, government control and legislation, etc.' Robert B. Harmon has a similar take on the subject: 'Broadly speaking, historical bibliography involves the history of books and of the people, institutions, and machines producing them. As a study, historical bibliography ranges from technological history to the history of art in its concern with the evidence books provide about culture and society. In this sense historical bibliography becomes archaeological in nature, with a never-ending amount of dated physical evidence.' These two authors are on the right track, but they do not go far enough in suggesting the range of disciplines that historical bibliography entails" (Berger, pp. 276–77, citing Stokes, *Bibliographical Companion*, p. 20, and Harmon, *Elements of Bibliography*, p. 86). Historical bibliography covers the globe of research. "To solve endless problems and answer endless questions about books, historical bibliographers can turn to endless sources of information. The keen researcher can identify the problem areas . . . , and can then figure out whom to turn to—what areas of inquiry must be approached—for answers. Worlds of knowledge can be opened through historical bibliography. People working with special collections and rare books, because of the materials they work with, and because of the very nature of their professions, must be historical bibliographers" (Berger, p. 278). (*See* History of the Book.)

5. Textual bibliography (sometimes called "textual criticism"). I have heard this branch of the discipline called "textual editing," but "editing" by itself is a bit narrow here since that practice entails the broader realm of textual bibliography, which uses features of the other three branches and applies it to the establishment of reliable, AUTHORIAL texts. A reliable text is one that a scholar can rely on to be as free of textual errors as possible. "[T]extual editing" is more a designation of the activity (editing), while "'textual bibliography' implies the application of scientific method, and understanding of technical issues and practices, writing and publishing, and a knowledge of the basic 'solutions' and 'theoretical approaches' to establishing reliable texts. The textual bibliographer cannot merely get a graduate degree in some discipline and then become a responsible editor of works in that field. He first needs a grounding in bibliographical theory, in the history of this discipline, in the related fields of bibliography (especially descriptive and historical), and in PALEOGRAPHY, printing history, the history of the manufacture of paper and ink, in the history and practices of bookbinding, and much more—including a thorough analysis of the biography of the person whose work he is editing and the history and condition of the world in which that author lived" (Berger, p. 279).

The goal of the textual bibliographer is to produce what is variously called a "definitive edition," a "critical edition," an "authoritative edition," an "eclectic edition," or sometimes a "scholarly edition"—a version that has been fully edited in the scholarly sense of having been produced by a careful comparison (COLLATION) of all versions the author could have had a hand in the production of. The textual bibliographer (i.e., the textual editor) gathers a listing of all VARIANTS, compares them at each CRUX, and selects the one that she thinks is the preferred one for the new edition she is preparing. The newly edited text, then, will be an amalgamation of readings from a COPY-TEXT and from all other versions from which readings have been drawn. (But see the entry for Copy-text, in which it is revealed that a copy-text may not be necessary for a responsibly edited text.) Since the editor is drawing readings from more than a single source, the product of her labors is sometimes called an "eclectic edition." Further, the newly edited definitive edition will have a scholarly apparatus containing such things as a general introduction to the work(s) under scrutiny; a textual introduction explaining the nature of the edition and the sources the editor has used for EMENDATION, with a discussion of the basis for her decisions; a list of variants (ACCIDENTALS and SUBSTANTIVES)

> that exist in all the collated versions; a table showing which variants were used for emendation; another table showing other variants that were not used for emendation but could have been; perhaps a notes section explaining particular editorial decisions, words or phrases, historical phenomena, or anything else to elucidate the text and how it came to be edited; and whatever else the editor deems necessary. There will also be a chart revealing end-of-line hyphenations in the newly edited volume (showing how hyphenated words or phrases at the ends of lines in the present edition should be styled if they are to be quoted). The new edition can be printed as a clear text or with the editorial information at the foot of the pages (as in a variorum edition). It should be noted that, as G. Thomas Tanselle has propounded, it is not necessary to use a copy-text in editing. (See Tanselle, "Editing without a Copy-Text.")

(An overview of the field can be seen in Berger, "Bibliography," pp. 249–96. See also Baker and Womack, comps., *Twentieth-Century Bibliography and Textual Criticism*; Bowers, *Bibliography and Textual Criticism*; Brack and Barnes, eds., *Bibliography and Textual Criticism*; Gaskell, *A New Introduction to Bibliography*; McKerrow, *An Introduction to Bibliography for Literary Students*; and Tanselle, *Essays in Bibliographical History*, *A Rationale of Textual Criticism*, and *Textual Criticism since Greg*. And, for overall comprehensiveness, Tanselle's Syllabus for his bibliography course at Rare Book School is a must; see Tanselle, *Introduction to Bibliography*.)

BIBLIOGRAPHY (the reference tool). A list of sources, sometimes at the end of a text, sometimes an entire volume devoted to a topic. (And also possibly online.) Hence, "The article contains a bibliography" or "The volume is a bibliography." A reference listing, guiding readers to published and unpublished sources of information.

BIBLIOGRAPHY OF AMERICAN LITERATURE. (Ed. Jacob Blanck and Michael Winship; referred to as *BAL*.) *See* Blanck, Jacob.

BIBLIOKLEPT. A book thief. *See* Book theft.

BIBLIOLATRY. Excessive love of books. Such an affliction is not as commandeering as is bibliomania, but it can cause people to do strange things.

BIBLIOMANCY. Foretelling the future and seeking guidance by opening a book (often the Bible) at random and interpreting an arbitrarily located passage.

BIBLIOMANIA. The love of books or, at the level of mania, the excessive love of books—taking bibliophily to another level. While the bibliophile simply loves books, and the person smitten with bibliolatry can wax poetic about them *ad nauseum*, the bibliomane might do foolish things for this love—like spending more money on them than he or she can afford. (See Jackson, *The Anatomy of Bibliomania*. See also Munby, *Portrait of an Obsession*; Wroth, "The Chief End of Book Madness"; and Beros, "Bibliomania.")

BIBLIOMYSTERY. A mystery novel—often a murder mystery—in which the plot revolves around books, libraries, librarians, archives, bookstores, booksellers, publishers, or printing, or some other book-related theme. The volume can also be a collection of similar book-related short stories. There are hundreds of these. (See Listopia, "Best Bibliomystery Books"; Mystery Readers International, "Bibliomysteries.")

BIBLIOPEGY. *See* Binding.

BIBLIOPHILE/BIBLIOPHILIA OR BIBLIOPHILY. A book lover/the love of books. (*See* Bibliomania.)

BIBLIOPHOBE. A person suffering from bibliophobia: an irrational fear of books. A person who will probably not acquire this dictionary.

BIBLIOPOLE. A dealer specializing in rare books.

BIBLIOTHÈQUE NATIONALE DE FRANCE. The national library of France, often referred to merely as the BN, tracing its roots to the 14th century. Its English website says, "The Bibliothèque Nationale de France collects, preserves and makes known the national documentary heritage. / The BnF's collections are unique in the world: 14 million books and printed documents, manuscripts, prints, photographs, maps and plans, scores, coins, medals, sound documents, video and multimedia documents, scenery elements. . . . All disciplines, whether intellectual, artistic or scientific, are represented in a comprehensive way. About 150,000 documents are added to the collections each year thanks to legal deposit, acquisitions and donations" (http://www.bnf.fr/en/tools/a.welcome_to_the_bnf.html [accessed 3 February 2015]).

BIFOLIUM. Two conjugate leaves; that is, two leaves connected by a fold (a bolt).

BIG BIG BOOKS. *See* Big Little Books.

BIG LITTLE BOOKS. (Sometimes abbreviated "BLB" in booksellers' listings.) Small (4½ × 3⅝ in.) hardbound books produced starting in 1932 (with *The Adventures of Dick Tracy*) by Whitman Publishing Company (in Racine, Wisconsin) aimed primarily at children. The format was full-page illustrations on RECTOS and prose text on VERSOS. The illustrations, all black and white, are usually drawings in printed black borders. The covers have a color illustration with the author's name, and with advertisements for other books in the series on the rear. And each volume had hundreds of pages. The books, in different series, were often abridged versions of popular children's fiction, along with texts on cartoon characters, TV show SPINOFFS, science fiction, and COMIC-BOOK and cartoon-strip characters. Whitman set the standard, and other companies, seeing the popularity of these little volumes, followed. "The various publishing companies that produced BLB-type books were Dell (Cartoon Story Books® and Fast-Action Stories®); Engel-van Wiseman (Five-Star Library Books®); Fawcett (Dime Action Books®); Goldsmith (Radio Star Series®); Lynn (A Lynn Book®); Ottenheimer; Saalfield (Little Big Books® and Jumbo Books®); Waldman (Moby Books®); Whitman (Big Little Books® and Better Little Books®); World Syndicate (High Lights of History Series®). In addition, a few premiums and other peripherally related items include Ice Cream Cup Lid Books; Top Ten Books; Wee Little Books; Penny Books; Nickle Books; Karmetz and Perkins Books; Big Big Books®; puzzles; cards; and so on" (Educational Research and Applications, "Learning About Big Little Books: What Are Big Little Books?"). The Educational Research and Applications website, listing all of the BLB titles, discusses the different phases of the publishing of these immensely popular books, and it highlights live links that delineate the sources of many of the titles, among other things. The site says, "When you look at the following listings, you will see that some titles are highlighted. These titles are programs derived from radio programs. Some titles are adaptations of radio scripts, some are stories about the radio characters. These titles are linked to a page describing the radio program, and if you click on the radio on the link, you can hear the introduction to the program." There is even a Big Little Book Club, with its own publications (http://www.biglittlebooks.com/club.html [accessed 26 February 2021]). (See Findlay, *Big Little Books: The Whitman Publishing Company's Golden Age, 1932–1938*; Borden, *Big Book of Big Little Books*; L-W Publishing, *Price Guide to Big Little Books & Better Little, Jumbo, Tiny Tales, A Fast-Action Story, Etc.*; James Stuart Thomas, *The Big Little Book Price Guide*.)

BIGMORE, EDWARD CLEMENTS, AND CHARLES WILLIAM HENRY WYMAN. Compilers of the celebrated text referred to as Bigmore and Wyman, *A Bibliography of Printing*, and reprinted several times (the most recent of which was in 1978). Originally published in three volumes, this giant volume of nearly 1,000 pages covers the broad history of printing, focusing on the major printers and publications, with extensive commentary for many of the entries. Scholarship on much of what is here has been superseded, but what Bigmore and Wyman have compiled is still a rich source of information. One indication of the meticulousness of their research may be found in their entry "Periodical Publications" (vol. 2, pp. 153–95). Their commentary begins, "The following is a list of Periodical Publications throughout the world devoted to Printing and the allied arts. It takes account of defunct as well as of existing journals, and gives the size, the interval of publication, the date of establishment, name of printer and editor, and other particulars, as far as obtainable. . . . This list will be found to be by far the fullest of the kind ever published" (p. 153). Bigmore and Wyman is still an oft-cited and quite rich resource.

BILINGUAL EDITION. An edition of a work, published in two languages, sometimes because the work is likely to be read by an audience fluent in one of the two languages, or because the work is co-published by two companies serving countries whose readers are conversant in the indigenous languages of the publication. Usually the text in the original language is printed facing the translated version, though in some volumes the original text in one language is followed by the text in the other. There are even INTERLINEAR texts, with the original, in one type size (or one TYPEFACE), running above the translated text in a contrasting face. (*See* Polyglot.)

BI-MONTHLY/SEMI-MONTHLY. (Added here because these terms are often confused for one another.) Bi-monthly means every other month. Semi-monthly means twice a month. Similarly, biennial means every other year. Semi-annual means twice a year.

BINDER'S BLANKS. *See* Blanks.

BINDER'S BOARD. "The wood, pasted paper, single- or multiple-ply sheets, or other base stock, for the covers of any bound or cased book, i.e., any book in hard covers. Boards, in one form or another, have been used to cover and thereby protect the leaves of codices since the earliest times of bookbinding" (Roberts and Etherington, "Binder's board"; https://cool.culturalheritage.org/don/dt/dt0299.html [accessed 28 January 2021]).

Though many a volume in BOARDS, especially in the earliest days of bookmaking in the Middle Ages and INCUNABULA period, was bound in real wood, either with the wood exposed or under leather or vellum, perhaps the most common form of a book in boards is that made with CARDBOARD (one term for which was "PASTEBOARD," since it was made from layers of paper pasted together). Also, a volume bound in boards made of paper only, and possibly with a paper cover on the boards, with no animal skin, is said to be in "paper boards."

BINDER'S CLOTH. The subject of an extensive literature, binder's cloth came into commercial use in the first quarter of the 19th century. Carter distinguishes this cloth from that used for whole editions. He says that binder's cloth can designate the cloth covering any book, whether or not it is the same as the cloth used for the entire edition (Carter, p. 46). He adds that such cloth may be used for pamphlet collections, French novels, or any volume that a collector did not wish to have bound in leather. He points out that for modern collectors, such a binding is less than completely desirable since the cloth binding will be neither attractive nor original. He adds that binder's cloth is clearly different from that used by the publisher and is thus often easy to spot since it is usually printed from metal type or from common metal dies that were not made specifically for the volume (though sometimes the cover lacks decoration completely). (See Carter, p. 46.) The distinction may have been sharp and understood in Carter's day, and it still holds. But today, most rare-book people do not understand this distinction, and they use "binder's cloth" to mean the cloth used on any publisher's binding. (*See also* Publisher's binding/Publisher's cloth.)

BINDER'S DUMMY. A group of LEAVES or SIGNATURES, possibly a full printed text of a book but more likely a batch of sheets (printed or blank) created to be the same size (horizontally, vertically, and BULKING) as will be the final published volume. The dummy is a copy that a binder uses in producing a preliminary binding for a book. The publisher may not wish to send a full printed text to the binder, so the binder is given (or creates him- or herself) the dummy of the same dimensions as the final volume. The binder does a binding on spec and sends it to the publisher for approval. The binder may produce more than one "practice" volume in numerous, variously colored, and variously decorated materials before the publisher settles on one or more for the commercial edition. For example, the final edition may have red cloth with one decoration on it, blue cloth with another decoration, and a tooled leather version. Assiduous collectors, wanting every manifestation of the volumes they amass, will want not only each of the final commercial versions but also the dummies, which show the evolution of the design of the bindings. (*See* Binder's sample.) These dummies seldom survive since, once they have served their purpose (giving the publisher a choice), they can then be discarded.

BINDER'S SAMPLE. A sample of the work of a bookbinder to show her skills: the quality of her work and materials. Created to showcase one option potential customers can avail themselves of. This is in contrast to a BINDER'S DUMMY, created for a publisher as an option for the binding of a particular text.

BINDER'S TICKET (sometimes called "binder's pallet")/ **BOOKSELLER'S TICKET.** A small LABEL affixed to a book (often on or below the front or rear pastedown) identifying the book's binder. Carter identifies three kinds of such tickets. From about 1725 to about 1825, they are small labels, ENGRAVED or printed LETTERPRESS, attached to the top outside edge of the front endsheets. Such labels identifying well-known binders can add considerably to the value of the books. This kind of label can be made by what Carter calls a "smoke-print stamp," and it might appear on either of the front endpapers (pastedown or free), or such a mark could be done from a PALLET, printed in ink, with gold leaf, or BLIND STAMPED, on one of the TURN-INS, usually at the very bottom of the binding. Carter adds that the label can be transferred from one volume to another and that the stamped kind cannot. A second version of binder's ticket, much the same as the first, was printed, and it appeared on edition bindings from the middle of the 19th century on. It usually appeared at the bottom of the rear endpaper. Carter points out that these kinds of labels may help scholars who wish to know whether the book is bound in a primary or a secondary binding. They should always be mentioned in a BIBLIOGRAPHICAL DESCRIPTION or library catalog of the volume. The third type is not from the binder but from the bookseller (as is shown in the illustration below). It was a form of advertising, and it could reveal whether the seller

Bookseller's Ticket on Henry Aldous Bromley, *Outlines of Stationery Testing: A Practical Manual* (London: Charles Griffin; Philadelphia: Lippincott, 1913). Photograph by Jeff Dykes.
Collection of the author.

was a stationer or a binder or merely a seller of the volume. (See Carter, pp. 46–47.) The uneducated, coming on such a phenomenon, will probably call it a "label," but the proper term (coming from who knows where) is "ticket." (And don't call a TYPE CASE a "tray" or a "drawer" no matter what it looks like.) What scholars can learn from these tickets is important: the existence of binders and booksellers, their location, and, by looking at the books they appear in, in some cases the dates of their work. As William Smith Mitchell reminds us, "A study of these labels shows that binding was carried on not only in the cities but also in some towns and villages from which bookbinders have now disappeared—for example, Brechin, Bruton, Penrith, Ulverston. This is a reflection of a social phenomenon, the disappearance of large private libraries in country houses, the binding for which was done locally, and not confined as it is now to a few centres mainly in large towns." And he also says that "these are worth examining for their intrinsic aesthetic interest, as examples in miniature of the art of the engraver and the craft of the printer" (Smith Mitchell, "Bookbinders' Tickets"). Readers of the present volume are in this wonderful world of the book for many reasons. One of those reasons is the pleasure of the physical objects; and these tickets, tiny though they are, have their own beauty that should be looked at with care when one sees one of them. The type was set or the plate was engraved to produce this ticket, and the work was not done haphazardly; it was *designed* to notify and to please. These tickets, additionally, constitute another area for collectors to indulge in.

BINDER'S-TITLE. It looks as if Jacob Blanck, in his *Bibliography of American Literature*, coined this term, designating a phenomenon that seems not to have had a term of its own. He says, "*binder's-title* indicates that the TITLE on the binding varies from that on the title page. Example: the binder's-title of T. B. Aldrich's *Pampinea and Other Poems* (1861) is *Poems of a Year*" (Blanck, *Bibliography of American Literature*, vol. 1, p. xxiii). More recently one might hear "COVER TITLE," indicating that the title on the cover differs from the one on the title page—or is the only title the volume exhibits.

BINDERS' WASTE. *See* Printers' overruns.

BINDING. (The old term was "bibliopegy.") The element of a book that holds all the parts together. The topic is so extensive that this short definition is clearly inadequate, especially since there are a great number of binding methods, materials, and styles. Thousands of books and articles have been written on the subject.

The complexity of the subject is reflected in Carter's entry (pp. 47–48) and by the 33 cross-references he has to other entries in his glossary. (See the Roberts and Etherington volume; Brenni, *Bookbinding*; Breslauer, *The Uses of Bookbinding Literature*; French, *Bookbinding in Early America*; Greenfield, *ABC of Bookbinding*; McLean, *Victorian Publishers' Book-Bindings in Cloth and Leather*; McLean, *Victorian Publishers' Book-Bindings in Paper*; Miner, *The History of Bookbinding 525–1950 A.D.*; Needham, *Twelve Centuries of Bookbindings, 400–1600*; Nixon, *Five Centuries of English Bookbinding*; Nixon and Foot, *The History of Decorated Bookbinding in England*; Pearson, *English Bookbinding Styles, 1450–1800*; and about 2,000 other titles.)

Roberts and Etherington, for the term "binding," give the following: "1. The style in which a book is bound, e.g., edition binding, library binding, etc. 2. The covers of a bound book. 3. The finished work resulting from the processes involved in binding a book. 4. The concept of securing the leaves or sections of a publication so as to keep them in proper order and to protect them. 5. The style in which a book is decorated, e.g., fanfare style, cottage style, etc." (p. 23). Each of these could generate a long essay or a series of monographs. Consult Appendix D for a list of all the terms in this dictionary that pertain to binding.

BINDING COPY. A copy of a book with its binding in such poor shape that it is not in COLLECTIBLE condition but would be worth rebinding. A term sometimes used by booksellers in describing CONDITION. The tendency of a bookseller to want to present a text in the best condition possible may lead her to take such a volume—with its cover in poor condition—and have it rebound in a splendid cover; but losing the original binding would be losing some of the original information the volume had that a researcher might be interested in, and could also diminish the value of the item since the original binding, even in poor condition, might be much more desirable to a collector than would be a fancy new cover. Carter says that the term has been supplanted, by the mid-20th century, by READING COPY.

BINDING VARIANT. *See* Variants.

BIRD & BULL PRESS. *See* Henry Morris.

BIRDCAGE. *See* Cobweb.

BISHOP'S FIST. *See* Fist.

BISQUING (or Bisking). An unbelievably obsolete word that is almost impossible to locate in a dictionary, but which Carter mysteriously has, which is defined as marking out a part of a text by painting it over. Here I should say that it was not Carter, but Nicolas Barker, who added it to the eighth edition of Carter's *ABC*. (It was not in his 7th edition of the work.) Barker is, to be sure, one of the great bibliographers and book historians of the 20th century. His knowledge in the field is great. He points out that the painting over could be done to censor and/or to CANCEL a passage. I guess it is appropriate in any dictionary about books since it is a term one may encounter somewhere. But a search of some unabridged dictionaries, even one from the 19th century, turned up nothing; only a foray into the *Oxford English Dictionary* turns up Edmund Calamy's 1713 *Abridgement Baxter's Hist. Life & Times*, in which one finds: "To be bisk'd, as I think the Word is; that is, to be rub'd over with an Inky Brush" (see the *OED* at https://www-oed-com.ezproxy.simmons.edu/view/Entry/19470?redirectedFrom=bisking#eid [accessed 5 January 2021]). Even Calamy himself seems to be unsure of the word. (A second citation from Robert Southey of 1838 is the only other use of the word recorded by the *OED*. The Southey text reads, "The chapter . . . has been not bisked, but semiramised"; whatever that means!) The *OED* lexicographer notes: "No etymology known: perhaps an error of Calamy's, followed by Southey." It is all the more to Barker's credit to know this word, obsolete as it was when the *OED* listed it. But more to the point for the present volume: What is it doing in Carter? How many of my readers (other than Barker himself) have ever encountered it? How many booksellers have used it in the last hundred years or are likely to use it now? If the idea of doing a new edition of Carter was to bring it up to date, Barker was going in the wrong direction.

As for "semiramised," Richard Hollick, on his Making Book website, says, "I'm struggling to come up with anything in the bisking world which might be derived from Semiramis, wife of Nimrod and later Queen of Assyria in her own right. Herodotus attributes the levees containing the Euphrates to her, and tells us there was a gate of Babylon named for her. She was alleged to have been raised by doves. Ammianus Marcellinus credits her with being the first person to castrate youths in order to create eunuchs" (https://rhollick.wordpress.com/2017/03/28/bisquing/ [accessed 24 January 2021]). Perhaps the cutting that creates eunuchs is used metaphorically for the cutting of the text, but that is pretty far afield. I'd like to delete this term from Carter, but since it is there, I guess I need to leave this entry here. We are more likely to use the common term "redacted," the blacking over of a text (or parts of it) for legal, moral, or security purposes. (*See* Caviar.)

BITE. The IMPRESSION of printing TYPE (or any other RELIEF printing method) in the paper. In relief printing, a surface that "sticks up" is inked and paper is pressed against it. Ideally, if the MAKEREADY is done properly and the printer is skillful enough, the type touches the sheet, not pressing into it. The old saying in the press shop is, "The type should kiss the sheet, not bite it." Such an impression, however, as three-dimensional as it is, is a sign of LETTERPRESS printing, suggesting handwork and value. So printers are not too likely to press out such bite. (*See* Unpressed.) A bookseller may say in a catalog, listing, for instance, a broadside, "A good clear impression, showing significant bite." The term has also been used for the impression made by copperplate engravings.

BLACK ART (printing). As one story goes, the medieval church would have frowned on any handmade objects that were identical. Two identical objects must surely have been the work of the Devil. Printing would have produced identical copies of texts, so it was looked on as the work of the Devil. Hence, printing was called the "black art," and much terminology related to printing reflects this. The BED of the press is the "COFFIN." The receptacle into which printers threw broken and unusable type (that was later to be melted down for the making of more type) was called the "hell box." The master's assistant was called the "PRINTER'S DEVIL." Pulling the BAR on the press was called "pulling the Devil's tail."

BLACKLETTER. *See* Gothic.

BLACK TULIPS. Exceptionally rare items that may appear once in a bookseller's or collector's lifetime (or not at all). Michael Vinson says about some of the forged items that were sold by John Jenkins, "The Texas forgeries were of the type that rare book dealers call 'black tulips.' The name comes from the Dutch tulip bloom speculation bubble of the 1600s and is a metaphor for something so rarely seen that a collector might have one chance in a lifetime to buy it" (Vinson, *Bluffing Texas Style*, p. 5).

BLAD. *See* Dummy.

BLADES, WILLIAM. (*Enemies of Books*, . . .) English bibliographer and printer (1824–1890) known for his excellent scholarship on WILLIAM CAXTON (see in the bibliography his *Life and Typography of William Caxton, England's First Printer* and, for his most enduring text, *Enemies of Books*).

BLAKE, WILLIAM (1757–1827). Writer, engraver, artist. After apprenticing with other engravers, Blake struck out on his own, developing a technique for creating his texts. "Blake's technique was to produce his text and design on a COPPER PLATE with an impervious liquid. The PLATE was then dipped in acid so that the text and design remained in RELIEF. That plate could be used to print on paper, and the final copy would be then hand colored. / After experimenting with this method in a series of aphorisms entitled *There is*

No Natural Religion and *All Religions are One* (1788?), Blake designed the series of plates for the poems entitled *Songs of Innocence* and dated the title page 1789. Blake continued to experiment with the process of illuminated writing and in 1794 combined the early poems with companion poems entitled *Songs of Experience*. The title page of the combined set announces that the poems show 'the two Contrary States of the Human Soul'" (Poetry Foundation, "William Blake"). Blake's method became his signature, and his books are tremendously COLLECTIBLE.

BLANCHED/BLANCHING. Said of whitish area on, say, the cover of a volume that shows a rather paled-out or whitish color, where the same material around it is darker. This is a defect that could have been caused by exposure to light or to moisture, or to a fast-evaporating solvent.

BLANCK, JACOB (1906–1974). American bibliographer and an expert on the printing of American authors. His monumental work *Bibliography of American Literature* (traditionally referred to merely as *BAL*) lists thousands of texts from hundreds of American authors, giving information on editions, printings, issues, states, and POINTS (*see* Edition, Impression [Printing], Issue, and State; Points). "Compiled by Jacob Blanck and completed by Michael Winship and Virginia L. Smyers, the *Bibliography of American Literature* (9 volumes, 1955–1991) provides more than 37,000 records of the literary works of 281 American writers from the period of the Revolution to 1930" (https://yalebooks.yale.edu/series/bibliography-of-american-literature-series [accessed 7 June 2021]).

BLANK. If it were not for the key word, the headline with the page number, and the present sentence, this would be a blank page.

BLANK(S). An unprinted sheet in a book or pamphlet. This can be complicated, for sometimes blanks are inserted by a binder after the front (and presumably an equal number before the rear) ENDLEAVES (sometimes called "binder's blanks," though the term is seldom used today). I have seen quite slender volumes with many such blanks inserted so that the bound volume has some BULK. If the source of the blanks is the binder, they are not strictly part of the printing of the book, and they should not be part of a COLLATIONAL FORMULA. A meticulous DESCRIPTIVE BIBLIOGRAPHY may list such blanks in a Notes section. If the blanks are the printer's contribution to the volume, they are thus part of the original printed part of the book, and they should be listed in the collational formula. As Carter points out, any volume with printer-created BLANKS WANTING is incomplete. He says that they often appear at the front of a book, sometimes in the text where one section is divided from another, and often at the back of the volume (Carter, p. 53). As I mentioned, in quite slender volumes—as with a LIMITED EDITION of a PRIVATE-PRESS printing of poetry—the binder may put a number of blanks in around the printed SIGNATURES—the same number of blanks at the front as at the back—to give the final bound volume added thickness.

Carter mentions the 17th-century (or earlier) practice of printing a SIGNATURE LETTER at the bottom of an otherwise blank leaf at the beginning of a volume. HARRY DUNCAN was known to have followed this practice. The signed leaf is thus not strictly a blank. WILLIAM MORRIS's Kelmscott *Chaucer* has a signature (only the single letter "a") on the very first printed leaf of the book (the first leaf of the "a" signature), the so-called blank—which is thus not blank. (This leaf is lacking in the World Publishing Company facsimile edition [1958], so the reader cannot see this nonblank leaf.)

If a scholar is preparing a descriptive bibliography and wishes to produce an accurate collational formula, blanks at the beginning of the volume (and even those at the end) could pose a problem, for it might not be discernible if they were part of the book's printing or of its binding. That is, did the printer include them as part of the printing of the book, or did the binder add them for one reason or another? Sometimes a published collation mentions a blank and a scholar's volume has one. Is the blank in the scholar's volume the same one that is mentioned in the published collation? That is, is the blank in the collation (presumably part of the book's printing) matched by the blank in the scholar's volume, which could have been added in a rebinding of the book? Carter says that the paper the blank is made from should be compared with the paper used for the printed text. The texture or weight of the paper of these leaves could differ. If the book is printed on LAID PAPER, the distance between the CHAIN LINES could differ. The WATERMARKS could differ (if any are present or discernible). If the blank is CONJUGATE with a printed leaf, it is certainly part of the printing of the book, and this blank must be mentioned in the collational formula. Carter also warns that sometimes the number of binder's blanks could vary from one copy to the next—that is, they are not always the same even for copies within an edition (see Carter, p. 53).

In some bibliographies I have seen, the owning library has disbound reference volumes and had them rebound with blanks throughout, allowing the library to insert additional entries (usually by hand) to bring the volume up to date with references the original compiler missed. These are blanks inserted for the sole purpose of adding information to supplement what was an incomplete listing. Computers have made this practice essentially obsolete.

Much has been made here of blanks, for they can be excellent evidence of publishing practices and can radically affect the value of books.

BLANK BOOKS. Volumes with no text of any kind. That is, all the pages are blank. These can be had in any brick-and-mortar bookstore. The aim of the item is to allow someone to fill the pages—writing, drawing, TIP-INS, and so on. One definition of "book" is this: an object with a text (verbal, pictorial, or both) in a container. Since the blank book contains no text, is it a book? This is getting too philosophical for me. It's a book.

BLEED. In printing, the bleed is the part of a text or picture that goes beyond the normal margins of the PAGE, sometimes off the page itself. It could also be the part of the LEAF that is to be trimmed off after the text is printed. If the original design was to have, say, a ¾-inch margin at the FORE-EDGE, the page may be printed with a 1-inch margin, allowing for the trimming of the extra ¼ inch. That ¼ inch is the bleed. It is not unusual for art or even sometimes actual text to be printed in the bleed area, even up to the very edge of the leaf.

The term also refers to pigments that have run, through having been exposed to water. A bookseller might describe the situation as follows: "Signature of former owner on front free endpaper with BLEED-THROUGH to verso of leaf and following leaf," indicating the damage, as the next term below indicates. Bleed-through generally indicates that the pigment has become visible on the verso of the leaf; straight "bleed" means it has run on one side of the leaf only. (*See* Feathering.)

BLEED-THROUGH. A situation in which ink from one side of a LEAF has soaked into the paper and shows on the VERSO of that leaf. This kind of "staining" could also be caused by an adhesive that shows on a side of the leaf opposite the one it was originally used on. (*See* Bleed.)

BLIND STAMPED. (Or Blind tooled.) Said of any printing or tooling that is done with no ink or foil. Hence, a binding can be blind stamped with a pattern on its cover (e.g., leather, paper, or cloth) or the pattern indented into the cover (but with no ink or foil used), or a page in a book (or a broadside) can have some of the text printed in ink and some additional blind stamping of the LEAF. Sometimes such printing is merely said to be "blind," as in "title in blind on cover." The blind text is usually done with binders' tools or printing type. Some Japanese prints are done from several WOODBLOCKS, each imparting a different color onto the substrate, and sometimes with a block (often the last printed) impressed into the sheet with no inking, imparting a texture to the sheet. This is a form of blind stamping. (*See* Tooling.)

BLOCK. A printer's or binder's tool used for printing a page or stamping a book cover—made from a variety of materials, as with a WOODBLOCK, a magnesium block, a zinc block, and so on. Booksellers will say, "Blocked in gilt on cover." (Note my objection to this locution; *see* Gilt.) Carter says that in the United States, the more common term for "blocking" is "stamping," but today that distinction is gone, and the two words are used pretty much interchangeably in both countries.

In books illustrated by woodblocks, the illustration is done on a block of wood, and one may see in a dealer's catalog or a librarian's MARC RECORD describing the images, "The blocks show much wear" or "The blocks were lost in the 1885 fire."

Carter offers a third definition in which blocks for printing were created through photoengraving, or blocks could be created with a screen, creating what is called a HALFTONE PROCESS. Others produced with no screen could be "line blocks" or "CUTS" (created with ZINC plates mounted TYPE HIGH). Carter calls these last "zincos"—what he calls the American term, but "zincos" is a fossil; the term in the United States was most often "zinc plates" or "zinc cuts." Here is a good example of a Carter term that one of his later editors should have brought up to date.

BLOCK BOOK. (Sometimes printed as a single word.) A book printed not from movable type but from woodblocks (possibly, later, from other materials, such as linoleum). Sometimes called "xylographica" (literally, "wood-printed"), these volumes date to after the introduction of printing from MOVABLE TYPE. The images and text (with images taking up more space than the text) were carved into blocks of wood and printed. These are usually fairly short texts, composed mostly of illustration, though they often had some short texts cut into the blocks. Most of the texts of block books were religious, to be shown to an illiterate audience (hence the predominance of picture over text). One old belief is that block books preceded printing in the West from movable type, but recent scholarship based on the paper used in them has suggested that they were all from the 1460s or slightly later, though a few may be from the 1450s. Carter says that occasional exemplars of these books show up and date to as late as about 1500 (p. 54), and he comments on their scarcity and high value. (Frederic Goudy, perpetuating the common error, says that block books are "typical of the books immediately preceding type printing" [*Typologia*, p. 11].) (*See* the entry for Stevenson, Allan H.; Allan H. Stevenson, *The Problem of the Missale Speciale*; *see also* Woodcut/Wood engraving/Woodblock.) (And in case you wanted to know, since most block books are printed on one side of a leaf only, they are known as anopisthographic books—a good word for after-dinner conversation, just in case you are a deipnosophist.)

BLOCKBUSTER. "Something, such as a film or book, that sustains widespread popularity and achieves enormous sales" (*American Heritage Dictionary of the English Language*, p. 197). Jessica Ruston delineates what makes for a blockbuster. Some of the characteristics of these works are that they are long (no one ever saw a short blockbuster); "These are big books not just physically, but in every way. The lives of the characters in a blockbuster happen on a grand scale. Poverty is extreme, the frequently chronicled rise to stratospheric wealth even more so. There is little in the way of middle ground. Addiction devastates, ambition turbo-charges, passion fuels an inferno. Whether it is the sexily scandalous Hollywood excesses of Jackie Collins, or the catastrophic meltdown of Atlantan titan of business Charlie Croker in *A Man in Full*, these are lives lived in technicolour. / Blockbusters often span both decades and continents, skipping through years and countries with ease. There is usually a major city involved, often counterpointed by a country escape, or a remote and exotic location" (Ruston, "The Ingredients for a Blockbuster Novel"). She adds that there are lots of unpleasant people, lots of detail, and extremes of poverty and wealth. And they are grand BEST SELLERS. When a publisher does not anticipate this popularity, it may have a small print run of the first impression. (*See* Edition, Impression [Printing], Issue, and State; Points.) Hence, the first edition, first impression could have strong market value while all later printings do not.

BLOCKING/BLOCKING PRESS. Impressing a design or a text into the surface of a cover. "The term applies to the impressing of type, blocks, etc., with foil, leaf, etc., or without (blind blocked)" (Roberts and Etherington, p. 26). Deep impressions can be made using a blocking press, and it can be done in an automatic press for edition binding. "The blocking press first came into use in England in the period

1830–31 for gold blocking on book cloths. Before this time books were blocked with a block that was heated off the press and then laid on the cover and pressed. Also called 'embossing press'" (p. 27). Booksellers often use the term "blocked in gilt" (when they should actually say "blocked in gold"). (*See* Gilt; *see also* Tooling.) The blocking press is the tool the binder uses to block the design.

Blocking is used in the world of conservation to indicate that two or more adjacent sheets have stuck together when they should not have. This can occur if the recently printed leaf is pressed tightly to another, with the ink still tacky; or if two leaves with adhesive or coating on their surfaces are pressed so tightly that the leaves adhere to one another. I have seen this kind of thing happen when there are TIP-INS, the adhesive on which is placed too close to the edge of the item tipped in; the adhesive squeezes out onto the SUBSTRATE, causing that leaf to stick to the facing one. This is not strictly blocking since only the point of sticking is attached, not the whole leaf. But it can be seen as related and might be called "blocking."

BLOCK-PRINTED PAPERS. To save money, bookbinders in the late 17th century looked for materials that were decorative and would substitute for leather in their bindings. Block-printed papers, printed from woodblocks, sometimes in several colors, were one of the answers. (Another was MARBLING.) Thousands of patterns were created throughout Europe but mostly in Germany and Italy. A six-color illustration took an equal number of blocks.

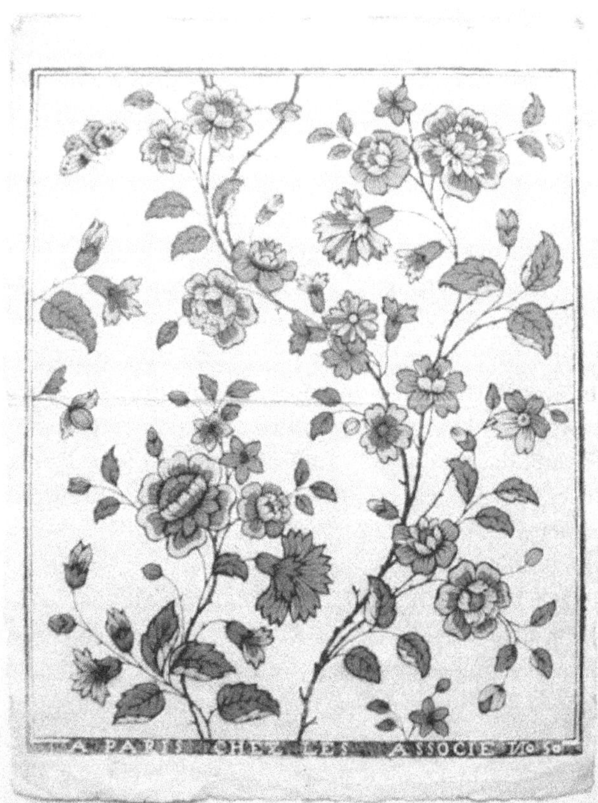

An 18th-century French block-printed sheet. Collection of the author.

An 18th-century wooden printing block. Photograph by Jeff Dykes. Collection of the author.

BLOOK. An item that looks like a book. Included here because, as explained in the new introduction to this volume, these things are likely to show up at book fairs—even the most exalted fairs. There is a massive world of blooks out there, including salt and pepper shakers, hot-water flasks, stone tablets, small boxes holding paper-related items (like repair tapes, alpha-numeric characters, hole reinforcements, photographic corners, and the like), cookie tins, cigarette lighters, and thousands of other items with titles, spines, and covers. This term was coined by Mindell Dubansky, a serious collector of blooks; her exhibition at the GROLIER CLUB in New York showcased about 200 pieces from her collection. Since these items have existed for centuries, since they are common items for sale by booksellers, and since there was no formal name for them until Dubansky named them, this dictionary offers to codify the term so that collectors, booksellers, librarians, and others will know what to call them. (Note: On 9 June 2021, Michael Laird Rare Books offered an item in an online catalog that he identified as a "blook." His description: "Arezzo, Italy: Sacchetti, n.d. Near Fine. Miniature silver 'blook' [28 × 22 × 7 mm], with blue enamel 'covers' and red enamel 'spine labels,' hinged at front cover which opens to reveal a tiny compartment, edges of 'text block' appropriately striated, and the latch on the 'fore-edge' in perfect working order. / Excellent, and highly curious silver 'Blook,' created out of sterling silver by a well-known Tuscan silversmith: Gianfranco Sacchetti Arezzo Italie" [https://fairs.abaa.org/item/1400066510 {accessed 9 June 2021}; but this will be a dead link since it is to a showing at the RBMS Booksellers' Showcase, which was held for only a few days.]) The word has made it into the trade!

BLOOM. A defect on the surface of some SUBSTRATE, like a film, binding of leather or cloth, or sheet of paper, that shows up as a sort of floral, whitish, opaque or semi-transparent stain, caused by mildew or some other problem. It can be powdery, waxy, or just cloudy, and it could obscure text beneath it or not.

BLOW BOOKS. (Also called "enchanted albums"; "flik-fliks"; "magic picture books"; and "trick magic books.") Volumes from the world of magic, immensely COLLECTIBLE (if you can find one). The magician riffled through the LEAVES of the book to show the audience page spread after page spread of black-and-white illustrations. Then after some gobbledygook and give and take with the viewers, he would riffle through the book again to reveal all of the images in full color. A third riffling might reveal only blank pages throughout. The trick was accomplished with the specially prepared volume, with every other leaf (or every third leaf) shorter at the FORE-EDGE than the intervening leaves. The Conjuring Credits website says: "Books with pages that magically change their contents—text, drawings, color, blank, etc.—began to be mentioned and explained in the 1500s. The earliest mention was by Gerolamo Cardano in his 1550 work, *De subtilitate*: 'Formas varias in uno eodemque libello ostendunt, semper prioribus abscedentibus.' (Conjurers show changing forms in one and the same book, with the earlier ones always vanishing.) . . . The name 'Blow Book' is said to have come from the practice of conjurers['] blowing on the book, or having spectators do so, as the magical means of effecting the transformations on its pages. The secret was a system of subtly (and sometimes not so subtly) trimmed page edges" (Conjuring Credits: The Origins of Wonder, "Blow Book"). (Kim Merker created the volume *Sequence, Sometimes Metaphysical*, poems by Theodore Roethke, in such a way that, if the book is riffled through in one direction, one sees the poems, in the other direction, one sees the illustrations. Though this was not done for the purposes of a magic show, it has the same effect as a blow book—and perhaps may be so designated.) Early volumes of blow books can command fairly high prices. The anonymous *De nieuwe Toverlantaarn* (Amsterdam: c. 1770) was offered by the bookseller Antiquariat F. Neidhardt at the "Firsts Online" book fair in May 2021 for £6800.

BLUE BIBLES. *See* Tijuana bibles.

BLUELINES. PAGE PROOFS. These are often created using a printing and photographic process that yields blue (or sometimes brown) proof sheets; hence the name. They come at the end of the proofreading of a text, after the GALLEYS, so authors are discouraged from making any (or too many) changes at this stage of a text's production. They are especially useful if the text has illustrations of any kind since, up to this point, the author would have been reading for textual problems, not the placement or actual printing of illustrations (that could be in the wrong place, the wrong illustration, or printed in reverse). Bluelines are expensive to produce, and many publishers do not supply them. (I wish they had for me: my chapter on "Endleaves" [*see* the bibliography] had two images reversed with one another.)

BLUESIES. *See* Tijuana bibles.

BLURB. The statement on a dust jacket about the book the jacket is on. Often written by impartial critics, these statements could also be penned by friends of the author or by the author him- or herself. Jeffrey A. Trachtenberg says, "Publishers have long counted on their best-selling authors to craft pithy words of praise to adorn the dust jackets of other writers. . . . [A] juicy blurb is considered essential for a fledgling author" (Trachtenberg, "What's an Author to Do With No Blurb on the Book Jacket?"). Naturally, blurbs are complimentary, for no publisher would ever put onto the jacket of a book a statement that would negatively affect sales. Thus, the veracity and impartiality of these statements are always suspect. In recent years, a flap in the book industry arose when professional writers with some reputation decided they would no longer write blurbs (blurb writing took time away from their own professional—and remunerative—writing) unless they were compensated. The conflict of interest this engenders is clear: "Pay me to write a blurb, and I will write a good one—no matter how bad I think the book is." (See Trachtenberg, "Authors Struggle to Get Blurbed.")

Carter identifies several styles of blurbs. The first is a quotation that comes off like an advertisement. The second is original prose from the critic who pens it, and it could be purely objective (but still complimentary). The third he calls "ostentatiously personal" (p. 55). His full entry is amusing and worth reading.

Since blurbs always praise, they are to be taken with a grain or a pound of salt.

BOARDING. "A method of producing a design on the grain side of leather, as well as softening it, by means of a series of creases produced on the surface of the skin. Boarding is accomplished by folding the leather, grain side to grain side, and working the fold board knife across its surface. A straight or 'willow' grain results when the skin is boarded on [*sic*] one direction, and a box or 'cross' grain when it is also boarded at right angles to the first. Boarding a third time in a direction diagonal to the first two produces a pebbled-grain pattern" (Roberts and Etherington, "boarding"; https://cool.culturalheritage.org/don/dt/dt0387.html [accessed 30 May 2021]).

BOARDS. The covers of a book. They can be made of wood or CARDBOARD. A book "in boards" is a hardcover volume. The boards can be bare, or they can be covered with vellum, leather, paper, cloth, or some other material (I have seen a binding with boards covered in TAPA CLOTH and one with AMATE). Carter has a long entry for this term, distinguishing various terms that include the word "boards," but today those fine points are pretty much lost on booksellers and collectors and librarians—even those with a good deal of knowledge of the terminology and experience in the trade. Today, "in boards" means "not a paperback," and it usually implies, for most books produced after about 1825, a hardbound volume with cardboard cover, covered in one of the materials mentioned above. "In boards" for books from the HANDPRESS PERIOD (up through about 1800) could mean that the boards were wood or cardboard, usually the latter. The term can be loosely used to mean "cover," as in "front board detached." Jacob Blanck points out that "[m]ost frequently books bound in paper-covered boards were issued with a printed label, or labels, which supplied the title and other pertinent information. . . . Books were also issued in printed boards with the title information printed directly on the paper covering. Such printing may occur on the spine, the side or sides, or on all three parts of the cover. Not infrequently books in boards were issued without any outer mark of identification" (Jacob Blanck, *Bibliography of American Literature*, vol. 1, p. xxx).

BOARD SHEAR. A large paper or board cutter used to trim the materials the binder uses. There are many models, most of which are able to cut quite large boards or sheets. They are hand operated.

Board shear.

Photograph by Dan Goldberg. Courtesy of American Bookbinders Museum; https://bookbindersmuseum.org/ (accessed 10 August 2021).

BODLEIAN LIBRARIES/BODLEIAN LIBRARY. A consortium of 28 libraries throughout Oxford University, including the Central Library. Their special collections and rare book libraries are world renowned for their holdings, which include "manuscripts and archives, rare books, printed ephemera, maps, music and digitized collections" ("Bodleian Libraries, University of Oxford"; https://www.bodleian.ox.ac.uk/home#/ [accessed 23 April 2021]). The Bodleian Libraries website says, "Oxford's libraries are among the most celebrated in the world, not only for their incomparable collections of books and manuscripts but also for their buildings, some of which have remained in continuous use since the Middle Ages. Libraries in the Bodleian Libraries group include major research libraries; libraries attached to faculties, departments and other institutions of the University; and, of course, the principal University library—the Bodleian Library—which has been a library of legal deposit for 400 years" (Bodleian Libraries, "Visit").

Distinct among these libraries is the Bodleian Library, the main research library at the University, with more than 13 million printed items—the largest of the 28 libraries in the institution (and second in size in Great Britain only to the BRITISH LIBRARY). The library's roots go back to the 1320s; over the next century and a half it suffered because of political and religious fervor against Catholicism. "The library was rescued by Sir Thomas Bodley (1545–1613), a Fellow of Merton College and a diplomat in Queen Elizabeth I's court. He married a rich widow (whose husband had made his fortune trading in pilchards) and, in his retirement, decided to 'set up my staff at the library door in Oxon; being thoroughly persuaded, that in my solitude, and surcease from the Commonwealth affairs, I could not busy myself to better purpose, than by reducing that place (which then in every part lay ruined and waste) to the public use of students'. / In 1598, the old library was refurbished to house a new collection of around 2,500 books, some of them given by Bodley himself. A librarian, Thomas James, was appointed, and the library finally opened on 8 November 1602" (Bodleian Libraries, "Visit"). Today the library is looked upon as one of the great treasure houses in the world of rare books and manuscripts.

BODONI, GIAMBATTISTA (1740–1813). Italian printer, type designer, and publisher from Parma, Italy. "He left home for Rome when he was just 18 years old, and found work as an apprentice at the press of the Propaganda Fide (the missionary arm of the Vatican). There he learned the art of PUNCH cutting and refined his skills as a COMPOSITOR and designer. In 1768, he was called to Parma to set up and run the royal press for Ferdinando I, the duke of Parma" (blurb for Valerie Lester's book, *Giambattista Bodoni*, http://www

.valerielester.com/bodoni [accessed 3 October 2015]). His books were elegantly printed with generous margins, and his typefaces were also elegant and legible, with a sharp contrast between thin and thick strokes. (See Lester, *Giambattista Bodoni: His Life and His World.*)

BODY OF TYPE. The main shaft of a SORT, that is, the metal that makes up the sort, from front to back and side to side. When one talks of the body of type, however, he generally means the size of the type—the size from front to back. Lawson defines "body" as "the size of the physical type as measured from back to front" (*Printing Types*, p. 25). Avis has "the depth of shank upon which the printing character is cast, as 12pt. (body), 10pt., etc." (Avis, *The Bookman's Concise Dictionary*, pp. 39–40). (*See* the image in Appendix B.)

BOLTS (in an UNOPENED book). Refers to the folds along the edges of LEAVES in a bound book. If the volume is a QUARTO, the original leaf is folded twice, producing four leaves. The first and second leaves are CONJUGATE (and the third and fourth leaves are conjugate) through the bolts at the HEAD of the leaves. Eventually, the bolts are removed—either slit through as with a letter opener or chopped off as with a guillotine-type paper cutter. A volume with its bolts still in place is said to be UNOPENED. When the bolts are removed, the formerly joined leaves are still said to be conjugate despite the removal of the bolt. (*See* Cropped; French fold.) The folds at the GUTTER, where the sewing is, are not strictly "bolts"; they are "spine folds."

BOND PAPER. SIZED paper. In paper with no sizing (WATERLEAF), ink will FEATHER. Sizing fills the infinitesimal air pockets around all the fibers so that no capillary action will draw ink into the sheet where the air pockets no longer exist. The sizing fills these pockets and binds the fibers to one another, hence "bond paper." (*See* Sized/Sizing.)

BOOK. I begin my "History of the Book" course by asking the students, "What is a book?" This engenders a discussion that goes on for more than an hour. We never come to a perfect consensus. The issues are grand: What *form* does a book take that distinguishes it as a book? What *contents* does a book have that make it a book? If you go into a *book*store, what do you expect to find on the shelves? What can you buy there? The discussion eventually gets to the following two statements: "Yesterday I bought a book" and "Yesterday I read a book"—showing that books have texts and containers, even if the text is blank. For the purpose of this dictionary, the foregoing is enough of a definition. If you are reading this volume, I assume you know what a book is. After all, you will know it when you see it. (*See* E-readers.)

BOOK AUCTION RECORDS (often referred to simply as *BAR*). *Book Auction Records* began in 1903, published in book form, and the series survived, a volume a year, until 1996. Individual volumes of *BAR* can sometimes be found on the web. One bookseller has for sale volume 93 (1995 [published in 1997]). (See http://www.stylophile.btinternet.co.uk [accessed 18 March 2012]. This site says, "The last available volume was published in 1996 and the new team will soon be releasing details of new multimedia developments." To date, I have not been able to discover a replacement. And this 2012 link seems to have perished.) Each volume listed items that had a HAMMER PRICE of £70 or more for books sold in the United Kingdom; it also listed maps, charts, plans, and atlases (this last in the regular listing of books sold); it did not list manuscripts or autograph letters. As with ABPC, the *BAR* volumes had their drawbacks. Of course, no pricing guide can be complete, and these volumes merely listed items that came up for AUCTION, not the millions of titles that did not. Thus, a search in *ABPC* and *BAR* might yield no mention of a volume that a librarian wanted to know the value of. Further, and a serious drawback, was that even if a librarian found the title she was looking for, there was no way to see the book that was at auction, so whether the item she was holding was the same as the one listed in the volume was impossible to determine. And even if they were the same, there was no way to compare CONDITION, bindings, or other copy-specific features since the *ABPC* and *BAR* texts did not always give enough information to describe the copy auctioned. They even skimped on a description of condition, which, as noted, is an important part of the value of a book. Further, it was not always clear from the price realized at auction whether the price listed included the buyer's premium. (*See* Buying at auctions.) The digital version of *ABPC* explains that all prices given are hammer prices (i.e., the final bid price), not showing the buyer's premium. If that premium was low or high (12 or 25 percent), the actual price paid was significantly different from the hammer price. Thus, the listing in these volumes was approximate at best and quite misleading at worst. *ABPC* and *BAR*, it must be remembered, were not published as price guides per se. They were simply notices of prices realized at auctions. But they were always used by librarians, booksellers, and collectors as one of the first things to consult for prices. Booksellers liked to say something like, "This is a scarce book; no copies have been on the auction block in the last 25 years." Of course, not being offered at auction was not necessarily a mark of rarity. (*See also American Book Prices Current.*)

BOOK AWARDS. The number of book awards given each year worldwide is astonishing—in the hundreds. There is no room here to recount them all, nor even to mention individual ones. The point is that when a book wins an award, it is presumably for something superior in it: the text, the illustrations, the adaptation to a particular audience, the preeminence in a particular genre, and so forth. Such recognition often means that there will be an increase in sales of the title, and the award then enhances the library of those who own a copy—especially a FIRST EDITION, FIRST IMPRESSION. Sometimes a publisher will have a seal or label TIPPED ONTO the DUST JACKET (or will print a new, augmented dust jacket) to indicate the award and entice buyers in a brick-and-mortar store. But by the time the book has won the award and these seals are applied, the book could be in its second or a later impression, and the collector will want a copy of the first impression of the first printing. (In fact, if the collector is a COMPLETIST, she will want a copy of both impressions, and certainly one with the seal.) (*See* Edition, Impression [Printing], Issue, and State; Points.) Booksellers may wish to research titles to see if they are award winners, and then mention this in their write-ups. For a startling view of many of the awards for books that are "out there," look at the amazing website "List of Literary Awards," showing the prizes in many countries: https://en.wikipedia.org/wiki/List_of_literary_awards (accessed 29 July 2021).

As an aside, a book-award-winning volume does not guarantee anyone that the title will achieve perpetual fame. Take a look at the Pulitzer Prize list and see how many titles you recognize. Under Pulitzer Prize for Fiction, how many of you have read (or even heard of) the following: Ernest Poole, *His Family*; Margaret Wilson, *The Able McLauchlins*; Louis Bromfield, *Early Autumn*; Julia Peterkin, *Scarlet Sister Mary*; Oliver La Farge, *Laughing Boy*; Margaret Ayer Barnes, *Years of Grace*; T. S. Stribling, *The Store*; Caroline Miller, *Lamb in His Bosom*; Josephine Winslow Johnson, *Now in November*; Harold L. Davis, *Honey in the Horn*; Martin Flavin, *Journey in the Dark*? This is not to say that these books were not worthy of the prize. But a Pulitzer (or any book prize) does not guarantee eternal fame. Even the coveted Newbery and Caldecott Prizes for children's books, that may spur sales, do not guarantee long-lasting fame. There are many books that have won these awards that are now obscure. Only the universal and timeless messages in the books themselves can give them long-lasting renown.

BOOKBINDER'S LABEL/BOOKSELLER'S LABEL. *See* Binder's ticket/Bookseller's ticket.

BOOK CLUBS/BOOK CLUB EDITIONS. Many book clubs arranged with publishers to sell at a reduced price (or to give away as premiums) copies of the publishers' popular books. These "clubs" were actually subscription services, offering at low prices recent or popular titles to members of the club. Sometimes the publisher would merely make a large number of copies of a title available to the club for distribution to its members, with no variation in the printing or the physical object, with the possible exception of a DUST JACKET that varied from that of the regular commercial version. The dust jacket may have "Book Club Edition" printed where the price would have gone on the FLAP of the jacket of the regular version. In the middle of the 20th century, some book clubs impressed into the lower right corner of the back cover a blind-stamped circle, diamond, or square (or some other geometrical shape—called a "dimple") beneath the dust jacket, indicating that this was a book club edition (though the word "edition" would be a misnomer; *see* Edition). (These subscription clubs are not related to members of the FELLOWSHIP OF AMERICAN BIBLIOPHILIC SOCIETIES [also known as FABS], which are BOOK COLLECTORS' CLUBS.)

In many cases, the book club versions were printed in a smaller size than were the first printings from the publisher, on cheaper paper, and with thinner BOARDS. They also might have had cheaper, uncoated dust jackets and possibly a different text on the jacket. The most famous of these is the Book of the Month Club, which was emulated by many other clubs purveying their own niche titles. (*See* Appendix E, "Book Collectors' Clubs and Societies." *See also* Limited Editions Club.)

THE BOOK COLLECTOR. One of the longest-running and most important book-related periodicals. The journal's website says, "Beloved by BIBLIOPHILES for nearly seventy years, The Book Collector is a quarterly journal and digital archive filled with erudite articles, beautiful illustrations, reviews, news, AUCTION results and more" (*The Book Collector*; https://www.thebookcollector.co.uk/ [accessed 28 July 2021]). The journal was founded in 1952 by Ian Fleming. (Today it is run by James and Fergus Fleming, Ian Fleming's nephews.) In 1965, "The Book Collector's then editor, John Hayward, . . . died and after a brief interregnum Nicolas Barker took up the reins as owner/editor. It is to Nicolas that this journal owes its continued existence. His was the inspiration and the hard work that kept it going. In 2016, after 50 years at the helm, he called it a day and handed it over to the founders' nephews, James and Fergus Fleming. / Today it remains the only journal in the world that deals with all aspects of the book, covering subjects ranging from typography to national heritage policy, from medieval libraries to modern first editions" (The Book Collector, "About: Starting Something"; https://www.thebookcollector.co.uk/about [accessed 28 July 2021]). And it may be the longest-running book-collecting journal in English.

BOOK COLLECTORS' CLUBS. (Grolier, Caxton, Roxburghe, Zamorano, Ticknor Society, etc.) Organizations whose members are usually collectors, producers (printers, publishers, binders, authors, or illustrators), or sellers of books. Not to be confused with clubs of readers who gather to discuss titles they have all (presumably) read. They are loosely gathered under the umbrella of the FELLOWSHIP OF AMERICAN BIBLIOPHILIC SOCIETIES. They charge dues and sometimes create their own publications (newsletters, books, or pamphlets). Some have clubhouses; some use the facilities of other organizations. Some have their own libraries, and most of them hold somewhat regular meetings, offer programs of various kinds (lectures and visits to important libraries and private collections, local and distant), and have a social media presence. Most of them have gone co-ed, though a few are still single-gender clubs. Since membership in some of these organizations is not guaranteed but must be voted on and the number of members in some is strictly held to a specific number, membership in some can carry a good deal of prestige in certain circles. Some of these clubs are members of the Fellowship of American Bibliophilic Societies (other such clubs are not members of FABS). FABS also has 22 international affiliates and clubs in other countries (see http://www.fabsbooks.org/Pages/InternationalAffiliates.aspx [accessed 25 January 2015]). THE GROLIER CLUB in New York is the oldest of these in the United States, founded in 1884. (*See* Appendix E, "Book Collectors' Clubs and Societies.")

BOOK CURSES. *See* Curses.

BOOKDEALER. *See* Dealer/Bookdealer.

BOOK FAIRS. Events at which books (and other library materials) are on display, for order or purchase. In this sense, they are commercial; hence, they differ from exhibitions, at which books are on display for enjoyment and education. There is no room in a single entry to do justice to this topic. Fairs have a long and distinguished history. The most famous of the early fairs is that in Frankfurt, Germany, the Frankfurter Buchmesse (the word, of course, means book fair), first held in the 1460s or 1470s (the date of its founding is uncertain). The aim of these expositions was for publishers to show their wares. They also were the venue for deals to be made for the acquisition of authors' new works to be published or translated. Fairs of all kinds of books, and at all levels (from the cheapest to the most expensive), have proliferated, and they are held all over the world. The publishing industry holds a huge such fair in the United States, in a sense modeled on the one from Frankfurt: open to commercial publishers at all levels of sales. Many countries have their own antiquarian bookselling organizations, and these have fairs. There were nearly 100 such fairs scheduled for 2020 (see Kotobee, "The Comprehensive List of International Book Fairs in 2020"). In Great Britain there is the ABA book fair, held since 1957 (see Fletcher and Harrington, "History of the Book Fair"). In the United States the ABAA holds a few fairs yearly, in New York, Boston, and California (the last of these alternating its venue from Northern to Southern California—lately in Oakland and Pasadena, but the venue is subject to change for economic and convenience of access reasons). And the antiquarian-book sellers may also hold mini-fairs at appropriate meetings. A small coterie of ABAA booksellers have such a "pop-up" fair at the annual meeting of RBMS.

Local and regional chapters of book organizations also hold fairs, parallel to those held by purveyors of EPHEMERA. But thanks to the COVID-19 pandemic, most fairs were canceled in 2020. (The splendid New York ABAA fair—the organization's 60th one—was the last major one held in the United States in that year, from 5–8 March 2020. As usual, at that fair, I spent more money than I had.) And the major fairs are usually accompanied by parallel ones at nearby venues—the so-called shadow fairs.

During the COVID pandemic lockdown, most such enterprises have been shut down, but the almost irresistible lure of these events to serious collectors and librarians (and to booksellers themselves) has spawned a new generation of book-fair operations, with online sales keeping many a bookseller afloat. Booksellers had sometimes immensely expensive bills to show at the fair: buying space for a booth; cataloging, packing, and shipping their wares; transportation to the fair's venue; paying for local assistance to get the goods to the booth (and home again); food and lodgings; evening drinks with colleagues and clients; and so forth. COVID spawned a new phenomenon: the online book fair. Most of the expenses just delineated were reduced or removed completely, the sellers could display one or 50 choice items, and their clientele was not limited to those "in the room"; they now had a worldwide audience. Anyone with a computer and access to the Internet could pop into the fair and see what was for sale. And instead of doing a single fair a year, they could do one each week. It was no more work than was their normal activity of selling their books on the web through any one of the ONLINE BOOK SALES sites. The convenience and affordability of this method of purveying books (and other materials) has changed the game for good, and these fairs will be with us henceforth.

BOOKFINDER. Like ABEBOOKS, an online search service selling hundreds of millions of volumes. The site lists volumes from over 100,000 booksellers worldwide. The Book-

Finder site claims to list more than 150 million books, and it is a good site to use for pricing, listing copies from least to most expensive. It also lists each item with its postage, showing the total for the volume and the additional cost of shipping. It lists books in most European languages along with English. (*See* Internet; Online book sales.)

BOOK FONT. A collection of all the SORTS of one TYPEFACE in a single size, packaged as a single lot, with the sorts in the numbers predetermined to be the optimum quantity based on their statistical frequency of use. (*See* Job font.) The term implies that the typeface will be used for written text, not for display. (*See* Display type.)

BOOK FORM. If an author publishes her work serially in a magazine over a number of issues, the publication of that text is said to be published "IN PARTS," not in "book form." Bibliographers, booksellers, collectors, and librarians who are describing FIRST EDITIONS generally refer to the first appearance of a work in book form, not in parts. (*See* Parts/In parts.) This can be tricky, however. If Edgar Allan Poe's "The Raven" appeared a hundred times in magazines and anthologies—over, say, a hundred years—and then a publisher decided to issue a volume containing only the poem with many illustrations, would that be considered a first edition? It would certainly be the first edition *in book form*.

BOOK JACKET. *See* Dust jacket.

BOOKKEEPER. *See under* Deacidification. (Probably the only word in English with three sets of double letters in a row.)

BOOK LABEL. A printed LABEL affixed to a book, usually on the front pastedown (*see* Endpapers), identifying an owner of the book. It is distinguished from a BOOKPLATE in that the label has only a name, while a bookplate will have some graphic device and the name or monogram of an owner and sometimes other text (e.g., "Ex libris," "From the books of . . . ," or perhaps a saying or motto).

BOOKMAN'S PRICE INDEX. (Often referred to merely as *BPI*; subtitled *A Guide to the Values of Rare and Other Out of Print Books*.) One of the old, often-consulted pricing guides for books being sold by dealers through their catalogs. "Established in 1964, Bookman's Price Index is an index to rare and ANTIQUARIAN books offered for sale in the catalogs of 100–200 book dealers in the U.S., Canada, and the British Isles. The number of titles listed in each volume is approximately 15,000; in the course of a year some 50–60,000 books are described. Volumes do not supersede previous volumes. Each volume covers catalogs from the previous 4 to 6 months. Entries Include [*sic*]: Title and author, edition, year published, physical description (size, binding, illustrations); detailed description of the book's condition including flaws, amount of wear, comment on scarcity; price as listed in catalog; catalog source and number. Included are three appendixes: 'Association Copies' (Listing books by significant people who have owned them); 'Fine Bindings' (Listing books that have had special bindings applied, arranged by the name of the binder; 'FORE-EDGE PAINTINGS' (Listing books that have had scenes painted on the edge of the book, listed by the name of the artist)" (see https://www.amazon.com/Bookmans-Price-Index-Guide-Values/dp/1414406606 [accessed 2 June 2021]). It is still being published in book form twice a year.

A problem with this source is that the prices listed were for specific copies, the condition of which was not always perfectly explained since the editors of *BPI* had to rely on the expertise of the booksellers whose catalogs the items were listed in. Some of the dealers were not experts in the book world and described condition poorly. Further, there was no way for *BPI* to determine if a book so listed was actually sold. It could have been listed by a bookseller at a grossly high price (there were no online services to consult when *BPI* was published), and the book could have languished on the dealer's shelf for decades.

BOOKMARKS. Bookmarks, or bookmarkers, are items usually loosely inserted into a book to mark a particular place for reference or for easy return and continued reading. They can also be sewn in, as was popular for certain kinds of reference or religious books, when a colored silk ribbon was sewn into the volume—sometimes two or more. Often the pigment in these sewn-in ribbons was acidic, or the dye in them was not fixed, and the dye or acid in them migrated to the leaves they touched. Peter Beal notes that their use is quite old, some from as early as the 12th century. They could have been made of VELLUM, leather, paper, or strings or ribbons. (See Beal, *A Dictionary of English Manuscript Terminology, 1450–2000*, p. 45.) Further, many bookmarks are used by dealers (of books and any other kind of product or service) as advertising, and they can be a great source of information. Publishers create bookmarks by the thousands advertising new volumes. There are serious bookmark collectors, and their holdings may wind up in special collections departments.

BOOK OF HOURS (the plural is often used: Horae). A medieval Christian devotional volume guiding the prayers of the devout, revealing what prayers to say at what time of the day and during what religious season. There were typically eight times of the day at which to pray (called the canonical hours); they were matins, lauds, prime, tierce, sext, nones, vespers, and compline. Prayers differed by the religious season and by the place (e.g., prayers in Paris differed from those in Bologna), hence scholars' ability to determine the place of use of an undated, unsigned book of hours. A typical purveyor's note in a catalog would say, "Use of Paris." (*See* How-to books.)

Many of these volumes were illuminated (*see* Illumination), some quite sumptuously. (There is a tremendous literature on this genre of books, including a great number of facsimile versions of books of hours. See Christopher de Hamel, *A History of Illuminated Manuscripts.*)

One of the disgraces of the book world is the wanton destruction of these books, often by BREAKERS, who take the books of hours (and other illustrated volumes) apart to sell the illuminations. Some have gone so far as to remove individual illuminated MAJUSCULES from leaves, to sell only the single letter. This abominable practice—a form of BIBLIOCLASM—would die of its own accord if there were not equally unscrupulous purchasers of these orphaned leaves and pieces. The religious (or antireligious) fanatics who destroyed books of hours for doctrinal reasons have their 19th- and 20th-century counterparts in the biblioclasts who profit from this practice.

BOOK OF MANNERS. *See* Courtesy book.

BOOKPLATE (sometimes hyphenated) (also called an "Ex libris"). A label (usually paper, though I have seen leather and vellum ones) pasted into a book (usually on the front pastedown [*see* Endpapers] or the front free endpaper), identifying the book's owner. An immense literature on bookplates exists, along with a great many collectors of these items. There is even the American Society of Bookplate Collectors and Designers (see http://bookplate.org [accessed 15 July 2021]) and an international equivalent, the Bookplate Society (http://www.bookplatesociety.org [accessed 2 June 2021]). This society's site says, "Bookplates, also known as ex-libris, have since the 15th century been placed in books to declare ownership. Many artists, some famous such as William Hogarth, Aubrey Beardsley and John Piper, have designed bookplates, and many significant people (e.g. Samuel Pepys and Rudyard Kipling) have used them, but a personal bookplate has been available to anyone owning a library and wishing to place in the books a printed design as a mark of possession." They can be produced with various kinds of printing, and they can be rectangular or other shapes. They may be printed in color, or be hand colored. And a brick-and-mortar bookstore will usually have for sale a selection of commercially printed, stick-on plates for anyone to use.

Bookplate of William J. Thoms on a volume with gilt dentelles. Alexander Pope, *The Dunciad. An Heroic Poem. In three books.* (London: Reprinted for A. Dodd, 1728.)

Courtesy of the Rare Book and Manuscript Library of the University of Illinois at Urbana–Champaign.

Bookplates can have extraordinary value (intellectual and fiscal), for they can show the PROVENANCE of the book to which they are affixed (though a bookplate adding value to a book could have been tipped into a volume by an unscrupulous bookseller or collector—creating a false provenance), and they could be created by collected artists or printers. (*See* Book label; Ex libris.) (See Allen, *American Book Plates*; Castle, *English Book-Plates*; Lee, *British Bookplates: A Pictorial History*; Lee, *Early Printed Book Labels*, Lee, *British Royal Bookplates*; and many more.)

BOOK SAFE. A book that has been hollowed out so that it sits on a shelf looking like an ordinary book but is designed to hide valuables (jewelry, money, or miniature books). As it is done to deceive, the title page and several of the front pages will usually be left intact so that someone opening the volume will see what looks like an ordinary TEXT BLOCK. All of the other LEAVES of the volume might be glued together, with that little boxlike opening additionally glued to the rear board. It is a form of an ALTERED BOOK but not for artistic purposes. It is also possible that a BLOOK can be used to keep valuables safe, so it too may be called a book safe. In fact, I would like to be given credit for the coinage "Blook safe."

BOOK SALE. Really! do we need an entry for this? Let's give it a go: A commercial event at which books are sold. The sale can be in an analog venue or one online. For instance, a shop may have all of its stock (or part of it) listed on the web at their regular prices, or they all could be on sale for 25 percent off their regular marked prices. This latter is a "SALE."

The difference, then, is between items "for sale" and items "on sale." The generic term "book sale" implies the latter: discounted items. This distinction obtains for sales in shops or for ongoing ONLINE BOOK SALES, in which 1) booksellers list their wares in any of several databases (the selling of books in an online environment), 2) specially coordinated sales of books, like those held by the ABAA or one of the Getman's fairs, and 3) sales of discounted items (either in a shop or online, in both cases in which booksellers have special sales at reduced prices. That is, a bookseller may have an online presence with its catalogs or its complete stock listed, but may have a "sale" of portions [or all] of its stock at, say, 20 percent off the stock's regular prices). Book sales, of course, can also be held by various institutions (a university selling off its duplicates and discards, for instance), thrift shops, or estates. Public libraries are famously the hosts of book sales—of duplicates or discards from their collections or from hosts of books donated to them for the sale purpose. The "on sale" type of sale purports to offer bargains, and it is true that occasionally a valuable volume may appear for a reasonable price. But just the notion of "sale book" does not guarantee that the item is really a bargain. (*See* Remainders.) (In walking through a shopping mall, one will invariably see signs that say "Up to 75% off on selected items." Some purveyors of books do the same in their announcement to their online [or even in-person] customers that discounts of 75 percent can be found in the stock. The least they can do is print the discount information in all one size of type.)

BOOK SCOUT. A bookseller at the lower end of the profession but not necessarily one who acquires books of poor quality or low value. Book scouts generally do not have their own book businesses; they acquire, for fairly low prices, good books that they sell to established booksellers with "storefronts" (which could imply dealers whose business is fully online). The scout buys low and sells for a medium price—close to wholesale—letting the established booksellers realize a retail price. The scouts may go to Goodwill or other such thrift shops, garage/tag sales, flea markets, regional bookstores or book fairs, ephemera fairs, estate sales, antiques malls, or anywhere else where they can find library materials. A good scout can recognize a good book regardless of the item's subject area. Scouts can be exceptionally knowledgeable about the trade, and good ones have supplied libraries and also booksellers at the top of the profession.

BOOKSELLER. *See* Dealer/Bookdealer.

BOOKSELLERS/BOOKSELLING. With the coming of the Internet, anyone can be a bookseller. The term, however, implies that the seller is a professional with some good experience in the trade, though it does not automatically guarantee this. Bookselling, naturally, goes back as far as books go, and where there is profit to be made, people will enter a trade sometimes with no experience or training. *Caveat emptor.* There is an extensive literature on bookselling. For a historical angle, see Duff, *A Century of the English Book Trade.* (For other titles on the subject, see the bibliography for works by Charles B. Anderson and Nat G. Bodian.)

BOOKSELLER'S CATALOG. A publication from a bookseller listing a portion of her stock for sale, with such information for each entry as author, title, place and date of publication, publisher, condition, presence of illustrations, number of pages, size, and, for certain items, much more. Most items will be priced, though occasionally, to keep the reader (i.e., the customer) from gawking, squawking, or fainting because of a tremendously high-priced item, the dealer will write "POR" (PRICE ON REQUEST). The catalogs can be extremely brief and perfunctory, or they can contain mini-essays of great learning, with extensive references, color illustrations, and dealers' personal commentaries. (*See* Internet.)

Carter points out that such catalogs can be simple and inexpensive or elaborate and costly (and pompous). They come in many sizes and can list a few or thousands of items. Some reveal the compiler's personality, with much humor, sarcasm, or self-deprecation. Some have extensive commentary, with great detail, and some are so spare that the reader gets little more than title, author, and publication information. Some give extensive description of CONDITION, and some give a mere letter ("g"—for "good," which means little). The order of entries can be alphabetical by author, alphabetical by subject, alphabetical by printer (whatever the cataloger thinks the customer may seek alphabetically—possibly a combination of all these), chronological, or, occasionally, with no discernible organization.

Today, a single dealer's catalog can be a listing of his entire stock, completely accessible online from anywhere in the world where there is a computer and an Internet connection. (See Berger, appendix 3, "Booksellers' Catalogs and the Business of Selling," pp. 493–504.) That is, a bookseller can list, on the web, every item she has for sale. The listing can be at the bookseller's site, or all the items can be on the web as part of a larger search service, like AddAll or VIALIBRI, in which case the dealer's "catalog" would be essentially invisible, with many entries dispersed into a larger searchable database.

For most collectors (and librarians in charge of collection development), the bookseller's catalog is enjoyable reading, and it is certainly educational: What is available on the market? What books and other materials have been produced? Who are their authors and editors? What are they worth? (This is not always discernible since some items may be grossly under- or overpriced.) What are the current collecting trends? What booksellers are carrying what kinds of books? And endless other information can be gleaned from these tools. In fact, just how learned the trade of booksellers—especially those at the highest level—is can often be seen in the meticulous scholarship that goes into these volumes. The catalogs' compilers often have substantial reference libraries available to them, and their entries in the catalogs are sometimes accompanied by bibliographical references to show where the information in the catalog entries comes from.

Catalogs were often issued with a few black-and-white pictures showing an item or three. But with advances in printing technology, it has become relatively inexpensive to produce catalogs with full-color images of selected items. One bookseller in particular, Between the Covers, set an early standard of showing a color image of just about every item listed. The idea was not only to entice the buyer with a view of the coveted piece but also to give a more accurate indication of condition than words could sometimes convey. Many booksellers now use this method of selling.

(Footnote: Some booksellers enjoyed compiling and sending out their catalogs, and their delight was reflected in some of their entries. Jim Presgraves, proprietor of Bookworm and Silverfish, wrote in an entry of one of his catalogs that this book "attracted dirt like the Veep's friends attract bird shot"—with reference to Dick Cheney's shotgun blast. See Bookworm and Silverfish catalog 551 [Item 126] of about 2006 [the accident took place 11 February 2006].)

BOOKSELLER'S TICKET. *See* Binders' ticket/Bookseller's ticket.

BOOKS FOR SAMMIES. In World War I, British soldiers were referred to as "Tommies," so someone named American soldiers "Sammies" after Uncle Sam. The American Library Association lobbied successfully to get books to them. In 1917, when the United States entered the war, "ALA undertook to supply books and periodicals to military personnel, at home and overseas. The initial campaign raised $1M for camp libraries, as well as including a book drive. . . . The Association was one of seven welfare groups affiliated with the Commission. ALA's wartime programs, known as the Library War Service, was directed by Herbert Putnam, Librarian of Congress, and later by Carl H. Milam. Between 1917 and 1920, ALA, whose membership was just over 3,300 in 1917, accomplished the following: / mounted two financial campaigns and raised $5 million from public donations / erected thirty-six camp libraries with $320,000 in Carnegie Corporation funds / distributed approximately 7–10,000,000 books and magazines; and / provided library collections to over 500 locations, including in military hospitals. / There were nearly 1,200 library workers [who] served in libraries sponsored by the Association" (American Library Association, "1917"; https://www.ala.org/aboutala/1917 [accessed 30 July 2021]). (See Young, *Books for Sammies: The American Library Association and World War I.*) (*See* Armed Services Editions.)

BOOK SHOE (sometimes hyphenated). An old device, not much in use today but important enough in its time to have merited an entry in Carter, who calls it an "open box"; he says that it has an open front and can be used to hold up a book with loose boards caused by damaged hinges. It cannot be seen when it is on the shelf. It is useful for volumes

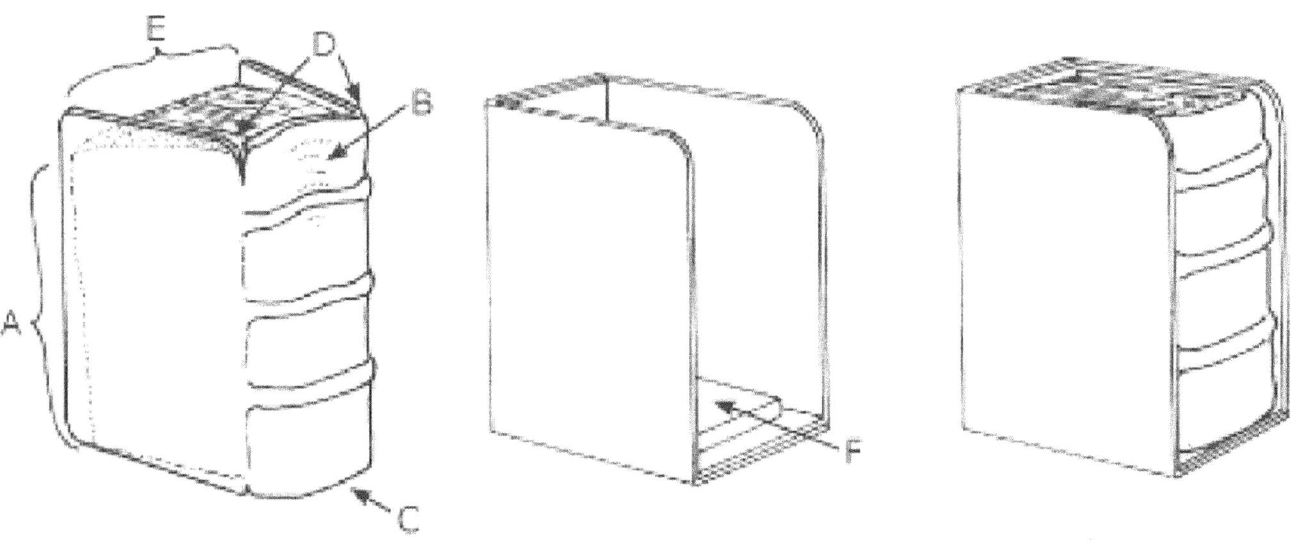

"The Book Shoe."

Courtesy of NEDCC; https://www.nedcc.org/free-resources/preservation-leaflets/4.-storage-and-handling/4.7-the-book-shoe-description-and-uses (accessed 2 June 2021).

that are not used often since the aim of the book shoe is to let the volume sit comfortably on the shelf without deteriorating further and to allow the spine of the volume to show (see Carter, p. 59). The website of the Northeast Document Conservation Center says, "The book shoe was developed to supply an almost invisible container to carry out at least some of the functions of a conventional box. It is also inexpensive and simple to make" ("The Book Shoe: Description and Uses," https://www.nedcc.org/free-resources/preservation-leaflets/4.-storage-and-handling/4.7-the-book-shoe-description-and-uses [accessed 10 July 2021]). They are much like PRINCETON FILES, only open fully at the spine.

BOOKS IN PRINT. An annual publication by R. R. Bowker listing all books available in the United States that are still IN PRINT. There is also a Global Edition that "[o]ffers global coverage, including U.S., U.K., Canadian, European, and Australian publications" (http://media.bowker.com/documents/booksinprint_brochure.pdf [accessed 22 August 2015]). Begun in 1948, it now is available digitally. The most comprehensive (though not complete) resource of books printed in the United States, "Books In Print® contains over 20 million global titles (in print, out of print, and forthcoming), including books, ebooks, audio books, and multimedia titles" (brochure of *Books in Print*, https://pq-static-content.proquest.com/collateral/media2/documents/booksinprint_brochure.pdf [accessed 2 June 2021]).

BOOK SIZES. *See* Quarto; Size (of books).

BOOK STAMP (sometimes hyphenated). A stamp (the tool that does the work or the stamped image) showing ownership of a volume or broadside—or other library object. Academic and public libraries (and even private libraries), to deter theft, will stamp their books along their edges, on the ENDLEAVES or FLYLEAVES, on TITLE PAGES, on the backs of PLATES, or elsewhere. The stamping could be done from metal or rubber stamps, and, if from metal, could be BLIND STAMPED. As a security measure, the embossed sheet or the indelible ink should prevent an item's removal from the collection. But I said "should"; though the stamping usually reduces the fiscal value of the item, an enterprising thief might not care that the stamp is there. In fact, BIBLIOKLEPT Steven Blumberg removed all traces of these stamps from the books he stole. If the book stamp is from a noted person (e.g., Thomas Jefferson, Thomas Edison, Albert Einstein), the value of the item could be increased.

BOOK THEFT. An age-old and perpetual problem in the book world. Where there are commodities worth something to someone (intellectually or fiscally), there is the possibility of theft. Libraries and collectors, booksellers and museums, and any other party collecting books and manuscripts have spent untold amounts of thought, money, and time trying to secure their holdings. TATTLE TAPES, alarm systems, marking practices and supplies, security devices, armed guards, "secure" buildings and rooms, safes and vaults, and on and on, are some of the expensive and sometimes futile ways book owners have tried to secure their collections. Thieves are conniving, often intelligent, clever, determined, and resourceful and sometimes just outright pugnacious and can sometimes defeat the most "secure" system. Thus, constant vigilance is in order to safeguard our collections.

This entry is included here because it is one of the most longstanding issues in the book world. It is part of the "vocabulary" of the trade. There are many ways of dealing with theft. "When an item in the collection cannot be found, even after a sustained, thorough search, the librarian [or collector, or bookseller] should suspect theft. And the librarian should not spend a lot of time trying to verify this suspicion. The longer the time spent verifying the loss, the more time the thief has to sell the stolen item. It is better to report a theft and then find the item that was missing than to wait until it is too late to notify potential buyers of the loss. Unfortunately, learning that a book is missing is not usually a soon-after-the-theft occurrence" (Berger, pp. 201–04).

An extensive literature (much of it on the web) is available on book thieves. It is riveting and dispiriting reading, with names such as Stephen Blumberg, THOMAS J. WISE, E. Forbes Smiley, Farhad Hakimzadeh, Marino Massimo De Caro, Barry H. Landau, and dozens of others.

One final note: Anyone contemplating buying a book with clear library PROVENANCE on it should be particularly wary, perhaps contacting the library, if this is feasible, to make sure the book was legitimately deaccessioned from the collection. An old method that libraries used was to give each removed item a "Deaccessioned" or "Withdrawn" stamp. But with libraries now deaccessioning thousands of volumes at a time, this practice has not been followed. Fairly common books of no great value will probably not raise any questions; but particularly valuable ones should raise red flags, and responsible potential buyers should contact the library to make sure it was legitimately removed.

BOOKTIONARY. A dictionary of terminology related to books: their manufacture, materials, tools, machinery, acquisition, cataloging, evaluating, researching, selling, coveting, stealing, preserving, repairing, and much more. This includes legal issues such as copyright and repleven; important libraries; publications about books and book people; prominent scholars and historians involved in the book world; influential binders and papermakers; inventors; and a host of others whose work has influenced the lore of the book through history. Perhaps the most important reference tool in the booksellers', book collectors', and librarians' holdings.

BOOK TRAVELLER/TRAVELLER'S SAMPLE. A traveller (or traveler) is a door-to-door salesman. (*See* Salesman's dummy/Salesman's sample book.) As Bruce Bleven says, a more elegant way of denoting this person is "publisher's commissioned representative" (Bleven, *Book Traveller*, p. 12). The subject of Bleven's book, one such seller, George Fabian Scheer, refined the sales to an art. I have a separate entry for "Book traveller" here, but more can be found at the Salesman's dummy entry referenced above. The point here is that these canvassers did not always need copies of their wares (samples) to be successful. Nor was the "door-to-door" to private homes; it was often to small independent bookshops that did not have arrangements with particular publishers or their distributors. When the travellers carried actual samples, they could be as described at the entry for Salesman's dummy.

BOOKWORM. A jargony word for an avid reader, though the term can also be used for a serious collector. One who "burrows into books" for the pleasure of reading or collecting them.

BOOKWORMS. *See* Worm holes.

BORDERS (in printing and binding). (1) In printing, a frame—plain or decorative—around the printed TEXT BLOCK. (2) In binding, also a frame—plain or decorative—that encloses the "text" on the covers of a book. (See McKerrow and Ferguson, *Title-Page Borders*.) Of course, a border does not have to be a full frame; it can be a plain or decorative line running parallel to any of the edges of a page or the edges of anything on the page. For instance, an illustration in the middle of a page can be surrounded by a border, or it can have a border above or below it (or both). A simple border can be composed of a single or double (or triple) RULE, or it can be a series of FLEURONS; and the border can be an unbroken or broken pattern. A border can also run vertically between columns of text on a page. And, as with medieval manuscripts, the borders can be zoomorphic (with animals in the decoration), anthropomorphic (with human beings—or animals exhibiting human features—in the decoration), or zoo-anthropomorphic (showing animal and human imagery). They can also contain GROTESQUES and BABEWYNES.

BOSSES. Metal knobs, often decorative, affixed to the corners (and occasionally in the center) of the front and rear boards of books in such a way that when the book is sitting flat on a surface, the cover is raised from the surface since the book will be sitting on the bosses. The aim, of course, was to protect the surface of the boards, though they could also be ornamental. (For more information, see Roberts and Etherington, p. 37.) (For an illustration, *see* Clasps.)

BOSTON PUBLIC LIBRARY. "Established in 1848, by an act of the Great and General Court of Massachusetts, the Boston Public Library (BPL) was the first large free municipal library in the United States" ("Boston Public Library: A Brief History and Description," https://www.bpl.org/bpl-history [accessed 2 June 2021]). It is also "the Library for the Commonwealth" (Wayne A. Wiegand and Donald G. Davis, *Encyclopedia of Library History*, pp. 85–86). It opened to the public in 1854. It claims holdings of "approximately 23 million items encompassing all formats including books, DVDs, maps, music scores, and visual materials" ("BPL by the Numbers: FY2014," https://www.bpl.org/about-us/ [accessed 2 June 2021]).

BOUDOIR PHOTOGRAPHY. Photography of intimate subject matter, with romantic, sensual, or outright erotic imagery. Though this kind of photography can be created in a bedroom, it is often done in a studio, but for the private use of the subjects and their partners. Nino Batista explains, "Almost all boudoir photography subjects are seen wearing intimate apparel, which can range from simple underwear to elaborate lingerie ensembles to totally nude. . . . A boudoir client generally meets these criteria: Has never posed for a camera beyond family, school or vacation photos. / Has never posed in front of a camera in anything but being fully clothed. / Has never posed in front of a camera in intimate apparel. / Is generally a bit nervous to utterly frightened of posing in intimate apparel on camera, let alone 'looking sexy'. / Spends some or no time on their physique because they don't pose in front of cameras for a living. / Are mostly in their late 20s or older" (Batista, "Boudoir Photography"). Most such photographs are done for women who want to give them to their mates, especially when the mate will be absent for a while. (See Surina, "Boudoir Photographs Turn the Girl Next Door into a Sexy, Confident Pin Up"). This term is included here because these kinds of photos often appear at booksellers' booths at book fairs.

BOUGHT IN. A book that does not sell at an AUCTION, usually because the bidding does not reach the level of its RESERVE, is withdrawn and returned to its consignor. It is said to be "bought in" (though I have heard people who should know better call it "brought in"). An enterprising collector or bookseller could contact the auction house and ask it to contact the consignor to see if he or she would be willing to sell the lot at some level agreed on by the two parties. Hence, books that were "bought in" could eventually be sold after the auction is done. Of course, the fact that an item was bought in might not be announced until the auction house publishes its list of "prices realized," but with online tools what they are today, this information can be had soon after the auction is complete—if the auction house is assiduous in publishing these data.

BOUND. Carter's definition of this word says that a bound book is one in which the SIGNATURES are sewn onto cords or bands and the ends of these bands or cords are pulled through holes in the cover boards and attached. He says that the covers and the TEXT BLOCK become a single unit, with the covering material glued to the boards (p. 61). This definition describes a composite of LACED-IN and CASED-IN binding. As such, it is a bit misleading. And this definition may have obtained when he was writing, but today the term merely signifies that a volume has a text block in some kind of protective cover, and usually that it is affixed to that cover (not merely LAID IN as in a PORTFOLIO). That is, the word "bound" does not necessarily imply sewing—since there are many kinds of bindings that are not sewn—and the binding can be "hard" or "soft" (boards or paper).

BOUND GALLEYS. *See* Galley proofs.

BOWDLERIZED. (Dr. Thomas Bowdler, 1754–1825.) Said of a text that has been censored. Typical is to have an editor remove material that is "sensitive" with respect to religion, profane language, bodily functions, politics, or sex. The word comes from Thomas Bowdler, who edited *The Family Shakespeare* (1815–1818) and who deleted anything he thought would be objectional in "polite company." (*See* Expurgated; Unexpurgated.) Literary, religious, and political texts (and images of all kinds) have been subject to bowdlerization over the centuries. The term is sometimes used merely to refer to an inferior version of a text, but censorship is the usual implication.

BOWED. The shape of the BOARDS on a binding that have warped, with the outer edges splayed away from the TEXT BLOCK or with the center part of the boards so warped, such that the fore-edges of the boards touch the text block, but their central part splays away from it. This means that the grain of the wood is vertical, and the warping is vertical. The warping could be because of the moisture in the wood (or CARDBOARD) of the cover, or because the cover material (like VELLUM) is too dry and has contracted, pulling the boards into the warp. Binders also can get the boards on incorrectly, with the grain of the wood or cardboard running horizontally, at right angles to the SPINE. I have a book in my library with the board bowed such that the HEAD and TAIL of the boards have splayed away from the text block, tearing the paper that covers the spine.

BOWERS, FREDSON THAYER (1905–1991). One of America's premier and most prolific bibliographers. His contributions to the field of BIBLIOGRAPHY—especially to descriptive and textual bibliography—are legion. Following on the work of W. W. GREG and RONALD B. MCKERROW, Bowers understood the need for a codification of bibliographical principles, especially in descriptive bibliography. (*See* Bibliography.) It is difficult to call his excellent and almost impenetrable *Principles of Bibliographical Description* his magnum opus since he produced such a huge body of scholarship. Flawed as it is (it could never be the comprehensive text it set out to be since Bowers could never have encountered all the variations in bookmaking over the centuries that needed *description* using his code), this volume raised the bar for scholars, booksellers, collectors, librarians, and anyone else trying in print to describe the books they were observing. In 1948, he founded the journal *Studies in Bibliography*, the premier publication in its field, still being published out of the University of Virginia, where Bowers was one of the founding members of the Bibliographical Society of the University of Virginia (founded in 1947). His theoretical essays on textual editing (for a discussion of textual bibliography, *see* Bibliography) were greatly influential in the shaping of this branch of bibliography. (The full text of back issues of *Studies in Bibliography* is available online at http://bsuva.org/wordpress/studies-in-bibliography [accessed 2 June 2021].) (See Tanselle, *The Life and Work of Fredson Bowers.*)

BOXES FOR BOOKS (and other library materials). Some books need extra protection. Particularly valuable or vulnerable volumes are often boxed, the container made of sturdy cardboard (though real wood is sometimes used), and lined with a smooth material: paper or padded cloth (even silk). And the volume may also be enclosed in a sheath of paper, sometimes with a ribbon attached to the box, under the volume, used to help the user pull the book up and out of the box.

The box could be open at one end or completely closed. Roberts and Etherington mention the CUT-CORNER PAMPHLET FILE; PULL-OFF BOX; SOLANDER BOX; PHASE BOX; and SLIPCASE. There is also the Tao Box, which consists of a four-flap sleeve; the book or pamphlet is placed in it and the four triangular flaps fold over it, sometimes with the flaps overlapping, sometimes with them meeting at the apexes of the triangles. This is then slipped into a slipcase or an envelope. It is particularly good for pamphlets and loose documents.

Carter says that enclosing a book for preservation cuts "it off from the circulation of air" (p. 70), as if this is not a good thing to do. In fact, air can be a pollutant, and removing the book from circulating air, as long as you don't seal it hermetically, is not bad at all. And he mentions that cloth boxes on a shelf do not look too good; nor do leather ones. But they are protective, and I submit that I'd rather have my books look less than stellar on a shelf while they are in boxes than have them damaged by not being so protected. But it is also true that sometimes the boxes can be quite lovely, even looking like books on the shelf. It is true, as he suggests, that an item in a box does seem to elicit special handling from someone taking the item in hand. Finally, boxing or casing a book that is in poor condition—even if you merely use a phase box—is a practical and relatively inexpensive way to protect an item that needs protection; it is far cheaper than paying a conservator to create a REBACKED, REBOUND, or RECASED book. (*See also* Enclosures for books.)

BRACES. Marks that function as parentheses or that enclose several lines of text or several items to show that they are a single unit. They are like curved SQUARE BRACKETS: { }.

Braces come in many sizes and shapes; image from "TEX"; http://tex.stackexchange.com/questions/212311/change-the-shape-of-the-curly-braces-of-the-newtxmath-package (accessed 2 June 2021).

Courtesy of DepositPhotos.

BRACKETS. *See* Square brackets.

BRADEL BINDING. "A type of binding having a hollow back, and not unlike a LIBRARY BINDING, except that it is considered to be temporary. The style was originated in Germany by Alexis Pierre Bradel, also known as Bradel l'aîné, and also as Bradel-Derome, son-in-law and successor to Nicholas-Denis Derôme. The style was taken to France sometime between 1772 and 1809. Bradel bindings generally have split BOARDS into which are attached the extensions of the spine lining cloth. The edges are UNCUT, sometimes with the HEAD edge being GILT. They generally have a LEATHER or linen spine. In France the style was known as 'Cartonnage à la Bradel,' or as 'en gist'" (Roberts and Etherington, "Bradel binding"; https://cool.culturalheritage.org/don/dt/dt0459.html [accessed 9 March 2021]). (*See* Hollow spine/Hollow back binding.)

BRAILLE. *See* Printing for the Blind.

BRASSES. *See* Thins.

BRAYER. *See* Roller.

BREAKER. One of the pariahs of the book world—a true BIBLIOCLAST. A person, not necessarily a bookseller or a print dealer, who breaks apart books to sell the pieces. A book with fine hand-colored plates, historic maps, or fine engravings could fetch, say, $500 on the rare-book market, but its plates could be pulled out, matted, and/or framed and sold for an amount that would net far more than $500. (The act of doing this is called "breaking" or "breaking up," and for some vandals, breaking up is easy to do.) The purist's notion is that a book is sacrosanct and that any damage done to it is anathema. Thus, a breaker takes a volume, with whatever information that volume has, and essentially destroys it, sometimes throwing away the text, only to keep the salable parts. Information is lost, and our cultural heritage is lesser for that. However, money—possibly greed or need—drives many a transaction and transgression, and the breaker can usually justify his actions (if only to himself). Carter also mentions breakers who take apart a SAMMELBAND, often a volume of tracts or plays, broadsides, or posters, assembled by some collector; the breaking is usually to pull out the truly valuable items to sell them at premium prices, with the remainder dealt with separately. There is also the breaker who, in compiling a LEAF BOOK, is just as guilty and condemnable. Finally, there is the breaker of medieval manuscripts, "harvesting" individual LEAVES, the elegant MINIATURES, and other artistic elements, discarding the rest, and essentially destroying the volume. Maybe there is a special place in the afterworld for breakers. (Parenthetically, the ABAA looks down on the practice to such an extent that the first person ever to be ejected from that organization was a breaker.) (*See* Book of hours; Disbound; Ege, Otto; Fragmentology; Leaf books.)

It is worth mentioning that in 1976, Margaret Haller said that "breaker" was "slang for a book more valuable broken up than preserved as a unit. Book dealers generally want to keep a book together in one piece as long as possible and will tenderly describe a book which is falling apart as 'needing rebinding'; on the other hand, art dealers are always on the lookout for just such books, which they have no compunction about tearing apart for the separate sale of any plates, illustrations, or maps" (*Book Collector's Fact Book*, p. 62). She probably means print dealers (not "art dealers"). The term, today, refers to the person, not the shabby book, though one might hear, "This book is a breaker," or it is a "BREAKING COPY." (*See* Fragmentology.)

In discussing this term (and practice) with a number of booksellers, I have heard the justifications: "The book was already in pieces," or "The volume had many of its illustrations missing," or "I never do this to a complete volume, regardless of its condition." Or some such other excuse to justify the breaking. But most scholars, booksellers, and librarians would say that the volume even in its fragmentary condition contains information that scholars need and that would be lost if the parts are separated from one another and disseminated to the four corners of the world. Is it greed that leads to breaking? Only the Shadow knows.

BREAKING COPY. Sometimes also called a "BREAKER," this is a copy of a book in such poor condition that it would be difficult for a dealer to sell it, so he may feel justified in breaking it up for its parts. For printed books that exist in many copies, there may be some justification for doing this, though it is still looked down on since any individual copy, no matter how common the title and edition, is still unique, and to break up even a defective copy may be jettisoning evidence of some kind that could be valuable to a scholar. Certainly, manuscripts should not be so treated, though these volumes have been prime targets for such vice. Stories abound about the defective copies of Gutenberg Bibles that booksellers decided were breakers, so they thought nothing of selling the volumes one LEAF at a time, Gabriel Wells's *A Noble Fragment* being perhaps the best-known example. (The story is told at the Wikipedia article on Wells: http://en.wikipedia.org/wiki/Gabriel_Wells [accessed 2 June 2021]). A volume as important as a Gutenberg Bible, regardless of its condition and what leaves it lacks, should never be considered a breaker. Carter points out that picture books and volumes lacking leaves, especially those from the first few centuries of printing, might be candidates for breaking up. They are often marketed (often in groups of leaves drawn from several sources) as being appropriate for people studying early printing, and booksellers putting together "teaching collections" might justify such BIBLIOCLASM. Carter's entry (p. 61) does not hint at disapprobation for such an amputation of leaves, though many in the book world today would not approve. Even a defective volume, lacking parts, contains information that would be lost with the dispersal of the pieces that are there. (*See* Cannibalization; Ege, Otto.)

BREVIARY. "A book containing the hymns, offices, and prayers for the canonical hours" (*American Heritage Dictionary of the English Language*, p. 230). "The Roman Breviary, which with rare exceptions (certain religious orders, the Ambrosian and Mozarabic Rites, etc.) is used in this day throughout the Latin Church, is divided into four parts according to the seasons of the year: Winter, Spring, Summer, and Autumn. It is constructed of the following elements: (a) the Psalter; (b) the Proper of the Season; (c) Proper of the Saints; (d) the Common; (e) certain special Offices" (see Catholic Encyclopedia, "New Advent," http://www.newadvent.org/cathen/02768b.htm [accessed 2 June 2021]). The books contain sung and spoken text (the sung text includes hymns and psalms but usually without musical notes), and they also show the readings for the same hours of the day that one finds in BOOKS OF HOURS: matins, lauds, prime, terce, sext, none, vespers, and compline. The users of these books were religious figures—someone in the church or outside it. They were produced for local use, so it is often possible to locate the area for which they were made by the prayers they contain, the feasts they celebrate, and the saints they mention. (*See* Religious books.)

BRIGHTBACKS. Volumes with highly decorated or pictorial cloth bindings, with a good deal of gold stamping or ENAMELED.

BRIGHT COPY. A frequently seen term in a bookseller's description of a volume that is fresh and clean and like new. Usually said of an older volume that one may often see in shabby or less-than-clean condition. The brightness refers not merely to the colors of the binding materials (cloth especially) but also to the soundness of the binding (JOINTS, TIPS, SPINE).

BRIQUET, CHARLES-MOÏSE (1839–1918). The compiler of the standard reference for WATERMARKS for more than a century. His four-volume *Les Filigranes: Dictionnaire Historique des Marques du Papier dès Leur Apparition vers 1282 jusqu'en 1600* lists and depicts with line drawings more than 16,000 watermarks from 1282 on. While Briquet did not examine papers from Great Britain, Portugal, Spain, Scandinavia, or other countries, it is still one of the premier resources for watermarks, so well known that it is referred to simply as "Briquet." At the time of this writing, a project titled Briquet Online is being prepared (see https://briquet-online.at/ [accessed 9 June 2021]), which aims to offer images of the complete corpus of the Briquet volumes.

BRISTOL; BRISTOL BOARD. "A lightweight board that can be made on either a FOURDRINIER or cylinder papermaking machine. There are three types of bristols: 1) index, 2) mill, and 3) wedding. They range in thickness from 0.006 inch and greater. The original bristol board, made in Bristol, England, was a pasted board made of rag content paper, but very little bristol today is of this character. Bristols are sometimes filled, but are more commonly pasted or plied, the thicker sheets being made by pasting sheets of the same stock together until the desired thickness is attained. They are designated as 2-ply, 3-ply, etc., according to the number of sheets used. The highest grade of bristol is wedding, followed by index and mill" (Roberts and Etherington, "Bristol board"; https://cool.culturalheritage.org/don/dt/dt0482.html [accessed 28 May 2021]). Bristol is used for the BOARDS in bindings, and it is also used as a substrate for TIPPING on art and other library materials (broadsides, illustrations, posters, and so forth). It can be archival, so it is used in conservation for various applications.

BRITISH ASSOCIATION OF PAPER HISTORIANS. "[A] national association which aims to bring together individuals, companies and institutions with a common interest in the following areas: paper in all its forms and diversity / papermaking by hand and machine / CONSERVATION / mill and company histories / papermakers, their families and communities / machinery manufacture and development / WATERMARKS" (British Association of Paper Historians website; http://www.baph.org.uk/ [accessed 27 July 2021]). The organization "was founded in 1989 after the successful congress of the IPH (International Paper Historians) in Durham and the celebration of 500 years of papermaking in Britain in 1988." They publish an informative *Quarterly* along with a regular newsletter and a host of books and PAMPHLETS concerning many areas of papermaking; and they hold annual meetings. Their members are immensely learned and willing to share their knowledge, their meetings are friendly and informative, and their publications are exemplary.

BRITISH LIBRARY. The British Library is the national library of the United Kingdom, holding nearly 200 million items from all over the world. There are more than 14 million volumes, and 3 million new items are added every year (see the British Library site "About Us," http://www.bl.uk/aboutus/quickinfo/facts/index.html [accessed 23 October 2015]). The British Library site also says, "We have manuscripts, maps, newspapers, magazines, prints and drawings, music scores, and patents / The Sound Archive keeps sound recordings from 19th-century cylinders to CD, DVD and MD recordings / We house 8 million stamps and other philatelic items / . . . We have on-site space for over 1,200 Readers / Over 16,000 people use the collections each day (on site and online)." The library's website (http://www.bl.uk [accessed 2 June 2021]) has many links to additional information.

BRITISH LIBRARY CATALOGUE. As the entry says, this is the catalog (I'm using the U.S. spelling) of the British Library, originally in book form, until 1975, but now a fully online database that is a wonder of information. As the previous entry indicates, the library is one of the most extensive in the world, and to have a catalog of its holdings at our fingertips is a boon. Some of the library's classical catalogs, in book form, are worth using (*see* the next entry, with a note about the obsolescence of that tool). And the specialty reference database *Catalogue of Chinese Printed Books* is also available online. (See https://www.bl.uk/catalogues-and-collections; and http://www.bodley.ox.ac.uk/rslpchin/search.htm [accessed 17 January 2021]).

BRITISH LIBRARY DATABASE OF BOOKBINDINGS. *See* Database of Bookbindings.

BRITISH MUSEUM CATALOGUE OF BOOKS PRINTED IN THE FIFTEENTH CENTURY (BMC). A specialty catalog of INCUNABULA that was often referred to by librarians, booksellers, and scholars. It is now relatively obsolete, having been replaced by ISBC (*INCUNABULA SHORT TITLE CATALOGUE*), a much more comprehensive and easier to use database. This excellent listing supplants the work done by ROBERT PROCTER.

BRITTLE. Said of any material, but usually paper, that will break with any manipulation. Most common, of course, is the yellowed paper of commercial paper mills—paper made with acidic materials that have dried out, turned yellow, and have become fragile and breakable with even gentle touching. One means to determine brittleness was called the "Double Fold Test," in which a piece of paper was folded, then back-folded against the first fold. If the folded piece broke off on a single double-fold test (or the test repeated once or twice), the paper was seriously brittle. The problem with this was that if the paper was so brittle to break, the test itself destroyed the item so tested. At one point, LAMINATION was used to protect such fragile papers, but it was deemed an inadequate method, and it would not work for entire books. (See Nicholson Baker, *Double Fold: Libraries and the Assault on Paper.*) Other strategies include DEACIDIFICATION and REFORMATTING.

BRITTLE BOOKS PROGRAM. "[A]n initiative carried out by the National Endowment for the Humanities at the request of the United States Congress. The initiative began officially between 1988 and 1989 and was to involve the eventual microfilming of over 3 million endangered volumes," endangered because the paper they were printed on was BRITTLE. "[I]t was estimated that there were 80 million brittle books in North American libraries, 12 million of which were unique titles. As MASS DEACIDIFICATION efforts proved costly and inconsistent, librarians and archivists began looking for more practical ways to preserve the intellectual content of the decaying material. Microfilm, one of the most stable and durable mediums around at the time, was seen as the most reasonable alternative" (enacademic.com. "Brittle Books Program.") The program advocated a variety of ways to deal with books in danger of being lost, including microform REFORMATTING (from paper to other formats, primarily digital), photocopying, paper splitting, and DEACIDIFICATION. With digitization the formal program has now relatively disappeared, though the need to preserve remains, and these brittle books continue to be "saved" with the expansion of digitization programs at institutions worldwide. There is currently a push to digitize microforms, and good machines have been developed to scan microfilm.

BROADSHEET. A LEAF of paper on which text is printed on both sides (as opposed to the BROADSIDE, that has text on only one side). What constitutes "text" is referred to under "Broadside."

BROADSIDE. A sheet of paper (usually intended to be shown unfolded) with text on only one side. A broadside was intended to be posted on a wall or other upright surface, so whatever text it was to convey would have to be printed on the side facing out. However, many printers issue broadsides as part of their corpus of printing (the broadside ballad or poem being exceptionally common), and sometimes they put their COLOPHONS or other text on the VERSO. Whether this qualifies the item still to be called a "broadside" is not worth debating (though *see* Broadsheet). If the main text is on one side of the sheet, it is still basically a broadside and should be called that. Carter adds that the term "broadside" should be applied to words *printed* on a single side of what he calls "a whole, undivided sheet" (p. 63). Technically, this is incorrect since it is not the *words* that constitute the broadside but rather the sheet of paper or other material that is the broadside. Also, it is possible to have a manuscript (or pictures only) that is in the form of a broadside, so his insistence on printed words may be ignored. Further, if the printer takes a full sheet and divides it into smaller parts (halves, quarters, or thirds) and prints a text on one side with the aim that it be seen from that side only, it is still a broadside no matter how small it is. Following this logic, a business card printed on one side only is a little broadside. That, at least, would be the way a bibliographer would designate the FORMAT of the card. We generally think of a broadside as something to be posted on a wall or framed, so it is usually large enough to be read from a distance, hence Carter's idea that the sheet should not be divided. But as I have said, the term can (and actually is) applied to smaller formats, made from parts of sheets. And I guess it is possible to have an enormous broadside composed of two (or more) pieces of paper glued together. If the text that it contains is still on a single side of the giant leaf, it is still a broadside.

BROCADE PAPERS. *See* Dutch gilt papers.

BROCHURE. A PAMPHLET, often (but not necessarily) in paper WRAPPERS. The French word *broché* may be used in a bookseller's catalog if it is describing such a volume; and it means, specifically, a volume sewn (or possibly stapled) and covered with a paper wrapper, not in BOARDS. Carter's entry says that "in America a brochure is a folder" (p. 63). What he means is that many a brochure is bi-folded or tri-folded, though it can also be a thin bound pamphlet. Today a brochure is usually thought of as an advertising piece, but they can also be small printed items holding information about a narrow topic. A library may have a brochure about its collections and another, more narrowly focused one, on a single collection in its holdings. A steamship line may have a brochure about one of its ships. A hospital may have a number of brochures about various diseases and conditions, their treatment and cure. Libraries and private collections and the shelves of many a bookseller will have hosts of brochures among their EPHEMERA holdings.

BROKE. Paper of inferior quality—"paper with holes and tears" (Voorn, *Old Ream Wrappers*, p. 13). Labarre says, "a mill and a trade term for 'broken' paper," and, quoting MRR (*Mortimer's Ready Reckoner*), Labarre adds, "'Paper without defects is called *good*, that in which there is some slight defect *RETREE*, and when there are greater defects or mixed sorts in a ream, *broke*'" (Labarre, *Dictionary and Encyclopaedia of Paper and Paper-Making*, p. 33). Broke paper is often repulped, or it can be used as REAM WRAPPERS. (For a more recent edition of *Mortimer's Ready Reckoner*, see Mortimer in the bibliography.)

BROKEN. *See* Half-stuff.

BROKEN TYPE. Carter's entry is instructive. He says that broken type is most often the result of damage caused by repeated use of the type. Thus, if one has a copy of a book printed early in the PRESSRUN and one printed late, he or she may observe broken type at the end of the run. This may help the bibliographer distinguish between an early printing and a later one, an early issue and a later one, or a variant state of the edition. (*See* Edition, Impression [Printing], Issue, and State; Points.) He warns—and rightly so—that this kind of evidence (broken type) may be seriously unreliable to reveal these things. As with misprints (he calls them "misgrints"), broken type in the hands of an ISSUE-MONGER can lead to incorrect or unreliable conclusions. (See Carter, p. 63.) (In the printing of Carter's entry, "broken" and "faultily" are printed with broken letters.) (*See* Battered.)

This entry encompasses a large body of writing that discusses, among many other things, printing house practices. Broken "type" could actually be damaged STEREOTYPE or ELECTROTYPE plates. A text with a piece of broken type could have been printed *before* one with the same type unbroken. Determining the order of issue of two volumes of the same edition on the basis of broken type is not always possible. As an assistant to Kim Merker at the Windhover and Stonewall Presses, I was charged with examining with minute detail (and an eight-power loupe) every SORT in the HANDSET TYPE. Kim and I began many a pressrun, ran off a number of sheets on the WASHINGTON PRESS, and then spotted a sort with a broken character. We did a STOP-PRESS CORRECTION and continued to print. Hence, sheets printed earlier had the broken type, and those printed later had perfect type. This shows that broken type can be an unreliable witness for the order of impressions, issues, or states.

BROKEN VOLUME. One that has had its innards eviscerated, with parts removed. The volume is often said to be "broken up for its parts." (*See* Breaker.)

BRONZE VARNISH PAPER. *See* Dutch gilt papers.

BRUNET, JACQUES-CHARLES (1780–1867). Compiler of several important French bibliographies. He "published a supplement to the *Dictionnaire bibliographique des livres rares* (1810; 'Dictionary of Rare Books'), brought out a few years earlier. The first edition of Brunet's *Manuel du libraire et de l'amateur de livres* (1810; 'Bookseller's and Book Lover's Manual') rapidly became the standard French bibliographical dictionary. Among Brunet's other works are *Nouvelles recherches bibliographiques* (1834; 'New Bibliographical Studies') and a study of the early editions of François Rabelais" (*Encyclopaedia Britannica*, https://www.britannica.com/biography/Jacques-Charles-Brunet [accessed 17 January 21]). Brunet's *Manual* went through five editions in his lifetime, going from three to five volumes, and containing thousands of entries. The entries in this massive reference tool offer annotations about the fiscal and informational values that books have. With the coming of digital tools, much of the bibliographical information these volumes have is now online, and there is a Brunet presence of the early printings on the web in full text. (See volume 3 of the 1820 text at https://books.google.com/books?id=BtTwGi-SpAIC&printsec=frontcover&sorce=gbs_book_other_versions_r&cad=4#v=onepage&q&f=false; other copies and editions also available on the web [accessed 17 January 2021].)

BSA. *See* Bibliographical Society of America.

BUCKRAM. "A book cloth made from cotton or linen, usually the former, and closely woven, occasionally with a double warp. It is filled or coated and calendered to give it a smooth finish which blocks well and is reasonably durable" (Roberts and Etherington, p. 400). In libraries, it is commonly used in binding groups of issues of periodicals, and since it comes in many colors, full runs of serials can be coded by color. In the 20th century, libraries often rebound great numbers of books in buckram, the aim being to extend the longevity of these volumes since the buckram is sturdy. But in so doing, they discarded the original bindings, eliminating the original information that the books' covers revealed. (*See* Library binding.)

BULGED RULE. (*See* Tapered rule)

BULK/BULKING (in binding). The thickness of the text block (including all of the printed leaves and the endpapers), not including the covers. I once had a "first edition" of a Hemingway novel—which turned out to be a North Korean forgery, detectable by the fact that the real first edition bulked to a particular measurement, while the forgery bulked to about ¼ inch less since it was printed on thinner paper. Also, often BOOK CLUBS (like the Book of the Month Club) may issue copies on thinner (i.e., usually cheaper) paper than was used for the true first. This may be the only sign that the item in hand is a BOOK CLUB EDITION. (*See* Size [of books].)

BUMF. (Sometimes spelled Bumph.) Short for "bum fodder," a British term for toilet paper. Any matter, printed on paper, considered not worthy to be kept. All kinds of such matter exists, much of which arrives daily as junk mail. However, even the most pestilential of bumf might have some intellectual merit, and the worst of this EPHEMERA could contain information of interest to a range of scholars. One odd person I know collects toilet-paper-roll wrappers and chopstick wrappers. The first of these comes really close to the etymology of "bumf," the latter not so much, but both may be considered bumf since these printed papers are generally discarded immediately before use, despite having information of various kinds on them that may be useful to future scholars. And collections of such printed materials wind up at antiquarian book fairs. (In an earlier incarnation, I bought for the library I directed a collection of tea-chest labels and one of rice-bag labels. It was amazing to see the kinds of information these contained, and the lovely art work they had, not to mention the printing techniques they exhibited. *Viva* bumf!)

BUMPED. A frequently seen word in a bookseller's catalog indicating that the item being described is imperfect, the imperfection being a dent or other DING caused by the item's having been banged against some hard surface. Bumps can be minimal, or they can be cataclysmal, in which case the description may be "seriously bumped," a much gentler description than the possibly more accurate "smashed." Where a "gouge" could imply something has been taken away from the volume, "bumped" implies that all of the original material is still there; but it also usually means that the item is unrepairable.

BUNDLES. According to Carter (in this instance Nicolas Barker, who added the term to the 8th edition), these are groups of volumes that are not worth auctioning individually, so they are gathered and sold in a single LOT. (*See* Auctions.) If this is the case, the auction house will try to bundle titles on a single topic. However, Ramanathan Subramaniam and R. Venkatesh speak of another situation: the sale of individual items that should be sold together but that are sold in separate lots. They offer a strategy to the auction house: "When the objects are asymmetric in value, it is optimal to auction the higher-valued object first." Auction houses on a stratum beneath Sotheby's and Christie's may be happy to take large numbers of items from consignors and bundle them, with 2, 10, or dozens of volumes in a single lot. As noted, the lots usually contain items of like subject matter, but that is not always the case, and the buyer wanting a single or a few titles in a lot may get "stuck" with a great number of items he did not want. (I once bought a lot of about 130 cookbooks just to acquire the one that I wanted. The rest I was able to sell to the underbidder.)

BURINS AND GRAVERS. Cutting tools used in ENGRAVING, composed of sharp-pointed steel shafts with a wooden handle, the points at various angles, and with varying thicknesses. (*See* Steel engraving.)

BURNISHED. Said of any surface that has been rubbed with a smooth tool to achieve an equally smooth surface, or to polish gold or other foil to brightness. This kind of treatment could be applied to the covers or edges of covers of leather-bound books; the foils used in manuscript illumination; or the surface of sheets of paper, to impart smoothness. The burnishing tool could be a bloodstone, an agate, or the tooth of any mammal. And burnishing marbled paper can give the surface a sheen that enhances the appearance of the pattern. (*See* Calendering.)

BUXTON FORMAN, HARRY. *See* Forman, Henry Buxton.

BUYER'S REMORSE. A waste of time. This is the feeling one has after purchasing anything and then feeling rotten for having done so. In the book world, this is a common feeling after one has gotten swept up by the frenzy of an AUCTION, then remembered that there are not-so-hidden costs to auctions: buyer's premium, taxes, and shipping, handling, and insurance (if the auction was online or the bidding was done from a distance), and so on. Or after one has bought something at a book fair, taken it home, and checked one's bank balance, or found out that the item was a DUPLICATE, or showed it to a disapproving significant other. Buyer's remorse is indeed a waste of time, since the feeling produces nothing but self-recrimination. And I can attest to the fact that in time this feeling fades and in the long run one is content—if not actually really happy—to have the item in the collection. This feeling runs parallel to non-buyer's remorse: the feeling one has for "the one that got away." (At an ABAA book fair, I saw two magnificent volumes I *should have* bought. I paused, walked away to think about it, turned around and strode back to the booth, and saw another buyer walk away with these prized volumes. That remorse has stuck with me for more than a decade, and I am sure it isn't going away. Ted Dunn has called this "Procrastinator's nightmare.")

C&P. *See* Collated and perfect.

CABS. *See* Colorado Antiquarian Book Seminar.

CAINS, ANTHONY ("TONY") (1936–2020). World famous conservator and binder. "The conservation and rebinding of the 8th Century Book of Mulling, the cleaning and rebinding of the early medieval Stowe Missal for the Royal Irish Academy, making and binding of the Great Book of Ireland (1989–1991) for University College Cork, and the conservation and rebinding of the 15th Century Ellesmere Manuscript of Chaucer's Canterbury Tales in the Huntington Library, San Marino, California (1994–1995) were among his most significant achievements. / In the 1990s, Cains was instrumental in the co-design (with Nathan Stolow) and development of the Book of Kells display system which combined security and environmental controls. He was also a founding member and director of the Institute for the Conservation of Historic and Artistic Works (now the Institute of Conservator-Restorers in Ireland). In 2014, that organisation gave him a Lifetime Achievement Award for his services to conservation. / Headhunted for the role of technical director of conservation at T[rinity] C[ollege] D[ublin], Cains designed and established the conservation laboratory in the attic of the Long Room Library building in the early 1970s. The conservation laboratory, which has since moved to the Ussher Library, won a Europa Nostra architecture prize when it was officially opened in 1974. . . . / The most significant development in his career came when he travelled to Italy with other expert conservators to respond to the catastrophic flooding of the River Arno in Florence in November 1966" ("Anthony [Tony] Cains: Book Binder and Pioneering Conservator"; obituary in the *Irish Times*, 9 January 2021; https://www.irishtimes.com/life-and-style/people/anthony-tony-cains-obituary-book-binder-and-pioneering-conservator-1.4452296 [accessed 25 March 2021]).

CALAVERAS. (Sometimes called "Day of the Dead broadside poems.") As a sub-genre of BROADSIDES, these items frequently appear at book and EPHEMERA fairs. They are satirical broadsides, usually in verse, in the form of mock epitaphs. Related to the Day of the Dead, they have skeleton illustrations in caricature. "A calavera, a representation of a human skull, is often applied to decorative or edible skulls made from sugar or clay during Day of the Dead" (López, The Newberry Library, "Satirical Calaveras and the Day of the Dead").

CALENDERING. The smoothing off of the surface of a sheet of paper or paperboard (or even cloth used in binding). A calendered sheet is polished, usually between smooth rollers of a calender (or calendering machine). If the top roller spins faster than the bottom one, the surface of the sheet that the top roller touches is BURNISHED to great smoothness. In a FOURDRINIER, the dry end of the machine may have a calender stack—several calender rollers one above the other, the sheet being run back and forth between all of them, polishing both sides of the paper. If the cylinders are heated, a sheet passing between them is said to be hot pressed; if the cylinders are not heated, the sheet is said to be cold pressed; if the sheet contains clay or other FILLER and then is calendered, it can become glossy, the calendering burnishing the surface of the sheet. Carter (9th ed.; hence, the term is added by its editor, Thadani; see bibliography) incorrectly says that calendered paper (and even cloth!) has "a high gloss." This is so only if the FURNISH that the paper is made from contains the proper ingredients to create a gloss. Most paper is calendered, removing the nap of the felts and the impression of the screen or laid wires (*see* Laid paper), but not adding any gloss to the sheet.

CALF (often decorated). The term used to designate perhaps the most common leather used in bookbinding. It is smooth, but it can be treated in many ways: dyed, textured, or grained to look like many other skins (snake, alligator, or lizard), or treated with acid to achieve various effects (SPOTTED, tree patterns [*see* tree calf], or MOTTLED). In the 19th century, paper manufacturers were adept at creating papers that looked like various materials, including calf and vellum, and sometimes they called their papers "calf" and "vellum." It is sometimes difficult to distinguish calf paper from the real skin. Roberts and Etherington say, "Books which are bound in calfskin may be described as being diced, grained, marbled, mottled, scored, sprinkled, stained, or tree, according to the form of decoration used. In addition, special styles are known as divinity, antique, law, reverse, or rough calf" (see pp. 44–45; this statement is on p. 45).

Carter distinguishes between "calf," "old calf," and "early calf," saying that booksellers may use these designations, showing how their descriptions indicate different qualities, conditions, or dates of the calf (shiny and not too old, not modern but not contemporary with the printing of the book, or for books printed before about 1750, respectively); however, the niceties of these distinctions are hardly referenced today. (See Carter, p. 64.)

CALIFORNIA JOB CASE. *See* Type case.

CALLED FOR. A term indicating that an item (book, BROADSIDE, or PAMPHLET) is generally seen with a particular feature ("TISSUE GUARDS on illustrations called for but WANTING"—"wanting" indicating "missing"; "containing extra FLYLEAVES, as called for"). Who has done the calling could possibly be in question. As Carter points out, if the person doing the calling is a named authority ("with the CANCEL called for by BLANCK"), one must trust the authority, but if no such expert is named, the feature's presence or absence may be a case for debate. (See Carter, p. 64.)

CALLIGRAPHY. Most simply, "fancy or beautiful writing." Sometimes an author inscribes a volume to someone, and her handwriting is elegant; so in a book description one can write, "Inscribed in the author's calligraphic hand." (*See* Script.) Mere "handwriting" is not necessarily calligraphy. Peter Beal says that the word usually implies elegant handwriting or design, and that the main focus of calligraphy is the beauty of the text, not its content. The final piece shows a great deal of attention paid to its attractiveness and the great skill of its making, and the work is a piece of art in itself (see Beal, pp. 56–57). Often calligraphic art included gracefully penned images of birds or human faces.

Martin Davies says that "the early Church Fathers, from Basil onward, preoccupied with the physical form of the Holy Writ, gave the word its modern sense" ("Calligraphy," in *The Oxford Companion to the Book*, vol. 1, p. 579).

As noted, calligraphy is not just handwriting. Beal says that often the purpose of the calligraphic document is the calligraphy more than it is the content. Hence, the beauty of the hand, in its artistry, is more the point of the origin of the piece than is the fact that it contains a text that someone might wish to read. Today, bookstore shelves will contain many recently published how-to books on elegant penmanship. Seemingly endless numbers of them have been published, and even today there are new texts coming out and societies of calligraphy with thousands of members. (e.g., The Society of Scribes and Illuminators [http://calligraphyonline.org/; accessed 3 June 2021]; The Calligraphy and Lettering Arts Society [http://www.clas.co.uk/; accessed 3 June 2021]; Society for Calligraphy [http://www.societyforcalligraphy.org/; accessed 8 June 2021]; The Friends of Calligraphy [http://www.friendsofcalligraphy.org/pages/resources.html; accessed 3 June 2021]; Portland Society for Calligraphy [http://portlandsocietyforcalligraphy.org/; accessed 3 June 2021]; and many others.) Under the calligraphy rubric are PENMANSHIP MANUALS, designed to train people in calligraphy, and WRITING BOOKS, that discuss the history and styles of writing.

CAMBRIDGE BIBLIOGRAPHY OF ENGLISH LITERATURE (*CBEL*). This excellent reference tool was published first in 1940 in four volumes, edited by F. W. Bateson, with a supplement coming out in 1957 edited by George Watson and a new edition (generally called *NCBEL*) edited by Watson and appearing in five volumes (1969–1977). Volume 4 of this set was issued in a third edition, edited by Joanne Shattock, covering 1800–1900 (published in 2000—and containing 1,536 pages!). This is the first volume to be published of the third edition. Others are possibly in preparation (but see below). The Cambridge University Press website says this about CBEL: "It offers authoritative individual bibliographies, compiled by specialists of international reputation, of writers in all genres—poetry, fiction, drama and the novel—together with sections compiled by specialists on children's literature, historical and travel writing, philosophy and science, political economy, the literature of sports, education, journalism, book production and literary relations with the continent" (https://www.cambridge.org/us/academic/subjects/literature/printing-and-publishing-history/cambridge-bibliography-english-literature-volume-4-3rd-edition?format=HB [accessed 3 June 2021]).

This grand reference set offers a broad survey of bibliographical sources of all of English literature, and it is cited as CBEL (sometimes in italics) in many a bookseller's catalog or in MARC RECORDS. It gives biographical sketches and bibliographical information for hundreds of authors' works, and (as noted above) it has separate sections (that would appeal to readers of this dictionary) on subjects such as book production, book collectors, libraries, newspapers, and others.

The PRELIMS of the text are available online at https://books.google.com/books?id=R0yHxY46E_IC&pg=PR7&dq=Cambridge+Bibliography+of+English+Literature+third+edition+volume+4&hl=en&newbks=1&newbks_redir=1&sa=X&ved=2ahUKEwjtwceFqvzwAhUVV80KHQiLA-4Q6AEwAHoECAUQAg (accessed 3 June 2021). Inasmuch as no volume has appeared on the market since 2000, it looks as if the series is no longer supported by the press.

There is also a shorter version, *The Concise Cambridge Bibliography of English Literature, 1600–1950*, second edition, also edited by George Watson. The Cambridge University Press website says this about the shorter version: "The Concise Bibliography begins with a general introductory section and the rest of the book is divided into six time periods. Each section begins with general bibliographies, literary histories and general works. Then the principal authors are listed alphabetically. Each has two sections, works 'by' and works 'about.' The first section gives the main works, with dates and editors. This is annotated by Mr Watson where necessary. In the second edition the emphasis is on books rather than articles. The authors chosen are British (although James and Eliot are included), not American or Commonwealth; but the biographical, critical and historical works take account of the scholarship of other English-speaking countries" (https://www.cambridge.org/us/academic/subjects/literature/printing-and-publishing-history/concise-cambridge-bibliography-english-literature-6001950-2nd-edition?format=PB [accessed 3 June 2021]).

CAMBRIDGE CALF; CAMBRIDGE SHEEP. "A method of decorating a calf- or sheepskin binding by sprinkling on two tints, leaving a rectangular 'pane' (panel) in the center of each cover. This technique was used extensively from the 1670s and again during the early decades of the 18th century. It was revived and used to a considerable extent during the second half of the 19th century" (Roberts and Etherington, "Cambridge calf (Cambridge sheep)"; https://cool.culturalheritage.org/don/dt/dt0560.html [accessed 18 January 2021]). Though the rectangular panel in the center of the front cover appears where a label might have been placed—that is, the panel sits in a spot where one might expect to see the title or author's name—that panel is usually left blank, merely as a decorative element.

CAMBRIDGE STYLE OF BINDING. "An English style of bookbinding practiced largely on theological works and in university libraries. Although used elsewhere, the style was so highly favored by binders in Cambridge in the early years of the 18th century that it became recognized as their speciality [*sic*], which probably accounts for the name. Books bound in this style were sewn on raised cords, covered in calfskin that was masked and sprinkled in such a manner as to leave a stained central rectangular panel, a plain rectangular frame, which, in turn, was surrounded by a stained outside frame. The books had Dutch marble endpapers and red edges. The spine was pieced with red russia leather labels and had double blind lines at head and tail on each side of the raised bands. The covers were decorated with a two-line FILLET close to the edges and on each side of the panel, and with a narrow flower roll worked on each side of the panel close to the lines. There were many variations of this style, including some books tooled in gold, and some with marbled covers and sprinkled panels" (Roberts and Etherington, "Cambridge style"; https://cool.culturalheritage.org/don/dt/dt0561.html [accessed 18 January 2021]).

CAMEO BINDING. "A style of Italian binding of the first half of the 16th century, which was imitated by French binders and also by ROGER PAYNE at a later date. The style consisted of designs in relief made from dies cut intaglio, somewhat in imitation of gems or metals. Leather was the medium most often used, although vellum was also used, being pressed while wet on the die, and with the cavities being filled with a composition of lacquered paste to preserve the shape of the figures. After being attached to the center of the leather cover, they were sometimes gilt and painted" (Roberts and Etherington, "Cameo bindings"; https://cool.culturalheritage.org/don/dt/dt0562.html [accessed 21 February 2021]). The designs that constitute the "cameo" of the binding are sometimes called "medallions."

CAMERA-READY COPY. Text printed out for a publisher (usually by an author—often with no training in book design—who has produced the text on a PC) and sent it to be printed from pictures made from the printed-out version. (*See* Desktop publishing.) As noted, the copy sent to the publisher was created by an author, often with no sense of design, so great numbers of books produced this way were quite unattractively designed. Also, when PCs first made it to the market—when publishers, knowing they could save money by having the authors do the design and printing, began requiring camera-ready copy—they did not have many handsome typefaces available, so not only were the books poorly designed, but the TYPEFACES were hardly anything beyond typewriter faces, and some of these were printed from the greatest invention since the shoehorn: dot-matrix printers. Also, since the publishers did not have to set any type (a process that could have introduced TYPOGRAPHICAL ERRORS), many of them assumed that the copy received from the authors did not need much (or any) proofreading. Big mistake! (*See* Repro.)

CAMOUFLAGED BOOKS. A genre familiar to many an intransigent student: a volume that looks like one thing from the outside (the side seen by an observer who can see only the cover), but that contains a text viewable by a reader who does not want the other party to know what she is looking at. This is not, however, for instance, a magazine of approved readership that covers an inserted one that is not approved. That would merely constitute a hidden text. A camouflaged book is bound to look like what it is not, and it will contain a text that is not approved by powers which could censure or punish the reader if that reader is caught. The German word, according to bookseller Simon Beattie, is *Tamschrift*, and he says it is "a pocket sabotage guide produced by the Resistance for distribution among French workers" (Beattie, "Never Judge a Book by Its Cover," Short List 1; *see* Bibliography; the volume referenced is *Dictionnaire Poucet*).

CANADIAN FEDERATION OF LIBRARY ASSOCIATIONS. "The Canadian Federation of Library Associations (CFLA-FCAB) is the united, national voice of Canada's library community. As the national voice of Canada's library communities, CFLA-FCAB will work to: / advance library excellence in Canada; / champion library values and the value of libraries; and / influence national and international public policy impacting libraries and their communities" (http://cfla-fcab.ca/en/about/ [accessed 8 June 2021]). This is the successor organization to the CANADIAN LIBRARY ASSOCIATION. Information about its strategic plan, Indigenous Resources, publications, programs, committees, and other data is available at: https://cfla-fcab.ca/en/about/ (accessed 15 July 2021).

CANADIAN LIBRARY ASSOCIATION (CLA). This was the professional association for librarians in Canada. Its old charter said, "The Canadian Library Association / Association canadienne des bibliothèques was founded in Hamilton, Ontario in 1946, and was incorporated under the Companies Act on November 26, 1947. CLA is a non-profit voluntary organization, governed by an elected Executive Council, which is advised by over forty networks and committees. / CLA members work in college, university, public, special (corporate, non-profit and government) and school libraries. Others sit on boards of public libraries, work for companies that provide goods and services to libraries, or are students in graduate level or community college programs" ("Canadian Library Association," http://www.cla.ca/AM/Template.cfm?Section=About_CLA [accessed 23 October 2015]). The CLA site added, "The CLA membership consists of a diverse group of individuals and organizations involved or interested in library or information sciences. . . . Membership categories of the Canadian Library Association / Association canadienne des bibliothèques include: Personal, Institutional, Corporate, and Associate." The organization gave out many grants and awards, had an advocacy program, had an annual national conference, helped its members with career placement, and much more.

However, on 27 January 2016, the organization decided to disband, with the aim of being reconstituted as the CANADIAN FEDERATION OF LIBRARY ASSOCIATIONS (CFLA, "For Immediate Release," http://cla.ca/canadian-library-association-results-of-the-special-general-meeting/ [accessed 8 June 2021]). (*See* ALA; Australian Library and Information Association; Chartered Institute of Library and Information Professionals.)

CANCEL. An alteration in a book from its original production, occasioned by the removal of something from the physical text; that is, any change that has been made to a volume that makes it differ from the way it was originally produced. R. B. MCKERROW says, "A cancel is any part of a book substituted for what was originally printed. It may be of any size from a tiny scrap of paper bearing one or two letters, pasted on over those first printed, to several sheets replacing the original ones. The most common form of cancel is perhaps a single LEAF inserted in place of the original leaf" (McKerrow, *An Introduction to Bibliography for Literary Students*, p. 222). But bibliographers recognize two phenomena with cancels: parts removed and replacements. The most common kind of cancel is a cancellandum, the removal of something from a book, as with the removal of a leaf (a bibliographer may say, "Leaf G3 has been canceled, as seen by its STUB," G3 being the third leaf in the G SIGNATURE)—though what has been removed does not have to be a whole leaf. In the Windhover Press volume *Kenny's: Twenty Poems for a Lost Tavern*, most of a paragraph had to be excised from the text of the FOREWORD. This excision is a cancellandum; what booksellers and collectors might refer to simply as "a cancel." But there is also a cancellans, an addition to a text that replaces what has been removed. In the Windhover book just mentioned, the printer was not able to remove the entire incendiary paragraph because of text on the VERSO of that leaf, so he pasted a strip of paper over a single line that had to be canceled. This strip was a cancellans—an addition to the text—though it was just a blank strip of paper.

A leaf in an early printed volume may be removed and replaced with another, corrected leaf—though the word "corrected" may not be strictly proper since what was removed may not have been an error. It could have been perfectly "correct" textually, but it may have contained something objectionable to the author, the printer, the church, or the authorities, and replacing it might have saved the printer's/publisher's neck. McKerrow says, "Cancels have been common at all times in the history of printing" (p. 222). (*See* Stop-press correction.) (See Berger, "Stop the Presses!") The simplest form of a cancel is a leaf cut from the text in such a way that a STUB is left. If the leaf is cut at the fold where the sewing is, the CONJUGATE LEAF would fall out. The stub could also be used to glue on a replacement leaf (the cancellans). And a final note: a volume could also contain a tipped-in piece of paper that covers over the original printed text. In Catalogue 188 from the British firm Peter Murray Hill, page 28 (for item 97) contains a tipped-in facsimile of a title page of a 1755 volume, covering what had been incorrectly shown in that place on the catalog's page. Item 20 in the catalog had a facsimile of its title page printed on page 8. That image was incorrectly printed again on page 28; so the bookseller carefully printed the correct image for page 28 and pasted it meticulously over the wrong one. Strictly speaking, this would not be a "replacement"; so it might not be seen as a cancel. But it has the weight of a cancellans in that it is an addition to the volume done to correct an error. Clearly, the phenomenon of cancels is complex. (See Chapman, *Cancels.*)

CANCEL TITLE. A title page added by a publisher that was not the original or primary publisher of the volume. Philip Gaskell explains, "Cases of *separate issue* would be: the alteration of title-pages to suit the issue of a book simultaneously in two or more different forms" (Gaskell, *New Introduction to Bibliography*, p. 315). If a printer prints a book for two or more publishers, one may have one publisher's name on the title page; the other publisher(s) would sometimes remove the title page and replace it with a new page showing their own name. This is a cancel title.

Carter mentions another kind of cancel title that results when a publisher cannot sell copies of a volume and tries to sell it later with a new title page. This would constitute a later issue (*see* Edition, Impression [Printing], Issue, and State; Points) of the book, with a cancel title. Another possibility that Carter talks about is when copies of a volume were sold (or traded or given) to another publisher, the latter substituting a new title page for the original. Naturally, the new publisher would want his own publishing house represented on the title page and would want the original publisher's information expunged. This was done by substituting a cancel title for the original one. Carter mentions examples of both kinds of cancel titles. (See Carter, p. 66.) F. C. Avis's definition raises another issue: "A title page bearing the name and address of a publisher other than those of the original publisher when a book is sold abroad" (Avis, *Bookman's Concise Dictionary*, p. 50). Strictly speaking, the original title page must be a CANCEL—that is, removed and then replaced—for it to be a "cancel title." But in today's more technological world of printing, it is easy for a publisher to contract with a foreign publisher and issue a volume with identical text blocks but only a variant title page with the foreign publisher's imprint. This is not really a cancel since no leaf has been removed and replaced by another.

I have seen yet another phenomenon: a title page printed by one publisher but with a small piece of paper pasted over the IMPRINT on the title page with a different publisher's (or bookseller's) imprint covering the original. This addition is a cancellans, but it does not quite constitute a "cancel title."

CANNIBALIZATION. Carter's entry states, "The vice of breaking up two (or more) copies of a book to achieve a complete set of variants never otherwise found within the same covers" (p. 67). The term is much out of use these days. It is closely related to BREAKING. In the few instances in which I have heard this term used, it has not meant precisely what Carter indicated: breaking up copies to make up a complete copy of a text. It has meant merely the disgraceful act of breaking up a volume. I have heard a bookseller say, "He cannibalized that book and sold the PLATES." That is, the party spoken of ripped or sliced the plates from a book to sell the illustrations or maps, for example, presumably discarding the rest of the volume. The power of the image of a cannibal shows how reprehensible and repugnant the practice is.

CANVAS. "A firm, closely woven fabric, usually made of cotton, hemp, or linen, in plain weave, and produced in various weights. Canvas has been used as a covering material for books for centuries, and was one of the principal fabrics used for embroidered bindings. Its greatest use historically, however, has been for rough job bindings, certain varieties of CHAPBOOKS, textbooks published between 1770 and about 1830 in England, and some types of reference books. Today its use is virtually limited to the covering of very large books, newspapers, etc., and as a CHEMISE for leather-bound county record books and other large stationery bindings" (Roberts and Etherington, p. 46).

CANVASSING BOOK. *See* Salesman's dummy/Salesman's sample book.

CAOUTCHOUC BINDING. *See* Gutta-percha.

CAPITAL FIGURE. *See* Lining figure.

CAPITALS. *See* Uppercase.

CAPTION. As Carter says, the term originally applied to a chapter title or the heading of a section of a text. We use it today to indicate a heading for something in the book: a chart, picture, drawing, or PLATE, for example. Let the reader beware, however, because while the author may write the text and the captions for the plates, he might get proofs only for the text, so he will sometimes not see how accurately the text of the captions was produced. Further, the author almost never has anything to do with the final makeup of the volume, so the placement of the illustrations and their accompanying captions must be left to the designers and printers. Case in point: my chapter on "Endleaves" (chapter 21, Duncan and Smyth, *Book Parts*, pp. 275–85) is accompanied by five plates (##8–12); the one putting the volume together reversed the order of the last two captions, and I found out only after the book was in print. No proofs of the plates were sent out to the authors of the chapters of the book.

CARBON PAPER. *See* Typescript.

CARDBOARD. A material used in bookbinding (in which it is called "BOARDS"), made by COUCHING several sheets of freshly made paper on top of one another until the desired thickness is attained. (*See* Post.)

CARET. A symbol (^) that is used to show where texts or corrections are to be inserted.

CAROUSEL BOOK. (Also called a "star book.") A three-dimensional book form that can be viewed one section at a time, and also opened fully to create a book in the round. This is a Victorian-era novelty, often used for souvenirs. Today the structure is most often used for children's books. The front cover of the book attaches to the rear cover, often with a string on both covers that can be tied so that the object is kept open. The ties also keep the volume shut when the carousel is closed. When it is open, the volume creates a 360-degree structure that, viewed from above, looks like a carousel, or a star with the same number of points as the volume has sections. As Ellen G. K. Rubin says, it is necessary for the item to be openable to 360 degrees for it to be called a carousel book; and the panels that open usually have pop-ups in them (personal communication; see Rubin, *Ideas in Motion: The History of Pop-up and Movable Books: Books & Ephemera from the Collection of Ellen G. K. Rubin*; see also Rubin, "Pop-up and Movable Books in the Context of History").

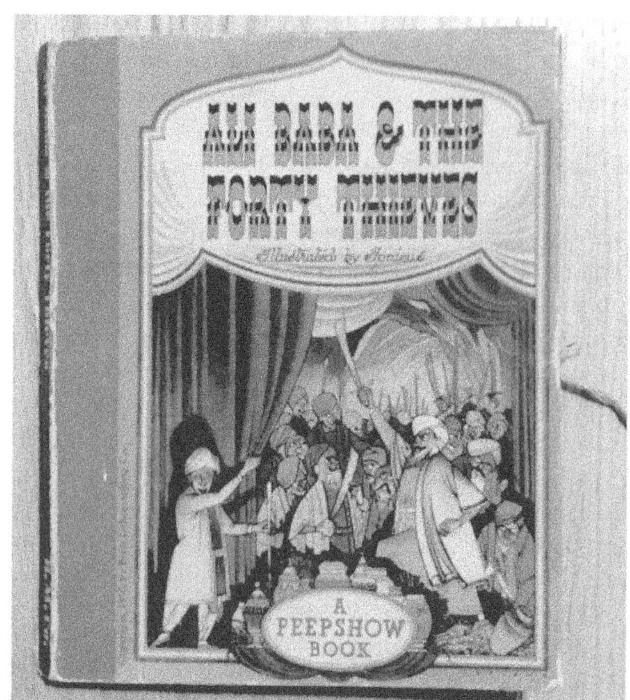

Carousel book. *Ali Baba & the Forty Thieves* (Boston: Houghton Mifflin, 1950). Though it calls itself a peep show book, the structure is that of a carousel.

Collection of the author.

Carousel book. (*See* caption for the previous figure.) This is a side view, showing that this specimen is related to a tunnel book.

Collection of the author.

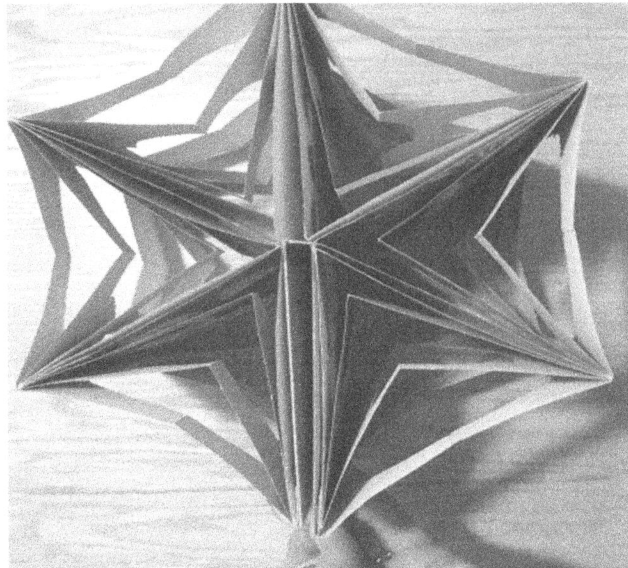

Carousel book opened, seen from above. (*See* caption to figure at the top of the previous page.)
Collection of the author.

CARPET PAGES. Pages in medieval manuscripts—or, later, in printed books—that are completely (or almost completely) decorated (with no written text). The decoration is usually geometrical, though it could include images of animals, birds, or flora. They generally appear at the beginning of the Gospels in the Christian Bible, though they appear in the books of other religions. Their patterns, usually symmetrical, are drawn or printed in bright colors, much like those in Oriental carpets. Similar patterns may appear stamped into the leather of bindings. Pages in the *Book of Kells* and the *Lindisfarne Gospels* are perhaps the best known and most recognizable.

CARRIERS' ADDRESSES. (Also called "bellman's verse"; "newscarriers' addresses.") BROADSIDES or pamphlets, often in poetry, given by newspaper carriers to their patrons, usually in late December or in the new year (almost always printed and distributed on New Year's Day), to solicit an annual gift. They "were published by newspapers, usually on January 1, and distributed in the United States for more than two centuries. The custom originated in England and was introduced here during colonial times. The newsboys delivered these greetings in verse each New Year's Day and the customers understood that a tip was expected. The poems, often anonymous, describe the events of the past year, locally, regionally, and nationally, and end with a request for a gratuity for the faithful carrier. Often the poem referred to the carrier's diligence and hardships during winter weather. Illustrated with wood-engravings and decorative borders, carriers' addresses are distinctive examples of popular publishing in nineteenth century America" (Brown University Library Center for Digital Initiatives, "Carriers' Addresses"). These pieces of EPHEMERA have become seriously collectible. Important gatherings of them are available at Brown University and the American Antiquarian Society.

CARTA RUSTICA. A form of binding in which rough handmade paper is pasted over flexible covers. As the Italian term indicates, the binding is usually associated with Italian volumes. Nicholas Pickwoad explains: "There is no rule of thumb and very little serious historical research into these very common and remarkable bindings. From my own research I have arrived at the following tentative conclusions: / It is apparent that they had appeared in the Italian book trade by the 1520s, possibly somewhat earlier, though in their first version, they use a stiff, often quite thick, hard-sized CARTONNAGE without TURN-INS, but with cut bookblock edges and sometimes with ENDBANDS. They will occasionally have FORE-EDGE cover extensions (often erroneously called YAPP EDGES). / At some point in the mid-sixteenth century, a thinner cartonnage was introduced which required turn-ins to stabilise the edges of the cover, and it also appears from the number of examples with deckle edges on all four turn-ins that these sheets were made for bookbindings in standard format sizes. / Unfortunately, once the standard pattern was established by the end of the sixteenth century—i.e. laced-case cartonnage covers, uncut edges (hence no endbands), two parallel creases on each joint about 1cm apart (the joint crease and the spine crease, made to ease the opening of the cover), no adhesive on the spine, no ties—they look much the same until the end of the eighteenth century and beyond (the latest I have seen is on an edition of 1856)" (Jeremy Norman's HistoryofInformation.com, "Nicolas [*sic*] Pickwoad's Tentative Observations on Dating Carta Rustica Bindings"). Pickwoad's statement that they are quite common necessitates an entry here. Since there is no standard English term for them, the Italian term must do.

CARTE-DE-VISITE. (Sometimes spelled unhyphenated, as three separate words.) A visiting card, somewhat akin to today's business cards but usually bearing only the name of the person (and possibly other information, such as an address or title) who bestows it to another. The card was sometimes given for business purposes but more often merely to announce one's presence. The original cartes-de-visite had photographs on them. "The carte de visite ('visiting card' in French) was a format for small photographs mounted on cardstock invented (and patented) by French photographer Andre [*sic*] Adolphe Eugene [these three names sometimes hyphenated] Disdéri in 1854. They became hugely popular worldwide, both for images of family members and of celebrities and royalty. Photographs about 2 × 3½ in. were pasted onto a cardstock mount about 2½ × 4 in. With the invention of photography, for the first time in history likenesses other than commissioned, painted portraits were available to—and affordable by—the masses. CDVs were small enough to be mailed, carried in a pocket or billfold, or gathered into parlor albums fifty or a hundred at a time" (The Ephemera Society of America, "Cartes de visite [CDV])." These have become COLLECTIBLES, and they can be found at EPHEMERA fairs and in library collections.

CARTER, JOHN (WAYNFLETE) (1905–1975). Prominent bibliographer, having learned his trade at King's College, Cambridge, and in the bookselling firm Scribner's. Well known for a host of his publications, the most important of which are (with GRAHAM POLLARD) *An Enquiry into the Nature of Certain Nineteenth Century Pamphlets*, *Taste and Technique in Book Collecting*, and *ABC for Book Collectors*. (See the bibliography.) His fame was ensured early in his career when he and Pollard exposed THOMAS J. WISE as the purveyor of a series of spurious "first editions." (See Dickinson, *John Carter*.)

CARTONNAGE. A term originally used to designate the "covering" of Egyptian mummy cases. The Merriam-Webster online dictionary says, "[T]he material of which many Egyptian mummy cases are made consisting of linen or papyrus glued together in many thicknesses and usually coated with stucco" (Merriam-Webster online dictionary, "Cartonnage"; https://www.merriam-webster.com/dictionary/cartonnage [accessed 2 March 2021]), but in the book world it has been used to describe PASTEBOARDS, so used because of the resemblance of pasteboards to the multilayered Egyptian material. Michèle V. Cloonan says of the term "cartonnagio": "Pasteboards used by the printer Giambattista Bodoni for his bindings in boards—*rilegatura della bodoniana*" (Cloonan, *Early Bindings in Paper*, p. 102). The term can often be found in booksellers' descriptions, especially for books from Italy.

CARTONNAGE À LA BRADEL. *See* Bradel binding.

CARTOON STORY BOOKS. *See* Big Little Books.

CARTOUCHE. A frame, usually decorative, used around a title, often seen on maps. The cartouche would contain the title of the map or text and might be decorated with animals, landscape scenes, or heraldic designs. As Roberts and Etherington point out, the term means a scroll or paper with the ends rolled up, bearing a title or other information. On a binding, it is "[a]n elaborate style of decoration popular in Italy about the middle of the 16th century. The decoration consists of elaborately interlaced fillets filling the entire field of the covers, and sometimes accompanied by arabesques, worked in a single line with tools cut in the shapes of flowers" (p. 47).

CARTULARY. A collection of charters, or official records and other papers, often relating to the operation of a monastery or estate, or any institution in which records are kept.

CASE. The cover of a book, composed of BOARDS (usually stiff) and a covering material, such as paper, cloth, or leather. The case is made separate from the TEXT BLOCK, which is eventually attached to the case. (*See* Cover.) There is also the SLIPCASE, a box into which a book slides. Old-time bibliographers may have said that a case-bound book was not really bound since the text block was not sewn to the covers; but the case made EDITION BINDING possible.

CASE. *See* Type case.

CASE BOUND/CASE BINDING/CASED-IN. Said of a volume that has had its TEXT BLOCK prepared for binding (sewn or glued or both) and that has been glued into a CASE that was prepared separate from the text block. Such a book is said to be in a case binding or is cased-in. Casing-in is far less expensive than LACING-IN, for it takes much less time and can be done in mass numbers, so it is popular for EDITION BINDING, especially beginning in the 19th century with PUBLISHER'S BINDINGS. The cloth or other covers of the case can be elaborately decorated fairly inexpensively and quickly. The problem with case bindings is that they can be flimsy and weak, and millions of them have deteriorated over the decades.

Cased-in binding.
Collection of the author.

CASE DUSTER. A tool used for blowing dust out of TYPE CASES. *See the image at* Fillets.

CASE LABEL/CASE MARK. *See* Pressmarks.

CASES (FOR BOOKS). *See* Boxes for books; Enclosures for books.

CASLON, WILLIAM (1692/1693–1766). "Mid-eighteenth century British punchcutter and typefounder, who solidly established British typefounding with well-crafted copies of earlier Dutch designs. / Caslon started work as apprentice to a London gunsmith, and set up his own business in 1716 engraving gunlocks and bookbinding tools. In 1720 William Bowyer the elder took him to see the respected James foundry, and subsequently helped Caslon set up as a type founder himself. His great reputation stems largely from his specimen of 1734, showing types that were (and often still are) reckoned to be superior to the Dutch types that inspired them. Indeed, his success meant the English reliance on Dutch types came to an end. He cut many non-Latin types (including Greek, Arabic, Hebrew, Coptic and Armenian) and some beautiful ornaments. His types were just as highly regarded in colonial America, and the Declaration of Independence was set in Caslon" (MyFonts, "William Caslon").

CASTING OFF COPY. The printer's practice of figuring out what text will begin on what page. That is, if a printer is setting type for a long text, say in a FOLIO in 10s (this format generates 20 pages of text for each SIGNATURE), and does not have enough type to set all 20 pages that that signature would need, he can figure out in advance what text will be needed on later pages and can set type for those later pages without having to set the intervening pages. Casting off is also used to figure out how many pages a book will be. "This is a very difficult problem. Should the copy be reprinted, it can be done quickly, a few lines of it being composed and the result noticed. But in manuscript it is not so easy. It may be in several handwritings and on pages of different magnitudes" (see *American Dictionary of Printing and Bookmaking*, p. 87). The importance of this subject can be seen by the fact that the *American Dictionary* just cited has more than a full page in small type devoted to it. Improperly cast-off copy can result in pages of text with blank space, tightly set type on some pages, or even full pages left blank. Carefully cast-off copy will tell a printer how many pages he will create using a particular size of type and can influence him to choose a smaller or larger font (depending on how large a volume he wishes to print), or can inform him of how much paper he will need for the edition.

CATALOG. *See* Bookseller's catalog.

CATALOGING IN PUBLICATION (CIP). Information in many books published in the United States and elsewhere, usually on the VERSO of the TITLE PAGE, giving Library of Congress and Dewey cataloging numbers. This was instituted for the convenience of libraries acquiring the volumes, but it also adds to the uniformity of cataloging records wherever the volumes are to be added to a library database. (*See* Library of Congress Subject Headings [LCSH]).

CATALOGUE RAISONNÉ. A comprehensive listing of the works of any artist, artisan, writer, or musician, for example. The volume (or volumes) purport to be complete and scholarly, though much debate could ensue when, for instance, two scholars individually do a catalogue raisonné of an artist or printer and their works do not match in content. The catalogs are systematic and often annotated, and contain a great deal of information about the party who is the subject of the catalog. Since these volumes often take years to compile and produce, and since the audience for them is generally not broad, they will usually be done in small numbers and be sold at high prices. They usually command a high price on the book market.

CATCHLINE. The printed line on a page that contains the CATCHWORDS. Sometimes other printing exists in this line as well. (*See* Direction line.)

CATCHPENNY PRINTS. (Sometimes "catchpenny" is hyphenated.) The reading matter of the poor in 18th- and 19th-century Europe. "They were cheap, mass-produced sheets printed on one side on unfolded sheets of paper. Because they were sold for one or more cents, they were known as catchpenny prints or 'centsprenten' in Dutch. The prints of about 30 × 40 cm [11¾ × 15¾ in.] size contained one or more images and a short accompanying text, often written in rhyme and secondary to the images. Retailers or merchants sold the prints per piece and teachers sometimes gave a print as a reward to students. . . . / Catchpenny prints cover all kinds of subjects. There are prints with images of ships, soldiers, animals, tools, people in other countries, but also board games and narrative prints with fairy tales, murder stories, farces, stories from Dutch history, Bible stories and more. A popular theme on catchpenny prints are [*sic*] children's games: next to marbles and riding in a goat cart, also less charming games such as knocking off a goose's head and shooting birds are depicted. / At the end of the eighteenth century, the 'Maatschappij tot Nut van 't Algemeen' (Society for Public Welfare) began to encourage publishers to produce prints with more educational value. The images became neater and the language of the prints was cleaned. It was the intention or the hope that both children and parents would become more aware of important civil norms and values" (Karin Vingerhoets, Europeana, "Catchpenny Prints in The Netherlands"). Millions of these inexpensive BROADSIDES were produced, usually in black and white, though later they were done in color. This is another genre of printed material that often shows up at antiquarian book fairs and EPHEMERA shows.

CATCHWORDS. (Sometimes spelled as two words.) Words or syllables printed in the lower right margins of pages, outside the TEXT BLOCK, that indicate what the first words or syllables of the following page will be. In texts with footnotes on the page, the footnote and the text itself may each have a catchword. That is, the text's catchword will lead one to the same word as the first word of the text on the following page; the catchword for the note will lead one to the first word of the note on the following page. It is not at all uncommon for a COMPOSITOR to set a catchword, then, remembering that he set that word already, begin the text on the following page not with the catchword but rather with the next word in the text. Also, as mentioned, sometimes the "catchword" is only a few letters of the word, not the full word. The catchword may be "ent," while the word at the top of the next page may be "entertain." In early printing, catchwords may be used only on the VERSO of the last leaf of a SIGNATURE, leading the reader

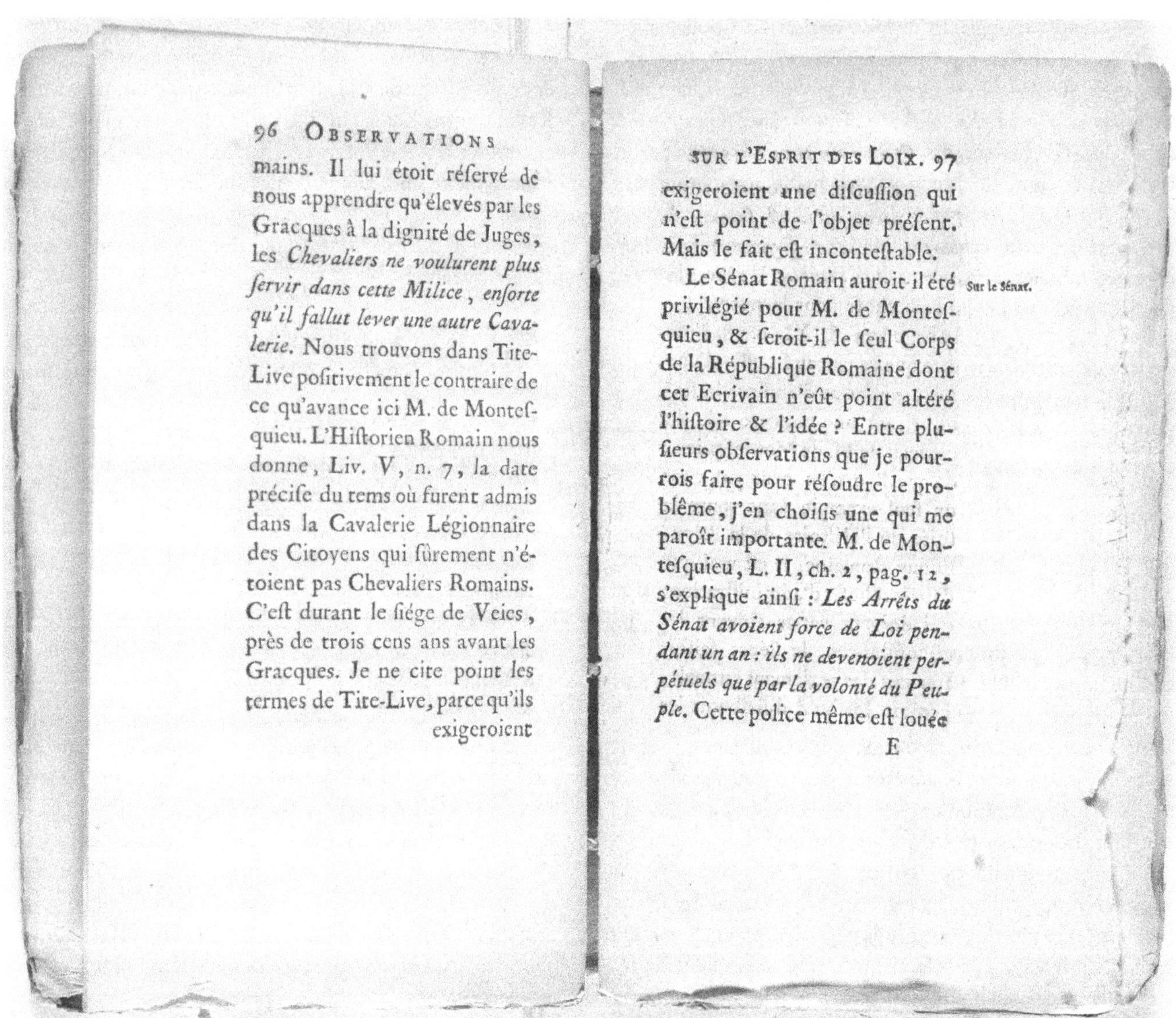

96 OBSERVATIONS

mains. Il lui étoit réſervé de nous apprendre qu'élevés par les Gracques à la dignité de Juges, les *Chevaliers ne voulurent plus ſervir dans cette Milice*, *enſorte qu'il fallut lever une autre Cavalerie.* Nous trouvons dans Tite-Live poſitivement le contraire de ce qu'avance ici M. de Monteſquieu. L'Hiſtorien Romain nous donne, Liv. V, n. 7, la date préciſe du tems où furent admis dans la Cavalerie Légionnaire des Citoyens qui ſûrement n'étoient pas Chevaliers Romains. C'eſt durant le ſiége de Veies, près de trois cens ans avant les Gracques. Je ne cite point les termes de Tite-Live, parce qu'ils

exigeroient

SUR L'ESPRIT DES LOIX. 97

exigeroient une diſcuſſion qui n'eſt point de l'objet préſent. Mais le fait eſt inconteſtable.

Le Sénat Romain auroit-il été privilégié pour M. de Monteſquieu, & ſeroit-il le ſeul Corps de la République Romaine dont cet Ecrivain n'eût point altéré l'hiſtoire & l'idée ? Entre pluſieurs obſervations que je pourrois faire pour réſoudre le problême, j'en choiſis une qui me paroît importante. M. de Monteſquieu, L. II, ch. 2, pag. 12, s'explique ainſi : *Les Arrêts du Sénat avoient force de Loi pendant un an : ils ne devenoient perpétuels que par la volonté du Peuple.* Cette police même eſt louée

Sur le Sénat.

E

Page with catchword (on the verso) and the facing page with the signature "E." Also, the loose binding shows how the text block was sewn to cords. (Jean Baptiste Louis Crevier, *Observations sur le livre l'Esprit des loix* [Paris: Desaint & Saillant, 1764]) (For other images of catchwords, *see the images at* "Drop cap" and "Headpiece.")

Courtesy of the Rare Book and Manuscript Library at the University of Illinois, Urbana–Champaign.

and the binder to the first word of the next signature. According to Berry and Poole, the first use of catchwords in a dated, printed book was in 1472 (*Annals of Printing*, see their entry for Balthasar Azoguidus, p. 27). Colin Clair gives the same date (spelling the printer's name Baldassare degli Azzoguidi, p. 15) but adds that the first book to have printed catchwords on each page was *Historia ecclesiastica*, by Eusebius Pamphilius Caesariensis, printed by Johann Schall in Mantua in 1479 (Clair, *A Chronology of Printing*, p. 22). With the end of the HANDPRESS PERIOD, with machine printing of books and the automatic gathering of the printed signatures, there was no need for such a device, and the practice ceased, except in a few volumes with pretentions to antiquity. In doing a COLLATION of a book from the handpress period, a bibliographer should observe catchwords carefully since they could be areas in the TYPOGRAPHY in which TYPOGRAPHICAL ERRORS could appear, possibly signaling a point or a CANCEL. (*See* Edition, Impression [Printing], Issue, and State; Points.)

CATHEDRAL BINDING. A binding "executed between about 1810 and approximately 1840 in England and France. The name derives from the motifs of the embellishment, e.g., Gothic architecture, rose windows, and the like. The design was either blocked on the cover, as in France, or built up by means of separate tools, as in England" (Roberts and Etherington, p. 49).

CATHOLICON. A 13th-century Latin dictionary (whose formal title is *Summa grammaticalis quae vocatur Catholicon*), generally referred to as the *Catholicon* (from the Greek word Καθολικόν, meaning "universal"). It contained definitions and a Latin grammar. It was "written by Johann Balbus a Genoese Dominican" to help scholars interpret the Bible (Glaister, *Glaister's Glossary*, p. 870). The first printing of the text was in Mainz in 1460, but the printer does not identify himself. As one of the first books printed from movable type, this text may have been printed by JOHANN GUTENBERG. Its often-quoted COLOPHON says, "With the help of the Most High at whose will the tongues of infants become eloquent and who often reveals to the lowly what he hides from the wise, this noble book *Catholicon* has been printed and accomplished without the help of reed, stylus or pen but by the wondrous agreement, proportion and harmony of PUNCHES and TYPES, in the year of the Lord's incarnation 1460 in the noble city of Mainz of the renowned German nation" (quoted in Steinberg, *Five Hundred Years of Printing*, p. 23).

In the world of books, the printing of the *Catholicon* has generated a good deal of controversy, mostly as to who the printer of it was and on the method of printing. Was the text printed from standing type or from some kind of printing plates? (For just two publications showing the sides of the debate, see Hellinga, "Das Mainzer Catholicon und Gutenbergs Nachlaß," and Needham, "Johann Gutenberg and the Catholicon Press." See also Kapr, *Johann Gutenberg*, pp. 226–34.)

CAT'S PAW CALF. "An acid-stain pattern on a calfskin binding, somewhat resembling the paw marks of a cat" (Roberts and Etherington, "Cat's paw calf"; https://cool.culturalheritage.org/don/dt/dt0619.html [accessed 20 April 2021]).

CAVIAR. (*See* Bisquing.) A metaphorical term for ink used to censor documents in the Soviet Union. The term is highlighted in Maryanna Tax Cholden's article "Access to Foreign Publications in Soviet Libraries." She says that in many Soviet books the text was "covered with caviar"—that is, obliterated with black ink by censors. She says that there was also "invisible caviar"—that is, passages removed, for one reason or another, from a text, and she cites the example of a book that had about four-fifths of its text removed. "A hefty, English-language copy of [Studs Terkel's 'Working,' in an exhibition] stands beside a skimpy authorized translation. Only about one-fifth of the original text . . . made it into the Soviet edition. . . . This is invisible caviar-censorship by translation. Most Soviet readers would be completely unaware that anything was missing" (quoted in Gallagher, "Scraping away the 'Caviar.' ")

CAXTON, WILLIAM (ca. 1422–ca. 1492). England's first printer. He was a merchant and diplomat working in Bruges. His travels exposed him to printing, and in 1475 he and a partner, Colard Mansion, created the first book printed in English, *Recuyell of the Historyes of Troye* (see Chappell, *A Short History of the Printed Word*, p. 73). When he returned to England, he published the first book printed there, *The Dictes or Sayings of the Philosophers* (1477). Chappell says that the BLACK LETTER type that he used in the nearly 100 volumes that he printed was influenced by his having learned the craft probably from a German printer and that he may have used a different face and come up with a completely different look to his publications had he learned to print in Italy or France (Chappell, pp. 74–75). (For Caxton's logo, *see* Printer's mark.) The name, by extension, has come to mean a volume printed by this printer: "I bought a Caxton the other day, and I won't eat for a year."

CCAHA (Conservation Center for Art and Historic Artifacts). "Based in Philadelphia, PA, CCAHA is a nonprofit facility specializing in paper conservation. / With conservators trained in paper, photograph, and book conservation, we treat every kind of paper, from family photographs to the nation's founding documents. Our mission is to provide expertise and leadership in the preservation of the world's cultural heritage, and our clients range from large institutions to private individuals" (http://ccaha.org [accessed 3 June 2021]). (*See* NEDCC; Regional Alliance for Preservation.)

CEAA (Center for Editions of American Authors). An organization founded in 1963 to promote the creation of definitive editions (*see* Bibliography) of the works of American authors. "Organized by the Modern Language Association to promote textual and bibliographical study and to oversee the creation of approved texts for definitive editions of classic American authors, including Cooper, Stephen Crane, John Dewey, Emerson, Hawthorne, Howells, Irving, Melville, Simms, Thoreau, Mark Twain, and Whitman. Its publication program was later directly overseen by the National Endowment for the Humanities" (http://www.oxfordreference.com/view/10.1093/oi/authority.20110803095558311 [accessed 3 June 2021]). In 1976, this organization was succeeded by the CSE (the Center for Scholarly Editions—today called the Committee on Scholarly Editions). The aim of the organization was (and still is) to create, for the texts of important writers, editions that can be relied on as the most scholarly, AUTHORITATIVE, and AUTHORIAL possible, having been edited under strict conditions and with the most up-to-date editorial practices. (*See* Bibliography, especially the section "Textual Bibliography.") The efforts were supported mainly by the National Endowment for the Humanities, but they cut off their support after some criticism of the editors' methods was pilloried by critics such as Edmund Wilson. His now-famous essay, "The Fruits of the MLA" (which appeared in the *New York Review of Books* [issue 11, no. 5 (26 September 1968), and issue 11, no. 6 (10 October 1968)], criticized the editors for some of their practices. Wilson, for example, criticized the experiment, carried out by one of the collation groups at the University of Iowa's Center for Textual Studies, of reading the texts backward to see if accurate COLLATIONS could be produced. The practice was abandoned, but Wilson, in his ignorance (he really knew nothing about such matters and was quite ignorant about the CEAA and its use of extremely high bibliographic/textual-editing standards), embarrassed the CEAA. (See Berger, p. 283.) Today, the CSE carries out the same kind of endeavors but with a different funding structure and for many authors, not merely American ones. ("Tanselle points out that the CEAA concentrated its efforts on American writers, but its successor, the CSE, had a wider charge: to edit the works of any important author"; see Berger, p. 295, n. 48; and Tanselle, "The Editing of Historical Documents," p. 3). (See Bruccoli, "What Bowers Wrought." See also *Recovering and Preserving the Author's Intentions* in the bibliography.)

CELESTIAL ATLAS. Also called a "Sky atlas." A map of the heavens: sun, stars, constellations, galaxies, and other phenomena. As the website "Celestial Cartography—Maps of the Heaven" explains: "The earliest printed depictions of the constellations were not true maps of the sky. Constellation figures were produced as woodcut diagrams with stars positioned to adorn the figures, but these stars were not positioned to accurately portray the heavens. / It was not until 1515 that the first printed maps of the heavens appeared that accurately portrayed the night sky. In that year, the celebrated artist Albrecht Dürer produced a pair of woodcut northern and southern planispheres (hemispherical views of half the heavens). His planispheres included a coordinate system and attempted to accurately position the stars of the 48 constellations based on the star catalog contained in Ptolemy's 2nd century Almagest. . . . / Early planispheres and celestial globes were popular, and it was only a matter of time until a true celestial atlas was to appear on the cartographic scene. / The year was 1540, and the place was Venice. Italian cardinal Alessandro Piccolomini was a prolific writer who turned his attention to the production of a book about the constellations and their mythical lore. . . . / The first celestial atlas with an accurate coordinate system and constellation figures did not appear until 1588. In that year, Giovanni Gallucci published an atlas of 48 woodcut constellation charts. In addition, his atlas included nebulae—a generic term for faint milky or cloudy objects in the sky. Ptolemy had identified seven such objects in the Almagest, and Gallucci included all of these" ("Celestial Cartography—Maps of the Heaven"; http://www.berksastronomy.org/starcharts.htm#:~:text=The%20first%20celestial%20atlas%20with,cloudy%20objects%20in%20the%20sky [accessed 12 August 2022]). These highly COLLECTIBLE volumes are often the victims of thieves or fools who remove particularly beautiful, important, or valuable plates to hang on the wall or to sell for their ill-gotten gains.

CELS. Small pieces of transparent celluloid onto which pictures of various kinds are painted or drawn and arranged in a sequence. Subsequent ones are drawn with slight variations in the image. When a light shining through the cels projects the images sequentially onto a surface, movement results. We see this principle in FLIP BOOKS, in which a cartoonlike motion is created. While not strictly "books," they belong in a dictionary of the book since they are frequently sold at antiquarian book fairs. They have become serious COLLECTIBLES in the book and EPHEMERA world. Dave O'Brian says, "Those colorful celluloid paintings from which cartoons are made were once trivial pieces of pop art that ended up on the walls of children's rooms. Now these comic drawings, used to create motion in animated films, have become high-priced objets d'art" (Dave O'Brian, "The Daffy Demand for Cels.")

CENSORSHIP. The suppression of anything that is considered morally, legally, politically, or otherwise objectionable. In the world of books, censorship has been around for centuries. As early as 1559, the Catholic Church published its *INDEX LIBRORUM PROHIBITORUM*. An extensive literature deals with censorship, but for the present purposes, it is enough to say that thorough censorship can indeed wipe out all traces of a text, but it can also have the opposite effect: raising the curiosity of a large audience and leading to the wide dissemination of a text, if not publicly, then under the radar of the censors. (*See* Expurgated.)

CENSUS. In the book world, a census is a listing of known copies of a text or edition. (*See* Edition, Impression [Printing], Issue, and State; Points). It is one thing for a scholar to identify a particular item useful for her research, another thing to be able to find a copy. Certain bibliographies may list institutional holdings of items, this listing constituting a census of copies. Thanks to OCLC (*see* the entry for this utility; Online Computer Library Center), holdings are now available through its WorldCat database, constituting a massive and growing census of items. While no bibliography is complete, the WorldCat census contains billions of citations. Carter missed this one. So did those who edited his *ABC*. Carter had an excuse: OCLC was in its infancy at the end of his career.

CENTERFOLD. The two-page spread at the center of a signature—usually in a publication like a magazine that is only a single SIGNATURE. Thanks to at least one well-known periodical publication, the term has taken on a prurient meaning. (Think "stapled navel.")

CENTERPIECE. "A finishing stamp, usually arabesque, BLOCKED in the center of the COVER and generally used in combination with center pieces or corner stamps. It was a popular form of decoration in the late 16th and early 17th centuries. Also called 'centerstamp'" (Roberts and Etherington, "centerpiece"; https://cool.culturalheritage.org/don/dt/dt0639.html [accessed 31 March 2021]).

CHAINED LIBRARIES. Libraries in which books were attached to their shelves, tables, desks, pulpits, or other furniture with chains, the obvious aim of which was to prevent theft. The chain was long enough for the volume to be taken down and placed on a platform or desk. Richard A. Linenthal says, "The earliest evidence for chaining dates from the 13th century (e.g. several Oxford and Cambridge colleges, and the Sorbonne). Most surviving chained books were so fitted in the 16th and 17th centuries; the practice had stopped by the second half of the 18th century" (in *The Oxford Companion to the Book*, vol. 1, pp. 599–600). The paucity of chained libraries remaining in the world may be a testament to how effective it was to chain the books in the first place.

A 14th-century volume from a chained library.

From the University of Kansas, Kenneth Spencer Research Library; http://blogs.lib.ku.edu/spencer/unchained-melody-or-how-to-house-a-chained-book/ (accessed 11 July 2021).

CHAIN LINES. (Sometimes styled as a single word.) When a piece of LAID PAPER is held up to the light, LAID LINES are visible. With a full sheet in landscape FORMAT, held up to a backlight, one will see lines where the sheet is thin enough to let light through. All the lines are called "laid lines." Horizontal lines, close together, are called "WIRE LINES." (*See* the entry for Laid lines.) Vertical ones, made where the laid wires are sewn to wooden supports beneath the surface of the MOLD, are called chain lines. They are apart by ½ inch or more, depending on where the wooden supports are, since the wires are sewn to the supports using a chain stitch that protrudes above the surface of the mold. This protrusion of chain stitches creates a long raised area above each support, making the paper fibers fall more thinly on the chain stitches than on the wires around them. The thin area, running the length of each support, vertically on the mold, allows light to shine through the sheet, creating chain lines. (For an image, *see* Laid paper.)

The phenomenon was a by-product of a handmade sheet, and for that reason the paper was often quite expensive. In the world of the FOURDRINIER, with paper made by machine, manufacturers were able to create a wire screen with the pattern of chain lines and wire lines on it (or they were able to employ a DANDY ROLL that imparted the laid lines on the machine-made sheet), so chain lines and wire lines could be "faked." They were real laid lines, but they were not created with a hand process. (See Berger, pp. 84–89.) (*See also* Antique laid paper; Modern laid paper.)

If a leaf in a volume is a cancellans (*see* Cancel), the bibliographer may be able to discern this if the added leaf is on laid paper and the chain lines are a different distance apart from those in the rest of the book. Since there was no standard for the distance between chain lines (i.e., between the supports in the paper mold), paper stocks could look alike and even be identical in measurements, but their chain lines could vary considerably.

Carter mentions only that the chain lines are "made by the wire mesh at the bottom of the tray in which [the sheet] is made" and they are "visible in the texture of laid paper" (p. 74). It is possible that the texture of the paper still shows the effects of the chain stitching, but more often than not (probably about 99 percent of the time) the paper has been CALENDERED and the sheet is smooth—the texture is gone. He really needed to say that the chain lines are visible when the sheet is held up to a light. Also, to call the laid mold a "tray" is seriously wrong, and laid paper—the kind with chain lines—was not made on a "mesh." Here is an example of Carter's expertise running a bit thin.

CHALKING. The turning white and powdery of something in a volume, usually the adhesive used for the binding, for SILKED LEAVES, or in any other place in which an adhesive has dried out and turned white and flaky. In silking, the chalking can actually become opaque and cover up printed text or illustrations.

CHAMPLEVÉ BINDINGS. "Bindings produced between the 11th and 13th centuries. The process involved cutting designs into a thin sheet of gold or copper, which formed the cover, with cavities filled with enamel. Sometimes the enamel was limited to the decoration of borders and corners" (Roberts and Etherington, "Champlevé bindings"; https://cool.culturalheritage.org/don/dt/dt0659.html [accessed 21 February 2021]). Also called "enameled bindings."

CHAPBOOKS. As the word indicates, these were items sold by chapmen, peddlers who peddled inexpensive items, sometimes on the street, sometimes in shops. In the book world, they usually purveyed children's texts or sensational or educational PAMPHLETS, often with a moral focus. The chapmen were not primarily booksellers. As the Incline Press website once said, "Chapbooks are small publications of a popular nature (often poems or stories) common from the seventeenth to the nineteenth centuries. They get their name from the chapmen who hawked them door to door along with other small items such as ribbons, laces, and pins from a tray slung across the shoulders" (http://www.inclinepress.com/Chapbooks.html [accessed 21 February 2016; this site no longer carries this information]). (See the Barry McKay volume cited in the bibliography.) Although Carter (p. 74) says that the term has not been used too much since about 1830, a good deal of recent scholarship on these publications has brought the word into much modern use. The pamphlets were generally sheets folded once, containing moral stories, almanacs, popular tales, jests (sometimes these were "gestes" in the older sense of "tales," not the "jests" that we today think of as humorous), fables, ballads, historical tales, and the like. (See the Brian Findlay article, "Chapbook," in *The Oxford Companion to the Book*, vol. 1, pp. 601–02.)

CHARTERED INSTITUTE OF LIBRARY AND INFORMATION PROFESSIONALS (CILIP). Great Britain's primary organization for library and information professionals, established in 2002 with the merger of the Library Association and the Institute of Information Scientists. The Library Association was founded in 1877; the Institute of Information Scientists was formed in 1958.

The CILIP website said, "CILIP is the leading body representing the information professions. We believe in a literate, knowledgeable and connected society. We build the professionalism of our members by supporting the development of skills, knowledge and excellence. We provide unity through shared values and advocate on behalf of the information professions" (http://www.cilip.org.uk/cilip/about [accessed 23 October 2015]). Its updated site says that they are "a professional body for librarians, information specialists and knowledge managers in the United Kingdom. It was established in 2002 as a merger of the Library Association (LA, sometimes LAUK) and the Institute of Information Scientists (IIS). / CILIP in Scotland (CILIPS) is an independent organisation which operates in Scotland in affiliation with CILIP and delivers services via a service level agreement. / CILIP's 2020 goal is to 'put information and library skills and professional values at the heart of a democratic, equal and prosperous society'" (https://en.wikipedia.org/wiki/Chartered_Institute_of_Library_and_Information_Professionals [accessed 28 June 2021]). The organization publishes a magazine, holds conferences, grants several awards, has a job information service, and promulgates policy and practices for its members and for others working in the profession who are not CILIP members. It is roughly equivalent to the American Library Association. (*See also* Australian Library and Information Association, though in the United States, information scientists tend to belong to the Association of Information Science and Technology that is headquartered in the States. *See also* Canadian Library Association.)

CHASE. The rectangular metal frame in a handpress that holds the forme. On standard handpresses, the chase was removable; it was taken to a composing stone, and the composed (set) type would be imposed (*see* Imposition) into the chase, along with anything else that was in the chase (e.g., illustrations, furniture, and quoins). (By the way, some mechanical presses also had a chase.)

CHASED EDGES. *See* Gauffered edges.

CHEAP COPY. This entry is here because Carter has an entry for this term. But this is not really a formal "book term"; it is merely a designation of an inexpensive copy of an item (book, pamphlet, broadside, etc.). As he indicates, the key feature of the item under scrutiny is that it is not expensive, implying that it is in less than ideal (read "shabby") condition. If it is cheap, one may assume that more expensive copies are available. And it is true that some collectors would rather have a cheap copy than no copy at all, while some would rather wait for a good copy to come along. (I searched for nearly two decades for a book, and then, in Hay-on-Wye, found a "cheap copy" with a quarter of its front cover bitten off by a hound of some large breed. It could not have been cheap enough. I passed on it.) Carter thought it necessary to have an entry for this made-up term, but I would add to his definition that "cheapness" is not necessarily the result of being in poor condition; it also implies inferior quality. A "bargain book" looking like a remainder could be inexpensive because it is on poor-quality paper, because it has a flimsy binding, or because it is perfect bound with inexpensive adhesive.

CHECKLIST. (Dictionaries give this as one word or two; Carter hyphenates it.) A "list of items, as names or tasks, for comparison, verification, or other checking purposes" (dictionary.com; https://www.dictionary.com/browse/checklist#:~:text=noun,verification%2C%20or%20other%20checking%20purposes [accessed 18 January 2021]). In the book world, the term has come to mean something like a short bibliographical listing, perhaps as a want list for a collector or bookseller. For many years I kept a checklist in my wallet of a series of paperback books that our son was reading—my list consisted of the numbers of all the ones he wanted, along with the ones he had wanted but that he had acquired along the way—these latter checked off so that I would not get him duplicates.

CHEMICAL WOOD PULP. "A paper pulp prepared from both coniferous and deciduous trees, in which the lignin and other undesirable materials are removed by cooking the wood with an alkaline sodium sulfide solution, or a sodium sulfite solution, leaving the cellulose fibers in an aqueous suspension of the dissolved lignins, etc. The fibers are washed and are then used 'as is' to produce unbleached paper or are bleached to produce white paper" (Roberts and Etherington, p. 52). The bleaching, which was common for papers used for books, left the paper with a low pH (hence the paper was acidic). (*See* Mechanical wood pulp.)

CHEMISE. A cover into which a book is placed for protection. In early printing, the cover could be made from silk or chevrotain (a soft deerskin). Roberts and Etherington say that the chemise can also be "[a] loose cover for a book with pockets [i.e., the chemise has pockets, the book does not] into which the boards are inserted" (p. 52). Today, any kind of soft cloth "bag" or other covering into which a volume can be slipped is a chemise. Michelle Brown says that the chemise could be made of leather or textile (like velvet or linen). "Chemises varied in form from high-grade luxurious embellishments for books of hours and prayer books to functional wrappers for administrative records and library books" (*Understanding Illuminated Manuscripts*, p. 38). (*See* Pull-off box.)

CHEVRON-SHAPED QUOTATION MARKS. *See* Guillemots.

CHIAROSCURO WATERMARK. *See* Light-and-shade watermark.

CHICAGO MANUAL OF STYLE. Perhaps the premiere style guide in the United States. Now in its 17th edition, the volume has grown to nearly 1,150 pages, and it aims to help writers of all stripes (and their editors and publishers) create reliable and readable texts. It now also has an online version (see the citation in the bibliography), at which site one finds: "*The Chicago Manual of Style Online* is the venerable, time-tested guide to style, usage, and grammar in an accessible online format. / It is the indispensable reference for writers, editors, proofreaders, indexers, copywriters, designers, and publishers, informing the editorial canon with sound, definitive advice" (accessed 1 February 2021). It covers so much territory that trying to find specific things in it can be a challenge, despite its extensive index. And with the evolution of technology and the world of information, it cannot cover every kind of information tidbit, so one may be left to falling back on one's own resources to create citation styles that seem not to be covered in this massive tome. It is circumspect in offering alternate styles for the presentation of bibliographic information.

CHINA PAPER. (In a sentence, "china" is not capitalized; *see* Japan paper.) A vague term in that originally it was a thin paper made in China, but all thin, strong papers came to be called "china paper" regardless of the country of origin. It could have been made from bamboo or KOZO or other fibers. Typically, it was used for fine prints (COPPERPLATE and STEEL PLATE), and it was TIPPED IN to illustrated books, the thinness of the paper allowing the book to be bound with no bulging where the plates were "stacked up" in the book and the smoothness of the surface being ideal for illustrations with fine lines. The paper was also used for proofs of engravings. The confusion about its origin led some people to call it "India paper" or "India proof paper." Although Carter says that this paper was from China, if it was made from bamboo, and its color was like straw or gray or yellow (p. 75), it could be from any country and made from many other fibers, and it is often quite white. The paper, because of its strength and imperviousness to ink, was often used as OFFSET SHEETS. It is sometimes called "Bible paper" since its thinness and strength made it ideal for printing the full text of Bibles that could be bound into fairly small, thin volumes. (*See* Rice paper.)

CHIPBOARD. A heavy board, made of layers of paper (even recycled or repulped paper), used for covering boards. "In library binding and craft binding, however, it is never used for anything but lining board" (Roberts and Etherington, p. 53).

CHIPPED. A term often used to describe the CONDITION of a DUST JACKET or book binding. Such a description implies that pieces are missing—chipped off. It can also be used for damaged photographs.

CHIRIMEN-BON. *See* Crepe paper.

CHITSU. A book-covering case made of flaps that fold over the volume, usually open at top and bottom, though there are variations with four flaps covering the book on all sides. One variation has four triangular flaps, folding over to cover the book completely but with no overlap. This is sometimes called a "Tao box." The word "chitsu" is from the Japanese meaning "vagina," so when booksellers present books so covered, they use the Japanese word for the case.

A simple chitsu, covered in chiyogami, with a bone clasp; http://darkroompaintings.blogspot.com/2009_11_01_archive.html.

Exhibited on Creative Adventures: The Guest Blog of the Book; http://darkroompaintings.blogspot.com/search?updated-max=2010-01-22T20:30:00-07:00&max-results=7 (accessed 10 August 2021).

CHIYOGAMI. Japanese papers, decorated with WOOD BLOCKS or stencils. The earliest of these, from the Edo period (1603–1868), were done with blocks; from the Meiji period on (1868–1912 to date), stencils were used. Each stencil imparts a single color; and some of the chiyogami had as many as 30 colors. The stencils are called KATAZOME. The number of patterns and pictures on these papers is truly astonishing, as is the stunning result of such decoration. The papers are often seen on bindings and SLIPCASES and for CHEMISES wrapping books. (One often sees the redundancy "chiyogami papers," redundant since the "gami" part of the word means "paper." I did not make that mistake when I wrote the book *Chiyogami Papers*; the publisher added that word to the title page without my knowledge, and when my copy of the book arrived at publication, its author was not pleased.) (See Berger, *Chiyogami Papers*; Herring, *Chiyogami: Hand-printed Patterned Papers of Japan.*) (*See* Washi.) As with the word "washi," not all chiyogami papers are Japanese. They are produced with great beauty and quality in Korea; and some of lesser quality can be had from China, Nepal, and Tibet.

CHRESTOMATHY. A gathering of snippets of texts from an author (or authors) that are usually on a single topic or gathered for a single purpose, as to teach language or to instruct on the topic of the passages. Similar to a COMMONPLACE BOOK. The collection could be a selection of stories or essays by a single author, along with a selection of correspondence or notes by that writer.

CHROMOLITHOGRAPHY. Printing in color from a stone or other flat surface. (*See* Lithography.) Invented in the second decade of the 19th century, it became one of the most popular and employed forms of printing, especially for children's books and for books with color PLATES. It is a form of PLANOGRAPHIC PRINTING. Since printing from a lithographic stone yields only a single color, to print in colors using a flat surface, the artist needed to have one stone for each color to be overprinted. With the primary colors, printers could achieve multicolor images. But some artists employing the medium wanted greater and greater depth and brilliance in their compositions and overprinted many colors. For example, in 1870, Louis Prang was able to produce a brilliant reproduction of a painting of Beethoven using 25 stones, each imparting a different color to the final image. (*See* Progressives.) (The standard and most exhaustive text on the subject is that by Michael Twyman. See his *A History of Chromolithography* in the bibliography.) In their catalogs, booksellers sometimes refer to prints made with this technique as "chromos."

CHRONOGRAM. A printed (or possibly MANUSCRIPT) text—usually a short statement or title—with key letters emphasized (as with red ink when the rest is in black, for example; or with UPPERCASE letters when the rest is in LOWERCASE), the emphasized letters being those used for ROMAN NUMERALS. These accentuated characters reveal a particular number. If they are on a title page, the number is usually the date of the item. The numbers can be in roman-numeral order (called a "natural chronogram"), as in "MaiDen Court / London / at the sign of the oX and IrIs" (MDCLXII = 1662), or they can be in any order, but adding up to the requisite number: "CaMDen: In boX Lane, over agaInst the quay" (= C [**100**] + M [**1000**] + D [**500**] + I [**1**] + X [**10**] + L [**50**] + I [**1**] = 1662). James Hilton says of most classical chronograms, that they often appear on stone monuments of various kinds, including gravestones. "The words composing a chronogram ought to convey a pertinent allusion to the event which it commemorates, the sentence should be concise, and should contain no more numerical letters than are necessary to form the date. . . . / Books . . . contain a great many chronograms. Some books require a most careful inspection in order to detect and regain the treasures which at one time delighted their readers, but which are now hardly within the knowledge of the modern student or 'bookworm.' Many books bear a chronogram on the title-page, or even on the back of it, in the place of figures, to tell the date of the publication; occasionally the title as well as the date is jointly expressed in that manner; some books again are full of chronograms from beginning to end, expressing the date over and over again, repeating it many hundreds of times in continual variety of words; entire odes and poems are thus composed, thoroughly fulfilling the strict rules of Latin versification, while cramped by the employment of words containing the needful date-letters. This is but an outline of the formerly extensive application of chronograms" (Hilton, *Chronograms: 5000 and More in Number Excerpted*, pp. vi, vii). And chronograms were not restricted to the Latin alphabet. (See Heller, *Studies in the Making of the Early Hebrew Book*, "Chronograms on Title Pages in Selected Eighteenth Century Editions of the Talmud," chapter 5, pp. 54–71).

CHRONOLOGICAL OBSESSION. Carter has an entry for this term—pretty much his own, since it is not truly a standard term in the book world. He says it is the preference of collectors (and others) for the earliest versions of texts—as in the first edition, first issue of a text. (*See* Edition, Impression [Printing], Issue, and State; Points). And he points out that such an obsession borders on lunacy, or at least can be used to ridicule the person so afflicted. (HENRY MORRIS of the Bird & Bull Press complained to me many times that his subscribers [*see* Subscription sales/Subscribers] asked to be sent the copy with the lowest number, that is, the earliest one "off the press.") Silly as this notion is (since the numbering of the volumes in a limited-edition run is usually irrespective of the item's chronological position), those low numbers seem to demand greater prices (at least in the minds of the collectors). (For one of his books, Morris numbered every copy "No. 1": *The World's Worst Marbled Paper*. See under Theodore Bachaus in the bibliography.)

Another issue with this obsession, to show its ludicrousness, is that books of a later printing, a later issue, or a later state may contain better texts (that is, with fewer flaws, later and more reliable readings, and authors' most recent thoughts) than those produced earlier. But collectors often do not care about such matters; they want the earliest copy they can get their hands on. THOMAS J. WISE certainly understood this when he was producing those "PRE-FIRSTS" for the people he was cheating. (They were a different kind of *dupes* than are dealt with under DUPLICATES later in this volume.)

Carter's making fun of those who have this obsession may be unfair in many instances. Earliest versions are likely to be closest to the AUTHOR'S FINAL INTENTIONS, and thus may have a great level of authority in the editing of a text that has VARIANTS in its later incarnations—even in incarnations that are later in the same PRESSRUN. Though Carter was having some fun here, playing with the possible foolishness of some collectors (and possibly the booksellers who supply them), there is something to be said in favor of this predilection ("obsession" is too harsh for what could be a perfectly justifiable inclination). It is okay to have this condition (says he who has it!).

CHRYSOGRAPHY. Literally "writing in gold." The term is used to designate such writing in ILLUMINATED MANU-

SCRIPTS. Powdered gold is mixed with a binding agent like a gum or GLAIR to make an ink.

CIGARETTE PAPERS. (Also called "cigarette tissue." In the United States, the uninitiated, not knowing the proper terminology, may call this "rolling paper.") Small LEAVES of paper in which tobacco is rolled. "[A] specially made tissue paper, very pure chemically, UNSIZED, odourless and tasteless, also while burning, is made in WOVE, which the manufacturers call vélin, and LAID, termed verge as this paper was formerly made chiefly in France, but this indicates a difference in appearance only, not in quality. It is rarely WATERMARKED except with laid lines, also impressed, but sometimes even highly glazed and transparent, as preferred in Russia" (Labarre, *Dictionary and Encyclopaedia of Paper and Paper-making*, p. 48). These papers have a long history, as Labarre says: "The first cigarette paper mill/factory was erected at Tarbes (France) in 1824 and it was only in 1842 that the idea occurred to make small booklets for making cigarettes by hand instead of inconveniently large sheets" (p. 49). Packages of these, with their typography and design, can be found at EPHEMERA fairs.

CILIP. *See* Chartered Institute of Library and Information Professionals.

CINII. The online database used by most Japanese libraries, similar to OCLC, but for books, articles, and dissertations of Japanese origin. "CiNii is a bibliographic database service for material in Japanese academic libraries, especially focusing on Japanese works and English works published in Japan. The database was founded in April 2005 and is maintained by the National Institute of Informatics. The service searches from within the databases maintained by the NII itself [NII Electronic Library Service (NII-ELS) and Citation Database for Japanese Publications (CJP)], as well as the databases provided by the National Diet Library of Japan, institutional repositories, and other organizations" (Word Finder, "What Is CINII?"). The database is searchable by title, key words, authors, and, for many items, full text, along with ISSN. Instructions for the use of the database can be found at "Searching CiNii for Japanese Periodical Articles" (https://www.sciping.com/wp-content/uploads/2018/08/SearchingCiNii-for-Japanese-Periodical-Articles.pdf [accessed 28 August 2022]).

CIP. *See* Cataloging in Publication.

CIPHERING BOOKS. *See* Writing books.

CIRCUIT BINDING. For "circuit edges," Roberts and Etherington say, "The projecting flexible covers of limp bindings turned over to protect the leaves and edges of books, usually of a devotional nature. The circuit edge differs from the YAPP EDGE in that the overlap of the cover is not continuous. The covering leather is turned over at head and tail, with an independent flap at the fore-edge. The corners are square. This technique allows the flaps to fold flat onto the edges. Sometimes called 'divinity circuit,' or 'divinity edges'" (p. 54). The projecting edges are sometimes called "circuit cover extensions." (*See* Yapp binding/Yapp edges.)

CIRCULATING LIBRARIES. Carter's entry says that these libraries were founded in the 18th century in England by groups of subscribers who paid for the volumes in the collection, allowing them the privilege to use the books. The practice was copied in the United States (with the founding of the Library Company of Philadelphia in 1731; see http://www.librarycompany.org [accessed 3 June 2021]). Carter adds that either these libraries got their books already bound or the volumes were bound specifically for the library, and he says that many of these libraries had their own bookplates and lists of subscribers/donors and that their borrower lists can be useful to scholars today. (See Carter, p. 75.)

Scott Lewis says that booksellers or publishers were the proprietors of most circulating libraries, and that "[p]atrons obtained books either by periodic subscriptions or by fixed fees per volume" (*Oxford Companion*, vol. 1, p. 612). He concludes, "Changes in readers' demands, the publishing trade, and copyright laws, eventually led to the decline of circulating libraries, giving way to the rise of public lending libraries" (p. 613). Also, some lending libraries were run out of other businesses as (modest) profit-making operations. In the 1940s, a stationery and office supplies store in Brooklyn, New York, had a lending library for its customers, charging a penny a day for books borrowed. (See Griest, *Mudie's Circulating Library and the Victorian Novel.*)

CIVILITÉ TYPE. Calligraphic typefaces were meant to resemble 16th- and 17th-century handwritings of northern Europe. "It was in France that the first type for this handwriting was made" (Carter and Vervliet, *Civilité Types*, p. 11). The typeface was designed in 1557 in France by ROBERT GRANJON. It is a calligraphic face, emulating the cursive French calligraphy of the Renaissance. Since the handwriting had a great deal of swash and flourish, it was popular because of its elegance; the typefaces—imitating the CALLIGRAPHY—had many SWASH characters and LIGATURES. The number of different characters was one of its shortcomings, as Carter and Vervliet say: "The type has severe handicaps, and Granjon must have known it, enough to make printers loath to invest in it and to account to some extent for the limited use to which this and other designs like it were put.

Civilité type.
Courtesy of Luc De Vroye.

The first Civilité had at least 138 SORTS, as compared with some 120 usual at the time for Roman or Italic, and the Civilité had no SMALL CAPITALS and, as a rule, no numerals" (pp. 13–14). It also had 30 ligatures, and "two dozen extra sorts for the initial, final, and other alternate forms of the lower-case letters" (Carter and Vervliet, p. 14). Elegant as it is, it was extremely difficult for the PUNCHCUTTER to make the punches for the type, and it also had "fine minims projecting from the letters on either side [i.e., KERNS], making the type difficult to cast and to rub and quick to show wear" (Carter and Vervliet, p. 14).

CLAMSHELL BOX. (Sometimes called a "tray case.") A box to protect all kinds of library materials. It is structured in two main parts: a closed four-sided box with a hinged cover, opening and closing like a clam's shell. (*See* Drop-spine box.) Some are made with acid-free, lignin-free, archival materials, and are excellent for storage of books, photographs, and documents. Some, especially millions made in the first three-quarters of the 20th century (with green or gray paper covers), are seriously acidic and should be gently recycled or burned.

CLAMSHELL PRESS. A printing press that swings open and closed like the shell of a clam. The original clamshell presses were hand-fed—that is, the printer would feed a sheet of paper onto the TYMPAN while the "clam shell" was open, and while ROLLERS were inking the type in a CHASE, the press would close, pressing the paper against the inked type. When the press opened, the printer would pull the printed sheet or card out with her left hand and replace it with an unprinted one with the right hand, as the press continued to move. The shell would close to print the new sheet, and the operation would continue like that. The sheets or cards to be printed were set onto the tympan against REGISTRATION PINS or GAUGES, carefully placed onto the tympan to guide the printer to the precise placement of the sheet. As the press closed, a roller (or two) would pick up ink from an inking plate above the type; as the press opened and while the operator pulled the newly printed sheet off the tympan, the roller(s) would descend and ink the type. The presses were originally run by foot with a treadle, but they could also

A clamshell press. This one is the Columbian Jobber. "The Columbian jobber was manufactured from 1878 to 1891 by Curtis & Mitchell of Boston. Although a clamshell press, this Columbian No. 2 jobber has a device which provides a pause in the action of the platen to facilitate feeding. (49 inches high)." The International Printing Museum, Carson, California; see their website at https://www.printmuseum.org/collection/equipment/platen-job-floor-6-x-9 (accessed 3 June 2021).
Courtesy of the International Printing Museum, Carson, California.

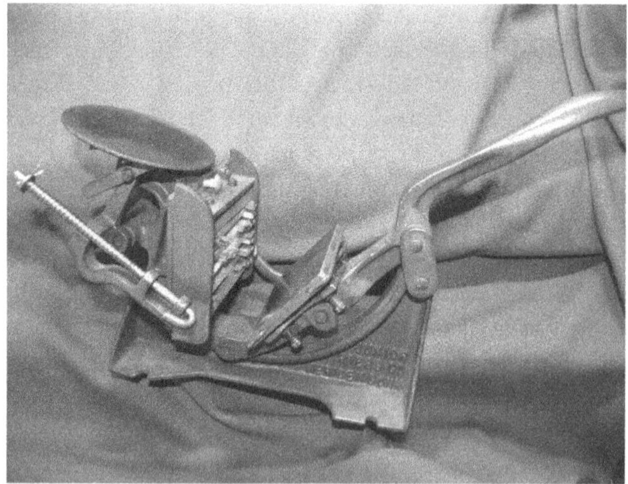

A Kelsey Junior press—a miniature clamshell—showing the miniature printing type in the chase. This press is only about 5 inches high.

Courtesy of Alan Runfeldt.

have a belt wound around the large wheel that turned while the press was in motion, and a motor could drive the press. A governor on the press could be adjusted to regulate the speed of the opening and closing of the press.

More and more elaborate and automatically fed clamshells were made, speeding up the printing. Also, tiny "toy presses" were manufactured for children to print up little cards—like calling cards. These tiny presses came with appropriately small printing type. They were clamshell presses, too.

CLANDESTINE PRESS. *See* Underground press.

CLARKSON, CHRISTOPHER (1938–2017). A "noted conservator of parchment and paper manuscripts, early printed books and book-bindings. . . . Mr. Clarkson was an authority on bookbinding structural history, specialising in the period from the birth of the codex to the early Renaissance. He gave lectures and workshops in many countries. In 2004 he was awarded the Plowden Gold Medal of the Royal Warrant Holders Association in recognition of his significant contribution to the advancement of the conservation profession. / In November 1966 he went with the English Government team to the City of Florence, where the flood had devastated many libraries and archives. / Since 1972 he held senior posts in the conservation of rare books and special collections at the Library of Congress, Washington DC, the Walters Art Gallery, Baltimore and the Bodleian Library, Oxford. He then started and ran a book conservation internship programme at West Dean College, West Sussex. / Since 1998 he worked as a private conservator mainly concentrating on the conservation of parchment and paper manuscripts and documents" (see "Christopher Clarkson, Book Conservator"; http://www.clarksonconservation.com/ [accessed 23 March 2021]). Trust in his work can be seen in his being asked to work on the *Codex Sinaiticus* (*see* Saint Catherine's Monastery.) (See also Clarkson, *Limp Vellum Binding* in the bibliography; Pickwoad, "Clarkson Festschrift.")

CLASPS. "The hinged fasteners of brass, precious metals, iron, etc., often elaborately chased, and intended to secure the covers of books, ledgers, albums, etc. They are sometimes provided with a lock, and are designed to hold the covers of a book closed, or when provided with a lock, to prevent opening by unauthorized persons. Clasps are attached after FORWARDING is completed except for the board papers, because by that time the final thickness of the book is known and any rivets on the inside of the boards will be covered by the board papers. Because a single clasp has a tendency to distort the boards, two are generally used, and are usually placed opposite the centers of the second and fifth panels of the spine. All metal-hinged clasps have to be made to fit the individual book, as a perfect fit is necessary; however, where the hinge consists of a leather strap, adjustments can easily be made. Stretching of the leather with use, thus causing looseness, can be overcome by making the strap of leather over vellum, which also provides additional strength" (Roberts and Etherington, p. 55). Sturdy as clasps

A book with clasps: *Das neue und verbesserte Gesagnbuch, worinnen die Psalmen Davids . . .* (Germantaun: Michael Billmeyer, 1807).

Collection of the author.

An unidentified medieval manuscript with fairly unusual clasps, consisting of straps that are attached to the rear board and extend up to the upper board. The straps have holes in them, the holes reinforced with metal panels. The straps fit over metal rods protruding from the upper board. Only three of the original straps have survived. Note also the simple, relatively unadorned bosses on the corners and center of the cover.

Courtesy of Phillips Library, Peabody Essex Museum.

are, they are often missing from books, either completely gone, or with their leather straps wanting. (The long entry by Roberts and Etherington is worth consulting.)

CLAY TABLETS. Inasmuch as the present volume is primarily aimed at book collectors, booksellers, and librarians, the present entry covers items occasionally seen in the possession of these parties, collected and sold by them, written about by scholars, and coveted by many who are outside the rare book community. Clay tablets are perhaps the earliest form of "books"—that is, surfaces containing texts. They are made from panels of clay incised with a STYLUS, the incised characters, thanks to the shape of the writing end of the stylus, taking the shape of wedges (hence the name CUNEIFORM). The pliable clay was then hardened by being dried in the sun or in an oven. Mary Alexandra Agner says, "Clay tablets in the ancient Near East were smaller than today's computer tablets. They most often fit into the palm of a hand, to be read as you would look into a compact mirror, large enough to hold, on average, up to 60 lines of cuneiform, the writing system used thousands of years ago by the peoples living between the Tigris and Euphrates rivers" (Agner, "Using Chemistry to Learn the Provenance of Clay Tablets"). Modern copies abound; genuine ancient ones still appear on the market, and they can be seen at antiquarian book fairs at appropriately "antiquarian" prices. If an institution owns any of these, they will usually be kept in the library's rare book department.

CLEAN COPY/CLEAN PROOF. A text at the proofreading stage that has no (or quite few) errors. For longer texts, it is exceptionally difficult to reach the "clean copy" stage after only two proofings (say, at the GALLEY PROOF and the PAGE PROOF stages). As Kim Merker said, "There is no plethora of perfection in the world." (*See* Dirty proof.)

CLEAR TEXT (edition). A scholarly edition of a literary work with all of the appropriate apparatus (tables of textual variants, lists of emendations, textual introduction, etc.) but all of that apparatus printed in the back of the volume so that the publisher can produce a clear text—that is, one with no notes or other textual information on the page of the main text. The purpose is to be able to produce two versions: one with the apparatus for scholars, the other for a general reading public. For the latter, who need no such apparatus, the clear text can be offered at a much lower price than can the scholarly version. Strictly speaking, the two versions are the same EDITION, so a more accurate term would be "clear text version" or "clear text printing." (*See* Bibliography; Critical apparatus.)

CLEAVAGE. It is tempting to say that one sees this in naughty photographs—for it is true. Cleavage is the separation of one surface from another to which it was formerly "permanently" adhered. So in a gelatin silver print photograph, if the emulsion begins to separate from the SUBSTRATE paper, there is cleavage (despite what the image of the photo contains!). That is, the naughtiness is in its separation, not in its content. If a TIP-IN in a volume is fully pasted down over the entire surface of the LEAF that is tipped in, and that tip-in begins to separate from the sheet beneath it, there is cleavage. (The term is not applicable to a leaf that is tipped in only along an edge or two.)

CLIPPED/PRICE CLIPPED. Said of a DUST JACKET that has had something (usually the price) trimmed off—usually manifested by a small triangular deficiency in the upper corner of the front flap of the jacket. Naturally, a price-clipped jacket reduces the value of the volume, which is not in PRISTINE condition. Important is the information that has been removed: it could be that the price would reveal a later impression or issue (*see* Edition, Impression [Printing], Issue, and State; Points) if later issues had higher prices. Also, some books were reissued as fake REMAINDERS, and the corner of the dust jacket's flap might say, "Originally issued at $35.00." This was accompanied by a lower price, making the buyer think that she is getting a real bargain. But the remainder could be much more cheaply produced.

CLIPPER SHIP CARDS. An immensely popular COLLECTIBLE, these cards were advertising pieces for clipper ship companies, announcing the availability of these ships to carry passengers and cargo of all kinds from the United States to the Far East, with many ports of call on the way. "The publication of clipper ship sailing cards began in 1853 and continued through the Civil War, reflecting the enormous increase in commerce between the east and west coasts after the discovery of gold at Sutter's Mill in California. During the four years following the 1848 discovery, as many as 160 ships were launched and set sail as opposed to only two ships that regularly sailed from Atlantic ports to San Francisco before then. In the one and one half years after 1848, seven hundred vessels stopped in the California harbor with estimated cargoes of 100,000 people and supplies. . . . The onset of steam transportation both by rail and sea caused the decline of the fleets of clipper ships. As the new modes of travel developed, the clipper ship industry faltered. / Clipper ship sailing cards featured full color illustrations illustrating the names of the ships, some of which created great opportunities for designers. For example, a ferocious tiger ornaments the card advertising the ship Bengal. A scene featuring a hot air balloon, a train on a bridge, bustling mills, and two sailing and one steam vessel under the spread wings of a bald eagle illustrates the advertisement for Comstock's clipper ship Enterprise. The imprints of the cards reveal that just three printing offices issued most of the hand-held advertisements: Nesbitt & Company and Watson & Clark of New York and John H. Bufford of Boston. Many lack an imprint. There is a pleasing mixture of styles that range from simple, but attractive, black and white letterpress printing to magnificent pictures of ships in full color. Generally, the cards were printed on one side of a piece of glossy card stock measuring 4 × 6½ inches. Rarely is anything printed on the reverse, although occasionally information about the ship is continued" (American Antiquarian Society, "Clipper Ship Cards"; https://www.americanantiquarian.org/clippershipcards.htm [accessed 13 March 2021]). These cards were also issued by companies whose ships sailed to the Far East. They can be a golden source of information: names of the ships; names of the captains; names of the companies of ownership; types of cargo carried; destinations; dates of departure; estimated return dates; availability of berths for passengers; names of printers and artists (artists seldom); prices of services; and much more. The best collection of these expensive cards is at the Phillips Library at the Peabody Essex Museum.

CLOSED TEAR. A tear in a LEAF or DUST JACKET that has both sides of the tear sitting properly on the untouched paper. That is, the tear does not look ragged and unsightly, and all of the original material is still there. It is nonetheless a tear, and will devalue the item in which it exists. The tear is not necessarily repaired with tape or mending tissue for it to be a "closed tear," but some booksellers use the term only for tears that have been repaired. (*See* Open tear.)

CLOSEOUT. In the book world, this is a title of in-print text that the publisher decides not to print further copies of, so it is being sold at a substantially reduced price. It is common, however, if the publisher has a large number of copies, for it to sell the volumes to a REMAINDER house, and they often wind up on tables of BARGAIN BOOKS.

CLOTH. A generic term for all the kinds of cloths that books are bound in. From the first quarter of the 19th century, with the invention of a cloth that could be used for binding, thousands of cloths have been employed, in many colors, using a host of fibers, treated in a great number of manners. Booksellers' catalogs will often say that a volume is "in cloth," indicating it is a CASE-BOUND volume with cloth over BOARDS.

The number of cloths used for books is seemingly endless, with variations in their materials (cotton, linen, burlap, silk, synthetics, and on and on), colors, textures, weights, thicknesses, and so on. Carter's entry for "Cloth Grains and Fabrics" (pp. 76–78) mentions the difficulties of describing all of the possible variations that can exist in book cloths, and it also mentions the attempts by scholars to standardize such descriptions using specimens from various companies' sample books. Carter concludes his entry with the information that one system, that was used by JACOB BLANCK for his multivolume *Bibliography of American Literature*, has been adopted by the Bibliographical Society of America. But in all the years I have been perusing booksellers' and library catalogs, I have hardly (if ever) seen this use. The seemingly "standard" way for booksellers to describe cloth is not to turn to Blanck, which requires that they have a copy on hand, that they are familiar with his method, and that their patrons equally have access to this information, but to just describe what they are looking at: "Bound in blue cloth, stamped in gold on spine." That sort of description, delineating shades of color, may also be imprecise but useful: "bound in robin's egg blue cloth" distinguishes that volume from one "bound in royal blue cloth."

Textures, too, can be mentioned, though the vocabulary for them is as imprecise as is that for color.

This is not to say that such descriptions are not important; they are quite important to collectors and scholars. Sanford and Helen Berger, who collected the works of WILLIAM MORRIS (their collection is now at the HUNTINGTON LIBRARY), had volumes 1 and 3 of one of Morris's TRIPLE-DECKERS. When I called to tell them that I had found volume 2—and in the same color cloth that their volumes were in—they were ecstatic. But they called me crestfallen when they received the volume: the blue cloth was the same as theirs was bound in, but the cloth on the volume I had sent had vertical ribbing, while theirs had horizontal ribbing. It was not the missing volume. Such distinctions make a big difference to serious collectors. (See Allen and Gullans, *Decorated Cloth in America*; Krupp, *Bookcloth in England and America, 1823–50*; Morris and Levin, *The Art of Publishers' Bookbindings, 1815–1915*; and Tomlinson and Masters, *Bookcloth, 1823–1980. See also* Tanselle, "The Bibliographical Description of Patterns"; and "A System of Color Identification"; Sadleir, *Evolution of Publishers' Binding Styles*; Carter's *Binding Variants* and *More Binding Variants*.)

A final note: When a bookseller says that a book is "in cloth," it means that the book is HARDBOUND with a cloth cover.

CLUB OF ODD VOLUMES. *See* Odd volumes.

CLYMER, GEORGE/COLUMBIAN PRESS. The inventor of the Columbian press, one of the handsomest and easiest to use iron handpresses of the 19th century. Clymer (1754?–1834), from Philadelphia, developed a press around 1813 that made printing large FORMES much easier than was possible on presses up to that time. In a traditional press, pulling the BAR to lower the PLATEN onto the FORME was relatively easy since gravity would pull the platen down. Getting the platen up again was more difficult with the screw or the toggle arrangement on the press. Clymer's Columbian press had a set of weights and counterbalances that made pulling the bar easy and getting it to go up again just as easy. Easy as it was to print on this press, printers were set in their older ways, and Clymer's presses did not sell well in the United States, so in 1817 he went to England, where his Columbian sold well in competition with the ALBION and other presses available there. When he died, his company continued to sell the Columbian. (See Oldham, "The Columbian Press at 200.")

The 6 years that I printed on a WASHINGTON PRESS did more damage to my back than was done in the 18 years that I printed on a Columbian.

A Royal Columbian Press, invented by George Clymer. International Printing Museum, Carson, California; see their website at https://www.printmuseum.org/collection/equipment/columbian-press/ (accessed 3 June 2021). The gold eagle flies (is raised) when the printer pulls the bar on the press. (See Kainen, *George Clymer and the Columbian Press*.)

Courtesy of the International Printing Museum, Carson, California.

COATED PAPERS. Papers can be coated with a variety of materials and can then be treated in several ways, allowing the paper to vary in smoothness, weight, gloss, texture, rattle, wet strength, or ink absorbency. When clay is added to the paper, the sheet can be burnished to a fine gloss, as is common for magazines or PLATES in books. If the paper gets wet, the clay softens and blends with the clay in neighboring sheets, and if these dry, they can become a single block of paper. When a book with coated papers gets wet, it should be interleaved with dry towels or some other materials to keep the leaves from touching one another. Cloth, also, can be coated, though it is not usually referred to as "coated cloth."

One may also see the abbreviations C1S/C2S, meaning paper that is Coated one side / Coated two sides.

COBDEN-SANDERSON, THOMAS JAMES (1840–1922). (Doves Press and Bindery.) Although Cobden-Sanderson practiced law, he was unhappy in that profession. He was guided to take up bookbinding, and he found his métier. In 1884, after a stint with Roger de Coverly, he set up the Doves Bindery, and in 1900 he joined with Emory Walker to found the Doves Press, which produced a host of uniformly designed, elegant, and well-received titles. Their Doves Bible is still one of the iconic publications in the FINE-PRESS world. (He was born Thomas James Sanderson, and in 1882 he wed Anne Cobden; both used the combined surname.)

In 1909, Cobden-Sanderson and Emery Walker, his partner at the press, fought over ownership of the Doves type rights; it led to the termination of their partnership. "By 1908, despite successful Milton prints & the aforementioned Bible, the Press was in dire financial difficulty. Subscribers began melting away after Walker had effectively left in 1906 as the bitter & acrimonious dispute took hold between the partners. On finally dissolving their partnership in 1909, Cobden-Sanderson began attempts to wriggle out of an earlier promise that, should the partnership cease, Walker would receive a fount of type 'for his own use.' Walker retaliated, issuing a writ insisting that the Press shut down completely and he receive 50% of remaining assets. In 1909, the Press's only valuable asset was the type. / A compromise was reached, brokered by their exasperated friend Sir Sydney Cockerell, which allowed Cobden-Sanderson uncontrolled use of the type for as long as he lived, at which time it would pass to Emery Walker, if he did not die first. / The thought of 'his' typeface being used by anyone else, and in a manner beyond his control, prompted Cobden-Sanderson's now infamous course of action. Only the Doves Press, run exclusively by him, could be bestowed the honour of printing his type. And so the mission to destroy it, beginning with the PUNCHES and MATRICES on Good Friday 1913, began. On an almost nightly basis from August 1916 the ailing septuagenarian dumped the type into the Thames, wrapped in paper parcels and tied with string; 'bequeathed to the river' as he put it in his personal diary. Every piece of this beautiful typeface, more than a ton of metal, was destroyed in a prolonged ritual sacrifice" (Robert Green, "New Font Releases/The Doves Type™ revival/Raised from the dead: Doves Type in digital form," Typespec; http://www.typespec.co.uk/doves-type-revival [accessed 3 June 2021]).

The well-known story of Cobden-Sanderson's feud with his partner Emery Walker and the disposal of the type into the Thames has recently been corroborated by the recovery of some of that type in November 2014. (See "Recovering the Doves Type," Typespec; http://www.typespec.co.uk/recovering-the-doves-type [accessed 22 August 2015].)

The Doves Press "formula" for designing a page (actually a two-page spread) yielded an elegant, spare, and beautifully laid-out text. Some have criticized the press for the uniformity of all of its volumes—a formula used over and over to produce books that were cookie-cutter designed, all bound in simple plain vellum, and, from a distance, indistinguishable from one another. But the formula worked, and the books are still beautiful and highly collectible, as are the volumes that received the Doves Bindery covers. (See Tidcombe, *The Bookbindings of T. J. Cobden-Sanderson*; Tidcombe, *The Doves Bindery*; and Tidcombe, *The Doves Press.*)

COBWEB. (Also called "birdcage," "beehive," or "flower cage.") This is a configuration of cut paper that might be used in a greeting card or an ALBUM AMICORUM, for instance. It consisted of a flat sheet of paper, often circular, and attached around its perimeter to another sheet; the top sheet was cut with many slits in a circular pattern (with no slit going all the way to the edge of the sheet or to a neighboring slit) in such a way that when a string attached to the middle of the top sheet was pulled up, the slits opened up, allowing someone to peer through the slits to the substrate, onto which would be a text or image (or both), hidden until the cobweb was raised in its middle. Nancy Rosin explains: "Cobwebs—also known as beehives, flower cages, or birdcages—are a rare example of a mechanical or movable valentine consisting of a minimum of two layers of paper. First, a web or cage would be cut from a piece of paper by making a pattern of concentric circles, leaving attachment points at regular intervals. In the center of the spiral, a delicate thread would be attached and its outer edges would be pasted directly on top of a second sheet on which an image or message would be written, painted, or printed. / As a cover, the cobweb formed the perfect sanctuary to enclose a private message that could only be revealed when the recipient of the card carefully pulled up the thread, causing the concentric circles of the web to rise and magically expose its hidden compartment. . . . Cobwebs could be made by hand or bought as a machine-made product, both with various levels of intricacy" (Rosin, "Valentine's Day and the Romance of Cobwebs"). (*See* the images on the following page and also at Album Amicorum.)

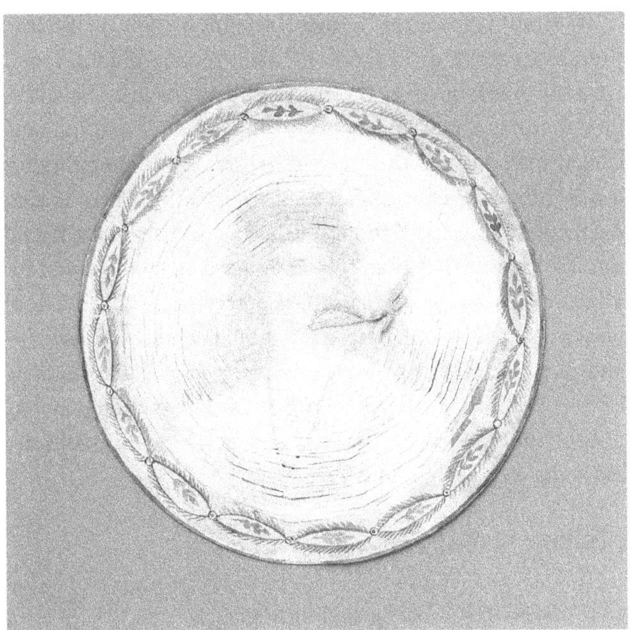

Cobweb Valentine's Day card, 1830–1840, closed.
Courtesy of Metropolitan Museum of Art, New York.

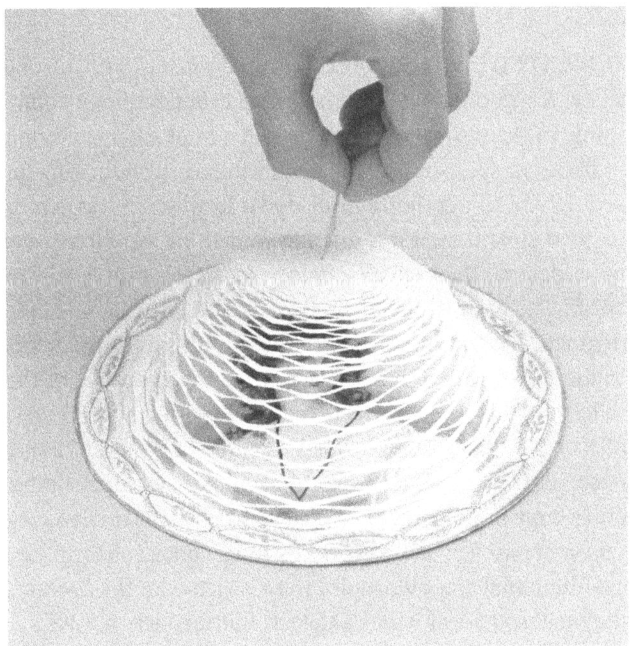

Cobweb opened.
Courtesy of Metropolitan Museum of Art, New York.

COCKED. Said of a volume that has been stored for long enough leaning over (and crooked in its binding) to have assumed that shape permanently. If such a volume is stood up vertically on its tail edge, one board will be crookedly raised from the shelf. It is possible to straighten out this volume, but it takes a good deal of "anti-cocking" by forcing the raised board of the cover down and the straight board up, clamping it that way to undo the distortion, and hoping that this works. It usually does not, and such manipulation could damage the binding. Best not to store books leaning over in the first place.

COCKLED. Said of paper that has a wavy, wrinkled, or puckered surface. If paper gets wet and then is dried, it may cockle. Also, if a book gets wet and then is dried, the whole text block could cockle—that is, become "puckered" or askew. Short of soaking and then pressing a sheet or volume, the cockling could be permanent.

CODES. *See* Library Codes.

CODEX. The form of a book that has been created from folded leaves, sewn through the folds at the inner margins of the leaves near the SPINE. Traditionally, the term was used to describe a manuscript volume, but today any book bound at the gutter, with sewing through the folded leaves (and by extension all books that look like these—even PERFECT-BOUND volumes), is now referred to as a codex since to read them, one flips one leaf, then another and another. This "reading motion" of "page turning" looks the same for sewn or perfect-bound books, so they all now are called codices. It is distinguished from volumes that preceded it in roll (or scroll) form. The word derives from the Latin *codex*, meaning "trunk of a tree" or "wooden tablet," and it hints at the material used in early bookbindings. To say that a volume is "IN BOARDS" originally meant that it had a wood cover (the wood possibly covered by vellum or leather).

CODEX FOUNDATION. The organization overseeing the "trade fair" called "Codex." The foundation's website says: "The Codex Foundation was conceived in 2005 by Peter Rutledge Koch, fine-press printer, and Susan Filter, paper conservator. Its purpose was to create an environment for promoting the book as a work of art. They accomplished this by bringing together the Best of the Best book artists and fine-press printers from around the world to share their work, explore new and old concepts, and to start an on-going conversation about the fate and future of the book as an essential art form. / The first CODEX Book Fair and Symposium took place over three days in February of 2007 in Berkeley, California, with 120 exhibitors showing their work at the Fair to approximately 750 visitors. Held biennially, the Book Fair has grown from three days to four, with over 200 exhibitors and almost 3000 visitors. It is ranked as one of the top three book fairs in the world. The Symposium, which features keynote speakers and book artists, is now the hottest ticket around for printers, artists, collectors and librarians and is sold out every year" (Codex Foundation, "Codex"; https://www.codexfoundation.org/about [accessed 4 May 2021]).

CODEX SINAITICUS. *See* Saint Catherine's Monastery.

CODICOLOGY. Simply, the study of the codex, but, more strictly, the study of medieval manuscripts. This is a broad field, for it entails their writing, editing, binding, reading, ILLUMINATION, DATING, and much more. Such intensive study requires a knowledge of authorship; VELLUM, PARCHMENT, and PAPER; QUILLS and INKS; writing styles (PALEOGRAPHY); the languages that MANUSCRIPTS are written in; editing practices over the years; audiences for the manuscripts; scribal practices (were they produced in a monastic scriptorium, in a school, by a STATIONER?); did SCRIBES work after dark?; did they copy from EXEMPLARS or from dictation?; did they copy verbatim and *ad literatim*, or were they free to "invent"?, and so on; the Stationers Company and the PECIAE SYSTEM of manuscript production; the manufacture of inks and writing instruments; page design, PRICKING, and RULING; illumination practices and styles—country to country and year to year; binding practices, styles, and materials; FORMATS and QUIRING; readership and the nature of the commissioning of manuscripts; use of CATCHWORDS, MARGINALIA, and annotations; COLOPHONS; and much more. It also includes a knowledge of all the kinds of things that might wind up in textual illuminations and marginal drawings: religious and historical figures and incidents; animals, plants, and insects (real, imaginary, and extinct); costume; architecture; the planets and stars; and a host of other images that inhabit the pages of manuscripts. And there is also the issue of RECENSION—part of the editing process of manuscripts.

COFFEE TABLE BOOKS. Volumes set out on tables where guests are likely to see them—perhaps the idea being to impress the visitors with the elevated aesthetics, affluence, cleverness, or intelligence of the owners. Such volumes could be on the coffee table simply because they are OVERSIZE and do not fit on the shelves in their library. Knowing of the many reasons that such books wind up on coffee tables, publishers of REMAINDERS (real and FAUX) have produced an entire section's worth of these for brick-and-mortar bookstores, the section variously called "remainders," "bargain books," or "exceptional value." These volumes, then, are often inexpensively produced, with many color photographs (people do not really *read* a coffee table book; they may thumb through it) and a minimal verbal text, and with a DUST JACKET carrying a high printed price on its FLAP—though the volume will be sold at a bargain price.

To show the appeal of these volumes, look no further than the website of *Elle Decor*: "They're meaningful, inspirational, and best of all: beautiful! Giving the gift of a coffee table book is a failsafe way to bring aesthetic (and literary) charm into the mix this year. Whether you're shopping for a new homeowner who's looking to warm up their spaces, or are browsing for a thoughtful—and stylish—best friend gift, look no further than the almighty coffee table book for all your holiday needs. Baubles and accents aside, a stack of books can give an uninspired tabletop a new sense of style—and purpose, so why not be the one to kick-start someone else's collection?" (Tonelli, "The 50+ Best Coffee Table Books to Gift in 2020"). The point is that coffee table books are more decorative than intellectual.

COFFIN. *See* Bed [of press]; Black art.

COIL BINDING. *See* Spiral binding.

COLD PRESSED. *See* Calendering.

COLD TYPE. *See* Hot metal.

COLLATED AND PERFECT (abbreviated C&P). In one sense, a collation is a careful, minute examination of something, in this instance a book. When a bookseller, collector, or librarian, for instance, collates a volume, she is looking for a variety of things, but it boils down to whether the item is in good condition, if it is missing something, or if it has any other defects. Booksellers' catalogs will often have "C&P" in an entry to indicate that the seller has carefully examined the item and has found nothing that might diminish the item's value. A potential buyer must rely on the expertise of the seller to know what "perfect" means. A perfectly good copy of KIM MERKER's Windhover Press book *Kenney's: Twenty Poems for a Lost Tavern* may look imperfect since almost every copy has a paragraph excised from the text. Knowing this, a bookseller may say "C&P" in the book's description, assuming that since all copies were issued with the CANCEL, the hole in the leaf is not a defect. But the lack of a WRAP-AROUND BAND would indicate that the volume is missing a key piece of paper that all copies were issued with.

COLLATING MACHINES (sometimes called "optical collators"). Machines used to compare one printing of a text with another. Usually, the machines allow the collator to compare text from a single setting of type or from type that was set line for line to match another setting. (See Berger, pp. 265–66.) (*See* Hailey's Comet; HINMAN COLLATOR; LINDSTRAND COMPARATOR; MCLEOD COLLATOR.) The Hinman, the Lindstrand, and the McLeod machines operated in such a way that two texts—purportedly from a single setting of type—were optically superimposed, differences between them made manifest in different ways. The machines allowed the collator to compare two pages of text in a few seconds, far quicker than was possible with an oral collation, in which a reader speaks the text aloud while another (or others) looks on other printed versions of the same text. Oral collation will not reveal broken type or reset type, but the machines show these quickly.

COLLATION. The word has at least four distinct meanings:

1. If a volume is sent to a binder IN SHEETS, she must gather all the SIGNATURES and arrange them in the proper sequence for binding. This is collating the signatures.
2. To a bibliographer, a collector, a librarian, or a bookseller, to collate a volume means to examine it with particular care, especially with an eye to its completeness. The collation will reveal missing (and/or replaced) leaves, the presence or absence of all the parts that should be there, and so on. A minute collation reveals the item's CONDITION. A bibliographical term one may encounter is "collated and perfect" (often, in dealers' catalogs, abbreviated "c&p" or "c. & p."). One aim of collation is to compare one copy of a volume with another. (*See* Collating machines.)
3. To a textual bibliographer, a collation is the careful comparison of multiple versions of a text against one another, the aim being to locate all variations of SUBSTANTIVES and ACCIDENTALS in preparation of the production of a new edition. The collation yields a chart or table listing all VARIANTS; the editor takes this table and decides, on the basis of many things, which reading of each variant is to be used for EMENDATION in the final edited version. Some of the things she considers are the authority of each reading (how likely is it that the author was responsible for the variation and whether there is any evidence that the change was directly from the author), the date of the reading (earlier readings are likely to be closer to the author's original than are later readings that have gone through the hands of editors and COMPOSITORS and PROOFREADERS), whether there is any internal or external evidence that the author made the changes, and so on.
4. To a descriptive bibliographer, a collation is an examination of a volume that yields a listing of all the signatures in a book using standard bibliographical notation. This listing is expressed in the "COLLATIONAL FORMULA." (*See* Bibliographical description; item 3 delineates the collational formula.) A potential buyer of a book could ask of the bookseller, "Please send me a collation; I want to compare this volume to the one I already own." (*See* Bibliography.)

COLLATIONAL FORMULA. The bibliographer's and bookseller's formulaic notation delineating the QUIRES or SIGNATURES or GATHERINGS in a book—usually employed for books of the HANDPRESS PERIOD. As part of a complete BIBLIOGRAPHICAL DESCRIPTION, the collational formula describes the "IDEAL COPY," but as part of that description, it also delineates the makeup of the copy under scrutiny, distinguishing that copy by its imperfections (if it has any).

Since booksellers and bibliographers need to be conversant with the collational formula, so do librarians and collectors, for they will encounter this formula in the catalogs and reference works they use. The formula goes back to the 1860s; it was adapted and enhanced by W. W. GREG and other bibliographers, and it was brought into the neon lights by FREDSON BOWERS in his massive and almost impenetrable *Principles of Bibliographical Description*.

Since the collational formula is employed primarily for books from the handpress period, it uses the alphabet of that period: all of our common letters except J, U or V (it uses one of these), and W. These letters—which are also called signatures—appear at the foot of the opening LEAVES of each signature, a different number of leaves being "signed" (i.e., with these letters) in different FORMATS. Hence, in delineating signatures, only 23 letters are employed. The PRELIMS are often signed with lowercase letters, the main text with uppercase letters. (Note that a leaf with these signatures is said to be "signed." Thus, in a quarto—a signature with four leaves—it is common to have the first two leaves signed.)

Printers in the handpress period were not constrained by any "standard practices." The purpose of the signing was strictly to help the binder get the signatures (the quires or gatherings) in the proper sequence in the binding. Thus, while the common practice was to use lowercase and uppercase for prelims and main text, respectively, there are great numbers of variations in this. Sometimes prelims are not signed at all (in which case bibliographers use the Greek letter *pi* [π] to show an unsigned signature), or signatures could be signed with arbitrary symbols, such as a dagger or double dagger, a squiggle with no name, or an ASTERISK. To guide the binder, then, who would know his alphabet but would not know in what order the non-alphabetic symbols were to be used, the volume would have a register (or REGISTRUM). (For a typical collational formula, *see* Bibliographical description; *see also* Blanck, Jacob.)

COLLECTED EDITION. A term used by publishers to designate a series or cluster of volumes published under a single imprint—of the works of a single author—issued as a set, usually in a uniform binding, and suggesting that the set is a complete corpus of that author (though this is often not the case). For "collected," Carter also says, "A poem, article or short story which had previously appeared in a periodical or anthology is sometimes said to be 'first collected' when it is republished in a volume devoted exclusively to its author's work" (p. 80).

COLLECTIBLE. A term occasionally encountered in the CATALOGS or listings of neophyte booksellers, where it implies that the seemingly high price being asked for this item is justified since there are those out there vying for it. In fact, just about anything is collectible, regardless of its intrinsic value, condition, age, materials or methods of manufacture, or commonness. There is probably someone out there who collects fingernail shavings. All who encounter this term should pretend they did not see it and assess whether the item is worth their investing in it based on its other merits, not on this vacuous word.

Worth adding is that any volume in shabby condition may be collectible if it is quite scarce and in high demand; so any copy is usually better to a collector than no copy at all.

Having said this, I want to add that there is a legitimacy in the use of the word when one is talking in broad terms. Many children's books are collectible, as are other genres of "collectibles." The word merely implies, in its broad sense, that the collectible is worth owning for one reason or another.

COLLECTING/COLLECTORS. In the book world, there are different kinds of collectors, private and institutional. Booksellers who are collectors are still private collectors, for despite their business, if they collect items that are not for sale, they are private collectors. There is a tremendous literature on book collecting, focusing on taste and technique (see Carter, *Taste and Technique in Book Collecting*), basic practices (Ahearn and Ahearn, *Book Collecting*; Brook, *Books and Book-Collecting*; Peters, ed., *Book Collecting*; Rees-Mogg, *How to Buy Rare Books*; Uden, *Understanding Book-Collecting*; Winterich and Randall, *A Primer of Book Collecting*), pricing (Ahearn and Ahearn, *Collected Books*), collection as an addiction (Raabe, *Biblioholism*), collecting antiquarian books (Lewis, *Antiquarian Books*; Rees-Mogg, *How to Buy*), the pleasure of collecting (Iacone, *The Pleasures of Collecting*), collectible books (Peters, *Collectible Books*), guide for beginners (Wilson, *Modern Book Collecting*), collecting as a fine art (Franklin, *Book Collecting as One of the Fine Arts and Other Essays*), first editions (Ahearn and Ahearn, *Collected Books*; Underhill, ed., *Henry S. Boutell's First Editions of Today and How to Tell Them*; Zempel and Verkler, *First Editions*), and many other topics. There are also great numbers of books on book collecting, memoirs of people well known in the book world, and biographies of famous booksellers and collectors (Arnold, *Ventures in Book Collecting*; Carter, *Books and Book Collectors*; Magee, *Infinite Riches*; Randall, *Dukedom Large Enough*; Rosenbach, *Books and Bidders*; Rostenberg and Sterne, *New Worlds in Old Books*; Sowerby, *Rare People & Rare Books*; Wolf and Fleming, *Rosenbach*; Basbanes, *A Gentle Madness*). One excellent essay on the topic is Tanselle's "A Rationale of Collecting." Also worth reading is Tanselle's "The Literature of Book Collecting."

A coordinating topic is: When does an accumulation become a collection? When people acquire books they know they will not read but merely because they *must* have them, they are serious collectors. And for a serious collector, there is usually no difference between appreciating a book and coveting it. Also, there is usually some focus to the collection—an author or topic or some other principle that brings books (and other materials) together with some like characteristics.

COLLECTOR'S CONDITION. A book in PRISTINE CONDITION, CRISP, and new, as if it had just been issued by the publisher, is said to be in "collector's condition." That does not mean that collectors will not collect items in poor(er) condition, especially if they are willing to add to their holdings a shabby copy of a title they have sought for decades and have not been able to find *any* copy until the shabby one came along. Also, if a book was issued with a prospectus and the copy presented to the collector—an absolutely BRIGHT and clean and perfect one—lacks the prospectus, is this in collector's condition? Only the collector can answer that. (*See* Used copy.)

COLLECTOR'S ITEM. Something that collectors eagerly seek and are glad to get their hands on. A fairly broad category, since just about anything can be a "COLLECTIBLE," as the florid prose on eBay will attest to. In the book world, inexperienced (read "neophyte") sellers on the web (*see* Online book sales) will claim, "This book is truly a collector's item," implying that the strangely high price I have put on it is justified since the laws of supply and demand will prove that the item offered here is in demand and you better grab it before all those other collectors out there hungering for it learn of its existence. Such ploys don't make true, knowledgeable collectors' juices flow. However, there is really a category of collector's items in books: so-called HIGH SPOTS, scarce and rare pieces that do indeed fall under the low-supply and high-demand category, and items in certain collecting genres that are always sought after. (Another definition, to bring the discussion to a close, is that a book that is a collector's item is one in the possession of a collector. This puerile definition holds true in its obviousness, but belonged in parentheses.)

COLLOTYPE. "A printing process employing a glass plate with a gelatin surface that carries the image to be reproduced. Also called *photogelatin process*" (*American Heritage Dictionary of the English Language*, p. 363). The process is expensive, but the images produced with it are of high quality.

COLONIAL EDITION. Carter has an entry for this term—emanating from England, where publishers may issue a text for the English and a cheaper version for the colonies, a practice that was in place for about 25 years, from the 1880s on. The cheaper versions were still the same edition, having been printed from the same setting of type. (*See* Edition, Impression [Printing], Issue, and State; Points.) But they were sometimes printed on lower-quality paper and bound in less expensive materials. Since saving money was the object, if the book were in STANDING TYPE, the LEADS (interlinear spacing) would be removed to allow for a tighter-set text, and thus a reduction in the space taken for printing the whole text. This way a multivolume set could be produced in a single volume. This was called a *colonial edition.* As Carter says, they have become COLLECTIBLE, and for good reason since with the manipulation of a text in standing type, variants can be introduced that would be of interest to bibliographers, and COMPLETIST collectors would want every manifestation of the work.

COLOPHON. From a Greek word meaning "finishing touch." A note, usually at the end of a manuscript or printed book, giving various kinds of information, such as the name of the scribe or printer, the name of the binder, the materials used in the production of the book (paper, vellum, inks, and types), dates (e.g., the date the scribe finished writing or the printer finished the printing), places of production, or other information. Some colophons are quite brief. (Vance Gerry's *Flowers on a Table: A Study of an Imprudent Wood Engraving* has the following colophon: "125 copies.") Some contain many sentences. (Walter Hamady's *In Sight of Blue Mounds* has a colophon that explains the title of the book, how the paper was made, who the artist of the frontispiece is, what the typeface is, how the ink signals seasons in the text, and so on.) The colophon in printed books was often accompanied by the PRINTER'S MARK. In the modern FINE-PRESS world, most printers have a colophon, usually stating, among other facts, the limitation of the pressrun and the number of the present copy. It is also a common place for principals (author, illustrator, printer, and binder) to sign the volume. In early printed books, the colophon may also contain the volume's REGISTER.

THE COLOPHON: A BOOK COLLECTOR'S QUARTERLY (usually referred to only as *The Colophon*). One of the premier book collectors' journals in the United States. Its first issue was in February 1930. The small advertising piece accompanying this first issue says that "its sponsors are supported by the conviction that America never has sheltered such a host of understanding book collectors as it does today. It is an audience that merits such a service as the editors of The Colophon hope the quarterly will render. / The reader to whom The Colophon will be directed already collects books and knows why. Its appeal, therefore, cannot be elementary, nor will it be a vehicle of collecting propaganda. Its tastes will be as catholic as the tastes of The Colophon's readers, as catholic as the tastes of all its contributors. / The Colophon's primary concern will be with collected and COLLECTABLE books—FIRST EDITIONS, FINE PRINTING, INCUNABULA, ASSOCIATION books, AMERICANA, bibliography and manuscripts. The subject of book illustration will receive attention, and significant examples, whether in COPPER PLATES, LITHOGRAPH or WOODCUT, will be printed either from the original plates or blocks or reproduced in FACSIMILE by one of the photo-mechanical processes. / The Colophon will have at least eighty pages of text, frequently with special INSERTS exemplifying experiment and achievement in book design from important American and foreign presses. The cover of each number will be from a special drawing by some distinguished American artist." And so on.

An important feature of this publication was that many perspectives were presented in its pages. The editorial board and cadre of contributors comprised a Who's Who of important people in the book world—the most prominent writers and practitioners, artists and scholars of the day—with many women editors and writers.

Forty-six volumes were issued, along with an index of the first volumes from 1930 to 1935. There was also a supplementary index published by Scarecrow Press in 1968, covering all the volumes after those covered in the first index (for *The Colophon, New Series*, *The Colophon, New Graphic Series*, and *The New Colophon*). One of the quirks of the periodical was that some of its FASCICLES were printed independent of one another, so there was no pagination in some of the volumes. It is worth adding here that, while the publication has never fallen out of favor with readers and collectors, it was printed in sufficient quantities that most of the volumes are readily available today on the web, save for part 5 (1931) of the original series, which contains an engraving by the Canadian artist David B. Milne, *"Hilltop: A Drypoint in Two Colors"* (bound in after the first two essays in the volume [which is unpaginated]). (See Silcox, *Painting Place*, p. 223.) Milne (1882–1953) was a fairly popular artist, and this print commands a high price today; hence, many copies of part 5 of *The Colophon* lack the print. Further worth noting is that since the print was a DRYPOINT, the very method of printing made it impossible to get as many copies in good condition (i.e., with sharp lines in the print—the issue was produced in 3,000 copies) as the *Colophon* publishers needed, and Milne had to redo the image several times. Hence, the print exists in a number of states. (For a discussion of states, *see* Edition, Impression [Printing], Issue, and State; Points.)

COLORADO ANTIQUARIAN BOOK SEMINAR. A long-standing "workshop" for booksellers to prepare them for the antiquarian book trade. "The Antiquarian Book Market Seminar began in 1978 as the result of a collaboration between Dean Margaret Goggin of the Graduate School of Librarianship and Information Management at the University of Denver and Jacob L. Chernofsky, editor and publisher of AB Bookmans' Weekly." (*See AB/BW.*) "Today the Antiquarian Book Seminar is a nonprofit organization, offering nearly a dozen scholarships annually. Nearly 3000 students have graduated from the seminar since its inception, many of whom have gone on to become prominent members of the bookselling community." (See Antiquarian Book Seminars at https://www.bookseminars.com/ [accessed 18 January 2021].) Despite the name of the event, in 2022 the seminar was given in St. Olaf College, Northfield, Minnesota.

COLOR-PLATE BOOKS. *See* Plates.

COLORS. Carter has an excellent entry for "Colours of Cloth and Leather" (pp. 82–83). For the present purpose, it is enough to say that in any kind of cataloging, BIBLIOGRAPHICAL DESCRIPTION, book collecting, bookselling, and the like, it is important to be accurate in describing color. (And we should add "paper" and other phenomena to this equation, for while Carter is describing cover materials, bibliographers also need to describe paper, ink, and the stamping that goes onto bindings.) The difference between a light blue and a dark blue, a Kelly green and a forest green, or a shade of light red and dark pink can be the difference between an AUTHORITATIVE edition and a shoddy one, a genuine first edition and a PIRATED version, or a valuable book and a cheap one. Naturally, there are problems with color description since all people do not perceive colors the same; there are literally endless shades of colors; dye lots from one batch of cloth or paper will produce different shades in the next batch; there are no industry, institutional, or national standards for colors or their names; colors can fade, so two identically colored volumes stored in different conditions may eventually be of different shades; colors that start out looking identical but made from different dyestuffs may evolve in different ways and at different speeds; SUBSTRATES (e.g., leather and paper) can make the colors on them change in different ways, so the shades of a QUARTER-BOUND book with uniform colors on its covers and spine may eventually look quite different; and so on. One tremendously insightful bibliographer (among several others) has approached the topic, and his work should be studied by anyone describing books: G. Thomas Tanselle, "The Bibliographical Description of Paper," and "A System of Color Identification for Bibliographical Description."

COLOR SEPARATION. Figuring out how to print a color image by analyzing the original and determining what colors, overprinted, will yield the final color image. Using the primary colors (along with black), printers can get a full range of tints. It takes a great deal of knowledge and experience to know how to separate out individual colors, what colors to use, how dense to print them, where to print them on the page (to get proper REGISTRATION), and in what order to print them to produce the final image. Today, the task can be accomplished with computers.

COLPORTEUR. An itinerant bookseller, often of devotional books, but also ALMANACS, CHAPBOOKS, BROADSIDES and prints, and instructional books for children. The *American Heritage Dictionary of the English Language* says, "influenced by *col*, neck, from the idea that peddlers carry their wares on trays suspended from straps around their necks" (p. 366), though "col" usually refers to the collar and "cou" to the neck.

COLUMBIAN PRESS. *See* Clymer, George.

COMB BINDING. "A form of mechanical binding consisting of a plastic strip on the SPINE from which curved prongs extend. They are inserted into holes punched into the leaves to be held. The name derives from the resulting 'comb' appearance of the binding. This type of mechanical binding provides a more or less solid spine on which the title of the publication may be printed. Its disadvantages, however, are many: leaves may be removed quite easily by unauthorized persons, and groups of leaves often slip from the grasp of the flexible prongs. In addition, leaves tend to tear from the binding because the large, usually rectangular, slots leave relatively little paper along the line of the punched holes" (Roberts and Etherington, p. 62).

COMIC BOOKS. A genre of publications, intended for children and adults (depending on the subject matter of their texts), usually heavily illustrated in color, often printed on inexpensive paper, and bound with staples or perfect binding. The artwork in them is usually in color, with an emphasis on pictures, with a good deal more image on the page than verbal text. The pictures are usually in small panels on each page, running sequentially through the volume.

In the West, they first are seen in the 1930s, an offshoot of the comic strips that appeared in newspapers from decades earlier. The word "comic" in the name implies that there is humor in the text, and that may be the case for many of these publications aimed at children. But the genre also contains "comics" that have to do with history, science fiction and fantasy (and "superhero" stories), mystery, and romance, among many other subjects. (See the Charles Hatfield entry in *The Oxford Companion*, vol. 1, pp. 626–28.)

As COLLECTIBLES, these have a grand and extensive presence, with some of the earliest of these selling for over $1 million. (In 2011, the first issue of Action Comics sold for $2.1 million. See Dave & Adam's Card World, dacardworld.com, "The 20 Most Expensive Comic Books Ever Sold.") Hence, they have found their niche in the antiquarian book world among serious booksellers and collectors. They can be found all over the world, with the greatest number being sold in Japan and in English-speaking countries. Anthony Gramuglia says that "a new market for comics aimed at juveniles has opened up. That, combined with the ever-increasing mainstream popularity of MANGA, has revolutionized what material fans want to read. . . . [As of 2019], 41% of comic sales are juvenile fiction, 28% are manga, while only 10% are superhero comics" (Gramuglia, "Why Manga & Comics for Kids Outsell Superheroes"). With Marvel and DC leading the way as the top comic book publishers, and joined by scores of smaller publishers, comic books by the thousands are produced every year.

COMMERCIAL EDITION/COMMERCIAL PUBLISHER. A designation to distinguish an item from another edition or editions, presumably ones more expensive. The term thus indicates that cheaper and more readily available copies may have been produced for wide distribution—the commercial copies. To be distinguished, for instance, from a LIMITED EDITION. As noted at that term, and also at VERSION, the word "edition" could be a misnomer since the limited and commercial manifestations of a text could have been printed from the same setting of type. (*See* Edition, Impression [Printing], Issue, and State; Points.) The publications would then have been done by a "commercial publisher." HARRY DUNCAN and KIM MERKER hand-printed *Golden Child* for Joyce Hall (owner of Hallmark) in an edition of about 110 copies. Hall then released a commercial edition—a perfect FACSIMILE—in untold numbers. Hallmark is a commercial publisher, and the commercial edition was priced at only a few dollars, commanding not much more today; the FINE-PRESS version sells today for many hundreds of dollars.

COMMISSION, ON. *See* Auctions; On commission.

COMMISSION BIDDING. *See* Auctions.

COMMONPLACE BOOK. A collection, in book form (printed or manuscript), of excerpts, sayings, quotable passages, extracts from other texts, or whatever else interested the compiler. The compilation need not be of elegant or highly literary pieces, as is the case with a FLORILEGIUM. Popular from the 15th century on in Europe, the commonplace book would be filled with sententious and witty sayings, recipes, verses, tables of measurements and weights, religious sayings and prayers, information about laws and regulations, lists of important dates (e.g., holidays and feast days), and whatever else was of interest to the compiler. Hence, no two commonplace books are alike since they are created by the single person putting them together. Any literate person might compile one as a memory aid or merely as a record of what interested him or her. The hodgepodge nature of the commonplace book shows that such compilations often had no theme or unifying subject matter other than the personal interests of their compilers. (*See* Analects; Chrestomathy; Miscellany; Scrapbook.) (See Havens, *Commonplace Books*.)

COMMON PRESS. A wooden handpress, like the one used in Western printing from the 15th to the 19th centuries. It had a BED, a PLATEN, a BAR to pull to make the platen descend onto the inked type, and so on. (For an illustration, see below; *see also* Handpresses.)

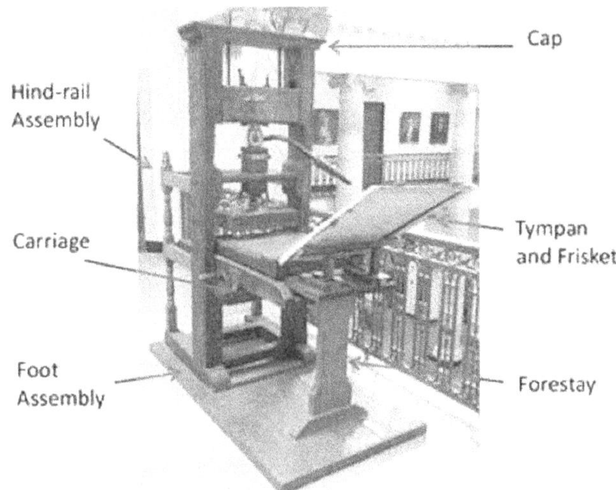

Common press; http://commonplace.online/article/pressing-matters/ (accessed 11 July 2021). This is the press used by Isaiah Thomas, founder of the American Antiquarian Society in Worcester, Massachusetts, where this press is on display. The tympan is opened, but the frisket is still folded down onto the tympan and is thus not visible in this view. Photo by Jeffrey D. Groves.

Courtesy of American Antiquarian Society.

COMPANION VOLUME. A volume that accompanies something else, like a suite of PRINTS or photographs ("the engravings accompanied by a companion volume by the artist"), or one that adds commentary and explanation for, say, a movie or television show ("the companion volume to *Gone with the Wind* was included in a box holding the DVD of the movie"). Ken Burns (with Geoffrey C. Ward) published *Baseball: An Illustrated History* as a companion volume to his PBS series on the sport.

COMPARTMENTS. *See* Panel/Panel binding.

COMPENSATION. A word with two meanings in the book world. 1) If an item has been damaged in some way, with the loss of materials—especially supporting materials like the sheet on which text is printed or the leaf onto which tip-ins have been attached—"compensation" is the conservation treatment that may be rendered to replace the missing support. One may, for instance, replace part of the paper on a leaf from a book by using LEAFCASTING to fill in a hole. (*See* Compensation guard.) And 2) A topic that could yield a 50-page essay: concerning what proper compensation (monetary) would be for one working in the book world. Does an antiquarian-book seller deserve compensation a thousand times as great as that for his employees? How much should one charge (or pay) for a given item? Where do librarians fit in along this spectrum of incoming and outgoing resources? And so forth. Such issues are hinted at in other entries in this dictionary. (*See*, for instance, Appraisal; Condition; Price.)

COMPENSATION GUARD. "A thickness of linen or paper, usually the latter, bound into a volume to compensate for the thickness of folded maps, charts or other bulky material within the text block, or pocket material, so as to incorporate such material without distorting the shape of the book. They are sometimes made by binding in a full section of blank leaves placed ahead of the bulky material, and then cutting out all except a narrow portion after binding. The more common method, however, is to bind in folded strips of guard paper when the book is to be sewn through the folds, or strips of paper when the book is to be oversewn or otherwise sewn through the sides of the leaves" (Roberts and Etherington, "compensation guard"; https://cool.culturalheritage.org/don/dt/dt0802.html [accessed 12 March 2021]). The purpose of these guards is to allow the front and rear boards of the volume to be parallel with one another once the volume is fully "finished"—that is, once it contains all the tipped-in and otherwise added materials that it will have when all that is scheduled to be mounted is there.

COMPILER. When a volume is composed of many pieces textually—as with a collection of essays or a gathering of jokes or photographs—the person responsible for bringing them all together and organizing them is the compiler. In a bibliographical description, the abbreviation "comp." indicates the role of that person: "*Essays on 20th-century American Architecture*, Steven Wright, comp."

COMPLETE. Used to describe a book that contains all the parts it is supposed to have—particularly everything between the covers. When a binder gets the loose sheets, he examines them to make sure everything the printer supplied (printed LEAVES, ILLUSTRATIONS, BLANKS, OFFSET SHEETS, and anything else that was intended to be bound in) is there. If so, he can call the volume "complete." A bibliographer may call a volume "COLLATED and complete"—meaning that the book was carefully examined and determined to have all that should be there.

If a volume is made up of FASCICLES published and issued separately, the volume may be lacking, say, a chapter or a part, but if that part or chapter was never printed, then even though the texts may be lacking that piece, it is still "complete," and the bibliographer can say of the bound volume that it is "ALL PUBLISHED."

COMPLETIST. A collector (private, library, or other) wishing a complete collection of whatever is collected. If a journal exists in 35 volumes and the collector owns only 34, the completist spirit drives him to fill in the gap, sometimes even being willing to spend far more than the missing volume is worth on the retail market just to complete the set. This goes too for the collection of, say, a 5-volume set of history or literature; most collectors will be reluctant to fill a gap in their collections when they are offered 4 of the 5 volumes. (Finding the ORPHAN—the ODD VOLUME—can be infuriating and fruitless.)

Completism can border on the manic, and it can make otherwise rational collectors do irrational things. The impulse is good: if you are collecting for some high moral purpose, such as to increase the intellectual value of your holdings and thus to allow scholars to have as much information as possible on whatever the collection focuses on, completism allows you to approach this ideal. But if the completism is driven by the saw that nature abhors a vacuum and the vacuum is a missing volume or two, beware the unscrupulous seller who can take advantage of this urgency. (I once asked a bookseller if she had a particular volume. She said she did, and, seeing how eager I was to get it to fill a gap in my collection, she offered it to me at more than twice its market value—and *at a price more than twice what she had originally quoted me.* I rejected it. Later that very copy came to me through another buyer at the much lower price that it should have been [and actually *was*] quoted at in the first place. Completism worn on the sleeve can be detrimental to one's budget.)

COMPOSING STICK. (Sometimes called a "type stick.") A handheld device, like a small tray, with a fixed or an adjustable ELBOW for composing (setting) type. The COMPOSITOR takes type from the TYPE CASE, usually one SORT at a time, and places each sort in the stick (as it is sometimes called)—letters, numbers, punctuation, spacing, and other sorts—until a full single line has been set. Additional lines are set in the stick until it is full, and then the type is transferred to a GALLEY or directly to the BED of the press. Early ones were made of wood, and they had a single fixed measure. Later ones, especially from the 19th century on, were made of metal and had various means of adjusting the elbow (to allow for longer or shorter line measures to be set) and locking it into place. (See Speckter, *Disquisition on the Composing Stick.*)

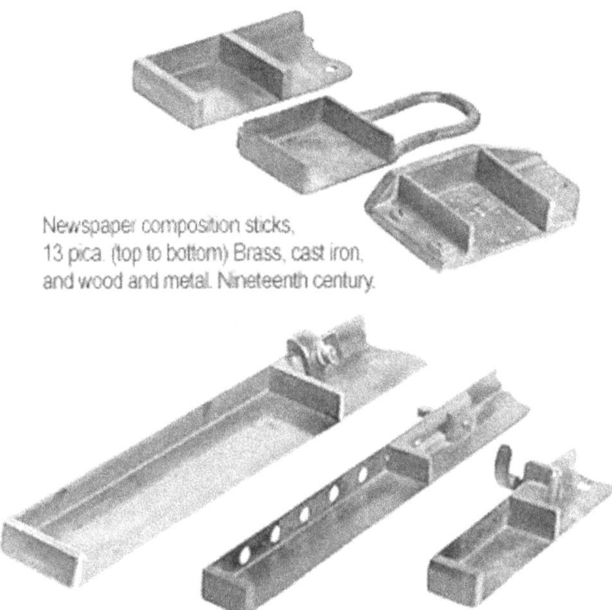

Composing sticks. International Printing Museum, Carson, California; http://www.printmuseum.org/museum/collection/ (accessed 22 April 2015)

Courtesy of the International Printing Museum, Carson, California.

COMPOSING STONE/COMPOSING TABLE. A large perfectly flat stone (on a table) that the COMPOSITOR uses in imposing (*see* Imposition) the type into the CHASE. The chase is removed from the BED of the press and placed on the stone. The FORME is composed on the stone and locked into the chase. Then the chase is returned to the press. Sometimes called an "imposing stone" or a "turtle," though the turtle was a movable table—on wheels—with a composing stone on top, for transporting the forme to the handpress. The turtle did not have a large surface, so it was useful for fairly small chases. The chase would be filled with type and everything else in the forme and then transferred to the press. The turtle was used to make the transport easy and to prevent the chase from being bumped and the type PIED if it had to be carried a long distance.

COMPOSITION. Typesetting. The art (or craft) of assembling SORTS into text. This requires some skills and some basic education, for COMPOSITORS need to spot errors in the texts they are setting, to divide words at the end of the line properly, to spell correctly, and so on. In printing establishments in which hand composition is the rule, setting type can be fatiguing (though for some it is energizing). As this definition began, there is an art to good composition: being able to set CLEAN COPY, with no typos, no RIVERS, fairly even spacing between words, good LETTERSPACING for uppercase text, consistently JUSTIFIED lines (optically and in the COMPOSING STICK), and so on. And the composition also includes the skill of transferring the set type from the stick to a GALLEY without PIEING the type and knowing how to tie it up with string. Before the mechanical means of typesetting, it was all done by hand, one sort at a time. Machine composition comes about in the 19th century. After much experimentation and various levels of success, the LINOTYPE machine effectively solved the problems of machine setting. (See Huss, *The Development of Printers' Mechanical Typesetting Methods, 1822–1925.*)

COMPOSITOR. A typesetter. As the *American Dictionary of Printing and Bookmaking* notes, "There are three divisions of workmen in a printing-office . . . : compositors, pressmen and readers. The compositor is the one who gets the form ready for printing" (p. 111). (*See* Forme.) The setting of type is a glorious activity; distributing it is scut work, too menial for the compositor. DISTRIBUTION is often left to the apprentices. The compositor stands before a TYPE CASE, takes SORTS from their compartments in the case, and places them into the COMPOSING STICK. In the era of machine typesetting, the compositor may sit at a keyboard (as with LINOTYPE or MONOTYPE setting or for a computer). In the handpress period, a compositor might set a number (his own) into the lower margin of the page, beneath the TEXT BLOCK, to identify him- or herself as the setter of the type for that page. (*See* Printer's mark.)

Since composition is an individual practice (i.e., some compositors have habits unique to their work), careful examination may reveal to a bibliographer certain patterns of setting practice, revealing that a particular text was set by a particular compositor. As Shef Rogers points out, "Such patterns then assist editors in determining the probable source of a particular textual reading" (see "Compositorial Analysis" in *The Oxford Companion*, vol. 1, p. 631). Rogers adds that the analysis is not merely of observing spelling or spacing habits, but "tracking specific pieces of broken type over several FORMS." (*See* Hinman Collator.)

It should be added that when OTTMAR MERGENTHALER invented the Linotype machine, the keyboarder who "set the type" was also called a compositor, though he was producing slugs of text, not type in individual sorts.

CONCERTINA FOLD. "A method of folding a sheet of paper, first to the right and then to the left, so that the sheet opens and closes in the manner of a concertina. Also called 'accordion fold,' or 'zig-zag fold'" (Roberts and Etherington, p. 63). Another word occasionally used for this kind of folding technique is "leporello." (*See* Orihon.)

CONCISE EDITION. *See* Abridged edition.

CONCORDANCE. An alphabetical list (or a whole volume) of all of the words (or all the key words) in a text (or in a body of texts). There are concordances to the Bible, to the works of Chaucer and Shakespeare, and to hundreds of other works and authors. The concordance usually gives the full line or the full context in which the key words are used (called KWIC [Key Word In Context] concordances). Before computers, concordances were scholars' primary search tools for finding key words or phrases in large bodies of text. Today, these tools are made obsolete for online texts by computers, which allow for searches by any combination of keystrokes.

CONDENSATION/CONDENSED BOOK. *See* Abridged edition.

CONDENSED TYPE. A narrow TYPEFACE, usually part of a family of faces, one of which is designed to have more characters per line than does the regular FACE. "In typography, descriptive of the relative narrowness of all the characters in one typeface. Condensed type is used when large amounts of copy must fit into a small space, such as in tabular composition. / There are four basic gradations of condensation beyond the 'normal' typeface: semicondensed, condensed, extracondensed, and ultracondensed. *Narrow* and *compressed* are often used synonymously with one or more of these degrees of condensation" ("Condensed," at PrintWiki, http://printwiki.org/Condensed [accessed 3 June 2021]).

Poster Tall Condensed type. iStock; https://www.istockphoto.com/vector/poster-black-tall-condensed-font-and-numbers-gm502346657-43724634 (accessed 3 June 2021).
Courtesy of iStock.

CONDITION. In appraising books, many a book person uses the phrase "condition is all," indicating that the shape a book (or other library material) is in carries a great deal of weight in its value and whether a collector or librarian or bookseller chooses to acquire it. A book in PRISTINE condition will obviously be worth more than the same item in average condition. The top two criteria for evaluating books are (1) supply and demand, and (2) condition, usually in that order.

There are no standard terms for book conditions. The publication *AB/Bookman's Weekly* once printed in each issue the following statement:

> A thriving antiquarian book trade is largely dependent on the effectiveness of catalogue and mail-order bookselling. Transactions by mail are possible as long as buyer and seller recognize the importance of accuracy in describing the condition of the books offered for sale.
>
> Terms used to describe condition of books are as varied and numerous as the creativity and imagination of bookmen can produce. When confusion reigns over descriptions by advertisers or quoters, dissatisfaction is the inevitable result. . . . A revised list of terms used in describing books is now published here in each weekly issue of *AB* to serve as a suggested guide and reference for bookmen.

[See "Condition" in the bibliography. *See also AB/BW.*]

The *AB/Bookman's Weekly* text cites nine levels of condition: As New, Fine, Very Good, Good, Fair, Poor (READING

Copy), Ex-Library, Book Club, and Binding Copy. One problem is that all such descriptions are subjective, and what could be *mint* to one person may be *pristine* to another and *very good* to a third. Also, a bookseller may have "poor eyesight" and describe almost all of his offerings as *fine* or *as new*, while another may have his own vocabulary altogether. "One catalog used the phrase 'a very near fine copy.' It is debatable whether this is distinguishable from 'near fine,' from the same catalog. Other terms in this listing are 'overall, less than very good,' 'a much nicer than average copy,' 'otherwise about very good,' 'collectible condition' (a terribly muddy term since a horrible copy of an almost impossible to find book may be 'collectible' to some), 'wear to extremities, thus very good or a bit better,' 'a passable copy,' 'else a bright near fine copy,' 'a less than very good copy,' 'near fine,' 'very near fine,' a 'very good+ or better copy,' an 'only about a very good copy,' and about another dozen variations on these terms" (Berger, p. 495). (*See* Crisp.)

The imprecision of booksellers in describing condition can almost be excused when one understands the entire range of "conditions" that books can be in and that there is, as I have said, no codified vocabulary for describing the state a volume is in. One would assume that "good" means "good," but what does it mean in the following context (culled from a reputable and justifiably revered bookseller): "Cocked, light wear to corners, small split to head of rear joint, two small white stains to rear board, text block slightly shaken, front hinge cracked but firm, occasional light spotting; still, a very good copy"? (This taken from Peter Harrington, describing Robert Louis Stevenson, *Island Nights' Entertainment*.) It doesn't sound "very good" to me. Perhaps the cataloger at Harrington has seen many other copies of this book in this edition and these others were shabby; so one in the condition that he was describing was "pretty good" considering that this book rarely surfaces in a condition as "good" as the one he has. Likewise, we have another fine bookseller, John K. King, offering Mark Twain's *Innocents Abroad* with this description: "covers worn and a bit soiled, extremities bumped and chipping, outer hinges cracking, former owner's private library bookplate inside front cover, pp a bit toned with some finger soiling, still a pretty good copy" (offered on abe: https://www.abebooks.com/servlet/SearchResults?yrl=1869&recentlyadded=all&prevpage=1&bx=off&bi=0&bsi=30&sortby=1&tn=innocents+abroad&an=mark+twain&yrh=1869&ds=30 [accessed 1 June 2021]). It doesn't sound "pretty good" to me. I wouldn't use the word "good" at all in describing this copy. But there it is. What does "pretty good" mean to you? Would you accept service from a "pretty good" doctor or hair dresser? The language of *condition* needs to be refined and codified. But that is nigh impossible.

One term related to condition that is amusing at best and stupid at worst is "else fine," a phrase that comes at the end of a list of a book's flaws. For example, "Ex. lib. Corners bumped. Green calf on spine and top half of front cover faded. Headcap worn, with loss of headband. Joints starting. Front free endpaper, flyleaf, and half-title wanting. Minor crayon writing on rear flyleaf. Sporadic underlining of text throughout. Two-inch tear in title page and first two leaves of Introduction, not affecting text. Three of six plates skillfully razored out. Some slight worming throughout. First and last dozen or so leaves lightly foxed. Else fine." The phrase is the bookseller's way of saying, "Despite its faults, this would be a good purchase for your library." (See Berger, "Else Fine," p. 42.) The use of the word "else" has always puzzled me. "Otherwise" makes more sense and is more idiomatic.

Condition is so important in the selling and collecting of books that John Carter has a whole chapter on it in his classic *Taste and Technique* (see the bibliography). Another crucial point is that a volume could be in absolutely pristine condition, but it has been rebound or has undergone restoration to make it as new. In such a situation, even its pristineness or as-new-ness will not enhance its value. Most collectors would prefer a volume in its shabby original binding to one in a binding that has been altered from its original materials. Running alongside this is the fact that books centuries old are practically impossible to be found in their original materials *in their original conditions*, and serious collectors would be happy to have, say, a 15th- or 16th-century book in scruffy condition rather than no copy at all.

In the world of paperbacks, some booksellers have come up with their own grading system, using the terms "A grade," "B grade," and "C grade" to designate levels of quality. "A grade" is like new: with no stamps or damage or deterioration of any kind. Of course, since paperbacks are fragile, if the text of the volume was read, there would be some sign of this desecration, reducing the volume's value. With the use of fairly cheap and acidic paper from the 1870s on, almost all paperbacks printed on this pulp will show the yellowing endemic to the inherent vice in the paper. Even the most beautiful copy of an old paperback (dating from, say, before 1980) will likely have yellowed paper. So a pristine copy would still be considered A grade, even with some yellowing of the paper, if there are no other signs of use. "B grade" paperbacks may show some sign of use, like a name of an owner or a reading crease at the spine. A "C grade" book will have a serious reading crease, quite brittle and discolored paper, a chipped (and possibly detached) cover, and various other defects. It is not really collectible (unless it is particularly scarce, and in great high demand); such a volume would be considered a reading copy.

One additional point: The more a collector deals with a bookseller, the more he will perceive the predilections and practices of that seller; so if that purveyor of volumes consistently describes books as "fine" or "PRISTINE" when the buyer perceives them to be "so-so" or "good+," he will know what to expect if he buys a book from that bookseller. Since there really is no formal standard of vocabulary used universally by the book trade, condition is in the eye (and judgment) of the beholder.

(See Berger, pp. 494–95; and Carter, pp. 84–87, where he discusses terms that are "descriptive" and "enthusiastic." *See also* Collector's condition; Crisp; Good for its age; Reading copy; Secondhand copy; Sharp copy; Used copy.)

CONDITION REPORT. In a library, this is a report covering the CONDITION of the physical facility and the books, manuscripts, and other materials it houses. For a single VOLUME, it is an assessment of its completeness, all defects it has, and anything else worth mentioning. Such a report can be done by a conservator for a bookseller who is contemplating CONSERVATION work, or for a librarian or collector contemplating the item's acquisition.

CONDUCT BOOK. *See* Courtesy book.

C1S/C2S. Designations of "coated one side" and "coated two sides"—in reference to the coating on the surfaces of sheets of paper.

CONFRATERNITY BOOK. *See* Liber Vitae.

CONJUGATE (as LEAVES in a bound book). Said of leaves joined through a fold; leaves attached to one another (or formerly so attached). In a simple FOLIO, with a single sheet folded once to produce two leaves, these leaves are said to be conjugate through that fold. In a QUARTO, with a sheet folded twice to yield four leaves, the first leaf is conjugate with the second (through the fold at the HEAD) and with the fourth (through the fold at the spine). A key point (that Carter ignores) is that conjugacy is not merely vertical (leaf 1 in a simple folio is conjugate with leaf 2, thanks to the vertical fold at the SPINE), but also horizontal—that is, folds (also called BOLTS) at the top (head) of a quarto volume yield conjugate leaves. Even if the bolts are removed, the formerly attached leaves are still said to be conjugate. To remember what this term means (or to help you recall the term), just think of a prisoner who is allowed a conjugal visit, which does not mean that they practice safe distancing or that they merely shake hands. (*See* Integral.) For booksellers or collectors, the term often comes up when they are looking at leaves in a volume that are now (or once were) attached, like those in the PRELIMS (especially HALF-TITLES and TITLE PAGES, but also FLYLEAVES and SINGLETONS). One of MARK HOFFMANN's insidious practices was to remove BLANKS from old volumes to acquire paper of the right age for his FORGERIES. In a COLLATION, a bibliographer will look for all leaves that should be there—to determine the completeness of the volume. Singletons could indicate missing conjugate leaves, like those for advertising; or they could signal a CANCEL (either a CANCELLANDUM or a CANCELLANS).

CONSERVATION. The treatment of individual items in a collection to extend the useful life of these items, as distinguished from PRESERVATION, which is the treatment of collections as a whole. The aim of the conservator is not to make items look good; it is to address areas in which items are deteriorating and to halt the deterioration. (Reversing deterioration is impossible.) (See Berger, chapter 12, esp. pp. 384–90.) The conservator, usually working with a curator (librarian, bookseller, or private collector), comes up with a conservation plan that extends the life of an object while retaining as much as possible all of the information contained in that object. For example, information resides in bindings, so if a book needs to be rebound, whatever information the original binding has may be retained with careful notes, photography, and a meticulous BIBLIOGRAPHICAL DESCRIPTION, even retaining the original binding even if it has been removed from the TEXT BLOCK and replaced. (*See also* Restoration.)

There is also the term "collections conservation": conservators care for entire collections—they address the physical needs of collections as a whole. In this, the term has much in common with "preservation."

CONSERVATION CENTER FOR ART & HISTORIC ARTIFACTS. *See* CCAHA; Regional Alliance for Preservation.

CONSIGNMENT. Some books are sent from a bookseller to a potential purchaser "ON APPROVAL"; this is one form of consignment. But more common in the book world is the situation in which a bookseller takes a volume (or many) from its owner and offers to sell it for the owner, usually at a price that the owner and dealer decide is appropriate. The customer who wishes to buy it from the dealer can ask for a discount, but if the volume is on consignment, the dealer often does not have much wiggle room in adjusting the price. On the other hand, a bookseller not wanting to come down on a price may say that the book is "on consignment" (whether it is or not), implying that the price is firm. The customer can then ask the dealer to ask the owner if he or she is willing to horse-trade. It is a game for two (or three). (Parenthetically, I do not like to bargain with booksellers. Booksellers are "professionals who should be shown the respect of their expertise. They have profits to make, lives to live, and books to sell. If they come up with a particular price, you either pay it or you do not. If you do, then the price was right for you. If you do not buy the item because of its price, then maybe someone else will at the price you thought was too high. If that is the case, then, again, the bookseller has priced the book appropriately. Someone bought it at whatever price the dealer had on it, so the book was priced right. Sometimes the price the dealer asks is too high, and he may look at that volume on his shelf for years. And if the dealer did indeed pay a lot for it, he may not want to sell it at a loss, so the price stays high. / Professional booksellers should be given credit for the expertise they have acquired over the years at their own expense. . . . One good practice is to assume that the dealer has a good reason for the price he is asking, and then say Yes or No to the purchase. Do not ask for 'accommodations'" [Berger, pp. 304–05].)

CONSIGNOR. At an AUCTION, the auction house sells items it does not own—items consigned to it by the consignor. As the owner, the consignor must pay the house for its services, so the consignor takes only a portion of the hammer price, the house takes the rest.

CONSOLIDATION. The bringing together of parts of an item that either were once all together or that will be beneficial to be together. If there is RED ROT on a leather binding, a consolidant can be used to stop the flakes from falling off and hold the ones that remain firmly to the binding. If a volume was issued with a host of tip-ins or items that were laid in, and all of these things are now loose, it may be a good idea to consolidate them by housing them all in a single sleeve or other container that is kept with the volume (though reattaching loosened tip-ins may be best for them, and is one level of consolidation). Any treatment to conserve library materials should be done by (or under the auspices of) a professional conservator.

CONTEMPORARY. Said of any feature of a book when that feature's contemporaneity with the publication of the volume may be seen as an asset and can thus command a higher price than a similar volume with a later such feature. One might see for a medieval manuscript, "With contemporary marginalia." The word in this context implies that the marginal notes or scrawls were done close to the book's production. The word, of course, could mean "contemporary" to the writing of this book description, but, though it is not used in that sense, the ambiguity is still there. A contemporary binding means one that was original to the volume or was at least done soon after the book was produced. Such attributions are sometimes made by booksellers who are not really experts in this kind of thing, and what they really mean is, "This is a pretty old binding—not done in this century." That does not automatically mean that the binding is actually contemporary to the book's production.

CONTRIBUTOR. In the composition of any text for a book (or a text in any other format), a person who adds her part of that text. A single volume can contain, say, 30 essays, each by a different contributor. Contributions can be of any kind, depending on the nature and subject of the volume. And contributions can be in verse or prose, tables, charts, maps, or photographs. They can be columns in newspapers, journals, or magazines; entries in a dictionary or encyclopedia; or suggestions or ideas that an author adopts but does not use verbatim from their source. By extension, a contributor can even help with the production of the volume, as with someone setting the type for a FINE-PRESS book. Contributors are usually cited somewhere in the work, usually as part of the BACK MATTER, as in a COLOPHON or afterword. Booksellers may even credit contributors to one of their catalogs.

COOKBOOKS/COOKERY BOOKS. Books that show a huge variety of things that are supposedly done in a kitchen or other area in which food is prepared. The early ones are referred to as "cookery books"; they might include all kinds of household recipes, not merely for cooking but also for curing illnesses, getting stains out of anything that got stained, and running a household. (The old profession of running a home engendered the term "domestic economy," which created a rash of books on how to run a home—volumes that included much about cooking.)

In the world of book collecting, immense collections of cookbooks have been amassed, partly because they are useful and often attractive—and often inexpensive—and partly because there are so many of them. There are volumes that are comprehensive, showing how to prepare all kinds of foods for all kinds of meals and those that are on a single subject. (*See* How-to books.) The number of foci of these books is astounding, and many of them are revelatory of domestic culture through the centuries.

COPINGER, W. A. *See* Hain, Ludwig.

COPPERPLATE. (Sometimes hyphenated.) Shorthand for "copperplate illustration," an image (verbal, pictorial, or both) made from an INTAGLIO plate of copper, with the image ENGRAVED or ETCHED into the PLATE and with the plate put through a COPPERPLATE PRESS. Usually, the plate is smaller than the sheet that the image is printed on so that the edges of the plate press into the dampened paper and leave a PLATE MARK (an indented line) around the image.

Of course, the phrase could mean the actual plate used for printing, as in, "[t]he illustrations were done from copperplates." And the word could also refer to "[t]he regular round-hand script developed from italic in Holland for commercial and other use, and standardised in England by the end of the 17th century" (Carter, p. 87).

COPPERPLATE PRESS (rolling press). The press on which COPPERPLATES are printed. It consists either of a flat BED that rolls under rollers (which press the paper onto the plate) or a flat bed that is stationary, on which the plates sit, and a roller rolls over the plates.

Copperplate press. International Printing Museum; https://www.printmuseum.org/collection/equipment/copperplate-9-x-10/ (accessed 3 June 2021).

Courtesy of International Printing Museum, Carson, California.

COPPERS. *See* Thins.

COPTIC BINDING. "Bindings produced by the Copts, or Egyptian Christians. The Coptic style . . . is . . . in the form of chain stitch linkings appearing as so many braids across the spine of the book. In addition, the covers of Coptic bindings were frequently sewn or laced by a number of hinging loops. Some Coptic bindings had wooden boards (from about the 4th century to the Middle Ages), but the majority had boards built up by layers of waste papyrus" (Roberts and Etherington, p. 65; see this source for further description of these bindings).

Michelle Brown explains that "the QUIRES are sewn together by thread carried by two needles working in a figure-eight movement from quire to quire. The boards are then laced onto the loose ends of these threads" (*Understanding Illuminated Manuscripts*, p. 45). (See Szirmai, *The Archaeology of Medieval Bookbinding.*)

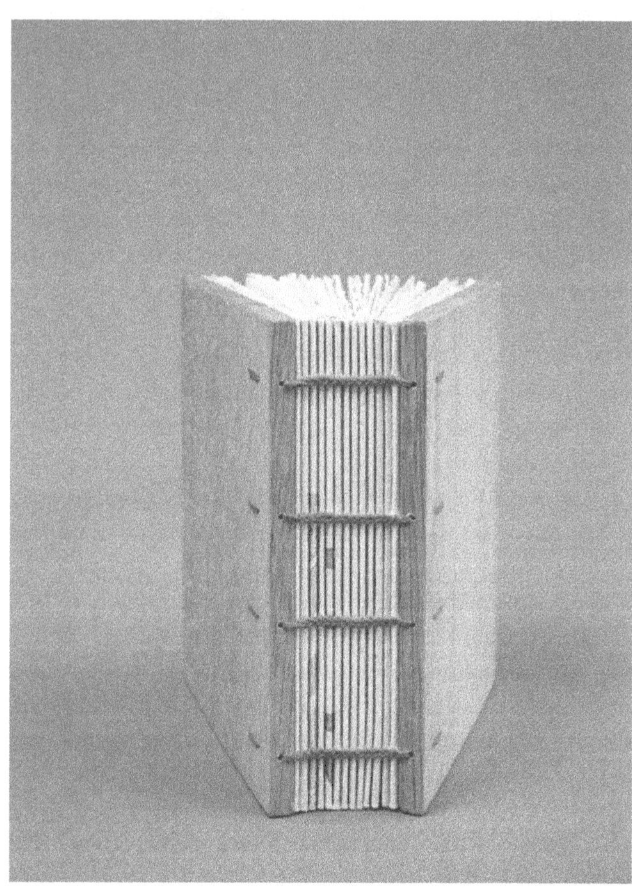

Coptic binding with the typical exposed sewing. Mika Bar-Chaim et al., Manuscript. (Claremont, CA: Scripps College Press, 2011). Photograph by Jeff Dykes.

Collection of the author.

CO-PUBLISHED. Said of a work that has more than one publisher, especially when that publication is in a single volume or set, and is a single edition, most often when the work appears in two countries. Such a text would normally have on its title page the name and location of the publisher in the country of origin. Other copies would have a different title page, showing the co-publisher, either as sole publisher or as a co-publisher. Some publishers like Oak Knoll Press often co-publish, as with the volumes they did with the British Library.

COPY. A single exemplar of a volume or pamphlet. ("I bought this copy from Dawson's.") Also, the original (printed or manuscript) version used by the compositor to set the type for a text. ("The typesetter affixed his copy to the wall above his case.") As a verb, it means to reproduce something as a scribe does in a scriptorium. ("The scribe must copy his source with accuracy.") But in the Middle Ages, copying did not have the same sense of responsibility as it does today—or as it has had since the dawn of Western printing. Medieval scribes could "copy" the sense of the original, not following that original *ad literatim* or even verbatim. Hence, a copy of a text in early manuscripts may not be an exact copy of the original.

The term also is used to delineate textual matter: "The COMPOSITOR created several errors when he did not follow his copy"; this means the text that was presented to him from the author and editors. A textual editor (*see* Bibliography) also creates copy for the compositor to set into type. And authors are asked to submit copy (that is, their complete text—e.g., article or book) to a publisher using that publisher's HOUSE STYLE.

COPYBOOK. (Sometimes written as two words.) (Also called an "exercise book.") A blank book (or one with ruled lines) used by students to practice all kinds of things taught in the classroom. In 18th-century America (and later), they were a primary way of teaching calligraphy, arithmetic, navigation, drawing, punctuation, reading, spelling, and other skills. Students would have before them a separate EXEMPLAR (or text or numbers printed onto the top of some of the pages) as the model to copy, and they would write—sometimes over and over—the text as they saw it in the model. The text could be an alphabetic sentence ("Pack my box with five dozen liquor jugs") or a moralistic sentence ("The early bird gathers no moss" or "Always obey your parents when they are present"). Some of the work of the students is exceptionally beautiful, showing great skill in writing, calculating, and art.

COPY BOOKS. *See* Copying press.

COPYEDITING. *See* Proofreading.

COPYING PRESS. Long before the Xerox machine and other kinds of copying, a kind of copying method was invented, to be used with a special kind of ink. "First the letter (or document) to be copied had to be written with a special soluble ink and allowed to dry without blotting to ensure that it would have a thick ink deposit. . . . Copies could be made for up to about 24 hours but the best were made within the first few hours. Next a copiest [*sic*] would prepare a 'sandwich' to place in the copy press. It consisted of a sheet of oiled paper followed by a water dampened sheet of thin tissue paper, then the original document with the inked side facing the tissue paper and finally another sheet of oiled paper. The 'sandwich' was then placed in the copy press and pressure was applied usually by turning a screw or using a lever. After a short time the pressure was released and enough of the ink from the original would have wicked into the tissue paper to make a copy. Thin tissue paper was used so the document could be read through the paper. The oiled paper prevented the ink from transferring to any other documents if multiple copies were being pressed at the same time" (Larson, "Before There Were Paper Jams"). The paper was strong, but very thin. Since the text was transferred to the underside of the sheet (the "VERSO" side), the text was readable through the paper from the "RECTO" side; it was right-reading. Companies used this method to make file copies of documents and correspondence, while the originals, on regular commercial paper, could be sent. Not only were the firms able to keep copies of important documents (without having to copy them out by hand), but they also saved space since the copying papers were especially thin. Companies would be able to store, perhaps, a thousand sheets in a single copy book. These presses were small enough to sit on a table, though they were made of cast iron, and when the practice of making such copies waned—especially with the coming of typewriters and carbon paper (*see* Typescript)—the presses passed into the hands of bookbinders, who used them to press volumes. Hence, they took on the name "binders' presses," though that was not what they were originally called. Larson says that James Watt invented the method in 1780. (This date comes from Rhodes and Streeter, *Before Photocopying: The Art & History of Mechanical Copying, 1780–1938*, pp. 8–9.)

COPYRIGHT. A tremendously complex and evolving subject. In its simplest form, the word means ownership of the rights to a text or image. Those rights imply control of making copies of the text. A copyright holder may give or deny permission to someone else to reproduce the work she owns. The copyright holder may be anyone—not necessarily a person: the original author or creator, an heir to that person, a publisher, a law firm, an organization that the legitimate copyright holder has given the rights to, a sports team, an academic institution, and so on. (See Berger, chapter 8, "Legal Issues," esp. pp. 212–24.)

The subject has become increasingly complicated with digital texts (those digitized from analog sources and those born digital) and with the proliferation of technologies on which texts can be created, stored, moved, and shared—and manipulated. At root is the creator's (or copyright holder's) ability to control use in order to create income or for other reasons. (*See also* Fair use; Permissions.)

Also, copyright is not uniformly interpreted internationally: different countries have their own copyright laws. There are international copyright conventions. The U.S. Copyright Office website says, "Original works of expression that are eligible for copyright protection are protected under national copyright laws. Protection against unauthorized use in a particular country depends on the national laws of that country; in other words, copyright protection depends on the national laws where protection is sought. International copyright conventions and treaties have been developed to establish obligations for treaty member countries to adhere to, and implement in their national laws, thus providing more certainty and understanding about the levels of copyright protection in particular countries" (U.S. Copyright Office, "International Issues"; https://www.copyright.gov/international-issues/ [accessed 28 August 2022]). This is an important issue for booksellers, collectors, librarians, and others to know about since use of copyrighted materials for various purposes may be restricted.

COPYRIGHT EDITION. Carter mentions a special use of the term. To guarantee copyright protection of a work, the publisher may produce some copies before the commercial copies are released, and these few copies can be copyrighted though not made available through any formal (or even informal) channels. The copyrighted copies, of any kind of text, secure publishing rights for the publisher and will be deposited in the appropriate library (*see* Copyright library), with a filing of the proper paperwork and payments, with the U.S. Copyright Office, that of Great Britain, or both. (See Carter, p. 88.) One point that this raises is that copyright differs from one country to another, and securing copyright in the United States does not protect a text from being printed (PIRATED) in another country. Mark Twain, for example, sought simultaneous publication in the United States and England for *Pudd'nhead Wilson* so that he could have copyright protection in both countries. In effect, the edition published in Hartford, Connecticut, was a copyright edition (as it gave him copyright in the United States), and the text published by Chatto & Windus in London was another copyright edition, for it gave him control in Great Britain.

Also, as clarified in Berger (p. 263), "Carter's explanation is fine, but he needed to explain that most of the time the 'edition' sent in to gain copyright was not really a different edition at all; it was a printing of the very edition that would eventually come out that the 'copyright edition' was protecting. A more accurate term would have been *copyright version of the edition*." Additionally, the version sent to the copyright office (in the U.S., for may years, usually two copies were sent) was often an early printing of the edition. That is, publishers wanted the copyright to be in effect as soon as the text was published. For *Pudd'nhead Wilson and Those Extraordinary Twins*, the two copies sent to the copyright office had a text that differed from the one eventually published as the "first edition." The two copies for the copyright office had 433 pages; the rest of the edition had 432 pages. (See Berger, "Editorial Intrusion in *Pudd'nhead Wilson*.") (*See* WATCH.)

COPYRIGHT LIBRARY. A deposit library that receives copies of books and other copyrightable materials from publishers that wish to secure COPYRIGHT. The practice is old, going back to the 17th century in Great Britain. Its copyright libraries are the BRITISH LIBRARY, the National Library of Scotland, the National Library of Wales, the BODLEIAN LIBRARY in Oxford, the University Library in Cambridge, and Trinity College, Dublin (see British Library website, http://www.bl.uk/aboutus/legaldeposit/introduction [accessed 3 June 2021]). Copyright laws in the United States now inhere rights to any creation, whether copies are deposited in the Library of Congress or not. However, until that practice became law, two copies of books had to be sent to the Library of Congress along with a certain legal form and a payment of a fee. Today, a sketch on a restaurant napkin is under copyright the moment it is made, as are notes or drawings or anything else created by an author or artist or anyone else.

In the United States, according to the website Copyright.gov (an arm of the U.S. Copyright Office), "All works under copyright protection that are published in the United States are subject to the mandatory deposit provision of the copyright law (17 USC section 407). / This law requires that two copies of the best edition of every copyrightable work published in the United States be sent to the Copyright Office within three months of publication. Works deposited under this law are for the use of the Library of Congress. / Mandatory deposit applies to works first published in a foreign country at the point at which they are distributed in the United States" (see http://copyright.gov/mandatory [accessed 3 June 2021]). However, this "requirement" is loosely followed by many since copyright law in the United States protects items the moment they are created, without formal deposition of copies in the Copyright Office. Also, many a FINE PRESS or ARTIST'S BOOK creator cannot afford to give up two copies of extremely expensive books merely to obtain copyright protection. Further, as suggested above, "[a] work does not need to have been published for it to be under copyright protection" (see Berger, p. 212).

In Great Britain, "[b]y law, a copy of every UK print publication must be given to the British Library by its publishers, and to five other major libraries that request it. This system is called legal deposit and has been a part of English law since 1662. / From 6 April 2013, legal deposit also covers material published digitally and online, so that the Legal Deposit Libraries can provide a national archive of the UK's non-print published material, such as websites, blogs, e-journals and CD-ROMs" (see the British Library website cited above).

The early practice of depositing two copies has been useful to some scholars, for publishers may have sent to the Library of Congress early versions of texts so that copyright would be in place on publication. Early versions could represent texts before they were finally "settled upon" by their publishers or authors. (See Berger, "Editorial Intrusion in *Pudd'nhead Wilson*.")

COPY-TEXT. The version of a text chosen by a textual bibliographer (*see* Bibliography, especially the section "Textual bibliography") that is used as the basis for a new edition. The editor must have a base text to use into which she inserts EMENDATIONS. A substantial literature exists explaining what "copy-text" means and how an editor chooses an appropriate one. (See, e.g., Baender, "The Meaning of Copy-Text"; Bowers, "Current Theories of Copy-Text, with an Illustration from Dryden"; and Greg, "The Rationale of Copy-Text.") The copy-text could be a printed volume or a manuscript—or a combination of these. (See Berger, ed., "Textual Introduction," pp. 189–98.) It should be added that modern editorial practices may not require the editor to work from a copy-text. (See Tanselle, "Editing without a Copy-text.")

CORANTO. A single sheet of paper offering its readers news. Strictly speaking, this was not a BROADSIDE since it had text on both sides of the LEAF, while a broadside generally had text on one side only. "The general newsletter gradually became known as a coranto. A coranto consisted of a single leaf with the text in two columns on both sides. (The term 'coranto' comes from the French 'corante,' running or dance. In turn this came to mean anything done swiftly and currently. News printed quickly took the form of a courante, couranto or corant.) It flourished throughout Europe during the first part of the sixteenth century, but generally became an obsolete term by the seventeenth century. / The first extant coranto is the Strasbourg *Relation*, published in 1609. (An earlier version was probably published in the Netherlands in 1605, but no copies are extant.)" (Katz, *Cuneiform to Computer*, p. 337.)

CORDOBAN LEATHER. "Originally, a 'leather' that was basically alum-tawed hair sheepskin, usually of a naturally white color but also dyed red. It was first produced in Córdoba, Spain, by a combination of Arab and Spanish craftsmen following the Moorish invasion of the 8th century. Sometime during the 14th and 15th century the method of producing Cordoban changed from tawing to vegetable tannage. . . . The terms 'Cordoban,' 'Cordovan,' and 'Spanish leather' have been used in England for centuries to denote indiscriminately several kinds of leather, some imported from Spain, others from France and Holland, as well as some actually produced in England and called 'cordwain,' which is probably a corruption of the French *cordouan*" (Roberts and Etherington, p. 65).

CORDOVAN LEATHER (also called "Spanish calf"). "A soft, fine-grained, colored leather produced mainly from the shell of a horse butt, but now also produced from goat- and pigskin" (Roberts and Etherington, p. 65). Commonly used in bookbinding.

CORDS (in binding). "The cotton, hemp, linen, or silk cords or bands, of varying thicknesses, which extend across the backs of the gathered sections and are used in sewing books through the folds. They are either sunk into saw cuts in the sections, as in recessed-cord sewing, or rest against the sections to form the raised cords or bands used in flexible sewing" (Roberts and Etherington, p. 65). Note that three kinds of materials are drawn across the backs of the SIGNATURES: cords, tapes, or thongs. Cords are self-explanatory, TAPES are flat pieces of material, and THONGS are made from thin strips of leather. But the term "cords" is used generically to refer to all three. (*See* Endbands.) (For an image, *see* Catchwords.)

CORNERPIECE. A decorative stamp on the corners of the covers (front and back) of a binding, usually impressed with gold though often BLIND STAMPED. Sometimes the corner decorations match other stamping in the center of the cover. The term can also be used to mean pieces of metal that cover the corners of the book's boards to protect the volume from damage. BOSSES will protect the surfaces of the covers from being scuffed; these metal cornerpieces protect the corners if the volume is dropped.

CORNERS. This refers to the upper and lower, right-angled outer edges of the BOARDS of a hardcover book. Mentioned in BOOKSELLERS' CATALOGS usually when they are damaged. (Why bring them up if they are perfect? No book description would say, "Corners in fine shape" unless they are traditionally in poor condition on most of the copies of this item.) They might also be mentioned if they are decorated in some way: "Corners in red vellum." (*See* Tips.)

CORRIGENDUM/CORRIGENDA. Corrections made in a volume, usually printed after the whole text has been printed. The corrigendum (singular) or corrigenda (plural) are TIPPED IN, LAID IN, or printed in, almost always at the end of the volume (though tipped-in or laid-in slips of corrections can be placed anywhere). (*See* Addendum/Addenda; Erratum/Errata.) In the production of a book, a printer might spot an error and stop the press to correct it. (*See* Stop-press correction.) This creates a second state of the text since the text now exists with some copies containing the error, some without it. (*See* Edition, Impression [Printing], Issue, and State; Points.) In fact, with many stop-press corrections and many errors corrected, the text can exist in many states.

COSWAY BINDINGS. "Leather bookbindings produced in the usual manner, except that they have miniature paintings inset into their covers. They are named after Richard Cosway (c. 1742–1821), the English miniaturist. Cosway actually had nothing to do with the execution of these bindings, as they were not introduced until early in the 20th century. They were probably the invention of the firm of Henry Sotheran, booksellers, or their manager, J. Harrison Stonehouse. The books were bound by Robert Rivière, in good quality Levant morocco, with morocco joints, watered-silk linings, and the miniatures painted on ivory, glazed, and insetted in the covers" (Roberts and Etherington, p. 66). Because these volumes are in high demand, a host of such bindings are "out there," and it is sometimes difficult to determine whether such a binding is a true Cosway (i.e., from Sotheran's).

COTTAGE BINDING. A style of decoration on a book cover that looks like a cottage. That is, in the stamping into the cover, "the top and bottom of a center rectangular panel slope away from a broken center, producing a kind of gabled effect. . . . Although this style of decoration may have originated in France, perhaps as early as 1630, it is most characteristic of English binding of the late 17th century (c 1660) to about 1710. The style was still being used on pocket almanacs and devotional books as late as, or even later than, 1822" (Roberts and Etherington, p. 66).

COUCH/COUCHING/COUCHER. The couch (in papermaking) (rhymes with "mooch") is the flat (or sometimes slightly convexly curved) surface on which the VATMAN presses the paper MOLD that has a recently formed sheet of paper on it. The couch has a FELT on its surface to which the wet sheet is transferred. The process is called "couching" (rhymes with "mooching"), and the word can be a verb: "to couch a sheet." The activity is done by a coucher. As the vatman forms the sheets, she hands the mold to the coucher for couching. As the couching is done, the pile of newly formed sheets, interleaved with felts, creates the POST of papers.

COUNTER (in a piece of type). The area of a SORT that is surrounded by the printed character. That is, letters, numbers, and other figures with an open, nonprinting bowl have a counter: A, B, C, D, G, O, P, Q, R, S, U, a, b, c, d, g, h, m, n, o, p, q, s, u, 4, 6, 8, 9, ?, and others. The nonprinting area need not be fully enclosed to have a counter. (*See* Appendix B.) *Counter* was also the title of a short-lived (1994–2001) bibliographic newsletter from the University of Iowa Center for the Book, edited by KIM MERKER.

COUNTERMARK. One of two WATERMARKS in a sheet of paper. Many sheets will have two separate watermarks, one in the center of each half of a sheet. The primary one (e.g., with an image of an animal, a building, a crown, etc.) is the watermark, and the other (e.g., the name of the papermaker, date, city of manufacture, etc.) is the countermark. (For an image of a countermark, *see* Laid paper.)

COUNTERPUNCH. In type making, the COUNTER is an open area in a character. The punchcutter (*see* Punch/punchcutter) must remove the metal on the end of the punch from the character's counter. It is difficult or impossible to do this with files and other standard punchcutting tools, but another punch, the shape of the counter, is created and used to "punch out" the metal in the counter on the punch. The second punch, in the shape of the counter, is called the "counterpunch."

COUNTERSUNK. "A bookbinding having a panel sunk or depressed below the surface of the covering material, and designed to take an inlay, label, or the like" (Roberts and Etherington, p. 67). The idea is that whatever is added to the binding's cover will be flush with the rest of the cover's surface.

COURTESY BOOK. (Also called a "book of manners" or a "conduct book.") From time immemorial, some people have been boors. They needed to be shown some manners, and, necessity being the source of invention, books were created to show them the error of their ways. (I have always believed, Once a boor, always a boor; and such people would not take kindly to being told, "You're being an ass; read this book and it will help you to be a better person.") The earliest such book is possibly that of the ancient Egyptian 12th Dynasty (1938–c. 1756 BCE) volume *The Teachings of Ptahhotep*, the words of an older person to guide youth in their thinking and actions. (See "Teaching of Ptahhotep," https://www.ucl.ac.uk/museums-static/digitalegypt/literature/ptahhotep.html [accessed 21 January 2021]). In the Middle Ages a whole genre of books emerged to guide society on education, morals, and proper conduct in all social realms. (See Clark and Ashley, *Medieval Conduct.*) Some were more narrowly directed, as were those aimed at women. (See Hallissy, *Clean Maids, True Wives, Steadfast Widows: Chaucer's Women and Medieval Codes of Conduct.*) One of the most famous of these books was that of Baldassare Castiglione, *Il Cortegiano* (The Book of the Courtier), containing conversations about what constitutes the perfect courtier or Lady (with a capital "L"). As a fairly ancient genre, these books have had a long run—with those of Emily Post leading the modern pack. Her first one was *Etiquette in Society, in Business, in Politics, and at Home* (1922), and her influence has been pervasive ever since. In all matters of manners, one might ask, "What would Emily Post say?"

COVER. The outer binding of a book. A book is "in covers" when it has a hard or soft binding around the TEXT BLOCK. Covers can be of wood, cardboard, leather, vellum, paper, stiffened cloth (stiffened by being lined with some material, such as paper), metal, plastic, or other material. (There is a book whose semi-circular covers are made from vinyl—they come from a vinyl record.) The cover often has on it some kind of "text," such as a title, author, publisher, date, or image, and it can be used for advertising purposes (as with a BLURB). Roberts and Etherington say, "In edition and library binding, the term *CASE* is more appropriate" (p. 67). Although booksellers will often say, "In paper covers," the term should be construed as singular. (*See* Wrapper.)

In the plural, a bookseller may say "Covers bound in" when a volume has been rebound for some reason (to repair a damaged copy; to remove an inexpensive binding and replace it with a more sumptuous one), and the binder has saved the original cover for any reason. It is particularly common in academic libraries that acquire PAPERBACKS and have them rebound in BUCKRAM. If the paper cover contained important information of any kind, the library may wish to retain that information.

CPSCM. (*Cum privilegio Sacrae Caesaris Maiestatis.*) The term was added to the abbreviations of the ninth edition of Carter's *ABC*, with the note that it means "privileged within the jurisdiction of the Holy Roman Emperors" (p. 18). This is all that is given, and it needs expansion to explain what that jurisdiction is, what years are referred to, and what that PRIVILEGE meant. Apparently it meant that publishers were granted permission to go to press with the text to which this was attached.

To elucidate the abbreviation, I googled it and found (after the entry for Center for Primary Care and Sports Medicine and for Catholic Pastoral Committee on Sexual Minorities) a reference to CPSCM on the website of the Malta Map Society: "Used in the area within the jurisdiction of the Holy Roman Emperor," the apparent source of the Carter reference. (See Malta Map Society, https://maltamapsociety.mt/glossary/terms-for-copyright/ [accessed 31 July 2021]). Modern booksellers, collectors, and librarians will probably not be using this term, nor the others cited in Carter (CPES and CPR [*Cum privilegio Excellentissime Senatus* and *Cum privilegio Regis*]). But they at least needed some explanation.

These terms *do* belong in Carter, however, and in the present dictionary since any bookseller, collector, librarian, scholar, or other reader working with old books and prints might find the terms or abbreviations in an old reference volume of some sort or printed in the original source, and we need to know where they come from and what they mean.

The jurisdiction of these privileges is international: anywhere in which the Holy Roman Church has its authority, which is where their ministers publish. Acquiring ecclesiastical PRIVILEGE was necessary for early book producers and print makers. Such privilege (permission to publish) could keep them in business—indeed, could keep their heads out of nooses. The terms apparently date to the 16th and 17th centuries, as Ad Stijnman shows. (See Stijnman, "Terms in Print Addresses.") He says that many of the abbreviations in his publication "can be found from 1500. . . . These expressions are usually found in the lower margins of ENGRAVINGS, ETCHINGS and LITHOGRAPHS, less in WOODCUTS and wood engravings, rarely in metalcuts" (p. 2 of the printed text that is referenced in the online source cited above). And they could also appear in printed books, on the images bound in or on the title pages. Privileges to publish seem to have begun around 1550. Stijnman adds that privileges were created "to secure copyrights; sometimes the number of years for which the privilege is valid is given . . ., sometimes the privilege is only given for a town; . . . also used for censorship." And there were different kinds of privilege: to print, "publication according to the law," "with imperial privilege ([as with the] Holy Roman Empire)," "with imperial (and royal) privilege," "with multiple privileges," specifically "with papal privilege," "with permission of Italian authorities," "with privilege (general)," with privileges of authorities in particular countries, and "without privilege" (Stijnman, pp. 10–13). Each of these had its own locutions and abbreviations. So for Thadani to have cited only a few was provocative but wanting. Readers will need to have access to the Stijnman text (as they now do, with its URL cited in the bibliography) if they wish to expand the abbreviations they find in these older texts. (The Index that Stijnman provides [pp. 18–53] shows hundreds of abbreviations and phrases with how they are to be interpreted. E.g., "ap nat. = "after nature"; "dddt" = "has dedicated.")

CRACKLE/CRAQUELURE. The network of fine cracks over the surface of a smooth image (often one in heavy pigments, printed or painted) caused by the drying out and cracking of the binding agents of the pigments. This can sometimes be seen in glossy photographs tipped into books or on the glossy surface of a painted binding. The English word is preferred, though the French word *craquelure* may show up in a catalog or book description. (See Getty Art and Architecture Thesaurus Online.)

CRASH. *See* Mull.

CREPE PAPER; CREPE PAPER BOOKS. A strong, thin paper that has been crimped in such a way that when it is stretched it has the feel of rubbery retraction. It has many uses, many of which are for celebratory purposes: garlands, ribbons, table fringes, hats, and so forth. It has been used in bookbinding, as well. But mostly—for the present volume—it was the primary material in the printing and binding of a host of volumes produced in Japan (where the paper was apparently invented) in the late 19th and early 20th centuries. The books were produced by several publishers, but the most famous of them was Takejiro Hasegawa, whose hundreds of titles were beautifully printed on KOZO paper. The paper was then creped, reducing the size of the sheet (copies of the texts on uncreped paper exist, and they are, of course, larger than the same titles on crepe paper). The creping also intensified the colors, while not affecting the sharpness of the illustrations. (See Frederic A. Sharf, *Takejiro Hasegawa: Meiji Japan's Preeminent Publisher of Wood-block-illustrated Crepe-paper Books.*) (These volumes are called *Chirimen-bon* in Japanese.) The books were mostly small (c. 6 × 4 in.), though there were larger ones of various sizes and some MINIATURES as well, including calendars. The original series, in English, German, and French, were retellings of Japanese children's fairy tales. Eventually Hasegawa expanded the line to create the volumes in other languages. (George C. Baxley cites publications in English, French, German, Spanish, Danish, Dutch, Swedish, Portuguese, Italian, and Russian. He also cites at least 10 other publishers of these books, beside Hasegawa.)

The foremost expert on these beautiful volumes is George C. Baxley, whose collection is one of the most complete in the United States (along with that of the Phillips Library at the Peabody Essex Museum in Salem, Massachusetts). Baxley says: "Takejiro Hasegawa (1853–1938) had a long association with Western missionaries and Westerners in Tokyo. It is through this association that he started printing WOODBLOCK illustrated books in the Western languages. Initially Hasegawa's books were published under the 'Kobunsha' imprint (Minami Saegi-cho and Maruya-cho, Kyobashi-ku, Tokyo) but in the 1889–1890 period the name was changed to T. Hasegawa (Hasegawa & Co.) and a number of addresses appear over the years. Books are found that were published ca 1928 which bear the imprint of 'T. Hasegawa & Son, Publishers & Art Printers' or 'T. Hasegawa & Son' with the 17 Kami Negishi, Tokyo address. On Hasegawa's death in 1938 (but perhaps as early as 1917/18) the firm operated under the name of Hasegawa and Nishinomiya, and subsequently Nishinomiya and Hasegawa" (George C. Baxley, "Takejiro Hasegawa/Kobunsha Publications: 'Chirimen-bon' [Crepe Paper Books] and Plain Paper Books").

Hasegawa "was inspired to publish seven of these stories in his own series. Hasegawa realized that as Japan was opening its doors to foreign commerce, a new market was emerging in Japan for educational books in English, French and German. In 1884, he started his own publishing business to help Japanese students learn western [*sic*] languages. The first 12 volumes of his Japanese fairy tale series were published in the mid-1880s, with the cover title printed in English to reach a Western market. Hasegawa's work was well-received due to the growing Western market for published material about Japan. / Additionally, at the time of the series' publication, Western interest was drawing from Japanese aesthetics, ideas, and artistic techniques, resulting in a genre known as Japonisme. Artists in the West pulled from and reflected Japanese culture in their interpretations on canvas. The trend was appreciated and consumed by the higher society of the Western hemisphere" (Linda Lear Center, Digital Collections and Exhibitions, "Takejiro Hasegawa and the Production of Crepe Paper Books"). The crepe paper books have become immensely COLLECTIBLE. (See Riccardo, *Takejiro Hasegawa e le fiabe giapponesi del Museo Stibbert* [Takejiro Hasegawa and the Japanese Fairy Tales Collection of the Stibbert Museum]; and Espinosa and Cruz, comps., *Cuentos del Japón Viejo*; Byrne, "Chirimon-bon or Crêpe Paper Books.")

CRIPPLES. *See* Used copy/Used-book store.

CRISP. Carter has an entry for this word, designating the texture of paper, which he linked to "unpressed." The word "crisp" occasionally appears in the vocabulary of book people today; one might hear someone talk about the RATTLE of paper that is stiff, as with heavily SIZED LEAVES of a book. The word is also featured in descriptions of volumes that are PRISTINE, their "crispness" being metaphorical for fresh and new, as with "a crisp new 20-dollar bill." I would rather have a crisp copy of a book than a wilted one.

CRITICAL APPARATUS. The non-textual part of a critical edition. (*See* Bibliography.) The editor takes a COPY-TEXT and edits it. The editorial practices the editor has employed must be delineated. All EMENDATIONS entered into the copy-text must be recorded for the reader's edification and information. All emendations that could have been made from textual VARIANTS but were not should be listed. Editorial decisions that need to be explained should be recorded in notes. And a great deal more information than this should be presented to a reader to reveal the extent of the editor's contributions to the final edited version of a text. All of this, along with an introduction, preface, and explanation of other work done in the production of the published version constitute the critical apparatus—often referred to merely as the *apparatus*.

CRITICAL EDITION. *See* Bibliography.

CROPPED (in binding and rebinding). Trimmed, as with the DECKLES from a sheet of paper or from a volume printed with deckle-edged paper. The term means that the deckles have been removed. The term is also used to indicate when any other part of a book has been trimmed in its production, as in "tipped-in copperplates, cropped to the PLATE MARKS." The aim of cropping is to remove some of the edges of the LEAF (or leaves), but there are times when a binder or butcher goes overboard, and one might see, "Cropped at the HEAD, removing most or all of the RUNNING HEADS" or "Margins cropped, removing contemporary MARGINALIA."

Books may be delivered IN SHEETS to a binder. The sheets may be folded or not, but if they are, BOLTS are created at the head, FORE-EDGE, and/or FOOT of the SIGNATURES, and these bolts must be removed. Hence, the cropping cuts them away, with the possible loss of more of the margins than the printer desired, affecting the layout of the page and possibly removing some of the printing from the pages. A book with its bolts intact is said to be "UNOPENED." A book with its deckles in place is said to be "untrimmed" or "UNCUT."

Cropped text. An example of a manuscript leaf cropped at the head, with the loss of some of the foliation. From an unidentified manuscript at the Phillips Library, Peabody Essex Museum.

Courtesy of Phillips Library, Peabody Essex Museum.

An example of a manuscript leaf cropped at the foot, with the loss of pretty much the entire last line. From an unidentified manuscript at the Phillips Library, Peabody Essex Museum.

Courtesy of Phillips Library, Peabody Essex Museum.

CROWN. The top edge of a book's SPINE. (*See* Headcap.)

CRUSHED (as in leathers for binding). A term designating the surface texture of certain leathers, as with crushed morocco or crushed levant. The crushing leaves the leather perfectly smooth. Roberts and Etherington say, "Such leather has an unnatural appearance and is now seldom used in craft bookbinding" (p. 69).

CRUSHED LEVANT. *See* Crushed.

CRUSHED MOROCCO. *See* Crushed.

CRUX. *See* Bibliography.

CRYODESICCATION. *See* Freeze drying.

CSE (Center for Scholarly Editions). *See* CEAA.

CUALA PRESS. An Irish PRIVATE PRESS, established in 1908 by Elizabeth (Lolly) Yeats, with support from her brother, William Butler Yeats. It was first called Dun Emer Press (from 1903–1908, having been established by Evelyn Gleeson). It played an important role in the Celtic Revival. The press closed in 1973. Gleeson's original impetus was to train "women to work in a useful trade while at the same time preserving Irish cultural heritage." When the Yeats sisters took over Dun Emer they continued her work. "[T]hey produced and printed numerous Celtic-themed works and materials by well-known Irish authors including WB, Lady Gregory, Frank O'Connor, J. M. Synge, and Douglas Hyde" (Villanova University, Falvey Memorial Library, "Jack Butler Yeats"). (See Miller, *A Brief Account of the Cuala Press Formerly the Dun Emer Press, Founded by Elizabeth Corbett Yeats in 1903.*)

CUIR-BOUILLI. "A method of decorating a book utilizing the capability of a vegetable tanned LEATHER to be molded when wet. After being thoroughly softened in water the leather can be formed or molded into various shapes, which, on drying, retain those shapes with a remarkable degree of permanence. The wet-mold leather can be more permanently set by drying it under moderate heat, the degree of rigidity obtained being determined by the drying temperature" (Roberts and Etherington, "cuir-bouille"; https://cool.culturalheritage.org/don/dt/dt0921.html [accessed 11 March 2021]). As Roberts and Etherington say, another method is to soak the skin in boiling water, producing the same result (and giving the technique its name: boiled leather). The leather can be hardened in this three-dimensional form in such a way that it does not need to be attached to BOARDS.

CUIR-CISELÉ. "A method of decorating a bookbinding in which the design is cut into dampened leather instead of being tooled or blocked. The design is first outlined with a pointed tool and then dampened. It is then brought into relief by depressing the background, usually by stamping a succession of dots into the leather very close together by means of a pointed tool. Certain parts of the design are sometimes EMBOSSED from the flesh side of the leather, and in such cases the decorating must be done before covering. / This technique of embellishment, which may well have been the highest manifestation of the medieval bookbinder's art, was widely practiced only during the 15th century and only in certain areas, principally southeastern Germany and in Spain. No English and Flemish and practically no Italian examples are known" (Roberts and Etherington, "cuir-ciselé"; https://cool.culturalheritage.org/don/dt/dt0922.html [accessed 21 January 2021]).

CUMMINGTON PRESS. *See* Duncan, Harry.

CUM PRIVILEGIO. *See* CPSCM; Privilege/Privilege leaf.

CUNEIFORM. A system of writing that "flourished in the Near East from before 3000 BC to AD 75" (BLURB from rear cover of C. B. F. Walker, *Cuneiform*). The characters were incised into clay tablets, seals, or monuments. (The word itself means "wedge-shaped.") "Eighty-five per cent of the tablets from the early levels at Uruk [in Sumer] are economic and are concerned with the income and outgoings of the city's temples in terms of food, livestock and textiles. . . . [I]t has been possible to identify a large number of place names known from the later history of Sumer, mostly written within the vicinity of Uruk, but including Kish and Eshnunna to the north, Aratta (somewhere in the mountains of Iran), and Dilmun (modern Bahrein). Fifteen per cent of the texts are lexical texts, including the names of various commodities, animals and officials. These lists were presumably compiled to establish and teach a definitive system of writing recognizable to every scribe" (Walker, p. 5). Not all cuneiform texts have been fully understood. "The early texts are not written in neat lines with every sign in the appropriate order—that came later—but with all the signs for each sense unit (or sentence) grouped together in a box" (p. 5). (*See* Clay tablets.)

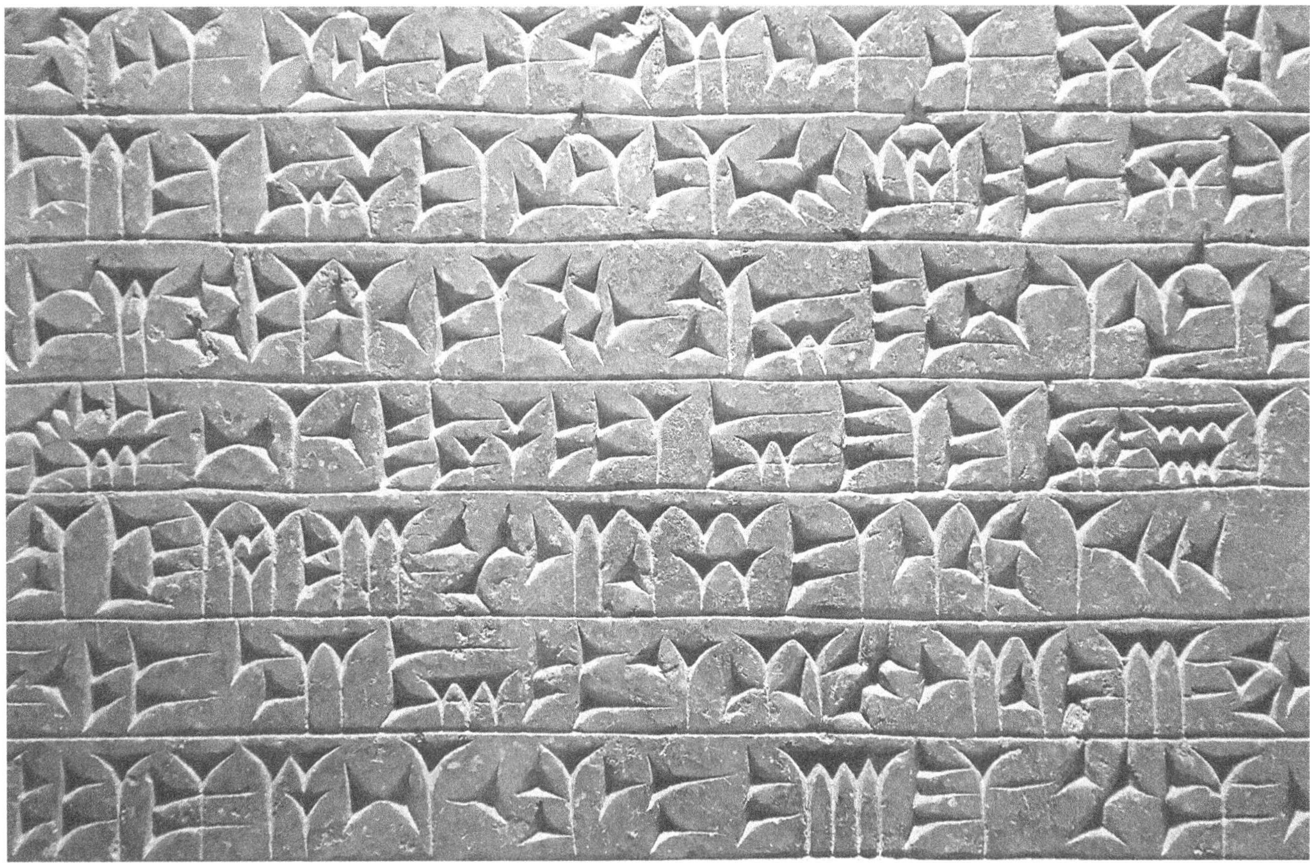

Cuneiform. Sumerian cuneiform writing.

Courtesy of iStock, https://www.istockphoto.com/search/2/image?phrase=sumerian%20cuneiform&family=creative (accessed 12 July 2021).

Modern facsimile of a cuneiform tablet, incised by Mark van Stone.

Collection of the author.

CURIOSA. A euphemism for items (books, pamphlets, prints, or other kinds of objects, such as decks of playing cards) that are of a risqué nature. If they are in a legitimate rare-book room or a serious collector's serious collection, they would not be called "pornography." "Curiosa" gives them a legitimacy. In the United States, following movie ratings, one might hear the term "X-rated" for pieces of curiosa. (*See* Erotica.)

CURSES (Book curses). Imprecations, often penned or printed into volumes, or TIPPED-IN on LABELS, warning people not to steal or disfigure the books the curses are in. The curse acted as a threat to potential thieves, warning them that if they stole or mutilated a volume they would be excommunicated or punished in some way. "If you steal this book may you suffer rabies; have harpies screech in your ears forever; have your eyes pecked out by ravens to perpetuity; suffer stomach cramps so severe that you can't stand up; have worms eat your entrails; have bill collectors knock on your door 24 hours a day; have to listen to your most hated TV station round the clock; and learn that the book you crave that has eluded you for decades has just been sold to another buyer" (or something like this). The Medieval Manuscript Blog of the British Library says, "During the Middle Ages, the fate of both your body and soul could have been at serious risk. Medieval librarians often added curses to their books upon those who did not return or damaged borrowed books, or stole them from their libraries. These curses usually invoked God, suggesting that these punishments would be made effective with divine authority" (British Library, Medieval Manuscript Blog, "Frying Pans, Forks and Fever: Medieval Book Curses"). The curses threatened physical punishments of the most gruesome sorts, and—even more frightening for many—eternal damnation and the scourging of the soul. The British Library blog entry concludes, "The use of these book curses seemingly sits at odds with the monastic lifestyle. Medieval monks dedicated their lives to imitating Christ, including his virtues of patience, forgiveness and love for mankind. The fact that monks used these curses testifies to the immense material and spiritual value that they attributed to their libraries: their books had not only been extremely costly and labour-intensive to produce, but often they also contained the only copies of a particular work to which their communities had access. The loss of a book did not only mean a material loss, but it could have permanently deprived a religious community of a work of knowledge that was essential for preserving or developing its religious identity. This may explain why some religious communities went to great lengths to protect their books. Book curses were a radical but effective way of preserving their book collections." (See *Steale Not Thys Book.*)

CURWEN PAPERS. *See* Curwen Press.

CURWEN PRESS. One of England's excellent fine and commercial presses, producing books and posters along with many kinds of ephemera. "John Curwen started his printing business in Plaistow in east London in 1863 to print music. It was incorporated as J. Curwen & Sons in 1897. Harold Curwen (1885–1949) took over the business in 1914 and began a specialism in well-designed jobbing work. After 1920, Oliver Simon (1895–1956) extended Curwen's reputation for good typography and design to book-work. The Press employed many important artists and designers, notable among whom were Claud Lovat Fraser, Barnett Freedman, Edward Bawden, Albert Rutherston, and Edward Ardizzone. The original directors were Harold Curwen, and Oliver and his brother Herbert Simon (1898–1974). The business suffered extensive war damage. Owing partly to its costs in London, the business was never highly profitable. In 1964 it merged with M. R. Harley & Co. and in 1965 Basil Harley became managing director. Under him, Curwen developed its business in high-quality colour lithography, notably for natural-history illustration. Letterpress work gradually declined in importance. Curwen Prints Ltd, a workshop for the production of artists' prints, became a separate business in 1968. In the 1970s various plans were considered, but never carried out, for the Curwen Press to be taken over by other printers. A merger of the letterpress department with the John Roberts Press was likewise planned then abandoned in 1981. The printers' strike of 1980 inflicted a final blow to the firm's financial position. It had a brief respite under a new owner Harry Myers in 1982, but finally went into receivership in 1984" (University of Cambridge, ArchiveSearch, "Curwen Press"). Others who worked at the press were Eric Ravilious, Paul Nash, and Barnett Freedman. "In 1933 the Curwen Press Ltd separated from J. Curwen & Sons which continued as a music publisher until 1969)." "The Curwen Studio survives as an independent studio" (RA: The Royal Academy, "The Curwen Press," https://www.royalacademy.org.uk/art-artists/organisation/the-curwen-press [accessed 29 June 2021]).

"1922 was the beginning of the Curwen Press's golden decade, during which it produced *The Woodcutter's Dog*, . . . the exhibition catalogue of books and manuscripts for The First Edition Club, Goldoni's *Four Comedies* and the delightful little pocket engagement book, *The Four Seasons*, and many other fine books. . . . Following restructuring in 1933 the Curwen Press had a further forty years of distinguished work" (Harold Curwen and Oliver Simon Curwen Press data sheet; http://www.accdistribution.com/uk/store/productdatasheet/9781851495719 [accessed 3 June 2021]).

When Oliver Simon joined the firm in 1920, the press output achieved great repute for the loveliness of its books. Further, Curwen papers, block printed in various designs and colors, became the rage in bookbinding, and they were sold to other publishers and bookbinders to adorn thousands of volumes. (See Gilmour, *Artists at Curwen*; Powers, *Art & Print*; and Webb and Skipwith, *Design*.)

One of the signature achievements of the press was its production of decorated papers. They were designed by many of the important artists of the day, including Enid Marx, Edward Bawden, Harry Carter, Lovat Fraser, Elisabeth Friedlander, E[mil] O[tto] Hoppe, Margaret James, Thomas Lowinsky, Paul Nash, Eric Ravilious, and others. These were used on countless books as binding papers. (See McKitterick, *A New Specimen Book of Curwen Pattern Papers*.)

CUT. An illustration, as in "ZINC CUT" or "WOODCUT." The implication is that the illustration has been done by hand (i.e., it was *cut* by hand), but the illustration could be done by photographic means as well.

The term can also apply to sheets of paper from which the deckles have been removed—usually in the negative: "With edges uncut." (*See* Uncut.)

CUT-CORNER PAMPHLET FILE. "A free-standing type of box, the upper rear corners of the sides of which are cut away to half its height, leaving the upper half of the back and the top open. It is generally used to house pamphlets and other such materials in the book stack" (Roberts and Etherington, "cut corner pamphlet file"; https://cool.culturalheritage.org/don/dt/dt0943.html [accessed 18 January 2021]). (*See also* "Princeton file" under Book shoe.)

CUT-IN INDEX. *See* Thumb index.

CUTTER EXPANSIVE CLASSIFICATION. A system of classification for book cataloging created by Charles Ammi Cutter (1837–1903). The system, of course, helps librarians arrange their holdings in a logical way so that they can be searched in a catalog and found on the shelves. "The system that Cutter developed was in seven stages (of which he fully developed the first six before his death in 1903), each geared to a different-sized library, and a library adopting one scheme could move easily to the next level as its collection grew. The system was logical and eminently implementable. The Library of Congress used many of the features of the Cutter system for its own Library of Congress Classification. Cutter died just before completing the full description of the system, and his system did not catch on as did Dewey's system because Cutter died before it was completely finished, making no provision for the kind of development necessary as the bounds of knowledge expanded and scholarly emphases changed throughout the twentieth century" (LaMontagne, *American Library Classification*, p. 226).

CYLINDER SEALS. *See* Seals.

D

DAGGER/DOUBLE DAGGER. *See* Footnote.

DAMP/DAMPING. Most printing papers are SIZED, mostly to prevent the FEATHERING of ink into the sheets that occurs on unsized papers. But sized paper can make it a challenge to get a good impression of the type since the sizing material can inhibit the ink from adhering to the somewhat "slick" surface of a sized paper. Damping the sheet softens the sizing and makes it easy for the ink to adhere to the sheet. Amateur (and often inexperienced) printers, having trouble getting a good impression in their printing, may increase the amount of ink they use. This might work to get an improved impression, but it can lead to exceptionally dark inking, with some of the ink filling the COUNTERS of the SORTS, and with smudging of ink that has taken longer to dry than the printer had left time for. Most of the time the printer needed only to dampen the sheets, and then she could actually *reduce* the amount of ink she used, and still achieve a superior impression. The operation, called "printing damp," has two possible drawbacks if it is done carelessly. First, too much damping and then improper handling of the sheet after the impression is made could leave the sheets COCKLED. Second, the sheets need to sit for some time under pressure before printing so that the water introduced into them (with a sponge, for instance) disperses evenly through each sheet and all of the sheets damped at one time for a single PRESSRUN. If the atmosphere is not properly vented and clean, and if the sheets are left for too long a time without being printed and interleaved with blotters (or hung up to dry) to remove the moisture, the sheets could mildew. (*See* Mold.) Some printers dampen their sheets one day and print the next, leaving the sheets in a special container called a "damp box," a closed box that may be lined with sponges or rags.

DANDY ROLL. On a FOURDRINIER—a papermaking machine—the dandy roll is a cylinder that hovers over the pulp that is forming the sheet on the mesh beneath it as the water drains out during sheet formation. The turning dandy roll has a raised pattern on it that disperses the fibers before the water has fully drained and while the fibers are still "dispersible," creating places in the sheet where the fibers are thinner than they are around where the pattern on the dandy roll is. That is, the sheet is created with a WATERMARK where the dandy roll has thinned out the fibers on the forming sheet. The paper made on such a machine is wove paper since the mesh of a fourdrinier is a woven screen, but the dandy roll can "imprint" the sheet with the pattern of LAID LINES, making the sheet look like MODERN LAID (i.e., HANDMADE) paper. The dandy roll cannot fabricate the look of ANTIQUE LAID PAPER, but it can make all sorts of watermarks. (*See also* Chain lines; Wire lines.)

DATABASE OF BOOKBINDINGS. A useful and extensive database showing images and giving descriptions of the bindings in the British Library. The Library's website says, "The British Library holds one of the world's leading collections of fine and historic bindings. Numbering in their thousands, the bindings are included in discrete specialist collections and dispersed individually throughout the Library's holdings. / The database is a work in progress and some records are incomplete. Amendments will be incorporated and additions made whenever possible. / At present, coverage includes selected bindings on western European printed books. . . . / Not all significant bindings have been included. Images have only been provided where condition and suitability for digitisation allow. Spines of bookbindings have not normally been digitised" (British Library, "Database of Bookbindings"). The site adds: "This database is a finding aid to the British Library's bookbindings. It aims to provide information and images of selected bindings of books printed in western Europe from the fifteenth century to date. Bindings of other formats (notably manuscripts) and from other regions (including Asia, the Middle East and Africa) will gradually be added, presenting a more representative sample from the Library's rich collection. The Library's partner, the National Library of the Netherlands has contributed some of its unparalleled Dutch bindings. The database is a work in progress and its scope will be widened as resources allow"; https://www.bl.uk/catalogues/bookbindings/Default.aspx [accessed 5 April 2021]). The site is searchable by many key terms, and almost every record retrieved has a thumbnail image (that can be enlarged), with information about the material of the binding, bibliographical data, the subcollection the item is in, and much more.

DATING. Ascertaining the dates of manuscripts or printed books can be a tedious and imprecise exercise. Even books with printed dates in them cannot always be trusted, as the publications (FORGERIES) of THOMAS WISE and HARRY BUXTON FORMAN showed. In an unpublished study (*The Dating of Medieval Manuscripts*), Berger demonstrated over a hundred means of determining a precise or (much more commonly) an approximate date of manuscripts. Any phenomenon that changes over time—handwriting, clothing, jewelry, architecture, type styles, sculpture, placement of text on a page, use of colors or particular materials, and scores of other things—can help a scholar narrow down a date for an undated (or inaccurately dated) piece. Carter and Pollard (*An Enquiry*) showed that the earliest use of esparto grass in papermaking could be dated and that any item printed on paper made from this grass but dated before this paper was commercially available could not be genuine; it had to be forgery. They also proved forgeries on the basis of the use of a typeface that was designed at a particular date but that was used in pamphlets with dates before that of the type's design.

Bibliographically, estblishing a date can be important to show where in a series of manifestations of a TEXT each such version belongs. (*See* Bibliography.) This can help the textual editor establish PRIORITY and thus help her to recognize AUTHORIAL readings (usually the earlier ones) from those introduced by an editor. And of course, most collectors are keen to acquire the items they seek in their earliest appearance, as the entry at CHRONOLIGICAL OBSESSION shows.

Handwriting is often the first thing that scholars turn to for MANUSCRIPTS to determine the date, but, as noted, there are many other features of manuscript (and printed) materials that can help one date a piece. Style of illustration, watermarks (if the item is on paper), and the placement of elements on the printed page (SIGNATURES, page numbers, CATCHWORDS, and RUNNING HEADS) may also be useful in determining a date. Binding styles and materials can be revealing. Also, certain technology can be employed, as with carbon dating, the use of other technology to reveal watermarks, or an examination of the materials that were used in an item's production. There are also stylistic/aesthetic features of items that can help one date a piece. Certain trends in printing, typeface design, page layout, illustration, language, ornaments, use of PAGINATION OR FOLIATION, and much more—all of which evolve over time and are tied to general periods of book creation—can be useful in showing (or suggesting) an approximate date. And external evidence can be extremely valuable—such things as the archives of printers and publishers, correspondence and biographical studies of authors, information gleaned from acquisition records of libraries (especially depository libraries [*see* Copyright library]), and so on—and a world of historical and scientific writing on all subjects may help one determine when a work was written or published.

A careful bibliographer seeking to determine the date of an item may have to consult experts in any of hundreds of disciplines. A scholar looking at a medieval manuscript showing a horseman may need to consult an expert in armor to find out when the weapons the rider is depicted with were in use or consult an expert in blacksmithing to see when a particular kind of stirrup or saddle was first used.

At best, a relatively close date may be determined (if it is not clearly written in the text). For example, in a manuscript illumination or in the written text, a historical figure may be depicted or mentioned at a particular event that can be precisely dated. That will give the scholar the *terminus a quo*—the earliest date at which the item could have been made. (This person could not have been depicted at this event *before it took place*.) Likewise, it is possible to show the latest date that a text could have been created (the *terminus ad quem*). For example, if a writer speaks of a person in the present tense and historical documents prove that that person died on a particular date, we can assume (but not with perfect certainty) that the person was still alive when the author was writing; hence, the person's death date would be the *terminus ad quem* for the piece if we presume that the author would have used past-tense verbs if the person he was writing about were deceased. Clearly, these examples show the imprecision of dating in many instances. (*See* Roman numerals.)

Another issue pertaining to date has to do with the calendars in use in the places in which dates are assigned. Scholars need to be aware of the difference between the Julian and the Gregorian calendar, the former promulgated by Julius Caesar and first used in 45 BC. The Julian calendar required a leap year to account for time gained each year.

Pope Gregory, in 1582, established the use of what came to be called the Gregorian calendar. It is "the most widely used calendar in the world today. It is a solar calendar based on a 365-day common year divided into 12 months of irregular lengths. . . . The Julian calendar's formula to calculate leap years produced a leap year every four years. This is way too often, and eventually the Julian calendar was 24 days out of sync with the fixed dates for astronomical events like equinoxes and solstices and important religious holidays, like Easter. The introduction of the Gregorian calendar allowed for the realignment with events like the Vernal equinox and Winter solstice" (timeanddate.com; http://www.timeanddate.com/calendar/gregorian-calendar.html [accessed 4 June 2021]).

Dates cited using the Gregorian calendar are designated "New Style" (often abbreviated "NS"), and those of the Julian Calendar are called "OLD STYLE" (or "OS"). A Jesuit mathematician, Christopher Clavius, working with other scholars, calculated that the Julian calendar had been so imprecise that the new one needed to bring its designations of dates "up to date." "In order to restore March 20 or 21 as the day of the lunar equinox, Clavius recommended that 10 days be skipped. Pope Gregory XIII issued an order that Oct. 5–Oct. 14 be dropped from the calendar in 1582" (see Finding Dulcinea; http://www.findingdulcinea.com/news/on-this-day/September-October-08/On-this-Day-In-1582-Oct-5-Did-Not-Exist-.html [accessed 4 June 2021]). The old trick riddle was, what happened between October 4 and October 14,1582? The answer was, *nothing*. Those were the dates that were dropped. Bibliographers may need to be aware of these issues in assigning a date to undated materials.

Booksellers, collectors, and librarians, among others, must be familiar with ROMAN NUMERALS, but they must also be alert to CHRONOGRAMS, a coded means of delineating dates. And they must also understand publishing practices, among which are the publisher's desire to offer the "latest" text to his buyers, so he "adjusts" the dates on title pages to make some copies look later than others when they were actually printed from the same setting of type (hence, they are of the same edition) and could even be issued at the same time. (*See* Edition, Impression [Printing], Issue, and State; Points.) Add to this the complexities of the dates of bindings. Trying to ascertain the date of a volume by its binding can be tricky. Dates stamped onto a binding, for instance, could indicate the date the binding was done or the date of the publication of the item. There is always the possiblility that the binder could stamp the wrong date; or the TEXT BLOCK could be be slipped into the cover of a different book. (*See* Remboîtage.) One must know about binding styles, materials, tools, and collectors' personal tastes and libraries, along with the practices and tools of particular binders, to try to figure out the date of a binding. And even then, a "figured-out" date could be widely inaccurate.

DAY OF THE DEAD BROADSIDE POEMS. *See* Calaveras.

DEACCESSIONING. Thought by many to be an evil necessity in a library, whether academic or private. This is the permanent removal of an item or items from the collection. Such activity is done for a number of reasons: items in such poor condition that they cannot be used or resuscitated, items out of scope, to raise money for what is perceived as more important than is retaining the item to be deaccessioned, to make space for more important materials, for political or moral reasons, or for other motives. Also called "weeding." (See Berger, pp. 37–40.)

DEACIDIFICATION. The removal of acid from whatever is acidic. The term, however, is used loosely, for some methods do not really remove the acid but rather neutralize it. One company claimed that its deacidification process strengthened the paper so treated, but if the paper was weakened, the deacidification process did not add strength to it. There are aqueous (water-based) and nonaqueous (non–water-based) methods. The process can be carried out on a single item (e.g., a sheet of paper) or in a mass operation (called "mass deacidification") in which large quantities of items are placed in a sealed chamber and treated at once. Many processes have been employed, but "only the Bookkeeper process, operated by Preservation Technologies, now [is] in use in the United States for mass treatment. . . . Deacidification is a boon to libraries and their patrons, for in its mass application it can extend the useful life of millions of books and other paper-based materials. It must be used with care, however, for some processes can discolor the items treated (it might change the color of illustrations or binding materials); aqueous methods can cause metal staples hidden in some bindings to rust; it may cause some volumes to cockle; if treatments are done en mass [*sic*], large numbers of items must be shipped to the company doing the work, and such shipping—especially of rare and valuable items—could be damaging and costly" (Berger, pp. 376–77). (*See* pH.) The practice is not much used today in the United States; limited resources are more likely to be allocated to DIGITIZATION, and from a bibliographical view, deacidification is not ideal because it can change the volume's physical characteristics (like the color of the paper, illustrations, or the original sizing). (*See* Mass deacidification.)

DEAD MATTER (as in a magnesium or ZINC PLATE or a WOODCUT). In a RELIEF block, any area that is below the printing surface. When one orders, for example, a zinc or magnesium plate, it is wise to specify "ROUT THE DEAD MATTER," meaning to remove the areas below the surface that is to print in such a way that the removed area is low enough not to receive ink and wind up printing. F. C. Avis gives another meaning for "dead matter": "type matter, correctly set, but no longer needed for printing" (*Bookman's Concise Dictionary*, p. 78).

DEALER/BOOKDEALER. Many moons ago I was told by a bookseller that he did not want to be called a "dealer"; he said it sounded as if he were doing something illegal. ("Jake is my dealer; I get many books from him.") So I almost always use "bookseller" or some other locution. I am not sure modern booksellers feel the same, but I think it is safe to avoid any term that could have a pejorative meaning. Saying "book dealer" is better than merely saying "dealer."

DEBOSSING. Impressing a sheet of paper or some other surface (as the cover of a book) so that a pattern or text is pressed below the surface. Opposite of EMBOSSING.

DECKLE. The frame that goes over a paper MOLD to hold the fibers on the surface of the mold while the fibers are settling onto the surface of the mold and the water is dripping through the wires beneath the sheet. The mold is actually composed of two parts: the mold and the deckle. The inner margins of the deckle determine the size and shape of the sheet that is formed. If a paper mold has a deckle with an opening in the shape of a duck, the sheet formed will be in that shape. Papermakers wishing to make round sheets on a square or rectangular mold need only create a deckle with a round opening on it. (For an image, *see* Laid paper.)

The edges of the deckle sit on the surface of the mold, and in hand papermaking, some of the fibers from the vat will get under these edges. This produces a sheet with an edge that is not perfectly straight—called a deckle (or deckled) edge. LEAVES with deckles are actually (or can be made in a machine to look like) sheets of handmade paper.

DECKLE(D) EDGE. The uneven edges of a sheet of paper, made by hand or by a machine that can impart this unevenness to the sheet. (*See* Deckle.) If a sheet or a volume still has its deckles, it is said to be "UNCUT" or "UNTRIMMED." (*See also* Cropped.)

DECKLE-FETISHISM. Carter's sardonic term for those who obsess over volumes that retain their original DECKLES. He calls this an "over-zealous, undiscriminating (and often very expensive) passion" (p. 92). Carter here was clearly indulging in one of his pet peeves, knowing that there really was no such formal term. I guess he was trying to create one, but it never actually caught on in the book world. When is the last time you heard a bookseller, collector, or, for that matter, *anyone*, use that term? This is a case of neologism fetishism. (*See* Cropped; Uncut; Unopened.)

DECORATED INITIAL. *See* Illuminated majuscule.

DECORATED PAPER. An exceptionally broad subject, to be treated here only cursorily. (Thousands of books have been written about the topic.) In the book world, to save money and time, publishers and binders turned to decorated papers to replace the more costly leather used for book covers and also to add elegance with ornamented endpapers (*see* Endleaves). "The earliest known specimen [of a paper-covered book], dated 1482, is a paper woodcut wrapper from Augsburg, where at least five were made" (Cloonan, *Early Bindings*, p. 5). Thus, from the 15th century on, decorated papers have been used in books and were also used for box liners and covers for slipcases.

Paper is decorated in many ways: MARBLING, PASTE PAPERS, inclusions in the pulp, block printing, stenciling, dyeing, surface treatments affecting the textures of the sheets, gilding and stamping with other metallic foils, hand-applied pigments, and many other methods. Even WATERMARKING is considered a form of decoration. The decoration can be done in the papermaking process, or it can be added after the sheets are formed and dried. As noted above, an extensive literature exists on decorated paper. See especially Wolfe, *Marbled Paper*; and Haemmerle, *Buntpapiere*. (*See* Block-printed papers; Chiyogami; Dutch gilt paper; Itajime; Kinkarakami.)

Since decorative styles have evolved over the centuries, it is sometimes possible to assign a broad date range to a volume or pamphlet based on the kind of decoration used on its papers. And because certain styles and techniques of paper decoration are identifiable, loosely, to a single country, the place of origin of a piece of decorated paper can sometimes reveal something about the volume it is associated with. However, centuries-old sheets still exist intact, and it is possible to acquire today an 18th-century German sheet and use it to bind any book. Thus, the contemporaneity of a binding, even with appropriately dated materials, is not guaranteed.

DECORATIVE TYPE. Printing type with ornate faces. Carter says of decorated type (his term, but more properly "decorative"), "[T]hough not unknown before 1700, [it] became more general in the 18th century, the taste for shaded, IN-LINE and floriated letters pioneered by P. S. Fournier *le jeune*. In the 19th century, a riot of new designs, sans serif, Egyptian, rusticated, even pictorial and in three-dimensional *trompe-l'oeil*, burst forth from the typefounders of Europe and the New World to meet the market, expanding with ever greater rapidity, for ephemera" (p. 93). What Carter does not say is that most of these types were garish and ugly, and they wrought the ire of such aesthetes as WILLIAM MORRIS, whose decision to start the Kelmscott Press was partly occasioned by his reaction to the poor TYPOGRAPHY he saw, often due to these types. Many FONTS were printed in two colors—that is, a single character with two colors on it (either top to bottom or IN-LINE. (See Johnston, *Alphabets to Order*; Loy et al., *Nineteenth Century American Designers and Engravers of Type*; and Twyman, *Printing 1770–1970*.)

DECORATOR BOOKS. There is a stale joke about the person who asks the bookseller for blue books. The bookseller asks, "The kind you take tests in?" and the customer replies, "No, ones to match our curtains." There is a world of books that are pretty, and their prettiness is the only thing they have going for them. They are not readable, valuable, or otherwise desirable. The term has come to describe just such items: books that look good on shelves, but that have no other redeeming quality.

DEDICATION/DEDICATION COPY. The part of a book, usually at the beginning (hence part of the PRELIMS), in which the author inscribes the volume to the honor of someone, possibly to a person who has made the volume possible (a loved one) or from whom the author is hoping to get some return patronage (a person of power or wealth, maybe one who made the book possible through largesse of some kind). The dedication can be incorporated into another part of the book (e.g., a preface, introduction, or foreword), but it is often a section of its own, sometimes only a few words ("To my mother"), but sometimes it can look like an essay ("This book is dedicated to my benefactor, the Count ———, whose generosity and guidance . . .").

Additionally, a dedication copy can be specially printed or in a unique binding, created for the dedicatee, and may contain extra materials and a handwritten INSCRIPTION, possibly on a leaf not in the regular version of the volume. Such copies, because they are unique (even if the author has made a dozen of them and has dedicated each to a different person), command high prices on the collectors' market, especially if the dedicatee is well known or one also collected.

DEFECTIVE. A term used by booksellers and collectors to indicate that there is a problem with the item described—the problem being that it is in some way not in good condition. The defect could be minor (a bumped corner), major (a lacking cover), or catastrophic (soaked and cockled or mildewed and foul smelling). Defects always affect value, and it is incumbent on the person using the term to describe the defect accurately. This is not always done. (A book I received from a vendor was described as in fine condition, but it had a single small defect. It arrived looking perfect but smelling like a fetid swamp. The defects can be olfactory as well as visible.)

DEFINITIVE EDITION. *See* Bibliography.

DEGRESSIVE BIBLIOGRAPHY. Carter has an entry for this kind of bibliography. He says that different periods of history should generate different kinds of bibliographical description. He points out that Falconer Madan described the principle in his commentary on a famous essay by A. W. Pollard and W. W. Greg, "Some Points in Bibliographical Description" (published by the Bibliographical Society in 1909 and reprinted in 1950). Madan said, "The idea [of Degressive Description] is that different periods of printing and different classes of books should meet with correspondingly varying treatment" (Madan, "Standard Descriptions of Printed Books," quoted by Ascher, "Progressing Toward Bibliography; or: Organic Growth in the Bibliographic Record," p. 98; at http://citeseerx.ist.psu.edu/viewdoc/download?doi=10.1.1.168.5254&rep=rep1&type=pdf [accessed 6 June 2021]). (See also Madan, Duff, and Gibson, "Standard Descriptions of Printed Books.") Madan's exact words describing degressive bibliography are "the principle of varying a [bibliographical] description according to the difference of the period treated or of the importance of the work to be described" (see Madan, "Degressive Bibliography," p. 53). In short, the principle was that the older a volume, the more description it merited; the younger, the less description it would get; and the more important the cataloger deemed an item, the more description it should get; the less important, the less description. While the notion was sensible to a point, it produced a level of bibliographical minutiae and complication that has not been seriously picked up by most scholars producing bibliographical descriptions. And such a notion ignored the importance of the text, the prominence of the author, or the influence the text had historically. Carter says that while the concept was "Newtonian in its simplicity, Einsteinian in its weight, it has yet to penetrate the consciousness of our more pachydermatous bibliographers" (Carter, p. 93). Included here to show Carter's erudition and humor, the term is seldom if ever used today. Carter seems to embrace it, though it has generally been discredited in bibliographical circles. And the whole idea of degressive bibliography was a bit skewed to the chronological rather than to the germane. And it relied, as well, on the personal tastes of the cataloger rather than on any truly "Einsteinian" approach. That is, it said older books deserve more bibliographic description than do "younger" ones, ignoring the fact that some older books were hardly worth describing, and that newer ones may have deserved a great deal of minute attention.

DELAMINATION. The coming apart of layers. It is sometimes a condition of a binding in which the covers are made of cardboard, the layers of which separate because of moisture or the failure of an adhesive. It is also common on DUST JACKETS that have plasticized surfaces. Early Dover PAPERBACKS, while exceptionally well bound and using archival, acid-free materials, often had delaminating covers—the shiny plastic coatings of their stiff paper covers separating from their substrates.

In conservation work, one way to preserve BROADSIDES and single leaves was to have them laminated—that is, bonded between layers of plastic. This was thought of as a good conservation technique, though it was not. (*See* Lamination.) Sometimes to reverse the damage, conservators tried to delaminate the item but not always successfully. (*See also* Encapsulation.)

DELUXE EDITION. A term used to indicate that the version in hand is in some way more luxurious (and thus more costly) than the more "regular" edition. The word "edition," of course, may be (and usually is) a misnomer in the strict sense in that no new *edition* may be indicated if the two versions are from the same setting of type. In such a case, "deluxe version" would be more apt. (*See* Edition, Impression [Printing], Issue, and State; Points.)

Deluxe editions (i.e., deluxe versions) were often given glitzy bindings, adding to the cost, but many of those—especially in the 19th century, when case binding was the norm—were merely fancy-looking cases made of inexpensive materials.

Often to add gloss to a volume or a set, publishers might use the French term "*édition de luxe*." Carter, however, points out that there is a distinction between a regular "deluxe edition" and an "*édition de luxe*." Creating the latter is a practice that has been around for centuries—as early as the 15th century. Gutenberg himself chose to print some of the copies of the Bible on vellum—clearly catering to an audience more affluent than those who could afford only copies on paper. Aldus Manutius used blue paper for some copies of his books to distinguish them from the "regular versions." And through the 20th century, printers may have a standard version and a LARGE-PAPER COPY of a text. All of these variations were designed to sell for more money than their "regular version" counterparts and can thus be called "éditions de luxe." Many a fine-press printer in the 20th and 21st centuries, likewise, will issue a volume in paper and in boards (often full leather) or with some copies with uncolored and some with hand-colored illustrations, often with "an extra suite of prints laid in" (for framing!). Some copies may be unsigned, and others may be signed by authors, illustrators, printers, binders, mothers-in-law, and marriage counselors. And some volumes may have 2 TIP-INS while the deluxe versions have 20.

With EDITION BINDING and the mechanization of book production, it was possible for publishers to print some copies of an edition on special paper and on larger LEAVES (*see* Large-paper copy/Large-paper edition) and bind those copies in fancier covers than were used for the standard copies. This does not guarantee that these so-called deluxe versions were made any more durable or of appreciably better materials than were the regular TRADE EDITION copies. Many a deluxe copy from the last half of the 19th century will be in wretched shape thanks to shoddy materials. On the other hand, collectors may have bought these attractive versions for their looks and placed them on shelves for display, not for use. Thus, it is possible that some of these copies have survived in somewhat better condition than their brethren that got read. Finally, true maniacal collectors will want all manifestations of an item, so it is incumbent on them to have each version—regular, deluxe, super deluxe, extraordinaire, and so forth.

DENTELLE. The French word for "lace" and used as a description of the ornate, usually gold-stamped outer margins of the covers of a book, around the pastedowns (*see also* Endleaves; Turn-ins). When leather is turned in on the inside of the covers, the end sheets are pasted down, leaving a border of the leather showing. Blank areas call out for decoration, so binders often decorated these leather borders with a lacelike gold stamping, usually referred to in dealers' catalogs as "gilt dentelles" (the word almost always, in the book world, appearing in the plural since the dentelles are on the front and rear boards). Roberts and Etherington say, "An 18th century style of book decoration, usually in gold, consisting of a combination of elliptical scrolls of slightly shaded leafy character joined to clusters and borders of great richness, resembling lace, and pointing toward the center of the cover" (p. 75). However, this overly precise description is not much heeded today, and catalogs will call "dentelles" any gold- or blind-stamped such decoration, no matter what it looks like or which way it points. (For images of gilt dentelles, *see* Bookplate; Signed binding.)

DEPOSIT COPY. (In Great Britain this is called "statutory copy.") Most countries have what is known as a COPYRIGHT LIBRARY or a depository library into which published items are deposited when their makers are seeking COPYRIGHT protection. Such deposit copies are often sent to the libraries before publication, and can thus be early printings (impressions) (*see* Edition, Impression [Printing], Issue, and State; Points) of the text. One particularly fascinating such copy is Mark Twain's *Pudd'nhead Wilson and Those Extraordinary Twins* (see bibliography under Sidney E. Berger), with two known deposit copies, both originally sent to the Library of Congress (which, at the time, required two copies of all texts to be deposited into LC for copyright purposes), containing 433 pages; all other copies of this first American edition with only 432 pages. (See Berger, "Editorial Intrusion in *Pudd'nhead Wilson*.") That editors mucked around with the author's text is clear, and the proper readings, for more than a century, could be seen only in the deposit copies (one of which is now at Harvard's Houghton Library), and, now, in the critical edition offered by W. W. Norton.

DEPOSITORY LIBRARY. *See* Deposit copy.

DE RICCI, SEYMOUR. Seymour Montefiore Robert Rosso de Ricci (1881–1942), with his Italian name, was an English-born scholar who became a French citizen. As a bibliographer he published, alone or as co-compiler, a host of reference works, some of which still have cachet. His most important work for today's bibliographers is probably his census of the printings of WILLIAM CAXTON (*A Census of Caxtons*), which, though now superseded by online databases, is still useful for showing where copies of this great English printer's volumes were at the time of the census. He also published *English Collectors of Books & Manuscripts, 1530–1930: And Their Marks of Ownership*.

DEROME STYLE. "A style of book decoration practiced by the Derome family of France in the 18th century. The most famous of the family was Nicolas Denis Derome (active 1761–c 1789)—Derome le juene—who was also known as the 'great cropper' because of his tendency to trim excessively. Nicolas Derome also used sawn-in [*see* Recessed-cord sewing] cords in order to obtain the hollow back [*see* Hollow spine], which prevents the SPINE of the book from flexing and thus possibly cracking the gold. He also achieved great fame by his use of the DENTELLE border, taking the dentelles of Padeloup as models. [This reference is to the 17th- and 18th-century family of bookbinders, the most famous of whom was Antoine Michel Padeloup (1685–1758).] His also are made up of dentelle tools in combination, rather than in repetition, and are represented by symmetrical corner tooling of a very richly engraved FLORIATED scroll work. An essential feature in Nicolas Derome's finest dentelles is a small bird with outstretched wings" (Roberts and Etherington, "Derome style"; https://cool.culturalheritage.org/don/dt/dt1005.html [accessed 21 January 2021]).

DESCENDERS. Portions of lowercase letters that descend below the base line of the body of the character. (*See* Ascenders.) The following letters have descenders: *f*, *g*, *j*, *p*, *q*, and *y*. In some FONTS, especially with CIVILITÉ TYPES, there could be SWASH LETTERS with descenders.

DESCRIPTIVE BIBLIOGRAPHY. *See* Bibliography.

DESIDERATA. *See* Want list.

DESIGNER BINDINGS. Volumes designed by artists and bound in elegant form, usually with high-quality materials, like fine leather and vellum. The decoration often has something to do with the contents of the volume, and the style is usually contemporary with binding styles in vogue at the time of the execution of the binding. From about the middle of the 19th century on, such bindings have become seriously COLLECTIBLE, usually enhancing the value of the volumes they adorn. In fact, sometimes a volume sells solely because of its binding, and the binding could add significanly to the cost of the volume (or be its only feature that is worth anything). Designer binders, however, should be careful not to put an elegant designer binding onto a volume that would be worth considerably more in its original skin.

DESIGNER BOOKBINDERS. A British organization whose work generally reveals artistic bindings in leather or vellum (or both), but not necessarily. Their website says, "Designer Bookbinders is one of the foremost societies devoted to the craft of fine bookbinding. Founded over fifty years ago it has, by means of exhibitions and publications, helped to establish the reputation of British bookbinding worldwide. Its membership includes some of the most highly regarded makers in the fields of fine bookbinding, book arts and artists' books, each with a passion for presenting the bound text as a unique art object" (Designer Bookbinders, "About DB"; http://www.designerbookbinders.org.uk/ [accessed 2 April 2021]). Their website adds: "The society evolved from The Hampstead Guild of Scribes and Bookbinders which was founded in 1951. Its name was changed in 1955 to The Guild of Contemporary Bookbinders. / Originally the Guild was an informal group of about a dozen practising bookbinders, but gradually an increasing number of people with an interest in bookbinding wished to be associated with the Guild's activities and so, in 1968, a formal constitution was drawn up and the present name, Designer Bookbinders, was adopted. In 1981 the society was accorded charitable [called "non-profit" in the U.S.] status" (Designer Bookbinders, "History"; http://www.designerbookbinders.org.uk/about_db/history.html [accessed 2 April 2021]). To become members, applicants must be elected, and they may be amateur or professional.

DESKTOP PUBLISHING. A term that emerged in the 1980s when personal computers (PCS) became available. The idea was that anyone with a PC could be one's own publisher since the hardware and software gave one the capacity to create a text and print it out in paper form. The ability to be a "desktop publisher" allowed people to produce the physical objects (books, pamphlets, broadsides, and so on) but did not automatically give them the ability to market what they had produced, nor did it automatically make them good designers since the defaults on the computers (for margins, typefaces, indentations, and so on) were not at all aesthetic. The very generic nature of desktop publishing made it such that almost all desktop-published items looked pretty much alike, with nonproportional types, uniform margins, RIVERS, and so on. Publishers capitalized on this by requiring authors to submit "CAMERA-READY COPY," and for at least a decade, a great number of books were published that were quite unattractive. The publishers seemingly did not care how repellent the text looked; they were saving a great deal of money in typesetting and proofreading—a saving not usually passed along to the author in her royalties or to the buyer in the price.

DEVICE. *See* Printer's device.

DEVIL'S TAIL. *See* Bar.

DEWEY CLASSIFICATION. The cataloging method devised by Melvil Dewey in 1876. Also called the Dewey Decimal Classification, it breaks all knowledge down into subject areas to allow items in a library collection to be locatable. It has gone through many editions, the most recent being the 23rd, published by OCLC and issued in January 2022 (see OCLC, "Organize Your Materials," oclc.org/en.dewey.html). The original version had fewer than 1,000 classes; the present edition has expanded to four volumes. The system is still in use throughout the world and is practical for smaller libraries. Larger institutions tend to use the LIBRARY OF CONGRESS CLASSIFICATION SYSTEM. (See UDC Consortium, "Universal Decimal Classification," in the bibliography.)

DIAMOND DASH. *See* Rule/Ruling.

DIAMOND SUTRA. The first printed book. "It was produced in AD 868 . . . and it is clearly the product of a mature printing industry in China" (Wood and Barnard, *The Diamond Sutra*, blurb; see also p. 64). It is one of the sutras, "being the discourses or sermons of the Buddha. It is just under five metres [about 16 feet] long [and 10½ inches wide] and has a beautiful FRONTISPIECE depicting the Buddha preaching amongst monks and flying 'angels.' . . . [T]he very end of the scroll contains the most important text since it gives us the date of production. A printed colophon reads: 'Reverently (caused to be) made for universal free distribution by Wang Jie on behalf of (his) two parents on the fifteenth day of the fourth month of the Xiantong reign,' a date equivalent to AD 868" (Wood and Barnard, p. 6). The printing was done from WOODBLOCKS (Wood and Barnard, pp. 63 ff.), and is on seven strips of paper glued together.

DIAPERED (in binding). "A gold- or blind-tooled decorative pattern, consisting of a motif constantly repeated in geometric form. The pattern may consist of figures such as diamonds, lozenges, or flowers, separated only by background, or by constantly repeating compartments, each filled with designs" (Roberts and Etherington, p. 76). The repeated pattern, especially when the pattern is diamond shaped, is sometimes termed "diced." The EMBOSSING can be done in leather or cloth—or even into a paper cover.

DIBDIN, THOMAS FROGNALL (1776–1847). One of the famous BIBLIOMANIACS, and author of *The Bibliomania, Or, Book-Madness; Containing Some Account Of The History, Symptoms, And Cure Of This Fatal Disease. In An Epistle Addressed To Richard Heber, Esq.* (1809), preceded in 1802 by *Introduction to the Knowledge of Rare and Valuable Editions of the Greek and Roman Classics.* His most engaging work is *The Bibliographical Decameron; Or, Ten Days Pleasant Discourse upon Illuminated Manuscripts, And Subjects Connected with Early Engraving, Typography, and Bibliography* (1817). His writings, especially in their first and early editions, are seriously collected, but not too seriously read, as he was only a so-so scholar. Despite the mediocre repute of his many writings, he is still known for his enthusiasm for books and bibliography, and for being the founder of the ROXBURGHE CLUB (1812) in England.

DICED. *See* Diapered.

DIDOT SYSTEM. A system of type measurement used in much of Europe, named after François-Ambroise Didot (1730–1804). It is "based on a unit of 0.0148 inches (0.3759 mm)" (Dictionary.com, http://dictionary.reference.com/browse/didot-point-system [accessed 4 June 2021]). The name "Didot" refers to a family of typefounders, printers, and publishers, among whom are Françoise-Ambroise, Pierre-Françoise (1732–1793), Pierre (1761–1853), and Firmin (1764–1836). Firmin Didot was a punchcutter, among other things, and "his series of modern face, shown in a specimen of 1819, remained the standard type used by most French printers throughout the 19th century" (Glaister, *Glaister's Glossary*, pp. 140–41). (See George, *The Didot Family and the Progress of Printing.* See also the brief biographies of the key Didot family members in BIGMORE AND WYMAN, *A Bibliography of Printing*, pp. 173–80.)

DIE-CUT. Shaped or otherwise cut with a metal die. Two main types are used for books: to create a shaped book or to cut through the cover or LEAVES of the volume to create a "window" through which the reader can see the substrate below the die-cut surface. Many children's books are cut to the shape of the subject of the volume. (Somewhere in my horde is a book about ducks die-cut into the shape of a duck.) A book cover can be die-cut to reveal the title on the HALF TITLE, for instance. (*See* Shaped book.)

Die-cut book: Donald Justice, *Banjo Dog* (Riverside, CA: Printed by the Doe Press for Thaumatrope Press, University of California, Riverside, 1995). The cover has had windows die-cut to reveal the printed ITAJIME paper beneath; with the original die used to make the cut.

Collection of the author.

DIGIT. *See* Fist.

DIGITAL PRESERVATION. A term bandied about a good deal in the book/ephemera/library/archives community. But it is a chimera: something hoped or wished for but impossible to achieve. At least to date, digitally captured or created information is excellent to access, but not capable of true "preservation" in the archival sense. "In a nutshell, many people think that digital is not preservation. Others think that the problem of impermanence of library materials has been solved by digital technology. One common notion is that digitally stored information is excellent for quick access, far more easily accessed than any data stored in analog formats. But to date there is no technology that guarantees long-term preservation in electronic form. / The term *digital preservation* has two meanings: 1) the use of digital technology to preserve things that were originally created in analog form; 2) the attempt to preserve information that was created in digital form (the current term is texts *born digital*). For both meanings, the key issue is trying to maintain access to information in a medium that has, to date, no secure, proven-long-term preservation tactics, though we seem to be getting closer with digital repositories. / A vast and rapidly growing literature on this topic exists—for good reason. The evolution of digital technology is faster than the evolution of practically any other technology in history. It is impossible for anyone to keep up with the changes. And there are so many changes that the literature on them comes pouring forth in articles, books, lectures, and symposia. With shifts from one platform to another, with changes in whole methods of creating and saving information, and with the steady evolution in software and hardware, the digital world itself has a built-in obsolescence factor that makes 'preservation' seemingly evanescent" (Berger, p. 391).

One additional factor is in play: Since most technology is created in the commercial sector, those profiting from it do not want innovations to cease coming out of their factories. It would mean a cessation of profits. So new technologies will continue to emerge in the name of progress: faster computers, greater storage capacities, more expeditious access to increasing amounts of information, more portability, and thus more (and continuing) profits. All this, of course, naturally leads to shorter intervals between one innovation and the next, and increasing obsolescence of existing hardware and software. And also the concomitant loss of support for the "obsolete" wares, even if these wares are only a few months old. On top of all this is the truly mind-boggling amount of information that is being produced today. No hardware or software can capture it all and store it all—even if it were worth saving in the first place. (But who decides?)

Texts in analog form have more of a chance to be around 1,000 years from now than does any piece of digital data. Yet the notion of "digital preservation" surfaces in the book world often.

DIME ACTION BOOKS. *See* Big Little Books.

DIME NOVELS. A form of popular reading in the 19th and early 20th centuries aimed at children and adults. Matthew Short says, "Between 1860 and 1933, publishers of cheap fiction in the United States produced thousands of what came to be known collectively as dime novels" (Short, "Blood and Thunder"). "Dime novels were short works of fiction, usually focused on the dramatic exploits of a single heroic character. As evidenced by their name, dime novels were sold for a dime (sometimes a nickel), and featured colorful cover illustrations. They were bound in paper, making them light, portable, and somewhat ephemeral. Publishers issued dime novels in series, numbering each novel individually. (This practice enabled publishers to take advantage of a postal loophole, and send their novels through the mail at the much cheaper rates established for periodicals.) Dime novels were read by literate adults of all ages, although over time young men and boys became the primary audience" ("Dime Novels," *The Newberry*, from the Newberry Library, https://www.newberry.org/dime-novels [accessed 23 October 2015]; a broken link. But see *The Newberry*, "The Cheap and Easy Room," 22 February 2012; https://www.newberry.org/cheap-and-easy-room, for a shorter paragraph about these publications [accessed 29 June 2021]; this site says that the term "dime novel" was synonymous with "cheap paperback trash").

They were often linked with "PENNY DREADFULS" (as they were called in Britain). "Both genres flourished from the middle to the close of the 19th century in America and England (where the novels were known as 'penny dreadfuls'), and benefited from three mutually reinforcing trends: the vastly increased mechanization of printing, the growth of efficient rail and canal shipping, and ever-growing rates of literacy. / The dime novels were aimed at youthful, working-class audiences and distributed in massive editions at newsstands and dry goods stores. Though the phrase conjures up stereotyped yarns of Wild West adventure, complete with lurid cover illustration, many other genres were represented: tales of urban outlaws, detective stories, working-girl narratives of virtue defended, and costume romances. / Story papers, weekly eight-page tabloids, covered much the same ground, but often combined material and themes to appeal to the whole family. The chief among them had national circulations greater than any other newspaper or magazine, some reaching 400,000 copies sold per issue. Unlike the dime novels, which generally confine illustration to the cover, the story papers integrate text and illustration (in the form of wood engravings) throughout" (Trujillo, "Dime Novels Full Text"; https://library.stanford.edu/collections/dime-novels-full-text#:~:text=Unlike%20the%20dime%20novels%2C%20which,form%20of%20wood%20engravings)%20throughout [accessed 29 June 2021]). Some of the major dime novel series were Frank Leslie's *Boys of America* and *Happy Days* and Beadle's *New York Dime Library*.

While the term "dime novel" has the specific meanings that are shown above, the term was also used more generically to denote all such cheap fiction. One manifestation is the "Nickel weekly," so named, of course, by its cost, but with the same features of the dime novel.

Thousands of these 10-cent (and 5-cent) paper-bound publications were issued from 1860 to 1920. And though they are still considered "dime novels," many of them cost up to 25 cents. They were produced in such large numbers, with reprints (and reprints of reprints) to such an extent that they are a bibliographer's nightmare. A single title may be sold to a second and then a third publisher, titles may change while the tales remain the same, reprints may have innumerable textual VARIANTS, and internal and cover art may change from one impression (*see* Edition, Impression [Printing], Issue, and State; Points) to the next. Nonetheless, they have been seriously collected, and even ones in less than perfect condition can be desirable and pricey. (See Bragin, *Dime Novels, Bibliography, 1860–1928*; Cox, ed., *Dashing Diamond Dick and Other Classic Dime Novels*; Cox, *The Dime Novel Companion*; Johanssen, *The House of Beadle & Adams*; and Pearson, *Dime Novels*. Also, from 1931 and for more than 70 years, the magazine *Dime Novel Round-Up* has been published.)

DIMPLE. *See* Book clubs/Book club editions.

DING. The informal term for a bit of damage in a book that has been struck here or there to leave a ding (a dent or nick, for instance). Though the term may not appear in the "literature" of the trade (booksellers' catalogs, auction catalogs, formal bibliographical descriptions), it will be heard at many a bookstore or fair: "This book has a ding on its fore-edge." "I do not want a dinged copy in my collection." The term is certainly in the active vocabulary of most book experts. (*See* Bumped.)

DINGBATS. *See* Fleurons.

DINKUS. Three ASTERISKS in a row (* * *), indicating a break between two parts of a text. When the asterisks are printed in a triangle, it is called an ASTERISM.

DIPHTHONG. A digraph—two characters printed together and representing a single sound). Though not common in English, and though representable as two separate characters, they are sometimes seen in such characters as Æ, æ, Œ, and œ (as in "encyclopædia" and "Œnology"). In printing type, since the two characters appear on a single SORT, they can be called LIGATURES.

DIPLOMA; DIPLOMATICS (text format). Literally "folded twice," though the term could mean that the piece called a "diploma" had any number of folds. The term has taken on specific meanings beyond those pertaining to books and documents. Etymologically, it refers to a document that is folded into thirds. In the world of manuscripts, "diplomatics" is "[t]he branch of paleography that deals with the study of old official documents and determines their age and authenticity" (*American Heritage Dictionary of the English Language*, p. 511). It also looks at the forms the documents take, the language(s) they are written in, and their meaning. Michelle Brown says that the word "diplomatic" is used as a noun, referring "to the study of documents and records, their form, language, and script" (Brown, *Understanding Illuminated Manuscripts*, p. 50). Diplomatics also refers to the study of the making of manuscripts and their authenticity and origin, possibly also focusing on paleography, the materials they are composed of, their language, the people involved in their being (the makers of the materials, the scribes and signers, those mentioned in them, witnesses to them, and so on), their date, the milieu in which they were produced, and many other phenomena that may help scholars in editing and understanding them. Scholars of diplomatics are experts in scripts, and they can often determine the country of origin and the approximate date of a manuscript on the basis of its handwriting, its language, and its content. They can thus authenticate documents. In the world of bibliography there is also the so-called "diplomatic transcription," one that comes as close as possible to the original; and the "diplomatic edition," "[b]eing an exact copy of the original" (*American Heritage Dictionary*, p. 511)—or as close to the original as is possible to produce in all of its words and spellings and punctuation.

DIPPER. *See* Vatman.

DIPTYCH/TRIPTYCH. A diptych is a text presented on two panels, usually connected to one another with hinges or some other attaching mechanism. A triptych is the same, but with three panels. The form is often used in ARTISTS' BOOKS, as with the fine work of Robin Price, *Altar Book for Gorecki*, presented in three panels (with the Polish poems on one side, the English translations on the other).

Triptych: *Altar Book for Gorecki* (Middletown, CT: Robin Price, Publisher, 1996).

Courtesy of Robin Price.

DIRECTION LINE. The printed line at the foot of a page beneath the printed text that can contain such things as a RUNNING HEAD; CATCHWORDS; SIGNATURES; page numbers; possibly volume number or date; or PRESS MARKS. For a brief time, a journal with this title was published at the University of Texas, Austin: *The Direction Line: A Newsletter for Bibliographers and Textual Critics*. Under the editorship of Warner Barnes, the journal (founded by Barnes and John Horden), calling itself "a newsletter for bibliographers and textual critics," ran from 1975–1982, and aimed to "deal with work in progress, the use of new techniques, and the minutiae of research." Sometimes only catchwords are printed in this line; if so, some scholars then prefer to call it a CATCHLINE.

DIRTY LITTLE COMICS. *See* Tijuana bibles.

DIRTY PROOF. (Also called "foul copy.") In the publishing industry, this is a PROOF copy sent to an author or reader with many TYPOGRAPHICAL ERRORS. (A clean proof is one that needs little or no correction. *See* Clean copy/Clean proof.) The filth indicated could be because of careless TYPESETTING, the heavy hand of an in-house editor, or an author who decides to make a host of changes at the proof stage. That is, the "dirt," indicated by many EMENDATIONS, could be because of what is going on at the publishing house (especially with a careless or inebriated COMPOSITOR), or because of an author who wants to make many changes at the proof stage. Either way, scholars would be interested in seeing such a copy as part of the evolution of a text, from an author's first VERSION to the final PUBLICATION. BOOKSELLERS and COLLECTORS love to get their hands on such versions, especially since they tend to be UNIQUE—and the RARITY of such copies (supply and demand being operative) can yield high prices and great bragging rights. (Parenthetically, just because a dirty proof exists does not mean that the emendations called for in a proofreader's marks were actually entered into the published text. For a variety of reasons, the publishing house may not follow the directions of the proofreader.)

DISBOUND/DISBINDING. Said of a book or pamphlet that was once bound and has been removed from its covers. As opposed to a text that is IN SHEETS, which has not been bound. The term could indicate that an item was in poor condition and had to be removed from its binding for repair, or it could mean that a composite volume, such as a SAMMELBAND, has been pulled apart for its pieces. This latter motive for disbinding (*see also* Unbound) is condemnable, for it removes an item from a collection; even if the item does not seem to fit thematically with the pamphlets it is bound with, such dismemberment loses some of the coherence its original owner (the one who bound the items together in the first place) thought appropriate. But sometimes a bookseller can make a good deal of money with the sale of a single pamphlet (or a few) from the sammelband, and the rest of the pieces in it are just taking up valuable space on his shelves. Another loss could be the original binding—which may just get thrown away when the collector or dealer has the one or few pieces he wants. The binding may itself have carried some good historical information. Serious collectors and responsible booksellers should shy away from such disbinding. (*See* Breaker; Fragmentology; Leaf book.)

Disbinding can also be removing a TEXT BLOCK from its covers, done usually for conservation purposes but also to rebind a volume into a different cover.

DISJUNCT LEAVES. LEAVES in a book not CONJUGATE with any other leaves in the SIGNATURE in which they appear. This could mean that they were TIPPED IN after the signature was printed and gathered. This term is (almost) never used in the book trade, but since it appears in the latest (9th) edition of Carter, I thought I'd pop it in here, too. The editor says that disjunct leaves "have no pair within a gathering" (p. 97). This odd wording seems to imply that the leaves were once attached to other leaves, but this is not clear from that wording.

DISPLAY TYPE. Large printing type used for headlines, titles, advertising pieces, and such. Since type is heavy, in the 19th century great numbers of FONTS of display type were made from wood (*see* Wood type). (*See also* Ludlow machine/Ludlow Typograph; Titling.) Eckersley et al. say, "A typeface designed for use in large sizes rather than for body text. A type family may include a display font as well as a text font; the boldness and stroke and weight of the display font will differ from those of the text font. In computer composition, a font should be called a 'display font' only if it is set from a master (usually an 18-point master) different from the one used for the text (usually a 12-point master). Some typefaces designed exclusively for display setting are limited to capitals and LINING FIGURES (also called titling fonts)" (*Glossary of Typesetting Terms*, p. 31).

DISSOLVING PICTURE BOOK. (Usually) a children's book that contains images on the surface of a slit leaf, the slits allowing other images beneath the sheet to appear (and cover up the ones on the surface) and create a new picture; this effect created with the pull of a tab that pulls the embedded sheet to move through the slits. Peter Haining says about publisher Peter Nister: "Nister's major contribution to the field was a large number of 'dissolving' picture books—developing further the rather rudimentary items produced by Dean—in which an illustration changed into a completely different scene at the pull of a tab" (Haining, *Movable Books*, as cited by Simon Curtis, Quagga Rare Books & Art; "Firsts Online" book fair, 20 May 2021; https://www.firsts-online.com/highlights/in-wonderland-and-what-is-to-be-seen-there-a-book-of-revolving-pictures?q= [accessed 20 May 2021]; this link disappeared after this online fair closed). (*See* Movable book; and see the Haining book in the bibliography.) The reference in the quotation is to *Dean's New Book of Dissolving Views* (London: Dean and Son, 1861). The company was founded by Thomas Dean about 1856. (See "Thomas Dean"; https://library.unt.edu/rarebooks/exhibits/popup2/dean.htm [accessed 31 July 2021]).

DISTRIBUTION. Returning set type to its TYPE CASE. The COMPOSITOR sets the type, but more menial employees in the printing house (if there are any) distribute the printed type. Careless distribution can lead to a FOUL CASE and may cause typos in future setting. I said "set type," but putting PIED type into a type case may be called "distribution," too.

DITTOGRAPHY. The accidental repetition of a letterr, word word, or phrase or phrase in a text. One may find this kind of error in handset type at the end of one line and beginning of the next. Modern software on a computer will flag such repetition. (Also called "double" or "doublet.") Such errors appear in manuscripts as well as in printed texts.

DIVINITY CALF. "A plain, drab, khaki-colored calfskin binding, popular in the mid-19th century for theological and devotional books. The style was particularly popular in the rebinding of books of an earlier time. The bindings were tooled in BLIND with single lines terminating in Oxford corners. / The style sometimes also featured beveled boards and red edges. Sometimes called 'Oxford style'" (Roberts and Etherington, p. 78).

DIVISIONAL TITLE. *See* Fly title; General title.

DOCTORED. *See* Sophisticated.

DOG-EARED. Said of LEAVES in a book that have had their corners turned (folded) over, often by readers who wish to mark where they stopped reading or to mark a page to return to. This practice turns the stomachs of bibliomanes (*see* Bibliomania), and, if the practice is done to cheap PAPERBACKS printed on acidic paper, it has led to the loss of the little triangular tip of many a leaf. I am sure there is a special place in the otherworld for people who dog-ear their books. The term can also mean merely shabby, or ragged, showing signs of having been rubbed or otherwise mishandled. Since dogs are man's best friends, they should not have had one of their most sensitive and adorable attributes sullied by using it in a phrase of defectiveness. At the moment I cannot think of a better term, and since this term has been in use for a long time, we are stuck with it.

THE DOLPHIN: A JOURNAL OF THE MAKING OF BOOKS. A bibliographical and typographical periodical published irregularly from 1933 to 1941. It has four volumes, the last published in three parts. "It was published by the LIMITED EDITIONS CLUB . . . and contained contributions from many of the persons who had been involved in the Club's publishing program" (Jeanne Somers, *Index*, p. xii). It contained articles (and was designed) by some of the premier book designers and scholars of its day, including Frederic Goudy, Paul Koch, Alfred W. Pollard, Lawrence Wroth, Paul Bennett, and many others.

DONKIN, BRYAN. *See* Fourdrinier.

DOS-À-DOS BINDING. (Sometimes called "back-to-back binding.") A binding of two volumes using three BOARDS, the rear of each volume being the same board. In a standard such construction, the reader holds volume one and reads it to the end, with the front and back boards containing the text block. He then turns the volume—still upright—around 180 degrees, with the HEAD still at the head, and is faced with another volume, with a front and back cover, but the back cover of this second volume is the same board as the back cover of the first one. Hence, this is a binding of (usually) two texts in two volumes but with a total of three boards. The two texts are usually related in some way—as is common with two religious texts (e.g., a book of prayers and a psalter). The volumes are usually small—perhaps the size of a 16mo (*see* Sextodecimo). The preferred material for such bindings is leather, though there are examples in paper and cloth as well.

Another similar construction, though not strictly a dos-à-dos binding, is a pair of volumes with three boards, but the rear board of volume 1 is the front board of volume 2. (In square dancing, a do-si-do move is when two dancers face each other and then circle one another, with their backs "facing" each other in the circling. Hence, the two backs of a true dos-à-dos binding retain their backs as one.) I know

Dos-à-dos binding. Jean Cabriès, Saint Jacob. (Hautes Plaines des Main, France: Robert Morel, 1968). (The French term for this kind of binding is *reliure siamoise*.) (*See also* the image at "Embroidered binding.")

Collection of the author.

Two volumes bound together as one, sharing a board between them, but not in the dos-à-dos configuration. *The Order for the Daily Evening Prayer, Also the Hymn Called Benedictus as Set Forth for the Use of the Church by the General Convention of 1886* (New York: E. & J. B. Young & Co., 1886); and *Hymnal: According to the Use of the Protestant Episcopal Church in the United States of America* (rev. ed., New York: E. & J. B. Young & Co., 1890). Though the photograph does not show it clearly, all edges are gilt over red.
Collection of the author.

of no specific book term for a situation just described, when the first volume's rear board and the second volume's front board are one and the same. (*See also* Tête-bêche.)

DOUBLE; DOUBLET. *See* Dittography.

DOUBLE DAGGER. *See* Footnote.

DOUBLE ELEPHANT FOLIO. *See* Elephant folio.

DOUBLE-FAN-ADHESIVE BINDING. *See* Perfect binding.

DOUBLE FORE-EDGE ILLUSTRATION. *See* Fore-edge illustration.

DOUBLE-PAGE SPREAD; DOUBLE SPREAD. *See* Two-page spread.

DOUBLURES. Often heavily ornamented panels pasted into the inner covers of deluxe-bound books where one would normally find pastedown ENDLEAVES. The panels can be made of silk or leather, and they can sometimes extend to the free endpaper (*see* Endleaves). Heavy leather doublures can substantially thicken the BOARDS and add weight to the volume, so such treatments will require especially strong JOINTS (or thinner boards) to keep the covers attached to the rest of the binding.

DOVER PUBLICATIONS (also called Dover Books). A U.S. publishing company, founded in 1941, noted for its reprints (and some original titles), usually on subjects having to do with art, illustration, or the book arts, produced with high-quality materials (sewn SIGNATURES on archival, acid-free papers) and at reasonable prices. Most Dover publications were bound in paper covers (some of the early of which had a tendency to DELAMINATE). Their texts were often music or literature, especially works not under copyright; hence, it is mostly a reprint publisher, though some of its titles were original to Dover. It often targets its reprints at a niche market, such as woodworking or artists or designers who want to use decorative elements in their work—hence Dover's use of materials in the public domain, requiring no permissions for use. Important to present readers is that Dover has published original texts and has reprinted many volumes of import to those interested in the book—volumes by Edith Diehl on bookbinding and by Dard Hunter on papermaking (see the bibliography) and reprints of book-related images: *A Diderot Pictorial Encyclopedia of Trades and Industry 485 Plates Selected from "L'Encyclopedie" of Denis Diderot*, Cennini's *The Craftsman's Handbook* (see the bibliography), Thompson's *Materials and Techniques of Medieval Painting*, and many others. They were able to produce their volumes relatively inexpensively by merely making photographic reproductions of the originals, and some of the volumes had new introductions putting their texts into the context of their original publication and the more modern one that the reprints were aimed at. One thing that this practice of using facsimiles did was to keep the pagination in the reprint the same as it was in the original editions.

DOVES PRESS AND BINDERY. *See* Cobden-Sanderson, Thomas James.

DPI. *See* Resolution.

DRAWER-HANDLE TOOL. "A finishing tool often used in England and the Netherlands during the second half of the 17th century. It was generally used in groups or sequences, and is so named because of its similarity to the handle of a drawer" (Roberts and Etherington, "drawer-handle tool"; https://cool.culturalheritage.org/don/dt/dt1081.html [accessed 18 May 2021]).

Binding decorated with drawer-handle tool blind blocking. AIC: A Collective Knowledge Resource, https://www.conservation-wiki.com/wiki/File:Drawer_handle_I_ftcover.jpg (accessed 18 May 2021).

Courtesy of the Harry Ransom Humanities Research Center, University of Texas, Austin.

DRESSED PRINT. An illustration—usually an ENGRAVING—onto which fabric fragments have been TIPPED. In a booksellers' catalog, titled *CTRL + P*, issued by Heather O'Donnell, Ben Kinmont, Simon Beattie, and Justin Croft, item 6, labeled "Dressed Print," describes a picture of Mary Magdelene: "[Probably French, but the print Augsburg: Martin Engelbrecht, mid-eighteenth century] . . . cut, hand coloured and dressed with several fabric fragments. . . . A striking and well preserved 'dressed print' . . . The fashion for dressing prints existed probably from the origin of printed illustrations themselves, though it was a widespread, predominantly female recreation during the seventeenth and eighteenth centuries, often with a devotional intent." (See under Justin Croft, *CTRL + P* in the bibliography.)

DROLLERY. *See* Babewynes.

DROP-BACK BOX. *See* Drop-spine box.

DROP CAP (i.e., drop capital letter; also called drop initial). An uppercase (often decorative) letter, such as the first one on a page or at the beginning of a paragraph or section, that is printed with a character of a point size much larger than that of the text, usually with the first characters of lines beneath the first removed to make room for the larger letter. Sometimes the drop cap also extends above the first line of the text. Some drop caps take two lines, some take three, and so on. (See R. M. Ritter, *The Oxford Guide to Style*, pp. 16–17.)

A drop cap.

From Sidney E. Berger, *Rare Books and Special Collections* (Chicago: American Library Association, 2014), 187. Reprinted with permission.

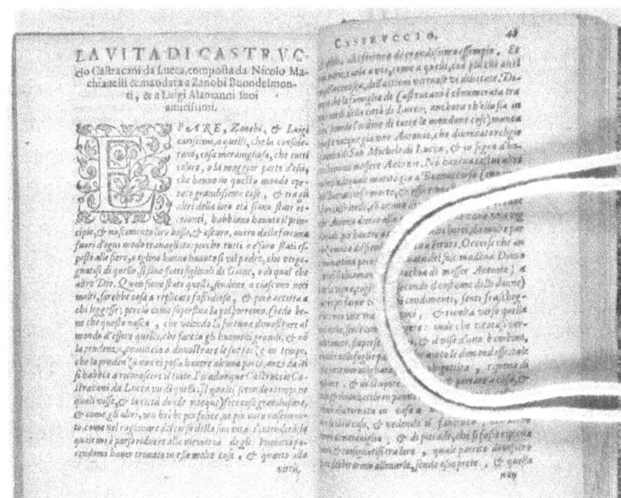

Drop cap. An 8-line drop cap FLORIATED initial; also showing CATCHWORDS on VERSO and RECTO. Niccolò Machiavelli, *I discorsi di Nicolo Machiavelli: sopra la prima deca di Tito Livio* (London: J. Wolfe, 1584). False imprint on title page: Palermo: appresso gli heredi d'Antoniello degli Antonielli a xxviii di Genaio, 1584. / One of the famous forgeries of John Wolfe, a London printer, who had traveled in Italy and invented a printer, "Antoniello," in order to publish Machiavelli's works, which had been banned in Italy since 1559.

Courtesy of the Rare Books & Manuscript Library at the University of Illinois, Urbana–Champaign.

DROP-FRONT BOX. A container for holding books that looks like a CLAMSHELL BOX, but that has a front panel (at the FORE-EDGE of the container) that folds down, allowing the user to remove the contents easily. With the front of the container folded down, contents of the box can be lifted or slid out.

DROPPED HEAD (or drop-head title, or drop title). The title of a work that lacks a title page. That is, the title appears on the first page of the text, not on a title page. For convenience and cost-saving, this phenomenon is likely to appear on pamphlets, but not too often in bound volumes. To a book designer who decided to use this unusual and annoying phenomenon I would say, "Dropped head." The term could also be used to indicate a headline (or a title) of a chapter that is printed partway down a page rather than at the top line of the page.

DROPPED LETTERS AND NUMERALS. Carter points out that it was not uncommon in the HANDPRESS PERIOD for a SORT to be pulled out of the FORME during printing or for one to be lacking from the beginning of a PRESSRUN. The result is a dropped sort (letter, number, piece of punctuation, or other printing character). The error can be spotted during the pressrun, so the missing character can be replaced. This yields three states of the text: the state with the text correct from the beginning, the state with the sort missing, and the state with the sort replaced. (*See* Edition, Impression [Printing], Issue, and State; Points.) It may be impossible to distinguish the first from the third of these. It is also possible for a sort to be missing from the first part of a pressrun and replaced for the rest or for the text to be complete for the first part of the pressrun and the dropped sort missing from the rest. Either way, this yields some copies with the text complete and some with the sort missing, and there is no way of discerning what happened first—that is, which copies were printed before the others. That is, priority of state (*see* Edition, Impression [Printing], Issue, and State; Points) might be indeterminable. Collectors and booksellers often glory in the knowledge that such points exist, and they can make good use of this in bragging about their holdings. (I am guilty of this sin, so I know.) (Carter, pp. 98–99.)

DROP-SPINE BOX. (Sometimes called a "drop-back box" or "fall-down-back box.") A (usually) cardboard box, covered in cloth or leather, with three main parts: 1) a front section that fits over 2) the back section (holding the well into which the volume is set), and 3) a SPINE attaching the two other parts. That is, the spine is a separate piece of cloth- or leather-covered cardboard, and will take a label or stamping for identification of what is inside the box. It could be designed to look like the spine of a book. Since the box looks like a clamshell in the way it opens and closes, it is sometimes called a "CLAMSHELL BOX." (*See* Boxes for books; Enclosures for books.)

DROP TITLE. *See* Dropped head.

DRYPOINT. "A technique of intaglio engraving in which a hard steel needle is used to incise lines in a metal, usually COPPER PLATE, with the rough burr at the sides of the incised lines often retained to produce a velvety black tone in the print" (*American Heritage Dictionary*, p. 551). In the 20th century, zinc, acetate, or Plexiglas could be substituted for the copper. Early in a PRESSRUN, when the burr is still firmly attached, the line it produces is generally visible. But since copper is soft, the burr can be pressed down or can become detached, and the velvety look that the burr produced would no longer be produced. The technique traces back to 15th-century Germany, and Rembrandt was one of the more accomplished artists to use it.

DRYPOINT RULING. *See* Hard point ruling.

DUCK-FOOT QUOTES. *See* Guillemets.

DUMMY. (Sometimes called a "blad" or "peddler's sample book.") A copy of a volume that is made up by a publisher to show what the final published version of the book will look like. There are two kinds. The first kind is created with the cooperation of the printer and the binder, the former supplying blank or possibly partially or fully printed sheets to the latter in the number that the final volume will have; the latter putting onto this TEXT BLOCK a mock-up binding to show what the book will be like in its published form. (This is sometimes called a "size copy" or "thickness copy." See Jacoby, *Some Notes on Books and Printing*, pp. 85, 86.) The second kind is a salesman's dummy (also called a "SALESMAN'S SAMPLE BOOK"). As just noted, sometimes the dummy copy is made from partially printed sheets, showing an early version of the text, and it can be useful to bibliographers if the author intervenes (at the point when the dummy is composed) to make substantive changes in the text. (*See* Book traveller/Traveller's sample; Subscription sales/Subscribers.)

DUNCAN, HARRY (1917–1997). One of the foremost printers and book designers of the 20th century. Duncan taught many to print, and a genealogical chart showing those he influenced includes many fine-press printers. "Harry Duncan began printing at the Cummington School of the Arts in Cummington, Massachusetts, in 1939. Using a HAND PRESS, he published books of contemporary poetry under The Cummington Press imprint first in Massachusetts, then in Iowa and Omaha, Nebraska. / From 1956 until 1972, Mr. Duncan directed the typographic laboratory and taught typography, book design and production full-time at the School of Journalism of the University of Iowa in Iowa City. / In 1972 he [went] to the University of Nebraska at Omaha where his full-time position was half teaching and half printing. He founded Abattoir Editions [there], publishing three or four titles a year. Following his retirement from teaching in 1985, he resumed printing under The Cummington Press imprint from his shop on the university campus in Omaha" (http://www.unomaha.edu/nbac/cmgt.html [accessed 26 March 2015]; this link is dead; but see https://archives.nebraska.edu/agents/corporate_entities/215 [accessed 16 July 2021]).

His books were models of design, with remarkable use of illustration, well-proportioned pages, handsome types, good paper, and attractive bindings. Equally important, Duncan was a poet with a good eye for talent. He published the first books of many poets, and he printed "the writings of some of the most prominent poets in America: Allen Tate, R. P. Blackmur, Wallace Stevens, Robert Penn Warren, . . . Robert Lowell, Richard Eberhart, [William Carlos Williams], and Marianne Moore, to name a few" (Berger, *Three Fine-Press Printers*, p. 7; see also "The Cummington Press," in *The New Colophon* 2.7 [September 1949]: 221–34, reprinted in Duncan, *Doors of Perception*, pp. 5–18; Bright, *No Longer Innocent*, pp. 52–56; and Dana, *Against the Grain*, pp. 43–86.)

DUODECIMO (also called a twelvemo). A book format formed when the original full sheet is folded into thirds and twice into halves, producing 12 leaves and 24 pages. Booksellers like to say that a duodecimo is a small format, but, as with other formats, size is only incidental, the real quality of a duodecimo being the 12 leaves formed in its composition. If the printer starts out with a large sheet, the twelvemo will be fairly large. "Different folding patterns are possible, but the more common ones produce a printed sheet that is torn or cut into two parts after printing. One part has 8 leaves, the other has 4 leaves, and these two parts are bound with the 4-leaf part preceding, following, or nested into the 8-leaf part. The format was extremely popular for it produced small volumes that contained substantial texts, and the books were easy to put into a pocket" (Berger, p. 259). The *American Heritage Dictionary of the English Language* gives the standard layman's error in its definition: "The size (5 × 7¾ inches of book pages formed by folding single sheets from a printing press into 12 leaves each" (p. 555). And many a novice bookseller adopts this definition based on the size of the volume. Serious bibliographers, booksellers, collectors, librarians, and catalogers know better.

DUOTONE. A two-color printing process, usually done for illustrations, in which a pair of halftones of the same subject—usually one in black and the other in another color or in a different tone of black—are printed at the same time. This adds a richness to a halftone image. It is sometimes called "duplex printing."

DUPLEX PRINTING. *See* Duotone.

DUPLICATES. When a colleague said to me, "We have a lot of dupes in this library," my response could have been, "And they should all be fired." But I knew she meant duplicate copies of books. These are problems because for a living library—one with a growing collection—space is (or will someday become) an issue, and duplicates take up space. They also might represent items acquired in quantity when they were first needed (as with a hot new novel for a public library or an important academic title acquired to help students in a class) and then, after their need is past, when only a single copy would suffice for the collection, they are taking up space that could be used by volumes seriously needed. And libraries, receiving large collections through purchase or gift, may acquire copies of items already in the cataloged collection. Collectors will wind up with duplicates, too, for a few reasons. At an auction, I bought one lot of books, wanting only a couple that were in the lot; the rest were duplicates. People, knowing a collector's interests, will give these collectors books that they assume the other would want; true enough, but the collector may already have the title. And I have seen quite a number of items seriously underpriced, so I got them even though I already owned a copy (or two) of the title.

Eventually duplicates can take their toll. They might need to be deaccessioned from the collection, through sale, trade, auction, bookseller arrangements, or trash. The psychological stress that collectors experience when faced with the prospect of parting with books deserves a textbook in itself. Institutions often have a weeding (*see* Appraisal) policy delineating what to do with duplicates.

But a serious issue for all concerned with dupes is: "Is this item truly a duplicate?" One line of bibliographical pronouncements is that there is no such thing as a duplicate—every copy is different from all others. This may be true for books produced in the handpress period, or possible for books that got extensive use (since these would show various signs of use and wear and would thus not be like any other copies). But for books produced during the Industrial Revolution and beyond, this might not be true (although some publishers like to issue books with variant covers—so textually two copies might be true duplicates, but the overall volumes would, of course, not be). Librarians and scholars are interested in not only the main texts but often in the variations from one copy of a text (or of the container for that text—the book or BROADSIDE itself, for example) to another. Information, of course, lies in variation, and scholars want information. A copy of a book that is worn, clearly from having been read, says something about that text. If every copy of a text shows absolutely no sign of wear of any kind, that says something, too. And for books produced in the handpress period, how can one determine if two copies are truly identical? of if they vary in some way? Variant copies are not duplicates. Should they thus be retained? Variations exist in texts, paper, binding, dust jackets, and in many other areas of the item.

(A number of years ago a publisher came out with a first edition of a novel by a prominent author. The book was issued in a hardcover with a DUST JACKET, and in PAPERBACK form with five distinct covers—each with a different-colored background. The texts within were identical; only the covers differed. As far as the text was concerned, these were duplicates. As far as a serious collector was concerned, they were not duplicates, and the collector needed to buy seven copies: the hardbound one; a copy of each of the five paperbacks; and a READING COPY. Sometimes such "duplicates" are carefully designed for a collectors' market.)

What to do with dupes is the subject for much more analysis than can be given here. We must know that they exist, learn how to identify them, decide what the variations in them mean, and decide whether to keep or part with them—and if they are to be jettisoned, we need to come up with a thoughtful plan to do so. (See Berger, *Rare Books*, pp. 37–40.)

One more note for booksellers: If a bookseller has two or more copies of an item, the pricing of it may need to be carefully thought out. One bookseller I know acquired about five copies of a scarce book (from the book's author). The first one he sold had a solid, fairly high price on it since it *was* a rare book, and in demand. The second he sold went for a higher price; and so forth. When he was down to only one copy—and there were still none for sale on the web—he could command whatever he thought the market would bear. Booksellers do not like to have duplicates of common books on their shelves; but they seldom have any problems with having dupes of treasures. (As a collector, I feel the same way.) (*See* Unique.)

DUST JACKET/DUST WRAPPER (also called "book jacket"). A usually unattached cover of a book, generally made from paper (a fairly heavy stock) or paper lined with cloth (possibly, today, from synthetic materials) used to protect the volume.

Tanselle's preferred term is Book-jacket, and he explains that "[a]lthough the terms 'book-WRAPPER' and 'dust wrapper' have sometimes been employed to refer to detachable jackets, they should be avoided because 'wrapper' is well established as a term referring to a paper cover that is physically attached to the sheets it encloses (whether it went through the press as part of those sheets or was printed separately and then attached to the folded sheets). 'Jacket,' on the other hand, has been in use at least since the 1890s to refer to a *detachable* paper covering for a book" (Tanselle, *Book-Jackets*, p. 3, n. 1), and he makes it clear that a jacket is "physically separate from the book it covers" (p. 3). The earliest jackets appear in the first third of the 19th century, and Tanselle cites the John Carter piece "Earliest Dust-Wrapper" that discusses one from 1832, covering *The Keepsake*, issued in 1832 for the following year (Tanselle, *Book-Jackets*, p. 5).

One reason there is a paucity of information on the early history of these covers is that they were not collected for much of their existence, with many a serious collector discarding them when an item with such a protective covering first came into their possession. Tanselle has the most thorough discussion of jackets, along with a discussion of related detachable book protection phenomena, like boxes, envelopes, slipcases, and cloth jackets.

The jacket has a long history, originally being used merely for protection but eventually coming to carry a great deal of information: title, author (biographical information and photograph), publishing information, BLURBS, illustrations, biographies of principals involved with the volume (author, illustrator, binder, and publisher), advertisements for many kinds of things (other works by the same author, other works by the same publisher, authors' dedications, family members, pets, and so on), price, and ISBN. (See Tanselle, *Book-Jackets*.) Often the jacket contains information not available anywhere else in the volume it covers, and the common practice in many libraries (especially academic libraries) of discarding these covers—while somewhat understandable—is nonetheless something of a disgrace in the loss of information that such trashing engenders. The argument that putting a call number on a dust jacket will not protect the item from theft is specious at best. The complaint that these things, in toto, take up valuable shelf space is equally foolish, especially in light of the fact that removing it (to save space) is discarding information.

As there are variant states of texts that can reveal much to the bookseller and bibliographer, so can there be variants in book jackets. They can sometimes be used in dating the issue (*see* Edition, Impression [Printing], Issue, and State; Points) of a volume, showing the number of copies sold, or revealing a historical occurrence (as with the book's receiving some award, being made into a movie, or being subject to a legal case)—not to mention that books in dust jackets command higher prices than the same volumes lacking these covers. Collectors want their holdings to be in as PRISTINE a condition as possible, meaning the way the volumes were issued from the publisher. If the original volume had a jacket, the collector wants it, and she is sometimes willing to pay a great deal for a copy with one. Booksellers, not being able to find a copy on the web with a jacket, may advertise a copy they are trying to sell with the words "No jacket, AS ISSUED." Or an unscrupulous book person may take a jacket from a copy and put it on his own volume. Since these covers exist in various states, a careful librarian or collector must try to figure out if the cover was original to the volume it is on.

And it bears repeating that the value of dust jackets lies not merely in the information they contain but also in the insistence by serious collectors (and the booksellers who supply them) that the jacket be present if the item is to be had in its ORIGINAL STATE OR CONDITION. On the day I wrote this paragraph, I searched the web for copies of John Steinbeck's *Grapes of Wrath*. A first edition, first printing lacking the dust jacket was available for $800; one with its dust jacket was $15,000 (https://www.biblio.com/the-grapes-of-wrath-by-steinbeck-john/work/4224 [accessed 23 January 2021]). Other copies with the jacket ranged from $1750 to $6000. If "clothes make the man," the jacket makes the book!

DUTCH FLORAL PAPER. *See* Dutch gilt papers.

DUTCH GILT PAPERS (brocade papers). A term used to describe two kinds of decorated papers, one of which is a true "dutch gilt." (The other is gold-varnished paper [see below].) A sheet of paper that has been decorated with a

An 18th-century sheet of dutch gilt paper: soldiers, gold-stamped over a blue paste wash. In the Berger-Cloonan Collection of Decorated Papers, Cushing Library, Texas A&M University.

Courtesy of Cushing Library, Texas A&M University.

foil-stamped pattern. These were first used in the 1690s, and they are generally products of the 18th century, mostly from Germany, though some were also produced in Italy. Their production died out in the early years of the 19th century, when book cloths came to be used for binding. The term comes either from the word *Deutsch* ("German") or from the fact that in Western Europe, where they were used, much of the supply outside of Germany came from the Netherlands since the Dutch got them from the Germans. This paper is frequently called "dutch floral," and applies, of course, only to dutch gilt papers with a floral pattern.

Perhaps because the papers exhibited decoration that looks like brocades, the German term *Brokatpapier* is used, engendering an English term, "brocade paper." This locution is used by many a bookseller and others in referring to these papers.

The paper usually had a wash of colored paste brushed over the surface (as with a PASTE PAPER; and the paste could be a single color or several, stenciled on in a geometrical pattern), and the gold image would be stamped over that, though many sheets have the patterns stamped over a plain, uncolored sheet. The foil was not real gold but some golden metal, sometimes mixed with copper to give the pattern a reddish/coppery cast. A silver foil was also used. The patterns were stamped onto the sheets with metal or WOODBLOCKS, and the technique was truly a RELIEF process, for in many sheets one can discern the DEBOSSING that such printing yields.

There were many patterns: geometrics; animals; birds; natural scenes; people doing all kinds of things; professions; alphabets; trees, plants, and flowers; scenes from legends and tales; soldiers; saints (particularly popular); brocades; myth-

An 18th-century sheet of dutch gilt paper: checkerboard pattern, gold-stamped over an orange paste wash. In the Berger-Cloonan Collection of Decorated Papers, Cushing Library, Texas A&M University.

Courtesy of Cushing Library, Texas A&M University.

ological beasts; and many others. The paper has many uses, including, for our purposes, book covers. They were a cheap alternative to leather, and the decorations could be quite beautiful. They were especially popular coverings for dissertations and almanacs, but they were also used as ENDPAPERS and linings for boxes and musical instruments, among many other things. Today they are scarce in full sheets, but they often turn up on the bindings of 18th-century books. (See Berger, "Dutch Gilt Papers as Substitutes for Leather"; Haemmerle, *Buntpapier*; and Wolfe, *Marbled Paper*.)

The term has also, incorrectly, been applied to another kind of paper decoration that is more properly called "gold-varnish paper." In this form of decoration, the sheet is prepared as it is for dutch gilt sheets (with the paste wash in one or more colors brushed over the sheet), but no stamping is done. The sheet then has a mordant stenciled or printed onto the surface in whatever image is desired (as above but usually floral or geometric patterns), and then a powder of metallic foil is introduced to the surface of the sheet. The finely ground powder sticks to the sheet where the mordant is, and the rest is brushed away, leaving the pattern on the sheet only where the mordant was. Since no pressing is used, there is no three-dimensionality on the sheet, as is evident in a dutch gilt sheet. Finally, a fine varnish is brushed over the sheet, which is discernible on close inspection. The two decorative techniques are quite different from one another, and anyone familiar with them will easily be able to distinguish a dutch gilt from a gold-varnish sheet—though they look from a distance quite similar. But many a bookseller or collector does not know the difference and will describe a binding's cover paper as "dutch gilt" when it is not. The technique was also used with silver and bronze powders, yielding "silver varnish paper" and "bronze varnish paper." (The German words reflect the techniques and colors: *Giltvernispapier*, *Silbervernispapier*, and *Bronzevernispapier*.) (*See* Kinkarakami.)

E

EARLY PRINTED. Carter's definition mentions INCUNABULA and then books printed before 1600 (p. 101). Today these distinctions hardly apply, and when a bookseller speaks of "early printed," she is more likely talking about books from the HANDPRESS PERIOD. I have even heard relative newcomers to the book world say of a 19th-century Bible, "This is an early printed book." It's all a matter of perspective. "Early printed" is not a formal bookman's term, as Carter seems to suggest.

EBAY. The premier online AUCTION site for all kinds of goods, including books and other paper-based collectibles. Brian O'Connell says, "Originally called Auction web, eBay was founded by [Pierre] Omidyar on Labor Day weekend in 1995, when he listed his laser printer for $1. For a week, there were no takers, then bidders began weighing in and driving the price of the battered printer up to $14.83. Immediately, Omidyar knew he was on to something big. / And 25 years later, history has proven Omidyar right. The company has a market capitalization of $29 billion at the end of 2019, and the company's founder now has a net worth of $13.1 billion" (Brian O'Connell, "History of eBay: Facts and Timeline," *The Street*, 18 December 2019, https://www.thestreet.com/markets/history-of-ebay#:~:text=1995%20%E2%80%93%20The%20company%20is%20founded,aboard%20as%20CEO%20in%201998 [accessed 30 May 2022].)

eBay was originally set up (and still operates) as an auction operation, though it allows its users, for many items, to "Buy It Now," meaning that if a patron sees an item on the eBay site, he can order it instantly, without going through the bidding process. The seller, in other words, puts the item up for bid, but is willing to sell at a price he has determined. And for many items for sale, the buyer can also "Make an Offer," hoping that the seller will take less than his "Buy It Now" price.

As with all ONLINE BOOK SALES, offerings on eBay can be tricky. The caveats noted at the "Online book sales" entry apply to sales from eBay. (Parenthetically, the level of professionalism of the eBay sellers ranges from the highest ABAA practitioners, to the mom-and-pop operations where retirees are trying to make some pocket change, to the outright criminal. With the hundreds of millions of items offered on this site, the proprietors of eBay cannot monitor everything. As a library director, I acquired on eBay a group of photographs that had been stolen from my library perhaps decades earlier than my acquisition. eBay responsibly assisted me in "straightening out" this sale. The relative anonymity of the sellers [when they want to remain in the shadows] makes it difficult to police the sales of *everything*. As with all commerce, and especially with e-commerce: *caveat emptor*.) But it is worth noting that eBay carries untold numbers of items that readers of this dictionary will be interested in, and often at bargain prices. Users of the site must be on their toes since most of the auctioned items have a time limit, and there is a worldwide competition for everything that the site lists. And since eBay acquired PayPal in 2002, and since more than 70 percent of eBay sellers use that payment method, it is dangerously easy to buy on the site.

E-BOOKS. *See* E-readers/e-books.

EBRÛ. (For convenience, it is spelled in Western scripts without the diacritic over the u.) Turkish MARBLING; or the Turkish word for marbling. The word, of Persian origin, and used in Turkish to designate the whole field of marbling, means cloud, or "looking like cloudy" (Muin Nursen Eriş, *Mustafa Esat Düzgünman ve Ebrû / Mustafa Esat Düzgünman and Ebrû*). The Turkish scholar and brilliant marbler Nedim Sönmez says, "The origin of the word Ebru is unclear. It may come from the Chagatay Turkish 'Ebre' (veined, not regular in colour) or from the Persian 'Ebri' (cloud)" (Sönmez, *From Ebru to Marbled Paper / vom Ebru zum Marmorpapier*, p. 7, n. 1). The word is often seen in English texts, used to give a sense of the exotic or simply because it sounds more elevated or intellectual to say that the binding was covered in ebru. (See Nedim Sönmez, *Ebru—The Turkish Art of Marbling.*)

ECLECTIC EDITION. *See* Bibliography, especially the section "Textual Bibliography."

EDGES OF BOOKS. The term, of course, refers to the three exposed edges of the TEXT BLOCK: the HEAD or top, the FORE-EDGE, and the FOOT or tail. These can be DECKLED, TRIMMED, or decorated in various ways, such as marbled, red, GAUFFERED, GILT, painted, or sprinkled. All of these decorative touches are called "edge treatments." Since edges are exposed (unless the volume is in some sort of protective enclosure, such as a SLIPCASE), they tend to be the first parts of books to become dirty, particularly along the top. This is especially true for millions of books from European and early American libraries shelved in homes heated with coal, which deposits a fine black layer on the tops of the text blocks. That coal dust can be acidic, and some damage may have occurred from this kind of exposure. Also, in moist climes, FOXING may be evident on the edges of books.

One popular treatment for edges is to gild them (top-gilded volumes are referred to as TEG; books with all edges gilt are referred to as AEG). And there are also the enhancements of creating FORE-EDGE ILLUSTRATIONS or gauffering, or the edges can be MARBLED sometimes using the same marbling bath in which the end sheets were decorated, achieving a harmony in patterns on the endleaves and the edges. In some early libraries, books were shelved with the fore-edges exposed, in which case the titles or authors' names (or some shelf numbering) may be written on them. (*See* Rough gilt.)

EDITION BINDING. The binding of an entire edition of a text in uniform (usually CASE) bindings. Until the first quarter of the 19th century—before the wide commercial use of cloth as a binding material—books were bound individually. With the coming of cloth for binding, case binding became the norm for its speed and low cost. Publishers could then order thousands of identical cases to be made for their TEXT BLOCKS, and entire editions could be bound uniformly. (*See* Binder's cloth.) These uniformly bound volumes are said to be in their "edition binding," but that does not mean that an entire edition is so bound. It is possible for the binder to run out of one color of cloth or for the publisher to decide to offer the edition in more than one design of cover (variations in cloth, paper, or leather are possible), or, for whatever reason, an edition could have two or more "edition bindings."

"The business of binding identical books in quantity, usually for a publisher or distributor, as opposed to binding done for an individual and library binding" (Roberts and Etherington, p. 86). The practice yields volumes that all look alike (unless there is some reason that the publisher decides to vary the looks of the bindings within the edition). It should be added, however, that the entire edition could be only a small number of copies (as with the work of a FINE PRESS that may produce an edition of, say, 20 copies). If all of these volumes are bound uniformly, this is still "edition binding." But Roberts and Etherington distinguish hand binding from edition binding in that the latter is done with "extensive use of semi-automatic and automatic equipment, some of which operates at very high speeds. This equipment is capable of processing thousands of books in a relatively short time" (p. 86).

ÉDITION DE LUXE. *See* Deluxe edition.

EDITION, IMPRESSION (PRINTING), ISSUE, AND STATE; POINTS. These terms must be presented in one place because of their relationship to one another. They are confusing to the novice and often even to the expert, as can be witnessed by their frequent misuse in dealers' catalogs and cataloging records.

"Strictly speaking, an *edition* of a text is composed of all copies of that text printed from the same setting of type. Although this is a simple concept, it is complicated by the fact that a text can be set into type and printed, and then the author revises two of his twelve chapters. The next printing is done from the 'same setting of type' for ten chapters, but a different setting for the other two. Is this still the same edition? The answer is that it is still the same edition for the first ten chapters. . . .

"[Also], a book can be printed from STEREOTYPE or ELECTROTYPE plates. These plates were created from standing type. Hence the printing of the text, done from the type, is identical to the printing from the plates. They are all the same edition. It is not strictly accurate, then, to call one the 'first edition' and the other the 'stereotype edition,' because there is no difference in edition. That is, they are both first editions. More accurate would be to say that one is the 'first edition' and the other is the 'stereotype version' (or printing) of the first edition.

"Likewise, a publisher can sell the standing type or the plates of an edition to another publisher and company number two can print a text, from the same type or plates, one hundred years after the first edition was printed. The publisher can even change the title page to reflect the new ownership of the work. If the rest of the volume is printed from that same setting of type, it is still the same edition.

"It is clear that an edition can have varying typography in some instances: a new title page, some typos corrected in later-printed versions, an added preface, or some other change in the original typesetting. But if the bulk of the second or subsequent printing of a text is from the first setting of type, the volume is essentially the same edition. How much change can be done that will yield the designation 'same edition' is up to the bibliographer. Maybe if half the book is printed from the original setting of type, the two copies will be of the same edition. Perhaps some scholars would say that much resetting constitutes a new edition. There are no 'industry standards' for such a decision on terminology. . . .

"So the printing of the text is the only thing that constitutes an edition, not the binding, the date of printing, the release of the text to the public, or the number of copies printed" (Berger, pp. 261–62). (*See* First edition.) It must be added as well that a publisher today, making an exact digital impression of a first edition of a book from, say, 1685 and then publishing that text using computer graphics (as a FACSIMILE version), is printing another copy of the first edition since it is printed from the same setting of type as was the 1685 edition. Modern publishers, not understanding this fine point, might advertise their work as a "new edition" when they really mean a new printing.

The *impression* (or *printing*) is all the copies printed at one STINT of the press. "All copies of a text that were printed at one time, without the printer's taking the type out of the press, are of the same impression or the same printing (in this context, the two words are interchangeable). Thus, a copyright page for a modern book (or a bibliographer with information about the printing history of an older book) may say, 'First edition, second impression.' In many books printed in the twentieth century, the copyright page may even give more specific information: 'Second edition, fifth impression; December 1945.' . . .

"Determining what printing a book is within an edition is not easy, though in recent years the copyright page of many commercially published books may have a string of numbers (e.g., '1 2 3 4 5 6 7 8 9 10' or numbers in reverse order); the lowest number showing usually indicates the printing. So the listing 4 5 6 7 8 9 10 would indicate that the volume in hand is the fourth printing of that edition. Not all publishers use this method of printing delineation, and often there is no way to know the impression of a book. For popular books that get many printings, the numbers might go 99 98 97 96 95 94 93, and so on. Again, the lowest number indicates the impression" (Berger, p. 266). (*See* Impression.)

"All copies released to the public at one time are said to be 'issued' on that date. They constitute the *issue* of the publisher of that title. A publisher could print twenty thousand copies of a book and issue half of them in April, five thousand in June, and the rest in September. This would constitute three issues of a volume. So a scholar could deduce that 'this copy is the first edition, second issue.' Usually, if the volume is indeed the same edition and the same printing [or impression], it is impossible to figure out what issue it is. Sometimes, however, the issue can be determined because the difference in issues is chronological. That is, one issue will precede the other, so changes could have been made between the issue dates. For instance, a first issue might be released in one kind of binding and the second issue in another. It may be possible to deduce the order of the issues: 'In the red binding of the first issue' as opposed to 'In the green binding of the second issue.' The cover art could have changed between issues. A publisher announcing the first issue of an edition might have an advertising piece that states, 'In a lovely gold-stamped, ribbed maroon cloth.' If the scholar finds the ad, and then sees a copy of the book in a binding of another color, she might deduce that the volume in the other color is a later issue. (This is not necessarily the case, of course, but it is food for thought.) . . .

"[V]ariations in typography, binding, or advertising matter may help the bibliographer distinguish one issue from another. But even the recognition of different issues may not allow the scholar to determine which issue came first. Hence a bibliographer might say, 'First issue with red cloth; second issue in blue cloth; third issue in wrappers. Chronological order of issues not determinable' (or 'Order of issues is arbitrary but used to distinguish different issues')" (Berger, p. 267).

"It was common in the HANDPRESS PERIOD for a printer to stop the press, make a change (usually a correction of a typographical error that he had spotted during the printing), and go on with the PRESSRUN. [*See* Stop-press corrections.] This operation created what is called a *state* variant, an alternate reading at one point in the text from how the text reads in another copy. . . . The result was a text in two states, one with the error, one with the correction. Often it is easy to spot such a correction and to determine which is the 'first state' and which is the 'second state,' for it would not make any sense for a printer to stop printing" in order to introduce a typo into the text. "The bibliographer could say, 'The text exists in two states,' and then delineate what they are, how they differ, and what order they came in" (Berger, p. 268). (*See* Corrigendum/Corrigenda; Erratum/Errata.)

This discussion about states (in Berger) goes on for many more paragraphs and is worth reading since not all state variants are corrections of typographical errors; some later states contain errors when the earlier states do not, and sometimes two perfectly good readings exist at one point in two copies of the same edition, and it is impossible to determine which came first and which was authorial, which compositorial or editorial, and so on. Further, state is not necessarily tied to typography—sometimes the bindings are in different states, or the dust jackets are, or the illustrations are. "And finally, the state of a text can be related to its completeness. For any reason, a publisher or an author may wish to remove an illustration, a page, even a chapter from a volume—or add something to the text in like manner. This, too, creates a different state from the one in which the book is complete. So a first edition, first state could lack three illustrations, while the second state has them tipped in where the publisher put them (and maybe where the author demanded they be put). These additions or subtractions may take place between the first and the second issue of a book, so it might be accurate to describe the book as 'first edition, second issue, second state.' In this instance the issue and the state are linked, but that is not always the case" (Berger, p. 269).

As Carter points out, different issues and different states can exist in a single edition. This could occur when some STOP-PRESS CORRECTIONS are made while a text is at press—hence, two or more states of the text would be created. Once the book is issued, the printer/publisher could find a particularly objectionable problem in the text. Thus, in the copies still unsold—that is, still in the hands of the publisher—the offending leaf can be removed and replaced with one fixing the problem. (This creates a CANCEL.) All those copies, with the cancellans (the replaced leaf) will then go on the market at a later time—that is, in a later *issue*. Copies from the first issue and from the second issue are still part of the *first edition*, and copies from both issues "are likely to show an indiscriminate mixture of variations of state" (Carter, p. 152). Carter concludes that it may be impossible, in many instances, to determine which issue came first.

The final term to learn here is *points*. When two texts vary at some specific spot, that variation is called a point. Points are any kind of variations that distinguish one copy from another. Usually the points are typographic: "With page 57 printed '75,'" "With the plate facing page 714 lacking the engraver's signature," or "With the last letter of line 7 on page 55 printed upside down." The points can be in the binding (variants in cover illustration, variants in endpapers, or variants in binding methods). Misprints are often corrected, yielding points that POINT MANIACS love to cite. Varying advertising in a volume (on the printed pages or in the inclusion of bound-in advertising brochures from the publisher) are points. And other kinds of differences (cancels, changes in text, and changes in illustrations [their images or their placement]) are also points. Sometimes the presence of a point can tell the scholar which copy of the volume was printed first, but that is not always the case. A case in point (pun intended) is the placement of the frog on the cover of Mark Twain's first published book, *The Celebrated Jumping Frog of Calaveras County, and Other Sketches*. If the frog is in the lower left of the cover, the book could be worth about $7,500 or more, depending on condition. But if the frog is in the center of the cover, the cost could be three or four times that. This is a grand point. Though there is no way to prove it, the version with the frog in the middle of the cover is almost certainly in the first state; the one with the frog in the lower left is the second state. (If you read the story about this frog, you will see why.)

Much more minor points have to do with broken type in some copies, a dropped letter, the color of the cover cloth, and so on. A dealer may say, "A good copy of the first edition, first issue, with all points," and the reader must know what those points are or where she can go (to which bibliography or other reference tool) to learn what these points are.

"The terminology can be confusing and bewildering, but a mastery of it is crucial if one is to be conversant with the language (and the concepts behind it) of the rare book world" (Berger, p. 269). (*See* Book club edition; First edition.)

***EDITIO PRINCEPS*.** Originally, the term indicated the first time a book was brought into print from manuscript form, but many a high-end collector, possibly taking his cue from an equally elevated bookseller, may use the term for any first edition. The implication is that this is not merely a first edition but also an *editio princeps*—hence particularly desirable and valuable. Happily, the term is slowly dying of its own weight, and it is not much in use these days. Though many a bookseller will use this term when they mean "first edition," especially for valuable and costly books, to give them the gloss of the exotic.

EDWARDS OF HALIFAX. P. J. M. Marks discusses the Edwards family of bookbinders in her "The Edwards of Halifax Bindery." "The story of the Edwards family of Halifax is the stuff of a Victorian three volume novel. William Edwards (baptized in 1722, died in 1808), a provincial publisher and bookseller, built up a firm which became influential in the book trade in England and abroad. William (1753–86), his first son, [was not involved in the family business]. Four other sons were partners in the bookselling business but were also known for their individual accomplishments. The second son, James (1756–1816), described as an 'EXOTIC bookseller,' was also a publisher, gentleman spy, and bibliophile; even his coffin was made from the empty bookshelves of his library. James and his brother John (1758–91) opened a London bookshop in Pall Mall in 1784 which continued until 1799. . . . Thomas (1762–1834) dutifully stayed at home and ran the Halifax shop selling books and patent medicines. . . . He also supervised trips to bind the libraries of local worthies, and was alleged to have been a local political activist. The youngest son, Richard Edwards (1768–1827), owned a bookshop; he was a patron and publisher of William Blake (Electronic British Library Journal, "Abstract," http://www.bl.uk/eblj/1998articles/article13.html [accessed 4 June 2021]; see bibliography).

James Edwards is the best known of the binders, but each of the sons had his own strength, and since many of their bindings are unsigned, booksellers and collectors are wont to attribute a binding to "Edwards of Halifax" when it is impossible to know who the actual binder was. One of the popular forms of decoration they excelled in was FORE-EDGE ILLUSTRATION (William and his son Thomas were particularly known for this kind of embellishment). They were also known for the Etruscan style of decoration (*see* Etruscan calf). Another innovation of the bindery was the creation of transparent vellum, which was painted on the underside—the technique allowing the painting to show through the vellum but be protected from abrasion since the painted surface was not exposed. This technique was patented in 1785 by James Edwards, though it was in use as early as 1781 (see Marks, cited above, p. 186). As Marks explains, "The painted vellum bindings were very popular and there is evidence that some were specially commissioned. This might explain the puzzling lack of references to painted vellum bindings in the sale catalogues issued by members of the Edwards family and other booksellers, which do refer to the other Edwards specialities, Etruscan calf and painted fore-edges" (p. 186).

These phenomena (fore-edge illustration, Etruscan-style bindings, and transparent-painted vellum) were so popular that they were copied—with fore-edge illustration by the thousands—and if a book with one of these embellishments dates to approximately when the Edwardses were in operation (ca. 1755–ca. 1834), a bookseller may well automatically attribute it to the Edwards atelier, though innumerable copies (even 20th- and 21st-century ones) abound that were not done in the Edwards bindery.

EGE, OTTO F. (1888–1951). One of the most notorious BREAKERS in book history. "In the late 1940s, longtime Cleveland resident and art historian Otto F. Ege selected fifty medieval manuscripts from his personal collection and removed several dozen individual pages from each one. He mounted each leaf onto a large paper mat using tape hinges, and added a descriptive label to the mat. He then put one leaf from each of the fifty component manuscripts into a durable portfolio box; each of the resulting boxed sets thus contained a different leaf from each of the fifty original manuscripts. Forty boxes containing fifty leaves each were made in this way, and were offered for sale to university and public libraries around North America" (Denison Library, Denison University, "Otto F. Ege Collection").

Ege repeated this kind of evisceration with printed books. The implications of this kind of BIBLIOCLASM are discussed at the entry for "Breaker." Often such actions are justified by the perpetrator with the stance, that Ege took, that many people can have the pleasure of owning a piece of history. (And as repugnant as the practice is, it does yield some valuable teaching tools.) But it was clear that he was in it for the money. His portfolios occasionally surface on the rare book market, though in a bizarre form of retribution—or maybe it is a compound fracture—individual leaves now surface, Ege's original portfolios having been broken, certainly for monetary gain. Attempts to reunite the stray pieces digitally to reconstitute the original manuscripts or printed volumes are under way (mostly for the manuscripts), but those efforts have been made much more difficult with the fracturing of the portfolios. (Parenthetically, I have seen individual leaves of printed books from Ege's gatherings selling for hundreds of dollars.) (*See* Fragmentology.)

EGYPTIAN TYPE (slab serif). A typeface with a slab serif—that is, with serifs that are square or rectangular, not ones that are thin or tapering. The serifs are almost of the same weight (or *are* of the same weight) as are the strokes of the rest of the character. The type was frequently used for display, not always for printing extended texts, and most typefounders of the 19th century produced a version of it. Lawson (*Printing Types*) says the first showing of them was in 1815, and he discusses their popularity (or lack thereof among many detractors of these "fat faces"; p. 93). He points out that "[b]y 1825, slab-serif types were brought out with lowercase characters. Further experiments with the form produced serifs which were bracketed slightly, and by 1850 they were available in several weights and widths from all typefounders. . . . The popularity of square serif types declined severely during the first three decades of the twentieth century, but the sans serif revival after 1926, along geometric lines, carried over to a renewed interest in similarly designed square serifs. . . . Although these styles were far removed from their nineteenth-century counterparts, the Egyptian terminology hung on" (pp. 93, 95). (See also Lawson, *Anatomy of a Typeface*, pp. 310 ff.)

EIGHT-PAGERS. *See* Tijuana bibles.

EIGHT UP. *See* Up (as in "two up," "four up," "eight up").

ELBOW (in a composing stick). The part of a COMPOSING STICK that is movable, adjustable to the length of the line the COMPOSITOR wishes to set. It is also sometimes called the knee. There are several locking mechanisms to hold the elbow in place, including levers that fold down over the edge of the stick, clamps, screws, and clips that screw on tightly. A loose elbow could cause lines in the composing stick to be set at different measures, so it is essential that the elbow be immobile and perfectly squared off from the opposite part of the stick, the head.

ELECTROSTATIC PRINTING. *See* Xerography.

ELECTROTYPING (electros). "The art of taking one metal, and, after placing it in a state of solution, causing it by electric or galvanic action to spread itself over the surface of a MOLD of whatever design, and there be deposited in a film or sheet" (*American Dictionary of Printing and Bookmaking*, p. 157; this source has a superb article on the process with relation to printing: pp. 157–66). In printing, the "mold" is a page of set type or an illustration, and the resultant PLATE, called an "electroplate" or an "electro," is a RELIEF plate with an exactly replicated text of what was in the type or image. The PLATES, made of a harder metal than type metal, can print many thousands of impressions without damage, and the plates not only weigh a fraction of what a page of set type weighs and take up only a fraction of the space that type occupies, but they also free up the type for DISTRIBUTION and use for other projects. "The process was first announced in 1838 by M[oritz] H. von Jacobi, a German working in St. Petersburg, Russia" (*Encyclopaedia Britannica*, "electrotyping"; http://www.britannica.com/technology/electrotyping [accessed 4 June 2021]).

"In brief, the process is, after the page or cut is made ready and perfectly clean, to impress it with great power into a sheet of wax; then this sheet, after having had its surface equally and thinly covered with powdered plumbago, is suspended in a galvanic bath in which copper is present in a state of solution; the copper being affected by electricity leaves the solution and deposits itself evenly over the face of the mold; the film or sheet is removed when it is thought to be thick enough, and is covered on the back with tin or a compound into which tin enters, which serves as a solder to which electrotype metal, or a compound closely resembling type metal, will adhere. Enough of the latter is added to make a thoroughly sound, stiff plate from one-tenth to one-sixth of an inch in thickness, and it is then planed, trimmed, beveled or has other operations performed upon it to increase its evenness or the ease with which it can be used" (*American Dictionary of Printing and Bookmaking*, p. 157). The printing plate looks much like a STEREOTYPE PLATE, but it is covered with a fine layer of copper, while the stereo is made basically from type metal with no surface on it.

Books printed from electrotype plates cannot be distinguished from those printed directly from STANDING TYPE. In fact, as the book *Basic Requirements for Better Electrotypes* points out, the method was so accurate that if there were even the smallest "imperfection" in the original—a printed dot, an area in a CUT that was high enough to receive ink and print—the electro would pick it up, so the plates had to be "tidied up" after the electrotyping was done. "[T]he electrotype reproduces not only the printing surface of the original from which it is made, but all other conditions below the printing surface, including 'shoulders' or any imperfections not obvious from a proof of the original. This means that the bad as well as the good features of the original sometimes are reproduced. / Consequently, the quality of an electrotype depends on the care with which the customer, photoengraver, COMPOSITOR and electrotyper do their work" (p. 3). (*See* Stereotyping.) (See *Basic Requirements for Better Electrotypes*.)

Also, it must be remembered that any text printed from electros is of the same edition as is the text printed from the original type from which the electros were produced. (*See* Edition, Impression [Printing], Issue, and State; Points.)

ELEPHANT FOLIO. The generic term for an enormous volume but more specifically a book that is a FOLIO in manuscript, or printed on exceptionally large sheets. Since paper sizes were never standardized, what constituted a volume that would merit the adjective "elephant" is not clear. But Labarre states: "Elephant is the name of a size of all kinds (writing, drawing and wrapping) of paper, varying between 28" × 23" and 34" × 28". . . . *Double Elephant* (also termed Grand Eagle in Boards) varies from 36" × 24" to 46" × 31", in 1784 also in Writings 40" × 26¾" while *Long Double Elephant* (in Boards) is 50" × 27½". This is probably another example of the watermark having given its name to a size of paper; though rare, an Elephant as watermark was used as early as 1366 at Brussels and in 1484 at Venice" (*Dictionary and Encyclopaedia*, pp. 87–88). Perhaps the best known double elephant folio is John James Audubon's *Birds of America*, published in FASCICLES from 1827 to 1838. (See Roger Tory Peterson and Virginia Marie Peterson, *Audubon's Birds of America*.)

ELSE FINE. *See* Condition.

ELZEVIER. (Also spelled Elzevir.) A distinguished family of 17th- and early 18th-century Dutch printers and booksellers, the earliest of whom was Louis, who was active from 1575 to 1617, early on as a bookbinder and bookseller but from 1583 as a publisher. (See Lankhorst, "Elzevir Family.") As Lankhorst points out, the family over several generations published hundreds of books, academic texts, books on science and philosophy, and books on many other topics. "The Elzeviers' vast international trade network is demonstrated by their numerous book lists, such as the impressive *Catalogus Librorum qui in Bibliopolio Danielis Elsevirii Venales Extant* (1674), which contains some 20,000 books on all subjects in many languages" (p. 695).

EMBLEM BOOKS. A 16th-century and later genre of books in which an image (an emblem) would be paired with a written text that commented in some way on the picture. As Alvan Bregman explains, in speaking of the first printed emblem book, done by Andrea Alciato (printed in 1531 in Augsburg, and titled *Emblematum Liber*), "If we look at the earliest printed versions of his work, we will see that each emblem in the collection has three inter-related parts, namely, from top to bottom, (1) a title, (2) an illustration, (3) a descriptive or moralizing verse. . . . [T]he illustration within an emblem has always been of keen interest to readers, and for modern readers especially, the chief charm of the emblem is the illustration" (Bregman, *Emblemata*, p. 38). The genre became tremendously popular, with more than 170 editions of Alciato's text alone being published. One important collection of these books is at the University of Illinois, Urbana–Champaign. The website for that collection says, "Since the 1940's the University of Illinois at Urbana–Champaign Library has been building a collection of emblem books written from 1540–1800, published in Germany, France, Italy, Spain and England. Emblem books can be considered the multimedia publications of the 16th through the 18th centuries. Each emblem is composed of three constitutive elements—a motto, an illustration or 'pictura' in the form of a woodcut or engraving, and an explanatory poem or 'subscriptio.' An emblem is more than the sum of its parts, because the interplay between text and image produces a greater meaning than any of the individual components can provide. Since 1998 the Rare Book & Manuscript Library has been enhancing access to the German emblem books through digitization. The digitization efforts are now being coordinated with the Herzog August Bibliothek, Wolfenbüttel. These two institutions are cooperating on the Project 'Emblematica On-Line,' funded by an NEH/DFG digital humanities grant to present emblem books in an innovative digital environment and to develop a portal for a key genre of Renaissance texts and images. The OpenEmblem Portal hosted at Illinois offers the ability to search and browse emblems from a variety of perspectives" ("Emblem Collection of the University of Illinois," https://archive.org/details/emblem [accessed 4 June 2021]; see "Emblematica Online" at http://emblematica.grainger.illinois.edu/projectHistory.html and http://emblematica.grainger.illinois.edu/otherProjects.html [accessed 4 June 2021]). (See also [Robin Raybould], *Emblemata: Symbolic Literature of the Renaissance, from the Collection of Robin Raybould.*)

EMBOSSING. Creating a pattern in relief—as on a sheet of paper or cover board. The surface is stamped between the faces of a male and female die, and the result is a raised "text" on one side and a depressed (DEBOSSED) "text" on the other. The method mimics the raised surface of ENGRAVING but often with much more pronounced results. That is, an engraved text is raised above the surface a small amount, while embossing can produce a much more pronounced raised surface. It was much used in the printing of ephemeral materials in the 19th century.

EMBRITTLED/EMBRITTLEMENT. A term popular in the literature of PRESERVATION, denoting the brittle nature of something—often paper. Because of the ACIDITY of paper starting during the last quarter of the 19th century, paper tended to turn yellow and become quite fragile and have practically no folding strength. A single fold could split the paper at that fold—the ultimate embrittlement. (Predictions of paper's turning so brittle that it turns to dust were grossly exaggerated to make a point to potential U.S. funding agencies in the 1970s and 1980s to support preservation microfilming efforts, but that often reproduced, iconic picture of Peter Waters crushing paper in his hand and blowing it away persists in the popular imagination.) Nonetheless, collectors of certain genres should understand that the items they collect may be composed of brittle papers.

EMBROIDERED BINDING. As the name says, a binding with embroidery or other kinds of needlework on it. As this definition shows, bookbindings have been decorated with several kinds of stitching, not merely embroidering, but many a bookseller, seeing, for example, a binding with cross-stitch on it, might call it an "embroidered binding" because the term has become a shorthand for any kind of textile work on a book cover. The more generic terms are "textile binding" or "needlework binding," for these cover all kinds of handwork. The practice of using embroidery goes back to the Middle Ages. (See Coron, ed. *Livres en Broderie.*)

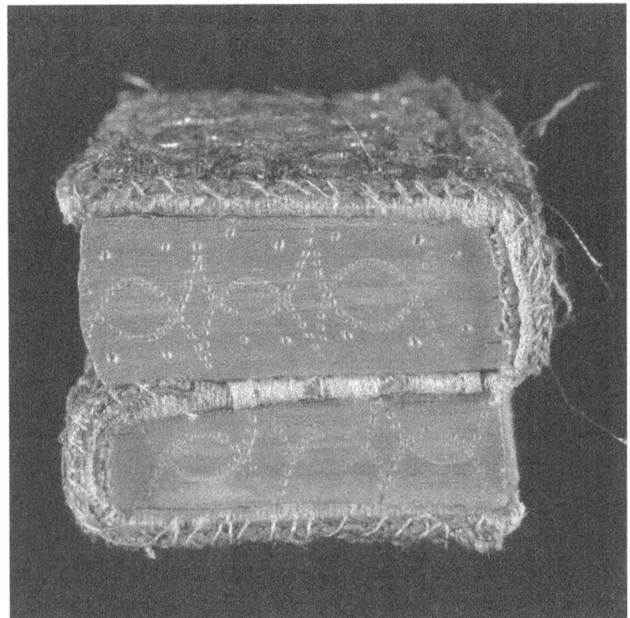

An "embroidered" binding—actually with needlework and beads (*see* next image). Also, this is a DOS-À-DOS binding with GAUFFERED edges. *The Whole Booke of Psalmes / Collected into English Meeter* (London: Imprinted [by Felix Kingston] for the Company of Stationers, 1630); bound with *The New Testament of our Lord and Sauiour Iesus Christ* (London: Robert Barker, Printer to the Kings Most Excellent Maiestie and by the Assignes of John Bill, 1630).

Courtesy of the Rare Books & Manuscript Library of the University of Illinois at Urbana–Champaign.

Another view of the needlework binding. (*See* previous image.)

Courtesy of the Rare Books & Manuscript Library of the University of Illinois at Urbana–Champaign.

EMENDATIONS. In creating a definitive edition (*see* Bibliography), the editor chooses a base text to work from (the so-called COPY-TEXT) and, after locating (in various versions of the text being edited) all variants that might be used to change the copy-text, emends the text with variants that seem to be more AUTHORIAL than the readings in the copy-text. These changes are called "emendations." (But see the note at the end of the entry for copy-text.) The selection of readings for emendation is a highly developed practice (*see* Bibliography). (*See* Accidentals; Recension; Substantives.)

EM QUAD/EN QUAD. QUADS (short for "quadrats") are spacing matter in printing type. The em was approximately the width of a capital *M* (from which the SORT gets its name), which meant that the nonprinting sort was square, and that is the shape that em quads were for all sizes of type. The sort was used as a unit of measurement, and a printer could be said to have set a certain number of ems per STINT. The en was half the size of an em. (The en was sometimes called a "nut" or "nut quad.") Naturally, one can set many ems of type for a large font (say, 18-point type) much more quickly than one could set ems for smaller fonts.

ENAMELED (spelled with one or two l's). "Originally, a supercalendered printing paper coated on both sides with a pigment such as satin white or blanc fixe; today, enamelled is considered to be any coated paper" (Roberts and Etherington, "enamelled"; https://cool.culturalheritage.org/don/dt/dt1182.html [accessed 18 July 2021]). Books are often bound in these exceptionally smooth and bright papers, sometimes with lithographic or other printed text on them. We might thus see the word "enameled" in a binding description for this kind of cover paper.

ENAMELED BINDINGS. *See* Champlevé bindings.

ENCAPSULATION. Enclosing documents or other materials in a protective covering. While Carter says that sheets so treated are vacuum sealed in what he calls "inert plastic" (p. 106), he is actually describing LAMINATION. The modern practice distinguishes encapsulation from lamination. The latter, creating a vacuum-sealed enclosure, creates a microclimate in this enclosure that can be damaging in that changes in temperature or humidity can cause the sealed item to be exposed to condensation. Modern conservation treatments that encapsulate create an enclosure that is not hermetically sealed but is open to allow air exchange. Encapsulation allows for the handling of the item with not much added deterioration, but INHERENT VICE in the item should be neutralized, if possible, before the encapsulation is done. Also, it is important to encapsulate with acid-free, archival materials. In modern practice, encapsulation is reversible; lamination usually is not. (*See* Delamination.) A final note:

despite Carter's claim, not all plastics are inert. Many are quite acidic.

ENCAUSTIC BOOKS. "Encaustic" is "[a] paint consisting of pigment mixed with beeswax and fixed with heat after its application" (*American Heritage Dictionary*, p. 586). Encaustic books are those made with this technique. The term (and the method) seem to derive from the work of Richard H. Turnbull of Furious Day Press, New York. His flyer states, "At an encaustic painting workshop at Snow Farm in Williamsburg, MA, I wondered about the possibility of making books with pigmented wax. After some experiments with how best to apply wax to folded paper, I realized that the accordion fold structure perhaps lent itself best to encaustic. Even there, however, the process of making an encaustic book turns out to be a bit counterintuitive to the way we normally make books, in the sense that all gluing and weighting down of covers has to be done *before* the application of wax, lest one wind up with a pressed block of wax between wooden covers." Though there seems to be a paucity of such books in the world, it *is* a term from the book world, and should anyone encounter one of these pigmented wax books, she will now have a proper term for them. (See Richard H. Turnbull in the bibliography.)

ENCLOSURES FOR BOOKS. Books are fragile. And particularly valuable or fragile volumes often wind up in some kind of enclosure for protection or preservation. The various common types are discussed at the appropriate place in the present volume: BOOK SHOE; CUT-CORNER PAMPHLET FILE; DROP-SPINE BOXES; SLIPCASES; WRAPPERS; and so on.

ENDBANDS/RAISED BANDS. The raised sewing supports of material on the back of (usually leather-bound) books (formed by the use of CORDS or alum-TAWED goatskin or vellum strips under the leather spine). If the binder has used three such bands and has not made them SAWN IN, there will be three raised strips on the spine, forming four PANELS (little compartments) into which the binder can place a label or can stamp information, such as the book's title, author, publisher, date—or all of these. The bands are either laced into the boards (*see* Laced in) or glued to the boards (*see* Cased in), holding the book's component parts (covers and TEXT BLOCK) together. If the bands were sunk into grooves sawn into the text block, genuine endbands could be present, but no raised bands would be visible. The presence of raised bands was once an indication of a hand-bound book and could then command higher prices than were asked for case-bound volumes. The raised bands created by pasted-on strips across the spine might produce the bulging strips, and they might look like the real thing (created by sewing over cords), but they had no structural integrity as did the genuine ones. (See the Carter entry in his *ABC*.) (*See* Bands; *see also* Headbands; Raised bands.)

ENCHANTED ALBUMS. *See* Blow books.

ENDLEAVES (also called endpapers or end sheets). LEAVES at the front and back of a volume that are not part of the printed TEXT BLOCK but are used by the binder. In a CASED-IN book, the endleaves are the prime connector of the binding to the text block. The endleaves consist of the ones pasted down to the inside of the covers (called the "pastedowns") and the free endleaves, those CONJUGATE with the pastedowns. Sometimes the binder uses additional BLANKS as fillers to bulk up the text block, perhaps to give the reader sheets for notes or TIP-INS or for other reasons. Strictly speaking, only the pastedowns and free endpapers are "endleaves," and additional ones are called "blanks" or "FLYLEAVES." Endleaves are often decorated: colored, MARBLED, with PASTE PAPERS, BLOCK PRINTED, or with other ornamentation. Occasionally, they are covered with cloth—as with a silk cover that was popular from the 17th century on. Extremely ornate endleaves are DOUBLURES. (*See* Inserted endleaves; Silk moiré.) (See Sidney E. Berger, "Endleaves.") The term "endleaves" is preferred over "endpapers" since the leaves are not always made from paper, and the former works for all kinds of materials. These leaves can be quite beautiful, and they have spawned a wonderful phenomenon: a group of people who are enamored of them. One can see their work at their aptly named site, We Love Endpapers (see https://simonbeattie.co.uk/blog/archives/4570/ [accessed 30 May 2022] and their direct site https://www.facebook.com/groups/WeLoveEndpapers/ [accessed 30 May 2022]).

ENDMATTER. According to R. M. Ritter (*The Oxford Guide to Style*), "A book is composed of three main segments: the preliminary matter (*PRELIMS* or *front matter*), the text, and the endmatter." The endmatter may contain some or all of the following: endnotes (*see* Footnote), APPENDIX or appendices, INDEX or indices, GLOSSARY, BIBLIOGRAPHY (THE REFERENCE TOOL), COLOPHON, ERRATA; author's biographical note, and, especially in the 18th and 19th centuries, ADVERTISEMENTS.

ENDNOTE. *See* Footnote.

ENDPAPERS (end sheets). *See* Endleaves.

ENDPIECE. *See* Tailpiece.

END SHEETS. *See* Endleaves.

ENGLEGRECHT, MARTIN. *See* Peep shows.

ENGLISH SHORT TITLE CATALOGUE. *See ESTC.*

ENGRAVED TITLE. From the 16th century on and for at least three centuries, printers sometimes used an engraved rather than a letterpress-printed title page—or sometimes both. The ENGRAVING lent the volume a sense of sumptuousness, for using that technique, printers could impart a level of artistry that printing type alone was incapable of creating. Part of the artistry was in the three-dimensionality that the engraving had, and part was the artist's (i.e., the engraver's) ability to decorate with scrollwork, fancy calligraphy, pictures, and abutting or overlapping text, text that was not bound by the linearity of printing type, and so on. It must be remembered that an engraved title, produced on a ROLLING PRESS, was not part of the printing of the rest of the text, which came from a different press altogether.

ENGRAVING. INTAGLIO PRINTING, done from a PLATE that has had its images, words, or both cut into the surface of the plate. It is "[t]he art of representing, by means of lines or points produced on a wooden or metallic substance by cutting or corrosion, the figures, light and shades of objects in order to multiply them by means of printing" (*American Dictionary of Printing and Bookmaking*, p. 174). This definition has the phrase "or corrosion," indicating that the surface can be entered by means of acids, in which case the image produced is more an ETCHING than an engraving. Engraving was a tremendously popular means of decoration for title pages (*see* Engraved title) or illustration. BURINS AND GRAVERS are used to "dig out" the material (e.g., copper or wood) from the surface of the plate or BLOCK, and stippling tools can be used to create dots that can be closely placed to create darker shaded areas in the printing. (*See* Woodcut/Wood Engraving/Woodblock.) Since an engraving is usually done from a plate that is smaller than the sheet on which it is printed, the PLATE MARK will be visible around the image. Sometimes later processes, such as LITHOGRAPHY or STEEL-PLATE ENGRAVING, both of which lack these plate marks, will have artificially impressed ones stamped around their images to give the impression (pun intended) that the original was done from a copperplate—a more costly means of printing. (For images, *see* Rolling press.) (See Hind, *A History of Engraving and Etching from the Fifteenth Century to the Year 1914.*)

In about the 1990s, Richard Woodman of Redwood City, CA, invented a synthetic wood-engraving medium that he called Resingrave. It replaces the more difficult to work on boxwood that was becoming short in supply, and it allows the artist to produce images with the same fineness and sharpness as was possible with real wood. Barry Moser was perhaps its most brilliant artist working with Resingrave. Unfortunately, when Woodman retired, he stopped making the product. (See McClain's Printmaking Supplies; https://www.imcclains.com/catalog/blocks/resingraveplate.html [accessed 1 June 2022].) (See also Richard J. Woodman and Peter J. Woodman, *Relief & intaglio printmaking methods on Resingrave blocks.*)

ENLARGED. A publisher's term meaning that an earlier edition is now being issued with new material. The term has been in use for centuries; witness Thomas Wright's 1630 text *The passions of the minde in generall In sixe bookes. Corrected, enlarged, and with sundry new discourses augmented.* The enlargement could be of text or images, and it could be a few pages or several chapters. Theoretically the process produces a more thorough and informative text, though as a later edition, it will probably still command a price lower than the unenlarged, inferior text of the FIRST EDITION.

EN QUAD. *See* Em quad/En quad.

ENSCHEDÉ. A line of Dutch printers and publishers who have been in operation since 1703, founded by Izaak Enschedé. They were printers of banknotes and stamps as well as books, newspapers, and many other materials, and their typefaces (which they have been producing since 1743) have become some of the most revered and copied over the centuries. One of their designers, Jan van Krimpen, produced for Enschedé some of the most honored typefaces in the 20th century: Lutetia, Spectrum, Romulus, Cancelleresca Bastarda, Romanée, and Open Roman Capitals—all particularly featured by fine-press printers.

ENUMERATIVE BIBLIOGRAPHY. *See* Bibliography.

EPHEMERA. Printed and other materials that—as their designation indicates—are not meant to last—that is, anything produced for short duration. In the world of the book, this category of materials is so extensive that it defies definition. There are hundreds of kinds of things that can be labeled ephemera (with the singular being "ephemeron"). The *American Heritage Dictionary of the English Language* definition is "[p]rinted matter of passing interest" (p. 598), an ambiguous explanation at best. "Passing interest" gets to the heart of the matter only in terms of the short-lived nature of the ephemeron—brief in its use (as with theater tickets, can labels, cigarette packs, or train tickets). But the phrase "of passing interest" suggests "of minor interest," and this cannot be further from the truth. Witness the establishment of ephemera societies and a massive literature on the subject, not to mention the great number of ephemera fairs at which millions of pieces of ephemera are for sale to an endless stream of collectors of such materials. Some of the great library collections in the world are the result of the insight and assiduity of ephemera collectors whose hunger for labels, ballads sold on the street, and anything having to do with tobacco or transportation or insects or witches or greeting cards or anything else imaginable that has appeared in ephemeral form, have amassed major collections that are the source of a world of scholarship.

Volumes in my own collection are instructive. There are the books. But tucked into them are ephemera of various kinds: a postcard announcing the publication, a prospectus issued by the publisher, a card with a note it in from the printer, a review of the volume cut out of a magazine, a downloaded e-mail message from the printer, a printout from the web containing a bookseller's description of the book, a letter from another bookseller quoting a copy to me, a copy of the publisher's letterpress-printed label that was on the package that held the book when it was shipped to me, a bookmark from the bookseller, and so on. All of these items carry information of one sort or another that the book itself does not have (dates of publication, prices, descriptions of illustrations or paper or printing types, personal assessments of the objects, and so on), and this information can be a rich source of scholarly inquiry. Hence, most rare-book and special collections departments the world over have substantial holdings of ephemera. (See Clinton, *Printed Ephemera*; J. Lewis, *Collecting Printed Ephemera*; J. Lewis, *Printed Ephemera*; and Rickards, *The Encyclopedia of Ephemera*.) (*See* Almanacs.)

EPHEMERA SOCIETY OF AMERICA. The primary scholarly (and also casual) organization in the United States whose members are dealers, scholars, researchers, archivists, and collectors of EPHEMERA, along with other members who are interested in these "short-lived" items. The organization was established in 1980, and since 1987 they have published their *Ephemera News*, and their newsletter and directories of members.

EPIGRAPH. A short statement, motto, quotation, or piece of verse at the beginning of a chapter or sometimes printed on the title page. "An epigraph can serve different purposes such as it can be used as a summary, introduction, an example, or an association with some famous literary works, so as to draw comparison or to generate a specific context to be presented in the piece" (Literary Devices: Definition and Examples of Literary Terms, "Epigraph"; http://literarydevices.net/epigraph [accessed 4 June 2021]).

ERASURES. *See* Sophisticated copy.

E-READERS/E-BOOKS. Electronic books (also called "e-books"). (*See* Book.) There is a distinction to be made between the "e-book," which is the text, and the "e-reader," which is the device that text is read from. The Nook; the Kobo Clara, Forma, and Nia; the eReader of Sony; Apple's iPad; the Onyx Book Note Air; and the Kindle, for example, are e-readers. The concept probably goes back to 1930 and may have been inspired by movies with sound. "In 1930, Bob Brown predicted that the printed book was bound for obsolescence. The time has come, he insisted, 'to rid the reader of the cumbersome book.' He invented a machine that would allow one to read books and any text extremely fast and in a hyper-abbreviated form. He called these abbreviated texts, with em-dashes replacing words, 'readies.' He envisioned sending the condensed texts through wireless networks" (see Google Books, "The Readies"; https://books.google.com/books?id=1FjLoAEACAAJ&dq=%22The+readies%22++Google+books&hl=en&sa=X&ved=0CDAQ6AEwAGoVChMI7fajj9rbyAIVxj0-Ch3Jgg2W [accessed 4 June 2021]). *The Oxford Companion to the Book* has a short article by Eileen Gardiner and Ronald G. Musto on this subject (vol. 1, chapter 19, pp. 164–71), not mentioning Bob Brown but giving a good background and recent history of the phenomenon.

The likelihood that e-readers will supplant books is rather small. But their convenience, their relatively low price, and the great numbers of texts available on them make them excellent traveling companions for readers. Some readers, however, say, "I like to read books and own books. Once I have read the text on my e-reader, I don't have a book to show for it—to put onto my shelves." As with the prediction that paper will be supplanted by the computer, that proved foolish and shortsighted, so is the prediction that e-readers will put books—real books—out of business. More millions of physical books are being produced today than ever before in history. Like paper and computers, e-books and books will run parallel courses. Neither shows any sign of dying away.

EROTICA (sometimes called "CURIOSA," "exotica," or "FACETIAE"; also termed "X-rated"). Material of a sexual nature, written, pictorial, or a combination of these, whose main aim is to arouse the reader/viewer sexually. This, of course, is an oversimplification, but "erotica" is extremely difficult to define. In a famous legal decision, "Supreme Court justice Potter Stewart [said]: 'I know it when I see it' (*Jacobellis v. Ohio*, 1964)" (cited by Peter Lattman, Law Blog, "The Origins of Justice Stewart's 'I Know It When I See It,'" http://blogs.wsj.com/law/2007/09/27/the-origins-of-justice-stewarts-i-know-it-when-i-see-it [accessed 4 June 2021]).

In the world of the book, erotica (perhaps a gentler term than "pornography" but meaning the same thing) takes many forms, including books, magazines, photographs, drawings, tabloids, and many other formats, and presenting as legitimate forms of reading such genres as Japanese shunga, sex manuals, books on anatomy, and other medical texts, among others. In Asia, shunga have a long history, going back to ancient Chinese medical volumes. The term "pillow book" is often used to describe shunga or manuals that purport to teach people about sexual acts. I have also seen a "pillow book" that is nothing more than a volume of 20 explicit erotic WATERMARKS, with no printed text. (On shunga, see Aki, "The Reception of Shunga in the Modern Era: From Meiji to the Pre-WWII Years"; Clark and Gerstle, *Shunga*; and Illing, *Japanese Erotic Art and the Life of the Courtesan*.)

As an extremely popular genre, erotica can be found—often uncataloged (or cataloged in such a way as to refer only obliquely to the subject matter)—in many of the great libraries of the world. See the entry "Pornography" by Nicole Moore in *The Oxford Companion to the Book* (vol. 2, pp. 1043–44). (*See also* Curiosa.)

One particular subgenre of erotica is the pillow book. As its name implies, a book to be taken to bed. This is a manual showing sexual positions. It falls, also, into the category of HOW-TO books, though I suspect no one would catalog it as such.

ERRATUM/ERRATA. A listing (often at the end of a text) of the error(s) in the work in question. Sometimes the list is inserted or TIPPED IN to the volume on a separate sheet of paper, and sometimes it is actually printed in the text. The related term "CORRIGENDA" means "a list of errors in a book along with their corrections" (*American Heritage Dictionary of the English Language*, p. 412). These too can be printed in the volume or LAID IN or tipped in. Carter says that errata are blunders or typographical errors spotted after the printing of the text. He says that they were sometimes called "corrigenda" or "faults escaped," and publishers sometimes had them corrected by hand (see Carter, p. 109). Often, however, the corrections were made during the printing, with "STOP-PRESS CORRECTIONS," and the printer either tipped in errata sheets or printed the corrections at the end (sometimes at the beginning) of the text. (Remember, PRELIMS were generally printed after the text was printed, so it is practical and practicable for printers to add the corrections to the prelims.) If the errata appeared somewhere in the text, they would generally appear in all copies issued, even in those in which the corrections had been made during the printing. When corrections are made during the printing of a text, different states of that text are created. (*See* Corrigendum/Corrigenda; Edition, Impression [Printing], Issue, and State; Points.) It is also possible that a printer, for one reason or another, makes a change in the text when the original was not strictly in error. As noted at stop-press correction, the change might not actually be a correction (of an error), but merely an alternate, revised, text. (We see this in some of the chapters of Peter Watson's *Sotheby's: The Inside Story*, a text with some revisions originally published as *Sotheby's: Inside Story*. The slightly later text brings some of the chapters up to date, so there are no errors to record.)

If a volume is lacking its errata slip (or page), it must be considered incomplete and thus a defective copy, for collectors want the volume as it was issued from the press. But an added complication could obtain, as Kim Merker explains about his printing of *The Collected Poems of Weldon Kees*: "If you look at the various copies of this book, on the back of the title page there is an errata statement showing all the mistakes that were made in that particular copy. What happened was this: as we were printing we would find mistakes and correct them—make what the bibliographers call 'stop-press corrections.' Those sheets with the errors were separated from the rest, so the errata page in nearly every [copy of the] book is different" (pp. 10–11). Errata, then, as mentioned above, wind up as points.

ESPARTO (grass). A fiber from a northern African grass and southern European grass imported to the United States for use in papermaking. It has been used for papermaking since as early as 1856. "The first really successful conversion of Spanish esparto was carried out by [Thomas] Routledge and his first patent is dated 1856. Thereafter, its use in papermaking increased slowly but steadily" (*Esparto Paper*, p. 3 [which is at the end of the volume]; see the bibliography). R. H. Clapperton says, "It was now, in 1857, that Thomas Routledge patented his process for preparing bleached pulp from esparto grass" (Clapperton, *The Paper-Making Machine*, p. 191). When the volume *Esparto Grass* was published (1956), a hundred years after Routledge's patent, the grass was still going strong as a paper-producing fiber.

For the present purpose, esparto grass was used as a fairly high-grade book paper, and it was the subject of intense scrutiny by Carter and Pollard in their unraveling of the FORGERIES of THOMAS WISE, who (along with Harry BUXTON FORMAN) used this paper in many of his spurious pamphlets. (See Carter and Pollard, *An Enquiry into the Nature of Certain Nineteenth Century Pamphlets*, especially pp. 42–44.)

ESTC. *English Short Title Catalogue*, a bibliographic compilation of books, periodicals, pamphlets, and other printed materials that "lists over 460,000 items . . . published between 1473 and 1800 . . . mainly, but not exclusively, in English

. . . published mainly in the British Isles and North America . . . from the collections of the British Library and over 2,000 other libraries" (http://estc.bl.uk/F/?func=file&file_name=login-bl-estc [accessed 4 June 2021]).

The database was first conceived as the *Eighteenth-Century Short Title Catalogue*, the aim being to record all 18th-century imprints. It was to continue the work of Alfred W. Pollard and G. R. Redgrave, whose SHORT TITLE CATALOGUE (2nd ed.) came out between 1976 and 1991, and also Donald G. Wing's bibliography, also a *Short Title Catalogue*, that covers 1641–1700 (it was issued from 1945 to 1951, and it had later supplements and addenda). Eventually, the work of these bibliographers was consolidated into the database now called simply the *ESTC* ("English Short Title Catalogue"), conveniently not requiring a change in the acronym. The database is now computerized and is available in digital form.

The project to compile this database began in 1976. "The aim of the original project was to create a machine-readable union catalogue of books, pamphlets and other ephemeral material printed in English-speaking countries from 1701 to 1800. . . . An ESTC team was established at the British Library in 1977, under the direction of Robin Alston, and began work on the Library's extensive holdings of in-scope material. . . . In 1978, Henry Snyder was appointed to direct the ESTC project in North America. An American cataloguing team was established in 1979, and the North American Imprints Project (NAIP) began at the American Antiquarian Society in 1980. The International Committee of the ESTC (IESTC) was established in 1980, with a membership drawn from the UK and the USA, chaired by the British Library" (Jeremy Norman's *History of Information*). The database also lists false imprints—those that were not printed in English-speaking countries but that claim to be. When the database was renamed in 1987 (to the *English Short Title Catalogue*), it stretched its coverage to pre-1701 items. Until 1987, the excellent work of Pollard and Redgrave (in their *Short Title Catalogue* for the period 1475–1640), and the Wing catalog (which covered 1641–1700) kept the project from going back to 1475 in the first place, but the work of these scholars clearly needed to be supplemented since many publications not listed in their volumes had surfaced, so their work was incorporated into the *ESTC* database, and the name and focus changed from "Eighteenth Century" to "English." (See Pollard and Redgrave and also Wing in the bibliography.)

Since the publication of the data quoted at the opening of this entry, all numbers have gone up.

ESTEEMED. Carter's entry for this term says that this epithet for an author or an edition indicated that the person or text so described was held in high regard at one point. The term is now pretty much out of favor, though it could appear in older catalogs, especially when high regard is a selling point. A quick search on the web shows that the word can be applied to any purveyor of goods: made by the esteemed silversmith; an esteemed hairdresser; an esteemed plumber. There are also esteemed collections of mattresses and an esteemed method of learning to play the piano. The term supposedly conjures up high quality. We see the word in catalog 338 of the esteemed bookseller Maggs Bros: *First Editions of the Works of Esteemed Authors and Book Illustrators of the XIXth Century / Association Books and Mss. / Sports and Pastimes* (1915). If the authors and illustrators listed in this volume were esteemed, you would be doing yourself great honor to have their books on your shelves.

ESTIMATES. *See* Auction catalogs.

ETCHING. The use of acids to eat into metal PLATES to create text, images, or both. (*See* Aquatint; Engraving.) The entry in the *American Dictionary of Printing and Bookmaking* (pp. 179–80) explains the process. The most common metal used for etching is the same as used for engraving: copper. Hence, an etching will usually have the telltale PLATE MARK around it. Etchings are printed from ink that is below the surface of the plate; hence, it is a form of INTAGLIO printing. (*See* Engraving; Steel engraving.)

ETHERINGTON, DON (1935–). One of the United States's important bookbinders and conservators, and a scholar in these related fields. He "began bookbinding at the age of thirteen as a student at the Central School of Arts and Crafts and later went on to study bookbinding and design at the London School of Printing. Since then, he has held positions at the Biblioteca Nazionale in Florence, The Library of Congress, the Harry Ransom Humanities Research Center at the University of Texas at Austin, Information Conservation, Inc., and . . . Etherington Conservation Services in Browns Summit, NC" (GoodReads, "Don Etherington"). Along with Matt Roberts, Etherington compiled the remarkable volume *Bookbinding and the Conservation of Books: A Dictionary of Descriptive Terminology*, quoted extensively in the present volume.

ETHICS. While not a formal term restricted to the book world, the issues implied by this word have a powerful impact in any profession in which actions have fiscal implications. The bookseller brought in strictly as an appraiser and who winds up acquiring items from the collector has come to the border of propriety and has crossed it—and as the amount of profit he makes from the transaction goes up, the more he has acted unethically. The bookseller who purchases a volume suspecting (or knowing) it was obtained illegally, who doctors it to remove traces of PROVENANCE and ownership, and who sells it for a profit has equally acted unethically—if not illegally. The collector who buys a book from a dealer or an auction house and then has post-transaction BUYER'S REMORSE, damages the item, and claims he has a right to return it because it was a damaged copy has also acted unethically. The donor who gives valuable books and manuscripts to a library year after year and then grossly overestimates their value on his tax returns so that he can maximize his tax returns has gone beyond ethics and is breaking the law, but the librarian receiving these materials, knowing of this illegal practice, and saying nothing because he wants the gifts to keep coming is bordering on the unethical and the illegal (in that he or she sees a crime being committed and says nothing). In fact, the opportunities for unethical behavior in all fields—but especially in the art and book world—are many. And the border between unethical behavior and illegal behavior can be a matter of inches.

Professional societies, such as auction houses and bookselling organizations (ABA, ABAA, SNEAB, and dozens of others), often have published guidelines on ethical behavior. Book buyers/collectors do not. But that does not mean that the lack of such formalized standards for them gives a buyer the right to act unethically. In fact, in a field in which trust is the basis for the relationships among sellers, buyers, librarians, archivists, scholars, and others, to betray that trust is damaging to all involved.

The Rare Books and Manuscripts Section (RBMS) of ACRL (the Association of College and Research Libraries—part of ALA [*see* American Library Association])—and the ABAA have published guidelines that, rudimentary as they are, do hold their members to certain standards that are to engender trust in those who have dealings with them. Perhaps the way to prevent—or at least to try to deter—unethical behavior is for all of us in the field to call to account those whose actions are objectionable.

Such "calling to account" is difficult. It means being a tattletale, a squealer. It means exposing one of our colleagues or the professionals we must deal with, and must face if there is a reckoning. Even if the one reporting unethical behavior can remain anonymous, gossip can be the result. Seeing a friend or colleague punished in some way can be painful. But not saying anything, not taking action of some kind to prevent such behavior, is like condoning it and allowing it to continue. Organizations have whistle-blower opportunities that allow the whistle-blower to be anonymous.

What does it mean to "face the reckoning"? Each organization must decide how to deal with those who are proven to have acted unethically. There are ethics committees who deal with such things. The ABAA expelled a BREAKER, and more recently a bookseller who for many years sold books that he knew were stolen from a nearby library.

The thief who steals prints and hand-colored plates from a library's volumes is breaking the law. The bookseller who buys these from this thief is also breaking the law—receiving stolen goods—though he can pretend that the items were legally acquired. But the customer buying from that bookseller, not knowing the provenance of those illustrations, can assume the items were acquired legally—but knowing in his heart that they were not. Is his buying—which merely encourages the corrupt system to progress in its corrupt way—ethical? Pretending ignorance is no justification to promulgate further corruption. If there were no market for those stolen illustrations, the thieves would stop stealing those things.

ET INFRA. Latin for "and below," pointing to something below on the same page or on a subsequent page or pages. Carter says that the phrase can be used to indicate a set of volumes of various sizes; the one describing the set would describe the largest volume and then say "et infra" to mean that the others are smaller. This is not what the Latin means (i.e., it does not mean "and smaller"), and the term used this way must be fairly rare. The term wound up in Carter possibly because of the William Loring Andrews volume *Sextodecimos Et Infra* of 1899 in which he is discussing smaller-format and MINIATURE books. Carter was a good deal closer to 1899 than are the bibliographers, catalogers, and booksellers of the 20th and 21st centuries, so it is no wonder that the term appeared in the *ABC* but has not been used too much since the first edition of Carter was issued in 1952.

ETRUSCAN CALF. "A method of decorating calfskin bindings by acid staining, so called because of the contrasting colors or shades of leather (light brown or terra cotta) in conjunction with dark brown or black tooling. The terra cotta shades and decoration represent Greek and Etruscan vases. Etruscan bindings usually have a rectangular panel on each cover, or, occasionally, a plain oval with a classical urn in the center. They are tooled in black, surrounded by a border of Greek palmate leaves, which are also in black, and with outer borders of classical design (Grecian key or Doric entablature) tooled in gold. The spines are also decorated with classical ornaments. Many 19th century authorities attributed this style to John Whitaker; however, it seems more likely that it was the creation of William EDWARDS OF HALIFAX. There appears to be no very conclusive evidence as to the origin of the style, but it is known that Edwards employed it at an early date, circa 1785. It was popular during the period 1785–1820" (Roberts and Etherington, p. 94). (*See* Edwards of Halifax.)

EVANS, CHARLES (1850–1935). "[O]ne of American Libraries' 100 most important library and information science leaders of the 20th century" (Kniffel, Sullivan, and McCormick, "100 of the Most Important Leaders We Had in the 20th Century," p. 38) and one of the foremost American bibliographers of the 20th century. He is best known for his massive bibliography *American Bibliography: A Chronological Dictionary of All Books, Pamphlets, and Periodical Publications Printed in the United States of America from the Genesis of Printing in 1639 Down to and Including the Year 1820, with Bibliographical and Biographical Notes*, published beginning in 1903. It is often referred to simply as "Evans." (One might hear, "Is that in Evans?")

Evans's work, filling 13 volumes (with volume 14 being the index by Roger Pattrell Bristol, also published by the American Antiquarian Society) and listing items only up to 1800, was completed by C. K. Shipton in 1955 (and a supplement was done for it by Roger Bristol; see the bibliography). It was controversial because Shipton "preferred to travel around the United States in order to actually see the books he was including in his work, though when he wasn't able to travel, he was known to include 'ghost' titles, as well as skip publications altogether due to the amount of space, and therefore money, they would take up in his printed book. It is said that American Bibliography lacks a proper representation of Harvard dissertations and broadsides" (*Dictionary of Literary Biography*, Vol. 187, *American Book Collectors and Bibliographers*, Second Series, "Charles Evans," pp. 92–102). This massive undertaking is still used by scholars, though thousands of additional publications that Evans and Shipton "missed" have been identified. (See Reese, "The First Hundred Years of Printing in British North America." See also Shipton and Mooney, *National Index of American Imprints through 1800*.) (*See* Shaw and Shoemaker.)

Evans was one of the cofounders (along with Melvil Dewey [*see* Dewey Classification]) of the American Library Association. (See Holley, *Charles Evans American Bibliographer*.)

EVEN NUMBERS. Just an observation that for most books printed from the period of INCUNABULA on—volumes with actual PAGINATION—almost always the page numbers of the VERSOS are even numbered; the page numbers of the RECTOS are odd numbered.

EVEN WORKING. Publishers do not want to waste paper, since that is one of the principal costs in the making of books. The aim is to have every leaf carry text, with no leftovers. If the number of pages of text in a book is divisible by 16 or 32, for instance, and the book has 254 pages of text, that is called "even working." A book with 265 pages was not produced with even working. R. M. Ritter says, "While publishers try to keep ENDMATTER to a minimum, as with PRELIMS, an even working can result in spare pages at the end of a work. These are sometimes filled with a publisher's advertisements for related books or series" (*The Oxford Guide to Style*, p. 20).

EXCESSIVELY. Carter lists this as a term he dislikes. When it precedes "rare," it makes little sense, he says, since there are already levels of rarity that imply "excessively not available." If something is not available, is it sensible to say "very not available"? But as a sales tactic, emphasizing rarity allows for a bulge in the price of an item, and the phrase "excessively rare" has come across our line of vision regularly over the decades, with no hint that the use is diminishing. It is excessively common.

EXEMPLAR. A copy of a text, manuscript or printed. In the copying of manuscripts, an exemplar is the version used by a scribe to make his own copy. Peter Beal adds to this that a stationer who commissions copies to be made has his scribe use an exemplar—an official version sanctioned by a university (see Beal, *A Dictionary of English Manuscript Terminology, 1450–2000*, p. 147).

EXEMPLUM. In bibliography, the word (from the Latin meaning "example") means a specific copy of a book. Peter Beal says that the word is used rather than "*copy* of a book" so that one will not confuse this term to mean a copied text (i.e., a transcript). In the literature of the Middle Ages (and later), an exemplum is a story that illustrates some moral or demonstrates a truth of some kind. In this latter sense, the term also refers to part of a medieval sermon. The sermon opened with a "text"—that is, the statement of some moral principle that should guide us. Then it went on to the biblical passage that discussed it or a discussion by the sermoner on the meaning of that text, drawing on religious teachings. The exemplum followed, being a story or tale that illustrated the moral teaching embodied in the text. This is followed by the peroration—the summing up and concluding passage reiterating the text and pointing out how the exemplum has proved the veracity of the text. Chaucer uses this structure in "The Pardoner's Tale." And in an elegant and ironic twist, the same structure is used in a host of medieval fabliaux—the erotic stories that contain the same elements. The exemplum is the most entertaining part since it is the story that everyone can understand and can "relate to."

EXERCISE BOOK. *See* Copybook.

EXHIBITION CATALOG. As the term says, this is the volume, pamphlet, or checklist showing (and sometimes discussing in great detail) the items in an exhibition. Since exhibitions often try to deal with newly recognized genres, new areas of collection, or original takes on older areas of exhibition, many an exhibition catalog is a true contribution to scholarship, with the exhibition having been conceived and mounted by one or more experts on the topic. So these catalogs can be groundbreaking in several ways, and can thus be highly sought after. One supreme example of this is the catalog (or, more properly, "catalogue") done for the exhibition titled *Printing and the Mind of Man*. Even if the catalog does not present anything new in the way of scholarship, it may be a fine scholarly source in itself since many of these publications draw upon (and cite) reliable sources.

In the United States, RBMS offers prizes for the best exhibition catalogs issued each year, in inexpensive, medium-priced, expensive, and online versions, along with brochures and student exhibitions that accompany exhibits, and, in their final category, shows that reveal "innovation." Their RBMS Exhibition Awards Committee honors the makers of these by giving The Katharine Kyes Leab & Daniel J. Leab American Book Prices Current Exhibition Awards, named after the people who founded the competition. (See https://rbms.info/committees/exhibition_awards/ [accessed 1 June 2022].)

EX LIBRARY (abbreviated "ex. lib."). Said of a volume that was once in a library, noticeable by whatever the library did to mark the book as its own: edge stamps, labels, penciled-in information about acquisition or call numbers or prices, bookplates, pockets holding check-out slips, rubber stamps, spine labels, and the like. Regardless of the condition of the volume, the signs that the book was once in a library will almost always reduce its value considerably. And beware of the bookseller who uses the ABBREVIATION "XL," as I once encountered in a catalog. The way it was printed in the bookseller's catalog, I thought it meant "excellent" or something like that. The book came with all the signs of a library on it. If the library that once held the book was famous, as with, for instance, the Doheny Library (with its small leather BOOKPLATES), the value of the book could be enhanced. Also, ENGRAVED bookplates on 17th- or 18th-century volumes may not affect the value of the item, especially since it is sometimes possible to trace owners from those centuries and say something penetrating about them: "Once resident of Henchley Manor, and clearly a significant book collector." An ex. lib. copy from a lending library (*see* CIRCULATING LIBRARY) would not have such a cachet. Conservators (along with booksellers and collectors) may try to remove all traces of a book's having been an ex library copy, but such traces are difficult to remove. And such a removal would be reducing the information about the item's PROVENANCE.

EX LIBRIS. A BOOKPLATE. Also, a phrase meaning "from the books of," indicating that the item under scrutiny is from a particular library or collector. The term has come to mean "a bookplate" because these words often appear on those LABELS.

EXOTIC. A term used to designate a non-Latin alphabet. Hebrew, Arabic, Cyrillic, Chinese, Japanese, and Korean are exotics. But since the coming of digital FONTS, and a younger generation of those who use them, the term "exotic" has taken on the meaning of "unusual," "strange," "bizarre," "weird," or just plain "ugly." A search of "exotic fonts" on the web will bring up scores of TYPEFACES that most people would be hard put to find a serious (or *any*) use for.

EXOTICA. *See* Erotica.

EXPLICIT. A statement at the end of a text, often a COLOPHON, that announces that the text is at an end. As a colophon, the explicit may show where the work was produced, who is responsible for it, where it was written or printed, its date, and so on. In many manuscripts or incunabula—and even in later printing—the term could refer to the kind of information that one might find in a colophon, or in the text just before the colophon, including the name of a scribe or printer, the place of publication, the date, the name of the publisher, and so on. The website Dawn of Western Printing: Incunabula says: "At the end of each chapter appeared a sentence starting with the word 'explicit' ('Here ends . . .' in English). This sentence is referred to as the 'explicit.' As 'incipit' and 'explicit' are independent from the text, they are sometimes printed in red" (National Diet Library of Japan, "Glossary: Incunabula: Incipit"). (*See* Incipit.)

EXPUNGE. To eliminate, erase, strike out, or remove something from a text. In medieval manuscripts, one way to do this removal is to put dots under the characters to be taken out—hence, the term's origin: ex-punge (remove with the use of dots). (*See* Bisquing; Caviar.)

EXPURGATED. The removal of text for whatever reason the expurgator can justify: on religious, moral, political, sexual, or other grounds. Often the expurgation is done by someone who is merely "following orders," as with the CENSORSHIP of religious texts, as per the *Index Librorum Prohibitorum*. For many years the publication *American Libraries* ran a column on local censorship—especially in public libraries. There seemed to be no end to the actions taken against the presence of certain books (often children's and young adult books) by people in conservative communities based on what they saw as offensive. It was clear in many instances that they had not even read the texts they were asking (or demanding) to be banned. But banning is not exactly expurgation, which is the removal from a text of offensive material. (*See* Bisquing; Caviar; Censorship; Unexpurgated.)

EXQUISITE CORPSE. A work composed by two or (usually) more authors, each one being given the "rules" of what he or she was to write, but not necessarily seeing what came before. Hence, it is a composite text, the genre's name of which comes from the French term *cadavre exquis*, the opening words to a game played by the Surrealists: "The exquisite corpse shall drink the new wine"—with each participant in the game entering a specified word (noun, verb, adjective, and so forth) without having seen what came before. "This technique was invented by surrealists and is similar to an old parlour game called Consequences in which players write in turn on a sheet of paper, fold it to conceal part of the writing, and then pass it to the next player for a further contribution. Surrealism principal founder André Breton reported that it started in fun, but became playful and eventually enriching. Breton said the diversion started about 1925, but Pierre Reverdy wrote that it started much earlier, at least as early as 1918" (see "Exquisite Corpse" in the bibliograhy).

EXTENDED. "An addition to the inner or binding margin of a leaf of a book. This procedure is more often required for title leaves, plates, the last leaves of a book, etc., than elsewhere, as these are most likely to become detached, frayed, or otherwise damaged. Occasionally, however, if a book has to be made up from a narrower copy, the narrow leaves may be extended so that their outer edges are even with the other leaves" (Roberts and Etherington, "extended"; https://cool.culturalheritage.org/don/dt/dt1226.html [accessed 13 January 2021]). These authors also reference the practice of EXTRA-ILLUSTRATION, also called "extended."

EXTENSION TAB. *See* Finger tab.

EXTRA BINDING. Originally the practice of putting a volume into a sumptuous, usually all-leather, binding. Now any kind of fancy binding (still usually with a leather spine) may be called "extra binding." The volume *Extra Binding at the Lakeside Press* (see the bibliography) depicts both of these options, with an additional decorative element—a FORE-EDGE PAINTING. This volume explains that the best extra-bound books follow the practice of the 16th and 17th centuries in FORWARDING, "so that the book will stand the test of time. . . . [but they at that bindery] have not neglected the study of artistic and original designing, as well as a new conception of end papers which our friends have found a pleasing variation from the marble papers of the past" (p. 5).

EXTRACTS. Text taken ("extracted") from longer texts and printed separately. The extracted texts could be parts of essays or whole essays, chapters from books, stories from volumes or serials, and other kinds of scholarly or non-scholarly sources. The term is often used bibliographically to mean a passage taken out of a text and quoted in another. Normally, short quotations are printed along with the prose in which the text is being quoted, but a passage of three lines or more may be printed indented (and possibly in smaller type than the text around it and with no quotation marks since the indentation shows that it is quoted) and is called an "extract." One proofreader's direction to the printer is, "Print as extract." (*See* Offprint.)

EXTRA-ILLUSTRATED (Grangerized). Enhanced with materials not in the original. That is, an extra-illustrated book may have TIPPED-IN plates, drawings, maps, letters, tickets, or many other kinds of enhancements that were not part of the volume as it was issued from the publisher. The practice is also called "grangerization" or "grangerizing," after James Granger, "(1723–1776), an English clergyman whose *Biographical History of England* (1769) was arranged for such illustration" (WordReference.com, "Grangerize"). That is, the volume was published with no illustrations, but space was left—with blank leaves bound in—for the owner to augment the volume as she wished. In the 18th century, there was already a strong market in PRINTS—usually ENGRAVINGS—but collectors sometimes went berserk and added leaves removed from other books, leading to the existence of thousands of otherwise fine volumes but with their illustrative material WANTING. A volume could also be rebound with extra blank LEAVES added for such added material; such a volume could also be called "extended." The HUNTINGTON LIBRARY in San Marino, California, has an exceptional collection of these volumes. Sharon Mizota, from an interview with the Huntington's Steve Tabor and Professor Lori Anne Ferrell, says that "[a]lthough the books were created in the 18th and 19th centuries, many include much older works of art. Collectors also typically neglected to record the sources of the artworks they incorporated" (KCET, "Everything Is Illuminated: Extra-Illustrated Books at The Huntington"; http://www.kcet.org/arts/artbound/counties/los-angeles/extra-illustrated-books-huntington-museum.html [accessed 4 June 2021]), so grangerized books led to the partial (or complete) destruction of thousands of other volumes, and they also led to the existence of innumerable "ORPHANS"—all of the tipped-in materials with no known parents. (See also the website by Tabor and Ferrell about the exhibition they held at the Huntington: "Illuminated Palaces," http://enfilade18thc.com/2013/08/05exhibition-illuminated-palaces

-extra-illustrated-books [accessed 4 June 2021].) A single volume could be broken apart and rebound with its text spread out over dozens of volumes, interspersed with BLANKS that were then filled with these orphans. Or the volume itself could have been designed for grangerization. Robert Rulon-Miller, in one of his catalogs, lists a copy of Mitchell Stace's book *Cromwelliana: A Chronological Detail of Events in Which Oliver Cromwell Was Engaged; From the Year 1642 to his Death, 1658, With a Continuation of Other Transactions to the Restoration*. He says, "LOWNDES notes that 'the volume was printed almost expressly for illustrations; accordingly it often occurs filled with engravings.' Here the book is in its unadorned state, with only the 5 engravings, AS ISSUED" (Rulon-Miller Books, Catalog 151, Saint Paul, 2015, pp. 30–31, item no. 217). (See Tredwell, *A Monograph on Privately Illustrated Books*.)

EXTRA NO. 1. *See* Rag paper.

EXTREMITIES. A term used only in dire situations. The outermost portions of a volume or pamphlet, for example. This usually refers to the edges of the BOARDS or the edges of the DUST JACKET. They are mentioned only when they are necessary to mention—and that is when the seller, in honesty, is pointing out defects: "Extremities scuffed." No bookseller would normally say "Extremities in good condition" unless they are usually found damaged and she is pointing out the rarity of finding a copy without that damage.

FABLIAUX. *See* Exemplum.

FABRIANO. Purportedly the oldest business in the Western world with unbroken production, this paper mill was founded in 1264 (see http://fabriano.com/en/327/fabriano_today [accessed 4 June 2021]). Although now a large commercial mill using FOURDRINIERS, it still has a hand mill, and it is still producing beautiful papers for artists and printers, along with its regular lines of commercial papers. Two of the company's claims to fame are its invention of the WATERMARK and the development and use of gelatin SIZING. Its SHADOWMARKS are quite lovely, and its papers are still of very high quality.

FABS. *See* Fellowship of American Bibliophilic Societies.

FACE (of type). The surface of the piece of type that is to be printed. It is inked with a ROLLER or a set of INK BALLS. The term is also used to mean the design of a FONT of type, as in "Bembo is a lovely face." (*See* Typeface.)

FACETIAE. A term designating various genres of books, including books of humor, or books about strange, abnormal, or bizarre phenomena. It is also used for books of salacious nature, and the term sounds more elegant than "pornography." (*See* Erotica.)

FACSIMILE. A copy of some original, often done by photographic means. It is not to be confused with a FAKE. The facsimile may aim to be indistinguishable from the original, but in fact most facsimiles are different in being on a different SUBSTRATE (e.g., a different kind of paper) or in a color that does not perfectly match the original. Many a facsimile is so designated on the item itself. However, a really well-made facsimile can be quite convincing and can sometimes be passed off as an original, and the collector or librarian, bookseller, or historian can be fooled. There is a strong market, for example, in early BROADSIDES, some of which can be quite valuable. Where there is a market for such things, facsimiles can be created and passed off as genuine, wreaking havoc on the market. The item can be a broadside, a playbill, a book or pamphlet, any kind of EPHEMERA, or even a photograph. Detecting these can be a nightmare.

The extraordinary length of the entry on facsimiles in Carter reveals the complexity of this phenomenon. For example, Carter mentions those that have been doctored to look aged, those that are bound into a volume surrounded by genuine pieces, individual LEAVES that are created to make up a defective copy of a book or pamphlet (*see* Sophisticated), or others that were made in full innocence and presented as copies of important letters or other documents, revealed as such in their first incarnation but then taken from that incarnation and presented as the genuine article. G.Thomas Tanselle points out that reproductions of many kinds (e.g., on paper or film) can be looked at as facsimiles and that those made with photographic processes can be flawed. He says that the literature on this "does not allude to the possibility of inaccurate or misleading reproduction. Indeed, what is often stressed is the absolute fidelity of photographic copies" (Tanselle, "Reproductions and Scholarship," p. 27). He cites several scholars who swear by photographic copies, and he calls their praise of this form of facsimile "blind faith in the virtues of photography, on the part of those who should know better" (p. 27). He then cites W. W. GREG, who, as early as 1925, "said simply that 'no process but in some measure obscures what it reproduces'" (Tanselle, p. 29), and Frederick George Kenyon (speaking at the same conference as Greg, said "that photographic copies 'should be regarded not as substitutes for the originals, but as approximations only helpful in suggesting points which must subsequently be verified'" (p. 29). (See Tanselle, "Reproductions and Scholarship.") It is clear that facsimiles are useful in scholarship up to a point but that they need to be scrutinized for their accuracy and supplemented, if possible, by an examination of the original. Only such an examination can show paper texture, WATERMARKS, stains, signs of use, and so on. (See also Weitenkampf, "What Is a Facsimile?") (*See* Type facsimile.)

As a footnote: I saw a copy of a 17th-century book at a book fair that was priced far below what I had thought it should be. It didn't seem to be defective, but the seller told me that the title page was a facsimile, actually done by hand. That is, though it looked like a printed page, it was actually done with pen and ink, right down to the serifs of every character. This was a manuscript facsimile, done on paper that was contemporary with the original volume, and it was completely convincing. One does not even need a camera to produce a good facsimile.

FACSIMILE REPRINT. As the phrase says, a reprint of an original (from a manuscript or printed source) reproducing the original by photographic means—or at least in such a way that the features of the original (such things as line breaks, spelling, punctuation, typographical errors, illustration, and so on) are as close to the original as possible. They can be produced by photographing or scanning the original or with a new setting of type that mimics the setting of the original—sometimes, if possible, even using the same font. Such editions may be published to commemorate an anniversary of the original or of its author or for scholarly purposes. (*See* Facsimile.)

FACTOTUM. "An ornamental block having a space in the centre for the insertion of a capital letter of an ordinary fount of type is called a 'factotum initial', or more properly a 'factotum'" (McKerrow, *Introduction to Bibliography for Literary Students*, p. 26). Philip Gaskell says that the factotum was a "square ornamental block with a hole through the middle into which a piece of type could be wedged, one block thus serving for any initial letter" (Gaskell, *A New Introduction to Bibliography*, p. 155).

FAHN LIBRARIES (FOLGER, ANTIQUARIAN SOCIETY, HUNTINGTON, NEWBERRY). Despite the acronym, this is a group of five private research libraries: the Folger Shakespeare Library (Washington, DC), the American Antiquarian Society (Worcester, MA), the Huntington Library (San Marino, CA), the Newberry Library (Chicago), and accompanied by the MORGAN LIBRARY AND MUSEUM (New York City), each with world-class holdings in their collecting areas.

FAIR COPY. "A legible manuscript of a written work, often in the author's own hand and usually representing the work's revised and corrected form prior to publication" (*American Heritage Dictionary of the English Language*, p. 634). The fair copy is often made from earlier drafts; its aim is to present a clear and legible copy for a reader or COMPOSITOR. As this definition suggests, the fair copy need not be in the author's hand, nor does it have to be free of EMENDATIONS; it may have penned-in changes of various kinds, but the key issue is that it be a legible and fairly clean copy.

FAIRS. *See* Book fairs.

FAIR USE. In the world of publishing and COPYRIGHT, the condition under which any copyrighted work (or part of it) may be used without the user's having to get PERMISSION, even if the copyright for that work is still active. Under several circumstances, copying a work (or some of it) would not be an infringement of copyright—if the use is for criticism, new writing, teaching, scholarship and research, comment, or some other protected use. "It is a general right that applies even—and especially—in situations where the law provides no specific statutory authorization for the use in question. Consequently, the fair use doctrine is described only generally in the law, and it is not tailored to the mission of any particular community" (*Code of Best Practices in Fair Use for Academic and Research Libraries*, p. 1). The complications are many, and what one person calls fair use, a court of law may say is PLAGIARISM. Publishers are particularly leery of allowing their authors to use the work of others without clear permissions. In the book world, however, booksellers (in the catalogs they issue offering items for sale) often quote extensively from their sources without getting permission. Whether this use falls under the fair use doctrine may be debatable, but the bookseller is fairly (but probably not *completely*) safe from litigation in such use. At least one bookseller I know has extensive passages in his cataloging of the items he is purveying—passages of scholarship that he himself has written. And he warns his readers not to lift passages from his catalogs since his scholarship is under his legal control. Fair use does not allow anyone, then, to use his prose or other data without his permission.

FAKE. Any item (for our purposes, a book, PAMPHLET, document, photograph, or piece of EPHEMERA) that purports to be something that it is not, and for which there is no genuine original. For example, a "Wanted" poster or other BROADSIDES from the 19th century can be faked, as can letters or other manuscript documents of all kinds. These can wreak havoc on the collectors' market and in the world of scholarship, for good ones can be taken as genuine and their content believed when it is completely spurious. MARK HOFFMANN fakes fooled many people. (*See* Facsimile; Faux; Forgery.)

FALL-DOWN-BACK BOX. *See* Drop-spine box.

FALSE BANDS; FALSE RAISED BANDS. Fake RAISED BANDS on the SPINE of a binding. In a genuine stitched, LACED-IN, binding, the sewing goes around cords or thongs on the spine. When the cover material, usually leather or vellum, is glued down over the spine, the cords force the leather to stand up across the cords, creating genuine raised bands. They are a sign of a high-quality, sturdy binding. When cased-in bindings appeared in the 19th century, they were made as cheaply as possible, sometimes with rudimentary or no stitching at the spine. (*See* Case bound.) To simulate high-quality binding, strips of cardboard (or other material, like strips of leather) could be glued down to the spine where the cords would have been adhered with thread. When the cover material was glued down over the spine, false bands were the result, making the volume look laced-in. The term "false bands" is really a misnomer, since they were actually real bands, just not made in the traditional laced-in way. As with the distinction between *functional* and *ornamental* HEADBANDS, the false bands were ornamental. The only function they served was to extract money from the pockets of buyers who were willing to pay for a more expensive laced-in binding.

FALSE DATE. Not all books are dated, nor are all dates in books accurate. Undated items could be REPRINTS or merely not dated by their makers. Items with incorrect dates could be printed in one year and issued in another, so the publisher gives the year of issue rather than the year of printing. (*See* Edition, Impression [Printing], Issue, and State; Points.) Or the inaccurate date could simply be a TYPOGRAPHICAL ERROR or intentional. In a bibliographic record, the compiler, learning of the inaccuracy, may wish to signal the correct date with SQUARE BRACKETS: "London: Hastings, 1799 [1801]." Scholars, suspecting the inaccuracy, may be able to ascertain the actual date by looking into reliable published bibliographies, doing research in publishing history for the item under scrutiny, or accessing such bibliographic utilities as WorldCat (*see* OCLC). Many a scholar, wanting to supply a date where one is lacking, does this: "C1907" (or "c.1907"). This means "circa [about] 1907," indicating an approximate date. But I have seen this interpreted as "Copyright 1907," turning an approximation into an accuracy. If a date is unknown but can be approximated, the best way to treat it is to say "about 1907." False dates, in some cases, are related to FALSE IMPRINTS.

FALSE IMPRINT. (Also called "fictitious imprint.") The practice of disguising a book's true place of imprint by printing a fictitious or inaccurate place of imprint. Mitch Fraas explains, "Title pages can be deceiving. Bibliographers have long learned not to trust colophons and other declarations of place and date. . . . Most literature on false imprints has focused on their use to avoid censorship or sidestep national laws, for example the numerous books printed in 16th-century London which bore imprints of a variety of continental cities" (Fraas, "Don't Believe That Imprint"). Intentionally using a false place of publication, then, generally is the result of a printer's trying to hide his identity to protect him from authorities who would not sanction the work in question. Fraas adds, "Bibliographers have also noted the use of false imprints to bolster the 'brand' of a book—if books from Germany are known for their quality and craftsmanship then as an English printer why not try to boost sales with a little deception?" And he points out that, to an American audience in the 18th century, a European imprint, especially for a religious text, would have a different meaning if it were London, France, or Germany, than it would have if it were Philadelphia. In one famous example, the last 10 volumes of the Diderot *Encyclopédie* were published with a false imprint since the publisher faced opposition from state and church. And the Columbia College (at Columbia University) website notes, "The first Italian edition of Machiavelli's Complete Works (*Tutte le Opera*) was released in 1550 or MDL in Roman numerals. But the volume here is not that edition, but rather a seventeenth-century 'false imprint.' In the course of the 1550s, Machiavelli's (1469–1527) works were put on the Pope's Index, or list of forbidden books (Galileo's *Dialogi* also made the list). This imprint—published between 1628 and 1660 A.D.—used the earlier date to avoid censorship" (Columbia College, "Machiavelli False Imprint, RBML 2011"). (*See Index Librorum Prohibitorum*.) (*See ESTC* and the caption for the second image at "Drop cap.")

FANFARE BINDING. A binding exhibiting "[a]n elaborate style of decoration consisting generally of geometrically formed compartments of varying sizes, each bounded by a ribbon consisting of a single FILLET on one side and a double fillet on the other, each of which, with the exception of the center compartment (which is larger or otherwise distinguished), being filled with leafy spirals, branches of laurel, and other sprays, floral tools, and the like. . . . It was imitated with varying degrees of fidelity, throughout Europe from about 1570 until well into the 17th century, although its elements were largely imitative of previous styles of embellishment" (Roberts and Etherington, pp. 96–97). The decoration could also consist of ONLAYS and INLAYS in various colors.

Fanfare binding on Hesiod, *Ta sôzomena tôn palaiotatôn poiètôn Geôrgika, Boukolika, kai Gnômika* [Greek]. / *Vetustissimorum authorum Georgica, Bucolica, & Gnomica poemata quae supersunt.* Para Krispinôi [Greek], *OGinevra!*: Para Krispinoi, 1570 (the bibliographical information from WorldCat; this copy offered for sale by Floristaus Fine Books at the Firsts Online book fair, May 2021).

Courtesy of Edwin Bloemsaat, Florisatus Fine Books, Manuscripts & Musicalia, Den Haag, Netherlands.

FAN STYLE; FAN BINDING. "A style of decorating a book characteristic of Italian bindings of the 17th century, and also Scottish bindings of the 18th century (usually referred to as Scottish 'wheel' bindings). In this style a design in the likeness of a fan is tooled on the covers of the book making a full circle in the center of the cover, and often quarter circles in the corners" (Roberts and Etherington, "fan style"; https://cool.culturalheritage.org/don/dt/dt1269.html [accessed 23 February 2021]).

FANZINE. A portmanteau word for "fan magazine." This is a publication of a fan group of a usually inexpensively produced magazine on a certain topic or in a particular genre. Fanzines exist in many areas, the most famous probably being in the realm of science fiction, in which the term appeared (about 1940—though fanzines existed a decade earlier than this) and which was the first genre to see such publications. Writers, especially young ones with no track record of publication, start these publications, or they offer their work to established fanzines. *The Encyclopedia of Science Fiction* says, "The first known sf fanzine was *The Comet* (May 1930) edited by Raymond A Palmer for the Science Correspondence Club, followed by *The Planet* (July 1930) edited by Allen Glasser for the New York Scienceers. However, both of these were mainly about science, although the second did include reviews of the professional sf magazines. Some regard the first true fanzine—certainly the first major one—as *The Time Traveller* (January 1932 #1) edited by Julius Schwartz and Mort Weisinger" (*The Encyclopedia of Science Fiction*, "Fanzine").

They are usually printed on inexpensive paper, originally using such early printing techniques as MIMEOGRAPH machines or early XEROGRAPHY from typed copy, and binding the LEAVES with staples. These publications were usually produced and authored by people not out to make a profit, and they were mostly traded or sold for nominal amounts. From science fiction, the fanzine format expanded out to other literary genres. They have been the stomping ground for unknown writers, many of whom went on to great careers. Ray Bradbury, Terry Carr, Harlan Ellison, and Robert Silverberg are a few of the many writers who have had stellar (literally and figuratively) careers in publishing, and who started and published extensively in fanzines. Despite their cheap production values, they have become highly COLLECTIBLE, especially those with the works of the more famous writers. (*See also* Zine.)

FASCICLE. A section of a work (as with a SIGNATURE of a book or a part of a magazine), usually issued at one time. Many books in the 19th century were issued in PARTS, with the purchaser receiving one fascicle at a time. The fascicle could consist of printed text, illustrations, or a combination of these. (*See* Serials/Serialization.)

FAST-ACTION STORIES. *See* Big Little Books.

FAUX. A word that has taken off in the language of advertising. It is French for "fake," but it does not have the negative connotations that "fake" has. Who wants a book bound in "fake leather"? But "faux leather" is okay. The Merriam-Webster website says, "made to look like something else that is usually more valuable" (https://www.merriam-webster.com/dictionary/faux [accessed 28 February 2021]). When the word first came into common English usage—as expected, in advertising—possibly people were taken in by it. Today it has become an English euphemism, not precisely apologizing for the shoddiness the word "fake" implies. It is fairly uniformly used for "imitation" or "artificial," which, also, have a ring of cheapness. (See Kanigel, *Faux Real: Genuine Leather and 200 Years of Inspired Fakes*.)

Imitation materials have been with us in the book world for more than a century. An early catalog of decorated papers from the Aschaffenburg paper factory lists dozens upon dozens of artificial materials—that is, papers that have the look of many kinds of leather, porcelain, wood, fabric, and other materials. The papers were used in bookbindings, and they showed up in sample books that are sought after by collectors and librarians, among many others. (See Berger, "Dutch Gilt Papers as Substitutes for Leather.") (*See* Graining; Kinkarakami; Leatherette.)

FAVORITE EDITION. Carter mentions this term—often used by booksellers to indicate an edition that they wish to sell, but that is not a more desirable one, like the first edition, or a limited edition signed. The term, of course, could also be used by a collector or reader who has a preference for one edition over others. But as a selling device, the phrase may not carry much weight since anyone seeing it might ask, "Who is to judge?" Is it the favorite of the bookseller, the bookseller's aunt, the general public, a particular scholar, or someone else? Tastes change, people have different aesthetic and literary senses, and the general public can be fickle. The term is unlikely to be much used today, though it belongs here in case someone comes across it in an old catalog and wants to know what it means.

FEATHERING. The dispersion into paper of the ink used to print on it—or any other liquid. A drop of water that falls onto a piece of NEWSPRINT, for example, will feather out into the sheet. (*See* Bleed.)

FEET (in type). The surfaces on which SORTS stand. When a sort is hand cast, it has a JET, extra metal attached to the bottom of the piece of type. When this jet is removed, a rough spot is left where it was attached. This rough spot is filed or planed down, leaving a small groove at the bottom of the sort, on either side of which are the feet of the piece of type. Type must be set into the bed of the PRESS so that every sort is flat on its feet, or the type will be askew and will not ink or print fully. Sorts cast by machine (as in a Monotype caster) also have feet. (*See* Plow.)

FELLOWSHIP OF AMERICAN BIBLIOPHILIC SOCIETIES (FABS). A "loose association of book collecting clubs. We are a non-profit 501C (6) organization, and do not seek any control or authority in any of the member clubs' policies or activities. Our mission is to communicate, share, and support bibliocentric activities, experience, and ideas among member clubs for mutual benefit and pleasure. / In furtherance of our mission we publish the FABS Journal, organize study tours to different cities in the U.S. and Europe, sponsor events and publications, create bibliophilic programming designed to connect bibliophiles across clubs, and hold annual meetings during a major antiquarian book-fair. Our website is designed to serve as a hub for communication for and about member clubs, affiliates and events" (http://www.fabsocieties.org [accessed 11 June 2022]). Founded in 1993, this organization is associated with clubs from coast to coast. As the organization's history says, "The seven founding member societies were The Grolier Club (New York City), The Club of Odd Volumes (Boston), The Rowfant Club (Cleveland), The Philobiblon Club (Philadelphia), The Caxton Club (Chicago), The Roxburghe Club (San Francisco, California), and The Baxter Society (Portland, Maine)" (see their website, "History of FABS"; http://www.fabsocieties.org/history-of-fabs [accessed 11 June 2022]). Many other book-collecting clubs exist that are not members of FABS. With the wish for inclusivity and social propriety, the organization rewrote its charter in 2021. The membership of this organization is in flux. See Appendix E for more information.

FELTS. In papermaking, the cloth surfaces onto which newly formed sheets are COUCHED. Felts are usually made of wool (or have some wool in them) so that the sheet will adhere to them and be pulled off the MOLD. This gives each sheet a "felt side" and a "mold side," distinguishable in some papers, especially handmade sheets that have not been CALENDERED. (*See* Post.)

FESTSCHRIFT. (Literally "celebration writing.") A collection of essays in a published volume, most or all of which have never been published before, and all dedicated to some person (usually a scholar) who has, in one way or another, influenced the writers of the essays. The dedicatee of the volume is being so honored because she is having a birthday, is retiring from a position, or simply because she is becoming superannuated and her peers want to thank her for her work and help. Or the work can be commemorative after the death of the honored person. The contributors to the volume are usually colleagues, friends, or students of the honoree, or others prominent in the honoree's field.

FICTITIOUS IMPRINT. *See* False imprint.

FIFTEENERS. A seldom-used term for INCUNABULA.

FILIGRANOLOGIST/FILIGRANOLOGY. An expert on the study of WATERMARKS. From the French word for "watermark," *filigrane*. There is no word in English for a watermarkologist, despite your seeing it in this sentence.

FILLER. Anything in paper besides the water and pulp of which the basic sheet is composed. Filler can be clay (for gloss), calcium carbonate (for longevity and alkalinity), glitter (for decorative purposes), or anything else in the VAT that goes into the paper. (*See* Furnish; Stuff; Waterleaf.)

FILLET. "A wheel-shaped FINISHING tool having one or more raised bands on its circumference. It is used to impress a line or parallel lines on the covering material of a book, usually one bound in leather" (Roberts and Etherington, p. 101). The term is also used to designate the lines that this tool imparts, so a book description may say, "With gilt fillets front and back." (*See* Pallet.)

Case Duster, wood, nineteenth century. (To eradicate type lice.)

Bookbinder's gold stamping tools, nineteenth century.

Fillets for bookbinding. The tool above it is a case duster, used to blow dust out of type cases.

Courtesy of International Printing Museum, Carson, CA.

FINE BINDING. Carter has this term, which is rather self-explanatory. In bookselling/book-collecting terms, it means the covering on a book that is far grander than the one used for most or all other copies of the same edition. A book issued in cloth may be presented in a fine binding of tooled leather (*see* Tooling), with elegant DOUBLURES, GILT EDGES, and a bound-in bookmark. While there is a strong market for fine bindings, and there is no shortage of experienced and superb bookbinders to produce them, it should be emphasized that to take an original binding off a COLLECTIBLE book and replace it with a costly fine binding could seriously reduce the value of the volume—such is the lure and importance of a volume in its ORIGINAL STATE.

FINE BOOKS & COLLECTIONS. A magazine featuring articles by many writers on the subjects of the magazine's title. Scott Brown and Dee Stewart were the founders and editors of *OP Magazine*, short for *Out-of-Print*. In 2004, Stewart left and Brown took on a new partner, Webb Howell, and they changed the magazine's name to *Fine Books & Collections*. *OP Magazine* was in print for only one year (2003). The first issue of the newly minted publication was for September/October 2004, and it has been going strong since.

The magazine has articles on all kinds of bookish topics, with a leaning toward the fine and rare materials. And its color photography, advertisements, regular columns, book reviews, announcements of book-related events, and other information make it the number one publication in the field at present.

FINE-PAPER COPY. A copy of a book printed on better paper than is used for other copies in the edition. Carter's entry says that in the 17th and early 18th centuries, printers used cheap and substandard paper, but they may have printed some volumes of a PRESSRUN on higher-quality paper, often from the Netherlands. He adds that later printers followed this same practice, offering the copies on better paper at a higher price. If this were the case, the ones on better paper would be advertised as being on "fine paper" (see Carter, p. 118). To be able to make the claim that a copy of a book is a "fine-paper copy," the person describing it must know that other copies are on inferior paper. Perhaps advertising literature will reveal that some copies are on fine paper, but this is rare to find. Sometimes LARGE-PAPER EDITIONS will be printed on a better stock than are the copies from the rest of the edition. One FINE-PRESS printer, needing a certain amount of paper for an edition and not finding enough in his cabinet of any one kind, used three different papers left over from previous titles. A bookseller or collector holding two copies of the final volume, each on a different paper, may assume that one was a fine-paper copy, the other not. The colophon merely says "printed . . . on various handmade papers," so there is no way to discern from any single copy in hand whether it is a fine-paper copy. (See Berger, *Printing and the Mind of Merker*, entry 58, p. 56.)

FINE PRESS BOOK ASSOCIATION (FPBA). "[A]n organization of individuals interested in the art of fine printing, formed with the goal of promoting the appreciation of beautiful books and printing skills. / Today it has a worldwide membership of those interested in the fine book and contemporary fine printing: collectors, printers, artists, illustrators, museums, libraries, and dealers. / It publishes *Parenthesis*, a journal devoted to fine printing and bookmaking, issues an occasional e-newsletter, organizes events for members and non-members, and has run competitions in book design. / *Parenthesis* is published twice a year and is free to members" (http://www.fpba.com [accessed 4 June 2021]). The organization is based in the UK and the United States, each of which produces an issue of *Parenthesis* yearly.

FINE-PRESS PRINTING. The printing done by a private (as opposed to a commercial) press. Certain characteristics of fine presses are that they are usually under the proprietorship of a single person or a small group of people who have full say in what is printed, what materials are used, and how many copies are done (hence the alternative designation "private press"); monetary profit is not necessarily the goal; usually high-quality materials are used for the papers, inks, and bindings; the typesetting and the printing are often done by hand; texts are printed LETTERPRESS; PRESSRUNS are short, ranging from a small number to, say, a few hundred (though a fine press may exceed this considerably); since profit is not usually a motive, the time it takes to create the final product is not generally an issue unless there is some other deadline that forces the printer to produce the volume before a certain date; because of the nature of the work (much of it done by hand), fairly short texts are often chosen, such as books of poetry; handsome typefaces (usually in excellent condition) are favored; presswork is careful; often, but by no means universal, the printer wishes to present an important text (sometimes reprints of classic works, more often volumes of verse from poets the printer deems "important" or "promising"); many have original artwork in them; volumes are often numbered and signed (by the author, illustrator, printer, binder, or anyone else of importance); these books can be quite expensive when they are produced for any of several reasons (they are in limited supply and high demand; they cost a good deal to produce; certain presses, authors, or binders are highly collected; or there is a market for fine-press, illustrated, signed books); because the production values are high for materials, there is a concomitant generosity in the layout and printing of the text, with good margins, proper LEADING, and good LETTERSPACING; and so on.

The printer KIM MERKER, proprietor of two such presses (Stone Wall and Windhover), would expatiate on the so-called artificial rarities that these presses produced, knowing that short pressruns and a strong audience will automatically make these books COLLECTIBLE and valuable. He hoped that the works he chose to print were of high literary quality, and he also hoped that they would be widely read. But he understood that these hopes were essentially dashed by the lack of ubiquity his books had because they were printed in small numbers and because they wound up in the collections of people who wanted them for their ARTIFACTUAL VALUE (not their literary value), and also in rare book collections in libraries, where they were somewhat sheltered from a general reading public. (*See* Limited edition.) (See Cave, *The Private Press*; Franklin, *The Private Presses*; and Ransom, *Private Presses*.) (*See also* Artists' books.)

FINE PRINT. One of the most important bibliographic journals in the United States focusing on fine printing, typography, and collectors' books. "The celebrated San Francisco–based journal *Fine Print: The Review for the Arts of the Book* (1975–1990) dealt broadly not only in its titular subject matter, the contemporary book arts, but also in the history of books and printing, typography, bookbinding, and related areas. Its many contributors included Martin Antonetti, John Dreyfus, Paul Hayden Duensing, Colin Franklin, Steven Heller, Janet Ing, Paul Needham, Stan Nelson, and Benjamin Vorst. The journal suddenly ceased publication (with volume 16 no. 3) in 1990 because of the unexpected ill health of its founding editor, Sandra Kirshenbaum" (Book Arts Press, "Back Issues of *Fine Print*," https://rarebookschool.org/2005/pbns/fineprint.html [accessed 6 June 2021]).

The articles that *Fine Print* published were usually by the most prominent people in their fields, and their collection *Fine Print on Type* is an excellent compendium of articles on printing types. (See Bigelow et al., eds., *Fine Print on Type*.)

FINGERPRINT. A term added by Nicolas Barker to Carter's original text (Barker's is the 6th edition [New Castle, DE: Oak Knoll Press, 1992], p. 97). Barker defines it as a "device" that bibliographers use to try to determine if a text has been reset. He says that bibliographers might compare characters in adjacent lines of text to see if they line up precisely in one copy with the same characters in another copy. The method I have used, similarly, charts the placement of characters: the bibliographer draws a line from the first printed character on a page to the last—running down the page diagonally from the farthest up and left spot of ink of the first character on the page to the lowest and farthest right spot of ink on the last character on the page. That line crosses characters (or goes between characters) in every line on the page. If the diagonal line hits all of the characters on one page in the exact same place as it does on the comparison page, it is likely that the type for that page has not been reset. "Fingerprint" seems to be Barker's adaptation for this kind of test. It is certainly a usage that appears exceptionally seldom in the literature of bookselling, collecting, or bibliography. I am glad that we now have a term for this phenomenon. Now we have to get all sellers and collectors, scholars and catalogers to read Carter in the later editions (6th through 9th), to memorize the term and its meaning, and use it consistently. As a footnote: The comparison, of course, must be done with copies from the same edition (*see* Edition, Impression [Printing], Issue, and State; Points). Photocopies, of course, will work fine, since we do not wish to deface the original. But with two copies of a text side by side, laying the straight edge onto the pages of both is all one needs to do, without drawing in lines. And if a bibliographer is keen on knowing about the RESETTING of type, this method works fairly well, with no fancy machinery necessary. If a HINMAN COLLATOR or a LINDSTRAND COMPARATOR is available, such "fingerprinting" can be done with a machine.

FINGER TAB. (Sometimes called an "extension tab.") Affixed to the fore-edge of a volume, a finger tab is a small marker that allows a user to locate a passage or part of a text. In medieval manuscripts, they were made of a variety of materials (paper, vellum, parchment, cloth), sometimes even as a knotted cord. Today they could also be made of cardboard or plastic. The tabs can have on them a designation of what they are there to locate: a letter of the alphabet, a number, or even words designating a subject or name, for instance. Another device used to help a reader locate a particular place in a text is the THUMB INDEX.

FINISHING (in binding). After a TEXT BLOCK is sewn and bound, it can be decorated—or finished. The work up to the finishing is FORWARDING. There are many methods of decoration, including lettering, stamping with various tools, GILDING, using DECORATED PAPERS, enhancing with fancy DOUBLURES, FORE-EDGE PAINTING (though this may not strictly be part of finishing), polishing, INLAYING and ONLAYING, and anything else the binder does to enhance the beauty of the binding. But the term is usually used for TOOLING that takes special skill. Traditionally, different people in the bindery sewed, forwarded, and finished. (See Fahey and Fahey, *Finishing in Hand Bookbinding*.) Finishing precedes forwarding in the binding process.

FIRST AMERICAN EDITION. *See* First edition; First English edition.

FIRST AND ONLY EDITION. A common bookseller's locution. If the book in question is the only edition, it is necessarily the first edition. But the magic of the word "first" may be too tempting to leave out, and some booksellers want that word in the book's description. It is irresistible—for the bookseller to use it and (he hopes) for the buyer, who may be a "firsts" collector. John Crichton of the Brick Row Book Shop, however, says that this phrase "is simply to clarify that there were no subsequent editions." He adds that "'Only Edition' would suffice, perhaps, but it is not part of the nomenclature, and to state that something is the 'first and only edition' is clear" (personal communiqué, 18 December 2017).

FIRST APPEARANCE. A term indicating that a text had never appeared in print before the one being considered. "First appearance of *It's Too Much for Me*" implies that that text had never before seen the light of day. A text could appear in a SERIAL version before being issued by itself in a bound volume. Or it could have been issued in a small PAMPHLET in a FINE-PRESS PRINTING in, say, only 20 copies (what some might call a "PRE-FIRST") before being issued in a larger edition of scores or hundreds of copies. The "first appearance" has some magical ring to it, as if its early issue makes it better in some way. It might be priced accordingly higher than would a copy of the FIRST EDITION. The term may also apply to a smaller portion of a text, as in, "This volume contains the first appearance of this famous poem," or, "This is the first appearance of this author's most famous character," thus appealing to a certain kind of collector, and making that volume special in its own way and perhaps commanding an enhanced price. A case in point: The first appearance of Superman, in comic book form, in *Action Comics* #1 (April 1938), will sell for hundreds of thousands (if not millions) of dollars. A bookseller, scholar, library cataloger, or collector may claim that such and such a text or character appears for the first time in a particular work; but such attributions could be incorrect, and some caution must be taken in making such statements. For example, "Those unfamiliar to comics may assume that Iron Man's first appearance is *The Invincible Iron Man* #1 (May 1968). However, in the golden and early silver ages of comic books, few superheroes debuted in magazines carrying their names. More often a character first appeared in a generically titled anthology series. If the character proved popular, a new series was launched. For example, Iron Man first appeared in *Tales of Suspense* #39 (March 1963) and appeared regularly in that series for five years before Marvel launched a series properly named *Iron Man*. Wonder Woman, Spider-Man, The Mighty Thor and many others also first appeared in anthology series" (Wikipedia, "First appearance"; https://en.wikipedia.org/wiki/First_appearance [accessed 24 February 2021]).

FIRST EDITION. An exceptionally complicated term bibliographically. Carter gives a long explanation to show the ins and outs of "first editions." As he says and as most bibliographers concur, the first edition of a text is that appearing for the first time in its own binding. But this is simpler than the situation really is. There are many instances in which what looks like a first edition is not one and in which one that does not look like one really is one. Carter lists a host of terms that show why the notion of "first edition" is imprecise at best and exceptionally complicated at worst. As all of these terms indicate, the notion of "first edition" is protean. Is a little pamphlet printed by a poet in, say, 1885 in a PRESSRUN of 50 copies for distribution to her friends (or a small number of copies printed for critics or reviewers) a true first edition, or is the commercial version issued the following year by a major publisher in an edition of 2,000 copies the real first? (For a reminder that an edition consists of all copies printed from the same setting of type, *see* Edition.) Is a book printed in 2015 from STEREOTYPE PLATES (made from standing type set in 1900 for the first edition) still a first edition? What about a text set into type twice—once by an English publisher, once by an American publisher—and printed in those two countries, with the final volumes released to the world on the same day? Which is the "first edition"?

There are no simple answers to the question "What is a first edition?" The cult of first-edition collectors, stemming from the book-collecting passions of the second half of the 19th century, has made that phrase ring like magic, and many an unremarkable text might command a remarkable price when "first edition" is attached to it. And collectors should be particularly wary of the use of the phrase in such locutions as "First edition thus," which means that the volume in question has never before been presented in the way this one was. This could mean nothing. It could be the first time the book was printed on extremely acidic paper, the first time it was issued with a particularly ugly and cheap binding, or the first time it came out with no DUST JACKET. "Thus" could mean anything. (*See below*.)

For most of us, the first definition given above (the first time a text appears in its own covers) will suffice. Hence, if a text of a novel appears serialized over many months in a magazine—a common form of publication in the 19th century—while this text appears for the first time *in print* in the magazine, it does not appear *in its own cover*, so most booksellers would not offer a run of the serial's issues containing the full text of the novel as a "first edition." They may say, "First printing," "The full text in its first appearance in print," or something like that.

Carter has a separate entry for "First published edition," a term that implies that the work in question was actually printed (and possibly bound) at one point but not offered to the public. It might have been created by an author in small numbers to be given to friends or relatives before the appearance of the text in a version offered by a publisher to the public. The "first *published* edition," then, might not be considered the real *first edition* since an edition preceded it. But to most booksellers and collectors, the commercial version in a large number of copies will probably merit being called the "first edition." A case in point is the volume published by HARRY DUNCAN and KIM MERKER, Paul Engle's *Golden Child*. The bibliographic record of this book reads: "Kansas City, Missouri: Hallmark Cards, 1960." But the first printing was from handset type and printed in a run of 105 copies for Joyce Hall, owner of Hallmark. Merker says, "Hall wanted copies of the libretto in book form to give to friends as a Christmas gift" (Berger, *Printing and the Mind of Merker*, p. 8). Joyce Hall liked the handmade, limited edition so much that he had a FACSIMILE version made on cheaper paper and in a much cheaper binding, which was offered for sale. The first can be called the "first edition" or even the "first printing" since it preceded the commercial version. But the commercial one should be called the "first published edition."

(As I was writing this, the term made it to the news. Jennifer Lopez, as a classics teacher in a high school—in the movie *The Boy Next Door*—is having a "flirtation" with a 19-year-old boy. He brings her a copy of Homer's *Iliad* in a lovely PUBLISHER'S BINDING and she asks him with wonder, "This is a first edition? It must have cost a fortune." The screenwriters and their continuity experts really messed up on this one.) (*See* Book form; Edition.) (See also Zempel and Verkler, *First Editions*.) (For more on this complex issue, *see* Advance copy; Authorized edition; Book form; Copyright edition; Edition, Impression [Printing], Issue, and State; Points; First separate edition; Follow the flag; Parts/In parts; Pirate; Pre-firsts; Secondary binding.)

As noted above, the term "first edition thus" is common but illogical. Booksellers, to capitalize on the magical phrase "first edition," will use any excuse to add those words to a description. "Thus" implies that there is something about their copy that had never been released to the public before. It could mean that this is the first time the text was issued with illustrations, the first with a DUST JACKET, the first in FOLIO FORMAT, the first with every copy in the edition water stained and mildewed from a flood at the publisher's warehouse, or anything else that makes this edition different from all that came before it. For many a collector or librarian, the "thus" is a red flag.

FIRST EDITION THUS. *See* First edition.

FIRST ENGLISH EDITION. Carter's entry for this term tells us that it refers to a copy of a text published in England, but the term implies that it is not the first one published. Equivalent terms could be created: "First _____ edition," fill in the blank with the name of any country. The appearance of an edition of a text in a given country—one that is not the original country of the "true FIRST EDITION"—says nothing about rarity, value (fiscal or intellectual), or anything else other than that the item is not a true first edition. Then why would a bookseller mention this in a book's description? Perhaps to get that magical word "first" in there, with its hint of specialness. In some circumstances the term is justified. When Mark Twain published *Pudd'nhead Wilson* in book form, to secure copyright protection in England and the United States, he sent a PRINTER'S COPY to his American publisher (American Publishing Company in Hartford, CT) and another printer's copy to his English publisher (Chatto & Windus in London). He instructed both publishers to release the book to the public on 28 November 1894. This simultaneous issue (*see* Edition, Impression [Printing], Issue, and State; Points) yielded a little bibliographical conundrum: Which was the first edition? One could claim that since the sun came up in England before it did in Hartford, the English edition was issued first and is thus the real first edition. Or one could say, "FOLLOW THE FLAG," and claim that the U.S. edition is the "true first." A better way around it is simply to call the Hartford version the "First American Edition"; the other the "First English Edition." This is another reason for this term to exist. Finally, there is the "First Published Edition," which is, as the term says, the first one published, regardless of the form in which it appeared, the country in which it was published, the publisher, and so forth. The text could have appeared in a SERIAL (*see* Serial/Serialization) before it was issued in its own covers. The serial version would be the First Published version of the text, but not formally a first edition in the bibliographical sense.

FIRST PRINTING. As Carter points out, the term means either the first time a text appears in print or the first impression of a text within an edition. (*See* Edition, Impression [Printing], Issue, and State; Points.) In this second sense, "printing" and "impression" are synonyms. In the former sense, for a novel that appeared serially, the bibliographer could say that the serial version was the "first printing" of the text.

Carter mentions one particular instance that is not unique: that of the publisher Victor Gollancz and others in the 20th century, who sent to a printer an order of only a small number of copies of a text and—if they needed additional copies later on—ordered more. They might do this several times. He says that the volumes so produced were called "second, third, nth printing before publication," and he adds that today one might see "first printing" or "first and second printing before publication" (Carter, p. 119). More recently, the novel *While England Sleeps* by David Leavitt was recalled after being on the market only a short time. The recall came because Stephen Spender recognized some of his own text (from his book *World within World*) embedded in Leavitt's work, and he threatened to sue, so Leavitt was forced to revise some of his text. The "first printing" was on the market for only a short time, but some copies have "second printing" on their copyright pages—possibly this second impression was made before the book was released to the public. (*See also* First edition.)

FIRST PUBLISHED EDITION. *See* First English edition.

FIRST SEPARATE EDITION. This is the first printing of a text that had appeared printed along with other texts in the past. A short story may appear in a collection (or in many collections) and then later get printed as a volume all its own. This would be the first separate edition.

FISH PRINTS. Prints made by inking the surface of a fish and pressing paper over that inked surface. The image transferred to the paper is of the entire inked surface of the fish. The technique has been used in some FINE-PRESS PRINTING, as with Carol Schatt's poem *House of Cods*, bound in a fish-printed paper. (See Schatt in the bibliography.) The technique developed in the middle of the 19th century in Japan, where it is called Gyotaku (Gyo = fish; taku = printing or rubbing). Tradition has it that Japanese fishermen wanted to record their catch, so they made prints directly from the sea creatures they caught. Three traditional methods of making these prints are described at the KCP International, Japanese Language School website ("Gyotaku: The Traditional Japanese Art of Fish Printing" (December 16, 2019; https://www.kcpinternational.com/2019/12/gyotaku-traditional-japanese-art-fish-printing/ [accessed 2 March 2021]).

FIST (also called a "manicule," "index," "printer's fist," "bishop's fist," "digit," "mutton-fist," "hand," "hand director," "pointer," and "pointing hand"). A printer's character or a drawn insertion into a manuscript or printed book that looks like a pointing hand. (See Sherman, "Toward a History of the Manicule.")

As William Sherman explains, "In fact, while the printers' manicules tend to be restrained in style and rigidly locked into their horizontal position alongside the texts they are highlighting, manuscript manicules often played with the space of the page. In some cases they are intentionally made to look like they're extending in from a now invisible reader's body off the edge of the margin—almost like a comic version of the hand of God coming down from the clouds in Renaissance emblems and in rings with moving dials and pointers" ("Toward a History of the Manicule," p. 12; citing Karr, "Constructions Both Sacred and Profane," especially pp. 124–27). And he says, "The primary functions served by the manicule are, on the one hand, designed to clarify the

Fists. Printing type (*see* Sorts) with fists.
Collection of the author.

organization of the text and, on the other, to help individual readers to find their way around that structure and put their hands on passages of particular interest (especially when they return to a book after some time). On the most general level in other words, the function of the manicule is to prevent the text from getting out of hand" (pp. 14–15).

FIVE-STAR LIBRARY BOOKS. *See* Big Little Books.

FLAP BOOK. A book with layered text or illustrations, as with medical volumes showing, for instance, a human body part from the outside of the body, a layer beneath that showing the structures immediately beneath the skin, a layer underneath showing muscles or bones, and so on. The pieces of paper one lifts to reveal the several layers are called FLAPS. They can be conjured up on the web under the term "flap books" or "lift-the-flap books."

FLAPS. The turned-in panels of a DUST JACKET that fold over and sit between the front and rear free and the pastedown ENDLEAVES when a book is closed. They have become the venue for all kinds of information: SHORT TITLE; a precis of the content of the book; BLURBS; photo and bio of the author or editor; ISBN; ADVERTISEMENTS; price; date of issue; and whatever else the publisher decides to put there. Flaps are also the pieces of paper layered over other pieces in an illustrated book; the flap has some kind of text or image on it; when it is lifted, one sees another printed or illustrated surface. (*See* Flap book.)

FLAT BACK (in binding). A binding, usually done by hand, that "has not been rounded and backed before the boards are attached" (Roberts and Etherington, p. 103). They add, "The spine of a flat back binding has a tendency to become concave." (*See* Recessed-cord sewing; Rounding and backing.)

FLATSIGNED. Signed. The simplicity of that definition sort of says it all: that a book that is flatsigned is merely signed with no inscription or other notation from the signer—presumably the author. And it generally means signed on the book itself, not on any LAID-IN or TIPPED-IN leaf or on a BOOKPLATE.

The Alibris website says that such a volume "was autographed in person, or that someone witnessed the book being signed" (Alibris; "Glossary of Book Terms"), but I cannot corroborate this with any other source.

The term seems to be of fairly recent coinage, and I must admit that I don't like it; but there it is, and one can find it on a quick web search, accompanied by "About 105,000 results (0.46 seconds)" (searched on 4 May 2021). OMG! In under a half second Google pulled up over 100,000 hits. I guess it belongs here.

FLESH SIDE. The side of an animal skin that was opposite to the HAIR SIDE. (*See* Hair side; Parchment; Vellum.) In preparing a text, the scribe wanted all flesh sides to be folded on the outside (or all on the inside) of each folded skin since the hair side tended to be darker than the flesh side. By folding all skins the same way (e.g., with all hair sides inside the fold), all facing pages would be about the same shade. In most skins, the hair side would be discernible by its slightly (or much) darker color and by the pores and other markings—e.g., scratches that the animal had—that might still be visible in the prepared skin. In well-prepared or dyed parchment, the hair side and the flesh side might not be distinguishable from one another.

THE FLEURON. One of the premier though short-lived bibliographic periodicals of the 20th century. It came out in seven issues from 1923 to 1930. "The Fleuron Society was formed in 1922 by Holbrook Jackson, Francis Meynell, Bernard Newdigate, Stanley Morison and Oliver Simon. [Their plan was] to produce one book a year to demonstrate that a machine-set book could rival the work of a private press" (Somers, *Index to* The Dolphin *and* The Fleuron, p. vii). Morison and Simon founded *The Fleuron* in 1923. The goal of the journal "was to examine problems of type and book design, and to encourage mutual understanding by establishing relations between printers, readers, bookmen and artists" (p. vii). It was printed by the Curwen Press. The periodical published a host of important articles by the most influential designers and typographical scholars of its day. Oliver Simon edited numbers 1 to 4; Stanley Morison edited numbers 5 to 7.

FLEURONS. Decorative elements used to embellish a page or a binding. In fact, they can be used anywhere in a book—on its covers, end sheets, or printed pages. (*See also* Dingbats; Printer's flowers; Type ornaments.)

Fleurons.
Getty Images; iStock.

They also can be the central reason that a book exists. Witness the Gehenna Press books *Flosculi Sententiarum* and *Cancelleresca Bastarda*, florilegia (*see* Florilegium) that were built around the decorative distribution of fleurons. (See also Berger, *Fleuronologia*, and Meynell and Morison, "Printers' Flowers.") (For another image, *see* Rule.)

FLEXIBLE SEWING. "A method of sewing the sections of a book to cords or bands which are above the backs of the sections and rest against them, instead of being recessed into the paper. [*See* Recessed-cord sewing.] / The sewing thread is looped completely around the cords, instead of passing in front of them. This type of sewing may be done on single or double cords and is one of the strongest forms of hand sewing known. The method was in use in Europe as early as the 8th century, and represents the foundation upon which hand bookbinding was built and developed for a thousand years. / The number of bands, which were always double (i.e., two cords or thongs adjacent to each other and almost touching), on which 12th and 13th century books were sewn varied from two to five (in the latter case the cords being spaced so there was a greater space between the cords than between the end bands and the head and tail of the book), although examples of books sewn on as many as fourteen cords are known. The use of double cords gradually diminished, however, and by the middle of the 16th century the technique of sewing on single cords had become fairly well established, although largely for smaller books and economical bindings. / The use of flexible sewing has been dominant in fine binding until the present day; however, its use declined sharply from the end of the 18th century until the end of the 19th century, when it was revived to some extent due to the efforts of T. J. Cobden-Sanderson and Douglas Cockerell. / Flexible sewing is not suitable for books printed on very heavy paper, nor in cases where the book is made up of very thick sections. It is also unsuitable for use with coated papers. If used on small volumes, the sewing thread and, therefore, the cords, must be proportionally thinner; otherwise there will be a reduction in flexibility" (Roberts and Etherington, "flexible sewing"; https://cool.culturalheritage.org/don/dt/dt1365.html [accessed 26 January 2021]). The term "flexible binding" is sometimes used to denote either a cover that is not rigid, or a volume that lies flat when it is opened, without springing shut. (See Charles T. Jacoby, *Some Notes on Books and Printing*, p. 78.)

FLEXOGRAPHY. "Flexography [often shortened to 'flexo'] is the major process used to print packaging materials. Flexography is used to print corrugated containers, folding cartons, multiwall sacks, paper sacks, plastic bags, milk and beverage cartons, disposable cups and containers, labels, adhesive tapes, envelopes, newspapers, and wrappers (candy and food). . . . [Using a flexible plate with an image in relief], [i]n the typical flexo printing sequence, the substrate is fed into the press from a roll. The image printed as [a] substrate is pulled through a series of stations, or print units. Each print unit is printing a single color. As with Gravure and LITHOGRAPHIC printing, the various tones and shading are achieved by overlaying the 4 basic shades of ink. These are magenta, cyan, yellow and black. Magenta being the red tones and cyan being the blue" (HT Labels, "Flexographic Applications"). Four rollers are used: 1) the ink roller that transfers ink from a pan to a 2) meter roller (also called an Anilox roll); it evens out the ink on the roller to transfer it to the 3) plate cylinder, which receives one color of the ink. The surface to be printed progresses between the plate cylinder and the 4) impression cylinder, which applies pressure to the plate cylinder, transferring the image onto the printed surface, which then goes to a dryer so that the ink is dry before it goes on to the next printing unit. Once the several colors are printed there may be another feeding of the printed material through a drying area of the press to remove any residual water or solvents. The printed material is then fed onto a take-up roll or is sent to a cutter. If the definition of the word "flexography" is extended to the relief printing from any flexible medium, then PHOTOPOLYMER PLATE printing may be seen as a form of flexography, even though the photopolymer plate is mounted to a TYPE-HIGH block and is not flexible at the time of its printing.

FLICK BOOK OR FLICKER BOOK. *See* Flip book.

FLIK-FLIK BOOKS. *See* Blow books.

FLIPBACK BOOKS. A new "genre" of books geared to commuters and others who wish to take their books with them. These are small, landscape orientation volumes with the spine at the head of the volume. They slip into pockets easily. They are geared to several audiences, many for the young adult reader. Shahrzad Warkentin says, "Mini pocket books or flipback books originated in the Netherlands where they are known as 'dwarsligger.' These tiny versions of regular paperback books, which are hugely popular across Europe, are designed to be small enough to fit inside your back pocket for easy carrying and are about the size of your smartphone" (Warkentin, "Flipback Books Make It Easy to Read with Just One Hand & Lit-Loving Moms Can So Relate.")

FLIP BOOK (also called a "flick book" or "flicker book"). A volume with illustrations on its pages that, when the pages are riffled through, reveals the images as a moving picture. (The Wikipedia article is illuminating: https://en.wikipedia.org/wiki/Flip_book#cite_note-2 [accessed 26 January 2021].) (*See* Cels.) In the past, a flip book was a volume with leaves that had been cut such that parts of each leaf could be flipped over to reveal a text beneath it that meshed textually (or visually—or both) with the text on the un-flipped parts of the leaf. *The Mix or Match Storybook* is one such volume, boasting that it contains over a million stories, once all of the combinations and permutations of flipping and mixing have been added up. (See Gantz, *The Mix or Match Storybook.*) (*See* Metamorphic books.) This construction, however, is no longer called a flip book, the term being reserved for the kind of volume that has leaves that are flipped with the fingers to reveal a "moving image." (*See* Metamorphosis books; Movable book.)

FLOATED. Said of a leaf of a text that has been attached to another (usually heavier) sheet in such a way that the attached leaf, glued to a window that has been cut in the SUBSTRATE sheet, can be seen on both sides. That is, a window is cut into the substrate that conforms to the edges of the leaf to be read (or viewed, if images, not text, are to be seen). The leaf to be viewed is glued down along its edges onto the substrate. In this situation, one can read the text, turn the pages (so to speak), read what is on the opposite side of the floated item, and not touch the leaves one is reading. This method, employed to protect fragile and/or damaged leaves, was popular at the end of the 19th and into the 20th century, before the invention of translucent plastic sheets (like MYLAR), which held the more fragile leaves in a way that allowed them to be seen on both sides but not touched. I encountered this floated phenomenon in working on the *Pudd'nhead Wilson* manuscript. Every page of that manuscript (at the MORGAN LIBRARY) was bound that way. It is also used to secure PAPYRUS fragments.

FLOCK PAPER/FLOCKED PAPER. (Sometimes hyphenated.) Showing the original use of this kind of paper, E. J. Labarre says, "A kind of wallpaper, now no longer in general use, prepared by being sized, either over the whole surface or over special parts constituting the pattern only, and then powdering over it flock—hence [as a verb] 'flocking', also 'velveting'—powdered wool or woolen waste . . . which has been previously dyed. Sometimes also impressed with a pattern. Earliest specimens known date from middle of 16th Cent. and were intended to imitate tapestry and Italian velvet brocades" (Labarre, *Dictionary and Encyclopaedia of Paper and Paper-making*, p. 106). (Flock is short-cut fine fibers finished with an electrostatic coating; it has many applications, but especially as a surface coating for functional and decorative purposes.) This paper was used in the 19th century, and has reappeared in abundance in the 20th and 21st centuries on all kinds of EPHEMERA, especially greeting cards, and even on some garish bindings. Its primary characteristic is its velvety texture.

FLONG (in stereotyping). A PAPIER-MÂCHÉ "sheet" of paper pulp pressed firmly over a page of STANDING TYPE. When this sheet has dried, it contains a perfect DEBOSSED image of the type. This is the flong, which is used as a MATRIX for TYPE METAL, that is poured in to make a STEREOTYPE PLATE and that can be used for printing instead of the type. Since type metal melts somewhere between 240°C and 360°C and paper burns at a much higher temperature than it takes to melt the type metal, the flong will not be damaged when it receives the molten metal. Brian Palmer says, "Older textbooks report a range of numbers for the auto-ignition point of paper, from the high 440s to the low 450s, but more recent experiments suggest it's about 30 degrees hotter than that" (Palmer, "Does Paper Really Burn at 451 Degrees Fahrenheit?"; http://www.slate.com/articles/health_and_science/explainer/2012/06/ray_bradbury_death_does_paper_really_burn_at_451_degrees_fahrenheit_.html [accessed 8 June 2021]). So the flong would be a perfectly solid material to receive the molten type metal for casting the stereotype plate. (*See* Stereotyping.)

FLORIATED. Decorated with flowers. Said of a MAJUSCULE or borders that have such decoration. It was common in medieval books to decorate with extensive vines and flowers in the margins or the capital letters of manuscripts. Floriated initials or borders would sometimes have additional ornamentation, such as insects, animals, human figures, GROTESQUES, and many other things. (*See* Illuminated.) (For a floriated initial, *see* Drop cap.)

FLORILEGIUM. An anthology of "flowers" of writers; that is, a collection of passages from writers that the compiler finds uplifting, perceptive, intelligent, or elegant. (*See* Commonplace book; Miscellany.)

FLOWER CAGE. *See* Cobweb.

FLOWERS/PRINTER'S FLOWERS. *See* Fleurons.

FLUSH LEFT/FLUSH RIGHT. *See* Justification (in typesetting). Also, if the leaves of a TEXT BLOCK are the same "length" as the covers of the book, as is the case in PAPERBACKS, they are said to be flush with the cover.

FLYER. An advertising piece, usually in the form of a BROADSIDE, LEAFLET, or PAMPHLET. It can be sewn or stapled, but it does not have to be. As a single sheet, it can be printed on one or two sides; it might be called a "fly-sheet," though this term is seldom used.

FLYLEAVES. Blank leaves used at the front and back of the bound volume. Strictly speaking, an ENDLEAF, either pastedown or free, is not a flyleaf, though the terminology has been muddied over the years, and some commentators will call the free endpaper a flyleaf. (*See* Endleaves.)

FLY-SHEET. *See* Flyer.

FLY TITLE. Some volumes have a HALF TITLE (also called a "bastard title" or sometimes a "divisional title") before the regular title page and another before the main text (but after the PRELIMINARIES). The latter is called the fly title. (*See also* Divisional title; Subtitle.)

FOLDED AND DYED PAPER. *See* Itajime.

FOLDED AND GATHERED. Once the SIGNATURES of a book are printed, they are sent to the binder for SEWING. The printer can send the SHEETS unfolded or folded. If unfolded, the binder did the folding. Then the signatures would be brought together in GATHERINGS so that they could be bound. It happens that full texts of books, in folded and gathered form, but unbound, survive. They are said to be "folded and gathered," which implies UNBOUND. Such groups of loose signatures from a book that was once bound are not said to be "folded and gathered"; one would say that the TEXT BLOCK has been DISBOUND.

FOLDOUT. Part of a LEAF in a book or PAMPHLET that is folded over when the volume is shut and that unfolds to be observed. Foldouts can be on a single leaf or on several leaves glued together to yield quite large images. The folds could be vertical, horizontal, or both. When they are both and when the book has a tight binding (so it does not lie flat when it is open), the foldout will be stressed in its unfolding and could tear. (*See* Gatefold.)

FOLGER SHAKESPEARE LIBRARY (Washington, DC). Named after Henry Clay Folger and his wife Emily Jordan Folger, a collection that is a "research center on Shakespeare and on the early modern age in the West" (http://www.folger.edu [accessed 8 June 2021]). Opening in 1932, the library now contains "the world's largest Shakespeare collection and . . . major collections of other rare Renaissance books, manuscripts, and works of art" ("About the Folger," http://www.folger.edu/about [accessed 8 June 2021]).

FOLIATION. The numbering of leaves in a volume, not pages. Before page numbers became common (in the HAND-PRESS PERIOD), each LEAF of MANUSCRIPTS could be NUMBERED, with designations of RECTO and VERSO indicating the front and back of the leaves. So a reader being directed to what would be page 6 in a printed book would be sent to leaf 3v, indicating the verso of the third leaf. The term comes from the fact that an old way to designate a leaf was "FOLIO." So a volume with its leaves numbered is said to be "foliated," *not* "paginated." (*See* Pagination.)

FOLIO (book format). A volume in which the TEXT BLOCK is formed from having the original full sheets that make up the volume folded only once. If the paper in the book was LAID, the CHAIN LINES in the book's leaves will be vertical. If the paper had a WATERMARK and a COUNTERMARK, these will appear in approximately the center of each leaf. The SIGNATURES in a simple folio will consist of two leaves. Other folio volumes are Folio in 4s (with two simple folios, one nested inside the other, the "4s" indicating that there are four leaves in the signature), Folio in 6s (three nested folios, with six leaves in the signature; *see* Ternion), Folio in 8s (*see* Quaternion), and Folio in 10s. It is possible to have a Folio in 12s also, but with this many leaves nested, the center one will stick out at the FORE-EDGE, so this format is uncommon (*see* Sexternion). Note that since the format is created by the single-folded full sheet, the volume is likely to be large—depending, of course, on the size of the original sheet. So there is a tendency among those who do not know how folios are created to call any large book a folio. And in libraries in which large books need to be shelved apart from smaller ones, the area in which they are shelved is often called "folios," though large QUARTOS and other large volumes could be shelved there. The term has evolved to mean "a large book."

Additional note: A papermaker I know, on a tiny MOLD, makes tiny sheets the size of a business card. If she folds those sheets in half to create a MINIATURE book, she has created a folio—tiny though it is—since the folio is composed of full-size sheets folded only once. In the bibliographical sense, size is not an issue in determining the FORMAT of a book.

FOLIO (leaf in a book). One old way to designate a LEAF in a book, hence the term "FOLIATION," the numbering of the book's leaves (as opposed to pagination, or numbering the pages). Sometimes the number on the leaf is called the "folio." In medieval manuscripts and early printed books, neither the pages nor the leaves might be numbered, so the numbers were put in by hand by a later user/owner. This kind of foliation is quite common. So one could say that "the folio (the leaf number) on the volume's third folio (the third leaf) is in red in this folio (the large book)." (*See* Format.)

FOLLOW COPY. Carter has an entry for this term that is not strictly a bookman's term, but it does raise a key issue in the bibliographic world: Does a copyist or SCRIBE or a COMPOSITOR setting type reproduce accurately the text he was given to reproduce? In the medieval period, before the beginning of standardized spelling and punctuation, a scribe would write down more what he heard than what he saw—how the text would have sounded to him had it been read aloud. That is, scribes were not constrained to follow copy with perfect fidelity. In the world of printing, following copy was not a mandate until, perhaps, the 19th century, and there are instances in which compositors or editors clearly thought they knew better than the author whose works they were responsible for. In a letter about *Pudd'nhead Wilson*, Mark Twain says that his "deeply thought out, and laboriously perfected" punctuation had been altered "by some imported proof-reader, from Oxford University. . . . I said I didn't care if he was an Archangel imported from Heaven, he couldn't puke his ignorant impudence over *my* punctuation, I wouldn't allow it for a moment. I said I couldn't read this proof. I couldn't sit in the *presence* of a proofsheet where that blatherskite had left his tracks" (see Berger, *Pudd'nhead Wilson*, "Textual Introduction," p. 192). Clearly some writers want their copies followed with precision.

One problem arises when an American author is having his text set by a compositor in England. With respect to ACCIDENTALS (punctuation, spelling, and so forth), the English typesetter may be constrained to follow the HOUSE STYLE of the publisher, and thus will change the styling of the author. Could that lead to a reinterpretation of the text in some way? And what does a compositor do when he sees a blunder in the text he is to follow? Reproduce the error? Try to seek out the author? (Using a Ouija board if the author is deceased?) Try to locate the editor for advice? Silently make the change? Assume the author would have wanted him to make the change? Run the risk of changing what he thinks is an error but was not? Following copy can have its challenges.

FOLLOW THE FLAG. The long entry on this term in Carter indicates the complexity of the issue. If an author publishes her work in a country other than her own and then publishes a different edition in her own country, which is the FIRST EDITION? There are two considerations: chronological priority and "homeland priority." With the cult of the first-edition collector, the true first edition may carry more weight than does any other edition as far as how much he will pay for the item goes, so there is a fiscal—if not an emotional and intellectual—issue with determining what the first edition really is. The second of the considerations, "homeland priority," is what engenders the term "follow the flag." That is, some, such as the French, deem the first edition of a French author to be the first French edition regardless of whether other versions were published in other countries before the first French one was published. Pirated versions (*see* Pirated edition) present their own problems, especially depending on what the pirates used as their PRINTER'S COPY, which could be an authoritative (*see* Authoritative edition) version, received directly from the author. As Carter points out, a serious collector will want all the editions, but this skirts the issue, as Carter knows. He says that collectors may be willing to pay more for one or the other of these—the "native first" or the "actual first." And he adds what I have already observed, namely, that a true collector will want all manifestations of the texts of the authors they collect, even copies created by a pirate that have no textual authority or authorial sanction. (See Carter, pp. 122–23.)

Carter then points out that there are also various editions created in different countries to secure copyright or copies created all printed from the same setting of type but with variant title pages to satisfy more than one publisher/bookseller (the title page being a CANCEL in some copies). (See Carter, p. 123.) Mark Twain made sure that his *Pudd'nhead Wilson* was issued on 28 November 1894 in London and Hartford, securing copyright in both countries simultaneously (see Berger, "Textual Introduction," p. 192), but those two versions had two different settings of type.

Then there are the situations of expatriates (e.g., T. S. Eliot and W. H. Auden) and also a writer such as B. Traven, who claimed birth in the United States, Mexico, and Germany. (Keeping his true identity a secret—even his own wife didn't know where he was from, and to this day no one seems to know what the "B" stands for in his name—he led a life of surreptitious identity.) Thus, for Traven's novels, "follow the flag" has another layer of complication to it. In fact, at least one of his novels was first published in Sweden.

FONT (spelled "fount" in Great Britain). In TYPOGRAPHY, a complete set of SORTS, including everything designed for that set that could be used for printing: letters (upper- and lowercase), numbers, punctuation, special characters (LIGATURES, decorative elements that go with that typeface, and others), diacritics, and anything else the set contains. The printer ordered type by the font, which means a separate font for one typeface of one size of type. Carter, showing his British bias, complains that the word "font" to mean a particular typeface is illiterate (p. 128). However, the term has gotten strong roots, and it is not uncommon to hear one say, "I really like this font" (i.e., this typeface). The usage is general and is no longer to be disparaged.

FONT SCHEME. Since different languages use characters in different numbers, the font scheme is designed to give a printer who orders a font the most likely distribution of SORTS she will need. That is, in broad terms, the printer would get more E's and T's than X's and Z's. Some printers, knowing that a particular text will require an extraordinary number of not-often-used characters, may ask the foundry to modify the font scheme to include extras of those characters.

FOOLSCAP. A size of a sheet of paper, so named because the watermark in the leaf shows a person wearing a fool's cap, usually with bells on the cap. Of course, such watermarks could be seen in sheets of many such sizes—not a specific size. Sheets of about this size were common for printing and writing. And not all of them of this size had the foolscap watermark. Labarre has the size of foolscap sheets "varying from 15½ × 12¾ inches to 18½ × 14½ inches" (Labarre, *Dictionary and Encyclopaedia of Paper and Paper-Making*, p. 110). He also cites Clarence West's *Classifications and Definitions of Paper*, which gives 16 × 13 inches as the size of a foolscap sheet. Labarres's long entry (pp. 110–11) mentions many variants, such as double flat foolscap, large foolscap, double foolscap, broad foolscap, littris foolscap, quad small foolscap, and so on. I have taken this much time on this sheet to indicate the wide range of variation in the designations of sheets, brought about by the complete lack of standardization in the paper industry with respect to paper sizes. The size of any handmade sheet was determined by the inner dimensions of the DECKLE on the MOLD on which the sheet was made. Machine-made paper could be cut to any size. Names indicate only approximate sizes. (*See* Appendix C.) The imprecision in terminology in paper names and paper sizes is fully discussed by Labarre (particularly worth reading is his discussion, pp. 268–72). (For a foolscap watermark, *see* Watermark.)

FOOT. *See* Tail.

FOOTLINE. The bottom line of text on a page. It could mean the last line of the *text*, but sometimes it designates the DIRECTION LINE.

FOOTNOTE. A note written or printed at the foot of a page. If the note is given at the end of the chapter or the end of the volume, it is called an "endnote." There are two kinds of such notes—bibliographical and informational—or a combination of the two. When an author cites sources, bibliographical information appears in the notes. But if the author wants to comment on the text at the point at which the note is inserted, the note can contain prose to the tune of hundreds or even thousands of words, depending on the prolixity of the writer and the need for such information at that point in the text. The cost of setting footnotes before the computerization of typesetting made it economical to use endnotes, allowing the publisher to cluster them all in one place and not "muck up" the design of the printed text page. Readers might have complained that flipping back and forth from the text to the notes was inconvenient, but it did leave a well-designed page unencumbered with the notes. (KIM MERKER solved the problem by printing one of his texts with all endnotes on a foldout leaf [a FLAP], allowing the readers to fold the leaf out and see the notes while they read or not to do so and have the experience of the aesthetically laid out page alone [see his *Völuspá*]). If there are only a few of these, symbols such as the ASTERISK (*), the dagger (†), or the double dagger (‡) may be used; otherwise, numbers (usually Arabic numerals) are used to mark notes. The asterisk, it is to be noted, is a sign that there is a footnote but not a numbered one. Bibliographical footnotes have been much supplanted in the past few decades by the use of internal citation (citations given in parentheses in the text and leading a reader to a section called "Works Cited," "Bibliography," or "References" in which the source information is given). (See Grafton, *Footnote*.)

FOOTNOTE CALL. "The number or symbol used in a text, table, or illustration to indicate that there is a note to what is being discussed and to identify which note. There are certain general practices: (1) When numbers are used, they should be SUPERSCRIPT LINING FIGURES . . . (2) If superior figures are used for the note number (as well as the call), the size should be the same unless there are specific instructions to the contrary or unless there is more than a 2-point difference between text type and note type. . . . (3) All note calls in a sequence are the same style of type" (Eckersley et al., *Glossary of Typesetting Terms*, pp. 43–44). In most book people's parlance, we would use the term "footnote number" to designate such things as "happiness[12]"; however, as already explained, not all notes are signaled by numbers (e.g., "happiness[*]"). So the more generic term "footnote call" is used to cover all such superscripts. Also, not all superscripts are footnote calls: "$7^2 = 49$"; "the 4th person"; "it was 80°."

FORE-EDGE. The edge of a CODEX opposite the SPINE. In a volume in which the text reads left to right, the fore-edge is on the right. Titles, in early-printed books, could be written onto the fore-edge; they are obviously referred to as "fore-edge titles."

FORE-EDGE ILLUSTRATION/FORE-EDGE PAINTING. A picture painted on the FORE-EDGE of a volume, most often under a GILT EDGE and made visible only when the TEXT BLOCK is fanned out. To be strictly accurate, the image is not really on the fore-edge but is on the very edges of the surfaces of the PAGES. When the book is "at rest," the surfaces of the sheets are not visible. But when the text block is fanned out, the surfaces of the pages are revealed, and the painting comes into view. It is possible that the illustration is actually on the fore-edge itself, in which case it is visible without any fanning out. But when the image is not on the fore-edge itself but is on the front of the LEAVES (sometimes on the RECTO, sometimes on both sides if two images appear when the volume is fanned out in both directions—in a "double fore-edge illustration"—and becomes visible with the fanning out), it is still called a "fore-edge painting." And, in fact, the fanned-out version is what most people refer to when they speak of a fore-edge illustration. It is possible, also, to have two separate images painted on a fore-edge, both visible when the leaves are fanned out in one direction.

A variation of this technique of decoration is called a "panoramic fore-edge illustration," created when the HEAD and TAIL edges of the volume are also painted with some image, usually one that "spills over" from the image on the fore-edge.

To produce such a picture, the artist fans out the leaves of the book, fixes them in a press of some kind, and exposes the very edges of the pages' surfaces, onto which the picture is painted. Carter points out that the technique was popularized by John Brindley and EDWARDS OF HALIFAX in the 17th century (see Carter, p. 108). (See Carl J. Weber, *Fore-Edge Painting*, and Jeff Weber, *An Annotated Dictionary of Fore-Edge Painting Artists & Binders*.) As Roberts and Etherington point out, though the practice of decorating the fore-edge of a volume goes back "perhaps as early as the 10th century" (p. 107), most of these pictures "are the work of the late 19th and 20th centuries, mainly on books dating from the early 19th century" (p. 107). That is to say, most of these enhancements are not contemporary with the volumes they are on. In fact, there is nothing to stop an artist today from painting the fore-edge of a volume from 1800. Modern artists can forge such work. If someone in 2020 paints an illustration under the gilt edge of a book from 1790, it is still a fore-edge illustration, and an "original" one at that—though not one contemporary with the production of the book. Undoubtedly, there are innumerable examples of recently done illustrations passing themselves off as old ones. But as Carter says, the market for such phenomena is strong, so booksellers and collectors should be suspicious of any such illustration. He adds that truly accomplished artists (actually miniaturists since these pictures are quite small) can mimic the work of 18th-century artists, making it difficult to discern an old from a new work; he calls modern examples "bogus" (Carter, p. 125), but it is to be noted that what is "bogus" is the age of the image, not the fact that it is a fore-edge illustration. That is, the painting is real, but its proposed date (offered by a bookseller or collector) could be off by a century or more. Nonetheless, even modern ones are in demand, and the market for them is strong. The appeal of fore-edge illustrations is partly in their novelty, partly in the skill of their execution, but also in their "wow factor." Show a fore-edge illustration to anyone not expecting a picture to "pop out" of the edge of a book, and the response is always awe, amusement, and pleasure.

One more thing: Publishers today can actually print a text onto the fore-edge of a volume, in which case calling it a "fore-edge painting" is inaccurate. That is why "fore-edge illustration" may be a better term. But to complicate matters, the fore-edge may not have an "illustration," but a text. The volume by Stefan Sagmeister *Made You Look* (see bibliography) has a double fore-edge enhancement under silver edges. Fanned out in one direction is the title; in the other direction are images of three dog bones. Perhaps the best generic designation for all such treatments is "fore-edge enhancements," which covers them all. "Fore-edge painting" can, of course, be used if the description is of an actual painting.

Fore-edge-illustrated volume, closed. Photograph by Jeff Dykes.
Collection of the author.

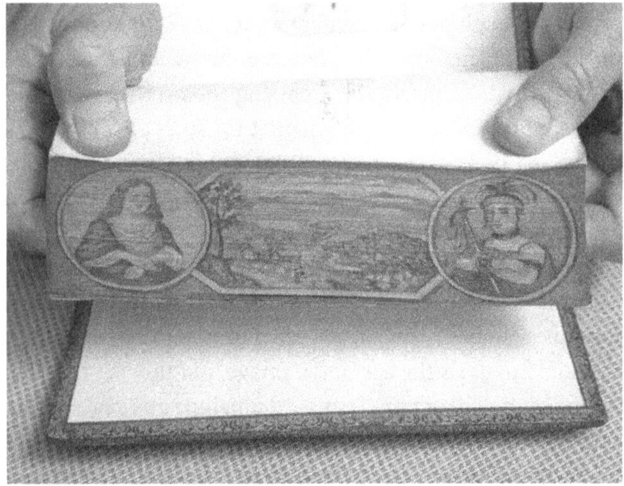

Fore-edge illustration, with the leaves splayed out to display the painting. Photograph by Jeff Dykes.
Collection of the author.

FORE-EDGE TITLE. *See* Fore-edge.

FOREL. (Sometimes spelled "forrel" or "forril.") "A grade of PARCHMENT made from a split SHEEPSKIN and dressed in imitation of VELLUM. / It is not a strong skin and tends to be greasy, which causes difficulties in trying to make it adhere to the boards of a book" (Roberts and Etherington, "forel"; https://cool.culturalheritage.org/don/dt/dt1416.html [accessed 26 January 2021]).

FOREWORD. One of the possible "prelims" of a volume in which an author can reveal the topic of the following text, perhaps its etiology, and other things. As with an ACKNOWLEDGMENTS, this part of the book may reveal information important to a scholar. Forewords can also be written by someone other than the volume's author. (Also, this is one of the words that undergraduates frequently misspell.)

FORGERY. A copy of some original (document, volume, pamphlet, broadside, photograph, signature, etc.) that purports to be original and genuine but is a duplicate (sometimes not a successful duplicate) of an original. This is opposed to a FAKE that purports to be genuine but is not and is not a copy of anything. (See Berger, pp. 204–07.) Sometimes the word is misapplied, as with the THOMAS WISE "forgeries"; these were more properly fakes.

FORM. *See* Forme.

FORMAN, HENRY BUXTON (1842–1917). (Nicknamed Harry.) (An appropriate entry to follow the previous one!) Well-known bibliographer of Shelley and Keats and also biographer of William Morris. He worked for nearly half a century for the British Postal Service, all the while working on his scholarship on these two poets. In 1934, JOHN CARTER and GRAHAM POLLARD's research revealed a great number of faked pamphlets, implicating THOMAS JAMES WISE, and subsequent research showed that Forman was Wise's accomplice. His collection of 19th-century books, manuscripts, and correspondence was excellent, and it sold at auction after his death. (See Freeman, "Conners of the Connoisseurs"; see also Berger, "Harry Buxton Forman," and Collins, *The Two Forgers*.)

FORMAT. A term that has a specific meaning in the world of books and also many generic meanings, depending on the knowledge and the intent of the one who uses it. Its specific meaning is the makeup of a volume, depending on the number of times the original sheets from which it was composed are folded. Its generic meaning—used by many in the trade because they simply do not know the formal meaning—is a particular size of a book. In fact, size is not an issue at all. If a book is made from extremely small

Wikipedia gives the following chart:

Book Formats and Corresponding Sizes

Name	Abbreviations	Leaves	Pages	Approximate cover size (width × height)	
				inches	cm
folio	2° *or* f°	2	4	12 × 15	30 × 48
quarto	4° *or* 4to	4	8	9½ × 12	24 × 30
octavo	8° *or* 8vo	8	16	6 × 9	15 × 23
duodecimo *or* twelvemo	12° *or* 12mo	12	24	5 × 7⅜	12.5 × 19
sextodecimo *or* sixteenmo	16° *or* 16mo	16	32	4 × 6¾	10 × 17
octodecimo *or* eighteenmo	18° *or* 18mo	18	36	4 × 6½	10 × 16
trigesimo-secundo *or* thirty-twomo	32° *or* 32mo	32	64	3½ × 5½	9 × 14
quadragesimo-octavo *or* forty-eightmo	48° *or* 48mo	48	96	2½ × 4	6.5 × 10
sexagesimo-quarto *or* sixty-fourmo	64° *or* 64mo	64	128	2 × 3	5 × 7.5

(See Wikipedia article on "Book Size" at http://en.wikipedia.org/wiki/Book_size [accessed 15 March 2015].)

sheets of paper, each of which is folded once to produce a tiny book with two-leaf signatures, the book is a folio. I know someone who has a paper mold that makes sheets the size of business cards. These are full sheets, and when they are folded and sewn into a text block, the resultant book—a miniature—is a folio.

Most sheets of paper produced by hand in the handpress period, when folded once, would produce a relatively large volume; hence, the term "folio" usually means a large book, and, in fact, libraries often shelve their large books in a section they might call "folios," even if many of the books therein are not true folios.

This chart offers information about the imprecise and generic terms for formats, not the bibliographical use of the term in which the number of folds in the original sheet is key. (For information on the most common formats in the handpress period, *see* Duodecimo; Folio; Octavo; Quarto; Sextodecimo.) (See also Berger, "Book Format, Part 1" and "Book Format, Part 2"; Gaskell, *A New Introduction to Bibliography*, pp. 80 ff.; and McKerrow, *An Introduction to Bibliography for Literary Students*, pp. 164 ff.)

FORME. (Sometimes spelled Form.) All of the type and other matter that gets locked up in the chase (the metal frame on a press that holds pages or other matter to be printed). The forme will contain the type, furniture and reglets that hold the type in place, quoins (these are metal [originally wooden] wedges that tighten up the type and furniture against the inner edges of the chase), and anything else. The forme could also contain illustrations or a counting device that advances while the printing progresses and prints numbers on the sheets.

When a sheet is printed, one surface will be on the outside when it is folded. The type used to print that side of the leaf will be in the chase along with the furniture and other things—and all this is called the "outer forme." The side of the sheet that is printed from the outer forme is also called the outer forme. There is also an inner forme, when the sheet is perfected (i.e., when the second side of the sheet to be printed is printed, the inner forme will be on the inside of the folded leaf). The outer forme of the sheet will always contain the lowest page number of that signature and will usually also contain the highest page number on a leaf conjugate with the first leaf of the signature. (*See* Imposition.)

FOR STOCK. An item that is said to be "purchased for stock" is one that the bookseller does not have an immediate sale of; there is no customer in mind whom the bookseller can interest in buying the item. Especially for high-ticket items (that is, quite expensive books, for instance), a bookseller who has a quick sale may be willing to pay more than what she would pay for the same item that may sit on her shelves for days or months or years. Hence, in weighing purchases, booksellers must adjust what they will pay for things based in part on how long they might have to hold on to them before making a sale. The item could be acquired for quick sale or "for stock.

FORTHCOMING (also "at press" or "in press"). Soon to be published. The term implies that a text has been accepted by a publisher and is going through the process of being readied for publication—or will soon be in that process. But such a designation can be misleading and frustrating for the bookseller and collector since a contract or promissory letter to publish can be reneged upon, and the author who has been salivating to see his work in print can continue to salivate till he runs out of saliva. The term, then, can truly indicate that some text will be out for all to have; or it could mean that there is a GHOST BOOK.

The fault could lie with the publisher in not publishing a volume they announced as "forthcoming," or it could be the author's fault. The publisher, with a signed contract in hand from the author, could announce the coming title, but the author for one reason or another does not produce the text. For whatever reason, an announced book does not materialize and the ghost is created.

Ashling Press issued a PROSPECTUS for the forthcoming volume *The Introduction of Linen Paper* (Mountcashel Castle, Kilmurry, Ennie, Co. Clare, Ireland: Ashling Press, 1977 [in association with Stinehour Press, Lunenberg, Vermont]). The book was never issued. In my own career, a publisher issued a prospectus for a book I wrote on papermaking. The publisher went belly up, and though the "forthcoming" volume had more than a score of buyers (a dozen or so who sent in checks to cover the cost of the volume plus shipping), the book never came forth. The term, then, should be used with some care, and followed up on—and retracted if it proves inaccurate.

42-LINE BIBLE. Term used for the GUTENBERG BIBLE because on most of its pages, there are 42 lines of text.

FORWARDING (in binding). "The processes or steps involved in binding a book. It has been variously defined as: 1) all of the binding processes following gathering, including covering; 2) the processes following sewing and up to covering; and 3) the processes following sewing and including covering. In edition binding, the term 'sheetwork' is usually used in lieu of forwarding." (Roberts and Etherington, "forwarding," https://cool.culturalheritage.org/don/dt/dt1428.html [accessed 1 August 2021]). Forwarding is often followed by FINISHING, in which the binding is decorated.

FORWARD SLASH. *See* Virgule.

FOUL CASE. A TYPE CASE containing poorly DISTRIBUTED type—SORTS in wrong compartments or from a FONT different from the one that is supposed to be in the case. Foul cases can be a monstrous headache for the proofreader and can yield many a TYPOGRAPHICAL ERROR or the appearance of a sort from a wrong font on the printed page. (*See* Pied/Pieing [type].)

FOUL COPY. *See* Dirty proof.

FOUNT. *See* Font.

FOURDRINIER (Henry and Sealy Fourdrinier). The fourdrinier is a papermaking machine, named after the brothers Henry and Sealy, who bought the patent for its construction from its inventor, Nicolas Louis Robert, in 1798. The first operating fourdrinier was made in about 1803. "Henry and Sealy Fourdrinier, London Stationers, became interested in the development of the new machine, and . . . Bryan Donkin, an ingenious mechanic, was induced to build a papermaking machine patterned entirely after the plans of Robert" (Hunter, *Papermaking*, p. 349). Today's fourdriniers are massive machines, creating paper at the wet end (at which WATERMARKS and LAID LINES could be incorporated into the sheets with a DANDY ROLL) and finishing it off at the dry end. And "finishing it off" could mean sizing it, coloring it, CALENDERING it, putting textures into it, trimming it, and so on—right to the final process of forming sheets and packaging it. The creation of this machine was made possible by Baskerville's having designed a typeface that had fine serifs (*see* Baskerville) and needing a paper with no laid lines, so he and James Whatman created a woven mesh rather than a mold with wooden frame and supports—a mesh that could be freestanding and be formed into a large loop, allowing for the mechanization of the papermaking process. Despite requiring a woven wire mesh to form the sheets, necessitating the production of WOVE PAPER, artificial laid lines (CHAIN LINES and WIRE LINES) can be produced on the fourdrinier with a dandy roll or by having the wove screen contain the laid lines on its surface. (For more on wove paper, see the discussion at WHATMAN, JAMES.) (See Maureen Greenland, *Bryan Donkin*.)

FOUR UP. *See* Up (as in "two up," "four up," "eight up").

FOXING. The splotches (in various colors but usually brown, orange, or black) possibly caused by mildew or acid in materials (e.g., paper or vellum) exposed to moisture. Foxing tends to occur on pages with illustrations or on the facing pages, though it can occur throughout any volume exposed to excessive moisture. Some inks make the paper more vulnerable to the effects of high humidity. Roberts and Etherington say, "The cause or causes of foxing, which usually occurs in machine-made paper . . . are not completely understood, but in all likelihood, it is fungoid in nature. Fungi, however, are not necessarily visible on foxed areas, nor does prolific growth necessarily imply excessive discoloration, and vice versa. . . . / Two significant differences between foxed and clean areas of a paper are the higher proportion of acid and iron in the former, although there does not seem to be any clear and definitive relationship between iron and foxing. Insofar as the acid is involved, it is not clear whether this is produced chemically or as a byproduct of the life function of the organisms present. Iron is attributed to impurities present in the paper, and this conclusion seems to be based largely on the fact that it is seldom found in papers produced before the introduction of papermaking equipment made of iron, e.g., the beater, and improvements in techniques, including bleaching and other forms of chemical treatment. But what role iron has in accelerating foxing, or causing a change from the invisible to visible state, has yet to be demonstrated" (p. 109).

Roberts and Etherington also mention high relative humidity as a cause. "The fact that foxing generally starts from the edge of the leaf and spreads inward would seem to indicate that something in the atmosphere is relevant, although air borne organisms may be adequate as an explanation for this effect. In addition, it must still be explained how the center of the leaf is affected most in occasional instances. Perhaps the most logical explanation is that infection by air borne organisms (or by organisms that are natural to the paper) may occur if the conditions, and especially the R.H., are favorable, and that growth, resulting in the generation of fox marks, then occurs. The acid subsequently renders any iron in the paper soluble and therefore visible, with its color being intensified by the presence of organic matter" (p. 109). Foxing can be cleaned but usually not completely.

FOXON, DAVID FAIRWEATHER (1923–2001). "David Foxon was perhaps the most distinguished British bibliographer of the second half of the twentieth century. His general contribution to bibliography has been widely admired and honoured, and his catalogue *English Verse, 1701–1750* (1975) has given his name to half a century of separately published poems. But, while his work has been influential, particularly on the study of the book trade, on the history of pornography, and on eighteenth-century editing, it has been little discussed. This neglect is at least partly due to the fact that Foxon founded no school of bibliography, formulated no theory of bibliographical enquiry, and initiated no general programme of research. Yet the body of his work as a whole displays an impressive consistency of approach and an awareness of the values, motivations, and intentions directing it" (McLaverty, "David Foxon, Humanist Bibliographer").

FPBA. *See* Fine Press Book Association.

FRAD. *See* MARC records.

FRAGMENTOLOGY. "[A]n emerging subfield of manuscript studies invested in the reconstruction of medieval books and the recovery of their dispersed LEAVES and lost (or obscured) histories" (Eric J. Johnson, "Students as Curators: Manuscripts in the Classroom at Ohio State University"). The name of the field comes from the journal *Fragmentology*, "an international, peer-reviewed Open Access journal, dedicated to publishing scholarly articles and reviews concerning medieval manuscript fragments. . . . [the journal was] founded in 2018 as part of *Fragmentarium*, an international research project at the University of Fribourg (Switzerland) funded by the Swiss National Science Foundation, the Stavros Niarchos Foundation, and the Zeno Karl Schindler Foundation" (*Fragmentarium: A Journal for the Study of Medieval Manuscript Fragments*). This is a small but growing field necessitated by BREAKERS of all types. The work of people like OTTO F. EGE, and booksellers all over the world who specialize in the sale of manuscript leaves and fragments, have necessitated this new discipline. (*See* Breaker; St. Catherine's Monastery.)

FRAKTUR (type). The often barely legible family of TYPEFACES based on a calligraphic model from the manuscript period. The word comes from the Latin *frangere* (to break)—an appropriate etymology for a typeface that will break a reader trying to master it, though it means that the smooth lines of some scripts are broken into angles in this family of faces. It is a form of BLACKLETTER.

Capital letters		Lower case letters	
𝔄 = A	𝔑 = N	𝔞 = a	𝔫 = n
𝔅 = B	𝔒 = O	𝔟 = b	𝔬 = o
ℭ = C	𝔓 = P	𝔠 = c	𝔭 = p
𝔇 = D	𝔔 = Q	𝔡 = d	𝔮 = q
𝔈 = E	ℜ = R	𝔢 = e	𝔯 = r
𝔉 = F	𝔖 = S	𝔣 ƒ = f	𝔰 = s ſ = s ß = ss
𝔊 = G	𝔗 = T	𝔤 = g	𝔱 = t
ℌ = H	𝔘 = U	𝔥 = h	𝔲 = u
ℑ = I	𝔙 = V	𝔦 = i	𝔳 = v
𝔍 = J	𝔚 = W	𝔧 = j	𝔴 = w
𝔎 = K	𝔛 = X	𝔨 = k	𝔵 = x
𝔏 = L	𝔜 = Y	𝔩 = l	𝔶 = y
𝔐 = M	ℨ = Z	𝔪 = m	𝔷 = z
These images are copyrighted by IconBAZAAR and are permanently licensed to me for my use in any educational or institutional non-profit application.			

Fraktur type; chart.

Courtesy of Michelle Koth, Yale University Music Library.

FRAME. A rectangle (or square) made up of straight lines or decorative BORDERS that are around an area that could be decorated or into which information like a title or a text could be stamped or printed. A binding or a title page, for example, can have a frame surrounding decorative stamping (on the binding) or the title and other bibliographical and illustrative material (on the title page).

FRBR. *See* Anglo-American Cataloguing Rules; MARC records.

FREE ENDPAPERS/FREE ENDLEAVES. *See* Endleaves.

FREEZE DRYING. (Sometimes referred to as "vacuum freeze drying.") One of the two clever inventions from the food industry that has been adopted into the book world (the other being SHRINK WRAPPING). If books are wet through some disaster, mildew could form. If they are quickly frozen, they can be freeze dried—that is, they can have the moisture removed while they are still frozen, not giving mildew an opportunity to form. The result can be slightly warped or COCKLED volumes, but that mild deformation is far preferable to mildew, which can destroy the volume. A cockled book can still be used, and it poses no health risks. The *New World Encyclopedia* article says, "Freeze-drying (also known as lyophilization or cryodesiccation) is a dehydration process typically used to preserve a perishable material or make the material more convenient for transport. Freeze-drying works by freezing the material and then reducing the surrounding pressure to allow the frozen water in the material to sublime directly from the solid phase to the gas phase" (http://www.newworldencyclopedia.org/entry/Freeze_drying [accessed 8 June 2021]). In the food industry the process is often accompanied by the removal of air from the freeze-dried product—a process called "vacuum freeze drying." This can also be done for books. (See the Northeast Document Conservation Center website for its pamphlet on "Freezing and Drying Wet Books and Records.")

FRENCH FLAPS. On a paperbound volume, cover materials extended beyond the TEXT BLOCK that are then folded over to look like the FLAPS on a DUST JACKET, but which are part of the cover. Sometimes these flaps are quite large, perhaps even the full size of the cover, giving the cover a second layer of stiff paper for strength, and offering the publisher much space for text, BLURBS, advertising, and so forth.

FRENCH FOLD (in text, not capitalized). A format in which a single sheet of paper is folded twice (as with a QUARTO), producing four leaves, but is printed on only one side. Hence, the outer forme (*see* Forme) is printed or written on, the inner forme is not, so the BOLTS are left UNCUT.

FRENCH SEWING. "A method of sewing a book adapted by French bookbinders in the 16th century, which is essentially the same as the sewing employed in COPTIC BINDINGS. / Unlike the traditional Western method of sewing on raised cords [*see* Flexible sewing], each section was sewn through the fold and attached to the next section by a loop similar to a KETTLE STITCH. / Cords were not employed. The first and last sections were then laced tightly to the boards. In modern usage, French sewing is the same technique as done by a sewing machine, without the attachment of the boards. Modern French sewing is the principal method employed in edition binding" (Roberts and Etherington, "French sewing"; https://cool.culturalheritage.org/don/dt/dt1454.html [accessed 26 January 2021]).

FRISKET. The part of a HANDPRESS—a metal frame—that folds down over the TYMPAN, holding the sheet to be printed onto the tympan. The frisket, attached to the frisket frame, starts out as a full sheet of paper or VELLUM, and then it has holes cut in it where the sheet of paper will be printed on. (For an image, *see* Common press.)

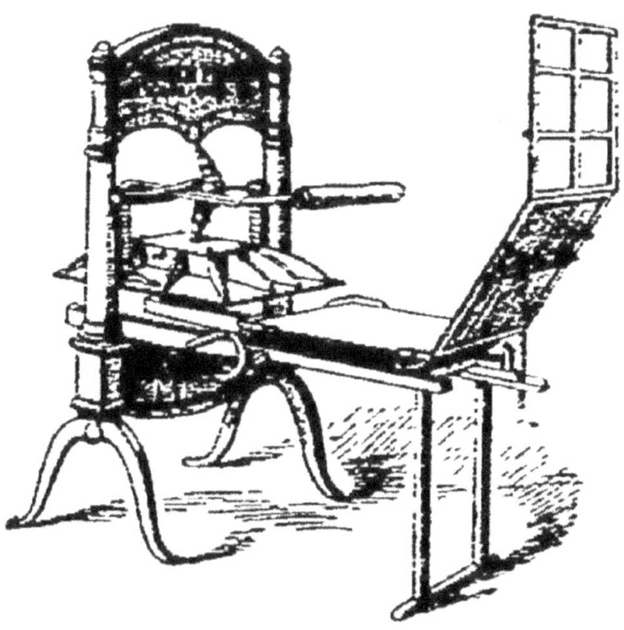

An iron handpress with its tympan and frisket open. The frisket has 6 panels open.

From Yesteryear Once More, https://yesteryearsnews.wordpress.com/tag/printing-press/ (accessed 12 July 2021).

FROM ENGLISH SHEETS. In the 18th (and even in the 19th) century, books may be bound in the United States but using a TEXT that was printed in England. It is thus said to be "Published in Boston, from English sheets." (The reverse is also true: "Published in London from American sheets.") The bookseller in the country in which such a volume was to be sold would have acquired the volume(s) from an English printer, usually with a title page stating who the original printer/publisher was; the title page would either be replaced with a new one to indicate the American publisher or company, or it would have a label pasted over the English publisher with the American publisher or distributor on it.

FRONTISPIECE. A page—usually with an illustration—that usually faces the title page. As the two "usually's" in that sentence imply, sometimes the frontispiece is some illustrative matter but not a picture, and sometimes it is on a RECTO, so it precedes the title page but is not visible when one is looking at the title page; what one sees is the VERSO of the frontispiece. The page contains something that is relevant to the book, such as a picture of the author or of a character in the volume. The LEAF could be part of the printing of the book's text, or it could be on a special (e.g., coated) paper and TIPPED ONTO a FLYLEAF or bound in. Hence, it could have been printed on another press, using another printing method (LITHOGRAPHY or ENGRAVING) and have nothing to do with the COLLATION of the volume that would wind up in the COLLATIONAL FORMULA (*see* Bibliography), though it would be mentioned in the notes section of a BIBLIOGRAPHICAL DESCRIPTION. A bookseller might refer to it thus: "With engr. front."

FRONT MATTER. *See* Prelims.

FRSAD. *See* Anglo-American Cataloguing Rules.

FUGITIVE. An adjective, used to describe colors (inks or dyes, for instance) that tend to fade. Green and some blues are particularly fugitive colors in cloth or leather bindings. The term is also sometimes used to designate materials that usually are thrown away, as is the case with EPHEMERA.

FUKUROTOJI. *See* Oriental binding.

FULL BINDING. Bound in a single material. The binding can be all cloth, all paper, all leather, or all vellum (or some other material; I have a volume bound in full metal and another one in wood). (*See* Half-bound; Half cloth; Quarter-bound; Three-quarter bound.) Roberts and Etherington say, "In a strict sense, the term is applied only to leather bindings" (p. 111), but this stricture is not much heeded today, and a bookseller's catalog may say, "In full cloth" or "In full paper binding."

FUMIGATION. Exposing things to a toxic vapor to kill deleterious elements, as with the desire to rid a volume of infestation with bookworms (*see* Worm holes) or MOLD.

FURNISH (in papermaking). Everything in the VAT from which a sheet of paper is formed. The furnish will include water, PULP, and whatever other things the papermaker has decided to put into the sheets: perfumes, glitter, pieces of bark, SIZING, dyes, and so on. (*See* Stuff.)

FURNITURE. Rectangular pieces of wood, metal, or plastic that hold type in the CHASE. Since the set type is composed of thousands of SORTS, the composed pages would fall apart if all the sorts are not held together in some way. When the type is imposed (*see* Imposition) into the chase, furniture is put all around the pages and squeezed against the type with QUOINS. Once the FORME is so prepared, it can be lifted without the type's falling out, and the chase can be taken to the press. Furniture comes in many lengths and widths, and it is stored in a furniture rack. (*See* Reglets.)

FUST, JOHANN, AND PETER SCHÖFFER. Johann Fust (ca. 1400–1466) was involved with GUTENBERG in the latter's printing experiments. The development of the whole art of printing, with printing's promise of bringing great wealth to its inventor, was kept under wraps for probably more than a decade while Gutenberg did his experiments. Hence, there is a great deal we do not know about what went on, who was responsible for what, and who should be given credit for what. It is clear that Fust loaned Gutenberg money at least twice and that once the printing operation was under way, in 1455, Fust asked for the debt to be repaid. When Gutenberg was unable to repay Fust, the latter took over the printing operation with his son-in-law, Peter Schöffer (ca. 1425–ca. 1503), and the two of them, in partnership, completed the printing of the Bible.

Schöffer is credited with being the first to date a printed book in the West, the first to print with Greek type, and the first to print in more than one color. The fact that he had a relationship with Johann Fust leads some scholars to speculate that Fust planted Schöffer in Gutenberg's workshop to learn everything there was to know about printing so that Fust could foreclose on the loans he made to Gutenberg. No documentary evidence supports this theory, however.

The truth about all these things will probably never come to light fully. As noted, most of what we "know" about Gutenberg is speculative, though many a scholar will proclaim suppositions as facts. (For the best treatment of the whole picture, see Kapr, *Johann Gutenberg*. Even Kapr, who knows just about as much as anyone else, must lard his text with "it is likely that," "Gutenberg probably," "we must suppose," and many other such locutions.)

G

GALLEY. The metal tray on which set type is placed before printing, and stored after printing. The galley has three raised sides, allowing the tied-up type to be slid off the end with no raised side directly onto the BED of the press or onto the PRINTER'S STONE when the FORME is being IMPOSED. The type is held as it was set in as many lines as the compositor decides to line up on the galley. For smaller fonts of type, the compositor may assemble 30 or 50 lines of type, one on top of the next (as many as the galley can conveniently hold) for the text she is setting. First PROOFS of the text will be taken on the galley ("GALLEY PROOFS"), because if changes need to be made to the type, it is easier to do it while the type is still in the galley than it is later when it is locked up in the CHASE. Eventually, the type will be removed from the galley and broken down into pages to be put into the forme, at which time more proofs will be taken (*see* Page proofs). A single galley may hold enough type for a half page, one page, or several. Once the book is printed, the publisher may wish to store the type on galleys, with the idea that later impressions can be taken. (*See* Edition, Impression [Printing], Issue, and State; Points.) Thus, STANDING TYPE can be used over and over again (or converted into plates [*see* Electrotyping; Stereotyping]) and would usually be stored with the text broken down into pages. Galleys come in many sizes, including ones quite small or those large enough to hold a full-sized newspaper page.

GALLEY PROOFS. (Often referred to simply as "galleys.") In the HANDPRESS PERIOD (and beyond), PROOFS that are taken when the type is still on the GALLEY. They are generally the first proofs of a text; corrections are easier to make when the type is still in the galley than they are when the type is in the FORME, locked into the CHASE. With modern technology—with texts created and proofed in digital form—the physical galley has become obsolete, but the term "galley proofs" has remained to indicate the first proofs of a text, preceding the second stage of proofs, the PAGE PROOFS. The shorthand term is "galleys" ("He read the galleys").

Since the publisher is at the galleys stage when these are produced, it is possible that several copies of the galleys are produced, one for the author, one or more for the in-house editor(s), and perhaps many more to send out to readers. So it is possible that galleys will be bound. Remember that these proofs are not at the page-proof stage, so bound galleys will often contain leaves that have many more lines per page than will the final bound volume. This is the stage in the volume's production that allows the author to make substantial changes in the text. Once the text is at the page-proof stage, the author can make only very minor changes—ones that do not add lines to (or subtract lines from) the page.

GALLEY RACK. A cabinet with narrow slots in which galleys are stored. If a printer wanted to keep the STANDING TYPE for a possible later IMPRESSION, it would be stored on galleys that are kept in a rack.

Galley rack.
Courtesy of Briar Press.

GALLEYS. *See* Galley proofs.

GALLOWS (on a handpress). "In a wooden hand-press, the frame at and beneath the end to hold up the TYMPAN, so that it may not fall flat, but shall be raised to an angle of twenty or thirty degrees. It has two legs and a crosspiece at the top, and bears some resemblance to a gallows" (*American Dictionary of Printing and Bookmaking*, p. 223). One of the many terms having to do with death associated with the "BLACK ART." (*See also* Coffin; Hell box; Printer's Devil; Pulling the Devil's tail.) The gallows was essentially a rack that the tympan and FRISKET rested on when they were open. This part of the press was used in some iron HANDPRESSES, but they were superseded by any of a number of devices or configurations that held the tympan and frisket when they were open.

GAMPI (papermaking). One of the three main fibers used in Japanese papermaking. The others are KOZO and MITSUMATA. This shrub, whose Latin name is Wikstroemia, is difficult to cultivate (much more difficult than is kozo), but it makes lovely, fine, smooth paper, excellent for printing and printmaking. (See Barrett, *Japanese Papermaking*; Kyoko Ibe, "On Gampi.")

GARAMOND, CLAUDE (ca. 1480–1561). (Some typefaces named after him are spelled Garamont.) "French 16th-century type designer and founder. His influence extended to all of the Latin countries and to Holland, Belgium and England" (*American Dictionary of Printing and Bookmaking*, p. 223.) He was the first to specialize in making type and selling it to others. His roman, italic, and Greek types were elegant and in demand.

GARLAND. A collection of encomia compiled to commemorate the work of someone; or an anthology that contains "flowers"—beautiful pieces—on a topic. To honor the printer HARRY DUNCAN, W. Thomas Taylor published *A Garland For Harry Duncan: Minister Erato Ministrorum.* Typical of the genre, it contains a collection of poems assembled in honor of this famous FINE-PRESS printer. As in this volume, the garland does not have to contain items pertaining to the volume's dedicatee.

GASKELL, PHILIP (1926–2001). One of the premier bibliographers of the 20th century. His influential and meticulously researched and clearly written *A New Introduction to Bibliography*, updating and improving on MCKERROW's *An Introduction to Bibliography for Literary Students*, was published in 1972 and is still the best text on the subject as an introduction to the field. It is filled with useful information and illustration, and anyone in the book field will profit from a familiarity with this important volume. It is so important that one might hear a collector or bookseller or librarian say, "Look it up in Gaskell." This was not his only publication, but it is the one he is most identified with.

GATEFOLD. Sometimes something in a VOLUME must be printed on a LEAF larger than those used for the rest of the volume, as with a chart that contains a great deal of information and that cannot be broken up to be shown on two or more pages. The solution may be to use a gatefold: a LEAF that folds out, sometimes into one twice the normal size of the leaves of the book. In printing *Völuspá: The Song of the Sybil*, KIM MERKER did not want to encumber the pages of the text with scholarly notes, which he thought would deface the elegantly laid-out verse. So he printed the notes on a separate leaf, bound into the rear of the volume. But he did not want to inconvenience his readers by making them flip back and forth to the notes, so he printed them on a gatefold so that they could be folded out and observed while a reader took in the text; or they could be kept folded and out of sight if the reader did not need to see the notes. (See Berger, *Printing and the Mind of Merker*, p. 33.) (*See* Foldout.)

GATHERINGS. SIGNATURES in a book. Although a simple FOLIO is composed of signatures of only two leaves (created from a single LEAF folded once), these signatures have not strictly been "gathered." But the pair of CONJUGATE leaves may still be called a "gathering." A folio in 4s or 8s, on the other hand, requires the requisite number of printed folios to be gathered in the correct order, and all of those needed for the volume to be gathered in the right sequence for binding. Each gathering is sewn into the book with a single sewing operation. As a verb, the word means the act of assembling and arranging in the proper sequence all of the folded sheets of a publication. (*See also* Quire; Section.)

GAUFFERED EDGES (also spelled gauffred, goffered, or gaufré). "The edges of a book, usually gilded, which have been decorated further by means of heated FINISHING tools or rolls which indent small repeated patterns" (Roberts and Etherington, p. 114). Note that the patterns are usually created first, sometimes with the artist carving the edges of the volume, and the gilding applied over that. But Roberts and Etherington say, "It may be done directly on the gold, or by laying a different colored gold over the first, and tooling over the top gold, leaving the pattern in the new gold impressed on the original metal" (p. 114). Not all gauffered edges are gilded; some are covered in a red (or other color) pigment. The word comes from the French *gaufre*, meaning "honeycomb" or "waffle," in reference to the look of the gauffered pattern (*American Heritage Dictionary of the English Lan-*

guage, p. 754). (For an image, *see* Embroidered binding.) (Sometimes called "chased edges.")

GAUGE PINS (in printing). Metal contraptions that are composed of two parts: one that pierces (or is glued or otherwise affixed to) the TYMPAN and the other a small sliding part. The pins are usually used in threes. Paper being laid onto the tympan is placed against two pins that the sheet rests on and a third, at right angles to the other two, adjusting the sheet to the proper placement. Fine adjustments can be made left to right with the sliding part of the pin. These were easier and more expeditious to use than were REGISTRATION PINS. (Some gauge pins are a single piece, with no sliding part.)

GAUZE. *See* Mull.

GBW. *See* Guild of Book Workers.

GED, WILLIAM (1690–1749). Supposedly the inventor of STEREOTYPING in 1725. "His work was opposed by typefounders and compositors, and the process was abandoned until the early 1800s. . . . Although Ged's system made fair copy, the opposition to his work resulted in its complete rejection by printers. He then became a goldsmith and jeweler" (*Encyclopaedia Britannica*, http://www.britannica.com/EBchecked/topic/227656/William-Ged [accessed 8 June 2021]).

GEHENNA PRESS. *See* Baskin, Leonard.

GENERAL TITLE. The main title page of a book, especially one in which there may be other "title pages" delineating separate sections in the volume. The ones at the internal sections are called "divisional titles." (*See* Fly title.)

GEORGE BAXTER/BAXTER PRINTS. *See* Baxter print; Hand-colored.

GERALD R. FORD CONSERVATION CENTER. *See* Regional Alliance for Preservation.

GERMAN MARBLE PAPER. *See* Annonay paper.

GESAMTKATALOG DER WIEGENDRUCKE. A publication of the Staatsbibliothek in Berlin—a UNION CATALOG of INCUNABULA. Often referred to simply as "GW" or "GKW." The project to compile a listing of all incunabula in German libraries began in 1925 but was halted by World War II and its aftermath, especially with the splitting of Germany into East and West. It started up again in 1972. The project to create this large catalog is ongoing; it is now available in digital form. (See this title in the bibliography.) (*See also* Hain, Ludwig.)

GESSO. A thick paint, made from chalk, gypsum, or plaster mixed with water, and used as a base for GILDING and other raised writing or illumination in manuscripts. Its raised surface is excellent for TOOLING or BURNISHING. Sometimes when the pigments or foils flake off, the SUBSTRATE of gesso shows.

GETTY RESEARCH INSTITUTE. The library/research center of the J. Paul Getty Museum in Los Angeles. "The Getty Research Institute library collections include over one million books, periodicals, study photographs, and auction catalogs as well as extensive special collections of rare and unique materials. Focusing on art history, architecture, and related fields, they begin with the archaeology of prehistory and extend to the contemporary moment" ("The Library," http://www.getty.edu/research/library [accessed 8 June 2021]). The museum has a superb collection of medieval illuminated manuscripts, among many other treasures. The GRI "conservation collection includes more than 45,000 titles and 60,000 volumes of primary and secondary sources related to the conservation, management, and protection of cultural property from paintings to architecture. . . . The special collections contain rare and unique materials in selected areas of art history and visual culture. . . . The Photo Archive contains approximately two million study photographs of art and architecture from the ancient world through the 20th century" ("Library Overview," http://www.getty.edu/research/library/overview.html [accessed 8 June 2021]).

GHOST BOOK (*see also* Advertisements). A volume for which there is some seemingly credible reference for its existence but that was never produced—or, possibly, that was produced but no copy of it survives. "A nonexistent publication listed in bibliographies" or other lists (The Free Dictionary, "ghost"; http://www.thefreedictionary.com/ghost [accessed 8 June 2021]). (See Berger, *The Anatomy of a Literary Hoax.*) A catalog of such books was published in 1967 by DONALD WING (as a supplement to his short title catalog) titled the *Gallery of Ghosts*. (See Wing, *A Gallery of Ghosts.*) A good example is the volume announced in a PROSPECTUS: *The First English Binding & Marbling Manuals*, to be published by W. Thomas Taylor of Austin, Texas. The four-page prospectus has a full description of the "FORTHCOMING" book, but no copy seems to have been printed.

GHOST MONEY. *See* Joss papers.

GHOSTWRITING. Writing a text to be published under the name not of the actual writer but of someone else. In the world of legal issues, someone who is hired to write a text for someone else creates a "work for hire," and the person paying him (if the contract between them so stipulates) may publish the text as her own. Strictly speaking, a ghost-written work is not one published anonymously or under a pseudonym. Those are properly labeled "anonymously published" or "pseudonymously published," respectively. Hence, all of the volumes emanating from the STRATEMEYER SYNDICATE were pseudonymously written, not ghostwritten. Many celebrities, wanting to get their names on books, hire ghostwriters to do the composition, sometimes giving that person credit with such locutions as "by Big Name Person, with the assistance of Mr. Ghostwriter." The ghostwriter can merely be used to edit a writer's copy, can do some or all of the research for the author, or can create the final text from start to finish, doing all the research, interviewing, writing, and editing. They can be paid by the word, the page, the chapter, or the project, and they may share in the royalties, though the contract they sign with the author for whom they are working will spell out what their compensation will be and where it will come from. And whether the ghostwriter is acknowledged will also be spelled out in the contract.

One common arrangement, mentioned above, is called "work for hire," in which the ghostwriter is hired to do all the work—doing all the research, writing the entire work, doing the "final" editing, and turning it over to the person who hired him to do it. The ghostwriter hands over everything, including all rights, and is then no longer "connected" to the work in any way. The ghostwriter is not party to any profits (or expenditures) for the work he has produced.

GIFT BINDING. *See* Gift book; Presentation binding.

GIFT BOOK. A common 19th- and early 20th-century phenomenon: a volume created to be given as a gift or prize, usually in a lovely binding (even if the binding itself is a cheap publisher's cloth, elaborately decorated, though many were in leather or silk). Such bindings are called "gift bindings." They contained the typical poetry of the 19th century, short stories, essays, and pictures, and the bindings were often quite attractive, with elaborate designs and gold work, usually stamped onto cloth-covered boards. Despite the glitzy nature of the bindings, the books were commonly quite cheaply made, and most of them are falling apart today. Sometimes they were printed as ANNUALS, as with diaries or ALMANACS, and they were often issued in the fall to be given as gifts for the upcoming holidays. These volumes were well illustrated, usually with STEEL PLATE ENGRAVINGS, printed in black, but encouraging their owners to color them. They were often edited by women, and they contained sentimental verse and prose or religious material. In the 20th century, the Lakeside Press books (1903–) may fall into this category: Thomas E. Donnelley had them published as holiday gifts for his customers. (See Spolsky, *Iconotropism* in the bibliography.)

GILDING. *See* Gilt.

GILL, ERIC (1882–1940). A prominent figure in the Arts and Crafts movement, well known for his sculptures, typeface designs, and prints. In the 1980s, biographer Fiona McCarthy revealed his sexual abuse of his daughters, sisters, and dog. His predations are in contrast with his religious art. While his artistic legacy survives, our appraisal of the man is changed. (See MacCarthy, "Written in Stone.") In the book world, Gill is known for his illustrations of books, his type designs (Perpetua and Perpetua Greek, Gill Sans, Humanist, Joanna, Gill Floriated Capitals, the Golden Cockerel Press Type, Bunyan, Aries, Solus, and Jubilee), and his *An Essay on Typography* (see the bibliography). (See *Eric Gill*; Gill, *Bibliography of Eric Gill*; MacCarthy, *Eric Gill*; and Speaight, *The Life of Eric Gill*.)

GILT. Done with gold. Hence, a title page can have a gilt title; a binding can have gilt stamping or gilt DENTELLES. And tops and all edges of books can be gilt (and they are so designated in booksellers' catalogs as "TEG" and "AEG," respectively). Note that the word is an adjective, though many booksellers and library catalogers like to say "BLOCKED in gilt" when they mean "Blocked in gold." (I have also seen scores of instances of "lettered in gilt.") This error has been perpetuated for so long that the phrase has become an idiom in the book world and has thus gained some legitimacy—over my own better judgment.

GILT EDGES. Said of a TEXT BLOCK that has had its edges (head, fore, and foot [or tail]) gilded. Usually, this means that the edges have been trimmed (removing the deckles) so that there is a smooth edge where the gilding is. It is possible, however, to have the deckles left intact and the edges gilded (hence the fairly obsolete term "gilt on the rough"). (*See* AEG; Gilt; Rough gilt; TEG.)

GILT ON THE ROUGH. *See* Rough gilt.

GILT TOP. *See* Top edge gilt.

GIRDLE BOOK. "A book which has an extra protective covering of soft leather made in such a manner that the book can be hung from the girdle or habit cord of a cleric and

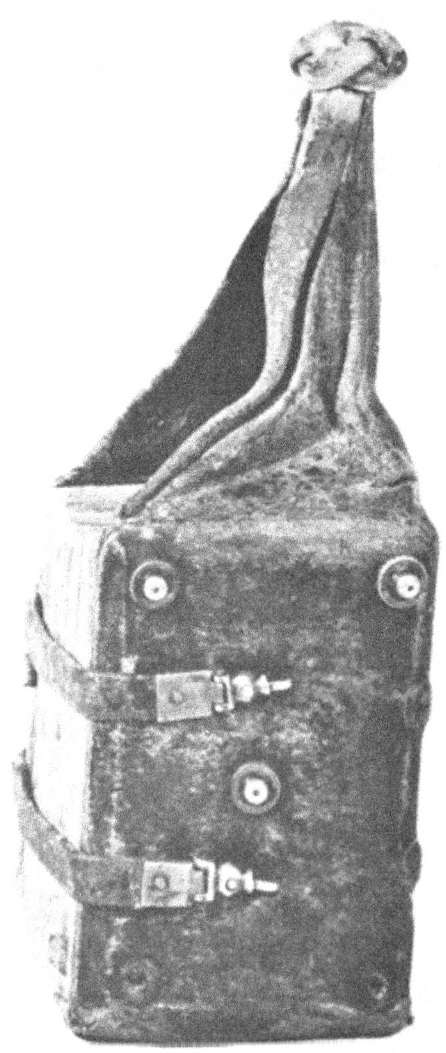
Girdle book.
Courtesy of the New York Public Library.

swung upward for reading while still attached to the girdle or cord" (Roberts and Etherington, p. 116). (*See* Vade mecum.)

According to Margit J. Smith, these books were produced between about 1450 and 1650. There were two types: one-cover books with only a single cover and two-cover books with a primary and a secondary cover. She says, that girdle books are "[s]hown in many medieval paintings, carvings, prints, etc. to have been used by clerics, law-clerks, knights, noble ladies. . . . Symbolically used by saints, especially the four evangelists, the virgin Mary, angels and the devil" (private correspondence to the author; notes for a talk she gave at the Third Annual Conference on the Book, Oxford, UK, September 2005). (See Smith and Bloxam, "The Medieval Girdle Book Project"). J. A. Szirmai says, "Most of the 23 original extant girdle books . . . contain religious works, four legal texts; 11 cover manuscripts on parchment, seven cover manuscripts on paper, five are on printed works" (Szirmai, *The Archaeology of Medieval Bookbinding*, p. 237). And he says that there are over 800 images of these volumes "in paintings, sculptures or in graphic art" (p. 236).

GIRTHS. *See* "Rounce.

GKW/GW. *See Gesamtkatalog der Wiegendrucke.*

GLAIR (or glaire). A mordant (i.e., a substance used to fix colors or dyes) used, for example, for gold tooling on leather bindings or in manuscripts under gold leaf; it is made from egg white. It is also used on book edges to make the gold leaf adhere with edge gilding (*see* Gilt). When the gold leaf is applied, heat is used to melt the leaf, and the glair melts as well but then sets instantly once the gold is applied. As Roberts and Etherington explain, "Two methods of applying glair are generally employed. If the slight gloss produced by the glair is not objectionable, the glair may be sponged over the entire surface to be tooled, and would in any case be applied over the entire edge of the book; however, if the gloss is objectionable, the design and/or lettering are TOOLED in BLIND and the glair is then applied to the blind impressions with a gilder's tip" (p. 117).

GLAISTER, GEOFFREY ASHALL (1917–1985). (*Encyclopedia of the Book/Glossary of the Book*). Glaister was a British Council librarian who compiled his much-used reference *An Encyclopedia of the Book: Terms Used in Paper-Making, Printing, Bookbinding, and Publishing, with Notes on Illuminated Manuscripts, Bibliophiles, Private Presses, and Printing Societies*, revised and expanded as *Glaister's Glossary of the Book: Terms Used in Papermaking, Printing, Bookbinding and Publishing with Notes on Illuminated Manuscripts and Private Presses.* Long out of print, this volume was a handy guide to much of what the titles and subtitles indicated, though each edition had its detractors for various reasons: the length of entries, inaccuracies, poor illustrations (in the second edition), weaknesses in the coverage of some topics, and so on. The second edition has 3,932 entries in its 551 pages (see its preface, p. xi); it contains 390 entries that are the work of others, with many translated from Swedish.

GLASSINE. A fine, smooth, semitransparent paper often used as a dust jacket for a book; but because it is light and not terribly sturdy, it may be seen as temporary, just to get the book to its owner in decent condition. The paper was clearly used for protection for only a short time since it was fairly fragile and would usually be thrown away once the book was delivered to its destination. Many issues of the *COLOPHON* still retain their glassine WRAPPERS, indicating, for most of them, that the volume was hardly read. Booksellers will often highlight the presence of the glassine wrappers as a way of pointing out that the volume in question is still in excellent condition: "With original glassine, AS ISSUED." They may even stress to collectors that other copies on the market, lacking the glassine, are incomplete and seriously less desirable than the one that they have with this wrapper. On a rare occasion, the glassine wrapper may be printed with a title, an author's name, or both. In this case, the lack of the wrapper is truly a devaluing phenomenon. Ironically, while the glassine was designed as a protection, it was sometimes made with acidic paper and it turned brown and became brittle, with occasional ACID MIGRATION to the very materials it was designed to protect. Even acid-free glassine is not recommended for photographic materials.

GLOSS. A note, somewhere on a page (between the lines or in the margins), explaining, summarizing, or translating something on that page. This kind of note was particularly common in religious texts, and in the world of printing, sometimes large margins were left specifically for the reader to add glosses. Texts were also created with printed commentaries on the same page as the text, usually in a smaller type, running parallel to the main text or surrounding it typographically. These printed notes are also called glosses. A glossary is a collection of glosses—or explanations. The most common kind of texts that are glossed are theological or legal, and sometimes the glosses are quite extensive, filling all the blank space on a page.

Gloss is also a term used in bookbinding and papermaking for a shiny surface: "The surface characteristic of a material which enables it to reflect light . . . and which causes it to appear shiny or lustrous" (Roberts and Etherington, p. 117). Many papers or leather bindings exhibit this trait.

GLOSSARY. A listing of words or phrases with definitions and possible examples. The arrangement is generally alphabetical, though it could be in the order in which words appear in a text. It can be a separate volume, with a single focus (a glossary of shoemaking terms), or it can appear as part of the ENDMATTER of a volume. As part of a volume on a given topic, sometimes the compilers of glossaries select only words they assume readers need to have explained. Any volume with the word "glossary" in its subtitle is certain to be authoritative and reliable.

GOATSKIN. Used in fine binding. Several species of goats' skins are used. Roberts and Etherington explain that "goatskin is tougher and more tightly fibred than sheepskin, has a hard-wearing grain, and, when properly tanned, can last for centuries. It colors beautifully and has a distinctive texture identified by ridges and furrows in the grain, and hair pits in groups all over the surface. . . . MOROCCO . . . , the best known goatskin . . . did not become common until the first half of the 16th century in Italy and was not common in France until the second half of the 16th century" (p. 119).

GOFF, FREDERICK R. (1916–1982). Compiler of *Incunabula in American Libraries*. Goff worked in the Library of Congress for many years, including a stint as assistant chief of the Rare Book Division for four years before becoming chief in 1945. He was head of RBMS (the Rare Book and Manuscript Section) and president of the BIBLIOGRAPHICAL SOCIETY OF AMERICA. The volume on INCUNABULA was, of course, not complete, but it was so revered and used by so many scholars and other book people that it was referred to simply by his last name. "Not in Goff" was often a way to designate a rare incunabulum. Note that the Kraus 1973 reprint of the 1964 edition (*see* citation below) contains Goff's own annotations. Goff says, "From the time the Third Census was published in 1964, it became my practice to annotate a personal copy as additional information regarding ownership, corrections, and new references became available from a variety of sources. Also a record was maintained of dealers' offerings both at home and abroad with the prices quoted as well as those copies that were to come under the auctioneer's hammer. For some of these the galleries' estimates were given, and this information was added when available. Between 1964 and 1972 an astonishing number of incunabula copies were added to libraries and collections in the United States. The great increase is reflected in the fact that the Third Census of 1964 recorded 47,188 incunabula in the United States, whereas the annotated copy records more than 51,000. A new feature of the present volume is a list of the dealers and auction houses whose names appear within the text" (taken from the introduction to *Incunabula in American Libraries* [Millwood: Kraus Reprint, 1973]). (*See also* Hain, Ludwig.)

GOLD BLOCKING. *See* Blocking.

GOLD STAMPING. Printing on the surface of a material (cloth, leather, vellum, or paper) in gold. This kind of printing does not impress the "text" into the surface as does BLOCKING.

GOLD TOPS. *See* Top edge gilt.

GOLD VARNISH PAPER. *See* Dutch gilt papers.

GOOD FOR ITS AGE. Said of a book that is in as good a shape as one can imagine despite how old it is. (Though this is a term once applied to me.) Odd as this term is, it appears now and then in the cataloging records of fairly naïve or inexperienced booksellers. As descriptive of CONDITION, it is not too transparent or revealing. All it means is that the item has flaws, but no one should complain, for anything (or, for that matter, any*one*) of a given age would have flaws. Richard Murian of Alcuin Books (Scottsdale, AZ) suggested this term—one that some of us have seen over the decades. (*See* Condition.)

GOTHIC TYPE. "A name given sometimes to blackletter . . . [or to] SANS SERIFS" (Avis, *Type Face Terminology*, p. 24). Lawson says, "The first movable types were exact copies of the manuscript hand of fifteenth-century Germany. Europeans properly call these first types Gothic, but terminology problems developed when in the United States this name was assigned to the early sans serif types of the 1830s. An argument against using the term Blackletter is that it could mean simply a description of a bold-faced character. . . . Probably the most common name for this style of type is Old English, but this term specifies a single model of blackletter rather than a whole group" (Lawson, *Printing Types*, p. 47). He distinguishes the following groups of gothic types: Textura (or Text), Gothic-Antique (also called, in the United States, Blackletter-Roman), Rotunda (or Round Gothic), and Bastarda (pp. 47, 49, 51). Gutenberg's type for the Bible is sometimes called a Textura Blackletter ("Blackletter" and "Gothic" are synonyms, and "Textura" is another name for "Gothic," so "Textura Blackletter" is a pleonasm).

As early as the 15th century, the word "Gothic," originally designating this heavy script, was used to describe this script in Italy, and humanists in the Renaissance thought it was barbaric. As Alexander Lawson says, the term is often used in the United States for sans serif types (*Printing Types*, pp. 97–98). (*See* Fraktur [type].) (See Bain and Shaw, *Blackletter*).

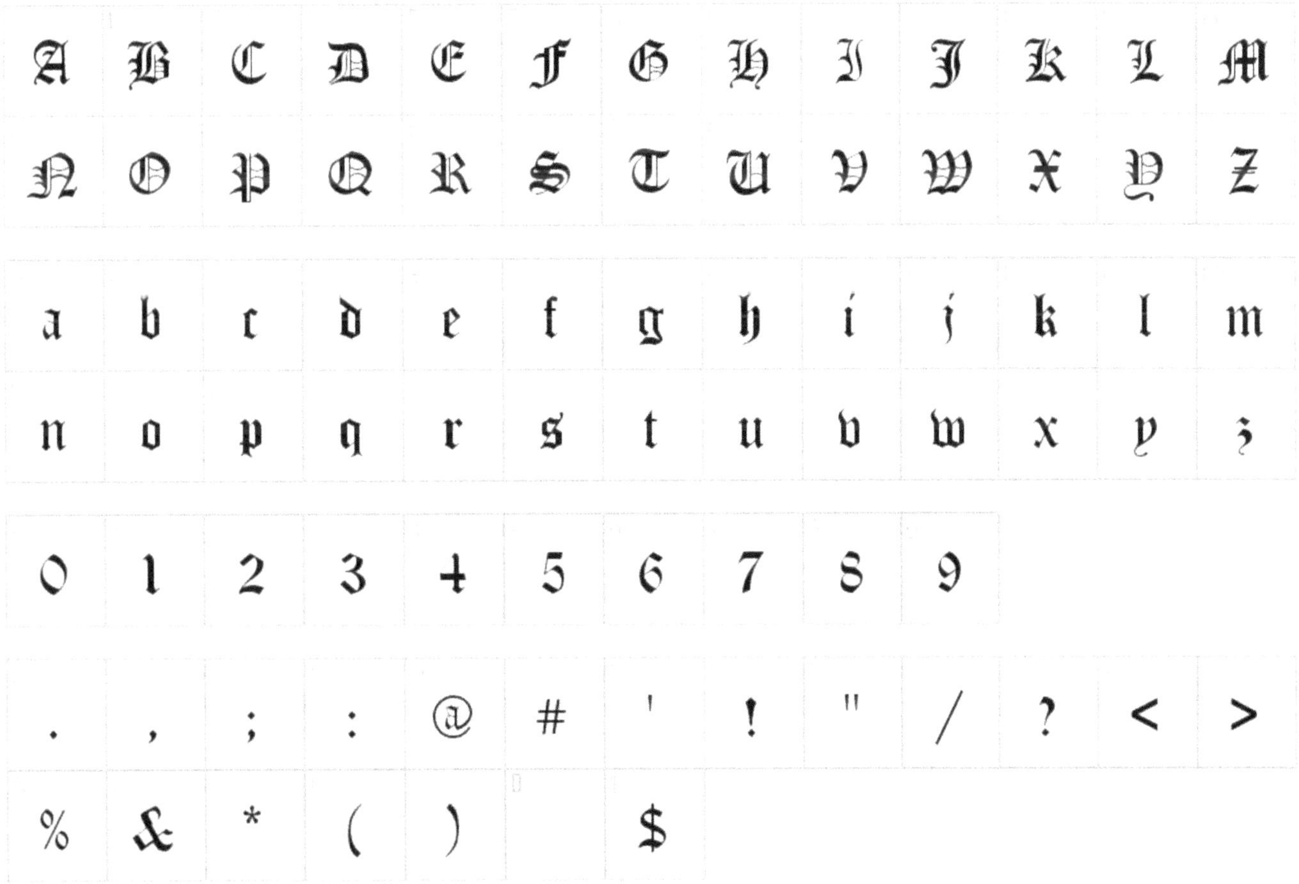

A	B	C	D	E	F	G	H	I	J	K	L	M
N	O	P	Q	R	S	T	U	V	W	X	Y	Z
a	b	c	d	e	f	g	h	i	j	k	l	m
n	o	p	q	r	s	t	u	v	w	x	y	z
0	1	2	3	4	5	6	7	8	9			
.	,	;	:	@	#	'	!	"	/	?	<	>
%	&	*	(	)		$						

Gothic typeface, "Canterbury."

1001 Free Fonts; https://www.1001freefonts.com/canterbury.font (accessed 10 August 2021).

GOUDY, FREDERIC WILLIAM (1865–1947). One of the most prolific type designers in history. Working independently, he sold many of his designs to the AMERICAN TYPE FOUNDERS while being an adviser to the LANSTON MONOTYPE COMPANY. (See Goudy, *Goudy's Type Designs*.) He founded the Village Press (with his partner Will Ransom) in Illinois in 1903, later moving to the Boston area and then to New York. "At the beginning of his career Goudy designed typefaces as an outgrowth of his work as a lettering artist. In this he was no different from Eckmann, Auriol, Otto Hupp, Peter Behrens and a host of other commercial artists in Europe and America. None of these individuals was a type designer per se. With the possible exception of Rudolf Koch, Goudy is the only one of this generation—or of the succeeding generation—to go on to devote his career to type design. / Between 1902 and 1911 Goudy designed many of his typefaces not for type foundries but for businesses. He pioneered the idea of the custom or bespoke typeface with his work for the Pabst Brewing Company, the clothier Kuppenheimer & Company, Mandel Brothers department store, financial news publisher Clarence Barron, Baltimore printer Norman Munder and, most importantly of all, book publisher Mitchell Kennerley. Essentially Goudy took the notion of the private press typeface inaugurated by William Morris and extended it beyond the insular Arts & Crafts community to the larger world of commerce. Kennerley, the typeface designed for *The Door in the Wall* by H. G. Wells (published by Mitchell Kennerley, 1911), was the turning point in his career, the moment when type design began to overtake lettering and private press printing as his principal activity" (Shaw, "An Appreciation of Frederic W. Goudy as a Type Designer"). Shaw speaks of Goudy's lack of appreciation in the printing world: "Contemporaries like D. B. Updike and Stanley Morison found Goudy insufferable. They disliked his typefaces—though Morison did say nice things about Goudy Modern—and especially what they saw as his endless self-promotion (and the hagiographic attitude toward him of many in the American printing trade). Their antipathy was partially due to snobbishness: they viewed Goudy as a rube from the American Midwest who lacked their printing history erudition; and they viewed his typefaces as part of the grubby world of advertising rather than the rarefied one of books. / Although there is no defense for the nauseating hero worship that many lavished on Goudy in his lifetime, there is a straightforward defense for Goudy's own self-promotion: economic survival. Without it the Village Letter Foundry would never have lasted for thirty-six years. Unlike Morison, who had the sales resources of the Monotype Corporation and the publicity efforts of Beatrice Warde to sell the fruits of his typographic program, Goudy had only himself and his wife Bertha in the early years. In this he was in the same position as the plethora of small digital foundries today who use any means available—print magazines, blogs, Facebook, Twitter, etc.—to promote their typefaces" (Shaw, "An Appreciation of Frederic W. Goudy as a Type Designer"). This explains the great number of typefaces that Goudy designed; chief among them are Kennerly Old Style, Goudy Old Style, Goudy Modern, Deepdene, Californian, and Village. (See Beilenson, *The Story of Frederic Goudy*; Bennett, ed., *Goudy's Type Designs*; Bruckner, *Frederic Goudy*; and Tracy, *Letters of Credit*, pp. 121–52.)

GRABHORN PRESS. A fine press and commercial enterprise founded in 1919 by Edwin Grabhorn with his brother Robert. The hundreds of books they produced were designed in the fashion of their day but were made mostly with high-quality materials, generous margins, careful letterpress printing, and attractive bindings. Their books became COLLECTIBLE over the years, though the passion for them has somewhat died down. Their MAGNUM OPUS is probably their edition of Walt Whitman's *Leaves of Grass*. Edwin Grabhorn himself even said, "I think that Leaves of Grass is the most perfect book we ever printed" (see Grabhorn, "Recollections of the Grabhorn Press," section 23).

The Santa Clara University Library website says, "In 1965 Edwin retired and Robert went into business with Andrew Hoyem, who had worked in a nearby printing shop and had later worked for the Grabhorns. They started the Grabhorn-Hoyem Press (1966–1977). In 1974 Andrew Hoyem established ARION PRESS to continue the work of Grabhorn Press and Grabhorn-Hoyem, including the collection of type, which was an extremely unique and historically significant collection from a working press. In 2000 Andrew Hoyem and his ARION PRESS established the Grabhorn Institute to continue the unbroken tradition of using the typefoundry [*sic*] amassed by the Grabhorns" (Santa Clara University, University Library, "Grabhorn Press: Home"; https://libguides.scu.edu/grabhorn [accessed 18 July 2021]).

GRAIN (in paper). The direction in which the fibers line up in a sheet of paper or in cardboard. Also called the "machine direction." Printers and binders must pay attention to the grain in the machine-made materials they use, for sheets and boards will tend to curl along the grain. A book bound IN BOARDS with the grain at right angles to the SPINE may, if the humidity gets low, curl in such a way that the top and bottom JOINTS could split as the boards bend. "Grain" is also used to describe the pattern of follicles in leather, and some ribbed cloths may be said to have a grain, in the direction of the ribbing. When someone tears a sheet of paper *with* the grain, the sheet will tear in a relatively straight line; but *against* the grain, the sheet will tear unevenly—as we have all observed when we try to tear something out of a newspaper. Hence, "against the grain" means in a messy or uneven fashion; and, by implication, it means in an unnatural way ("It goes against the grain to fight with one's friends"). "Against the grain" could also mean in an unconventional way; innovative; so it is not always a negative trait. But in bookmaking, it usually means someone has made a blunder. In an image printed from a metal plate, GRAINING is a means of creating shading in the image. The graining can be done manually or mechanically with printing plates or rollers, or it can be done with chemicals that etch the plates.

GRAINING. "1. The process of applying an all-over pattern to cloth, either during manufacture or by rolling the cloth between embossing plates. 2. The process or result of printing various designs on paper or board to simulate various wood grains, marble, etc., generally for use as cover papers" (Roberts and Etherington, "graining"; https://cool.culturalheritage.org/don/dt/dt1613.html [accessed 10 May 2021]). On cloth or paper, the number of graining patterns is great. In specimen books from 19th- and 20th-century paper and cloth companies, one may find hundreds of such patterns. (*See* Faux.)

GRAIN SIDE. *See* Hair side.

GRANGERIZED. *See* Extra-illustrated.

GRANJON, ROBERT (1513–1590). French type designer and printer and the one who created CIVILITÉ TYPE and fonts for printing music. He was one of the most productive and original type designers in history. "Granjon was innovative, talented, and amazingly productive. An approximate count of his production amounts to nearly ninety typefaces: thirty Italics, twenty Romans, seven civilités . . . nine Greeks, a dozen exotics, half a dozen music faces, a few Hebrews, and an undefinite [*sic*] number of initials, arabesque ornaments and fleurons. All were qualitatively outstanding" (Vervliet, *The Palaeotypography of the French Renaissance*, p. 321).

GRAPHIC NOVELS. Texts that may look like comics but are not "comic" in the sense of humorous; they often contain serious stories in pictorial versions, where the images and printed text compete for prominence but the pictures win out. That is, the texts are primarily pictorial. They are usually fiction (hence the term "novel"), but the volumes can just as well be nonfiction. In fact, the term cannot be clearly defined since these publications can have a wide range of content. The graphics make them look like comic books, but they can have many kinds of texts: adventure, horror, humor, romance, sexuality, science fiction, mystery, and so forth, but all having images and a narrative. They are usually bound IN BOARDS, though they can also be in paper covers. They are what Gene Luen Yang has called "thick comic books," but clearly they stand out from comic books in their binding and the higher-quality materials they are made of. (See Yang, "Comic Heroes.")

The French term, also sometimes used in English-speaking countries, is *bande dessinée*, and there is an International Bande Dessinée Society (see https://ibds.arts.gla.ac.uk/?page_id=154 [accessed 30 June 2021]). (See also O'English, Matthews, and Lindsay, "Graphic Novels in Academic Libraries.") The genre is associated with ANIME and MANGA.

GRAVERS. *See* Burins and gravers.

GRAVURE. "[A]n INTAGLIO printing process. The image carrier has the image cut or etched below the surface of the non-image area. On the gravure image carrier (usually a copper cylinder), all the images are screened, creating thousands of tiny cells. During printing, the image carrier is immersed in fluid ink. As the image carrier rotates, ink fills the tiny cells and covers the surface of the cylinder. The surface of the cylinder is wiped with a doctor blade, leaving the non-image area clean while the ink remains in the recessed cells. Substrate is brought into contact with the image carrier with the help of an impression roll. At the point of contact, ink is drawn out of the cells onto the substrate by capillary action. . . . Gravure is used for publications, catalogs, Sunday newspaper supplements, labels, cartons, packaging, gift-wrap, wall and floor coverings, and a variety of precision coating applications." (See "What Is Gravure?" in the bibliography.)

GRAY LITERATURE. *See* Grey literature.

THE GREAT OMAR. One of the most famous and storied bindings in history. It was a copy of Elihu Vedder's edition of Omar Khayyam's *Rubaiyat*, bound by SANGORSKI & SUTCLIFFE. "Their most famous work was The Great Omar—a copy of The Rubáiyát of Omar Khayyám commissioned by Sotherans [*sic*] Bookshop, where he indicated that the cost of the book was not to be a consideration. With that carte blanche, they outdid all previous efforts. Sangorski & Sutcliffe worked for two and a half years to create a sumptuous binding containing over a thousand jewels. The front cover was adorned with three golden peacocks, their tails made of inlaid jewels and gold, as were the vines winding around them. / When the book was finally completed in 1911, it was listed for sale at £1,000 and shipped to New York for display. The trouble began when customs demanded a heavy duty on the shipment and Sotherans refused to pay.

The Great Omar was returned to England, where Sotherans had it sent to Sotheby's auction, where it sold to an American named Gabriel Wells for £450, less than half of its initial reserve amount. The first ship scheduled to transport the Great Omar sailed without the book, so it was packed safely into the very next option, a luxury liner called the Titanic. The book went down with the ship in 1912, and weeks later, a distressed Sangorski drowned as he tried to rescue a drowning woman. / Sangorski & Sutcliffe continued successfully after the lost [*sic*] of Sangorski. Sutcliffe created a second copy of The Great Omar to replace the first. As soon as it was completed, it was stored in a bank vault for safety. Unfortunately, the bank, vault, and book were destroyed in the bombings of World War II." (See "The Great Omar: The Jewel of Sangorski & Sutcliffe" in the bibliography. *See also* Jeweled bindings.)

GREEK FRET (OR GREEK KEY). *See* Meander.

GREEK STYLE. "A 15th and 16th century style of BLIND tooled binding in which the books had spines rising at head and tail to protect the thick double HEADBANDS which were striped in bright red and blue. The thick wooden BOARDS had grooved edges, and clasp straps of triple braided thongs fastened to pins set in the grooves. Greek texts, or even translations from the Greek, were bound in this manner in France and Italy, probably by Greek craftsmen" (Roberts and Etherington, "Greek style"; https://cool.culturalheritage.org/don/dt/dt1634.html [accessed 17 May 2021]).

GREG, W[ALTER]. W[ILSON]. (1875–1959). One of the foremost textual bibliographers in the 20th century. As a scholar of Shakespeare and 16th-century drama, he is noted for his four-volume *Bibliography of the English Printed Drama to the Restoration*. Also of significance are his publications *The Editorial Problem in Shakespeare*, *The Shakespeare First Folio*, and *Some Aspects and Problems of London Publishing, 1550–1650*.

His work in this field convinced him of the importance of having reliable, scholarly editions and of focusing on textual editing as a means of creating them. One cannot underestimate the importance of his seminal (and often anthologized) article, "The Rationale of Copy-Text," which spawned a host of commentaries and generations of textual editors. (*See* Bibliography.)

GREY LITERATURE. Unpublished work from the academic world. The term originally meant any unpublished material, such as notes, informal reports, and interoffice mail. It also includes such things as patents; technical reports about products or services, people or events, or proposed policies and procedures; scientific findings from individuals or groups; committee papers; and PREPRINTS. It can also include WHITE PAPERS.

The fact that grey literature, by definition, is unpublished makes it a particular challenge for information institutions to acquire it. And its being unpublished does not mean that it is in the public domain, so it presents copyright issues as do other texts. It also poses challenges with respect to making it accessible either in a private collection or in an academic library. There are no specific standards for the processing and cataloging of this kind of material, and its marginality may make it a low priority for cataloging for most holders of these materials. The fact that it is unpublished is no indication of its accuracy or importance. Moya K. Mason says, "The grey in grey literature refers to the brain's grey matter since so much of it is highly intellectual, and is significant for research and development in many subject areas" (Mason, "Grey Literature"). And with technology what it is, grey literature exists in the digital world as well. As Claudia Marzi, Gabriella Pardelli, and Manuela Sassi show, "The conventionally accepted definition of Grey Literature, as Information produced and distributed by non-commercial publishing, does not take into consideration either the increasing availability of forms of grey knowledge, or the growing importance of computer-based encoding and management as the standard mode of creating and developing grey literature" (Marzi, Pardelli, and Sassi, "A Terminology-Based Re-Definition of Grey Literature").

One of the joys of collecting (for private as well as institutional collectors) is acquiring rare and unusual materials related to the collection. Grey literature abounds in many collections, if only in the correspondence that collectors have from the booksellers, authors, artists, photographers, and anyone else who has produced a "grey" piece in a collection. And it is just this kind of material that adds to the delight of collecting and to the substantive intellectual quality of collections. (The early versions of this book—many as handouts for the classes I have taught—are all grey, as I am myself.) (See Debachere, "Problems in Obtaining Grey Literature," 94–98.)

GRIMOIRE. One aim of this dictionary is to offer its readers definitions of terms they may find in booksellers' catalogs. On a recent online book sale, this term appeared, offered by the writer of the catalog—with no explanation of the term—as if his readers knew what it meant. So here goes: *The American Heritage Dictionary* says, "A book of magical knowledge, especially one containing spells" (p. 774). It tells its readers how to create the spells; call up angels, demons, genii, and other supernatural creatures; conjure up magical items like amulets and talismans; and cast charms (and release people from them). Like a cookbook, a grimoire can have recipes for achieving magical ends. The books are the vehicle for this information, but they themselves can be seen to have such powers. Almost all cultures worldwide have such volumes. (*See* How-to books.)

GROLIER CLUB. A private book-collectors club in New York City, founded in 1884, and the first such club in the United States. Its members have been some of the premier book collectors, booksellers, scholars, and artists of the past century and more, and its publications, lectures, symposia, and exhibitions are well known in the book world as scholarly and important. It calls itself "America's oldest and largest society for bibliophiles and enthusiasts in the graphic arts" (see http://www.grolierclub.org [accessed 8 June 2021]). The club's website says, "On the evening of January 23, 1884, New York printing press manufacturer and book collector Robert Hoe invited to his home eight fellow bibliophiles to discuss the formation of a club devoted to the book arts. Although the nine men differed in age, occupation and social position, they shared the opinion that the arts of printing and typography in late 19th-century America were in need of reform." The club was formed and has been a beacon of scholarship in book history ever since. Their aim is "to foster the study, collecting, and appreciation of books and works on paper, their art, history, production, and commerce." Their library of more than 50,000 booksellers and auction catalogs (and many thousands of other scholarly volumes, mostly on the book arts) is one of the best in the world. They currently have more than 700 members worldwide. The club was named after Jean Grolier.

While the club has published hundreds of important volumes and exhibition catalogs, perhaps its most famous and cited is *One Hundred Books Famous in English Literature*. It includes Chaucer's *Canterbury Tales* (1478), the King James Bible (1611), Shakespeare's First Folio (1623), Milton's *Paradise Lost*, works by Longfellow, George Eliot's *Adam Bede*, Frances Hodgson Burnett's *Little Lord Fauntleroy*, Jane Austen's *Pride and Prejudice*, Thackeray, and Tennison, Elizabeth Barrett Browning's *Sonnets*, Charlotte Bronte's *Jane Eyre*, Harriet Beecher Stowe's *Uncle Tom's Cabin*, and Whittier's *Snowbound* (1866), to name just a few. The volume is a listing of highlights of English publishing and high spots in collecting. The book is so well known that it is referred to as the Grolier List, with little more identification than that. And by itself, it can be seen as a collector's guidepost.

GROLIER, JEAN (Jean Grolier de Servières, Viscount d'Aguisy) (1489/1490–1565). One of France's best-known bibliophiles, a serious collector of Aldines. (*See* Aldus Manutius.) One of his claims to fame is the quality of the bindings he had executed for his books, exhibiting elaborate geometric patterns. "The designs generally consist of a geometrical pattern, occasionally colored, combined with arabesque work, which is solid, azured, or only outlined. On some of his bindings, however, the geometrical pattern has no arabesques, while in others the arabesque work is found without the geometrical design. Nearly all of the books of the first class, as well as many of those of the second, include the altruistic inscription, *Io. Grolierii et Amicorvm* (of Jean Grolier and his friends), usually at the tail edge of the upper cover, which he apparently borrowed from his contemporary, [Thomas] Mahieu. Both covers of most of Grolier's bindings feature a central compartment, usually containing the title of the book on the upper cover, and the expression *Portia Mea, Domine, Sit in Terra Vivetivm* (Let my portion, O Lord, be in the land of the living), on the lower cover. Other legends also at times appear on his bindings" (Roberts and Etherington, p. 123). Most of his books had vellum pastedowns (*see* Endleaves) and gilt edges.

GROOVES. Roberts and Etherington give the following three phenomena: "The V-shaped or rectangular incisions made on the outside of the boards connecting the holes made for lacing-in with the edges of the board," "[t]he depression along the binding edge of the upper and lower covers of a book," and "[t]he space between the board and spine of a book having an open joint" (pp. 123–24).

GROTESQUE. "A hybrid and comic figure, often combining elements from various human and animal forms. Grotesques often bear no obvious relationship to the texts they embellish, although they can carry a commonly understood meaning derived, for example, from bestiary-related [*see* Bestiary] texts" (Brown, *Understanding Illuminated Manuscripts*, p. 63). (*See* Babewynes.)

Grotesque from the *Luttrell Psalter* (fol. 27r).

Wikipedia article on *Luttrell Psalter*; https://en.wikipedia.org/wiki/Luttrell_Psalter (accessed 8 June 2021).

GROTESQUE TYPE. *See* Sans serif type.

GUARD BOOK. A volume created with GUARDS onto which LEAVES were intended to be tipped (*see* Tipped in). Also, "[a] book containing compensation guards equal to the anticipated thickness of the additional matter to be added at a later time. The guards are sewn with the book and are intended to prevent gaping of the boards or damage to the spine when the book is filled with photographs, clippings, etc. Also called a 'stub book'" (Roberts and Etherington, p. 124).

GUARDS. "A strip of cloth or paper pasted around or into a section of a book so as to reinforce the paper and prevent the sewing thread from tearing through" (Roberts and Etherington, p. 124). Carter adds that a leaf or an illustration included in a volume as a PLATE can be "guarded" if it is pasted into the volume along the inner edge of that LEAF—and it is pasted onto a guard, as Roberts and Etherington describe. (See Carter, p. 135.) The guard can be added to reinforce the connection between the volume and a leaf that is about to (or has) become detached. The guard is folded, the sewing goes through the fold, and the loose leaves are pasted to the guard(s). (*See* Tissues/Tissue guards.)

GUEST BOOKS. (Sometimes printed as a single word; and also called "VISITOR LOG, VISITORS' BOOK, or VISITORS' ALBUM.") Volumes with BLANK (or RULED, or decorated) LEAVES created to be signed by guests at a home or other venue (wedding chapels, museums, funeral homes, businesses, schools, or just about anywhere else where visitors' names are recorded). Most of these are signed by the unknown masses, and, other than for their sometimes lovely bindings, can be relatively worthless, intellectually and monetarily. But if the guests include anyone important or famous, that person's signature can be COLLECTIBLE. Also, occasionally one encounters accomplished artwork or elegant CALLIGRAPHY that could have some worth.

As a genre, these albums were published as BLANK BOOKS, often with attractive designs but quite shoddy materials. They can be found in used-book stores (*see* Used copy/Used-book store), falling apart, and with brittle leaves coming loose. Nonetheless, there is a good market for them as examples of 19th-century PUBLISHERS' BINDINGS and volumes with faded glory.

GUIDE LETTERS. Small letters—often barely visible—written or printed into a volume in a space left for larger, decorative initials to be inserted. Putting in guide letters was common in the manuscript period, when ILLUMINATED MAJUSCULES (or letters larger than those of the regular script of the text) were to be added by an artist, not by the original SCRIBE. The practice extended into the world of print, especially in the 15th century, when many volumes were illu-

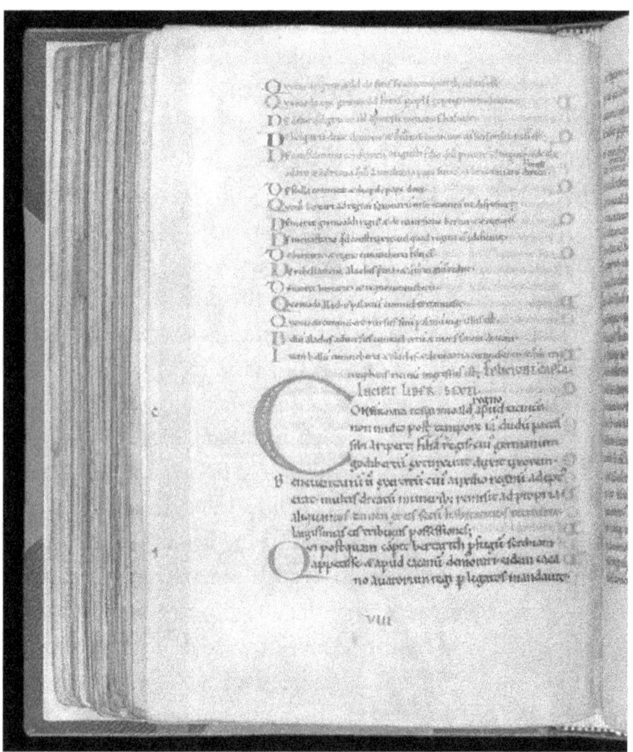

Guide letters "C" and "Q" in a manuscript, written on the far left side of the leaf; possibly the scribe anticipated their being trimmed off.

https://medievalfragments.wordpress.com/2013/03/15/image-interrupted-the-unfinished-medieval-manuscript/ (accessed 8 June 2021).

Printed page showing a guide letter ("a") that was not "covered."

http://yorktown.library.pitt.edu/libraries/is/enroom/pathfinder/guide.jpg (accessed 22 March 2015).

Guide letter for a majuscule "T." From a manuscript at the Phillips Library, Peabody Essex Museum. It served its purpose since the artist/scribe added the correct letter in red. It was not a problem to leave the guide letter still visible.

Courtesy of Phillips Library, Peabody Essex Museum.

minated with the same kind of decorations found in manuscripts. Untold numbers of these guide letters are still visible in texts in which the larger letter was never completed. Often the larger letter *was* completed and those responsible for the creation of the manuscript did not expunge the guide letter.

GUILD OF BOOK WORKERS. An American organization "founded in 1906 to 'establish and maintain a feeling of kinship and mutual interest among workers in the several hand book crafts.'" The guild believes "that there is a responsibility among civilized people to sustain the crafts involved with the production of fine books. Its members hope to broaden public awareness of the hand book arts, to stimulate commissions of FINE BINDINGS, and to stress the need for sound book CONSERVATION and RESTORATION." Their mission statement is the following: "The Guild of Book Workers promotes interest in and awareness of the tradition of the book and paper arts by maintaining high standards of workmanship, hosting educational opportunities, and sponsoring exhibits." Their 10 chapters "produce newsletters, sponsor exhibitions and hold local meetings that feature tours, talks, lectures, demonstrations and workshops" (https://guildofbookworkers.org/about [accessed 18 July 2021]).

GUILD OF WOMEN-BINDERS. (Note the hyphen in the name.) "The Guild of Women-Binders was a collective of female artisans who created a variety of FINE BINDINGS in the period from 1898 to 1904. The Guild was set up by Frank (Francis) Karslake (1864–1917), an antiquarian and second-hand bookseller with a shop in Charing Cross, London. Karslake viewed several bindings by women binders at the 'Victorian Era Exhibition' at Earl's Court in 1897, and decided to promote the work he had seen as EXEMPLARS of a new interest in handicraft. 'The Exhibition of Artistic Book-bindings by Women' was displayed at his shop (November 1897–February 1898), and thereafter he decided to act as an agent for several of the binders. The final stage was the creation of the Guild in May 1898, which he based partly in his bookselling premises and partly at the Hampstead Bindery, in which he also had a financial interest. The venture had two dimensions: Karslake sold the work of experienced binders such as Florence de Rheims, and established the Guild as a teaching institution which trained new entrants. Students were instructed in the principles of handicraft binding and employed on a piece-meal basis once their studies were completed" (Cooke, "An Introduction to the Guild of Women-Binders"). As Marianne Tidcombe points out, the so-called guild was not a real guild, but a business venture created for profit by Karslake. Tidcombe mentions many women who joined the "guild." (See Tidcombe, *Women Bookbinders, 1880–1920*.) Most of their work was in leather and vellum, and the volumes they bound are now COLLECTIBLE as much for their bindings as they are for their texts or editions. (Readers may wish to hunt up a copy of the excellent Oak Knoll Books Special Catalogue 30, "The Guild of Women-Binders," issued in 2020, with a short but fine introduction by Rob Fleck. The catalog shows about 2 dozen bindings done by members of the guild.)

GUILLEMETS. Punctuation marks used to indicate quotations, used in many languages. Sometimes they are «chucked in» as double-chevrons; sometimes they are <popped in> as single right- or acute-angle lines to indicate quoted matter within other quoted matter. (Sometimes called "angle-bracket quotation marks," "chevron-shaped quotation marks," or "duck-foot quotes.") They are used in Arabic, Bulgarian, Chinese (for book or album titles), French, German, Greek, Italian, Norwegian, Polish, Russian, Swiss languages, Turkish, Vietnamese, and more than two dozen other languages. They are also reversed »like this« to quote speech in several languages, like Czech, Danish, Polish, Serbian, Swedish, and others.

GULF COAST/SOUTHERN U.S. MEMBERS. *See* Regional Alliance for Preservation.

GUM TRAGACANTH. The gum of any of several spiny Asian shrubs that is used as a SIZING to thicken water for various uses. For the present purposes, it is one of the substances used to prepare the bath for MARBLING.

GUTENBERG, JOHANNES (ca. 1400–1468) (Gutenberg Bible). Through ignorance, many people call Gutenberg the inventor (or father) of printing. He did not invent printing. Through equal ignorance, others call him the inventor of the printing press. He did not invent the press. The *Oxford Companion to the Book* wisely uses the phrase "Inventor of printing in Europe" (see Wagner, "Johann Gutenberg"; this statement is on p. 771).

What is known for certain about Gutenberg would fill a quite small PAMPHLET. He led much of his working life in secrecy, employed with the complexities of the craft he was perfecting. His three great achievements are the development of an adjustable mold for casting type (*see* Mold [type casting]; Type casting), TYPE METAL, and the ink he used in his printing. (See Berger, "Reconsidering Gutenberg."). We do not have any of his printing type, but to have figured out what metals to use, in what combinations, probably took more of his time than did devising the adjustable mold. And his ink had to be his own formulation since there was no need for such an ink before his work on printing from metal types was perfected. Scientific studies of his inks have revealed much about why the images on the page are as sharp and black and legible today as they were when he first printed them. Albert Kapr's excellent biography, *Johann Gutenberg*, with more than 300 pages, is filled with words and phrases such as "probably," "it is likely," "he must have," "it is almost certain that," "we can surmise," and so on.

Gutenberg's great achievement, the printed Bible, was probably (I do it, too!) completed by FUST AND SCHÖFFER since the former foreclosed on the loans he made to Gutenberg and took over his printing operation. Whether Gutenberg printed after Fust and Schöffer took over his press is a matter of debate. Also, a debate has simmered for many years about whether he devised a way to cast text in blocks of lines, not just in individual SORTS. The many theories and the ongoing debates and the continuing conversations about Gutenberg's role in the history of printing are beyond the scope of this dictionary. Kapr's volume is an excellent starting point. The Gutenberg Bible is also known as the Mazarin Bible, the 42-line Bible (since almost all of its pages have 42 lines of text), or B42. (See also Ing, *Johann Gutenberg and His Bible.*) (On Gutenberg's possibly printing from two-line slugs, see Needham, "Johann Gutenberg and the Catholicon Press." See one response to this theory in Mosley, "Fallen and Threaded Types." Several articles by Lotte Hellinge disputed the "cast slug" theory, including "Das Mainzer Catholicon und Gutenbergs Nachlaß.")

GUTENBERG-JAHRBUCH. An annual bibliographical serial, published since 1926 and filled with extensive, scholarly, historical research on all aspects of printing (mostly early printing), including such topics as paper decoration and papermaking, book design, illustration, type design and casting, and much more. The articles are mainly in German and English, though it also publishes items in French, Spanish, and Italian. It is published by the Internationale Gutenberg-Gesellschaft. The design, printing, and binding are of high quality, as befitting such a journal.

GUTTA-PERCHA BINDING (also called "caoutchouc binding"). A "form of adhesive binding, invented by William Hancock, and patented in 1836" (Roberts and Etherington, p. 46). It is the first so-called PERFECT BINDING, in which the folds at the spine are guillotined off, leaving a smooth surface on the edges of the LEAVES of the volume. The leaves "were secured with a rubber solution obtained from the latex of certain tropical plants. . . . [T]he edges of the assembled leaves were roughened and then coated with caoutchouc, which, when dry, was followed by one to five coatings of a stronger rubber solution" (Roberts and Etherington, p. 46).

Great numbers of books were bound this way, primarily because in cutting out the sewing operation, publishers could save a great deal of money. This form of binding was popular on fancy GIFT BOOKS, even large FOLIO-sized volumes. But predictably, the adhesive dried out, and the bindings fell apart. The method was revived in the 20th century with the extensive growth of the PAPERBACK book trade and with improved adhesives. (*See* Perfect binding.)

Julia Miller, in her excellent volume *Books Will Speak Plain*, says of caoutchouc binding that it is "incorrectly called *gutta percha binding*" (p. 421), but she does not say why it is incorrect. The word "caoutchouc" means rubber. (She also says that the word is pronounced "cow chuck.")

GUTTER. The inner MARGINS of facing pages in a CODEX. Also called the "inside margins." They are between the TEXT BLOCK (the part of the page containing the printed text) and the point of the LEAVES where the leaves are attached (in the binding). In a tightly bound book, as is common in some French bindings, the gutter margin cannot be observed fully since part of it is in the tight, unprinted opening space. A bookseller's description may say, "tight gutters."

GYOTAKU. *See* Fish prints.

HAGGLING. *See* Appraisal; Cost; Price.

HAGS. Brass projections protruding from the two halves of the type mold used to pull from the mold the newly formed SORT. The sort will stick in one side or the other of the "funnel" of the mold, and it will be too hot to touch with one's hands. The hags make it easy to pry the sort loose. (For an image, *see* Mold [type casting].)

HAILEY'S COMET (collating machine). An optical COLLATING MACHINE that allows a scholar to compare two printed texts with one another. As Sebastiaan Verweij explains, "'Hailey's Comet' [is] a so-called optical collator. In short, this is a set of portable mirrors on anglepoised stands which allow me to see simultaneously a page in front of me (the actual book in question), and a reproduction on a laptop screen of another copy of the same book. By superimposing the two images (rather like using transparencies) by endlessly twisting and turning the mirrors, and by unlearning my dominant eye's impulse to see one but not the other image, my brain finally marries both images, after which any variant on the page jumps out in full 3D" (see Verweij, "Through a Glass Darkly"). The machine may work well for someone with decent vision in both eyes. (*See* Hinman collator.)

HAIN, LUDWIG (1781–1836). German bibliographer and specialist in INCUNABULA whose *Repertorium Bibliographicum, in quo Libri Omnes ab Arte Typographica Inventa Usque ad Annum MC Typis Expressi recensentur* (a listing of all the incunabula he was able to observe, mostly at the Bavarian State Library in Munich) was a reliable source of information for many years. It was published from 1826 to 1838 (reprinted by Josef Altmann in Berlin in 1925 and in other reprints). This was a SHORT-TITLE CATALOG, listing 16,311 volumes. W. A. Copinger did a supplement to Hain, in three volumes (published from 1895 to 1902), generally referred to as "Hain-Copinger." Today, scholars do not turn much to Hain since the *INCUNABULA SHORT TITLE CATALOGUE* (ISTC) is now available through the British Library, and the *GESAMTKATALOG DER WIEGENDRUCKE* (GW) is also available at the Staatsbibliothek in Berlin. (*See also* Goff, Frederick R.)

HAIRLINE RULE. The finest rule in the printer's arsenal. (*See* Rule/Ruling.)

HAIR SIDE. The side of an animal skin that was opposite to the FLESH SIDE. (*See* Parchment; Vellum.) The hair side of the vellum was likely to be somewhat (or much) darker than the flesh side. Sometimes the follicles of the animal are visible on the hair side, possibly giving an indication of the kind of animal that was the source of the skin. (Sometimes called "grain side.")

HAIR SPACES. *See* Thins.

HALF-BOUND. Descriptive of a hardbound volume with one material over the boards and another over the spine and corners. (*See* Full binding; Half cloth; Quarter-bound; Three-quarter bound.) A half-bound book could also have a spine covered in one paper (or one cloth)—wrapping around and protruding onto the front and back covers—and another paper (or cloth) covering the rest of the boards.

HALF CLOTH/HALF LEATHER. "Half cloth" describes a hardbound volume with cloth over the boards but a different material over the spine and corners—sometimes another cloth, sometimes vellum or leather. (*See* "Full binding"; "Half-bound"; "Quarter-bound"; "Three-quarter bound.")

Similarly, "half leather" refers to a volume with leather over the SPINE (and sometimes also the TIPS) and another material over the BOARDS.

HALF-SHEET IMPOSITION. A common form of printing in the HANDPRESS PERIOD. The printer imposed the type into the CHASE in such a way that when the sheet was printed and PERFECTED (i.e., the sheet was printed on both sides), it would be cut in half, producing two SIGNATURES of half as many LEAVES as were printed. For example, in an OCTAVO IN HALF SHEETS, the fully printed sheet has 8 leaves (since it *is* an OCTAVO); the sheet is cut into halves, producing two identical 4-leaf signatures. This extremely common FORMAT was practical for volumes (mostly PAMPHLETS but also for much longer texts) produced in printing shops with limited amounts of type, but it was occasioned even more by the fact that if a particular format would have entailed printing any number of signatures plus a half signature (to finish off the text), the half-sheet imposition saved a full pressrun for that last half signature. To illustrate, if a text of a pamphlet would come to 24 pages of printed matter, an octavo format would yield 8 leaves and therefore 16 pages for each printed SIGNATURE. Hence, the printer, needing only 24 pages of text, would need to print one octavo signature (16 pages) and then, in another full pressrun, a half of an octavo signature (8 more pages). To avoid this, the printer would print the octavo in half sheets, each yielding only a 4-leaf signature and therefore 8 pages per signature. Three such half-sheet signatures would yield the desired 24 pages. This method may have increased the number of signatures the binder needed to sew into the volume, but in the long run it was less expensive in the printing. Half-sheet imposition is also called "work-and-turn." (See Berger, pp. 257–58.) (*See* Imposition.)

A bit more clarification: In regular imposition, the text on one side of the full printed sheet differs from the text on the verso of that sheet. In half-sheet imposition, the printer prints the same text on both sides of the large sheet, then cuts it in half to produce two signatures with different text on the opposite sides of each half sheet. (For an illustration of a sheet printed in half-sheet imposition, see Berger, p. 258.)

If someone is trying to determine the format of a book printed in the handpress period, she would start by counting the number of leaves in a signature, then observing the direction of the CHAIN LINES, and also looking at the general proportions of the leaves of the book. Eight leaves in a signature, vertical chain lines, and a fairly upright volume (with the same proportions as those in a FOLIO, not one that is rather squat) generally indicates an octavo. If the volume has only four leaves in each signature, vertical chain lines, and the same proportions as a folio, it is almost certainly an octavo in half sheets. (If the paper the volume is printed on has WATERMARKS, these could be visible in the upper, inner corners of the sheets—another clue that the book is an octavo in half sheets.)

HALF-STUFF (in papermaking). "[A]ny partially broken and washed stock (rag pulp or other material) and thus reduced to a fibrous pulp, usually before it is bleached, the finished pulp, ready for the vat or paper machine, being termed 'whole-stuff'" (Labarre, *Dictionary and Encyclopaedia of Paper and Paper-Making*, p. 122). "Broken" here means macerated—hence, "partially broken" means with the fibers not fully prepared for the papermaking process. (*See* Stuff.)

HALF TITLE (also called "bastard title"). In many books there is a leaf—the first printed one in the volume—that has a part title (i.e., an abbreviated title) of the book, with sometimes other information, such as a date or a volume number if the book is part of a multivolume set. This is the half title. The regular TITLE PAGE will have additional information, such as the publisher and date, an illustration, and so on. Occasionally, the half title will have printing on its VERSO, such as ads for other books by the publisher or a list of other titles by the same author.

Some books may also have a half title after the PRELIMS and before the main TEXT BLOCK (called a "FLY TITLE"). Rarely, a book may have a second half title, as in the MINIATURE volume by Guus Thürkôw, *William Morris Wallpapers*, which has a first half title that says only "Wallpapers" and a second one with "William Morris Wallpapers."

Carter has a long discussion of the half title, explaining its use as originally a protective leaf and how binders sometimes removed them with the idea that once the book is bound, it no longer needs to be protected and also with the opportunity to sell them back to the papermakers as "waste paper." He also mentions that it is sometimes difficult to determine whether a book lacking the half title once had one and that a careful collation and a comparison with other copies may be revealing. (*See* Subtitle.)

HALFTONE ILLUSTRATION. "A picture in which the gradations of light are obtained by the relative darkness and density of tiny dots produced by photographing the subject [which can be another photograph] through a fine screen" (*American Heritage Dictionary of the English Language*, p. 792). The dots of the screen vary in size and spacing. So the density of the dots will allow gradations of light and dark areas on the original to be printed shading from light to dark on the substrate. The term can refer to the printing surface or to the printed-out image. (One can refer to the printing block as a halftone; or the image it prints can be referred to with the same word.) Since the image is printed from thousands of raised dots, it is a form of RELIEF PRINTING, though the plate from which the image is printed may feel smooth. In the production of halftones (as they are called), a benday screen is used; it is "a piece of film with a screen pattern that creates an overall pattern of halftone dots or lines. Benday screens may be used with either line cuts or halftones to change the value of tone or to alter the image of a line by reinforcing or lightening it" (Marjorie E. Killin et al., *Words into Type*, p. 536). (Etymological note: The so-called benday screen was named after Benjamin Henry Day, who invented it in 1879. It is the process used by Roy Lichtenstein in his exaggerated way in his illustrations that look like comic book pictures.) (See "Ben Day Process" at the Wikipedia site listed in the bibliography.)

HALKETT AND LAING. The shorthand designation for the work of Samuel Halkett (1814–1871) and John Laing (1809–1880): *Dictionary of Anonymous and Pseudonymous English Literature of Great Britain, Including the Works of Foreigners Written in, or Translated into the English Language.* The work was a tour de force of scholarship, identifying the authors of many anonymously published works or works published under pen names. In the 20th century, it was expanded to nine volumes. (See Carter, p. 139. See also the full text of Halkett and Laing's 1883 edition at Internet Archive, https://archive.org/details/adictionaryanon03laingoog [accessed 8 June 2021].) (*See also* Pseudonymous publication.)

HAMADY, WALTER (1940–2019) (Perishable Press). One of America's best-known FINE-PRESS printers, famous for his innovative designs, his papermaking (at his Shadwell Papermill), and the highly sought after books from his Perishable Press. Hamady, inspired by HARRY DUNCAN at the University of Iowa, taught at the University of Wisconsin, Madison, from the early 1960s until the 1990s. "His Perishable Press has designed and printed more than 130 limited edition books for well-known poets (Black Mountain Poets) and writers. Hamady also collaborates with visual artists. He has won over 13 AIGA (American Institute of Graphic Arts Fifty Best Books and Fifty Best Covers Awards). [*sic*] Hamady is known to be a passionate teacher and mentor. Many well known book artists studied with Hamady, including Barbara Tetenbaum, Walter Tisdale, Amos Kennedy, Caren Heft, Kathy Kuehn[, and Steve Miller]. One can say that Walter Hamady is the grandfather of current letterpress-bookarts-paper making students today" (Maria Lee, "Walter Hamady").

"In 1973 he began his first of eight (series) of *Interminable Gabberjabbs*. In the traditional sense, the Gabberjabbs have no category. In them he 'plays' with free association, found imagery and radical juxtaposition of TYPOGRAPHY and ephemeral images. In one such Gabberjabb, Hamady uses footnotes so extensively that eventually the poem disappears" (Maria Lee, "Walter Hamady"). His humor and inventiveness have hardly been equaled in the fine-press field. *I.D.: International Design Magazine* chose Hamady as one of the top 50 designers in the United States in 2004. John Della Contrada says, "Noted for its fine handmade paper, distinguished typography and unique COLOPHONS, Hamady's Perishable Press challenged traditional notions of the book. Over the years, his press has produced a body of work highly sought after by collectors—books prized for their meticulous and complex physical structures, quirkiness and inventive collaborations between typesetter, binder and illustrator" (Della Contrada, "UB's Hamady Collection to Be Exhibited at Grolier Club in NYC").

HAMILTON WOOD TYPE MUSEUM. (For the most part, this dictionary does not list all of the book-related museums in the world. But this museum represents an important and often neglected area of the book arts. Hence its inclusion here.) Museum in Two Rivers, Wisconsin, that has one of the most important collections of WOOD TYPE in the world. Its "mission is to advance the understanding of our printing and design heritage by documenting, archiving and reproducing the history and images of American letterpress printing. Our premier collection of printing type, engravings, library, prints and equipment support scholarship and education at all levels by preserving through use, research and demonstration. / The Hamilton Wood Type and Printing Museum is the only museum dedicated to the preservation, study, production and printing of wood type. With 1.5 million pieces of wood type and more than 1,000 styles and sizes of patterns, Hamilton's collection is one of the premier wood type collections in the world. In addition to wood type, the museum is home to an amazing array of advertising cuts from the 1930s through the 1970s, all of the equipment necessary to make wood type and print with it, as well as equipment used in the production of hot metal type, tools of the craft and rare type specimen catalogs" (Hamilton Wood Type Museum, "About"; https://woodtype.org/pages/about [accessed 3 May 2021]).

HAMMER PRICE. *See* Auctions.

HAND. *See* Fist.

HAND-COLORED. As the term indicates, the item so described is colored by hand. (How's that for a tautological explanation!) However, the text or image so described can be deceptive for a couple of reasons. First, what constitutes "hand" coloring? Is the use of stencils (as in POCHOIR) hand coloring? Yes, it is, in that stencils generally require handwork. (But not always.) But the term "hand-colored" implies that no two copies are identical, whereas with the use of stencils one can achieve almost perfect uniformity in coloring. Second, in the 19th century, printing techniques were developed in which a color image could be printed, as with CHROMOLITHOGRAPHY that produced remarkable hand-like results, especially when the printed image was touched up by hand. The observer could see, for instance, the sheen of an oil-based pigment over the color-printed surface. Third, beyond chromolithography, other methods of printing yielded remarkable color images, like those done by George Baxter (1804–1867), whose BAXTER PRINTS are called the first color printing (though they are not the first). Some of these prints, too, have a look of handwork to them, having been done with a combination of INTAGLIO and RELIEF methods. A careless cataloger might say that the picture was hand-colored when it was only partially done by hand. The message: be careful when describing something as "hand-colored."

HAND COMPOSITION. Setting type by hand rather than by machine. This takes patience, dexterity, and perseverance, and good letter- and word-spacing skills. COMPOSITORS were traditionally paid by the number of EMS they would set, and they had contests to see who could set the fastest. With the coming of high-speed printing presses, the manufacture of CASES for the rapid binding of books, the machine making of paper, and many other technologies that sped up the production of books, the need to set type by hand was the one thing that slowed down the entire bookmaking process. Only with the invention of the Linotype machine by OTTMAR MERGENTHALER did hand composition come to an end in commercial shops, though it is still carried out by hobby printers and FINE-PRESS operators. (*See* Handset type.)

HAND DIRECTOR. *See* Fist.

HANDPRESSES. Presses for printing type and cuts—generally RELIEF PRINTING—as opposed to ROLLING PRESSES. Originally, these presses were made of wood, but by around 1800, metal was incorporated into their manufacture, and for the most part all the handpresses of the 19th and 20th centuries were metal. The original term for them, especially when they were made of wood, is "common press."

There were thousands of designs of handpresses, and they came in sizes tiny enough to print only calling cards and large enough to print ELEPHANT-FOLIO sheets. GUTENBERG adapted a wine, olive, or papermaking press (with a screw to lower his PLATEN) for printing. He certainly did not invent the press. (For an image of a Columbian press, *see* Clymer, George.)

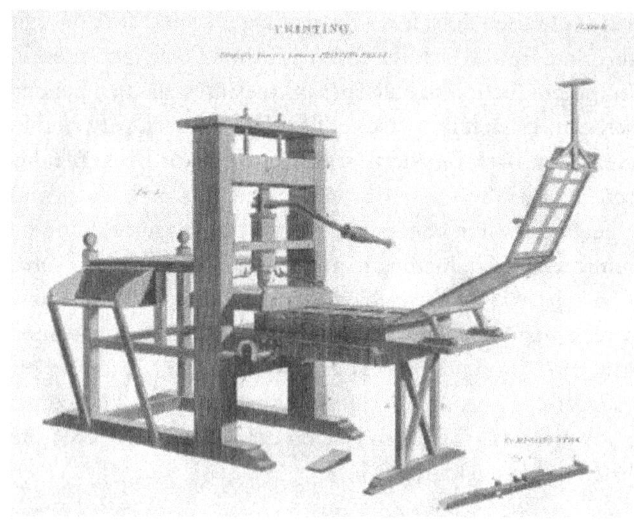

A wooden handpress (common press), with its tympan and frisket open.

http://www.zazzle.com/common_press_poster-228603975075116384 (accessed 8 June 2021).

(See Moran, *Printing Presses*; *American Dictionary of Printing and Bookmaking*, pp. 253–56; Harris and Sisson, *The Common Press*; Harris, *Personal Impressions*; and Sterne, *A Catalogue of Nineteenth Century Printing Presses*.)

HANDPRESS PERIOD. The time from the middle of the 15th century to about 1800 (though this termination date is quite imprecise, and some scholars say it ends about 1830 or even 1850). Almost all printing was done on HANDPRESSES during this period. With the coming of the industrial revolution in the first quarter of the 19th century—in which the world saw steam presses, automatic inking made possible by the invention of ROLLERS, the introduction of machine-made papers with the FOURDRINIER machine, the additional introduction of CLOTH that could be used for bookbinding in the 1820s, and the mechanization of other operations in the making of books (e.g., machine sewing)—and with all of these advancements, the handpress period is said to have come to an end. But, of course, there are still people today cutting their own PUNCHES, casting their own type, making paper by hand, printing on handpresses of many kinds, and doing hand binding. The handpress period is thus still with us in its own fairly quiet way. It is convenient to say that the handpress period ends in 1800 (the last year of the 18th century). (Probably not coincidentally, the end of the signing of the SIGNATURES of books, the practical disappearance of the use of CATCHWORDS, and the loss of the SWASH "S" are just a few of the features of books that mark the end of the handpress period.)

HANDSET TYPE. Printing type that was composed (*see* Composing stick; Compositor) by hand, as opposed to machine-set type (*see* Machine composition). LETTERPRESS PRINTERS usually proudly proclaim in their COLOPHONS that the type for their books was set by hand. The use of machines to do this (as with the MONOTYPE) results in a mechanical distribution of printed type and spacing and could result in RIVERS or other infelicities in the final printed text. Handsetting allows the compositor to adjust WORD SPACING and line length as he goes, producing a more evenly distributed image (printed type, spacing, punctuation, and so on). The phrase "handset" in a colophon usually (but not always) indicates a beautifully printed page. And, considering the human labor involved, it usually justifies higher prices for the items so produced. (*See* Hand composition.)

HANGING CAPTION. A caption or title printed vertically in the outer margin of a page, beside the text that it accompanies, and not horizontally across the page as is the usual placement for captions or titles. These may be traced to space left in the margins of medieval manuscripts for notes and annotations. And since the space in the margins is created (and reserved) for these captions, that particular layout could have been chosen by a printer or designer for texts that encourage such marginal notation.

HANGING INDENT. In printing, having a line of text flush left and all subsequent lines of that paragraph indented, as with this paragraph. In many bibliographies, the hanging indent—a form of SPATIAL CODING—is used to help the reader see where new entries of the bibliography begin.

HARDBACKS. Books IN BOARDS. (*See* Soft covered books.)

HARD COPY. Text on an analog surface (like paper or vellum), rather than one in an online/electronic version.

HARDCOVER/HARDBACK. *See* Boards.

HARD-GRAINED GOAT (HARD-GRAINED MOROCCO). "A vegetable-tanned GOATSKIN with the characteristic soft and small pinhead grain pattern produced by BOARDING in a wet condition in a minimum of four directions. The grain is much tighter than that of LEVANT and the leather itself is firmer and harder than NIGER" (Roberts and Etherington, "Hard-grained goat"; https://cool.culturalheritage.org/don/dt/dt1715.html [accessed 30 May 2021]).

HARD POINT RULING (also called "drypoint ruling"). Ruling (of a manuscript LEAF or leaves) using a hard point or stylus. This leaves no lines drawn on the LEAF, and it essentially rules both sides of the leaf at once, creating a groove on one side of the leaf and a ridge on the other, guaranteeing perfect REGISTRATION of text from front to back (RECTO to VERSO) on the leaf. With enough pressure, the scribe can rule two or more leaves at once. (*See* Lead point ruling.) (I have heard this called "blind ruling," though I cannot find this attested to in the literature.) (See Beal, *A Dictionary of English Manuscript Terminology, 1450–2000*, p. 128, who uses "dry point"; and Michelle P. Brown, *Understanding Illuminated Manuscripts*, p. 65.) (*See also* Metal point ruling; Rule [in manuscripts and in printing].)

HARLEIAN STYLE. "An English style of book decoration which came into vogue in about 1720. The name derives from the books of the Harleian library founded by Robert Harley (1661–1724) and expanded considerably by his son Edward (1689–1741). Although the name [Christopher] Chapman was once associated with these bindings, along with that of Elliott, it has been established that at least the more important bindings were probably executed by Thomas Elliott. The general characteristics of the bindings are the predominantly bright red color (and inferior quality) of the MOROCCO LEATHER used, and a three-line FILLET running around the edges of the covers. Within the fillet is a broad-tooled border made up of two or three sprigs of various patterns, and a large central ornament, usually in the shape of an elongated lozenge, built up from a number of small units" (Roberts and Etherington, pp. 128–29).

HARLEQUINADE. *See* Metamorphosis book.

HARRY RANSOM CENTER (formerly the Harry Ransom Humanities Research Center). The rare book library at the University of Texas at Austin. "The Ransom Center advances the study of the arts and humanities by acquiring, preserving, and making accessible original cultural materials. To this end, it provides access to extensive collections of rare books, manuscripts, photography, film, art, and the performing arts, while also supporting research and education through symposia, fellowships, exhibitions, and public programs. Originally founded in 1957 as the Humanities Research Center by Vice President and Provost Henry Huntt Ransom (1908–1976), it was renamed in honor of its founder in 1983. The Ransom Center's collections include many millions of manuscripts, rare books, photographs, and 100,000 works of art, in addition to major holdings in theater arts and film" (https://www.artstor.org/collection/harry-ransom-center-university-texas-austin/ [accessed 20 July 2021]). Among its many treasures and extensive holdings, it has the JOHN HENRY WRENN LIBRARY, the first named collection acquired by the University of Texas at Austin. This library is so well known in the trade that it is often referred to merely as the HRC (or, formerly, the HRHRC).

HASH CHARACTER (or hashtag). Also called the "hatch character," "hatchmark" or "hatch tag," "number sign," or "pound symbol": #. This character has many uses, including the proofreader's symbol meaning to insert a space and as a number (as in "Apartment #5"). In recent parlance, the term is used before a URL to indicate an Internet location.

HAWKER/HAWKING. A street peddler selling goods (for the present volume—the selling of books) in the streets. The hawker offers only so much as he can carry, of course, so lighter items would allow for handling a large number of pieces. Hence, PAMPHLETS and small books were more common for the hawkers to carry than were FOLIOS or QUARTOS.

HAYWARD, JOHN (1905–1965). Compiler of the exhibition catalog *English Poetry. A Catalogue of First & Early Editions of Works of the English Poets from Chaucer to the Present Day, Exhibited by the National Book League at 7 Albemarle Street, London*. The volume contains 346 illustrations of the exhibits, and is often cited by bibliographers. When one sees a citation that reads simply "Hayward," this is the volume referred to. As with all reference tools of this ilk, it has been superseded by online data. But any item listed in this volume has Hayward's recognition, so the item may be worth collecting, regardless of the current opinion of the quality of the verse it contains.

HEAD. The top of a book, hence "HEADLINE" and "HEADBAND." The opposite of the TAIL.

HEADBAND. "A functional and/or ornamental band at the HEAD and TAIL of a book between the sections and the SPINE covering, which projects slightly beyond the head and tail. Originally, the headband consisted of a thong core, similar to the bands on which the book was sewn, around which the ends of the threads were twisted and then laced into the boards of the book. Today, however, the headband is much simpler and is usually made of colored silk sewn to the book or simply attached after the volume has been FORWARDED. In EDITION BINDING they are almost always manufactured separately and then attached, while in library binding they have been replaced for the most part by a length of cord around which the covering material is rolled at both head and tail" (Roberts and Etherington, p. 129; their full entry [pp. 129–30] is worth consulting).

Roberts and Etherington's phrase "functional and/or ornamental" is telling. The original headband was composed of threads stitched around some core and then sewn through the folds of the TEXT BLOCK, and it was truly functional in that it added a good deal of strength to the binding. The ornamental kind (known as a "stuck-on headband") is merely a piece of cloth, usually with a pattern printed on it that looks like stitching but definitely is not. It is pasted to the head of the spine (and at the foot—once referred to as a "tailband"), and it could look like the "real thing," but it adds practically no strength. (*See* Endbands; Raised bands.)

HEADCAP. "The leather covering at the HEAD and TAIL of the SPINE of a book, formed by turning the leather on the spine over the head and tail and shaping it" (Roberts and Etherington, p. 130). It is one of the more vulnerable parts of the volume since it is often used to pull a book from the shelf. This part of the book almost never features in a bookseller's description unless it is defective, as in "torn headcap" or "headcap WANTING." (*See also* Crown; Oriental binding.) Strictly speaking, the term refers to a part of a leather spine, but that spot on the volume—the very top of the spine cover—is often referred to as the headcap, even if it is paper or cloth.

HEADLINE (also called a "running head"). A printed line of text above the main text of the TEXT BLOCK that may contain information about what is on that page, an author's name, the title of a chapter, a subject heading, the title of the section of the book, or other information. If the headline contains the title of the book, it is called a "running title." Carter points out that everything printed in that top line must be considered part of the headline, including the page number (p. 141).

HEADPIECE. (Sometimes hyphenated.) A decorative CUT at the beginning of a chapter, at the top of a page preceding a new section of the text, or anywhere else at which it precedes text (and often appearing at the top of a page). It could be pictorial or geometric. Sometimes called a "VIGNETTE." A vignette can also be a decorative cut printed, not necessarily at the head of a LEAF, but anywhere else on the page, as with

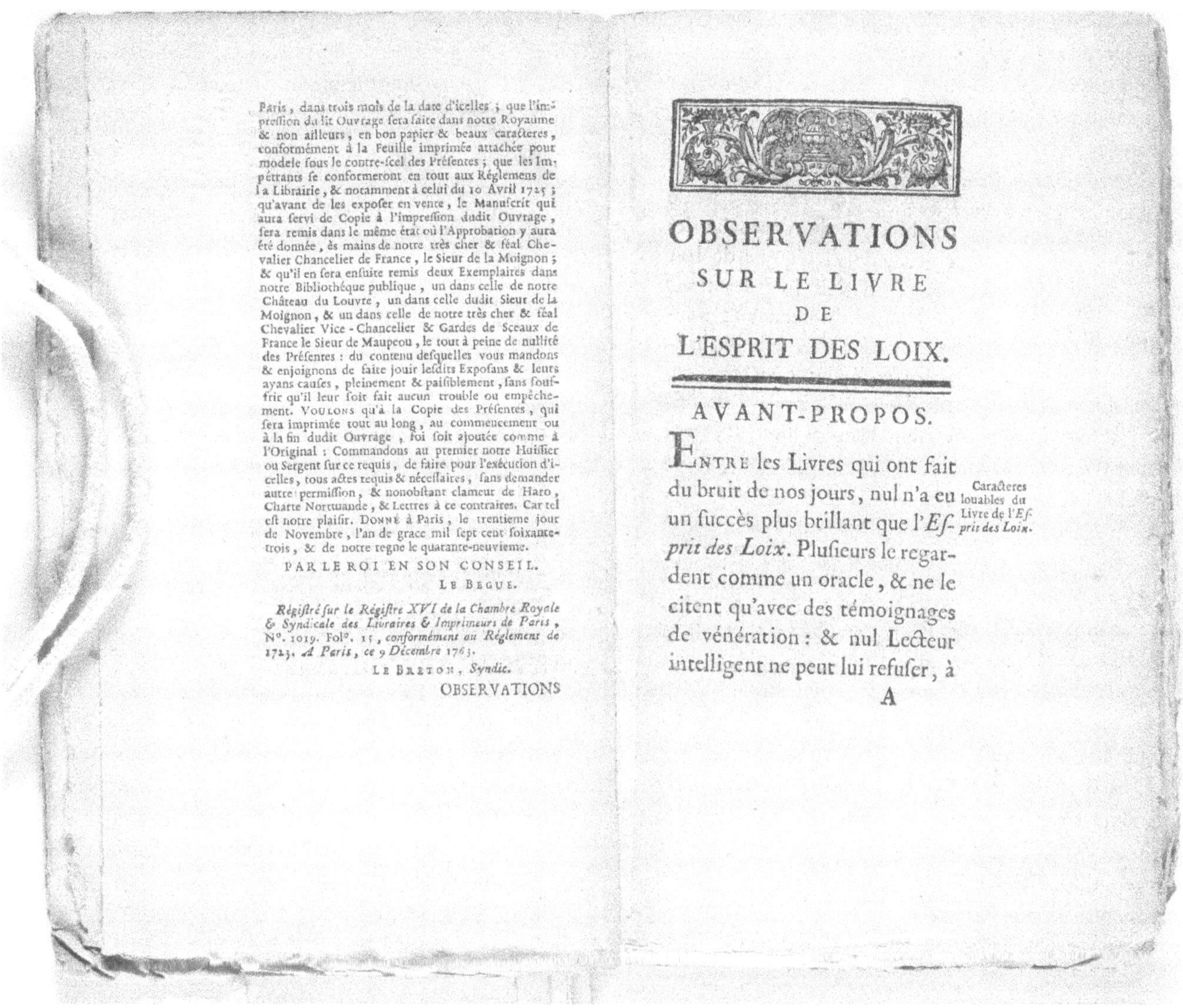

Paris, dans trois mois de la date d'icelles; que l'impreſſion dudit Ouvrage ſera faite dans notre Royaume & non ailleurs, en bon papier & beaux caracteres, conformément à la Feuille imprimée attachée pour modele ſous le contre-ſcel des Préſentes; que les Impétrants ſe conformeront en tout aux Réglemens de la Librairie, & notamment à celui du 10 Avril 1725; qu'avant de les expoſer en vente, le Manuſcrit qui aura ſervi de Copie à l'impreſſion dudit Ouvrage, ſera remis dans le même état où l'Approbation y aura été donnée, ès mains de notre très cher & féal Chevalier Chancelier de France, le Sieur de la Moignon; & qu'il en ſera enſuite remis deux Exemplaires dans notre Bibliothéque publique, un dans celle de notre Château du Louvre, un dans celle dudit Sieur de la Moignon, & un dans celle de notre très cher & féal Chevalier Vice-Chancelier & Gardes de Sceaux de France le Sieur de Maupeou, le tout à peine de nullité des Préſentes: du contenu deſquelles vous mandons & enjoignons de faire jouir leſdits Expoſans & leurs ayans cauſes, pleinement & paiſiblement, ſans ſouffrir qu'il leur ſoit fait aucun trouble ou empêchement. VOULONS qu'à la Copie des Préſentes, qui ſera imprimée tout au long, au commencement ou à la fin dudit Ouvrage, foi ſoit ajoutée comme à l'Original: Commandons au premier notre Huiſſier ou Sergent ſur ce requis, de faire pour l'exécution d'icelles, tous actes requis & néceſſaires, ſans demander autre permiſſion, & nonobſtant clameur de Haro, Chatte Normande, & Lettres à ce contraires. Car tel eſt notre plaiſir. DONNÉ à Paris, le trentieme jour de Novembre, l'an de grace mil ſept cent ſoixante-trois, & de notre regne le quarante-neuvieme.

PAR LE ROI EN SON CONSEIL.

LE BEGUE.

Régiſtré ſur le Régiſtre XVI de la Chambre Royale & Syndicale des Libraires & Imprimeurs de Paris, N°. 1019. Fol°. 15, *conformément au Réglement de* 1723. *A Paris, ce* 9 *Décembre* 1763.

LE BRETON, *Syndic.*

OBSERVATIONS

OBSERVATIONS SUR LE LIVRE DE L'ESPRIT DES LOIX.

AVANT-PROPOS.

ENTRE les Livres qui ont fait du bruit de nos jours, nul n'a eu un ſuccès plus brillant que l'*Eſprit des Loix*. Pluſieurs le regardent comme un oracle, & ne le citent qu'avec des témoignages de vénération: & nul Lecteur intelligent ne peut lui refuſer, à

Caracteres louables du Livre de l'*Eſprit des Loix*.

A

Headpiece; also showing a catchword (on the verso) and a signature ("A") on the recto. Jean Baptiste Louis Crevier, *Observations sur le livre l'Esprit des loix*. Paris: Desaint & Saillant, 1764.

Courtesy of the Rare Books & Manuscript Library at the University of Illinois, Urbana–Champaign.

one on a title page beneath the title but above the publication information. (*See also* Tailpiece.)

HEBER, RICHARD (1773–1833). One of the premiere British book collectors, whose library supplied information to countless scholars. W. Carew Hazlitt points out that Heber was not merely a collector, he was a devourer—he was conversant with the contents of just about every volume in his vast collection, and he shared the library with researchers: "[H]is most surprising and most interesting trait is his conversance with the interiors of so many of his treasures; nor should we ever forget his generosity in lending them to literary workers" (Hazlitt, *The Book-Collector*, p. 40). The sale of his massive collection of perhaps 150,000 volumes supplied the basis of the Britwell, Huth, and Daniel Libraries. (The Britwell Library was assembled by Scotsman William Henry Miller [1789–1848]; Henry Huth [1815–1878] was a prominent English book collector; George Daniel [1789–1864] was an English author and book collector.) Hazlitt says, "The FLYLEAVES of an enormous proportion of Heber's books are found enriched by his scholarly and often very interesting memoranda. . . . The notes are always pertinent and occasionally numerous; and the pages of the sale catalogue, of which we have no fewer than thirteen parts, are lifted above the mechanical common-place by the curious and varied matter interspersed from this source, as well as to a certain extent from the pen of John Payne Collier, who edited the early poetical and dramatic portions" (Hazlitt, *The Book-Collector*, p. 41). The Sotheby's sale at auction of the massive Heber collection, as Hazlitt says, is in 13 volumes, with 3 supplemental volumes—a treasure trove of information about one of the great treasure libraries of all time. (See Sotheby's, *Bibliotheca Heberiana*, in the bibliography.) As Seymour de Ricci notes: "The Dibdinian age may be aptly said to terminate with the dispersal of the gigantic library accumulated by Richard Heber . . . , a bibliomaniac if ever there was one. From 1800 to 1830, he purchased at every London sale, either in his own name or through agents like Triphook and Thorpe. He thought nothing of securing whole libraries at a time. When he died, his books filled two houses in London, one at Hodnet, one at Oxford, one at Ghent and one at Paris, not to speak of smaller stores at Brussels, Antwerp and other Continental cities. The total number of volumes in his library must have been between two and three hundred thousand, and it is doubtful whether any private individual has ever owned so large a library. / The dispersal of the Heber library took no less than sixteen sales, thirteen in London by Evans, Sotheby and Wheatley, two in Paris and one in Ghent. The Heber catalogues, although badly compiled and arranged in the most inconvenient manner, are daily consulted by every bibliographer. / Heber's library, although it contained books of every description and in every language, was especially strong in literature and in history. His series of Continental books, early Italian and Spanish works, later Latin poetry, humanistic treatises of the Renaissance, were unrivalled. He owned a very large number of early French books. / The real strength of Heber's library was, however, in the field of early English literature, especially poetry and the drama. For thirty years he collected systematically and purchased nearly every item which came on the market" (de Ricci, *English Collectors of Books and Manuscripts*, pp. 102–04).

HEIGHT-TO-PAPER. *See* Type high.

HELL BOX. *See* Black art.

HERBAL. A book of herbs, a popular genre from the manuscript and INCUNABULA periods onward. These volumes, often based on classical texts, were usually extensively illustrated with drawings (for manuscript volumes) or with woodcuts (*see* Woodcuts/Wood engravings/Wood blocks) in printed books. They might be considered medical or pharmaceutical in that often they showed the medicinal values of herbs. Such illustrations took time (and cost money) to produce, so they were often reused, even in one volume, to represent more than one plant.

HERMETICS. Books on alchemy or other occult "sciences." Named after Hermes Trismegistus, a legendary author, an amalgam of Greek and Egyptian deities.

HERZOG AUGUST BIBLIOTHEK (often referred to as the Wolfenbüttel Library). Known as the Bibliotheca Augusta, this library is internationally renowned. It was founded in the 16th century, and it took in the collections of other libraries in the 16th century and later. "The Herzog August Library is one of the oldest libraries in the world to have survived to the present day without sustaining any losses to its famous collections. The library can look back on a peaceful history of over four hundred years of book collecting to which many individuals have contributed, both members of the ducal family and the librarians and scholars in their employ. . . . The Wolfenbüttel collection was founded in 1572 by Duke Julius of Brunswick-Wolfenbüttel, but it was the systematic collecting activity of Duke August (1579–1666) which led to the creation of one of the largest European libraries of his day, composed of 135,000 valuable printed works and manuscripts and hailed by some of the Duke's contemporaries as another wonder of the world. Of the one million imprints which make up today's collection, 410,000 were printed before 1850. Of these works, 3,500 are INCUNABLES printed before 1600 [*sic*], 7,500 were printed in the sixteenth, 150,000 in the seventeenth centuries. / The Wolfenbüttel library has been open to the public since the death of the Duke August in 1666 and ever since its foundation it has been the location of research and intellectual activity" (Herzog August Bibliothek, "History of the Library").

Today in "the Herzog August Bibliothek there are approximately 1,000,000 units including approximately 11,800 manuscripts, incunabula and . . . more than 400,000 old PRINTS (appearance before 1830). Among the special collections . . . the library also includes 15 BLOCK BOOKS, over 4,000 ARTISTS' BOOKS, a Bible collection with more than 3,000 different editions, approximately 13,150 funeral sermons, 150 oil paintings, the collection of prints, 12,000 sheets [of] WOODCUTS, ENGRAVINGS, LITHOGRAPHS, drawings and illustrated PAMPHLETS, portraits, 3000 historical maps, 120 atlases and . . . globes from the 16th to the 18th century. The library also contains large collections of music, historical postcards, play-bills and cover rubbings" (Memim Encyclopedia; http://memim.com/herzog-august-library.html [accessed 24 October 2015; this is a dead link; but see the next sentence]). The library's most recent site says, "Wolfenbüttel's Herzog August library was founded in 1572. By the 17th century, it was considered the largest library north of the Alps and 8th wonder of the world. The library houses approximately 1 million media units, of which 11.800 are handwritten, 3500 incunabula and more than 400,000 prints published before 1830. The library's special collections also include several extensive art collections and historical maps, atlases and globes from the 16th to 18th century. Gottfried Wilhelm Leibniz and Gotthold Ephraim Lessing were among the many to walk and work in Herzog August library halls" (Herzog August Bibliothek, "In Between Future and Past").

HIDE. The generic word for an animal skin. As Carter notes, if a cataloger does not recognize the kind of animal skin a book is bound in, the general term may suffice for the catalog record.

HIGHLIGHTING. One of the depredations to which books have been subjected. For at least half a century, it has consisted of the use of yellow or pink (or pale blue) broad-nibbed markers drawn over the text that someone wished to make stand out. Students studying for exams are particularly guilty of such defacement. A book with such indelible marking has lost a good deal of its value, but the words, sentences, or passages so highlighted may be of interest to a scholar studying what others thought important in a volume. (*See* Marginalia.)

HIGHLIGHTS OF HISTORY SERIES. *See* Big Little Books.

HIGH SPOTS. Books (or other COLLECTIBLE matter) determined by someone to be of the highest importance (and usually of the highest value) to exist in a collection. Carter takes a provocative stance. He says that someone decides—with his or her own idiosyncratic aesthetic or criteria—what is most important, best, most essential for a collection, or the like. It may be merely the selector's favorite book or one that other people revere or admire. If the selector is well known and his or her views are publicized, others might then agree that these selections are truly the mark of a great collection. Carter condemns those who follow this kind of personal selectivity and make it their own. He points out that sometimes the criterion for selection to this list of "high spots" has to do with RARITY and not necessarily price or value, although, of course, many a volume on the "high-spot" list will be expensive. And Carter thus mocks high-spot collectors as having "more money than sense" (p. 142). In a more modern vein, high spots (which Carter hyphenates) are books in many fields that are seen as premier volumes for a collection, almost always scarce—hence the high prices they command. In other words, rather than being "dictated" by someone, the high spots are generally acclaimed to be of special desirability in a collection. Some people collect in a single field, which has its own high spots. Then there are the general collectors of high spots—that is, people who want the best books in all fields. These are the ones who merit Carter's opprobrium, for they certainly will not read what they buy—they have these books for bragging rights.

For this second edition I'd like to modify my last statement a bit: Collectors of high spots may well want bragging rights, but these collectors do serve some important functions. First, they identify and commemorate the books that have the right to offer bragging rights. Their collections can be like bibliographies that focus on important books. Second, they are often proud of their collections and like to share them with others—by private showings in their homes or by loaning to (or creating whole, original) exhibitions. In this way, they promulgate the notions that books are important, books are worth collecting, and we think many people should know about the ones we have collected. And third, they keep books moving through the world, helping booksellers and scholars (when the scholars are invited in to use the books), the librarians who may eventually get their collections, other collectors if they decide to sell their holdings, and the whole world of books, among whom high-spot collectors can be looked to with reverence. As I noted above, Carter says that high-spot collectors display "more money than sense" (Carter, p. 142). He may have taken a sardonic look at high-spot collectors; I do not.

HINGES. The connections of a book on the inner part of the binding where the covers and SPINE are attached to one another. (The outside junctures are JOINTS.) But, as Carter says, the word "hinge" is sometimes used for the outside connection, and the word "joints" is sometimes used for the inner connection, thus rendering them pretty much interchangeable, though, strictly speaking, they are not the same phenomena (Carter, p. 142). Hence, a book that is REHINGED is different from one that has been rejointed, and often booksellers know the distinction and get it right in their catalogs when they describe condition. Thus, if a bookseller says that the hinges of a book are compromised, she is probably speaking of the inner connections between the text blocks and the covers. And the phrase "JOINTS STARTING" will almost certainly refer to the outer connections. Carter adds that "the binder's term *morocco joints* refers to the inside, and there is enough room for confusion in current usage to make some clear ruling desirable" (p. 142). Roberts and Etherington say that a hinge is "[t]he strip of fabric (usually linen or cambric), or paper placed between the two parts of a library-style cloth-jointed endpaper, for the purpose of providing additional strength at the point of flexing" (p. 131). A conservation treatment for a book that has had its hinges replaced is called "rehinging." Another kind of hinges are those that are used for matting prints.

HINMAN COLLATOR. A machine used to compare two copies of what look like identical texts, the aim being to identify reset type or to locate textual changes in a printed edition. Invented by Charlton Hinman after World War II and based on the use of aerial photography that charted the movement of enemy troops, the machine operates on the principle that the eye can spot movement. The machine contains two lighted platforms on each of which the operator would place a copy of a volume—the two volumes being of the same edition (i.e., the same setting of type). Looking through a binocular eyepiece and thanks to a series of mirrors in the machine, the operator would optically superimpose one image on top of the other; since both were printed from the same setting of type, the superimposition would yield a view of what looked like a single sheet (a single page of text, though it was really two pages, one on top of the other). Note that the operator was actually seeing two pages, though it looked like one. The lights would be turned off, and then the operator would move a lever (located at the outside of the left knee) to the left, lighting up first one platform and then the other so that he would see first one page and then the other, alternately. If there was a difference between the type on the two pages, it would show up as movement. Thus, for example, if an upright lowercase *L* were perfect in one copy and broken over in the other, the collator would see the letter going from straight to bent to straight to bent while the lights alternated on opposite platforms. Similarly, a missing dot on a lowercase *i* would appear and disappear as the lights flashed left and right. One could

A Hinman collator. "The Collation: A Gathering of Scholarship . . . ," Folger Shakespeare Library; http://collation.folger.edu /2011/08/welcome-to-the-collation/ (accessed 8 June 2021). Courtesy of Folger Shakespeare Library.

COLLATE a whole page in a few seconds. Oral collations could not identify the resetting of or the damage to type, but the Hinman could do so quickly and unerringly. (See Smith, "'The Eternal Verities Verified.' ") Other collating machines, based on different principles, are those made by Gordon Lindstrand and Randall McLeod. (See Lindstrand, "Mechanized Textual Collation and Recent Designs," in which Lindstrand describes his own inventions, the Mark I and Mark II Comparators; and McLeod, "A New Technique of Headline Analysis with Application to Shakespeare's Sonnets, 1609." See also Dearing, "The Poor Man's Mark IV or Ersatz Hinman Collator"; and Smith, "A Collating Machine.") Note that Nicolas Barker's explanation (in the latest edition of Carter's *ABC*) that the Hinman collator has "a prism and mirrors" (p. 142) is inaccurate. There is no prism—just mirrors, lights, and a binocular device. (The Hinman is a miracle of efficiency in collating texts, though few of them are still in use.) (*See also* Hailey's Comet.)

HISTOIRE DU LIVRE. *See* History of the book.

HISTORIATED. A term used to denote any illustrated matter in medieval or Renaissance manuscripts in which people, events, or creatures are depicted. Michelle P. Brown says of a "historiated initial," "A letter [or a border] containing an identifiable scene or figures, sometimes relating to the text. Historiated initials, first encountered in insular illumination of the first half of the eighth century, became a popular feature of medieval illumination. BORDERS can also be historiated" (Brown, *Understanding Illuminated Manuscripts*, p. 68). (*See* Illuminated.) To be historiated, the initial must contain a figure who is recognizable. Brown says that such an initial or a border with figures or scenes that are not identifiable is called "inhabited."

HISTORY OF THE BOOK; *HISTOIRE DU LIVRE.* The English and French terms for a discipline that is exceptionally broad, encompassing as it does everything that relates to books as historic objects—containers of texts and information—in all of their manifestations. This includes, among a huge range of topics, their materials, manufacture, and use; economic, religious, and political issues; legal matters; printing, papermaking (and the manufacture of all the materials that go into book production); buying and selling; librarianship and library history; books as markers of commerce; reading and reception; criticism; restoration, preservation, and conservation; theft and suppression; description, cataloging, and access to information; and much more. Matthew Symonds and Earle Havens say, "The history of the book has its roots in bibliography, librarianship, and the intersections of social, cultural, and material history. It has emerged in recent decades as an academic discipline with its own undergraduate and postgraduate university courses, scholarly journals, monographic series, conferences, and research centers. It is methodologically diverse and interdisciplinary, situated between the worlds of scholarship and the physical collections of historical materials, the latter largely in the possession and care of universities and research libraries, as well as antiquarian booksellers and private collectors. It has as its subject a form of technology that has become so universal, chronologically and geographically, as to be considered almost natural: the material landscape within which the historical record is most clearly preserved and communicated across time" (Symonds and Havens, "The Archaeology of Reading"; https://archaeologyofreading.org/historiography/ [accessed 29 July 2021]). The French term is often used since many of the outstanding proponents of this discipline have been French.

The 1980s saw the birth and immediate growth of classes in this broad discipline—recognized as a discipline by itself, though in many academic institutions courses were taught before the History of the Book was recognized as a field in itself. Such classes were the rudimentary subjects of the field: bibliography, paleography, codicology, history (cultural and social), philology, textual editing, the history of art, language and literature, engineering, chemistry, and other sciences (especially those focusing on the machinery and materials that lead to the making of books), and others. And from the 1990s on, untold numbers of articles and books dealing with the History of the Book have been published. In their own way, booksellers' catalogs and the collectors' listings of their own holdings are part of, and contribute to, the field, as do the activities of librarians and scholars in the many fields delineated above. Even the psychiatrist who tries to break the BIBLIOMANE from his irrational habit is operating within this discipline. (*See* "Historical Bibliography" under Bibliography.)

HOFMANN, MARK (1954–). One of the great FORGERS of all time. Hofmann was at one time a bookseller and EPHEMERA dealer who "discovered" a copy of the "Oath of a Freeman," the first item printed (in 1639) in what is now the United States. According to CHARLES EVANS, in his monumental *American Bibliography*, this is Number 1. No copy is known, though Hofmann "found" a copy—that is, he created a forged copy—and tried to sell it to the LIBRARY OF CONGRESS and the AMERICAN ANTIQUARIAN SOCIETY. At the time, he fooled many people, who said that while they doubted its authenticity, they could not prove it to be forged. (See Gilreath, ed., *The Judgment of Experts*.) This was only one of many such forgeries Hofmann created. (See Sillitoe and Roberts, *Salamander*; Lindsey, *A Gathering of Saints*; Naifeh and Smith, *The Mormon Murders*; and Throckmorton, Christensen, and Casper, *Motive for Murder*.)

Hofmann was identified as a bomber who killed two people to whom he owed money. A third bomb (with the same characteristics as the other two) injured him, tipping off authorities that he was the creator of the other two. Knowing he was caught, he confessed to his crimes, including the forging of a host of documents other than "Oath of a Freeman." He had forged so many that he could not recall all of them, so documents—some of which maligned the Mormon Church and called its foundation into question—are "out there" that are forgeries but have not been identified as such.

His method of forgery was ingenious, for he was able to fool experts with respect to ink, paper, text, and typeface. He is serving a lifetime sentence in prison.

HOG (in papermaking). A device in the VAT that stirs the water containing the paper pulp. The pulp would settle to the bottom of the vat if the hog did not keep the water and pulp in motion. Labarre calls it a "mechanical stirrer, mixer or agitator" used to "keep the pulp of uniform consistency" (*Dictionary and Encyclopaedia of Paper and Paper-Making*, p. 126).

HOGARTH PRESS. *See* Virginia Woolf.

HOLD-TO-LIGHT. A genre of printed or painted (or both) LEAVES that show one image, but show an addition to that image when the leaves are back-lighted. That is, a blank sheet or one printed with an image embedded inside the leaf, invisible from either side of that leaf, an "addition" to what one sees on the sheet if a light shines through it. The method was applied to a variety of kinds of printed matter, but it was mostly used for postcards. Helmfried Luers explains about these hold-to-light cards: "Another quite popular novelty that turned up by early/mid 1898. D.R.G.M. no. 88077 was registered for the huge ('Luxuspapierfabrik') company of Wolf Hagelberg, Berlin. They produced quite a number of different designs and makes. / The second major hold-to-light card design was registered under D.R.G.M. number 88680, usually with the suffix 'Meteor'. They could best be described as 'transparency-type'. I strongly believe 'Meteor' was registered for E. A. Schwerdtfeger, also from Berlin. / The idea behind the Hagelberg design was quite simple. A[n] image was printed by CHROMOLITHO or COLLOTYPE process. Then a FORME had to be arranged to stamp out carefully windows, doors, the moon or whatever. The address side was printed separately, and between the image and the sheet carrying the address side a blank sheet, usually of bright yellow colour was put." These were glued and pressed together. "The 'Meteor' hold-to-light cards were done in a different way. No stamping-out [was] necessary, the cards have a smooth surface. How the impressive effect was arranged is unknown to me. However, it required motifs with some 'blank' areas, without heavy illustration. Postage stamps could ruin the effect a bit" (Luers, "The Postcard Album: Postcard Printer & Publisher Research"). Luers points out that such cards were also produced in other countries than Germany: One "card was published for the Hungarian market and the short message is dated 31 December 1899. The publisher (and printer?) was a company with the name KOSMOS and found at Budapest, Graz and Munich. I have seen other cards, usually fine chromolitho printed, with KOSMOS Munich on, all from about the turn of the century. / When held to light the image turns into a little bit different, coloured (!) view. The mythical fury is now an elderly woman, with a broom instead [of a] knife in her hand. Her husband has broken a mug in their bedroom. He is seen in front of her down on his knees and awaiting punishment. Typical humour of the time and many years to come." For the most part, the embedded image, invisible from both sides of the sheet when it was not backlit, had to be printed in such a way as to be revealed onto the front of the leaf where there was blank space. These collectible items show up at every book fair and ephemera show. This is related to the Shine-a-Light Books. (Thanks to Diane Deblois from aGatherin' for her assistance.)

HOLLANDER BEATER. A 17th-century invention from Holland—the machine that beats (macerates) fibers for papermaking. "The typical form of this machine is a longitudinal tank or vat, originally of wood but now of cast-iron or re-inforced [*sic*] cement, usually lined with glazed tiles . . . , with rounded corners, called the pan[,] divided lengthwise by partition, which does not reach the ends of the pan, called the mid-feather, thus forming a continual channel of regular width in which the stuff can circulate. / On one side of the partition there is placed between the mid-feather and the wall of the tank, a beater roll, acting in conjunction with the bed-plate let in the floor of the Hollander at what is termed the midpoint" (Labarre, *Dictionary and Encyclopaedia of Paper and Paper-Making*, p. 126). This beater roll, a cylinder running the width of the channel, has along its surface, parallel to the width of the roll, a series of blades that, when the roll turns, scrape against the bedplate beneath it. The raw pulp is put into the tank or trough in water, and the beater roll turns, grinding the pulp against the bedplate and breaking down the fibers to the desired length. The longer the beater roll turns and the pulp is ground, the finer become the fibers. This machine replaced the stamping mill in most paper mills. (*See also* Naginata beater.) (For images of Hollander beaters, see Lee, "A New Naginata Beater, in Cleveland!") (See Thomas, *Beater Time Tests.*)

HOLLOW SPINE/HOLLOW BACK BINDING. "A binding having a space between the spine of the text block and the spine of the cover, resulting from the covering material being attached at the joints (or a one-piece cover in the style of a case binding) and not glued to the spine of the text block. Sometimes a hollow is glued to the text block and covering material; in library binding, however, generally only an inlay is glued to the covering material, while in edition binding there is usually no support of any kind" (Roberts and Etherington, p. 133). When a book with a hollow spine is opened, a hollow space in the form of a half circle is formed over the spine. (*See* Bradel binding.)

HOLOGRAPH. Completely in an author's or scribe's handwriting, hence a holograph inscription or a holograph manuscript, the latter indicating that the whole text is in handwriting, not typed or computer generated and then merely signed. The phrase "autograph manuscript" may be used rather than "holograph manuscript," but it must be made clear that "autograph" here means that the entire text is handwritten. It is not a text that is printed and then "autographed."

HONEST COPY. The entry is here because Carter has a similar entry, though the term has pretty much disappeared from the book trade. Carter says that an "honest copy" is one with all of its faults manifest—not a sophisticated copy or one on which restoration work has been done that hides former flaws.

HORAE. *See* Book of hours.

HORIZONTAL FORMAT. *See* Landscape format.

HORNBOOK. (Sometimes hyphenated.) A primer for children composed of a small piece of paper or vellum on which is printed the alphabet (upper- and lowercase), sometimes common letter combinations (e.g., "ab," "eb," "ib," "ob," "ub," "ba," "be," "bi," "bo," "bu," and so on), maybe a line of prose (as in "In the Name of the Father . . ."), and the Lord's Prayer. This would be placed or pasted onto a little wooden board with a handle and then covered with a thin veneer of cattle horn (hence the name), tacked down with tiny brads. Sometimes the back of the hornbook was covered with leather. Similar devices for teaching could be made out of ivory, and because they have the same or a similar text, they might be called a "hornbook," though they have no horn.

Two 17th-century hornbooks.

Bookmaking with Kids; http://www.bookmakingwithkids.com/?p=716 (accessed 8 June 2021).

HORS DE COMMERCE. *See* Limited editions.

HORS TEXT. French for "outside the text." The term is used in the book world primarily for illustrations that were printed not with the text, but separate from it, usually on a different (and often glossy) paper, or on a press different from the one that was used for the text—as with a ROLLING PRESS. Sometimes these LEAVES are given ROMAN NUMERALS to distinguish them from illustrations printed with the text. (Those printed with the text would be given arabic numbers.) A bookseller may say "*Hors text*, VERSOS blank." (Parenthetically, when illustrations are so printed, with blank versos, libraries often mark them by stamping them on this blank surface with the library's identification, to discourage their being stolen. And this stamping would be done in the middle of the printed image, not in the margin, which could be trimmed off.)

HOT METAL (TYPE)/HOT TYPE. Printing type that is made of metal. It could be from a type foundry, from a MONOTYPE machine, from a Linotype machine (though this is not strictly "type"), or from any other kind of metal-casting process. It is often a sign of pride (and of high quality) to say that "this book was printed from hot metal," indicating, often, some handwork in the operation. Cold type refers to phototypesetting and other forms of printing that do not use metal. (See Merriam-Webster, http://www.merriam-webster.com/dictionary/cold%20type [accessed 8 June 2021].) (*See* Mergenthaler, Ottmar.)

HOT PRESSED. *See* Calendering.

HOUGHTON LIBRARY. The rare book library at Harvard University, opened in 1942. It was named after Arthur Amory Houghton Jr. (1906–1990), once the president of Steuben Glass. "After graduation [from Harvard] in 1929 he began collecting in earnest, stocking original manuscripts and letters of writers like Samuel Pepys, Robert Browning and Elizabeth Barrett Browning. . . . He donated his Keats collections, one of the largest anywhere, to the Houghton Library at Harvard University, which he had endowed in 1942 as a repository for the university's collections of rare books and manuscripts" (James, "Arthur Houghton Jr., 83, Dies"). (A capsule history of the library is available at *The Harvard Gazette*, "The History at Houghton," https://news.harvard.edu/gazette/story/2011/11/the-history-at-houghton/#:~:text=Harvard's%20neo%2DGeorgian%20Houghton%20Library,%2C%20and%20air%2Dfiltration%20systems [accessed 30 June 2021]).

HOUSE STYLE. The editorial and printing (and sometimes binding) practices of a particular publisher. Authors are asked to submit COPY to a publisher using that publisher's house style. To that end, publishers may say, in advice to prospective authors, "All submissions must be in our house style"; or that the publisher has chosen *Chicago* as its house style, in reference to the massive volume published by the University of Chicago Press: *THE CHICAGO MANUAL OF STYLE*. Not using the proper house style in a submission marks the author as ignorant of that publisher's standard practices and can make the recipient at the publishing house jettison the piece immediately upon its reception. House style includes such things as preferences in spelling, indentation, capitalization, word choice, and punctuation, along with source citation. For decades the *New York Times* house style looked like this: "The 1920's was a rip-roaring great decade"; "She was born in the permissive 1960's." They were just about the only major publisher using that silly apostrophe, which they eventually dropped. House styles are often idiosyncratic, so it is to the benefit of an author to learn the style of the publisher to whom she is submitting copy. (*See* Follow copy.)

HOWELL, DOUGLASS MORSE (1906–1994). One of the early 20th-century American papermakers who brought hand papermaking back from somnolence. As Roberta Smith says, Howell returned from World War II in 1946 and "built the first of several pulp beaters, a machine he continued to refine throughout his life. He used it both to create his own works and to make paper for other artists, especially in printmaking. The artists he worked with included

Jackson Pollock, Lee Krasner, Dorothy Dehner and Alfonso Ossorio. . . . Mr. Howell made paper in an astounding range of weights, colors, and textures. All sheets were distinctive and some . . . were three-dimensional" (Smith, "Douglas [*sic*] Morse Howell, 87, Artist and Papermaker"). One of his signature decorative elements was the cloths he embedded into his sheets. Sometimes there were snippets of cloth or ribbons, sometime pieces of lace. And since many (if not all) of his papers were not CALENDERED, they had a heavy nap—a highly textured surface.

In his bookmaking and in the papers he made for himself and others, Howell showed great artistry, and many of his papers have become available on the secondary market through his daughter's selling of them.

HOW-TO BOOKS. Volumes teaching readers the way to perform any kind of skill: how to give a tea party, how to make a dress, how to win an argument, how to lose your money in the stock market, how to say prayers. (In fact, the common BOOK OF HOURS is a sort of how-to book.) Most cookbooks are how-to books, but they fall into the more defined genre of COOKBOOK. There is no end to these, with untold numbers of experts or people just learning a new craft or way of bending their bodies or thinking about life and death—all wanting to write a book on how to do it. (*See* Grimoire.)

HOYEM, ANDREW. *See* Arion Press.

HRC. *See* Harry Ransom Center.

HUBBARD, ELBERT (1856–1917) (ROYCROFT PRESS). Hubbard was the founder of the Roycroft Community in East Aurora, New York. After a successful career for the Larkin Soap Company, he became a writer and publisher, using the Roycroft Community in East Aurora as his base. He used his traveling-salesman selling tactics on a broad middle-class public eager to embrace the finer things in life, which he produced at Roycroft in quantity and at prices aimed at this large middle class. With an Arts and Crafts sensibility, the community produced furniture, household goods, pottery, leather items, and books by the millions, still collected today despite the fairly poor quality of many of them. His series of volumes *Little Journeys to the Homes of the Great* was tremendously popular, and his little tale *A Message to Garcia*, espousing fidelity to one's employer (among other things), sold millions of copies. During World War I, Hubbard, a golden-throated orator, thought he could end the war single-handedly by talking to the heads of the warring nations, so he and his second wife, Alice Moore Hubbard, sailed off to Europe on the *Lusitania*. He went down with the ship, as it neared Ireland, when it was torpedoed by a German U-boat on 7 May 1915.

Hubbard's aim was to make money, but his public persona was of a philanthropist who brought literature to the common person in "elegant" and fine books. The community he started in 1895, "Roycroft," gave housing and training to many craftspeople and artists, including DARD HUNTER. The community survived with the sale of its pottery, printing, and books, among other things until its demise in 1938. Today one can visit the Roycroft Campus, a National Historic Landmark. (See Champney, *Art and Glory*; Hamilton, *As Bees in Honey Drown*; and Via, *Head, Heart and Hand.*)

HUNTER, DARD (1883–1966) (born William Joseph Hunter). Perhaps the premier paper historian of all time. For more than 40 years, Hunter traveled in search of papermakers and papers, and he produced a host of amazing books on the topics of all the areas of papermaking he researched, some commercially printed, some he did himself. His research brought to the West an extensive knowledge about papers and PROTO-PAPERS from Japan, China, Korea, Siam, Indochina, and the United States. He is noted as one of the few people ever to have made books from scratch: he designed his own FONT, cut the PUNCHES, struck the MATRICES, cast his own type, made the paper, did the research and wrote the texts, printed his own texts, and did some of the binding himself, almost always with samples of the papers he was writing about tipped or bound into the volumes. Some of his scholarship was printed by Pynson Printers (e.g., *Papermaking by Hand in India* and *A Papermaking Pilgrimage to Japan, Korea and China*). Many of his most valuable volumes were completely self-produced under the Mountain House Press imprint. For example, *Old Papermaking in China and Japan* was done in only 200 copies, a fourth of which were lost in a fire. And *Primitive Papermaking* was one of the early and most thorough treatments of proto-papers to be published. His monumental *Papermaking by Hand in America*, his swan song in the FINE-PRESS publishing field, is a tour de force of scholarship and bookmaking. And his most consulted book, *Papermaking*, was reprinted by Dover Publications and has been in print for nearly 40 years. (It was originally published in 1930 as *Papermaking through Eighteen Centuries.*) His *My Life with Paper* is a delightful read. (The best books on Hunter are by his son Dard Hunter II, *The Life Work of Dard Hunter*; Baker, *By His Own Labor*; and Hunter II, Hunter III, and Morris, *Dard Hunter & Son.*)

HUNTINGTON LIBRARY. The library and art gallery of Henry E. Huntington (1850–1927). The library is known mostly for its holdings on American and English literature.

"The Huntington Library is one of the largest and most complete research libraries in the United States in its fields of specialization. The Library's collection of rare books, manuscripts, prints, photographs, maps, and other materials in the fields of British and American history and literature totals more than nine million items. . . . The Library collections date from the Middle Ages to the 21st century. The greatest concentration is in the English Renaissance, about 1500 to 1641; other strengths include medieval manuscripts, INCUNABULA (books printed before 1501), maps, travel literature, British and American history and literature, the American Southwest, and the history of science, medicine and technology" (The Huntington, http://www.huntington.org/webassets/templates/general.aspx?id=17334 [accessed 18 April 2015]; this is a dead link; a more recent posting says, "At the heart of The Huntington is the Library, which contains nearly 9 million manuscripts, books, photographs and other works in the fields of American and British history, literature, art, and the history of science, medicine, and technology. Among the highlights of the collection are the Ellesmere manuscript of Chaucer's The Canterbury Tales (ca. 1410); a Gutenberg Bible (ca. 1450–55); a world-class collection of early editions of Shakespeare; original letters of George Washington, Thomas Jefferson, Benjamin Franklin, and Abraham Lincoln; an unsurpassed collection of materials relating to the history of the American West"; https://www.huntington.org/general-press-kit [accessed 30 June 2021]). The library has one of the largest collections of incunabula (nearly 5,500 items) in the United States, second only to the holdings in the Library of Congress.

I

IBID. One of a host of abbreviations used in texts to indicate that the work cited is the same as one cited previously. It is a space saver, allowing the writer to cite a reference without having to spell it out in full once again. Other more contemporary methods of citing sources are preferred in many STYLE GUIDES. The revered *CHICAGO MANUAL OF STYLE* says that such scholarly abbreviations "are typically found in bibliographic references, glossaries, and other scholarly apparatus. Some of them are no longer widely used and are listed here mainly as an aid to interpreting older texts" (pp. 589–90). The principle of listing obsolete terms to elucidate them for modern readers who may encounter them in their research applies to the inclusion of many obsolete terms in the present text.

ICE CREAM CUP LID BOOKS. *See* Big Little Books.

IDEAL COPY. In bibliography, the most perfect copy of a book—presumably the way the book was when it was issued directly from the publisher. In many cases, especially when a title is exceptionally scarce, only defective copies survive, but the descriptive bibliographer connotes a perfect copy with the COLLATIONAL FORMULA and then adds the notes to reveal the imperfections of the copy she is examining. (*See* Bibliographical description; Bibliography.) The term connotes what every serious collector wants: the ideal (i.e., the best) copy—without flaws. One problem, however, is that—especially for books from the HANDPRESS PERIOD—a publisher may have created a text in its first edition, first impression, first issue, but in more than one state (*see* Edition, Impression [Printing], Issue, and State; Points). What, then, is an "ideal copy"? Which state does the collector want? Of course, a COMPLETIST would want one of every variant manifestation, but these would be impossible to identify without an examination of every extant copy. Hence, the term remains current in the world of descriptive bibliography, but not in the realm of collecting.

IFLA (International Federation of Library Associations). Most countries have library associations. IFLA is the parent organization for them. "The International Federation of Library Associations and Institutions (IFLA) is the leading international body representing the interests of library and information services and their users. It is the global voice of the library and information profession. / [It was] [f]ounded in Edinburgh, Scotland, on 30 September 1927 at an international conference. . . . [It now has] 1500 members in approximately 150 countries around the world. IFLA was registered in the Netherlands in 1971" (http://www.ifla.org/about [accessed 8 June 2021]). The organization, divided into sections and divisions, has many institutional and private memberships as well as country members, and they hold an annual conference in major cities around the world. (The divisions and sections are delineated on their website at http://www.ifla.org/activities-and-groups#divisions [accessed 8 June 2021]). IFLA has five divisions (Library Collections, Library Services, Library Types, Regions, and Support of the Profession). Beneath this structure they have 43 sections, including Rare Books and Manuscripts and Preservation and Conservation.

ILAB (International League of Antiquarian Booksellers). (Also called LILA [Ligue Internationale de la Librairie Ancienne].) An organization of 22 national booksellers' associations from around the world, generally specializing in all the things that one expects to find in an antiquarian bookstore. (*See* ABAA.) The organization was founded in 1942, and it is composed of associations in Australia and New Zealand, Austria, Belgium, Brazil, Canada, the Czech Republic, Denmark, Finland, France, Germany, Hungary, Italy, Japan, the Republic of Korea, the Netherlands, Norway, the Russian

Federation, Spain, Sweden, Switzerland, the United Kingdom, and the United States. The league, like the ABAA, promotes antiquarian book fairs; they have a member directory; and they have published a multilingual glossary of terms relating to books and bookselling. Their website contains a wealth of information (https://www.ilab.org [accessed 8 June 2021]). The ILAB dictionary may be of use to readers of this dictionary (see Hertzberger, ed., *Dictionary for the Antiquarian Booktrade, in French, English, German, Swedish, Danish, Italian, Spanish and Dutch*).

ILLUMINATED. The word "illuminated" generally means decorated or embellished by hand, though printed books made to look like medieval manuscripts may also be called "illuminated" by the less scrupulous. Illumination that is floral is called "FLORIATED," and that with human beings is called "HISTORIATED." Michelle P. Brown says, "The illuminator could, on occasion, also be the SCRIBE. . . . Illuminators could be male or female and members of monastic or minor clerical orders; from about 1200 members of the laity increasingly took up the profession. By the late Middle Ages, most illuminators were lay people. Illuminators continued to practice their art, although to a limited extent, after the introduction of printing, sometimes embellishing early printed books, and often working in the field of professional calligraphy" (Brown, *Understanding Illuminated Manuscripts*, pp. 70–71).

ILLUMINATED MAJUSCULE. A capital letter decorated with any one of many kinds of embellishments: people, nature scenes, animals, flowers, and so on. Sometimes simply called a "decorated initial."

ILLUMINATED MANUSCRIPTS. Manuscripts embellished with artwork of various kinds. The artwork could be in the margins, in the MAJUSCULES, or in the lines of the text, or they could be full- or part-page MINIATURES anywhere on the page. (See Michelle P. Brown, *Understanding Illuminated Manuscripts. See also* De Hamel, *A History of Illuminated Manuscripts*; and Harthan, *An Introduction to Illuminated Manuscripts.*) There is a huge market for books about these volumes, and also an extensive market for FACSIMILE EDITIONS of them.

ILLUSTRATION PROCESSES. Carter mentions direct illustrations employing artists' tools (including cameras) and photoreprographic illustrations (which are "line-block, HALF-TONE, PHOTOGRAVURE, COLLOTYPE, photolithography, etc." [p. 145]). In his revision, reflected in the eighth edition of Carter's *ABC*, Barker has added that there are three other kinds—RELIEF, INTAGLIO, and PLANOGRAPHIC—along with "original, whether produced by an artist's tools or camera" (p. 145). (See Berger, "History of Three Basic Printing Processes.")

IMITATION. *See* Faux.

IMPENSIS. The Latin word in the dative plural (masculine, feminine, and neuter) of "impensa," meaning "cost," "outlay," "expense." It indicates who (a person or people—or possibly a corporate body or organization) or what (printer or publisher) paid for the volume in which this is printed.

IMPERFECT. Said of a volume with flaws in its text block. That is, it is usually not a word used to describe a damaged binding. (Though I have seen booksellers talk of a volume with some flaw in its binding as being imperfect.) The flaws can be missing or torn leaves or damaged or removed plates. Carter says that booksellers usually say "lacking" [or "wanting"] for missing blank leaves, half-title pages, slips showing errata, and other such pieces (see Carter, p. 145). As a guide to new booksellers, David Magee says about "flaws": "These are always 'natural.' Tears, holes, bites, thin spots, etc., found in any early printed books are, as it were, acts of God—never those of rats, mice, children or other desecrators of ancient tomes" (Magee, *The 2nd Course in Correct Cataloging, or Further Notes to The Neophyte*, pp. 10–11). Roger Gaskell says, "Strictly speaking a copy with worm-holes which damage even one letter is imperfect and so such defects should always be described" (Gaskell, "Terms of the Trade"). No matter what the problem is, no matter what is different from the volume the way it was issued or what was not there that was there when the item was issued, the mere absence of these things or alterations in any way that are different from the condition one finds in a PRISTINE copy make the item imperfect, and that will affect its price and desirability to the collector, bookseller, librarian, or scholar.

IMPERFECT LEAF. *See* Perfecting (in printing).

IMPERIAL PAPER COPY. A large copy of a volume. Labarre (*Dictionary and Encyclopaedia of Paper and Paper-Making*) says of "Imperial": "[A] large size of paper and boards, varying from 28" × 20½" (or 26" × 21") to 36" × 24"," and he identifies "Large Imperial," "Double Imperial," "Half Imperial," "Quad Imperial," and other such designations. The few people in the book world who now know the term may use it for its grand sound, but for the most part, all they mean when they say "an imperial paper copy" is "this is a large volume." The term is now obsolete, and not too many booksellers or collectors, librarians, or historians use it.

IMPOSING STONE. *See* Composing stone.

IMPOSITION (in printing). Placement of set type and other matter into the CHASE for printing. The type and all other materials set into the chase (e.g., FURNITURE, REGLETS, QUOINS, illustrative matter, etc.) compose the FORME. The *American Dictionary of Printing and Bookmaking* says, "The art of laying down pages so that when locked up and printed they will come in a regular consecutive order in the printed and folded sheet, with the appropriate margin" (p. 274).

This is a skill and an art, for a misimposed page will be printed either upside down or out of order. The former is easy to see; the latter may not be. For example, in the FIRST EDITION, first impression (*see* Edition, Impression [Printing], Issue, and State; Points) of Lawson's *Printing Types*, misimposition yielded a reversal of pages 60 and 61. Hence, it is essential that printers impose the type properly in the chase. To assist them, printers' manuals have imposition tables showing what pages are imposed in what order for various FORMATS. The manual will show the imposition for inner formes and outer formes. One format, for example, is OCTAVO IN HALF SHEETS, for which the printer must account for HALF-SHEET IMPOSITION. (See Gaskell, *New Introduction*, pp. 78–87.)

IMPRESSION. Carter gives four definitions for this term, which I have summarized here (with my own comments in [brackets]):

1. The printing of sheets during a PRESSRUN. [Definition added by Barker for the eighth edition. In effect, the term in this usage is synonymous with "printing"—as in the phrase "first edition, first printing"; *see* Edition, Impression (Printing), Issue, and State; Points. A related definition comes from the *American Dictionary of Printing and Bookmaking*: "The pressure applied to the form by means of a platen or cylinder to give a print from type or from a cut" (p. 285).]
2. A piece of paper containing the image printed—often a picture [though it could be a text as well]. Carter says that the *impression* will come from "a plate, stone or block" [but as I indicated, it could also come directly from type]. [Also Barker's addition and not too common. That is, who would ask a dealer for an "impression" when he means "a print"? Barker probably means that a printing of an illustration or a verbal text done as an INTAGLIO or from a PLANOGRAPHIC surface has the same status (i.e., is of the same ilk) as a sheet printed from type and thus should also be called an "impression."]
3. All of the copies of an edition that were printed in a single pressrun. [Thus, a bibliographer or publisher may say that the second impression consisted of 1,000 copies, or "early impressions had a Bewick cut on the half title; later impressions lacked this cut."] [*See* Edition, Impression (Printing), Issue, and State; Points. As noted in that entry, it is not always possible to determine what impression (within an edition) a text is. That is, the bibliographer may have to say, "priority of impressions is indeterminable."]
4. The quality of the image—whether the final image or text is printed with clarity and sharply or with signs of wear. [Thus, a descriptive bibliographer or bookseller may say that "the illustrations are excellent impressions," meaning that they are beautifully printed and implying that later *impressions* may lack the clarity and sharpness of the ones she is describing.] Also, Carter says that the term could also refer to the clarity of images impressed into covers. (See Carter, p. 146.)

IMPRIMATUR. "Official approval or license to print or publish, especially as granted by a censor or an ecclesiastical authority"—especially the Roman Catholic Church (*American Heritage Dictionary of the English Language*, p. 884). The word is from the Latin, meaning "let it be printed."

Britannica explains, "[I]n the Roman Catholic church, a permission, required by contemporary canon law and granted by a bishop, for the publication of any work on Scripture or, in general, any writing containing something of peculiar significance to religion, theology, or morality. Strictly speaking, the imprimatur is nothing more than the permission. But because its concession must be preceded by the favourable judgment of a censor (*nihil obstat*: 'nothing hinders [it from being printed]'), the term has come to imply ecclesiastical approval of the publication itself. Nevertheless, the imprimatur is not an episcopal endorsement of the content, nor is it a guarantee of doctrinal integrity. It does indicate that nothing offensive to faith or morals has been discovered in the work" (Britannica.com, Imprimatur). (*See Nihil obstat*; Privilege.) Though the original meaning of imprimatur had to do with permission, the word has taken on the meaning "sanction" or a more general "approval"; hence, the fact that a book is included in a published bibliography gives it the imprimatur of the compiler of that listing, despite the possibility that the item so included could be a royal dud.

One last point: If the imprimatur, as is sometimes the case, is printed on a separate LEAF of the volume, this is called the "license leaf." (*See* Privilege/Privilege leaf.)

IMPRINT. A statement in a volume or on any other printed matter that identifies the party or parties responsible for the item. The requisite information is usually the following: place of publication, name of the printer or publisher, and the date of publication. This information can appear on the TITLE PAGE or on its VERSO, though untold numbers of books lack some or all of these data. In early printed books, these data may appear in a COLOPHON, and many volumes had the information in both places. As Carter says, books printed early in the INCUNABULA period may lack all of this information. He adds that after that, until the end of the 16th century, information that one finds in an imprint may be found at the colophon. "Some of the earliest printed books bore no such note; but from about 1465 till late in the 16th century the printer's imprint was generally placed at the end of the book," and then, when title pages become standard features of printed books, the imprint information may be found on them (and possibly also at the end of the book) (Carter, p. 147). Thus, on a title page, one might find the name of the printer, the publisher, and the bookseller. And Carter explains that each of these pieces of information can be informative with respect to the making of the volume—who paid for it, who printed it, and who sold and distributed it (p. 147). The veracity of the information in an imprint must always be suspected, especially for works of a scurrilous nature (political, moral, sexual, or confrontational). As Barker added to Carter's entry, the word could also mean a volume, as in "The publisher released all 28 imprints of that author as a uniformly bound set."

In modern publishing, especially in some European countries, the imprint may be located at the end of the volume.

IN BOARDS. Said of a volume bound with wood or cardboard covers as opposed to a PAPERBACK. (Hence, sometimes called "HARDBACKS.") Roberts and Etherington, more specifically, say, "A term occasionally applied to an economical style of binding common in the 18th and early 19th centuries, consisting of pasteboards covered with paper, usually blue sides and a white spine" (p. 137). But today, when a bookseller says "in boards," the buyer knows it's a hardback book, regardless of what those boards are made of.

INCIPIT. "The opening words of a text, especially when used in place of a title to identify an otherwise untitled work" (*American Heritage Dictionary of the English Language*, p. 888). From the Latin *incipere*, "to begin." (*See* Explicit.) The word can also refer to the opening words to a part of a text, as with a new chapter or section. The incipit may contain an author's name or the work's title, and it can also refer to the initial letter (or letters) of a text, especially in a medieval manuscript when that MAJUSCULE is elaborately ornate.

INCUNABULA. (Sometimes referred to as "fifteeners"; i.e., from the 15th century.) Given here in the plural (the singular is "incunabulum"). Books or other matter printed in the West from MOVABLE TYPE in the 15th century—the so-called infancy of printing (hence the term, which means "swaddling clothes" or "cradles"). In their natural tendency to simplify the language (or possibly borrowing from the French equivalent of this word), booksellers—and hence others following their lead—have coined the word "incunable" (plural "incunables") for anything printed from movable type in the West before 1501. (Remember that 1500 is the last year of the 15th century.) Block books or engravings are not counted among incunabula since they are not printed from movable type. Some purists recoil at "incunable," but the term has been used so often by so many in the book world that it has now begun to inspire practically no opprobrium. And with the increasing familiarity of the word among the cognoscenti of the book world and even beyond, we now have experts in the field called "incunabulists." (Soon we will be seeing "incunabulophilia" and "incunabuloklept.")

There is no logical reason to have chosen 1500 as the last year of the incunabula period. It was merely a convenience. Books from that period cannot be distinguished from many thousands printed after 1500, but the fact that the cutoff date exists has created a class of (private and institutional) incunabula collectors. Also, the term "POST-INCUNABULA" was spawned by this craze, tacking on the notion of "incunabula" to works printed in 1501 and later. This latter term is not much in use today. The obsession for incunabula has led otherwise rational people to spend a good deal on a homely, shabby little volume printed in 1490 and spurn a lovely, elegant, fine copy of a book from 1502 selling for a fifth the price. *De gustibus. . . .*

No one can know how many titles (books, pamphlets, and ephemera of many kinds) were published during the incunabula period. Thanks to modern scholarship and the careful collecting and cataloging of the products of the press in the 15th century, we have more than 30,000 individual publications (some merely broadsides or short documents). The INCUNABULA SHORT TITLE CATALOGUE entry brings that number up: "The database records nearly every item printed from movable type before 1501, but not material printed entirely from woodblocks or engraved plates. 30,375 editions are listed as of March 2014" (see http://www.bl.uk/catalogues/istc [accessed 8 June 2021]). (See also the *Encyclopaedia Britannica* article at http://www.britannica.com/EBchecked/topic/284960/incunabula [accessed 8 June 2021].) One who studies these volumes is called an "incunabulist." There are many scholarly references to study on incunabula, possibly the chief of which is the *GESAMTKATALOG DER WIEGENDRUCKE*.

Two other terms employing the word are "Mexican incunabula," designating books printed in Mexico from 1539 to 1600, mostly religious and instructional works that Spanish missionaries printed for the native people, and "American incunabula," for books and other materials printed in what is now the United States, from 1639 to 1700. (Robert F. Roden uses the phrase in *The Cambridge Press, 1638–1692*, p. 18.) (For bibliographical information about printed items from this period, see the entries in the bibliography for Berkowitz, Copinger, Goff, Hain, Reichling, and Stillwell.)

INCUNABULA SHORT TITLE CATALOGUE (ISTC). A database hosted by the British Museum listing all known INCUNABULA. (*See also* Hain, Ludwig.) The ISTC website says, "The database records nearly every item printed from movable type before 1501, but not material printed entirely from woodblocks or engraved plates. 30,375 editions are listed as of March 2014, including some 17th-century items previously assigned incorrectly to the 15th century. Additions and amendments to ISTC are made frequently, and new information and comments and suggestions are always welcome. . . . Information on each item includes authors, short titles, the language of the text, printer, place and date of printing, and format. Locations for copies have been confirmed [in] libraries all over the world. Many links are provided to online digital facsimiles, and also to major online catalogues of incunabula such as the GESAMTKATALOG DER WIEGENDRUCKE[,] http://www.gesamtkatalogderwiegendrucke.de/GWEN.xhtml and the Bayerische Staatsbibliothek Inkunabelkatalog[,] http://inkunabeln.digitale-sammlungen.de" (http://www.bl.uk/catalogues/istc [accessed 8 June 2021]). (*See Short Title Catalogue*.)

INDENTATION. Space left at the beginning of a line of text. It is usually used to mark the beginning of a paragraph, though it has many other uses. In typing, we were taught to indent five spaces to delineate a new paragraph. The default on a computer yields approximately this much space, though it can be adjusted to the desire of the designer. In an enumerative BIBLIOGRAPHY it is a form of SPATIAL CODING. Inasmuch as an indentation is a marker of a new paragraph, those "in the know" about classical typography will usually not use that indent at the beginning of a text and the first paragraph after a section break, since it is clear that in those places a new paragraph is beginning.

INDEPENDENT ONLINE BOOKSELLERS ASSOCIATION (IOBA). As its name indicates, this is an organization of booksellers who are not affiliated with the formal associations of purveyors, like the ABAA or the smaller regional booksellers like SNEAB (Southern New England Antiquarian Booksellers). The organization was founded in 1999. It is possible that their members are as schooled and professional as one would expect from those in the more formal associations, but its own brochure incorrectly calls the group "the International Online Booksellers Association" (see its promotional pamphlet under IOBA in the bibliography), which does not bode well. However, I have used its site (http://www.ioba.org/pages/), which is easy to use, with good books, fine descriptions, and reasonable prices.

INDEX. *See* Fist.

INDEX. (Plural is indexes or indices.) An alphabetical (or sometimes chronological) list of something or several things in a volume: authors' names, titles, cities, dates, subjects, or something else of a special nature dictated by the text of the volume. The index is part of the book's ENDMATTER. In some instances, those putting the volume together may wish to create separate indices for various things. For instance, it might be useful to have one index for authors' names, another for titles, a third for illustrators, a fourth for translators, and so forth. As the following two entries indicate, an entire volume can be an index. (Footnote: After an emergency appendectomy I finally found time to create an index for one of my books. The long recovery gave me the time, so I asked the publisher if I could call it an appendix. They said no; it wound up as an index.)

INDEX LIBRORUM EXPURGATORUM (List of Expurgated Books). A list of books that needed amendments from the Catholic Church. This Index of Expurgated Books "was designed to allow books that were only partially objectionable to be circulated as soon as corrections by an ecclesiastical censor had been entered. Such Indexes listed the specific passages of books that required censorship in the expectation that all copies would be brought forward to the censor for physical correction. This correction usually took one of three forms: deletion of the text by applying ink over the printed passage, deletion of the text by gluing blank paper over the printed passage, or removal of the text by cutting the leaves containing the passage out of the book. In rare cases, the correct words were substituted in place of incorrect ones. Typically the censor would sign and date the book to certify that it had been expurgated correctly. Not all expurgated books were considered heretical. Many books of mainstream Catholic orthodoxy were expurgated simply because they contained errors" (White, *"Heresy and Error,"* p. 45). (*See* Bisquing; Caviar; Expurgated.)

INDEX LIBRORUM PROHIBITORUM (List of Prohibited Books). The *Index Librorum Prohibitorum*, a publication of the Catholic Church, listed texts thought to be heretical, anticlerical, or lascivious and thus proscribed by the church. The so-called Pauline Index of 1559 was disseminated by Pope Paul IV; Grendler says that that marked "the turning-point for the freedom of enquiry in the Catholic world"; under a year later it was replaced by the Tridentine Index (so called because it was authorized at the 1564 Council of Trent). Where the Pauline Index was never accepted by the church for its stringent views, the Tridentine Index was accepted (see Grendler, "Printing and Censorship," pp. 45–46).

"The 20th and final edition appeared in 1948, and the Index was formally abolished on 14 June 1966 by Pope Paul VI" (Jedin, Dolan, and Adriányi, *The Church in the Modern Age*, vol. 10, p. 168).

INDEX NOTCH. *See* Thumb index.

INDIA PAPER/INDIA PROOF PAPER. *See* China paper.

INEDITA. Literary material (or any written matter) that has not been published. The MANUSCRIPT papers of authors, for instance, or diaries, or business records of any kind, that may be found in special collections in libraries, are among several genres of inedita.

INFERIOR LETTERS; INFERIOR NUMERALS. *See* Subscripts.

INFERRED INFORMATION. A neologism (coined by the compiler of *The Dictionary of the Book*) for information not in a source but deduced from information that *is* in that source. The field of Historical BIBLIOGRAPHY takes scholars and booksellers outside the world of the book to discover needed information on a volume. In the Between the Covers online catalog 15 September 2020, the write-up of item #3 discusses a photographic postcard: "Real Photo Post Card of an Amateur Baseball Team likely from Bath, Pennsylvania. / Gelatin silver real photo post card. 5.5" × 3.5". . . . [C]ontemporary name of Ida A. Bensing on the verso. . . . Image of eleven men in full uniform and one man in street clothes, with bats and gloves. While the team is unidentified, the logo on the uniforms is of an Old English-style 'B' inside a diamond. It seems most likely that Ida A. Bensing (born c.1889) was a silk mill worker from Bath, Pennsylvania, in the Lehigh Valley, and it is likely the 'B' stands for Bath." This is a good example of research that reveals possible useful data. The information is inferred, and not provable. But many a bookseller does this kind of research to uncover data that could reveal the source of an item, explain something in the item, or make it increasingly salable.

INHABITED. *See* Historiated.

INHERENT VICE. The term used by conservators and others for any deleterious agent in any library materials. For example, there are the acids and lignin in wood-pulp-based paper. These substances, inherent in the paper, seriously damage the fibers of the sheet. (*See* Tanning; Wood pulp.) Sometimes the vice does its greatest depredations early on and then "eases up," as with the damage that acid does in paper. For instance, in the first few years of existence, the acid in NEWSPRINT will weaken the paper and turn it yellow. Fifty years and more along, the acid is still there and doing its evil thing, but not at such a pace. Some inherent vices can be neutralized or removed, as, for example, washing the acids out of a sheet of paper or introducing a neutralizing agent (like calciuim carbonate for paper), but the treatment generally cannot strengthen the substrate or reverse the damage.

IN-HOUSE EDITOR. *See* Reader, Press reader.

INITIAL. The first character of a text, a paragraph, or a word. Often, especially in ILLUMINATED MANUSCRIPTS, this first character was considerably larger than the handwriting of the text, and it could be decorated in many ways: with a color, fancy calligraphy, a picture, scrollwork, or other decorative elements. Such larger MAJUSCULES could also be printed—with varying sizes of characters at the opening of the text, the head of a chapter, the first paragraph of a section within the chapter, and so forth. Or the printer could leave a blank space for an artist to insert a decorative initial. Since the SCRIBE of the manuscript text would usually not be the artist who entered the decorated initial, a blank space would be left there for an artist to fill. In either case—manuscript or printed text—GUIDE LETTERS would often be inserted so the artist would know what letter to insert. (*See* Historiated.)

INK. The oil- or water-based liquid or paste used for writing or printing. Roberts and Etherington say, "A general descriptive term for a fluid or viscous material of various colors, but most often black or blue-black, that is composed essentially of a pigment or dye in a suitable vehicle and used for printing or writing" (p. 138). In Asia, where printing was invented, the inks were water based; in the West, they were usually oil based. Most printing inks, especially in the first few centuries of printing, were made basically of carbon (lampblack) and linseed (or some other) oil. Scientific examination of Gutenberg's inks showed that he incorporated various metals into his formula, and one batch of his ink can be distinguished from another by the type and quantity of metal used. (See Cahill, Kusko, and Schwab, "Analyses of Inks and Papers in Historical Documents through External Beam PIXE Techniques," and Schwab et al., "Cyclotron Analysis of the Ink in the 42-Line Bible." See also Bloy, *A History of Printing Ink, Balls and Rollers, 1440–1850.*) (*See* Iron-gall ink.)

INK BALLS (or "inking-balls"; and, in the proper context, they were simply called "balls"). "The earliest method whereby ink was applied to the forme was by the use of ink-balls. We may assume that the use of these implements dates from the inception of the press, as ink balls figure in a woodcut of a printing house of 1499" (Bloy, *A History of Printing Ink, Balls and Rollers, 1440–1850*, p. 53). Ink balls were made of untanned sheepskin stretched over some kind of batting (usually wool) and affixed to a wooden handle. They were used in pairs. The printer would pick up the ink on the balls from an INKING GLASS OR TABLE by rocking the balls over the inked surface, then rock the two balls' surfaces together to get the same amount of ink on each ball, then "beat the type"—that is, spread the ink onto the type by rolling the ink balls over it in a rocking motion. If the ink, during a PRESS-RUN, began to dry out, the ink would become tacky and could pull a SORT (a piece of type) out of the FORME. This would happen only if the type were not properly locked up in the CHASE. If the printer noticed this, he would replace the sort and tighten the QUOINS to make sure no other sorts were pulled out; and he would refresh his ink supply on the inking table. If he didn't notice it, the text would be printed with an error and would require an ERRATUM notice somewhere in the volume—if the printer eventually spotted this. The text would then exist in at least two states (*see* Edition, Impression [Printing], Issue, and State; Points), possibly three: the original impression, the impression lacking the character, and possibly the corrected text, which may be indistinguishable from the first. (See *American Dictionary of Printing and Bookmaking*, p. 35, under "Balls"; and Bloy, *A History of Printing Ink, Balls and Rollers, 1440–1850*, chap. 7, "Ink Balls, Rollers, Tables and Mechanical Inking Systems," pp. 53–65.)

Inkballs made by Richard Hicks.
Collection of the author.

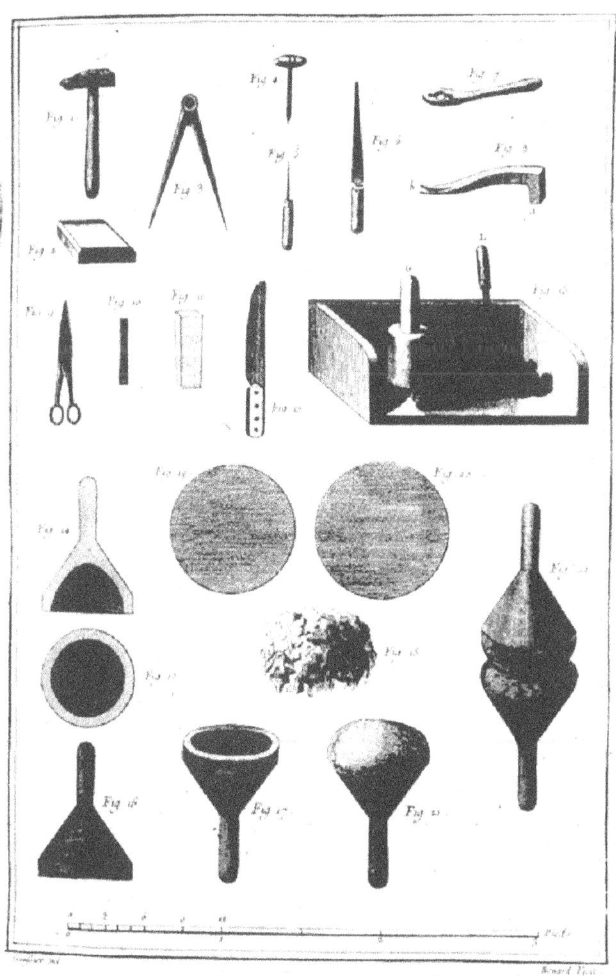

The plate showing the manufacture of ink balls.
From the Diderot *l'Encyclopédie*, vol. 6, plate 19.

INKING GLASS/INKING TABLE. A surface holding printing ink. This is a perfectly flat surface made of glass or stone, or possibly some other material. The printer rolls the INK BALLS or a ROLLER over this surface, picking up the ink, and then she distributes it to the type.

INLAID (BINDING)/INLAYS. Any substance (leather, cloth, paper, or other material) set into (below) another surface, as with leather inlays in a decorator binding. Roberts and Etherington say of an inlay, "A piece of leather, of the same thickness as the leather covering of a book, but usually of a contrasting color, grain, or both, cut to a desired shape for placing into the leather covering, from which a piece of the exact same size and shape has been removed. If the scheme of decoration calls for tooling over the area of the inlay, the leather for the inlay is cut on a bevel so that the grain surface is slightly larger than the flesh side, while the leather covering is cut in the opposite manner. If, however, the area of the inlay is not to be tooled, the inlay and leather covering are cut vertically. Inlaid bindings were produced in great numbers in the 17th and 18th centuries, especially in France" (p. 139).

Carter also recognizes another kind of "inlay" that was popular in the 19th century and practiced into the 20th. It entailed the practice of having a leaf or plate TIPPED ON to another larger one to give the smaller one wider margins, allowing it to be bound into a volume in such a way as to fit with the larger leaves of the volume. The smaller piece can be said to be "inlaid" onto a larger leaf. Carter says that a damaged leaf may have lost some of its margins, in which case a conservator could augment the leaf's original margins with new mending paper; this "re-margining" (as he calls it) may allow the repaired leaf to be said to be "inlaid." (See Carter, pp. 148–49.) This last use of the term is quite unusual (and is almost certainly no longer practiced) today. (*See also* Laid in; Onlay; Remargined.)

INLINE (sometimes hyphenated) (said of printing type) (also called "open face" or "outline"). A TYPEFACE with an open, unprinted area inside the printed surrounding lines for each sort. F. C. Avis says, "A type design into which a fine line appears to be engraved" (Avis, *Type Face Terminology*, p. 27). (*See* Decorative type.)

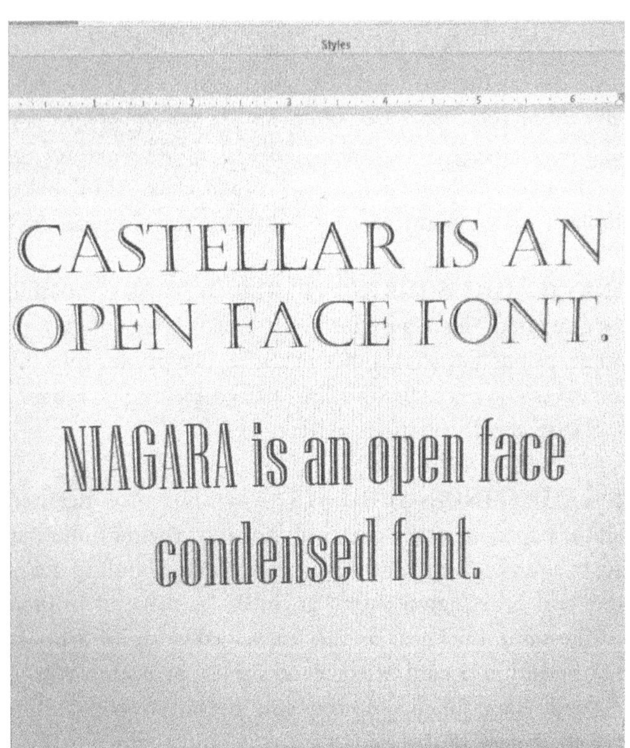

Two-line (open face) fonts: Castellar and Niagara.
Sidney E. Berger.

INNER FORME. *See* Forme.

IN PARTS. *See* Parts.

IN PRESS. *See* Forthcoming.

IN PRINT. Said of any printed item still available from its publisher. Presumably, any item still on the publisher's shelf is still in print, though from personal experience I can attest to the fact that some publishers do not want to be bothered by individual orders from private parties, so while they claim they still have copies of particular titles, they may not be willing to sell them. This makes the item OUT OF PRINT.

Also, the changes in tax laws in the United States created a disincentive for publishers to maintain stockpiles of books. The Internal Revenue Service would not allow publishers to "write down" or depreciate inventories to obtain tax deductions if they sold those books at market value. This loss of a tax benefit was a boon to the pulping industry, and also to the REMAINDER houses. The wholesale sale of these books put many a title into the "out of print" category.

BOOKSELLERS can tack the term "out of print" onto a description to make it seem that the item is no longer easy to acquire. But with ONLINE SALES, this ploy is difficult to pull off. Hence, "in print" does not mean that the item is available from the publisher, and "out of print" does not mean that the item is unavailable. (*See* Print on demand.)

IN QUIRES. *See* In sheets.

INSCRIBED COPY/INSCRIPTION. A copy of a book, PAMPHLET, illustration, photograph, or other kind of library material signed over to someone with an inscription—from one person to another. Although the term "inscribed copy" implies that the signature and note are those of the author, the inscription can indeed be from the author, or it can be from anyone giving the item to someone else. If from the author, it may be considered an ASSOCIATION COPY in that the author once held the piece. (*See also* Dedication/Dedication copy; Presentation copy; Signed copy.)

INSERTED. *See* Laid in.

INSERTED ENDLEAVES. "Additional ENDLEAVES that have been inserted into a binding after it [the binding] was completed. This may happen quite soon after the binding was finished or many years later at the request of an owner, either to supply new leaves where the originals have been lost or damaged or to add decorated paper to existing plain endleaves. Additional endleaves are most often attached by means of adhesive (tipped) and are therefore usually unsewn. It is however possible for inserted endleaves to have been sewn, especially when books have been repaired" (Ligatus. *Language of Bindings*. Ligatus Thesaurus, "Inserted endleaves"; https://www.ligatus.org.uk/lob/concept/2931 [accessed 25 March 2021]). Either way, such insertions are part of the binding of the volume and not part of its printing; so they should not be shown in the COLLATIONAL FORMULA (they should, however, be mentioned in the notes section) of a BIBLIOGRAPHICAL DESCRIPTION.

INSET. "1. A section placed within another section so that the subsequent sewing passes through the folds of both. The inset may be four pages only or multiples of four pages and may be placed in the center of the outer section, or on the outside, where it is wrapped around the main section. In rare cases it is sometimes located in some intermediate position. Insetting is of considerable importance as a method of incorporating PLATES into a section without resorting to TIPPING-IN. Where the plates are on the outside of the section they are sometimes referred to as 'outserts' or 'wrap arounds.' If the section to be insetted is required to complete the succession of pages, it is called an 'offcut.' 2. A small map, illustration, etc., set within the border of a larger one" (Roberts and Etherington, "inset"; https://cool.culturalheritage.org/don/dt/dt1868.html [accessed 19 February 2021]). In a folio of 4s, for instance, two CONJUGATE leaves are nested into two other conjugate leaves. The two nested leaves are "inset."

IN SHEETS. Said of a book or pamphlet that is unbound (and sometimes also unfolded). Often printers (especially in the world of FINE PRINTING) will issue some copies of a text in sheets, the idea being that the recipient can have her own binding put on it. (The older term "in quires" is no longer in vogue. It could have meant that the sheets had already been folded for the binder.) Bound copies will cost more than copies in sheets. If a full text is printed and folded but not bound, it is sometimes referred to as "in SIGNATURES." (See Roberts and Etherington, p. 140.) (*See* Cropped.)

INSIDE MARGIN. *See* Gutter.

INSIDE REAM. *See* Ream.

INSTRUCTOR'S EDITION. In educational publishing, students will purchase their textbooks in the form in which they were designed—with only the students in mind. The instructors will sometimes have a separate edition, designed for their use only, that will have additional matter: sample tests with all of the answers, lesson plans, questions for the instructor to ask the students, and so forth. It may even have a compact disk tipped in for the instuctor's use. The main part of the text will be the same edition as the one that the students have. (*See* Edition, Impression [Printing], Issue, and State; Points.) For the most part, textbooks are not particularly COLLECTIBLE. But a copy with the HOLOGRAPH notes of a famous person could be valuable, if not monetarily, then intellectually, depending on the nature of those notes.

INTAGLIO. One of the three basic printing processes. The process in which the text is printed from ink that has been squeezed into the grooves or dots below the surface of the printing medium, as with a copperplate or a woodblock. (The word, now English, is from the Italian, and it is pronounced without the "g": /in *tal* yo/.) The word also can be used to mean the item printed, as in, "This is an excellent intaglio, with fine lines and superb shading." (*See* Engraving.) The artist, using BURINS AND GRAVERS and other tools, incises grooves or creates dots indented beneath the printing surface. The "indentations" can also be made with acids, as in ETCHING. Ink is squeegeed over the surface and forced into the sunken areas of the plate. The plate is wiped off, removing the ink from the surface but not from the intaglio parts. Dampened paper is placed over the plate, backed with a blanket, and pressed such that the paper is forced below the surface to pick up the ink. (See Berger, "History of Three Basic Printing Processes.") (*See* Planographic printing; Relief printing.)

INTEGRAL. Integral leaves are those CONJUGATE with (joined to) others in a signature, as distinguished from leaves LAID IN. Also, BLANKS that are supplied by a binder and not part of the original printed signatures are not integral with the part of the volume that will be described in the COLLATIONAL FORMULA. Sometimes a leaf is printed and intended to be part of the full text of a volume but is INSET by the printer, or a printed advertising leaf is laid in; these two situations do not represent "integral leaves."

INTERLACE BINDINGS. *See* Strapwork.

INTERLEAVED. Said of a volume that has blank leaves bound in or inserted between printed ones. The interleaving could have been an intentional addition to a volume for allowing someone to take notes or to add TIP-INS, as with a scrapbook. (*See* Extra illustrated.) Or it could be the result of an owner's desire to create space for notes and other inclusions that the publisher did not account for. The AMERICAN ANTIQUARIAN SOCIETY (AAS), before computers were available, had some of its reference volumes DISBOUND and rebound with interleaving with BLANKS for the addition of notes about new acquisitions. Their copy of CHARLES EVANS's *American Bibliography* was disbound and rebound interleaved. Hundreds of new blank leaves were then annotated with acquisitions that the AAS made of items that were not listed in Evans.

INTERLINEAR. Between the lines. Anything that comes between the lines of type is said to be "interlinear." For example, there can be interlinear glosses, an interlinear transliteration, an interlinear translation, or interlinear SPACING. Generally, when text is printed between lines of type, the interposed text is set in a different (usually smaller) type.

ΚΑΤΑ ΙΩΑΝΗΝ

ACCORDING TO JOHN

1 Ἐν ἀρχῇ ἦν ὁ λόγος, καὶ ὁ λόγος
In beginning was the Word, and the Word
ἦν πρὸς τὸν θεόν, καὶ θεὸς ἦν ὁ λόγος.
was toward the God, and god was the Word.
2 Οὗτος ἦν ἐν ἀρχῇ πρὸς τὸν θεόν.
This (one) was in beginning toward the God.
3 πάντα δι' αὐτοῦ ἐγένετο, καὶ
All (things) through him came to be, and
χωρὶς αὐτοῦ ἐγένετο οὐδὲ ἕν.
apart from him came to be not-but one (thing).
ὃ γέγονεν 4 ἐν αὐτῷ ζωὴ ἦν, καὶ
Which has come to be in him life was, and
ἡ ζωὴ ἦν τὸ φῶς τῶν ἀνθρώπων· 5 καὶ
the life was the light of the men; and
τὸ φῶς ἐν τῇ σκοτίᾳ φαίνει, καὶ ἡ
the light in the darkness is shining, and the
σκοτία αὐτὸ οὐ κατέλαβεν.
darkness it not overpowered.
6 Ἐγένετο ἄνθρωπος ἀπεσταλμένος
Came to be man having been sent forth
παρὰ θεοῦ, ὄνομα αὐτῷ Ἰωάνης·
beside God, name to him John;
7 οὗτος ἦλθεν εἰς
this (one) came into
μαρτυρίαν, ἵνα μαρτυρήσῃ
witness, in order that he might witness
περὶ τοῦ φωτός, ἵνα πάντες
about the light, in order that all
πιστεύσωσιν δι' αὐτοῦ. 8 οὐκ ἦν
might believe through him. Not was
ἐκεῖνος τὸ φῶς, ἀλλ' ἵνα
that (one) the light, but in order that
μαρτυρήσῃ περὶ τοῦ φωτός.
he might witness about the light.
9 Ἦν τὸ φῶς τὸ ἀληθινὸν
Was the light the true
ὃ φωτίζει πάντα ἄνθρωπον
which is enlightening every man
ἐρχόμενον εἰς τὸν κόσμον. 10 ἐν
coming into the world. In

1 In [the] beginning
the Word was,
and the Word was
with God, and the
Word was a god.[a]
2 This one was in
[the] beginning with
God. 3 All things came
into existence through
him, and apart from
him not even one
thing came into existence.
What has come into
existence 4 by means
of him was life, and
the life was the light
of men. 5 And the
light is shining in
the darkness, but
the darkness has not
overpowered it.
6 There arose a man
that was sent forth
as a representative of
God: his name was
John.[b] 7 This [man]
came for a witness,
in order to bear witness
about the light,
that people of all sorts
might believe through
him. 8 He was not
that light, but he was
meant to bear witness
about that light.
9 The true light that
gives light to every
sort of man was
about to come into
the world.[c] 10 He

1[a] "A god." In contrast with "the God." See Appendix under John 1:1. 6[b] See Matthew 3:1, footnote[a]. 9[c] World=κόσμος (kos'mos), ℵBA; עולם (o·lahm'), J17,18.

417

Greek text printed with interlinear translation and with side notes.

Courtesy of Redeemer Theological Academy; http://www.redeemertheological academy.org/2013/05/29/ (accessed 10 August 2021).

INTERLINEAR SPACING. *See* Leading.

INTERMUSEUM CONSERVATION ASSOCIATION. *See* Regional Alliance for Preservation.

INTERNATIONAL ASSOCIATION OF PAPER HISTORIANS (IPH). As the name of the organization indicates, this is an association composed of members from all over the world who specialize in paper: its history, manufacture, collecting, decoration, and use. They have annual congresses at which dozens of experts speak on the work they are doing. The organization's website says, "The IPH integrates professionals of different branches and all friends of paper within the field of paper history. It coordinates all interests and activities in paper history as an international specialist association co-operating with international, regional and local organizations not only of paper historians but also of keepers of archives and libraries, conservators, arthistorians [*sic*], specialists in books, printing and technology, associations of the paper industry, the publishing trade etc., including handicraft and artistic activities in connection with paper. To reach these goals, IPH provides the necessary means. / The IPH brings together experts from the most varied of directions and the friends of paper around the topic of paper history. It coordinates all paper history interests and activities as an international, scientific specialist organization in cooperation with the relevant national and international professional associations not only of paper historians, but also of archivists, librarians, restorers, art, book and technology historians, the paper industry, the publishing industry, etc. Inclusion of the manual and artistic activities in connection with the material paper" (http://www.paperhistory.org/index.php [accessed 14 June 2021]).

INTERNATIONAL FEDERATION OF LIBRARY ASSOCIATIONS. *See* IFLA.

INTERNATIONAL LEAGUE OF ANTIQUARIAN BOOKSELLERS. *See* ILAB.

INTERNATIONAL ORGANISATION OF BOOK TOWNS. An organization of several towns in which the principal occupation of many of its businesses is selling books and purveying other services related to books. The organization's website says, "A book town is a small rural town or village in which second-hand and antiquarian bookshops are concentrated. Most Book Towns have developed in villages of historic interest or of scenic beauty. / The concept was initiated by Richard Booth of Hay-on-Wye in Wales. . . . / The book town offers an exemplary model of sustainable rural development and tourism. It is one of the most successful new tourism developments and it is being followed in many countries around the world. . . . / Members of the organisation may be associations, organisations, local governments, businesses or individuals in book towns" (http://www.booktown.net/). At the time of the writing of this entry, towns in the following countries were members: Australia, Belgium, Bulgaria, Croatia, Denmark, England, Finland, Germany, Italy, Malasia, Netherlands, New Zealand, Norway, Scotland, Sweden, and Switzerland. Interestingly, the original of these, in Hay-on-Wye in Wales, is not a member.

INTERNET (also called the "World Wide Web" or the "web"—and now so familiar that it is often not capitalized). (*See* Online book sales.) The entry in Barker's edition to Carter's *ABC* (p. 151 in the 9th ed.) speaks of the possibilities and problems of book sales and acquisition on the web. But for anyone in the book world, seeking out, buying, and selling are only a few aspects of the web's offerings. Equally important is the research possibilities that the Internet presents. There is hardly a topic under the broad rubric "Book" that is not covered on the web, and Internet searches for information have reached gargantuan levels. The Internet is now the number one go-to source for information for collectors and booksellers, librarians, archivists, and practitioners in the book arts. Barker decries the loss of booksellers' catalogs thanks to the web; but I see it differently: now the bookseller can put her catalog on the web with more photographs and more information than she could have fit into a paper catalog, and at a fraction of the cost. She can update the information in that catalog with a few keystrokes. She can remove from her catalogs items that have sold (or leave them up, so that we can still have the information she presented in the listings, and mark them "sold" so that we do not contact her with an order only to be disappointed). And rather than see a bookseller's catalog with a finite number of entries (10 or 50 or 500), we can see her entire stock. As television did not replace radio, the Internet will not replace booksellers' (or auction) catalogs. We can have both.

And as I hinted above, bibliographic information is researchable on the Internet, for it connects us to a huge number of dealer sites, academic libraries, WorldCat, individual scholars' papers, blogs, scholars, reference librarians, and many others.

INTERNET ARCHIVE. "[A] non-profit library of millions of free books, movies, software, music, websites, and more" (Internet Archive; https://archive.org/ [accessed 29 July 2021]). The website for this bibliographic utility has a masthead that says, "Search the history of over 591 billion web pages on the Internet." The Archive is the work of Brewster Kahle, who, in 1996, wanted to capture all knowledge in digital form and make it universally available. But as the entry at Universal bibliographic control says, this is obviously impossible. Nonetheless, the Internet Archive is digitizing hundreds of millions of books and pamphlets, much of which is no longer under copyright protection. To access it all, one merely needs to log in to its site, beginning with https://archive.org/?iax=newsletter052920%7ctxtlnk (accessed 29 July 2021), where there are links to American libraries, Canadian libraries, music, and a huge amount of other material that is available.

One key point is that this Archive has digitized many materials—ephemera, orphan films, periodicals, and much more—that are not owned or collected by libraries, materials that might otherwise have been lost. And they work with libraries to make their content freely available to anyone with access to the Internet.

As valuable and extensive as this endeavor is, it can never capture everything—or even a tiny percentage of everything. But it is one of the great information resources out there for people in the book world.

INTERROBANG (sometimes spelled interabang). A piece of punctuation that expresses a question asked in an exclamatory way, as in "What's going on here" or "You think I would do such a thing." Since the word conveys both emotional feelings (querelousness and insistence), the punctuation combines a question mark and an exclamation point. It looks like this: ? On many computers the mark is included under "special characters." In the past all we needed to do was print the two pieces of punctuation one after another ("He did that?!"), but someone decided to combine them into a single glyph. And we needed this?

IOBA. *See* Independent Online Booksellers Association.

IRON-GALL INK. "An ink produced by the reaction of tannic acid with an iron salt, such as ferrous sulfate (FeSO). The reaction produces no immediate change in the color of the solution, but, when the ink is applied to paper and is thus exposed to air, it darkens by oxidation, forming ferric tannate. The difficulty of writing with a colorless fluid was partially overcome by the addition of gum arabic to the solution, as well as some pre-exposure to air, so as to form of [*sic*] the ferric tannate before use. The gum arabic served to prevent the ferric tannate from settling out of solution. There were disadvantages to this procedure, such as the tendency of the ferric tannate to settle out despite the gum arabic, and the tendency of the ink to remain on the surface of the writing material instead of impregnating the fibers. . . . Iron-gall ink does have one serious disadvantage. Free acid is often present, which not only corrodes steel pens badly, but, far worse, attacks the paper, as well as certain of the dyes used to color them" (Roberts and Etherington, p. 141). Many a manuscript on paper is in poor condition due to these inks, which turn brown and, with age, eat into the substrate. This ink has been around since the 9th century (p. 141). It was used in Europe and America for many centuries though in diminishing amounts in the 20th century with the development of more affordable, higher-quality inks, and it is still used by artists who want to use traditional materials.

ISBD (International Standard Bibliographic Description). A set of rules produced by the International Federation of Library Associations (*see* IFLA) to create descriptions of bibliographic resources in any kind of catalog. Their "consolidated edition merges the texts of the seven specialized ISBDs (for books, maps, serials, sound recordings, computer files and other electronic resources, etc.) into a single text." (See www.ifla.org/publications/international-standard-bibliographic-description [accessed 8 June 2021].)

ISBN. The International Standard Book Number, a unique number assigned to a book or pamphlet or other published item, identifying it also by a bar code that accompanies the number. "In 1965, W. H. Smith (the largest single book retailer in Great Britain) announced its plans to move to a computerized warehouse in 1967 and wanted a standard numbering system for books it carried. They hired consultants to work on behalf of their interest, the British Publishers Association's Distribution and Methods Committee and other experts in the U.K. book trade. They devised the Standard Book Numbering (SBN) system in 1966 and it was implemented in 1967. / At the same time, the International Organization for Standardization (ISO) Technical Committee on Documentation (TC 46) set up a working party to investigate the possibility of adapting the British SBN for international use. A meeting was held in London in 1968 with representatives from Denmark, France, Germany, Eire, the Netherlands, Norway, the United Kingdom, the United States of America, and an observer from UNESCO. Other countries contributed written suggestions and expressions of interest. A report of the meeting was circulated to all ISO member countries. Comments on this report and subsequent proposals were considered at meetings of the working party held in Berlin and Stockholm in 1969. As a result of the thinking at all of these meetings, the International Standard Book Number (ISBN) was approved as an ISO standard in 1970, and became ISO 2108. / That original standard has been revised as book and book-like content appeared in new forms of media, but the basic structure of the ISBN as defined in that standard has not changed and is in use today in more than 150 countries. Today the ISBN Agencies around the world are administered by the International ISBN Agency, located in London, UK" ("ISBN History," ISBN.org by Bowker; http://www.isbn.org/ISBN_history [accessed 8 June 2021]).

The original configuration of 10 numbers (sometimes accompanied by a letter) was given to every edition, with separate numbers given to paperbacks and hardbound versions of the same work, and now also to digital versions of a text. "On January 1, 2007 the ISBN system switched to a 13-digit format. Now all ISBNs are 13-digits long" ("About the ISBN Standard," ISBN.org by Bowker; http://www.isbn.org/about_ISBN_standard [accessed 8 June 2021]).

In the United States, R. R. Bowker issues the ISBNs, representing all books submitted to them for such registration. But not all books get an ISBN, especially fine-press or privately published volumes. Every year in *Books in Print*, published by Bowker, there is a section of statistics, including the number of books published in the preceding year. Bowker can estimate the number (and they often give a quite specific [but not specifically accurate] figure) based on the number of ISBNs they have issued. But this number is always low because not all books get ISBNs.

ISSN. The International Standard Serial Number, a unique number assigned to serials throughout the world and run by the International Centre for the Registration of Serial Publications—CIEPS (Centre International d'Enregistrement des Publications en Série). The ISSN Network was established in 1975. "The ISSN International Centre was officially created in Paris in 1976, under the terms of an agreement signed between UNESCO and France, the host country of the International Centre" (http://www.issn.org/the-centre-and-the-network/our-mission/the-international-centre-for-the-registration-of-serial-publications-cieps [accessed 1 July 2021]). UNESCO is the custodian of the law and the decree that established the ISSN. Today there are 92 member countries, and the ISSN International Centre coordinates the activities of these countries. "An ISSN is an 8-digit code used to identify newspapers, journals, magazines and periodicals of all kinds and on all media—print and electronic" (http://www.issn.org/understanding-the-issn/what-is-an-issn [accessed 8 June 2021]).

ISSUE. *See* Edition, Impression (Printing), Issue, and State; Points.

ISSUE-MONGERS. On the term "issue-mongers," Carter has a long entry revealing his wit, his insight, and his ability to understand human psychology, particularly that of book collectors and others "devoted" to books. In effect, he says that the issue-monger is overly fastidious about the particulars of individual copies that have features that prove the volumes to be of an earlier (or later) issue (*see* Edition, Impression [Printing], Issue, and State; Points) than the issue of another copy.

Carter calls the issue-monger "one of the worst pests of the collecting world, and the more dangerous because many humble and well-intentioned collectors think him a hero to whom they should be grateful" (p. 153). This person could be anyone in the book world, and whoever he is, he can wreak havoc. Carter quotes Lathrop Harper in calling the issue-monger an advanced graduate of the "fly-spot school of bibliography," that is, a person who sees a fly spot on a printed page, sees it as a *POINT*, and claims that the copy he is observing is of a different STATE from others in the edition. These "bogus points" prove that the volume is a different issue from others, no matter how small or insignificant such a typographical (and not always typographical!) VARIANT might be. In the hands of an issue-monger, a typographical error or dropped page number will immediately be turned into an "issue-point." A change in the date of an advertising insert from one copy to another will yield a paragraph of "dubious inferences." Any variant, as in the wrapper of a proof copy, will make the issue-monger burst forth poetically that he has discovered a "'TRIAL ISSUE' or 'PRE-FIRST-EDITION'" (Carter, p. 153).

Carter says that such bibliographical minutiae influence the POINT-MANIACS and book collectors who will believe anything if the issue-mongers proclaim their findings loudly and authoritatively enough. Anything that proclaims "priority" and can make a collector's copy more desirable than that of another collector is welcome news. And though actual typographical variants do say something about the printing of a volume (and may well deserve to be recorded), not all of them are meaningful and merit being called markers of variant issues or states.

Barker concludes Carter's commentary by saying that today, issue-mongers are less common, self-assured, or persuasive than they were when Carter was writing, and he says that this is so because it is possible that those in the book world are more rational and levelheaded than were the collectors of Carter's day or that no books on the market today merit such treatment. (See Carter, p. 153.) (*See also* Point-maniac.) Barker's concluding paragraph offers those two reasons for the lesser number of point-maniacs than there were when Carter first wrote his definition for the 1952 first edition of his *ABC*. Another reason presents itself: that this newer generation of booksellers and collectors are less schooled in bibliography and the niceties of issues, points, states, and impressions, and they are not ready to be educated in such things. There are still highly educated booksellers, but perhaps they expect that their customers, as Barker suggests, would not care to know about all of the "issues" and the points that distinguish them.

One small concluding comment: TEXTUAL BIBLIOGRAPHERS sometimes cannot decide upon a particular reading when two or more present themselves at a point in a text. It is possible that an earlier issue (if it can be proved to *be* such an issue) contains a reading closer to the AUTHOR'S FINAL INTENTION than are the variants in later issues. If an earlier issue is identified, and it can be shown that its readings are closer to the author's preferred readings, the editor will know (not with complete, but with guarded, certainty) which variants to choose. So in rare cases, being an issue-monger can be productive.

ISTC. *See* Incunabula Short Title Catalogue.

ITAJIME. Folded and dyed papers. This method may be called "folded-and-dyed paper" in English, but the process, emanating from Japan, has become so well known in the English-speaking world, and under its Japanese name, that the preferred term for this process (and the papers produced with it) is "itajime." (A snippet of itajime paper is visible at the entry for "Die cut.")

A sheet of itajime paper. Berger-Cloonan Collection of Decorated Papers, Texas A&M University.

Courtesy of Cushing Library, Texas A&M University.

A sheet of orizomegami, a subset of itajime (folded-and-dyed) paper.

From Textile Studio, Singapore; http://www.maitextilestudio.com/orizomegami.html (accessed 4 June 2022); and https://en.pinkoi.com/store/maitextilestudio.

ITALICS. "A type inclined headwards slightly to the right (approx. 15°–17° from the perpendicular, after the first of such designs (Aldus Manutius, Venice, 1501)" (Avis, *Type Face Terminology*, p. 27). This definition is not perfect in that some italic typefaces were not merely roman types that were slanted over, and the degree of the slanting might be outside the numbers that Avis gives. Some italic types were designed to look like the cursive handwriting of scribes. Daniel Berkeley Updike explains, "Before 1500 Italy had no vernacular type simply because the current handwriting of Italy (which was not of the BLACK-LETTER school) was only translated into type-forms at the beginning of the sixteenth century. Italic was the Italian cursive vernacular type, and it ultimately drove out all other vernacular types wherever roman letters came into use" (Updike, *Printing Types*, vol. 1, p. 125). Updike makes it clear that "it was modelled so clearly on fifteenth century cursive hands" (p. 125). Thus, Avis's definition reflects the abilities of modern technology to be able to take a font of roman type and just "lean it over." The problem with this, of course, is that some romans do not translate well to italics by being skewed that way, and it is better, for many faces, to have new italics made for them, as matching italics, rather than merely skewing the roman. Centaur type, designed by BRUCE ROGERS in 1914, had no italic. Frederic Warde designed an italic to go with Centaur, which he called Arrighi (ca. 1925; see Lawson, *Anatomy of a Typeface*, pp. 92–94).

Times New Roman
italic type:
ABCDEFGHIJKLMN
OPQRSTUVWXYZ
1 2 3 4 5 6 7 8 9 0 &
abcdefghijklmn
opqrstuvwxyz

Alexander Lawson says, "To conserve space it appeared reasonable to use a type that was closer fitting than the roman, or upright, character. [Aldus's] punchcutter, Francesco Griffo, chose the informal cursive writing styles as a model, producing a font that was used by Aldus to print a small-format edition of Virgil in 1501. This was the first book to be set in an inclined letter, a style later given the name italic, from 'Italy,' its place of origin. This earliest italic differs from later models in the lack of the sloped form of capitals, roman being used in their place" (Lawson, *Anatomy of a Typeface*, p. 86). This use of roman capitals mixed with italic lowercase is reflected in the 20th century in the classical typography of such printers as HARRY DUNCAN and KIM MERKER, among others.

J

JACKET. *See* Dust jacket.

JACONET. *See* Mull.

JADE BOOKS. Volumes in which the text is incised onto panels of jade, with the incised areas GILT. The panels were either left in a stack or they were bound together into volumes. They were produced in the 17th and 18th centuries in China, and they have a Buddhist or secular text. These are exceptionally scarce and costly. (See Watson and Mish, *Chinese Jade Books in the Chester Beatty Library*.)

JANSENIST STYLE (in binding). Roberts and Etherington: "Originally, a French style of book decoration of the late 17th and early 18th centuries, named after the followers of Cornelius Jansen (1585–1638), the Bishop of Ypres, who advocated personal holiness and austerity. The books were embellished only by a centerpiece (often armorial) and corner fleurons, or by elaborate DOUBLURES tooled with DENTELLE borders but with no decoration at all on the spine and covers" (p. 143).

JANUS PRESS. *See* Van Vliet, Claire.

JAPANESE PAPER (in a sentence this is capitalized; *see* China paper). The Japanese are the most prolific and imaginative papermakers in history. They have made the widest range of papers—colors, textures, thicknesses, decorations, and inclusions—ever produced by a single culture. (The Germans are not far behind.) So to designate any paper "Japanese paper" really makes no sense because of its lack of specificity; the term can apply to thousands of kinds of paper, differing in manufacture, fibers, other materials, colors, decoration, thickness, and use. The term is useful in such phrases as "Japanese papers are made from three main fibers" or "There are so many kinds of Japanese papers that they are practically impossible to describe." On the other hand, like the term "rice paper" (a designation of a material that does not exist, except perhaps in the food industry [*see* Rice paper]), people have a general sense of what they mean, which is described in the entry on "Japan paper."

Since many Japanese papers are made from three basic fibers (MITSUMATA, KOZO, and GAMPI), and since these papers have a particular look and feel, many a writer will claim that such and such a book or BROADSIDE or map is made with "Japanese paper," when in fact the paper could be made in many other countries, either using the same fibers, or achieving the same look and feel as in papers from Japan.

As early as the 17th century, Japanese papers have been used in the West. "From at least 1647 onward, Rembrandt executed many of his prints on papers of oriental origin" (van Breda, "Rembrandt Etchings on Oriental Papers: Papers in the Collection of the National Gallery of Victoria.")

JAPANESE TISSUE. Very fine paper—usually from Japan but now made in Germany and other countries—used for conservation. Most of these tissues are made from KOZO, a long, strong, fine fiber that is flexible, white, and easily dyed. "It is a very versatile paper, and according to the thickness used, it can be employed for patching leaves, for overall lining of leaves as a reinforcement, for mending tears, for reinforcing the folds of sections, or for mending inner hinges" (Book Arts Web, "Glossary of Binding Terms"; http://www.philobiblon.com/gbwarticle/bindterm.htm [accessed 8 June 2021]).

JAPAN PAPER. A fine, strong, smooth, white paper made from KOZO; other, less strong but quite lovely, smooth paper is made from MITSUMATA, or GAMPI fibers (or a combination of these three—sometimes with other fibers added in), used for fine art. The last two are sometimes backed with cotton-fibered sheets to keep the mitsumata and gampi paper from shrinking. (More recently, wood-pulp-based paper can be used as a backing or the wood pulp added into the FURNISH in the making of the JAPANESE PAPER.)

Labarre says, "Japanese paper or tissue is a paper in varying substances of silky texture, hand-beaten from the bark fibres of the mulberry tree [KOZO] in Japan, or in imitation of it, used for artists' proofs of engravings, woodcuts, etc." (*Dictionary and Encyclopaedia of Paper and Paper-Making*, p. 139). The kozo fibers are long and strong, and if properly beaten, they produce a smooth, strong, thin paper. The fibers are so strong that even when they are made into paper of airy thinness, the sheets can be used for conservation as a cover sheet over thinning and deteriorated papers, the way SILKING was once done. Because of the smoothness of their surface and their strength, Japan papers are ideal for engravings or other prints TIPPED-ON to heavier paper for illustrated books. (*See* China paper; Rice paper.) It is worth reiterating that the "Asian" look that is distinctive of these papers will make people automatically call them "Japan(ese) papers," though they could well have been made in Korea, China, Germany, or other countries. Unless the one using the term is certain that they are Japanese, it is probably safer to say something like "Japanese-style paper," "Asian paper," or some other locution to show the uncertainness of the origin of the material.

JAPAN PAPER COMPANY (JPC). An important importer of Western and Asian papers for the use of artists, printers, publishers, and graphic designers. Founded in New York by Richard Tracy Stevens in 1901, the company began importing only Japanese papers, but they soon branched out into acquiring handmade, mold-made, and other high-quality papers from throughout Europe. To showcase their offerings, they produced a large number of beautiful, well-designed and -printed sample books that have become highly collectible. They commissioned some of the best designers and printers to produce many of these, and they advertised throughout the printing industry in the United States. Partly to reflect anti-Japanese sentiment in the United States and partly to show that their stock offered papers from a host of countries (not just Japan), they changed their name to Stevens-Nelson Company in 1938 or 1939 (one of their 1939 samples still uses Japan Paper Company), adding the name of George Nelson who had been their paper manager for 25 years by that time. In 1957, the company became Nelson-Whitehead and in 1962 Andrews/Nelson/Whitehead. The range of papers they offered from at least 15 countries was immense; some of those papers were commissioned by the JPC. Many thousands of books—especially of the FINE-PRESS kind—were printed or bound in papers from this company; and their papers saw a tremendous range of other uses: advertisements, PAMPHLETS, BROADSIDES, box liners, and others. (See Walsh, "The Japan Paper Company.")

JAPAN VELLUM (or Japanese vellum). A strong thick paper that looks like VELLUM, used in bookbinding. Roberts and Etherington say, "A thick paper produced in Japan from native fibers [usually KOZO] that are of relatively great length. The paper has a very cloudy formation and is tough and durable. The color is usually cream or natural, and the paper is finished with a smooth surface. Japanese vellum is suitable for ENGRAVINGS, etc., or where a very durable paper is required. An imitation, made by treating ordinary paper with sulfuric acid, is sometimes called 'Japon'" (p. 143). The paper is such a good imitation of vellum that, on a binding, it is hard to know whether one is looking at an animal skin or a piece of paper.

JENSON, NICOLAS (1420–1480). French printer and type designer. "[W]hen he was 38, Jenson worked as an engraver at one of France's mints. Charles VII sent him to Mainz to study the new art of movable-type printing, which was styled after the region's BLACKLETTER" (White, "Nicolas Jenson's Typographic Contributions"). "In 1468, Jenson moved to Venice, [where he] designed his own Venetian typeface" (White, "Nicolas Jenson's Typographic Contributions").

Jenson learned printing in Germany, and "[b]y 1468 he was established in Venice as a printer and by 1470 had printed his first book, Eusebius' *De Praeparatione Evangelica*, using a fine roman type clearly modeled on the elegant humanistic MANUSCRIPTS found in Venice at the time. Jenson's books were celebrated from the start. His typefaces were admired for their LEGIBILITY and elegance, and inspired subsequent generations of printers. . . . Jenson was the finest type designer of his day" (Mustain, *Monuments of Printing*, p. 24). Alex W. White says, "Jenson's type has been used continuously since its design in 1470: it has proven its worthiness through many interpretations. Some of Jenson's offspring are Golden (Morris, 1890), Kennerly (Goudy, 1911), Cloister Old Style (Benton, 1913), Centaur (Rogers, 1915), and Berkeley Oldstyle (Goudy, 1938)" (White, "Nicolas Jenson's Typographic Contributions"). (See Bullen, *Nicolas Jenson, Printer of Venice*; and Lowry, *Nicolas Jenson and the Rise of Venetian Publishing in Renaissance Europe.*)

JET (in type making). In casting type by hand (or in some machines), the type metal is injected or poured down the caster's funnel, filling the matrix at the bottom of the funnel, and forming the SORT but with more type metal than is needed for the sort. The remaining metal, attached to the base of the sort, is called the "jet." It must be broken off and where it was attached must be filed down, producing the FEET of the piece of type. The jet will be thrown back into the pot and melted to use in further casting. (For a depiction of a jet being created, *see* Mold [type casting].)

JEWELED BINDINGS. (Also called "treasure bindings.") Volumes bound in a sumptuous way, using jewels, pearls, ivory, gold or silver (or both), enamels, and other expensive materials. Often these were done with leather or velvet covers, and they had GILT EDGES, elegant DOUBLURES, bound-in silk BOOKMARKS, and other expensive touches. They are usually stored in protective cases or boxes. Such bindings adorned Medieval manuscripts, and they are still being produced. (*See* The Great Omar.)

JIGGS-AND-MAGGIE BOOKS. *See* Tijuana bibles.

JOBBING PRINTING. Work usually other than book printing, done for commercial purposes. The kinds of things a jobbing printer might do are business cards, signs, letterhead stationery, advertising pieces of various kinds, invitations and announcements, and other kinds of EPHEMERA. Sometimes the printing is done by a FINE PRESS, inasmuch as most such presses do not make much money and the income from jobbing can be useful to fund the more elegant items from the press. One might consider HENRY MORRIS's printing of *Tiller: A bimonthly devoted to the Arts and Crafts Movement* to be job printing. (The periodical lasted only 12 issues, vol. 1, nos. 1–6; and vol. 2, nos. 1–6. Morris's Bird & Bull Press printed the first 9 issues. The last 3 were done by the Stinehour Press.) Jobbing printing can produce important ephemera that winds up in private and institutional collections. And it could be done, as in this example, by a highly collected press. Such items can be found at antiquarian book fairs and in private collections.

JOB CASE. *See* Type case.

JOB FONT. "A small font of type used for display, distinct from a book FONT" (*American Dictionary of Printing and Bookmaking*, p. 308). When a printer orders a font of type, it comes with a preset distribution of characters—more *E*'s than any other letter since that is the most commonly used letter in English and with a proportionally smaller number of other characters depending on their statistical frequency of use. (The *American Dictionary of Printing and Bookmaking* has a chart showing the standard number of each character cast for each job font—as it was determined when that book was published in 1894. It does not give an equivalent chart for book fonts, though it does, in a sentence under "Job font," show [for a book font] the distribution of sorts from *Z* to *E*, the least to the most used characters in English; see p. 309.) Job fonts are usually used for advertising.

JOINTS. The junctures between the SPINE and COVERS of a CODEX on the outside of the volume. The inner junctures are HINGES. Carter's observation is worth noting: that the only time these parts of a book are mentioned in a description is when they are beginning to split (or when they have fully split), and the one doing the description has many adjectives to indicate how far gone they are: "STARTING," "RUBBED," "fragile," "weak," "split," and "WANTING." (See Carter, pp. 154–55.) (*See* Doublures; Rejointed.)

JO-JO BOOKS. *See* Tijuana bibles.

JOSS PAPERS. (Sometimes called "ghost money.") Chinese ceremonial papers, used by people to send goods and money (along with other good wishes) to departed ancestors—the method of sending was through burning the papers. These are printed on inexpensive paper (since they were to be burned), in one or more colors, often with bright gold or silver foil, and sometimes embossed or DIE-CUT. A piece of paper featuring a watch or stove, a house or clothing, when burned, would send these items to the ancestors. They are sometimes used in bookbindings, and collections of them wind up in libraries. (See Cave, *Chinese Ceremonial Papers*; Cave, *Chinese Paper Offerings*; Hunter, *Chinese Ceremonial Paper*; and Shucun, *Paper Joss*.)

JOURNEYMAN. In the world of printing, an itinerant printer who has finished serving his apprenticeship but is not yet a master. Apprenticeships last about six to eight years, after which the apprentice, no longer bound to a master, is released from that servitude and becomes a journeyman, implying that he is out on his own, journeying from one establishment to another, if he chooses, earning a living at the trade he learned as an apprentice. The ostensible aim of a journeyman—as the guild system directed—is to save up enough resources to start a shop of his own, becoming a master craftsman. The time for accomplishing this was anywhere from three to many years, depending on how successful and frugal the journeyman was. To become a master, however, meant submitting a body of his own work to the guild, to be voted on by the masters of the guild as to the worthiness of the candidate to become a master.

JUDGE A BOOK BY ITS COVER. How many times do we need to see this cliché? It's not cute anymore. I would have no qualms if I never saw it again.

JUMBO BOOKS. *See* Big Little Books.

JUSTIFICATION (in type casting). When a type caster strikes the PUNCH into the MATRIX, some of the metal of the matrix is displaced, leaving a bulge on the side of the matrix. The matrix, at this point in its creation, is called a STRIKE. The justification is done by filing down and removing the bulge. This is a delicate and precise skill, for the matrix must fit precisely in the right place in the MOLD so that the character is cast exactly where it needs to be on the SORT. A poorly justified matrix could result in a character that prints askew, too high, too low, or too far to the right or left. (For an image, *see* Punch [in type making].)

JUSTIFICATION (in typesetting) (also called "flush right"; *see* Letterspacing.). Justified text is text with all lines set to the same measure and the last printed character of all lines lining up at the right margin (or the left margin for languages that read right to left). This is easy to accomplish with a computer, but it was a test of the hand COMPOSITOR's skill to do this elegantly. Computers—or Linotype or Monotype machines—cannot "see the page" when the keyboarder hits the "justify" icon or instructs the machine to set the text flush right, so the result could be some lines with too much space between words, other lines with not enough. Also, automatic justification can result in the printing of RIVERS on the page. With Monotype, at least the printer had individual SORTS to reset, if needed, to eliminate these unsightly phenomena. But with the Linotype, resetting was often not possible, mostly because it would take time (which means it would cost money) and resetting would not guarantee the repair of the flaws. (*See* Unjustified.)

Flush left text is the norm for setting prose—that is, the first printed character in each of the lines of prose (except those indented for paragraphs or for EXTRACTS) is printed flush with the left margin.

JUVENILE PICTURE-BOOK BINDING. Roberts and Etherington say, "A style of binding in which the illustration of the book jacket is usually incorporated in the case and the book itself is given a sturdy binding suitable for use by children" (Roberts and Etherington, "juvenile picture-book binding"; https://cool.culturalheritage.org/don/dt/dt1937.html [accessed 30 May 2021]). The aim, of course, is to give the book the glitz that a colorful DUST JACKET offers without exposing that jacket to the depredations of juvenile hands and roughness. From the condition of most of these bindings, if they have survived at all, I would say that the publishers perhaps should have considered a steel binding. (I love exposing children to books and reading early in their lives—even at birth, as soon as they can focus their attention. But a gentle guide to how to handle books should be part of their education.)

JUVENILES/JUVENILIA. Books for children/books by children. As Carter points out, the more common term for "juveniles" is "children's books," though one still sees the word "juveniles" in booksellers' catalogs. The two terms are often used interchangeably, though the second ("juvenilia") can also (and properly does) mean the writing of children. Such writing can exhibit the authors' immaturity but also their enthusiasm and promise.

K

KARMETZ AND PERKINS BOOKS. *See* Big Little Books.

KATAZOME. The Japanese (and now an English) word for stencils used to decorate paper—as with those for producing CHIYOGAMI. The stencils are cut by hand, each one imparting a separate color to the sheet. A multi-color sheet of chiyogami may have as many as 30 colors, necessitating the cutting of that many stencils, and also necessitating a means of REGISTRATION to get the colors precisely placed on the sheet. The stencils themselves are made of WASHI (Japanese paper) that has been impregnated with persimmon juice to make the stencil waterproof. Small pinholes are placed on each katazome as registration guides. These stencils are common in the book world, for many books have been written about the technique of their use, sheets produced using them are used in bindings and slipcases (and for other things: CHEMISES, bookmarks, SOLANDER BOXES, LABELS, and so forth), and they themselves are collected as works of book-related art, since they are quite beautiful by themselves. The katazome were also used to decorate silks for kimonos and other textile applications. (See Berger, *Chiyogami Papers.*) And there is an active market for the collection of these items themselves.

KEEPSAKE. Any item retained for its memories. In the book world, this could include books, PAMPHLETS, or all kinds of EPHEMERA. A host of publications, usually in the 19th century, had that word in their titles. They were often well illustrated with sentimental images: flowers, trees, scenery, rural villages, and the like, along with religious topics. For this reason, they were popular GIFT BOOKS. There was John Keese's *The Floral Keepsake* (1850); Gilbert Thomas Burnet's *The Floral Keepsake: A Selection of Forty-eight Accurately Coloured Figures of Tender and Hardy Useful and Ornamental Plants* (1858); and the Rev. William Ellis's *The Christian Keepsake and Missionary Annual* (1837).

A second kind of keepsake is that handed out at an event, like a ceremonial dinner or the meeting of a book collectors' club, to commemorate the gathering of members. To encourage members to attend the club's events, the club solicits keepsakes to be created for each meeting. Only those in attendance receive copies of the keepsakes. These items, especially in areas with strong book arts communities, are often beautifully printed, LETTERPRESS, and are often on handmade or other high-quality paper, and done in LIMITED EDITIONS. They are sometimes illustrated and signed, and are true COLLECTORS' ITEMS.

KELMSCOTT PRESS. *See* Morris, William.

KER, NEIL RIPLEY (1908–1982). As with several other entries in the present volume, this one offers the reader an identification of a scholar whose work readers may find cited in a bibliography or BOOKSELLER'S CATALOG. Ker was a scholar of Anglo-Saxon texts. As a reader in PALEOGRAPHY at Oxford University and a fellow at Magdalen College in Oxford, he is famous for his *Catalogue of Manuscripts Containing Anglo-Saxon*, and for his *Medieval Libraries of Great Britain: A List of Surviving Books.* In my own career I was fortunate to have used his edition of *The Owl and the Nightingale: Reproduced in Facsimile from the Surviving Manuscripts, Jesus College Oxford 29 and British Museum Cotton Caligula A. ix.* His work on *Medieval Manuscripts in British Libraries* in five volumes (1969–1992) is still cited, though it has been superseded by online databases.

KERN/KERNED. A part of a character on a SORT that protrudes beyond the BODY of the sort. This is particularly common in ITALIC and SWASH types, where the "lean" of the character makes part of it reach beyond the body. (The most commonly kerned letter is probably the italic lowercase *F*, which in many fonts kerns at top and bottom.) If the kern reaches out to a neighboring character and would touch or even conflict with the space taken by any part of that neighboring character, the two would need to be recast on a single sort as a LIGATURE. This is particularly visible in the kerned version of the "Q," with its tail going beyond the body of the sort and pushing the "u" far away from the central part of the "Q." The two characters are often combined so that they wind up as a ligature (on a single sort).

The projection (the kern itself) is not backed by the body of the sort the character is on, so it is vulnerable to breaking. But the standard practice is to create all characters that would abut the kern with a SHOULDER the same height as the shoulder of the sort on which the kerned character sits; hence, the kern is backed by the shoulder of the neighboring sort, protecting it under the pressure of the press. In computer typesetting (and also in the initial designing of a type that was to be cast in metal), kerning (as a verb) is adjusting pairs of characters such that they appear to be equidistantly apart from one another as are other characters in the FONT.

The word can be a verb: to kern. This means to allow one character to be moved over in such a way that part of the printable surface lies over a neighboring piece of type. With metal type, for example, the two caps *A* and *V*, when printed side by side, would leave a fairly wide optical gap between them, so with metal type, the printer may kern them both a bit: shave off one side of each letter (the two sides that would abut) to bring the two close together and reduce the optical space between them. VANITY, printed with no proportional spacing (which brings the characters closer together) shows the problem. The distance between the *V* and the *A* is great; the distance between other pairs of letters is small. This word, printed in all caps, needs to be LETTERSPACED for consistency in spacing between each pair of letters. (For an illustration of kerning, *see* Raised initial.)

KETTLE STITCH. "The stitch made near the HEAD and TAIL of a book sewn on tapes or cords, and which holds the sections (other than the first and last) together. The term may be a corruption of 'catch-up stitch,' or 'Kettel stitch' (the stitch that forms a little chain). Sometimes called 'ketch stitch'" (Roberts and Etherington, "kettle stitch"; https://cool.culturalheritage.org/don/dt/dt1945.html [accessed 26 January 2021]).

KEY BOOKS. Carter's entry mentions this as a formal term that some like to use to indicate an essential book in a given field or on a given subject. Hence, one might say, "Labarre is a key book in the field of papermaking." Carter says that the term can be misused through ignorance or pretension but that anyone wanting to proclaim a title as being central to a collection on the subject might simply call it a "key book" and hope that others believe him. (See Carter, p. 155.)

KEY WORD IN CONTEXT CONCORDANCES. *See* Concordance.

KINKARAKAMI (also called "kinkarakawakami" or "imitation leather [wall]paper"). In the 17th century and after, many manor houses and public buildings had wall coverings of leather that were often elaborately carved, colored, and gilt. With the coming of the industrial revolution, acid rain attacked the leather, along with new methods of processing leather that left acids in it, often leaving it in crumbling condition and so deteriorated that it was unsightly and no longer served its original functions of being attractive and keeping the cold out. In the 19th century, the Japanese solved the problem of replacing the leather panels by producing a paper that looked and functioned like the original leather but was not subject to the same deterioration: kinkarakami (imitation leather paper). The craft was born during the Meiji era (1868–1912), but "it declined [at] about the start at the Showa era (1926–1989) and it became a lost craft" ("Kinkarakami," http://www5b.biglobe.ne.jp/~kinkara/english.html [accessed 9 June 2021]). It was revived by Takashi Ueda in Japan, and the paper is being made today. Paper sample books and sheets of the paper are available. (See Frazer, "Kinkarakami.") Since making kinkarakami is done completely by hand and since it takes great skill and a good deal of time to make a sheet, the papers are quite expensive, but they are beautiful and well worth the expense.

KNEE (in a composing stick). *See* Elbow.

KNOCKED DOWN. *See* Auctions.

KNOCKOUT. *See* Auction rings.

KOCH, RUDOLF (1876–1934). German type designer, artist, calligrapher, and book designer. Koch worked for the well-known foundry Klingspor, for whom he designed nearly 20 TYPEFACES, with Kabel and Neuland his most famous. Neuland was called "ugly" by some people, but it was popular and commercially successful. His much more readable Koch-Antiqua was "clean" enough to be made into a Linotype face. He was a strong proponent of the use of BLACKLETTER for reading matter, as is evident in his face called "Deutsche Schrift." Probably his best known book is his *Book of Signs*, showing nearly 500 old runes, symbols, and monograms. (See the bibliography.)

KOZO (papermaking). The most common fiber used in Japanese and Chinese papermaking. It comes from the plant *Broussonetia papyrifera* (the paper mulberry plant, in Hawaiian called *wauke*), and it is common anywhere that birds fly. It is the same fiber used for TAPA CLOTH. The plant's outer bark is stripped off, and the inner bark is peeled away, cleaned, hydrated, and then pounded or cut into pulp in a number of ways, such as using a stick on an anvil, a stamping-mill kind of contraption (*see* Stamping mill), or a NAGINATA BEATER. Once the fibers are to the length the papermaker wants, they are floated in a vat and formed into sheets. Kozo fibers are long and strong, and they make beautiful paper. The fibers are so strong that even quite thin kozo paper is used as CONSERVATION tissue to reinforce or repair damaged leaves. A seemingly endless number of kinds of kozo papers are produced in Japan, though for the last century or so, the fibers have sometimes been mixed with wood pulp fibers for economy. (*See* China paper. *See also* Gampi; Japanese tissue; Mitsumata.) (See Barrett, *Japanese Papermaking*; Neal, *In Gardens of Hawaii*.)

KRAFT PAPER. Coarse paper made of wood pulp. "It is a relatively coarse paper and is known especially for its strength. Kraft paper is usually manufactured on a FOURDRINIER machine and is generally given a regular machine finished or machine-glazed surface. It can be WATERMARKED, striped, or CALENDERED, and has an acceptable surface for printing. Its natural unbleached color is brown, but it can be produced in lighter shades of brown, cream tints, and white, by the use of semi-bleached or fully bleached sulfate pulps. Kraft paper is generally made in basis weights from 25 to 60 pounds (24 × 36) but it is also made in weights ranging from 18 to 200 pounds" (Roberts and Etherington, p. 147). Labarre points out that it was often made from ropes, and its name comes from the German word for "strength." He adds that it is made "from unbleached SULPHATE wood pulp by prolonged boiling under low pressure, thus preserving strength because the stock has received less drastic chemical treatment" (*Dictionary and Encyclopaedia of Paper and Paper-Making*, p. 140). "[I]n publisher's bindings [it is used] for lining the inside cover spine (spine strip) of a CASEBOUND book" (Book Arts Web, "Glossary of Binding Terms"; http://www.philobiblon.com/gbwarticle/bindterm.htm [accessed 9 June 2021]).

KRIMPEN, JAN VAN. *See under* van Krimpen, Jan.

KWIC (Key Word In Context) concordances. *See* Concordance.

L

LABELS. "A square, rectangular [or other-shaped] piece of leather, cloth, or paper, usually of a different color from that used for covering, and attached to the spine, or (occasionally) the upper cover of a book. Labels display, usually in gilt tooling or blocking, the title of the book, the volume number (if any), the author's name (sporadically before the late 18th century, but regularly since), and, since about 1800, the date of publication" (Roberts and Etherington, p. 148). On the spine of books, leather labels are called "letter pieces" or "lettering pieces." Carter mentions "bookbinders' labels" and "booksellers' labels," but the more common term in the trade is "BINDERS' TICKETS" and "sellers' tickets." (*See* Longitudinal labels.) Jacob Blanck mentions labels in his discussion of books in BOARDS: "Most frequently, books bound in paper-covered boards were issued with a printed label, or labels, which supplied the title and other pertinent information. These labels, though usually pasted to the spine, often occur on the side or sides" (Blanck, *Bibliography of American Literature*, vol. 1, p. xxx).

Blanck has insightful observations about the cover labels; for instance, they were often printed not by the printer of the volume, but by the binder. Also, variations in them can be observed. When the printer did the labels, he says, "Variations (frequent in labels) almost certainly do not indicate printings. [*See* Edition, Impression (Printing), Issue, and State; Points.] Labels were not always printed singly, but sometimes printed in sheets from duplicate or multiple settings and the printed result cut apart. In setting types for labels a printer out of SORTS would set from available types, thus producing variations. Lacking positive evidence no attempt should be made to establish a sequence on the basis of typographic variations or of spacing. The presence of a typographical error in a label is not necessarily proof of priority" (Blanck, *Bibliography of American Literature*, vol. 1, p. xxiv). Booksellers, for instance, want, of course, to be able to say that the copy they are trying to sell is a "first edition, first issue." And a collector is eager to get such a copy since it precedes other, later, copies, and thus is closer to the earliest version issued to the public. But such priority, Blanck warns, cannot be proven by the labels on the binding (unless there is some reason that such priority shown by the label can be proven).

LACED-IN (in binding). Said of a binding in which the TEXT BLOCK is attached to the boards by means of the tapes, cords, or thongs that were used in the binding of the leaves. Holes are punched or drilled into the BOARDS, and the tapes or cords used in the sewing of the text block are drawn through these holes, effectively uniting the leaves and the covers into a single solid binding structure. (For an image of a laced-in binding, *see* Coptic binding.)

LACE PAPER. Paper formed in such a way that the sheet looks like lace. This is a common form of Japanese paper decoration, manifesting in a host of beautiful patterns. The paper is made mostly of KOZO fibers, so it is soft and pliable—almost fabric-like. It is usually white, though it comes in many shades of colors. It is used in bindings, and for many other applications. Sample books of these papers are quite COLLECTIBLE.

LACQUERED BINDINGS. "A method of decorating bookbindings by means of scenes painted and then covered with lacquer. The technique was probably a Persian (Near Eastern) invention of the second quarter of the 16th century, and while they are still being produced today, the technique reached its pinnacle in the 16th century. Lacquered bindings are actually more the work of the miniature painter than the bookbinder. The designs were painted in watercolors on leather, and later pasteboard, that had been dusted with chalk and given a thin coat of clear lacquer. After painting had been completed several more coatings of lacquer were applied" (Roberts and Etherington, "lacquered bindings"; https://cool.culturalheritage.org/don/dt/dt1980.html [accessed February 25, 2021]).

LACUNA. (The plural is "lacunae" or "lacunas," but in the book world, the more sophisticated "lacunae" is preferred.) A lacuna is "an empty space or a missing part; a gap" (*American Heritage Dictionary*, p. 982). In the book world, it means a space left, usually in a manuscript but also in a printed volume, that is intended to be filled in with a letter or word. (*See* Guide letters.) A scribe may leave a lacuna at the beginning of a section of text for an illuminator to draw in a MAJUSCULE or picture. Peter Beal says that sometimes a scribe cannot decipher some word in the text he is copying from and may leave a lacuna. Or lacunae could be left if the scribe's EXEMPLAR itself has a blank space in the text or if that text is defective in some way. (See Beal, *A Dictionary of English Manuscript Terminology, 1450–2000*, p. 220.) A bookseller or bibliographer can also use the term to mean a missing LEAF or SIGNATURE in a volume.

LAID DOWN. Said of a print that has been backed by paper to strengthen it (see *American Dictionary of Printing*, p. 322). Also said of a part of a book's binding that has been removed in conservation, with a new SUBSTRATE replacing the old and the original cover pasted back down onto this new surface. A REBACKED volume may have its original spine cloth "laid down."

LAID IN. Inserted without adhesive or sewing. Anything that is loosely inserted into a volume—tickets, newspaper clippings, lottery coupons, and so on—is said to be laid in. This is opposed to something TIPPED IN (i.e., pasted in) or bound in (also termed "inserted"). Sometimes, laid-in items were part of the original volume's production, and their lack would reduce the value of the book to a collector—and will probably also reduce the amount of information the item has, so the missing "laid-in" piece could be quite a loss. Often items are laid in by the volume's owner who thinks the items enhance the volume, as with an invitation to a lecture on an author laid in to a copy of that author's book about which he was to speak at the lecture. Unfortunately, for whatever reason, millions of things are laid in to books that should not be there, such as newspaper clippings that are (or are not) germane to the topic of the book. Most newspapers for the past 125 years are on acidic paper, and the acid burn they leave on the LEAVES of a book can migrate to other leaves. Other common laid-in items are leaves, ferns, and flowers, which are also acidic and damaging. I am sure there is some bibliocurse for people who do such things. Laid-in items or leaves, then, are *inserted*, and this insertion may not have been done by the original maker of the book. On the other hand, many an inserted PROSPECTUS, laid in by the publisher, was not part of the book's printing and binding, but is clearly germane to the book, and its lack would be a mark against the volume if that prospectus was originally issued with the book. In the periodical *THE COLOPHON*, the publishers often laid in advertising pieces and newsletters when the volumes were originally sent out. Most copies lack these laid-in pieces.

LAID LINES. Areas in a sheet of LAID PAPER where the fibers are thin enough to let light shine through the sheet, the lines being formed by 1) the wires across the surface of the MOLD and the 2) CHAIN STITCHES that protrude above the wires where the supports in the mold are. Note that there are two kinds of laid lines: CHAIN LINES and WIRE LINES.

Laid lines were originally a by-product of handmade paper, made on a laid mold. The extra sumptuousness implied by a handmade product led paper manufacturers to create laid lines in machine-made paper, made possible when wove paper was invented in the 1750s. (*See* Baskerville, John. *See also* Antique laid paper; Dandy roll; Fourdrinier; Modern laid paper.)

One important note: I have seen many texts getting the definition of "laid lines" wrong—or at least used with less precision than many experts would like. Carter himself misused the term, and the later editors of his text did not correct his mistake. He equates laid lines with "wire lines." He says under "wire lines" that these are "called nowadays by paper experts *laid lines*" (p. 260). This is wrong: a true paper expert knows that laid lines are two things: wire lines and chain lines. At "laid paper" he comes closer to being correct: he says that there are close-set parallel wires in the mold which produce "wire (*or laid*) lines" (p. 156). "Wire lines"—yes; "laid lines"—no.

In Carter's day and beyond, this loose use of "laid lines" for "wire lines" was so common that to this day I hear people say, "this laid paper has chain lines and laid lines"—when many people would prefer "chain lines and wire lines." If the paper is "laid paper," that "laid-ness" is visible in the two kinds of lines one sees when the sheet is held up to the light: chain lines and wire lines. To say "chain lines and laid lines" is intuitively wrong, but there is a long history of that use, and when experts say it, the use (which gives me a headache) looks as if it is here to stay.

As of the writing of this entry in June 2021, I would like to add a note: At the congress held by the INTERNATIONAL ASSOCIATION OF PAPER HISTORIANS, several of the speakers—some of whom were not native English speakers—used "laid lines" when I contend they should have used the more precise "wire lines." One speaker actually said, "laid lines—I mean wire lines," correcting himself the way I believe he should have. In the name of precision, I advocate the use of "laid lines" to indicate the two kinds, chain lines and wire lines, and that those other two terms be used properly as I have indicated above. I may be fighting a losing battle on this.

LAID PAPER. Paper with CHAIN LINES and WIRE LINES at right angles to one another—visible when the sheet is backlighted. These lines are made by the wires running parallel to the long side of a rectangular sheet (these are wire lines) and chain stitches (raised above the wires) running at a 90-degree angle from the wire lines. The four pieces of wood that compose the PAPER MOLD are held in place and rigid with supports (or "ribs") running the short measure of the mold (and equally spaced apart); these supports are beneath the wires, which are stretched across the mold close together. The chain stitches, running above (and the full length of) each support, are raised enough that the fibers of the paper fall thinly on these stitches, and the paper is consequently thinner where the chain stitch is than it is elsewhere around the stitches.

It must be added that the supports in the hand mold could be anywhere from a short distance apart to a great deal of distance apart—as much as an inch and a half or more. There were no standards of paper-mold manufacture, and the mold makers could do what they pleased as far as spacing the supports. Thus, all paper made on a single mold would have the same (or almost exactly the same) distance between the supports (i.e., between the chain lines), but not all paper made at the same mill would have the same

Laid-paper mold showing the horizontal wires, wooden supports beneath the wires, and the chain stitches on top of the supports. Below the mold is the deckle.

Collection of the author.

A sheet of antique laid paper showing laid lines made up of (horizontal) wire lines, (vertical) chain lines, and shadows around the chain lines—indicating that the sheet was made on a mold with a single layer of wires. This sheet has a WATERMARK on the right and a COUNTERMARK on the left, showing that it was made at the Whatman mill in 1801. Modern laid paper has the laid lines but no shadows. Photograph by Jeff Dykes.

Collection of the author.

uniform spacing if the mill used more than one mold. Furthermore, a paper mold would usually be composed of two molds and one deckle. (*See* Mold [papermaking] [Western; Asian]; *see also* Laid lines; Wove paper.)

A final comment: Most definitions of "laid paper" begin with "handmade paper. . . ." But if we define "laid paper" as having this pattern of laid lines, then any such paper with those lines is laid paper. Since manufacturers for more than a century have been making machine-made paper with laid lines, *any* paper with laid lines is laid paper, not just handmade sheets.

LAKESIDE PRESS GIFT BOOKS. *See* Gift book.

LAMINATION. A one-time conservation treatment, no longer practiced because it usually is not reversible, and it often damaged the paper it was meant to protect. The technique involved fusing a sheet of paper between sheets of plastic, usually with adhesives and heat. Roberts and Etherington, writing in 1982, say about this treatment, "A method of protecting and preserving EMBRITTLED or otherwise weak papers, maps, etc., by placing them between sheets of thin, transparent thermoplastic material, which, when subjected to heat and pressure, with or without an adhesive, seals the paper in and protects it by making it more or less impervious to atmospheric conditions. It also increases its effective strength. / The paper is first deacidified and dried. It is then placed between two layers of cellulose acetate film approximately 0.001 inch thick. Layers of Japanese tissue or lens tissue are then placed over the film. The 'sandwich' is then fed through heated rollers under pressure, emerging as a sheet slightly thicker and heavier than the original document and considerably stiffer and stronger" (Roberts and Etherington, "lamination," https://cool.culturalheritage.org/don/dt/dt1991.html (accessed 4 June 2022). Today, the method has been recognized as a quite poor "conservation" or "preservation" technique, especially in that the so-called DEACIDIFICATION that they call for was not often successful and also that lamination is a permanent "sandwich." That is, once an item is laminated with the method they describe, it can never be unlaminated. If there were any INHERENT VICES that were in the original object at lamination, they were free to continue to damage the item. Further, lamination creates a micro-environment (the "package" is, after all, hermetically sealed); changes in temperature or humidity outside the package could cause a rise in humidity within (hence condensation), causing all kinds of problems. Lamination as a method of "conservation" has been fully superseded by ENCAPSULATION. (*See also* Delamination; Silking.)

Lamination can also be done on bindings. Paperback book covers are sometimes laminated at public libraries that wish to maintain the original covers. This is a more attractive binding than standard library bindings that use a plain cloth. The lamination preserves the cover art and printed information; the cloth covers, which are more expensive than lamination, dispose of these things. In the 1930s and later, some paperback publishers would issue their books with a laminated cover, the artwork on the cover "protected" beneath the lamination. Often these covers would delaminate, with the thin film peeling away from the stiff paper beneath.

LAMPBLACK. "Fine soot collected from incompletely burned carbonaceous materials" (*American Heritage Dictionary of the English Language*, p. 986). Lampblack is used as the basis for black ink and was often mixed with linseed oil to make the ink. "It may be prepared by burning organic matters rich in carbon with an imperfect supply of air and providing a means for collecting the dense smoke or coal produced" (*American Dictionary of Printing and Bookmaking*, p. 322).

LANDSCAPE FORMAT. (Sometimes called "horizontal format" or a book bound in this way might be called "oblong.") The configuration of a book or broadside such that, in normal use, it is wider than it is tall, as opposed to "PORTRAIT FORMAT." Strictly speaking, though this term is used frequently, the word "FORMAT" is not proper since, in bibliographical terms, this word has a particular meaning. More accurate would be the term "landscape ORIENTATION."

LANSTON, TOLBERT (1844–1913). Lanston Monotype Company. Inventor of the MONOTYPE MACHINE.

LARGE-PAPER COPY/LARGE-PAPER EDITION. A copy of a book printed on larger paper than the regular version is printed on. Sometimes the paper of a large-paper copy is of finer quality than that used for the other version. Dealers may use the term "large-paper edition," but this is a misnomer since all copies of a text printed from the same setting of type are of the same edition. (*See* Edition, Impression [Printing], Issue, and State; Points.) Publishers may wish to offer such limited-run copies as a way of increasing profits since collectors will pay a premium for a copy that is deluxe and in limited numbers—and the large-paper version certainly matches those criteria. But occasionally a copy of a book that never got properly trimmed at the bindery—perhaps a copy IN SHEETS—gets into the hands of a collector or bookseller who is tempted to call it a "large-paper copy" when it was never intended to be one. As Carter says, these special copies are produced "either for presentation, or for subscribers, or to be sold at a higher price" (p. 157). From an aesthetic perspective, I have often found that the large-paper version has poorly proportioned pages, with the printed TEXT BLOCK sitting in a sea of margins. This has not diminished collectors' coveting such versions, which is why they are created in the first place.

LARGE-PRINT BOOKS. As the name says, these are publications aimed at sight-impaired readers, printed with large-sized FONTS—at least 18-POINT type. Usually these publications are also larger than the normal-sized book, to accommodate the extra size of TYPE without having to increase the number of LEAVES in the volume.

LAW CALF. "1. A general term applied to an uncolored calfskin. 2. A cream-colored vegetable-tanned calfskin with a smooth grain surface, at one time used in covering the better grades of law books, but now largely superseded by BUCKRAM. Also called 'fair calf,' and, incorrectly, law sheep" (Roberts and Etherington, "law calf"; https://cool.culturalheritage.org/don/dt/dt2005.html [accessed 27 January 2021]).

LAYMAN. In making paper by hand, the team of workmen have specific tasks. The VATMAN dips the MOLD into the VAT and forms a sheet on the surface of the mold; the COUCHER transfers the newly formed sheet onto a FELT. Once a POST of sheets has been formed (made of newly couched sheets interleaved by felts), it is pressed to remove most of the water. "The third workman in the process of old papermaking was known as the 'layman,' and it was his duty to free each sheet of paper from the interleaving felts and to place the sheets in a neat and even pile, one upon another, on an inclined stool or bench" (Hunter, *Papermaking*, p. 185). Later, Dard Hunter gets more specific: the layman "separates the sheets of paper from the felts. This is done by taking each sheet by the two corners nearest to him and lifting the sheet so that it pulls away from the felt evenly and without strain. He places the sheets of paper in a pile, taking care that the four corners of each sheet fall directly over the corresponding corners of the sheet underneath" (p. 442). The post (with felts and sheets) is thus turned into a WHITE POST (i.e., the sheets with the felts removed), and it is then pressed a second time. If a sheet sits on top of another but not with the four corners perfectly superimposed, the edge of the top sheet will leave a crease in the sheet beneath it during the pressing. Thus, the layman must be precise in his placement of the sheets.

LAY OF THE CASE. *See* Type case.

LAYOUT. The general disposition of printed and illustrative matter on a page, with relation to such things as margins, RUNNING HEADS, page numbers, footnotes or SIDE NOTES, SIGNATURES, and anything else that might appear on a page. Some pages had main text in one typeface placed in a particular position on the page, notes (perhaps in a smaller typeface), and a commentary in another typeface or type size—all needing to be laid out so that the different parts of the text stood apart distinctly from one another. Layout can be quite complicated and requires a good sense of legibility and user-friendliness. The term can be expanded to mean the plan for the entire volume, the order of materials in the text, and so on.

For medieval manuscripts, a good literature exists on the way the text has been integrated with ILLUMINATIONS of various kinds. Page layout often resulted in what was called the 2-3-4-5 (or 2-3-4-6) margin, with the inner margins 2 units, the top margins 3 units, the margins at the FORE-EDGE 4 units, and 5 or 6 units at the foot of the leaves. Innumerable medieval manuscripts had these proportions for their written texts. How this was achieved was lost for centuries until Jan Tschichold re-exposed it in the 1940s, following the work of J. A. van de Graaf, Dutch book design historian and the originator of the Van de Graaf canon (Tschichold cites Joh. A. van de Graaf, *Nieuwe Berekening voor ve vormgeving* [A New Way to Compute Form], in Tété [Amsterdam (1946)]: 95–100). His long experimentation showed that these proportions were achieved by ruler alone (not the kind that measures, just the kind that draws in rule [i.e., straight lines]), as shown in the illustration.

This layout leaves room for the book to be held at the foot and outer margins, for notes, for illuminations, and for some trimming by a binder. Printers from the 15th century

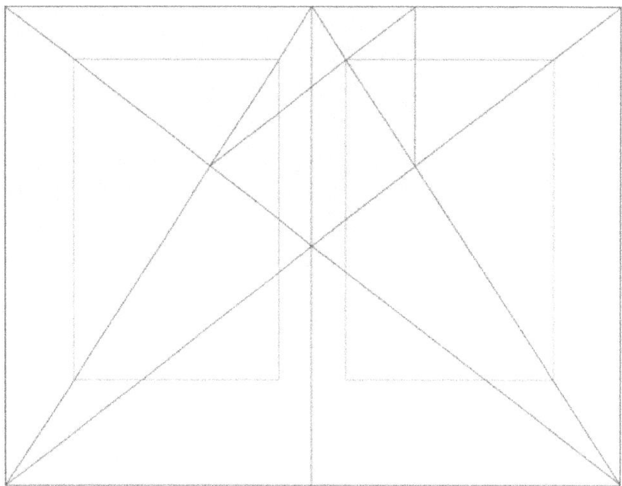

The "2-3-4-5" (or "2-3-4-6") layout, commonly used in medieval manuscripts. See Tschichold, *The Form of the Book*, p. 47.
Drawing by the author

on seemed to have lost this method and came up with other ways to lay out their pages. (See Biggs, *Basic Typography*. See also Wikipedia, "Canons of Page Construction"; http://en.wikipedia.org/wiki/Canons_of_page_construction [accessed 9 June 2021].) (*See* Orientation.)

LCSH. *See* Library of Congress Subject Headings.

LEADING (interlinear spacing) (rhymes with "wedding"). Strips of metal used to separate lines of type from one another. (*See* Leads.) The word can also mean the act of placing these strips between lines of type. In the world of computers, the act of separating out lines on a computer screen is still called "leading," with most people no more aware of the word's origins than they are when they say the phone is "off the hook." If the "leading" is done with thin strips of paper or cardboard, it is called "carding."

LEAD POINT RULING. Ruling (i.e., drawing the lines) in a manuscript to guide the scribe and artist(s), using a piece of lead. Lead can be used as a writing material and was such before graphite replaced it in pencils. (*See* Hard point ruling; Red ruling; Rule [in manuscripts and in printing].) A lead point was also called a "plummet."

LEADS (in printing) (rhymes with "weds"). Thin strips of metal usually made from the same material as type is composed of, used for various purposes in printing but usually used between lines of set type to add spacing between the lines (called "LEADING" [rhymes with "bedding"] or "interlinear spacing"). Leads come in 1-point, 2-point, and 3-point thicknesses; 6-point strips are called "SLUGS." In some cases, leading turns stories into novels and makes publishing profitable. Vladimir Nabokov died in 1977. To capitalize on his popularity, his family (specifically his son Dmitri) resurrected a long story that his father had written and then buried in a chest; Dmitri translated it into English and published it in 1986 as a novel. It could have been printed on about 35 pages, but it was stretched into novel status by virtue of taking up 127 numbered pages in a hardbound volume; it reached this many pages by being printed with 6-point leading and extra-wide margins, having the printed text for each new chapter begin in the bottom half of the page, and with the text pagination beginning on page 21. This was turning lead into gold.

LEAF. Carter calls a leaf the "basic bibliographical unit" (p. 158). The leaf is the sheet that contains a front and a back (a RECTO and a VERSO). An older term for a leaf and still used occasionally by modern printers, bibliographers, or bookbinders is "FOLIO," so one may encounter a statement such as "water stains on ll. 7–12" ("ll." is the abbreviation for "leaves"; "l" is the singular) or "one-inch tear in ff. 10–15" ("ff." is the abbreviation for "folios"; "f." is the singular). Carter rails against the inaccurate and careless use of the word "page" when "leaf" is intended, as in "the half-title page is WANTING" (when what is meant is that the *leaf* with the half title is wanting). And Carter also reminds us that the leaf is part of the larger sheet of which it is only one part. The tendency that Carter complained of is still to be encountered: people (even seasoned collectors and highly professional and knowledgeable booksellers) say things such as "The fourth page is torn." Shame on them.

LEAF BOOKS. Books containing a leaf or leaves from other books. The "other books" are often scarce and COLLECTIBLE, and the act of breaking them up to put their parts into other books is seen by some as unethical or even criminal. (*See* Breaker; Ege, Otto.) Perhaps the most famous of all leaf books is that published by bookseller Gabriel Wells, with A. E. Newton's introduction, *A Noble Fragment.* It allowed hundreds of buyers (academic and private) the thrill of owning a leaf from the first book printed from movable type in the West (the Gutenberg Bible), but it was a shame to break up the original volume; "it was missing 50 of its 643 leaves and some of those that remained had their illuminations cut out," but even a book in such "poor" condition has bibliographical evidence in it that is lost when the leaves are dispersed. (See De Hamel and Silver, *Disbound and Dispersed.*) (*See* Disbound; Fragmentology.)

LEAFCASTING. (Sometimes spelled as two words.) An old and now abandoned method of adding to a sheet of paper to extend its margins or to mend a hole in the middle of the LEAF. In the leafcaster (the machine in which this is done), paper pulp is created and used to fill the LACUNA in the leaf, while that leaf sits on a mesh. The paper fibers are pulled through the mesh with a vacuum pump or they settle onto the mesh with gravity. (See Futernick, "Leaf Casting on the Suction Table.") (*See* Remargined.) Included here in case one comes across a reference to it and wants to know what it means.

LEAFLET. A single sheet of paper folded once or twice (possibly more), usually printed on, and used for advertisements, menus, handbills, or flyers. A leaflet is not sewn, but it could be stapled.

LEATHER (in binding). "The outer covering from an animal (usually a mammal) tanned, or otherwise dressed and prepared in such a manner as to render it usable and resistant to putrefaction, even when wet. Leather is a unique and flexible sheet material that is somewhat analogous to textiles, and may in fact be considered to be the first and only *natural* fabric" (Roberts and Etherington, p. 152; this long entry [pp. 152–54] is worth consulting for its depth of coverage and its application to books and bookbinding). The skin can be of any animal, usually a mammal, though skins from fish, amphibians, and reptiles have also been used for binding. The most common leathers used for bookbinding are sheep (and lambs), cows (and calves), and goats, though a large number of other animal skins have been used. (Mel Kavin [1916–2006], of Kater-Crafts Bookbinders in Pico Rivera, California, had a wall of books [hundreds of them] bound from the skins of dozens of different animals.) One of the problems with leather is that if it is not prepared properly or if it is stored in an atmosphere that is too moist, the leather can deteriorate and wreak havoc on the volume it covers and smudge those it touches. (*See* Red rot.) Along with VELLUM, and PAPER, leather was the most common binding material until the commercial use of cloth from about 1830 on, at which time the use of leather declined steadily.

LEATHERETTE. Fake leather, made from plastics or plastic-coated cloth (though some are rubber-based), that look somewhat like leather, and is used as a substitute. For about two centuries such material has been in the wheelhouse of manufacturers, inventors, bookbinders, and shoemakers—and auto-upholstery makers. Some are remarkably leather-like; others are poor substitutes. (*See* Faux; and see Kanigel, *Faux Real: Genuine Leather and 200 Years of Inspired Fakes.*) Many readers may remember the buzz that Corfam caused when it was first announced as a substitute for leather (the rollout was in 1963; see Kanigel, p. 116), when it promised to replace leather as a shoe material. It had its drawbacks, as do all such fakes. "Leatherette" was a brand name for a product made by Harrington & Co., but "[t]oday, 'leatherette' can mean about any leatherlike material you like—vinyl, maybe, or coated paper, or coated fabric. . . . [and] thanks to that dismissive suffix *-ette* [we know] that it's not the real thing" (Kanigel, p. 25). Other "leatherettes" were Lorica, Ultrasuede, and Vinyl, all of which can be used for bookbinding. I have seen books bound in Ultrasuede.

LEDGIT. "A slip of paper or parchment projecting from the edge of a leaf in a book, upon which notes or memoranda may be written" (Wordnik, "ledgit"; https://www.wordnik.com/words/ledgit [accessed 26 May 2021]). These can be found attached to the leaves of medieval manuscripts, sometimes being a means to helping the reader find a particular place in the text, but also carrying notes commenting on the text or identifying a particular subject.

LEGIBILITY. The condition of being able to be read with minimal impediment. A broad literature exists on legibility (see Berger, *The Design of Bibliographies*, pp. 22–26). It is measured (with some level of accuracy and the hope that the features that are measured are accurate for such measurement) by means of speed of reading and retention. (See Luckiesh and Moss, *The Science of Seeing*, and Tinker, *Bases for Effective Reading* and *Legibility of Print*.) Many things affect legibility, including typeface (serif or sans serif, size of the type, and particular typeface); whether the type is printed in italics or boldface, in all caps, in all lowercase, or a combination of these; color of paper; texture and thickness of paper (sometimes allowing SHOW-THROUGH from the other side of the leaf); color of ink; line length; size and shape of margins; placement of headlines and page numbers; ambient lighting; angle of reading (whether the text being read is on a monitor—requiring a fairly steady positioning of the head—or on paper); LEADING (interlinear spacing); word spacing; page size and volume size; lengths of paragraphs; and more.

Book collectors who actually read their books might want to consider the legibility of the items they purchase. The comfort and pleasure of reading a well-designed book contrasts with the discomfort of having to cope with poorly designed text.

LENDING LIBRARIES. *See* Circulating libraries.

LEPORELLO. *See* Concertina fold.

LETTER. *See* Letters/Letterforms.

LETTERED DIRECT. A term generally used to describe bindings: when any kind of printing is done directly onto the substrate (the material of the binding, as with cloth or leather), and not onto a label which is pasted onto that substrate, it is said to be lettered direct: "Title lettered direct onto SPINE."

LETTERING. "The process of marking a binding with author, title, or other distinguishing bibliographical information, and, in a loose sense, with accompanying ornamentation, e.g., lines, library imprints, etc. The lettering of handbound books is usually done either with individual letters (as in the best work), or with type set in a pallet. It is also done at times with straight lines or gouges. . . . Edition and library bindings are usually blocked (stamped), either in an automatic or hand-blocking machine" (Roberts and Etherington, "lettering"; https://cool.culturalheritage.org/don/dt/dt2051.html [accessed 20 July 2021]). (*See* Blocking/Blocking press.)

LETTERING PIECES. *See* Labels.

LETTERLOCKING. "The technology of folding & securing an epistolary writing substrate to function as its own envelope" (Dambrogio, Smith, and Massachusetts Institute of Technology [M.I.T], "Letterlocking: Unlocking History"; http://letterlocking.org/about [accessed 22 May 2021]). This is a fairly new discipline, with a new designation of what it is—and a term that will probably have its permanent place in the collecting world once the concept described here is familiar to the book world. Letterlocking has been practiced for centuries, especially before the introduction of commercially made envelopes. Correspondence needed to be sealed in some way. Wax seals and glue, of course, have existed for centuries, but they were not necessary since the letters could be folded in such a way as to close them with parts of the sheets attaching to or folding or sliding into other parts of the sheets—either into other folds or into slits. And even with letterlocked documents, the texts can be read without scholars' having to open them, as Jana Dambrogio et al. explain (see "Unlocking History through Automated Virtual Unfolding of Sealed Documents Imaged by X-ray Microtomography"). (See Cain, "Before Envelopes, People Protected Messages with Letterlocking," Atlas Obscura, 9 November 2018; https://www.atlasobscura.com/articles/what-did-people-do-before-envelopes-letterlocking [accessed 22 May 2021].)

Abigail Cain says, "The practice of letterlocking in the Western world is roughly bookended by the spread of flexible, foldable paper in the 13th century and the invention of the mass-produced envelope in the 19th century. But it also fits into a 10,000-year history of document security—one that begins with clay tablets in Mesopotamia and extends all the way to today's passwords and two-step authentication" (Cain, "Before Envelopes, People Protected Messages With Letterlocking").

Collectors, booksellers, archivists, and librarians (primary acquirers of such documents) should be aware of the many methods that writers used, often not easily noticed if they are dealing with any document that was once folded and is now offered and stored opened and flat. The presence of small slits or holes, and the visible fold lines are what to look for. The fold lines are often on the outside of the folded document, so they might have faded or become stained in some way, leaving discolored lines in what looks like a geometric pattern on the leaf.

LETTER PIECES. *See* Labels.

LETTERPRESS. A term designating a method of printing from a RELIEF surface. "This card was printed letterpress" usually implies that the card was printed from metal type, but with newer technology it could also mean that it was printed from a PHOTOPOLYMER plate. Purists would insist that photopolymer is faux letterpress, but it *is* a relief process, and it leaves the same kind of impression in the printed surface as is left by metal type. "Letterpress" also implies the use of handwork and can often justify an enhanced price. Carter also says that the word "letterpress" is casually used to refer more to verbal text than to images in a book (p. 160), but this usage is not seen on the American side of the Atlantic.

LETTERS/LETTERFORMS. Under the heading "Letter," Carter says that up to the end of the 18th century, the word "letter" was used to mean a piece of printing type. So one might say, "The letters are in the type case." He adds that all of the types in a complete set constituted a FONT (usually spelled with the *u* in Great Britain). In Carter's day, maybe his use of this terminology was correct. Today we would not call a single piece of type a "letter"; it is a piece of type or a SORT (this latter word has been around for at least a quarter of a millennium). Nor would we say that "a complete set of multiple types was a fount" (Carter, p. 159); we would say that a complete set of sorts constituted a font. To repeat: Today, and also following historical models, we do not use the word "letter" to indicate a sort. A letter is a letter (*A*, *B*, or *C*), a piece of type is a sort, and we can use both of these terms ("piece of type" or "sort") to refer to this object. As just noted, in American English we use the spelling "font," but "fount" is also seen in the United States to designate the full set of characters that constitute a TYPEFACE, though the latter is "Chiefly British" (*American Heritage Dictionary of the English Language*, p. 693). It may be useful to know how the terms were once used historically if we are reading an old manual about printing or type manufacture. (There is no entry in Carter's volume for "sorts.") The obvious reason that "sort" is preferable is that a sort does not have to be a letter—it could be a number, a piece of punctuation, a FLEURON, or some special character created by a printer. "Letterforms" refers to the shape of individual letters (and may even refer to non-letter characters, like numbers and punctuation—and this segues to a complex discussion (beyond the purview of this volume) of type classification. (One excellent treatment of this can be found in Lawson, *Printing Types*, chap. 3, pp. 31–119.) The "formes" affect LEGIBILITY.

LETTERSPACING. The use of THINS to equalize the spaces between letters in a word, usually done with UPPERCASE letters. LOWERCASE letters are designed to sit beside one another with an equal amount of visual space between them when they are set. But uppercase letters are not designed to be read as a text, so when they are juxtaposed, the spaces between them will vary, as with the nearly touching "HI" or the optically wide apart "VA." (In computer printing—with proportional spacing—the V and the A will be printed fairly closely together [as you see here], but in metal type they will be far apart optically. *See* Kern.) If a COMPOSITOR is setting a line in all capitals using metal type, as with a headline or on a title page, she must letterspace the SORTS so that they look equidistant from one another. (*See* Justification [in typesetting].)

LEVANT (GOATSKIN used in binding). Roberts and Etherington say, "a leather having a characteristic drawn-grain pattern, originally produced by an astringent tannage, but now produced by hand or machine BOARDING of vegetable or semichrome tanned goatskins and sheepskins, or vegetable tanned sealskin. The traditional 'levant' used in bookbinding is a vegetable tanned goatskin. When the pattern is produced by embossing, as it frequently is, it is called 'levant grain.' The original levant, which during the past one hundred years or so was considered to be the finest of the MOROCCO family, was always goatskin obtained from the Near East. In recent years, however, the best levant has been tanned in the northern and northwestern areas of Africa and usually finished in France. Today the great bulk of genuine 'levant' goatskin comes from South Africa and is called 'cape levant'" (p. 157). The skin usually appears brightly polished, and for this reason a bookseller in a catalog may call any grained and polished leather "levant" when it might just as well be calf.

LIANHUANHUA. A tremendously popular and numerous form of Chinese book, small enough to put into one's pocket, and aimed mostly at middle- and lower-income readers and the young. "Lianhuanhua, literally 'serial pictures', means 'little character's book'; it was a major traditional Chinese art form, developed at the beginning of the twentieth century in Shanghai. Lianhuanhua is described as palm-size in a three by five inch picture book with sequential illustrated stories. The introduction of western [*sic*] printing technology and Japanese manga in the late nineteenth century, reveal [*sic*] that Lianhuanhua is similar to the comic-strip stylebooks of Western cartoons, comics, graphic novel and Japanese MANGA. . . . Although Western cartoons or comics and Japanese manga inspire the form of Lianhuanhua, it has . . . its own unique artistic style which uses a traditional Chinese line drawing technique. Chinese line drawing, also called 'Gong-bi', uses precisely detailed ink strokes in progressively thinner lines to depict the narrative figures" (Wu, "The Memory of Lianhuanhua"). R. Orion Martin calls them "Chinese Pulp Comics," and he says, "In 1985, there were 8.1 billion pulp comics (lianhuanhua) printed in mainland China. Most lianhuanhua were black and white paperbacks with a single illustration and a few lines of text on each page. They looked similar to the BIG LITTLE BOOKS published in the United States from the 1930s to 1950s, but they were published in quantities that make the US comics market look tiny" (Martin, "Lianhuanhua: Chinese Pulp Comics").

LIBER AMICORUM. *See* Album amicorum.

LIBER MEMORIALIS. *See* Liber Vitae.

LIBER VITAE (or Book of Life). (Also called a "confraternity book" and a "liber memorialis.") "The purpose of a 'Book of Life' (or 'Liber Vitae'), [*sic*] was to record the names of members and friends of monasteries or convents: the belief was that these names would also appear in the heavenly book opened on the Day of Judgement. Some lists from religious houses are neat and well-ordered, but [a] page—from the Liber Vitae of the New Minster, Winchester—has a distinctly cluttered appearance, with several different inks and scripts" (see British Library, "New Minster Liber vitae"). Michelle P. Brown says that the liber vitae is a "book listing the *familiares* ('members') and benefactors of a monastic community who were to be remembered in its masses and in other services and prayers. . . . Those listed were sometimes depicted in the manuscript" in which the names appeared (Brown, *Understanding Illuminated Manuscripts*, pp. 79–80).

LIBRARIES. *Webster's Third New International Dictionary of the English Language, Unabridged*, famous for its all-inclusive definitions, says of "library," "a room, a section or series of sections of a building, or a building itself given over to books, manuscripts, musical scores, or other literary and sometimes artistic materials (as paintings or musical recordings) usu. kept in some convenient order for use but not for sale" (p. 1304). But, of course, this definition is incomplete by leaps and bounds since what libraries collect and what they do cannot be captured in a single statement. In the book world, they are the source of huge amounts of information for collectors and booksellers, librarians, scholars, and anyone else moved to use their resources. The word also means a collection of books, as in that assembled by a private collector: "I have all of Dard Hunter's books in my library." A bookseller, on the other hand, would say "in my stock" or "in my inventory."

LIBRARY BINDING. A binding put onto a book by a bindery at the behest of a library—usually replacing the publisher's original binding—with the aim of giving the volume a covering with more strength and longevity than what the publisher's cover offered. Unfortunately, despite the longevity of the library binding, the original artwork and information from the first binding are lost. From a rare-books perspective, the loss of evidence is significant since DUST JACKETS, SLIPCASES, and covers are discarded in rebinding. Even though library binding is for general collections, any book can become rare, and its original binding carries information that could someday be valuable. Even the size of the original volume could be compromised if the binder trims the book down to fit new library binding BOARDS. However, this battle was lost long ago, and it has become standard practice in many libraries to have their own bindings placed on volumes when the original one is no longer "doing its job."

In the United States, the phrase "library binding" conjures up a monochrome, polished-BUCKRAM-covered volume, often bound with a tight spine so that the book is difficult to open. (*See* Library edition.) In a dealer's catalog, "ex lib." is often the kiss of death for a collector. Serious collectors do not want their books in library bindings. For the past, say, 20 years, some vendors that supply books to libraries are instructed by their clients to put a library binding on any paperback book when the hardbound version costs significantly more than the paperback. For example, if a title comes out in a $15 paperback version and a $35 version in boards, it is cheaper to put a $10 library binding on the paperback than to buy the hardbound copy.

LIBRARY CODES. When the LIBRARY OF CONGRESS (LC) decided to create a NATIONAL UNION CATALOGUE (NUC) for American library holdings, it solicited millions of images made from card catalog cards, copied onto large pages. It was not enough to indicate that such and such a volume existed—with all of its revealed bibliographical information; the LC wanted to help users of this massive database to locate copies. Every library contributing to this effort was thus given its own code letters, and those were appended to the cards that were photographed for the published volumes. Since these coded notes helped users of the volumes to locate copies, they are sometimes called "location symbols," the term that JACOB BLANCK used for entries in his *Bibliography of American Literature*. Blanck came up with his own codes for his bibliographical entries since his first volume was published in 1955—before the NUC volumes began to emerge. The Library of Congress used a fairly simple system: the codes consisted of (usually) three letters, the first designating the state in which the library resides, the second the name of the city, and the third the name of the library. Hence, Massachusetts, Worcester, American, yields MWA for the AMERICAN ANTIQUARIAN SOCIETY. Additional letters were necessary to distinguish libraries from other states beginning with *M* and for other libraries when there was a second, third, or subsequent library that would have generated the same combination of letters for its code. The codes were adopted by the Online Computer Library Center (OCLC) for its MARC records, and there is an online database to help scholars expand the abbreviated codes they see in such bibliographic records. (*See MARC Code List for Organizations*). Of course, the list of abbreviations also is printed in the first volume of the 754-volume set of NUC, just in case you have a copy of the set lying around in reach and you need to decipher the code.

LIBRARY EDITION. The creation of library editions is rare today, but Carter's definition is amusing and worth referring to. He calls a library edition a collected set of volumes printed in type big enough to be read comfortably, and he says that they were produced for gentlemen, noting that large-type volumes and gentlemen are pretty much obsolete (p. 161). Worth noting is that Carter's entry in 1952 spoke only of the collection and the size of the type (p. 114 of the first edition), and Barker added the last comment (about obsolescence) in his seventh edition. When Barker added to the definition for the 2004 edition, I am sure booksellers did label such volumes "library edition." But as early as the 1990s, Peter Briscoe of the University of California, Riverside, pioneered a new kind of packaging: he contracted with a distributor that sold books to the library to set up a bindery of their own, with the idea that all books that came out in paperback they would rebind in hardcover LIBRARY BINDINGS. (Though the practice is now almost obsolete, it is mentioned here to explain the existence of ex lib. copies in the world with such bindings. They did not come from the publishers, and booksellers and collectors may not be able to account for their existence without this knowledge.) The cost of turning a paperback into a hardbound book was far less than was the cost of the hardbound version, so the library saved money, and the vendor made another sale (or thousands of them) by providing this service. The technology to make this accommodation (with inexpensive and fairly durable binding materials and long-lasting, flexible adhesives) did not exist in Carter's day. Thus, the term "library edition" has taken on a new meaning since Carter wrote his definition in 1952. Barker, living in Great Britain, may not have known about this practice when he rewrote Carter's entry. Strictly speaking, this new binding should not be termed an "edition" since the text in a volume so designated would be the same EDITION as that of the regular version—both being printed from the same setting of TYPE.

LIBRARY OF CONGRESS. "The Library of Congress is the nation's oldest federal cultural institution and serves as the research arm of Congress. It is also the largest library in the world, with millions of books, recordings, photographs, maps and manuscripts in its collections. / The Library's mission is to support the Congress in fulfilling its constitutional duties and to further the progress of knowledge and creativity for the benefit of the American people" (Library of Congress website, http://www.loc.gov/about [accessed 9 June 2021]). This site adds, "An agency of the legislative branch of the U.S. government, the Library of Congress encompasses several integral service and support units," including units that deal with Congressional Research Services, copyright, the Law Library, Library Services, the Office of Strategic Initiatives, and much more. The LIBRARY OF CONGRESS CLASSIFICATION was developed here in the 19th century, and the library is a repository of untold numbers of books and manuscripts, PAMPHLETS, photographs, and an enormous number of other kinds of research materials.

LIBRARY OF CONGRESS CLASSIFICATION. "The Library of Congress Classification (LCC) is a classification system that was first developed in the late nineteenth and early twentieth centuries to organize and arrange the book collections of the Library of Congress. Over the course of the twentieth century, the system was adopted for use by other libraries as well, especially large academic libraries in the United States. It is currently one of the most widely used library classification systems in the world. The Library's Policy and Standards Division maintains and develops the system, posting lists of updates. / The system divides all knowledge into twenty-one basic classes, each identified by a single letter of the alphabet. Most of these alphabetical classes are further divided into more specific subclasses, identified by two-letter, or occasionally three-letter, combinations" (http://www.loc.gov/catdir/cpso/lcc.html [accessed 9 June 2021]). (*See* Dewey Classification.)

LIBRARY OF CONGRESS PRESERVATION DIRECTORATE. *See* Regional Alliance for Preservation.

LIBRARY OF CONGRESS SUBJECT HEADINGS (LCSH). "Library of Congress Subject Headings (LCSH) has been actively maintained since 1898 to catalog materials held at the Library of Congress. By virtue of cooperative cataloging other libraries around the United States also use LCSH to provide subject access to their collections. In addition LCSH is used internationally, often in translation. LCSH in this service includes all Library of Congress Subject Headings, free-floating subdivisions (topical and form), Genre/Form headings, Children's (AC) headings, . . . for which authority records have been created. The content includes a few name headings (personal and corporate), such as William Shakespeare, Jesus Christ, and Harvard University, and geographic headings that are added to LCSH as they are needed to establish subdivisions, provide a pattern for subdivision practice, or provide reference structure for other terms. This content is expanded beyond the print issue of LCSH (the 'red books') with inclusion of validation strings" (Library of Congress, "Subject Headings"; http://id.loc.gov/authorities/subjects.html [accessed 9 June 2021]).

LIBRARY STAMP. A stamp of any kind on any kind of library material that identifies the library that owned the item at the moment the stamping was done. The practice has raised hackles in the bookselling community because to vendors such stamps are equivalent to defacements, usually lowering the value of an item. On the other hand, the stamp of someone important, prominent, famous, or COLLECTIBLE may enhance the value by proving the sterling quality of the item's PROVENANCE. (*See* Bookplate.)

In the rare-book world, a small but important literature exists on marking books for security purposes. A book with a library stamp—especially an indelible one—is hard to sell, so the stamp discourages theft. The practice of marking books stems from libraries' long-sought desire to discourage theft. The argument that rare-book librarians put forth is that once an item enters a library, its monetary value is immaterial; its only value is intellectual: What research can the item support, and what information does the item have that scholars might need? Lowering the item's monetary value through a library stamp is not an issue. The only thing the processor must be wary about is that the stamping should be done in such a way that it does not cover up or conceal any information.

A related practice is to put a library stamp onto every PRINT, map, or illustration in a volume (or in the collection since not all prints or maps are in volumes)—again, not in any place that would obscure part of the image. Some booksellers are known to be purveyors of prints, and they can receive a supply of them from people who have surreptitiously taken them from library books. But if a print has a library stamp on it, a dealer may think twice about acquiring it (or offering it for sale). Stamps on prints and maps should be placed in the middle of the back of the image so that they cannot be trimmed off (as would be possible if the stamps were in the margins). An unscrupulous dealer may still acquire such stamped images, then mat and frame them such that the back cannot be seen without having the item taken out of its frame. Collectors and booksellers should inspect the backs of all such pieces before they acquire them. Buying stolen prints encourages their continued theft.

LIBRICIDE. *See* Biblioclasm.

LICENSE. *See* Imprimatur; Permission; Permissions.

LICENSE LEAF. *See* Imprimatur.

LIFT-THE-FLAP BOOK. *See* Flap book.

LIGATURE. In printing type, a ligature is the joining of two or more characters on a single SORT. In the Latin alphabet, because of the way characters sit on their bodies (*see* Body), the most common ligatures are "fi," "ffi," "ff," "fl," "ffl," upper- and lowercase "æ" and "œ," and a few others, especially in SWASH forms and in ITALIC typefaces. If there is a KERN on a sort, the type designer may create a ligature for it, as with the uppercase *Q* and the lowercase *u*. The ampersand is also the result of a ligature, where the two letters of the Latin *et*

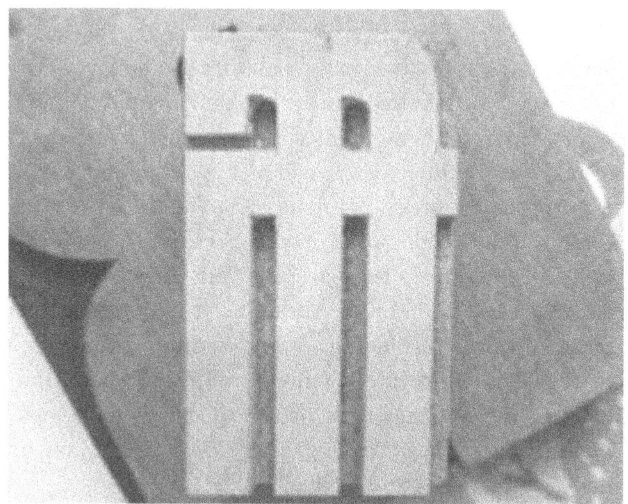

An "ffi" ligature in wood type.

Etsy; https://www.etsy.com/listing/197848743/letterpress-wood-type-printers-block-ffi?ref=market (accessed 9 June 2021).

are joined (for an illustration, *see* Ampersand) to form the character that we call "ampersand." In early printing—even through the 20th century—two particular ligatures were used for elegance: the "ct" and the "st" combinations.

LIGATUS RESEARCH CENTRE. A research unit (at University of the Arts in London) "in which the study of the history of bookbinding and the conservation of books is combined with research into modern digital data analysis and collection management tools. This is the first time that bookbinding and book conservation have been made the focus of a research unit and the first time also, therefore, that it has been combined with advanced data analysis. It is intended that Ligatus will provide a central resource for these two subjects and enhance their practice through the use of current digital technologies" (see their website at http://www.ligatus.org.uk/node/2 [accessed 9 June 2021]). Their aims are the following: "To produce internationally recognised research in the field of book history and conservation. / To produce a digital resource directly relevant to the history of bookbinding and conservation. . . . / [and] To develop these resources and expand research possibilities in the field of the history of bookbinding, book conservation and digital data structuring for the humanities within the wider academic world."

The website for the organization, in 2021 merely called "Ligatus," has links to its many activities, including the one most germane to the present volume: its "Language of Bindings" list (https://www.ligatus.org.uk/node/712 [all links accessed 25 March 2021]), searchable at "Language of Bindings Thesaurus (LoB) . . . a thesaurus of bookbinding terms for book structures dating from the ninth to the nineteenth century" (https://www.ligatus.org.uk/lob/). All terms are searchable by alphabet (https://www.ligatus.org.uk/lob/alphabetical) or by where the terms fall in the hierarchy (https://www.ligatus.org.uk/lob/hierarchy). A tremendously valuable resource for bookbinding terminology. As of March 2021, the aim of Ligatus was to prepare "a reference tool holding details and pictures of bindings from 19 European countries, dating from the ninth to the nineteenth century. While we continue to seek funding for this project, we received a further AHRC [Arts and Humanities Research Council] grant to pursue the THESAURUS element of the Language of Bindings project and the creation of a set of guidelines for the description of historic bookbindings (in preparation, under the title Coming to Terms)" (Ligatus, "Language of Bindings"; https://www.ligatus.org.uk/node/712 [accessed 25 March 2021]).

LIGHT-AND-SHADE WATERMARK (also called "chiaroscuro watermark" and "shadowmark"). A WATERMARK in

Light-and-shade watermark from Fabriano. Photograph by Jeff Dykes.
Collection of the author.

which the fibers run from thick to thin in a shaded fashion, producing an image with many shades of black and gray.

LILLY LIBRARY (Indiana University). One of the great rare book collections in the United States, founded by Lilly Pharmaceuticals founder Josiah K. Lilly Jr. in 1960. He was a serious collector of many kinds of things (weapons, coins and stamps, ship models, and much more, along with books and manuscripts). His own holdings "of books and manuscripts, totalling more than 20,000 books and 17,000 manuscripts, together with more than fifty oil paintings and 300 prints, were given by the collector to Indiana University between 1954 and 1957. These materials form the foundation of the rare book and manuscript collections of the Lilly Library" (http://www.indiana.edu/~liblilly/tour/foyer.shtml [accessed 25 October 2015; this link no longer retrieves this passage, but the information is available in this form on Wikipedia]). Today, "Lilly Library holdings include about 460,000 books, more than 120,000 pieces of sheet music, and more than 8.5 million manuscripts" (https://libraries.indiana.edu/lilly-library [accessed 2 July 2021]). The collections are particularly strong in a number of areas, including automobiles; Bibles; children's literature; early printing; film, radio, and television; fine printing and binding; food and drink; American, British, and Indiana history; American, British, and European literature; medieval and Renaissance manuscripts; medicine and science; music; mystery writing; puzzles; and voyages and exploration (see the Wikipedia article for a discussion of these collecting areas: "Lilly Library"; https://en.wikipedia.org/wiki/Lilly_Library [accessed 2 July 2021]). (See Silver, *Dr. Rosenbach and Mr. Lilly*, and Silver, *J. K. Lilly, Jr.*)

LIMITATION. The number of copies produced of an edition of a text of any kind. A book or a BROADSIDE, for instance, may show its limitation in a variety of ways. (*See* Limited editions; Limitation notice.)

LIMITED EDITIONS; LIMITATION NOTICE. A "limited edition" is a phrase used by booksellers and publishers to suggest RARITY and to allow them to charge a premium price. This is justifiable when the limitation is low (especially when the number of copies of the "limited" piece is in demand in numbers beyond the limitation). But when the number is high, no "limitation" should affect the price. "Limited to 12 million copies" is still a limited edition. Strictly speaking, every edition of every book ever printed was a limited edition since at some point the publisher stopped printing that edition. Sometimes a volume has a printed or LAID IN note that explains what the limitation is (often at the COLOPHON), and such a message is usually reliable. (Henry Morris numbered every copy of his *The World's Worst Marbled Paper* "No. 1." He told me that too many of his subscribers wanted the lowest number he could provide. They all got what they wanted.)

Carter gives several reasons for such limitations. First, if a volume is illustrated by a means with which the printing surface will deteriorate in the printing (as with COPPERPLATE ENGRAVINGS), only so many good copies can be made. Second, if the book is handmade, a printer may not have the stamina or inclination to stand at the press for great lengths of time and may keep the numbers low for her own sanity and comfort. Third, if the publisher prints up too many copies, the price may be low if too many are available, while a book in short supply could realize a higher price if buyers see it as scarce. (LEONARD BASKIN told me that early in the life of his Gehenna Press, he would produce large PRESSRUNS, often being saddled by many unsold copies and resulting in low prices for those he sold; later in his career, he understood the forces of the market, and he made many fewer copies to sell to his most ardent SUBSCRIBERS, allowing him to charge much higher prices and to have fewer unsold copies.) Fourth, the publisher decides to print only so many copies as he thinks will sell, and limiting his production to that many—and making a virtue of this by announcing that the book is "limited to × copies" (see Carter, p. 162). KIM MERKER called the practice of printing limited editions "the creation of artificial rarities," but the reasons Carter gives are valid: hand-produced volumes do create a physical and psychological burden on the printer, who can take only so much of the repetition of production before ennui, utter fatigue, or madness sets in. Another reason for limiting the number of copies is that a printer may want to use up a paper stock and has only so much paper to produce a limited number of copies. Also, the publisher/printer may wish to issue some copies for a commercial market, but, for a higher-paying clientele, a limited number—printed on a better paper, in a better binding, issued with a duplicate suite of prints, or with some other feature that makes the limited number special.

With this said, the phrase does carry a magic to it that is often justified, and FINE-PRESS publishers often will say, "The edition is limited to only ____ copies" (the word "only" conveying the scarceness of the piece), and sometimes with the added incentive that "after the printing, the type was distributed," proving that no additional copies would be created, thus increasing the sense of "limitation" and the desirability of the item so designated. The blank in the formula is the designation of what the limitation was, and the smaller the number, the more desirable the item. In the 19th century, publishers would issue the complete works of such and such an author, with the statement "limited to 2,500 copies." What was the veracity of this claim? If they numbered the copies, this would be "proof" of that limitation, but was this really proof? And if a publisher said only "limited edition" without giving the actual number of the limitation, the veracity of that claim was seriously in doubt.

Additionally, innumerable copies of "limited editions," from books with their copies numbered, exist with no numbering, presumably printers' OVERRUNS. These are called (sometimes by the printer him- or herself) "OUT OF SERIES" or "*HORS DE COMMERCE*" (the French term for the same phenomenon—meaning "out of commerce," that is, "not sold"—used by some booksellers to elevate the volume to suggest some mystic level of unattainability). Thus, if an edition was "limited to 150 numbered copies," there could be another 200 unnumbered out there, waiting to reduce the value of the copy you just paid a premium price for. Most book collectors, therefore, will want the copy that is numbered, which guarantees the limitation, over the unnumbered one, which lacks a shade of respectability in not being one of the chosen (numbered) copies. But, of course, the true COMPLETIST will want a copy of each.

It should be added that any item can be "limited," not just books. BROADSIDES, PAMPHLETS, photographs, and other COLLECTIBLES can be limited. Sometimes the indication is: "This is copy number XXX of 350 printed at the press." Sometimes the limitation is more succinctly delineated: "XXX/350."

LIMITED EDITIONS CLUB (known in the trade as LEC). A SUBSCRIPTION bookselling operation. "The Limited Editions Club was founded in 1929 by George Macy (1900–1956) to publish finely made and finely illustrated LIMITED EDITIONS of the classics of literature—and of a few carefully selected contemporary titles, such as *The Grapes of Wrath* by John Steinbeck. / Most of the books were beautifully illustrated with original artwork by leading book illustrators. In most cases, the illustrators handsigned each copy of the books that they illustrated for the LEC. Some books were published without that signature due to the unexpected death of the artist before publication, as happened with the *The Arabian Nights* illustrated by Arthur Szyk, *Comus* illustrated by Edmund Dulac, and the Arthur Rackham illustrated *Wind In The Willows*. / George Macy also commissioned some major fine art artists to illustrate LEC books with original finely printed etchings, lithographs, and engravings, which were bound into the books, including artists such as Henri Matisse, Pablo Picasso, Marie Laurencin and other members of the Paris School of Art. He also commissioned a number of American masters of that period, largely from the Social Realism and American Regionalism schools of art. Included were Reginald Marsh, Grant Wood, Thomas Hart Benton, and John Steuart Curry. In addition, he commissioned major photographers, including Edward Weston and Edward Steichen, to illustrate LEC books. Those artists and photographers handsigned all copies of the books that they illustrated" (Majure, "A Brief History of the Limited Editions Club"). All volumes were issued—as the name of the series indicates—in limited editions, though some of the limitations were high: as many as 2,000 copies. Most of the titles were reissued in cheaper, "unlimited" versions under the imprint of the Heritage Press or the Heritage Club, and these attractive volumes, issued in inexpensive slipcases, are themselves COLLECTIBLES though at a fraction of the prices of the LEC versions. Some of the LEC volumes have reached true HIGH-SPOT status because they were illustrated and signed by high-spot illustrators or were by high-spot authors. "The two most sought after (and valuable) LEC books published under Macy's leadership are *Lysistrata*, illustrated and signed by Pablo Picasso, 1934; and *Ulysses*, illustrated and signed by Henri Matisse, 1935. 250 copies of the 1500 copy limited edition of *Ulysses* were also signed by the author, James Joyce" (Majure, "A Brief History of the Limited Editions Club").

Majure continues, "After George Macy's death in 1956, his wife, Helen (1904–1978), took over and directed the operations of the LEC until 1968. From 1968 until 1970, the club was operated by her son, Jonathan Macy, and other family members. In 1970, the LEC (together with The Heritage Press and The Heritage Club), [*sic*] was sold to Boise Cascade Corporation. Boise Cascade sold it to Ziff-Davis Publishing Company. Ziff-Davis sold it to Cardavon Press. Cardavon operated the LEC with limited success for most of the 1970's, finally putting it on the block for sale. / Cardavon had raised the limitation to 2000 copies, and had sold The Heritage Press & The Heritage Club to The Danbury Mint (a sister company to The Easton Press) to generate needed cash. The Heritage Press and The Heritage Club were, respectively, the publisher and distributor of inexpensive, unlimited, and unsigned reprint editions of books which had previously been published by the Limited Editions Club. And as a result of that sale, today The Easton Press has the reprint publishing rights for those LEC titles. A great many of the Easton Press leather books are reprints of the great Limited Editions Club editions. / Sidney Shiff (1924–2010) acquired the LEC from Cardavon in 1978. Over the next decade, Mr. Shiff gradually changed the focus of the club, and eventually began producing only LIVRES D'ARTISTE illustrated with original artwork by major 'fine art' artists, rather than by major illustrators and graphic artists. And he also gradually reduced the number of copies printed. As of 2004, the limitation per edition was 300 copies, and the annual subscription rate was $5,000."

LIMP LEATHER/LIMP VELLUM. "Limp" says it all—floppy, flexible, bendable. The terms "limp leather" and "limp vellum" describe binding materials. While some of the ROYCROFT PRESS volumes were covered with truly limp leather (e.g., soft suede), "limp" is also used for such bindings as those on the common Doves Press volumes, which have a stiff but still flexible vellum with silk ties. The bindings could be LACED IN or CASED IN; the designation simply described the flexible covers. That is, the covers were not glued onto BOARDS. Without the boards, you have a loose structure. You can also have a semi-limp vellum binding where the boards are seated into the vellum case. Limp bindings were also done with cloth, and usually all of these materials (cloth, leather, and vellum) were lined. Roberts and Etherington say, "In the last quarter of the 18th century and the first quarter of the 19th, limp leather was commonly used for books to be carried in the pocket, but for the past century or so limp bindings have been largely restricted to devotional books, diaries, and sentimental verse, sometimes in the YAPP style" (p. 160). (*See* Suede; Vellum.) (See Clarkson, *Limp Vellum Binding and Its Potential as a Conservation Type Structure for the Rebuilding of Early Printed Books*, chap. 10, pp. 285–319.)

LINDSTRAND COMPARATOR. A small, portable COLLATING MACHINE that allows the user to ocularly superimpose one printed text upon another, revealing the differences between them. It was invented by Gordon Lindstrand around 1970 to rival the HINMAN COLLATOR, which is a large piece of furniture and is thus not portable. "The Lindstrand Comparator allows you to view two different pages simultaneously, with each image being fed to only one eye at a time through a series of mirrors" (Witmore, "Pre-Digital Iteration"; Steven Escar Smith, "'Armadillos of Invention': A Census of Mechanical Collators"; see also Lindstrand, "Mechanized Textual Collation and Recent Designs.") (A one-eyed person can use the Hinman Collator, but not a Lindstrand Comparator. The latter requires two well-functioning eyes.)

LINE GAUGE. *See* Pica stick; Type gauge.

LINEN PAPER. Originally this was paper made from linen rags. Made from flax, it had the off-white tint that the rags imparted to the pulp. Those ignorant of the origin of the paper may apply the term incorrectly to any paper made from rags, and many paper companies will call their products that contain any proportion of rags such names as "Linen BOND," "Linen LAID," "Linen ledger," or "Linen WOVE." With the use of specially designed DANDY ROLLS, paper manufacturers can impart texture to their machine-made papers that look something like woven fabric; such papers are also called "linen papers" or "linen-faced papers." Booksellers, in their descriptions, should be careful to avoid these loose uses when they should be saying something like "rag-content paper."

LINING FIGURE. "Also called *aligning figure, capital figure, Modern figure, ranging figure.* Lining figures are numerals all of the same height, usually the same as that of the capital letters in a TYPEFACE, though in some FONTS they are slightly shorter. Lining figures are generally used for tabular matter, for SUPERSCRIPTS and FOOTNOTE CALLS, with capital letters (in display or in constructions such as 'Interstate I-40'), and with mathematical expressions even when old-style figures are specified for the job" (Eckersley et al., *Glossary of Typesetting Terms*, p. 62). (*See* Display type.)

LININGS OR LINERS. Carter says that this is synonymous with ENDLEAVES, but the term is seldom used this way. More specifically, Roberts and Etherington explain that a liner is "[a] sheet of paper of an appropriate thickness attached to the inner surface of the board of a book, usually one that is to be fully covered in leather. The liner causes the board to curve convexly to the text block. This curvature will be straightened by the shrinkage of the leather which covers the outside of the board. In order to prevent warping of the cover at a later time, the grain direction of the lining paper should be parallel to the spine of the book" (Roberts and Etherington, "liner"; https://cool.culturalheritage.org/don/dt/dt3856.html [accessed 27 January 2021]).

LINOLEUM BLOCKS (linocuts). Linocuts are illustrations made from linoleum blocks, which are similar to WOODCUTS in that an image is drawn onto the surface of the block (which is a SUBSTRATE, such as wood or plastic, covered with a layer of linoleum) and everything else is removed from that surface (the artist using BURINS AND GRAVERS), leaving the image in RELIEF. The surface of the BLOCK is inked with a ROLLER, and then paper or cloth is pressed onto the block to print the image. (See Kafka, *Linoleum Block Printing.*)

LINOTYPE MACHINE. *See* Mergenthaler, Ottmar.

LINSEED OIL. "A pale yellow drying oil extracted from ground flax seed genus Linum, and especially L. usitatissimum, and used occasionally in the 19th century as a marbling size. It was never used as extensively as gum tragacanth or flea seed. / Linseed oil is also used in the manufacture of some printing inks and in some finishing processes in leather manufacture" (Roberts and Etherington, p. 160).

LINSON. A strong paper that is used in bookbindings. The paper is manufactured to look like CLOTH, and thus can have a pattern of cloth EMBOSSED onto its surface. Patterns can be of woven or ribbed textures, for instance. Sometimes there is a fine varnish on the paper; and the overall final product can sometimes be indistinguishable from cloth. It is manufactured in large enough rolls to be useful for covering the BOARDS of a book, or in strips to be used as tape, and it comes in many colors.

LIST PRICE. (Also called the "Published price," "Retail price," and "Sticker price.") The original full price of a book as charged by the publisher. This price is often printed on the dust jacket, though this could be deceptive, especially when the book is sold as a REMAINDER but is not a genuine remainder. For as long as publishers have been printing prices on DUST JACKETS, books have been available—even brand-new copies—for less than the printed price. The "list price" may appear in some list at the "original" price, but was merely a MSRP (manufacturer's suggested retail price) or RRP (recommended retail price). The vendor, then, can sell the item for whatever price it decides, with the idea that a small profit may be better than none at all.

LITHOGRAPHY. Literally, "stone writing." Printing from the flat surface of a stone, achieved by the natural opposition of water and oil. An oil-based ink called TUSCHE is drawn onto the smooth surface of the stone. The stone is covered

Lithographic stones. International Printing Museum, Carson, California; https://www.printmuseum.org/collection/equipment/lithographic-stones/ (accessed 9 June 2021).

Courtesy of International Printing Museum, Carson, California.

with water, which sticks to the stone except where the tusche is since the oil-based tusche repels the water. An oil-based ink is rolled over the stone, and the ink sticks to the places on the stone where the tusche is but not where the water is since the water on the surface of the stone repels the oil-based ink. The stone is now properly inked; a sheet of paper is placed on the stone's surface and pressed. The paper picks up the ink, and the operation can be repeated indefinitely.

Since the stone is perfectly flat, this method of printing is called "PLANOGRAPHIC"—printing from a flat surface. It was invented in 1798 by Alois Senefelder, an actor looking for an inexpensive way to reproduce scripts. The earliest lithography was done from a stone surface, but the technique works equally well from any flat impervious surface, such as metal. When the printing is from a metal surface, it is still called "lithography." (*See* Chromolithography.) (See Pennell and Pennell, *Lithography and Lithographers*; Twyman, *A History of Chromolithography*; and Weber, *A History of Lithography*.)

LITTLE BIG BOOKS. *See* Big Little Books.

LITTLE BLUE BOOKS. The Little Blue Books was an extensive series of small, inexpensive publications released by the publisher Haldeman-Julius in Girard, Kansas (though some were published under a different imprint: Appeal to Reason or the Appeal Publishing Company). The Kent State University Library explains: "Emanuel Haldeman-Julius (1888–1951) began publishing his 'Little Blue Books' in 1919 in order for classic works of literature to be available for a much lower price than usual, at five or ten cents each. His association with the Socialist party led him to buy the Socialist paper Appeal to Reason along with their printing press, which he used to publish a number of his books. The books became widely popular, and by 1949, over 300,000,000 had been sold. The series includes over a thousand titles spanning a wide range of material, from novels to philosophical tracts to advice manuals. The first several hundred books include mostly previously published pieces, but the series later expanded to include original works as well. Some of these are edited versions of more extensive pieces and some are completely original" (see bibliography under Haldeman-Julius). The booklets were about 3½ × 5 inches, and were usually stapled into light cardboard covers with simple titles and other information printed onto the covers. Though they were called "blue books," their covers were sometimes gray or other pale colors. Haldeman-Julius also released a number of Big Blue Books (from 1925 to 1950). In all, nearly 1900 titles were published. They are "COLLECTIBLE," though they are often faded or in poor condition, and they command (perhaps too bold a verb) only a few dollars apiece since they were published in massive quantities and almost no titles are of premium value. (A Google search in January 2022 brought up over 5,100 items.) (See Mordell, Comp., *The World of Haldeman-Julius*.)

LITTLE MAGAZINE. "[A]ny of various small periodicals devoted to serious literary writings, usually avant-garde and noncommercial. They were published from about 1880 through much of the 20th century and flourished in the United States and England, though French writers (especially the Symbolist poets and critics, 1880–c. 1900) often had access to a similar type of publication and German literature of the 1920s was also indebted to them. The name signifies most of all a noncommercial manner of editing, managing, and financing. A little magazine usually begins with the object of publishing literary work of some artistic merit that is unacceptable to commercial magazines for any one or all of three reasons—the writer is unknown and therefore not a good risk; the work itself is unconventional or experimental in form; or it violates one of several popular notions of moral, social, or aesthetic behaviour" (*Encyclopaedia Britannica*, "Little Magazine"). The *Britannica* article cites several important such publications, including *Poetry: A Magazine of Verse* (founded 1912); *Little Review* (1914–1929) of Margaret Anderson; *Transatlantic Review* (1924–1925); *The Kenyon Review*, founded by John Crowe Ransom in 1939; in Great Britain, *Scrutiny*, edited by F. R. Leavis (1932–1953), and many others. These publications were usually the work of a single editor/compiler. Today our newsstands (in such stores as Barnes & Noble) are filled with such publications—the analog world being the ideal venue for their dissemination. Inasmuch as the larger commercial publishers shy away from such magazines, the little magazine movement has been a strong force in presenting to the public a major literary and social movement. A substantial proportion of modern and avant-garde, and experimental, literary output, and an exceptionally wide swath of writers—in fiction, nonfiction, poetry, and drama, among other genres, including drawing and photography—appear in little magazines. "[L]ittle magazines have continuously rebelled against established literary expression and theory by demonstrating an aggressive receptivity to new authors, new ideas, and new styles. Such publications usually have very small circulations, and are frequently short-lived; many die after publishing only one or two issues" (University of Wisconsin–Madison, "Little Magazine Collection").

LIVRE D'ARTISTE. (Also called a *Livre de peintre.*) Distinct from the ARTIST'S BOOK, the *livre d'artiste* is a volume containing original works of art by an artist. W. J. Strachan in Grove Art Online says that the term is "used to define a variety of illustrated book that originated in France in the early 20th century. The essential feature of the *livre d'artiste* is that each illustration is an original work executed by the artist directly on the support (stone, wood, metal, linoleum etc[.]) from which it is printed. Its originator was the dealer Ambroise Vollard, who commissioned Pierre Bonnard to illustrate with lithographs *Parallèlement*, poems by Paul Verlaine, published in Paris in 1900. . . . Subsequently Vollard enlisted the services of other painters and sculptors, including Auguste Rodin, Maurice Denis, Picasso, Aristide Maillol, Georges Braque and Georges Rouault" (W. J. Strachan, "Livre d'artiste," Grove Art Online; https://www.oxfordartonline.com/groveart/groveart/view/10.1093/gao/9781884446054.001.0001/oao-9781884446054-e-7000051448 [accessed 4 June 2022]). The presence of original pieces of art—and the fact that no two copies are alike—usually makes these volumes extraordinarily COLLECTIBLE and expensive. (See also Adamowicz, "The livre d'artiste in Twentieth-Century France.") John Crichton of Brick Row Book Shop says the illustrations in such volumes are more important than the text (private communication).

LOCALIZED RARITY. *See* Rarity.

LOCATION SYMBOLS. *See* Library codes.

LOCK-UP. The act of tightening up the contents of printed matter in the CHASE (the metal frame that holds the type and other things) in the PRINTING PRESS. The lock-up is done with QUOINS and a QUOIN KEY (or, before the existence of metal quoins, with wooden ones and a SHOOTING STICK). With straight prose text, this lock-up can be simple, using one or two sets of quoins in either direction (vertically and horzontally). But with a complicated FORME, holding type of various sizes, illustrations here and there in the chase, maybe special areas of type in the chase for page numbers, headlines, or other features that do not align with the rest of the prose or verse set in the chase, and for other kinds of materials imposed (*see* Imposition), the lock-up can be quite complicated and difficult. (I once observed [and threw in my unneeded advice to] Harry Duncan, who was printing an immense BROADSIDE, a poem about Noah's flood, each stanza of which began with a different font of WOODEN TYPE; and those wooden SORTS were of at least a dozen different sizes, and appeared randomly throughout the chase. The lock-up, using perhaps 25 or 30 sets of quoins, took the better part of a day.)

LOGBOOK. A volume recording maritime and other activities on board a ship. The term, by extension, has been used to record activities in other contexts (a truck driver's logbook; an airplane pilot's logbook; and so forth), mostly in the realm of transportation. However, one may also encounter "a manicurist's logbook" in which that person's activities and clientele are recorded; "a concert pianist's logbook," recording gigs and pupils; or the logbook of a contractor hired to build a shed in someone's backyard, recording costs of materials, time worked, dates of beginning and completing the phases of (and the entirety of) the project, the people hired to work for the contractor, and so on. While all of these contain information that could be useful to scholars, for the purposes of the present volume, the original meaning yields a broad world of volumes in which are recorded names (and ranks) of personnel on board a ship, ship owners and investors, dates of operation and notable events related to the voyages of the ship, routes traversed, activities and incidents on the vessel, sights seen along the way, weather encountered, ports of call, cargoes taken on board and deposited from the inception of the journey to its conclusion, entertainment experience on the ship, financial data pertaining to the ship and its activities, and so forth. In the antiquarian book world, these volumes—especially manuscript ones from the age of sail—are sought after, usually with respect to local collecting needs. For instance, the Phillips Library at the Peabody Essex Museum has a large collection of logbooks focusing on maritime activities emanating from and returning to Salem, Massachusetts, where the museum is located. These are excellent sources of information about local history and finances, art, and culture.

LOGO (printer's logo). *See* Printer's mark.

LONGITUDINAL LABELS. In the 18th century, "trade bindings of the more expensive sort were given coloured leather LETTERING pieces from about 1700. The longitudinal LABELS printed on otherwise BLANK LEAVES of a few late-seventeenth-century English books may have been meant for use as FORE-EDGE labels, or they may have been intended for labelling the bins or shelves that contained a stock of books—whether the printer's, the wholesaler's, or the bookseller's stock is unclear" (Gaskell, *A New Introduction to Bibliography*, p. 152). Gaskell adds, "A greatly increased proportion of books were retailed in paper WRAPPERS and paper BOARDS, UNCUT to allow for the later REBINDING in leather. The wrappers of periodicals and EPHEMERA were often printed; and from the 1780s printed labels were sometimes stuck on to the SPINES of boarded books, being supplied by the printer on a spare leaf" (p. 153). These labels were printed vertically, but Gaskell also notes that some such labels survive in manuscript form (p. 153, note 13). William A. Jackson says, " Occasionally one finds traces of paste on the inside of the fore-edge of the back covers of early English books, indicating that at one time they had hand-written labels. . . . That any of these labels have survived is probably rather the result of their having been folded into the books than because of any especial tenderness with which they have been treated. . . . [There is a] common title-label, which, in various forms, can be found in English printed books from 1653 to 1691, although the period of its most general use appears to have ended about 1675. . . . These labels occur printed vertically on either the recto or verso of a leaf, otherwise blank, which is an integral part of some sheet or portion of a sheet which is a regular part of the book. Most of those observed are found in books of quarto or smaller sizes, but a few are found in folios" (William A. Jackson, "English Title-Labels to the End of the Seventeenth Century," pp. 223–24). He adds that they can be found printed vertically in the middle, the fore-edge, or the GUTTER side of the leaf. Since they were almost certainly created for use on spines (though that is unclear), their appearance in a volume does not add any special value to the book; nor does their absence in some copies detract from the volumes' value. For the present volume, the key issue is that they be called "longitudinal labels," more as a descriptive than as a formally accepted term.

LONG PRIMER. "A term used before the general adoption of the point system for a type size nearly equal to 10-POINT" (Eckersley et al., *Glossary of Typesetting Terms*, p. 64). Worth noting here to explain JOHN CARTER's and GRAHAM POLLARD's discovery of the THOMAS J. WISE FORGERIES, partly identified as forgeries by the TYPE that Wise used on many of his PAMPHLETS: Clay's Long Primer.

LONG REAM. *See* Ream.

LONG S. *See* Swash letters.

LOOSE. Said of a binding in which the TEXT BLOCK is not firmly attached to its cover. This is often the situation with CASED-IN BINDINGS in CLOTH covers. Publishers to save money attached the text blocks to the cases only with glue, and frequent handling loosens the block. Booksellers might say "loose in its covers" or "a loose copy." Though the word implies that the text block is still attached to the cover, it could also mean that there is no connection at all, with the cover still there, but on its own.

LOOSE-LEAF BINDING. A binding in which the LEAVES are not attached, but are held in on rings through holes punched in the GUTTER-margins of the volume. The structure allows leaves to be added or taken out, replaced or repositioned in the volume. The structure is common for business records, manuals of instruction, company catalogs, or any kind of application in which new or additional information is being generated, so that the new leaves supplement or supplant older ones, keeping the information in the volume up to date. The rings could be attached at the head of the binder, allowing leaves to be flipped upward. (*See* Ring binder.)

LOWER CASE/LOWERCASE. The lower case is the TYPE CASE that holds the small letters (as opposed to the capital SORTS). Since COMPOSITORS need to use the small letters much more often than they need to set the capitals, the small ones were placed in a type case at the easiest level to reach for efficiency of motion and ease of muscle strain in TYPESETTING. This case was beneath the one that held the capitals, so it is called the "lowercase" and the other the "uppercase." Lowercase (single word or sometimes hyphenated) letters are those in the lower case; they are also called minuscules (sometimes spelled "miniscules").

LOWNDES, WILLIAM THOMAS. Compiler of the influential (though today out of date) *The Bibliographer's Manual of English Literature*. Listing about 50,000 titles, this reference tool was once the first go-to volume for scholars and bibliographers who needed information on hundreds of authors' works. The entries, arranged alphabetically by author, give much information, including bibliographical data, size of the volumes, sometimes original prices or prices fetched on the open market, and so on. It is still a good source of information not available elsewhere in a single source; today it is much superseded by the *CAMBRIDGE BIBLIOGRAPHY OF ENGLISH LITERATURE*. But booksellers and scholars may still cite Lowndes in their work.

LUDLOW MACHINE/LUDLOW TYPOGRAPH. A machine for casting type into metal SLUGS, similar to the LINOTYPE but designed for the most part for DISPLAY TYPE. The type is cast from handset matrices (*see* Matrix) that are locked into a special COMPOSING STICK; the stick is placed

A Ludlow slug and the matrices it was set from. Note the thin shafts on which the printing surface sits.

Courtesy of Heritage Photos.

A parchment maker with a vellum skin stretched on a frame and a lunellum.

From Christopher de Hamel, *Medieval Craftsmen: Scribes and Illuminators* (Toronto and Buffalo: Toronto University Press, 1997), p. 12.

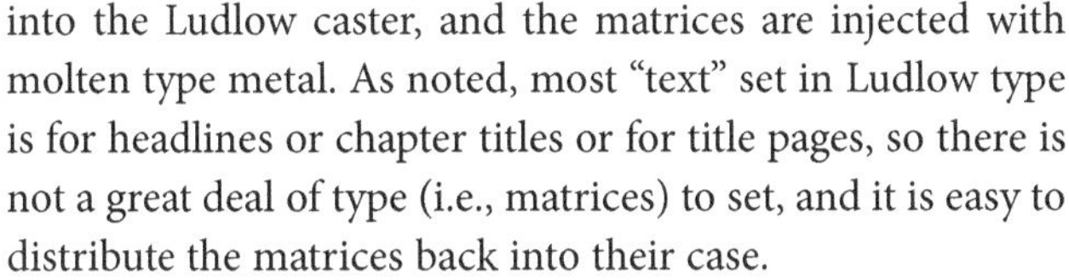

into the Ludlow caster, and the matrices are injected with molten type metal. As noted, most "text" set in Ludlow type is for headlines or chapter titles or for title pages, so there is not a great deal of type (i.e., matrices) to set, and it is easy to distribute the matrices back into their case.

Since Ludlow slugs contain large typefaces, the slugs could be quite heavy, but the shafts on which the printing surfaces of the text sit are cast with thin shanks, leaving the characters protruding far over the shanks, saving type metal and reducing the weight of the slugs. William I. Ludlow (along with a machinist, William A. Reade) created the Ludlow Typograph Company in 1906 in Chicago.

LUNELLUM. (Sometimes called a "lunellarium.") A moon-shaped knife used for scraping VELLUM.

LYNN BOOK. *See* Big Little Books.

LYONNAISE STYLE. "A 16th century style of book decoration featuring broad interlaced geometrical strapwork, usually gold tooled and then painted, lacquered, or enamelled in different colors. Lyonnaise was also a style in which the binding was decorated by blocking the cover with large corner ornaments and a predominant center design, roughly lozenge shaped, the all-over background being filled in with dots. The name is misleading, as neither style had any connection with Lyons" (Roberts and Etherington, p. 162).

LYOPHILIZATION. *See* Freeze drying.

LYRASIS. *See* Regional Alliance for Preservation.

M

MACHINE COMPOSITION. The setting of type using a machine rather than setting by hand. Such COMPOSITION is done with a LINOTYPE MACHINE, a MONOTYPE setter, a Ludlow machine (or LUDLOW TYPOGRAPH), or some other machine.

MACHINE DIRECTION. *See* Grain.

MACRON. A horizontal line over a letter (usually a vowel). In manuscripts, the macron was used as an abbreviation for many suffixes. It is also used to indicate a long vowel when it is placed over that character: "Pay is pronounced /pā/" (the VIRGULES are linguists' symbols to indicate pronunciation). (*See* Roman numerals.)

MADDEN, SIR FREDERIC (1801–1873). Influential and important bibliographer, paleographer, linguist, translator, printing historian, and librarian of the 19th century. He was keeper of manuscripts at the British Museum (1837–1866). "He edited for the Roxburghe Club *Havelok the Dane* (1828), discovered by himself among the Laudian MSS. in the Bodleian, *William and the Werwolf* (1832) and the old English versions of the *Gesta Romanorum* (1838). In 1839 he edited the ancient metrical romances of *Syr Gawayne* for the Bannatyne Club, and in 1847 Layamon's *Brut*, with a prose translation, for the Society of Antiquaries. In 1850 the magnificent edition, in parallel columns, of what are known as the 'Wycliffite' versions of the Bible, from the original MSS., upon which he and his coadjutor, [Josiah] Forshall [1795–1863], had been engaged for twenty years, was published by the university of Oxford. In 1866–1869 he edited the *Historia Minor* of Matthew Paris for the Rolls Series. In 1833 he wrote the text of Henry Shaw's *Illuminated Ornaments of the Middle Ages*; and in 1850 edited the English translation of Silvestre's *Paleographie universelle*" (*Encyclopaedia Britannica 1911*; http://www.theodora.com/encyclopedia/m/sir_frederic_madden.html [accessed 9 June 2021]). He was knighted in 1833. As a rival of ANTONIO PANIZZI, he made waves at the British Museum.

Madden oversaw a great deal of conservation of manuscripts, especially those of Robert Bruce Cotton (1571–1631) and his heirs, many of which were damaged in a fire. The collection contained the *Beowulf* manuscript, along with "more than 1,400 [other] manuscripts and over 1,500 charters, rolls and seals. These items range in date from approximately the 4th century to the 1600s" (British Library, "Cotton Manuscripts"), and Madden's work on them, along with his devising a whole conservation program, saved many of these priceless treasures. (See Prescott, "'Their Present Miserable State of Cremation,'" now available at http://www.uky.edu/~kiernan/eBeo_archives/articles90s/ajp-pms.htm [accessed 9 June 2021].) (See also Berger, "Sir Frederic Madden.")

(Personal note: I worked at the British Library's Manuscript Room for more than six months in 1972 on the original manuscript of Layamon's *Brut*, with a copy of Madden's amazing edition at my elbow—three giant volumes containing Madden's impeccable editorial and scholarly work. Overhead was an oil painting of Madden, watching me as I worked. What Madden did to produce that magnificent edition was nearly miraculous, and I have revered his scholarly abilities for decades.)

MADE-UP (copy) (sets). A volume or a set of volumes that is composed of parts brought together from pieces not originally part of one original volume or set. A single volume may have had a LEAF or a SIGNATURE missing, but the missing part is supplied from another copy. A multivolume set may be made up of volumes not originally issued together.

The fact that the volume or set is made up may not be discernible if the "replacement parts" are exactly like the ones that were missing and if the bringing together of the disparate parts is skillfully done. Carter points out that such "making up" is really "faking up," and this reprehensible practice is "valid grounds for divorce between buyer and seller" (p. 165). (*See* Sophisticated.) This implies that the faking up was done by the seller, and that it is always reprehensible. We know from history (as with Carter and Pollard's *An Enquiry into the Nature of Certain Nineteenth Century Pamphlets*) that collectors could also do the making up: THOMAS J. WISE was known to have sophisticated his own defective books with leaves from copies in the British Library. Sanford and Helen Berger, the great William Morris collectors, had a set of a Morris THREE-DECKER, lacking volume 2. I found a volume 2 in a used-book store and sent it to them. They called in appreciation when they got the book, but, though the cloth was identical to that used on their volumes 1 and 3, the ribbing on it was horizontal on the volume I sent them and vertical on their volumes. From a distance, the set was perfect; from close up, it was clearly made up. And it is worth adding that most collectors would rather have a made-up set than a set missing a part (or parts). The bookseller's efforts to make up a full set from disparate parts can sometimes be rewarded by the deep gratitude of the collector.

MAGIC LANTERN. A device that projects images onto a surface (like a screen or wall). A source of light is projected through some translucent material (like glass slides or film). Included here because the slides, which have become quite COLLECTIBLE, appear at antiquarian book fairs, sometimes accompanied by the projectors. They have become so popular as collectibles that a society was formed to memorialize them: The Magic Lantern Society of the U.S. and Canada.

MAGIC PICTURE BOOKS. *See* Blow books.

MAGNESIUM CUT. Illustration, text, or both printed from a magnesium PLATE. Magnesium took the place of ZINC at the end of the 20th century when zinc was prohibited due to the toxic fumes it produced in its own production. Both metals print well, but magnesium will corrode after a few years, developing a white flaky surface, and the image on the BLOCK, in RELIEF, will eventually break down.

MAGNUM OPUS. Literally, a "great work," especially of literary or artistic value, though (as any dictionary will say) it is also rendered "greatest work." That is, one might say that "Hamlet" is Shakespeare's magnum opus. The phrase also appears in booksellers' catalogs in reference to the work of a press: "The Chaucer is the magnum opus of the Kelmscott Press." (*See* Morris, William.) Such judgments often come from the notion that "all would agree" that this is the best, though there might be much debate over this. Unless there is clear universal agreement over what constitutes any person's (or press's) greatest achievement, the phrase should be used with great caution. Is *Ulysses* or *Finnegan's Wake* James Joyce's magnum opus? Only the Shadow knows.

MAJUSCULE. A capital or UPPERCASE letter. (*See* Illuminated majuscule.) Although it can mean any capital letter, it often implies an extraordinarily large one, with decoration of various kinds. Its opposite is the miniscule (*see* Lowercase).

MAKEREADY (in printing). The preparation a printer does on a press to create a perfectly even impression when the paper is pressed against the inked type—or whatever else is in the CHASE that is to be printed. (*See* Edition, Impression [Printing], Issue, and State; Points.) The *American Dictionary of Printing* says under "Making Ready": "Under this head are comprised all of the procedures necessary after the form [*see* Forme] is placed upon the press until a perfectly satisfactory impression is produced upon the sheet" (p. 358).

On a handpress, the type is in the BED, and the TYMPAN, with the piece of paper to be printed sitting on it, is folded over the type. Behind the tympan is PACKING, usually pieces of paper that sit behind the sheet to be printed. If there is an uneven impression—that is, if some of the type presses too hard onto the sheet, some not enough, the makeready has to be adjusted so that all of the type presses with the same level of pressure over the whole printed area of the sheet, not forcing the type to bite into the sheet and not pressing too little and thus not getting the ink onto the printed sheet properly. An improperly done makeready will create an improperly printed sheet, easily seen in the final product. This is noteworthy for this volume since such a visible sign as a poorly done makeready might explain sloppily printed pages, and this explanation may wind up in a dealer's catalog description or a library's cataloging record; it might also indicate where in a PRESSRUN the sheet was printed, and it may have other bibliographical uses. Similar packing can be done if the pressure comes when the paper to be printed is rolled over the type, as on a press with a cylinder (like a VANDERCOOK).

MAKEUP RULE. A printer's tool that is useful for many tasks. It is a small, flat, rectangular piece of steel with a sharp edge at the bottom of its blade and with a curved projection at the upper side of the blade for gripping with the thumb and fingers. It is one of the printer's most versatile tools. One patent explains, "The invention has for its object the provision of a unitary composing or makeup rule which is practically adapted for quickly JUSTIFYING type forms, for lifting column RULE, BORDER rule, page numbers, etc., for lifting CUTS or tight SLUGS in FORMS, for spreading type to facilitate the insertion of LEADS, for removing string from ads, and for removing burrs from LINOTYPE faces; the tool being of such size and shape as to facilitate work in narrow measures and to facilitate the work of pressmen on high leads or work-up type on flat bed presses" (patent, "Filed Nov. 13, 1937 INVENTOR. William C. Ed," http://www.google.com/patents/US2133501 [accessed 9 June 2021]). The tool also is useful for cutting string, inserting string ends into the wraparound strings that tie up blocks of set type, scraping ink off an inking surface, using in a COMPOSING STICK as a setting rule, and scratching itches. Makeup rules come in several widths. John Howells and Marion Dearman say, "The pre-machine printer needed few tools to practice his craft. All that was needed was a line gauge, composing stick, a makeup rule, and an apron" (*Tramp Printers*, p. 42). (*See* Setting rule.)

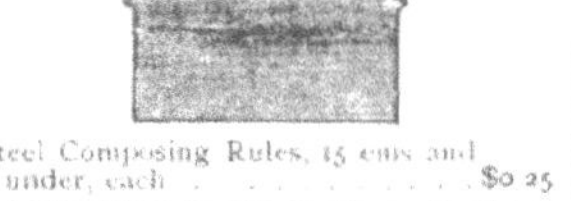

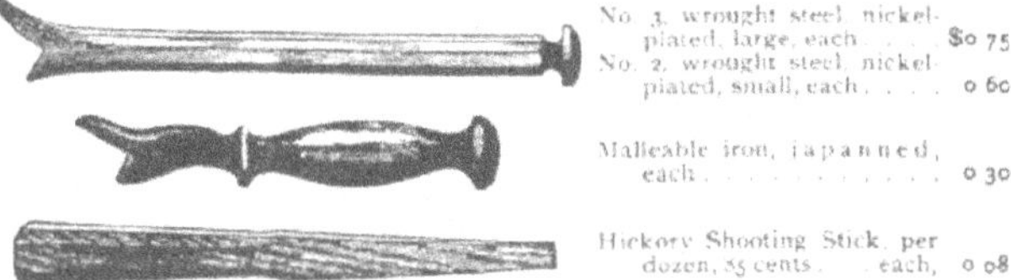

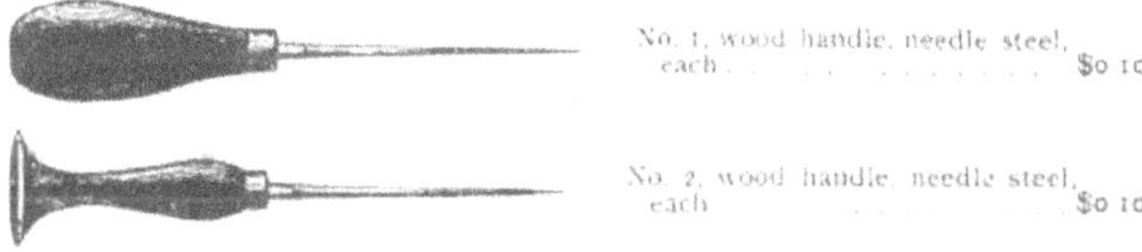

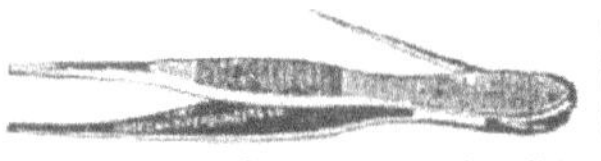

Printers' tools, including a makeup rule and shooting sticks; Letterpress Commons, "Compositors Tools"; https://letterpresscommons.com/compositors-tools/ (accessed 9 June 2021). These versatile tools are cast from steel in several widths, and they can be used, as just noted, as setting rule: metal strips, placed into the composing stick, against which the type is set.

Courtesy of Letterpress Commons.

MANDORLA. "A decorative motif in the shape of a pointed oval, used in bookbinding, usually as a centerpiece. . . . In medieval manuscript illumination, an almond-shaped aureole painted around the head or body of a deity or holy person (or group of holy figures), often ornamented with gilding" (Reitz, "Mandorla," *ABC-CLIO Online Dictionary for Library and Information Science*).

MANGA. The so-called comic books of Japan. Most of them are printed in black and white, but also with some color printing as well, and they cover many genres, including sexuality, history, suspense and mystery, business, romance, and adventure, among others. The range of subjects and the wide audience of these books make them much like Western (mostly American) COMIC BOOKS. And their popularity has led to their being available in many languages. There is a broad collecting populace of these volumes, as is the case with ANIME, comic books, and GRAPHIC NOVELS. (See Lent, *Illustrating Asia*, and Thorn, "A History of Manga.")

MANICULE. *See* Fist.

MANSELL. *See* National Union Catalog.

MANUFACTURER'S SUGGESTED RETAIL PRICE (MSRP). A term we have seen throughout the retail industries for the price that an item's maker says the item should sell at. This, of course, is one of the more abused terms in the selling world, for it is used with abandon to make buyers think they are getting a bargain when the actual asking price is considerably below this MSRP. And no commodity is immune from this lie. In the world of the book, REMAINDERS are often not really remainders, many BARGAIN BOOKS are not really bargains, and DUST JACKET copy is often written by people who are sometimes less than truthful.

MANUSCRIPT. Literally, "handwritten"; any text written by hand. The term is also loosely used to designate a text in general, as in "the manuscript was produced on a Brother printer." One might even encounter the seemingly contradictory "he sent in a typed manuscript of his novel." (*See* Typescript.)

MANUTIUS, ALDUS (1449–1515) (also called Aldo Manuzio). Other than GUTENBERG and FUST AND SCHÖFFER,

Aldus (as he is usually called) is perhaps the most celebrated printer of the INCUNABULA period and into the 16th century at his Aldine Press in Venice. At his death in 1515, the printing operation was continued by his grandson, Aldus Manutius, the Younger. The original Aldus was the first printer to use italic type, he was one of the first to use Greek type, and his small pocket editions of the classics set a very high standard in editing and printing. One of the true scholar printers, Aldus carefully collated multiple manuscript texts to produce the "DEFINITIVE EDITIONS" (*see* Bibliography) of his day. (See Barker, *Aldus Manutius*.) His anchor and dolphin PRESSMARK—which he used in several versions—was often copied by other printers.

MAPBACKS. As Rich Rennicks explains, the term "mapbacks" is "the informal name for a series of pulp paperback books published by Dell between 1943 and 1950. / Initially, the back cover of these books featured bland art, but starting with the fifth book in the series, *Four Frightened Women* by George Harmon Coxe, Dell added an illustration showing the locale where the book's events took place. (Note: the previous book in the series, *The American Gun Mystery* by Ellery Queen, was later reprinted with a map on the back cover, but it was the fifth book in the series that was the first to feature a map.) / The 'maps' were not all conventional maps by any means, with cut-away illustrations of buildings being a frequent option the various artists used when the action was largely confined to one house or building" (Rennicks, "Collecting Dell Mapbacks," The New Antiquarian blog, 9 July 2020; https://www.abaa.org/blog/post/dell-mapbacks [accessed 20 April 2021]). J. Kingston Pierce says that the company produced more than 570 of these volumes, and he adds that "the carefully executed scene-of-the-crime layouts—touted initially by narrow front-cover banners reading 'with crime map on back cover'—set Dell's paperbacks apart from the competition" (J. Kingston Pierce, "Dell Mapbacks: A History"). Most of these books were murder mysteries, and the maps were done in color, showing the physical setting of the action of the stories. Pierce says, "Early Dell maps most often concentrated on individual rooms, private dwellings, small communities, and parks or penthouses where murders, kidnappings, and other transgressions of societal order occurred. Fewer of them captured broad geographical territories and cities. However, as the series went on, the drawings became increasingly stylized and less tightly focused." As inexpensive paperbacks, these COLLECTIBLES are often in shabby condition, with yellowing paper, and not in COLLECTOR'S CONDITION. So they do not sell for much today. But they wind up in clusters at book fairs.

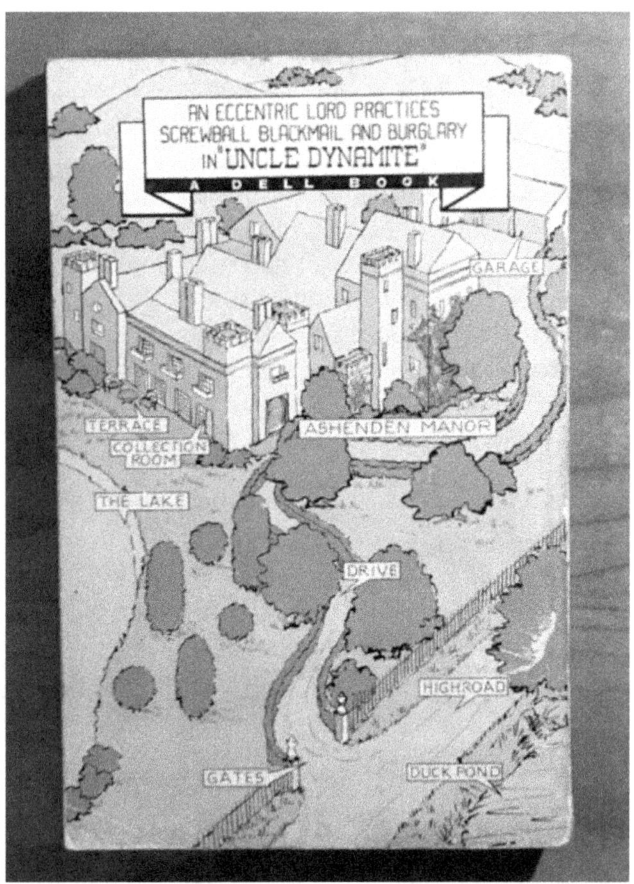

Mapback paperback book: P. G. Wodehouse, *Uncle Dynamite* (New York, Dell, 1948).
Collection of the author.

MAQUETTE. *See* Trial binding.

MARBLING / MARBLED PAPER / MARBLE(D) CALF. Marbling is a form of paper decoration (though the technique is used on other surfaces as well; see below), created by floating pigments on the surface of a SIZE, manipulating them into patterns (or just leaving the droplets in their stochastically fallen arrangement), and then transferring these colors to a sheet of paper by laying the sheet onto the surface of the size. The sheet is prepared with a coating of a mordant (usually alum, which is dissolved in water and then brushed over the surface of the sheet and left to dry). The pigments are mixed with ox gall, which makes the droplets spread out when they land on the surface of the size, and it also makes the pigments float and not blend with other, neighboring/touching drops. Once the sheet has picked up the pattern from the size, the marbler must repeat the process from scratch since only one sheet can be made from a single dripping of pigments. Sometimes, after the pattern was prepared on the surface of the size, the marbler would spatter the surface with tiny droplets of pigments to give another decorative element to the final pattern. Or the marbler could do the spattering onto the already-marbled sheet for the same effect. (*See* Spotted calf.)

The origins of marbling are obscure, though it seems to have been inspired by SUMINAGASHI, developed in Japan in the 12th century, which Europeans saw from goods that made it to the West on the Silk Road. Marbling was first done in the West in Persia or Turkey, possibly by the 15th century. (See Wolfe, *Marbled Paper.*)

Marbling was used for bookbinding (cover papers and endpapers and book edges) to replace the more expensive leather, and some GOATSKINS and CLOTHS were marbled for decoration. (*See* the images here. For more images, *see* Nonpareil marbling; Tiger-eye marbling.)

As noted, the technique could be used on other materials: wood, leather or vellum, or cloth, for instance. In the Berger-Cloonan Collection of Decorated Papers (in the Cushing Library at Texas A&M University), there is a series of marbled images done by Tom Leech on large panels of X-ray film. Marbled cloth was used in the 19th century, and in the 20th century marblers like Karli Frigge and Jan Sobota, among many others, created marbled cloths. Of course, many fabrics have been marbled, and silk scarves and shirts, for example, have proliferated. Any of these cloths can be used for bookbinding or for bookmarks bound into volumes. Goatskin has been marbled for centuries as a binding material, and other leathers are still receiving this treatment.

There is also a material called "marble (or marbled) calf," popular as a cover in bookbinding. But the leather is not really marbled; it has had an acid poured over it, and sort of "swirled around" (the artist shifts the angles of the leather so that the acid runs here and there), and creates a "pattern" that looks like marbling. The use of the acid is similar to that in the making of MOTTLED CALF and TREE CALF.

Carter says that marbling is done by drawing "a stick or comb into a pattern" (p. 166). "Stick" is not precisely the tool. It is called a rake (a tool looking like a comb, but with its "teeth" made not of fine needles or toothpick-shaped teeth, but with heavier pieces of wood, spaced far apart. The rake would allow for the first manipulation of the pigment droplets; the comb could then be used for finer lines in the resulting pattern. And not all marbling is produced this way, creating patterns. The stochastic distribution of drops of pigment over the surface of the size in the marbling bath can yield attractive sheets with no patterns at all. Further, there is oil-and-water marbling, the simplest kind, in which no size need be prepared. Oil-based pigments are dropped onto the surface of a bath of water. The droplets float and can be moved around a bit, but cannot really be combed into patterns.

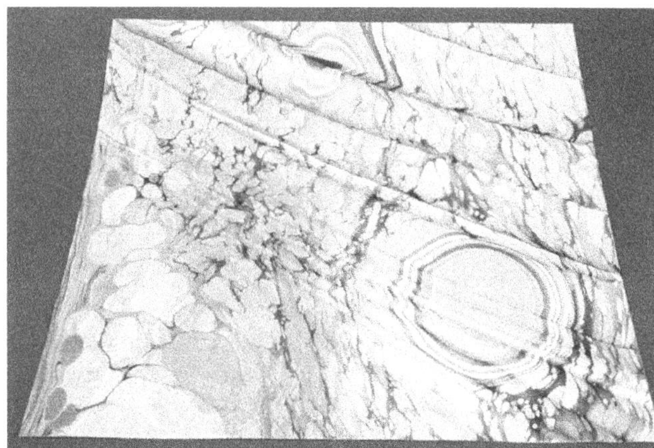

Marbled sheet; random distribution of pigments and with a Spanish wave. Photograph by Jeff Dykes. Berger-Cloonan Collection of Decorated Paper; Texas A&M University.

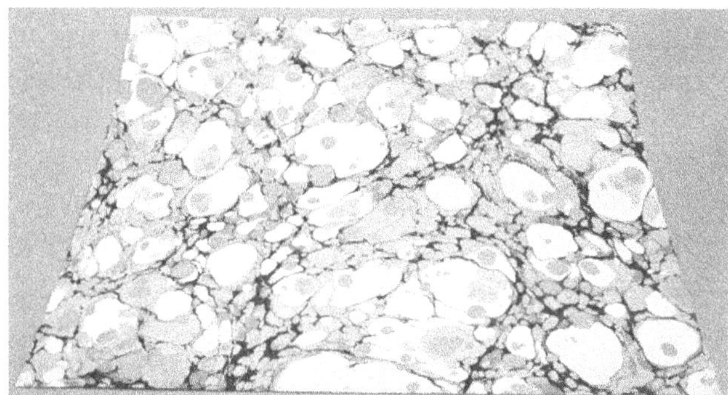

Marbled sheet; stone pattern. Photograph by Jeff Dykes. Berger-Cloonan Collection of Decorated Paper; Texas A&M University.

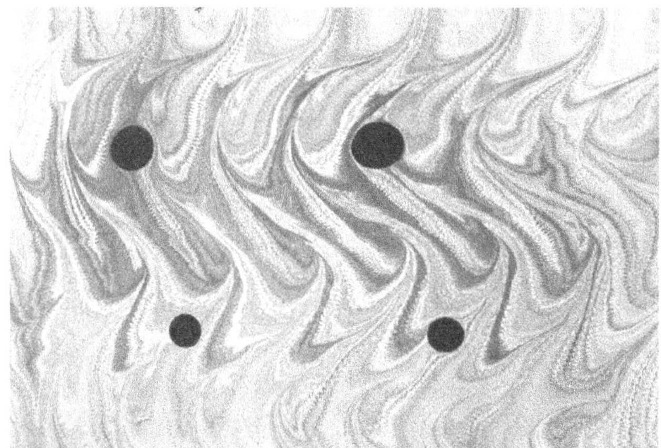

Marbled sheet by Karli Frigge; wings pattern. Photograph by Jeff Dykes. Berger-Cloonan Collection of Decorated Paper; Texas A&M University.

The basic techniques for traditional marbling (not the oil-on-water kind, but the method using a size thickened by carragheenin, Irish moss, or some other thickener) have not changed for centuries, and since the early 20th century, marbling has become a major occupation in Turkey, with more than 45,000 marblers practicing the craft. The Turks are particularly noted for their marbled flowers. There is an enormous literature about the craft.

MARC CODE LIST FOR ORGANIZATIONS. *See* Library codes.

MARC RECORDS. An acronym for MAchine Readable Cataloging, that is, the use of computers to record bibliographical data in cataloging. The system of MARC records was created by Henriette Avram, who "joined the Library of Congress in 1965. With no background in library work, she was assigned to develop an automated cataloging format where none had existed" (Schudel, "Henriette Avram, 'Mother of MARC,' Dies"). Schudel adds, "The MARC format was in use at the Library of Congress by 1970, and within a decade most larger libraries in the country had converted to the automated system, abandoning their manual card files." Today most libraries with online systems use one of the MARC versions in the United States, Canada, and Europe. (See Library of Congress, "What Is MARC Record, and Why Is It Important?")

The MARC records contain set data fields for recording a great deal of information, such as author, title, city of publication, publisher, date, holding institutions, pagination, content, language, media type, and so on. There is also a field for copy-specific information—showing what features a particular copy has that might differ from the features of other copies of the same item. Whether this complex cataloging system has a future is uncertain. It requires much training for one to create MARC records. Because these records are complex and do require special training to create, a new form of cataloging is being implemented in a host of libraries: RDA (Resource Description and Access). Libraries now shifting to RDA include the Library of Congress, the U.S. National Agricultural Library, the National Library of Medicine, the British Library, and libraries in Canada, Germany, and Australia. Hence, MARC may not have a solid future despite the existence of billions of records that exist today in the MARC format. RDA is "the successor to AACR2. Resource Description and Access (RDA) is a standard for descriptive cataloging providing instructions and guidelines on formulating bibliographic data. . . . [It] is a set of cataloging instructions based on FRBR [Functional Requirements for Bibliographic Records, 'a 1998 recommendation of the International Federation of Library Associations and Institutions (IFLA) to restructure catalog databases to reflect the conceptual structure of information resources'; see bibliography under FRBR] and FRAD [Functional Requirements for Authority Data, 'a highly theoretical, entity-relationship (E-R) model for authority data. Published in 2009 by the International Federation of Library Associations and Institutions (IFLA), FRAD extends and expands upon the FRBR (Functional Requirements for Bibliographic Records) model'; see bibliography under FRAD], for producing the description and name and title access points representing a resource. RDA offers libraries the potential to change significantly how bibliographic data is created and used. RDA is a standard for resource description and access designed for the digital world. It provides (i) A flexible framework for describing all resources (analog and digital) that is extensible for new types of material, (ii) Data that is readily adaptable to new and emerging database structures, (iii) Data that is compatible with existing records in online library catalogs. RDA is a package of data elements, guidelines, and instructions for creating library and cultural heritage resource metadata that are well-formed according to international models for user-focused linked data applications. RDA goes beyond earlier cataloging codes in that it provides guidelines on cataloging digital resources and places a stronger emphasis on helping users find, identify, select, and obtain the information they want. RDA also supports the clustering of bibliographic records in order to show relationships between works and their creators." For the latest information (as of 14 July 2021) on such cataloging, please see the entry for ANGLO-AMERICAN CATALOGUING RULES.

I have given a good deal of space to this entry because of the importance of all this information to booksellers, collectors, and librarians, in particular, and to researchers in general. Being able to access and interpret the records referred to here is becoming progressively crucial in a digital realm when an increasing amount of information is available online. We must often seek it out and be able to interpret it for us to become ever more knowledgeable about books and other formats of materials and the information they contain. (See Joudrey and Taylor, *The Organization of Information.*)

MARDERSTEIG, GIOVANNI (HANS) (1892–1977) (Stamperia Valdonega; Officina Bodoni). "Giovanni Mardersteig, original name Hans Mardersteig (born Jan. 8, 1892, Weimar, Ger.—died Dec. 27, 1977, Verona, Italy), printer and typographer who, as head of Officina Bodoni, created books exemplifying the highest standards in the art of printing" ("Giovanni Mardersteig, Italian Printer," *Encyclopaedia Britannica*, http://www.britannica.com/biography/Giovanni

-Mardersteig [accessed 9 June 2021]). After studying law and teaching, "In 1917 he joined the publishing house of Kurt Wolff, in Leipzig, where he was in charge of the publication of a series of art books and edited the art journal *Genius*. / 1922 Mardersteig moved to Montagnola, near Lugano, Italy, where he founded Officina Bodoni. His first book (1923) was an edition of Politian's *Favola d'Orfeo*; other early works included Shelley's *Epipsychidion*, Shakespeare's *Tempest*, and Dante's *Vita nuova*. These and other works were printed by Mardersteig alone, using his handpress, and they earned him an international reputation. Later, he acquired a few assistants. He received permission from the Italian government to cast type from Giambattista Bodoni's original matrices, and many of his editions used these Bodoni types" (*Encyclopaedia Britannica*). His books were elegantly designed and for them he usually used the finest materials. He published over 200 books and pamphlets. "The press specialized in small editions, printed with meticulous care on an old-fashioned handpress that occupied a room in his house. In addition to Fontana, he also designed the typefaces Dante, Griffo, and Zeno. / From 1947 Mardersteig also operated the Stamperia Valdonèga in Verona. This organization, continued after Mardersteig's death by his son Martino, became known for larger editions than those of the Officina Bodoni, but it, too, emphasized fine workmanship" (*Encyclopaedia Britannica*). He also printed volumes for the LIMITED EDITIONS CLUB. (See Barr, *The Officina Bodoni, Montagnola, Verona*; Dreyfus, *Giovanni Mardersteig*; Kelly et al., *Giovanni and Martino Mardersteig*; and Schmoller, *Two Titans*.)

MARGINALIA. Notes and other scribbles—and decorative elements—in margins of books and manuscripts, broadsides, pamphlets, and other printed and manuscript matter. In medieval manuscripts, marginalia can be planned by the original scribes and book designers—taking the form of all kinds of images, but the term usually implies words, squiggles, and artwork of various kinds added by later users of the volume. They can be commentary on the text, additional text, corrections, or anything else the writer deems important or necessary (shopping lists, curses, ruminations, and so on), or they can have nothing at all to do with the text they are written in. One common small piece of marginalia is the FIST (or manicule), pointing to what the annotator thinks is important or thinks he will want to locate quickly at a later time than when the mark is made. It is equivalent to modern HIGHLIGHTING.

In printed books, the same kinds of annotations can appear. For the most part, books that contain marginalia have lost some of their value since collectors want copies as PRISTINE as possible, and these scratchings can be looked on as defects or flaws. However, marginalia by recognized, important people (including the author of the volume itself) can enhance the item fiscally and intellectually. A copy of an edition with the author's marginalia correcting errors or in preparation for a new edition can add considerably to a volume's worth. A copy of Ezra Pound's *A Lume Spento* surfaced some years ago with his own HOLOGRAPH corrections and with a stanza crossed out and replaced with a new one. (See Berger, "Another Copy of Ezra Pound's *A Lume Spento*.") The notes of a scholar elucidating the text could add to the book's value, as can the underlining of a well-known author or other eminent person. (See also H. J. Jackson, *Marginalia: Readers Writing in Books*; Stoddard, *Marks in Books*.)

MARGINS. The areas in a printed or manuscript text that surround the printed or written text. Texts can be flush left, flush right, centered, or a combination of these. (*See* Justification.) The margins are usually delineated by where they are: HEAD margin, TAIL margin, FORE-EDGE margin, and GUTTER. In manuscripts of the Middle Ages, margins were often laid out geometrically, not by measure, so they were often in the so-called 2 / 3 / 4 / 5 proportions. (For an illustration and discussion, *see* Layout.)

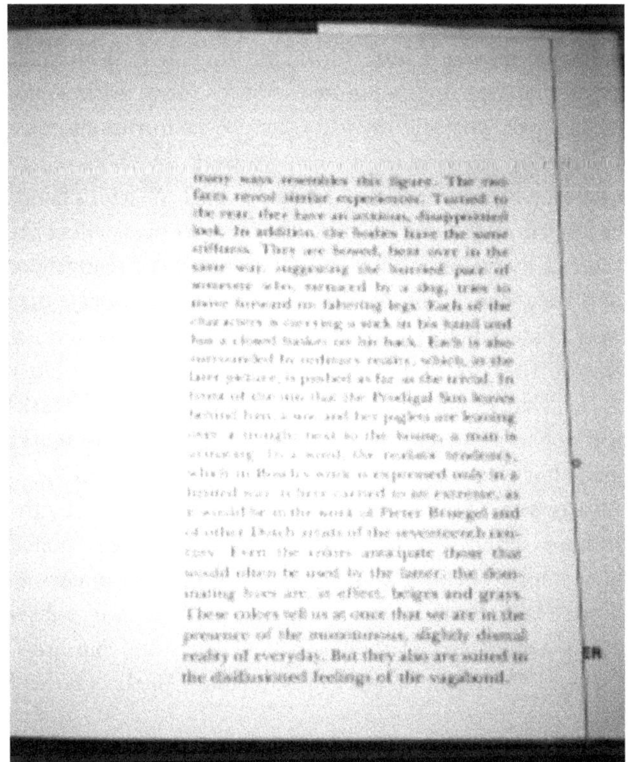

Odd margins in Joseph-Emile Muller, *Bosch* (New York: Leon Amiel, Publisher, n.d.).

Collection of the author.

In early books, generous margins made sense: to allow the reader to hold the volume without getting her hand in the way of the text, to leave room for notes and commentary, to give the binder some leeway in trimming the text to remove the BOLTS (i.e., the folds) and to make the TEXT BLOCK fit into the BOARDS, and to lend an air of sumptuousness to the volume with the extra space on the page. Wider margins enhanced the reading experience.

Modern publishers saw margins as costing money—space where text could be. The more text they got onto the page, the more paper they would save. By the middle of the 20th century, books were being produced as cheaply as the publishers could get away with, and shrunken margins were a way to achieve this. The reduction in the size of margins was sometimes occasioned by a scarcity in paper, as was the case during the Colonial period in U.S. history, and also during wartime. Margins were also places that designers could experiment. Sometimes the space surrounding a text was elegant, sometimes it was bizarre.

MARKS IN BOOKS. A term meaning "marks in books." Hmm. That is, any kind of marking that can be found on pages: underlining, HIGHLIGHTING, squiggles, drawings, annotations, explanations, critiques, crossing-outs (*see* Bisquing), censorship marks, crayon splotches from unruly offspring, coffee stains, tea stains, bourbon stains, diatribes, or something else. Clearly, the marks could have been made by *anyone*, and they could be useful for many reasons, not the least of which is PROVENANCE. These intrusions must be noted in any kind of cataloging record—in a bookseller's catalog, a library MARC RECORD, a personal collector's handlist, or an AUCTION CATALOG. They can seriously affect the value of the volume (intellectually or fiscally), negatively or positively, depending on who made the marks, when they were made, whether they are expungible, or for some other reason. The older the marks, the less offensive they are likely to be. That is, an INCUNABULUM with 15th-century marks will not suffer much in value; the same volume with marks made last week may lose a good deal of its value. As Pablo Alvarez says, "Mostly, these marks were not intended by the authors, scribes and printers as they originally envisioned their books, but were later included in the form of corrections, readers' marginalia, drawings, and traces of subsequent ownerships as shown in bookplates and bindings" (Alvarez, "Marks in Books"). (*See* Stoddard, *Marks in Books.*)

MARRIED. Used to indicate that one part of a VOLUME has been joined by another part that was not originally part of the very volume under discussion. For example, if a volume lacks its DUST JACKET, but someone has supplied one from another copy, they are said to be a married item. Sometimes it is not possible to spot such a marriage; but if a dust jacket from a later edition, printing, or issue winds up on a FIRST EDITION, first IMPRESSION of a text, that marriage may be easy to spot. (*See* Edition, Impression [Printing], Issue, and State; Points.)

The term is also used to indicate when volumes or fascicles of a set have been assembled from two or more sets. The Brick Row Book Shop description of a Charles Dickens first edition of *Dombey and Son* says: "A set of Dombey and Son in original parts, completely UNSOPHISTICATED. . . . Dickens novels IN PARTS with the evidence of the CONTEMPORARY ownership on each WRAPPER are scarce, and such PROVENANCE is virtually the only way to establish that a set has not been SOPHISTICATED, 'married' or 'MADE UP.'" (The Brick Row Book Shop; Miscellany Eighty-Three: An Antiquarian Sampler; Books@brickrow.com [accessed 9 November 2020].)

MASS DEACIDIFICATION. A technique developed in the 20th century to remove (or neutralize) the acid in library materials by subjecting large quantities of these materials all at once—in a large, sealed chamber—to a neutralizing agent. The deacidification uses a nonaqueous (gaseous) system, and its aim is to neutralize acids and leave an alkaline reserve in the paper sufficient to prevent future decay. (*See* Deacidification.) In the United States, only the Bookkeeper method was recently used—primarily at the Library of Congress.

Because of budget issues and the view that other methods of protection can extend the lives of books and other library materials, the Library of Congress is apparently phasing out its mass deacidification project. Its *Fiscal 2021 Budget Justification Submitted for Use of the Committees on Appropriations* recommends the cessation of the project: "Over 80 percent of the priority treatment goals are complete and overall need is declining. . . . For the deacidification program, PRES intends to continue with planned production through fiscal 2021, completing deacidification of approximately 170,000 book equivalent volumes and one million sheets of manuscript materials in the period of performance ending May 31 of 2022. At that time, the Mass Deacidification program will be at a level of substantial completeness for bound volumes, having treated over 90 percent of top priority materials and over 70 percent of the total projected need. From that point, the Library believes that the large scale program can be discontinued as the cost per unit becomes more prohibitive" (p. 157). The information here was accessed in July 2021. Gary Price, who writes the "info/docket" for *Library Journal*, posted on 5 November 2021 the following article: "The Library of Congress Awards $5.5 Million Contract For 'Mass Deacidification of Library Collection'" (see under Price in the bibliography). So it seems as though, despite what their own budget justification reported, the Library of Congress is proceeding with the mass deacidification project, at least for now.

MASS-MARKET. An adjectival phrase to indicate the commercial version of a text, produced in large numbers, that may have been issued in a LIMITED EDITION. Hence, one might see "mass-market paperback" or "mass-market version" to distinguish this item from a copy that was done in, say, only 100 copies.

MASTER PROOFS. *See* Proofs.

MASTHEAD. The area, usually at the top of the first page, of a newspaper, newsletter, or other publication (though the masthead can also appear elsewhere) in which the publication's name and other information are printed. Other information can include the place and date of publication, the number of the volume or issue, the name of the publisher, the price for the issue, the motto of the publication, names of editors or owners of the item, subscription information, or anything else the publisher wants to put there. The publication's logo (if it has one) is often in the masthead, as well.

MATRIX (in type making). The receptacle—like a mold—into which type metal is poured to form the SORTS. The matrix is like a gelatin mold: it contains impressed in it the shape of the character to be cast, right-reading (i.e., not in a mirror image). When TYPE METAL is poured into the matrix, the sort is formed, "backward" (i.e., in a mirror image); the sort will be inked and will print positive. The matrix traditionally was formed with a PUNCH, though in the 19th century, matrices could be made in other ways. The matrix is put into the bottom of a hand mold (*see* Mold [type casting]), the two parts of the mold are put together, a spring (or "bow") is moved under the matrix to hold it in place during the casting, molten type metal is poured into the funnel in the mold, and the metal casts into the matrix, forming the sort in a split second. The mold is opened, the sort is removed, and the process is repeated. When the matrix is struck with the punch, some of the copper of the matrix is displaced, leaving a bulge. This is called an "unjustified matrix"; the bulging metal must be filed away. When it is and the punch is perfectly squared off, the result is a "justified matrix." (For an image of a Linotype matrix, *see* the entry for Mergenthaler, Ottmar; for an image of a Monotype matrix holder, *see* Monotype; for an image of a punch and two matrices—one justified and one unjustified—*see* Punch [in type making]. *See also* Justification [in type making].)

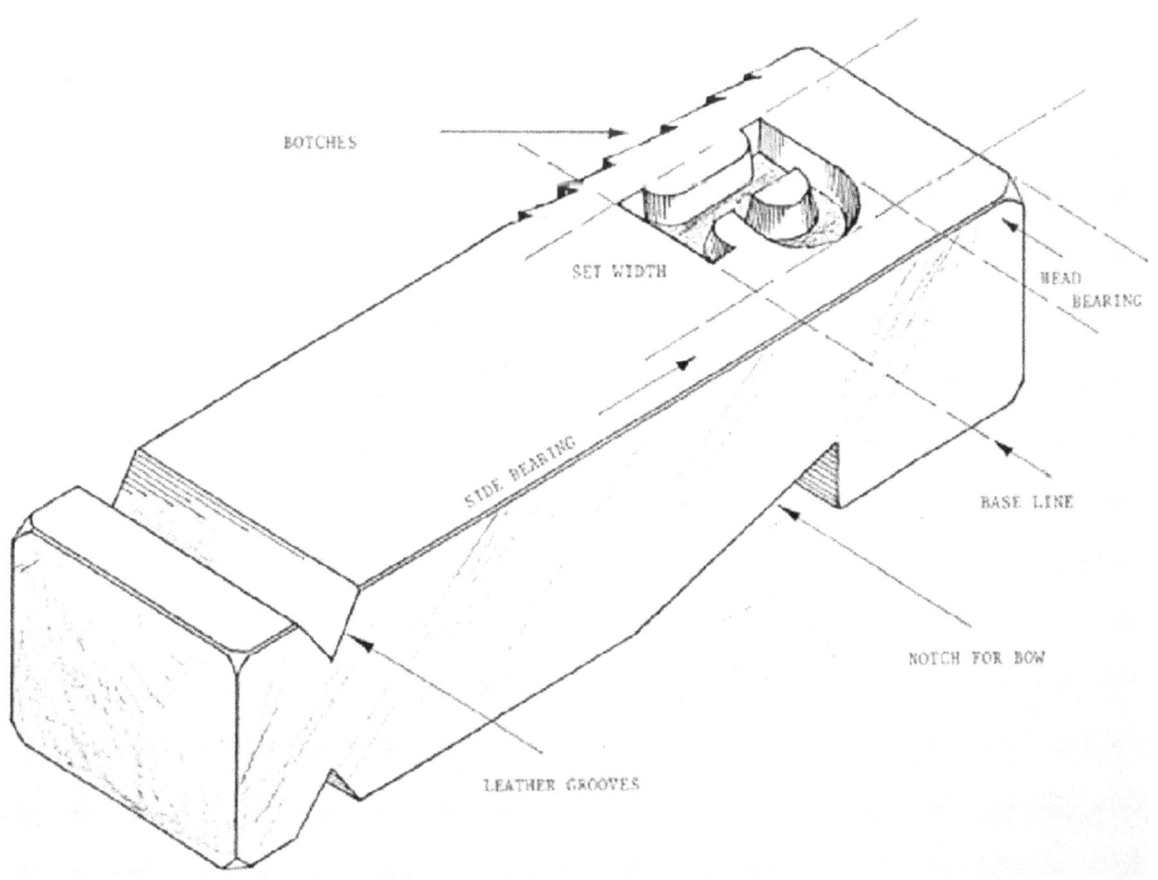

Drawing of a matrix with the parts delineated. Drawing by Stan Nelson.
Courtesy of Stan Nelson.

MATRIX (the journal). One of the premier bibliographic journals in history. Begun in the autumn of 1981 by John and Rosalind Randle, this annual is a compilation of items and illustrations about books—fine printing, presswork, papermaking, binding, editing, writing, biographies of important people in the book world, and other BOOK ARTS. The issues contain bound- or TIPPED-IN fliers, PAMPHLETS, photographs, WOODCUTS, BROADSIDES, and many other kinds of things, and the publication is issued in a regular version with a stiff paper cover and a deluxe version with a leather spine, paper over boards, and SLIPCASED, and with an extra portfolio containing a variety of kinds of other COLLECTIBLES. The articles are written by the most informed writers in their fields, the production values of the volumes are extremely high, and the text is a treasure trove of information available nowhere else. At the present writing (June 2022), 34 volumes have been issued. Considered by many the finest periodical on the book arts published in the 20th and 21st centuries, exceeding in importance *THE FLEURON*, *THE COLOPHON*, and *THE DOLPHIN*. Update: It has recently been announced that the publication of *Matrix* is now at an end. The loss of this giant in the book world will be mourned by many.

MAUCHLINE BINDING. A book binding in which the covers are made of a polished wood over which a transfer pattern has been adhered. Sometimes the boards were covered with a cloth tartan, and the transfer pattern, on a piece of wood, was adhered to the cover. Rather than a transfer pattern, in some cases a pattern is created on the wood (front and back covers) by exposing the boards to the sun and placing ferns or flowers over the cover, the sun darkening the SUBSTRATE, but the ferns keeping the areas they cover lighter in color. "A decorative technique that originated in the 1830s in the Scottish town of Mauchline in which a transfer print of a wood engraving, often a color design (tartan or floral motif), was applied to a lacquered wooden object, such as the boards of a bookbinding. In the 1860s, photographs and stencils began to be used in the design process. Mauchline ware reached a peak of popularity in the 1880s, disappearing in the 1920s" (Reitz, *Online Dictionary for Library and Information Science*). (*See* Transfer paper.)

Mauchline binding. "Collection of Burns's songs printed in Mauchline, Ayrshire (not far from the Burns birthplace at Alloway) in about 1854. The binding is an example of the cottage industry of wooden transferware, most often with a Burns connection, that developed in Mauchine [*sic*], and known, appropriately enough, as Mauchline Ware. . . . This binding has a full tartan pattern transferred onto it, with an inset Scottish landscape scene."

Image and description by Michael Weisenberg, "The Irvin Department of Rare Books & Special Collections Blog"; University Libraries, University of South Carolina; https://digital.library.sc.edu/blogs/rbsc/a-burns-gift-book-in-a-mauchline-ware-binding/ (accessed 12 July 2021).

Front cover of a "Mauchline Ware binding consisting of morocco-backed wooden boards, the upper cover with 5 vignettes of Melrose Abbey, Edinburgh Castle and Holyrood Palace, the back cover with a larger vignette central of the Scott Memorial, Edinburgh. . . ." (image and description by Rob Rulon-Miller, Rulon-Miller Books website: http://rbmsthesauri.pbworks.com/w/page/51851134/Mauchline%20ware%20bindings [accessed 12 July 2021]).

Courtesy of Rob Rulon-Miller.

MAZARIN BIBLE. *See* Gutenberg, Johannes.

McKENZIE, D[ONALD] F[RANCIS] (1931–1999). One of the prominent bibliographical and textual scholars of the 20th century. Born in New Zealand, he studied at Cambridge University in England. As a doctoral candidate he worked on printing history, immersing himself in the relatively unused archives of Cambridge University Press, which recorded publishing activities from the 1690s through the 18th century. "With its wealth of documentation and informed attention to the relationship between the finished books and the records of their production, he brought the printing house to life, disproved many old theories and assumptions about why books look as they do, and laid the foundation for much of the rest of his career. The resulting two volumes, *The Cambridge University Press 1696–1712: A Bibliographical Study,* published in 1966, remain the locus classicus on the daily running of an early printing house" (McKitterick, "Obituary: Professor Donald McKenzie"). His prominence in the field is based on a host of things, including his teaching, the many honors and awards he received, and his numerous publications. A lecture series, "The D. F. McKenzie Lectures at Oxford University," brings in major bibliographers yearly.

McKERROW, RONALD BRUNLEES (1872–1940). One of the premier bibliographers of the 20th century. His *Introduction to Bibliography for Literary Students* (see the bibliography) was the primary such text for decades until it was supplanted by Philip Gaskell's *New Introduction to Bibliography*. McKerrow was a scholar of book history, early English drama, and the early book trade. (See his other classical texts in the bibliography.) Many of us cut our bibliographical teeth on his *Introduction to Bibliography* and his equally insightful and influential *Prolegomena to the Oxford Shakespeare* (see the bibliography).

McLEOD COLLATOR. A mechanical collating machine invented by Randall McLeod. The device "uses the operator's two eyes viewing texts simultaneously. The two images are then superimposed by the human brain, trained for binocular vision. In McLeod's words, the images 'suddenly fuse [and] [t]he brain . . . sees only one page.' Where the two settings of type are identical, the image appears solid, but any differences appear to 'shimmer,' and gain depth, like the pictures seen through a stereoscope" (quoted from "Library Machines"; see also Randall McLeod in the bibliography).

McLOUGHLIN BROS. A prolific publishing house based in New York. "The McLoughlin brothers, John Jr. (1827–1905) and Edmund (1833/4–1889), were New York publishers who operated from 1858 to 1920. They produced books and games for children for over fifty years. As one of the first publishers to focus exclusively on products for children, McLoughlin Brothers was able to shape and define the American picture book market" (Hewes and Wasowicz, *Radiant with Color & Art: McLoughlin Brothers and the Business of Picture Books, 1858–1920*). The company produced thousands of titles of children's games, puzzles, chapbooks, and books, many of the texts taken from earlier works and rewritten and condensed (e.g., *Robinson Crusoe*, *Three Little Pigs*, and Mother Goose). There were also many ABCderia and other educational texts, fairy tales, and religious stories. The publications were mostly printed with chromolithography. The American Antiquarian Society website says, "The Society holds one of the major repositories of McLoughlin Bros. materials, including over 1,700 picture books, games, paper toys, publishers' catalogs, and original art work. McLoughlin publications are particularly well known for their use of colored illustrations, which were hand-stenciled during the firm's early years and printed using chromolithographs and photo engravings later on" (American Antiquarian Society, "McLoughlin Bros. Collection"). While the production values were fairly inexpensive, the pamphlets they published withstood the rigors of a fairly destructive readership, and untold numbers of these books (or, more properly, booklets) survived, though usually in poor condition. They have become serious collectibles, and those in good condition can command reasonably solid prices. They came in several sizes, and they were usually single-signature, stapled volumes.

MEANDER (or Meandros; also called the "Greek fret" or "Greek key"). A decorative border made from a repeated "continuous line that folds back on itself replicating the Maeander River which is located in Turkey" (Revolution Performance Fabrics, "The Origins of the Greek Key Pattern").

Variations of the Meander or Greek key border.

Laurel Home; https://laurelberninteriors.com/2018/07/03/greek-key-motif/variations-on-a-greek-key-motif-theme/ (accessed 2 February 2021).

This is one of the many decorative RULES used as BORDERS in printing. (*See* Rule/Ruling.)

MEARNE, SAMUEL (1624–1683). "An English publisher, bookseller, and bookbinder, about whom little definitive knowledge exists. While Mearne's name is associated with the splendid cottage style [*see* Cottage binding], some authorities have expressed doubts that he actually bound any books himself, but rather that the famous Mearne bindings were executed by the Dutch bookbinder Suckerman, and that Mearne was a publisher, not a bookbinder. It has been established, however, that Mearne's second apprenticeship was with Jeremy Arnold, a bookbinder and it is therefore argued that he must have learned the craft, the question being how many books he actually bound. It is probably unlikely that he would have taken the time to bind books following the Restoration, because he quickly became an important figure in the book trade" (Roberts and Etherington, "Samuel Mearne"; https://cool.culturalheritage.org/don/dt/dt2203.html [accessed 15 March 2021]). Mearne's importance in the book trade exceeded his importance as a bookbinder, for, though he studied binding, he never practiced it to the extent that modern book purveyors would have us believe. Many a 17th-century binding has been attributed to him with little evidence that he was responsible for it. The workshop he oversaw created elegant binding with ONLAYS and gold TOOLING. (See Nixon, *Five Centuries of English Bookbinding*, in which is revealed that many a binding can be attributed to Mearne's shop, pp. 32–33.)

MEASURE. The length of a printed line, usually measured in PICAS.

MECHANICAL WOOD PULP. The pulp used for extremely cheap paper; originally used extensively for newspapers, which are one major kind of EPHEMERA, so if the papers discolored and became brittle quickly, the companies that used it did not care since the papers were to be discarded soon after their use. But the cheapness of the material made it attractive to book publishers, who used it in PAPERBACKS. It is called "mechanical" because the fibers were prepared using mechanical means—being ground up as opposed to being broken down with chemicals. Roberts and Etherington say, "A papermaking pulp produced by mechanical means only. The resultant fibers, which are produced by abrading the de-barked logs against a grinding wheel, are short, the average length being about 3 to 4 mm, with an average diameter of about 0.03 mm. Paper made from 100% mechanical wood pulp has relatively low strength, discolors fairly rapidly upon exposure to air and light (possibly because no lignin is removed from the fibers), and has very little permanence. It does, however, possess good bulk, opacity, and compressibility, which are desirable characteristics in some BOARDS, book papers, and printing or writing papers" (p. 168). The pulp was full of lignin and some chemicals, and the resulting paper was highly acidic, beginning to turn yellow and brittle soon after being manufactured. This slight exaggeration suggests that most such paper was as inexpensive as it could be and was used for what publishers suspected would be books that were seen as ephemera. (*See* Chemical wood pulp.)

MEDALLIONS. *See* Cameo binding.

MENDING TAPE; MENDING TISSUE. Strips or sheets of material (usually paper) used to repair damaged LEAVES. Usually the tape, especially for the last, say, 50 years, has been fairly invisible when it is applied, as with JAPANESE TISSUE. Booksellers, conservators, librarians, and collectors—or anyone making repairs—should choose such papers carefully, being certain to use acid-free, archival tapes.

MERGENTHALER, OTTMAR (1854–1899). Inventor of the Linotype machine around 1884. The revolution in book production launched by GUTENBERG's inventions was practically equaled by that occasioned by the Linotype. With mechanical papermaking, automated printing, and many other parts of book production fully mechanized, the one thing slowing down the publishing process was TYPESETTING, which, despite many attempts to automate, resisted successful operation until the Linotype came along. (See Kahan, *Ottmar Mergenthaler*; Levine, *Miracle Man of Printing*; Schlesinger, *The Biography of Ottmar Mergenthaler*.)

Having used a Linotype as a youth, I have always been amazed at its versatility, its speed, and the noise it made. The machine casts full lines of type, mechanically, from matrices (*see* Matrix [in type making]) released from a magazine (a huge container holding hundreds of mats [as they are called]) as the operator struck the keys of a keyboard. The mats lined up as the keyboarder (whom we can call the "COMPOSITOR") keyed in the text. When the line was fully keyed in, the compositor "activated" the SPACEBANDS to JUSTIFY the line and then sent the mats to the casting position in the machine. The line of type, in the form of a SLUG, was cast in the machine and was released to a GALLEY-like tray in the order in which it was cast, one line at a time. The molten metal was kept in a cauldron at the back of the machine, and it was delivered in spurts to the casting part of the machine. Since each casting produces one line of type, it was only natural for Mergenthaler to call the machine a Linotype.

Mergenthaler worked on the machine for many years, from its invention in about 1884 until his death in 1899, constantly making improvements. A single magazine of matrices could hold more than one FONT. Matrices were created to cast ROMAN or ITALIC from a single matrix. Multiple magazines could be mounted to allow the compositor to set from more than one FONT of type—in more than one size (e.g., 12-point for text and 18-point for headlines)—without having to remove one magazine from the machine and replace it with another.

The speed with which compositors could "set type" with a Linotype outpaced the work of compositors setting from individual SORTS. Owners of newspapers, who saw the tremendous advantage of such speed, bankrolled Mergenthaler, and he rewarded them with a machine that had the capacity to allow their printers to publish two or more editions of newspapers each day, increasing their sales tremendously.

As previously mentioned, I worked briefly on a Linotype machine as a student reporter on my university's newspaper. I studied its miraculous workings, with its endless moving parts, the large ingot of type metal on a hook hanging into a pot and feeding the caster inside the machine, the matrices released one at a time by individual keystrokes of the compositor, the movement of these matrices into position ready to be cast, the sound of the casting and the parts rattling and hissing and the clank of all the moving parts, the click of the Linotype slug as it emerged still hot from the caster, the movement of the matrices to the top of the machine to be automatically dropped back into their magazine in the proper channels, and so on. It was indeed a miracle of invention, and it sped up typesetting to a pace that quickly put handsetting compositors out of business. Where it might take a compositor a few hours to set a page of type by hand, the keyboard compositor at the Linotype machine could do it in minutes. It is no wonder that newspapers and book publishers bought these machines by the thousands.

The set text emerges from the machine as slugs of TYPE METAL with the text in relief on its surface. Hence, it produces "type" that mimics LETTERPRESS (i.e., RELIEF) printing, and such printing is indistinguishable from the work done from individual sorts. (See Romano, *History of the Linotype Company*.)

Linotype machine.
Getty Images; iStock.

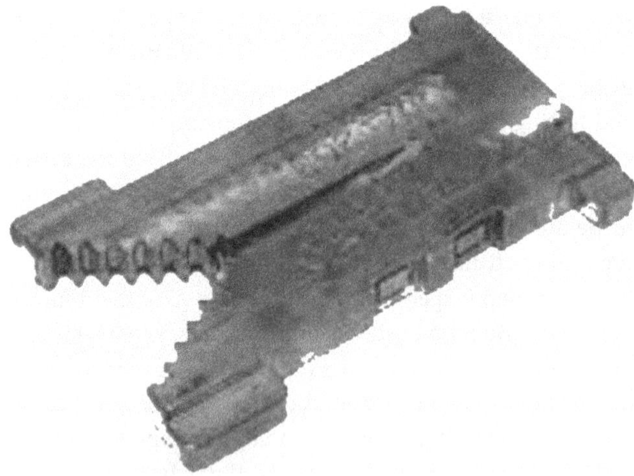

Linotype matrix, with the character to be cast along the edge. The V-shaped configuration of "teeth" at the bottom of the matrix differs from one matrix to another and these "teeth" instruct the machine which channel in the magazine above the machine to drop the matrix into.

Collection of the author.

Linotype slugs; from Frederick W. Warburton, "Composition by the Linotype Machine."

Hitchcock, ed., *The Building of a Book*, p. 64.

MERKER, KIM (1932–2013) (Stone Wall Press; Windhover Press). One of the premier fine-press printers in the United States in the 20th century. Proprietor of Stone Wall Press (his own imprint from 1957 on) and Windhover Press (the imprint he used at the University of Iowa from 1963 until a stroke ended his printing in 1996). He was HARRY DUNCAN's most accomplished student at the University of Iowa, where he went to enroll in the university's celebrated Writer's Workshop but where, under Duncan, he discovered printing, which changed the course of his life.

All of his printing was done on HANDPRESSES (mostly WASHINGTONS) and VANDERCOOKS, with handset type, and usually using dampened handmade paper. He was meticulous as a printer, using graceful TYPEFACES (Bembo, Cancelleresca Bastarda, Dante, Joanna, Lutetia, Romanée, Romulus, and other classical faces) and with spare, elegant TYPOGRAPHY. As a poet himself, he was a superb critic, and with the Writer's Workshop at his disposal, he was able to meet many young and upcoming poets with important careers ahead of them. He printed the first, or significant, volumes of Mark Strand, Donald Justice, Theodore Roethke, W. S. Merwin, George Bernard Shaw, Henry David Thoreau, Mona van Duyn, H. D. (Hilda Doolittle), Charles Olson, Ezra Pound, William Carlos Williams, Philip Levine, James Tate, Gary Snyder, Thom Gunn, Denis Johnson, Margaret Sunday, Dana Gioia, F. Scott Fitzgerald, and many others.

Merker started the Iowa Center for the Book (later the name was changed to the University of Iowa Center for the Book) in 1986, uniting the crafts of printing, printmaking, papermaking, and photography with academic disciplines in writing, literature, bibliography, and history, to produce what is still a popular academic program at the University of Iowa. His influence can be seen in the books he designed and printed, in the many writers he discovered and whose works he published, and in the following generation of printers he trained. (*See* Fine-press printing; see Berger, *Printing and the Mind of Merker*; O'Connell, "The Quality of Response"; and Vitello, "Kim Merker, Hand-Press Printer of Poets, Is Dead at 81.")

METAL POINT RULING. Ruling of a manuscript leaf using a hard metal point. Not the same as HARD POINT RULING in that metal point leaves marks that "are more discreet than those made with ink but more visible than those made with a hard point" (Brown, *Understanding Illuminated Manuscripts*, p. 86). Michelle P. Brown also says that the "mark [made with the metal point] varies in appearance according to the metal used (and any alloys present), with a ferrous point leaving a brown mark, silver and lead (LEAD POINT) leaving a silver-gray trace, and copper alloys sometimes leaving a gray-green mark" (p. 86). (*See* Rule [in manuscripts and in printing].)

METAMORPHIC BOOKS (or Metamorphosis books). A term used for books that contain metamorphic pictures: images that can be transformed into one or more other pictures by turning, folding, or sliding a section. They are part of the larger genre of MOVABLE BOOKS. The most common form is the volume with several (or many) leaves, stacked up in the book, with all of them slit all the way through the volume, creating a host of panels on each LEAF; the text or (more commonly) the image on each panel can be turned to reveal the equivalent panel beneath, that has a different text or image (or both). Each time a panel is turned, a new composite text is produced. (These are sometimes called

A metamorphic book: *Metamorphose* (France[?]: n.p., 1864). Images courtesy of Antiquariat F. Neidhardt, Böblingen, Germany.
Courtesy of Max Neidhardt, Antiquariat F. Neidhardt.

"slice books," as explained in a personal communiqué by Ellen G. K. Rubin, author of *Ideas in Motion*.) The form is distantly related to the EXQUISITE CORPSE. Since the possibilities of such combinations of disparate images can produce truly ridiculous pictures, the genre is particularly suited to children's books. The David Gantz volume *The Mix or Match Storybook*, with its eight leaves each cut into seven panels (each panel containing text and image), claims to yield 2,097,152 possible story combinations. Hervé Tullet's *The Game of Mix-up Art* contains no verbal text, only abstract art on each page; its seven cardboard leaves, illustrated on both sides, are cut into three panels each. A great number of illustrations—individual works of art—can be seen when one flips the individual panels and views the resultant abstract pictures, observing from the front of the volume or the rear. A similar technique, but with a slightly different structure, goes back at least as early as 1831, when the Harrisburg, Pennsylvania, publisher G. S. Peters published *Metamorphosis; or, a Transformation of Pictures, with Poetical Explanations, for the Amusement of Young Persons*. This little children's volume opens to a two-page spread; each leaf is slit horizontally down the middle of the sheet, creating a top and a bottom flap, the two pieces containing a full-page image. When the top flap is raised, an image beneath it is revealed and "completes" the picture on the bottom flap; and vice versa, with the bottom flap. The volume accordions out to four such panels.

Leaves from the metamorphic book shown in figure above: *Metamorphose*. (France [?]: n.p., 1864).
Courtesy of Max Neidhardt, Antiquariat F. Neidhardt.

This particular form of movables was called a "harlequinade." Ian Dooley explains, "A Harlequinade, so named because many works featured the comic Harlequin character, is created when two ENGRAVED sheets are pasted together. Each sheet contains four VIGNETTE engravings." (See Ian Dooley, "The Truth Within.") What makes the Harlequinade so unique, however, is that the top sheet is cut into eight separate sections which reveal the sheet beneath when one turns up the flaps of each section (thus, why the harlequinade is also called a metamorphic book, flap-book, or turn-up book). Each vignette is accompanied by simple verse, usually containing instructions to turn the flaps and reveal the transformative accompanying image (and last verse) underneath. Harlequinades are usually didactic and interactive.

On the web one can find such "cut-leaf, panelled books" that are called EXQUISITE CORPSE FLIP BOOKS (*see* these two terms individually), though the exquisite corpse is not necessarily a flip book, nor does it have to be a movable. There are also sets of individual cards, not bound, but in a decorative cover leaf, that have the same properties. At the "Firsts Online" book fair in May 2021, the bookseller Antiquariat F. Neidhardt was selling such a set of hand-painted cards titled *Metamorphose*, probably French, with no imprint, but dated 1864. The scarcity of such early examples justified the price of £980.

MEXICAN INCUNABULA. *See* Incunabula.

MEZZOTINT. "Mezzotint, also called black manner, a method of engraving a metal plate by systematically and evenly pricking its entire surface with innumerable small holes that will hold ink and, when printed, produce large areas of tone. The pricking of the plate was originally done with a roulette (a small wheel covered with sharp points), but later an instrument called a cradle, or rocker, was used. It resembles a small spade with a toothed edge, and its cutting action throws up rough ridges of metal called burrs. The burrs are scraped away in places intended to be white in the finished print. In the 21st century, the plate is often roughened by working over it in several directions with a carborundum stone. / The term mezzotint (from Italian *mezza tinta*, "halftone") derives from the capability of the process to produce soft, subtle gradations of tone. Used alone, however, mezzotint designs are often indistinct and, consequently, ENGRAVED or ETCHED lines are introduced to give the design greater definition. / Although the process of mezzotint was invented in Holland by the German-born Ludwig von Siegen during the 17th century, it was soon practiced enthusiastically and almost exclusively in England. The technique is laborious and, consequently, unsuitable for original work. But its rich blacks, its subtle gradations of tone, and especially its adaptability to making colour prints made it ideal for the reproduction of paintings" ("Mezzotint Printmaking," *Encyclopaedia Britannica*, http://www.britannica.com/topic/mezzotint [accessed 9 June 2021]). (See Wax, *The Mezzotint*.)

MICHEL, MARIUS. "The name employed by Jean Michel (1821–1890) and his son, Henri François (1846–1925), who were distinguished Parisian bookbinders. The work of the elder Michel, while technically excellent, was largely traditional. Henri François, on the other hand, was more enterprising, and used curved stamps instead of small dies and fillets to work exotic flower and leaf forms, and also attempted to relate the decoration of the book cover to its contents. He was the first bookbinder to suggest that the mood of the book should be continued in the design and color of the binding. He may, in fact, be called the founder of the 20th century French school of binding. The designs of the two binders were often based on natural forms and the ornament is often expressed in color, outlined in blind, and very often without the use of gold" (Roberts and Etherington, "Michel, Marius"; https://cool.culturalheritage.org/don/dt/dt2225.html [accessed 29 March 2021]).

MICRO-MINIATURE. *See* Miniature.

MIDDLETON, BERNARD (1924–2019) (binder). "One of the outstanding modernday bookbinders and conservationists, Middleton won a Trade Scholarship to the Central School of Arts and Crafts, Southhampton [*sic*] Row in 1938, and was apprenticed to the British Museum Bindery in 1940. He was a City and Guilds Silver Medalist in 1943. Middleton was later bookbinder at the Royal College of Art and, for a short time, managed the ZAEHNSDORF bindery. He started his own business as a book restorer in 1953. / Middleton's FORWARDING is considered to be superlative, while his designs and tooling, though restrained, are always in good taste and are superbly executed. . . . / Aside from being a gifted bookbinder, Middleton is recognized as an outstanding scholar in the field of bookbinding history, and is the author of a comprehensive work entitled *A History of English Craft Bookbinding Technique*, as well as *The Restoration of Leather Bindings* [see the bibliography]. He is unique among historians of bookbindings because he writes with such a vast knowledge of technique, largely overlooked by others" (Roberts and Etherington, p. 169).

MIDWEST ART CONSERVATION CENTER. *See* Regional Alliance for Preservation.

MILDEW. *See* Mold.

MILL REAM. *See* Ream.

MIMEOGRAPHED. Said of a document printed by mimeography, a printing technique that used a stencil wrapped around a drum. "Mimeograph, also called stencil duplicator, duplicating machine that uses a stencil consisting of a coated fibre sheet through which ink is pressed. Employing a typewriter with the ribbon shifted out of the way so that the keys do not strike it, the information to be duplicated is typed on[to] the stencil. The keys cut the coating on the stencil and expose the fibre base, making it possible for ink to pass through it" (*Encyclopaedia Britannica*, "Mimeograph"). Ernie Smith says that the mimeograph was "a stencil machine combined with an ink roller. Rather than using an additive process to make the necessary pages, the mimeograph relied on a master page, often made of wax, that had elements stenciled out. The ink was then forced through the holes in the master page, producing high-quality copies" ("How Mimeographs Transformed Information Sharing in Schools"). Smith also says, "Mimeograph machines shouldn't be (but often are) mistaken for another technology widely used in classrooms of the time: the spirit duplicator or ditto machine. This machine used a similar crank-based process, but involved the use of alcohol-based solvents, which dissolved the ink from a master sheet and transferred it onto other pieces of paper." The copies produced on these machines (especially spirit duplicators) often faded, sometimes so much that the texts could barely be seen. But they were inexpensive ways of making copies (dozens, hundreds, or thousands of them) quickly. They were used for school newspapers, all kinds of handouts, ZINES, church and others' newsletters, minutes, publications of the UNDERGROUND PRESS, and many other kinds of texts that wind up at antiquarian book fairs and in special collections departments and private collections.

MINIATURE (book). In the United States, officially, a book that has a maximum height, width, or depth of three inches or less. "Outside of the United States, books up to four inches are often considered miniature" (MINIATURE BOOK SOCIETY, http://www.mbs.org [accessed 9 June 2021]). (*See* Bibelot.) Patricia J. Pistner explains that there are four sizes of books that constitute the world of miniatures—three of which belong squarely in that world: 1) Macro-miniatures (over 3 inches but smaller than 4 inches); 2) Miniatures (under 3 inches); 3) Micro-miniatures (under 1 inch); and 4) Ultra micro-miniatures (under ¼ inch). (See Pistner and Storm van Leeuwen, *A Matter of Size: Miniature Bindings and Texts from the Collection of Patricia J. Pistner*, p. 7.) The printed volumes of the 15th century were preceded by miniatures of the manuscript period, as many religious texts on vellum were produced (several are shown in the Pistner volume, pp. 41 ff.).

The term also means an ILLUMINATION in the form of a picture in a manuscript. One might find in a bookseller's catalog (in a description of a medieval manuscript) "with twelve elegant miniatures." The term comes originally from the verb to *miniate*, which meant to color with red pigment. Hence, rubrication (*see* Rubric/rubricated) or illumination was often done in red. Over the centuries, the term "miniature" has come to mean the painted illustrations in manuscripts (not the decorations in borders or between lines or the embellishments that adorn initials—though some initials may have miniatures in them). The miniatures, as just noted, could be incorporated in ILLUMINATED MAJUSCULES, or they could take up substantial parts of (or full) pages. (See also Edison and Bromer, *Miniature Books: 4,000 Years of Tiny Treasures.*)

MINIATURE BOOK SOCIETY. A fellowship of collectors and makers of MINIATURE BOOKS. Their website says, "The Miniature Book Society (MBS) is a non-profit organization founded in 1983 in the United States which now enjoys a worldwide membership. The Society sustains an interest in all phases of miniature books and is a clearinghouse for information through its journal, the MBS Newsletter, published three times annually. The MBS is interested in promoting all aspects of the book arts with special affection for the small format" (see https://www.worthpoint.com/worthopedia/miniature-book-society-deluxe-487333668 [accessed 3 July 2021]).

MINISCULE. (A variant spelling of Minuscule). A LOWERCASE letter.

MINT. As Carter explains, this term is borrowed from numismatics, denoting a coin in perfect CONDITION. With the inconsistency in terminology of the book world, there are no standard words to describe what a book looks like. "Mint" might just as well be "CRISP," "perfect" or "PRISTINE" or "immaculate" or "unblemished" or "a really great copy." The term can be applied to the volume and to its DUST JACKET. (*See* Condition.)

MINUSCULE. (The preferred spelling, though miniscule is gaining favor as well.) A LOWERCASE letter.

MISBOUND. This term describes a volume in which a LEAF or several—or even a whole SIGNATURE or more—are bound into the volume out of sequence, or possibly upside down. This could be caused by the printer's (or binder's) having folded a large sheet incorrectly or having gathered the printed QUIRES in the wrong order. The result for a reader, as Carter suggests, is inconvenience (p. 169). But for a collector, this could be a valuable and desirable book: to have an unusual copy of a COLLECTIBLE volume. In fact, a misbound copy may be unique, and a collector may prefer that one to a perfect copy since unique ones are likely to be more desirable (and hence more valuable) than one of a large number of copies that are all the same. "I have the only copy" is the beginning of a sentence of a proud owner of a freak error made by a sleepy or inattentive binder. One kind of misbinding is having the TEXT BLOCK right-side up and the cover bound upside down. (Kim Merker accidentally misfolded a signature in one of his books, bound the volume, and realized too late that the copy was defective. It now resides appreciated and cherished in my library. So I know the frisson that a collector can have from what is otherwise a mistake.)

MISCELLANY. (Pronounced in the United States with the accent on the first syllable, though the variant pronunciation, with the accent on the second syllable, is often heard.) A gathering of various items, usually not related to one another in any determined order, and not necessarily on the same topic. In the world of the book, a miscellany could be something like a SCRAPBOOK in which someone has gathered all kinds of odds and ends: newspaper clippings, menus, autographs, drawings, pictures of various kinds, snippets of literary items, and so on. The content is usually drawn from several or many authors. Similar to a COMMONPLACE BOOK but not as focused as one. (*See also* Florilegium.)

MISE-EN-PAGE. A French term, used often by English writers and speakers, to indicate the LAYOUT of a printed page, referring to where on the page the MARGINS are, the indentations, the RUNNING HEADS, columns of printed text, interlinear spacing, spacing between paragraphs, the placement of page numbers, and so forth. A direct translation would be "putting-on-the-page." Use of the French phrase has the same impact as does "POCHOIR": it gives the user a sense of intelligence and worldliness, and therefore authority, where the English equivalents lack such sophistication. Rather than say, "The layout of the pages is elegant," one might say, "I love the book's mise-en-page," which, itself, has a ring of sophistication, though literally that suggestion is not in the original.

MISIMPOSITION. *See* Imposition.

MISPRINTS. This is perhaps the funniest entry in Carter, with its 12 misprints of the word "misprint" (see pp. 169–70). But Carter's entry is brilliant in its circumspection about and insights into what the implications are of misprints and how these implications can be misconstrued. Quoting McKerrow (*An Introduction to Bibliography for Literary Students*), Carter points out that printing errors are misprints, errors in wording are not. (Because of copyright restrictions, I unfortunately cannot quote the entire entry from Carter, but it is worth looking at. Here is a summary of his points.) Misprints in spelling or page numbering are common and may lead a scholar to claim that certain corrections can help us determine the priority of issue of one copy over another. Priority of issue means much to booksellers and collectors because the earlier the copy can be proven to be, the more valuable it is (at least fiscally). As mentioned under "FIRST EDITIONS," collectors are willing to pay more for the earlier copies than they are for later ones, even if later ones are superior textually, with misprints corrected and errors of fact "repaired." And in most cases, misprints in earlier versions are corrected in later ones, though that is not always the case. Is the "First edition, first issue, with page number 277 printed 217" a better text than "First edition, second issue, with page 277 correct"? Not really, but the collector will want the first issue rather than the second (actually, she will want both issues, if she is a COMPLETIST), and the bookseller is likely to price the first issue higher than he will the second issue.

Carter then makes the key point, in this part of his discussion, that a misprint or misprints (he calls them "midprint" and "milprints") should not be used to prove priority. In the HANDPRESS PERIOD, STOP-PRESS CORRECTIONS could be made at any time in a PRESSRUN, and in gathering the sheets, the binder or printer did not always line them up and bind them in the exact order in which they were printed. It is possible, for several reasons, that earlier-printed sheets had no errors and that later-printed ones had typos (as when some kind of damage takes place during a PRESSRUN and the type needs to be reset or if loose type needs to be reset). A correct reading in an early impression can be reset with a typographical error. Thus, priority of printing cannot be absolutely accurately determined by discerning the typos in the text. Also, state variants (*see* Edition, Impression [Printing], Issue, and State; Points) will present similar priority problems. The printed sheets will be gathered for binding regardless of what order they were printed in in their pressruns. Thus, as Carter shows, sheets with misprints and sheets with correct readings at the same places in the texts can be combined in no particular order in the final bound volume that gets sold to a customer, and even if it can be proved that a misprint has been corrected, all the scholar can say about it is that the version with the error is almost certainly earlier than the one with the correction. But even this cannot always be demonstrated, and the comment may hold true for the LEAF on which the misprint exists, not for the volume as a whole.

Carter concludes his discussion by saying that misprints (he calls them "masprints") have their use for bibliographers, but they cannot be relied upon to prove priority of issue. (See Carter, pp. 169–70.) The best we can say about misprints is that they are sort of fun to find; it's the "misery loves company" syndrome: I know I am fallible, and it is good to know that others are, too. Or, I am superior to the fool who made this mistake. Booksellers like to find them because there could be a fiscal implication to them, especially if they exist in some versions of an EDITION and not in others. And the collector can say, "I have the copy with the misprint!" Drawing again from Kim Merker's printing, I can say that in his printing of Levis's *The Afterlife*, Merker spotted the misprint "Captiviy" in the table of contents when he had printed off a number of copies of that SIGNATURE. He could not go back and print those sheets again—lack of paper, lack of time, and lack of opportunity if the sheets had already been printed on the other side and that type distributed. Thus, he issued the book with an ERRATA slip notifying the readers of the misprint. Those are the most desirable copies today since a COMPLETIST will want both versions (with and without the misprint), and the copies with "Captiviy" are mighty hard to come by.

MISSALE SPECIALE. *See* Stevenson, Allan [Henry].

MITERED. (The British spelling is mitred.) "1. A binding ornamentation on the SPINE or covers of a book, either in gold or BLIND, consisting of straight lines that meet but do not pass beyond the vertical panel or 'run-up' lines on either side. A FILLET or pallet may be used to make the lines; however, the fillet is not generally used on the spine of a book except when executing the run-up gilt back. 2. The juncture at the corners of the TURN-INS edged to an angle of 45°. . . . 3. The connection at the angles of an outer frame to an inner frame or panel by the diagonal use of a fillet or ROLL" (Roberts and Etherington, p. 170).

MITSUMATA (papermaking). One of the three most common fibers used in Asian papermaking (the other two being KOZO and GAMPI). The plant (*Edgeworthia chrysantha*, *Edgeworthia papyrifera*, or *Daphne papyrifera*) is a deciduous shrub with thick dark green leaves, and it makes a strong, smooth paper, making it ideal to use in currency and printmaking. (See Barrett, *Japanese Papermaking*.)

MOBY BOOKS. *See* Big Little Books.

MOCK-UP. A model made in preparation of the final product, created as a general guide to what that final item will look like. The mock-up will usually be the same size as the anticipated final VERSION, and it will have all parts that the final will have. In preparing a book on MARBLING, for instance, the marbler/artist may create a mock-up to help her decide how many samples to create, the size to make them, where they will be TIPPED IN, what the binding should look like and how heavy the BOARDS should be, and so on. Since mock-ups are often made of materials inferior to those of the final version and are thus more fragile or evanescent, and since they are UNIQUE, collectors covet them; and scholars can learn from them about the evolutionary process that went into the production of the final items. COMPLETIST collectors desire them as well since they want to have every manifestation of the items they collect. Being able to show a treasure and its mock-up confers bragging rights equal to those one can have with owning an author's unique PROOF copy.

MODEL BOOK (for ILLUMINATED manuscripts). (Also called a "Pattern book.") A volume exhibiting illuminations that were used by SCRIBES and artists as models for them to copy (in various ways), enabling them to transfer or reproduce an image from one MANUSCRIPT to another. Erik Kwakkel says, "[T]wo types of model books can be distinguished. Some functioned as instruction manuals. In such books, the drawings might be accompanied by a narrative or explanation that instructs the artisan how to proceed, usually in a step-by-step process. Other model books appear to have merely functioned as a source of inspiration: they present a wide array of shapes and drawings from which the artisan could take his pick" (http://medievalbooks.nl/2014/09/12/medieval-super-models [accessed 9 June 2021]). He adds, "On the lower end of the spectrum there are pattern books that merely show how to make enlarged letters with some minor flourishing. On the higher end, by contrast, there are copies with high-quality stand-alone designs and sophisticated HISTORIATED initials inhabited by figures and scenes." (See Ives and Lehmann-Haupt, *An English 13th Century Bestiary*; Lehmann-Haupt, *The Göttingen Model Book*; Muller, *The Use of Models in Medieval Painting*; and Scheller, *A Survey of Medieval Model Books*.) One form of model book used PRICKING and POUNCE.

MODERN FIGURE. *See* Lining figure.

MODERN FIRSTS. A term that Carter mentions, claiming it is often impossible to define the term owing to the idiosyncratic nature of its use. What is "modern" to one bookseller is not necessarily modern to another. He says that in the 1920s it meant books of the previous generation and that this definition still holds, even if the word "modern" there does not ring true to us since hundred-year-old volumes do not appear to be modern to us today. He suggests the use of "contemporary" as a replacement for "modern," but even that is too time-bound to have long-term usefulness. (See Carter, p. 171.) To bring Carter up to date, I offer that it has now been abandoned or is seldom used, and when it is, it is used rather generically to mean first editions that are relatively recent (and how recent is "recent" is fuzzy). If someone says, "I collect modern firsts," I think we all will understand what he says. But if he uses that term for a half century, still collecting the same things he bought 50 years earlier, the term loses its precision. The term usually implies that the items so spoken of are fiction, but it can be extended to any genre.

MODERN LAID PAPER. Paper originally made on a hand MOLD with two layers of wire over its surface. The paper, when held up to the light, shows the typical "LAID LINES" of LAID PAPER, but it has no shadows around the CHAIN LINES. With the coming of machine-made papers at the end of the 18th century, all mechanically produced paper was made on a woven mesh, which could be fitted with wires mimicking laid lines. Hence, machine-made paper (with laid lines visible when the sheet is backlighted) could have those laid lines artificially produced. It was also possible to produce laid lines using a DANDY ROLL. (*See* Antique laid paper; Chain lines; Fourdrinier; Laid lines; Wire lines.) (For an image of ANTIQUE LAID PAPER, *see* Laid paper.)

Modern laid paper, with the laid lines made up of (horizontal) wire lines and (vertical) chain lines, but with no shadows around the chain lines. Photograph by Jeff Dykes.
Collection of the author.

MOIRÉ. The word means having a rippled or wavy effect, and it applies specifically to a fabric, usually silk or rayon, that has such an effect. Such material can be found in bookbindings, usually on DOUBLURES—or lining boxes holding specially bound volumes. The effect can also be achieved on paper, which is stamped with male and female dies to produce the EMBOSSED effect of moiré.

MOLD (papermaking) (Western; Asian). The device used for making paper. There are so many kinds of paper molds that coming up with a generic definition and description of them is futile. The best one can do is give a general description that illuminates what is usually meant by the term "paper mold." (I will use the Japanese terms since molds from Japan are more commonly written about in the West than are those from China or Korea, and Japanese terminology is much more known than are the words from other Asian countries.) In Asian papermaking, the mold consists of two parts: the *su* (the surface on which the fibers settle and the sheet is formed) and the *geta* (or *keta*—the frame that holds the *su*). Hence, the entire apparatus is called a *sugeta* (or *suketa*). The *su* is detachable; that is, a sheet is formed on the mold, and the *su* is removed so that the sheet can be COUCHED onto a stack of like sheets. Chinese and other Asian paper molds can also have a cloth mesh on which the sheets are formed; the cloth is not detached. When a sheet is formed on it, it is set out to dry and the dry sheet is then peeled off the cloth.

Western paper molds consist of two parts: the mold and the DECKLE. (Yes, the whole two-part apparatus is called a

Western paper mold with the mold and deckle for making modern laid paper. Close examination will show that the mold has two layers of wires, so that no shadows will be produced when a sheet is made on it. This makes modern laid paper. Photograph by Jeff Dykes.
Collection of the author.

Paper mold for making wove paper, with the Doe Press watermark in wire on the screen. Photograph by Jeff Dykes.
Collection of the author.

Asian paper mold (the *sugeta* or *suketa*). The detachable screen is the *su*, the rest of the mold is the *geta* (or *keta*). Photograph by Jeff Dykes.
Collection of the author.

"mold," and one of those two parts is also called the "mold.") The deckle is the frame placed on top of the mold to hold the fibers on the surface of the mold after the VATMAN has dipped the mold into the VAT to form a sheet.

Further, in mills where handmade paper is produced in large quantities, one common practice is to have a vatman—the one forming the sheets at the vat—who has two molds and one deckle. He scoops up the pulp and forms a sheet on one mold, removes the deckle, hands the mold off to the coucher (*see* Couch), and receives from the coucher the second mold. (The deckle fits perfectly over both molds.) He is forming the next sheet while the coucher is couching the previous one. Hence, a "paper mold" consists of two molds and one deckle. (See Allan H. Stevenson, "Watermarks Are Twins." *See also* Watermark.)

Molds can be LAID or WOVE. That is, they can make laid paper or wove paper. (*See* Laid paper.) (See also Loeber, *Paper Mould and Mouldmaker.*)

MOLD (preservation of collections; mildew) (spelled "mould" in Great Britain). "Any of various filamentous fungi that grow on and contribute to the decay of organic matter" (*American Heritage Dictionary*, p. 1134). "Mold spores are everywhere. Mold and mildew are types of fungi, microorganisms that depend on other organisms for sustenance. There are over 100,000 known species of fungi. The great variety of species means that patterns of mold growth and the response of mold in a particular situation can be unpredictable. / Molds excrete enzymes that allow them to digest organic materials such as paper and book bindings, altering and weakening those materials. In addition, many molds contain colored substances that can stain paper, cloth, or leather. It is important to realize that mold can be dangerous to people and can in some cases pose a major health hazard. Mold outbreaks should never be ignored or left to 'go away on their own'" ("Mold Protection," Northeast Document Conservation Center [NEDCC], https://www.nedcc.org/preservation101/session-2/2mold-protection [accessed 9 June 2021]).

The growth of mold is facilitated by the presence of moisture in the air. Many kinds of molds can grow on (and damage) all kinds of library materials. Hence, it is desirable to keep these materials in a relatively dry environment—with a humidity lower than about 50 percent. If mold forms on library materials, these items should be isolated from the rest of the collection and taken to a CONSERVATOR. At the very least, as soon as the mold is discovered, affected items should be removed from neighboring items and laid out in a dry environment to stop the growth, and other treatments may be necessary. Even if the outbreak is spotted soon after it has begun and the materials are not physically compromised beyond use, mold can still leave unsightly stains on papers, cloth, and animal skins, sometimes impossible to clean off completely. (See also "Emergency Salvage of Moldy Books and Paper," NEDCC Leaflet 3.8, https://www.nedcc.org/free-resources/preservation-leaflets/3.-emergency-management/3.8-emergency-salvage-of-moldy-books-and-paper [accessed 9 June 2021]).

There is a difference between mold and mildew: "'Mold' and 'mildew' are terms that are used generally to describe growths of fungi on various surfaces. 'Mildew' also is a scientific term that describes a type of plant disease. In common usage, the difference between mold and mildew usually is in their appearance and the surfaces on which they are growing. Mold is often thicker and black, green, red or blue in color, and mildew usually is lighter, powdery and gray or white. Both mold and mildew often grow in moist and warm locations, but mildew is more often found in showers, on paper and on fabrics, and mold is often found on foods and in walls and other permanent structures" ("What Is the Difference between Mold and Mildew?" wiseGEEK, http://www.wisegeek.com/what-is-the-difference-between-mold-and-mildew.htm [accessed 9 June 2021]).

Like insects, mold is a family-oriented living organism. It does not come by itself; it lives in colonies. If mold is discovered in an item, the cause should be determined as quickly as possible, and all surrounding items should be carefully checked for like damage.

A final observation: Mold smells. It has that odor of damp basements and wet attics. It is not always visible, but it is detectable with our noses, and that scent can be difficult or impossible to get rid of without extensive CONSERVATION treatment. Any bookseller who has a volume that looks fine but smells like mold must mention it in her catalog description. Likewise, librarians may wish to add something about the volume's scent to the cataloging record.

MOLD (type casting). The tool used to cast type. It is in two parts, as the illustration shows. The parts slide back and forth against one another, allowing the "funnel" that they form between them to open and close, depending on the width of the MATRIX that is at the bottom of the funnel. Wider matrices will cast wider characters; narrower matrices will cast narrower SORTS. This is GUTENBERG's ingenious device that made printing alphabetical characters possible since the mold adjusts to accommodate the various widths of the characters. (*See* Type casting.)

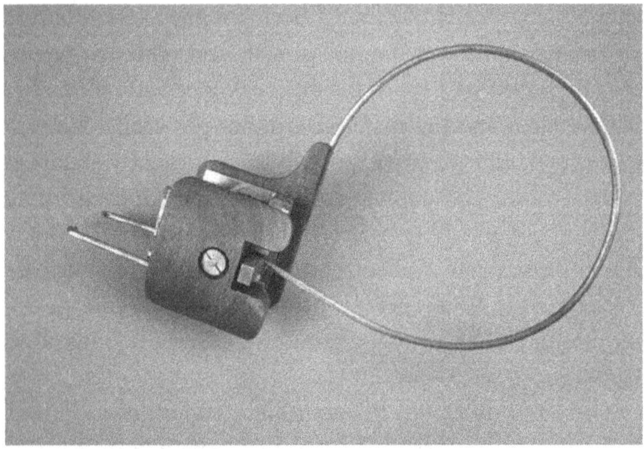

Type-casting mold, closed. Made by Stan Nelson. Photograph by Jeff Dykes. The two brass rods projecting from the two parts of the mold are the HAGS, used to help the type caster remove the newly cast (and quite hot) sort from the mold.

Collection of the author.

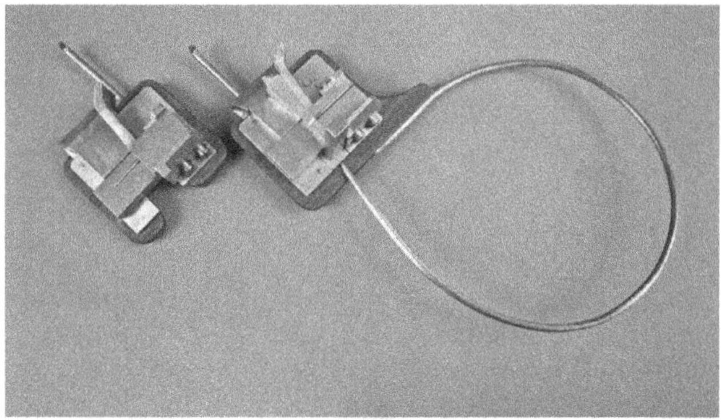

Type-casting mold, open, shown holding a matrix and a cast sort with its JET attached. Photograph by Jeff Dykes.

Collection of the author.

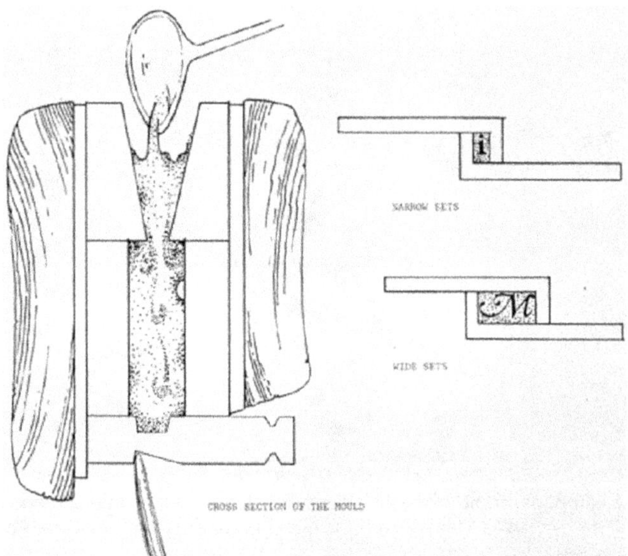

Drawing of the type-casting mold. The picture shows the "funnel" formed by the two halves of the mold, at the bottom of which is the matrix, receiving the molten type metal. The matrix is held in place with the spring (or "bow"). When the type metal is fully poured, the jet above the sort will be formed as well, and will need to be removed. Drawing by Stan Nelson.

Courtesy of Stan Nelson.

MOLDED-LEATHER BINDING. *See* Cuir-bouilli.

MOLD-MADE PAPER. "A deckle-edged paper resembling handmade paper but actually produced on a cylinder machine or a cylindrical mold revolving in a VAT of paper pulp. The sizes of the sheets are determined by dividing the surface of the cylinder with rubber bands which also create the DECKLE EDGES. The deckle edge may also be simulated by cutting the web with a jet of water. Mold-made paper is used in LIMITED EDITIONS where a handmade or simulated handmade paper is desired" (Roberts and Etherington, pp. 171–72).

MONOGRAPH. A book, as opposed to a serialized text, a PAMPHLET, a BROADSIDE, or some other short publication. The term refers specifically to a book with a single text, as opposed to one with a collection of shorter pieces (as with short stories).

MONOTYPE MACHINE. Actually a pair of machines that produce printing type as individual SORTS. The machines, invented by TOLBERT LANSTON around 1885, are a keyboard that, when keys are struck, produces a roll of punched paper, and a caster for casting the individual pieces of type. When the text is keyboarded, a roll of paper is punched with holes the configuration of which is unique for each character.

Once the roll of paper is fully hole-punched with the full text, it is taken to a casting machine that casts individual sorts from a set of matrices (*see* Matrix) in a matrix holder.

As a rival to the Linotype, the Monotype system yielded individual sorts, favored by many printers who wished to have more flexibility in the distribution of the type on the printed page than they had with the Linotype. (See Slinn, Carter, and Southall, *History of the Monotype Corporation.*)

Monotype casting machine.
Courtesy of Claire and David Bolton, Alembic Press.

Monotype keyboard, showing the roll of paper (above the keyboard) that will be punched with holes.
Courtesy of Claire and David Bolton, Alembic Press.

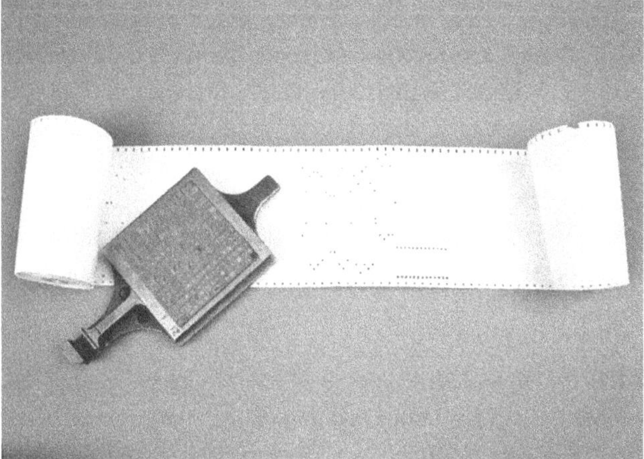

A roll of punched paper and a Monotype matrix holder.
Collection of the author.

MOOD-ALTERING BOOKS. A term coined by Kenneth Soehner (chief librarian, Thomas J. Watson Library, Metropolitan Museum of Art, New York) to indicate volumes that are uplifting—that make one feel good, that delight, amuse, and possibly enchant the observer. All book people—collectors, booksellers, librarians, or simply observers of fine and beautiful books—will know what this term means and how it applies to them. Certain categories of books stand out as mood altering: POP-UPS and others with moving parts, FLIP BOOKS, books with beautiful ILLUSTRATIONS, those with FORE-EDGE ILLUSTRATIONS, volumes with exquisite bindings, and many others. A mood-altering book usually makes the viewer smile and for some makes them covetous. The term should be in the vocabulary of all in the book world.

MOON SYSTEM OF READING FOR THE BLIND. *See* Printing for the blind.

MORGAN LIBRARY AND MUSEUM (J. Pierpont Morgan). "The Morgan Library & Museum began as the private library of financier Pierpont Morgan (1837–1913), one of the preeminent collectors and cultural benefactors in the United States. As early as 1890 Morgan had begun to assemble a collection of ILLUMINATED, literary, and historical MANUSCRIPTS, EARLY PRINTED books, and old master drawings and PRINTS. / Mr. Morgan's library, as it was known in his lifetime, was built between 1902 and 1906 adjacent to his New York residence at Madison Avenue and 36th Street. . . . Over the years—through purchases and generous gifts—The Morgan Library & Museum has continued to acquire rare materials as well as important music manuscripts, early children's books, AMERICANA, and materials from the twentieth century. Without losing its decidedly domestic feeling, the Morgan also has expanded its physical space considerably" ("The Morgan Library & Museum," http://www.themorgan.org/about/introduction [accessed 9 June 2021]). (See the library's website at http://www.themorgan.org/about/mission-statement [accessed 9 June 2021]. See also Strouse, *Introduction to the Morgan Library*.)

MORISON, STANLEY (1889–1967). "English typographer, scholar, and historian of printing, particularly remembered for his design of Times New Roman, later called the most successful new typeface of the first half of the 20th century" ("Stanley Morison," *Encyclopaedia Britannica*, http://www.britannica.com/biography/Stanley-Morison [accessed 9 June 2021]). He worked for the Pelican Press and then at the Cloister Press between 1918 and 1923, when he moved to MONOTYPE.

"In 1923 Morison was appointed typographic adviser to the Monotype Corporation, where he was instrumental in having many important typefaces of the past adapted to machine composition. For three years (1923–25) he was also a writer and an editor on the staff of the *PENROSE ANNUAL*, which he helped to broaden from its former stress on technical processes in the graphic arts. In 1923 he was appointed typographic adviser to Cambridge University Press, a position he held until 1959. From 1926 to 1930 he was editor of *THE FLEURON*, an influential typographic journal" (*Encyclopaedia Britannica*, "Stanley Morison"). (See also Appleton, *Writings of Stanley Morison*; Barker, *Stanley Morison*; Barr, *Stanley Morison*; Jones, *Stanley Morison Displayed*; and Moran, *Stanley Morison*.)

MOROCCO (leather). "A vegetable tanned leather having a characteristic pinhead grain pattern developed either naturally or by means of graining or BOARDING, but never by EMBOSSING. The most common and characteristic grain pattern is known as 'hard grain.' / By long usage, the term 'morocco' is taken to denote a GOATSKIN, tanned by any vegetable tannage, and boarded in the wet condition; in a more strict interpretation, however, morocco is defined as a goatskin tanned exclusively with SUMAC, and boarded in the wet condition. Leather made from vegetable tanned goatskin having a grain pattern resembling that of genuine morocco, but produced other than by hand boarding, is more properly termed 'morocco grained goat' or 'assisted morocco'" (Roberts and Etherington, p. 172). The leather is strong, flexible, and long wearing, and it takes dye well. Carter points out that the goats usually came from Anatolia, so the use of the word "morocco" is an error (p. 171). Roberts and Etherington add, "Alum-tawed 'morocco' stained pink, [*sic*] was first produced by the Moors, possibly before the 11th century. Vegetable-tanned morocco was in use in some part of Europe in the 16th century, particularly in Italy where the goat was more common than in the north of Europe, where calfskin was more abundant. Morocco leather was rarely used in England before 1600. / Straight-grained morocco was popular in the late 18th and early 19th centuries. Bright red and green were the most popular colors, with dark blue, black, citron, and even purple skins also being used. / Throughout the 19th century, morocco, in its various grain patterns, was used in the finest bookbinding, and it is still used for much of the better binding, although it is very expensive and is also becoming more and more difficult to obtain" (p. 172). This last comment, written more than 30 years ago, is no longer accurate. There seems to be a good availability of this leather today. (*See also* Levant.)

MORRIS, HENRY (c. 1925–2019) (Bird & Bull Press). Proprietor of one of the premier private presses in the United States in the 20th and early 21st centuries—Bird &

Bull Press. Morris specialized in books about books, mostly PAPERMAKING, but also BOOKBINDING, book ILLUSTRATION, and other book topics. The press was in operation from 1958 until 2013. In this 55-year run, Morris chose a field with a fairly niche audience—those who love books and people interested in papermaking and printing, book illustration, and printing TYPES. He used high-quality materials in the texts and the bindings, and he never compromised on page design. His LAYOUTS were generous, his use of illustration was excellent, and his personality was almost always evident, even in books written by others for him. His LETTERPRESS printing was also superb, and his books had a strong following from academic libraries (because of the scholarly content that could be found nowhere else) and from private collectors who loved the handsome volumes, many of which had TIP-INS and were presented in SLIPCASES and attractive bindings. Morris even made the paper for some of his books, and his research into perfecting that craft appears in one of his early, learned volumes: *Omnibus*. He wrote or published seminal texts on Japanese and Western decorated papers (especially marbled paper), DARD HUNTER, WATERMARKS, booksellers' trade tokens, and many other bookish topics—texts that would never have been issued by large commercial publishers because the market was too small. Morris's books are in major libraries around the world.

MORRIS, WILLIAM (1834–1896) (Kelmscott Press). "[A] major figure of the Arts and Crafts movement, a loosely-linked group of artisans, craftsmen, architects and writers who sought to elevate the status of the applied arts in the age of industrial manufacturing. . . . Passionately involved with the book arts as a writer, typographer, and designer, and a great book collector himself, Morris looked to the past for inspiration. He founded the Kelmscott Press in 1891 and endeavored to produce works of the style and appearance of books from the fifteenth century, the earliest days of printing" (Mustain, *Monuments of Printing*, p. 95; see also Peterson, *The Kelmscott Press*). Morris sought to create "the book beautiful" by overseeing every aspect of its production: type design, papermaking, page LAYOUT, printing, illustration, binding, and so on. He engaged the best craftsmen, designers, printers, and artists. Although he began making books at the end of his life and was at it for only about six years (1891–1896), the impact of the Kelmscott Press was great. The press produced 66 titles in that short time. He brought a lifetime of thinking about art to his work, and his insistence on the highest quality of production and design in all aspects of his printing has influenced innumerable printers since. PRIVATE PRESSES throughout the world strove to emulate Morris with respect to the extremely high standards he brought to his printing. The MAGNUM OPUS of the press is his volume of Chaucer, referred to as the "Kelmscott Chaucer," but properly titled *The Works of Geoffrey Chaucer Now Newly Imprinted*. The volume was ornamented throughout with WOODCUTS by Edward Burne-Jones. The Albion press (made by Hopkinson & Cope in England in 1891) used at the Kelmscott Press is now in the possession of the Carey Graphic Arts Collection at Rochester Institute of Technology in Rochester, New York.

Morris's books have a staid look about them and page and type designs not completely congenial to comfortable reading. Alan Bartram says that Morris used "darkly medieval types and overpowering, suffocating decoration" (*Five Hundred Years of Book Design*, p. 11). But Morris ushered in the modern fine-press movement at the same time that he stultified it. Many a book designer imitated his look, but that was short lived. The high standards he set had more influence than did the actual designs of his books. They wound up on collectors' shelves more for the ownership of them than for the reading of them. (Henry Herman Evans said, "Indeed, if the private owners of copies of the Kelmscott and Doves books were required to burn all the unread books contained in their collections, it is safe to say that the smoke and flame would rise in ominous judgement over the great libraries of our most affluent literary circles. How many persons have actually read the Kelmscott Chaucer or the Doves Bible? These rascally printing fellows have precipitated a rain of confusion into the book world, where they have no place or right to meddle. They have encouraged and promoted manufacture of planned scarcities, thereby strengthening the position of simple rarity as a basis for book collecting, and injecting an aroma of speculation into the literary scene which is not pleasant. All this claptrap and snobbery attendant on collecting rarities, whether in press books, old books, EDITIO PRINCEPS, or any other preference, exudes a strange odor which is foreign to literature, foreign to honest culture, and surely foreign to the sincere planes of human thought"; Henry Herman Evans, *First Duet*, ll. 6–7.) Nonetheless, Morris is looked upon as something of a progenitor of the modern fine-press movement, and the Kelmscott Press has found its way into the Empyrean of FINE-PRESS PRINTING.

(There is an extensive literature on Morris. A few important readings are MacCarthy, *William Morris*; Mackail, *The Life of William Morris*; Peterson, *A Bibliography of the Kelmscott Press*; Peterson, *The Kelmscott Press*; Robinson, *William Morris, Edward Burne-Jones and the Kelmscott Chaucer;* and Walsdorf, *William Morris in Private Press and Limited Editions*.)

MOSAIC BINDING. A binding decorated in patterns with multicolored materials (LAID ON, LAID IN, or painted on).

"This form of decoration has been used for a considerable length of time; examples of mosaics of INLAID leather, while extremely rare, date back to the 16th century. Painted mosaics consist of geometrical interlacings filled with a colored and varnished incrustation, with BORDERS of gold lines. Very brilliant when first executed, the composition in time cracks and peels off, thus damaging the line work of gold encircling it" (Roberts and Etherington, p. 173).

MOSHER, THOMAS BIRD (1852–1923). American publisher and one of the first (if not *the* first) to set up a PRIVATE PRESS in the United States. After a series of unsuccessful attempts to make a living, Mosher opened his own stationery business, with a sideline of printing/publishing (see Bishop, "Thomas Bird Mosher"). His printing of George Meredith's *Modern Love* (in 1891) was the first of his publishing endeavors and started him on a career of publishing literary texts in finely designed, well-produced books, all aimed at a general public (hence the affordability of his books). "That first book in 1891 heralded a flow of LIMITED EDITIONS that would reach a total of 730 titles and editions by the end of his publishing career" (Bishop, "Thomas Bird Mosher," p. 40). Among all of his other publishing efforts was the *Bibelot*, an ANNUAL volume and an anthology of literary pieces (coming out between 1895 and 1914). The *Bibelot* series were "tall slender volumes, modeled on the Aldine Books, and, like them entirely printed in Italics. It appears that his clientele heeded Mosher's warning, since the first six titles were sold out by 1896" ("The Fourteen Series and the Books for Private Distribution," http://www.thomasbirdmosher.net/exhibitions/onepage.htm#BIS [accessed 25 October 2015]). Most of Mosher's books were small (6⅛ in. × 4¾ in.) and portable, and they look like the work of a FINE-PRESS printer. They were printed (with two-color title pages) on fine paper with good MARGINS and TYPEFACES, and the bindings were more elegant than were those of other commercial publishers, retaining their DECKLE EDGES, and were bound with paper covers and "vellum" (i.e., cream-colored paper that looks like parchment) spines, with RAISED BANDS and paper LABELS on the SPINES. Mosher's PRESSMARK was an anchor and dolphin, reminiscent of that of ALDUS MANUTIUS. (See Hatch, *A Checklist of the Publications of Thomas Bird Mosher of Portland Maine*, and Vilain and Bishop, *Thomas Bird Mosher and the Art of the Book*.)

MOSLEY, JAMES. (1935–) One of Great Britain's important contributors to book history and scholarship in the 20th—and into the 21st—century. With primary foci on printing, TYPOGRAPHY, and letter design, Mosley influenced generations of scholars with his scholarship and—equally important—with his contributions to the ST BRIDE LIBRARY. Paul Barnes says, "Through his ideas, collecting and dogged research, the former St Bride librarian has shown that printing history can be both lively and opinionated. The world of typography owes him a great debt" (Barnes, "James Mosley: A Life in Objects"). Mosley's hands-on experience in TYPE CASTING and PRINTING made him an authority on these activities, and his heading up St Bride (from 1956 as assistant librarian and 1958 as librarian, retiring in 2000) exposed him to all of the BOOK ARTS. Too often people write about the book arts while never having practiced any of them. Hence, their writing is flawed. Mosley was not one of those, and his insightful writing drew on a great deal of practical experience and keen observation. Further, he had the resources of the St Bride Library at his disposal, and over the decades of his librarianship there he added significantly to that collection. Also, he spread information on the history of letterforms in the course he taught at the University of Reading for many years and in his many publications. (See Tuohy, comp., *James Mosley: Librarian, St Bride Printing Library, London: A Checklist of the Published Writings 1958–95*, with two essays by James Mosley.) One of Mosley's important contributions to St Bride came from his recognition that the library, strong as it was in its print collection, would become meaningfully more valuable to researchers if it collected non-book materials; and he added superior collections of printing items and other things having to do with the making of books: punches, type, paper molds, and many other kinds of objects. After his retirement from St Bride, he continued to publish his research, as can be seen by his valuable contribution on "The Materials of Typefounding," a remarkable compilation of information that is "[a] guide to the present location of typographical punches, matrices, drawings, type specimens and archives" (James Mosley, "The Materials of Typefounding"). In 1964 he was one of the founders of the Printing Historical Society in Great Britain. As of the present writing, Mosley continues to contribute to various publications.

MOTTLED CALF. The term used for a calfskin binding with dark splotches over it, created by the dabbing on of acid. Edges of books can also be mottled with a similar dabbing-on of pigments. (*See* Tree calf.)

MOUNTED. Said of any TIPPED-IN sheet, as a print mounted onto a LEAF of a book or a leaf of a book mounted onto a backing (e.g., paper or linen) in CONSERVATION work. Roberts and Etherington say of a PLATE that is mounted or tipped in, "A plate that is smaller than the leaf to which it is to be attached, and which is positioned above the caption and secured by tipping along the top or side edge, or at the corners. The entire plate is not usually pasted down because of the greater danger of COCKLING, particularly if the GRAIN directions of the two papers are in opposition" (p. 173).

MOUSTACHES. *See* Slips.

MOVABLE BOOK. A generic term for any book with movable parts. Several entries in the present volume discuss these. (*See* Carousel book; Dissolving picture books; Flap book; Flip book; Pop-up [book]; Metamorphic books; Shine-a-Light books; Volvelle.) The key feature of this genre is the interactivity of the object with the reader—beyond the simple fact of reading. Something in a movable book actually moves other than the leaves of the volume: FLAPS, wheels, sliding panels, or something else. Carol Barton delineates several kinds of three-dimensional and movable phenomena: boxes; triangles; combinations and variations; layered pop-ups; floating platforms; tabbed props; and spirals and straddles (Barton, *The Pocket Paper Engineer*).

David A. Carter and James Diaz, in *The Elements of Pop-Up*, say, "It wasn't until the 1700s that the focus of movable books turned to children's literature; a British bookseller created the idea of using movable flaps of paper to illustrate well-known children's stories" (p. [1] of text [inside front flap]). Of course, such hands-on, delightful movable items in the hands of children had a challenge surviving in decent COLLECTOR'S CONDITION, if they survived at all. Common genres of classic 19th-century movables (as they are sometimes called) are medical or astronomical volumes and children's books. (*See also* Cobweb.)

One prominent purveyor of these books was Ernest Nistor (*see* the entries at Dissolving picture books and Volvelle). Others included Lothar Meggendorfer, the most acclaimed creator of 19th century movables, and publishers Raphael Tuck, Dean and Sons, and McLoughlin Bros. The popularity of movable books has extended well into the 21st century with notable contributions by paper engineers such as Robert Sabuda, Matthew Reinhart, Bruce Foster and the aforementioned David A Carter among others. And booksellers like Larry Rakow of Wonderland Books specialize in these delightful items.

MOVABLE TYPE. A term used by FINE-PRESS printers and others to indicate that a text was HANDSET (or at least printed from MONOTYPE so that it could have had some HAND COMPOSITION). Some people may think that any text printed LETTERPRESS is created from movable type, as I have heard some say, but strictly speaking, to be printed from "movable type," a text must have come from individual SORTS. (Text from LINOTYPE, computer-set text, and that from PHOTOPOLYMER plates do not qualify.) (*See* Gutenberg, Johannes.)

MOXON, JOSEPH (1627–1691). "English hydrographer, printer, PUNCH cutter, globe maker, and instrument maker Joseph Moxon published in London his *Mechanick Exercises on the Whole Art of Printing* as part of his survey of the chief trades of his day. This was the first printing manual published in English, and the first comprehensive manual in any language published on printing—a trade that was passed down through apprenticeship, without truly useful printed manuals, since the mid-15th century" (Norman, "Joseph Moxon Issues the First Comprehensive Printing Manual [1683–1684]").

"The son of a printer, Joseph Moxon learned the trade of printing early, but also achieved expertise in other disciplines, including mathematics, astronomy, globe- and map-making, and wood-working. His greatest contemporary recognition came when he was appointed to the post of Hydrographer to the King, a position in which he was responsible for maintaining official charts of ocean navigation routes. Moxon's most enduring achievement and the source of his lasting fame was the *Mechanick Exercises*, a series of useful tracts on 'handy-works' published in two volumes. The second of these was devoted entirely to the arts of printing and typefounding. Herbert Davis and Harry Carter, in their exhaustively annotated 1962 edition of the *Exercises*, note that Moxon's book 'was by forty years the earliest manual of printing in any language, and it put in writing a knowledge that was wholly traditional. Though he did not himself live in a great age of printing, he described with great care the tools and the skilled movements that had produced the masterpieces of the craft in better days.' No manual ever provided more information about the construction and proper management of the printer's primary tool in those days, the wooden common press; a modern-day reader, caught long enough under the manual's spell, could still follow the directions and copper-plate diagrams and build such a press today" (Pankow, "The Printer's Manual"). If imitation is the best form of flattery, then Moxon was flattered over and over again by a long tradition of printers' manuals that shamelessly stole from his text (usually with no recognition of Moxon).

MULL. (Also called "crash," "gauze," "super," "scrim," and "Jaconet.") "An open-weave variety of coarse, sized fabric—usually muslin or something looking like cheesecloth—used for reinforcing or stiffening the TEXTBLOCK spine of a casebound book. [For several kinds of binding] [t]he super forms the first SPINE LINING on the textblock. The excess (super hinge) that extends (usually one inch) beyond the edges of the textblock SPINE is used to attach the textblock into its case" ("Glossary of Binding Terms," Book Arts Web, cited under "Super"; http://www.philobiblon.com/gbwarticle/bindterm.htm [accessed 9 June 2021]).

In innumerable cheaply bound volumes, the mull is visible under the PASTEDOWNS, running the full height of the BOARDS. It is especially useful in CASED-IN BINDINGS (since the cases are not sewn to the TEXT BLOCKS) because the mull gives the binding a bit of extra strength by being porous enough to hold more adhesive than would be possible without it.

MUTILATED. Carter says that the damage this describes was done intentionally, as by vandal or censor. (*See* Bisquing; Cancel.) But anyone (or any entity) could have mutilated a book. I have had umpteen books arrive in the mail having been mutilated by the United States Postal Service—and I assume it was not done intentionally. (One recent experience yielded the delivery by the USPS of an empty carton—one that had been sent full of valuable books. This is mutilation out of existence.)

MUTTON FIST. *See* Fist.

MUTTON THUMPER. "An old term for an incompetent bookbinder" (Roberts and Etherington, p. 173).

MYLAR. A plastic sheeting material used for several applications in the book world, mostly as a WRAPPER for a book but also as a sleeve into which photographs, PRINTS, PAMPHLETS, and other printed matter can be slid. "Some people use the word 'mylar' generically to refer to polyester film or plastic sheet. In reality, Mylar® brand is a registered trademark owned by DuPont Teijin Films for a specific family of plastic sheet products made from the resin Polyethylene Terephthalate (PET). The true generic terms for this material are either polyester film or plastic sheet" (Grafix, "What Is Mylar Plastic Film?"). Mylar can be archival, but not all of it is. (See Thomas O. "Tuck" Taylor, "Not All Mylar Is Archival.")

Many companies produce plastic sheeting, even sheets that look like Mylar. But not all of these products are archival, and unless a person describing the material knows for sure that it is Mylar, that brand name should not be used. (*See* Floated.)

N

NAGINATA BEATER. A machine used to produce paper pulp from raw materials, consisting of a series of blades protruding from a cylinder or core, the blades cutting the fibers rather than macerating them as is done in a HOLLANDER BEATER. The Hollander has parallel blades on a cylinder that rotates and grinds the fibers between the blades and a bedplate. "The naginata beater was designed with no bedplate and far fewer blades. These are paired and sickle shaped (named after curved swords used by Japanese warriors), lined up in the direction of the water flow. They are not sharp to the touch (unlike Hollander blades), and tease long strands apart to leave fiber length intact but allow for more even dispersion in the VAT. The usual Hollander beat time is most usually measured in hours; the maximum beat time in a naginata is 15 minutes" (Lee, "A New Naginata Beater, in Cleveland!").

Naginata beater with blades exposed. Paperslurry; http://paperslurry.com/tag/david-reina/ (accessed 28 June 2021).
Courtesy of May Babcock.

Naginata beater with top closed. Paperslurry; http://paperslurry.com/tag/david-reina/ (accessed 28 June 2021).
Courtesy of May Babcock.

NAMES. Carter has an entry under this rubric in which he somewhat jestingly speaks of dealers' predilection for dropping names into their catalog entries (names that refer to scholarly sources). He says that names quoted with no other information (e.g., no title or date or subject) in a catalog entry shows the reader the dealer's supreme expertise, the "wonderful sense of the solidity of his work, a foundation built of authoritative bricks" (Carter, p. 172). But he adds that collectors should not be overwhelmed or overly impressed with the names, partly because some of them may be irrelevant or not at all germane to the item in the dealer's catalog. Also, an expert collector will probably be knowledgeable him- or herself about the appropriate names to quote for information about the volumes in her collection (p. 172). That is, citing a source only by name assumes that the catalog compiler's extensive knowledge is shared by his readers, who will understand in a trice what the names refer to. And his concluding remark is telling: it indicates that sometimes a bookseller, trying to show how scarce an item is, says "Not in ———," implying that the item in question should be there—when it really should not and its absence from that source is no real proof that the item for sale is scarce. "Unknown to Blanck"—in reference to a book by Rupert Brooke—is no big deal since Jacob Blanck listed books by American authors.

NAME STRIPS. (For want of a better term.) A feature in the binding of some books is the addition of the names of owners usually along the tops of spines, and usually stamped in gold on strips of leather, often over vellum. They are particularly in evidence on sets of law volumes, as in the following figures. Not all such strips are at the tops of the spines, however. Catalog 255 (June 2022, on p. 34)

A name strip across the head of the spine, leather over vellum. R[obert] S[tewart] Morrison (and Emilio D. De Soto), eds., *The Mining Reports: A Series Containing the Cases on the Law of Mines Found in the American and English Reports, Arranged Alphabetically by Subjects, with Notes and References.* 22 vols. (Chicago: Callaghan, 1883–1906).

Courtesy of Stanley Dempsey.

Name strip at the head of the spine. Robert Stewart Morrison, *Digest of the Law of Mines and Minerals and of All Controversies Incident to the Subject-matter of Mining: Comprising the Cases in the English and American Reports, from the Year Books to the Present Time* (San Francisco: A. L. Bancroft and Co., 1878).

Courtesy of Stanley Dempsey.

from the bookseller Between the Covers, item 26 is a nautical journal of 1825–1827, "A Journal, Kept on Board the U.S. Frigate Constellation," showing the calf binding with the name strip of the writer, W[illiam] H. Alexander; the owner's name strip, a red morocco label, is tipped into a panel, vertically, in the center of the front cover of the volume. There seems to be no formal name for these points of identification, but as a phenomenon of provenance, they need a proper term. (Thanks to Stanley Dempsey Sr., we now have a formal term: "name strips.")

NARA. *See* National Archives and Records Administration.

THE NATIONAL ARCHIVES (formerly the Public Records Office). In Kew, Richmond, Surrey, United Kingdom. The massive repository of historical records. Formed April 2003 (see http://www.nationalarchives.gov.uk [accessed 28 June 2021]). Their site says, "We collect and secure the future of the government record, from Shakespeare's will to tweets from Downing Street, to preserve it for generations to come, making it as accessible and available as possible" (http://www.nationalarchives.gov.uk/about/our-role/what-we-do [accessed 28 June 2021]). And they say, "As the official public archive of the United Kingdom government, we hold records covering more than 1,000 years of history. Government records which have been selected for permanent preservation are sent to The National Archives" (The National Archives; https://www.nationalarchives.gov.uk/about/visit-us/researching-here/what-records-we-hold/#:~:text=As%20the%20official%20public%20archive,hold%20in%20Discovery%2C%20our%20catalogue [accessed 2 July 2021]). They collect all kinds of records from any government department and body whose records are public under the Public Records Act. They do not collect privately created records, though they may add to their collections materials from outside the UK government if those records complement holdings already in their collection. There is also a National Archives of Scotland and a Public Record Office of Northern Ireland, both separate institutions and facilities.

NATIONAL ARCHIVES AND RECORDS ADMINISTRATION, U.S.A. (NARA). The U.S. repository of U.S. archival materials—originally formed as a repository for government agencies. "The National Archives and Records Administration (NARA) is the nation's record keeper. Of all documents and materials created in the course of business conducted by the United States Federal government, only 1%–3% are so important for legal or historical reasons that they are kept by us forever" ("About the National Archives," National Archives; http://www.archives.gov/about [accessed 10 June 2021]).

"The National Archives was established in 1934 by President Franklin Roosevelt, but its major holdings date back to 1775. They capture the sweep of the past: slave ship manifests and the Emancipation Proclamation; captured German records and the Japanese surrender documents from World War II; journals of polar expeditions and photographs of Dust Bowl farmers; Indian treaties making transitory promises; and a richly bound document bearing the bold signature 'Bonaparte'—the Louisiana Purchase Treaty that doubled the territory of the young republic. / NARA keeps only those Federal records that are judged to have continuing value—about 2 to 5 percent of those generated in any given year. By now, they add up to a formidable number, diverse in form as well as in content. There are approximately 10 billion pages of textual records; 12 million maps, charts, and architectural and engineering drawings; 25 million still photographs and graphics; 24 million aerial photographs; 300,000 reels of motion picture film; 400,000 video and sound recordings; and 133 terabytes of electronic data. All of these materials are preserved because they are important to the workings of Government, have long-term research worth, or provide information of value to citizens" (National Archives, http://www.archives.gov/publications/general-info-leaflets/1-about-archives.html [accessed 10 June 2021]).

NATIONAL PARK SERVICE, MUSEUM CONSERVATION SERVICES. *See* Regional Alliance for Preservation.

NATIONAL UNION CATALOGUE (NUC). The Library of Congress's attempt to approach Universal Bibliographic Control. The effort was futile, of course, but in the meantime the Library of Congress engaged Mansell, the British publisher, to photocopy millions of library catalog cards and print them out on large pages. NUC, as it is often called, is a massive set of volumes (followed by microfiche "volumes") showing millions of titles in U.S. and Canadian libraries printed before 1956. It was begun in 1968, and the final volume of the first set (composed of 754 huge volumes) was issued in 1981.

The publisher, Mansell (hence, the set is sometimes referred to as "Mansell"), photocopied millions of card catalog cards from a great number of contributing libraries, printing the fronts of all the cards on the large pages in alphabetical order by author (or by title if the work did not have an author). The first set was followed by other sets of volumes, also in print form, and then by the microfiche versions of the same tool. Despite its flaws and failings (it did not show backs of the cards that had handwritten information that could have been useful to bibliographers and scholars, some of its cards were shown out of alphabetical order, it was not a comprehensive showing of U.S. and Canadian libraries since it included cards only from contributing libraries, and many thousands of titles were not listed), it was the number one bibliographic reference tool in the country for North American library holdings. With the coming of electronic librarianship, WorldCat and other online databases have taken the place of NUC for most scholars, but the giant set still contains information that can be found nowhere else, and while it takes up huge amounts of space, many reference libraries are retaining their sets for the convenience of scholars. (See Cole, ed., *In Celebration*.) Sad to say, however, many libraries, to reclaim the space that these volumes take up on the shelves, are jettisoning their copies, with few takers. So they are winding up in the recycle bins. The loss to scholarship (and to our culture) is inestimable. (*See* Library codes; OCLC; Union catalog.)

NATURE PRINTING. Creating images on a SUBSTRATE (like paper or wood). "Nature printing" is "the name given to the technique [of] using the surface of a natural object—like a leaf—to produce the PRINT. / The practice was developed in the Middle Ages to help those gathering medicinal plants, and evolved into a serious scientific process used to reproduce plants and build up collections of flora and fauna. During the 19th century, the technique drew on new photographic technology, and today, the long-standing art form continues to interest everyone from botanists to graphic designers and tattoo artists" (see Cave, *Impressions of Nature—A History of Nature Printing*). The substrate can be paper, AMATE (Mexican bark cloth), wood, or any other surface that will take printing of this kind. Several methods of nature printing have been used. Geoffrey A. Glaister describes a few of them: "As practised in the later 15th century[,] a lightly oiled leaf or plant was uniformly blackened over a flame, placed between two sheets of paper and rubbed. This left a lifelike impression of the veins and fibres. / . . . [Another] method was to place plants into a plate of soft lead and make an ELECTROTYPE of the resulting impression. The process was quick and gave a print of astonishing fidelity" (Glaister, *Glaister's Glossary*, p. 340). Other methods were developed as well (see the website cited at the Cave volume in the bibliography). Nature-printed book covers, ENDLEAVES, and internal decorations often command substantial prices in the antiquarian book world.

NCBEL—NEW CAMBRIDGE BIBLIOGRAPHY OF ENGLISH LITERATURE. Edited by George Watson, this five-volume bibliography is a standard and extensive reference tool. Volume 1 covers the years 600–1660 (2,491 pages), volume 2 covers 1660–1800 (2,092 pages), volume 3 covers 1800–1900 (1,956 pages), volume 4 covers 1900–1950 (1,414 pages), and volume 5 is the index (542 pages). A shorter (condensed) version came out in 1981 from the same press. "Its aim remains to list and classify the whole of English studies as represented by the literature of the British Isles, both in primary and in secondary materials, 'works by' and 'works about'. The main author sections begin with bibliographies (where they exist) and collections, followed by the primary section and its subsections, followed in turn by a chronological list of secondary material with works by individual scholars and writers grouped together" (from the book description of bookseller Wykeham Books, London, http://www.abebooks.com/servlet/SearchResults?bsi=30&sortby=1&tn=new+cambridge+bibliography+of+english+literature&prevpage=1 [accessed 10 June 2021]).

NEAT. For this term, Carter's entry says that the word implies a clean, solid, unsoiled copy, but it also implies that the volume is not PRISTINE or immaculate (see Carter, p. 173). The term is seldom used today by anyone describing books, possibly because it was co-opted by Valley girls and up-speakers to mean "nifty," "keeno," "spiffy," or (in today's parlance) "awesome." (*See* Condition.)

NEDCC (Northeast Document Conservation Center). An independent, nonprofit CONSERVATION laboratory in North Andover, Massachusetts. "Founded [by George Cunha] in 1973, the Northeast Document Conservation Center is the first independent conservation laboratory in the nation to specialize exclusively in treating collections made of paper or parchment, such as works of art, photographs, books, maps, manuscripts, and more. NEDCC . . . has treated some of the nation's most significant cultural heritage materials" ("Northeast Document Conservation Center," https://www.nedcc.org [accessed 10 June 2021]). NEDCC offers several workshops on preservation and conservation, and its many publications are kept up to date with frequent revisions. Their Preservation Manual, published as a series of leaflets, covers many areas of PRESERVATION and conservation. (Full texts are available free online at https://www.nedcc.org/free-resources/preservation-leaflets/overview [accessed 10 June 2021].) (*See* CCAHA; Regional Alliance for Preservation.)

NEEDLEWORK BINDING. *See* Embroidered binding.

NEWBERRY LIBRARY. One of the premier private research libraries in the country. The Newberry is a "world-renowned independent research library in Chicago . . . [offering] readers an extensive noncirculating collection of rare books, maps, music, manuscripts, and other printed material spanning six centuries" ("The Newberry," http://www.newberry.org/about [accessed 10 June 2021]).

The library's mission statement says, "The Newberry, open to the public without charge, is an independent research library dedicated to the advancement and dissemination of knowledge, especially in the humanities. The Newberry acquires and preserves a broad array of special collections research materials relating to the civilizations of Europe and the Americas. It promotes and provides for their effective use, fostering research, teaching, publication, and life-long learning, as well as civic engagement. In service to its diverse community, the Newberry encourages intellectual pursuit in an atmosphere of free inquiry and sustains the highest standards of collection preservation, bibliographic access, and reader services" ("The Newberry"). The Newberry's core collections are in the following areas: American history and culture; American Indian and Indigenous studies; Chicago and the Midwest; genealogy and local history; HISTORY OF THE BOOK; manuscripts and archives; maps, travel, and exploration; medieval, Renaissance, and early modern studies; music; and religion.

NEWSPRINT. The paper that newspapers are printed on. This is an exceptionally inexpensive (read "cheap") paper that has little or no SIZING, and is usually quite acidic. It has at least two outstanding characteristics that identify it. First, it will turn yellow when left in direct sunlight even for only a short time. Second, it is particularly subject to the FEATHERING of ink—especially ink that is thin or is mixed with too much solvent. It got its name from the fact that newspapers are printed on it, such paper being chosen since newspapers are generally considered to be EPHEMERA, so its longevity is clearly not an issue and the cheaper the paper, the more money the publisher saves. Because it is made primarily from WOOD PULP, it will also contain lignin, which adds acidity to the paper. Thanks to its cheapness, the paper is also used for other printed material that is considered ephemeral: inexpensive wallpaper, leaflets, flyers, tickets, magazines, COMIC BOOKS, and PAPERBACKS of the lurid or PULP FICTION sort that need to last through a single reading before being cast off.

NEW YORK PUBLIC LIBRARY (NYPL). The premier public library and also one of the most important research libraries in the United States. "Samuel J. Tilden (1814–1886) . . . upon his death bequeathed the bulk of his fortune—about $2.1 million to 'establish and maintain a free library and reading room in the city of New York'" ("History of the New York Public Library," http://www.nypl.org/help/about-nypl/history [accessed 10 June 2021]). Tilden was one of a host of civic-minded citizens who helped the city create this institution. Because New York's other two fine libraries (the Astor and the Lenox) were struggling financially, "John Bigelow, a New York attorney and Tilden trustee, devised a bold plan whereby the resources of the Astor and Lenox libraries and the Tilden Trust would be combined to form a new entity, to be known as The New York Public Library, Astor, Lenox and Tilden Foundations. Bigelow's plan, signed and agreed upon on May 23, 1895, was hailed as an unprecedented example of private philanthropy for the public good. . . . Today the Library's 92 locations include four research centers—focusing on the humanities and social sciences, the performing arts, black history and culture, and business and industry—and a network of neighborhood libraries throughout the Bronx, Manhattan, and Staten Island. Throughout the system, the Library provides free and open access to its physical and electronic collections and information, as well as to its services for people of all ages, from toddlers to teens and adults. Research and circulating collections combined total more than 51 million items, among them materials for the visually impaired. In addition, each year the Library presents thousands of exhibitions and public programs, including classes in technology, literacy, researching, and English for Speakers of Other Languages. The Library serves some 18 million patrons who come through its doors annually; in addition, the Library's website receives 32 million visits annually from more than 200 countries" ("History of the New York Public Library").

Beyond its function as a public library, NYPL has exceptional rare books and manuscripts collections and is truly one of the finest scholarly libraries in the country.

NICKEL WEEKLIES. *See* Dime novel.

NIGER. "A soft vegetable tanned goatskin that has a natural grain pattern resulting from the nature of the skin, the tanning processes employed, and, especially, BOARDING in the wet condition. Niger . . . is tanned and finished from native skins in Nigeria and surrounding districts by primitive methods, usually employing babul bark as the principal tanning material. The most common colors, which are seldom uniform, include crimson, orange to brick-red, green, as well as the natural buff. The slight variations in grain surface and color which give Niger its characteristic appearance, are seldom successfully imitated in other skins, such as that of the sheep, which is being increasingly offered as genuine Niger" (Roberts and Etherington, p. 176).

NIHIL OBSTAT. A Latin phrase meaning "nothing impedes," "nothing stands in the way." It is found on books from the Catholic Church to indicate that there is nothing in the way of publishing the volume's text. It is equivalent of an IMPRIMATUR, stating that doctrinally and morally the text is fully approved of by the Church. (*See* Privilege.)

NITROCELLULOSE. *See* Pyroxyline.

NIXON, HOWARD M[ILLAR] (1909–1983). One of Britain's renowned historians of bookbinding. He was librarian at the British Museum and, later, at Westminster Abbey from 1974 until his death. His many publications about bookbinding were models of scholarship, and are still consulted by researchers and historians. A few stand out: *Five Centuries of English Bookbinding*; (with Mirjam M. Foot) *The History of Decorated Bookbinding in England*; *Royal English Bookbindings in the British Museum*; and *Sixteenth-century Gold-tooled Bookbindings in the Pierpont Morgan Library.*

NO DATE. Abbreviated "n.d." in bibliographic references. This designation is sometimes followed by a date in brackets (e.g., "n.d. [1773]") when the bibliographer can establish a date that is not printed on the item. That is, the "n.d." means that the date is not stated on the item under scrutiny. The old method of indicating this was "s.d."—the Latin *sine datum* (without date). (Carter also gives "s.a." for *sine anno*, but this is exceptionally rare.) The same is true for "NO PLACE" and "no printer" (or "no publisher"). It is thus common to see a bibliographical entry like the following: "Howard, Frank. *My Best Post-Game Interviews*. N.p.: n.p., n.d."—where the first "N.p." refers to place of publication, the second to publisher. And likewise, one may see: "N.p. [Paris]: n.p. [Roret], n.d. [1845]."

NOM DE PLUME. *See* Pseudonymous publication.

NON-BUYER'S REMORSE. *See* Buyer's remorse.

NONPAREIL. This is an old-fashioned term for 6-point type. It is also a common pattern in MARBLING, showing closely aligned, fairly parallel lines in the pigments. The word is often mispronounced. It should be /non-pa-*rel*/. This and other named patterns can be found in many excellent texts. (See, e.g., Maurer, *Marbling*; Maurer-Matheson, *The Ultimate Marbling Handbook*; Miura, *The Art of Marbled Paper*; Schleicher and Schleicher, *Marbled Designs*; and Wolfe, *Marbled Paper*.) (*See* Marbling/Marbled paper.)

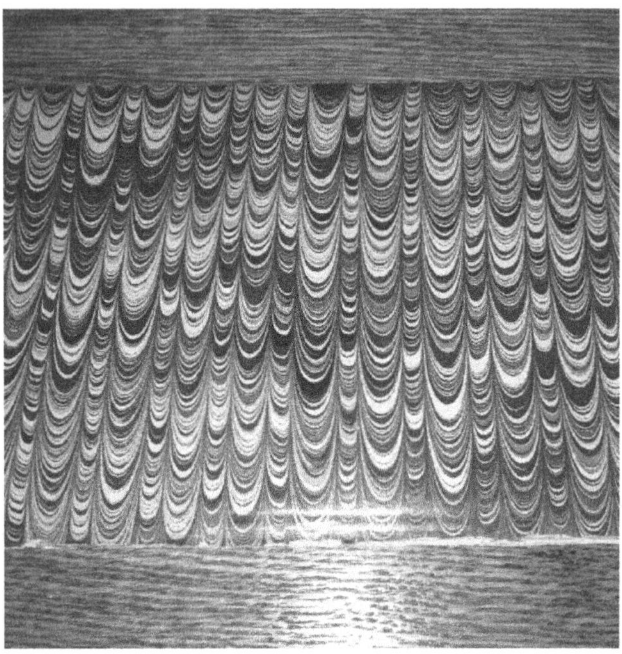

Nonpareil pattern on mid-19th-century marbled endpaper. Collection of the author.

NO PLACE (of publication). As with "NO DATE," no place of publication is printed on the item, though it is sometimes possible, from outside sources, to determine a publisher (and thus a place of publication), in which case that information can be supplied in brackets. Carter also gives "s.l." (for *sine loco*—no place) and "s.n." (*sine nomine*—no name), which are seldom seen today.

NO PRINTER/NO PUBLISHER. As with "NO DATE," no printer or publisher's name is printed on the item, though it can be supplied in brackets when this information can be ascertained.

NORMALIZATION. In TEXTUAL EDITING, the practice of the editor of changing words or punctuation, among other things, to a single style rather than leaving the text with various versions of that which is normalized. For instance, a writer with characters speaking in an American Southern dialect might have one say, "I'se goin' home"; another say, "I is goin' home"; a third say, "I'se gwyne home"; and a fourth say, "I is gwynne home"—all four spellings coming, say, in one conversation. And the variations could appear even in the speech of a single character. An editor, perhaps thinking that readers would be flummoxed by the variations, could choose to normalize the spellings to a single form. Mark Twain has such variations in his characters' speech, and also in his spellings. In the manuscripts for *Those Extraordinary Twins* and *Pudd'nhead Wilson*, he calls Angelo and Luigi "the Twins" and "the twins." In speech, the variations could signal differences in pronunciation; in the spelling of "twins," the capitalization is not tied to pronunciation. Normalization may make sense with capitalization and may not make sense where pronunciation is concerned.

NORTHEAST DOCUMENT CONSERVATION CENTER. *See* NEDCC.

NOT IN ———. A frequent bit of information given in booksellers' catalogs indicating that the volume in question is missing from some reference book or bibliographic database in which one would expect to find it. For example, "Not in *AI*" means that the book in question is unlisted in *American Imprints*. The implication is that it is a scarce item and that, also by implication, it is valuable. One bookseller many years ago compiled a catalog of items "Not in NUC" (the NATIONAL UNION CATALOG). But thousands upon thousands of items are not in NUC, and their not being listed in that seriously incomplete resource was not always an indication of rarity—or enhanced value. The "not in" formula can be abused when the bibliographer or bookseller claims a book is missing from a particular reference volume when that volume itself is seriously flawed or is on another topic altogether. For example, to say that Sarah Grand's novel *The Heavenly Twins* (1893) is "Not in BAL" (*see* Blanck, Jacob) is misleading because this volume should not be there. BAL deals with American authors; Grand was British. Or a volume of poetry may be said to be WANTING from a bibliography of the works of novelists. Or a work published in 1900 may be said to be lacking in a reference tool devoted to the 20th century when 1900 is actually the last year of the 19th century. There is also the possibility that the "not in" formula is simply incorrect: that the work in question is actually *in* the reference it is said to be missing from, as is often the case with NUC, which in some instances did a poor job of listing its entries. Carter's main heading for this term, "Unknown to," is a practical way of describing the phenomenon. It is listed here under "Not in" since this is the most common way it appears today. (*See* Unknown to; Unrecorded.)

NOT SUBJECT TO RETURN. A term often seen in auction catalogs indicating that once the purchase is made, the buyer may not return it. Carter mentions several classes of book that may not be returned to booksellers—fine bindings, ASSOCIATION books, atlases, magazines and periodicals, pamphlet collections, and sometimes books issued IN PARTS (pp. 173–74). Why he thought it necessary to enumerate these is beyond me. A dealer can arbitrarily say, "This book is not subject to return," for whatever reason he chooses, and the buyer must know that, when he buys the item, he is stuck with it.

NUC. *See* National Union Catalog.

NUMBERED. Said of a book, BROADSIDE, PAMPHLET, or any other item that is part of a LIMITED EDITION, showing the number of that item in the series. Many FINE-PRESS books or broadsides, for example, will be numbered, either in type, in the hand of the printer, or by the signer (as with an author). The binder might also do the numbering, but this is rare. If the number of the item is printed, there are two ways for this to be accomplished: 1) the really classy way, with the printer resetting the type for each IMPRESSION of the LEAF that holds the number, or 2) with an automatic numbering device that automatically advances the number with every impression of the PLATEN. The abbreviation "No." prints with each lowering of the platen, and the platen also is pressed into the device, triggering the advancement of the numbers.

NUMBERING. *See* Foliation; Pagination.

NUMBER LINE. *See* Printer's key.

NUMBERS. *See* Serials/Serialization.

NUMBER SIGN. *See* Hash character.

NUMERALS. These are numbers, but when we use the term, it is often with respect to ROMAN NUMERALS.

NUT; NUT QUAD. *See* Em quad/En quad.

OASIS GOAT (for binding). "A trade name for a second quality Niger GOATSKIN tanned and processed in England. It has a smoother surface than the usual goatskin" (Roberts and Etherington, p. 179).

OBLONG. Said of a book that is in LANDSCAPE FORMAT.

OBVERSE. Though seldom used in the book world, it means the "front" of a LEAF, or what is more often called the RECTO, as opposed to the reverse (or VERSO). Hence, in most Western books (with alphabets reading left to right), the obverse would be the right-hand page when the volume is open (and it would most likely be an odd-numbered page). (*See* Pagination.) The term is more often used in the world of numismatics to denote the "front" of a coin, as with one that has a bust of a person on it.

OCLC—ONLINE COMPUTER LIBRARY CENTER. (Originally Ohio College Library Center, when it was established in 1967. But from the very first, it was called "OCLC," and practically no one remembers what the acronym originally stood for or what it stands for now.) Its website says, "OCLC is a global library cooperative that provides shared technology services, original research and community programs for its membership and the library community at large. We are librarians, technologists, researchers, pioneers, leaders and learners. With thousands of library members in more than 100 countries, we come together as OCLC to make information more accessible and more useful" (OCLC, "Together We Make Breakthroughs Possible"; https://www.oclc.org/en/about.html?cmpid=md_ab [accessed 3 July 2021]). The utility's site adds: "OCLC libraries collectively steward a vast quantity of knowledge. Working together, we make this information more visible and accessible to end users through shared WorldCat data, syndication programs and partnerships. This sharing of ideas creates connections both inside and outside the library community. It unites thinkers and doers around common purposes. And it helps researchers and learners achieve their goals by putting the world's knowledge in reach" (OCLC, "About"; https://www.oclc.org/en/about.html [accessed 27 April 2021]). OCLC is the world's largest bibliographic utility, host to WorldCat, a UNION CATALOG recording the holdings of scores of thousands of libraries worldwide. The catalog is available on the web for free. (See worldcat.org.) By sharing bibliographic information, the members can "piggyback" on OCLC cataloging records in their own cataloging and thus save time and money.

One of the problems with this massive database is that it is sometimes difficult to determine whether a record in its database is of an original item, a reprint, a digital version, or something else. As Rob Rulon-Miller says in his "Note on OCLC": "As is now the norm, OCLC counts are tentative, at best, as we recognize that searches using different qualifiers will often turn up different results. Searches are now further complicated by the vast numbers of digital, microfilm, and even print-on-demand copies, which have polluted the database considerably, making it difficult, without numerous phone calls or emails, to determine the actual number of tangible copies. Hence, even though the counts herein [in his catalog] have been recently checked, most all should be taken as a measure of approximation" (Rulon-Miller, "A Note on OCLC"). Hence, as booksellers sometimes price items based on their RARITY, and that rarity is partly determined on the number of copies showing up in WorldCat, the actual rarity could be much less than is indicated by a careless WorldCat search. Though OCLC dates to 1967, "Open World Cat" was not launched until 2005. By then, booksellers had become accustomed to referring to the database as "OCLC"—as in, "Only three copies located in OCLC." Today most people familiar with this history think of OCLC as the bibliographic utility and WorldCat as the catalog revealing holdings and the libraries that are the holders. Hence, we now see, "Only three copies listed in WorldCat." But the older booksellers still cite it as OCLC. In such citations, both methods of designation of the database are used.

OCTAVO. A common book format. The term has a specific meaning, but it has been co-opted by those ignorant of that specific meaning, and in modern parlance that meaning—based on the number of times the original full sheet of printed paper was folded—has been debased and used to indicate the size of a volume.

An octavo is a volume in which the TEXT BLOCK is formed from having the original full sheets that make up the volume folded three times. If the paper in the book was LAID, the CHAIN LINES in the book's leaves will be vertical. If the paper had a WATERMARK and a COUNTERMARK, these will appear in the upper inner corners of each LEAF at the GUTTER. The SIGNATURES in an octavo will consist of eight leaves. In fact, the number in the name of the format (QUARTO [4°], OCTAVO [8°], DUODECIMO [12°], SEXTODECIMO [16°], and so on) will tell the number of leaves in the signature.

OCTAVO IN HALF SHEETS. A book format in which the original full sheets are printed OCTAVOS but are cut in half to create a pair of four-LEAF SIGNATURES, each a half octavo. A common format in the 18th century and beyond. (*See* Half-sheet imposition.)

ODD VOLUMES. Members of a bibliophilic society in Boston. Well, that's what they call themselves, anyway. (See Percival Merritt, "The Club of Odd Volumes.") In bookmen's parlance, these are single volumes of a multivolume set, unattached to the rest of the tomes in the set. Most collectors are COMPLETISTS, and will be reluctant to acquire single volumes of such sets. The ORPHANS (as these single volumes are often called) are often fairly worthless apart from the full set, and collectors who acquire them knowing they are odd volumes are setting themselves up for the frustration of having such a hole in the collection. (Footnote: At a flea market in Sacramento I bought a single volume—labeled "Vol. 1" on its spine and title page—of what looked like a valuable book. In fact, I bought four copies of it, since the price was excellent and even a single volume would certainly have been worth significantly more than I paid for these. It turned out that no subsequent volumes had been published. That is, this was "ALL PUBLISHED," and I was able to sell them to booksellers for more than what I paid for them. What looked like an odd volume was not.) The term can also be applied to more than a single volume if these are parts of still larger sets. Fifteen volumes of *THE COLOPHON*, offered by a bookseller, represent odd volumes of the nearly 50 volumes that constitute the full set. (Though the term generally refers to a single volume, not groups of them.)

As for the Club of Odd Volumes, they are one of the few such clubs that still refuse to allow women members, and thus they are not part of FABS. (*See* the entry for this organization; and *see* Appendix E.)

OFFICINA BODONI. *See* Mardersteig, Giovanni.

OFFPRINT. A separate printing of an article or chapter that appeared in a larger volume. Many scholarly journals used to supply the authors of the articles they print with offprints, sometimes with their own covers stapled onto sheets from the original journal. That is, the original setting of type is used for making up the copies of some offprints.

The world is replete with offprints, usually inscribed by the article's author to someone he or she thought would be delighted to have a copy of the piece. This is ostensibly the original impetus for creating the offprints: so authors can spread the word about their scholarship or literary creations. Carter says, moreover, that sometimes publishers of serials or volumes made up of parts from one or several authors will issue "EXTRACTS"—that is, issues of the work in small printings (see Carter, p. 175). Carter also says that the sharing of offprints among scholars encouraged their corresponding with one another about their scholarship. However, the cost of creating offprints and the conversion of great numbers of text to digital formats have driven most scholarly journals to abandon the practice of supplying offprints to authors. I remember publishing an article early in my career and being happy to get the offprints, then much more recently getting offprints (after not having seen one in decades) and thinking, "How quaint."

OFFSET. To smear or transfer to another surface. When recently printed text with wet ink has a surface laid over it (as with another piece of paper), the ink could smear or transfer to the other sheet. This is offsetting. (Sometimes called "set-off.") (*See* Offset printing; Offset sheets; Offsetting.) The offsetting could also happen when an oil-based ink with insufficient dryers transfers to the facing page, perhaps taking years to happen. The offset text is a ghost image of the original, in reverse (in mirror writing).

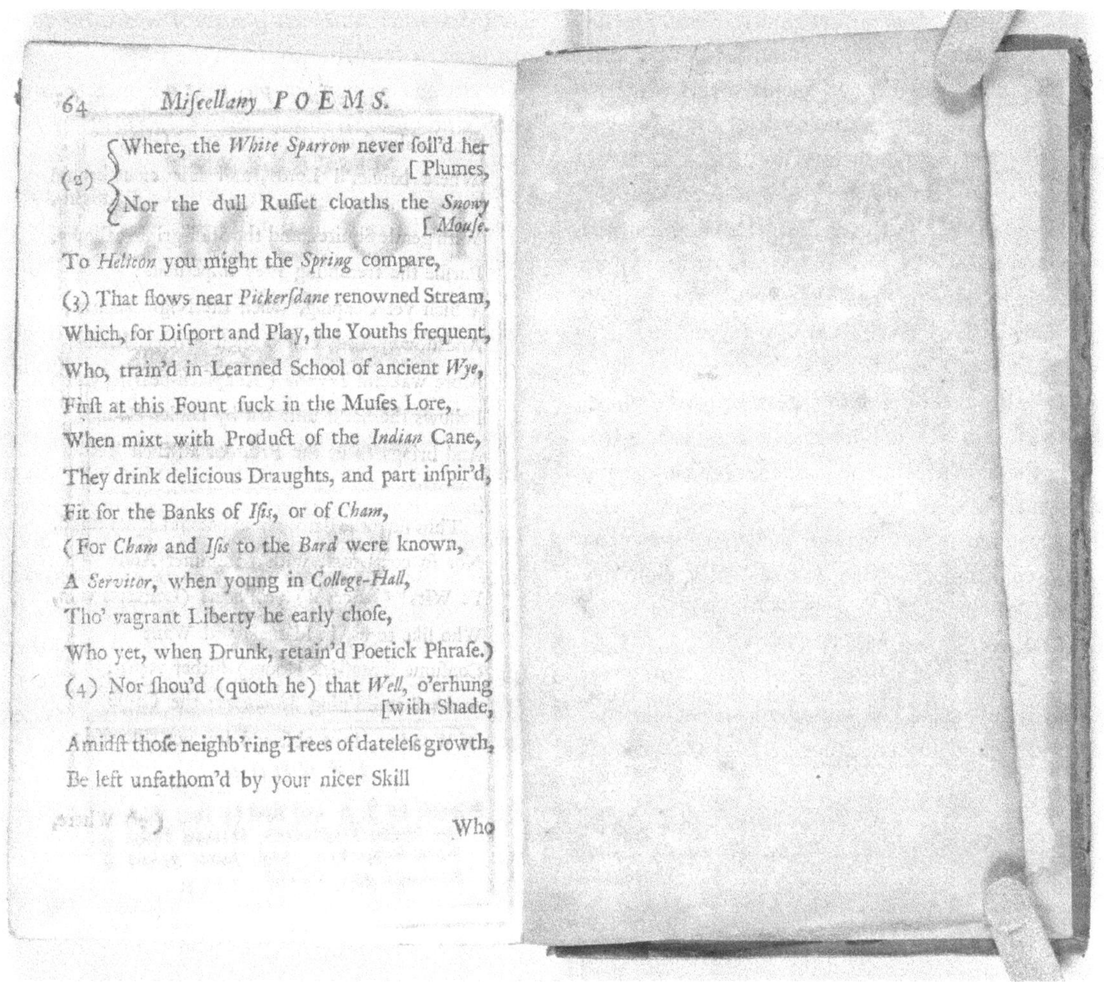

64 *Miſcellany* POEMS.

(2) Where, the *White Sparrow* never ſoil'd her [Plumes,
Nor the dull Ruſſet cloaths the *Snowy* [*Mouſe*.

To *Helicon* you might the *Spring* compare,
(3) That flows near *Pickerſdane* renowned Stream,
Which, for Diſport and Play, the Youths frequent,
Who, train'd in Learned School of ancient *Wye*,
Firſt at this Fount ſuck in the Muſes Lore,
When mixt with Product of the *Indian* Cane,
They drink delicious Draughts, and part inſpir'd,
Fit for the Banks of *Iſis*, or of *Cham*,
(For *Cham* and *Iſis* to the *Bard* were known,
A *Servitor*, when young in *College-Hall*,
Tho' vagrant Liberty he early choſe,
Who yet, when Drunk, retain'd Poetick Phraſe.)
(4) Nor ſhou'd (quoth he) that *Well*, o'erhung [with Shade,
Amidſt thoſe neighb'ring Trees of dateleſs growth,
Be left unfathom'd by your nicer Skill

Who

A printed page in a book with offset from a title page that had been laid over it. Also note the poorly trimmed volume (the head of the leaf is trimmed at an angle) and the foxing on the facing endpaper. Anne Kingsmill Finch, *Countess of Winchilsea, Miscellany: Poems, on Several Occasions, Written by a Lady* (London: Printed for J.B. and sold by Benj. Tooke, William Taylor, and James Round, 1713).

Courtesy of the Rare Books & Manuscript Library, University of Illinois, Urbana–Champaign.

OFFSET PRINTING. A type of printing in which the text to be printed, usually from a PLATE, is picked up by a rubber sheet and then is transferred to the surface that receives the image.

"Offset printing, also called offset LITHOGRAPHY, is a method of mass-production printing in which the images on metal plates are transferred (offset) to rubber blankets or rollers and then to the print media. The print media, usually paper, does not come into direct contact with the metal plates. This prolongs the life of the plates. In addition, the flexible rubber conforms readily to the print media surface, allowing the process to be used effectively on rough-surfaced media such as canvas, cloth or wood. / The main advantage of offset printing is its high and consistent image quality. The process can be used for small, medium or high-volume jobs. There are two types of offset printing machines in common use for publication today. In sheet-fed offset printing, individual pages of paper are fed into the machine. The pages can be pre-cut to the final publication size or trimmed after printing. / In web offset printing, larger, higher-speed machines are used. These are fed with large rolls of paper and the individual pages are separated and trimmed afterwards. Sheet-fed offset printing is popular for small and medium-sized fixed jobs such as LIMITED-EDITION books. Web offset printing is more cost-effective for high-volume publications whose content changes often, such as metropolitan newspapers" ("Offset Printing/Offset Lithography," WhatIs.com; http://whatis.techtarget.com/definition/offset-printing-offset-lithography [accessed 11 June 2021]). (*See* Xerography.)

OFFSET SHEETS. (Sometimes called "barrier sheets.") Thin papers laid or bound into books where printed text might OFFSET onto the opposite page. The papers are designed to prevent the ink from one sheet from transferring onto the facing surface. (*See* China paper; Tissue/Tissue guard.) Under the heading of TMI (too much information): If a letterpress printer wants to perfect his sheets while he prints the first side (i.e., if he wants to print both sides at once, printing the second side before the first has dried), he can use offset sheets as follows: Print side A. Take it out of the press, lay an offset sheet over the TYMPAN and invert the newly printed sheet so that it is laid onto the tympan onto the offset sheet. This prevents the wet ink from getting onto the tympan. Perfect the sheet (i.e., print side B). The wet ink from Side A gets onto the offset sheet and not onto the tympan. Take the sheet out of the press, printed on both sides (with the ink still wet on both sides). Then repeat this operation with the next sheet to be printed, each time using a new, dry offset sheet. This necessitates having as many dry offset sheets as you have sheets to be printed, but these offset sheets can be used over and over (of course, letting them dry between uses). This is another meaning (or use) of offset sheets. (*See* Slip sheet/Slip proofs.)

OFFSETTING. The (usually) unwanted transfer of ink from one surface to a facing surface, either because the ink was not dry when the facing surface was exposed to the sheet or because moisture softened the ink and caused it to offset. Offsetting can happen with pages printed from TYPE or with any kind of illustration (COPPERPLATE, STEEL PLATE, LITHOGRAPHIC, and so on).

Carter says that the offset text can offer bibliographical evidence because it could come from an early stage in the printing or gathering of SIGNATURES into the final volume (see Carter, p. 175), but this facile observation is suspect. The evidence might be there, and it might be valuable, but not because it derives from early stages in a book's assembly. Carter follows this with a more reliable statement—that the offsetting may be valuable if it comes from a page that was not related to the volume in which the offsetting took place.

From my own experience, offsetting can happen if a printer using a HANDPRESS inks the type and forgets to place a sheet of paper onto the TYMPAN, then pulls the BAR, printing the text onto the tympan. The ink is fresh on the tympan, and if another sheet is placed onto the tympan to be printed without the printer's cleaning the tympan, the ink on the tympan will offset onto the underside of the next sheet impressed.

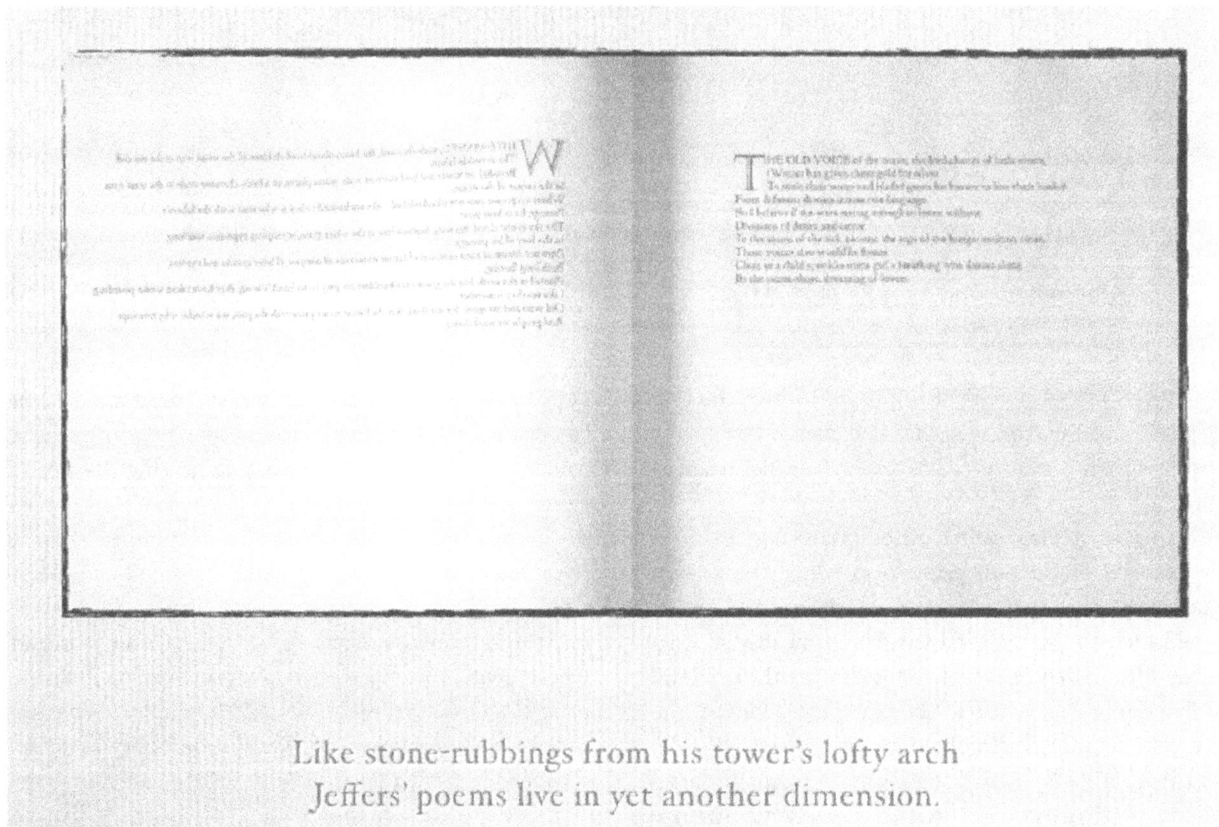

Two-page spread from Robinson Jeffers, *Granite & Cypress* (Santa Cruz: Lime Kiln Press, 1975). Note how the printer, William Everson, allowed the text to offset (printed in reverse) on the verso.

Collection of the author.

Printer and poet William Everson used this technique intentionally in printing his tour de force, Robinson Jeffers's poems *Granite & Cypress*. Everson printed onto the tympan, inserted a fresh sheet, inked the type again, and printed essentially both sides of the sheet at once, one side with the type, the other with the wet ink on the tympan. So the text on the RECTO perfectly superimposed with the type on the VERSO. He bound the volume with rectos facing reverse-printed texts on versos. That is, every printed page in the book has, on the opposite side of the LEAF, the same text printed in reverse, in perfect REGISTER. Offsetting is not always unintentional.

OLD BUT NOT RARE. A phrase occasionally encountered in the cataloging records of inexperienced booksellers. And also used by experienced ones when they are telling a patron that the book the patron has brought in for sale is not valuable. It goes without saying (and that is a phrase which goes without saying) that age has little to do with the value of a book. I once bought a 1517 folio in mint condition for $40. Demand for the title was essentially nil; hence, the value was close to nil, too. Unless the item is a piece of INCUNABULA, its age could add little or nothing to its value. (*See* Appraisal.)

This is a point worth reiterating since many people think that "this book is old, so it must be worth a lot"—when "old" to them is 50 or 75 years, or even from the 19th century. It's the Antiques Road Show Syndrome: "I found it in Grandpa's attic. I want to make a bundle on it." (Thanks to Richard Murian of Alcuin Books for this term.)

OLDHAM, J. BASIL. Author of three important studies of bookbindings, all of which are often consulted and cited.

1. *English Blind-Stamped Bindings* (not "British," as Barker has it in the 8th edition of Carter, and followed in the 9th edition). This volume depicts 1,089 photographic and rubbed examples of bindings, rolls, and ornaments—small stamps and roll tools, used by mid-15th- to 17th-century English binders.
2. *Early Stamped Bookbindings in the British Museum: Descriptions of 385 Blind-Stamped Bindings of the XIIth–XVth Centuries in the Departments of Manuscripts and Printed Books / Mainly by the Late W. H. James Weale. With 490 Illustrations of the Stamps Used on Them.*
3. *Blind Panels of English Binders*. In this volume, companion to the first one listed here, Oldham reproduces all the types of panels known, arranging them into a classification system that includes Acorn, Animal, Biblical, Heraldic, Rose, and several other classes. The 67 plates show about 250 panels. (*See* Panel/Panel binding.)

OLD STYLE AND NEW STYLE (DATES). The website ClearlyExplained.com says, "Old Style (O.S.) and New Style (N.S.) are sometimes used with dates to indicate whether the Julian year has been adjusted to start on 1 January (N.S.), even though documents written at the time use a different start of year (O.S.), or whether a date conforms to the Julian calendar (O.S.), formerly in use in many countries, rather than the Gregorian (N.S.). / Closely related is double dating, which uses two consecutive years because of differences in the starting date of the year, or includes both the Julian and Gregorian dates. / Beginning in 1582, the Gregorian calendar replaced the Julian in Catholic countries. / This change was also implemented in Protestant and Orthodox countries some time later. / In England and Wales, Ireland, and the British colonies, the change of the start of the year and the changeover from the Julian calendar occurred in 1752 under the Calendar (New Style) Act 1750. / In Scotland, the legal start of the year had already been moved to 1 January (in 1600), but Scotland otherwise continued to use the Julian calendar until 1752. / Many cultures and countries now using the Gregorian calendar have different old styles of dating, depending on the type of calendar they used before the change" (ClearlyExplained.com, "Old and New Style Dates"; http://clearlyexplained.com/old-and-new-style-dates/index.html [accessed 16 May 2021]).

ON APPROVAL. Some collectors (and librarians) do not wish to buy a pig in a poke—that is, they want to see an item before they commit to buying it. So they may ask the dealer to send it "on approval," meaning that they are asking to see the piece but letting the seller know that they are not guaranteeing a sale: they may send the item back if they are not satisfied with it. For inexpensive books and manuscripts, such an arrangement makes little sense. But for expensive items, it makes good sense. The recipients may already have a copy, but they want to see if the one offered differs in some substantial way from their own—in which case acquiring a second copy makes sense. They may wish to COLLATE the volume, not fully trusting the bookseller's description (of the text or of the condition). The buyer may wish to examine a particular aspect of the piece that the bookseller may not have known about—a phenomenon that makes the copy particularly desirable.

As Carter says, if a bookseller has a firm order, he is likely to send the book to that customer, for it is a guaranteed sale, while an "on approval" order is not. Also, it is poor form for a customer to receive the item on approval, decide he does not want it, and not return it immediately. The longer he holds on to it, the longer the bookseller cannot offer it to another customer. The moment the potential buyer decides the item is not for him, he should contact the bookseller and let him know and then return it quickly. Booksellers and customers should know in advance who is responsible for the postage and handling (and—for a valuable item—the insurance) in the shipping. It is customary for the dealer to pay for the first shipping, the customer for the return. (*See* Consignment.)

ON COMMISSION. One way that booksellers sell books. A bookseller may not want to buy a book from someone with the idea of selling it himself. The item could be on his shelf for a long time; it could cost him a good deal out of pocket with no guarantee that the item will sell. That is, for one reason or another, the item may be too much of a risk for the bookseller to take on. He might then tell the owner of the book that he will take it "on commission," meaning that he will take it and try to sell it, but without paying the owner for it until the item sells. This reduces the gamble for the bookseller, who can then sell it at his leisure with no pressure to make a quick sale or to feel the need to recoup his costs. The owner of the item, however, is then at the mercy of the bookseller. His precious volume is out of his hands, he cannot sell it through any other channels, and he must wait patiently until the bookseller sells the item and pays him what the two of them have decided upon, or until the seller decides that he is unable or unwilling to try to sell the item any longer and returns it to the owner. There is a bit of inconvenience on the part of both parties, depending on the arrangement.

Further, there must be a clear—even a contractual—understanding between both parties on the details of the arrangement. How much does the owner wish to realize on the sale? How much does the seller wish to realize? Is there a time limit on selling the item? If so, what is it; if not, how long must the owner have to wait? Who will pay for shipping and handling (either to a new owner or to the original owner)? Who will contact whom when there is a sale or when the time limit draws near? And so forth.

Finally, and emanating from a discussion I once had with a bookseller: Items on commission are often offered at a price set by the owner, so the bookseller has no room for discounts or negotiations (on price or payment options). One bookseller told me that he sometimes tells a prospective buyer that an item is on commission, so he cannot negotiate, when, in fact, he just does not want to negotiate on an item. Either way (on commission or not), people should not HAGGLE with a bookseller over price.

An older meaning for the term "on commission" is that an author has paid for the publication of her book (what we might today call VANITY PUBLISHING). A book so published—"on commission"—could be scarce, but it could also be hardly worth acquiring if the text was so bad that a commercial publisher would not touch it.

A further meaning of the term refers to the situation in which a bookseller represents a collector at an AUCTION, and is thus working on commission for that collector.

105 AD. The supposed date of the invention of paper. This is not accurate. Paper was invented in the second century BC. Don't let this often cited date mislead you. The literature on papermaking has promulgated this error for ages. (*See* Paper.)

ONE-OF-A-KIND BOOK. *See* Duplicate; Unique.

ONE-PULL PRESS. *See* Ramage press.

ONIONSKIN (also spelled as two words). "[A] very thin, hard, glazed translucent paper [so named] because of its resemblance to the dry outer skin of the onion; . . . it is used for permanent records where small volume is desirable, for duplicating purposes, . . . and for 'air-mail' postage. . . . Its particular characteristics are transparency, strength and thinness for the weight, and the fact that the paper will lie flat at all times" (Labarre, *Dictionary and Encyclopaedia of Paper and Paper-Making*, p. 176). For much of the 20th century, onionskin was used with carbon paper to make typed copies of documents and correspondence, so great quantities of it exist in archives and library collections. (Remember onionskin stationery for air mailing?)

ONLAID/ONLAYS (in binding). Said of any decorative or other pasted-on pieces of paper, leather, or other materials—adhered to the surface of a SUBSTRATE—as opposed to INLAID, which designates pieces laid into a well and made flush with the substrate's surface. With respect to bindings, Roberts and Etherington say, "A method of decorating a leather binding by means of thin, variously colored pieces of leather, usually of a different color than the covering leather, which are attached by means of paste or P.V.A. to the surface of the covering leather, thus giving it a kind of mosaic effect. The pieces of leather are usually, but not necessarily, of the same type of leather as that covering the book. The onlay was certainly in use in England by the 17th century and was also a technique occasionally adapted to publisher's cloth bindings between 1840 and 1860, with onlays sometimes made of paper" (p. 180).

ONLINE BOOK SALES. In any book on book terminology, there must be an entry for perhaps the greatest and most revolutionary means of book sales in history: online sales. DEALERS' CATALOGS, bookstores, and direct QUOTATIONS from booksellers, along with AUCTION sales (and their CATALOGS) and BOOK FAIRS, were the primary means by which books changed hands for centuries, along with garage sales, flea markets, and thrift shops. But these sales were of necessity of limited nature—that is, only a limited number of items could be purveyed these ways. Even a massive bookshop or a multisession auction would have books in the thousands. Now the Internet carries them by the hundreds of millions. A bookseller offering his wares in a shop could reach all those who visited the shop—hundreds or maybe thousands a year. The same dealer can reach a potential clientele of scores of millions online, 24 hours a day, year-round.

In the last decade of the 20th century, with the coming of the World Wide Web, online sales of books and manuscripts began to outstrip all other means of sales, and today more books and manuscripts and other library materials are sold on the web than are sold in any other way.

When online sales became a reality, booksellers were able to sell hosts of items that had languished on their shelves maybe for decades. With Michael Selzer's Bibliofind (ca. 1999), book sales went worldwide. With Amazon, eBay, ABEBOOKS, BOOKFINDER, Biblio.com, Bibliofind, VIALIBRI, Powell's, Barnes & Noble, and scores of other U.S. and international online utilities, one now has literally hundreds of millions of volumes available at the movement of a mouse—and in all languages in which books exist. BookFinder alone advertises that it has 150 million books to choose from, "from over 100,000 booksellers worldwide" (https://www.bookfinder.com/?mode=advanced&new_used=*&first_ed=&signed=¤cy=USD [accessed 5 June 2021]). Some sites, such as EBAY, are an amalgam of auction and sales ("your next bid" or "buy it now"), but most are direct sales from thousands of vendors.

Once the ability to sell online came to the masses, every mom and pop with a book to sell could become a bookseller. People not professionals in the book world saw the opportunity, and they began putting up for sale—direct or by auction—millions of titles, all in competition with the booksellers. A book that was hard to find, with perhaps only a few auction records in the last three decades and no more than that in *BOOKMAN'S PRICE INDEX*, may appear in dozens of copies, dredged up from private homes—attics and basements and crowded bookshelves—or thrift shops. This glut made prices drop, thanks to the competition, and it became a buyer's market. This is the situation today.

People comb garage and tag sales, thrift shops, estate sales, used-book stores, flea markets, and anywhere else they can find a volume that might sell. And some books are selling for one cent, with the vendors making a profit on their "shipping and handling" charges.

Obvious drawbacks are that (1) the amateur (now-turned-semiprofessional) booksellers who knew little about books were offering things with prices considerably off what their "normal" (pre-Internet) evaluations were, either too high or too low, setting pricing precedents that were difficult to change, and that (2) these neophytes also did not know the standard terminology of the book trade and were describing things that they did not understand. Hence, condition was often misrepresented; a second edition was called a first edition; a book club version was not recognized as such; a rebound book was not recognized as such; a book that said "first edition" on its copyright page may have been a facsimile edition, but those words were put into the description on the Internet with no hint that there was a real first edition that was the source of the facsimile; claims were made such as "with no DUST JACKET, AS ISSUED" when there really was a dust jacket on the book when it was issued; and other problems with veracity, accuracy, and thoroughness yielding the sale of many a volume as one thing when it was really another thing. Descriptions of binding, papers, decorations, condition, and editions are often misleading, uninformed, or just plain wrong. These unschooled booksellers are making it difficult for serious buyers (collectors, booksellers, librarians, scholars, and readers) to know exactly what they are getting.

Even photographs of the items for sale can be doctored. And one seller may borrow the photograph of a volume from another, not realizing that the two volumes represented by the two sellers are not really the same. As with so much more in the book world, buyers from online sellers—especially those with no "name" or reputation—must proceed with caution. On the other hand, online sales is the greatest boon to the book collector in the past 500 years, for the process exposes millions of copies of books that would have laid hidden on shelves without this electronic medium. And books that people might have sought for decades—unsuccessfully—may now appear in multiple copies thanks to the web. As noted, competition drives prices down. But the buyer must carefully weigh multiple copies against one another for differences in edition, condition, completeness, and other factors that make some volumes "COLLECTIBLE" and others mere READING COPIES.

Predictions were that the Internet would do away with dealers' catalogs, and it is true that many a dealer has gone from issuing catalogs to listing her whole stock online. It saves time and money, it eliminates the need to have an open shop, and it allows the seller to reach a worldwide audience, hundreds or thousands of times what she could reach without the web. On the other hand, dealers' catalogs are still around in abundance, and they remain a popular means of selling.

In the meantime, and perhaps for evermore, the Internet will be the number one way for books to travel through the world. Untold numbers of copies are available on the web, and there seems to be no diminution of them. The Internet has also become perhaps the premier means of pricing since it contains a convenient cluster of databases (e.g., AbeBooks, ALIBRIS, Bookfinder, viaLibri, and many others), listing hundreds of millions of volumes. (*See* Used copy/Used-book store.) (*See also* Amazon; Appraisal; Rarity.)

Running parallel to straight-up online book sales is the online auction, typified by eBay, but now picked up by a host of companies, especially during the pandemic when face-to-face auctions have been canceled by the dozens. Auction houses not specifically geared to book sales—as with those dealing with jewelry and antiques—can easily get into this game. The Rare Book Hub has a listing (as of the present writing) of "115 Searchable Auctions Upcoming / [with] 31,941 Searchable Lots" (see Rare Book Hub; https://www.rarebookhub.com/ [accessed 9 March 2021]). To repeat: online sales of books has never before been so tempting, widespread, and intoxicating.

ONLINE COMPUTER LIBRARY CENTER. *See* OCLC—Online Computer Library Center.

ONLY. As Carter points out, this word is sometimes used in a bookseller's description to indicate something not quite right. He cites the locution "with 48 plates (only)" or "9 volumes (only)," implying that there is something missing. (See Carter, p. 176.) (*See also* First and only.) This use differs considerably from the selling tactic "priced at only _____," that word implying that the price is a bargain. "We could ask $500 for this, but we are asking only $19.95." Don't be fooled by this "only."

OOZE CALF/OOZE LEATHER. "Originally, a leather produced from calfskin by forcing ooze [a vegetable tanning liquor] through the skin by mechanical means, producing a soft, finely grained finish like velvet or suede on the FLESH SIDE. The term is also used incorrectly with reference to SHEEPSKIN. Today, ooze leather is a vegetable- or chrome-tanned skin of bovine origin, generally calfskin, with a very soft, glovelike feel and a natural GRAIN" (Roberts and Etherington, "ooze leather [ooze calf]"; https://cool.culturalheritage.org/don/dt/dt2378.html [accessed 27 February 2021]).

OPACITY. The quality of paper that prohibits images or even light from shining through it. As E. J. Labarre says, "Opacity in papers is sometimes desirable in thin papers and is attained by special treatment and material, such as loading agents, waste paper, and careful selection of material, e.g. hemp and cotton" (Labarre, "Opaque," *Dictionary and Encyclopaedia of Paper and Paper-Making*, p. 176). In booksellers' catalogs and librarians' and scholars' bibliographic descriptions, it is sometimes useful to discuss the opacity of paper, perhaps to distinguish one version of a volume from another (e.g., a book-club printing from a first edition on the normal paper of the edition).

OPEN ACCESS. Since the inception of the creation of online content (information of all kinds), access to this content has often become monetized, to the great consternation of many. Countering this "pay to play" mode, open access is a movement to make all kinds of content free of charge and easy to locate and use. Perhaps mostly affected are scholarly journals and books, but open access can apply to any kind of information. The Open Knowledge Foundation summarizes it this way: "Knowledge is open if anyone is free to access, use, modify, and share it—subject, at most, to measures that preserve PROVENANCE and openness" (Open Knowledge Foundation, "Open Definition"; http://opendefinition.org/od/2.1/en/ [accessed 7 April 2010]). With respect to access, this website explains that "[t]he work must be provided as a whole and at no more than a reasonable one-time reproduction cost, and should be downloadable via the Internet without charge." A key proviso is that, while access may be open, the work in question may still be under COPYRIGHT, and users, who have free *access*, must still observe intellectual property rights, and will need to get PERMISSION to use the materials they have accessed.

OPENED. When a book is composed of folded LEAVES, for FORMATS other than folios (in which the original sheets of paper are folded only once), the resulting format will have BOLTS—folds at the HEAD, sometimes also at the FORE-EDGE, and even at the foot of the volume. If the book is bound and these bolts have not been slit open or sliced off, the book is said to be "UNOPENED." Hence, when anyone refers to an "opened book," it could mean one in which the bolts have been opened (or it could mean that the book has been opened to be read, the sign of which could be that that book has a tendency to open easily rather than be tight when the covers are parted).

OPEN FACE. *See* Inline.

OPEN TEAR. A tear in a LEAF with part of the leaf at the tear missing. In a CLOSED TEAR, all of the material of the leaf is present. In an open tear, what is missing could be of little consequence with respect to the completeness of the text; or the missing part(s) could be where text existed. In either case, especially the latter, the item is defective and its value will be effected.

OPISTHOGRAPH. "[A]n ancient manuscript or tablet written or inscribed upon both the back and the front" (Merriam-Webster online dictionary, "Opisthograph"; https://www.merriam-webster.com/dictionary/opisthograph [accessed 27 February 2021]).

OPTICAL COLLATORS. *See* Collating machines.

ORIENTAL BINDING (stab binding). Because Asian papers were made of fine fibers, the sheets were quite thin, and text written or printed on one side of a LEAF was visible on the other side (a phenomenon called "SHOW-THROUGH"). Hence, Asian books could be printed or written on on one side only. If the leaves were folded and sewn through the fold, the result would be two facing pages of text followed by a blank TWO-PAGE SPREAD. Hence, to hide the blank pages, binders sewed the books at the FORE-EDGE by stabbing holes through the entire TEXT BLOCK and sewing through the holes. This left all of the folds intact at the fore-edge, necessitating the volume's binding to be done through holes stabbed through this fore-edge and the sewing threads drawn through these holes. This Oriental binding (or "stab binding") structure was quite sturdy; in fact, it is one of the strongest kinds of binding. Sometimes the HEADCAP—that is, the top and bottom SPINE areas—was covered with a decorative cloth that would add some protection to these vulnerable corners. There is no proper English term other than "Oriental binding" or "stab binding," though there is a proper Japanese term for this: *fukurotoji.* Most *fukurotoji* volumes do not have page numbers, relying instead on FOLIATION. (*Fukurotoji* is sometimes hyphenated: *fukuro-toji.* It translates to "pouch binding." George C. Baxley explains: "In this binding process sheets of paper are printed [WOODBLOCK and/or text] on only one side. They are then folded in half with the printed side out. The folded printed sheets are then stacked together along with similarly printed and folded covers and the unit secured along the spine, which is the side opposite the folds, to form the book. This technique gives you the folded pages [double leaves] which are open at the top and bottom forming the pouch [*fukuro*] which the binding technique is named after" (Baxley, "Takejiro Hasegawa/Kobunsha Publications: 'Chirimen-bon' [Crepe Paper Books] and Plain Paper Books.")

Oriental binding.
Collection of the author.

ORIENTATION. Some books are taller than wide, when held with the SPINE to the left. Some are wider than tall. (Some are square.) These configurations are often incorrectly called, respectively, PORTRAIT FORMAT and LANDSCAPE FORMAT. As the notes at these terms indicate, the configurations so described are really not functions of format; they are more properly functions of the orientation of the volumes. I prefer "portrait orientation" and "landscape orientation." But dealers' catalogs for so long have used the terms with the word "format" that it is probably a fool's errand to try to change this habit. Old habits die hard, and sometimes they spawn new terms. I guess we are stuck with "portrait format" and "landscape format," though as a finicky old-fashioned purist, I wish they would go away.

ORIGINAL PARTS. A designation of the way a multi-part set of VOLUMES or FASCICLES was first issued. (*See* Parts.) A bookseller, extolling the virtues of such a set, will point out that all of the volumes or fascicles are "original parts." That is, the set is not made up of MARRIED pieces, and thus is not SOPHISTICATED.

ORIGINAL STATE/ORIGINAL CONDITION. Part of the problem with these terms (when we encounter them in dealers' catalogs, for instance) is: What is meant by "original?"; and "Does the word indicate that all EXEMPLARS in an edition must look alike?" Carter has a long entry for these terms. The main questions he raises are the following: What is original? How does the original state or condition vary from copy to copy? How do they affect COLLECTABILITY and value? Not easy questions to answer since the original state or condition can indicate several states or conditions;

and the original state is not always determinable, especially in an era when books were sold by printers/publishers in a variety of states (IN SHEETS, in paper wrappers with the intent that the buyer would have the volume bound to her own specifications, in leather but with various leathers used over a period of time as the books sold over that period, in custom-designed bindings for particular purchasers, or in various cloths, depending on what the binder had on hand or the customer ordered).

One form of bookselling, by canvassing (*see* Salesman's dummy; Salesman's sample book), yielded sample books that show that customers were often given two, three, or more choices for the volumes they were ordering. A salesman could offer blue cloth, green cloth, red cloth, leather, and other choices. So a book in its "original binding" would be in one color cloth, and a second book of the same edition would be in a different cloth or different material altogether. They differ markedly, but they are both in "original binding."

As Michèle Valerie Cloonan points out, early paper bindings were the "originals," but usually they were not intended to be the final ones, so an original binding on a volume that was issued in a paper WRAPPER might be impossible to locate. (See Cloonan, *Early Bindings in Paper.*) And, as for worth (always hovering in the air with respect to books), is an inexpensive, unadorned paper wrapper (the book's original cover) worth more or less than a sumptuous first "permanent" binding in leather? Only the collector knows for sure. If a book is taken from its state in sheets or paper wrapper, with its original DECKLES, and transmogrified into a glorious tome with trimmed and gilt edges and highly decorative MOROCCO cover, which state is more desirable to the collector? to the librarian? to the scholar? The last of these may not be interested in the monetary value of the volume; the value of the volume for the scholar is informational.

Carter points out that the designation "original" refers almost always to the exterior of the book, though with FINE-PRESS and ARTISTS' BOOKS, with various kinds of inclusions, and with imaginative boxes and other containers, the term could also refer to things inside the volume or to the books' housing. An original state may imply with a certain number of LAID-IN flyers or other inclusions. When issues of *THE COLOPHON* were sent out, they often had flyers in them with information about upcoming issues of the journal, with advertisements for other things published by the press, and with printed order forms. Hence, "original state" in this case could mean with all of these laid-in items. If there are none, how can booksellers (or others) know what was originally there so that they can claim "in original state" when no inclusions are present? Or, if there are inclusions in a volume, can a bookseller know for certain that these were part of the volume when it was originally issued, or were they inserted by an earlier owner? Or are the two present inclusions the only ones the volume was issued with? Also, some books are issued with a WRAPAROUND BAND. If the band is missing, is the book still in original condition? Additionally, if the item in question is a PAMPHLET or BROADSIDE, and the copy in hand is folded in half, does this mean that all copies sent out to buyers were sent folded? Is the folded piece in original condition? Or are they one step away from PRISTINE? Are there copies out there without the fold? In other words, "original condition" is a difficult proposition.

One last consideration: I have seen a number of fine-press books that got damaged (with water or with nicks in the bindings, for instance) at the press, before they were issued to the world—before they were formally "published." Does the original condition mean before they were damaged, or, since they were issued with the defect, does the damaged item still merit being said to be in original condition?

At any rate, when a bookseller says "in original condition," the potential buyer must weigh these issues, always with a skepticism that the dealer may not really know what that original state or condition was. "Original condition" may simply mean—to the bookseller—in excellent condition. If that is the case, she should say so.

ORIHON. Roberts and Etherington give the following: "A strip of paper, PAPYRUS or VELLUM accordion [i.e., CONCERTINA] folded so that writing or printing, which appears on only one side, is formed into pages or columns. The resulting 'book' is then secured by cord passed through holes punched along the length of the binding edge. Covers were also at times laced on. Single sheets, folded but also uncut, were also at times treated in this manner" (p. 182).

The concertina fold is easy to make, and as a book and binding structure, it is popular with neophytes learning how to make books. The accordion-folded sheet (with text or images or both on one or both sides of the leaves) can be attached to others until the desired length (i.e., the desired number of leaves) is achieved; then the ENDLEAVES of the accordion can be glued to BOARDS cut to shape and size, forming a simple and effective binding. Those new to bookmaking might call this an accordion-format book. Those wanting to impress will use "orihon."

ORIZOMEGAMI. *See* Itajime.

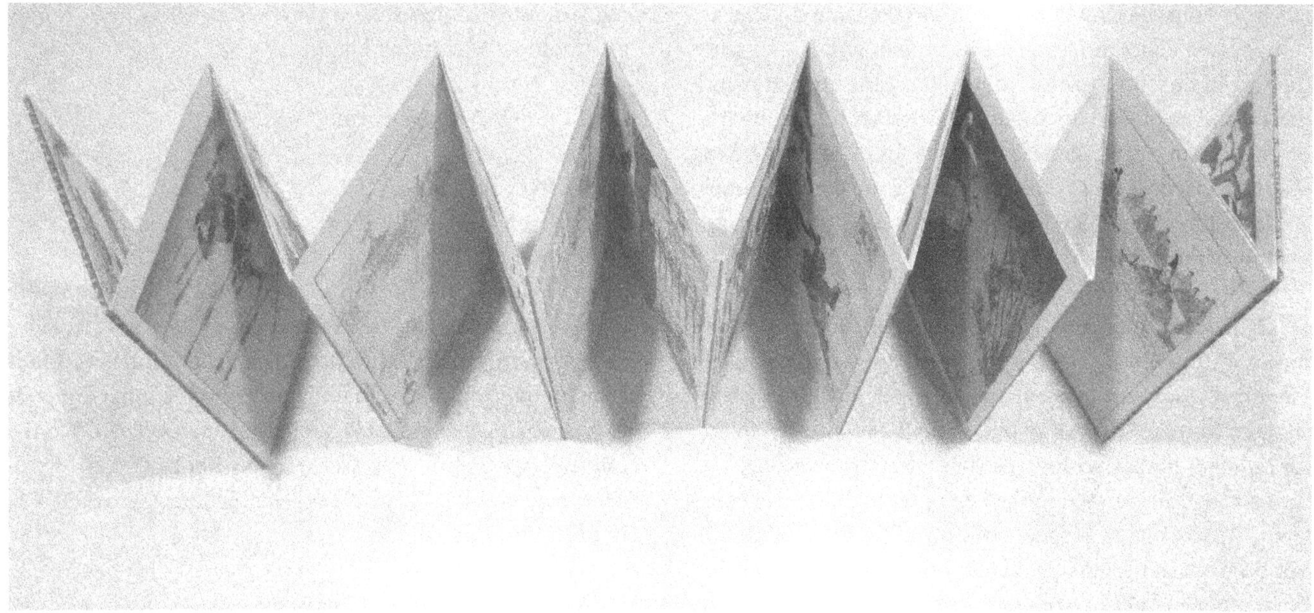

Orihon—a concertina-fold (accordion) binding.
From a private collection.

ORNAMENTAL TYPE. *See* Decorative type.

ORNAMENTS. *See* Fleurons.

ORPHANS (in printing). Lines of prose text that are the first words of a paragraph and that are single lines at the bottom of a page. Although there is nothing "illegal" about orphans—that is, there is nothing to prevent one of these things from remaining in a text, even by a keen designer they are mildly frowned on, enough that Microsoft Word has a feature allowing the writer to do away with them. This feature is called "Widow and Orphan Control" (it sounds like a military unit), and though WIDOWS are seriously frowned on and orphans are not, one can do away with both at a single click of the mouse. (There is no way that I have found to do away only with widows. You keep them both, or you eliminate them both. This relegates orphans to the same despised status as widows, an unfair assessment, if you ask me.)

The term can also apply to a single volume, unaccompanied by the rest of the volumes of a set. Volume 3 of a five-volume set, without its mates, can be called an orphan. (*See* Odd volumes; Orphan works).

ORPHAN WORKS. Books or other research material (music, photographs, research papers, moving images, time-based media, and literary texts) with no known COPYRIGHT holder are called "orphan works." Miguel Helft says that orphans are "books that the author and publisher have essentially abandoned. They are OUT OF PRINT, and while they remain under copyright, the rights holders are unknown or cannot be found. / While most orphan books are obscure, in aggregate they are a valuable, broad swath of 20th-century literature and scholarship. / Determining which books are orphans is difficult, but specialists say orphan works could make up the bulk of the collections of some major libraries" (Helft, "Some Raise Alarms as Google Resurrects Out-of-Print Books"). Even when an author is known, it is possible that the work can still be termed "orphan" if it is not clear that the author him or herself owns the rights to the work. The problem with orphan works is that they may have been produced recently enough to be under copyright protection, but extensive research does not reveal who the owner of the rights is. Sometimes a rights holder dies, and his heirs do not know that they have become the holders of those rights. This is the case, as well, for a company that goes out of business, ceding its rights to those who inherit the intellectual property but who are unaware that they are owners. It is also possible that a company dies and does not name anyone or any entity to take over ownership of the rights that that company controls. A potential user of the material, knowing she needs permission before using the text or image(s) she needs, is stymied since going to press with protected text could engender penalties. If full diligence is exercised in seeking the owner of clearly protected material and still no copyright holder emerges, the user can go to press with the text but with a statement like, "All avenues of inquiry to determine copyright holder have been unsuccessful." In a digital environment, any copyrightable material (such as software) for which there is no known owner is called "abandonware." (See Borgman, *Scholarship in the Digital Age*; see also "Orphan Works in the United States.")

The laws in the United Kingdom and the United States are complicated concerning the use of orphan works, and since they are in flux, it is unwise for anyone wishing to use a work under copyright for which the rights holder is unknown to do so without due diligence in finding the owner or seeking out the latest laws on such use. One database that could help those seeking copyright ownership is WATCH (*see* the entry for this organization).

OTHER PROPERTIES. A phrase from the AUCTION house meaning LOTS in the auction for which the consignor is not identified, especially in an auction in which the primary consignor is known. There might be a sale of a prominent collector or major library, so advertised in the auction catalog. The "other properties" noted in the title of the auction may come from anyone; that is, the PROVENANCE of the other items will not be given in the catalog, but that provenance implies that these other pieces are from a source as important as are the items from the person named in the catalog—whose sale is the main reason for the present auction. This association may enhance the value of items in the auction and might encourage more robust bidding than would happen if the lots came from someone of little public fame. Booksellers and others may wish to piggyback on this kind of sale by unloading from their stock volumes that they have had on their shelves for decades. The auction catalog may say, "Sale of an important collector," "From the library of the Duchess of So-and-Such," and then add in the catalog's title, "And other properties." The problem, of course, is that the other properties will not have the cachet of those from the important collector or duchess, but they may not be identified in the catalog. Certainly, the auction house offers consigners the opportunity to piggyback their items onto the more prestigious collection that forms the main focus of the sale.

OUTDENTED. Not really a bookish term, though it recalls a book-realm debate carried out decades ago by two printers (who must remain anonymous). One of them, in that person's printing, had a line protruding to the left of the left margin on a page of otherwise left-JUSTIFIED text. The printer mentioned that it was a single "outdented" line. Another printer, fully steeped in the tradition and vocabulary of the trade, published a critique of the first printer's work. One of the criticisms is that the notion of a *dent* was that it went *inward*, and there was no such thing as being *outdented.* It was possible to take an indented line and "outdent" it *to the margin*, but not past that margin and out into no-person's land. The first printer responded in print that the term clearly defined the phenomenon and would not have caused any readers to scratch their heads or rush to their glossaries. The second printer replied, again in print, that the word was pretty stupid, and then proceeded from there. In the literature of the book, that word, then, has some history, appearing a number of times. So it deserves an entry here, if only as a footnote to printing history.

OUTER FORME. *See* Forme.

OUTLINE. *See* Inline.

OUT OF PRINT. No longer available from its original publisher. This is different from "out of stock," which implies that the item will still be available from its publisher once new copies are supplied to them from the printers or binders. Out of print implies that the publisher no longer intends to reprint or make available additional copies. Thanks to the Internet (*see* Online book sales), many books that are out of print may be easily available on the secondary market. (*See* In print; Print on demand.)

OUT OF REGISTER. Said of any printed text or image when more than one color is printed and they are not lined up properly in the printing. For a page printed in black with red initials or other lines (as is fairly common on title pages of the 17th and 18th centuries), text printed out of REGISTER looks amateurish at best and ugly at worst. And with pictures, especially multicolored LITHOGRAPHS, out-of-register images will appear blurry and fuzzy.

Additionally, printers usually want to get good registration of text, with the lines on one side of the leaf registering perfectly with those on the verso of the leaf. Careless or hasty printers may not achieve this, and one could describe the printing as out of register.

OUT OF SERIES. In the printing of LIMITED EDITIONS of books, publishers could print more copies than are indicated by the limitation stated in the COLOPHON. There is likely to be spoilage; trial printings and TRIAL BINDINGS may be done, taking up some of these extra copies; the principals involved in the production (author, illustrator, printer, binder, and editor) may be given copies that are not part of the number stated; volumes may be created as ADVANCED COPIES, possibly for reviewers; and copies may be created to send to a philanthropist who supported the production or for COPYRIGHT purposes. These will not be NUMBERED, as will the volumes in the stated limitation, and they are called "out of series" (a slight misnomer since there really is not a *series* per se). Some collectors may see the out-of-series copies as not worth quite as much as those that are numbered (unless they are SIGNED or INSCRIBED by the author or some other important person); others may recognize that out-of-series copies exist in numbers far fewer than those for the numbered copies and may think they are scarcer and thus more desirable. A true COMPLETIST will want both. (*See* Printers' overruns/Overs. *See also* "Hors de commerce," under Limited edition.)

OUTSET (OR OUTSERT). In his chapter on "Imposition" (pp. 78–117; that is, the placement of the printing type into the chase for printing), Philip Gaskell explains, "Books were normally imposed in a series of regular sheets of the chosen format, the preliminaries being printed last, perhaps (if they were not extensive) filling up the last sheet of text and then being detached so that they could be placed at the front. Occasionally preliminaries were printed in a format different from that of the text, or even as part of an entirely different book that was under way at the same time and which happened to have an odd half or quarter sheet unused. Again, the preliminaries of pamphlets were sometimes arranged as an outset conjugate with the final leaves of the text, and wrapped round the rest of the gatherings" (Gaskell, *A New Introduction to Bibliography*, p. 108). That is, the pamphlet cover could be printed at the same time as part of the last-printed leaf of the text (saving the printer from having to do a separate pressrun just for the cover). The printed cover would be conjugate with one of the leaves of the text, and this cover would be called an "outset." The term was probably coined by Gaskell. Roberts and Etherington have a similar term, "Outsert," which they describe as follows: "An additional folio placed around the outside of a section" (https://cool.culturalheritage.org/don/dt/dt2404.html [accessed 28 January 2021]). The extra folio is not an insert—it is an *out*sert, probably where they get the term. It is convenient to have words for these particular phenomena.

OVERCASTING. "A method of hand sewing in which groups of single sheets [or separate signatures] are sewn together using a single length of thread which passes through the paper [or signature; and not through the fold] and over the back edges of the leaves" (Roberts and Etherington, p. 182). Sometimes a sammelband is composed of several pamphlets stitched together with overcasting. (*See* Oversewn; Stitched.)

OVERHEAD PREMIUM. *See* Premiums.

OVERLAY. A leaf in a book (or on a broadside) that is attached over another leaf, usually hinged so that the one on top can be peeled back to reveal something beneath. The overlay could be a protective leaf with information on it explaining what is beneath, or it could be transparent and printed with something that augments what is beneath when the overlay is laid flat onto the page beneath. There are also medical texts with layers of flaps of paper that show a body (when the flaps are down) and reveal the body's innards when the flaps are raised. These overlays could be in two or three or more layers.

OVERMARBLED PAPERS. Paper that has been printed on and then marbled. Sometimes a printer, for whatever reason, has printed sheets that he no longer needs: he printed more than he needed for an edition, he printed sheets for an upcoming title and then decided not to publish that title, or he had proof sheets of a book he was producing. Rather than wasting the paper, since paper was expensive and recycling was economical, he has the sheets marbled, (sometimes) obscuring the print, and he then can use the sheets for binding (covers or endpapers). This is called "overmarbling," and it was not uncommon in early American printing. Marbling can wear away from outer covers by abrasion, and the printing begins to show. Marcus McCorison wrote, "Two printed sheets bearing text from John Cleland's erotic novel *Memoirs of a Woman of Pleasure, Written by Herself* (1749), commonly known as *Fanny Hill*, found their way to AAS [the American Antiquarian Society] after being marbled, pasted as coverings for the boards used for binding material for Isaiah Thomas's collection of broadside ballads as well as for numerous other volumes now at AAS. Much remains unknown about the origins of these sheets. . . . The

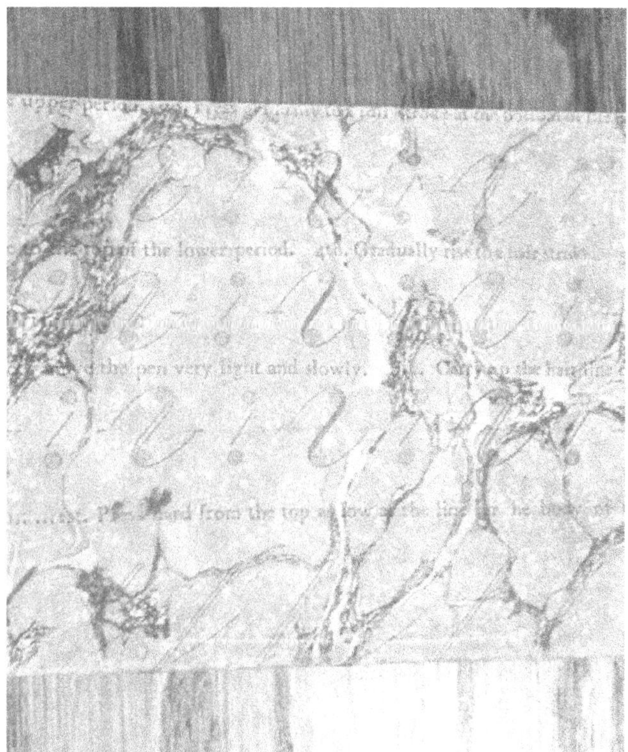

Overmarbled sheet on a small pamphlet: Robert Blair, *The Grave* (New-Ipswich, NH: Printed by Simeon Ide, 1815). The original printed text under the marbling is a calligraphy manual, and the sheet shows the calligraphic lines along with the printed directions on how to make them. Note that the marbling on the item shown in this figure does not nearly cover the printed text, nor was it the printer's (or binder's) aim to conceal the printed text. Clearly whoever chose this method of paper decoration merely wanted to adorn the sides of the volume, and the marbling achieved that—regardless of whether the text was still visible. Collection of the author.

Stormont pattern, blue and black marbling on the BOARDS themselves, has largely faded due to abrasion, so it is easy to see the columns of type from the waste paper" ("Fanny Hill and Thomas's Broadside Ballads").

The term is also used for sheets of paper with two marbled patterns, one on top of the other. This is a common phenomenon in paper marbling, but the former use is more thrilling to encounter since most of the time one cannot tell if a sheet is overmarbled over a printed text.

OVERPRINTING. The word has several meanings: 1) "[O]verprint is when colours are printed directly over each other which causes mixing of colours. This mixing of colours results in a different colour. For example, if yellow ink is set to overprint on top of the cyan print, the overlap would create green" (HelloPrint blog, "What is Overprint?"; https://www.helloprint.co.uk/blog/what-is-overprint/ [accessed 28 January 2021]). 2) A color can be printed directly over the same color to intensify the tone. This is sometimes done with black over black. 3) A text can be blacked out by having it fully covered with ink in a separate PRESSRUN to correct an error or to simply get rid of something objectionable. 4) Any printed item can have a word printed over it, as with a text sent to an editor marked "PROOF" diagonally printed over a page, or a page overprinted with a word or image that makes the rest of the text or image on the page unable to be copied (to prevent unauthorized use). (*See* Bisquing.)

OVERRUNS/OVERS. *See* Printers' overruns.

OVERSEWN. "A method of sewing the LEAVES of a book [or PAMPHLET] by hand or machine. . . . The sewing thread passes through the edges of each 'section' [i.e., SIGNATURE], in consecutive order, using pre-punched holes through which the sewing needles pass" (Roberts and Etherington, p. 182). (*See* Overcasting; Whip stitching.)

An example of oversewing on a manuscript that had been disbound, and then, casually and carelessly, the signatures were rebound with oversewing. From an unidentified manuscript at the Phillips Library, Peabody Essex Museum.

Courtesy of Phillips Library, Peabody Essex Museum.

OVERSIZE. A term to indicate that a given item is larger than most volumes and will probably not fit comfortably on most bookshelves. (*See* Coffee table books.) It would be useful for booksellers to mention this feature (along with dimensions) in their descriptions, partly to warn the potential buyer that such volumes may increase the cost of shipping, and partly to let the buyer know that he might be getting something larger than he can house.

In libraries one is likely to see a note like, "Oversize volumes are shelved on the second floor," and the fact that a volume is oversize will be noted in the cataloging record. It is common for oversize volumes to be shelved in an area of the library called "FOLIOS," though as the entry at the word indicates, this is a misnomer in the bibliographical world.

OWNERSHIP MARK. One of the signs of PROVENANCE that indicates that an item was once possessed by someone or some institution (a private party, a church, a company, a university or college, or some other owner). These marks can confer great value ("this is the ownership mark of Albert Einstein") or can reduce the value greatly ("this is the rubber stamp of former owner Frank Nobody"). The mark can be a stamp, signature, bookplate, embossed name, holes punched into the paper spelling out the name (or showing a logo), or some other identification device. Collectors and booksellers, among others, must proceed with caution here since it is possible for these marks to be faked. I once knew a BOOKSELLER who bought the library of a famous politician; among the books was a box of that person's BOOKPLATES. He destroyed them all, telling me that he didn't want them to fall into the hands of some unscrupulous person who could have affixed these to any old volume and passed it off as coming from that person's library.

OXFORD CORNERS. On the cover of a volume, TOOLED or STAMPED lines that cross one another at right angles at the corners, forming a small square at the very TIPS of the covers.

OXFORD STYLE. *See* Divinity calf.

P

PACK. *See* White post.

PACKING. The material—usually sheets or pieces of paper—that go between the two parts of the TYMPAN (the inner and the outer tympan). These pieces of paper are used to increase the pressure of the press at the spots in the FORME where the pieces are placed. For example, if the top three lines of type in a forme are not printing with sufficient "bite," the printer can add packing to add pressure to where those lines are. Doing this is called "doing the MAKEREADY."

PADDED BOARDS. (Sometimes called "padded binding.") Said of the covers in a binding that has some kind of batting, foam, or other compressible material between the cover material and the BOARDS. The softness and "give" of the cover add a sense of sumptuousness to the volume. It is sometimes found in real or imitation leather bindings. The technique goes back to the early 20th century, and possibly earlier, and can be seen today in children's books.

PAGE. One side of a LEAF in a CODEX. A BROADSIDE has two sides (front and back), but they are not generally called "pages." In books from the manuscript and HANDPRESS PERIODS, often the SCRIBES and printers did not number the pages; rather, they numbered the LEAVES (or did not number either), almost as if the concept of "page" was alien to them. In the parlance of such books, the "right-hand page" is called the "RECTO," and the "left-hand page" is the "VERSO."

PAGE PROOFS. In early book production, the proofs that are created once the set type has been divided into pages. As the entry at GALLEY PROOFS explains, the type is set and placed into a GALLEY, and proofs are taken. This, the first proof, is called the "galley proof" (or just the "galleys"). Once the galleys have been proofed and corrected, the type is broken down into pages—the pages that will be printed in the final volume—and proofs are taken at this stage. These are the "page proofs," a point at which printers strongly discourage extensive change or any changes that cause the addition (or subtraction) of even a single line that may require extensive RESETTING of type. (*See* Bluelines; Revise [noun].)

Although modern computer setting of type might make it simple to "reset" the text, such a resetting could still impact the LAYOUT of the page and adjacent pages, so even with modern printing technology, publishers strongly discourage extensive revisions at the page proof stage, and they sometimes impose a fee for such changes. This may not stop an author from revising, rewriting, removing, or rethinking his text, but he does so at the peril of raising the publisher's ire and possibly incurring a fee. Having to reset a page could mean having to change PAGINATION, HEADLINES, or SHOULDER NOTES or to reposition illustrations, charts, or tables. Page proofs, then, are the last stage before the final printing is done.

Additionally, if the author finds many errors at the page proof stage—or if the author makes substantial changes at that stage—the publisher or author may call for another set of proofs. These are also called "page proofs," but after the first set, they may be called "second page proofs," "third page proofs," and so on, though it is quite unlikely that proofs will go that many stages. (In the galleys and page proofs of a book I published several years ago, the COMPOSITORS continued to introduce new errors at every stage of proofing, and I kept asking for more proofs. After the fifth page proofs, the publisher said, "Enough," but I said that the fifth page proofs had many errors. There was no arguing, and the book went to press with many "infelicities"; I insisted that it be issued with an "ERRATA" sheet.)

Additionally, in the computer world, the first set of proofs are still called "galleys," though no metal tray (the galley) exists; and the second set of proofs is still called "page proofs," though the entire operation may be conducted on a computer—with no paper in sight.

PAGINATION. The numbering of the PAGES of a book. If the pages are not numbered but the LEAVES are, the book is said to be "foliated." (*See* Foliation.) In a normally paginated volume for alphabets that read left to right, the RECTO pages have odd numbers, and the VERSOS have even numbers, though careless or inexperienced designers may reverse this pattern. In most books, also, the main text is numbered with arabic numerals, and the PRELIMS use ROMAN NUMERALS. And it is not uncommon for the pages of END MATTER not to be numbered at all.

PAIGE TYPESETTER (also known as the Paige Compositor). The TYPESETTING machine (invented by James W. Paige between 1872 and 1888) that led to Mark Twain's bankruptcy. The aim of the machine, as was the aim of other attempts to mechanize typesetting, was to speed up the setting process. All other aspects of printing and bookmaking had been mechanized by the last quarter of the 19th century (papermaking, printing, inking, feeding paper into the press, and so on). The one impediment to speedy book production was the fact that type had to be set by hand. (*See* Mergenthaler, Ottmar.) The machine failed and took with it a good portion of Twain's fortune—some $300,000 (see "Paige Compositor," Wikipedia; https://en.wikipedia.org/wiki/Paige_Compositor [accessed 11 June 2021]). Two versions of the machine were built; one survives in the Mark Twain House in Hartford, Connecticut. "Stretching to 9 feet in length, the eventual machine contained 18,000 parts and weighted 50,000 pounds. Some $2,000,000 were invested in the project" (Wallis, *A Concise Chronology of Typesetting Developments, 1886–1986*, p. 1). (See also Huss, *The Development of Printers' Mechanical Typesetting Methods, 1822–1925.*)

The Paige Compositor.

Scientific American Magazine, March 9, 1901; American Society of Mechanical Engineers; https://www.asme.org/about-asme/who-we-are/engineering-history/landmarks/11-paige-compositor (accessed 11 June 2021).

PAINTED BINDING. As the term indicates, a book cover (almost always leather or vellum) that has been decorated with painting rather than in the more traditional way with tooled leather, fancy paper, or stamped cloth. This kind of decoration was popular in the late 17th and early 18th centuries, though there are exemplars from the 16th century

Painted binding, the painting over paper boards. Christoph Hermann Gottfried Demme, ed., *Altenburgisches Gesangbuch: nebst Gebeten: Zum Gebrauch bey der öffentlichen Gottesverehrung und häuslichen Andacht* (Altenburg: Herzogl. Sächs. Hofbuchdruckeren, 1825).

Collection of the author.

with painting over tooled leather; and 19th-century volumes were also so decorated. The decoration usually consisted of geometric patterns, landscapes, and floral designs.

PALEOGRAPHY. (In Great Britain spelled "palæography.") The study of handwriting, especially that of early writers. While the original meaning suggested that this was the study of old scripts, it has come to mean the study of handwritings in general. The original impetus for studying ancient writings was simply to be able to read the texts they displayed. But since handwriting as an art and craft evolves over time, a paleographer can often localize or date a manuscript by its handwriting—possibly even identifying a particular SCRIBE or SCRIPTORIUM.

PALIMPSEST. "A manuscript consisting of a later writing superimposed upon the original writing, which was first removed to the extent possible. A double palimpsest is one that has two subsequent writings, and therefore two removals. The extent to which the earlier writing could be removed depended to a great degree on the ink used. Early carbon inks, which merely lay on the surface of the parchment, could be removed more or less completely simply by sponging, but the later IRON GALL INKS were much more difficult to remove because of the interaction with the fibers of the tannin present in the ink. They had to be scraped and then treated with a weak acid, such as the citric acid of an orange. Even then traces of the original writing remained. Wetting the parchment in this manner softened it to such an extent that it was necessary to treat the skin with dry lime to make it dry and white once again. The word 'palimpsest' derives from the Greek roots meaning 'rub away again'" (Roberts and Etherington, p. 186). With modern technology, the removed texts can often become readable. The fairly recent example of the Archimedes Palimpsest is a case in point. (See Netz and Noel, *The Archimedes Codex*.) Peter Beal says that the word could also refer to a text that has several layers of meaning (*A Dictionary of English Manuscript Terminology, 1450–2000*, p. 280).

PALLET. "A FINISHING tool having a long narrow face bearing a line or design, and used for decorating books, usually those bound in leather. Straight-line pallets are available in various lengths, and a complete set, used for building designs, ranges from 1⁄16 inch to a maximum of 2, 3, 4, or more inches, increasing (in very complete sets) by as little as 1⁄16 inch at a time. Pallets are generally used to impress lines on the SPINES of books, although they are also used on the covers, especially to finish off lines impressed with FILLETS, or other tools. Very short pallets are usually referred to as 'short-line pallets' or, occasionally, as 'short-line tools.' The edge of the pallet is made very slightly convex in order to avoid cutting the leather in the process of TOOLING. A decorative pallet is called a 'band pallet,' while one with more than one line on its face is called a 'two-, 'three-, 'etc., 'line pallet'" (Roberts and Etherington, p. 186).

PALM LEAF BOOK. "A manuscript book, produced in India, Burma, and contiguous areas, consisting of strips cut from the leaves of the palmyra or talipot palm (*Corypha umbraculifera*). . . . The leaves were first inscribed with a stylus, the incisions then being filled with an ink prepared from charcoal and oil. The strips were then gathered, pierced through the middle, secured with cord or twine, and attached to a board" (Roberts and Etherington, pp. 186–87). Most such books were about 1½ inches wide and about 8 to 10 inches long, though they could vary in size up or down.

Palm leaf book.
Collection of the author.

PAMPHLET. A complete text, usually short—certainly not a full "book"—usually bound in WRAPPERS or stiff paper covers (though sometimes lacking any cover). The wrapper can be blank or printed. Roberts and Etherington say, "In a limited sense, [a pamphlet is] an independent publication consisting of a few LEAVES of printed matter stitched together but not bound, and with or without self-, or other paper, covers" (p. 187). Today, we need to add to "stitched" the words "or STAPLED." Most pamphlets have only one SIGNATURE, though they could have more than that. Roberts and Etherington add, "While independent in the sense that each is complete in itself, it is not uncommon to issue pamphlets in a series, usually numbered consecutively. In a bibliographical sense, a pamphlet has been variously defined as a publication of not more than 8 pages, one not exceeding 5 sheets, one not more than 100 pages, one less than 80 pages, one not less than 5 nor more than 48 pages, and as a publication consisting of one folded section (signature), regardless of the number of pages (but generally never more than 128). In early 18th century England, a pamphlet was described as work consisting of 20 leaves in FOLIO, 12 in quarto and 6 in octavo. A periodical issue is not generally regarded as a pamphlet."

It was once a fairly common practice—by libraries and private collectors—to bind groups of pamphlets into a single cover (*see* Sammelband), usually ones on a single subject or of one size—though these two features were not necessary. That is, many a sammelband is composed of pamphlets whose subjects have little or no relation to one another, and sometimes small and large, or FOLIO and QUARTO, pamphlets might wind up in the same covers. When such volumes survive (though many have been broken up for practical, cataloging, or commercial reasons), they could tell us something of their PROVENANCE.

PAMPHLET WARS. Generically, the term refers to any issue publicly debated through the medium of published PAMPHLETS. The NEWBERRY LIBRARY in Chicago has more than 2,200 pamphlets covering such topics as "the Civil War, Church of England doctrines, Acts of Parliament, and the Popish Plot. There are collections of pamphlets about the Stuart era monarchs as well as Cromwellian pamphlets. There are pamphlets in the form of letters, sermons, political verse, and drama. Authors include Defoe, Hobbes, Swift, Milton, Pepys. While the collection is rich, finding pamphlets can be a challenge" (Newberry Library, "British Pamphlets, 17th Century," Newberry Library, http://www.newberry.org/british-pamphlets-17th-century [accessed 11 June 2021]). In speaking of the pamphlet wars in England from 1640 to 1660, James Holstun says, "With the *de facto* breakdown in CENSORSHIP, the period saw a staggering output of more than 20,000 books, pamphlets, BROADSIDES and newspapers: sermons and scriptural commentaries mixed with satires and fictions, political theory and manifestos—a polyglot Babel of print." (See Holstun, ed., *Pamphlet Wars*, p. 1. See also Bloom, *English Tracts, Pamphlets and Printed Sheets*; Goodrich, *Debating England's Aristocracy in the 1790s*; and Pentland, *Edinburgh History of the Book in Scotland*, pp. 390–98.)

PANEL/PANEL BINDING. A panel is "[a] form of decoration consisting of single, double, or triple lines, rectangular in shape, formed by a FILLET or PALLET, in GILT or BLIND, either on the sides or between the bands [*see* Endbands] on the SPINE of a book" (Roberts and Etherington, p. 187). These panels form what is called a "panel binding"; and the panels are sometimes called "compartments." Since untold numbers of bindings from the HANDPRESS PERIOD were done in CALF, which is an easy material to STAMP, one is likely to see in a bookseller's catalog, "Bound in paneled calf."

Additionally, the front and rear LEAF of a DUST JACKET is a panel, as opposed to its FLAPS and spine.

PANIZZI, ANTONIO (1797–1879). Director of the British Library and one of the most influential librarians of the 19th century (whose influence is still felt). Panizzi fled from Italy to Switzerland and then to England. Through friends, he got the position (in 1831) at the British Museum, and thereafter he was made assistant librarian, keeper of printed books, and eventually principal librarian; the last of these he held for 10 years (1856–1866).

Despite some political tensions that he experienced, the library thrived under his leadership. "While at the library, Panizzi undertook the creation of a new catalog, based on the 73 rules which he devised with his assistants in 1839. These rules served as the basis for the 91 rules adopted by the British Museum in 1841, which became the foundation for all subsequent library catalog rules of the nineteenth and twentieth centuries, and are at the origins of the ISBD of the twenty-first century and of digital cataloging elements such as Dublin Core. Panizzi also instituted the COPYRIGHT system which, by law, made British publishers give the library a copy of every book printed in England. / In the early years of his tenure, Panizzi became aware that [the] library needed a new reading room. Due to lack of space to store books, purchases of new books were discouraged. Panizzi himself made a design for a new building—inside the Great Court, enclosed by existing museum buildings. The design was eventually perfected by architect Sydney Smirke and accepted by the museum trustees in 1854. The Reading Room was opened in 1857. Many great writers including Charles Dickens, Karl Marx, and Virginia Woolf are known to have used it" ("Antonio Panizzi," *New World Encyclopedia*, http://www.newworldencyclopedia.org/entry/Antonio_Panizzi [accessed 11 June 2021]). (See Panizzi, *Rules for the Compilation of the Catalogue*, pp. v–ix.) He was knighted for his extraordinary work in 1869. (See Miller, *Prince of Librarians*; and Panizzi, *Rules for the Compilation of the Catalogue*.)

PANORAMA. "A picture or series of pictures representing a continuous scene, often exhibited a part at a time by being unrolled and passed before the spectator" (*American Heritage Dictionary of the English Language*, p. 1274). In the world of the book, there are panoramic photographs, and also volumes that themselves are panoramas, often containing images printed on several panels that are glued together and bound as an accordion-folded CONCERTINA. A typical, and wonderful, example is that published by Samuel Leigh, *Panorama of the Thames from London, to Richmond,* composed of 45 hand-colored aquatints mounted on linen opening to nearly 60 feet in length. Such volumes appear at antiquarian book fairs, often at substantial prices.

Photographic panoramas date to early after photography was invented. The Library of Congress site says, "Shortly after the invention of photography in 1839, the desire to show overviews of cities and landscapes prompted photographers to create panoramas. Early panoramas were made by placing two or more daguerreotype plates side-by-side. Daguerreotypes, the first commercially available photographic process, used silver-coated copper plates to produce highly detailed images. . . . In the late nineteenth century, cameras were manufactured specifically for producing panoramas. These cameras were either swing-lens cameras, where the lens rotated while the film remained stationary, or 360-degree rotation cameras, where both the camera and the film rotated" (Library of Congress, "A Brief History of Panoramic Photography"; https://www.loc.gov/collections/panoramic-photographs/articles-and-essays/a-brief-history-of-panoramic-photography/ [accessed 23 May 2021]).

PANORAMIC FORE-EDGE PAINTING. *See* Fore-edge painting.

PANTOGRAPH. A tool for copying one image by tracing another, the copy being reproduced at the same, reduced, or enlarged size. The tool is composed of four pieces of wood (or other material), joined in the configuration of a parallelogram, with the connections changeable so that the image drawn at one end of the pantograph can be made smaller or larger depending on where the four pieces of wood are joined. One kind of pantograph has a stylus or pen or pencil on one end and another on the other end. When the operator draws with a pencil at one end, the other pencil is drawing a perfect copy at the other end. The operator need not have a pencil at the drawing end; it could be a stylus tracing over a pattern. This device was adapted to the making of WOODEN PRINTING TYPES and also for drilling matrices (*see* Matrix) for TYPE CASTING, eliminating the need for PUNCHES.

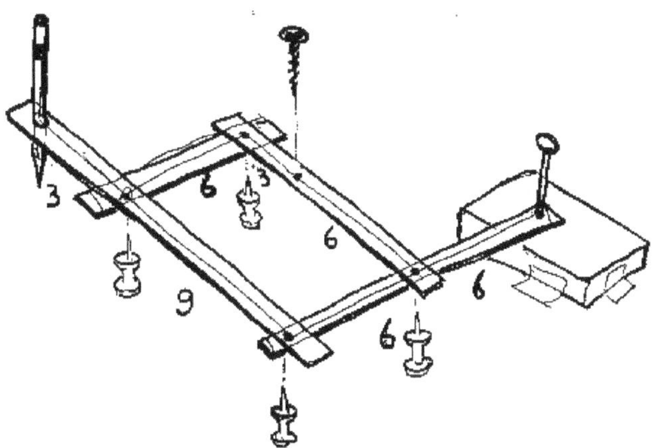

Pantograph.
Courtesy of Hubert van Hecke, Los Alamos National Laboratory.

PAPER. Perhaps the greatest and most important invention of all time. (Roger Levenson, proprietor of the Tamalpais Press in Berkeley, California, and once a professor at the library school [now the School of Information] at the University of California, Berkeley, said that any fool could have invented the wheel, but it took a genius to invent the alphabet and another genius to invent something to write or print it on.) Certainly, paper is the most important material in the history of the book.

It is composed of matted fibers. Any fibers will do, just so long as they can be broken into tiny lengths and matted together in some fashion. It is an extensive and complex subject, covering history, materials, manufacture, tools, decoration, and much more, each of these subtopics broken down to further subtopics. Only a cursory discussion is in order here.

One in the book world needs to know how to identify paper (types, fibers, date, manufacturers, decorative methods, and more). And one working with books needs the proper vocabulary so that he or she can communicate with clarity with others who know that vocabulary. The literature on paper is enormous, and anyone working with books should be familiar with some of the central texts and writers on the subject. The present volume has a bibliography listing many key volumes worthy of study, and it has nearly 200 entries throughout with the proper vocabulary that collectors, booksellers, archivists, bibliographers, librarians, and anyone else needs to know when speaking authoritatively about paper and PROTO-PAPERS. The entries to observe are listed in Appendix A.

PAPERBACK. A book bound with flexible paper covers, as opposed to one IN BOARDS. Roberts and Etherington's definition is telling: "A book generally defined as a flat back book with a paper cover that is usually, but not always, of a heavier stock than that used for the leaves of the publication itself. Paperback books are often made up of single LEAVES secured by a hot-melt adhesive. They usually have relatively narrow binding margins, are often printed on paper of poor to very poor quality (frequently with a high proportion of MECHANICAL WOOD PULP), and are generally cut flush" (p. 188). Paperback books can have sewn SIGNATURES (which is more common in European publications than in the United States), with the TEXT BLOCK glued into paper covers. But more often, the term refers to what Roberts and Etherington describe: PERFECT-BOUND TEXT BLOCKS made up of individual leaves glued at the SPINE and with the cover glued on. Their comment about small margins indicates that the books' publishers were trying to save money by getting as much text on a page as they could; this also led to their use of MECHANICAL WOOD PULP. For most of the 20th century, the word "paperback" meant "cheap"—in price and quality. Today, the adhesives are much better than they were in the 20th century, and many publishers are using good-quality paper, so a paperback book has a chance of making it through several readings, possibly more, without falling apart. But the notion of cheapness still lingers. As opposed to "HARDBACKS."

PAPERBACK CONDITION GRADING. *See* Condition.

PAPER BOARD. *See* Binder's board.

PAPERCUTS. Pieces of paper with patterns cut out of them. The art, which seems to have begun in China, has evolved in such a way that the final piece is usually cut from a single sheet. These usually show people, animals, or geometric designs, though they could depict anything in the physical world. Papercutting has been done in many countries, and by some famous artists, including Henri Matisse and Hans Christian Andersen. They can be tiny or immense. In the Berger-Cloonan Collection of Decorated Paper at Texas A&M University there is a papercut about 6 feet wide depicting women in a garden. And the Phillips Library at the Peabody Essex Museum has a collection of tiny papercuts, originally created for embroidery. A tiny cut in the shape of a flower, for example, would be placed on a piece of fabric and silk threads would be used to stitch the papercut to the fabric. The threads, thin as they were, would be so thickly stitched that the tiny papercut would be completely obscured. All the viewer would see is an embroidered pattern over the fabric, standing in relief (the thickness of the paper the cut was made from). The paper used for the cut was KOZO, which is strong and impervious to water, so the embroidered piece could be washed without damaging the hidden papercut. So the papercuts could be pieces of art in themselves, or they could be part of other works.

PAPER FILIGREE. *See* Quilling.

PAPERLESS SOCIETY. "With the coming of the computer, as long ago as the 1980s, we heard the phrase 'paperless society,' coined in 1982 by F. W. 'Wilf' Lancaster of the University of Illinois, who was talking about the possibility that almost every bit of information we had become used to seeing on paper could now—or in the near future—be storable and accessible in digital form. From the day he created that phrase, the amount of paper in use worldwide has gone up and up. . . . [M]any people have taken this phrase literally and expect that all department's holdings will eventually be digitized" (Berger, p. 50). Lancaster was visionary enough to know that his phrase was not to be taken at face value. He knew that paper and digital information would share the world henceforth. But many people in the general public, when the subject of books arises, will say, "Everything is online today, right!?" or, "Why do we need books? They and paper will soon be obsolete." Those in the book world, of course, know better. More physical books—*on paper*—are being produced today than ever before in history. We will never have a paperless society.

PAPERMAKER'S TEARS. *See* Vatman's tears.

PAPER MOLD. *See* Mold (papermaking).

PAPER-RULING MACHINE. *See* Ruling machine.

PAPERS OF THE BIBLIOGRAPHICAL SOCIETY OF AMERICA. *See PBSA*; *see also* Bibliographical Society of America.

PAPER SPLITTING. A technique in CONSERVATION work in which a LEAF of paper is split in such a way that the VERSO of the leaf and the RECTO are separated from one another, forming essentially two distinct parts. This is done for sheets that are in poor condition and need to be reinforced for them to be handled safely. The two portions of the original sheet can then be backed and preserved individually, or they can be reattached to one another with a thin, strong piece of mending tissue between them. The tissue adheres to both of the parts of the original sheet, and the final product looks and feels like a single sheet again, though strengthened by the tissue. This costly treatment can be valuable for expensive items. It is also useful to allow for both sides of the original sheet, each individually mounted onto a support, to be shown at once, as for an exhibition in which both sides of a leaf can be exhibited simultaneously. This remarkable but radical operation destroys bibliographical evidence, just as washing does. This practice is almost never used today.

PAPIER-MÂCHÉ. A "name given to the product of waste papers which have been repulped and, after being mixed with clay and rosin, pressed into moulds or stamped for trays, plates, etc." (Labarre, *Dictionary and Encyclopaedia of Paper and Paper-making*, 2nd ed., p. 184). This material is

"Relievo" or papier-mâché binding by Remnant & Edwards on the volume *Parables of Our Lord*. London: Longman & Co in London, 1847.

also made from any kind of macerated paper pulp that was mixed with an adhesive or starch that, when poured into a mold, would dry to a solid shape, retaining the pattern given it by the mold. Such stiff, hard panels were used as covers for books. These were sometimes called "relievo bindings."

Andrea Reithmayr, on the "Library as Incubator Project" website, describes another means of composition: "The English firm Jackson & Sons, makers of composition ornament for use in architecture, moldings, picture frames, carriages, and etc. [*sic*], held the patent for papier-mâché bindings. Imitating ebony or other hand-carved materials and evoking the medieval, they were made from a black plaster composition over papier-mâché. At least some examples were built up on a metal framework" (Reithmayr, Library as Incubator Project, "Owen Jones: Relievo and Papier-mâché Bindings" [Part 2]). Reithmayr says that Henry Noel Humphreys was the first to use this method of binding (Humphreys, ed., *Parables of Our Lord*). She says, "The account books of its publisher record that they printed 2,000 copies in 1847 and sold half the run to D. Appleton in New York with a changed title page." These heavy covers were attached to the TEXT BLOCKS with leather spines. And with RED ROT, time, and other sources of deterioration, the heavy covers of many of these bindings pulled off the volumes, while other covers split or cracked under use, mishandling, or poor environmental controls. Hence, most of these bindings show various forms of damage.

PAPIER PORCELAINE. A material used for printing (in LITHOGRAPHY) certain texts. In the booksellers' catalog from Heather O'Donnell, Ben Kinmont, Simon Beattie, and Justin Croft (the catalog titled *CTRL + P*), entry 9 is a menu from the Hôtel de Flandre Déjeuné. It is printed on this material. The booksellers say, "One of the most coveted of all types of menus are those printed on papier porcelaine. They were only produced for approximately thirty-five years and are always printed lithographically with special iridescent inks. Papier porcelaine is a coated paper that is highly polished and quite heavy. The technique to make the paper began in the early 1840s and it was primarily produced in northern France and Belgium; however, due to the toxicity of the process (lead was used to achieve the hard, white surface), it was abandoned in the late 1870s. The menus on papier porcelaine are from banquets organized to commemorate an important event such as a marriage, the completion of a monument, the appointment of a colleague to a new post, or a dinner prepared for a royal family, and they were given to those who attended the banquet." (See under Justin Croft, *CTRL + P*, in bibliography.) (*See* Porcelain cards.)

PAPYRUS. "A giant sedge, Cyperus papyrus, native to the region of the Nile, the pith of which was used to make a writing material by the ancient Egyptians, Greeks, and Romans. Papyrus was the forerunner of paper and the origin of the word, although it is not paper because it is not a matted or felted sheet made from a fibrous material" (Roberts and Etherington, p. 190). Up to the word "matted," this definition is fine. Roberts and Etherington are wrong, however, when they add "or felted sheet made from a fibrous material." The strips of the papyrus plant are indeed made from a fibrous material, and they are essentially felted in that the strips are laid one layer on another, with the strips on the top layer placed at right angles to those of the bottom layer. The strips are then placed between blotters or some other kind of blotting material and placed under pressure to squeeze the water out and to press the two layers of strips together. Inside, the stalks have the pithiness of watermelon and the stringiness of celery. The pith of the strips in the two directions fuses, holding all the long fibers together. German 19th-century scholars, trying to re-create papyrus after its disappearance for centuries, conjectured that the strips were beaten or hammered together, but this conjecture came from guesswork, and it would not have worked since such pounding would have dispersed the strips of fiber, disfiguring the final leaf. All they needed was to put the strips under pressure to allow the strips in the two directions to fuse with the blending of the pith. However, the scholars' conjectures evolved into

Leaf of papyrus. Note the horizontal strips of the plant on the upper surface, and the show-through of the vertical strips from the opposite side of the leaf. Photograph by Jeff Dykes. Collection of the author.

"facts," and—without much knowledge and without trying it for themselves—innumerable scholars took the German recipe as gospel and have repeated the error (about pounding) for more than a century. Another error that one sees in the literature is that the strips are glued together. Nonsense. The plant's natural pith is all that is needed to keep the strips together. We also encounter the error that the strips of the plant were woven together—another long-held blunder that persists. The experiments by Hassan Ragab, who wrote his dissertation on the history and manufacture of papyrus, dispelled the clouds of ignorance, and his work is important reading by those who want to know the real gospel about the manufacture of LEAVES of this plant. (See the two entries by Ragab in the bibliography. See also O'Casey and Maney, *The Nature and Making of Papyrus.*)

Papyrus was written on on one side since it could not be folded, so the standard form of the "book" was the SCROLL. If SCRIBES needed additional surfaces to write on once a papyrus surface was full, they could glue another leaf of the material to the earlier one(s), simply adding to the length of the scroll. With no INHERENT VICE, its light weight and portability, a surface that would take and hold pigments, and relative low cost, papyrus was an ideal SUBSTRATE for texts.

PARALLEL-TEXT EDITION. A volume in which more than one version of a text is printed in parallel columns. The multiple columns could have texts in one language, or they could show the same text in more than one language. The aim is to allow readers to examine differing versions of a text, one beside the other, to observe variations among the versions, or to compare translations to originals. An editor can use this to record all VARIANTS that exist in a work; scholars can perceive how a text has evolved over time. Perhaps the most elaborate of these is the remarkable Manly/Rickert edition of Chaucer's *Canterbury Tales.* (See Manly and Rickert, eds., *The Text of the* Canterbury Tales, *Studied on the Basis of All Known Manuscripts.*)

PARAPH. "A flourish made after or below a signature, originally to prevent forgery" (*American Heritage Dictionary of the English Language*, p. 1279). In a manuscript, it is a symbol, such as a double slash (//) or the so-called paragraph sign (¶), to show where a new section or paragraph begins. It was used for decoration or to discourage forgery. It was also used by printers in the HANDPRESS PERIOD to sign early LEAVES in SIGNATURES in a book (or those beyond the regular alphabetical sequence). (*See* Pilcrow; Virgule.)

PARCHMENT. The generic term for any animal skin prepared for many uses. In the book world, it is used for manuscripts, printing, and binding. The term refers to the skin of any animal; "VELLUM" is the specific term used to denote CALFSKIN, though the two words have been used for so long interchangeably that they have now become synonymous. The name evolved from the city in which the material supposedly was first made: Pergamon.

The making of parchment begins with the shepherd. The butcher then flays the animal, and the parchment maker scrapes the skins, HAIR SIDE and FLESH SIDE, and prepares it for its uses in books: LEAVES to write or print on and for binding materials. (See Reed, *Ancient Skins, Parchments and Leathers*; and Reed, *The Nature and Making of Parchment.*)

PARCHMENT RUNNER. *See* Punctorium.

PARENTHESIS. *See* Fine Press Book Association.

PARTBOOK (or part-book). A volume "in which vocal or instrumental polyphonic music was handwritten or printed in the 15th and 16th centuries" (*Encyclopaedia Britannica*, "partbook"; http://www.britannica.com/art/partbook [accessed 14 June 2021]). Usually the volume would have notation for a single voice—only one part of the music. Hence, each performer has his or her own volume. The *Encyclopaedia Britannica* site adds: "parts of madrigals, however, were sometimes published crosswise on single sheets, which allowed each of the singers seated around a rectangular table to sing from his particular part. Most commonly there were four partbooks: *cantus* (also *discantus* or *superius*), *altus*, *tenor*, and *bassus*; additional parts were either indicated *quinta vox*, etc., or were subdivisions of one of the principal parts—e.g., *cantus* I and *cantus* II. The practice of having musicians perform from their individual parts has continued in chamber and orchestral music." They were usually written or printed in the LANDSCAPE layout, and since they were created to be economical (not like a choir book containing all texts for all musicians for the piece being performed), they were fairly cheaply made and most have perished or survive in poor condition.

PARTS/IN PARTS. The individual installments of a text, issued to the public as they came off the press (rather than all of the text issued at the same time). From the 17th century on, texts were issued in parts to SUBSCRIBERS whose up-front payment for the early issues helped the publisher fund the production of the later parts.

Carter's long entry on this phenomenon is excellent. He discusses the kinds of texts so issued (e.g., encyclopedias and dictionaries, other reference books, and works of fiction). He points out that this kind of publishing generally was applied to texts that would have large audiences, but the method was also used for novels. (He cites Dickens and Thackeray as two authors whose works came out this way.) He also treats the bibliographic complications when collectors have MADE-UP SETS, especially when these sets have varying colors of papers; when the original covers, in various colors for different authors, are printed with ADVERTISEMENTS (or with ads LAID IN); and so forth. He says that works of fiction were usually issued with colored-paper covers, with illustrations on the covers and with ads on the back, the inside of the paper covers, and sometimes printed along with the text pages as well. The covers would have an indication printed on them of what issue number was within (sometimes also with a date given). If the text were issued later, the ads and dates would change. If the WRAPPERS got damaged, an owner might take a wrapper from a later issue and use it to replace the damaged cover of an earlier issue, so collectors and booksellers should be scrupulous in trying to determine what issue is in the covers. Carter says that a changed part numeral is generally easy to discern; such a change indicates that the front wrapper has been exchanged. But he adds that scholarly references describing the original covers usually do not exist, or, if they do, they may not be explicit enough for one to spot the change, especially if one is trying to use evidence that is inside the volume. (See Carter, p. 183.) He also points out that the SPINES of the volumes, perhaps the most vulnerable parts of the volumes, will often be repaired or replaced. And he concludes that a common practice has been to make up sets from parts taken from later or earlier issues, so it might be impossible to figure out what one has in front of him (with respect to issues and states) when it comes to full sets of books in parts.

One of the most famous of the "books" issued in parts is John James Audubon's *Birds of America*, issued from 1827 to 1838. "Prints were issued in sets of five every month or two. . . . In 1838, at the end of the thirteen-year project, 435 plates (87 sets of five) had been issued" (*The Birds of America*, Wikipedia; https://en.wikipedia.org/wiki/The_Birds_of_America [accessed 14 June 2021]). The works of many British authors were similarly released in parts, and making up a set, as Carter explains, can be difficult. Spotting a made-up set can be equally challenging.

Carter also has an entry on "part-issued books in volume form," in which he points out the practice of many publishers of issuing the complete text in a bound volume just before the last installment of the text issued in parts is released to its subscribers. He says that these bound volumes can be considered the first copies of the books in published form (p. 184). He then points out the complication that "this publisher's volume-issue would generally be made up from the last-printed sheets of text and PLATES; so that although issued before any set of parts could have been completed, it would be apt to exhibit the latest STATE of any particular variant" (p. 184). Another complication that he notes is that those buying the installments were often supplied with a CASE from the publisher into which their parts were to be bound (the case being in cloth or part leather). Thus, a copy so made up could contain the text and plates in their earliest state, and "it would be in publisher's cloth [*see* Publisher's binding]; yet as a completed entity (even if the local binder had not, as often, trimmed—or even sprinkled—the edges of the leaves) it is at some disadvantage *vis-à-vis* either a set of

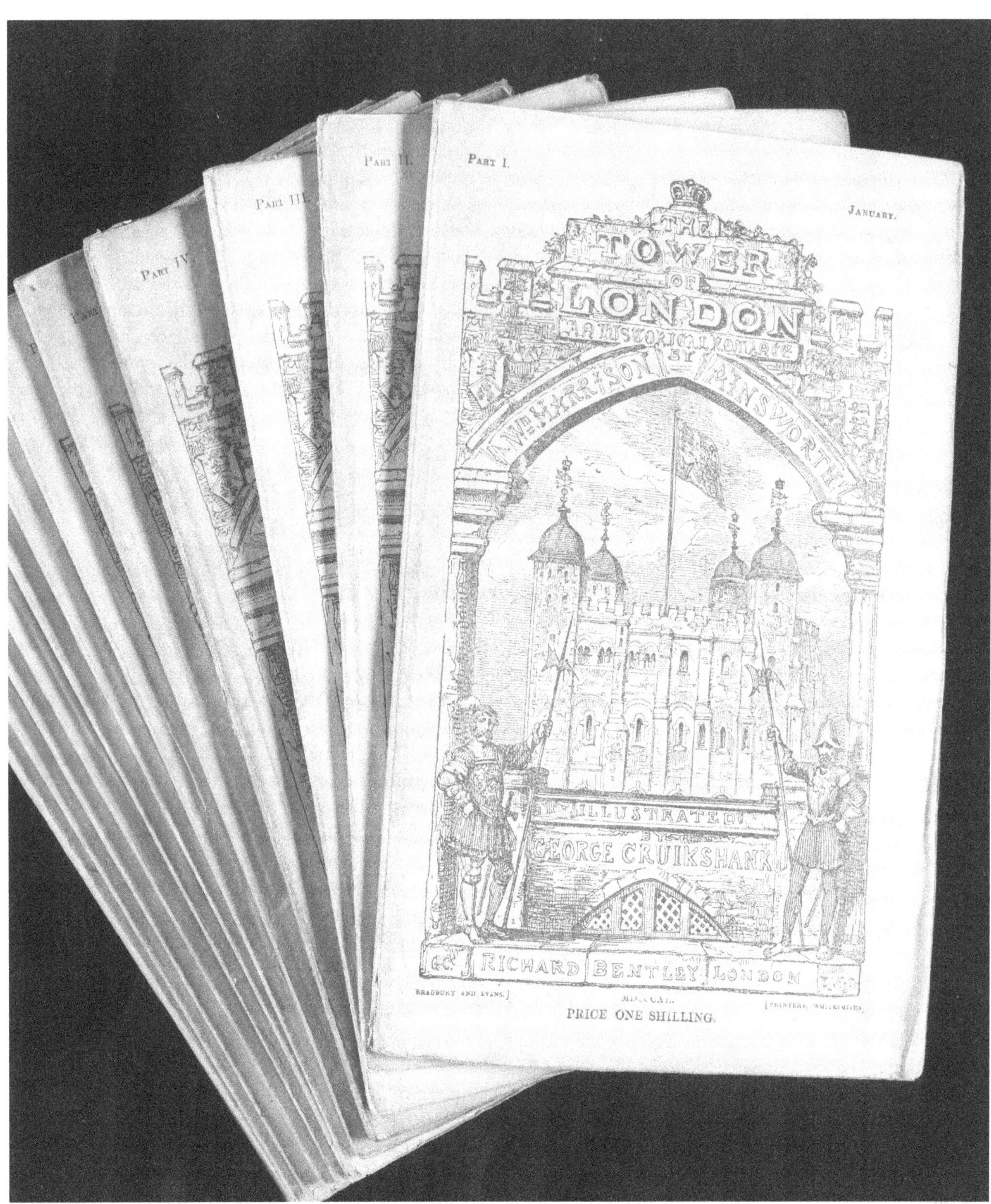

Book in parts. William Harrison Ainsworth, *Tower of London* (London: Richard Bentley, 1840).

Courtesy of the Rare Books & Manuscripts Library, University of Illinois, Urbana–Champaign.

parts or the publisher's volume-issue" (p. 185). He says these "cased-up sets" are generally easy to differentiate from the text issued as a volume by the publisher because the made-up sets would have stab holes where the original parts were bound. He concludes, "[W]hen the distinction is made, it yet remains for bibliographers and collectors to assess the difference" (p. 185). (*See* Book form.)

PASQUINADES. (Also called a "pasquil" or a "pasquino.") These BROADSIDES (sometimes in the form of short tracts) are satires or lampoons intended to be posted in a public place. There is a giant world of broadsides, covering a wide range of genres (wanted posters, announcements, advertisements, and so forth). Laurie Nussdorfer explains: "Pasquino, the remnant of an antique sculptural group unearthed and set up in downtown Rome in 1501, headed a small but audacious band of 'talking statues' who conversed publicly among themselves about the frailties of the city's great men. Anonymous satirical comments, often high literary, were placed secretly upon Pasquino. . . . Pasquino gave his name to the word for a mocking, clandestine lampoon, the 'pasquil' or 'pasquinade,' which entered several European languages in the sixteenth century" (Nussdorfer, *Civic Politics in the Rome of Urban VIII*, pp. 8–9). Of course, anyone talking about or offering or collecting one of these items can call it a broadside or PAMPHLET; but the more precise historical term is useful to show expertise.

PASTEBOARDS (sometimes hyphenated). "A class of board produced by LAMINATING (pasting) sheets of (brown) paper and used for the BOARDS of books, or, if lined, for printing. Originally pasteboards were generally of three types: 1) those made by pasting together sheets of plain paper, leaves of books, or printing spoilage; 2) a better grade produced by matting together sheets of newly made handmade paper; and 3) an inferior grade produced from shavings and even floor sweepings. The last named was not actually 'pasteboard,' by definition, as it was not built up of laminated layers" (Roberts and Etherington, pp. 192–93). (*See* Binder's board; Cartonnage.)

PASTEDOWNS. *See* Endleaves.

PASTE PAPERS. Sheets decorated with some kind of brushed- or dabbed-on colored paste. The paste can be left as is—merely brushed on, usually with the brushstrokes still visible—or, while it is still wet, it can be manipulated in a variety of ways to create various styles of decoration. The technique dates to the 17th century, and it was used extensively for bookbindings (usually for covers, though it

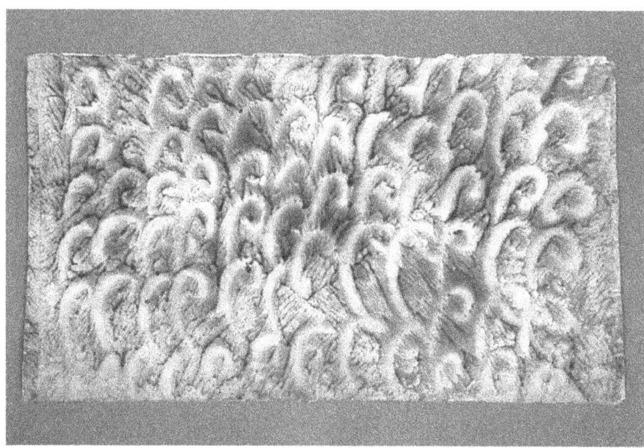

Paste paper, 18th century. Photograph by Jeff Dykes. Berger-Cloonan Collection of Decorated Papers, Texas A&M University.
Courtesy of Cushing Library, Texas A&M University.

was also used for end sheets) in place of the more expensive leather bindings.

While the paste is still wet, any way that it is touched will disrupt the smooth brushed-on paste and leave a little "hole" in it, revealing the paper beneath. An endless number of tools (or one's fingers) can be employed to disturb the paste. One technique was to cover a sheet with the colored paste and then fold it in half, with the two pasted LEAVES touching each other (or to place two sheets with the colored paste freshly brushed on face-to-face and touching one another), and then to pull them apart—producing what is called a "pulled paste paper." The striations left in the paste are attractive, and the sheets were often left to dry just as they were when they were pulled apart. While the two wet-paste surfaces are still touching, the pair of leaves can be pressed with fingers or tools to "disrupt" the paste within, creating a pattern that emerges when the sheets are pulled apart. And additional decoration can then be done to them since

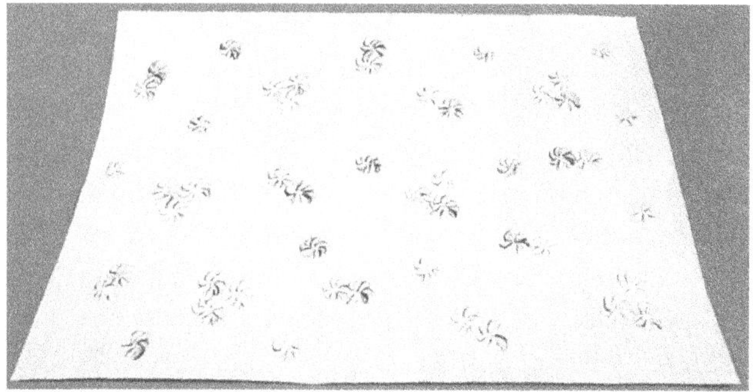

Paste paper by Susanne Krause, 20th century. Photograph by Jeff Dykes. Berger-Cloonan Collection of Decorated Papers, Texas A&M University.
Courtesy of Cushing Library, Texas A&M University.

Eighteenth-century *albums amicorum* showing marbled and paste papers.
Courtesy of Elizabeth Baird.

the sheets are still wet at the point at which they are pulled apart. Additional applications of other-colored pastes can be introduced to the sheet at any time during the decoration process. (*See* Pulled paste paper.)

PATTERN BOOK. *See* Model book.

PAYNE, ROGER (1738–1797). "The most accomplished and influential of the 18th century English bookbinders. . . . Roger Payne was an outstanding craftsman. His books were very well forwarded [*see* Forwarding] and his style of FINISHING displayed not only a high level of skill but also very good taste. He usually sewed his books with silk thread and lined the SPINES with LEATHER. He frequently used elaborately designed DOUBLURES, made his endpapers [*see* Endleaves] with leather JOINTS, and covered the books with RUSSIA leather or MOROCCO. . . . Payne developed a style of splendid simplicity, perhaps made necessary by having to cut his own tools, which gave his design a simplicity and individuality which they otherwise might have lacked. His style consisted essentially of the repetition of small floral forms in BORDERS of radiating corners, the background being formed with dots and circles. . . . He made his ornamentation appropriate to the subject matter of the book and while the SPINES were often richly embellished, the COVERS were generally quite simple. / The leathers he used were generally olive, red or blue morocco, or brown Russia. Payne's endpapers were nearly always solid in color. He preferred purple (sometimes pink) and generally used endpapers which clashed with the covers. His HEADBANDS were flat (upright) and sewn with green silk which sometimes had a gold thread in it. The edges of his bindings were ROUGH GILT or plain" (Roberts and Etherington, "Payne, Roger"; https://cool.culturalheritage.org/don/dt/dt2521.html [accessed 28 February 2021]).

Payne's fame as a binder has led many a bookseller to want to find evidence of his hand in the volumes they are selling, leading to a good deal of misattribution.

PBFA. *See* Provincial Booksellers' Fairs Association.

PBSA (*Papers of the Bibliographical Society of America*). The oldest bibliographical journal in the United States, published since 1906. "*The Papers of the Bibliographical Society of America* (*PBSA*) is the Society's distinguished quarterly journal; it has been an important avenue for scholarly communication on bibliographical matters since 1906. . . . *PBSA* welcomes scholarship that deals with the study of books and manuscripts from any period or geographical region. Of particular interest is work that examines the book or manuscript (the physical object) as historical evidence, whether for establishing a text or illuminating the history of book production, publication, distribution, or collecting, or for other purposes. Studies of the printing, publishing, and allied trades are also welcome. We will consider enumerative submissions as well, but such work should consist primarily of original scholarship and not a compilation from existing sources" (Bibliographical Society of America, http://bibsocamer.org/publications/papers [accessed 3 July 2021]).

PC (personal computer). One of the greatest boons in history for the production of books. The PC allowed Everyman to be his own author, editor, designer, and publisher. In the 1980s, when PCs were becoming more and more common and with the production of increasingly sophisticated (though to today's eyes fairly primitive) printers (most of which were dot-matrix), publishers, to save the cost of setting type and designing pages, required in their contracts with authors that the latter supply "CAMERA-READY COPY." This was copy, designed and printed out by the authors themselves, that was to be photographed and then printed by the publishers. The PC made this possible. Authors, however, experts in their subjects, were not book designers, so for about a generation (and still today), the world has seen a proliferation of text designed by design amateurs. The PC thus ushered in an era of ugly books. But it sped up production from the side of the authors (who could make corrections in editing their texts far faster than they could have in the typewriter era) and from the side of the publisher (who saved a great deal of time in typesetting and proofreading). (*See* Desktop publishing.) The PC is one of several tools used by those searching for books on the Internet and doing APPRAISALS.

PDF. An abbreviation for Portable Document Format. In 1992 the company Adobe developed this file format to present documents—verbal texts as well as images of all kinds—in such a way that it is not dependent on special software or hardware or on a particular operating system. Hence, a PDF file contains a full description of a fixed-layout flat document, delineating the full text, the typefaces used in the original, all kinds of graphics, and information that is necessary for a full display of the text. Tim Fisher says, "PDF files can contain not only images and text, but also interactive buttons, hyperlinks, embedded fonts, video, and more" (Fisher, "What Is a PDF File?"). Included here since books have been digitized by the millions as PDF files and are often available digitally on the web.

PEASANT BINDING. On Philip J. Pirages's website, we find offered a volume in a peasant binding. The catalog entry reads: "this volume is of considerable interest as an expertly made and decorated so-called 'Peasant Binding,' a colorful binding style that began in Hungary and spread through Germany, the Netherlands, and Scandinavia in the 18th century. The use of the word 'peasant' in this context is a reference to the obvious influence of folk art on this decoration, rather than to the clientele for which it was intended. Bibles, prayer books, and hymnals in the brightly painted and exuberantly decorated vellum bindings were popular wedding gifts among the bourgeoisie, who were both literate and sufficiently affluent to afford such luxuries" (Philip J. Pirages; the volume offered was BIBLE IN GERMAN: *Das ganze neue Testament. Der Psalter Davids. Die CL Psalmen David.* [Zurich: David Gessner, 1768]; https://www.pirages.com/pages/books/ST12938/bindings-peasant-bible-in-german/das-ganze-neue-testament-der-psalter-davids-die-cl-psalmen-david [accessed 1 March 2021]). (*See* Painted binding.)

A peasant binding. This also is a painted binding, a German Bible. *Das ganze neue Testament. Der Psalter Davids. Die CL Psalmen David.* (Zurich: David Gessner, 1768). From the website of bookseller Philip J. Pirages; https://www.pirages.com/pages/books/ST12938/bindings-peasant-bible-in-german/das-ganze-neue-testament-der-psalter-davids-die-cl-psalmen-david (accessed 1 March 2021).

Courtesy of Philip J. Pirages.

PEBBLED LEATHER. A leather surface containing a pattern of small, regular indentions stamped into the smooth surface (usually CALF). It looked something like MOROCCO. A pebbling effect can be introduced into paper or cloth also, for decoration, and a well-done pebbled cloth or paper, with good varnish, can be nearly indistinguishable from leather. This treatment was particularly popular in the last four decades of the 19th century in PUBLISHERS' BINDINGS.

PECIAE SYSTEM OF MANUSCRIPT PRODUCTION (sometimes spelled "petiae."). The method of copying MANUSCRIPTS in which the original texts were broken up into parts and copied, usually by more than one SCRIBE. The system was used from the 13th to the 15th centuries at the major universities (Paris and Bologna, and probably at Cambridge and Oxford). Faculty of the university would supply the STATIONERS (who regulated the system) with their own copies of their texts (their lectures at the schools), which would be the authorized versions that the Stationers would have copied by professional scribes. The lectures would be broken up into parts, and each part would be rented out to students (or to anyone else) to make their own copies from. The pieces (*peciae*) were small portions of the full text, and the students, once they made their own copies, would return the pieces to the Stationers and rent out others. The Stationer may have two or more copies of each piece, and these parts were not necessarily copied by a single scribe. The one who rented the piece would need to return it to get the next piece. The texts produced by the scribes working with the Stationers—and possibly also by the students who are doing their own copying—may be marked in the margin with the letter *p* or *pi*, *pij*, and so forth.

The resulting "complete" text, then—in the single hand of the person who rented all the parts and made copies from them—would be an amalgam of copies from perhaps several original pieces done by one or many scribes whose accuracy, from one scribe to another, was not consistent.

A modern editor working with a manuscript that was produced in this manner, then, has the task of trying to determine which parts of that manuscript came from reliably copied originals and which came from carelessly copied ones.

PEDDLER'S SAMPLE BOOK. *See* Dummy; Salesman's dummy/Salesman's sample book.

PEEBLES ISLAND RESOURCE CENTER (PIRC). A conservation center for the treatment of library and other materials. "For over thirty years, the Bureau's conservation laboratories have cared for the thousands of historic objects in New York's state historic sites. During this time, PIRC has extended its CONSERVATION services, under contract, to other governmental agencies within New York State. Conservators specializing in seven disciplines—archeology, paintings, gilded objects and frames, textiles, furniture, decorative arts and paper—provide a full spectrum of treatment and preventive conservation services such as general surveys and collection-specific surveys, conservation treatments, materials analysis, workshops and public presentations, and internship opportunities for undergraduate and graduate students" (Peebles Island Resource Center; http://rap-arcc.org/rap-members/peebles-island-resource-center [accessed 3 June 2021]). This is one of the smaller of the conservation centers, but it is included here as an example of the kinds of work being done around the United States—work that collectors, booksellers, and librarians may need to have done on their own holdings.

PEEP SHOWS. (Sometimes printed as a single word.) (Also called "tunnel books.") (And not to be confused with the "machine" called a peep show that consists of a box containing peep holes—unusually binocular—and internal pictures that the observer sees by looking inside.) Printed and/or painted items composed of several LEAVES (usually) of stiff paper, with the images (and possibly some text) as cutouts on the outer edges of the leaves, the inner parts cut away; housed with a rear panel, not at all cut away, but with a full-page image on it. They are bound onto a CONCERTINA FOLDed structure, with the leaves attached parallel to each other, and when they are pulled apart, the structure opens into what looks like a tunnel. The observer looks through the "tunnel" to see a three-dimensional view of a street scene, a natural setting, a long room in a palace, religious, mythical, or historical figures, or any other desired picture. (One theory is that the structure created a tunnel book because many of them were commemorative of the mid-19th-century construction of the tunnel under the Thames River in London.) The structure (often in book form) closes flat, but accordions out for the viewer to observe a whole scene in 3-D. In untold numbers of these, the "bellows" attachments, to which each of the leaves was attached, is missing, and what remains are only the individual leaves, which are then inserted into slots in a flat piece of wood or plastic, allowing them to line up and be viewed as they would have been in their original pull-apart concertina form.

These go back at least to the 17th century, as noted by Emily Martin and Alice Austin, who refer to one of the 1650s (Martin and Austin, "Book Theater: The History of the Tunnel Book," p. 215). Their popularity was broadened in the 18th century as witnessed by those published using hand-colored ETCHINGS by Martin Englebrecht in Augsburg, Germany, c. 1730–1750 (Englebrecht died in 1756);

Peep show of a printing workshop. (Augsburg, Germany: Martin Engelbrecht, c. 1750).
Courtesy of Justin Croft, Justin Croft Antiquarian Books.

Peep show. Martin Engelbrecht, *Concert in the Garden* (Augsburg, Germany: Martin Engelbrecht, c. 1750).
Courtesy of Antiquariat F. Neidhardt.

Peep show. *Concert in the Garden* (Augsburg, Germany: Martin Engelbrecht, c. 1750).
Courtesy of Antiquariat F. Neidhardt.

one of his shows "a library interior with shelves, numerous books, 10 figures (one holding an open book), two large table globes, library steps and two hanging wall maps" (Justin Croft Antiquarian Books Limited; https://fairs.abaa.org/item/1385776265 [accessed 4 March 2021]).

"Engelbrecht (1684–1756) produced many different designs of these sets in three sizes . . . . They were designed to be viewed when slotted successively into a perspective viewing box but can equally be appreciated when standing in simple slots or stands" (Justin Croft). Michael R. Thompson, Booksellers says, "Martin Engelbrecht . . . and his brother Christian (1627–1735) established their printing house in Augsburg in 1719. By 1730, Engelbrecht had innovated his miniature theaters, the earliest of their kind, and he and his printing house had produced thousands by the 1770s. Engelbrecht and his printing house produced thousands of these theaters with little to no competition, likely as a result of Engelbrecht's royal privilege for the exclusive production of cutout images. . . . Other examples showed Biblical events like Noah leading the animals to the ark and lavish scenes of bourgeoise amusement . . .; another series was devoted entirely to the Italian theater. Englebrecht's theaters were the forerunners of the peepshow books popularized by Dean & Son of London during the mid-nineteenth century" (Michael R. Thompson, Booksellers; https://fairs.abaa.org/item/1353468453 [accessed 4 March 2021]).

The structure has been revived in the 20th and 21st centuries. One book artist, Laura Davidson of Boston, for instance, has done these peep shows on Paris, Venice, Fort Point, Florence, and Fenway Park. The Victoria & Albert Museum in London has a collection of more than 400 of these fragile items (see Victoria and Albert Museum, "Paper Peepshows" in the bibliography; several of these structures are shown at their website; Richard Balzer's *Peepshows* is about the machines mentioned above, not about tunnel books). As this entry explains, there are two kinds of things called "peepshows," the tunnel type and the machines. For this reason, I prefer the term "tunnel book" for the items that booksellers and collectors, librarians and archivists may encounter. But in the literature I have encountered in the book-collecting community, "peepshows" seems to predominate. Hence, that is the key word chosen for the present volume.

PENMANSHIP MANUALS. Volumes that teach CALLIGRAPHY, a genre of books that has been with us for centuries. The *Encyclopaedia Britannica* online distinguishes two types: "From the 16th through 18th centuries two types of writing books predominated in Europe: the writing manual, which instructed the reader how to make, space, and join letters, as well as, in some books, how to choose paper, cut QUILLS, and make ink; and the COPYBOOK, which consisted of pages of writing models to be copied as practice" (*Encyclopaedia Britannica*, "Writing Manuals and Copybooks [16th to 18th Century]." The literature on these volumes is enormous, and hosts of people who have mastered some of the elements of calligraphy feel obliged to write books on the subject, so the level of expertise exhibited in them varies from brilliant to pedestrian. Penmanship manuals are related to, but a separate genre from, WRITING BOOKS, which discuss the history and styles of calligraphy. The manuals in the second sense delineated by the *Encyclopaedia Britannica* are synonymous with penmanship specimen books. (See Bickham, *The Universal Penman: Engraved by George Bickham, London, 1743*; Kapr, *The Art of Lettering: The History, Anatomy, and Aesthetics of the Roman Letter Forms*; and Nesbitt, *The History and Technique of Lettering*.)

PENNY BOOKS. *See* Big Little Books.

PENNY DREADFULS. A genre of cheap, late 19th- and early 20th-century British fiction, aimed at adults and young adults, printed on inexpensive paper and bound cheaply. They are often linked with DIME NOVELS—the U.S. equivalent. The term is derogatory (of course, as the word "dreadful" signifies) since the stories are often lurid, sentimental, or supernatural. Ben Zimmer says, "By the end of the 19th century, the noun *horrible* began showing up in the idiomatic phrase *penny horrible*, a cheaply published violent novel better known as a *penny dreadful* (or also sometimes *penny awful*)" (see his blog "Horribles and Terribles," Language Log, 14 April 2008, http://languagelog.ldc.upenn.edu/nll/?p=31 [accessed 14 June 2021]). Unlike dime novels, which were published as cheap monographs, the penny dreadfuls were issued IN PARTS, one FASCICLE a week. The tales were lurid and stimulating, so they appealed to boys, and the tales were serialized in a number of magazines and published in fascicles to an eager audience. They are highly COLLECTIBLE today. (*See* Dime novels; Sixpenny wonderfuls.) (See James, *Fiction for the Working Man, 1830–50.*)

THE PENROSE ANNUAL. A British bibliographical periodical that ran from 1895 to 1982, with single volumes issued in almost every year. The serial published articles by some of the most prominent writers, printers, bibliographers, designers, and typographers of its day, issued in a well-produced and strongly bound volume. Articles focused on printing arts, paper, illustration, the technology of the printing trades, and much more. The journal's production values were high, and even the advertisements were worth the price of the publication. Many of the volumes had TIP-INS of various kinds, individual SIGNATURES or LEAVES produced by printing firms, manufacturers of printing equipment, or paper companies.

PERFECT. A bookseller's term meaning that the item is as it was issued by the publisher—with no flaws and containing all of the materials (ERRATA slips, ADVERTISEMENT pieces like PROSPECTUSES, or anything else) that were with the item when it was issued to the public. A dealer's catalog may say "COLLATED and perfect" (or merely used the abbreviation "C&P" or "C/P"). A perfect item may be called "MINT" or "PRISTINE."

PERFECT (in printing). *See* Perfecting (in printing).

PERFECT BINDING. (One of the least appropriate names for a phenomenon.) (Also called "adhesive binding.") A binding method in which all of the folds at the GUTTER of the TEXT BLOCK have been guillotined off, leaving all the LEAVES unattached to anything (like a deck of cards); the slit edge is dipped into adhesive, binding all the leaves together. This produces one of the cheapest and least enduring (i.e., least perfect) bindings. The leaves are held together by all of the adhesive that will attach to each leaf; so the adhesive sticks to the leaf in an amount that is the same as the thickness of each sheet of paper. To add a bit of adhesion (to increase the area of the sheet on which the adhesive is applied), the text block can be fanned out, opening the surface of the page a small amount to receive the glue; it is then dipped into the adhesive, fanned in the opposite direction to add a bit of glue to the opposite side of the leaf, and dipped again. This is called "double-fan-adhesive (perfect) binding." In the 19th century, when perfect binding was developed, the adhesives were particularly poor, drying out, flaking, turning white or dark and staining the paper, and becoming brittle. This situation continued through the 1950s and later, and millions of books—in paper and in BOARDS—that were bound using this method split at the spine and produced leaves and clusters of leaves popping out of their covers. Even "deluxe" books, bound with leather SPINES and fancy covers, with fake RAISED BANDS, were bound this way. With tight bindings, the only way someone could detect the use of the perfect-binding method was to pull the volume apart—or let it run the course of its short life. But by the time these expensive volumes self-destructed, they were beyond the time that they could be returned to the publisher. (Around 1985, I bought a lovely facsimile of a medieval manuscript published by George Braziller. Within two years, it had destroyed itself because its perfect binding fell apart under the weight of its heavy coated paper. I sent it back to the publisher, who replaced it *gratis*, but with another copy of the book with a perfect binding.) (*See* Gutta-percha binding.)

A perfect binding. The only thing holding the leaves of this volume together and in its cover is glue.
Collection of the author.

PERFECTING (in printing). Printing the second printed side of a LEAF. The printer prints one side of a leaf that is destined to have both sides printed. Once the ink dries, he or she can perfect the leaf by printing the second side. Hence, an imperfect leaf is one printed on one side, waiting to be perfected. (*See* Offset sheets.)

PERIODICAL PRINTING. Carter's entry (p. 186) mentions the importance of first printings of many works, even if they are not considered "FIRST EDITIONS" since the issues in serials disqualify them from falling under the glorious rubric "first edition" because only texts issued in their own covers merit that distinction. From the perspective of the librarian or collector (and therefore also from the bookseller's angle), such publications can have great value—intellectual and fiscal. They could reveal authors' early views on their texts, they could contain readings more AUTHORIAL than are in later-printed versions of the work that could have corruptions or editorial or compositorial variations, and they could reveal (from the serials they were published in) a good deal about their original intended audiences. A true COMPLETIST collector will want to have in her library the original parts as they were serialized along with the other manifestations of the texts she collects.

PERIODICALS. In the world of the book, many periodicals play an important role. There are those that publish materials that eventually wind up in books (*see* Periodical printing), those that write about many of the BOOK ARTS that are at the root of book production, those that tell us of new volumes in many fields, and those that guide us to books to purchase in delineated collecting areas. About ten years ago, the bookseller Timothy Hawley sent out a catalog titled "Periodicals on Book Collecting, Bibliography, Printing and Book Arts," listing periodical issues for sale; astonishingly, the catalog had about 250 titles. He said that these represented only about 30 percent of the titles that he had in his holdings. Hundreds of these serials have been published. An abbreviated, short, and highly select list follows of some of the more important such periodicals, some still active. Those with entries in this volume are marked with an asterisk (*).

*AB/Bookman's Weekly**
ABA Newsletter
American Book Collector
Antiquarian Book Review
Antiques Trade Gazette
Biblio
Bibliography Newsletter (*BiN*)
The Book and Paper Group Annual
*The Book Collector**
The Bookdealer
Bookways
*The Colophon**
*The Dolphin**
*Fine Books & Collections**
*Fine Print**
*The Fleuron**
The Guild of Book Workers Journal
*Gutenberg-Jahrbuch**
Hand Papermaking
Journal of Library History (now titled *Information & Culture*)
The Library
Library Association Rare Books Group Newsletter
Library History
Library Trends
*Matrix**
The New Bookbinder
Papers of the Bibliographical Society of America (*PBSA*)*
*Penrose Annual**
Printing History
Private Library
Rare Book Review (now titled *Fine Books & Collections*)
RBML (*Rare Books and Manuscripts Librarianship*; now titled *RBM: A Journal of Rare Books, Manuscripts, and Cultural Heritage*)
Restaurator
Studies in Bibliography (*see under* Fredson Bowers)

There are also several newsletters of book collectors' clubs, such as those of the Caxton Club and the Grolier Club. (*See ABHB* and its entry in the bibliography.)

PERMANENT PAPER LAW. *See* Wood pulp.

PERMISSION/PERMISSIONS. In general, this word, in the book world, means allowance to publish. In a specific sense, there are IMPRIMATUR and *NIHIL OBSTAT*, both of which have the narrower meaning of the allowance to publish granted by religious authority (even more specifically, the Catholic Church), and "license," which could have religious overtones, but is more general. But equally important today is the relationship of this term to publishing the work of others, especially work under COPYRIGHT. As the Elsevier site explains, "permission should be sought from the rights holder to reproduce any substantial part of a copyrighted work. This includes any text, illustrations, charts, tables, photographs, or other material from previously published sources" (Elsevier,

"Permissions"). Without receiving permission, an author or publisher could be violating copyright and could be subject to litigation. Problems arise with FAIR USE, the definition of "substantial part" of a work, copyright ownership, and so forth. As the entry at copyright explains, copyright has become so complex that many publishers are especially leery about going to press with *anything* that could be under copyright. They usually want iron-clad assurances that permission from a rights holder has been obtained. And while in the past, most publishers helped their authors in identifying copyright holders and then getting permission to use the protected material, nowadays most publishers leave that chore to the authors themselves. If an author wants to use what looks like protected material, and cannot get formal approval for its use, the publisher is likely to require the author to strike the item from the text—or to paraphrase to avoid legal complications.

(Parenthetical story: When I was about to go to press with my edition of Mark Twain's *Pudd'nhead Wilson and Those Extraordinary Twins*—in 1979—I wanted to include in my CRITICAL APPARATUS passages from Twain's manuscript. My publisher required that I get permission from the rights holder; but no rights holder was evident. The University of California Press said they had the right to print the materials before anyone else, but they could not show any documentary evidence that they owned such rights. Since Twain died in 1910, and since copyright obtained for 70 years after the death of the work's creator, we were a year shy of that date. Since I could not get iron-clad permission from anyone, my publisher [W. W. Norton] took the conservative route, so I could not quote the passages in full; I had to give only prose summaries of them. When the second edition of the Norton text came out in 2004, I was able to quote the passages in full—no permissions needed. Note the use of the plural: one must acquire permissions [though the singular would also do in this context].)

Such permission is held by the copyright holder, and who (or what) that is might not be easy to determine. In fact, it might be impossible to figure out because of the way intellectual-property ownership moves through the world, from author to (publisher) (heir) (organization) (other party). And permissions to use can be granted for free or for a fee, to be determined by the copyright holder. There are no laws or regulations to draw upon in setting fees. Copyright inheres also for images, music, photographs, and other materials, not just verbal text.

PERSONAL COMPUTER. *See* PC.

PETIAE SYSTEM OF MANUSCRIPT PRODUCTION. *See* Peciae system of manuscript production.

PH (p[otential] of h[ydrogen)]). "A measure of the acidity or alkalinity of a solution, numerically equal to 7 for neutral solutions, increasing with increasing alkalinity and decreasing with increasing acidity. The pH scale commonly uses ranges from 7 to 14" (*American Heritage Dictionary of the English Language*, p. 1321). Relevant for anyone working with library materials since acidity (with a pH of under 7) causes paper to deteriorate. Books, BROADSIDES, PAMPHLETS, and anything else on paper may be tested for its pH. If an item is acidic, there are three things one can do: subjecting the item to DEACIDIFICATION if the pH is not too low, monitoring the environment in which the item is stored, or, in some cases, doing CONSERVATION work. Depending on the pH level (and sometimes other factors), the conservator might not be able to treat an item. Acid-testing pens and acid-testing strips are available from specialty supply houses. There are untold numbers of acidic boxes for library storage, SLIPCASES, and pamphlet covers in the world. Throughout the 20th century, millions of pamphlets were "protected" by being bound in pamphlet covers that were so acidic that they are crumbling today. Also, inks and leathers can be acidic. Roberts and Etherington point out, "Hydrogen-ion concentration is important in archival work because it has been adequately demonstrated that the presence of acid(s) in ink, leather, paper, etc., has or can have, [*sic*] a deleterious effect on such materials, the extent of the effect depending not so much on the volume of acid present, as on the type of acid and its concentration, i.e., a large volume of a relatively weak organic acid, such as formic acid, is less harmful than a smaller amount of a powerful, inorganic acid, such as sulfuric acid. As a decrease of pH means a logarithmic increase in acid concentration, levels of concentration below pH 5.0, or under certain circumstances, even 6.0, become important. Conversely, although not as serious a problem, a high concentration of hydroxyl ions, corresponding to a pH of 10.0 or above, can lead to serious oxydization of cellulosic materials" (p. 134). Testing for pH may help the collector and librarian preserve valuable materials.

PHASE BOX. A container for damaged volumes. These are usually made to order for volumes that must be protected, either because they are falling apart or because they can be a danger to neighboring volumes. The boxes are made (presumably) from archival materials, with a central panel, four sides, and four flaps that fold over the top of the book, with ties or magnetic or Velcro closures. They are so called because they are only one phase of CONSERVATION—the first phase. However, since the cost of conservation is high and most libraries have many more things to conserve than they have money for, the phase boxes become the long-term housing for the damaged volumes. Their benefits are many: they consolidate the parts of the volume so that these do not get detached and removed from the book; they protect neighboring volumes from RED ROT and other damaging protuberances; they are archival, so no damaging materials are introduced to the item to cause it to deteriorate further; they are not hermetically sealed, so no microenvironment is formed inside in which condensation could form; they shield the item from light and dust; and they are fairly inexpensive and easy to make. Also, if a library is fortunate enough to be able to do a serious, extensive conservation project on its damaged books, the phase boxes are easy to locate on the shelves.

PHÉNAKISTOSCOPE. (Sometimes spelled Phenakistiscope.) A device that optically creates the illusion of movement. The Colossal website says: "Nearly 155 years before CompuServe debuted the first animated gif in 1987, Belgian physicist Joseph Plateau unveiled an invention called the Phenakistoscope [*sic*], a device that is largely considered to be the first mechanism for true animation. The simple gadget relied on the persistence of vision principle to display the illusion of images in motion" (Colossal, "Phénakistiscope"). The Juxtapoz site adds: "It was invented by Joseph Plateau in 1841. The phenakistoscope used a spinning disc attached vertically to a handle. / Arrayed around the disc's center were a series of drawings showing phases of the animation, and cut through it were a series of equally spaced radial slits. The user would spin the disc and look through the moving slits at the disc's reflection in a mirror. The scanning of the slits across the reflected images kept them from simply blurring together, so that the user would see a rapid succession of images that appeared to be a single moving picture. A variant of it had two discs, one with slits and one with pictures; this was slightly more unwieldy but needed no mirror. Unlike the zoetrope and its successors, the phenakistoscope could only practically be used by one person at a time" (Juxtapoz, "A Short History of the Phenakistoscope," 28 June 2014; https://www.juxtapoz.com/illustration/short-history-of-the-phenakistoscope/ [accessed 1 May 2021]). The discs, and sometimes also the devices that they attached to, are often to be seen at antiquarian book fairs and EPHEMERA fairs. The booksellers Honey & Wax, at one of the online book fairs in early 2021, had a "Group of ten hand-colored nineteenth-century phénakistiscope discs" showing the kinds of animation common to these devices: "the blacksmith at his anvil, the man with a ball and racket, the bassist with a Cossack dancer, the tightrope walker, the dancer with her cornucopia, two dancers twirling, and two men playing leapfrog. / Three are more abstract in design: a windmill turning, a ball flying through a hoop, a chromotrope kaleidoscope." (See Selvin, "A Passionate Collector's Pre-Cinema Objects Will Go to Academy Museum, Illuminating Early Film History"; referencing the Richard Balzer Collection.)

PHILLIPPS, SIR THOMAS (1792–1872). One of the most lunatic but important book collectors in history. His motto was, "I wish to have one copy of every book in the world," and he set out to achieve this aim. Thomas loved vellum, and he tried to collect every piece of it he could find, from bookstores and printing establishments and even from butchers who were using it to wrap their products. He spent most of his life collecting every volume he could get his hands on, and "[w]hen he died . . . his affairs were in chaos. He had antagonized his family, tradesmen, and almost everyone he knew; he had also accumulated the largest collection of manuscripts, medieval and modern, ever put together by one man and an almost equally large collection of printed books. . . . [And] he also found time to carry on a ceaseless battle against the booksellers he bought from; against public officials who, he considered, were less careful than they should be to preserve records; and, most of all against his son-in-law, James Halliwell, Shakespearean scholar and (to his father-in-law's undying horror) thief of manuscripts" (blurb on the dust jacket of Munby, *Portrait of an Obsession* [see also p. 268]). His collection contained about 50,000 books and 60,000 manuscripts, many of extreme rarity and exceptional value. Those in the world of books, speaking of BIBLIOMANIA, think first of Sir Thomas Phillipps with awe and wonder and with gratitude, for he saved from extinction untold numbers of important manuscripts and books. A. N. L. Munby says that Phillipps "spent perhaps between two hundred thousand and a quarter of a million pounds altogether—four or five thousand pounds a year, while accessions came in at the rate of forty or fifty a week. For thirty years he conducted single-handed the administration of a library which ranked as a national institution" (*Portrait of an Obsession*, p. 268). Phillipps's collection was so large that when the family finally sold it off at auction, the sales lasted into the 20th century.

PHOTOENGRAVING (also called "LETTERPRESS platemaking" or "process ENGRAVING"). "The process of reproducing graphic material by transferring the image photographically to a plate or another surface, which is then ETCHED for printing" (*American Heritage Dictionary of the English Language*, p. 1328). "The original copy for reproduction may be a photograph, transparency, painting, ink drawing, pencil sketch, PRINT, water colour, print of type matter, music, an actual object, or a combination of these" (Glaister, *Glaister's Glossary of the Book*, p. 374).

PHOTOGRAVURE. "The process of printing from an INTAGLIO PLATE, ETCHED according to a photographic image" (*American Heritage Dictionary of the English Language*, p. 1329). Henry Fox Talbot patented the process in 1852 (see Glaister, *Glaister's Glossary of the Book*, p. 374). "The image (type or picture) to be reproduced is photographed to obtain a negative from which a document print (a continuous tone positive) is then made. . . . The positive is then printed on a sheet of pigmented gelatin-coated sensitized carbon tissue. After exposure the tissue is mounted on a copper cylinder and developed by rotation in hot water. It is varnished in any areas which are not to be etched, fanned dry, and etched with ferric chloride. Fundamental to the printing process is the division of the picture to be etched in the cylinder into a number of small cells which hold the ink" (*Glaister's Glossary of the Book*, p. 375). Glaister explains that the "positives are mounted on glass, the glass plate is put on the bed of a vacuum frame, the screened and coated carbon tissue is fitted to it, and an exposure is made." The carbon is put onto a printing surface; "all parts of the cylinder surface which are not to be etched are covered with an acid-resist. . . . Photogravure work is identifiable by the fine screen network which is faintly discernible in the finished print and in the lack of sharpness of accompanying type" (p. 375).

PHOTOPOLYMER PLATE. A flexible plastic PLATE that is used for LETTERPRESS printing. According to some purists, the more accurate way of describing the use of the photopolymer plate is that it is used for RELIEF printing since "letterpress" implies the use of metal type. The plate is covered with a stencil or other light-resistant substance, then it is exposed to light, which etches the plastic where it is not protected, leaving some areas of the plate in relief. The raised areas constitute the printing surface. This is a form of FLEXOGRAPHY.

TYPESETTING using metal type requires the printer to print in straight lines (with some virtuoso printers being able to curve lines or set in circles but with great effort). With photopolymer, the pages can be designed by hand or on a computer, with lines going every which way and overlapping and crisscrossing. The photopolymer plate is then etched through a printout of the text onto a plastic sheet that is laid over the plate, which is then exposed to light. Modern FINE-PRESS printers have embraced photopolymer for its flexibility and for the clarity of image that can be achieved with its use. They also like the impression that this relief method makes in a printed sheet for its resemblance to printing from metal type.

Some people in the letterpress world think of the use of photopolymer as a form of "cheating." In a recent article in *MATRIX* (see Docter, "Bradley Hutchinson"), Catherine Docter asks the printer Brad Hutchinson, "From some in the letterpress book world I detect an attitude, verging on hostility, toward photopolymer plates. What's your take on that?" His answer is typical of some in the letterpress world: "Since I make my living using them I'm obviously biased. But clearly it depends on your purpose and your level of interest in digital typography. If you're in it for the rhythms of handling metal type and the satisfaction of working with traditional techniques, then photopolymer plates have little appeal. Making those plates is utterly without charm, and printing with them requires a very different approach to LOCK-UP [of the type in the CHASE] and IMPOSITION and many of the other technical aspects of traditional letterpress printing. . . . But if you're interested in contemporary typography and working with living type designers, as I am, then some sort of photomechanical process is necessary to print those letterforms, and photopolymer plates can be made in-house, unlike photoengravings. In the digital environment you can work at such a granular level with type, so if you pay attention to details like proper optical scaling and understand how to control KERNING and hyphenation and JUSTIFICATION in your page LAYOUT program, then you can achieve some excellent typography with a level of control not available in HOT METAL. I see the techniques as complementary, not contradictory" (pp. 78–79).

PICA. A printer's measure equaling about one-sixth of an inch. Also, the designation of a TYPEFACE that has six lines to an inch. The pica is broken up into POINTS, with 12 points to a pica. To be precise, "Six picas equal 0.996 inch, though personal computer systems round this off to an exact inch. This system of measurement is used primarily by typesetters, but also by many printers and binders" (Eckersley et al., *Glossary of Typesetting Terms*, p. 80). You will hear, for instance, a printer say that he is setting his prose to 48 picas.

PICA POLE. A wooden measuring stick, the cross section of which is in the shape of a square, used by printers. A cursory search of the web shows that this rare and quite antique tool is no longer understood: many a steel PICA STICK is being sold as a pica pole by people unaware of the difference. (*See* Type gauge.)

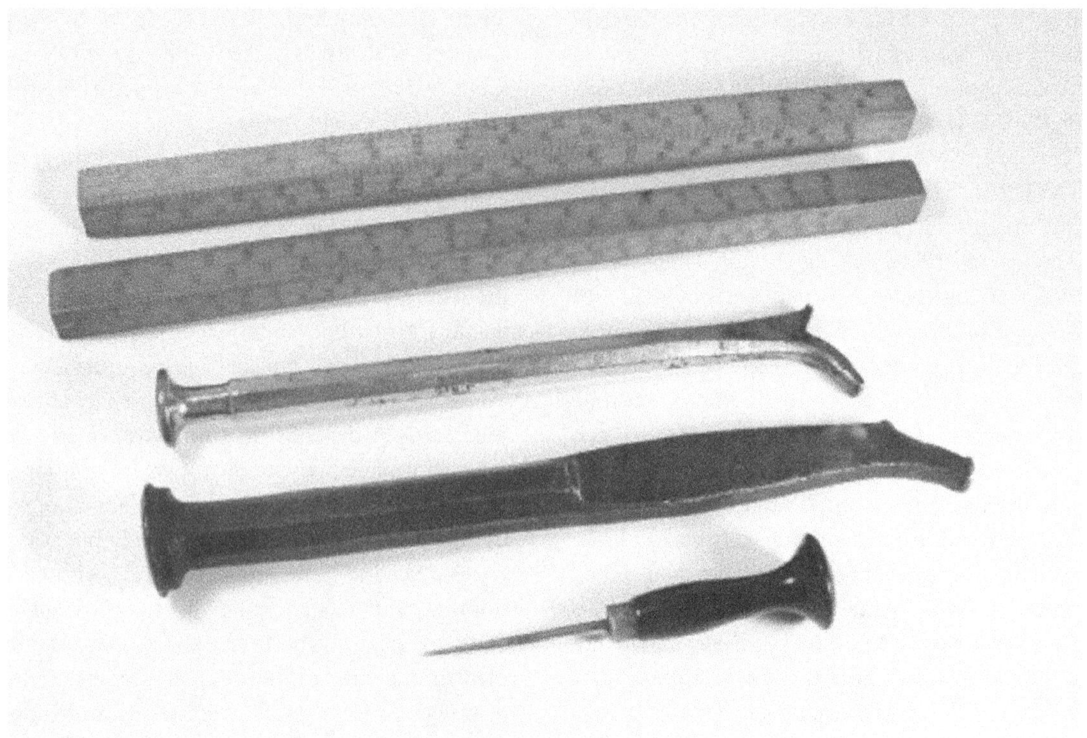

Two pica poles, two shooting sticks, and an awl (or bodkin, used for pulling SORTS out of set type); "Letterpress Commons," https://letterpresscommons.com/compositors-tools/ (accessed 14 June 2021).

Courtesy of Letterpress Commons.

PICA STICK. A printer's measuring device composed of a flat metal, wooden, or plastic piece with printers' and other measurements delineated on one or both sides. (*See* Type gauge.)

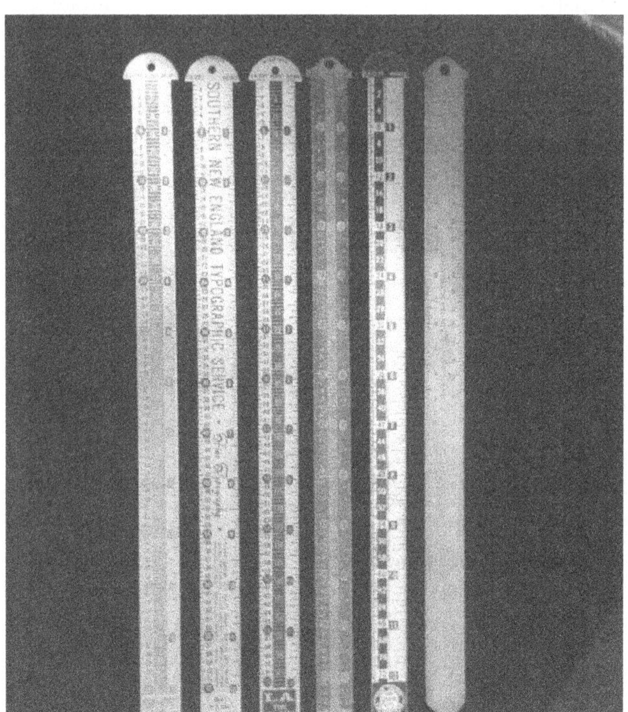

Pica sticks.

Collection of the author.

PICK. "A speck or blur caused by dirt or badly distributed ink on the face of a letter" (Paekakariki Press, "Printers' Vocabulary"). The speck can appear anywhere on a printed LEAF, but it will most often be seen in the COUNTERS of LETTERS and NUMBERS.

PICKERING, WILLIAM (1796–1854). "[P]ublisher and bookseller . . . born on 2 April 1796 into 'humble circumstances,' although he was apparently the son of an earl and lady, who were not married to each other, and he was put out to be raised by a tailor and his wife [Keynes, *William Pickering Publisher*, p. 9]. He was apprenticed at the age of 14 to Quaker booksellers John and Arthur Arch, and the arrangement may have been made by his biological father. Pickering's early publications carry the coat of arms of the Earl of Spencer, as well as a dedication to him, and are cited as sufficient evidence that the Earl was, in fact, Pickering's father" (see "William Pickering," http://www.orgs.miamioh.edu/anthologies/bijou/youngcd/pick.html [accessed 14 June 2021]). "By 1820, at the age of 24 he had started a bookselling business on his own. His business prospered, and as a[n] ANTIQUARIAN bookseller he was knowledgeable and acted as a buyer and advisor for libraries and private collectors. This interest and success in older books probably influenced the style of his later publication catalogue" (*see* citation above).

Pickering became a successful publisher, issuing his well-known Diamond Classics, with cloth bindings (possibly the first publisher to use cloth for EDITION BINDINGS). (Jeremy Norman's HistoryofInformation.com says of Pickering's printing, "The Earliest Publisher's Cloth Bindings, Issued by William Pickering"; see http://www.historyofinformation.com/expanded.php?id=2071 [accessed 14 June 2021].) Their small size and the reliable texts he printed led to their great popularity despite the fact that they were printed in extremely small type. He specialized in classic texts of literature and published works by Chaucer, Boswell, Shakespeare, Marlowe, Blake, Isaac Walton, Coleridge, and many other prominent authors.

PICOTAGE. The use of brass pins in a WOOD BLOCK to create the look of STIPPLING, allowing the artist to produce shading. The closer together the pins are, the darker the shading. This was a practice employed in the 18th century in the production of decorated papers. The technique was also used for decorating fabrics. Woodblock-printed papers will often have hundreds of tiny dots as part of the decoration. These could not have been carved into the blocks; they were created with these small pins with round, flat heads which received the ink along with the RELIEF parts of the block. The pinheads took the ink and printed in whatever configuration and density they were arranged. These "picotaged" (how is that for a new adjective!) papers are used in abundance as WRAPPERS for all kinds of books and PAMPHLETS, and they are particularly common on 18th-century dissertations and ALMANACS.

PICTORIAL COVER. Said of the cover of a book or pamphlet with some form of picture on it. The image can be in color or black and white on a tinted paper or cloth. In fact, one common phrase in the description of PUBLISHERS' BINDINGS is "pictorial cloth."

PIED/PIEING (type). Said of printing type that has been spilled and mixed up. Pied type can result from careless handling, being poorly tied up in a GALLEY, being dropped from a COMPOSING STICK or from any other surface on which it is stored, being improperly transported, or from other depredations of the printing house. Type that is all set and ready to be printed that gets pied can hardly be reconstituted. It will need to be DISTRIBUTED back into its TYPE CASE and RESET. When set type is redistributed, the person doing the task lifts a word (or a part of a long word) from the set line of type, reads it, and can then drop the SORTS back into their proper receptacles in the type case. But distributing pied type back into the case does not allow the person doing it to read words, so it is possible that sorts will be put into the wrong receptacle in the case—especially with sorts that can be misread, such as b, d, n, p, q, and u. This results in a FOUL CASE and could manifest itself in typos in the next text set from that type. The greatest chance that this will happen is when more than one font existed in the set type that got pied. That is, a page of type could have had ROMAN, boldface, and ITALIC type in it, along with sorts from a different FONT altogether.

Another thing could happen when type is pied: If it is dropped onto a hard surface, the soft metal could be damaged—something not always discernible to the person returning the type to its case. The damage will be visible when the type is next printed. This can be useful bibliographical evidence for determining the STATE of a text or the date of the printed item.

PIGEONHOLE. *See* River.

PIGSKIN. "A leather produced from the skin of the domestic pig (*Sus scrofa*). For use in bookbinding, it is vegetable tanned (or alum tawed). Pigskin has the characteristic GRAIN pattern produced by the hair follicles, which are arranged in (roughly) triangular groups of three. The nature of pigskin is such that the holes remaining following removal of the bristles can be seen on the FLESH SIDE as well as the grain side. Pigskin is a tough and durable leather (and is even more durable perhaps when alum tawed) but is somewhat stiff and intractable. In addition, it does not tool readily, except in BLIND, although very fine bindings tooled in both blind and gold have been produced. It is a rugged leather best used on large books which can more readily emphasize its rugged characteristics. Pigskin was used extensively as a bookbinding leather in Germany from about 1550 to 1640, usually on books having wooden BOARDS" (Roberts and Etherington, p. 198).

PILCROW (¶). The name of the "paragraph sign." *See* Paraph.

PILLOW BOOK. *See* Erotica.

PIRATE/PIRATED EDITION/PIRACY. A publisher who steals the text of another publisher and reprints it without PERMISSION. The laws about ownership of intellectual property were fuzzy in the first few centuries of printing, and catching and prosecuting pirates was not easy. The situation exists to this day with piracies emanating from countries that do not adhere to international conventions concerning COPYRIGHT. (See Baines and Rogers, Edmund Curll; A. W. Pollard, *Shakespeare's Fight with the Pirates*; Ralph Straus, *The Unspeakable Curll*.)

PITH PAPER. Sometimes called "RICE PAPER" (a misnomer in that there is no such thing as rice paper). Pith paper is a thin sheet of PROTO-PAPER made by slicing thin layers of the pith of the plant *Tetrapanax papyrifera*, or other plants.

Labarre says, "The substance which has received this name in Europe, through the mistaken notion that it is made from rice, consists of the pith of a small tree, *Aralia* (also *Fatsia*) *papyrifera*, which grows in the swampy forests of Formosa. . . . The cylindrical core of pith is rolled on a hard flat surface against a knife, by which it is cut into thin sheets of fine ivory-like texture" (*Dictionary and Encyclopaedia of Paper and Paper-Making*, p. 227). Note that real paper is made from macerated fibers; pith paper (the proper designation for this material, *not* "rice paper," which Labarre emphasizes is a mistake) is merely sliced pith.

Thin sheets of this lovely material are common in Asian books, in which they are used for beautiful, fine paintings. Most of them are only a few inches in width and height, though some can be 7 or 10 inches high; but the larger they are, the more fragile they are. Subjects of these MINIATURES—for they are necessarily small since the pith is quite brittle and cannot be made into large pieces—are many: plants and flowers, costumes, trades, tortures, weapons, and many other images of cultural significance. They are often gathered into albums, with a few to scores of these fine artworks. Because of their fragility, they are wont to crack and split.

PLAGIARISM. Passing off as one's own the work of another. The key point here is that if a library or bookseller, collector, or any other party owns a physical document (book, manuscript, letter, photograph, drawing, notes, work of art, or recorded sound of any kind), that owner does not necessarily (and usually does not) own the intellectual property in that item, unless the owner is the maker of the item—and even then, physical ownership does not automatically confer ownership of the intellectual property. COPYRIGHT laws were designed to protect the interests of the copyright holder, and anyone using the work of someone else, while that work is still protected by copyright, is committing plagiarism, except under certain circumstances. If the user gets PERMISSION from the copyright holder, if the work is used under FAIR-USE provisions, or if the work is an ORPHAN (i.e., it may have a copyright holder, but the person wanting to use the work has been unable, after diligent searching, to find that owner—and no one else knows who that owner is), the user may publish from the work and not be plagiarizing.

The intricacies of copyright, plagiarism, and fair use and the notion of "public domain" are complicated and have been made even more complex than ever before with the coming of texts in digital form. (See Berger, pp. 212–24.) Plagiarists perhaps expect not to be caught (or merely hope they won't be), but when they are, they could be subject to various legal issues. Witness the cases of Kaavya Viswanathan and David Leavitt. (See Mehegan, "Harvard Author's Apology Not Accepted"; and Spender, "My Life Is Mine: It Is Not David Leavitt's.")

PLANING/A PLANE. Tapping down the type with a plane to make sure that every SORT is the same height, in preparation for inking and printing. The plane is a tool (usually made of wood and sometimes with a piece of leather tacked to the top) that is placed over the set type and tapped so that all the sorts are tamped down so that their feet (*see* Feet [in type]) are touching the flat surface beneath. Sorts that are not tamped down so that their face is flush with all of the other type in the CHASE, and so that their feet are firmly touching the BED of the press, will be locked into place "sticking up" above the rest of the type. These sorts will bite into the sheet being printed. The simple plane is a crucial tool.

Printer's plane.
Collection of the author.

PLANOGRAPHIC PRINTING. Printing from a flat surface. The other two basic methods of printing are RELIEF (printing from a raised surface, as with printing type) and INTAGLIO (printing from "beneath the surface" of a plane, as with ENGRAVING). (*See* Chromolithography; Lithography.)

PLANTIN-MORETUS MUSEUM. A museum in Antwerp, Belgium, named for two of the great printers of that city: Christophe Plantin (1520–1589) and Jan Moretus (1543–1610). Moretus worked for Plantin and took over the printing business when Plantin died. Plantin founded the company in the mid-1550s, and he printed a host of French and Latin texts. "When Antwerp was plundered by the Spaniards in 1576 and Plantin had to pay a ransom, he established a branch office in Paris and then, in 1583, settled in Leiden as the typographer of the new university of the states of Holland, leaving his much-reduced business in Antwerp in the hands of his sons-in-law, John Moerentorf (Moretus) and Francis van Ravelinghen (Raphelengius). But in 1585 Plantin returned to Antwerp and Raphelengius took over the business in Leiden. After Plantin's death, the Antwerp business was carried on by Moretus, but it declined during the second half of the 17th century. All was religiously preserved, however, and in 1876 the city of Antwerp acquired the buildings and their contents and created the Plantin-Moretus Museum" ("Christophe Plantin," *Encyclopaedia Britannica*, http://www.britannica.com/biography/Christophe-Plantin [accessed 14 June 2021]). (See also Clair, *Christopher Plantin*; De Vinne, *Christopher Plantin and the Plantin-Moretus Museum at Antwerp*; Imhoff, *Jan Moretus and the Continuation of the Plantin Press*; Voet, *The Golden Compass*, vol. 1; and Voet and Kaye, *The Golden Compass*, vol. 2.)

The museum, in the very house that Plantin and Moretus used for their shop, shows the full range of bookmaking, and it contains a great number of copies of the books they printed, along with much of their original equipment and the house's furnishings. On my visit there, on a bitterly cold, blustery, snowy day, I nearly froze my fingers off and was grateful to have reached the door of the museum—only to find that the temperature inside was not much warmer than it was outside. But the array of printing presses and the displays of type casting materials and books were worth the visit.

PLATE. This refers to a medium of printing an illustration or text ("the plate was made from copper") and the printed result of that printing ("it was a HAND-COLORED plate"; "the volume was lacking all of its plates"). Books illustrated with plates, especially plates created by hand, are often treasured by collectors. And occasionally such volumes are offered in a DELUXE or super-deluxe VERSION with one of the printing plates included, usually in a box that contains the volume. LEONARD BASKIN's Gehenna Press volume *Fleuronologia* was issued in a deluxe version with a copper plate of one of Baskin's fleurons that had been printed in the book. (*See* Berger, *Fleuronologia*.)

PLATE MARKS. The indented lines showing on a LEAF (possibly of a book) around a PLATE that has been printed in (or TIPPED INTO) the volume. (*See* Copperplate; Engraving; Etching; Intaglio.) Since the copperplate is usually smaller than the leaf that it is being printed on, the edges of the plate make an indentation on the leaf in the printing process. These plate marks can be faked. On a sheet with a prominent texture (as on a ribbed or an uncalendered paper [*see* Calendering]), the smooth area of an intaglio plate may smooth out the printed sheet, leaving the mark of the plate, but this is not strictly a "plate mark."

PLATEN. The flat plate on a HANDPRESS that descends when the BAR is pulled, pressing the sheet of paper to be printed (the sheet that is lying on the TYMPAN) down onto the inked type. When the IMPRESSION is made, the bar is returned to its original position, and the platen ascends, releasing the BED of the PRESS to be rolled out so that the operation can be repeated. Such presses are appropriately called "platen presses."

PLATE NUMBERS. Carter (who hyphenates the term) gives two definitions. In engraved music, these are numbers at the bottom of the pages showing where in the corpus of the publishing house the score appears numerically. These numbers can be used for dating the scores. Also, these can be an indication of the number in a sequence of engraved plates (illustrative, textual, or both) in a volume. It is possible, Carter adds, that the plates could be reengraved and the numbers burnished out and reengraved if the number of order of the plates in the text changes. The state of the plate can sometimes be discerned if one has a record of all the variations that appear in these plate numbers. (See Carter, pp. 189–90.) Of course, any volume with plates may also have them numbered on the page onto which they were pasted and not necessarily numbered in the plates themselves. As with all such bibliographical information, such variation must be approached with great caution. Priority of state may not be determinable from the plate numbers and their variations over time. If a copper plate wears down (as it is wont to do since copper is a soft metal), later impressions will show the wear. So it will be clear which are earlier and which later impressions. But at that point the artist can touch up the plate in such a way that a beautiful and "un-worn" image is the result. At this point, new impressions will look crisp and sharp, and it may be impossible for one trying to determine which came first: the original sharp images from the original run or the new sharp images from the retouched plate. A cautious bibliographer, in this situation, may merely have to say, "The plate exists in two versions (or two states); priority is indeterminable." In the touch-up, if the plate numbers get changed, there may be some evidence of which state was earlier.

PLATES. The generic term for various kinds of printing surfaces that are on flat pieces of metal or plastic or other material. (Plates could also be on curved surfaces to be fitted over a cylinder for printing.) The term also means "[a]n illustration printed separately from the text of a book, often on a different type of paper" than the book is printed on (Roberts and Etherington, p. 199). "Plates may be bound into a book, tipped onto a blank leaf (or a leaf bearing a printed caption), loose in a pocket or portfolio, or bound in a separate volume. Plates are not generally included in the pagination of a book" (Roberts and Etherington, p. 200). The printing item called a "plate" could be on wood, any metal, plastic, rubber, or other material, and the plate could be in RELIEF, INTAGLIO, or PLANOGRAPHIC. Sometimes when a volume is printed from STEREOTYPE or ELECTROTYPE plates, a description of the item may say "printed from plates."

Carter has a separate entry for "color-plate books" in which he discusses these volumes with respect to their genre and whether the plates are printed in color (from any kind of surface) or whether the color is applied manually in some fashion. (See Carter, pp. 82–83.) Of course, the subject areas he lists (picturesque, sports, natural history, and satire) are only a few of those in which color-plate volumes exist, and the methods of color he mentions (printed, AQUATINT, HAND COLORED, ENGRAVED, and LITHOGRAPHED) do not exhaust the possibilities of ways color plates are created—especially today when Xerox, laser, and ink-jet printers can produce excellent color images. For more than a century and a half, there has been a vogue in collecting books with color plates, and the ones with such illustrations done by hand generally command the highest prices. Whether the coloring was done when the book was originally created or more recently may be extremely difficult to determine. What is to stop a modern owner of an uncolored *Nuremberg Chronicle* to have it colored? I once met a collector who bought 17th-, 18th-, and 19th-century books with black-and-white plates and had an artist color them. She did a lovely job, and the plates looked as if the coloring was done when the books were first produced.

PLAYING CARDS. These are cards, usually made from paper, marked in various ways to allow games to be played with them. They were also used for conjuring, cheating people, performing tricks, and fortune-telling, and to show sleight of hand. In the world of EPHEMERA, these cards are immensely popular, and they appear often at book and ephemera fairs. They have a long history, though as Will Roya repeatedly says on his website (PlayingCardDecks.com), there is no documentary evidence of their origin, and all such histories are speculative. He says, "There is clear historical evidence that playing cards began to appear in Europe in the late 1300s and early 1400s . . . . They seem to have come from somewhere in the East, and may have been imported to Europe by gypsies, crusaders, or traders. The common consensus appears to be that an early form of playing cards originated somewhere in Asia, but . . . solid historical evidence is lacking. / Educated guesses have made links to the cards, suits, and icons of [the] 12th century and even older cards in China, India, Korea, Persia, or Egypt, which may have been introduced to Europe by Arabs. Some scholars believe that playing cards were invented in China during the Tang dynasty around the 9th century AD. There does seem to be evidence of some kinds of games involving playing cards (and drinking!) from this time onward, including cards with icons representing coins, which also appear as icons on playing cards later in Western Europe. If correct, it would place the origins of playing cards before 1000AD, and it would see them as originating alongside or even from tile games like dominoes and mahjong. Some have suggested that the playing cards first functioned as 'play money' and represented the stakes used for other gambling games, and later became part of the games themselves. . . . It is very possible that playing cards made their way from China to Europe via Egypt in the Mamluk period, with decks from that era having goblets (cups), gold coins, swords, and polo-sticks, which represent the main interests of the Mamluk aristocracy, and bear parallels to the four suits seen in Italian playing cards from the 14th century" (Roya, "The History of Playing Cards: The Evolution of the Modern Deck," PlayingCardDecks.com, 16 October 2018; https://playingcarddecks.com/blogs/all-in/history-playing-cards-modern-deck [accessed 2 August 2021]). An extensive literature exists on these cards, with publications showing historical decks from around the world. Yale University, with its huge collection of them, published an illustrated catalog. (See the bibliography: Keller, *A Catalogue of The Cary Collection of Playing Cards in the Yale University Library*; see also Hargrave, *History of Playing Cards and a Bibliography of Cards and Gaming*; and Tilley, *History of Playing Cards*.)

PLOW (also spelled "plough"—the British spelling). "A device used for trimming the LEAVES of a book, usually one bound by hand. It consists of two parallel blocks of wood about 4 inches wide and 8 inches long connected by two guide rods and one threaded rod, with a cutting blade attached to the lower edge of one of the blocks. The left hand part of the plow fits into a runner on the left cheek of the lying press while the other block is fitted with the adjustable knife. The knife is generally moved inward by the turn of a screw, cutting into the leaves as the plow is moved back and forth" (Roberts and Etherington," p. 200). Hence, a bookseller may say something like "fore-edge and foot of volume plowed" when the marks of the tool are visible.

A similar device is used for finishing hand-cast type. When the SORT is removed from the MOLD, the JET is still attached. The jet will be broken off, leaving a rough spot at the foot (*see* Feet [in type]) of the sort where it was attached. Rather than filing down each sort one at a time to remove this rough spot (which would prevent the sort from standing perfectly on its feet), a large number of the sorts can be lined up in a holder and clamped together, then a plow can shave off the rough spots all at once.

PLUG. A favorable reference to a commercial product, as when a lecturer slips into his talk mentions of his own published books. A shameful practice. (*See* the caption to the entry for Two-line character.)

PLUMMET. *See* Lead point ruling.

PMM. *See Printing and the Mind of Man.*

POCHOIR. Printing using stencils. "Pochoir (French: 'stencil'), as distinguished from ordinary stenciling, is a highly refined technique of making fine LIMITED EDITIONS of stencil PRINTS. It is often called hand colouring, or hand illustration" ("Pochoir," *Encyclopaedia Britannica*, http://www.britannica.com/art/pochoir [accessed 14 June 2021]), though the color is imparted with brushes or sponges or other implements. As with the use of stencils, there is a good deal of handwork in such coloring, and the final product has more of a look of hand coloring than does color printing, no matter how fine that is. But, as with the term MISE-EN-PAGE, "pochoir" has a ring of elegance and expensiveness that "stencil-colored" lacks. Many FINE PRESS books contain pochoir ILLUSTRATIONS. (See Wallen and Greengard, *Pochoir*; and Gerry, *Pochoir*.)

POCKET-BOOK. Carter has two definitions for this term. The first claims that the book is an OCTAVO printed from a fairly small sheet and able to be put into one's pocket. The second is a small book combining the functions of a yearbook, a personal journal or diary, and a billfold, common from the late 17th to the 19th centuries. (See Carter, pp. 190–91.) The generic term that Carter defines here was adopted as the formal company name, Pocket Books, the firm founded by Robert F. de Graff in 1939 (see "Robert F. de Graff Dies at 86; Was Pocket Book Founder," *New York Times*, Obituaries, 3 November 1981, http://www.nytimes.com/1981/11/03/obituaries/robert-f-de-graff-dies-at-86-was-pocket-books-founder.html [accessed 14 June 2021]). While de Graff was not the first to publish small paperback books in extremely inexpensive versions (it had been done in Germany under the Albatross imprint and in England with Penguin Books), de Graff chose popular fiction that appealed to millions of readers and had it printed up in small cheap copies with glitzy art on the covers and selling for 25 cents or so. "The 10 initial titles of reprints of best sellers and classics on the Pocket Book list were offered in 1939 at 25 cents apiece. Each title had a first printing of about 10,000 copies. The extent of the demand is shown in the sales figures: *Lost Horizon*, James Hilton, 2,514,747 sold. *Wake Up and Live*, Dorothea Brande, 570,843. *Five Great Tragedies*, Shakespeare, 2,862,792. *Topper*, Thorne Smith, 1,546,000. *The Murder of Roger Ackroyd*, Agatha Christie, 961,967. *Enough Rope*, Dorothy Parker, 210,000. *Wuthering Heights*, Emily Bronte, 1,666,262. *The Way of All Flesh*, Samuel Butler, 338,279. *The Bridge of San Luis Rey*, Thornton Wilder, 1,189,764. *Bambi*, Felix Salten, 289,000" (*New York Times*). Hundreds of millions of these inexpensive paperbacks were produced, so many that "pocket book" became a generic term for a cheap paperback that had little more than a single reading in it before it destroyed itself. Surviving Pocket Books are on yellowed, brittle paper, and few are in any condition to be read without falling to pieces (if they are not already in pieces). The company had a good track record for sales since it could spot titles that would sell. Dr. Benjamin Spock's *Baby and Child Care* sold 28 million copies, and "[b]y 1964, when Pocket Books celebrated its 25th anniversary, annual sales totaled 300 million volumes" (*New York Times*).

Carter's statement that the books were octavos is disheartening since the name of that format designates a particular structure, not a size; and even if it designated a size, Pocket Books were smaller than most octavos. The PERFECT-BINDING nature of these cheap PAPERBACKS defy a FORMAT designation, and they should be described by their dimensions. Carter was perpetuating the notion that statements of format conjure up an item's size. In the bookselling world, this is somewhat defensible if the seller is describing fairly modern books (made, say, from 1850 on). But bibliographically, and historically, the name of the format has little to do with size.

P.O.D. *See* Print on demand.

POINTER. *See* Fist.

POINT HOLES (also called "registration marks"). In positioning a sheet onto a TYMPAN in a HANDPRESS, the printer would lay the paper over two pins protruding vertically from the tympan. These were called "REGISTRATION PINS." The pins were positioned such that they would fall directly between two TEXT BLOCKS of the type representing the text to be printed on opposing pages. This was done so that when the tympan was folded down over the FORME, the pins would not hit any type, and also because the pins had uses after the printing. Two holes were pierced in the sheet to be printed. The registration pins held the sheet in place on the tympan, and they also aligned the sheet perfectly to be printed. Once the sheet was printed on one side, it needed to be PERFECTED—printed on its opposite side. The printer would take the sheet from the press and let the ink dry. When it was time to perfect the sheet, the printer removed the type from the forme but not the FURNITURE, which was left in exactly the same position that it was in when the first forme was printed. The printer replaced the type from the first forme with the type needed to perfect the sheet. Since the furniture was not disturbed, this positioned the type for the second forme in exactly the same place that the type for the first forme was in. The printer then placed the sheet of paper to be perfected over the registration pinholes (unprinted side facing the type, printed side facing the tympan), positioning the sheet in exactly the right place to allow the type from the second forme to be superimposed over the same area where the type from the first forme was, on the opposite side of the sheet—achieving perfect registration on both sides of the sheet. That is, no new holes were punched in the sheet after the first side was printed; the sheet was turned over and placed onto the tympan with the pins going through the same holes that were formed for the printing of the first side.

The pins were left in place for subsequent SIGNATURES so that the RECTOS and VERSOS of all signatures registered. Hence, there was not only perfect registration from one side of each sheet to the next but also perfect registration for the last page of each signature and the first page of the following signature. If the point holes were carefully measured out, they could be used, in a FOLIO, to guide the person folding the leaves in preparation for binding. Fold the LEAF through the point holes, and the type on facing pages within the signature would register, as well as text blocks on opposite sides of the leaf and last and first pages of signatures. Further, the point holes could be used as two of the sewing holes for the binder. For signatures that required more folds than the one that formed a folio, the point holes would wind up along folds that were BOLTS—that is, folds that connected CONJUGATE LEAVES. So the point holes were guides for precise folding. Eventually, the bolts would be sliced open or guillotined off, essentially making the point holes disappear.

If the bolts were sliced open (as with a letter-opener action), sometimes a trace of the point holes would be visible (along the edge of the book that once had the fold) to those looking carefully for them. So the point holes guided registration and folding and assisted in binding.

POINTILLÉ. "1. A luxurious style of FINISHING consisting of dotted lines and curves impressed on the covers of a book. In the first half of the 17th century, pointillé was used by numerous French bookbinders and/or gilders, including Florimond Badier and Macé Ruette, although in terms of sheer magnificence of execution, it reached its pinnacle earlier in the bindings associated with the name (Le) Gascon. 2. A generic term indicating a form of dotted book decorations. 3. A small dotted finishing tool" (Roberts and Etherington, p. 201).

POINTING HAND. *See* Fist.

POINT-MANIAC. The discussion of "points" (*see* Edition, Impression [Printing], Issue, and State; Points) explains that these are places in which one printing of a text varies from another printing of the same text from the same setting of type—that is, in the same EDITION. The change from "flittering candles" in one copy of a text to "flickering candles" in another (constituting a STATE VARIANT) is a legitimate point. A stray spot of ink that appears in the middle of a linocut in one copy and not in another is not a legitimate point. Carter coined the term "point-maniac" to indicate the collector (or bookseller) who is crazy about points—even tiny and relatively insignificant typographical variations between one copy and another. At what place does a point not constitute a significant variation but be simply a flyspeck on the page?

Carter says that point-maniacs love points excessively, and he rightly explains that it is a great pleasure to discern bibliographical history in the complex distinctions between one fine point and another in printing history—and to be able to draw useful conclusions about such things. (See Carter, pp. 192–93.) The case expressed in the preceding paragraph (concerning candles)—from a textual analysis of copies of the first edition of Mark Twain's *Innocents Abroad*—reveals two of several states in which that volume exists, and such analysis is revealing about an author's methods and possibly printing-house practices. Having spotted such a *point* is indeed a pleasure, and it leads to an important decision that an editor must make (and an equally important explanation of how such a point could come about). But the maniac goes further, exhibiting his brilliance and unparalleled understanding of the world of printing and the importance of a particular copy of a text by expatiating on the ink smudge after the page number on such and such a page of a copy in his possession. Where does bibliographical intelligence let off and point-mania begin? (*See also* Author's corrections; Issue-monger; States; and State variants.)

POINTS. Printers' measurements equaling 12 to a PICA. Hence, a point is about 1⁄72 of an inch.

In bibliographic terms, points are places in particular volumes in which the text or other parts of the book vary from the same places in what look like identical copies. (For a discussion of points, *see* Edition, Impression [Printing], Issue, and State; Points; and Point-maniacs.)

Points are also the metal pins protruding from a TYMPAN that pierce a sheet of paper to be printed as it is laid onto the tympan. (For an explanation of this, *see* Point holes.) The holes made in the sheet guide the binder in folding the sheet, and they can sometimes be used as two of the sewing holes in the binding. (*See* Gauge pins.)

POINT SYSTEM. The system of measurement for type in which there are 12 points to a PICA and 6 picas to an inch. "The present-day system upon which all printer's type measurements are based; also known as the American Point System" (Avis, *The Bookman's Concise Dictionary*, pp. 227–28).

POISON BOOK PROJECT. *See* Arsenic.

POLISHED CALF. Calfskin that has been varnished and polished to a high sheen.

POLLARD, ALFRED WILLIAM (1859–1944). British scholar and bibliographer who helped 20th-century researchers develop the field of systematic BIBLIOGRAPHY, especially known for his textual scholarship on the works of Shakespeare (see Wilson, "Introduction," in Roper, comp., *Alfred William Pollard*, pp. 1–57; the section on Pollard's Shakespeare work is on pp. 36–48). He was "keeper of the Department of Printed Books at the British Museum, 1919–24. He edited several volumes of Chaucer's *Canterbury Tales* (1886–7) and the 'Globe' Chaucer (1898), published other pioneering works which influenced the study of medieval literature, and also made important contributions to Shakespeare criticism. He was largely responsible for the completion of the *Short-title Catalogue of Books, Printed in England, Scotland and Ireland . . . 1475–1640* (1926)" ("A. W. Pollard," Oxford Reference, http://www.oxfordreference.com/view/10.1093/oi/authority.20110803100334954 [accessed 14 June 2021]). (*See* Wing, Donald G.)

POLLARD, (HENRY) GRAHAM (1903–1976). English bibliographer and bookseller, famous for, inter alia, exposing, with JOHN CARTER, the FORGERIES of THOMAS J. WISE. Pollard became part owner of Birrell and Garnett, booksellers in London, and in 1927 became managing director. Some of the catalogs he produced with the company became important reference works. (See Collins, *The Two Forgers*, and Pollard and Redgrave, *A Short-Title Catalogue of Books Printed in England, Scotland, & Ireland*.) (*See ESTC*.)

POLYGLOT. A term that designates a volume that is presented in more than one (and usually several) languages, usually printed in parallel columns for easy comparison. "In the printing of polyglot works, when two or more versions of the same work are on one page in parallel columns, each paragraph begins on a line with the other paragraph in the other part. If one of the texts is more important than another it may be in large type, wider measure and LEADED, while that which is less important is solid [*see* Set solid], in small type and narrow measure. In three languages it is usual to put the main text in the center and the others at each side" (and so on; *American Dictionary of Printing and Bookmaking*, p. 441). This article concludes, "Should any printer to whom this work is unfamiliar receive an order to print a book of this kind he will find it worth while [*sic*] to visit a theological seminary and ask the librarian for permission to look at some of his polyglot books. Some of these are miracles of typographical ingenuity" (p. 441). Setting in columns is difficult enough; setting with different typefaces in columns—or with different leading and line measures—is even more troublesome.

POP-UP (book). A volume in which some of the "text" pops up—extending in three dimensions from the flat surface of the page—when the TWO-PAGE SPREAD is opened. There can also be pop-ups attached to a single LEAF. The term, however, has also been used for any book in which other kinds of movable parts can be engaged by a user: the inclusion of VOLVELLES, FLAPS that can be lifted, or tabs that can be pulled to make elements of the opening move in one way or another. (*See* Movable book.) That is, "pop-up" now does not always designate things that pop up. Perhaps a more appropriate term would be "books with movable parts." Gay Walker, in an exhibition at Yale University, called these "eccentric books," her clever title wrapping around from the rear cover to the front—so on the front cover we see "tric books"! And indeed, they are like tricks in the response they elicit from people. (See Walker, *Eccentric Books*.) These books have had a strong following, with many collectors (private and institutional), for more than 150 years.

P.O.R. *See* Price on request.

PORCELAIN CARDS. Cards printed on a white paper that looks like porcelain. These collectibles are usually trade cards, often printed in CHROMOLITHOGRAPHY. Anita van Elferen at Knuf Rare Books says, "Porcelain-cards were mainly produced in Belgium in the nineteenth century (between 1825 and the 1870's). They are called porcelain-cards because they look a bit like porcelain. They were printed in LITHOGRAPHY on a white background of paper with kaolin or lead white. Their production gradually stopped in the 1870's because of the health hazards for printers" (Anita van Elferen, Knuf Rare Books, E-Catalogue, May 2021, item 2, Trade card for D. & J. Bevernaege, lithographic printers in

Oudenaarde. No place, no date [but Oudenaarde, c. 1850]; http://www.fritsknuf.com/Ecat12_hd.pdf [accessed 25 May 2021]). This is yet another term that shows up occasionally in booksellers' catalogs. (*See* Papier porcelaine.)

PORNOGRAPHY. *See* Erotica.

PORTFOLIO. A case that is made of two boards that wrap around whatever it contains: PRINTS, correspondence, a bound volume or PAMPHLET, maps, charts, and so on. The portfolio often has some kind of device to hold it closed (strings for tying, Velcro tabs, magnets, loop and ivory [or plastic] piece that fits into the loop [*see* figure at "Chitsu"], or possibly a third board that wraps around the portfolio). All of the DELUXE issues of *MATRIX* are issued in a SLIPCASE with a portfolio of extra pieces that the regular version lacks. Sometimes a portfolio will have a pocket on one or both of the boards (usually inside).

PORTMANTEAU TITLE. A title printed onto a volume containing several smaller, individually published pieces—as with a SAMMELBAND. The binding of a volume that is sitting on a shelf needs to guide the browser as to what the volume holds. The sammelband could have dozens of pamphlets, so it would be impossible for the binding to show them all. WorldCat lists, for instance, a single volume; the cataloging record says, "27 tracts and chapbooks, most by women printers and women in the printing trade bound into one volume with a portmanteau title." The title on the volume is *Bookmaking on the Distaff Side*. (Thanks to John Crichton of the Brick Row Book Shop for calling this to my attention.)

PORTOLAN (or portulan). Maps used to aid sailors in navigation. They help to steer the ship by compass directions and distances, as reported by those who have sailed particular routes in the past. The earliest portolans (from Italy) date to the 13th century. Those from Portugal and Spain, being made by highly experienced sailors, were amazingly accurate, even as early as the 15th century. The opportunities afforded by accurate maritime charts made them particularly valuable, and countries did their best to keep the information they held from those of other countries.

"[T]he word 'portolan' derives from the word 'portolani' which is translated into English as 'pilots' or as 'rutters'" (see "What is a portolan chart?"; https://apps.lib.umn.edu/bell/map/PORTO/INTRO/intro2.html [accessed 22 July 2021]). Julie Rehmeyer, in "The Mystery of Extraordinarily Accurate Medieval Maps," says that the word is from the Italian *portolano*, "meaning 'a collection of sailing directions.'" "These texts list places, with distances and directions to reach them. / Portolan charts were made to get seafarers from home to another place and back again safely. On portolan charts prior to 1500, distance, direction, and coastal features were provided for navigators, with information to enable them to calculate and measure the progress and direction of their vessels during a voyage; mariners still had to rely on experience and common sense, however. Modern sea charts have many of the characteristics that the early portolan charts have—scale, compass, details of coastlines and harbors and little detail in the interior" (James Ford Bell Library, University of Minnesota, https://www.lib.umn.edu/apps/bell/map/PORTO/INTRO/intro2.html [accessed 14 June 2021]). The site of the previous passage says that all portolans had characteristics similar to those of modern maps: "a network of lines made within a circle; coastlines of lands, place-names; scales of distance; a compass showing cardinal directions; and indications of shoals, reefs, and islands along coastlines."

PORTRAIT FORMAT. The LAYOUT of a volume such that it is taller than it is wide. (*See* Landscape format, where the use of the word "format" is discussed.) Better would be the term "portrait ORIENTATION."

POST (in papermaking). A stack of freshly made sheets of paper, interleaved by woven FELTS. The newly dipped sheets are COUCHED onto felts; if they are couched directly onto other sheets of paper, the sheets will fuse and make multilayer papers—with enough of these eventually making CARDBOARD. Hence, felts are used to interleave the couched sheets, preparing them for their first pressing to remove the water from the sheets and to help the fibers mat together. After the pressing of the post, the felts will be removed, and the sheets will be stacked up on top of one another (forming the "WHITE POST") for a second pressing and will eventually be dried. (*See* Layman.)

POST BINDING. A binding consisting of heavy BOARDS from which protrude a number of metal posts (often with threads on their ends). LEAVES of paper with holes punched in them are placed into the binding, with the posts going through the holes and the leaves stacking up until they reach the height of the post. At this point, the volume can be considered full, or another set of posts can be added onto the top of the others by being screwed onto the first ones, increasing the thickness of the volume and allowing more hole-punched leaves to be added to the volume. These volumes were common in the stationery trade, used by companies that kept files of invoices or other business papers, and also used by entities producing an ongoing set of publications that needed to be added to and bound into a single volume. Post binders are also used for leaves that have been ENCAPSULATED, in which case holes are punched through the encapsulating materials and not through the item itself.

POST-INCUNABULA. A term from Carter designating printed items each of which looks like an INCUNABULUM but that were printed after 1500 (the last year of the incunabula period). He says that the term seems to have been created by Wouter Nijhoff about 1900. He adds that in the Netherlands (and possibly in other European countries), it refers to books printed in the first four decades of the 16th century, possibly because the books printed then would have still looked much like those of the incunabula period. He says that the term was used in England for books printed in the first two decades of the 16th century. (See Carter, p. 193.) The term may have been so used in England when Carter wrote that entry, but I have seen it only once (in a European bookseller's catalog) in the past 45 years. That all things printed from 1501 on—by any means—are "post-incunabula" and that the term is almost never used today mitigates against its present use, though we may encounter it here and there, so it merits mention in this dictionary.

POST-IT NOTES. The brand name (developed in the United States by 3M) of a product referred to generically as "sticky notes"—sheets of note-sized paper (issued in many sizes) treated with a removable adhesive, allowing the user to stick the note to a surface and then remove it with "no damage" to the other surface. The quotation marks indicate that there is a problem: These notes leave an invisible residue of the adhesive, which is acidic. If the SUBSTRATE is paper, eventually the acids will make the paper turn brownish, a stain that may be impossible to remove. The Post-it Note user who decorates books with these will wind up in the same place as will the one who DOG-EARS the LEAVES of his books. (*See* Pressure-sensitive adhesives.)

POUNCE. White powder burnished over the surface of vellum to smooth it out and act as a mordant on both sides of the skin. Also used in transferring images or MAJUSCULES from one manuscript leaf to another. The image (e.g., a picture or decorative letter) was PRICKED (or a piece of TRACING VELLUM was laid over the original image, with a copy being drawn onto the tracing vellum and then pricked), and then pounce was dabbed over the pricked holes, depositing an outline in small dots of white powder onto the surface beneath, to be used as a guide to re-create the original image.

POUND SIGN. *See* Hash character.

POUPÉE, À LA. *See under* À la poupée.

POWELL, ROGER (1896–1990). "An English bookbinder and restorer, born in London and educated at Bedales. Powell did not become seriously interested in bookbinding until 1930, when he studied for a year at the Central School of Arts and Crafts under Douglas Cockerell and others. In 1931 he established his own bindery in Welwyn Garden City and maintained it for 4 years, before joining the firm of Douglas Cockerell & Son in 1935. The following year he became a partner, continuing on with the firm until 1947. He succeeded Douglas Cockerell as tutor in charge of bookbinding at the Royal College of Art, remaining there until 1956, when he left formal teaching to devote himself full time to his bookbinding and RESTORATION business. / Powell has maintained a long standing interest in the field of restoration and repair, together with an abiding interest in problems relating to the durability and permanence of materials, sewing methods, and FORWARDING in general. Because of this, as well as his outstanding craftsmanship, he has been commissioned to restore many priceless (and irreplaceable) volumes, including *The Book of Kells*, for the Trinity College Library in Dublin (1953), *The Book of Durrow* (1954), *The Book of Armagh* and *The Book of Dimma* (1956–1957), as well as numerous comparatively early books in the Aberdeen University Library. In recognition of his outstanding service, he was awarded the degree of Master of Arts, *honoris causa* (1961), from Trinity College, Dublin, and the O.B.E. (Officer of the Order of the British Empire) in 1976. / Roger Powell places soundness of construction, in both materials and method, ahead of decorative design. He believes that the actual design of a binding must be an integral part of the binding itself, because a book is a tangible object meant to be used. His desire to make bookbinding a work of artistic merit, and his ability to carry out this desire have made him one of England's outstanding bookbinders" (Roberts and Etherington, "Roger Powell"; https://cool.culturalheritage.org/don/dt/dt2659.html [accessed 23 March 2021]; see also Petherbridge, "The Compleat Binder: The Arts and Crafts Legacy of Roger Powell").

PREFACE. One of the possible "PRELIMS" of a volume in which an author introduces the subject of the volume, explaining his intention and scope. The preface usually explains why, when, and how the book was written, and it may offer acknowledgments and explain how the text differs from the work of others (or from earlier editions by the same author).

PRE-FIRSTS (pre-first editions). "I have an aversion to the airplanese term *pre-boarding*. When a passenger boards the plane, he boards it. What goes on before (pre-) boarding? How can anyone board the plane before boarding the plane? What does pre-boarding look like? It looks like boarding. It *is* boarding. Many professions have terminology that borders on the ridiculous. 'Pre-first' is one of those words, but it sounds impressive and rare and exclusive. So collectors and booksellers like to use it to enhance the aura and the value of their books" (Berger, p. 264). If an author printed a few copies of her work for private distribution to friends and family, before the commercially issued TEXT was printed, these "pre-firsts" might also be called "first printed edition" (*see* First printing), as distinguishable from "first published version," since the notion of "published" implies released to the public. As for the bizarre term "pre-first," Carter says the term contradicts itself and does not really have a logical meaning. He says that the use of the term is a sign of what he calls the "CHRONOLOGICAL OBSESSION" in which collectors are obsessed with having the earliest version of a text—a TRIAL ISSUE or ADVANCE COPY, an early version created to secure COPYRIGHT, an edition printed privately, a PIRACY, a SERIALIZED version, or any other version that might predate the "first edition." (See Carter, p. 193.) If the phrase "FIRST EDITION" has some magic to it, "pre-first" must add to that magic. One can see why the Wise FORGERIES caused such a stir—since they were all "pre-firsts" and thus must have had some cachet for collectors. (*See* Copyright edition.)

PRELIMS (also called "front matter"). The preliminary printed LEAVES in a book—those preceding the main text. The prelims can consist of HALF TITLE, FRONTISPIECE, TITLE PAGE, COPYRIGHT PAGE, DEDICATION, PREFACE, FOREWORD, ACKNOWLEDGMENTS, TABLE OF CONTENTS, table of illustrations or figures, a second half title, an ADDRESS TO THE READER, and so on. If a printed LEAF in the prelims is CONJUGATE with a BLANK, that blank is properly part of the prelims. Not included in the prelims are blanks inserted by the binder. Prelims are often numbered with ROMAN NUMERALS. This was an issue of practicality. In the HANDPRESS PERIOD, if a volume had a table of contents, it almost always was printed after the main text was printed so that page numbers could be put into the table of contents. Since the table of contents was printed later than the text, the page numbers it gave could not be the regular arabic numerals of the text since that text had yet to be printed. It was easy and necessary to give the prelims roman numerals. (*See* Back matter.) (See Ritter, *The Oxford Guide to Style*, pp. 1–13.)

PREMIUMS. At an AUCTION, the auction house does a good deal of work for the CONSIGNOR, so it charges the consignor for its efforts by taking a portion of the hammer price. That portion is called the seller's premium. The buyer, too, must pay for the efforts the house has gone through to get the items to the auction block. The final bidder will pay what is known as the buyer's premium. The amount paid is a percentage of the hammer price, determined by the auction house and agreed to by the consignor and buyer. That percentage was once fairly low—about 10 percent or so. Today the premium could be as much as 25 percent, more or less. Further, the higher the hammer price, the lower the premium could be, on a sliding scale. For example, Sotheby's website delineates what this scale is: "Sotheby's Buyer's Premium for all categories excluding Wine and select Online-Only sales will be: 25% of the hammer price up to and including $400,000/£300,000; 20% of amounts in excess of $400,000/£300,000 up to and including $4,000,000/£3,000,000, and 13.9% of any amounts in excess of $4,000,000/£3,000,000" (Sotheby's, "Update Regarding Sotheby's Buyer's Premium").

Additionally, at least one auction house has initiated a new charge: an "overhead premium." Sotheby's says: "Starting 1 August 2020, Sotheby's will be implementing a new fee—an Overhead Premium—payable by all auction buyers in Sotheby's global salesrooms and online sales. The fee will be 1% of the hammer price. It's the fifth time that the auction house has increased the buyer's fees between 2015 and 2020" (Sotheby's, *TheValue.com*). The site shows what the premiums will be at Sotheby's various auction venues, including a 26 percent premium in the United States and other countries, and the site explains, "The Overhead Premium is a separate fee from Buyer's Premium, which will both be included in the final price realised. Simply put, generally speaking, the newly-added Overhead Premium is similar to a 1% increase in Buyer's Premium." My own term for this added 1 percent is "Premium Creep," referring partly to the slight increase, partly to the person who thought it up. (Is it fair to say that another word for this new premium is "greed"?)

PREPRINT. A copy of an article or chapter from a book that is printed and, often, bound with staples or sewn (sometimes into its own cover) that is sent to an author to distribute to anyone he or she wishes to send it to. It could also be printed for distribution to reviewers or readers for their commentary. The cover may be the journal's own cover LEAF or a separate leaf printed just for the article or chapter. The preprint is usually composed of pages of the actual published journal or volume, so it may have the last paragraphs of a preceding article (and the first paragraphs of a following one) as part of its text. (*See* Reprint.)

PRE-PUBLICATION PRICE. The price a publisher will charge to a buyer who pays in advance of the book's publication. (This is fairly common in the FINE-PRESS world.) A publisher may announce an upcoming publication with a PROSPECTUS, enticing buyers to pay in advance for the coming book, helping the publisher to finance the production of the volume. With cash in hand, the publisher may be able to afford to create a more sumptuous volume than he or she would have been able to do without that money. Hence, pre-publication prices reflect a discount for the buyer, who sends in his cash on the speculation that the volume will indeed be published. The lower price, of course, is an inducement to buy.

PRESENTATION BINDING. A binding of a volume done (usually) on a single copy of a book so that copy can be presented to a special recipient—as a gift, a commemoration, or an award, for instance. In the world of commercial binding, the term has come to mean a binding that has either a clear cover that reveals the title page of the volume, or a one-off cover with decorative elements that make the book stand out in some way. The presentation could be by the volume's author or by the publisher, and the fact that it is "presentation" is clear from the information showing somewhere on the cover rather than on the inside, in which case it would be a PRESENTATION COPY. (Also called a "gift binding.") An author or publisher may even create dozens of such bindings for a single title, one for each person listed, for instance, in the ACKNOWLEDGMENTS.

PRESENTATION COPY. A copy of some item (book, BROADSIDE, PAMPHLET, or photograph) with someone's HOLOGRAPH statement on it showing that it was presented by the signer to some recipient. "Presentation" implies that the *author* is presenting the piece to someone, but it could be anyone doing the presenting: a publisher, printer, illustrator, aunt or uncle, or pastor. The presentation copy's value will be enhanced or diminished by who the presenter and the (supposed) recipient are. A copy of a nondescript and valueless volume presented by its relatively unknown author to Albert Einstein may have some added value if we can prove that the volume was once in Einstein's library—that he held it, read it, or borrowed from it. The presentation could be a fake, the recipient mentioned in the inscription may never have seen the volume, and the whole inscription could be the joke or the ruse of an owner trying to increase the value of a worthless volume. I have seen booksellers say of a presentation copy of an important author giving the book to another important person, "With a sterling PROVENANCE," but with no documentary evidence that the two mentioned parties ever had anything to do with the volume in question.

Further, the implication with the phrase "presentation copy" is that the author has, on her own, chosen to give the volume to someone—as opposed to an INSCRIBED COPY, with a holograph note from the presenter to someone else, the volume having been brought to the inscriber just to get the signature and inscription.

Carter grades presentation copies into six levels of desirability: those with inscriptions from the author to an identified recipient, with the signature dated close to the publication of the volume; the same, but with a much later date or with no date; the same, but with no signature, just a statement that it is "from the author"; with no inscription but revealing that the author (or the publisher at the author's behest) sent the volume; with a manuscript memo in the collector's handwriting saying that the volume came from the author; and with a later memo, with the same information but written by someone else (as by a family member). Carter then says there are other situations in which the volume could be called a "presentation copy," but no matter the classification, a bookseller will want to emphasize the *presentation* nature of the item, and the collector will be happy to have it. (See Carter, pp. 194–95.)

PRESERVATION. The aggregate care of a collection that aims to maintain the body of material in usable condition for as long as possible, as opposed to CONSERVATION, in which individual items are treated (though conservators also monitor environmental conditions and develop strategies for collections care). "Preservation is a global activity—or, really, a series of global activities. That is, caretakers of the library doing preservation work are protecting the collection as a whole by taking a number of steps, all of which, working together, will maintain and protect the holdings over a long period of time. As with conservation, the aim is to keep everything in usable condition. Use is the key here. If an item is preserved in a condition in which it cannot be used, it might as well not exist" (See Berger, pp. 357–84).

These efforts include having (1) a good HVAC (heating, ventilation, and air conditioning) system, (2) good air filtration, (3) controlled lighting, (4) effective pest control, (5) thorough training of staff and patrons on how to use a collection, and so forth. (See Northeast Document Conservation Center, "Preservation Leaflets," https://www.nedcc.org/free-resources/nedcc-publications [accessed 14 June 2021].)

Nicolas Barker introduced this term into the seventh edition of the *ABC* (in 1998), with the opening statement that "preservation" is a newish word in the bibliophilic vocabulary" (7th ed., New Castle, DE: Oak Knoll, 1998; p. 166), a surprising statement since the term and the notion of "preservation" has been applied to books for many decades before that edition was issued, and since he was head of preservation at the BRITISH LIBRARY.

PRESS. The machine used for printing. Thousands of designs of presses have been created, but the basic requirements for an operating press are 1) a place to put the TYPE or other things to be printed (PLATES and illustrations), (2) a means of getting ink onto the surface(s) that need to be printed, (3) a place to put the surface to be printed (e.g., paper, vellum, or cloth), and (4) a means of pressing the printing surface onto the inked surface. Gutenberg's adaptation of a wine or olive press did the trick, and the press has evolved over the centuries to make printing faster and cheaper—but not necessarily better. (See Moran, *Printing Presses*; Perry, "Early Depictions of the Printing Press"; and Sterne, *A Catalogue of Nineteenth Century Printing Presses*.) "Press" is also an old word for a bookshelf, and we thus may hear the word "pressmark" meaning a designation on a book to show where in the bookshelf that volume was to be shelved. The term also could mean a PRIVATE PRESS, as in "she was the proprietor of that press for three decades. (*See also* Pressmarks.)

In the bookbinding realm, there are also various kinds of presses: screw, arming, backing, bundling, nipping, finishing, lying, copy, standing; and also those used in papermaking, to squeeze water out of recently COUCHED or recently SIZED sheets, and to flatten papers. (Descriptions of the binding presses are available at Roberts and Etherington, "Table of Contents"; https://cool.culturalheritage.org/don/toc/toc1.html [accessed 2 August 2021].)

PRESS BOOKS. A broad term for books printed by private presses. (*See* Fine-press printing.) A strong passion for press books over the centuries has yielded a great number of these COLLECTIBLES. Commercial presses may even issue a small number of copies of an edition in a special version—with a slipcase and signed by the author—to make these almost the equivalent of press books. Also, the true press book publishers (of which there are many) are rivaled by hobby printers whose efforts yield some of the same kinds of volumes: issued in short numbers, using good materials (though not always), the edition signed and NUMBERED, with original illustrations, and so on. These hobby printers, however, sometimes produce relatively unattractive pieces with imperfect presswork, amateurish designs and bindings, and an overall look of second-quality work. Whether these fit properly under the rubric "press book" is anyone's opinion. Some hobby printers, on the other hand, produce truly lovely volumes and BROADSIDES. (See Cave, *Fine Printing and Private Presses*; Cave, *The Private Press*; Franklin, *The Private Presses*; Will Ransom, *Private Presses and Their Books*; and Will Ransom, *Selective Check Lists of Press Books*.) For the most part, press books are in the long tradition begun by WILLIAM MORRIS: they are printed LETTERPRESS from HANDSET TYPE (sometimes machine-set types, or, more recently, from PHOTOPOLYMER PLATES) on handmade paper; they often contain original illustrations, done for the edition; many of them use beautiful types; they are bound by hand using the best LACED-IN techniques or with imaginative and decorative bindings; they are often numbered and signed by the printer, author, illustrator, binder, or whoever else had a hand in the production (photographer, papermaker, mother-in-law); and they usually command fairly hefty prices. Some academic institutions have (or have had) their own fine presses, and since the proprietors of them receive their income from the universities or colleges (i.e., they do not need to make a living from their printing), they can issue books at fairly reasonable prices. (See Berger, *Printing and the Mind of Merker*, and Duncan, "Bookworms and Type Lice.")

PRESS CORRECTIONS. *See* Stop-press corrections.

PRESS FIGURES. Numbers, letters, or other symbols in the lower margins of pages—often but not necessarily on VERSOS—that indicate how much type was set by a particular COMPOSITOR or how many IMPRESSIONS were made by a PRESSMAN, both of whom were paid by how much work they produced. "From the late seventeenth until the end of the eighteenth century, British pressmen sometimes set an arabic figure or other symbol at the bottom of a page of the FORME they were about to work off; they would put it in any page that did not already have a SIGNATURE in it. . . . Press figures appear to have been used for two very different purposes. One . . . was to enable pressmen to identify their own work, probably so that they could keep a check on their wages. The other . . . was to enable the master to identify the pressman's work so that he could penalize individuals in cases of bad workmanship. In the first case the pressman voluntarily put his mark on the sheets he printed; in the second the master compelled his pressmen to mark their work . . . fining them if they failed to do so" (Gaskell, *A New Introduction to Bibliography*, p. 133). Carter points out that an examination of these figures could reveal much in terms of the impressions and IMPOSITION of printed books and may explain things about FORMAT, the number of copies printed, and the practices of printing in early shops. (See Carter, p. 196.)

PRESSMAN. A PRINTER. The term "printer," however, can refer to anyone working at the PRESS—including the person who places the paper onto the TYMPAN and then removes it while the pressman is inking the FORME and pulling the Devil's tail. (*See* Bar.) As with the term VATMAN, the implication is that the activity is done only by a man, while history has proved this seriously wrong: some of the important presses in the world have been run by women. However, the term "pressman" is so engrained, and the alternative "printer" is so vague, that an alternative non-sexist term is hard to come by. "Press person" is awkward and cumbersome; "woman printer" does not solve the problem; and "press operator," while doing the trick, still sounds wordy and unwieldy. It may be all we have, unless we understand that when we say "pressman" we are speaking generically, not with any gender in mind.

PRESSMARKS (sometimes hyphenated). A term sometimes used to indicate printers' logos but more properly used to indicate a mark on a volume that designates the location in a library of a particular volume. In early libraries, bookshelves were called "presses." Books were sometimes cataloged by press, shelf, and item number on the shelf. The marks could be letters, numbers, or both, and they might appear on the SPINE of the book or inside on one of the ENDPAPERS, written on the LEAF or TIPPED IN as a LABEL. Because they indicate the place on the shelf where the volume sits, they can be called "shelfmarks" or "case-marks." One famous instance of these marks is the system used by Sir Robert Cotton, whose presses were accompanied by busts of Roman emperors. He designated the presses by the 12 Caesars and two imperial ladies (Julius, Augustus, Tiberius, Caligula, Claudius, Nero, Galba, Otho, Vitellius, Vespasian, Titus, Domitian, Cleopatra, and Faustina; see "Cotton Manuscripts," British Library, http://www.bl.uk/reshelp/findhelprestype/manuscripts/cottonmss/cottonmss.html [accessed 14 June 2021]). Hence, the manuscript containing the works of the *Gawain* Poet was "cataloged" "Cotton Nero A.X"—the shelf beneath the bust of Nero, the first shelf, the 10th volume from the left.

Another kind of press mark (now printed as two words), which appears during the HANDPRESS PERIOD, is a number that might appear in the lower margin of a page, almost certainly indicating the printing PRESS on which the text on that page was printed. According to the Wordnik website, a press-mark (hyphenated) is "[t]he letter or number, printed on the margin of a newspaper, that specifies the press on which it was printed" (Wordnik, "Press-mark").

PRESSRUN. All of the sheets of a single LEAF printed at one time: "The pressrun of this signature was 500 pages." The term also means the total number of copies printed for an item: "The pressrun of the BROADSIDE was 750 copies," or "The volume had an initial pressrun of a million volumes."

PRESSURE-SENSITIVE ADHESIVES / PRESSURE-SENSITIVE LABELS OR TAPES. Any material that causes one SUBSTRATE to adhere to another using pressure rather than chemicals, heat, or water. Booksellers and others often use POST-IT NOTES, to the detriment of the surfaces they adhere them to. LABELS and tapes of all kinds can be had with a slick backing; once the backing is removed, the adhesive is revealed and the label or tape can be pressed into place. The problem with most of these is that the adhesive is not necessarily archival, nor are they removable, except possibly with expensive CONSERVATION. They could damage the substrates also in being much stiffer than, say, a LEAF in a book, so they pose a tearing hazard along their edges, and the adhesive could discolor in time. Their ubiquity, cheapness, and ease of use make them appealing to booksellers and collectors, but their long-term "issues" should be carefully considered before they are employed for BOOKPLATES or labels of any kind, or for repair tapes.

PRESSWORK. The actual work of printing. The term is used almost exclusively in an assessment of the quality of the work being done: "with excellent presswork" means that the item is beautifully printed, with even inking and no great bite into the paper. (The old printer's adage is that fine presswork means that the printer got the type to kiss the sheet, not to bite it.) Bad presswork shows, with uneven inking on a single page and from one page to another; the deep impression the type makes on some or all leaves; the TEXT BLOCK that may not be perfectly squared off on the page, the BACKUP is off, yielding much SHOW-THROUGH; COUNTERS in SORTS that are filled with ink; and so on.

PRICE. In the world of any commodity, prices play a major role. With books, booksellers buy the volumes at one price and sell them at another (presumably higher) price. Though I know a bookseller who bought high and had to sell low to rid himself of his misguided purchases. How prices are determined is a complex matter. (*See* Appraisal.) One piece of information is in order here: A bookseller has overhead that is often invisible to a purchaser—or to someone selling a book to a proprietor of a shop. Since that overhead can be extremely high, the bookseller must factor it into the prices he puts onto the items for sale or how much he pays for items he buys. A canny collector may be able to determine what a fair retail price is for an item, but he cannot expect that a bookseller will give him anything close to that retail price if he decides to sell it to the bookseller. A bookseller must make a profit or he will soon be out of business and on the government dole. If a bookseller pays, say, 50 percent of the retail value of an item, he will usually not be making enough for that item to keep him in business. Hence, I tell my students not to HAGGLE with a bookseller unless there is a good reason to. For instance, if a bookseller is asking $1000 for a book that should sell for $75, the buyer may say something like, "Really?!" That is a subtle way of haggling. Of course, the item may be on the web at a much more reasonable price, and the buyer should just keep his mouth shut and get the copy from the online seller. I once asked a bookseller, "How do you know what a book is worth?" and he replied, "It is worth what anyone is willing to part with for it." I might not pay more than, say, $15 for a book that someone else would pay $100 for—depending on the circumstances. For example, I might not pay $15 for a copy of the COLOPHON if I already owned a copy. But another collector may be lacking a volume from his otherwise complete set, and may be willing to pay $100 for the volume to complete his set. In other words, the price a person is willing to pay can be circumstantial or situational. Hence, the book has two values, one for each of us. Haggling over the price of a book can create bad feelings all around, and can sour the relationship between buyer and seller.

One bookseller told me he acquires an item, figures out how much it cost him, decides what kind of profit he would like to get for it, and prices it accordingly, regardless of its market value. Another bookseller said that he does lots of research about an item so that he knows exactly what its market value is, and then puts a price on it that maximizes his profit. A third told me, "I know what this book's market value is. But I also know that the very best place to acquire this book (a public university) cannot afford it at that value. So I will offer it to that institution at a price I know they can afford." Similar lucubrations go through the mind of a collector.

Books and other library materials have two kinds of value: monetary and intellectual. The price of an item can be affected by both of these, or by other market influences. Does the price paid for an item at an AUCTION determine that item's intrinsic value? Not necessarily. It could be the result of two maniacal collectors "going at it." Does the price listed in a bookseller's catalog determine that item's intrinsic value? Not necessarily. The bookseller, never having seen the item before he acquired it and finding no record of it on the web or in WorldCat [*see* OCLC], may price it ridiculously high or embarrassingly low. And what does CONDITION have to do with price? Plenty. Final word (here—but there really is never a final word about this complex subject): Every item for sale must be priced; every seller must come up with a price that he can live with; every buyer knows if that price is reasonable or not *for her*. And when an item sells at a particular price, both parties must be content: the seller in that he got what he was willing to take; the buyer in that she was willing to part with that much for the item. The seller may learn after the sale that he has seriously underpriced the item. Too late. He has made his profit and that should suffice. The buyer should never think she has been taken ("I paid too much for this."). Too late. At the point of decision-making, she decided it was "worth it," and that is all there is to it. BUYER'S REMORSE will only yield lost sleep, and that is a waste of time and brain power.

PRICE CLIPPED. *See* Clipped/Price clipped.

PRICE CODES. Many a collector will receive a volume from a bookseller with a penciled-in code of some kind and might wonder what that cypher means. The book is priced at $65.50. The code is "RMPE." Many a bookseller will take a 10-letter word with no repeating characters and assign a number to each letter, indicating what the book cost him. If the code word is "trampoline," with t = 1, r = 2, a = 3, and so forth, RMPE = $24.50. The code could also include some indication of date purchased, percentage of markup (e.g., "a" could mean I am doubling the price I paid for the book, "b" = tripling, and so on), or other information. If a customer can figure out the code, he has one foot in the door to being able to ask for a discount if he so chooses. (But see my notes under "Consignment" and "Price.") The word the bookseller chooses could be an indication of where he lives (or wishes he lived: CHARLESTON; BEACHFRONT), what he would rather be doing (LUMBERJACK; EDUCATION), what he is fond of (GODPARENTS; GREYHOUNDS), his mood on the world (DESPICABLY; PHLEGMATIC; SHOCKINGLY; COMPLAINTS), things he likes (ARTICHOKES; FLAMINGOES), or how business is (BANKRUPTCY; MALNOURISH; NIGHTMARES). (See Jackson, *The Price-Codes of the Book-Trade.*) As noted, the code will usually be penciled in on the PASTEDOWN or free ENDLEAF, and a fastidious collector may wish to erase it to remove this "blemish." But the code is part of the book's history—its PROVENANCE—and perhaps some future scholar doing research on book prices may be able to figure out who the bookseller was and to decipher the code. In fact, a penciled-in code does not really deface the volume or reduce its value for most serious book people.

PRICED CATALOGS. *See* Auction catalogs.

PRICE GUIDE. A volume or listing of some sort in which values are given for various kinds of materials. In the book world, these reference tools are in book or pamphlet form, and they can often be had online. (*See* Ahearn Price Guides; *American Book Prices Current*; *Book Auction Records.*) Of course, as the entry at ONLINE BOOK SALES says, increasingly people are turning to the Internet for their appraisal information. Can we then say that the web is a "price guide"? Technically, it is not one, nor do all the sites selling books purport to be price guides. But that is how they are being used. And in their up-to-the-minute nature—what is selling *right now*—they are more current than any volume or database that claims to be a price guide.

PRICE ON REQUEST (P.O.R.). In some dealers' catalogs, when an item or lot is so expensive that the dealer is shy about asking what might seem like an exorbitant price, when the bookseller does not want to shock the potential buyer or scare him away, or for other reasons, the seller may not want to put a price on the item(s), so he instead puts in P.O.R. This is a good ploy, for if anyone is interested enough to call about it, the dealer has identified someone who is interested in it and can then give the caller a pitch to make the sale, justifying the price before he names it.

PRICES REALIZED. *See* Auctions; Auction catalogs.

PRICKING (in manuscripts). The use of a STYLUS, needle, knife point, or other sharp instrument to make holes in a LEAF (or several leaves) of VELLUM or paper. The holes surrounding an image will allow an artist to transfer a copy of that image to another leaf. Also, the pricking can be used to guide the scribe or illuminator in RULING the leaves. (*See* Punctorium.) For instance, the artist can prick holes through the vellum on which is a picture of a lion, the holes made all around the border of the lion image. A piece of vellum or other SUBSTRATE would be placed under the pricked leaf, and POUNCE would be dabbed through the holes to show on the substrate the outline of the image to be copied. The fine details of the picture will not transfer, but the actual size and shape of the original will be delineated by the little dots of pounce.

PRIMARY BINDING. The first binding that a book is given by the original publisher. Carter points out that the term should be used only for books bound in an edition binding and that the term almost always refers to books in publisher's cloth, "though it would be correctly applied to a boards-and-label copy of a book published between 1820 and 1830 if later-issued copies were known to have been put up in gilt-lettered cloth (i.e. after 1832)" (p. 197). Though Carter says that the term is usually used for publishers' cloth volumes, this is tricky since many publishers issued books in more than one color or type of cloth. The "primary" binding may be represented by (i.e., two or more copies were issued with) two or more colors of cloth (e.g., some copies in blue cloth, some copies in red cloth) but with identical decoration and SPINE information. If Carter is correct—that the term is used only for edition-bound books—then it may also be applicable to 20th-century paperbound volumes, and I have seen the term used for this. One of Stephen King's novels was issued by the publisher in five colors of paper wrappers—the artwork and typography otherwise identical on all five. The obvious aim was to sell multiple copies to serious collectors, who would want one of each (along with a hardbound version and a reading copy!). Thus, what is the "primary binding"? It is a term fraught with possibilities, so it has seldom been used in recent times.

PRIMER (rhymes with "simmer"). "An elementary textbook for teaching children to read"; more generally, it is "a book that covers the basic elements of a subject" (*American Heritage Dictionary of the English Language*, p. 1399). These were produced for children in abundance, and in the 19th century they were a major genre of some publishing houses. They consisted of simple reading exercises, stories—usually with a moral to instruct young people—poems, and illustrations. (*See* Hornbook.)

PRINCETON FILE. *See* Book shoe.

PRINTER. The person who runs the printing PRESS. The printing operation in the HANDPRESS PERIOD was usually run by two people: the one who places the paper onto the TYMPAN and then removes it while the PRESSMAN is inking the FORME and pulling the Devil's tail. (*See* Bar.) The term is also loosely used for one who owns a printing establishment, even if that person did not do the actual printing. I have heard people say that WILLIAM MORRIS was a great printer—all you have to do is see the output of his press; but he didn't do the printing.

PRINTER'S COPY. (*See* Follow the flag.) The text (MANUSCRIPT, TYPESCRIPT [from a typewriter], or printed—or some combination of these) that the COMPOSITOR uses to set a text into type. The practice for centuries was for printers to take the manuscripts from authors or editors, set the text into type, and discard the original, the thought being that once the text was available in print in multiple copies, there was no need for the manuscript version. However, a surviving printer's copy for many a volume reveals that compositors err and that authors' original texts are not always faithfully reproduced. The value of a printer's copy, then, can be immense, especially for an editor trying to establish an AUTHORIAL, AUTHORITATIVE EDITION and for the scholars who are the beneficiaries of such an edition. (See Gaskell, *A New Introduction to Bibliography*, pp. 40–42.)

PRINTER'S DEVICE. *See* Printer's mark.

PRINTER'S DEVIL. (*See* Black art.) An assistant in a print shop. The printer's devil could be an apprentice, one who merely washes the type and sweeps the floors, or another worker assigned relatively menial print-shop tasks. As setting type was glorious and remunerative and DISTRIBUTING it menial, the devil was usually given the latter task.

PRINTER'S DUMMY. *See* Dummy; Salesman's dummy/ Salesman's sample book.

PRINTER'S ERRORS. Typographical mistakes made by the PRINTER, as with incorrectly set type, misimposition (*see* Imposition), incorrect PAGINATION, and the like. As Carter says, if the errors are made by an author (or the author requests that the text be changed because he or she is revising), their correction can be charged to the author; printer's errors are the responsibility of the publisher and cannot be charged to the author.

PRINTER'S FIST. *See* Fist.

PRINTER'S FLOWERS. *See* Fleurons.

PRINTER'S KEY. (Also called a "number line.") Beginning in the 1940s, publishers adopted a method of showing where a volume stands in its printing history. The printer's key is a series of letters or numbers on the COPYRIGHT page (usually the VERSO of the TITLE PAGE) indicating the impression of a book. (*See* Edition, Impression [Printing], Issue, and State; Points.) Numbers can be in regular numerical order (1 2 3 4 5 6, and so on), reverse order (10 9 8 7 6 5, and so on), to indicate the PRESSRUN of a book. Letters of the alphabet can be in UPPERCASE or LOWERCASE, and can be in regular or reverse order (A B C D E F G or z y x w v u). Sometimes the numbers alternate from odd to even (or even to odd): 1 3 5 7 9 11 13 15 14 12 10 8 6 4 2. Or they can start at, say, 100, and then descend: 100 99 98 97 96 95. . . . The lowest number (or the letter lowest in the alphabet) visible designates the impression. So a book that has as its lowest number 5 tells us that this is the 5th impression of that book's edition. It is possible, also, that somewhere in this formula a date is given, indicating the year of that impression (6 7 8 9 10 11 12 13 14 15 10 09 08 07 06 05 [referring to 2005, 2006, and so on—with the lowest number shown being the year of printing]). If the book goes into another impression, the "5" is removed from the key, leaving a 6 as the lowest number. Not all publishers use this key, and even those that do use it do not always have such a key since they know the text will not go into a subsequent impression.

PRINTERS MANUALS. Volumes of instruction for printers telling them a great variety of things: sometimes the history of their craft, information on printing practices, presses (making and use of them), ink manufacture and use, how to lay out pages, IMPOSITION for various FORMATS, the operation of a print shop, and much more. The first great such manual was by JOSEPH MOXON, his *Mechanick Exercises on the Whole Art of Printing* (see the bibliography), which was borrowed from and PLAGIARIZED for centuries by innumerable others creating their own such manuals.

PRINTER'S MARK. (*See* Pressmark.) A number, appearing beneath the TEXT BLOCK of a page of type, set by the COMPOSITOR to identify him- or herself as the one who set the type for that page. It can be instructive to a bibliographer trying to figure out who set certain text, the size of the printing establishment, the amount of type a compositor can set at a STINT, and so on. The term (in a different meaning, called "printer's DEVICE") is also used to designate a logo used by a printer to distinguish his work from that of others. As the note at Pressmark says, the number could also refer to the work done by a pressman. Supposedly the first one ever used was by Johann Fust and Peter Schöffer (*see* Gutenberg, Johannes) in the Mainz Psalter of 1457. Hence, the term has come to mean a printer's logo. (See Victoria and Albert Museum, *Early Printers' Marks*; and Winger, *Printers' Marks and Devices*. See also Davies, *Devices of the Early Printers, 1457–1560*; and Moran, *Heraldic Influences on Early Printers' Devices*.) (For a printer's mark, *see* Register [in printing].)

Printer's mark of William Caxton, England's first printer. Reproduced from Henry R. Plomer, *A Short History of English Printing, 1476–1898* (London: Kegan Paul, Trench, Trübner, 1900).

Courtesy of Project Gutenberg; http://www.gutenberg.org/files/20393/20393-h/20393-h.htm (accessed 14 June 2021).

PRINTERS' OVERRUNS/OVERS. Printed sheets from a PRESSRUN that were more than the printer needed and were never used for the final project. Printers wanting to publish an edition of, say, 500 copies may print 550 or more of each SIGNATURE in case of spoilage, damage of some kind (as in folding or binding), or for some other reason. The edition would be bound, and leftover sheets would remain. These "printer's overruns" sometimes wind up as full copies of the published volume but IN SHEETS; they could enter the library of a collector as an unbound copy or as individual LEAVES. They could be used as spine liners in the binding of books or could be used as TIP-INS for a LEAF BOOK. They could be MARBLED over and used as cover papers or ENDLEAVES. (*See* Overmarbled papers.) Or they could have many other uses. (*See* Limited edition.) Sometimes these sheets are called "printer's waste," though they may not be wasted. And if the scrapped pieces are used in bindings, they are called "binder's waste." If the overruns come from an edition of numbered copies, the overs would not be numbered. Bound into covers, they could look like part of the authorized edition (and they are of the same edition in that they are printed from the same setting of type as were all of the other, numbered, volumes of the edition), but they could wind up in the marketplace as "OUT OF SERIES." (*See* Edition, Impression [Printing], Issue, and State; Points.)

PRINTER'S REAM. *See* Ream.

PRINTER'S WASTE. *See* Printers' overruns.

PRINTING (as in "printing a book"). In the HANDPRESS PERIOD and later, the act of pressing onto a SUBSTRATE a text or images or both. The process involves setting the text into type or creating it on any of several kinds of printing PLATES, inking the type or plates, and delivering a sheet of paper, vellum, or cloth (or other material) over the inked surface, then pressing this sheet onto the inked surface to transfer the ink to the substrate.

(For the use of the word "printing" [as in "2nd printing"], *see* Edition, Impression [Printing], Issue, and State; Points.)

Modern folks can now use the word "printing" in a completely new sense, thanks to modern technology. We have all kinds of printers, including older ones (dot-matrix) and newer ones (ink-jet and laser), and many others. The result that all printers produce is text or image (or both) on a substrate.

PRINTING AND THE MIND OF MAN (*PMM*). The title of an influential exhibition held at the British Museum and in Earl's Court in 1963 (see *Printing and the Mind of Man* in the bibliography) and also the title of the catalog published for that exhibition. The catalog has endured as one of the great monuments in the history of printing. The paperback version proved so popular that an expanded version was created, adding significantly to the entries, adding images, and published in hard covers; a second edition also was published. (See Carter, Muir, et al., eds., *Printing and the Mind of Man.*) The exhibition presented the equipment developed over the centuries and the most influential volumes published between the earliest printing and when the exhibit was put on. This monumental exhibition has taken on fabled status, and scholars, booksellers, collectors, and librarians refer to it simply by *PMM*. Booksellers like to emphasize, when they are offering a volume that made it to this exhibition, that the offered volume is from *PMM*. The exhibit had three foci: "to illustrate the internal development of [printing], in the technical progress of printing as a craft; the external development, in the finest achievements of printing as an art; and, beyond the limits of the art and craft of printing, to demonstrate the impact of printing on the mind of man and the effect it has had on the history of the last five hundred years" (*Printing and the Mind of Man*, p. 7). The catalog contained a listing of all the books in the exhibition along with dozens of illustrations of tools and equipment. The standard volume is in two parts. The first is *Printing and the Mind of Man: Assembled at The British Museum and at Earls Court London, 16–27 July 1963* (125 pages plus 32 plates); the second part, bound with the first, is *Printing and the Mind of Man: An Exhibition of Fine Printing in the King's Library of The British Museum, July–September 1963* (62 pages plus 16 plates). The latter of these was also issued as a separate volume—that is, without the British Museum and Earl's Court section. The illustrations show TYPE-CASTING MOLDS, a PUNCHCUTTER at work, PUNCHES, MATRICES, printing PRESSES, printing and type-casting machines and equipment, and much more. Items chosen for the exhibit are seen as so important that they merit mention in dealers' catalogs with a reference to the exhibit: *PMM* 204 (item 204 in the catalog).

PRINTING DAMP. *See* Damp/Damping.

PRINTING FOR THE BLIND. (This is the generic term for printing for anyone who has visual impairments of any kind that make reading difficult or impossible. Though organizations that have been around for a long time have the word "blind" in their name; nowadays one might see such phrases as "printing for the sight impaired" or some other term. The idea is to be more inclusive.) Over the centuries, various methods have been developed to help the sight-impaired to read. Other than printing characters quite large and in dark ink, which works for many people who have partial vision, the most common form of such printing is in tactile characters, made "visible" manually with embossing and using what is referred to as "tactile alphabets." Braille is the most widely used (and best known), though several others were developed, mostly in the 19th century, such as the Moon system (developed by Dr. William Moon), the Valentin Haüy system, and those of several others. (See Lorimer, "A Critical Evaluation of the Historical Development of the Tactile Modes of Reading. . . .")

PRINTING PRESS. *See* Press.

PRINT ON DEMAND (P.O.D.). With modern technology, one can feed a computer a text on a thumb drive or from a computer and generate a bound copy of a printed book. A publisher, not knowing how many copies of a book to print and not wanting to create far more copies than it can sell (and thus have many unsold leftovers—REMAINDERS—on its warehouse shelves), can print only as many as it has orders for: print on demand. This saves money and time, and it is an excellent business model.

Further, P.O.D. publishers can grab any text that is in the public domain—that is, no longer protected by COPYRIGHT—and can offer it for sale as if it has a copy (or many copies) on its shelves, where in reality all it has is a single (analog or digital) copy, from which it can generate as many copies as it has orders for: one or a thousand. The market is now seeing a proliferation of these P.O.D. publishers (Nabu Press, Virtual Bookworm, Lulu, Kessinger, Literary Licensing, Booklocker, CreateSpace, AuthorHouse, Aventine, and many others). These publishers come and go, and there is no guarantee that by the time the present volume is in print, they will still be in operation.

Additionally, authors wanting to self-publish (*see* Vanity publishing) can arrange with a P.O.D. publisher to print up as many copies as they wish to have on hand, paying the publisher only for the copies it supplies. Or they can do the printing themselves, again creating only as many copies as they need. This is especially attractive for authors whose titles fall into narrow niches in the publishing world in which it is difficult to find a commercial publisher to take their works. P.O.D. is inexpensive, relatively quick, and practical for such writers. And with modern printing technology what it is, the products of these P.O.D. publishers are fairly good quality—on archival paper and in decent bindings.

One feature of the P.O.D. environment is that some books are always available—all one needs to do is order a volume, and it can be generated instantly. Thus, titles are always available, that is, "IN PRINT." And a last feature of this phenomenon is that companies in India are able to supply many titles in leather bindings at remarkably low prices. The bindings are no great shakes, but they are leather, and fairly well done.

PRIORITY. A term used by bibliographers to designate the printing of one copy of a text before the printing of another in that edition. (*See* Edition, Impression [Printing], Issue, and State; Points.) How one determines the priority of one copy over another can be tricky. If one copy of a text in an edition has a word spelled "hte" and another copy has the word spelled "the," one might think it is safe to assume that a STOP-PRESS CORRECTION fixed a TYPOGRAPHICAL ERROR. And that might be a good assumption in many cases. But it is possible that a printer had to loosen the TYPE in the CHASE for some reason, and PIED THE TYPE; in resetting the line he could have introduced the typo. Hence, the version with the correct reading is prior to the one with the error. Priority may not be determinable. JACOB BLANCK himself, in compiling his wonderful *Bibliography of American Literature*, sometimes had to say that one volume that differed from another may be earlier or later, but he had to assign them a designation of order. So he called one State A and the other State B, but the priority is indeterminable.

A good example, as alluded to at POINT MANIAC, concerns a change in a copy of Mark Twain's *Innocents Abroad* (the word "flittering"—referring to the sight of distant candles) to the same word in another copy of the same edition ("flickering"). Both words were current in the 1860s when Twain was writing. Which came first, "flittering" or "flickering"? Which impression has *priority*? It is indeterminable, though we can conjecture about one over the other.

Priority inheres as well in DUST JACKETS, ADVERTISING matter, and any other ephemera, but beware! A first edition, first impression could be issued with a particular dust jacket that differs from those on copies of later impressions. An unscrupulous person can take a dust jacket from a first impression (a damaged copy of the book, with, say, water stains on all the leaves) and put it onto a copy of a later printing. (*See* Plate numbers.)

PRISTINE (collector's term). A term some booksellers and collectors use to describe an unblemished copy of a COLLECTIBLE. Other terms that they could use are "like new," "mint," "perfect," or "immaculate." But the suggestion of holiness in the term "pristine" gives it a gloss that proves the point and lends an air of extra value to the piece. (*See* Condition.)

PRIVATE LIBRARY. A library not under public auspices, that is, one whose expenses are covered by private funds. A book collector has her own library—her private collection. And such entities as the HUNTINGTON, the FOLGER, or the NEWBERRY are private libraries. They are governed by their own set of rules, they can regulate who is permitted to use the collection, and they do not need to answer to the city, state, or federal government, except in such matters as are covered by the laws of these bodies. If they use external funding from a government agency, they may be subject to state or federal laws. There is a Private Libraries Association: "Founded in 1956, the Private Libraries Association is an international society of book collectors—collectors of rare books, fine books, single authors, special subjects, and, above all collectors of books for the simple pleasures of reading and ownership. / The Association publishes a well regarded quarterly journal, *The Private Library*. It prints essays on members' libraries, specialised collections, the work of the private presses, illustrators and, indeed, any aspect of the mania likely to appeal to collectors. Reviews of new books are a regular feature" (http://www.plabooks.org [accessed 14 June 2021]).

PRIVATELY PRINTED. Published by a private party, as opposed to publication by a commercial entity. But, as Carter says, often such printing is not done actually privately (and he adds that the term often refers to things not actually published) but was done for an author, not for a commercial publisher, though it could have been produced by a private press. (*See* Fine-press printing.) Sometimes such works are circulated privately or made available by means other than the way commercially published texts are. (See Carter, p. 199.) Carter also mentions the possibility that a commercial publisher who might fear being punished for libel or obscenity may publish a text "privately"—that is, not through its normal public channel but essentially through another means not necessarily traceable to the publisher itself. Many books, intended to be sold, would thus be advertised as being for private circulation. And Carter adds that such volumes are often quite rare, regardless of the size of the original PRESSRUNS.

Of course, Carter is speaking historically. Today, "privately printed" usually means printed by a private press, and it thus has all the implications of that distinction: not necessarily created for profit, done using high-quality materials, with much handwork involved, done in small numbers, often SIGNED and NUMBERED, with special bindings, and intended for a particular discerning audience. And since it was usually done without regard to the costs, the final products could be quite expensive—and desirable to a collector.

One genre of book, EROTICA, along with books on "naughty" or uncomfortable topics were often "privately printed" to save the printer some embarrassment that he had produced such a socially awkward text. Mark Twain's *1601* has appeared in many privately printed versions. In their description of *Amish Love: Adventures in a Puritan Cult* (Florence, Italy: Michael Angelino Press, c. 1930s), Bromer Booksellers says, "This book is part of the swelling trend in the 1930s for 'privately printed' erotic books, which would often be published by anonymous or PSEUDONYMOUS authors and illustrators and printed with fake publication information in order to protect the creators from public backlash" (information sheet from the booksellers).

PRIVATE PRESS. *See* Fine-press printing.

PRIVILEGE/PRIVILEGE LEAF. Carter talks of the 1709 COPYRIGHT Act that solidified, to some extent, the protection an author or publisher had in a published work. Before that, however, PERMISSION had to be sought from some "competent authority" (Carter, p. 199) for the right (or privilege) to print a text "within the area of the authority's jurisdiction"; such permission was given for a specified amount of time. The privilege would be noted in the published work by words like "cum privilegio," printed somewhere in the volume or on a separate leaf laid or TIPPED IN (a "privilege leaf"). Carter also points out that there are some examples after 1700, but mostly the practice precedes the 1709 date mentioned above. The privilege was also granted, in some limited cases, for the right to reproduce a pattern on a decorated sheet, as with the example shown below. (*See* CPSCM; Imprimatur; *Nihil obstat*.)

Sheet of dutch gilt paper with the "privilege" stamped in the block. The sheet is exhibited in Albert Haemmerle, 2nd ed., No. 130, p. 207: "Cum Privilegio Sac. Caes. Mai. Anno 1723 Jos. Frid. Leopold Excud. Aug. V." Berger-Cloonan Collection of Decorated Papers, Texas A&M University. The notion of privilege, it is clear from this sheet, extends to works of visual arts, not merely written texts.

Courtesy of Cushing Library, Texas A&M University.

PRIZE BINDING; PRIZE BOOKS. A decorative binding, usually in CALFSKIN, placed on a volume that was given to a recipient (usually a student) as a prize for some achievement. The recipient's name would be displayed somewhere on the volume, often on a BOOKPLATE TIPPED IN to the ENDPAPER, and the reason for the prize would be stated on the plate. Roberts and Etherington say, "A style of fine binding employed in northern France and the Netherlands as early as the 17th century, in Ireland (Trinity College, Dublin) from the 18th century, and in England from the last quarter of the 19th century until the First World War. In England, the bindings were produced in a common pattern consisting of a full calfskin cover (usually of a dark color), worked HEADBANDS, run up GILT backs and colored title LABELS, two-line FILLETS on the covers ending with a rosette, and with the arms of the particular school BLOCKED on the upper cover. The endpapers and edges were MARBLED, often matching in both color and pattern, while the TURN-INS and edges of the BOARDS were decorated with a ROLL in BLIND. The books often included, inserted before the title page, a printed or manuscript form giving the subject in which the prize was awarded, the name of the recipient, the date, etc." (Roberts and Etherington, "School prize binding"; https://cool.culturalheritage.org/don/dt/dt2975.html [accessed 1 March 2021]).

These bindings were used on prize books, though not all such books were in special bindings. As Christian Coppens explains, "Most of the time the binding indeed plays an important role, but a binding does not always identify a book as a prize book. Usually the binding for a prize book was specially made for it, but sometimes it was not, when an old book in its original binding was simply recycled to serve as a prize" (Coppens, "The Prize is the Proof: Four Centuries of Prize Books" in Mirjam M. Foot, ed., *Eloquent Witnesses: Bookbindings and Their History*. London: The Bibliographical Society of The British Library; New Castle, DE: Oak Knoll Press, 2004). The Coppens article is the most circumspect on the subject.

PROCRASTINATOR'S NIGHTMARE. *See* Buyer's remorse.

PROCTER, ROBERT GEORGE COLLIER (1868–1903). Bibliographer and librarian, working at the British Museum from 1893 till his disappearance and presumed death in 1903. (His hike in the Austrian Alps was the last known sighting of him.) Procter was one of the most authoritative scholars on INCUNABULA and early 16th-century printing. He organized the British Museum collection of early books into a new arrangement, "A system of classification according to geographical origin, printer, and chronology for early printed books, first used in Proctor's Index" (Lexico: Oxford English and Spanish Dictionary, Synonyms, and Spanish to English Translator, "Procter Order"; https://www.lexico.com/en/definition/proctor_order [accessed 6 June 2022]), a method still referred to as "Proctor order" (or "Proctor's order). The index referred to is the massive 908-page volume *An Index to the Early Printed Books in the British Museum: From the Invention of Printing to the Year MD*, with Notes of those in the Bodleian Library. The work that Procter (and by Francis S. Isaac, who compiled a supplement) did has been superseded by the BRITISH MUSEUM CATALOGUE OF BOOKS PRINTED IN THE FIFTEENTH CENTURY, a fully online database.

PROGRESSIVES. A series of printed leaves of an item that is printed in more than one color, the individual leaves showing, first, the single color of the first-printed image and, second, the image with all preceding colors printed one upon the other. Hence, if a chromolithograph is printed in, say, 10 colors, the first of the progressives will show color 1; the second will show color 2; the third will show colors 1 and 2 printed together; the fourth will show color 3; the fifth will show colors 1, 2, and 3 printed together; and so on. The final product will be the multicolor image, and the progressives will be the full set of single-color and multicolor prints. If the final picture is composed of 25 colors, there will be 49 progressives (one for color 1 and two for every additional color). (*See* Chromolithography.)

PROOF BEFORE LETTER(S). A "PROOF taken before the title or INSCRIPTION has been ENGRAVED" (Merriam-Webster online, "Proof before letter"; https://www.merriam-webster.com/dictionary/proof%20before%20letter [accessed 15 March 2021]). When an engraver is preparing a PLATE, she may take a series of proofs of the image only (whether that image is verbal or pictorial—or both). There was no need to do the extra work necessary to engrave the title of the print, the name of the publisher, the name of the engraver, the image number if it was to be in a series in a volume or set, the date, and so forth. That kind of information is the last to be added to the plate. Such a state of the plate would be called the "proof before letter." (*See* Edition, Impression [Printing], Issue, and State; Points.) Also, if the publisher aimed to have a DELUXE or super-deluxe VERSION of the text, she may wish to have the images bound into the volume, but a separate suite of the prints could be inserted into a pocket or envelope in the book or the box housing the book. Those prints (as the old advertising ploy used to state, "suitable for framing") may be taken before letter.

PROOF COPY. *See* Proofs.

PROOF PRESS. A printing PRESS designed to print PROOFS, usually while the type is still in a GALLEY. In the United States, type height has for more than a century been .918

A table-top proof press, "Introduction to Letterpress Printing in the 21st Century; http://www.fiveroses.org/intro.htm (accessed 14 June 2021).

Courtesy of International Printing Museum, Carson, California.

inch. If the type is in the BED OF THE PRESS, the distance between the bed and the PLATEN had to be .918 inch for the type to print. It was easier to make corrections for set type while it was still in a galley, so presses were developed that would take the set type, still at the proof stage, so that the distance between the foot of the type and the platen would be .918 inch plus the thickness of the bed of the galley. To take proofs, printers did not need perfect REGISTRATION, so they could merely lay a sheet of paper over the type to do the printing. Mechanical proof presses were developed for more sophisticated printing, especially for multicolor work. "Proof presses print four or more color jobs one color at a time, registration being accomplished with a scope or other device. Proof presses are used to check the color balance and the efficacy of ink color mixing" ("Proof Press," PrintWiki, http://printwiki.org/Proof_Press [accessed 14 June 2021]). (See also Moran, *Printing Presses*, pp. 249–52.)

PROOFREADER'S SYMBOLS. The marks a proofreader uses to tell the COMPOSITOR what changes must be made in PROOFS to achieve a perfectly printed TEXT. An elaborate set of symbols has evolved, each indicating changes that need to be made. For example, a single underline means "ITALICIZE." Two underlines mean "print in SMALL CAPS." Three underlines mean "print in UPPERCASE." A CARET (^) means "insert."

PROOFREADING (also called "copyediting"). Checking a text for TYPOGRAPHICAL ERRORS and other things that need to be fixed before a text can "go to press." The proofreader looks also for problems with the text—its intellectual as well as its mechanical parts. (*See* Proofs.)

Having worked as an editor for half a century and more, I know that "perfect proofreading," especially for longer texts, is a most difficult goal to achieve. After more than a dozen proofreadings of a text I did many years ago—and add to that the parallel proofreading done at the publishing house—the final text had at least two typos, discovered during a casual reading after the publication of the volume. There is an old adage that an author cannot proofread his own text perfectly, for the errors he makes he will overlook in his proofing. This may be so for some writers; others are exceptionally careful and can proof their own work with as much accuracy as can anyone else looking at the same text. Proofreading is a chore, a task, and an art. From what I see in today's newspapers and magazines, it is becoming a lost art. (See Simpson, *Proof-Reading in the Sixteenth, Seventeenth and Eighteenth Centuries.*)

PROOFS (uncorrected; corrected). Printed matter that needs to be proofread for errors or other kinds of changes. There are traditionally two levels of these: GALLEY PROOFS and PAGE PROOFS. Once the proofs have been read and the corrections made, the text can be printed from what are called the "corrected proofs," presumably error-free copy. The author's set of proofs, if they survive, are likely to show EMENDATIONS as well as REVISIONS and can be eminently collectible. A proof copy with emendations in the author's handwriting, showing PROVENANCE and the care with which the author saw her text through to publication, is obviously UNIQUE and thus quite desirable to the collector, especially for major authors. (For more, see Carter's discussion, pp. 178–79. See also Gaskell, *A New Introduction to Bibliography*, pp. 110–16.) (*See* Advance sheets.)

As Gaskell points out, in early printing, "it had been the COMPOSITOR's duty to correct or NORMALIZE the spelling, punctuation, and capitalization . . . of the MANUSCRIPT" (*A New Introduction to Bibliography*, p. 110), so variations in PRINTER'S COPY and the final printed version were expected. The compositor, however, was not expected to change the substantive readings of the text. He adds that "in the HAND-PRESS PERIOD, when the printed text was not a literal reproduction of the manuscript but a normalized version with much alteration of detail, the corrector preferred to have the copy read aloud to him by his reader while he followed the proof and marked the mistakes" (p. 112).

It is to be noted that sometimes several sets of proofs will be made—and *read*. One kind of proof is sometimes called the "author's proofs" (or the "master proofs"), those sent to the author. These would be the same as those sent to others (as for an in-house editor, for instance), but if they contain marks from the author, they are clearly "author's proofs," as mentioned above, and they carry much weight—and can be quite valuable, textually and monetarily. And also if one is dealing with compositors whose native language is not the same as your own, you cannot guarantee that the corrections delineated by the author will be made.

The term is often used in the phrase "proof copy" of a book—an early printing of a text, the copy to be sent to a proofreader or reviewer. (*See* Review copy.) Sometimes such early printings will be issued in an inexpensive paper cover and with some kind of statement such as "If the reviewer wishes to quote from this book, please do not do so from this proof copy. Contact the publisher for an approved text."

PROPRIETARY TYPE. A TYPEFACE commissioned by a private party, a press, a publisher, or anyone else to be designed for that party's use only. Presses, such as the Kelmscott and the Doves and that at the University of California, designed their own typefaces or had them designed for them. (*See* Morris, William; Cobden-Sanderson, Thomas James.) On the basis of the proprietary type designed for R. Clay and Sons, Printers, GRAHAM POLLARD and JOHN CARTER were able to prove that many of the pamphlets produced by THOMAS J. WISE were FORGERIES. As noted, anyone—or any entity—can commission a proprietary typeface. Ernst Detterer created one for the bindery at the NEWBERRY LIBRARY. (See Clarke, "Just Our Type.)

PROSPECTUS. An ADVERTISEMENT for a volume usually sent out in advance of the publication of the book to announce the book's impending availability. They take many forms, but most often are single- or two-leaf items. Prospectuses are, for the collector, almost an essential appendage of the book since a copy of the book without its prospectus will be worth less than one with it. The prospectus will often be printed on the same kind of paper used in the book, will have an illustration that will appear in the volume (if it is an illustrated book), and will contain information that the book itself will not have: date of completion, number of copies printed, price(s) (e.g., there may be a "PRE-PUBLICATION PRICE"), biographical information about the author or illustrator, binding information (binder and materials used), and so on. A well-conceived prospectus, sent out plenty in advance of the book's publication, will be revelatory to the publisher of what the interest in the volume might be and could influence the number of copies the publisher prints. Also, if the prospectus generates enough advanced sales, the publisher may have additional cash on hand to justify creating an even more sumptuous volume than they could have afforded without the advanced sales income. As an advertising piece, however, a prospectus may be seen as a piece of EPHEMERA, but the kinds of books that generate prospectuses are collected by the kind of people who know the importance of these pieces and who are likely to keep them with the published volume. Sometimes, as with some of the volumes published by HENRY MORRIS at his Bird & Bull Press, the number of subscribers to the press obviated the need to send out such advanced notice since the entire edition would have been sold upon publication; so no prospectus was needed. But Morris produced one anyway, explaining to me that his subscribers expected a prospectus with each book, so he printed one up and inserted it into the volume when it was mailed out to the subscribers. (*See* Laid in.) Further, I have in my collection a prospectus for a book that was never issued (and the proof of another prospectus from a different press for another book that was never issued). In both cases, the prospectus exists, but no publication exists for either of these texts. So a prospectus could generate a GHOST BOOK. Finally, if a prospectus is issued laid in to the volume, a bookseller may have in her description of the book, "With the prospectus laid in, AS ISSUED."

Additional note: I recently discovered an elaborate prospectus in my library for an expensive book—the prospectus being a stapled pamphlet of many pages. It is a full text in itself, and while it has all the requisite information to sell the book (it is, after all, an advertising piece), it can be seen as a work of scholarship on its own. A search of the web revealed two copies on offer, each for over $120.

PROTO-PAPER. A material that is not paper (i.e., it was not produced from macerated and matted fibers) but that looks like and can function like paper. Such SUBSTRATES as AMATE, TAPA CLOTH, and PAPYRUS are proto-papers.

PROVENANCE. The lineage of ownership (or at least the handling) of a book or other item. The fact that a book was once in the hands of such and such a person is part of the volume's provenance, even if that person was not the item's owner. Provenance is discernible by a number of clues: ownership stamps or LABELS, SIGNATURES, library cataloging or PRESSMARKS, marginal notes, bindings (e.g., with a family crest), insertions, external evidence (e.g., a letter from an author stating that he or she has had a particular binding put onto a volume, family papers showing purchases and other acquisitions, or from AUCTION records), or some other information. The former owner could be anyone: the author, a well-known scholar, a politician, a bookbinder, a teacher, an actor, an aviator, a prominent collector, or anyone else who might be COLLECTIBLE in her own right—apart from the subject matter of the book. Or the provenance can be shown to be of no consequence at all—an obscure shoemaker, a teller in a bank, or someone else of like anonymity.

As with other things that affect a book's fiscal and intellectual value, provenance can be enhancing or detracting.

From a librarian's or scholar's perspective—and often from the collector's view as well—provenance information should not be removed when the book is changing hands. However, a thief will want to remove provenance information, and someone wishing to make money on the volume may wish to remove the BOOKPLATES and penciled-in notes of a previous owner whose marks would detract from the book's value or prove the item to be stolen. Equally, adding in spurious provenance information (as with a signature or a bookplate) could add to the value of the item, so buyers must be wary of such enhancements.

Obviously, provenance can seriously enhance a volume—in terms of its fiscal and its intellectual value, regardless of whether the provenance markers are contemporary with the book when it first appeared in the world or whether they are modern. That is, a volume's value could be enhanced if provenance information shows that it was handled by Voltaire, but it could be equally enhanced if we can show that Albert Einstein owned it. It could also be increased by showing provenance information as having been in a prestigious library. (For an excellent treatment of provenance, see Pearson, *Provenance Research in Book History*, in which the many kinds of things that show provenance are discussed; see also de Ricci, *English Collectors of Books & Manuscripts [1530–1930] and Their Marks of Ownership*.)

The Society of American Archivists defines "provenance" as "1. The origin or source of something. 2. Information regarding the origins, custody, and ownership of an item or collection" and adds that "[p]rovenance is a fundamental principle of archives, referring to the individual, family, or organization that created or received the items in a collection" ("Provenance," Society of American Archives, http://www2.archivists.org/glossary/terms/p/provenance [accessed 14 June 2021]). In the art world, the word has different shades of meaning: "Art provenance is the history of a painting, its creation and ownership used to help establish its authenticity. Documents used for provenance include sales receipts, auction and exhibition catalogs, gallery stickers on the painting, letters from the artist, statements from people who knew the artist, or circumstances of the painting. These must mention the painting specifically enough for it to be identified, not in vague or broad terms" (Cook, "Art Provenance," https://adcook.com/provenance/ [accessed 3 July 2021]). Since special collections in libraries are often linked with archives, with overlapping holdings, and since many pieces of art exist in special collections and rare book libraries, curators must be sensitive to all of these meanings.

And an additional note: If a valuable volume of a scarce and collectible book surfaces, booksellers, librarians, and collectors must try to determine its provenance. The appearance of something sought after by collectors and librarians must raise suspicion, especially if the item has no known provenance. Signs of the removal of ownership information should be looked for carefully.

PROVINCIAL BOOKSELLERS' FAIRS ASSOCIATION. From 1972 until today, an organization in Great Britain that takes books to the people. "The idea of bookseller Gerry Mosdell was to take books out to the people with 'Book Fairs'. The first event was held in the Hotel Eden in Kensington in 1972. / The Fairs expanded rapidly and after the first York Book Fair in October 1974 the Provincial Booksellers' Fairs Association or PBFA was founded. / Our fairs now cover the length and breadth of the country. Our members display a wide variety of books both second-hand and ANTIQUARIAN and often with PRINTS, maps and EPHEMERA. Our Code of Practice ensures all items are correctly described and fairly priced. / We are a 'Not for Profit' association and our fairs are run by volunteers and supported by staff at our Royston offices. / The Association continues to show resilience and initiative in challenging times. Our new website, using the latest technology, helps us to keep in touch with a modern world. . . . Affiliated Membership is open to bookbinders, conservators, FINE-PRESS publishers, packaging suppliers and others who supply the book trade" (https://www.pbfa.org/about [accessed 3 July 2021]). The organization's original "intention [was] providing a group of twenty or so British provincial second-hand booksellers with a shop window in London by organizing book fairs. From such modest beginnings, it grew to have more than 600 members and has become an organization capable of mounting some 100 book fairs a year across the whole of the UK. It is the largest association of its kind in the world, and its annual September fair in York is the largest such event in Europe" (Worms, "Provincial Booksellers Fairs Association [PBFA]").

PSEUDANDRY. "[U]se of a masculine name by a woman as a pseudonym" (Merriam-Webster Online, "Pseudandry"; https://www.merriam-webster.com/dictionary/pseudandry [accessed 2 March 2021]). The English Project website says, "When women first came to publish, they often adopted a man's name. That practice is called pseudandry: Greek for 'false-man'" (The English Project, "The Woman's Page"). Perhaps the most famous of these women are Charlotte, Emily, and Anne Brontë (who published as Currer, Ellis, and Acton Bell) and Mary Ann Evans (George Eliot). More recently there is Robert Galbraith (that is, J. K. Rowling of Harry Potter fame).

PSEUDONYMOUS PUBLICATION. The publication of an item under an assumed name. (The assumed name is often called a "Nom de plume.") For a host of reasons, works can be published with a false name credited with authorship. (*See* Halkett and Laing; Stratemeyer Syndicate.) (See Wikipedia, "Pseudonym," https://en.wikipedia.org/?title=Pseudonym [accessed 14 June 2021]). The pseudonymity gives a volume an air of mystery, and, of course, it allows a writer to (try to) conceal himself. Thanks to works like Halkett and Laing (the way this famous reference tool is generally referred to) and others, the identity of the pseudonymous author can often be revealed. In 1994, Shadow Books of Philadelphia issued a catalog (No. 50) with 75 pseudonymously published items. The catalog reveals that N. W. Clerk was actually C. S. Lewis; Geoffrey Crayon, Gent. was Washington Irving; Christopher Crowfield was Harriet Beecher Stowe; and Jedediah Cleishbotham, School-Master and Parish-Clerk at Gandercleuch, was Sir Walter Scott. (The proprietor[s] of Shadow Books, himself/herself/themselves are not identified and tried to remain in the shadows. But thanks to James N. Green, Emeritus Librarian of the Free Library of Philadelphia, we learned that the catalog was done by David J. Holmes, proprietor of David J. Holmes Autographs of Philadelphia. His name and the name of his firm are not printed anywhere in the catalog, but a search of his catalogs in the Columbia University Libraries online catalog reveals that they hold Holmes's catalogs 8–49 and 51–78. When they were cataloging the collection of these booksellers' catalogs, they may have come upon "Shadow Books, Catalog 50" and not recognized it as that of Holmes. Here we have yet another reason that authors remain anonymous: for fun.)

As the entry at STRATEMEYER SYNDICATE indicates, some writers made their living (or a good portion of it) creating stories pseudonymously. For example, J[ohn] W[illiam] Duffield wrote 115 volumes of young adult fiction for Stratemeyer, using the pseudonyms Franklin W. Dixon (under which name he wrote Hardy Boys books), Richard H. Stone (Slim Tyler Air Stories), Allen Chapman (The Radio Boys series), Victor Appleton (the Don Sturdy sequence), and Roy Rockwood (Bomba the Jungle Boy). (See fadedpage.com, https://www.fadedpage.com/csearch.php?author=Duffield%2C%20J.%20W.%20%28John%20William%29 [accessed 26 July 2021].)

PUBLICATION. The releasing to the public of a text. Most definitions say that a *book* is given to the public, but the item published could be a BROADSIDE, a PAMPHLET, a photograph in a folder, or something else. The act of release is called "publication," but so is the item so released. Hence, "The publication of this publication took place on Father's Day."

Carter points out that even if a copy of a book is created only for COPYRIGHT purposes (*see* Copyright edition), if it was PRIVATELY PRINTED or was issued only for subscribers (*see* Subscription sales), the release of the item to the public constitutes *publication*. (See Carter, p. 203.) I am not sure this distinction holds today—despite the fact that "publication" and "public" are cognates. When I print a small run of a volume of verse that I give to my friends, I still think of this as publishing. But for the British audience, Carter says that "publication" implies that the item is offered to the public for sale. He says that for an item to be considered published, in British law, copies of the item must show proof of being sold or offered for sale in the public. The fact that an item is registered with the STATIONERS Company or is deposited in the nation's copyright library (the British Library) has no bearing on its status as being "published." And he says that the day an item is first made available to a buying public can be considered its day of publication since those copies are to be considered those that the publisher wishes to be seen as being published in its publisher-approved final form. ADVANCE COPIES, proof copies, and TRIAL ISSUES, and the like—usually getting out into the world before the to-be-sold copies are made available—are not strictly to be considered published (see Carter, p. 203).

A key consideration, then, is whether the item is (1) offered to the public and (2) for sale. In the United States, I am not sure this distinction holds as a definition of "publication." If publishing is getting materials to the general public, who is the general public? If I give a copy of my own "publication" to some friends—or even to just one friend—is that person part of the general public? Is this publication? Is dissemination to a single person enough to constitute publishing? And is sale, as Carter emphasizes, necessary? What about a run of books—say, 10,000 copies—that are printed and bound and then *given away*? By Carter's definition, these are not published since they were never sold or offered for sale.

Also, a publisher can be the company that creates the item so published or the person who owns the company. ("The American Library Association is an important publisher of books on librarianship." "David Godine is a keen judge of what will sell; he was a successful publisher.")

PUBLIC DOMAIN. When a work is not protected by COPYRIGHT, it is said to be in the public domain. Various kinds of works are in the public domain, including, in the United States, works for which copyright has expired; items published by the federal government (since taxpayer funds have paid for the publication of these works, the text belongs to the taxpayers); and titles (of books, plays, movies, and the like). If a bookseller wants to use in a catalog anything in the public domain, she is free to do so without needing to obtain PERMISSION. Scholars may quote freely without permission from anything in the public domain. But determining when something is in the public domain could be difficult in some circumstances. In the United States, for instance, copyright inheres for 70 years beyond a maker's death; sometimes determining when a person died can be challenging.

PUBLIC LIBRARY. A library open to all, funded by and thus accessible to all those who contribute (through their taxes) to the library's existence and operation. The public library is one of the great inventions of humankind, offering information to all regardless of social status, wealth, or education level. Many are run by professional librarians, though in some communities that cannot afford such positions, they may be run (on a curtailed schedule) by paraprofessionals or others. Their main aim is to serve the public, and all members of their public may avail themselves of their services at no cost to them.

Their holdings are eclectic and wide ranging. They, of course, will have books, usually recently published and selected by the people who work there with the interests of their immediate clientele in mind. But they will also have music in various formats, books "on tape" (i.e., digital books), and many other materials for their patrons to check out. Some have framed artwork that they loan out for people to take home. They will have computers for patrons to use to access their catalogs but also for them to do research on—especially useful for people who cannot afford computers and for those who are unemployed to seek jobs. Hence, they are especially vital in financially hard times (when governments, in their bizarre and perverse wisdom, wish to close down libraries and cut back on their resources).

Carter says that the proliferation of public libraries in the 19th century powerfully increased literacy and strongly escalated the publication and sale of books. And he extolls Andrew Carnegie, whose largesse led to the building of more than 2,500 such libraries in the United States, the United Kingdom, Ireland, Canada, Australia, and other countries. (See Carter, p. 203.)

PUBLIC RECORDS OFFICE. *See* National Archives.

PUBLISHED PRICE. *See* List price.

PUBLISHER. "A person or business that produces and distributes something, such as a book or magazine, in printed or electronic form" (*American Heritage Dictionary of the English Language*, p. 1424), for distribution to some audience—public or private. In the first two centuries of printing, publishers and printers (and, hence, booksellers) were one and the same. Eventually, these became separate trades. As the *American Heritage* definition says, the publisher can be a person, and indeed there has been for centuries a practice of self-publishing (*see* Vanity publishing), culminating in today's inundation on the market of self-published books. The word could also mean a person who is at the head of a publishing house ("Alfred Knopf was a great publisher"), and that house could be the disseminator of books, magazines, newspapers, flyers, or any other printed matter that "goes public." And, more recently, the term has been used to refer to people who publish on the World Wide Web (*see* Online book sales), as with a blog or a producer of electronic games or as someone with her own website from which text of one kind or another is disseminated. In the world of the book, we can identify the "publishing house," the way we refer to a publishing business. "Scribner's was a great publishing house." And emanating from that locution, since publishers had their own style sheets, the publisher may be seen as shaping communication in its own preferred way.

PUBLISHER'S BINDING/PUBLISHER'S CLOTH. (*See* Binder's cloth.) The binding placed on books by the publisher, not by a later binder. This simple definition is complicated since a publisher may issue a volume in 2 or 3 or 10 different bindings, either at the volume's initial issue (*see* Edition, Impression [Printing], Issue, and State; Points) or over time. And while the term could be used for any standard binding that publishers used (including leather or paper), it has come to designate almost exclusively the kind of cloth bindings that came into general use in the 1820s. (See Morris and Levin, *The Art of Publishers' Bookbindings, 1815–1915.*) Where once such bindings could be had inexpensively, there has been a vogue in collecting these sometimes quite beautifully designed and executed books, and their prices have risen dramatically for good copies in the past two decades. The possibility of covering their books with pretty cloth and with multicolored and gold-foil-stamped cloth led publishers to adopt this medium, which, not coincidentally, was far less expensive than leather. Such bindings became popular with publishers, also, because the new cloths that were developed at the beginning of the 19th century allowed for inexpensive cases to be made. (*See* Case bound.) So the cheapness of the product was enticing to publishers and to collectors who saw the attractiveness of the books without seeing their cheapness, which manifested itself over time. (*See* Trade binding.)

PUBLISHER'S DUMMY/PUBLISHER'S SAMPLE BOOK. *See* Dummy; Salesman's dummy/Salesman's sample book.

***PUBLISHERS WEEKLY*.** One of the most important and long-serving periodicals in the United States that serves the publishing industry and all associated with it. "First published in 1872, the magazine began as The Publishers' Weekly [*sic*; no itals.], a collective catalogue for publishers to pool their resources. That listing of books enabled

BOOKSELLERS to learn about FORTHCOMING titles, and eventually the publication expanded to include features and articles. / Publishers Weekly attempts to serve all involved in the creation, production, marketing and sale of the written word in book, audio, video and electronic formats" (Publishers Weekly, "About Publishers Weekly"). The information published in *PW* (as it is often referred to) can help bibliographers, booksellers, and other researchers in identifying and dating untold numbers of books. But as the note at "Forthcoming" says, such information is not always reliable since *PW* could announce the publication of a book based on the information they received from a publisher only to find that that volume never made it to print. Or items could have made it to print but were not picked up by (or announced in) *PW*.

PULLED PASTE PAPER. Decorative PASTE PAPERS made by applying colored paste to the surfaces of the sheets, placing these wet surfaces together, and then pulling them apart. The result is a striated "pattern." Additionally, while the two sheets are still touching, the artist can manipulate the paste by applying various kinds of pressure to them so that when they are pulled apart, the patterns created by this pressure are visible. They were made with one or more colors of paste, and the designs could be somewhat controlled by the way the pressure was applied.

PULLING THE DEVIL'S TAIL. *See* Bar; Black art.

PULL-OFF BOX. "A simple or elaborate bookshaped box designed primarily to hold a book, but also used to contain PAMPHLETS, MANUSCRIPTS, etc. Occasionally it opens at the side or front, but it more often consists of two separate parts, one telescoping over the other, hence its name. In its most elaborate form, it often has a rounded back (SPINE) with RAISED BANDS, projecting squares, a leather covering, and possibly one or more spring catches. When properly constructed, it provides nearly air-tight protection. The book is generally provided with a separate WRAPPER. Also called 'pull-off case' or 'pull-off cover,' and frequently, though incorrectly, a SOLANDER BOX" (Roberts and Etherington, "pull-off box"; https://cool.culturalheritage.org/don/dt/dt2717.html [accessed 18 January 2021]). Two points to make: First, this description says "nearly air-tight." Books and other library materials generally should not be put into completely sealed containers since changes in humidity or temperature could cause condensation inside the container, leading to the formation of mold. Second, this kind of box is often the repository for books in PARTS. Innumerable 19th-century serial publications like the works of Charles Dickens were issued over many months in FASCICLES; once the text was complete, the owner had a pull-off box made for them, with a CHEMISE encircling the fascicles so when they were removed from the box they would not rub against the sides of the container. These boxes contained the full text of a book; and though the parts were all separate pieces, the owner took the opportunity of having a protective enclosure made to make the whole package look like a book. The binders carefully constructed the top part of the box (the one that got pulled up to reveal all the pieces inside) to fit over what looked like raised bands on the lower part of the box, thus concealing the opening where the two parts of the box separated from one another. Seen on a shelf, then, this pull-off box looked like a leather-bound volume with raised bands.

PULP FICTION/PULP MAGAZINES. A genre of publishing—developed in the United States at the end of the 19th century—in which the final product is printed on extremely cheap paper, made from wood pulp and, hence, with a fairly short life. (*See* Sulphate and sulphite.) "The age of the pulps lasted roughly from 1896 to 1955. (Frank Munsey's *Argosy Magazine* [1896] is considered the first of the pulps.) By the fifties the pulps were being replaced either by illustrated men's magazines, usually in the large flat FORMAT, or digest magazines in the smaller format, roughly 7 × 5 inches. Both of these are sometimes also referred to as pulps. The digests often used pulp paper, but strictly speaking they are a different category" (The Pulp Magazines Project, "Mike Ashley's 'The Golden Age of Pulp Fiction' "; http://pulpmags.org/history_page.html [accessed 14 June 2021]).

The common genres were crime and detective magazines, science fiction, war stories, and westerns, and once the pattern was set, by the 1920s, they were usually illustrated with garish cartoon images, often featuring women in distress (usually with not too much clothing on), nasty criminals, good guys versus bad guys, and so on. The covers were festooned with lurid pictures, promising sensational stories within. They were read with gusto by adults, and collections of these cheap magazines survive, usually not in good condition, in many libraries. (See Ellis et al., *The Adventure House Guide to the Pulps*; Goodstone, *The Pulps*; Goulart, *Cheap Thrills*; and the extensive online site The Pulp Magazine Project, http://www.pulpmags.org/default.htm [accessed 14 June 2021]. For a bibliography of works on pulps, see ThePulp.net, http://www.thepulp.net/pulp-info/pulp-bibliography/pulps-in-general [accessed 14 June 2021].)

PUNCH/PUNCHCUTTER. The metal bar on the end of which is the character, in RELIEF, that will be struck into a MATRIX for casting TYPE. The character's design is drawn onto the flat tip of the punch, and the punchcutter carves and files away everything else, leaving the character in

Punch of a dollar sign. The difficulty of creating such a punch—with its little counters and all of the counter punches necessary to fashion it, made the creation of this a tour de force of the punch-cutter's skill. Photograph by Jeff Dykes.

Collection of the author.

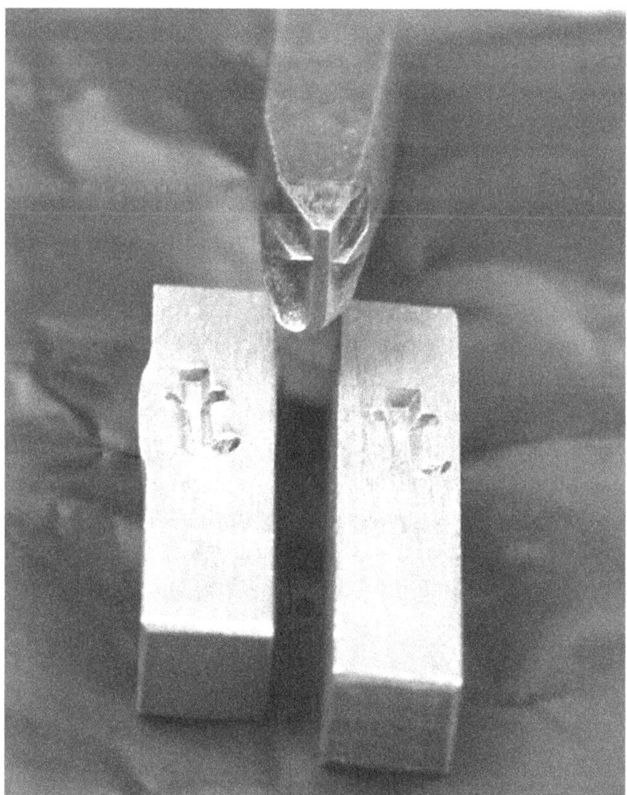

Punch, with unjustified and justified matrices. (*See* the entries for Justification [in type making] and Matrix.) The unjustified matrix on the left is a "strike." Photograph by Jeff Dykes.

Collection of the author.

relief. The punchcutter may also need a COUNTERPUNCH to remove the metal from the punch where a COUNTER will be in the cast SORT. While the punchcutter (the person making the punch) is doing his work, as he approaches the final look of the character being prepared, he holds the punch into the smoke above the flame of a candle to deposit some of the flame's soot onto the face of the punch. He then presses the punch against a piece of paper, essentially "printing" the character on the sheet. This is called a "SMOKE PROOF." After several smoke proofs are taken and the character is now shaped at the end of the punch exactly as it should look when it eventually becomes a sort (a piece of type), the punch is now ready to be hardened. It is held in a flame and then plunged into cold water (the "Bessemer process," by which iron is hardened into steel). The steel punch is now hard enough to be used over and over again to make matrices.

PUNCTORIUM. The tool used by scribes to punch holes into VELLUM for ruling and for copying images and MAJUSCULES. (*See* Model book.) The tool, like an awl, usually had a wooden handle and a sharp metal point. It could pierce several pieces of vellum at once. Cheryl A. Rychkov says, "Once the QUIRE was assembled, the pages needed to be pricked. This series of tiny holes running the vertical length of the margins, was created by a scribe using a punctorium (a stylus) or a 'star-shaped wheel mounted on a handle, which when pushed or pulled along a surface would prick it quickly and consistently'" ("Medieval Manuscript Production"; Rychkov cites Vladimir Baranov, "Materials and Techniques of Manuscript Production," Medieval Manuscript Manual, http://web.ceu.hu/medstud/manual/MMM/about.html [accessed 4 July 2021], p. 4; see also Diringer, *The Book before Printing*, p. 210). (*See* Pricking [in manuscripts]; Rule.) The wheel looked like a small circular blade of a pizza cutter (also on a handle), with needlelike teeth projecting out from the wheel. It could be run up (or down) the right and left margin, piercing the vellum with equally spaced holes that would be used as guides for the one ruling the pages. Since most ruled leaves have vertical rule as well as horizontal, the pricking is sometimes done along the top and bottom margins as well as vertically.

The tool was also used for pricking holes in leather, as for use in shoemaking, and—more to the point [pun intended] for this dictionary—it could be used in copying a character or image from one manuscript into another. (The method is described at POUNCE and PRICKING.) That such wheels were used in manuscript ruling is attested to by the fact that many manuscripts survive with marginal pricking still in place; and a recurring "mispositioned" hole recurs. That is, for instance, if one "needle" on an eight-pin wheel was slightly

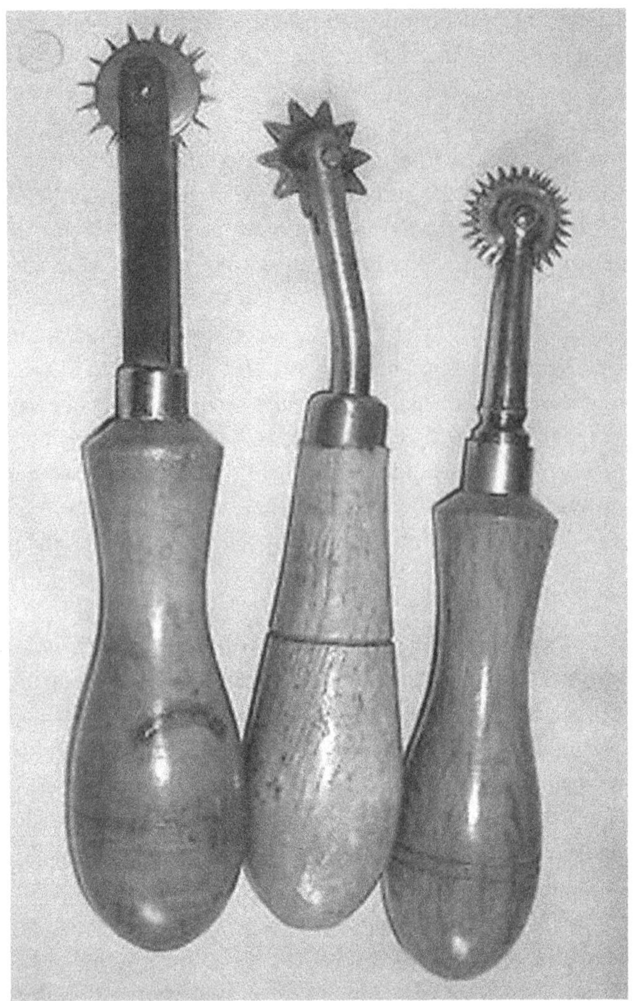

Three wheel-style punctoriums used for pricking to rule manuscripts. The ones shown here were designated for leather work, but the same principle works for paper or vellum ruling and decoration. Each of these shows a different spacing for the holes to be punched.

Exhibited on WorthPoint; https://www.worthpoint.com/worthopedia/x-vintage-leather-work-stitch-marker-531856485 (accessed 10 August 2021).

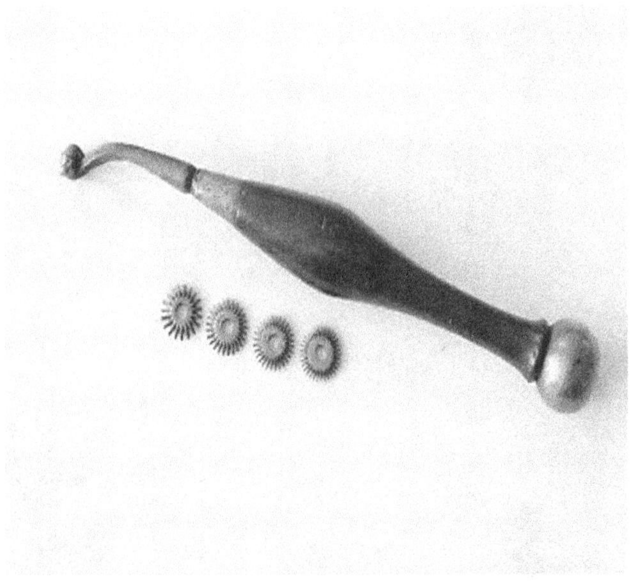

A vintage tool with four pricking wheels, giving four different distances between the pricked holes.

"Vintage Vergez Blanchard Pricking Wheel"; https://picclick.com/Vintage-Vergez-Blanchard-Pricking-Wheel-275cm-4-323470984866.html (accessed 4 July 2021).

bent out of place, it would punch a hole slightly off where it should be; and every eighth hole along the margin of the LEAF would show this "defect." (See also Gould, "Terms for Book Production in a Fifteenth-Century Latin-English Nominale.") (Peter Beal calls this a "parchment-runner." See *A Dictionary of English Manuscript Terminology*, p. 283.)

PYROXYLIN. (Also spelled pyroxyline. Also called "nitrocellulose.") A chemical substance used to make lacquers, plastics, and artificial leathers, among many other things. It is used to strengthen papers, but, most important for the present dictionary, by the end of the third decade of the 19th century it was used to coat or impregnate CLOTH to add strength and "body" and improve durability. The extensive use of pyroxylin in the book world made cloth bindings durable, and it changed the world of bookbinding. The cloths can be stretched over BOARDS, stamped in gold or printed on, or have LABELS pasted on. Pyroxylin brought a whole new world to PUBLISHERS' BINDINGS. (See BPG [Book and Paper Group] Cloth Bookbinding in the bibliography.)

Q

QUADRILLE. Also called "graph paper." Paper ruled horizontally and vertically. Used by book designers, especially those who design using the grid system. (See Berger, *The Design of Bibliographies*, pp. 15–16.)

QUADS (quadrats). Printer's measures, equal to about the size of an uppercase *M*. Hence, a cross section of a quad is a square. A quad is also called an EM QUAD. Half the width of the em is the EN QUAD. It was used as spacing and to fill up a line of type in the COMPOSING STICK. There are also 3-to-em, and 4-to-em quads (i.e., 2 en quads make up an em, 3 3-to-em quads make up an em, and 4 4-to-em quads make up an em).

QUARTER-BOUND. Bound with the SPINE and small triangular areas of the corners on the front and rear covers using one material, the rest of the BOARDS using another. Traditionally, the spine and corners were leather or vellum, and the rest of the binding was paper or cloth, but any combination of materials was possible. A volume could also be bound with the corners and spine of one kind (or color) of paper, the rest of the binding in another color of paper. (*See* Full binding; Half-bound; Half cloth; Three-quarter bound.)

QUARTO. A book FORMAT in which the original full sheet has been folded twice to produce a relatively squat volume with horizontal CHAIN LINES (if it is printed on LAID PAPER), with four LEAVES to a SIGNATURE. There were no standards of paper sizes, so a quarto—which one might expect to be smaller than a FOLIO (since the folio was produced from sheets that were folded only once)—could be larger than a folio. That is, a quarto produced from a very large sheet could be larger than a folio produced from a much smaller sheet. Once books were produced—from the early 19th century on—from high-speed presses, the distinctions among formats became unclear, and booksellers and collectors (and even librarians, who should know better) started calling books by the names of the formats based on their size rather than on the number of times the original sheets were folded. Since the "original sheets" were massive rolls of paper, the original terms for formats were based on size, not on the number of times sheets were folded. The term derives from the Italian, meaning "one-fourth" (of the original sheet). (*See* Size [of books].)

QUATERNION. "A gathering consisting of four sheets folded once, and insetted" (Roberts and Etherington, p. 210). "Insetted" means "nested." As such, this term—used in the world of medieval manuscripts—is essentially the same as a folio in 8s. (*See* Format; Quinion.)

QUESTION MARKS. The use of this piece of punctuation in bibliographical or cataloging records generally means that the immediately preceding statement (like a date or place of publication) is in question. "Freiburg (?): 1774 (?)." It could also signal the laziness of the cataloger who has not troubled to try to find out the accurate place or date, especially when that information is often available in a database like WorldCat (*see* OCLC).

QUILL. A bird's feather, used as a writing instrument. In fact, the modern "pen" comes from the Latin word *penna*, meaning "feather." Quills were in use from at least the 6th to the 19th centuries. And modern calligraphers may still use one. A slightly curved segment at the tip of the quill is sliced off, and a small slit is made in the center of the remaining tip, parallel to the shaft of the feather. The slit allows the ink to flow. To prepare the feather, the quill maker removes the feathery part (the "barbs")—which is not needed and can be a nuisance in writing. Once the tip of the feather is sliced off, some of the barbs part can be stuffed into the hollow shaft of the feather, the perfect material for soaking up and holding the ink. With the quill filled with the barbs, ink will stay in the barrel of the quill, and the SCRIBE does not need to dip and write, dip and write, dip and write too frequently. In movies we see the frequent dipping and the barbs wafting back and forth. (The moviemakers are taking the stance, "Aren't we smart! We know that this author used a quill to write with, and we will show you how clever we are by leaving that feathery part showing." This is a historical blunder since the exposed barbs serve no function, and they are in the way. Practically all medieval depictions of scribes show a barbless quill in use.) Feathers from swans, turkeys, ducks, geese, crows, and other birds were used, and they were usually the largest from each wing. Peter Beal says that the flight feathers were used. Scribes could create extremely fine or quite broad written lines, depending on the size of the feathers and how the quill was cut.

To sound especially knowledgeable, some people claim that only the left wing of certain birds can be used for writing since it curves in a particular direction such that it does not obscure the vision of the scribe. (See Brown and Lovett, *The Historical Source Book for Scribes*, where, on p. 8, they say, "Feathers from a bird's right wing curve naturally to the left and so are best suited to left-handers.") But the actual part of the quill that is used is quite short—only about six inches long. This is far too short for any curvature to figure into the use of the feather. As noted above, some of the barbs may be shoved into the open tip of the quill to help the quill retain ink, but practically all medieval depictions of scribes show a barbless quill in use.

QUILLING. (Also called "paper filigree.") An art form in which the maker rolls thin strips of paper, manipulating them into various shapes, and gluing them down into patterns. "Quilling was first practiced [in the West] by Renaissance nuns and monks, who made artistic use of the gilded edges of worn-out bibles, and later by eighteenth-century ladies, who made artistic use of lots of free time" (Helen Hiebert, *Playing with Paper*, p. 124). A craft used in ARTISTS' BOOKS and the making of other kinds of paper art likely to be found at ANTIQUARIAN BOOK and EPHEMERA fairs. Eugene Aronsky says, "Quilling began as an art form in the ancient world. Although its exact origins are unknown it is believed that Quilling began in Ancient Egypt. The etymology of 'Quilling' is thought to have originated from the bird feathers, or 'quills' that were used as a primary tool to roll the strips of paper. Although this artform has ebbed and flowed throughout the centuries, Quilling makes many appearances throughout history and gave birth to spinoff artforms such as metal filigree, a popular artform used in Renaissance churches" (Aronsky, quillingcard, "The Mighty Quill: The Art of Quilling"). Of course, the "ancient Egypt" dating is inaccurate if paper was the medium, but the art does seem to predate its European appearance.

QUINION (also called a "quinternion"). A volume may be made up of SIGNATURES containing 10 LEAVES each, each signature composed of five FOLIOS (since they are folios, the original sheets from which they are made are folded only once), nested into one another to form a GATHERING of those 10 leaves (yielding 20 pages). Each gathering (signature) is a quinion. The term, from the world of medieval manuscripts, means the same as a folio in 10s. (*See* Format; Quaternion.)

QUIRE. In the composition of books, the same as a GATHERING, a SECTION, or a SIGNATURE. In the world of paper, a quire is "a twentieth part of a ream, the number of sheets in a quire varying with the nature of the ream (*Mill*, *Perfect*, *Inside*, etc. . . .), but usually taken to mean 24 sheets of paper probably due to the old method of counting in dozens, now 25 in reams of 500 sheets, of any size, folded to half-length, that is, once in the middle of the long way" (Labarre, *Dictionary and Encyclopaedia of Paper and Paper-Making*, p. 218). Labarre points out that such folding yields the verb "to quire"; "Hence, 'to quire', vb. to fold two or more sheets together in the centre so that they will lie one within the other" (p. 218). He points out that the phrase "in quires" means "IN SHEETS," and he adds that "[t]he word is derived from *O. Fr.* [Old French] *quaier*, *Med. Lat. quaternus*, a set of four, and originally meant a set of four sheets of parchment or paper, a common unit in medieval manuscripts, so as to form 8 leaves = 16 pages" (p. 219).

QUOINS/QUOIN KEY. (Sounds like /coins/.) Metal wedges used in the CHASE to tighten up the TYPE against the inner walls of the chase. The original quoins were made of wood, and they were tapped into place with a mallet tapping a SHOOTING STICK (for an image of shooting sticks, *see* Pica pole). So-called high-speed quoins, developed to hasten the lockup of the type, come in several lengths.

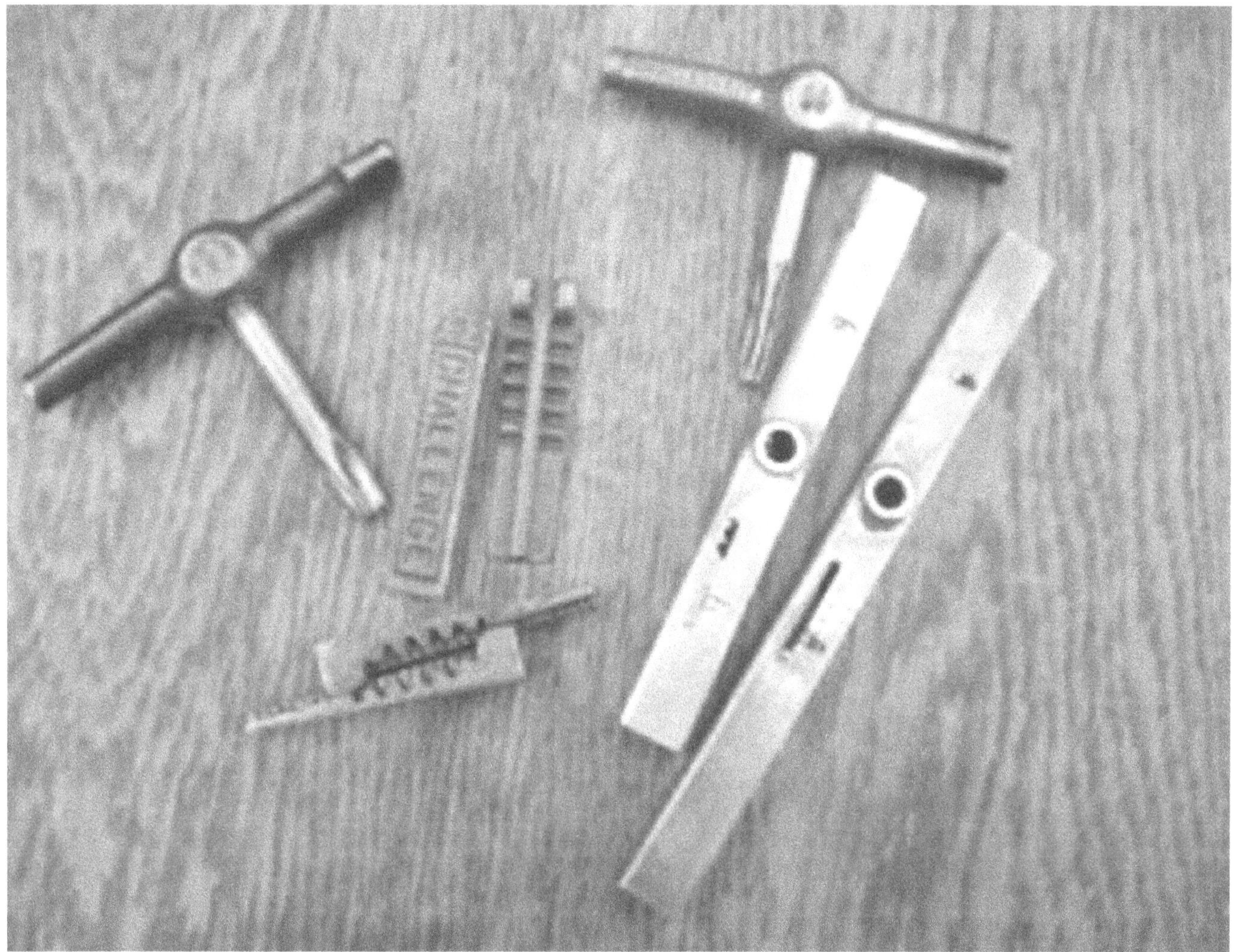

Challenge metal wedge-shaped quoins on the left; high-speed quoins on the right, and quoin keys for each.
Collection of the author.

QUOTES (a bookselling term). Offers made to potential buyers from booksellers. If the bookseller has a particular item that she knows would be perfect for an institutional or private buyer, rather than listing it in a catalog or online, she might quote it directly to that customer. This arrangement works well for many buyers and sellers. For the seller, it saves the time and effort of listing it in a public forum (in a catalog or online), and it maximizes the chance that the item will sell if the buyer is well chosen and carefully thought out as being interested in the item(s) quoted. And it gives the buyer RIGHT OF FIRST REFUSAL for the item—so that he does not have to compete with all the others out there who might be interested in the piece. The quotes will typically have a full description of the book or manuscript (or whatever!), along with a price. The bookseller will usually expect a "yes" or "no" from the person quoted in a reasonably short time (a few days) so that if the item is not of interest, the seller can then quote it to others or list it publicly.

R

RADIO STAR SERIES. *See* Big Little Books.

RAG BOOK. A children's book printed on rag (that is, cloth). The idea, of course, is that cloth has more chance of surviving the depredations of little hands than does paper. Don't count on it! Have you seen what little hands can do?! For this reason, finding these—especially those from the early 20th century—in good condition is a challenge.

RAG PAPER. In the Middle Ages, a guild called the Rag Pickers was active, supplying paper mills with whatever they could scrounge up. "Rags, formerly the principal, if not the only, source of raw material for the manufacture of paper, are now rarely used except in the highest grades of writing and printing papers (hand-made & machine)[,] blottings and parchment stocks. Hence 'rag' paper, 'rag content' implies a large proportion of rags in the paper" (Labarre, *Dictionary and Encyclopaedia of Paper and Paper-Making*, p. 219). Roberts and Etherington say of rag book paper, "A wide range of book papers having a cotton fiber content of 25, 50, 75, or 100%, the one with 100% being known as 'Extra No. 1.' Such paper is used for currency, ledger, manifold and ONIONSKIN, blueprint and other reproduction papers, maps and charts, etc." (p. 212). Until the almost complete takeover of wood pulp for making paper, most papers through the first three-quarters of the 19th century were made of rag. Books and other documents made with this paper, if properly stored, will be in good condition today since the papers had no INHERENT VICE, unless the rags were bleached and the bleach was not properly removed during the papermaking process.

RAGGED RIGHT. *See* Unjustified.

RAISED BANDS. "The cords or thongs on which the sections of a book are sewn. The cords, of which there are traditionally five (but which historically have varied from two to as many as fourteen) are seen as ridges across the SPINE of the covered book. Raised bands have long been associated with the best of fine hand binding and the tight back. False raised bands, which are generally glued to the hollow of the spine, are sometimes used to give the impression of flexible sewing" (Roberts and Etherington, p. 212). (*See* Cords; Endbands; Headbands; Recessed-cord sewing.)

In the 19th century, with the coming of book CLOTHS and the development of CASED-IN BINDINGS, quite beautiful bindings were executed, but with inexpensive materials and techniques. Binders, knowing that their customers would see raised bands as a sign of a handmade (i.e., expensive and quality) product, developed the false raised bands that Roberts and Etherington speak of. The only way to see if the raised bands in a tight binding were genuine was to take the volume apart.

RAISED INITIAL. The first letter of a text (at the beginning of a chapter, section, paragraph, and so on) that has its

From fairest creatures we desire increase,
That thereby beauty's rose might never die,
But as the riper should by time decease,
His tender heir might bear his memory:
But thou contracted to thine own bright eyes,
Feed'st thy light's flame with self-substantial fuel

Raised initial that has been kerned (*see* Kern; kerned)—that is, after the opening letter "F," the letters "rom" have been moved over to the left to prevent the text from having a large space between the "F" and the "rom."

From Allan Haley, Fonts.com, "Raised and Dropped Initials"; https://www.fonts.com/content/learning/fontology/level-4/fine-typography/raised-and-dropped-initials (accessed 12 July 2021).

Starbuck was no crusader after perils; in him courage was not a sentiment; but a thing simply useful to him, and always at hand upon all mortally practical occasions. Besides, he thought, perhaps, that in this business of whaling, courage was one of the great staple outfits of the ship, like her beef and her bread, and not to be foolishly wasted. Wherefore he had no fancy for lowering for whales after sun-down; nor for persisting in fighting a fish that too much persisted in fighting him. For, thought Starbuck, I am here in this critical ocean to kill whales for my living, and not to be killed by them for theirs; and that hundreds of men had been so killed Starbuck well knew. What doom was his own father's? Where, in the bottomless deeps, could he find the torn limbs of his brother?

Raised initial.

W3C; https://www.w3.org/TR/2014/WD-css-inline-3-20141218/ (accessed 12 July 2021).

baseline at the same level as that of all the other characters in the line but that is larger than the rest of the type and thus stands above the other characters. (*See* Drop cap.)

RAMAGE PRESS. A completely or mostly wooden common press, built by Adam Ramage (1772–1850). In America, he was a prolific manufacturer of presses for many years. The earliest ones were made all of wood. "[A]fter a time they were constructed of wood and iron, and toward the close of his life they were made entirely of iron" (*American Dictionary of Printing and Bookmaking*, p. 484). All of Ramage's presses—especially the wooden ones—were light, fairly portable, sturdy, and serviceable. The BED of the press was either small enough that it could be a one-pull operation (i.e., the entire FORME could be printed with a single pull of the BAR) or large enough to be a two-pull press (i.e., requiring the printer to roll the bed under the PLATEN halfway, pull the bar to print the first half of the sheet, then roll the bed the rest of the way to allow the printer to pull the bar a second time to print the rest of the sheet). Thus, some Ramage presses are called "two-pull presses." Ramage invented a good number of presses, and since his work was copied by others, the presses from the end of the 18th century and the first quarter of the 19th (especially wooden ones) are often called "Ramages," though many of them were not of his manufacture. "[I]t is clear that the use of the generic term, 'Ramage Press,' is quite misleading" (M. Hamilton, *Adam Ramage and His Presses*, p. 27). Milton Hamilton concludes, "He was a pioneer in the spread of printing. More than other American pressmakers he paved the way for the early printers, and his widespread manufacture made his name a household word" (p. 29). (See also Moran, *Printing Presses*, p. 47; and Saxe, "Ramage Proof Press.")

RANGANATHAN, SHIYALI RAMAMRITA (1892–1972). "Indian librarian and educator who was considered the father of library science in India and whose contributions had worldwide influence" ("Shiyali Ramamrita Ranganathan," *Encyclopaedia Britannica*, http://www.britannica.com/biography/Shiyali-Ramamrita-Ranganathan [accessed 14 June 2021]). Ranganathan's chief technical contributions to library science were in classification and indexing theory. His *Colon Classification* (1933) introduced a system that is widely used in research libraries around the world and that has affected the evolution of such older systems as the Dewey Decimal Classification. Later, he devised the technique of "chain indexing" for deriving subject-index entries. Other works of his include *Classified Catalogue Code* (1934), *Prolegomena to Library Classification* (1937), *Theory of the Library Catalogue* (1938), *Elements of Library Classification* (1945), *Classification and International Documentation* (1948), *Classification and Communication* (1951), and *Headings and Canons* (1955). His *Five Laws of Library Science* (1931) was widely accepted as a definitive statement of the ideal of library service and still influences librarianship worldwide. The five laws are as follows: books are for use, every reader his (or her) book, every book its reader, save the time of the reader, and the library is a growing organism.

RANGING FIGURE. *See* Lining figure.

RAP. *See* Regional Alliance for Preservation—Association of Regional Conservation Centers.

RARE BOOKS AND MANUSCRIPTS SECTION. *See* RBMS.

RARE BOOK SCHOOL/RARE BOOK SCHOOLS. When someone in the U.S. rare-book field uses the phrase "Rare Book School," the first thing that comes to mind is the school at the University of Virginia. It was founded by Terry Belanger at Columbia University in 1983. After Columbia closed its library school, RBS (as it is often called) moved to Virginia in 1992. The school offers a wide variety of classes to guide those in the field of rare books (librarians, booksellers, students, collectors, and faculty). Today, other Rare Book Schools offer similar courses, such as the one at the University of Illinois, Urbana–Champaign, which at one time gave a certificate in rare books, and California Rare Book School at the University of California, Los Angeles. Other schools around the United States—while not formally "rare-book schools"—offer courses of value to those in the field: the University of Utah, the University of Alabama, the University of Iowa, Simmons University, the Claremont Colleges, Colorado College, the Texas A&M Book History Workshop, Wellesley College, and several others. The University of London Institute of English Studies sponsors The London Rare Book School, a series of courses—online—throughout the year. There are also other programs in Europe, Australia, and New Zealand. See the Internet for these constantly changing programs.

RARITY. In a glossary about books, one can hardly find a more germane term than "rarity" since many of the readers of this volume are concerned about values of their holdings, and this is tied closely to rarity. It is no wonder, then, that this term generates one of Carter's longest entries, in which he expatiates on this concept, and it is worth reading for his knowledge and biting wit. His opening statement, typical of his approach, calls rarity "the salt in book-collecting," but he points out that too much of that seasoning will ruin the food and it could make one sick. And he is biting about collectors who value rarity over other criteria in collecting (see Carter, p. 206). The key points are that there are degrees of rarity, it is partly a function of how hard it is to acquire a copy of an item, rarity is sometimes (often) not at all related to the intellectual value of a book, the notion that a title is easy to procure undercuts that item's rarity and interest in it as a COLLECTIBLE, and so forth.

He then distinguishes several kinds of rarity: absolute rarity (books produced in small numbers), relative rarity (the number of copies that survive, even if the original PRESSRUN was large—measured by how often an item appears on the book market), temporary rarity (caused by a shortage of a title that only recently has become COLLECTIBLE), and localized rarity (referring to scarcity of a title beyond the geographical area in which it was produced or collected) (Carter, p. 206). I would like to add to this categorization, *perceived rarity*—that is, the general notion of booksellers and collectors that a particular item is hard to come by based on their own experience. But this last category is being undercut—as are many of these types of rarity—by the truly miraculous availability of items on the web. (*See* Online book sales.) My own search for volumes that were once impossible to find has yielded sometimes several copies of what I thought I would never see. Certainly, I can cite many titles that I know are not available on the web (or possibly anywhere else), but I can also show the existence of a host of copies of books I searched for unsuccessfully for decades before the coming of online sales. That is, for any given title, its originally perceived rarity is possibly undercut by the unbelievably high number of items that are now available on the Internet.

Also, Carter says that rarity inheres in some titles that have not been sought after, so no one has kept (or even recalls seeing) a copy. Thus, rarity in such an instance has no bearing on value. What he is obviously implying is that supply and demand are at play here and that a book that is invisible because no one has ever wanted to collect it (hence, one that is exceptionally scarce) may have no value, while a volume that is scarce because there are more people searching for it than there are copies available could command quite high prices. And Carter cites Charles Lamb's observation that 10th editions are harder to find than first editions (see Carter, p. 207). One way to assess the rarity of a volume is to check its availability on the web. How many copies are listed in, say, VIALIBRI? When was the last time the item came up at an AUCTION? How many copies are listed in WorldCat (*see* OCLC)? (Booksellers often say, "Only two copies listed in WorldCat." This could mean that the item is quite rare or that it is a book that practically no library would have—like some of the romance or science fiction volumes of the 1950s and 1960s, in acidic paperback versions, brittle and falling apart, books that many libraries never collected. It is perhaps ironic that titles originally intended for the masses tend now to be found in libraries' special collections departments.)

Carter's entry also divulges the several ways that booksellers (and others) express the rarity of a volume: by pointing out the low number of the title in published sources (as just noted, now we can look to online bookselling sites and to WorldCat), by saying that the bibliographer whose work would normally include the volume in question has overlooked (i.e., was unaware of) the volume, by showing how seldom the item appears on the market (especially at auction), and so on. Carter points out that scarcity is relative to other features: a book could be quite rare in one state (*see* Edition, Impression [Printing], Issue, and State; Points) and not in another, rare in fine condition (one might see a bookseller's description that says, "without the usual fading of the publisher's cloth—rare in this condition"), rare with its dust wrapper (*see* Dust jacket), or rare with certain accompanying materials ("seldom seen with its original laid-in PROSPECTUS"). And Carter concludes that all statements about rarity are subjective, often coming from sources who are not too well informed or experienced, and that the words used to express levels of rarity are not fixed in the vocabulary of the book world, so terminology may be imprecise when it comes to accurate delineations of what is rare (see Carter, p. 207). One bookseller's "exceptionally rare" could be another's "uncommon; I have had only three copies of this in my 20-year career."

Carter, in chapter 12 ("Rarity") of his *Taste and Technique in Book Collecting*, says there is "localized rarity" (as noted above)—meaning that a volume may be rare in one geographical place and not rare in another. A volume published in Paris might be easily obtainable there but difficult to find in London. He says, "The great body of books of . . . localized reputation . . . will naturally remain rarer of occurrence outside their own area of demand" (p. 141). This whole notion was worth noting in Carter's day, but the concept melts away in an online environment, when books are now available worldwide from any computer with Internet access. (*See* Online book sales.)

As I already noted, however rare an item is may have little to do with its fiscal or intellectual worth. A MANUSCRIPT—which by definition exists in only one EXEMPLAR—may be worthless, depending on who the writer is, the condition of the piece, the nature of its content, and, ultimately, the demand for it on the market. Supply and demand will dictate value. No demand = no value, regardless of how rare an item is.

I recently uncovered in my own library three early 20th-century publications—8½ × 11 inch pamphlets, two that were done for advertising purposes, the third an issue of a newsletter from an arts club in Philadelphia. Each is beautifully produced, on high-quality paper, with good text and many clear and informative illustrations. I can find no record of these anywhere, though for the newsletter I can find a record of a notice that the club planned to issue such a newsletter. I have looked through every online database I can find to see if I can locate copies of these pieces: no luck. Even the Free Library of Philadelphia did not seem to know of the newsletter from a club in their own city. These might qualify to be called "rare," though since they are "UNKNOWN," there is no demand for them. If they were made known to a wide audience, would there be a demand? Does demand that exceeds supply automatically yield rarity?

RATTLE. "The sound produced by snapping or shaking a piece of paper . . . indicative of hardness and, generally speaking, of quality. The hardness is due to the degree of wetness of hydration of the pulp, and linen rags will give a toughness and rattle to papers which (are said to) distinguish them from that made from cotton" (Labarre, *Dictionary and Encyclopaedia of Paper and Paper-Making*, p. 220). Rattle is also affected by the amount and kind of sizing a sheet has and the weight of the sheet. (*See* Weight [of paper].)

RBMS (Rare Books and Manuscripts Section). (Here listed under the acronym since it is the standard way of referring to this organization.) The section of the Association of College and Research Libraries (a division of the American Library Association [ALA]) that "strives to represent and promote the interests of librarians who work with rare books, manuscripts, and other types of special collections" (http://rbms.info [accessed 28 June 2021]). RBMS holds its own conference annually (preceding the annual ALA conference), focusing on issues in the rare-books field; it has several standing committees; it offers scholarships; and it publishes its own journal (*RBM: A Journal of Rare Books, Manuscripts, and Cultural Heritage*; formerly titled *RBML* [*Rare Books and Manuscripts Librarianship*]). "The roots of RBMS go back to 1948, when an ACRL University Libraries section meeting was devoted to the topic of rare books. In 1955 an ACRL Committee on Rare Books, Manuscripts, and Special Collections was formed 'to promote wider understanding of the value of rare books to scholarly research and to cultural growth, [and] bring improvement to the care, use and recognition of rare books in all libraries.' As part of a 1958 reorganization of ACRL, the Committee became the Rare Books Section. / From its inception, RBMS has attempted to foster communication between special collections librarians and assist in their professional development. To this end, it first held a preconference in 1959 and has held one annually every year since 1961" (http://rbms.info/history [accessed 14 June 2021]).

RBMS THESAURI. As early as 1979 the RESEARCH LIBRARIES GROUP petitioned the Rare Books and Manuscripts Section (*see* RBMS) of the AMERICAN LIBRARY ASSOCIATION to create tools to assist librarians in cataloging their rare materials. Over several years, RBMS created six THESAURI, each containing the terminology needed for such cataloging. The thesauri covered the various kinds of information needed for rare book records: Binding; Genre; Paper; Printing and Publishing; Provenance; Type Evidence. Other areas of cataloging needs may be satisfied by other thesauri, as, for instance, with the ART & ARCHITECTURE THESAURUS done by the Getty Research Institute (see https://www.getty.edu/research/tools/vocabularies/aat/ [accessed 29 July 2021]).

Regular library cataloging, then, is supplemented or aided by the six RBMS documents, which have much more specific terminology than standard library records offer. "The RBMS thesauri provide standard terminology for access to these items as called for in the Independent Research Libraries Association's Proposals for Establishing Standards for the Cataloguing of Rare Books and Specialized Research Materials in Machine-Readable Form (Worcester, Mass., 1979). There is the possibility of overlap among the six RBMS thesauri; some terms may be repeated in more than one thesaurus" (RBMS, "RBMS Manual / Thesaurus Construction and Maintenance Guidelines"; https://rbms.info/rbms_manual/thesaurus_construction/ [accessed 29 July 2021]).

For most of the years of the existence of these thesauri they were not set in stone: anyone could suggest adding a term or recommend a correction to the scope notes (the short notes explaining what a given term meant and how it was to be used). At the time of this writing (July 2021), adding to these thesauri has been suspended while the RBMS Bibliographic Standards Committee is working on combining all six documents into one.

Behind all of this is the aim of the present dictionary: having the proper terms used for describing the materials in our holdings. For cataloging purposes, it is desirable for all of us to be using the same terminology for the same phenomena: don't call an UNOPENED book "UNCUT." Also, if there are two separate terms for one phenomenon, the thesauri tells the cataloger which is the preferred term—the one to be used in the cataloging record: don't use "Dutch curl"; rather use "French snail" when describing a particular MARBLING pattern.

Anyone in the rare book world—and of course that includes collectors and booksellers, along with librarians—

should know the content of these thesauri since they offer the "preferred terms" for describing all kinds of things that need description with respect to books, ephemera, and other kinds of collectibles in the book world. The thesauri can be accessed free at https://rbms.info/vocabularies/paper/alpha betical_list.htm (accessed 29 July 2021).

Two observations: First, since many book-realm items move through the world from BOOKSELLERS, and since these parties supply all in this world, it is incumbent on them (the sellers and their customers) to be conversant with the wide vocabulary of these commodities and to use it correctly. Second, to be able to use all the terms correctly takes a good deal of education, training, and experience. The thesauri go a long way in supplying the vocabulary (though they themselves are not as comprehensive as I think they need to be). But they contain so many terms, coming from so many realms, that it is near impossible for anyone to master them. It is important for a cataloger or bookseller, for instance, to know a word and need to know its meaning and how it is used; and they can consult the thesauri for guidance. But what if one of these people needs a term for a phenomenon and does not know where to find it in the thesauri? A volume with the TETE-BECHE structure might need to be entered into a catalog. How does the possessor of it know where to look? Perhaps the person will know to look into the thesaurus of bookbinding terminology. But where do you look in there? You have to read every entry before you come up with the right term. Unfortunately, it is not there. But even if it were, seeing the term in the alphabetical list would not help since the word in that list is not presented with a definition. (The clarifications of what the terms mean come in their "scope notes" or their "use for" explanations). You get the definition of what certain binding structures are once you click on the entry. The only way these thesauri can become fully useful is for the user to read and memorize pretty much all of them. Or take courses in one of the RARE BOOK SCHOOLS, hoping that all the words one needs are in the vocabularies of the instructors and that they present them all, correctly and thoroughly. These thesauri are brilliant reference tools, produced by smart and experienced people, but they are not easy to use or to learn from, especially for one coming to the field afresh, and even for people who have been in the book world for decades. They are nonetheless essential tools in the bookperson's library.

RDA (Resource Description and Access). *See under* MARC records.

READABILITY. Not to be confused with LEGIBILITY, readability refers to the ability of a text to be understood without much hair-pulling effort. Good prose, like John Steinbeck's, need not be larded with polysyllabic words seldom encountered in normal discourse—locutions culled from a thesaurus and not from informal speech.

READER, PRESS READER. Nicolas Barker added these terms to the eighth edition of the *ABC*. The first refers to a proofreader working as a copy editor for a publishing house; the second refers to an expert to whom the publisher sends a prospective text—one offered to the publisher for publication. This person reads COPY for all kinds of mechanical and intellectual things. She finds typos (i.e., TYPOGRAPHICAL ERRORS), suggests better wording, cleans up grammar, deletes redundancies, and suggests several other kinds of changes. She may also find errors of fact or interpretation. These readers, working in parallel to the PROOFREADING that the author does, sometimes overstep their boundaries and begin to rewrite the text, to the bewilderment and infuriation of the author. In the past (through most of the 20th century), these readers were called "in-house editors" in that they were part of the professional staff of publishing houses. But following astute (and sometimes heartless) business models, most of these editors/readers were fired and then the publishing house offered to hire them as independent readers, thus eliminating for these people full-time positions, regular salaries, benefits, office space, computers and office supplies, and so forth. There is now an extensive world of independent readers and a large number of publishing houses happy to hire them.

The press reader vets (evaluates) the submitted MANUSCRIPT and says to the publisher one of three things: 1) reject; 2) accept as is (very rare); or 3) publishable, but needs revisions as follows"; and then gives an analysis of what the author needs to do to make the text acceptable for publication.

READER'S EDITION. *See* Advance copy.

READING COPY. A copy of a book that is in such poor condition that it would fetch next to nothing on the retail market but is fine if all the possessor wants to do is read it. (Sometimes called a "working copy" or "BINDING COPY.") (*See* Condition.) The term, of course, implies that the copy is complete, despite its shabby state.

READING CREASE. The crease down the SPINE of a book that indicates the volume has been opened enough to have caused a permanent crease. Though exceptionally common on PAPERBACKS, where one might find two or more such creases, these also can be seen on some 19th-century cloth-bound volumes (and even books in leather). There is, in most cases, no remedy for this defect, and a collector with such a damaged volume in her possession may bemoan the fact that the book shows signs that it was used for something so damaging as having been read. Perish the thought that a COLLECTIBLE book was actually read!

REAM. Labarre says, "Ream is the most typical and most ancient word in the papermaker's vocabulary and is the universal term for a quantity of paper. . . . / The actual quantity of paper in a ream gradually became fixed through the centuries . . . probably in some relation to the amount of paper a VATMAN could make in a day, and has been in the neighborhood of 500 sheets for the last 3 or 4 centuries, though it may still contain, according to the class of paper, 472, 480, 504, or 516 sheets (and other quantities in various countries" (*Dictionary and Encyclopaedia of Paper and Paper-Making*, p. 222). He then cites the different kinds of reams: "Inside ream, contains 480 sheets. . . . Mill ream, (of hand-made paper) consists of two grades of the same paper, whether the paper is bought as good or as RETREE, formerly referred to as an 'imperfect' ream. If the paper is good it will consist of 18 QUIRES of insides or perfect paper, each quire containing 24 sheets, and two quires of outsides or inferior, broken, or damaged paper, of only 20 sheets each, one on the top and one at the bottom, making a total of 472. . . . Perfect ream, same as printer's ream, and used to distinguish it from Mill ream. . . . Printer's ream, contains 21½ quires of 24 good sheets, i.e. 516 in all to allow, after making ready [*see* Makeready] and spoilage, of a product of at least 508 good (printed) copies. . . . Standard ream, a term used in US for a suggested 'standard' ream of 500 sheets measuring 40" × 25", all sizes and weights to be calculated in terms of this standard" (p. 222). (One might also see the term "long ream" to indicate one with 500 or 516 sheets.) To elaborate on one point that Labarre makes, Henk Voorn says, "It was a long established custom that the top and bottom quires [in a ream] were of inferior quality" (Voorn, *Old Ream Wrappers*, p. 12).

REAM WRAPPERS. "[S]heets of coarse wrapping paper used to wrap up REAMS; in hand-made papers such wrappers are frequently typical and bear labels or imprints with old marks" (Labarre, *Dictionary and Encyclopaedia of Paper and Paper-Making*, p. 223). ("Frequently typical" means "of a type": that many of them will look pretty much alike: on inexpensive, coarse paper, and stamped—often in red ink—with a logo of the paper mill.) Henk Voorn says, "Ream-covers are an important source of historic information" (Voorn, *Old Ream Wrappers*, p. 7). The American Antiquarian Society website says, "The pictorial art on the [ream] labels has provided historians with views of both the interior and the exterior of extinct mills, including employees at work, equipment and the basic layout of the mill and its surrounding lands. Papermakers hoped that buyers would appreciate the sense of artistic quality of the pictorial label. Many of these illustrations were elaborate and realistic in content. Symbols such as the phoenix and the eagle were common on ream wrappers" (http://www.americanantiquarian.org/reamwrappers.htm [accessed 14 June 2021]). (See Schlieder, *Riesaufdrucke*, and Schlosser, ed., *Paper in Printing History*; pamphlet VII is on ream wrappers.)

REBACKED (binding). "The renewal or replacement of the material covering the SPINE of a book. The term is used primarily with reference to books covered in leather . . . or a publisher's cloth (edition) binding, unless the book is rare or has a binding of unusual attractiveness. Used in a strict sense, however, it refers to the renewal of the original spine covering" (Roberts and Etherington, p. 213).

Originally, "rebacking" was a term used for leather bindings. The rebacking was done with another piece of leather. After the new leather was inserted, the binder would use as much of the original spine as possible, depending on how much was left after the original was removed. If the volume was being restored as for a private collector or bookseller, the binder would try to do some retooling to fill in where the original was gone. The book conservator's goal, on the other hand, is to make the book usable (*see* Conservation), so less attention would be paid to restoring missing pieces. Binders ran into problems with rebacking when the quality of leather on the market began to decline. They needed to turn to high-quality cloth or paper as a substitute for the leather. Additionally, as collectors began to value 19th-century publishers' cloth bindings, whose spine could also come apart, conservators used high-quality handmade papers toned to the color of the cloth. This is a newer form of rebacking, and it is practiced today. Rebacking was a repair that was used for centuries, and sometimes it was so skillfully done that the repair was barely (or not at all) visible. Thus, it is important for collectors to look carefully at the bindings of volumes offered to them for their collections. Booksellers themselves may not even see the rebacking and will thus not mention it in their descriptions.

(In David Magee's *A Course in Correct Cataloguing, or Notes to the Neophyte*, in which he is teaching new booksellers how to describe books in their catalogs, we find under "Rebacked" the following: "Qualify with 'skillfully' or 'neatly' to prove that you don't send your books for repair to the local blacksmith," p. 11.)

REBOUND (binding). Said of a volume that has its original cover removed and completely replaced by another. (Sometimes a rebinding is done to an already rebound book.) Naturally, a second cover brings the volume to a condition removed from its original state and thus reduces its value—often the case even when the rebinding is in a sumptuous new cover. Most collectors want their volumes in the condition they were in when they were issued by the publisher. If the new binding is truly sumptuous and by a well-known (and collected) binder, the volume's value may not plummet much or may even go up. But rebinding removes information from the original package, and thus scholars may object to the practice. The process of rebinding, however, may offer the binder the opportunity to observe previous binding materials or techniques, and this could be quite educational. In the rebinding of the Ellesmere Chaucer at the HUNTINGTON LIBRARY, original sewing holes could be detected. (*See* Stab holes; see also Cains and Fredericks, "The Bindings of the Ellesmere Chaucer.") Sometimes DESIGN BOOKBINDERS give a volume of no particular value a new, artistic cover; the value of the book inheres in its binding, and many collectors (including libraries) will pay premium prices for bindings by famous or skilled binders. (*See* The Great Omar.)

RECASED. (Sometimes hyphenated.) Said of a volume that has had its case replaced. (*See* Case bound.) Roberts and Etherington say, "In a strict sense, a TEXT BLOCK that is separated from its case, and, following repair to the text block and case, is then placed back into the *same* case, perhaps with new endpapers, or possibly simply with new hinges. In a more general sense, a book is recased when the text block is removed from its original case (usually a publisher's binding) and placed in a new case made specifically for it" (p. 213). Carter's entry discusses the ease with which a volume—especially one in a PUBLISHER'S BINDING—can be recased and how such treatment affects value; also, an unscrupulous bookseller can fake up a "beautiful copy of a first edition" with a carefully recased second edition by using a good case of a first edition. Carter says that we should be particularly wary when an immaculate copy of a book that often appears in less than good condition shows up; he says there are many books that have been recased, with practically no trace of the recasing. And he raises the issue of value between a SHAKEN copy in its unrepaired state as opposed to a much tighter copy that has been recased. Which is preferable? Only the buyer can say. And as noted, it is not always possible to spot a recased copy. (See Carter, pp. 210–11.) (*See* Reset.)

RECENSION. "A critical revision of a text incorporating the most plausible elements found in varying sources" (*American Heritage Dictionary of the English Language*, p. 1467). Although some take the term to mean the establishment of a reliable text, recension is the part of that process in which the base text (*see* Copy-text) is emended (*see* Emendations) to contain readings that the editor deems more AUTHORITATIVE than the ones being replaced. Strictly speaking, the word is used mostly in the realm of manuscripts; in the world of printing, the term used would be "emendation." Also, the act of making the changes is called "recension," but the term applies also to the finally "corrected" text. Peter Beal says that the recension is the actual text that has been revised, the product of the meticulous examination of many texts in the same STEMMA of the work (or of printed works possibly derived from that stemma), and the emendations that are made by the editor. Hence, recension is a wide-ranging view of all extant texts (manuscript or printed) with a view to identifying those that are authoritative (and authoritative readings in those that are not so authoritative) and trying to reconstruct the earliest version possible (or the archetype), for the earlier the text, the closer to the author's original it is likely to be. As Beal indicates, the editor examines all versions of the text (and anything external to it) that can shed light on the transmission of that text from the author to the latest version—especially any version that the author could have had a hand in the production of. Multiple versions are COLLATED, lists of VARIANTS are created, and the editor then creates a new version by selecting the readings she deems most authoritative and AUTHORIAL. (See Beal, *A Dictionary of English Manuscript Terminology, 1450–2000*, pp. 333–34.) The result of the recension is a new, presumably authoritative, edition. (See Maas, *Textual Criticism*, section B, pp. 2–9; and Moorman, *Editing the Middle English Manuscript*, pp. 48–54.)

RECESSED-CORD SEWING. "A method of sewing a book by hand which involves cutting grooves into the SPINE of the gathered sections and recessing the cords into those grooves. A single length of thread is carried from kettle stitch to kettle stitch, as in FLEXIBLE SEWING, but passes across the cords instead of encircling them" (Roberts and Etherington, p. 213). Also called "sawn-in" binding since the cords are laid into a groove (that is made with a saw) in the TEXT BLOCK. Roberts and Etherington point out the advantages of this kind of binding: it is faster to do than the sewing that must be done for a flexible binding, it is less expensive, and "in combination with the hollow back, it usually allows more throw-up ['the rising up or buckling of the spine of a book when it is opened'; Roberts and Etherington, p. 264], thus facilitating opening of the book" (p. 213). The volume with this kind of sewing will not have RAISED BANDS—it will have a FLAT BACK.

RECTO. The right-hand page of a TWO-PAGE SPREAD when a CODEX is open. From the word that means "right." For alphabets that read left to right, the recto may be considered the front of the LEAF; on the opposite side of this, backing up the recto, is the VERSO, so named because it is the reverse of the leaf. Versos are on the left of a two-page spread. Normally, rectos are odd-numbered pages, versos are even-numbered pages, though careless, ignorant, or defiant book designers may reverse this. Before pages were numbered—in the Middle Ages and in the early days of printing in the West—rectos and versos were designated by the superscripts "R" and "V" in bibliographic descriptions. Hence, what would later be pages 7 and 8 in the "A" SIGNATURE of a book would be the front and back of the fourth leaf and would be designated A4^{r} and A4^{v}, respectively. (Sometimes shown with the "r" not as a superscript: "A4r.")

REDACTED/REDACTING. *See* Bisquing.

RED EDGES. Said of a volume that has had its edges smoothly cut and covered in red pigment. Roberts and Etherington (p. 214) say that it is most common for only a single edge (at the head of the volume) to be so decorated, but I have seen many volumes with all of their edges colored red—and other colors, such as green or gray. It adds a decorative touch to the volume at a small fraction of the cost of gilding. (*See* Gilt.)

RED ROT. The condition of a leather binding in which the leather dries out and turns powdery, flaking off and staining anything that touches it. It is caused by the acids imparted to the leather in tanning, by exposure to deleterious light (especially lighting that gives off ultraviolet rays), and by exposure to pollution, as well as by being inferior leather to begin with, as with much sheep leather. With the coming of the Industrial Revolution, which pumped acid into the atmosphere (hence the spread of "acid rain"), and with no air conditioning in most homes and libraries, prompting people to open windows to cool their spaces, the damaging air entered libraries and the acids it carried attacked the leathers, creating the red rot (also known as "red decay"). (See "Red Rot," AIC Wiki, http://www.conservation-wiki.com/wiki/Red_rot [accessed 14 June 2021].) The "rot" that rubs off onto one's sleeves (and onto neighboring volumes or anything else it touches) is not necessarily red; it is most often brown. But "red rot" is the term, and there it is. (The term goes back to at least the 16th century in English.)

Short of replacing the leather altogether on the volume, there is no perfect solution to the problem. Isolating the volumes exhibiting red rot is a start—so that they will not transfer the reddish-brown powder to neighboring volumes or to the clothes of those who brush by. They can be placed in PHASE BOXES, SHRINK-WRAPPED, or covered with acid-free paper. One product on the market, Klucel G, is a consolidant for leather that, once applied to the powdery binding, allows the leather to remain flexible and stops the flaking, but it does not strengthen the binding. (See Kite and Thomson, eds., *Conservation of Leather and Related Materials*.) (*See* Consolidation.)

RED RULING. One of the three methods of ruling lines to guide SCRIBES of manuscripts. Lines were ruled using red ink and lead (as in "lead pencil," in which the writing is actually done with lead as opposed to graphite) and with a stylus, leaving a groove but no actual drawn-in line. Carter points out that the use of red lines transferred over to the world of printing: he says that such lines, made with ink or a roll, surrounding the printed text on a page and sometimes drawn into the margins, added elegance to the page, especially to deluxe copies, done from the 1500s on, though these volumes are uncommon after 1740, and they were no longer done in the 19th century. He adds that account books and journals continued to have red ruling later on. (See Carter, p. 211). (*See* Rule [in manuscripts and in printing].) Carter (that is, Barker, who added the entry in Carter) is not fully correct insofar as his 19th-century comment goes. Many a publisher thought that printing a text within red borders added a level of sophistication or beauty to the page. Among several 19th-century books with red-printed borders in my own collection, there is a copy of *Poems* by William Cullen Bryant with red rule on every page, including the title page.

RED UNDER GOLD EDGE (Sometimes called "red under gilt edge.") This term describes a volume with GILT EDGES on which the gilding was done over edges stained or painted red. The technique is usually employed only on the HEAD edge, but one may see the word "edges" (in the plural) used inaccurately.

REED PENS. Writing implements made from reeds or bamboo that are cut the same way a feather is cut to make a QUILL. "Various instruments have been used for writing. The early Egyptians used a slender rush. From about 300 BC the thicker reed pen was used. The reed was in general use in the Greco-Roman world" ("Reed Pen," *Encyclopaedia Britannica*, http://www.britannica.com/topic/reed-pen [accessed 14 June 2021]). They are easy to cut. (I did one in a workshop and wrote with it for some time, but since it was quite stiff and inflexible, the writing tip eventually broke and split, so it would have to be recut regularly.) (See Finlay, *Western Writing Implements*.)

REFERENCES. The word has more than one meaning in the world of the book. 1) A bibliographical listing at the end of an article or book showing the sources used in the text. Sometimes referred to as "Works cited"—though this term refers specifically to sources that were actually used and cited in the text, while "References" is more generic and is equivalent to "Bibliography," meaning works not necessarily used in the text but on topics related to the topics of the text. 2) In a bookseller's catalog, there are often references to scholarly works from which the bookseller took information for the write-up of the item(s) being described. In some bookseller catalogs, there is a list of references elucidating what those references at each entry of the catalog refer to. But many booksellers assume that their customers will recognize the sources by the shortcut references at the entries, so they do not have a listing of those sources. If, for example, a bookseller is offering the classical reference text *Bibliotheca Classica, Or a Classical Dictionary* by John Lemprière (Reading: Printed for T. Cadell, London, 1788), all she needs to say at the end of the entry in her catalog is *PMM*, 236, a reference to *Printing and the Mind of Man*. With such a citation, the bookseller is showing expertise and authority, though it may be in the buyer's interest to check out the source to see how accurately it is being quoted or how carefully the bookseller has used that source.

REFORMATTING. In the library world, this means transforming a text from one medium to another: microfilming a printed text; digitizing an analog text; using Xerography to capture photographed or printed material. The aim of reformatting is usually to preserve the original, with the greatest amount of fidelity to the original in terms of capturing the information the original contains. But reformatting by its very nature yields a text with some loss of the information the original had. For instance, reproducing a book in digital form will remove information about its printing and binding, watermarks and illustrations from the reader. Collectors want originals. Reformatted versions may suffice if there is no other way to access the content of the original, but the collector knows that she is getting only a partial commodity.

REGIONAL ALLIANCE FOR PRESERVATION—ASSOCIATION OF REGIONAL CONSERVATION CENTERS. (Known in the trade as RAP.) An umbrella group in the United States for organizations that provide conservation and preservation services to libraries (and sometimes others). The "others" is a key issue here since some of these organizations offer collectors and booksellers conservation services and more. For instance, a library or bookseller (or even a private party) may hire someone in one of these centers to do a collection survey or to repair a valuable book or document. Many other services are also available. (The website for RAP can be seen at https://www.connectingtocollections.org/regional-alliance-for-preservation-_-association-of-regional-conservation-centers/ [accessed 3 June 2021].) Their mission statement says: "RAP is a national network of nonprofit organizations with expertise in the field of conservation and preservation. Through coordinated outreach activities, educational programs, and publications, RAP organizations foster awareness about preserving our cultural heritage." For the most part, the conservators and preservation experts at these organizations are highly trained and superb in their work. Anyone needing advice about preservation or conservation of library materials, their storage and care should look to the professionals in these organizations. Each of these has its own website. In this dictionary, typical offerings of these groups can be seen at four of them (chosen at random), marked with an asterisk (*) below.

The parent group, RAP, has had many affiliates over the years, listed by region. It is an organization in transition.

Eastern Seaboard Members
Conservation Center for Art & Historic Artifacts*
Library of Congress Preservation Directorate
National Park Service, Museum Conservation Services
Northeast Document Conservation Center*
Peebles Island Resource Center*
The Textile Conservation Workshop
Williamstown Art Conservation Center
Gulf Coast / Southern US Members
Amigos Library Services, Inc.
LYRASIS*

Midwest Members
The Gerald R. Ford Conservation Center
Intermuseum Conservation Association
Midwest Art Conservation Center

Western & Pacific Members
Balboa Art Conservation Center
Western States & Territories Preservation Assistance Service

As a footnote: When I was the director of a rare book library, I hired a consultant from NEDCC (Northeast Document Conservation Center) to do a collection survey. Her work was impeccable; and the report she provided led the administration to make changes that had been needed for decades. The work these professionals do is excellent and carries much weight.

REGISTER (in printing). The term has three uses. First, register means printing with accurate placement on the page, especially a second and subsequent color after the first color is printed. If a text is printed in black but all of its majuscules are printed in red, the printer will strive for perfect register (or "REGISTRATION") so that all the red characters fall exactly where they ought to on the page, lining up properly with the rest of the text. Good register also means getting text on facing pages and on opposite sides of a LEAF to line up properly. This also applies to the printing of illustrations: the illustrations, if printed in a separate PRESSRUN from the rest of the text, should sit on the page exactly where they are intended to be, not too close to (or overlapping) the text, and multicolor illustrations need perfect register for the printing of each color. (*See* Out of register; for a more detailed explanation, *see* Point holes; Registration.)

Second, a register (or registrum) in some early printed books (and even earlier in manuscripts) is a guide to the binder to show the order that the SIGNATURES must be bound in. The binder, receiving printed sheets from the printer, will need to fold and gather all of the signatures into the proper sequence for binding. It will not always be obvious what that order is. If the signatures are SIGNED with letters of the alphabet, the binder simply arranges the signatures in alphabetical order (usually with lowercase letters first and uppercase ones following—if the printer used these characters in that order). But sometimes printers used odd characters, not alphabetical, along with those of the alphabet, so no logical sequence was discernible. To guide the binder, the printer would print out, at the COLOPHON, a chart of the signatures that appear at the foot of each signature, in the order that they are to be bound in. This listing is called a "register" or "registrum." Philip Gaskell says, "The precise form of the signatures varied from time to time and from place to place. It was common in the sixteenth century to begin the series of signatures for the text with a lower-case alphabet, a–z, and to continue with A- or aa- (or less commonly with Aa- or AA-). . . . / The signing of preliminary leaves varied even more widely. . . . It was [common] to use symbols in forms such as * ** ***, or even (without logical order) * † ¶ § (etc.). During the fifteenth and sixteenth centuries printers got over the resulting difficulties by adding (usually adjacent to the colophon) a summary of the signatures called the register" (*A New Introduction to Bibliography*, pp. 51–52).

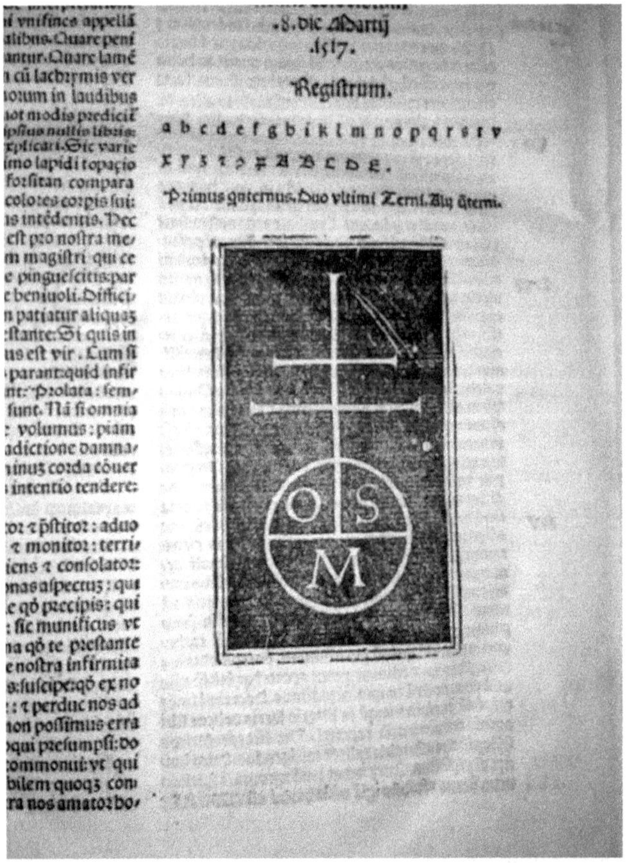

The register at the colophon of Flavius Magnus Aurelius Cassiodorus, *Cassiodori clarissimi Senatoris Romani in Psalterium exposition* (Venetiis: Octaviani Scoti, 1517). Note that in the register, the lowercase letters are followed by three non-alphanumeric symbols, corresponding to the symbols found on the signatures in the volume.

Collection of the author.

The third use is a reference to the records kept by the STATIONERS' COMPANY regarding ownership of texts. The company kept a register (known, appropriately enough, as the Stationers' Register), listing volumes published by printers who needed the Stationers' permission to publish. It was a precursor to COPYRIGHT, and the Stationers had the right to prohibit certain publications, and to seize volumes that did not meet their standards of morality or for political or other reasons. Books had to be licensed by the Stationers' Company before they could be printed. (See Blagden, *The Stationers' Company*.)

REGISTRATION (*See* Color separation.). The placement of text on a sheet such that it falls exactly where it is supposed to fall, especially when it is in synchronization with text on the opposite side of a LEAF (*see* Backup) or when several colors are printed on one side of the sheet, when they must print exactly where they need to. Registration is also important in printmaking when the artist is using multiple stones (*see* Lithography) or BLOCKS or printing from stencils. (*See also* Register.)

In printing, registration can be achieved by the use of pins that attach to or protrude from the TYMPAN. (*See* Point holes; Registration pins.) In lithography, registration is achieved by having separated colors carefully marked with small "plus signs" on the stone, outside the printing area. Small, strategically placed holes in stencils aid the artist in registering many-colored prints. For example, a carelessly registered CHROMOLITHOGRAPH will have colors improperly overlapping (or printing too far from) where they were intended.

Similarly, with poor backup, TEXT BLOCKS on opposite sides of the sheet will SHOW THROUGH. Masters of WOODBLOCK, stenciling, or lithographic printing will be able to achieve perfect registration.

REGISTRATION MARKS. Marks of one kind or another (often in the printing of multicolor images) that help the printer align the various colors properly on the SUBSTRATE. Usually, the registration marks are so far outside the image that they can eventually be trimmed away, leaving the multicolor image perfectly registered and with satisfactory margins.

REGISTRATION PINS. (*See* Gauge pins; Point holes.) The pins that printers used to REGISTER text from one side of the LEAF to the other and from one SIGNATURE to another. (For an explanation of the method, *see* Point holes.)

REGISTRUM (in or near a colophon). (*See* Register [in printing].)

REGLETS. Thin pieces of wood, of varying length, used to lock up the TYPE in the CHASE in preparation for printing. (*See* "Furniture.")

RE-HINGED (binding). *See* Hinges.

REISSUE. The second or subsequent release to the public of a text. Philip Gaskell says, a "[r]eissue normally involves a new or altered TITLE-PAGE, and includes cases such as CANCELLATIONS of the title-page to bring old sheets up to date; a new impression [*see* Edition, Impression (Printing), Issue, and State; Points] with a new title-page; and collections of separate pieces with a new general title" (*A New Introduction to Bibliography*, p. 316). Carter points out that the word is used carelessly by many a purveyor, as in "the book was reissued in paperback," showing that the writer meant that the book was created in a new form (see Carter, p. 212).

REJECTION SLIP; REJECTION LETTER. You know what this is! If an author's submission to a publisher received bad reviews from the publisher's READERS, the author will often get some kind of response telling him that the item is not for them. The terms "slip" and "letter" are used interchangeably, but they differ in that the slip is merely a form that the publisher's representative sends, sometimes with boxes checked off: Not for us or our readers; Too long; Too short; Badly written; Never submit to us again; Needs serious editing; or some other excuse for rejection. Living with rejection is not easy, so sometimes the publisher actually writes a letter explaining their disinterest. Authors might feel the rejection viscerally, and trash the letters or slips. But when they survive, especially for an author who becomes prominent and has the very item rejected published to acclaim elsewhere, these can be quite COLLECTIBLE, revelatory of the first publisher's ignorance or error or stupidity. Isaac Asimov said, "Rejection slips, or form letters, however tactfully phrased, are lacerations of the soul, if not quite inventions of the devil—but there is no way around them" (Asimov, "Literature/Rejection Slips"). And while sometimes hurtful, they can spur a writer to improve—or to give up writing.

REJOINTED. Said of "[a] leather binding that has had one or both JOINTS repaired or replaced. Replacement joints are the length of the book and about ¾ inch wide, the exact width being determined by the size of the book and the distance the strips are to extend underneath the SPINE and sides. The strips, which are pared moderately thin, have a long feathered bevel on all sides. While paring does weaken the leather, if it is too thick along the line of the joint, it will tend to lever itself off the spine each time the cover is opened" (Roberts and Etherington, p. 215).

RELIABLE TEXT. *See* Bibliography, especially the section "Textual Bibliography." *See also* Recension.

RELIEF PRINTING. One of the three basic methods of printing, the other two being INTAGLIO and PLANOGRAPHIC. The printing is done from a raised surface, as with PRINTING TYPE or a WOODBLOCK. In the book world, this form of printing is often called "LETTERPRESS." The raised surface can be any material: metal, wood, linoleum, plastic, rubber, or others. The printing surface can receive ink in a number of ways, and the ink can be transferred to the printed SUBSTRATE through some means—rubbing, pressing, or rolling on. Often the paper used in letterpress printing—especially with printing on a handpress—will be dampened, softening the SIZE in the paper and making the surface more receptive to ink than in paper that is not wet. The softer paper, then, in taking the IMPRESSION, also takes the raised surface into the paper's surface. The old saying in printing circles was that a good letterpress printer has the type kiss the paper, not bite it. The "kiss" deposits ink onto the sheet, creating no indentations in the sheet; the "bite" leaves a three-dimensional indentation in the sheet, palpable and even visible in raking light. Hence, though we think of relief printing as producing an almost three-dimensional effect, with the text pressing into the substrate, this is not always the case. For centuries, from at least the time of GUTENBERG to the middle of the 20th century, relief was the primary form of printing in the West.

RELIGIOUS BOOKS. The number and type of religious books is huge. The list below is a selection from that number, focusing only on Christian, Jewish, and Islamic books. No attempt has been made to represent all types of such volumes. Booksellers will need the precise term to designate the specific item they are cataloging. Only a brief description of each is given. Booksellers and collectors will encounter many of these kinds of volumes. The parenthetical definitions (where they are needed) may help them to distinguish one from another.

Christian texts

Antiphonal; Antiphonary (bound collection of antiphons—responsive musical texts)

Bead-roll ("a list or catalogue of persons for whose souls prayers are to be said in the Catholic Church" [Beale, *A Dictionary of English Manuscript Terminology*, p. 33])

Beatus MS (illustrated compilation of allegorical commentaries or passages from the Apocalypse, the revelation of the second coming of Christ experienced by St. John the Evangelist)

Benedictional (volume of benedictions or blessings, usually collected from the sacramentary)

Bible

Breviary (book containing hymns, offices, and prayers for the canonical hours)

Bullary ("a volume or collection of transcripts of papal bulls, including those that appeared in print from the late sixteenth century onward" [Beale, *A Dictionary of English Manuscript Terminology*, p. 53])

Choir book

Chrestomathy (selection of literary passages or passages designed to help with language study; not necessarily religious, but often the passages are drawn from religious texts)

Collectarium (service book containing collects [brief formal prayers] and chapters [short lessons])

Decretals (decrees, often Papal, giving decisions on religious points or canon law)

Enchiridion (manual or handbook; not necessarily religious, but many were books of devotion)

Epistolary (liturgical book containing readings for church services from the New Testament Epistles)

Evangelary (Evangelistary) (book containing selected pericopes [selections] from the Gospel, arranged to be read at the Eucharistic Liturgy or Liturgy of the Hours for the feasts and seasons of the liturgical year)

Exultet roll (scroll in manuscript that celebrated the return of light to the world, combining words, music, and pictures)

Gospel

Gradual (book of chants for the Mass)

Hagiography (book of saints)

Homiliary (book with homilies or sermons)

Horae (books of hours) (*See under* Book of hours)

Hymnal

Lectionary (book of readings from the Scripture; part of the Breviary with lessons, saints' lives, and homilies)

Legenda (book with sermons, biblical lessons, and saints' lives)

Manuale ("As used in the Catholic Church, the Manuale, or *Manuale* [*sic*] or *manual*, is the small handbook—which was circulated in many manuscript copies, with variations—containing the forms of the rituals to be observed by priests in the administration of the sacraments [Baptism, Confirmation, the Eucharist, Penance, Extreme Unction, Order, and Matrimony], in churchings [women's obligatory appearances in church to give thanks for successful childbirth], in burials, and in most of the blessings that priests can give by ordinary or delegated authority" [Beale, *A Dictionary of English Manuscript Terminology*, pp. 243–44].)

Martyrology (Passionale) (volume listing martyrs and saints and their sufferings)

Menologium (service book, arranged by months, for the Eastern Orthodox Church and the Eastern Catholic Churches)

Missal (book containing the year's services for the Mass)

Partbook (musical) (volume showing a single part of music; other volumes supplemented this one to add up to the full sound of all contributing parts; not necessarily religious, but many were)

Penetential (book of rules of the church concerning penance)

Plenarium (a book containing the complete text of religious doctrine that might otherwise be scattered in several texts; as opposed to a volume of pericopes [or selections])

Pontifical (book of forms for ceremonies performed by a bishop)

Portas (small portable manuscript breviary)

Prayer book

Primer (Medieval devotional book of hours)

Processional(e) (book with hymns, psalms, and litanies)

Psalter (Book of psalms)

Pye book ("The term . . . as used at least by the seventeenth century, means an alphabetical index to rolls and records. In earlier, pre-Reformation times, it was also a book concerning regulations for the celebration of saints' days as affected by the moveable feast of Easter" [Beale, *A Dictionary of English Manuscript Terminology*, p. 326])

Rituale (book showing the form and the order of the religious service)

Sacramentary (a missal without epistles or gospels)

Septuagint (translation into Greek of the Pentateuch and the Apocrypha)

Sequentiary ("A book [or portion of a Gradual or Troper] containing sequences [extended melodies] sung by a soloist between the alleluia and the Gospel lesson at Mass"; vhmml (Hill Museum and Monastic Library), "Sequentiary"; https://www.vhmml.org/lexicon/definition/14951 [accessed 28 May 2021])

Service book (generic term for many of the items listed here)

Summa (collection of religious treatises)

Synaxary (collection of saints' lives; hagiography)

Tetraevangelium (a book containing the four gospels; in Greek)

Tonary ("a liturgical book in the Western Christian Church which lists by INCIPIT various items of Gregorian chant according to the Gregorian mode [tonus] of their melodies within the eight-mode system. Tonaries often include Office antiphons"; Definitions; https://www.definitions.net/definition/TONARY [accessed 30 May 2021])

Totum (a complete Roman breviary)

Troper ("A book of liturgical music containing tropes or sequences, used during services in the medieval Christian Church"; Lexico; https://www.lexico.com/en/definition/troper [accessed 30 May 2021])

Jewish texts (taken from "Jewish Sacred Texts"; https://embassies.gov.il/mumbai/AboutIsrael/People/Pages/Jewish-Sacred-Texts.aspx#:~:text=The%20Jewish%20Bible%20is%20known,and%20the%20Writings%20(Ketuvim [accessed 2 August 2021])

Bible (Holy Scripture; also called "the Tanakh, an acronym of the three sets of books which comprise it: the Pentateuch [Torah], the Prophets [Nevi'im] and the Writings [Ketuvim].")

Halakhic (legal literature)

Mishna (interpretations of the law)

Responsa (Jewish "common law")

Torah ("the basis of all Jewish sacred texts is the Torah. In its most basic sense, the Torah is the Pentateuch—the five books of Moses, which tell the story of the Creation of the world, God's covenant with Abraham and his descendants, the Exodus from Egypt, the revelation at Mt. Sinai (where God enunciated the Ten Commandments), the wanderings of the Israelites in the desert, and a recapitulation of that experience shortly before the entrance to the Promised Land.")

Islamic texts

Book of John the Baptist ("a scripture that is alluded to in Qur'an 19:12: "[To his son came the command]: 'O Yahya [John]! take hold of the Book with might': and We gave him Wisdom even as a youth." Most scholars and Muslims believe that the verse is referring to the Torah [Tawrat], but some scholars suggest that it could be referring to Mandæan scriptures such as the Ginza Rba or the Draša d̲-Iahia" ("Islamic Holy Books"; https://en.wikipedia.org/wiki/Islamic_holy_books [accessed 2 August 2021])

Hadith ("sayings, acts or tacit approvals ascribed to the Islamic prophet Muhammad") ("List of Islamic Texts"; https://en.wikipedia.org/wiki/List_of_Islamic_texts [accessed 2 August 2021])

Injil ("the holy book revealed to Jesus [Isa], according to the Quran. Although some lay Muslims believe the Injil refers to the entire New Testament, most scholars and Muslims believe that it refers not to the New Testament but to an original Gospel, given to Jesus as the word of Allah") ("Islamic Holy Books"; https://en.wikipedia.org/wiki/Islamic_holy_books [accessed 2 August 2021])

Quran (Koran) ("central religious text of Islam, which Muslims believe to be a revelation from God") ("List of Islamic Texts"; https://en.wikipedia.org/wiki/List_of_Islamic_texts [accessed 2 August 2021])

Scrolls of Abraham ("believed to have been one of the earliest bodies of scripture, which were given to Abraham [Ibrāhīm],[22] and later used by Ishmael [Ismā'īl] and Isaac") ("Islamic Holy Books"; https://en.wikipedia.org/wiki/Islamic_holy_books [accessed 2 August 2021])

Scrolls of Moses ("some of the revelation of Moses, are understood by Muslims to refer not to the Torah but to revelations aside from the Torah") ("Islamic Holy Books"; https://en.wikipedia.org/wiki/Islamic_holy_books [accessed 2 August 2021])

Sunnah ("denotes the practice of Islamic prophet Muhammad") ("List of Islamic Texts"; https://en.wikipedia.org/wiki/List_of_Islamic_texts [accessed 2 August 2021])

Torah ("the Torah was revealed to Moses [Musa][12] but Muslims argue that the current Torah has suffered corruption over the years, and is no longer reliable.") ("Islamic Holy Books"; https://en.wikipedia.org/wiki/Islamic_holy_books [accessed 2 August 2021])

Zabur ("often interpreted as being the Book of Psalms,[14] as being the holy scripture revealed to King David [Dawud]") ("Islamic Holy Books"; https://en.wikipedia.org/wiki/Islamic_holy_books [accessed 2 August 2021])

[Another list of nearly 150 additional texts ("List of Shia Books") can be found at https://en.wikipedia.org/wiki/List_of_Shia_books (accessed 2 August 2021).]

REMAINDER BINDING. The binding of REMAINDERS, "unsold copies of a book that are in sheets or gatherings. These are sold to a jobber, bound in a different FORMAT from the original binding, and offered for sale, sometimes with a different title" (Roberts and Etherington, p. 216). Roberts and Etherington point out that remainder bindings are usually much cheaper (in price and quality) than was the original binding. They add, "For 19th and 20th century books, the term 'remainder binding' is used correctly only with reference to a book bound for the wholesale book trade by someone other than the original publisher of the book. A later (and sometimes less expensive) publisher's binding was a SECONDARY BINDING" (p. 216). Sometimes the remainder bindings look exactly like the original ones, but they are still made from cheaper materials. The aim of creating remainders in the first place is to maximize profits, so the cheaper the binding, the more profit that can be realized. Also note that Roberts and Etherington's "format" above is a loose use of the word since the format of the remainder volume would be the same as that for the original publication.

REMAINDERS. Books that the publisher could not sell at full LIST PRICE and that languished in the publisher's warehouse. These were sold to a remainder house—a vendor that buys such books at a fraction of their original list price and then sells to a big-box store or directly to the public—and then are sold at remainder prices. The books could be in their original binding, or they could be IN SHEETS. For example, the publisher prints 10,000 copies of a book, makes its profits by selling half of them at their $20 list price, and then sells the rest to a remainder house at, say, a 90 percent discount, or $2 each. The publisher clears its shelves of deadwood (books that are costing the publisher money since it pays taxes on unsold inventory and is paying for the storage) and earns something on the books that were bringing in no income at all. The remainder house sells the books at 60 percent off the list price ($8 each). The publisher makes some money on these remainders, the remainder house makes money on them, and the public get a bargain, being able to get a $20 book for $8. The *American Dictionary of Printing and Bookmaking* says that "remainders are disposed of at very low prices to booksellers who have such a trade that they can dispose of them. If bought in sheets they are often given new titles and new bindings, so as to increase their chances of sale" (p. 487). Often remainders are marked in some way, as with an ink marking on the bottom edge of the TEXT BLOCK.

If a publisher is not sure how many copies of a book it will sell but prints up, say, 20,000 copies, it may not bind them all. If the publisher sells only half, it will have saved the binding costs on 10,000 copies. So it is possible for the unsold copies to be in sheets in the publisher's warehouse. The remainder company buys what is available—bound or unbound copies. If the latter, the remainder company has the sheets bound in a "REMAINDER BINDING."

The catch comes when publishers realize that remainders sell, so they print books on cheap paper and sell them to the vendors or the remainder houses as "remainders" when in fact they are just cheaply made books. They may even put dust jackets on the volumes with the original list prices of the genuine first editions—sometimes even saying "originally issued at $20." These are not really "remainders," and the big-box stores that are famous for their "Remainders" tables know this, so they have changed the signs over these tables to read "Bargain Books." Are they a bargain? Only the Shadow knows.

Carter has an entry for "remainder binding," a binding put onto volumes that have reached the remainder status but that were never bound by their original publisher. The remainder house needs to bind them to make them salable. Often these later bindings, which go onto volumes of a text block of genuine first-printing books, are cheap. The volume, then, may be a true first edition but with a later binding—what Carter says should be called a "SECONDARY BINDING."

A case in point: Quayle's *A Collector's Book of Books* came out at something in the neighborhood of $20. It was remaindered at $1 (at which time I bought a stack of copies as gifts for friends). The remaindered price climbed to $5 and then to $10 as supplies dwindled quickly. Then it was $15, and then it really went out of print. The publisher saw the market for this book, so another printing was done (but on cheaper paper), and it sold as a bargain-priced book for about $17.50. (*See* Bargain books; Closeouts.)

The complexities revealed in this entry—genuine printings of an edition; later printings of that edition but on inferior paper; text blocks in sheets of the genuine printings but with later, cheaper bindings; volumes that are printed up to look like genuine printings but starting out in life as bargain books; dust jackets with genuine pricing; dust jackets with deceptive pricing; remainder books; bargain books; genuine remainders that sell for a fraction of their original price and then "catch on" with the public and begin to climb in price, as remainders, back toward their original list prices; and other permutations and combinations—all of these complexities show why it is important for a buyer (collector, librarian, scholar, student, archivist, or investor) to be well informed in the world of book collecting. (*See* Clipped/Price clipped.)

REMARGINED. "The replacement or restoration of part of one or more of the outer MARGINS of a LEAF, either by means of paper cut to size and pasted to the leaf or by LEAFCASTING. If all four margins are replaced, the leaf is said to have been INLAID" (Roberts and Etherington, "remargined"; https://cool.culturalheritage.org/don/dt/dt2826.html [accessed 1 February 2021]).

REMBOÎTAGE. From the French word *remboîter*, meaning "to fit back into." Carter points out that there is no equivalent term in English for this phenomenon. Remboîtage is the removal of a text block from its original binding and placement into a more elegant one—or one more sympathetic to a binding that might have been in existence when the volume was first produced or a binding more in spirit with the text of the book. The aim, of course, is often to put the text into a binding that is more valuable, in better condition, or more beautiful than the one that it had before the transfer. Carter says that such a transfer may be quite difficult to spot. (See Carter, pp. 213–14.) The goal, of course, is to enhance the value of a volume, sometimes fraudulently. One danger is that if a book is taken from its original shabby binding and put into a fancy one, the original ugly one could be more valuable, especially with the information it contains. Collectors want books in as close to their original being as possible; a book that has "suffered" remboîtage may lose its value, regardless of the sumptuousness of the replacement cover it is given.

REMONDINI PAPERS. Decorated papers made by the Remondini family, a printing establishment (founded in 1649) in Bassano, Italy, that sold their operations in 1861 (after that date, the firm of Giuseppe Rizzi took over the making of the papers; see Schmoller, *Remondini and Rizzi*). The papers, printed by WOODBLOCK, were decorated with religious designs, along with florals, geometrical patterns, landscapes, architectural scenes, and fruits. "The printing was generally done in up to five colours, although the 1791 catalogue [of the firm] mentions papers in seven colours. To help REGISTER the designs correctly pins were placed in the corners of each block. Frequently the paper would first be brushed with a background tint of either red, green, yellow, brown, blue or grey. Some papers were later waxed so they could be sponged clean" (Schmoller, *Remondini and Rizzi*, p. 26). The sheets were used for bookbindings—covers and endpapers—and they were popular for pamphlets. (See Infelise and Marini, *Remondini*.) They are so beautiful and desirable that a coterie of paper collectors eagerly seeks out full sheets, which occasionally come onto the market.

REMOVED. A word indicating that the item so described was removed from some other item—as with a collection of sheet music that was bound, but a single item is being offered having been "removed" from the original volume. It does not necessarily indicate that the volume was once published with all of its pieces bound in; it indicates that there is some sign that the item was once attached to something. (One bookseller whose catalog this term appeared in says about the term: "Once a separate item then bound up, now free again." See Bookworm & Silverfish, Catalog 342, n.d. [c. 1995].)

REPAIRING. Carter has an entry for this term; it is fairly well covered in this dictionary (*see* Restoration; Sophisticated). If a bookseller wants to maximize his profits on a damaged volume, he must weigh (the costs of repair + sale) with (the income he can get from leaving the volume in its damaged condition + sale). It is a balancing act. The same balance obtains for the collector who is trying to decide whether to buy a damaged volume: How much am I saving by buying a defective copy, and what would it cost to have it repaired to mitigate the damage? (Or he may be deciding whether to buy a copy that has already been fixed up.) For many collectors, having damaged books on their shelves is nettlesome, to say the least, and even if the cost of fixing them exceeds the rise in valuation for the items, it is worth it to them psychically to have the repairs done. I once acquired a damaged copy of a wonderful Cummington Press book. I loved having the book, but I hated having it on my shelves in its crumbling state. I had a conservator consolidate its loose parts, making it possible for me to handle it without fear of the loss of additional parts and knowing that the chemise she made for it will protect it on my shelves and give it an appearance of respectability. I can now sleep with ease, at least with respect to that volume.

REPLEVIN. The seizure of any item (or items) with the aim of returning it to its rightful owner, but only after the legal ownership is determined through proper channels. The book world being what it is, over the decades and even centuries, books as valuable commodities have been stolen by the millions. What does one do when a volume surfaces owned by some person or institution but claimed by its ostensible legal owner? The challenges, court cases, and dispositions can be protracted and costly. Hence, booksellers must be leery about acquiring an item with cloudy PROVENANCE; collectors (private or institutional) have a right to ask for that provenance if there is any suspicion about ownership. The *Encyclopaedia Britannica* online says, "Replevin, also called revendication, a form of lawsuit in common-law countries, such as England, Commonwealth countries, and the United States, for return of personal property wrongfully taken and for compensation for resulting loss. Replevin is one of the oldest legal actions, dating to the 14th century.

It is now called 'claim and delivery'" (*Encyclopaedia Britannica* online, "Replevin" [https://www.britannica.com/topic/replevin; accessed 20 March 2021]).

REPOUSÉ. "A book cover of metal, usually silver, produced by hammering or shaping the metal into a design from the reverse side, generally into a mold of wood, or other solid material, that has been carved INTAGLIO. The metal is then attached to the book BOARD, which is usually made of wood" (Roberts and Etherington, p. 216).

REPP. (Also spelled rep, rip, or reps.) A ribbed cloth, made of cotton, wool, or silk, often used for bookbindings. One might see in a bookseller's catalog, "Bound in blue repp"; sometimes followed by the word "finish" ("In a blue repp-finished cloth" [though the word "cloth" here is redundant]). This finish was also imparted to papers—especially in the 19th century when many kinds of paper decoration became possible and the sophistication of making DECORATED PAPER hit a peak at the end of that century.

REPRINT. A second or subsequent printing of a text—not the first printing. The term implies that the later printing is from the same EDITION (i.e., the same setting of type), but the term is often used loosely to mean a later printing, regardless of the edition. Thus, strictly speaking, a reprint is a reimpression (for a discussion of "impression," *see* Edition, Impression [Printing], Issue, and State; Points).

In collecting terms, the reprint is never as sought after as is the first printing (*see* First edition), but sometimes a reprint is all that a collector can get. One excellent example is the reprints done for the first two volumes of the journal *Matrix*. Finding copies of the first printing of these volumes is akin to finding the cliché needle in a haystack. Even the reprints are practically invisible on the market. Thus, just because a volume is a reprint does not mean it is not worth a good deal.

Sometimes a volume contains a straight reprint (that is, a later impression) of a text, but with a changed title, so it is not immediately recognized as a reprint. Also, reprints that are actually new editions (that is, they are not printed from the same setting of type as that used for the earlier edition), from fully reset type, or even those that are merely later impressions of an edition, may have textual variants that are ACCIDENTALS or SUBSTANTIVES. So the designation "reprint" does not guarantee a text identical to the earlier one that was the basis for the reprint.

Finally, a FACSIMILE edition, done from a photograph of the original edition, or a copy printed from STEREOTYPE PLATES where the first edition, first impression was printed from STANDING TYPE, is still a reprint since it is of the same edition as the original.

REPRO (reproduction proof). Proof copies created so that the copy of the text can be photographed and turned into printing plates. The repros would be checked for textual accuracy and also, usually, for the clarity of the printing—are all the SERIFS and COUNTERS printing clearly? Is the inking sharp and not smudged or too heavy (or too light)? Repros were common after personal computers came in, for publishers saw an opportunity to save a great deal of money in TYPESETTING by having the authors "set their own type" by requiring what was called "CAMERA-READY COPY" from the authors. The writers made their own repros, but while they may have been experts in their own fields, they were usually not book designers, so books printed from repros were often quite poorly designed.

When KIM MERKER of the Windhover and Stone Wall Presses was printing the first edition of Henry David Thoreau's *Huckleberries* for the New York Public Library (which owned the original manuscript), the library asked Merker to set the type without the illustrations so that they could issue a commercial edition after the LIMITED EDITION was released. I set the type for the text and took sharp repro proofs on special repro paper. (Later, the text was reset to incorporate the illustrations for the HAND-PRINTED version.) The repro proofs represent the true FIRST EDITION for much of the text; the LETTERPRESS version was printed from the second setting of type for those pages. (Incidentally, the commercial version was never published, so the repros are the only record of that setting of type. And after writing to the New York Public Library to ask them about their failed printing of the text, I learned from them that they had no record in their files of such a project. The repros seemed to have dematerialized.)

RESEARCH LIBRARIES GROUP (RLG). "The Research Libraries Group (RLG) is a not-for-profit membership corporation of 150 universities, independent research libraries, archives, historical societies, museums and other institutions devoted to improving access to information that supports research and learning. Since its founding in 1974, RLG has been a pioneer in developing cooperative solutions to the acquisition, access, delivery, and preservation challenges those institutions face. RLG provides a forum for collegial sharing of resources, costs, experience, and shaping of the future. RLG membership is open to any not-for-profit institution with an educational, cultural, or scientific mission and a commitment to improving access to research materials. Access to the wealth of information resources, however, is not restricted to RLG members. . . . First, to build a union catalog, the Research Libraries Information Network (RLIN), of over one-hundred-million bibliographic records from over 250 sources describing books, journal articles, dissertations, and rare materials in over 365 languages. The RLIN databases form a one-of-a-kind resource for technical services librarians as well as for researchers" (Erway, "Digital Initiatives of the Research Libraries Group"). "RLG is founded by three universities—Columbia, Harvard, and Yale—and The New York Public Library" ("History of the OCLC Research Library Partnership," http://www.oclc.org/research/partnership/history.html [accessed 14 June 2021]). In 2006 RLG and OCLC voted to merge the two organizations, and "[o]n 1 July 2006, RLG Programs is formed and becomes part of the OCLC Programs and Research division. [In 2009] OCLC Programs and Research consolidate further under the name of OCLC Research, and RLG Programs becomes known as the RLG Partnership. [Then in 2011] [t]he OCLC Research Library Partnership replaces the RLG Partnership" ("History of the OCLC Research Library Partnership," as above). As of 2021, "The OCLC Research Library Partnership is a venue for research libraries to undertake significant, innovative, collective action to benefit scholars and researchers everywhere. The Partnership magnifies the leadership and direction provided by innovative libraries" ("The OCLC Research Library Partnership," OCLC, http://www.oclc.org/research/partnership.html [accessed 28 June 2021]). The partnership has about 125 members as of July 2021. (See "OCLC Research Library Partnership Roster"; https://www.oclc.org/research/partnership/roster.html [accessed 21 July 2021].) The Research Libraries Group no longer exists as a stand-alone organization; it is part of OCLC.

RESEARCH LIBRARIES INFORMATION NETWORK (RLIN). *See* RLG.

RESERVE. *See* Auctions.

RESET (in binding). Said of "[a] LEAF, leaves, or an entire section of a book which has become detached and has been glued back into place. Although the technique is used by some bookbinders, it is a poor and usually ineffective method of repair. The term is also used (improperly) to describe an entire TEXT BLOCK that has become loosened in its CASE and has been reset" (Roberts and Etherington, p. 216). This latter use should more properly be "RECASED." (*See also* Reset/Resetting [in printing].)

RESET/RESETTING (in printing). The term refers to printing type that has had to be constituted at least once after its first setting. If type is PIED or distributed back into the TYPE CASE or for any other reason needs to be reconstituted into its proper order to compose the text, the COMPOSITOR must reset it. Resetting is sometimes more challenging than was the initial setting. First setting would be fairly simple if the compositor is taking the type from an ordered type case. But pied type needs to be carefully examined if it is jumbled on a GALLEY or in the BED of the press. With a HINMAN COLLATOR, it is usually possible to discern when type has been reset. If the type for a text has been distributed into its cases and the publisher decides to print up more copies, the new setting can be called a "resetting," and it yields a new edition since an edition is a new setting of type. (*See* Edition, Impression [Printing], Issue, and State; Points.)

The term is also used to indicate the matter so printed, as in the following sentence: "This is a resetting of the original text."

RESEWING. "The process of removing a text block from its case or covers, removing the SPINE LINING (if any), old adhesive, as well as the original sewing thread, and then resewing the sections. In conservation bookbinding, 'resewing' usually implies the same method of sewing as the original; in library binding, however, the term generally implies the substitution of OVERSEWING for edition sewing" (Roberts and Etherington, p. 216).

RESIZING. *See* Size (in paper formation).

RESOLUTION. "The number of lines or dots (per unit of measurement) used to form an image. For computer monitors and photocomposition [and for scanning on a digital scanner] in the United States, this is lines per inch or dots per inch (DPI). Theoretically, the more lines or dots per inch, the higher the quality of the image" (Eckersley et al., *Glossary of Typesetting Terms*, p. 88). Some institutions, wanting to share their holdings but not wanting those holdings to be used without PERMISSION, may scan texts at a low resolution—not good enough for reproducing for publication. Users, then, need to get high-resolution images from the holders of the original materials.

RESTORATION. The treatment of a damaged item such that the effort is made to make it look "as good as new," or it can be restored to some known state. "In fact, for special collections librarians and many others in the rare book world, the term 'restoration' is hardly used except in possibly nefarious situations, because such treatment that leads to the hiding of defects can be deceptive. Restoration of an item allows its owner to pass it off as 'like new' or 'in excellent condition,' when in fact its defects have been hidden by the restorative treatment. Hence, the concept of 'restoration' is usually frowned upon in the rare book world. / On the other hand, if you are a bookseller and you live from your profits, and if you can maximize your profits by 'getting rid of' imperfections in something you want to sell and thus be able to raise your price considerably, having an item restored may be quite lucrative. It is not illegal to repair a binding, clean up smudges, erase underlinings, or replace a missing leaf with a FACSIMILE that cannot be detected. But it may be illegal—and it is surely unethical—to pass off as PRISTINE and original something that was not so fine before its treatment. Hence, the concept of restoration is usually looked down upon by ethical people in the rare books world" (Berger, p. 355).

Carter's long entry on this falls under his rubric "repairing." He says that repaired copies are looked upon with suspicion by collectors, who are inclined to let defects stand in an imperfect copy because even a copy with damage is closer to its original state than is a repaired one. (See Carter, p. 215.) This being said, however, booksellers, collectors, and librarians are likely to prefer fixed-up copies to shabby ones, partly because a repaired item is more useful—that is, it is sturdier and more easily handled and used—than is a copy falling apart. Also, it looks better, and usually a bookseller can more easily sell a restored copy than he can sell a damaged one. Recognizing this, Carter adds that fixed-up copies are not automatically SOPHISTICATED or faked up, and a keen collector will be able to see where a repair was done not to make the volume look better (and thus sell for a higher price than it would have if it were still unrepaired) but rather to make it usable. He says that responsible collectors will thus give their damaged books to a binder who understands the difference and will not try to hide any repairs but will record the repairs so as to keep whatever bibliographical evidence the volume had in its damaged state (see Carter, p. 215). Carter, in this paragraph, is describing more the CONSERVATOR than he is the restorer. The point is that a "restored" book tries to hide the defects that brought it to the restorer; a conserved book may cover up some of the defects, though that is not the aim of CONSERVATION, but the treatment of a conservator is to make the object useful for as long as is possible, without taking any information away from the book. Restoration removes information (about the book's history and use); conservation extends use with a minimal loss of information.

RESTRIKE. An IMPRESSION of a print made after the first edition of impressions have been made. (*See* Edition, Impression [Printing], Issue, and State; Points.) If the first edition of the PRINT is NUMBERED or signed (or both), often the restrike will not be—one way to distinguish it from the earlier printing. Printing PLATES from, say, the 17th century could be used in the 21st century to make restrikes. If they are done on the appropriate paper, it may be difficult to determine when the images were printed. I have a copy of a Rembrandt print done on WOVE PAPER—clearly a restrike since the original dates to long before wove paper was invented. With photographic technology it is possible to create a modern plate of a 16th-century picture with perfect fidelity. A printing from that plate would not be a restrike; it would merely be a modern reproduction or a FACSIMILE.

RETAIL PRICE. *See* List price.

RETREE. "A term applied to (slightly) defective sheets of paper, mostly used in reference to hand-made papers, to distinguish them from good or perfect sheets. Retree sheets are not broken [*see* Broke] . . . but contain defects indicated by such terms as: B [as in "B-grade" as opposed to "A"], back mark, bell, blackening, blister . . . poor colour or defective sizing, which do not necessarily prevent the sheets from being used, especially if printed" (Labarre, *Dictionary and Encyclopaedia of Paper and Paper-Making*, p. 226). Although the sheets are still usable, often retree would be repulped, and the new pulp would be used for wrapping or other papers, not usable for fine work. And I have heard the term "retree" used for paper made from repulped defective sheets.

RETOUCHED. Said of any text, illustration, or photograph, for instance, that has been "improved" by hand to mend a flaw of some kind, to add color, to add a detail, or to make the original sharper than it was. It is often a way to create a SOPHISTICATED COPY.

REVENDICATION. *See* Repleven.

REVERSE/REVERSE CALF. (Sometimes called "reverse skin.") "Reverse" is the back side of a LEAF. In a CODEX, the front of the leaf would be the RECTO, and the reverse is the VERSO. The word is also used in the phrase "reverse calf," in which the skin is "finished on the flesh side by light buffering. Reverse calf was sometimes used in place of SUEDE leather as a covering material for ledgers and BLANK BOOKS during the latter 18th and early 19th centuries" (Roberts and Etherington, p. 218). The term "reversed skin" is sometimes used for "suede." (It is also called "rough calf.") (For some reason Carter says it is called "reversed calf.")

REVIEW COPY (also called "ADVANCE COPY," "advance reading copy" or "uncorrected proofs"). A copy of a book sent out to a critic for review—the review presumably to be published, though it is possible that a publisher just wants a review so that it can take a BLURB from it to print onto the DUST JACKET (or the cover of a paperback). Although these volumes could be EXEMPLARS of the final version of the text in the regular commercial binding, they are more often printed on inferior paper, bound cheaply in paper covers, and labeled in some way to indicate that it is a review copy. (Or the volume may merely have a REVIEW SLIP laid in indicating that it is a review copy.) Inasmuch as the text in the copies is often early in the book's production and the final published version may go through subsequent PROOFREADINGS and contain EMENDATIONS, the review copies may have a statement to the effect that quotations (for publication or review) should not be taken from that version. (*See* Proofs.) A copy of Hook's *Breakfast at Sotheby's*—on cheap paper and in a paper wrapper—says on the front cover, "Advance Printing Copy / Uncorrected Proofs / Not for sale," and it gives a publication date of October 2014 (though I acquired the book in June 2014). On the back cover is this statement: "Unrevised and unpublished proofs. Confidential. Please do not quote for publication until verified with a finished book. Not for distribution to the public." The text on this rear cover also lists contact people and their contact points for publicity, sales information, and rights information, none of which will be on the published hardback version of the book. Another volume, listing itself as "Advance Reading Copy / Not For Sale" on the front cover and "Advance Uncorrected Proof" on the rear cover, gives a summary of the plot, a statement of the intended audience, blurbs, a short biographical note about the author, and "Marketing and Publicity" information, including the intended date of publication, the size of the published version (which differs from that of the review copy), the number of pages the book will have (which is also different from the review version), and so forth. And it says, "Please do not quote for publication without checking against the finished book." Also, the cover design of the review copy differs from that of all the other published versions, even those from the same publisher. (See in the bibliography Eli Gottlieb, *Best Boy*.)

Since only a limited number of such copies are produced, these could be quite desirable on the collector's market, regardless of the cheapness of their production and the fact that they could be rife with typographical or other errors. The value, of course, is usually related to other things than whether this is a review copy, but for COLLECTIBLE authors, those gathering their publications will want every manifestation of those authors' books, and the review copies are sure to be much less numerous than are copies of the regular edition.

REVIEWS. Evaluations of books that are published in appropriate venues—that is, the review will be on a text covering a subject that the audience of the review might be interested in. Hence, a book on printing may be reviewed in *PBSA*. (See Law's good overview of reviews in *The Oxford Companion to the Book*, pp. 1091–92.) In assessing a review, the reader must always be aware of who the reviewer is and what level of impartiality he can be shown to have. Author A writes a book that could undercut the sales of the work (or the reputation) of Author B. Author B reviews Author A's book. Will it be an impartial review? Authors A and B could have been longstanding rivals. Or they could be longstanding friends, and one could give a glowing review for his friend's fairly poor book.

Reviews should ultimately give a summary of the contents of the item under review and a fair judgment of the work's quality, with a recommendation of who should buy the book, who should not, and under what circumstances. The review should also be thorough, giving the reader a fair appraisal of the quality and breadth of the work under scrutiny. Presumably, the reviewer was chosen because she is an expert in the field of the volume. But too many reviews allow the reviewer merely to recap what the book says, with no indication that the reviewer knew anything about the subject matter of the book before taking on the job, and many reviews damn with no praise when some praise is due, praise only when some criticism is in order, or do not praise or condemn at all, just recount content.

Sometimes, the audience (the potential buyer) is not given a hint of the worth of the volume, so the reviewer has not done his job. Good reviews can increase sales. Bad ones can be devastating to the sale of books.

REVIEW SLIP. A printed slip LAID INTO (or sometimes TIPPED INTO) a volume indicating that the copy was sent out as a REVIEW COPY. The text on the slip is often addressed to an editor at a publication (newspaper, magazine, or other news medium) that tries to encourage him to publish a review of the book—thus garnering free advertising. Some presses might issue a version of the text with a label pasted onto the cover (or onto an endleaf) showing that the copy is being sent out for review. This is not technically a "review slip," it is a review label, though both terms might be used for this paste-on.

REVISE (noun). The version of a text sent to a reader (e.g., the author or editor) for PROOFREADING after the first proofreading has been done and corrections entered. The publisher may send the author the GALLEY PROOFS; the author reads and corrects them and returns them to the publisher. The publisher makes the called-for changes and then sends the revise to the author for another reading. (*See* Page proofs.) The author, editor, or other proofreader may get a revise—even two or more of them, depending on how many changes take place in each iteration of the proofreading. Some scholars use the term to indicate the version of the proofs that already has corrections in them; some more specifically say these pages have the author's corrections.

REVISED EDITION. Generally, a second or later edition of a text—one that has been revised and thus, presumably, is different from *and better than* the earlier edition. But what constitutes "better" is anyone's guess. Although the revision is often by the author or editor of the original, that is not always the case, and a revision without the author's consent might yield readings quite different from what the author might have wanted. The revision, if minor (and with basically the same setting of type), will generally keep most of the text of the earlier version; if it does not, then a true second (i.e., new) edition is produced.

In the world of textbooks, publishers ask authors of popular volumes to revise regularly. With students selling their textbooks to vendors and with a growing number of used copies on the market, the publisher stands to lose a great deal of money if students buy used copies only. But a revised edition instantly makes copies of the earlier edition obsolete and worthless (so the students will get nothing for selling them), and the authors will begin to get ROYALTIES for a new edition where royalties of the earlier version have dried up. With textbooks, revised editions may sometimes have more a fiscal than a pedagogical reason for being created, and revised editions are not necessarily better than the versions they replace.

REVISIONS. (*See* Proofs.) Changes made in a text. The notion of "revision" implies that improvements are being made to the original, though what constitutes an improvement is up for debate. Revisions can be minimal, resulting in a "REVISED EDITION," or extensive, resulting in a new edition. The authority (and therefore the reliability) of revisions can be debatable: Were they done by the author, an editor, a proofreader, a COMPOSITOR, or someone else?

REWARDS OF MERIT. Printed or manuscript certificates created to congratulate the young on their performance in or out of school. The awarding of these small pieces of EPHEMERA "was most popular during the nineteenth century when printing techniques evolved to make this form of ephemera more readily available. A majority of the surviving rewards of merit are printed, as opposed to hand drawn and painted examples that involved significant artistic effort. The earliest rewards of merit were almost always purely of a religious nature, depicting the benefits of piety. Beginning in the early nineteenth century, the rewards of merit gradually became more secular, touching lighter topics such as polite behavior, patriotic awareness, and children's games and other activities. [The American Antiquarian Society has] nearly 2,000 hand painted, ENGRAVED, printed, and CHROMOLITHOGRAPHED examples [that] provide a glimpse into education and cultural issues over a span of almost one hundred years" (American Antiquarian Society, "Rewards of Merit"). (See Fenn and Malpa, *Rewards of Merit*.)

RIBS. (Sometimes called "supports.") The wooden supports beneath the wires on which paper is made in a paper MOLD. Ribs run the short dimension of the mold, and are usually equally spaced. In a mold on which LAID PAPER is made, the ribs will have wires drawn through tiny holes, and on the top of the ribs, above the wires that will yield WIRE LINES in the paper made on the mold, will be the chain stitches that will produce the CHAIN LINES in the laid paper. The chain lines in the sheet are the result of the chain stitches formed along the length of the ribs, where the stitches sew the wires to the ribs.

RICE PAPER. There is no such thing as rice paper. Paper cannot be made from rice, which is a starch. This misnomer has existed for a long time. People seeing extremely thin paper, some of which was made in Japan, assume it is (and therefore call it) "rice paper," possibly thinking that there is a connection between Japan and rice. It is possible the starch from rice could be used as a binding material or SIZING in paper, but this is not enough to label such sheets as "rice paper."

Labarre mentions that rice straw was used as the basis of paper "in oriental [*sic*] countries and in Italy" (*Dictionary and Encyclopaedia of Paper and Paper-Making*, p. 227; he cites an early source for this: Julia de Fontenelle and P. Poisson, *Nouveau Manuel Complet du Marchand Papetier et du Régleur*), but the paper was not made of the rice itself. Hence, a proper designation for this would be "rice-straw paper." A material that looks much like paper but is merely the sliced inner pith of a plant has also been called "rice paper," though it is also not paper. (*See* Pith paper.)

What most people who use the term "rice paper" are referring to is actually JAPANESE PAPER or CHINA PAPER. It is thin, strong, and durable, and often, but not always, translucent. Early editions of the *Encyclopaedia Britannica*, for example, were printed on such paper, the thinness desirable since it allowed the publisher to have many LEAVES in a volume with not much BULKING. Such papers are also used as OFFSET SHEETS.

In the food industry, a flat edible material used (like seaweed) to wrap some hard candies or rice or other sushi-like rolls can be made from rice starch and is sometimes called "rice paper." But it is not paper, and it has no application in the world of books except to feed those who make, buy, sell, and collect them.

Thanks to Phil Salmon of Bromer Booksellers, I learned of a new use for the term "rice paper"—for cosmetic purposes. In France at the turn of the 20th century, manufacturers purveyed a product marketed as "Papier Poudre de Riz" (powder rice paper). These are small, soft, thin pieces of paper bound into a little booklet, with directions for use printed onto the rear PASTEDOWN in Spanish, Italian, and Portuguese. (One French company, J. Lesquendieu, had these papers with the directions in 6 languages.) The user was to remove a leaf from the book and rub its powdered side onto the face. Here "rice paper" was used almost certainly because the paper was very much like the soft, thin KOZO papers from Japan. (It is possible—and even likely—that the powder itself was made of rice. It is not clear from the name of the product. There *was* a product called "Poudre de riz." But another product, marketed by Palladio, on the cover of its packet has "Rice Paper," with a drawing of the face of an Asian woman. And the company Burt's Bees sells Wings Of Love Rice Paper Powdered Facial Tissues. Looks as if the word "rice" has transferred from "powder" to "paper." You can decide.)

RIGHT OF FIRST REFUSAL. An arrangement, whether contractual or not, in which a seller offers an object to a potential buyer before offering the object to anyone else. Booksellers may have preferred customers (i.e., ones who get preferential treatment); or they may have an item that would be well placed in the collection of a small number of people. They may choose one party to offer the item to first, before making it available to others. The one so offered has been given the right of first refusal—the first opportunity to acquire the item or to refuse to acquire it. The offer, then, rather than being made to two or more parties, is offered as a QUOTE.

RINCEAU. (Plural: Rinceaux.) "[I]n architecture, decorative border or strip, featuring stylized vines with leaves and often with fruit or flowers. It first appears as a decorative motif in Classical antiquity. Roman rinceaux most often consisted of an undulating double vine growing from a vase. Branches, vines, and thistles are mixed together in Gothic rinceaux, and in Renaissance examples tiny animals or human heads appear" (*Encyclopaedia Britannica* online, "Rinceau"; https://www.britannica.com/technology/rinceau [accessed 2 March 2021]). This kind of decoration, popular in 14th- and 15th-century ILLUMINATED MANUSCRIPTS, appeared in abundance on the title pages of 18th-century printed books.

RING BINDER. A volume with two or more heavy metal (or sometimes plastic) rings that open into two parts, allowing hole-punched LEAVES to be inserted. The rings then snap shut, allowing the leaves to be turned like leaves in a book. The rings are usually fixed into a strong, heavy metal or plastic SPINE, and the COVERS are often heavy BOARDS, though they can also be flexible. Often there are heavy metal tabs at the HEAD and TAIL of the spine that can be pressed to separate the two parts of the rings; or the rings can be pulled apart manually. This BINDING structure is useful for gatherings of leaves that need to be pulled out—or added to—as individual parts (or groups of leaves). They are sometimes called "LOOSE-LEAF BINDERS," though hole-punched file folders can be used in them, and a folder does not constitute a "leaf."

RINGS. *See* Auction ring.

RITTENHOUSE, WILLIAM (1644–1708). The first papermaker in North America. He set up the first mill in 1790 in Germantown, Pennsylvania. The mill was in operation until 1855. (See Green, *The Rittenhouse Mill and the Beginnings of Papermaking in America*.) His partners were "linen draper and landowner Robert Turner, ironmonger Thomas Tresse, and printer William Bradford" (Bidwell, *American Paper Mills 1690–1832*, p. 1).

RIVER. (Sometimes called a "pigeonhole" or a "staircase.") A line of blank spaces running through a page of set type, formed where blank spaces between words line up in successive lines of text. A "river" of two or three lines may be excusable in elegant COMPOSITION, but four or more lines of blank spaces can leave a trail of space that can be unsightly and distracting to a reader. A good COMPOSITOR knows how to avoid such unsightliness, even if it means RESETTING lines by hand. (*See* Justification [in typesetting].)

piscing elit. Pellentesque viverra
n nunc. Nam sed nisl nec elit susc
llamcorper. In leo ante, venenati
ıtpat ut, imperdiet auctor, enim.
avida. Suspendisse molestie sem
esent a lacus vitae turpis consec
mper. Integer porta. Donec sit am
aesent a eros. In hac habitasse pl
ctumst. Suspendisse fermentum.
em ipsum dolor sit amet, consect

A river in the set type, running down from the word "leo" in the third line to "amet" on the bottom line.

Wikimedia Commons, "Typographic river.svg"; https://commons.wikimedia.org/wiki/File:Typographic_river.svg (accessed 12 July 2021).

RIVIÈRE, ROBERT (binder) (1808–1882). "One of the great names in English bookbinding for about a century until the firm ceased business in 1939 and its tools passed to Bayntun's of Bath" (Nixon, *Five Centuries of English Bookbinding*, p. 218). Rivière set up his bindery in 1829 in Bath and then moved to London around 1840. "When the eldest son of [his] second daughter, Percival Calkin, was taken into partnership in 1881 the firm's name became Rivière & Son, and it subsequently remained in the hands of the Calkin family until it closed down in 1939" (Nixon, *Five Centuries of English Bookbinding*, p. 218). "The excellent workmanship and good taste displayed in his bindings gradually won for them the appreciation of connoisseurs, and he was largely employed by the Duke of Devonshire, Mr. [Samuel] Christie-Miller, Captain [Francis Capper] Brooke and other great collectors. He also bound for the queen and the royal family. In the Great Exhibition of 1851 he exhibited several examples of his skill, and he obtained a medal. He was chosen by the council to bind one thousand copies of the large 'Illustrated Catalogue,' intended for presentation to 'all the crowned heads in Europe' and other distinguished persons. It is said that two thousand skins of the best red MOROCCO, as well as fifteen hundred yards of silk for the linings of the covers, were used by Rivière for this undertaking. He also restored and bound the famous Domesday Book, now preserved in the Record Office, an excellent piece of work. / While the binding of Riviere, like that of his equally celebrated fellow-craftsman, Francis Bedford, is deficient in originality, it is in all other respects—in the quality of the materials, the FORWARDING, and in the finish and delicacy of the TOOLING—deserving of almost unqualified commendation. Taking into consideration the fact that he was entirely self-taught, his bindings are wonderful specimens of artistic taste, skill, and perseverance" (*Dictionary of National Biography*, 1885–1900, "Riviere, Robert"; https://en.wikisource.org/wiki/Dictionary_of_National_Biography,_1885-1900/Riviere,_Robert [accessed 4 July 2021]).

"Rivière was an accomplished craftsman and excelled in imitating the best historical styles with a fidelity and technique that have not often been surpassed" (Roberts and Etherington, p. 219). "You can date Rivière bindings by their stamp [usually inside the front covers]. / 1829–1832—Bound by R. Riviere, Bath / 1832–1840—Bound by R. Rivière / 1840–1860—Bound by Rivière / 1880 and on—Bound by Rivière & Son" (Biblio.com., "Bayntun-Rivière Bindery"; https://www.biblio.com/book-collecting/what-to-collect/bayntun-riviere-bindery/ [accessed 4 July 2021]).

RLIN (Research Libraries Information Network). *See* Research Libraries Group.

ROAN. "A variety, or varieties, of leather produced from a superior grade of unsplit sheepskin. Roan is softer than BASIL, and is colored and finished in imitation MOROCCO. / The typical roan has a close, tough, long, BOARDED GRAIN, a compact structure, and is usually dyed a red color. Originally, roans were leathers tanned exclusively with sumac (as were the moroccos); however, in later years they were often tanned with other vegetable tannins. They were used extensively for covering books from about 1790 until well into the 19th century, but have been seldom used since that time" (Roberts and Etherington, p. 219).

ROGERS, BRUCE (1870–1957). "[T]ypographer and book designer, highly influential in fine book design in the United States during the early 20th century. . . . In 1895 he moved to Boston, where he met a number of men who were revolutionizing the book publishing industry, including George Mifflin of Houghton Mifflin, who offered him a job at the Riverside Press. When the press opened a LIMITED-EDITIONS department in 1900, Rogers was put in charge and given responsibility and freedom to design and print fine books. During the next 12 years he produced more than 100 Riverside Press editions, which are still highly esteemed and valued. / He designed the Montaigne typeface in 1901 and the Centaur in 1915, both inspired by NICOLAS JENSON's roman type of 1470, and he also designed Riverside Caslon. In 1912 he left Boston to travel and to do freelance work. While in England in 1916 he served as adviser to the Cambridge University Press, and after returning to the United States in 1919 he held an advisory post at Harvard University Press until 1934. At the same time, he was designing distinguished books for the William E. Rudge printing plant in Mount Vernon, N.Y. As adviser to the Oxford University Press he directed the preparation of the monumental Oxford Lectern Bible (1935). His other fine books and limited editions included the *Odyssey*, *Pacioli*, an edition of Shakespeare, the Boswell Papers, and an American Folio Lectern Bible" ("Bruce Rogers, American Typographer," *Encyclopaedia Britannica*, http://www.britannica.com/biography/Bruce-Rogers [accessed 15 June 2021]). Perhaps his greatest achievement was this Lectern Bible. "The Oxford Lectern Bible, published in 1935, was a massive project, but amazingly Rogers still found time to put out other pieces during its production. But it was the Bible that would leave his largest artistic thumbprint on the world; hailed by critics from around the globe as a masterpiece, the Bible flung Rogers into the realms of typographical immortality. Sixty of his friends, among them George Ade, Edward C. Elliott, John T. McCutcheon and David Ross, donated funds for a special printing of the Bible on a small quantity of unique Japanese paper. This one-of-a-kind treasure was donated to the Library of Congress in Washington, D.C.

The Library honored Rogers in turn by putting his printer's emblem on two of its bronze door panels, the first time a living printer had been so recognized" (Amanda Grossman, "Bruce Rogers Papers, 1889–1957, Purdue University Libraries, Archives and Special Collections," https://archives.lib.purdue.edu/fa/bruce_rogersP.pdf [accessed 15 June 2021]). The Bible was printed in what to some is another of Rogers's great achievements, Centaur type, which Rogers designed as TITLING CAPITALS in 1914 and as a full FONT in 1915. (See Lawson, *Anatomy of a Typeface*, pp. 67–73.)

ROLL (scroll). The form of the "book" before the codex. Rolls could be in PAPYRUS or vellum, leather or silk, or other materials, and they were written on one side only. Also, in bookbinding, this is "[a] FINISHING tool consisting of a brass wheel, the circumference of which is engraved so as to impress a continuous repeating pattern as it revolves under (considerable) pressure" (Roberts and Etherington, p. 219). The word is also used to designate "[t]he design impressed by a roll" (Roberts and Etherington, p. 219).

ROLLER (brayer). The device that transfers ink from an inking source to the face of the printing type. Invented in about 1810, this tool enabled the automatic inking of type and thus the automation of printing. It is made from various substances (glue and molasses or glycerin or glue, molasses, and plaster of Paris [as per the *American Dictionary of Printing and Bookmaking*, pp. 490–91]). (See Bloy, *A History of Printing Ink, Balls and Rollers, 1440–1850*, pp. 53–65.) Today they are usually made from rubber. Albert S. Burlingham says, in his somewhat florid way, "Notwithstanding the fact that no one thing connected with the art of printing has done more toward the advancement of that art than the simple inking appliance familiarly and commonly known as 'the printer's roller,'—without which, indeed, the evolution of the power printing press from the primitive hand machines of the fathers would not have been possible,—it is an inexplicable truth that historians and encyclopædia makers who have made investigation of the origin and progress of the art seem to have attached so little of importance to the invention or introduction of the composition roller that only meagre and casual reference is made to it" (Burlingham, "The Printer's Roller," p. 144). He adds, "There is no record in any of the histories of printing, or in encyclopædias, of who it was that introduced the composition roller into use in this country, or any reference to the date when it came into service" (Burlingham, p. 150). But the point he makes is crucial: without the roller, automatic inking would have been impossible, and all inking would have to be done with INK BALLS, slowing down the printing considerably. With the roller, mechanized high-speed printing is made possible.

ROLLING PRESS (COPPERPLATE press). A press used for making images from ENGRAVED or ETCHED PLATES or from LITHOGRAPHY stones, so called because the plate is placed on the BED of the press, the bed is rolled under ROLLERS that press blankets against the paper, and the paper is pressed onto the plates. Sometimes also called a LITHO PRESS or an etching press.

A rolling press.

Image from the Diderot Encyclopédie, Vol VIII.

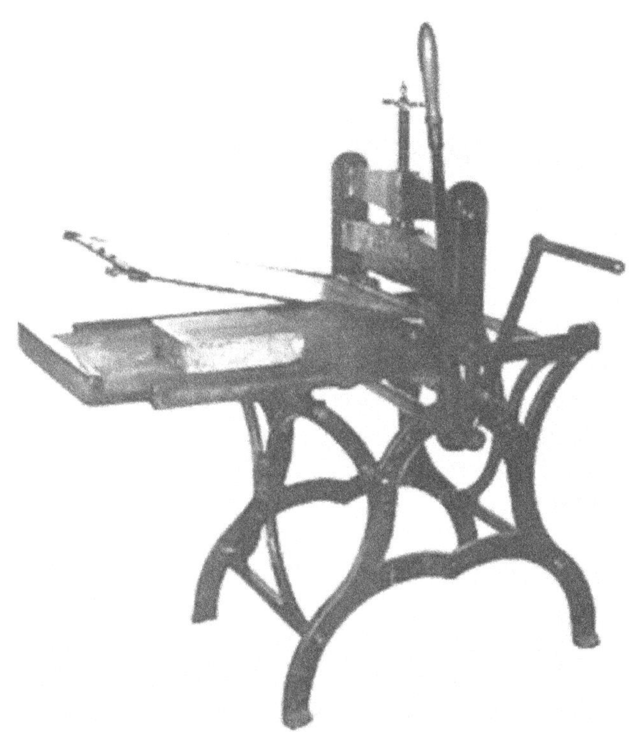

A rolling press specifically used for lithography, showing the litho stone on its bed. (*See also* figure at Copperplate press. *Also see* Handpresses.)

Courtesy of Bracken Press.

ROLLINS, CARL PURINGTON (1880–1960). Book designer; as "printer for Yale University (1928–48), he designed over 2,000 volumes and lectured on TYPOGRAPHY; he wrote a column for the *Saturday Review of Literature* called 'The Compleat Collector'" ("Rollins, Carl Purington," *The Free Dictionary*; https://encyclopedia2.thefreedictionary.com/Rollins%2c+Carl+Purington [accessed 15 June 2021]).

"He attended Harvard University from 1897 to 1900, and worked for the Georgetown Advocate, a small country newspaper, before obtaining a position with D[ANIEL] B[ERKELEY] UPDIKE at the Merrymount Press in Boston. . . . [I]n 1908, Rollins . . . established an arts and crafts cooperative at Dyke Mill where furniture, textiles, and printed works were made and sold. Eventually, the business became a press exclusively, the Montague Press. In 1918, Rollins joined the staff of the Yale University Press and was appointed Printer to the University in 1920. . . . Rollins taught a course in BIBLIOGRAPHY and established the Bibliographical Press in the University library for student use. . . . He was the recipient of numerous awards and prizes, including the highest award of the AMERICAN INSTITUTE OF GRAPHIC ARTS in 1941. He received honorary degrees from Yale and was named Printer Emeritus when he retired from the University in 1948. . . . He died in New Haven, Connecticut, in 1960" ("Rollins, Carl Purington," SNAC; https://snaccooperative.org/ark:/99166/w6f774pj [accessed 14 June 2021]). (See Megan Benton, "Carl Purington Rollins and the Design of Scholarly Books," http://link.springer.com/article/10.1007%2FBF02678331#page-1 [accessed 15 June 2021].)

ROMAINE, LAWRENCE B. *See* Trade catalogs.

ROMAN (type). Upright printing type with SERIFS. As opposed to BLACKLETTER, SANS SERIF, or ITALIC TYPES. Some of the features of roman types over the centuries, as Bringhurst shows, are vertical stems, circular bowls (*see* Counters), modulated strokes, modest contrast, modest X-HEIGHT, and so on. (See Bringhurst, *The Elements of Typographic Style*, pp. 112–19.) Popular roman TYPEFACES include Palatino, Bembo, Baskerville, Caslon, Century, Bodoni, Times New Roman, and Garamond.

ROMANESQUE (bindings). "A group of bookbindings dating from the 12th and early 13th centuries. These bindings, of which more than a hundred examples are recorded, are always in leather, usually of a dark brown color. Their decorative patterns were not incised with a knife or graver, as was common in that time, but were produced by means of repeated impressions made with engraved metal stamps. The finest examples are of French or English origin, but the style was also prevalent in Germany, although not in Italy or Spain. Romanesque bindings are the earliest of the BLOCKED bindings and represent a fully developed art of book decoration by means of deeply engraved metal dies, which left excellent impressions in RELIEF in the leather. These 12th century stamps are well engraved, and seem to have no known antecedents. There is evidence indicating that they were produced by the members of a small group of monasteries, and within a relatively short period of time. Most of the extant examples are bindings of individual books of the Bible, each usually having a different design on the upper cover" (Roberts and Etherington, p. 220).

ROMAN NUMERALS. Numbers based on those used in ancient Rome, with letters (upper- or lowercase) from the roman alphabet representing numbers. They are often used to indicate dates (especially on title pages) in books from the HANDPRESS PERIOD and later and also used to number pages in PRELIMS, before the main body of the text, which will use arabic numerals.

The system is simple, with some basic principles (shown with lowercase letters here though in dates usually shown with capitals): i = 1; v = 5; x = 10; l (lowercase *L*) = 50; c = 100; d = 500; m = 1,000. If a larger number is followed by a smaller one, the smaller one is added onto the larger one (vii = 7). If a larger number is preceded by a smaller one, the smaller one is subtracted from the larger one (ix = 9). These are the "additive" and the "subtractive" forms (with smaller numbers added to or subtracted from the larger ones, depending on their positions relative to the larger ones). If the additive form is used exclusively, then one could encounter four identical numbers in a row (so 9 will be rendered "viiii"). The subtractive form will not use four identical numbers in a row. It is not uncommon to find four identical numbers in a row in dates (MDCCCC = 1900). And "'Double subtractives' also occur, such as XIIX or even IIXX instead of XVIII" (Wikipedia, "Roman numerals"; http://en.wikipedia.org/wiki/Roman_numerals [accessed 15 June 2021]).

i	=	1	xv	=	15	ccxxvii	=	227
ii	=	2	xvii	=	17	cccxliv	=	344
iii	=	3	xix	=	19	cdlv	=	455
iv	=	4	xxi	=	21	id	=	499
v	=	5	xxx	=	30	dxciii	=	593
vi	=	6	xxxviii	=	38	dcccxxvii	=	827
vii	=	7	xl	=	40	md	=	1500
viii	=	8	xlvi	=	46	mm	=	2,000
ix	=	9	lxxxviii	=	88			
x	=	10	xcii	=	92			

In early printing, roman numerals were sometimes shown in a stylized way, with the capital *M* being made with a forward *C*, a vertical line, and a backward *C*: C I Ɔ. The spaces between the strokes can be confusing to someone who does not know that the three strokes represent a single character. Similarly, the *D* can be rendered: I Ɔ. So a date might look like this: C I Ɔ I Ɔ C C C I I I I (= MDCCCIIII =1804).

Larger numbers could be rendered by having a macron (a straight line: ¯) placed over a number to multiply it by 1,000. Hence, Ī = 1,000. This form is not used in the dates of books.

ROSENBACH LIBRARY. (A[braham] S[imon] W[olf] Rosenbach) (1876–1952). A private research library in Philadelphia, now merged with the Free Library of Philadelphia. "On December 3, 2013 the Chairs of the Boards of the Free Library of Philadelphia Foundation and The Rosenbach Museum & Library jointly signed an agreement approving and making official the affiliation that was announced in April. This partnership brings together two of the world's preeminent collections of rare books, MANUSCRIPTS, AMERICANA, and art anywhere in the world, offering new and exciting opportunities for the future" ("The Rosenbach Museum & Library Completes Affiliation with The Free Library of Philadelphia Foundation," Rosenbach of the Free Library of Philadelphia, https://www.rosenbach.org/learn/news/rosenbach-museum-library-completes-affiliation-free-library-philadelphia-foundation [accessed 27 October 2015]; this is no longer a live link, but information about the library can be had at https://rosenbach.org/about/ [accessed 4 July 2021]). The Rosenbach was the collection of Philip (1863–1953) and A. S. W. Rosenbach, brothers who were distinguished booksellers dealing in rare books and manuscripts. "[T]he brothers played a central role in the development of private libraries that later became our nation's most important public collections of rare books, such as the FOLGER and HUNTINGTON Libraries. The brothers' own personal collection, now the core of the Rosenbach, features treasures the brothers were unable to part with, including the only surviving copy of Benjamin Franklin's first *Poor Richard's Almanac* and the manuscript of James Joyce's *Ulysses*" (Rosenbach of the Free Library of Philadelphia, https://rosenbach.org/about/mission-history/ [accessed 15 June 2021]). The library's holdings focus on American and European culture. (See Silver, *Dr. Rosenbach and Mr. Lilly*.)

The Free Library of Philadelphia is the general public library system of that city, chartered in 1891. It opened in 1894. (See https://www.freelibrary.org [accessed 14 June 2021].)

ROTARY PRESS (sometimes referred to as a "web press"). A press on which the text to be printed is attached to a revolving cylinder. Rotary presses in hundreds of designs were developed in the 19th century to speed up printing. It is a "printing press that prints on paper passing between a supporting cylinder and a cylinder containing the printing plates. It may be contrasted to the flatbed press, which has a flat printing surface. It is primarily used in high-speed, web-fed operations, in which the press takes paper from a roll, as in newspaper printing. Many of these large presses not only print as many as four colours but cut and fold and even bind in a cover—in one continuous automatic process. Paper passes through some presses at nearly 20 miles (30 km) per hour, the speed limited partly by the tensile strength of the paper; large presses can print up to 60,000 copies of 128 standard-size pages in an hour. / In its simplest form a rotary press consists of two cylinders turning in opposite directions, with the plate cylinder having curved printing plates attached to its surface and the impression cylinder working to press the paper to the inked plates as the paper passes between the cylinders. A simple two-colour rotary press uses two plate cylinders in succession, each bearing a different typeform and each having its own inking system. The same side of the same sheet of paper receives two successive impressions of two different colours as it passes through the press. Printing on both sides of a sheet of paper and printing in three, four, or even five colours can be achieved in a rotary press by using different combinations and successions of plate and impression cylinders. Extremely high rates of production can be achieved in very large, highly automated roll-fed rotary presses. These machines have cylinders with a circumference large enough to accommodate two or more plates, so that with each revolution the cylinder prints two or more copies of the same page. Similar arrangements enable a cylinder to print eight copies of the same page in a single revolution" ("Rotary Press," *Encyclopaedia Britannica*, http://www.britannica.com/technology/rotary-press [accessed 15 June 2021]).

ROTOGRAVURE. "An INTAGLIO printing process in which letters and pictures are transferred from an ETCHED copper cylinder to a web of paper, plastic, or similar material in a rotary press" (*American Heritage Dictionary of the English Language*, p. 1516). The term is also used for anything printed by this process ("I clipped the rotogravure out of the magazine") and also for the section of a magazine or a newspaper that uses this printing method ("The rotogravure in today's paper had 24 pages").

ROUGH CALF. *See* Reverse/Reverse calf.

ROUGH GILT. (Also called "GILT in the rough.") "The edges of a book that have been cut solid and gilded before sewing, so that when the book is later sewn the edges are slightly uneven (rough), although usually to an almost imperceptible extent. This technique has been widely used in England and

America, especially by those bookbinders who do not care for the solid 'block of metal' appearance of edges gilt subsequent to sewing" (Roberts and Etherington, "rough gilt"; https://cool.culturalheritage.org/don/dt/dt2905.html [accessed 26 January 2021]). There are also volumes with their deckles still in place, printed on heavy paper—heavy enough that the edges can be gilt, regardless of the fact that the edges are not smoothly cut. This may also be called "rough gilt," though it is not precisely what the term originally meant.

ROUNCE. A handle on a HANDPRESS that, when turned, runs the BED of the press under the PLATEN and out again. The rounce has affixed to it leather straps—called "girths"—that are attached to the bed. The girths could also be made from heavy cloth straps. (The bed of the press is also called the "coffin," hence the name of the book appreciation club in Los Angeles: Rounce & Coffin Club, in existence from 1931 to 2007.)

ROUNDEL. "A FINISHING tool consisting of a double ring, usually surrounding a dot in the center" (Roberts and Etherington, "roundel"; https://cool.culturalheritage.org/don/dt/dt2915.html [accessed 21 March 2021]). Of course, Roberts and Etherington are speaking specifically of the use of this shape in bookbinding; but the shape appears also in art of various kinds, on flags, in heraldry, on aircraft, and in many other applications.

ROUNDING AND BACKING (in bookbinding). Rounding is "[t]he process of molding the spine of a TEXT BLOCK into an arc of approximately one-third of a circle, which in the process produces the characteristic concave FORE EDGE of the book. Rounding takes place after the SPINE has been given a light coat of adhesive, and is accomplished by means of light hammering along the spine with a round-headed hammer. It may also be done by pushing in on the fore edge while holding the sides of the text block firmly" (Roberts and Etherington, pp. 221–22). Backing is "[t]he process of shaping a ridge or shoulder on each side of the spine of a text block prior to the application of the SPINE LINING material. The backs of the sewn sections or LEAVES are bent over from the center to the left and right until shoulders are formed against which the boards will fit" (Roberts and Etherington, p. 15). These authorities explain at length the benefits that these operations have on the book. (See especially p. 15.)

ROUT THE DEAD MATTER. The direction to a platemaker to make sure that nonprinting surfaces are removed sufficiently so that a ROLLER or other inking device will not get ink in that area of a BLOCK for printing. If a drawing is sent to a platemaker to have an illustration or text converted into, say, a ZINC or MAGNESIUM CUT, areas of the block that are not intended to print are sometimes created in the metal lower than TYPE HIGH but still high enough that they could receive ink during the inking process. The thickness of the paper, and the fact that in much letterpress printing paper is printed damp and is thus somewhat flexible, may cause the paper to "reach down" into this supposedly nonprinting area of the block and pick up ink. The direction "rout the dead matter" tells the platemaker to be sure to grind this area ("dead matter" is the area in the block that is not meant to print) extra deeply. (This entry was written from the memory of my cursing at the problem in my own printing. When I called the company that supplied the plate, they told me, "You should have told us to rout the dead matter"—a lesson I never forgot.)

ROXBURGHE STYLE/ROXBURGHE CLUB. "A particular style of QUARTER BINDING characterized by plain flat SPINES covered with brown and green calfskin, no RAISED BANDS, and dark red cloth or paper sides. The lettering, which is in gilt, is near the HEAD within a BORDER. Only the head edge was gilt and the other edges were rough cut. The style was originally designed for the publications of the Roxburghe Club, founded in England in 1812 by a group of wealthy bibliophiles, and named in honor of John Kerr, Duke of Roxburghe" (1740–1806) (Roberts and Etherington, p. 222). "Its membership is limited to 40, chosen from among those with distinguished libraries or collections, or with a scholarly interest in books" ("The Roxburghe Club," http://www.roxburgheclub.org.uk [accessed 15 June 2021]). Each member is expected to publish a book at his own expense. "Since its foundation, almost 300 volumes have been published on a wide range of subjects and scholarship" ("The Roxburghe Club," as above), and the volumes are bound in the "Roxburghe Style."

Carter's entry names members of the original club, including the 2nd Earl Spencer, Joseph Haslewood, and the Rev. THOMAS DIBDIN. And he says that the club's membership, composed of wealthy and not so affluent, is pretty much the same today as when the club was founded. They still publish FINE-PRESS books, and they are still quite active. (See Carter, pp. 219–20.) (This club is not to be confused with the Roxburghe Club of San Francisco, a member of the FELLOWSHIP OF AMERICAN BIBLIOPHILIC SOCIETIES.)

ROYAL BINDINGS. "A general term applied to bindings which have a sovereign's arms in the upper or upper and lower covers. Despite the presence of a sovereign's arms, so-called royal bindings did not necessarily have any royal PROVENANCE, as such bindings were produced rather frequently, especially in the 16th and 17th centuries. English bookbinders used royal arms indiscriminately as a means of decorating their books well into the 19th century. The blind-stamped bindings produced in the reign of Henry VIII, for example, which are embellished panels of the royal arms, are all trade bindings, as are almost all of the plain calfskin bindings bearing the arms of Queen Elizabeth, or her crowned falcon badge. Large prayer books or Bibles with royal arms may have come from one of the Royal Chapels, or they may have been bound for any (loyal) local parish" (Roberts and Etherington, p. 222).

ROYALTIES. Money paid to authors of works (or to those designated by the author to receive that money) by the entity that makes money for those works. An author may publish a book with a publishing house; the two parties sign a contract that designates what royalties the publisher will pay the author or her designee for the privilege of publishing the book. An author, if he is the copyright holder, normally expects his publisher to pay him royalties on the sale of his work. If the author relinquishes these rights—say, by giving intellectual control over to someone else—he may also be relinquishing the royalties to the other party. How much the publisher pays the copyright holder will be determined by the negotiations carried out before the rights holder signs the contract with the publisher. An extremely popular author, whose work the publisher knows will sell in the hundreds of thousands or millions of copies, may be able to negotiate a strong royalty (20 percent or so), while a neophyte writer may be happy merely to get his work into print and will settle for a much more modest royalty (e.g., 7½ percent). Authors often work through agents who can negotiate licenses for them and possibly maximize the royalties but who also take a percentage of the profits (or a negotiated set fee) for their efforts. The owner of the rights may draw up an agreement with a publisher with no intermediary or may employ legal (or other) counsel for assistance. The actual royalties are generally spelled out clearly in a contract, and they are usually based on the actual amount the publisher realizes in the sale of the volumes (cover price, net price, price after giving discounts to vendors, and so on).

An author may sign a contract that has escalating royalties: 7½ percent for the first 5,000 copies sold, 10 percent for the next 5,000 copies, and 15 percent for all copies over that. And royalties may be different for hardback and paperbound copies (and digital copies). Sometimes authors are given an advance (i.e., royalties paid before the book is published), and as the book sells, the royalties are deducted until the advance is paid off, but if the book does not sell enough to cover the costs of the advance, the author keeps the advance anyway, if that is the way the contract is written. If there are certain publishing costs, as for permissions (what the author pays for permission to publish the work of others that is still under copyright), the publisher may pay the permissions up front and then take their payment out of the royalties they would otherwise be sending to the author. (It is possible, however, for an author to negotiate for the publisher to pay for all permissions—and for other things, such as the costs of creating illustrations for a volume or compiling an index—and not to have to pay for them out of future royalties. Or the publisher will pay for a certain amount or percentage of the permissions.) Also, if the work in question has more than one maker (for instance, with two authors, a photographer, and another graphic artist), the royalties may be split among all of them, the percentage to be determined by the makers and the publishing house. Or they may be sent to the primary author (if there is one), and she then distributes the shares to the others.

ROYCROFT PRESS (Elbert Hubbard). The Roycroft community in East Aurora, New York, was founded in 1895 by Elbert Hubbard, who wanted to run what looked like a Utopian commune, though it was actually a for-profit community. He brought in craftspeople from anywhere they would come from, gave them food and lodgings, trained them in crafts, and sold the products of their labor. He gave them lectures, took them on health walks, and provided health care and good food in exchange for their loyalties and efforts. They were called the Roycrofters, and they worked to Hubbard's standards or were shipped out.

The products they made—housewares, furniture, pottery, and printed books, among other things—were strongly influenced by (and themselves strongly influenced) the Arts and Crafts movement in the United States. One of the operations at the community was the Roycroft Press, which produced books and serials printed letterpress, often on handmade or other fine papers. Their bindings were fairly shoddy, and much of the leather they used—including the limp suede of many of their books—became subject to red rot. The style of binding that was popularized in the community was called Roycroft bindings: "An old term applied to full leather or paper-bound books bound by the Roycroft Bindery, in East Aurora, New York. . . . The books were not backed and had the covers glued to the lined spine. The covers were flexible and were not turned in but overlapped the head, tail, and fore edge. Sometimes the covers were not attached to the text block by any other means other than cords laced through holes drilled from front to back of the entire text block at the binding edge. This style was popular for suede leather bindings" (Roberts and Etherington, p. 222).

Hubbard was influenced by William Morris and his Kelmscott Press, but his own publications were clearly aimed at the masses, while Morris's were aimed at a more elite clientele. There is a market of collectors for Roycroft books, but finding the volumes in fine (or even good) condition is a challenge.

As a footnote, Hubbard was the cliché soft-soap salesman, having made his first "fortune" in the Larkin Soap Company as a golden-throated salesman. He was a strong rhetorician, and he believed he could convince almost anybody of anything. On the strength of this belief, he and his second wife sailed to Europe in May 1915 believing that he could convince the warring powers of Europe to stop the war. He was killed when the ship he was on, *Lusitania*, was sunk by a German U-boat. The community was overseen by their son Bert until it closed down in 1938.

RUBBED. A typical descriptive word in a bookseller's catalog—often for leather bindings but for any binding that shows the feature. Rubbing shows as wear along any part of a book that might protrude (even slightly—as with BOARDS that have bowed out a bit, on which the rubbing could be in the center of the cover's boards). Common are rubbed corners or the cloth or leather at the foot of a volume. Sometimes the term is modified: "slight rubbing." And sometimes the word covers a multitude of sins and is used as a euphemism for "royally scraped" or "leather abraded down to the boards." David Magee says that the word, when used for illuminations in manuscripts, should "always be qualified by 'slightly.' If all gold and paint have vanished, you may say 'shows evidence of great devotional love by former owner'" (Magee, *The 2nd Course in Correct Cataloguing, or Further Notes to The Neophyte*, p. 10). (*See* Scuffed.)

RUBRIC/RUBRICATED. A rubric is a "part of a MANUSCRIPT or book, such as a title, heading, or initial letter, that appears in decorative red lettering or is otherwise distinguished from the rest of the text" (*American Heritage Dictionary of the English Language*, p. 1532). The word "rubric" comes from the Latin *rubricare* meaning "to color red" (or to a word meaning "red chalk")—hence the use of red ink to mark letters, words, or passages in red in the manuscript. (Some early printed books were equally rubricated.) The one doing the rubrication is the rubricator.

"Rubric" has come to mean introductory materials in a text—not part of the main text; and it is not necessarily written or printed in red (it usually is not). The term is also used to indicate a title or heading, as for a chapter or section in a book or PERIODICAL; and it is printed in such a way as to distinguish it from the rest of the text. For instance, it could be printed in all CAPS, **boldface**, or in red. Although rubrication usually manifests itself with the addition of touches of red ink to already written letters, sometimes the rubricator may use blue ink (or alternate blue with red). This is strictly not rubrication in its etymological sense, but the practice is the same, and one may say "rubricated in blue" (oxymoronic as that is). Also, rubrication influenced early printers, who frequently opened a new chapter or section in their text with a red letter.

RULE / RULING / TAPERED RULE / BEVELED RULE / BULGED RULE / DECORATIVE RULE. In MANUSCRIPTS, a rule is a line drawn on the writing surface, the person doing the ruling guided by a straight edge. (Note that the word "ruler" originally referred only to a device for drawing straight lines, not a measuring tool.) In manuscripts, the ruling guided the SCRIBE and the artists for writing the text and placing the illustrations. To guide the person doing the ruling, the one preparing the vellum would use a PUNCTORIUM to pierce a series of holes into the LEAF on all sides—vertically left and right (and also at the HEAD and foot if vertical ruling was called for). Then the ruling was done with red lines (*see* Red ruling), with black lines using lead (*see* Lead point ruling), with another metal tool (*see* Metal point ruling), or with a stylus, producing grooves and ridges rather than drawn-in lines (*see* Hard point ruling; Layout).

The manuscript leaves are generally pricked along their edges (*see* Pricking), and more than one leaf can be pricked at once, so successive leaves would have the holes in the same position on each leaf, allowing for perfect REGISTRATION on both sides of the leaves (and hence on facing pages) and on successive leaves. Similarly, with the use of a stylus, grooves would be created on one side of each leaf and ridges on the opposite side—also yielding perfect registration.

In printing, rule is a "horizontal or vertical line, either typeset, computer generated, or hand-drawn, that can be included in copy as type or added as art. If typeset, the thickness of the rule is usually measured in POINTS, the length in PICAS" (Eckersley et al., *Glossary of Typesetting Terms*, p. 89). The rule itself was made from brass or TYPE METAL, and it often contained more than a single line; hence, double- (or triple-) rule lines were possible, with the multiple lines the same thickness or varying. There is also the so-called TAPERED RULE (also called "beveled rule," "bulged rule," or "swelled rule"), a piece of thick rule that tapers at the ends (or a thin rule that bulges or swells in the middle—it depends on which way you are describing it). More decorative rule exists in printing metal, as with what is called the "diamond dash"—"A rule of brass or type metal, designed as a diamond in the middle of a straight line" (Wijnekus and Wijnekus, *Elseveir's Dictionary of the Printing and Allied Industries*, p. 272). That is, a rule does not need to be simple straight lines; it can be double and decorative in many ways. For instance, the rule can have a flower pattern, the "MEANDER" (or Greek key) design, or a series of dots. Thousands of decorative rules with adornments of endless patterns were

Printers' ornaments with decorative rule.

From iStock, Getty Images, https://www.istockphoto.com/vector/set-of-calligraphic-and-decorative-design-elements-gm493612089-40369990 (accessed 15 June 2021).

issued by many type foundries. There is also the hairline rule, the thinnest of all lines, which is about 1 POINT thick. Rule this thin can be printed from regular type metal, but brass rule was sturdier and withstood the pressure of the PLATEN better than did type-metal rule. And as the entry at "Red rule" explains, in early printing, and even through the 19th century, many publishers used red borders on all of the pages of their books to enclose the printed text.

RULING. *See* Rule / Ruling / Tapered rule / Beveled rule / Bulged rule.

RULING MACHINE. A machine that rules pages. Invented in the 18th century, this machine was used to rule pages for books for music, school books, stationery, accounting, business and bank records, and other kinds of pages that needed rows and columns. The ruling could be fine or broad; single, double, or triple; in black or in colors (with colors mixed when needed), and vertical as well as horizontal.

RUNNERS. Numbers printed vertically down a margin to show the line number beside which each number is printed. This kind of reference is used for long poems, and also for plays, especially when the printer expects the text to be referred to in scholarly works. The numbers help the scholars to guide readers to specific lines in the text. It would make no sense to write about a 1,200-line poem, "Poet Smith indicates in line 577 that . . ." and then make the reader try to find that allusion. The runners are a swift guide to the correct place in the text.

RUNNING FOOT. Though this sounds like part of a Nike advertisement, it is actually a line of text at the foot of the page that serves the same function as the HEADLINE, giving information such as the title of the volume, the name of the author, the title of the chapter, an indication of what information is on the page on which the running foot appears, a page number, or other information. Some bibliographers may want to call this a headline, but since it appears at the foot of the page, it must have a name that indicates its placement. In the plural, however, it can be amusing.

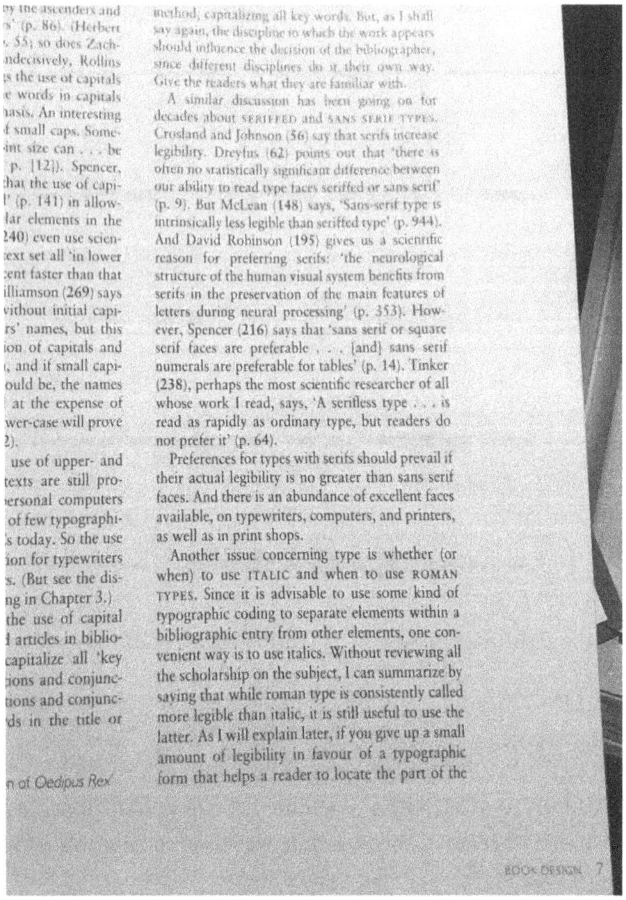
method, capitalizing all key words. But, as I shall say again, the discipline to which the work appears should influence the decision of the bibliographer, since different disciplines do it their own way. Give the readers what they are familiar with.

A similar discussion has been going on for decades about SERIFFED and SANS SERIF TYPES. Crosland and Johnson (56) say that serifs increase legibility. Dreyfus (62) points out that 'there is often no statistically significant difference between our ability to read type faces seriffed or sans serif' (p. 9). But McLean (148) says, 'Sans-serif type is intrinsically less legible than seriffed type' (p. 944). And David Robinson (195) gives us a scientific reason for preferring serifs: 'the neurological structure of the human visual system benefits from serifs in the preservation of the main features of letters during neural processing' (p. 353). However, Spencer (216) says that 'sans serif or square serif faces are preferable . . . [and] sans serif numerals are preferable for tables' (p. 14). Tinker (238), perhaps the most scientific researcher of all whose work I read, says, 'A serifless type . . . is read as rapidly as ordinary type, but readers do not prefer it' (p. 64).

Preferences for types with serifs should prevail if their actual legibility is no greater than sans serif faces. And there is an abundance of excellent faces available, on typewriters, computers, and printers, as well as in print shops.

Another issue concerning type is whether (or when) to use ITALIC and when to use ROMAN TYPES. Since it is advisable to use some kind of typographic coding to separate elements within a bibliographic entry from other elements, one convenient way is to use italics. Without reviewing all the scholarship on the subject, I can summarize by saying that while roman type is consistently called more legible than italic, it is still useful to use the latter. As I will explain later, if you give up a small amount of legibility in favour of a typographic form that helps a reader to locate the part of the

BOOK DESIGN 7

A page with a running foot, in the lower, outer corner of the page.

Sidney E. Berger, *The Design of Bibliographies* (London: Mansell, 1991), p. 7.

RUNNING HEAD. *See* Headline. *See also* Direction line.

RUNNING TITLE. *See* Headline. *See also* Direction line.

RUSSIA/RUSSIA CALF. A term still occasionally seen in booksellers' catalogs and in older descriptive bibliographies. It is "[o]riginally, a leather produced in Russia from CALFSKIN, vegetable-tanned with tannin obtained from the bark of willow, poplar, or larch trees, curried from the FLESH SIDE with a mixture containing birch-bark extracts—which gives it the characteristic odor for which it was famous—and dyed red or reddish brown. It was often given a grain pattern of latticed lines. Genuine Russia calf was at one time highly valued as a bookbinding leather, particularly between 1780 and 1830, partly because its pleasing odor was supposed to repel insects. It was first introduced into Europe before 1700" (Roberts and Etherington, p. 224).

S

S. A. A. (*See* Society of American Archivists.)

SABIN, JOSEPH (1821–1881). American book dealer and bibliographer (though born in England) who is best known for his extensive bibliography *Bibliotheca Americana: Dictionary of Books Relating to America* (see the bibliography), listing books and pamphlets and other publications about the Americas from about 1500 to 1926. Edward E. Dunbar says that "Sabin" (as the work is referred to) "is rich in original accounts of discovery and exploration, pioneering and westward expansion, the U.S. Civil War and other military actions, Native Americans, slavery and abolition, religious history and more. Sabin Americana offers an up-close perspective on life in the western hemisphere, encompassing the arrival of the Europeans on the shores of North America in the late 15th century to the first decades of the 20th century. Covering a span of over 400 years in North, Central and South America as well as the Caribbean, this collection highlights the society, politics, religious beliefs, culture, contemporary opinions and momentous events of the time. It provides access to documents from an assortment of genres, sermons, political tracts, newspapers, books, pamphlets, maps, legislation, literature and more" (Edward E. Dunbar, "American Pioneering: An Address before the Travelers' Club"; listed on Amazon at https://www.amazon.com/American-pioneering-address-before-Travellers/dp/127563625X [accessed 4 July 2021]). Sabin's monumental work has been digitized and is now available online. (Some of the text above comes from the advertisement from the company that digitized the work: Gale: A Cengage Company; see their ad at https://www.gale.com/c/sabin-americana-history-of-the-americas-1500-1926 [accessed 4 July 2021].) (See Krummel, "Early American Imprint Bibliography and Its Stories.")

SADDLE STITCHING. "The process of securing the leaves of a section, e.g., a periodical issue or PAMPHLET, through the center fold by means of wire STAPLES. The term 'saddle' derives from the saddle of the machine. The machine cuts the wire, forms the staple, drives it through the paper and clinches it from the other side. The section is [usually] stitched in two or more places depending on the height of the publication. The number of leaves that can be satisfactorily stitched in this manner depends to a great degree on the thickness of the paper" (Roberts and Etherington, p. 225). One bookseller used a single, centered staple in his low-budget catalogs—adding another category to the list of "EPHEMERA." (*See* Stapled.)

SADLEIR, MICHAEL T. H. (1888–1957). A "book collector, publisher, bibliographer, biographer, essayist and novelist. . . . His work as a bibliographer of Trollope and 19th century fiction in general turned academic attention to the book as physical object rather than text alone" (UCLA Library Special Collections, "The Michael Sadleir Collection of 19th Century Fiction"). In this realm, his major publication, *XIX Century Fiction. A Bibliographical Record Based on His Own Collection*, while obviously not a comprehensive listing, is an excellent record of authors and titles from that period.

SAINT CATHERINE'S MONASTERY (also called the Holy Monastery of Mt. Sinai). The monastery's own site says, "The Greek Orthodox monastery of the God-trodden Mount Sinai is located at the very place where God appeared to Moses in the Burning Bush, beneath the Mount of the Decalogue. . . . [I]t is at this site also that the holy relics of Saint Catherine are enshrined. This is the oldest continuously inhabited Christian monastery [constructed between AD 548 and AD 565], with a history that can be traced back over seventeen centuries. The monastery predates the divisions of the Christian world, its origins extending to late antiquity" (https://www.sinaimonastery.com/index.php/en/1 [accessed 15 June 2021]). The monastery has the world's oldest continually operating library, and it holds the precious *Syriac Sinaiticus* and, until 1859, the *Codex Sinaiticus*. (See Saad El Din et al., *Sinai*; and Schrope, "Medicine's Hidden Roots in an Ancient Manuscript.")

The "Codex Sinaiticus is one of the most important books in the world. Handwritten well over 1600 years ago, the manuscript [from the fourth century] contains the Christian Bible in Greek, including the oldest complete copy of the New Testament. Its heavily corrected text is of outstanding importance for the history of the Bible and the manuscript—the oldest substantial book to survive Antiquity—is of supreme importance for the history of the book" ("Codex Sinaiticus," https://codexsinaiticus.org/en/ [accessed 15 June 2021]). "The hand-written text is in Greek. The New Testament appears in the original vernacular language (koine) and the Old Testament in the version, known as the Septuagint, that was adopted by early Greek-speaking Christians. In the Codex, the text of both the Septuagint and the New Testament has been heavily annotated by a series of early correctors. / The significance of Codex Sinaiticus for the reconstruction of the Christian Bible's original text, the history of the Bible and the history of Western book-making is immense" ("What Is Codex Sinaiticus?" https://codexsinaiticus.org/en/codex/ [accessed 15 June 2021]).

The manuscript was broken into four parts: "The principal surviving portion of the Codex, comprising 347 leaves, is now held by the British Library. A further 43 leaves are kept at the University Library in Leipzig. Parts of six leaves are held at the National Library of Russia in Saint Petersburg. Further portions remain at Saint Catherine's Monastery" ("History of Codex Sinaiticus," https://codexsinaiticus.org/en/codex/history.aspx [accessed 15 June 2021]). The parts will be brought together digitally thanks to a cooperative program among the four libraries holding the parts (see "The Codex Sinaiticus Project," https://codexsinaiticus.org/en/project/ [accessed 15 June 2021]). The significance of the present entry is to indicate how modern technology is helping people in the book world: One of the most important books in the world of religion was dispersed to several venues. Scholars needing to see the text had the expenses of time and funds to work with these parts. With digitization and international cooperation, the parts are being brought together so that the entire text can be worked on from anywhere in the world where there is a computer and Internet access. (*See* Fragmentology.)

SALESMAN'S DUMMY/SALESMAN'S SAMPLE BOOK. (Also called a "canvassing book," a "peddler's sample book," a "printer's dummy," or a "publisher's sample book"—or some combination of these.) (*See also* Dummy.) A partial copy of a book, put together by the publisher for the use of door-to-door salesmen, so that they can show prospective buyers what the final published book will look like. The dummy will have a title page; a selection of printed pages; another selection of illustrations (if the book was to be illustrated); samples of various bindings, including the one the dummy is in along with others tipped into the dummy (sometimes on foldout flaps); and a few ruled sheets at the back of the abridged text for the names and addresses of people who subscribe to the volume. By selling by subscription this way, the publisher will get a good idea of the number of copies to print up and will know what bindings to put on the volumes. (See Arbour, *Canvassing Books, Sample Books, and Subscription Publishers' Ephemera 1833–1951 in the Collection of Michael Zinman*.)

These dummies are often accompanied by notes from the publisher (printed right on the dummy—e.g., on the END SHEETS—or LAID IN in a small BROADSIDE or PAMPHLET) telling the salesman what to say to prospective buyers. Dummies often represent early printings of the text, sometimes with title pages that vary from those that wind up on the final published copy. Only a sampling of the pages and illustrations will be in these abridged versions, but they can contain readings that vary from those of the actual published edition, so they could be of great interest to textual scholars. The dummies have become serious COLLECTIBLES among bibliophiles, especially those wanting to acquire all manifestations of the books they collect. (*See* Book traveller/Traveller's sample; Subscription sales/Subscribers.)

SALTING (at an auction). *See* Auctions.

SAMIZDAT. "The secret publication and distribution of government-banned literature in the former Soviet Union" (*American Heritage Dictionary of the English Language*, p. 1550). The word comes from *sam* ("self") and *izdatel'stvo* ("publishing house") (*American Heritage Dictionary of the English Language*). The term also, by extension, means the underground circulation of dissident texts. These were often quite cheaply produced, using a typewriter (with carbon copies) or a MIMEOGRAPH or XEROX machine.

"Samizdat began appearing following Joseph Stalin's death in 1953, largely as a revolt against official restrictions on the freedom of expression of major dissident Soviet authors. After the ouster of Nikita S. Khrushchev in 1964, samizdat publications expanded their focus beyond freedom of expression to a critique of many aspects of official Soviet policies and activities, including ideologies, culture, law, economic policy, historiography, and treatment of religions and ethnic minorities. Because of the government's strict monopoly on presses, photocopiers, and other such devices, samizdat publications typically took the form of carbon copies of typewritten sheets and were passed by hand from reader to reader" (*Encyclopaedia Britannica*, "samizdat"; http://www.britannica.com/technology/samizdat [accessed 15 June 2021]). (*See* Underground press.)

SAMMELBAND (plural is Sammelbände, though in English the tendency is to say Sammelbands). From the German words *sammeln* ("to collect") or the noun *Sammeln* ("gathering") and *Band* ("volume"). In one sense, the word means an anthology, but it is more used for a volume made up of parts, collected or brought together. Collectors might amass a group of thin publications—PAMPHLETS on many kinds of subjects: sermons, speeches on various holidays such as Thanksgiving or Easter, political or controversial topics, instruction manuals as for cooking or making dolls, and so on. They would have all of these bound into a single volume to keep them together. This volume is a sammelband. Not all of the items in this collection are necessarily on the same topic, though they may be. The pieces may have been gathered and bound together merely because the collector wanted to consolidate into a single volume a group of pamphlets that were the same (or about the same) size.

Sometimes a collector or bookseller spots a particularly valuable item in the volume and disbinds it to have the one piece. This BREAKER might profit in some way from the breaking, but she does a disservice to scholarship, for the sammelband is a record of one person's view of what belongs together (logical or not), and the disbinding takes away the information about the original collection. Sometimes the items in the volume have little or no relationship to one another, and one might wonder why anyone would have put them together in the first place. But often there is a thematic unity in the collection, and it is a crime (not literally) to break the volume. (*See* Breaker; Disbound; Pamphlet.)

SAMPLE BOOK. In general, a salesman's or company's advertising volume showing actual products for sale—not merely pictures of them. The term implies that real samples are bound in or TIPPED IN, or are LAID IN in some way, as in a pocket or sleeve. The use of these books was clearly commercial: showing potential customers products that they can order or buy immediately. These collectibles are important for many reasons, not the least of which is as a record of the kind of objects they display, many of which could no longer be available. The sample books may have the only known reference to them or to the company that manufactured or sold them, important for the study of material culture. And they are appealing because the original materials they contain are usually the best the companies have to offer, so they represent good things beautifully presented. Since tip-ins almost always have to be done by hand, the hands-on aspect of the sample books' creation makes them desirable. (Henry Morris of the Bird & Bull Press once told me that if he does a book on any subject, he might not be able to sell it; but if the book contains tip-ins, it flies off his shelves. Such is the nature of collectors.) And untold numbers of these books are simply beautiful: well designed, printed on and bound with good materials, elegantly illustrated, and a pleasure to hold. Not to mention that many of them have information about the materials and manufacture of the products they are displaying, along with data about the companies themselves.

SANGORSKI, FRANCIS (1875–1912)**, AND GEORGE SUTCLIFFE** (1878–1943). Principals in the bookbinding firm Sangorski & Sutcliffe, an English firm noted for its beautiful and high-quality bindings—especially jeweled bindings, of which the GREAT OMAR is the most famous. The firm, founded in London in 1901, is known for its exquisite bindings, using gold and precious and semiprecious stones, pearls, and other valuable materials. Sangorski & Sutcliffe is "one of the oldest bookbinding companies in England specialising in fine binding, restoration and the conservation of books and manuscripts" (http://www.bookbinding.co.uk/index.htm [accessed 15 June 2021]). They merged with ZAEHNSDORF's bindery in 1988, and 10 years later, they were acquired by Shepherds. (The website refers to the firm as Shepherds Sangorski & Sutcliffe; their website says, "The workshop now incorporates the long established firms of ZAEHNSDORF, founded in 1842, and Sangorski & Sutcliffe, established in 1901" (Shepherds / Sangorski & Sutcliffe, "The Bindery"; http://www.bookbinding.co.uk/The%20Bindery.htm [accessed 4 July 2021]).

SANS SERIF TYPE. Typefaces with no SERIFS. "The types that Americans call gothic and that Europeans call grotesque were the first serifless letters to achieve popularity as printing types. Now, more than a century and a half since their introduction, their appeal has not diminished in the eyes of most typographic designers . . . [and] they continue to flourish and fulfill a substantial niche in the typographic requirements for commercial printing" (Lawson, *Anatomy of a Typeface*, p. 337). As Lawson says, the sans serifs are popular in commercial printing (especially in advertising), though they are also seen in other contexts. (For an image, *see* Serif/Sans serif.)

SAWN IN (in binding). *See* Endbands; Recessed-cord sewing.

SCALEBOARD. (Also called "scabbard" or "sca'board." [Inexplicably spelled "scabboard" in the 9th ed. of Carter]). "Scaleboard, also known as scabbard, is thin wood that was used for bindings in Europe and Britain until around 1600 and much less so thereafter. Scaleboard was used in America for bindings in the 1680s and earlier, and the thin wood covers continued to be used until at least the 1840s. Scaleboard was used in place of paste or pulpboard long after those materials were widely available in America" (Non Solus Blog, "Julia Miller: Scaleboard Bindings and a Visit to RBML"). Scabbard was "[u]sed in Colonial America from the 16th to the 19th century. The grain of the wood was usually at a right angle to the spine in Boston," so it was sometimes possible to pinpoint the origin of a scaleboard-bound book not identified by place of publication (Jane Greenfield, *ABC of Bookbinding*, p. 59). In my years of working with early American imprints, I saw scores of these bindings, almost all of which were in less-than-perfect condition. The thin papers covering the boards were almost always rubbed away, torn, and peeling; and the boards themselves, thin as they were, were often cracked. An inexpensive leather usually covered the SPINE (creating QUARTER-BOUND volumes), and that leather, too, was generally in wretched condition. Because of the fragility of the binding, covers were loose, detached, or STARTING.

SCHEIDE LIBRARY (Princeton University). The rare book library at Princeton University. "The Scheide Library has been housed in Princeton's Firestone Library since 1959, when William H. Scheide [1915–2015] . . . moved the collection from his hometown of Titusville, Pennsylvania. It holds the first six printed editions of the Bible, starting with the 1455 Gutenberg Bible, the earliest substantial European printed book; the original printing of the Declaration of Independence; Beethoven's autograph (in his own handwriting) music sketchbook for 1815–16, the only outside Europe; Shakespeare's first, second, third and fourth folios; significant autograph music manuscripts of Bach, Mozart, Beethoven, Schubert and Wagner; a lengthy autograph speech by Abraham Lincoln from 1856 on the problems of slavery; and Gen. Ulysses S. Grant's original letter and telegram copy books from the last weeks of the Civil War" ("Scheide Library," https://library.princeton.edu/special-collections/divisions/scheide-library [accessed 15 June 2021]). In February 2015, Scheide gave his collection to Princeton's Firestone Library: "Musician, musicologist, bibliophile and philanthropist William H. Scheide, a 1936 Princeton University alumnus who died in November at age 100, has left his extraordinary collection of some 2,500 rare printed books and manuscripts to Princeton University" ("Scheide Donates Rare Books Library to Princeton; Collection Is Largest Gift in University's History," *News at Princeton*, October 24, 2015, https://www.princeton.edu/news/2015/02/16/scheide-donates-rare-books-library-princeton-collection-largest-gift-universitys?section=featured [accessed 15 June 2021]). (See Tanselle, "William H. Scheide [1994].")

SCHOENBERG DATABASE OF MANUSCRIPTS. A database of information pertaining to MANUSCRIPTS produced up to the end of the 16th century. "The Schoenberg Database of Manuscripts (SDBM) provides an incomparable resource for the study of the provenance of manuscript books produced before 1600. The SDBM is the largest repository of descriptive data on medieval and early modern manuscripts freely and openly available online. With a continually expanding database of over 225,000 records representing data drawn from over 12,000 AUCTION and sales catalogues, inventories, catalogues from institutional and private collections and other sources that document sales and locations of manuscript books since as early as the fifteenth century, it serves a wide range of users: an international body of scholars, book collectors and booksellers, students at various levels and citizen scholars interested in the movement of manuscript books across time and geography" (National Endowment for the Humanities, "Products for grant PW-51580-14: The New Schoenberg Database of Manuscripts: A Research Tool for Tracking the Current and Historic Locations of Manuscripts"; https://securegrants.neh.gov/publicquery/products.aspx?gn=PW-51580-14 [accessed 25 July 2021]).

SCHÖFFER, PETER. *See* Faust, Johann.

SCHOLARLY EDITION. *See* Bibliography.

SCHOMBURG CENTER FOR RESEARCH IN BLACK CULTURE. A division of the New York Public Library, the Schomburg Center is "a world-leading cultural institution devoted to the research, preservation, and exhibition of materials focused on African American, African Diaspora, and African experiences. . . . the Schomburg Center features diverse programming and collections spanning over 11 million items that illuminate the richness of global black history, arts, and culture. / Established with the collections of Arturo Alfonso Schomburg 95 years ago, the Schomburg has collected, preserved, and provided access to materials documenting black life in America and worldwide. It has also promoted the study and interpretation of the history and culture of people of African descent. In 2015, the Schomburg won the National Medal for Museum and Library Service and in January 2017, the Schomburg Center was named a National Historic Landmark by the National Park Service, recognizing its vast collection of materials that represent the history and culture of people of African descent through a global, transnational perspective.

Today, the Schomburg continues to serve the community not just as a center and a library, but also as a space that encourages lifelong education and exploration" (New York Public Library, "About the Schomburg Center for Research in Black Culture"; https://www.nypl.org/about/locations/schomburg [accessed 2 August 2021]).

The Center has several important collections (books, manuscripts, art and artifacts, photographs, prints, moving images, sound recordings), it offers educational programs, and it has a research and reference division.

SCHOLIUM. "An explanatory note or commentary, as on a Greek or Latin text" (*American Heritage Dictionary of the English Language*, p. 1569). They can be original notes written in the margins by a scholar or quotations taken from other sources. In either case, they are intended to expand the text, the suggestion being that the scholiast (the writer of scholia) is inserting information that he or she thinks the authors would have added had they had the extra wisdom and experience of the commentator (not always an accurate supposition) and that a reader would probably want to know (also not always the case).

SCHOOL PRIZE BINDING. *See* Prize binding.

SCORED; SCORING. To assist a binder (or anyone else) to fold a sheet of paper, the printer, using a metal RULE, can "print" in BLIND (or even in ink) onto the sheet a crease or groove where the fold is desired. I have seen advertising pieces so scored but never folded. It is possible that one collector could say, "I have the folded PROSPECTUS for the book," while another boasts, "I have it, too, but mine is scored but not folded!"—implying a better copy [?] and thus more valuable [?]. For extremely fine and small folding, as for doing complicated origami, artists can use lasers to do the scoring. (See Andreas Bastian, "Laser Etched Paper for Folding Complex Forms.") (As a slang term, this also means acquiring for a drastically low price what is worth a great deal more than what was paid: "I got that Dard Hunter at the garage sale for only $50; I really scored!")

SCORED CALF. "A calfskin subjected to an EMBOSSING process (subsequent to the covering of the book) so as to produce on the grain surface an indented effect that was supposed to simulate straight-grained MOROCCO. This type of embossing was popular in England from about 1800 to 1830" (Roberts and Etherington, p. 226).

SCRAPBOOK. "A book with blank pages used for the mounting and preserving of pictures, clippings, or other mementos" (*American Heritage Dictionary of the English Language*, p. 1575). The popularity of such collections goes back centuries, as COMMONPLACE BOOKS were kept as early as the 15th century. In the 20th and 21st centuries, the popularity of this genre has been strong, with scrapbooking clubs, businesses purveying a wide range of paper goods for the craft, and no shortage of volumes to use and people to fill them.

In the 19th century, travelers would bring home a wide array of goods from their trips and mount them in scrapbooks—items that were not necessarily paper based. One scrapbook at the Peabody Essex Museum contains coins, photographs, stones, and many artifacts from a visit to an international exposition. (*See* Miscellany.)

SCRATTED CALF. *See* Spotted calf.

SCRATTING (over leather; over MARBLING). Scratting is splattering droplets of a pigment (or an acid) over a surface to leave a spotted pattern on the surface. It is also called "spotting," "speckling," "spattering," "splotching," and "sprinkling." It is used over calf (*see* Spotted calf) or other leathers on bindings and is also a popular way of finishing off a marbled, paste, or other patterned paper. The scratting may be done in the marbling bath before the sheet is laid over the surface, or it can be done on the already-marbled sheet. (*See* Annonay paper.)

SCREEN PRINTING (also called "serigraphy" [i.e., silkscreen printing]). Printing through a mesh, which transfers ink to some other surface (paper, plastic, VELLUM, CLOTH, or other material) in all areas exposed by the mesh but not where the mesh is blocked off. The ink is squeegeed onto the surface through the mesh onto the SUBSTRATE. Multicolor printings can be done with additional screens, one screen for each color (unless a single screen is used, with parts masked off to let through one color, then having the screen masked off where that color was used and another part of the screen opened for another color, and so on).

The term is also used, as Carter points out, for LETTERPRESS and PLANOGRAPHIC printing using a screen that breaks up the images into dots, printed in varying sizes, and allowing for variations in density of the image. The dots range from 65 to 300 lines to an inch (see Carter, p. 224). A different kind of screen (a benday screen) is used for the production of HALFTONE ILLUSTRATIONS.

SCRIBAL COPY. A copy written by a SCRIBE, either from dictation or copied from some analog source. It is distinct from one in the hand of the author. Authors may have used WAX TABLETS or written on VELLUM or paper, and then, for one reason or another, had the text copied by a scribe. The AUTHORIAL copy is likely the most AUTHORITATIVE; a scribal copy likely to contain VARIANTS that were not authorial.

SCRIBE. From the Latin word *scribo, scribere* (to write); the word designates a writer, but more strictly a copyist, professional or amateur (though the suggestion is the former). As a professional, the scribe would work in a SCRIPTORIUM, for instance, in a monastery or for a Stationer, in a law practice, or in a commercial business—the scriptorium being a room or series of rooms set aside for copying. Professional scribes were taught particular hands (that is, particular scripts), and their training, aimed at producing legible text, yielded a script that could be fairly uniform from one scribe to another. (*See* Paleography.)

SCRIM. *See* Mull.

SCRIPT. The generic term for "handwriting" (what in schools may be called "cursive" writing), but in the study of MANUSCRIPTS it means a particular form of handwriting with identifiable features that distinguish it from other hands from different places and times. Hence, there are CUNEIFORM script, Carolingian script, italic script, and so forth. (*See* Paleography.) Some calligraphic TYPEFACES are called scripts. In reading about a FONT, one might see, "Under this title [i.e., 'Script'] a number of faces are comprised. They are all designed to imitate handwriting." (See the *American Dictionary of Printing*, pp. 503–04.)

SCRIPTORIUM. A room in which writing is done—as in a monastery where the monks copy MANUSCRIPTS. The room can hold a single SCRIBE or many, and a particularly busy scriptorium can be composed of several rooms. And the scriptorium may also house artists who ILLUMINATE the manuscripts (though I would love to have someone create the word "illuminatorium").

SCROLL (roll). *See* Roll.

SCUFFED. A common term to describe CONDITION. It means that a volume has been rubbed in such a way as to remove some of its surface. Scuffed leather will show the rubbing where, for instance, with a dark leather, the scuffed area is light or flaking. Scuffed CLOTH will lose some of its color, too, and perhaps some of its surface decoration (colored or gilt illustrations), ribbing, or other texturing, and the cloth could be frayed or torn—even to the point of showing the CARDBOARD beneath. Paper covers will likewise show scuffing in various ways. The scuffing takes the volume from PRISTINE and FINE down to GOOD or worse, and it should thus not be priced among the better copies. As with "SHAKEN," a volume described as "scuffed" may be more than merely (lightly) scuffed, and should be ordered "ON APPROVAL." (*See* Rubbed.)

S.D. *See* No date.

SEALED-BID AUCTIONS. In sealed-bid AUCTIONS, the bidders present their bids to the auctioneer in sealed form (as with a sealed envelope, but of course, it can be done electronically, just not under the purview of others). That is, they do not know what other bidders have bid, since all of the offers are sealed. There is thus no back and forth among several bidders for any given lot. The sealed bid is the only bid each party makes. When the auction is "over," the auctioneer opens the "envelopes" and the highest bidder is the winner of the lot. Such auctions are often used when there is a single item being offered, as with a house or piece of property.

SEALS. An ancient method of proving the authenticity of a document was to have it sealed shut by means of melted wax (though clay was also used), usually impressed with a pattern imparted by a signet ring or cylinder in which the pattern was carved or cast. A broken seal meant that the document had been tampered with. The method goes back to quite ancient times. "Seals with designs carved in INTAGLIO were used throughout antiquity. They were of two main types—the cylinder and the stamp. The cylinder first appeared in Mesopotamia in the late 4th millennium BC and continued to be used there until the 4th century BC. It was also widespread in Elam, Syria, and Egypt (3rd millennium BC) and in Cyprus and the Aegean (2nd millennium BC). Stamp seals preceded cylinders, first appearing in Mesopotamia in the 5th millennium BC and developing over a period of about 1,500 years until largely replaced by the cylinder in the 3rd millennium" (the term "sigillography" means the study of seals; this passage is from the online *Encyclopaedia Britannica*, "Sigillography," at http://www.britannica.com/topic/sigillography [accessed 15 June 2021]). Note that the term means the tool that is impressed into the wax or clay and the wax or clay piece itself.

In the last two centuries, seals have been used to seal envelopes, the practice—at least in the 20th and 21st centuries—being an archaism. And many a stationery store will sell seals with monograms or pictorial elements, along with sticks of red wax. A broken seal, however, may be an actual indication of tampering with an envelope, scroll, or package. (Or that the United States Postal Service had done its typical destroyer act.) There are also tools available today for EMBOSSING paper with one's monogram, producing a seal-like impression in paper. (*See* Clay tablets.)

SECONDARY BINDING. "A second or subsequent binding of a publication. Although the term may also be applied to hand or library bindings, it is used principally with reference to different times of EDITION BINDING. When a publisher does not know how many copies of an edition will be sold, and does not want to assume the cost of binding and inventorying copies which may not sell, he may have copies bound in segments, and, as this may spread the binding of the full edition over a period of time, the different bindings may vary because of changes in CLOTH color, SPINE lettering, etc. The practice of deferred binding was more prevalent, and the periods of time much longer, in the 19th century than today, as edition binding is now very highly mechanized and standardized. A REMAINDER BINDING is not a SECONDARY BINDING" (Roberts and Etherington, p. 227).

Sometimes a binder may have the same cloth for the secondary binding as was used for the initial binding, but for the secondary binding he may put the cloth onto the volume with the ribbing at right angles to the ribbing of the cloth used for the initial binding. When one holds two copies of a book with differences in their bindings, it may be impossible to determine which is the primary and which the secondary binding. Also, a secondary binding may be exactly the same as the primary one, and there may be no way to distinguish them from one another. So the fact that a primary and a secondary binding exist may be indeterminable.

Additionally, if a binder runs out of one cloth during the binding of an EDITION, she may simply take a second cloth and continue the work. All of the binding, then, may have been done in one operation. Which is the primary and which is the secondary binding? To complicate matters, if such a situation obtains, the binder using first red and then blue cloth, and if the copies with the blue cloth are issued to the public first, followed, say, six months later by copies in the red cloth, which is the primary and which the secondary binding? (*See* Edition, Impression [Printing], Issue, and State; Points, especially the section "Issue.") (*See also* Remainders; Trial binding.)

SECONDHAND BOOKSTORE. A shop selling secondhand books. (So obviously, the "secondhand" refers to the books, not the store.) (*See* Secondhand copy.) Such a store might have for sale some high-end volumes, but most of its stock will be run-of-the-mill copies of common (and not terribly desirable) books, usually exhibiting signs of their use. The leap from "secondhand bookstore" to "ANTIQUARIAN bookseller" is partly a function of the quality of the books for sale and partly a function of the bookseller's confidence and advertising. Further, such stores may get in PRISTINE copies of books, but it is unethical (and possibly illegal) to sell them as new copies. In the automotive world, "used cars" have disappeared; we now have only "preowned vehicles." There is no sign that the equivalent shift will be taking place in the book world. "Preowned books" may be difficult to sell.

SECONDHAND COPY/SECONDHAND BOOK. A USED BOOK—one that has had at least one previous owner. (*See* Secondhand bookstore.) The term "secondhand copy" implies a book not in PRISTINE condition. (Though *see* Secondhand bookstore.)

A bookseller acquiring volumes in pristine condition from a collector or library (copies with no markings at all and looking as if they had just come from the publisher) may wish to sell them as new copies. Most booksellers, however, will sell them as secondhand volumes, with the appropriately lower price than a new copy would command. It is a matter of honesty and professionalism. In a catalog of used books, the bookseller might describe a pristine copy "AS NEW."

SECTION. A SIGNATURE (also called a "GATHERING" or a "QUIRE") of a book. A bookseller, not knowing the more bibliographic terms, may say that a section of a book is loose, but today's more sophisticated and better-educated booksellers and collectors are more likely to use "signature" or "quire." (*See* Opened.)

SECURITY PAPER. Paper with special properties (e.g., secret fiber content, embedded foils, or WATERMARKS) that make counterfeiting difficult. The aim of security paper is to make counterfeiting impossible, but counterfeiters are ingenious. Papers with special watermarks, embedded strips of various materials, secret-formula inks, and special inclusions and colors of fibers make counterfeiting difficult but not impossible, for all of these can be copied. (*See* Security printing.)

SECURITY PRINTING. Printing techniques and materials that aim to make counterfeiting impossible. Such printing is done on papers that, themselves, are valuable (currency and stock certificates) or other kinds of official papers (passports and other kinds of identity documents, LABELS, postage stamps, tamper-resistant/tamper-evident papers, and the like). To prevent forgery, many methods have been created that may fall under the wider rubric of "security printing." Naturally, SECURITY PAPERS with special fiber composition and WATERMARKS have been tried. So have special inks, complicated and intricate ENGRAVING PLATES, holograms, special dyes in papers, and much more. While these techniques and materials add levels of security enough to keep most forgers away, they are not always enough. The North Koreans are brilliant counterfeiters, and the effort to create increasingly sophisticated security printing has merely spurred on an increasingly sophisticated world of counterfeit printing. (See Mihm, "No Ordinary Counterfeit"; and Rose, "North Korea's Dollar Store.") (*See also* Xerography.)

SEE-THROUGH (as with paper). *See* Show-through.

SELF-PUBLISHING. *See* Vanity publishing.

SELF-WRAPPER. Jacob Blanck explains: "The self-wrapper is the paper cover of a book or of a pamphlet and it is an integral part of the book itself. For example, a self-wrappered pamphlet of thirty-two pages would be one in which the first and last leaves (*i.e.*, pp. 1–2, 31–32) serve as the cover. The self-wrapper may be (and usually is) printed. / Confronted with what appears to be a self-wrappered pamphlet one cannot be certain that the publication was so issued; it may well be an imperfect or incomplete copy lacking the wrapper" (Blanck, *Bibliography of American Literature*, vol. 1, p. xxx). If a volume can be ascertained to be in self-wrappers or not, the fact that the printed pages (1–2 and 31–32) are part of the original format of the volume means that those pages are not part of the binding that the binder would have supplied. Hence, the self-wrapper belongs in the collational formula.

SEMÉ. Roberts and Etherington say, "An heraldic term indicating a form of decoration consisting of a scattered (sown) pattern of diminutive figures—flowers, leaves, sprays, etc., often repeated at regular intervals by means of one, two, or three small tools, resulting in a sort of powdered effect. Sometimes a coat of arms, or other vignette, is added in the center of the cover, or at the corners. There may also be a tooled fillet around the edges of the cover. Early examples of this style date from 1560 on books bound for Charles IX of France" (p. 228). It is included here because Carter has a brief entry for it, but it is not a term I have seen used in the past five decades. As generations pass, so do the terms that earlier ones used. It barely made the present text. (However, if scholars are using old sources, the term may appear in them, so it is probably prudent to leave it here.) Scholars today may encounter it in older literature.

SEMI-LIMP VELLUM. *See* Limp leather/Limp vellum.

SEMI-MONTHLY. *See* Bi-monthly/Semi-monthly.

SENEFELDER, JOHANN ALOIS (1771–1834). German playwright and actor who, needing an inexpensive way to reproduce scripts for the troupe, developed lithography. (See Twyman, *A History of Chromolithography.*) (*See* Chromolithography; Lithography.)

SERIALS/SERIALIZATION. Publications issued at (usually) regular intervals. Strictly speaking, magazines and newspapers are not serials, but scholarly journals are usually called "serials." The term is commonly employed for longer works that are issued over a period of months. A serialized text is released one or more chapters at a time in parts (also called "numbers"), printed as separate fascicles or in a periodical publication, such as a magazine or newspaper. (See Law, "Serials and the Nineteenth-Century Publishing Industry," and Law, *Serializing Fiction in the Victorian Press.*)

Some of Charles Dickens's novels were serialized, usually in 32-page fascicles. So was Mark Twain's *Pudd'nhead Wilson*—released a few chapters at a time in the *Century Magazine* from December 1893 to June 1894. While the more common practice was to issue the first printing of a work in parts, then gather the text and release it as a single volume, Carter points out that from the early 18th century, another common phenomenon was to reprint an already published text in parts in a serial. He cites *Robinson Crusoe*, published in the *London Post* (1719–1720). And he says that the first novel to be released in installments was Tobias Smollett's *The Adventures of Sir Launcelot Greaves* (which appeared in 1760 and 1761 in *The British Magazine*). In the 19th century, the practice took off, and innumerable texts were printed serially in magazines. (See Carter, p. 226; *see also* Parts/In parts.) (See Wiles, *Serial Publication in England before 1750.*)

SERIF/SANS SERIF. A serif is "[t]he beginning or terminal stroke drawn at right angle or obliquely across the arm, stem, or tail of a letter" (Lawson, *Printing Types*, p. 26). Serif types, thus, have these terminal strokes, while sans serif types lack them. In one way, serifs changed the course of the history of the book, if the traditional story is correct. (*See* Baskerville, John.) (See Catich, *The Origin of the Serif.*)

Following are three serif typefaces (on the left) and three sans serifs (on the right, after the virgule):

Serif/sans Serif

Serif/sans Serif

Serif/sans Serif

Three serif typefaces (on the left), and three sans serifs (on the right, after the virgule.)

SERIGRAPHY. *See* Screen printing.

SET-OFF. *See* Offset.

SET SOLID. Said of type that is not LEADED—that is, with no interlinear spacing.

SETTING RULE (in typesetting). (*See* Makeup rule.) A metal SLUG, usually made of brass (though it could be of other metals), used in a COMPOSING STICK by the COMPOSITOR, against which she sets type. When a single line has been set into the stick, the "bottom" of each sort is exposed (at the foot of each character). Since for most typefaces the sorts have exposed grooves, the surface all these sorts create is not smooth. The compositor wants a smooth surface to set type against, so she inserts a setting rule into the stick, covering the exposed surface of all of the type from the already set line in the stick, and she sets a second line against this rule. Once the second line is set, the setting rule is pulled out by small flanges projecting from the two sides (left and right) of the rule, and it is placed over this second line, giving the compositor another smooth surface to set the third line into the stick and so on until the stick is full.

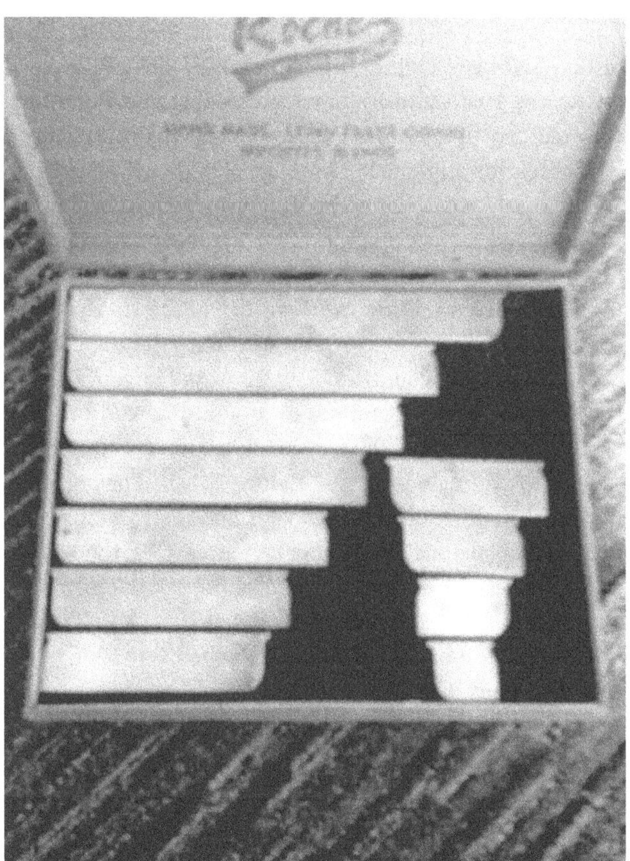

A set of brass setting rules for setting type.
Collection of the author.

Since the setting rules are of varying widths, the compositor can choose the one that is of the same measure as the lines she is setting (e.g., 15 PICAS, 20 picas, etc.) and use it to adjust the ELBOW of the composing stick to the desired line measure. So even the first line of type to be set will be placed into the stick against a setting rule.

Setting rules usually come in sets of, say, a dozen or more lengths—the most common line lengths a printer is likely to need. Printers do not need such formal tools; they can use LEADS or slugs just as well, though these will not have the convenient flanges to lift them out of the composing stick. If they do use slugs, for example, they can cut the slugs to whatever length they need, not being constrained by the standard setting-rule lengths.

SETTLEMENT. *See* Auction rings.

SEWING STATIONS. Places along the SPINE of a sewn VOLUME at which the thread of the binding appears. A LACED-IN binding may have, for instance, five genuine RAISED BANDS, each of which reveals that many sewing stations on the spine.

SEXTERNION. "A GATHERING composed of six sheets, each folded once and insetted" (i.e., nested into one another; Roberts and Etherington, p. 232). This is equivalent to a folio in 12s. (*See* Folio.)

SEXTODECIMO (sixteenmo). A book FORMAT created by folding the original sheet in half four times to create 16 LEAVES and 32 pages, with horizontal CHAIN LINES.

SHADOWMARK. *See* Light-and-shade watermark.

SHADOWS (in antique laid paper). *See* Antique laid paper.

SHAGREEN. "A somewhat obscure and ambiguous term which seems to have been used, at different times, for very different materials. The word, along with its French and German equivalents, chagrin, is said to have been derived from the Persian expression saghari, which applies to a leather produced from an ass, and which had an indented GRAIN surface caused by spreading seeds of Chenopodium (goose foot) over the surface of the moist skin, covering the skin with a CLOTH, and trampling them into the skin. When the skin was dry the seeds were shaken off, leaving the surface of the leather covered with small indentations. / In the 17th and early 18th centuries, however, the term 'shagreen' (or 'chagrin') began to be applied to a leather made from sharkskin having a curious grain surface of lozenge-shaped, raised and spiny scales of minute size, the character of which is difficult to perceive without optical assistance.

The term was also applied to the skin of a rayfish (probably Hypolophus sephen), which is covered with round, closely set, calcified papillae resembling small pearls. In its natural form it has been used for many years in both the East and the West for a variety of purposes, including bookbinding; however, in the early years of the 18th century it became the practice to grind the surface flat and smooth, leaving only the pattern of small contiguous circles. The leather was dyed from the FLESH SIDE so that the dye did not reach the small circles of calcified substance but only colored the epidermis where it could be seen between the circles. This is the leather which for a century has been called 'shagreen'; how confusion arose with sharkskin, which is completely different both in character and in appearance, is not clear" (Roberts and Etherington, "Shagreen"; https://cool.culturalheritage.org/don/dt/dt3058.html [accessed 3 March 2021]).

SHAKEN. A term used to indicate the loose condition of a book's binding. This is common for CASED-IN books bound in CLOTH, for the inherent weakness of that structure allows the BOARDS to be jolted in such a way that the inner JOINTS (where the pastedown is CONJUGATE with the front free ENDPAPER) will split. Also, the sewing holding the SIGNATURES together may be "shaken," and one or more signatures may be loose in a shaken volume. The term "shaken" may be accompanied by the modifying "slightly," but this does not mean that the volume is in a condition a collector would want. "Shaken" may be a euphemism for "poor." Any volume that was described by its purveyor as "shaken" should be ordered "ON APPROVAL," or should be expected to be loose in its boards and not in true COLLECTOR'S CONDITION. (*See* Scuffed.)

SHANK. The basic shaft of a SORT. The shank sits on its FEET, and it has the character protruding (in RELIEF) from its upper surface (unless the sort is a piece of spacing, in which case no character is there).

SHAPED BOOK. (Also called a "shape book.") A volume that does not have the traditional rectangular or square shape with straight sides, the vertical and horizontal dimensions at right angles to one another, but is configured in a way that conforms to an illustration on the cover, a shape related to the content of the book, or is in some way "out of square." Most of these volumes are children's books, though there are many for others as well. In my library is a volume made from a vinyl, long-play record that has been cut in half, with one half used as the front cover, the other the rear cover, and all the pages semicircles onto which the text has been printed. It is literally a "record book." (*See* Die-cut.)

A shaped book: Michael Heatley, *Guitar Trivia* (N.p.: Metro Books, 2010).

Photo by the author.

SHARP (Society for the History of Authorship, Reading and Publishing). An international organization focusing on book history and print culture throughout the world. "The Society for the History of Authorship, Reading and Publishing was founded [in 1991] to create a global network for book historians working in a broad range of scholarly disciplines. Research addresses the composition, mediation, reception, survival, and transformation of written communication in material forms from marks on stone to new media. Perspectives range from the individual reader to the transnational communication network. With more than a thousand members in over forty countries, SHARP works in concert with affiliated academic organizations around the world to support the study of book history in all its forms" (http://www.sharpweb.org/main [accessed 17 June 2021]). The organization holds annual conferences with hundreds of attendees, and smaller regional focused conferences. (See the American Historical Association website, http://www.historians.org/about-aha-and-membership/affiliated-societies/society-for-the-history-of-authorship-reading-and-publishing [accessed 17 June 2021].)

SHARP COPY. A term I saw in a bookseller's catalog: a copy that is bright and PRISTINE. Included here to reiterate what I said in the entry on CONDITION: there is no standard and sanctioned vocabulary for describing books. One can only hope the bookseller's readers will know that the copy so described will not cut their fingers, but will look great on their shelves.

SHAVED. Said of a volume that has had parts of LEAVES sliced off by a careless binder. Carter may have invented this use of the word "shaved," partly to show his humor and partly because it is an apt metaphor for the phenomenon. To him, a shaved page has had some ink sliced off but not necessarily the full characters so affected. As he says, a bookseller might describe a text as having a "slightly shaved" RUNNING HEAD or CATCHWORD, indicating that most of the affected characters are still visible and legible (Carter, p. 227). Although there are thousands of books for which this can be said, the occurrence is not great in most people's experience, so the term seldom appears in dealers' catalogs or bibliographic records. More common is to see "leaves trimmed, affecting some text"—or something more descriptive when there is a true loss of printed material. Seldom will anyone encounter "text trimmed by an over-ambitious binder [read 'bloody butcher'], with the loss of one to three lines on many leaves." "Shaved" is certainly a useful euphemism.

SHAW AND SHOEMAKER (Ralph R. Shaw [1907–1972] and Richard H. Shoemaker [1907–1970], comps.). Shaw and Shoemaker took over where Evans left off (*see* Evans, Charles), compiling BIBLIOGRAPHIES for *Early American Imprints* (second series), one volume for each year from 1801 to 1819. Their aim was to have a bibliographic entry for every book, PAMPHLET, BROADSIDE, and any other printed item from the first 19 years of the 19th century. They recorded about 36,000 titles, and while this was a monumental and tremendously valuable undertaking, they clearly could not "get them all," so the work needed to be supplemented by additional titles discovered after their volumes were published. The Readex company eventually microfilmed the full text of all of the Shaw and Shoemaker volumes (and included the full text of other items discovered after Shaw and Shoemaker's work was in print) as part of a two-part series, the first being the volumes listed by Charles Evans; the set is now available in digital form. The old Readex site said, "With more than four million pages from over 36,000 items—including 1,000 catalogued new items unavailable in previous microform editions—this digital edition from Readex is an essential complement to *Early American Imprints, Series I: Evans, 1639–1800*, the definitive resource for researching 17th- and 18th-century America" (Readex, "Early American Imprints, Series II: Shaw-Shoemaker, 1801–1819"; http://www.readex.com/content/early-american-imprints-series-ii-shaw-shoemaker-1801-1819 [accessed 9 October 2015]). Readex also writes, "This incomparable digital collection contains virtually every book, pamphlet and broadside published in America during the first two decades of the 19th century. Providing complete digital editions of more than 37,000 printed works, Series II covers subjects ranging from history, literature and culture to politics, government and society" ("Early American Imprints, Series II: Shaw-Shoemaker, 1801–1819"; https://www.readex.com/sites/default/files/productflyers/EAI-SeriesIIShaw-flyer.pdf [accessed 4 July 2021]). The value to scholars of these bibliographers' work is inestimable, and their volumes came to be known simply as "Shaw and Shoemaker." One might hear a librarian say, "Is it in Shaw and Shoemaker?" or even more simply, "Is it in AI?" (meaning *American Imprints*). Their work was carried on by other scholars, with subsequent volumes for subsequent years.

SHEEPSKIN. Roberts and Etherington say, "A soft, porous leather produced from the skins of wooled or hair sheep. It is usually vegetable-tanned and grained in imitation of other (more expensive) skins, e.g., MOROCCO, a process to which it lends itself very well. The term 'sheepskin' always indicates an unsplit skin, and is not applied to split sheepskin or SKIVER. Split sheepskin is the traditional material used in producing PARCHMENT. / Sheepskin is somewhat difficult to describe because the individual skins differ so greatly in size, fat content, and general quality of the dermal network. From the standpoint of leather, the closer a sheepskin approaches the hair sheep, the tighter and firmer the fiber network, and, therefore, the better the skin for producing leather. This is the case because the numerous fine wool fibers, as opposed to the lesser number of coarse fibers of the hair sheep, cause the skin to be more open and loose in texture" (p. 233). They add that "[s]heepskin is a reasonably durable leather if properly prepared and cared for. It has been used as a covering for books for more than 500 years" (p. 233). But as Carter points out, the term has come to mean really cheap material, for it abrades easily and will tear in strips as if layers are being stripped off. And sheep is weak enough that it will deteriorate at the joints (see Carter, p. 228). Through much of the 20th century, the term "sheepskin" also meant a DIPLOMA, for many institutions actually issued diplomas on this material. With varying levels of support to academic institutions (tending to the more penurious rather than to the more generous), the use of sheep's skin for diplomas has pretty much disappeared, though the term has held on as a quaint archaism. My own sheepskins were made from papers of diminishing quality and size over the decades. (My high school diploma was twice the size of the one for my Ph.D.)

SHEET (of paper). The basic unit of paper. Sheets are measured in size (*see* Appendix C, "Paper Sizes") and in number (*see* Ream). Printers begin with (presumably blank) sheets.

They print them on one side to create a BROADSIDE or on both sides (when called for) to produce various FORMATS of books and PAMPHLETS. With machine-made papers, a single sheet can be miles long, but the term is generally used for papers cut to "standard" sizes (though for centuries, there were no standards for sizes, as Appendix C explains). Books not bound, but fully printed, may be said to be IN SHEETS.

SHEETS. *See* In sheets.

SHELF MARK. *See* Pressmarks.

SHELF WEAR. Deterioration of a book along the TAIL on the edges of its binding, where the volume is slid off and back onto the shelf. The deterioration could also be to a DUST JACKET, or to any part of the book that has been RUBBED during use. The term has become generic to describe any volume not in good condition, regardless of where on it the deterioration exists.

SHELL GOLD. Gold that has been reduced to a powder. It is usually made as a byproduct of GILDING, with the "leftovers" from gold leaf stamped onto book covers or from the gilding of other surfaces; these tailings or skewings (the leftovers) are collected, mixed with honey so they can be powdered by a pestle in a mortar, and then the honey is processed away by putting the powdered gold and honey in a container with hot water. The gold sinks to the bottom and the rest is poured off. The gold is then mixed with gum arabic to form a paint. This gold is used in bindings, being brushed onto leather, mostly to repair gilding that has flaked off. It is also used in the production of manuscripts. The name comes from the mussel shells that were used as a container for the powdered gold.

SHINE-A-LIGHT BOOK. A volume that has pages with certain images on one side of a LEAF that "complete" an image on the opposite side of that leaf only when a light is shone behind the leaf. This type of book, aimed primarily at children, can be seen in the publications of Kane Miller, A Division of EDC Publishing. (They seem to have coined the term, as their series are called "Shine-a-Light Books.") The blurb on the front cover of many of these volumes says, "Hold the page to light to reveal hidden secrets." This is a sub-genre of MOVABLE BOOKS, and it is related to HOLD-TO-LIGHT cards. The difference is that in Shine-a-Light Books, the image seen when the sheet is backlighted is printed clearly on the VERSO of the LEAF, whereas in a Hold-to-light item, the image that is added to the picture or text on its front is not visible on the verso but is embedded inside the sheet.

SHOOTING STICK. A metal or wooden tool used by a printer in making up the FORME; the shooting stick is a shaft that is placed against the end of a quoin (in a pair of QUOINS) and tapped with a mallet so that the two halves of the quoins push together with their outer (parallel) surfaces spreading apart, thus wedging the type tightly into the CHASE. (For an image, *see* Makeup rule; Pica pole.) It is described by Joseph Moxon: "The *Shooting-stick* must be made of *Box* [wood], which Wood being very hard, and withal tough, will best and longest endure the knocking against the *Quoyns*. Its shape is a perfect Wedge about six Inches long, and its thicker end two Inches broad, and an Inch and a half thick; and its thin end about an Inch and a half broad, and half an Inch thick" (*Mechanick Exercises on the Whole Art of Printing*, p. 40). (See "shooting stick" at http://languagehat.com/shooting-stick [accessed 28 June 2021].) (See Gaskell, *A New Introduction*, pp. 79–80.)

SHORT-TITLE CATALOGUE. When printed in italics, the title refers to *A Short-Title Catalogue of Books Printed in England, Scotland and Ireland and of English Books Printed Abroad 1475–1640*, compiled by A. W. Pollard and G. R. Redgrave and others. It is often abbreviated *STC*. It is an important and frequently cited bibliography, appearing in several editions, including the one reedited by W. A. Jackson and Katharine F. Pantzer (1976–1991).

And as Carter points out, the notion of "short-title" emanates from an attempt to give as many entries as possible in as economical a space as possible, but (as Barker adds) with computers now in the bibliographical picture, scholars are able to have much longer entries than they were in an analog environment. The idea of a short-title text stretched to many other projects, including the *ESTC* (*see ESTC*) and the *ISTC* (*see Incunabula Short Title Catalogue*). (*See also* Evans, Charles.)

STCs were excellent bibliographic tools in the era of print, and they are still tremendously useful in a digital environment. They were quicker to produce than were catalogs containing all of the MARC RECORD data fields that rare-book cataloging encourages. Thus, they saved time and money in their production. In an electronic environment, there may be a shift away from STCs. Full cataloging records are more useful, for they contain information that modern scholars need. Full titles tell us a good deal more than do short ones. And full records should contain copy-specific information that is vital for security and that tells us about the provenance and use of volumes. This does not at all undermine the usefulness of STCs, which will be with us for a long time.

SHOULDER (on a piece of type). (*See* Kern.) "The non-printing area on the physical type [i.e., on the SORT] between the base-line and the front of the type. In certain styles capitals may be shorter than ascending lowercase letters, creating a shoulder between the face of the letter and back of the type" (Lawson, *Printing Types*, p. 25). If a neighboring sort has a kern, the kern rests on the shoulder of the next sort so that it does not break off under the pressure of the PLATEN. (*See* Appendix B.)

SHOULDER NOTES. Printed notes in the outer MARGINS, at the top of the page opposite the first printed line of the text. (*See* Side notes.) Shoulder notes are often brief summary statements (in a few words) of the contents of the page on which they appear.

SHOW-THROUGH (sometimes called "see-through"). The visibility of text on one side of a sheet from the other side of that sheet. Thin paper (or paper with little OPACITY) may have much show-through. This makes it imperative for printers either to achieve perfect BACKUP or to print on only one side of the sheet, as is the norm in Asian printing. (*See* Oriental binding; Registration.)

SHRINK WRAPPING. One of the two adaptations from the food industry, this is a temporary method of handling books that are not in good condition. (The other is FREEZE DRYING). Damaged volumes, with loose parts or with desiccating leather covers and SPINES, can be encased in archival plastic wrap. This holds the volume's parts together, keeps the book rigid so that further movement-generated deterioration does not happen, and encloses the flaking or powdery materials so that they will not transfer to other surfaces and will not be breathed in. The process is excellent for moving collections from place to place, and since the wrapping can be removed quickly, the volume can be easily accessed and then inexpensively and quickly rewrapped. Proper shrink wrapping should allow the item to breathe: that is, the shrink-wrapped package should not be hermetically sealed, but should have a hole in the wrapping to let air in so a micro-climate will not form. Though not everyone likes it, it has many advantages, and it is much cheaper than making PHASE BOXES for damaged items.

SHUNGA. *See* Erotica.

SIC (usually spelled with lowercase *S* and often in italics). Latin for "thus" or "so" and used in quoted matter that looks as if it is (or actually is) an error to indicate to the reader that the error is in the quotation as it is copied, not made by the person doing the copying. Since it is usually used in the quotation itself, it will normally be printed in square brackets: "To be or not to be: what [*sic*] is the question." An author's temptation may be to make the correction silently, not noting it in any way. But that would then produce a quotation that does not show the original *exactly as it is*. Usually better to use "[*sic*]" than to be accused of quoting inaccurately. Also, the error that occasioned the "[*sic*]" may be a state variant (*see* Edition, Impression [Printing], Issue, and State; Points) that could be useful to a textual or other scholar. And there is the possibility, also, that the passage that looks like an error is not, so leaving it as is (with the [*sic*]) is the safest way to handle an "errir" [*sic*]. On the Continent in Europe, the exclamation point is used the same way as is the "*sic*."

SIDEBAR. Text printed somewhere on the page that is not part of the main text, but that comments on it, adds to it, or clarifies it. Usually this text is printed in a parallel margin, hence the *side* in the word; but the sidebar could also be printed in a shaded area (or inside a printed box) on the page to distinguish it from the main text.

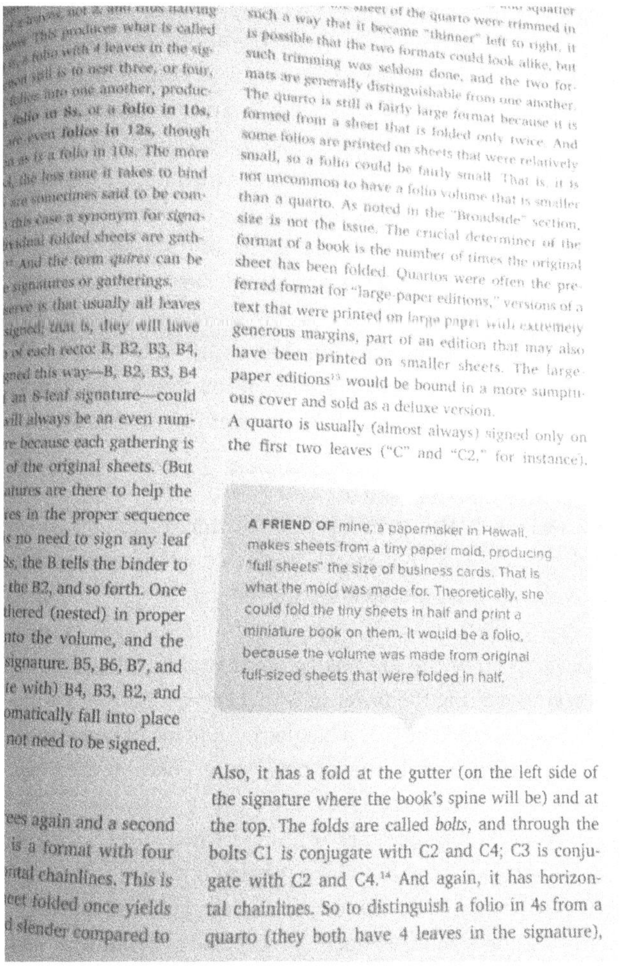
such a way that it became "thinner" left to right, it is possible that the two formats could look alike, but such trimming was seldom done, and the two formats are generally distinguishable from one another. The quarto is still a fairly large format because it is formed from a sheet that is folded only twice. And some folios are printed on sheets that were relatively small, so a folio could be fairly small. That is, it is not uncommon to have a folio volume that is smaller than a quarto. As noted in the "Broadside" section, size is not the issue. The crucial determiner of the format of a book is the number of times the original sheet has been folded. Quartos were often the preferred format for "large-paper editions," versions of a text that were printed on large paper with extremely generous margins, part of an edition that may also have been printed on smaller sheets. The large-paper editions[13] would be bound in a more sumptuous cover and sold as a deluxe version.

A quarto is usually (almost always) signed only on the first two leaves ("C" and "C2," for instance).

A FRIEND OF mine, a papermaker in Hawaii, makes sheets from a tiny paper mold, producing "full sheets" the size of business cards. That is what the mold was made for. Theoretically, she could fold the tiny sheets in half and print a miniature book on them. It would be a folio, because the volume was made from original full-sized sheets that were folded in half.

Also, it has a fold at the gutter (on the left side of the signature where the book's spine will be) and at the top. The folds are called *bolts*, and through the bolts C1 is conjugate with C2 and C4; C3 is conjugate with C2 and C4.[14] And again, it has horizontal chainlines. So to distinguish a folio in 4s from a quarto (they both have 4 leaves in the signature),

A page with a sidebar that is incorporated into the text.

From Sidney E. Berger, *Rare Books and Special Collections* (Chicago: American Library Association, 2014), 255. Reprinted with permission.

SIDE NOTES. Notes printed (or in MANUSCRIPT) in the outer MARGINS, opposite the place in the text to which the notes refer. (*See* Shoulder notes.) These notes can contain bibliographical references, citations to another text (e.g., biblical references or scholarly sources), glosses on key words in the text, or other information. (For an image, see figure at the entry for Interlinear.)

SIDES. A term used in booksellers' catalogs to mean the faces of the covers of the book, as in: "fine copy, ruled, in old French red MOROCCO, gilt edges, with Arms of Bishop De La Tour in gold on sides." (This description comes from the auction catalog of Sotheby, Wilkinson & Hodge *Catalogue of the Towneley Library*, [London: 1883]. p. 11, Item 227: *BREVIARIUM ROMANUM, cum Calendario* [Paris, 1647].) (Available at http://www.atoz.myzen.co.uk/towneley/downloads/books_1883sale.pdf [accessed 15 May 2021].)

SIDE STITCHING. "A method of securing the LEAVES or SECTIONS of a book with wire staples, from front to back of the entire thickness of the TEXT BLOCK. Side STITCHING is one of the strongest forms of construction and is frequently used in binding textbooks; it is also a common method of binding periodical issues made up of leaves or more than one section, and which, therefore, cannot be SADDLE STITCHED. The stitching is done by means of a machine that cuts the wire, forms it into a staple, drives it through the paper, and clinches it from the other side. Flat-wire staples of galvanized iron or aluminized iron are usually employed. Flat staples are used to provide flatter surface on the side of the publication than could be obtained with round staples" (Roberts and Etherington, "side stitching"; https://cool.culturalheritage.org/don/dt/dt3104.html [accessed 26 July 2021]).

SIGNATURE. The term has three distinct meanings in the book world: (1) a section of a book that will be bound into the volume with a single sewing operation, (2) the mark printed at the bottom of a page (in the HANDPRESS PERIOD, usually on all of the RECTOS before the fold of the gathered sheets) indicating the order in which the signature (in sense 1) is to be bound, and (3) a handwritten name of someone—such as a former owner or donor—somewhere in the book, often on the front ENDPAPER.

In sense 1, the signature is formed when sheets of paper are folded (*see* Format); to bind these folded (and sometimes gathered) LEAVES, the binder sews through the fold at the SPINE of the volume, attaching successive signatures with additional sewing operations. The signature is also called a "GATHERING," a "QUIRE," or a "SECTION."

In sense 2, the signatures at the bottom of the page are usually characters of the alphabet, but some printers, for various parts of the volume, may use other characters (e.g., numbers, punctuation, or special characters such as ASTERISKS OR PILCROWS, or some other character made up specifically for the volume) or none at all (common for the opening leaves of a volume). (*See* Register [in printing].) (For images, *see* figures at the entries for Catchwords and Headpiece.)

Sense 3 is either an enhancement or a defect of a COLLECTIBLE book. (*See* Signed copy.)

SIGNED BINDING. A bookbinding that has the name of the binder somewhere in the binding materials. "Several forms of 'signatures' have been used over the years, including: 1) the initials, cypher, or name of the binder tooled in BLIND on the outer surface of one of the covers, either by means of a tool or with a roll; 2) BINDER'S TICKET; 3) a stamped name, mainly on the inside edge of the lower cover, but also at the TAIL of the SPINE, inside the upper cover, on the inside of the front HINGE, and, in modern times, in ink at the edge of one of the FLYLEAVES; 4) a note inserted in the book by the owner; and 5) sometimes external evidence, such as a description of the work done, as with Roger Payne, or correspondence; or a famous style—Edgar Mansfield, Paul Bonet, etc." (Roberts and Etherington, p. 235). Carter has a long examination of unsigned bindings that can possibly be attributed to particular binders but with his typical cautionary remarks about not trusting suppositions of who a binder was based on stylistic or other criteria. He also notes that between 1835 and 1850, cloth PUBLISHER'S BINDINGS may be signed by a binder. (See Carter, pp. 230–32.) Two now-well-known designers are Sarah Wyman Whitman and Margaret Armstrong. From about 1850 on, *designers* of publisher's cloth bindings might sign their work, sometimes worked into the design on the front cover. (Margaret Armstrong used her initials on many of her bindings.) (See Boston Public Library, "Sarah Wyman Whitman Bindings"; and the Allen and the Gullans and Espey items cited below.)

Publisher's cloth bindings can be quite beautiful and can be strong selling points, so publishers often hired excellent artists to design their volumes. Thousands of these are unsigned, but many are signed by their designers, such as the ones by Margaret Armstrong, whose monogram "MA" appears (sometimes subtly) worked into her decorations. (See Gullans and Espey, *Margaret Armstrong and American Trade Bindings*. See also Allen, *The Book Cover Art of Sarah Wyman Whitman*; Allen and Gullans, *Decorated Cloth in America*; and Morris and Levin, *The Art of Publishers' Bookbindings, 1815–1915*.)

Binding signed by "S. Wright, Binder." On Thomas Campbell, *The Poetical Works of Thomas Campbell* (London: Edward Moxon, 1843). Note the gilt dentelles.
Collection of the author.

SIGNED COPY. A book, PAMPHLET, photograph, or other piece of library material that has been signed. The implication is that the copy has been signed by the author, but it could have been signed by anyone (the publisher, the illustrator, the binder, or a former owner), and the description "signed copy" should be clear as to who the signer is. If the SIGNATURE is accompanied by a note, it becomes an "INSCRIBED COPY." If the signature is from an important person, it becomes an "ASSOCIATION COPY." On the other hand, a signature by an unknown could reduce the value of a volume significantly. That is why some booksellers will minimize the impact of a signature by researching the signer to find out who he or she was and giving a short biography of the one who defaced the book.

SILKING. (*See* Japan paper; Lamination.) In CONSERVATION, the covering of a LEAF (of a BROADSIDE or a book) in a thin layer of silk on one or both sides. The aim was to strengthen a fragile or damaged sheet. The silk, along with the thin paste that was used to adhere it to the sheet, became invisible, so the text or images on the page were perfectly visible. Over time, however, in most cases, the paste dried out and turned powdery, and the silk gauze started to DELAMINATE. This was obviously an imperfect conservation treatment, but fortunately the process was mostly reversible since the adhesive was water based and the silk gauze could be removed. The term may occasionally be found, used incorrectly, to mean laminated with a fine conservation tissue. Strictly speaking, however, silking was done with silk. (*See* Chalking.)

SILK MOIRÉ. A so-called watered silk that has a wavy or ripple effect, used for the PASTEDOWNS and sometimes also the free ENDPAPERS in fancy bindings. Roberts and Etherington say about moiré book cloth: "A book cloth having an irregular, wavy finish produced by EMBOSSING in such a manner as to resemble watered silk. Prayer books and Bibles sometimes have endpapers consisting of a folded sheet of black moiré cloth mounted on a paper flyleaf. Moiré book cloth was at one time used fairly frequently for DOUBLURES. It was also one of the earliest decorative effects applied to the calico used for publishers' bindings" (p. 171). The pattern was also applied to papers. (*See* Moiré.)

SILK-SCREEN PRINTING. *See* Screen printing.

SILVERFISH. "Any of various small wingless insects of the order Thysanura, having a silvery body and a three-pronged tail, especially *Lepisma saccharina*, which feeds on the starchy material in bookbindings, clothing, and food" (*American Heritage Dictionary* online, "silverfish"; https://www.ahdictionary.com/word/search.html?q=silverfish [accessed 5 March 2021]). These nasty little bugs are partial to moist environments, so though they can be controlled with any of several insecticides, the best treatment is keeping the environment dry. However, once they have established a colony, more drastic measures are often in order. They are particularly drawn to the starches in papers and some of the adhesives in bindings, and their "trails" of munching can often be seen along the cloth covers of books and in areas over the surface of photographs.

SILVER VARNISH PAPER. *See* Dutch gilt papers.

***SINA NOTA*.** The bookseller Bernard Quaritch published his *Catalogue of the Monuments of the Early Printers in All Countries . . . Offered for Cash at the Affixed Net Prices* in 1888. On page 3592, Item 36233 is a book by Jacobus D. Cessolis. The line in the catalog for publication data has "*Sina nota* (about 1480)." Item 36234 (page 3592) is a volume by Hemmerlin (the full name given). That entry has "S.n. (*circa* 1480)," the "S.n." the abbreviated form of the Latin phrase. (He uses the spelled-out and the abbreviated version many times in this catalog.) *Sina nota* means without any information concerning the publisher: no city or publisher's name appears on the item; it is used for INCUNABULA and other EARLY-PRINTED books. The Quaritch catalog has a good deal of information about the volume (its FORMAT, its SIGNATURES, its COLLATION, its TYPEFACE, and its RARITY—and its mere existence), and it is just the kind of source one might seek out for publication and other information. The term is used by the more learned booksellers of the late 19th and early 20th centuries in their descriptions, and anyone encountering it should know what it means. If they look here, they will be enlightened. Quaritch assumed his readers knew what the term (and its abbreviation) meant.

Additionally, the Quaritch catalog has, at several entries, "s.n. & l." meaning "without a publisher or place"—implied by "s.n." by itself, but made more explicit with the addition of the "L" for "*locus*."

SINGLETON. Carter says that this term refers to a LEAF placed in a volume in an irregular place among the SIGNATURES. It might be a leaf that was once CONJUGATE to a removed leaf (one that has been removed to be placed elsewhere in the book) or an extra leaf that needed to be added to the text for one reason or another. (See Carter, p. 232.) As with many of Carter's terms, this one is not often used, but the commonness of singletons should give the term an opportunity to make a comeback. They are likely to be referred to by modern booksellers in a slightly more generic way: "with a loose leaf laid in" or "with G2 unattached to its conjugate leaf" ("G2" referring to the second leaf of the G signature).

SIXTEENMO. *See* Sextodecimo.

16-PAGERS. *See* Tijuana bibles.

SIXPENNY PUBLICATIONS. At the end of the 19th century and into the 20th, a host of publishers, mostly British, recognized the possibilities of selling cheap books to a newly literate readership. Many of the books, as typified by the SIXPENNY WONDERFULS, were sold—with texts that would appeal to people of moderate means and drab lives. In the 20th century, Penguin became the number one purveyor of such volumes, but there were many predecessors to Penguin, and they led the way. Chatto and Windus, Routledge (with its Sixpenny series), the Daily Mail and its Sixpenny Novels, Hutchinson's Famous Sixpenny Novels, and Viztelly's Sixpenny Series were among the more prosperous sellers. A writer who is identified as jojoal, on a blog called Paperbackrevolution (dated only February 28), says, "The success of Penguin was so overwhelming that in retrospect it has obscured what went before and rather created the impression that Penguins appeared out of nowhere. In practice Penguins evolved from a long history of sixpenny PAPERBACKS going back to Victorian times. I've already written about the Chatto & Windus series that ran from 1893 to the 1920s and about the Hutchinson series that ran roughly from 1925 to 1935" (jojoal, "Collins Sixpenny Paperbacks from the Pre-Penguin Era"). On a separate blog (dated only Oct. 12) this writer says, "Believe it or not, there were paperbacks in the UK before Penguin. There were even sixpenny paperbacks. There had been for a very long time and they were particularly plentiful in the first thirty years or so of the twentieth century, before Allen Lane [of Penguin Books] came along to transform the market. Lane's paperback revolution changed many things, perhaps most notably in getting rid of cover art, but also in changing the size of paperbacks. Before 1935, the standard size for a paperback was roughly 15 cm by 22 cm, or 6 inches by about 8.5 inches, considerably larger than the standard size ushered in by Penguin. What Penguin didn't change was the price" (jojoal, "Hutchinson's Famous Copyright Novels"). There was also Macmillan's reprint series called the Three & Sixpenny Novels series issued from the late 1880s to about 1935 or so. There were over 400 titles consisting mostly of fiction by scores of writers, including Mrs. Oliphant, Cruikshank, Dickens, Sir Walter Scott, H. G. Wells, and many others.

SIXPENNY WONDERFULS. Like their cousins the PENNY DREADFULS, these were inexpensive lurid publications, printed in color on cheap paper, and sold as escapist literature to the masses. Since most of them were priced at six pennies, they got their name. As the book *Sixpenny Wonderfuls* explains, a new reading class emerged at the end of the 19th century in Great Britain (the first was issued in 1893), and "Reading was a ticket to a different life, an exciting adventure or the promise of a bright future" (p. 8). These cheap volumes were issued by Chatto & Windus, one of England's premiere publishers, who saw the opportunity of tremendous sales to this burgeoning audience. "Chatto's directors were among the first publishers to move toward this new market. The intention was to republish some of their most successful hardbound novels in new, paper covers with bright colourful designs, and at a much cheaper price. The illustrators were commissioned to choose exciting and dramatic moments to attract the customers" (*Sixpenny Wonderfuls*, p. 8; see *Sixpenny Wonderfuls* in the bibliography). These publications often had lurid covers, but the texts were not necessarily lurid. They were of romance, westerns, detective fiction, stories taking place in exotic lands, and classics of literature. The series had, for instance, Mark Twain's *The Adventures of Tom Sawyer*, *The Prince and the Pauper*, and *Huckleberry Finn*, along with works by Émile Zola, A. Conan Doyle, Robert Louis Stevenson, Wilkie Collins, and Charles Reade.

Seeing the popularity of these volumes, and recognizing that six pennies was a price point that encouraged the public to buy books, another publisher, Ernest Benn, issued its own Sixpenny Library, about 250 titles, mostly of reference books. They were cheaply produced, with simple, unillustrated printed covers, with the titles and other publishing information printed inside elaborate borders. The titles were on history, art, nutrition, the natural world, architecture, famous people, economics, science, astronomy, education, literature, and the like.

SIXTIES BOOKS. Included here as an example of the kind of terminology that Carter thought important because literature *of his day* covered it. His entry says the term refers to the work of English illustrators working in the 1860s. The now-defunct website "Sixties Books: A Collector's Guide" said that the term refers to "the unique set of illustrated books, produced in the middle years of the 19th century, using the technique of reproductive WOOD-ENGRAVING" (https://4d30eded3a46eee17b113ef47ff4be07c388f4c1.googledrive.com/host/0BxcALKfrokYfflAzRXNYVGVndTh2bzFmUTR2amhPdWIwa0lRdkNsWWNpajRKMDVGUUgtVTA/page2.html#PG [accessed 5 March 2016, but no longer accessible]). Carter adds that volumes of this decade may have been issued in sumptuous bindings, with gilt edges, BEVELED boards, and GUTTA-PERCHA covers. (See Carter, pp. 232–33.) These are poor-quality bindings, so many of them perished.

Although Carter says that the term was somewhat common when he wrote his entry (p. 232), today the term is seldom seen, and, lacking Carter's knowledge and historical perspective, modern commenters on books would probably more likely describe the books in terms of their PUBLISHER'S BINDINGS since that was one of the markers of an 1860s book rather than understanding that the illustration of the book, not its binding, was the primary characteristic of the sixties books. The term is so rare in the book world—and in the world in general—that I could not find it on the web. But in keeping with the philosophy of selection for the present volume, it must be included here since it may appear in the literature of Carter's day, and readers need to know what it refers to. (See Goldman, *Victorian Illustrated Books 1850–1870*; Houfe, *The Dictionary of British Book Illustrators and Caricaturists, 1800–1914, with Introductory Chapters on the Rise and Progress of the Art*; and White, *English Illustration, "The Sixties"; 1855–1870.*)

SIZE (in MARBLING). To marble a sheet in the traditional Western fashion, the marbler needed to have a trough of slightly thickened water onto which to drop the pigments that would form the pattern on the sheet. This thickened water is called the "size." The thickening agent (e.g., gum tragacanth, Irish moss, or some other material) allows the droplets of pigments to sit on the surface of the size and not float around, allowing the marbler to manipulate the drops with rakes and combs and other tools.

SIZE (in paper formation) (also called "sizing"). Additive to paper that bonds all the fibers together and fills in the tiny air pockets around the fibers. When a sheet is made with just water and pulp, the resulting sheet—called "WATERLEAF"—will be porous; ink (especially water-based ink) will be pulled into the sheet by capillary action, FEATHERING into the LEAF where the air pockets are. Size fills in these pockets, binding the fibers together, hence "BOND PAPER." The additive, usually an animal glue, is added either in the VAT when the sheet is being formed ("vat sizing") or in a tub after the sheets have been dried ("tub sizing"). The latter is more common than the former, for if the sizing is done in the vat, the glue gets into the FELTS onto which the just-formed sheets are COUCHED, and the felts will need to be washed to remove the size before they can be used again.

Carter says that the only time a collector or bookseller would be interested in size is when a conservator has washed a leaf (or a volume) and removed the size. In such a case, the paper might be flaccid and not too strong. Many a conservator might add new sizing to the washed leaf (or leaves). When this occurs, the collector might not be willing to acquire the item since it is removed from its original condition—and thus one further degree less in value, if the resizing is visible.

One further note: The size strengthens the paper, but it also makes it marginally more difficult to print on than is waterleaf. Ink will not always adhere easily to sized paper. Inexperienced printers would often use additional ink to achieve a good image. For centuries, printers, to deal with this, would dampen their sheets, softening the size, and making it possible to get excellent IMPRESSIONS by even *reducing* the amount of ink they were using.

SIZE (of books). This topic yields two sub-topics: 1) how to denote size with respect to FORMAT, and 2) how to denote books with respect to measurement. 1) In the HANDPRESS PERIOD, the format of books was determined by the number of folds made in the original full sheets that made up the books. Size was absolutely not the issue. Small sheets folded once would yield small FOLIOS, for instance. Hence, the size of the volume was determined by the size of the original full sheets. So one could not say with perfect accuracy, "This is a large book; it must be a folio," since it could have been a large QUARTO. Nor could one say with accuracy, "This is a tiny book; it could not possibly be a folio," because the printer could have been using quite small sheets, made on a tiny PAPER MOLD. Hence, for books produced in the handpress period, rather than denote the size of a volume by designating its format, one should do so by giving its dimensions (*see* 2, below), perhaps also by mentioning its format, though this is not really necessary if the size is all one wishes to show. For books printed after the end of the handpress period, when they were produced on automatic presses using large rolls of paper, designations of the format have essentially lost their meaning. The idea of the size of the "original full sheet" no longer obtains. So those describing the *format* of books from the machine-press period might use terms for format based on size. Geoffrey Ashall Glaister has a chart of 18 "American Book Sizes" (*Glaister's Glossary of the Book*, p. 8), and another of "British Book Sizes" (p. 71), with their commonly used names and their dimensions. For instance, for the American ones, a "Thirtysixmo" book is 4 × 3½ inches. A "Royal Octavo" would be 10 × 6½ inches. All BOOKSELLERS or BIBLIOGRAPHERS had to do was measure the volume, find a dimension close to one listed in Glaister's chart, and they had a name for the format. It is clear, from this, that the whole classical notion of *format* has changed from a designation of *number of times a sheet was folded* to *a particular size*. For a classical approach to books printed beyond the handpress period (and especially those CASE BOUND), naming the format makes no sense. The best thing to do is simply give the dimensions. 2) Denoting the size of volumes with respect to their dimensions cannot be simpler: measure them with a RULER. (And remember that sheets could have been trimmed by the binder.) Traditionally the height is given first, followed by the width. And in some cases, to emphasize the weight and heft of a substantial tome, the depth or BULK of a volume may also be given. In the United States, since most of a bookseller's audience will probably be American, it is traditional to use inches. But if the seller has a substantial number of non-U.S. clients, centimeters may be preferred, or both can be given. European booksellers (and many U.S. ones as well, who want to look worldly, I suppose) almost uniformly use only centimeters.

SIZE COPY. *See* Dummy.

SIZED. Said of paper that has been impregnated with glue. (*See* Size [in paper formation].) Sized paper, in this respect, is BOND PAPER, and is the opposite of WATERLEAF.

SKELETON FORMES. When a printer is running off one SIGNATURE after the next for a book, she will pull type from the press once the pages have been printed off, replacing it with the type needed for the next PRESSRUN. But part of the page will not change: decorative or plain RULES, ORNAMENTS, and HEADLINES, for example, and the line that contains the page numbers. There is no need to remove those parts of the FORMES from one pressrun to the next. The part of the forme that stays in the CHASE is called the "skeleton forme." It saves the COMPOSITOR time in setting type, and it helps the printer achieve good REGISTRATION if the lines of type from one forme to the next are kept in the same position forme after forme. Philip Gaskell says, "Every forme of a book was arranged essentially the same way. The number and pattern of the pages were regularly and exactly repeated, and it saved labour to re-use the chase, QUOINS, FURNITURE, headlines, and regularly repeated rules or ornaments [*see* Fleurons] from a forme that had been printed off, rather than to find or set them afresh for each new forme. All these re-usable parts, the typographical parts which left their mark upon the paper, and the chase, quoins, and furniture which did not, are known collectively today as the 'skeleton forme'" (*A New Introduction to Bibliography*, p. 109). Gaskell discusses the bibliographical information that can be gleaned by studying skeleton formes (pp. 109–10).

SKIVER. "The outer GRAIN split of a sheep-, lamb-, or (occasionally) GOATSKIN, vegetable-tanned, and usually from 0.25 to 1.0 mm thick. Skivers are finished in a wide variety of colors and EMBOSSED grains, as well as with a plain, smooth surface. At one time skiver was used very extensively for LABELS of many kinds of bindings, e.g., the red and black labels of law books" (Roberts and Etherington, p. 238). The word has a suggestion of cheapness and lack of quality, especially when a volume is bound in it, since it is a thin and thus not terribly durable material.

SLA. *See* Special Libraries Association.

SLAB SERIF. *See* Egyptian type.

SLAM BOOK. A volume, kept by children and teenagers, usually SPIRAL BOUND, that contains questions written at the tops of pages; the books were handed around for others to answer the questions. (See Mansour, *From Abba to Zoom: A Pop Culture Encyclopedia of the Late 20th Century*, p. 436.) The term is also used for similar volumes, but to gather insults and deprecatory statements about classmates and others. Sam Oglesby explains, "The format of the slam book was simple enough. At the top of each page, the name of a student was written in large letters. The blank page below invited brief but biting comments, something on the order of what today might be a Tweet or a Facebook comment, except that these were scrawls in pencil or ballpoint" (Oglesby, "Before Facebook Bullying, There Was the Dreaded Slam Book"). As with the unbiquitous AUTOGRAPH ALBUM, these can be valueless or tremendously COLLECTIBLE, depending on the owner or the people written about in the volumes.

SLASH. *See* Virgule.

SLEEPER. In the commercial world, a book that has slow sales when it is first released, but later has substantial sales over months or years. Because of its initial lethargy, such a volume could become a REMAINDER and go OUT OF PRINT. When the publisher sees this, he may issue a new edition or create a new impression. (*See* Edition, Impression [Printing], Issue, and State; Points.) In the ANTIQUARIAN book market, a sleeper is a volume that is underpriced at a BOOK FAIR or in a BOOKSELLER's source (printed or online catalog). This may happen when the book does not show up in any online selling site, and the bookseller, unaware of the volume's actual retail value, must try to figure out what it is worth, and guesses wrong. Many a sleeper is snapped up by a bookseller from another bookseller's booth at a book fair before it opens to the public, and the sleeper is awakened—a term I just coined for a volume that was underpriced at one booth and repriced at another once the book fair opened. "I have for sale an awakened book." It often happens, and sometimes the signs of it are visible in the imperfectly erased price on the front free ENDLEAF. Sleepers also appear at AUCTIONS, when the cataloger for the sale has come upon a volume outside her area of expertise and her write-up does not reveal the item for what it really is: worth a good deal more that the cataloger has recognized.

One source of the sleeper could be that an item is by an author publishing under a name unfamiliar to the cataloger and to most others. Bradford Morrow, in his post "In Search of America's Rarest Unknown Books by Renowned Writers," mentions, for example, a volume titled *Verses* by Edith Newbold Jones. It is the first book published by Edith Wharton. On a bookseller's shelf, this modest volume might be priced quite reasonably, the seller not realizing its great worth since he did not recognize who its author really was.

SLEEVE. In their desire to protect DUST JACKETS, booksellers might encase these WRAPPERS in transparent covers, made of some kind of presumably archival plastic (like MYLAR). Such covers are called "sleeves," since the jackets slide in the way an arm slides into the sleeve of a jacket. The sleeve does protect the jacket from abrasion and other mechanical attacks, but if the sleeve is acidic, it attacks the jacket in its own way. Collectors must be particularly careful about keeping the sleeve on the jacket for the long term, in case the sleeve offers up its own deleterious material. (Sleeves do make a volume look spiffy when they contain a handsome dust jacket over a good copy of a hardcover volume. But they can be a false luxury.)

SLICE BOOKS. *See* Metamorphic books.

SLIP. A piece of paper that is LAID IN or TIPPED IN to a volume that has some connection with that volume. The slip could be printed or have MANUSCRIPT material on it (as with a SIGNATURE of an author or printer). It may be a review slip, a presentation slip, an ADVERTISEMENT, an ERRATA sheet, or an invoice. Or it could be a cancellans (*see* Cancel). Sometimes the slips are part of the original publication, as with an errata slip. Sometimes they are part of the package of the book but not connected to its text proper, as with an inserted advertising piece. Sometimes they are merely laid-in pieces of paper with a tenuous relationship to the volume, as with an advertisement by the publisher of a book, say, by a different author from the one who has written the volume in which the slip is placed. If a volume is released from the publisher with a slip, then copies lacking this are WANTING and the value of the copy could be seriously compromised. Most issues of *THE COLOPHON* contained various slips, mostly advertising pieces or order sheets, and to many a bookseller or collector, a copy of an issue that usually has these slips but is lacking them could be considered incomplete. Some of these insertions, however, were folded pieces of paper, and therefore, strictly speaking, they are not true slips.

SLIPCASE. (Sometimes hyphenated.) A box open at one end used for holding a book. When the book is slipped into the case, its SPINE (or FORE-EDGE) will be exposed. Roberts and Etherington say, "A more-or-less elaborate box made to order for a specific book, or other archival material, and used for protection. The simplest form of the slipcase is a cloth- or paper-covered box with one open edge into which the book is slipped with its spine exposed. The addition of a cloth dust wrapper or CHEMISE affords additional protection; however, since the spine is then covered, the title must either be BLOCKED directly on the closed edge of the box or a label must be attached to the chemise. The substitution of an inner box for the chemise is a further elaboration. The inner box is usually made of chipboard covered with cloth, and frequently it is lined with felt or a felt substitute to protect the contents against friction within the inner box. A cloth tab [or ribbon] may be attached as a means of pulling the inner box from the case, or the sides of the case may be thumb-notched to permit grasping of the inner box. Simple slipcases, which have no inner box or chemise, should not be notched as this places considerable strain on the JOINTS of the book when it is removed and also causes soiling of the covering material. . . . The booklike appearance may be further enhanced by attaching false bands to the closed edge to give the effect of sewing on raised bands, and by covering the case with a leather spine and cloth sides" (p. 239).

SLIPS. "The free end of the cords, thongs, or tapes on which a book has been sewn, that are used to attach the boards (or case) to the next [*sic*; that should be "text"] block" (Roberts and Etherington, "slips"; https://cool.culturalheritage.org/don/dt/dt3163.html [accessed 12 March 2021]). Roberts and Etherington discuss the various ways these binding materials are attached to the BOARDS. The slips can often be seen in a binding in which either the pastedown ENDLEAVES are so thin that the slips show through, or in which the pastedowns have come loose, revealing the boards beneath them. If the slips were made of cord, they were traditionally frayed out so that when the endleaf was pasted over them, the full dimensions of the cords were not visible under the pastedowns; the cords' ends were distributed under the endleaves. Such "spread out" cords were sometimes called "moustaches."

SLIP SHEET/SLIP PROOFS. "A blank sheet of paper slipped between newly printed sheets to prevent OFFSETTING" (*American Heritage Dictionary of the English Language*, p. 1649). Also, as Philip Gaskell explains, in newspaper printing, "[S]lip proofs were taken from the type while it was still in GALLEY, a practice that was normal in news work by the 1820s" (*A New Introduction to Bibliography*, p. 194). (*See* Offset sheets.)

Roberts and Etherington give a third definition (with the word spelled "slipsheet"): "In terms of the preparation of copy, 'slipsheet' means to insert pages into proper sequence to indicate the placement of illustrations that have not yet been prepared. Each page, or slipsheet, identifies its particular illustration, along with information as to whether the illustration is line or HALFTONE, foldout or horizontal, as well as the size, the negative or art file number, the figure number and titles, and any other information that might serve to key illustration to its proper page for printing or COLLATING" (p. 239).

SLUGS. Strips of TYPE METAL that can be cut to any length for TYPESETTING or for filling the CHASE to tighten the type in the FORME. Slugs are 6 POINTS thick. They can be used between lines of type or in place of REGLETS. They can also be used as SETTING RULE. (*See* Leads.) Naturally, they are not TYPE HIGH, for they are not meant to print.

The term also means a solid line of type metal with a text of some kind in relief on it, set type high, as with a LINOTYPE slug.

SLUNK. *See* Uterine vellum.

SMALL CAPS. Capital letters that are approximately the height of the X-HEIGHT of the LOWERCASE letters (though usually just slightly taller than lowercase characters). Small caps are sometimes used as the first letters of lines of poetry and in the abbreviations BC and AD. Sometimes a printer, not wanting words or titles in all caps that appear in prose paragraphs to look too large, will use small caps; note the difference in readability between the two following sentences: "The type was named CANCELLERESCA BASTARDA" and "The type was named CANCELLERESCA BASTARDA." Small caps can also be used to key a reader to certain things, as is done here to indicate that any word(s) in small caps will have their own entries in the dictionary. Or they may indicate that a particular illustration spoken of in the prose text may be seen or otherwise dealt with in a section of images or in a glossary or appendix.

A PRINTER MAY signal the opening lines of a chapter or a section of a chapter with small caps, more as a sign of designerly elegance than to key the reader into the fact that a new section or chapter is beginning. In a reference tool, small caps may be used consistently from one entry to the next to call attention to the same element in each entry—like an author's name: JAMES FENIMORE COOPER. *Last of the Mohicans*. HERMAN MELVILLE. *White-Jacket*.

Matthew Butterick says about the creation of small caps on a computer, "Small-cap formatting works by scaling down regular caps. But compared to the other characters in the FONT, the fake small caps that result are the wrong height, and their vertical strokes are too light. Whereas with real small caps, the color and height have been calibrated to blend well with the normal UPPERCASE and lowercase letters" (see http://practicaltypography.com/small-caps.html [accessed 17 June 2021]). Hence, the computer method of achieving small caps merely downsizes regular caps without adjusting the weight of the strokes of each character.

SMALL PRESS. A publishing house releasing to the public only a few titles per year. How few is not specifically delineated in the literature of small press production, but these presses are distinguished from the large commercial publishers that control most of the book-publishing market. As Kate Sullivan says, "The standard industry definition for a small press in the US is any publisher with annual sales below $50 million, or those that publish on average 10 or fewer titles per year." She adds, "Small presses are abundant throughout the US and beyond, and they're powerful drivers of the written word. They can be more responsive and take bigger risks than the major houses, making them an excellent resource for beginning authors" (Sullivan, "Complete Guide to Small Press Publishing: The Good, The Bad, and The Ugly of Small Presses for Writers"). The rise of the small press—in the last half of the twentieth century—came about with the consolidation of publishing houses under larger holding companies. The major publishers often jettisoned the publishing lines that produced little or no income, leaving small companies to pick up these specialty lines. Some of the larger publishers like to maintain small press names in their lines. The Fantasy publishing line started out as a small imprint of Penguin Books.

SMITH, PHILIP (1928–2018). One of England's premiere bookbinders, creator of hundreds of elegant DESIGNER BINDINGS. "Born in 1928, Philip began his career in bookbinding and book art in 1949, graduating from the Royal College of Art in London with First Class Honours in 1954. He was an internationally renowned designer bookbinder and book artist. He designed and created intricate and fascinating bindings for well over 50 years and was awarded gold and silver medals in several international competitions. In 2000 he was awarded an MBE for services to Art. Philip was a great innovator, having invented and pioneered several groundbreaking and influential techniques and structural developments. His work is represented in many private collections and can be seen in several public collections overseas and in the UK including the V&A National Art Library and the British Library" (PhilipSmithBookArt blog; "Announcement" [obituary]; http://www.philipsmithbookart.com/ [accessed 23 April 2021]). One of his famous techniques is the "book wall" on which a large number of books are shelved together, with "the images on each book flowing on to the covers of adjacent books, front and back, yet also integral across each component book. The first book walls were developed around the text of The Lord of the Rings, by JRR Tolkien; in 1973, he and Tolkien were invited to present one of those special bindings to the Duke of Edinburgh, and it is now in his personal library" (Jason Smith, "Philip Smith Obituary"; *The Guardian*, 26 March 2019; https://www.theguardian.com/books/2019/mar/26/philip-smith-obituary [accessed 23 April 2021]). The technique is related to SPINESCAPING in that the overall picture developed in the several volumes can be observed when all of the volumes are placed in proper sequence on shelves.

SMOKE PROOF. In cutting a PUNCH, the craftsman puts the character on the end of the punch and removes everything else. He uses a COUNTERPUNCH and files, slowly removing metal, coming closer and closer to the final character desired. As he forms the character, he places the face of the punch into the smoke from a flame of a candle, gathering onto the surface some carbon (lampblack), and then presses it onto a sheet of paper to see how it prints, revealing where the punch needs more filing. The images made with these pressings are called "smoke proofs." (See Avis, *Edward Philip Prince*, p. 89.)

SOCIETY FOR THE HISTORY OF AUTHORSHIP, READING AND PUBLISHING. *See* SHARP.

SOCIETY OF AMERICAN ARCHIVISTS (SAA). As the name indicates, this is an organization representing the wide archival community in the U.S. The society's website explains: "Founded in 1936, the Society of American Archivists is North America's oldest and largest national professional association dedicated to the needs and interests of archives and archivists. SAA represents more than 6,200 professional archivists employed by governments, universities, businesses, libraries, and historical organizations nationally. / All of the work undertaken by SAA on behalf of its members and archives users is guided by the following vision, mission, and core values: / VISION: The Society of American Archivists empowers archivists to achieve professional excellence and foster innovation to ensure the identification, preservation, understanding, and use of records of enduring value. / MISSION: SAA is a vital community that promotes the value and diversity of archives and archivists and serves as the preeminent resource for the profession. / CORE ORGANIZATIONAL VALUES: The Society of American Archivists is committed to: [1] Advancing the public standing of archivists. [2] Ensuring the diversity of its membership and leaders, the profession, and the archival record. [3] Fostering an open and inclusive culture of creativity, collaboration, and experimentation across the association. [4] Providing excellent member service. [5] Ensuring transparency, accountability, integrity, professionalism, and social responsibility in conducting its activities." (See their website at https://www2.archivists.org/aboutsaa [accessed 17 August 2022].)

SOFT COVERED BOOKS. As opposed to HARDBACKS (or books IN BOARDS), these are bound in flexible covers. (Also called "PAPERBACKS.")

SOLANDER BOX/SOLANDER CASE. "A more or less elaborate book or document box invented by Dr. Daniel Charles Solander, a botanist, during his tenure at the British Museum (1773–1782). The Solander box, which is generally of a drop-back construction, is made of wood, has dovetailed joints and a back shaped from a single piece of wood. The top and bottom are held in place by screws and glue. The box is secured by two spring catches fixed in the 'FORE EDGE' frames near the HEAD and TAIL. When properly constructed the Solander box is very nearly dustproof and almost waterproof. The box, which can be made as elaborate as the maker desires, is generally covered in cloth, or, in more elaborate instances, full MOROCCO. It may even have RAISED BANDS on the back (corresponding to the SPINE of a book)

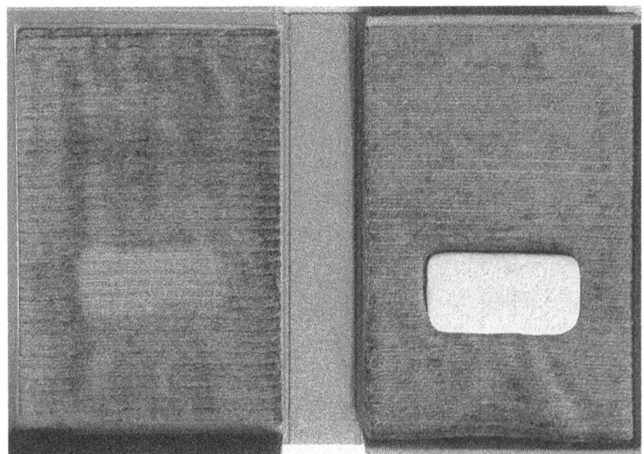

Solander box, made by the author.
Collection of the author.

and may be tooled. / The drop-back Solander is intended to house a book. For document storage, specifically to facilitate removal from the box, a DROP-FRONT BOX may actually be preferable, although in a strict sense it may be argued that such an arrangement is not really a Solander box. Aside from this, however, the DROP-BACK BOX has a distinct advantage over the drop-front type in that the former imposes virtually no strain on the hinge of the box because it is in a right-angle position when closed and assumes a straight line position when opened. The drop-front box, on the other hand, with its fixed back, strains the hinge at the back because of the approximate 60° angle at the top when the box is open. If the top is accidently struck when the box is open the top may break off" (Roberts and Etherington, p. 243).

More recently, Solander boxes are made not of wood but of cardboard covered in cloth and, as has been the case since their first use, can be constructed with fake raised bands to look like a book. (*See* Slipcase.)

SOLID. *See* Set solid.

SOLIDUS. *See* Virgule.

SOPHISTICATED COPY. A copy of a book or other item that has been repaired or "tidied up"—but to such an extent that the repair is fairly invisible. Also called "doctored." A librarian with a defective item wants it conserved so that the treatment extends the useful life of the item with minimal loss of the information that inheres in it. This often means creating a copy in which the repairs are visible. A bookseller or collector, on the other hand, may wish to have his copy sophisticated—restored in such a way that the mends and "fixes" are not visible. This may increase the apparent (and actual) value of the piece, but it may be seen as a form of deception: here is a perfect copy (when it was not at one time perfect). The sophistication can take many forms, as with cleaning off dirt, replacing the binding, removing torn sheets and replacing them with perfect FACSIMILES or identical ones taken from other copies, replacing missing leaves (i.e., creating a MADE-UP COPY), washing out stains, or the like. There is nothing to stop an unscrupulous person from removing a TITLE PAGE from a true first edition and sophisticating his own copy of the second edition with this LEAF. Carter treats one form of sophistication in his entry on erasures (p. 93), in which he points out that such changes sometimes hide the fact that the words "2nd edition" (or a later edition) are removed, sometimes a former owner's name is expunged, or a library stamp has been rubbed out. In any event, some of the PROVENANCE of the volume is lost, and, when the erasures are visible, the value of the item may be diminished. Sophistication may not be considered dishonest if the sophistication is not hidden in any way and a prospective buyer is made aware of it. But if the sophistication is not mentioned in a bookseller's description and the buyer notices it, that makes returning the volume to the seller justifiable. (*See* Restoration; Washed.) (Parenthetically, Carter, through all editions of his work, has what seems to be a blunder when he says that one form of sophistication is having "a first edition re-cased in second edition covers" [p. 93], when it looks as if he should be talking about a second edition recased in first-edition covers. Am I reading something wrong? Carter and his later editors should have rethought—or reworded—that one.]

SORTS (type). Individual pieces of TYPE. They were produced from matrices (*see* Matrix [in type making]). Each sort could be TYPE HIGH, so it would print, or it could be shorter than type high (e.g., as with SPACING to be used between words), so it would not print. The ones that print could contain UPPER- or LOWERCASE letters (or both in the case of LIGATURES, as with a *Qu* ligature), numbers, punctuations, special decorative or bibliographical images, or anything else the printer needed. In setting the type, if the COMPOSITOR ran out of one or more of these, she was "out of sorts," the origin of that idiom. (*See* Letter.)

SOUND COPY. A volume that is stable in its binding and in fairly good condition. Carter says that the term means no more than this, for if it were PRISTINE, the bookseller would have said so in his description. So when you see this phrase in a bookseller's catalog, you know that the copy is not perfect. Rob Rulon-Miller advertised a volume as "rubbed and worn, but sound" (online catalog of "New Acquisitions," 15 September 2020, Entry #21).

SPACEBAND (Linotype machine). A wedge-shaped device inserted between matrices (*see* Matrix [in type making]) at the ends of words on a LINOTYPE MACHINE for JUSTIFYING the lines of text. The story of the invention of the spaceband is riveting reading. (See Kahan, *Ottmar Mergenthaler*, pp. 30–31, 97 ff.) Mergenthaler did his best to justify lines, but another inventor (Jacobs W. Schuckers) developed the spaceband just when Mergenthaler did. (See also Kahan, *Ottmar Mergenthaler*.) Basil Kahan says, "The two justifiers were developed simultaneously, and probably independently, but Schuckers had filed his [patent] application on 27 February 1885, 49 days before Mergenthaler" (p. 30). The Mergenthaler Linotype Company had to buy the patent from the other inventor.

SPACING (in printing). There are at least three kinds of spacing in printing: LETTERSPACING, WORD SPACING, and interlinear spacing (LEADING). In a bookseller's catalog, one might find, "title poorly letterspaced," or a bibliographer might say, "the word spacing in paragraph 3 on page 225 seems to indicate that the text has been RESET."

SPANISH CALF. *See* Cordoban leather; Cordovan leather.

SPANISH FORGER. The name given to a forger of medieval MANUSCRIPTS—full texts and individual MINIATURES. He always did his work in original medieval manuscript leaves, sometimes creating a PALIMPSEST by scraping off the original text and doing his artwork over the newly cleared-off page. "The Spanish Forger painted numerous miniatures and panels in a late-medieval style at the end of the 19th and into the 20th century. No one knows who he was, but given the number of leaves and panels attributed to him, he must have made a significant amount of money selling his forgeries to an unsuspecting audience" (Davis, "Manuscript Road Trip"). Lisa Fagan Davis points out that Belle da Costa Greene, curator at the J. P. Morgan Library in New York, was the first to recognize the FORGERY of this person (she is the one who named him). Davis says, "While preparing a major exhibit of the Forger's work for the Morgan Library in 1978, curator William Voelkle discovered that the Forger had based much of his work on illustrations found in five volumes on medieval and Renaissance life and culture by Paul Lacroix (published between 1869–1882); many of his paintings are clear copies of Lacroix illustrations."

The first of the Spanish Forger's works to be identified as fake was "The Betrothal of St. Ursula," on a wood panel. "After the St. Ursula panel was later tested using neutron activation analysis, it was discovered that the green pigment in the painting was copper arsenite a.k.a. Paris Green, which was not available before 1814, confirming Greene's suspicions. Because French newsprint has been found behind some of his panels, it is suspected that he actually worked in Paris, but the name Greene gave him has stuck" (Davis, "Manuscript Road Trip"). And Davis points out that several things give him away, like his use of gold: "In a genuine medieval manuscript, the gold leaf would have been applied before the colors. The Forger tended to apply his gold as a final step; a close examination of his work often finds gold overlapping the color rather than the (correct) other way around." (See Voelkle, *The Spanish Forger*.) Sometimes the forger added images that had nothing at all to do with the text, hoping that his buyers would be acquiring the leaves for their beauty and would not notice the disconnect between the text and its accompanying image.

There are more than 200 known forgeries by this person, many of which have wound up in major collections, and his work is now collected in the same way that Wise forgeries have been. (*See* Wise, Thomas J.)

SPANISH MARBLE (sometimes called "Spanish ripple"). "A MARBLE pattern of soft colors, including pale green, old rose and brown (or fawn), with a moiré effect. It was used in Spain from the early 17th century and is found on the more familiar later Spanish marble papers that have been used in both England and the United States since the end of the 18th

Spanish marble on a mid-19th-century endpaper.
Collection of the author.

century" (Roberts and Etherington, p. 244). One of the signature characteristics of Spanish marble is that these sheets have a ripple in their pattern, produced when the marbler lowers the sheet in a staccato fashion onto the SIZE in the MARBLING BATH, producing a wave that disrupts the pigments on the surface of the size into a wavy configuration. The effect can be quite attractive (or particularly disagreeable, depending on the skills of the marbler), so it has been used for sheets of a great variety of color combinations, not merely the originally preferred ones that Roberts and Etherington refer to. Since marblers usually lower the sheet to be decorated onto the size from opposite diagonal corners, most Spanish marbles have the ripples running diagonally on the sheet. But changing the direction of the sheet as it is being placed over the surface of the bath can allow the marbler to redirect the waves to random patterns or to directions parallel to the edges of the sheets.

SPATIAL CODING. The use of space on a page to key a reader into certain features of a text. For example, in a bibliography, space in the form of LEADING and HANGING INDENTS may show a reader where a new entry begins and where data fields in each entry begin. Spaces between entries may also code the move from one entry to another. (*See also* Typographic coding.) (See Berger, *The Design of Bibliographies*, pp. 40–43.)

SPATTERED CALF. *See* Spotted calf.

SPECIAL LIBRARIES. Libraries that are usually not affiliated with academic institutions or part of the public library system (though see below). They have special collections focused on the interests of their founders, such as those for law, government documents, corporate libraries, some libraries in museums, and nonprofit organizations (and there are many other categories). In an academic institution, a specialized law library or chemistry library may also be considered a "special library." Access to these libraries is usually restricted to scholars with the proper credentials who make appointments to use the collections, though some of these institutions do allow "drop-ins" to have access. Sometimes people from the general public may avail themselves of some of these special libraries but only after the proper introductions and advanced requests. (See Shumaker, "Special Libraries," pp. 4966–74.) (*See* Special Libraries Association.)

SPECIAL LIBRARIES ASSOCIATION (SLA). An organization with members worldwide whose members represent all kinds of libraries, including those from government, law, some academic divisional libraries, the business and financial world, nonprofit organizations, and others. "John Cotton Dana, 1856–1929, American librarian and museum director, . . . was one of the founders of the Special Libraries Association and its first president" (Encyclopedia.com, "Dana, John Cotton"; https://www.encyclopedia.com/reference/encyclopedias-almanacs-transcripts-and-maps/dana-john-cotton [accessed 5 July 2021]). "The Special Libraries Association 'SLA' is a specialized global organization founded in 1909 with Head Office in the United States. It adopts innovations of specialists and professionals in the field of information and libraries. SLA serves more than 12,000 members in 83 countries in the information profession, including corporate, academic and government information specialists. SLA promotes and strengthens its members through learning, incentives, and networking initiatives. / SLA members are professionals working in economic firms, private companies, Governmental Departments, Scientific Centers and Institutes, museums, Medical Service Centers and consulting agencies. The mission of SLA is developing the concept of professional leadership for the Specialists in libraries and information centers including shaping information policies for serving our communities" (Special Libraries Association, Arabian Gulf Chapter, "Special Libraries Association"; https://slaagc.org/ [accessed 5 July 2021]).

SPECIAL SORTS. SORTS (as any reader going sequentially through this volume will have recently learned) are individual pieces of type. In the standard FONT, there are the standard characters: the alphabet A–Z (upper- and lowercase), numerals, punctuation, and a few LIGATURES. Some TYPESETTING will require the COMPOSITOR to use other characters, like those from foreign languages, mathematical or medical or astronomical symbols, characters from botany, chess, foreign currencies, the copyright symbol, and many others. The computer offers hundreds or even thousands of them at one's fingertips; but those printing from HOT METAL will need to find a foundry able to supply these oddball or uncommon sorts. When publishers and printers were one and the same—in the period of INCUNABULA and into the 16th century—many printers were their own type "foundries," so if they needed a special sort, they would design it themselves and have it made by a PUNCH created by their own PUNCHCUTTER. (*See* the figure accompanying the entry for "Register [in printing]" shows the registrum for a 1517 volume containing special characters.)

The COMPOSITOR at the keyboard of a LINOTYPE machine had, for many fonts, a set of special MATRICES for these special sorts. When one of them was needed, the compositor took it and inserted it manually where it needed to go, in the line-up of the regular matrices for the line. Any given font may have had as many as 200 of such sorts.

SPECIMEN BINDING. *See* Trial binding.

SPECKLED. *See* Scratting.

SPINE (of a book or a box). The part of a CODEX formed where the original sheets of paper have been folded and through which the sewing goes to bind the volume. In a perfect-bound (*see* Perfect binding) book, it is the part of the volume that receives the glue that holds the LEAVES together and the cover on. Roberts and Etherington add to this, "That part of the covering material of a book which covers the folds of the sections of a book and which is the part usually visible as it stands on the shelf. It generally bears the title, author, name of the publisher (when an edition binding), and (in a library) frequently a location (classification) number, or a symbol of some kind. Also called 'back,' 'backbone,' or 'shelfback'" (pp. 244–45). Sometimes called the "back" of the book (*see* Back). On a DROP-SPINE BOX, there are front and back covers and a spine to which these are attached.

SPINE FOLDS. *See* Bolts.

SPINE LINING. "Any material used to line the SPINE, or back, of the sewn TEXT BLOCK. The purpose of lining is to reinforce the back during the mechanical operation of opening and reading the book. Linings often extend to each side of the spine and form part of the text-to-cover attachment. The term for the lining found on the inside of the spine of a CASE BINDING is *inlay*" (Miller, *Books Will Speak Plain*, p. 469). VELLUM/PARCHMENT and paper are the most common materials used for lining, though cloth has also been used. In REBINDING or CONSERVATION work, the lining is often revealed, and what the technician finds can be important, for it might reveal pieces of discarded monographs or other documents—manuscript and printed.

SPINESCAPING. A term to describe a phenomenon in bookbinding—the term coming from the *World Book Encyclopedia*, though the phenomenon has existed before *World Book* started using it. It means the arrangement of images across the spines of a multivolume set that, when the volumes are properly arranged on a shelf, show a picture: a landscape, a scene of activities or of nature, or anything else that can be seen as an illustration of some kind. "The Spinescape is World Book's trademarked method of printing a unique image across the spine of the 22-volume encyclopedia set" (*World Book Encyclopedia*, "World Book Readers Choose Design for Next Encyclopedia"). The British bookbinder PHILIP SMITH produced his "wall of books," bound in leather, such that a picture was produced when the bound volumes were placed properly on shelves. And more recently, collections of Harry Potter books use this method of binding; the publisher, Scholastic, issued the seven volumes with spines that reveal—when all the volumes are properly arrayed—an image of Hogwarts.

SPINOFFS. In the book world, the meaning of this term differs somewhat from that in the world of entertainment. For instance, the TV show *All in the Family* introduced characters George and Louise Jefferson, whose popularity yielded a spinoff show *The Jeffersons*. In publishing, the term "spinoff" can denote a volume that was inspired by a TV show. In fact, myriad spinoffs were produced, original pieces of literature, not directly related to the television production, but presenting texts whose main characters were created from those in the TV shows. "Two dozen novels were based upon *Man from U.N.C.L.E.* and published between 1965 and 1968. Unhampered by television censors, the novels were generally grittier and more violent than the televised episodes. The series sold in the millions, and was the largest TV-novel tie-in franchise until surpassed by *Dark Shadows* and *Star Trek*" ("Wikipedia: All 24 Man From UNCLE Novels"; http://manfuncle2014.blogspot.com/2016/12/wikipedia-all-24-man-from-uncle-novels.html). For the most part, these were published in cheap PAPERBACK editions, meant to be read and passed along—or discarded. They are the prototypical PULP FICTION, on acidic paper, with fragile PERFECT BINDINGS. In the 1970s—long before there were ONLINE BOOK SALES—I was tasked by Herb Kaplan of Argus Books in Sacramento to acquire as many TV spinoff novels as I could find. Over about three years he and I were able to amass well over a thousand titles, most of which cost 25 cents or less. There were at least 90 such series that spawned printed versions, as the Wikipedia site shows. (See "List of television series made into books"; Wikipedia; https://en.wikipedia.org/wiki/List_of_television_series_made_into_books.) Some of the more prominent of these series are *The Avengers*; *Bewitched*; *Buffy the Vampire Slayer;* several of the *CSI* series; *Dallas*; *Dr. Who*; *Murder She Wrote*; *Sabrina, the Teenage Witch*; *Six Million Dollar Man*, *Star Trek*; *Twin Peaks*; and *The X-Files*. (*See* Big Little Books.)

SPIRAL BINDING. (Sometimes called a "coil binding.") A means of attaching the LEAVES of a volume to one another using a metal or plastic spiral-shaped wire or coil that threads through holes drilled into the TEXT BLOCK along the GUTTER. One advantage of this kind of binding is that the leaves will lie flat when the volume is open. A drawback is that the coil may cut through the paper if the volume is frequently used. The term sometimes is (incorrectly) used to denote a binding with a plastic strip that runs the full height of the volume, the strip having right-angle-protruding circular-configured plastic tabs that thread through holes in the leaves of the text block. This latter is a "COMB BINDING."

SPIRIT DUPLICATOR. *See* Mimeographed.

SPLIT BOARDS. "The BOARDS of a book that are made up of two or more plies of board glued together, except for a distance at the inner edge into which the SLIPS or TAPES are glued when the boards are being attached. Generally, if two boards are used they are of different thicknesses, with the thinner of the two adjacent to the TEXT BLOCK. If three boards are used, the thinnest is placed in the center and does not extend all the way to the inner edge, thus providing the space for the tapes or slips. In the past some 'split boards' were made by splitting a single ply board, either by hand or by machine, thus eliminating the cost of LAMINATING. / The split stopped an inch or so short of the HEAD and TAIL of the board (in case binding), which made it possible to make the CASE separately and then attach it to the text block by gluing the tapes into the splits of each board. / Split boards are used today almost exclusively in hand binding and then only for books sewn on tapes, although the technique has also been used occasionally for books sewn on RECESSED CORDS" (Roberts and Etherington, "split boards"; https://cool.culturalheritage.org/don/dt/dt3263.html [accessed 4 April 2021]). If the boards are too thin or the volume experiences the stress of mishandling, the cover may crack verticlly.

SPLITTING. *See* Starting.

SPLOTCHED CALF. *See* Spotted calf.

SPOTTED CALF (sometimes called "scratted," "spattered," "splotched," or "sprinkled"). CALFSKIN decorated with small spots created by dropping a coloring matter onto the leather. Roberts and Etherington say that a common material for the drips is ferrous sulfate (p. 247), which gives the leather (not necessarily calf) a spattering of places darkened by the acid. They say, "It has been used in England since the 17th century, if not earlier" (p. 247).

The technique is also used on the edges of books, often using a red or green dye to achieve the spotting. And it is used as well on papers, especially MARBLED PAPER or PASTE PAPER, which has been sprinkled over another pattern to put tiny colored dots over the first application of decoration.

Under "sprinkling," Roberts and Etherington say, "The process of sprinkling or spattering irregularly shaped spots or splotches or coloring matter on the leather covers of a book, usually calfskin or SHEEPSKIN, or on the edges, to achieve a decorative effect" (p. 247). In some older bindings, it is clear that the effect was achieved with an acidic liquid that has eaten through the leather to the underlying BOARDS.

Spotted calf cover. On Catharine Macaulay, *The History of England from the Accession of James I to the Elevation of the House of Hanover* (London: Printed for Edward and Charles Dilly, 1769). Collection of the author.

SPREAD. *See* Two-page spread.

SPRING-BACK BINDING. "A device or technique invented by the Englishmen John and Joseph Williams, in about 1799 and used ever since in the binding of large blankbooks [*sic*]. The spring-back consists of a strip of millboard, or other hard binder's BOARD, the length of the boards of the book and of a width that, when curved, will fit around the SPINE and onto the sides of the text block at least one fourth of an inch on both sides. The board is first soaked in water and a strip of KRAFT PAPER four times its width is then glued around it. The purpose of the paper is to stiffen the board further so that it will maintain its form after it is curved to the proper shape. The assembly is curved around a core (the thickness of the book), or by means of a back-molding iron. A cloth liner is then glued to the interior of the curve, overlapping the edges by inches on either side. These overlaps are glued to the levers. After the spring-back is attached, both ends are softened, paste is applied, and the ends of the spring-back are bent over to form the HEADCAPS. / The purpose of the spring-back is to cause the book to lie flat so as to facilitate its being written in. It acts as a spring, and its pressure on the sides of the book near the spine causes the book to snap open and shut. The levers assist in this snapping effect, which is enhanced by the fact that the machine direction of the lever boards is at right angles to the length of the spine" (Roberts and Etherington, "spring-back"; https://cool.culturalheritage.org/don/dt/dt3277.html [accessed 21 March 2021]).

SPRINKLED CALF. *See* Spotted calf.

SPRUNG. Said of a volume in which the TEXT BLOCK is separate from its binding. For instance, in the commonest case, a CASE-BOUND book will have its case no longer attached to its text block. Since the only thing that holds a case to the rest of the volume is the glue that attaches to the PASTEDOWN endleaves, a single dropping of the book onto the FORE-EDGE of the cover might detach the two parts in one second. It sounds less cataclysmic and is more concise to say that the volume is sprung than to describe the "springing."

SQUARE BRACKETS. Used like parentheses, pieces of punctuation used in texts of many kinds to indicate information supplied that was not in the original. For example, for a volume that has no printed date but that can be dated from external sources, one might see "London [1776]." An anonymously published book for which we know the author may be styled in a bibliography as "*Tamerlane*, by a Bostonian [Edgar Allan Poe]." Such brackets are also used in quoted matter when the writer wants to add something to the source that was not in the original: "His automobile rolled over when he took the hairpin [turn] at 50 miles an hour"; or when a correction needs to be shown in the quoted matter: "Smith says 'The book was published in 1931 [1913] before the first big war.'" Similarly, the word *sic* is inserted in brackets in quoted matter to show that an error or some oddity was in the original, not included in the passage by the person doing the quoting (e.g., *see* the entry for "Spring-back binding" above). And brackets are also used as parentheses inside the curved parentheses.

SQUARES. "The marginal difference between the edges of the TEXT BLOCK and the edges of the CASE or BOARDS of the book. Normally, squares vary both in proportion to the size of the book and according to taste. They are described relatively from the least extensive, or *pinhead*, to the most extensive, *bold*, with *neat*, *ordinary*, and *full* being intermediary sizes" (Roberts and Etherington, p. 248; "squares"; https://cool.culturalheritage.org/don/dt/dt3289.html [accessed 3 February 2021]). If the text block aligns perfectly with the edges of the boards, there are no squares.

STAB BINDING. *See* Oriental binding.

STAB HOLES. The holes made in the fold at the GUTTER of a SIGNATURE through which the thread of the binding passes. DISBINDING a rebound volume for any purpose may reveal the original stab holes of the book's first (and possibly subsequent) binding and could guide CONSERVATORS or binders on how to REBIND the volume in a manner closer to its original than the way it was with its later bindings. This kind of information guided the rebinding of the HUNTINGTON LIBRARY's Ellesmere Chaucer. (See Cains and Fredericks, "The Bindings of the Ellesmere Chaucer.") Observing the stab holes of books bound in PUBLISHER'S CLOTH may show that the volume was composed of collected installments that were issued IN PARTS, as opposed to a volume of the complete text that was issued in its own binding with the text complete at issue.

Stab holes are also made in the creation of an ORIENTAL BINDING.

STAMP. "A FINISHING tool, cut in brass, bearing figures or patterns in RELIEF. Stamps range in design from a simple dot to the most intricate lacework design, and can be used by hand or in a BLOCKING machine" (Roberts and Etherington, p. 249).

STAMPED. Carter says this word is not a formal term in the world of bookbinding, though it has taken on a specific meaning to describe bindings. It refers to the pattern on a BLOCK that has been ENGRAVED to decorate a cover (or the impression itself). Hence, one describing a book may say, "stamped with the family crest," the stamping showing that the pattern was made not by a FILLET or by the work of a binder who cut the leather by hand. There are panel-stamps, armorial stamps (for an illustration, *see* figure at "Armorial bindings"), and others (see Carter, p. 236). (*See* Blocked.)

STAMPING MILL. A machine used in papermaking to pound the pulp, fibrillating and separating the fibers. The stamping mill is composed of a single mortar-and-pestle configuration (or a row of several of them), the wet pulp being placed into the mortar, the water-, wind-, animal-, or human-driven pestles raised and lowered strongly into the mortars to beat the fibers. (*See* Hollander beater.)

Stamping mill (water-wheel driven).
From Denis Diderot's *Encyclopédie*, 1767.

Image of a water-driven stamping mill.

From Vittorio Zonca, *Novo Teatro di Machine et Edificii per Uarie et Sicure Operationi* (Padua: Pietro Bertelli, 1607).

STANDING ORDER. This is basically the same thing as a SUBSCRIPTION: the arrangement with a press that a buyer will acquire everything that that press produces. The buyer has a "standing order" for everything from the press. (I chose to have this as a separate term so that I can expatiate on one of the problems with standing orders—drawn from real life [though the principals must remain anonymous].) Some collectors gather all of the work of a press, being collectors *of that press*. Some collectors go after items in a certain and somewhat well-defined subject area. If a press publishes in that particular area or in a cluster of related topics, it may get a standing order from a collector wishing to reap the benefits of having a subscription *to that press*. But it sometimes happens that that press, being, after all, a PRIVATE PRESS and producing texts at the whim of its proprietor, chooses to print a text completely outside the purview of its normal topics. The subscriber can be upset that she, a standing-order customer, *must* buy the item even though it does not fit into her collection. That is the nature of subscription sales: standing orders are just that—automatic acquirers of whatever the press creates. And one of the features of such an arrangement—the feature that gives the subscriber the perquisites of subscription—is that the subscriber must take all that the press prints. The press I am referring to had a habit of publishing on topics outside its long-established norm, and thus alienating its subscribers. The proprietor confided that they [I apologize for the plural and gender-neutral pronoun, necessary to conceal the party involved.] lost many a subscriber this way, and when they were approached to sell to former subscribers subsequent books, they refused to do so. Standing orders can cause discontent and outright animosity, depending on the personalities of those involved.

STANDARD REAM. *See* Ream.

STANDING TYPE. Printing type that has been set into a text and is ready to be printed or type that has been printed and is then stored, not distributed (*see* Distribution) back into its TYPE CASE. Keeping the type in GALLEYS is done with the idea that it is cheaper to keep the standing type for a later IMPRESSION than it would be to reset (*see* Resetting) the text. If a publisher prints a certain number of copies of a book, for example, and thinks he may need to print further copies, he may wish to keep his text in "standing type," ready for another impression. (*See* Edition, Impression [Printing], Issue, and State; Points.) The implication is that the type has been stored out of its CHASE, possibly in a GALLEY RACK.

STANHOPE PRESS. This is "the first all-iron printing press . . . invented in about 1800 by Earl Stanhope" (Moran, *Printing Presses*, pp. 48 ff.). Stanhope's press, incorporating as it did only metal in its construction, allowed for a larger BED than most other presses had; this required a larger PLATEN,

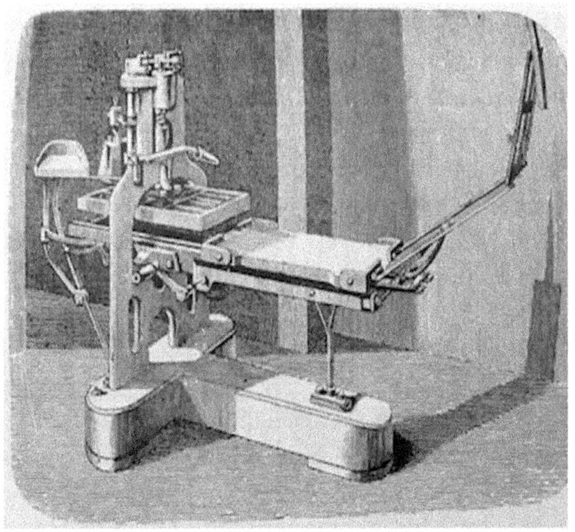

Stanhope press.

Image from Stower. *Printer's Grammar* (see bibliography). Note that on the press the tympan and frisket are open, the frisket showing four openings, probably indicating the printing of a quarto.

which increased the size of the sheets it could print. It comes at the end of the so-called HANDPRESS PERIOD, though HANDPRESSES have never really "come to an end"—as they are still employed today.

STAPLED. Said of a volume that uses metal staples for its binding. As distinguished from SADDLE-STITCHED volumes with the staples piercing the SIGNATURES at the inner folds (at the SPINE), stapled volumes had their folds trimmed off, and the staples went through the LEAVES a short distance in from the spine. This kind of binding was much quicker and cheaper to produce than was sewing with threads, and it came into frequent use in the last quarter of the 19th century. It was often used for periodicals and inexpensive PAPERBACK volumes, which had a TEXT BLOCK stapled and paper covers glued over to conceal the staples. The drawback for many a volume is that the staples could rust, damaging the paper and weakening the binding; also, with modern methods of book CONSERVATION (especially with MASS DEACIDIFICATION), if the stapled volumes are conserved with water-based treatments, the staples could rust. This, of course, could not have been anticipated in the 19th century when staples were first used.

STAR BOOK. *See* Carousel book.

STARTED. An indication that at least one SIGNATURE of a book is sticking out of a volume at the FORE-EDGE, indicating a poor binding job, or that the signature is pulling loose. Such damage may require a full resewing of the volume.

STARTING. A bookseller's term indicating that JOINTS in a volume are beginning to split. The term is less dramatic than "splitting," so its use is common in booksellers' catalogs. The splitting can be incipient—that is, only a slight hint of tearing is visible—or it can be extensive, in which case the person describing the damage should be honest: "joints split halfway down the spine." But I have seen "starting" used as a euphemism for covers that are barely attached to their volumes. The covers have not only started but are nearly finished. (For an image that shows a binding that is "starting"—and that is pretty well along—*see* figure at "Spotted calf.")

STATE (as in "condition"). A term used to indicate the CONDITION of a volume, as in "this volume is in its original state, before the CANCEL" or "a tight copy in excellent state."

STATES (as in "first state," "third state"). *See* Edition, Impression (Printing), Issue, and State; Points.

STATE VARIANTS. Typographical variations that exist within a single edition of a work. (*See* Author's corrections; Edition, Impression [Printing], Issue, and State; Points; *see also* the entry for Points; and Stop-press corrections.) A state variant exists when stop-press corrections are made. Additionally, bindings can be distinguished by states: "binding in the first state, with the frog in the center of the cover" as opposed to "binding in the second state with the frog in the lower left corner of the cover." States in bindings can be with the cloth used, the decoration on the covers, the ENDPAPERS that were used, the method of sewing or gluing, or any other variation that distinguishes one manifestation of an edition from another. Bibliographers do not refer to state variants *from one edition to another*. There can also be state variants in DUST JACKETS.

STATIONERS' REGISTER. *See* Register.

STATIONER/STATIONERS' COMPANY. From 1403 on, a commercial company that worked with universities in the production of books. They oversaw the commissioning, writing, copying, illustrating, binding, sales, and mending. Their name comes from the fact that they were stationed (not mobile) outside the major universities, where they plied their trade. Peter Beal says, "By the mid-seventeenth century, and especially since the eighteenth century, stationers became largely distinct from booksellers, even though still selling some books, by concentrating more on the purveying of miscellaneous writing materials and 'stationery'" (*A Dictionary of English Manuscript Terminology, 1450–2000*, p. 397). Until 1937, their title was the Worshipful Company of Stationers, but their proper title today is the Worshipful Company of Stationers and Newspaper Makers. Beal adds that Queen Mary I, in 1557, granted the company its first royal charter. From then until 1911, the stationers were "subject to government licensing, CENSORSHIP, and other changing regulations, [but] the company was the principal body officially empowered to control printing and COPYRIGHT, enforce trading monopolies, and regulate the book trade" (p. 397).

The company essentially regulated English printing. Carter says that the Stationers' Company required publishers to record in the Stationers' Register any text they wanted to print, and these registers are a rich fount of information about early English printing. Copies of many of the books listed there do not survive. Between 1875 and 1894, Edward Arber published *Transcript of the Registers of the Company of Stationers of London, 1554–1640* (the publication of which was made possible by stationer George Eyre). Carter adds that the Copyright Act of 1709 required publishers to list their books in this register, but in the 19th century, this practice was not followed too much by many publishers. (See Carter, p. 237.) (See Arber, *Transcript of the Registers of the Company of Stationers of London, 1554–1708*; Blagden, *The*

Stationers' Company; and Blayney, *The Stationers' Company and the Printers of London, 1501–1557.*)

STATIONERY BINDING. Binding for volumes not intended to be read in the way one reads a fiction or nonfiction text, but to be consulted for various kinds of information, as with tabular figures, purchase or sales records, or other business records. Ledgers, for instance, are one form of stationery binding, as are account books, and other forms of volumes holding business records of many kinds. In this sense, then, a stationery binding will be on a volume meant to be written in. Their frequent opening for consultation and for adding to their pages required a sturdy form of binding, as one finds in POST BINDINGS. The term "also encompasses the binding of manifold and duplicate books, receipt books, check books, passports, bankbooks, loose-leaf volumes, and other forms of mechanical binding, as well as punching, perforating, padding, ruling, and other miscellaneous binding operations" (Roberts and Etherington, "stationery binding," https://cool.culturalheritage.org/don/dt/dt3321.html [accessed 16 February 2021]).

STATUTORY COPY. *See* Deposit copy.

ST BRIDE LIBRARY. A library and quasi museum in London whose holdings present great amounts of information on all of the book arts. "St Bride Library (formerly known as St Bride Printing Library and St Bride Typographical Library) is a library in London primarily devoted to printing, book arts, typography and graphic design. The library is housed in the St Bride Foundation Institute in Bride Lane. . . . It is centrally located in the area traditionally synonymous with the British Press and once home to many of London's newspaper publishing houses. The Library is named after the nearby church, St Bride's Church, the so-called 'Cathedral of Fleet Street'. . . . / St Bride Library opened on 20 November 1895 as a technical library for the printing school and printing trades. The library remained, as the school relocated in 1922 to become what is now known as the London College of Communication. The library's collection has grown to incorporate a vast amount of printing-related material numbering about 60,000 books and pamphlets, in addition to back issues of some 3,600 serials and numerous artefacts. Among its extensive collection the library houses: an Eric Gill collection, a William Addison Dwiggins collection, a Beatrice Warde collection, types of the Oxford University Press, and punches of the Caslon and Figgins foundries. / On 30 July 2015 the long-term closure of the library was announced as a result of major funding issues. The library staff were made redundant and the future of the collections appeared in doubt. After a change of management in late 2015 the Trustees took the decision to allow limited access. No charge is made for access to the reading room but a fee of £1 per item is levied for titles retrieved from closed access storage. The limited Reading Room study space means that potential visitors must email the library in advance of their visit to ensure that they may be accommodated on open days. / The library is currently open each Wednesday from noon" ("St Bride Library," Wikipedia [accessed 9 June 2022]).

As of the writing of this dictionary, St Bride's is back in business. Their website says, "We are delighted to announce that in line with Government advice and guidance, St Bride Foundation is open. The Foundation doors are open for venue hire from Monday 19 July without any restrictions and St Bride Library from Wednesday 2 June. The team is looking forward to welcoming you back!" (St Bride Foundation, "About Us"; https://www.sbf.org.uk/about/ [accessed 25 July 2021]). The posting announces future workshops—into 2022—and this excellent collection that has something for everyone interested in books is available again. (*See* Mosley, James.)

STC. *See* Pollard, Alfred William; Wing.

STEEL ENGRAVING/STEEL-PLATE ENGRAVING. Illustrations or text (or both together) printed from a steel PLATE rather than from wood or copper, as was traditional. While copper was the most commonly used material for creating artistic images, steel was the preferred material for commercial printing in the 19th century because of its sturdiness. Copper will yield only a limited number of good-quality prints before the soft metal will began to break down. Steel ENGRAVINGS can be done in the many thousands without any discernible deterioration of image.

"Steel engraving was introduced in 1792 by Jacob Perkins (1766–1849), an American Inventor, for banknote printing. When Perkins moved to London in 1818, the technique in 1820 became adapted by Charles Warren and especially by Charles Heath (1785–1848) for Thomas Campbell's *Pleasures of Hope* with the first published plates engraved on steel. The new technique only partially replaced the other commercial techniques of that time such as wood engraving, copper engraving, and later LITHOGRAPHY" (Wikipedia, "Steel Engraving"). The now defunct website of Peters Engraving adds, "All the illustrations of the Encyclopedia [*sic*] Britannica of 1911 are steel engravings. / Steel plates can be case hardened to ensure that they can print thousands of times with little wear. Copper plates cannot be case hardened but can be steel-faced or nickel-plated to increase their life expectancy. / During the 1820s steel began to replace copper as the preferred medium of commercial publishers for illustration, replacing etching but rivalled still by wood engraving and later lithography. This produced plates with sharper, harder, more distinct lines. Also, the harder steel plates produced much longer wearing dies that could strike thousands of copies before they would need any repair or refurbishing engraving. The hardness of steel also allowed for much finer detail than would have been possible under copper which would have quickly deteriorated under the stress" ("Engraving Illustration," http://www.petersiu.com/engraving.asp [accessed 21 October 2015]). Steel plates were also adaptable to ROTARY PRINTING, and since images could be printed mechanically in high-speed presses, they no longer had the PLATE MARKS that were produced with COPPERPLATE ENGRAVING. (See Griffiths, *Prints and Printmaking*.)

The method is an INTAGLIO form of printing, and while the term "engraving" implies much hand work with BURINS AND GRAVERS, acids were often used to etch the plates. Nonetheless, images from etched plates are often referred to as engravings.

STEELS. *See* Thins.

STEMMA/STEMMATICS. The stemma is a chart showing the genealogical relationships among MANUSCRIPT or printed EXEMPLARS. For example, an author writes a text in manuscript (the "archetype"). It is copied by two scribes (A and B), each entering readings that differ from one another (or not). The manuscript of scribe A is then copied by three others and that of scribe B by four others. There are now three generations of manuscripts at this point: that of the author, that of scribes A and B, and that of the other seven scribes. Other "layers" or "branches" on the stemma will be created with the subsequent copying of these seven scribes, and so on.

Stemmatics is the study of the manuscripts in such a way as to determine where in the stemma each exemplar fits. The discipline of stemmatics was developed in the 19th century by biblical scholars and then codified by Karl Lachmann (1793–1851) to assist editors in determining the authenticity and accuracy of each exemplar and to use this information to produce a scholarly edition (*see* Bibliography) of a text. Presumably, the exemplar closest to the author's original had fewer transcription VARIANTS than did exemplars lower down on the stemma, so the scholar creating and examining the stemma would also want to date each exemplar if possible. However, the date of an exemplar was not always a reliable feature since a manuscript dated, say, 1500 could be three genealogical levels down from the earliest known (the one at the top of the stemma), while a manuscript dated 1650 could be only one level down. (See Maas, *Textual Criticism*.) As noted above, the "science" of creating the stemma is called "stemmatics," and the quotation marks around the word "science" shows that there was nothing purely scientific about this discipline. Two scholars, working with the same cluster of manuscripts, may well—for various reasons and with various scholarly rationales—produce stemmas that differ from one another, depending on the complexity of the manuscripts in the mix and the number and nature of the variations they exhibit.

STEMS. "All vertical strokes of a letter, and full-length oblique strokes as in V, W, and Y" (Lawson, *Printing Types*, p. 26). Alexander Lawson also explains "flared stem": "A stem that thickens at either terminal, or both. They are used in such Romans as Bernhard Modern and Egmont, and in such SANS SERIF types as Optima, Stellar, and Pascal" (p. 26). (See Appendix B, on "Typeface Terminology.")

STENCIL. *See* Pochoir.

STEPHENSON BLAKE & CO. One of the world's most revered and important type foundries. The Monotype MyFonts website says, "Sheffield typefoundry started in July 1818 by silversmith and mechanic William Garnett and toolmaker John Stephenson, financially supported by James Blake, seemingly with little prospect for success. / However in November of that year news came that the breakaway Caslon foundry (formed when WILLIAM CASLON III left the original Caslon foundry in 1792) was put up for sale by William Caslon IV. In 1819 the deal was concluded and Blake, Garnett & Co. were suddenly in charge of one of England's most prestigious typefoundries. In 1829 Garnett left to become a farmer. The company was renamed Blake & Stephenson in 1830, but Blake died soon after. It became Stephenson, Blake & Co. in 1841. John Stephenson died in 1864, the year after he handed control to his son Henry. / Over the years the company has acquired: Fann Street Foundry (1906); Fry's Type Street Letter Foundry; H. W. Caslon & Sons (1937); Miller & Richard (1952). Thus it inherited almost the entire British fine printing industry. / In recent years the MATRICES and other typographic equipment, by then of little commercial value (but of great historical value), were passed to Monotype and now form a key part of the Type Museum in London. Members of both the Stephenson and Blake families still sit on the board of the present company. / In 2001, according to managing director Tom Blake, the foundry was still producing some type in ZINC, but by 2005 the company was wound up" (Monotype MyFonts, "Stephenson Blake"). The company also manufactured printing equipment and composing room furniture.

STEREOTYPING (stereos). "The art of producing from WOODCUTS or pages of type in RELIEF a solid block or PLATE which is an exact replica of the original. It is usually done by casting, but in ELECTROTYPING, a species of stereotyping, it is produced by galvanic action. In ordinary stereotyping a mold is taken of the page of type, which, when dried, is used as a MATRIX in which to cast TYPE METAL or metal somewhat resembling it. This being trimmed, shaved and mounted upon a BLOCK, is used for exactly the same purpose as the original" (*American Dictionary of Printing and Bookmaking*, p. 526). The stereotyping mold can be made from plaster of Paris or from paper; that made from paper pulp is called a "FLONG." (See the long entry on this method of printing in the *American Dictionary of Printing and Bookmaking*, pp. 526–29.) The method was invented by WILLIAM GED in 1725 (see *Encyclopaedia Britannica*, "William Ged"; http://www.britannica.com/biography/William-Ged [accessed 17 June 2021]). However, according to Douglas C. McMurtrie, an earlier form of this process was in use in the 16th century in the printing of a map that had WOODCUT illustration mixed with printing type. (See McMurtrie, *Stereotyping in Bavaria in the Sixteenth Century*.)

Millions of books were printed from stereotype plates (called "stereos"). They will often show this with a small printed notice that may say the name of the company supplying the stereo plates, sometimes at the very end of the printed text. (Occasionally the fact that the book was printed from such plates is noted on the title page, as is the case with Charles Turner Thackrah's *The Effects of the Principal Arts, Trades, and Professions*, published in Philadelphia in 1831, and announcing on its title page "Stereotyped by L. Johnson.") A book could be printed in its first impression (*see* Edition, Impression [Printing], Issue, and State; Points) from STANDING TYPE, then, in subsequent impressions, from stereotype plates made from that type. It is to be remembered that if this is the case, there will be a difference in *impression* but no difference in *edition* since all copies printed from the same setting of type are of the same edition. In this example, the copies printed from the stereo plates came from the same setting of type as were the copies made from the first impression, printed from the original type. (See Brightly, *The Method of Founding Stereotype*; Hodgson, *An Essay on the Origin and Progress of Stereotype Printing*; and Newell, *Stereotyping and Electrotyping*.)

STET. An order to a COMPOSITOR or editor to ignore a change that has been written into a PROOF. If anyone "corrects" a text and then decides that the correction was improper, "stet" means "[leave it as] it stands" (i.e., the way it was before the correction). (From the Latin third-person singular, present active indicative of *sto, stare*—meaning "to stand.") The person using that word may also put dots beneath any character that should be left as it originally was. Authors will often look with bewilderment at the work of their editors, and put in "stet" to mean, "I do not approve of the change you are making. Use the text the way I submitted it."

STEVENSON, ALLAN H[ENRY] (1903–1970). American paper historian and researcher whose work opened up a new avenue of scholarly approach to paper analysis. "He was an [e]xpert on paper history; scholar on the works of Renaissance dramatist James Shirley. / [He] was best known for his innovative work on WATERMARKS as a means of DATING early printed books. . . . In 1952 he left teaching to continue his research as a professional bibliographer. His research was supported by a number of grants (e.g. from the Folger Shakespeare Library, the Huntington Library, the Newberry Library, the Fulbright Commission, and the Bibliographical Society of the University of Virginia) as well as by his wife, Rachel Waples Stevenson, a pioneering television producer in Chicago. / . . . Stevenson developed a new method for the bibliographical description of botanical books while cataloging the collection of Rachel McMasters Miller Hunt between 1956 and 1961; his best-known work was a study of the Constance *Missale Speciale*, using watermark evidence to prove its date. Stevenson was [a] member of many learned societies and was particularly active in the Bibliographical Society (London), the International Association of Paper Historians, and the Paper Publications Society" ("Inventory of the Allan H. Stevenson Papers, 1944–1970, Bulk 1952–1970"; https://i-share-nby.primo.exlibrisgroup.com/discovery/fulldisplay?vid=01CARLI_NBY:CARLI_NBY&docid=alma998294418805867&context=L [accessed 9 June 2022]). The "problem" with the *Missale* was that some scholars claimed that it was printed before GUTENBERG, FUST, and SCHÖFFER printed the Bible; Stevenson showed from paper evidence that the *Missale* actually came much later, perhaps around 1473. Similarly, he showed that BLOCK BOOKS, which scholars assumed predated printing from MOVABLE TYPE, were actually later than the Bible as well, certainly after 1460. (See Stevenson, *The Problem of the Missale Speciale*, and the review of this important volume in Tanselle, "Review of *The Problem of the Missale Speciale*.")

Another important "discovery" was Stevenson's recognition that paper molds were not composed merely of a MOLD and A DECKLE but were actually two molds and one deckle, allowing for an increase in speed in hand papermaking. (*See* Mold [papermaking] [Western; Asian].) (See Stevenson, "Watermarks Are Twins." See also Needham, "Allan H. Stevenson and the Bibliographical Uses of Paper.")

STICK. *See* Composing stick.

STICKER. A LABEL pasted onto a book to show its asking price, or possibly the name and other information of the seller. Stickers could also be pasted onto a DUST JACKET to announce that a book has recently won a prize (the prize coming after the dust jackets were printed), or that the book has been made into a "Major Hollywood Movie." Collectors may wish to retain those announcement labels, but other kinds—like those showing the book is EX LIBRARY—may reduce the value of a volume and the owner may wish to remove them. The label may leave some residue of its adhesive, and if this is not removable (or if the sticker causes some damage in its removal), the "sticker damage" can reduce the value of the volume. The damage may be what is called a "sticker ghost," where the adhesive has penetrated into the paper, cloth, or leather, leaving a stain. And such damage, while often on the outside of the volume, can also be inside, on an ENDLEAF. Stickers are not to be confused with tickets, as in "BINDER'S TICKET."

STICKER PRICE. *See* List price.

STICKING THE TYPE. *See* Typesticker.

STILTED. "The SQUARES of a book that are unusually extensive. A book is stilted so as to make it of the same height as other books on the same shelf. [As if the book is on stilts.] Stilting may be required when one volume of a set is rebound (and trimmed), in order to make it range with other volumes of the set. In addition, books issued in parts were sometimes stilted by a binder who trimmed excessively" (Roberts and Etherington, p. 251). Carter adds that stilting can be a sign that a book's TEXT BLOCK has been moved from one cover to another. (See Carter, p. 238.) (*See* Remboîtage.)

STINT. The length of time a COMPOSITOR or printer spends at his craft in a single stretch. (This explains the pun in the E. Raffe poem of around 1861: "I must confess / I love my press / For when I print / I know no stint / of joy." Done from my memory. Not sure I got it verbatim.)

STIPPLING. Irregular spots impressed into leather bindings or into PRINTS (*see* Copperplate) to create shading. The dots, often thousands of them, allow for subtle shading, from one color or tone to another, in ENGRAVINGS. The technique is also used on covers, with decorative stamping consisting of the same kind of use of dots—often in gold. The term can be used in the description of an engraving which is made with this technique: "The stippling in the sky of the print creates the extensive shading of the clouds." Or a bookseller's catalog might extol the beauty of a binding: "Panel stamp in the center of the upper cover, with shaded stippling borders at the edges of the cover."

The same effect can be achieved on paper. In the 18th century BLOCK PRINTED papers sometimes had shaded areas in their decoration, the dots made by pins that were hammered into the blocks, with their tips at the same level as the rest of the printing surface. The pins got inked at the same time as did the block's pattern. The technique was called PICOTAGE.

STITCHED. Sewn, as of a binding (e.g., a book or PAMPHLET). Carter seems to distinguish between books sewn through the fold and those that were stitched, apparently meaning OVERSEWN, visible by the presence of holes stabbed through the LEAVES or SIGNATURES (not through the folds at the spine). But most people would not make this distinction. If a pamphlet is stitched, it is stitched, regardless how the stitching was done. One can, however, delineate SADDLE STITCHING and SIDE STITCHING, the former using metal staples rather than thread. (*See* Oriental binding; Overcasting.) "Stitched" is sometimes used for side sewing.

One authoritative text, by Julia Miller, says that stitching is "[a]nother term for side-sewing, stabbing, or stab-sewing" (Miller, *Books Will Speak Plain*, p. 471). The use of thread, then, in these instances, qualifies an item as "stitched."

STONE (printer's stone). *See* Composing stone.

STONE PRINTING. *See* Lithography.

STONE, REYNOLDS (1909–1979). One of England's great CALLIGRAPHERS, letterers, and ENGRAVERS. As Honor Clerk wrote, "You may not know the name of Reynolds Stone, but it is almost impossible that you haven't come across his designs. If you're familiar with the masthead of the Economist or remember the clock on the top of the front page of the Times; if you've seen the COLOPHON on a book published by the Folio Society or Hamish Hamilton or owned a Penguin edition of Shakespeare; if you've borrowed something from the London Library; if you had a £5 note in your wallet in the 1960s, if you've walked over the memorial to Winston Churchill on the floor of Westminster Abbey or if you own a passport with the royal coat of arms on the front, then you've been in close contact with the work of this wood engraver, typographer, letter-cutter and watercolourist" (Clerk, "The Genius of Reynolds Stone: A Private Man in a Public World"; *The Guardian*, 21 December 2019; https://www.spectator.co.uk/article/the-genius-of-reynolds-stone-a-private-man-in-a-public-world [accessed 15 May 2021]). Stone's work was picked up in the United States, and he created many a BOOKPLATE and logo for American collectors and printers. (*See* Victoria and Albert Museum, *Reynolds Stone 1909–1979 An Exhibition*; *Reynolds Stone, 1909–1979*; Humphrey Stone, *Reynolds Stone: A Memoir*; Reynolds Stone, *Reynolds Stone: Engravings*.)

STOP-PRESS CORRECTIONS. Changes in type made during a PRESSRUN. The pressrun constitutes all the sheets to be printed in that IMPRESSION, and stop-press corrections yield STATE VARIANTS (*see* Edition, Impression [Printing], Issue, and State; Points) within that edition. While such VARIANTS are often termed "corrections," the term is not always accurate since a change of a perfectly good reading can yield another perfectly good reading. For example, a change from "flittering" to "flickering"—or the other way around—is an instance of a stop-press "correction" when neither word needs correcting (*see* Point maniac). (For discussions of author's corrections and states and state variants, *see* Edition, Impression [Printing], Issue, and State; Points.)

Stop-press corrections can be made by a printer who spots what he considers a TYPOGRAPHICAL ERROR, by an editor who thinks that something needs to be changed in the text while it is at press, or by an author who intrudes on the printing process. The textual editor's job is to determine the nature and source of the correction and to decide whether it is AUTHORIAL or not. (*See* Bibliography.) Further, if two readings are discerned, one may presume that a typographical error precedes a correct reading, but this is not necessarily the case. Type made loose by the improper tightening of QUOINS may occasion a printer to stop the press and RESET a line, introducing an error where one did not exist. Damage in the FORME could equally require resetting—another opportunity for errors to be introduced. The utter complexity of the entire printing process, which could vary from shop to shop and even from printer to printer within a single shop, could make "stop-press changes" (a preferable term) happen for many reasons.

STORY PAPERS. *See* Dime novels.

STRAIGHT-GRAIN MOROCCO. "Ostensibly, a GOATSKIN having creases in one direction on the GRAIN surface. The term is generally applied to leathers other than goatskin, which makes the expression 'MOROCCO' virtually meaningless. . . . The technique dates from the second half of the 18th century" (Roberts and Etherington, p. 252). Booksellers and bibliographers, seeing a straight grain in a leather, are often wont to call it "straight-grain morocco" despite the inaccuracy of this locution.

STRAPWORK. Decorative elements on bindings or in printed (or, more commonly, ENGRAVED) pages consisting of interlaced lines (sometimes double lines), forming a pattern that is usually geometrical. The use of this kind of design was popular in the 16th and 17th centuries on leather bindings. (Strapwork bindings are sometimes referred to as "interlace bindings.")

Strapwork on a 19th- or early 20th-century binding: John Hill Burton, *The Book-Hunter* (Edinburgh and London: William Blackwood & Sons, 1862).

Courtesy of Phillip J. Pirages, Fine Books & Medieval Manuscripts.

STRATEMEYER SYNDICATE/EDWARD STRATEMEYER (1862–1930). Edward Stratemeyer was the founder (in 1883) of a syndicate that hired freelance writers to produce novels for young adults based on plots that the syndicate supplied (*see* Greenwald, *The Secret of the Hardy Boys*, p. xiii). Although Stratemeyer himself wrote some of the earlier volumes, for the most part he hired out the writing to many freelancers who were paid by the novel—work for hire (*see* Ghostwriting)—so they did not own the intellectual property rights of the works. Some of the series have reached iconic status as the prototypical fiction for the young, and some of the series have endured for generations. Among them are the Hardy Boys, some of the Tom Swift books, Nancy Drew, the Rover Boys, the Bobbsey Twins, Bomba the Jungle Boy, and several others. "Not including graphic novels and planned releases, there have been well over 450 Hardy Boys titles published since their 1927 debut. This rough sum includes 38 titles from the original series that were entirely rewritten after 1959, releases by Grosset & Dunlap and digests from Simon & Schuster publishers, and the spinoff Clues Brothers, Undercover Brothers, Casefiles, Super Mysteries, and Adventures series, among others" ("15 Mysterious Facts about 'The Hardy Boys,'" Mental Floss; http://mentalfloss.com/article/66089/15-mysterious-facts-about-hardy-boys [accessed 17 June 2021]).

"As a result of the 1953 United States Senate Subcommittee on Juvenile Delinquency, many publishers of children's media worked hard throughout the '50s to get their stories in line with new legal and social standards for kid-appropriate material. Like other Stratemeyer Syndicate series, Hardy Boys books had often contained negative racial and gender stereotyping among its supporting and minor characters, many of which would shock modern audiences, but which were also considered unpalatable by readers in 1959. . . . That year, the Syndicate started rewriting 38 of its original Hardy Boys titles to remove objectionable material, including many of the books' most violent moments. Writers also tried to give the books a more modern feel with fewer tough words, streamlined action plots, and generally updated language" ("15 Mysterious Facts," cited above). (See Romalov and Dyer, eds., "Children's Series Books and the Rhetoric of Guidance"; see also Billman, *The Secret of the Stratemeyer Syndicate*; Johnson, *Edward Stratemeyer and the Stratemeyer Syndicate*; and Keeline, "Edward Stratemeyer & the Stratemeyer Syndicate.") (*See* Pseudonymous publication.)

Bibliographically, the output from the syndicate is a nightmare. Each series had perhaps dozens of authors, and every edition could have one or several rewrites, depending on all kinds of things, but mostly having to do with updating plots and language to remove stereotypes and offensive action. Cover art changed. Characters changed. Authors changed, as did those doing revisions.

STRAWBOARD. "A coarse, yellowish board produced largely from straw pulp" (Roberts and Etherington, "strawboard"; https://cool.culturalheritage.org/don/dt/dt3358.html [accessed 6 February 2021]). It came into use in the 18th century, and though it has never been extensively used for binding, it was so inexpensive that the publishers of YELLOWBACKS chose to use it for most of their publications. As Roberts and Etherington say, "[I]t has been demonstrated that strawboard is less likely to form sulfuric acid because it contains a lower percentage of iron impurities than does millboard, and it is alkaline, which in itself promotes greater permanence."

STRIKE. The MATRIX after it has been struck with the PUNCH, with the bulge where metal has been displaced by the punch. The strike must be justified for it to be usable for casting. (*See* Justification [in typecasting].) (A strike can be seen in the figure at "Punch.")

STUB. The thin strip of a LEAF left when the rest of the leaf has been removed from a volume. If the leaf is removed at the fold, its CONJUGATE LEAF will no longer be attached to the binding and will fall out. Thus, when a leaf is removed, a stub is left to keep the conjugate leaf bound into the volume and also to be used to attach a replacement leaf, if desired. (*See* Cancel.)

A stub is also present if an illustration, (usually) printed on a different press from that used for the type of the volume, has been bound in (rather than TIPPED IN). For example, a COPPERPLATE ENGRAVING may be bound in as a FRONTISPIECE, its stub extending around the SIGNATURE that carries the TITLE PAGE.

Carter says that sometimes an additional leaf (not part of the original plan for the book) might be printed up to be added to a volume. It will have a stub so that it can be bound into the volume with the other signatures. But sometimes a stub exists that cannot be explained by such a simple addition to a book. Other stubs could indicate a cancel (which, he points out, is often quite hard to see), and such a situation requires some careful analysis by the bibliographer. (See Carter, p. 239.)

Additionally, a volume could be bound with a series of stubs with the intention of having leaves tipped onto them—thus forming what is called a "GUARD BOOK."

press alive in Bristol, to
printing to its citizens a
change in the city. Letter
of Bristol's working popu
I am both a cyclist an
when I was sixteen, I stu
I spent a year in the prin
and a printer, both craft
seven-year apprenticeship
pride in letterpress as a cra
graphic designer since th
working with computers
better, but I do know that
a day, however interesting
somewhere in my head sin
About five or six years a
ing less time on computer
distances on my bicycle an
who make things with thei
are the most inspiring fol
some of them in my book
cluding Dominique Lieb's
pp. 81-84]. A year or two
thusiast, Cally Callomon, p

Stubs, indicating conjugate leaves of illustrations that were bound in with this signature; *Matrix* 33 (2015), between pp. 8 and 9 (between the first and second signature of the volume).

Courtesy of John and Rosalind Randle, Whittington Press.

STUCK-ON HEADBAND. *See* Headband.

STUDIES IN BIBLIOGRAPHY. *See* Bowers, Fredson.

STUFF (in papermaking). Originally, the pulp for papermaking, beaten and ready to use. But it is also used to mean anything in the VAT from which the paper is made. (*See* Filler; Furnish; Half-stuff.)

STYLE GUIDE; STYLE SHEET; STYLE MANUAL. Publishers (of all kinds of texts) generally follow a particular style in the works that they publish. And they ask their authors (and require their editors) to create for the COMPOSITOR clean COPY to be set into type—copy that conforms to the publisher's textual standards. Such things as spellings, punctuation practices, and the use of ITALICS, for example, may be part of the style that the publisher wishes to have. The aim is to produce as clear and readable a text as possible, with uniformity in the publications from this press. Many publishers rely on what is briefly called "Chicago"—*THE CHICAGO MANUAL OF STYLE*, now in its 17th edition. In the sciences and social sciences, the American Psychological Association has its *APA* guide, with its idiosyncratic styling, adopted by hosts of publishers. Other publishers have their own styling, referred to as "house style." Hence, a publisher may say in its advice to authors who wish to submit text for publication, "All submissions must follow house style." (*See* Reader; Press Reader.)

Another kind of style guide exists in newspaper publishing. The aim of this kind of reference is to get journalistic entries to conform to the house preferences of the news medium. How does the newspaper, for instance, want to style the name of this country: United States; United States of America; U.S.; US; or in some other way? They might list preferred hyphenations, forms of address, the presentation of statistical matter, and other kinds of things that newspapers prefer. Prominent among these guides are *The Associated Press Stylebook*, *The New York Times Manual of Style and Usage*, and *The Washington Post Deskbook on Style*. (Though paper-based versions of these are listed in the bibliography, online versions are available for at least the first two of these.)

A last note: magazines, journals, publishers, and any other publishing entity may have their own guides to style that do not conform to the styles of any other entity. Their aim, of course, is to have all items published with them to have a uniform usage of spelling, word choice, and other phenomena, issue after issue.

STYLUS. Peter Beal thinks that this could be the earliest tool for writing, examples being used in Mesopotamia as early as 3500 BC. It was made of various materials (wood, metal, or bone) and had a flat broad point at one end for incising characters in some soft material, like wax or clay. (*See* Cuneiform; Wax tablet.) Beal adds that some had triangular heads that could be heated to melt the wax and smooth it out if the scribe wanted to change or "erase" the text. (See Beal, *A Dictionary of English Manuscript Terminology, 1450–2000*, p. 402.) "A stylus could also be used for PRICKING and ruling [*see* Rule] a MANUSCRIPT" (Brown, *Understanding Illuminated Manuscripts*, p. 119). (*See* Clay tablets.)

SUBSCRIPT. (Also called "inferior letters," though they are not necessarily alphabetic.) A number, figure, symbol, or other character set below the line, beside the character to which it is attached. Subscripts are used in chemistry (H_2O) and "to distinguish between different versions of a subatomic particle. Thus electron, muon, and tau *neutrinos* are denoted ν_e ν_μ and ν_τ" ("Subscript and Superscript," Wikipedia, https://en.wikipedia.org/wiki/Subscript_and_superscript [accessed 17 June 2021]). The Wikipedia article adds, "Subscripted numbers dropped below the baseline are also used for the denominators of stacked fractions, like this: $\frac{67}{68}$." (*See* Superior letters and figures.)

SUBSCRIPTION SALES/SUBSCRIBERS. Selling items (for our purposes, books) by means of advanced orders. The orders are sometimes generated by door-to-door salesmen (*see* Salesman's dummy/Salesman's sample book). The aim of such sales is manifold. The publishers can get an idea of how many copies of a title to print. If advance payment is required, the publishers can have some cash in hand to produce the books. Signing up subscribers—who might be offered discounts for a permanent subscription—will guarantee sales of further publications of the press. (*See* Standing order.)

This method is common today with some FINE-PRESS publishers whose customers wish to get all publications from the press. If a modern fine press issues its publications through a distributor, the distributor will take a certain percentage of the profits. By selling directly to subscribers, the press can pass off a smaller percentage of the profits to the buyers, cutting out the middle person (the distributor). The press makes more income from this method, and the subscriber gets a discount that he would not have gotten from the distributor. The current system works well for particularly expensive books, for a "PRE-PUBLICATION PRICE" might entice a purchaser who might balk at paying the "regular price" or who might be seduced into buying at a special low price with the knowledge that the volume will appreciate as soon as it is issued to the public. There may be the added bonus of having one's name printed in the volume in a "Subscribers List."

A drawback might be that a publisher prints up only enough copies for his subscribers and a few extra copies and the book "takes off," with demand far beyond the numbers in the first PRESSRUN. It might be unfeasible to print additional copies of an expensive book that took special papers and inks, hand-done illustrations, special bindings, and so forth. The volume then goes OUT OF PRINT, and the demand—exceeding supply—drives prices up considerably. This situation obtains with the early volumes of *MATRIX*, for example, produced before this journal had built up its subscriber list.

Another drawback could be that a collector subscribes to the work of a press, liking the topics of the books that that press issues. Then the press issues a title that is outside the subscriber's interests and collecting. The subscriber is obliged to take the volume or be jettisoned from the subscriber list.

SUBSIDY PUBLISHING. *See* Vanity publishing.

SUBSTANTIVES/SUBSTANTIVE VARIANTS. In the world of BIBLIOGRAPHY, substantives are VARIANTS in a text from one version to another, the variation carrying meaning. Hence, a variation between two texts like "The man was here" to "The fellow was here" is a substantive variant. These differ from ACCIDENTAL VARIANTS, which generally do not carry meaning. Textual editors (*see* Bibliography, especially the section "Textual Editing") usually attribute accidentals to COMPOSITORS and editors and substantives to authors—though this is not always an accurate assumption. (See, e.g., Berger, "Editorial Intrusion in *Pudd'nhead Wilson*"; *see also* Author's corrections.)

SUBSTRATE. In simplest terms, this means an underlying layer or material. In the world of books it is often used to designate whatever surface a text or images (or both) appear on. Common, of course, are paper and VELLUM, but substrates of many other kinds are used for books: AMATL, metal, TAPA CLOTH, plastics, PAPYRUS, and others.

SUBTITLE. A secondary title to a volume. It is usually printed below the main title though with "bright typography" (the term used sarcastically by STANLEY MORISON in his "First Principles of Typography"), the subtitle may wind up anywhere—even with its words interspersed between the words of the main title. The subtitle is usually printed directly onto the TITLE PAGE (though sometimes it is printed on the page facing the title page, giving a bibliographer pause as what constitutes the subtitle and which is the main title). Carter says that the subtitle usually explains the main title, as with Grant Barrett's *Hatchet Jobs and Hardball: The Oxford Dictionary of American Political Slang*. Sometimes it is the other way around, as with Scott McCloud's *Understanding Comics: The Invisible Art*.

In the 20th century, especially in the realm of scholarly writing, the subtitle has taken on a life of its own, with the possibly annoying practice of having a cutesy title followed by an explanatory subtitle (as in the first example above). In fact, there is even a literature on the "colonated title"—the title with a colon, preceded by some outrageous, sickening, or insipid title and followed by the main title: "Damn Your Eyes: A Study of *Oedipus Rex*."

SUEDE. (Sometimes called "reversed skin.") "[A] leather finished on the FLESH SIDE by buffering so as to raise a velvet-like nap. The typical suede leather is produced from the smaller skins, such as CALFSKIN, kidskin, lambskin, and GOATSKIN, although cowhide has also been used" (Roberts and Etherington, p. 253). The feel of the suede made it popular for what tried to pass as deluxe bindings, but often the process, hastily or carelessly done, yielded an acidic skin that eventually began to powder and flake, as can be seen by innumerable "LIMP LEATHER," ROYCROFT bindings. (*See* Roycroft Press.)

SUGETA (OR SUKETA). *See* Mold (papermaking).

SULPHATE AND SULPHITE (pulps used in papermaking). "Sulphate process is a method of cooking wood chips, to produce CHEMICAL WOOD PULP, first introduced by Dahl in 1883/84, under pressure and high temperature" (Labarre, *Dictionary and Encyclopaedia of Paper and Paper-Making*, p. 298). "Sulphite process, invented by Tilghmann in 1863/66, is the method of reducing wood to pulp suitable for the manufacture of paper, and consists in general terms in submitting the wood to the action of sulphurous acid and its acid salts" (Labarre, p. 298). The point here is that acids are used in the papermaking process, and if they are not washed out of the pulp—or neutralized in some way—they yield an acidic paper that will become yellow and/or BRITTLE over time. Untold numbers of books, newspapers, and magazines published from about 1875 on—and for about a century or more—are printed on such papers. Millions of PAPERBACKS and magazines, printed on this weak paper, are called "pulps." (*See* Pulp fiction/Pulp magazines.)

SUMINAGASHI. Japanese paper MARBLING. First used in the 12th century, this kind of paper decoration is created with inks floating on the surface of a bath of water. (The word itself means "the floating of colors.") The artist touches the pointed tip of a brush soaked with pigment to the surface of the SIZE, imparting a circular drop of the pigment to the surface; then he touches the surface with another brush—usually in the middle of the first drop—imparting either another color of pigment or a drop of water, either of which forces the first drop to expand into a ring. Further such applications create multiple concentric rings—or, alternatively, other neighboring rings that abut (or are separated from) the first group. When the artist is satisfied with the number and placement of the rings, he "moves" them across the surface using a paper fan, his hand, or his breath until a "pattern" is formed. Since the bath has not been thickened as is done in Western marbling, there is not much control of the movement of the pigments, but, nonetheless, lovely arrangements of them can result. A sheet of paper is then placed over the surface of the size, and the pattern transfers to the sheet. If the paper is WATERLEAF or contains only a small amount of SIZING, the pattern will soak into the sheet, making it visible from both sides of the sheet. Scholars assume that the movement of suminagashi papers to the West inspired Western marbling. (See Chambers, *Suminagashi*; Guyot, *Suminagashi*; Wolfe, *Marbled Paper*, pp. 5–7; and Yagi et al., *Suminagashi-Zome*.)

SUNNED. Said of any volume showing fading (usually) to its binding, or to any other part of the volume. A DUST JACKET could be sunned, as could be the exposed part of a bound-in ribbon BOOKMARK. Of course, the fading could have come from indoor lighting (especially fluorescent lighting, which emits strong UV rays) or just from the evanescence of the dye in a book cloth; but the word "sunned" is used for any kind of fading—caused by any source. Common is the sunning of leather or cloth on the SPINE (of the binding or the dust jacket), where the volume is most exposed to light and the deleterious effects of pollution.

SUPER. *See* Mull.

SUPERIOR LETTERS AND FIGURES. (Also called "superscript numbers and figures.") Small letters, numbers, or other characters printed above regular-sized characters. There are hosts of these, as with 1st, 2nd, 3rd, and 4th, and such common characters as 98.6^{o}; $4^3 = 64$. In French one will see Mlle (mademoiselle) and Mgr (monseigneur), along with 1^{e} (first) and XXIIe (twenty-second), and others. They appear also in other languages, but these are the most common ones that we are likely to see.

FOOTNOTE CALLS (i.e., footnote numbers or ASTERISKS[*]) are printed as superscripts.

Certain scholarly disciplines, of course, have their own superscripts, as with astronomy, mathematics, and physics, not to mention the hordes of them in MANUSCRIPTS of early texts. Manuscripts in Latin and Italian have scores of them, as one can see from the volume compiled by Adriano Cappelli, *Dizionario di Abbreviature latine ed italiane*. These represent abbreviations employed by the SCRIBES to save space in a line or to enable words to fit in at the end of a line.

(And while I have the chance, I might as well throw in one of my pet peeves: These superscripts are redundant and superfluous in dates. "The meeting will be on April 8th, 2022." When we see "April 8," we pronounce this "/April eighth/," so there is no need to put the superscript in there. It is akin to "What is your PIN number?" [which means "What is your personal identification number number?"])

SUPERSCRIPT. (*See* Superior letters and figures; Subscript.)

SUPPORTS (in a paper mold). *See* Ribs.

SUPPRESSED. Said of a text that is withdrawn from publication for any of several reasons. Carter has a long entry explaining the reasons for suppression, which can be done for a passage or a whole volume. Passages can be removed between impressions (*see* Edition, Impression [Printing], Issue, and State; Points), after a book has been published, or before it is released to the public. (The instance from

Kenney's: Twenty Poems for a Lost Tavern [*see* Cancel] shows prepublication suppression of a passage from the text.)

Carter cites the 1865 *Alice's Adventures in Wonderland* as a volume suppressed before it was published. And he comments on the rarity of such books—with perhaps only a tiny number surviving and thus being true collector's items. He points out that sometimes a book is published and then gets suppressed, and the number of remaining copies could be substantial, depending on how many got out into the world and how many were successfully retrieved and destroyed. He points out that a popular book could have been suppressed soon after its publication but that a great number may have been distributed and might still be extant. (*See* my comment on *While England Sleeps* below.) Hence, just because a book is suppressed does not automatically mean that it is scarce.

As Carter says, there are several reasons for suppression, and suppressed volumes, often, then, in short numbers, become serious collectors' items since the scandal surrounding the removal of the text from the public often engenders a desire to own what is scandalous or scarce. As mentioned above, sometimes the suppression takes place after the volume is released to the public, the suppression being carried out by a recall from vendors of unsold copies. This means that copies in the original state—with the objectionable material—will exist on the market, as happened with David Leavitt's *While England Sleeps*, recalled for copyright infringement reasons when Stephen Spender noticed Leavitt's use of Spender's materials, or the case of Kaavya Viswanathan's *How Opal Mehta Got Kissed, Got Wild, and Got a Life*, also recalled for COPYRIGHT infringement. The Leavitt volume in its objectionable form (with the PLAGIARISM still evident) was on the market long enough for Spender to have received a copy, read it, and have it recalled. Thus, the number of copies on the market of this suppressed volume must be quite large. The point is that, while Carter speaks in historical terms of suppression, such things are still taking place today. (See Berger, p. 218.) (Parenthetically, the Leavitt volume, suppressed not too long after its release, was out long enough to make it to a second printing [*see* Edition, Impression (Printing), Issue, and State; Points]. That is, copies of this suppressed version exist in two impressions: first and second. Hence, suppression did not necessarily limit the number of copies on the market to a small number.)

One short addition: as noted above, a whole volume can be suppressed, but so can a part of it. A single chapter or part of a chapter can be suppressed in printings subsequent to the first.

SUPRALIBROS. As an EX LIBRIS is a sign of ownership, so is a supralibros, the latter, however, being stamped or attached to the front cover of a book (the word formed from "supra" + "libros" = on top of the book). The name of the owner is signaled with its being spelled out in part or in full, or shown in a monogram, a coat of arms, a heraldic device, or in some other way. The information is usually stamped in gold, though it could be BLIND STAMPED as well, and it could be a personal or family name or the name of a library or other institution. (See The Private Library, "In Search of Supralibros at The Private Library").

Supralibros of King Charles II; on *Book of Common Prayer: The book of common prayer: and administration of the sacraments: and other ceremonies of the Church of England.* INCLUDES: *The psalter or Psalms of David after the translation of the great Bible, pointed as it shall be sung or said in the churches* (London: n.p., 1660). Offered for sale by Florisatus Rare Books at the Firsts Online book fair, May 2021.

Courtesy of Florisatus Rare Books.

SWASH LETTERS (in type). Alphabetic characters (though numerals can also be displayed as swash characters)—usually in roman but sometimes in ITALIC TYPEFACES—that have a CALLIGRAPHIC touch such that extended, graceful lines are formed from the simple letterform. Some typefaces have dozens of such embellishments (*see* Civilité type). The use of swash characteristics in ROMAN type appears in the employment of the so-called long *S*, the lowercase *S* that looks like a lowercase *F* (ſ), the difference being that the crossbar on the *F* goes through the main STEM (the upright stroke) and that the crossbar on the swash *S* goes up to but not through the upright stroke.

SWELLED RULE. *See* Tapered rule.

Swash letters. http://www.martinmajoor.com/images/nexus_arrighi_nexus_swash.gif (accessed 17 June 2021).
Courtesy of Martin Majoor.

T

TACKETING. "A method originally employed in non-adhesive binding to secure the SECTION (or sections) and covers of LIMP VELLUM bindings. The technique was later used to secure the loose, jacket-like cover to the TEXT BLOCK of some bindings, and, from late medieval times, as a method of decorating the covers of STATIONERY BINDINGS. Tacketing in one form or another dates back to at least the early 12th century. In the past 100 years or so, tacketing has been used to reinforce the sewing of large blankbooks [*sic*]. The tackets are secured around the FOLIO, webbing, and clothings of the spine. In this latter use, it was restricted to the better grades of stationery bindings. Over a period of some 800 years, therefore, tacketing has evolved from a method of constructing a bookbinding to a method of reinforcing and decorating the spine and covers of a book" (Roberts and Etherington, p. 258). (See also Espinoza and Barrios, "Joint Tacketing," where the method is explained and depicted.)

TAIL. The lower part of a book or page. Hence, a TAILPIECE appears at the lower part of a page; a tailband (*see* Endbands) is at the bottom of the volume. The opposite of the HEAD. Also called the "foot."

TAILBAND. *See* Endbands.

TAILLE-DOUCE. A term one might find in a bookseller's catalog when she is describing French books: it is the French term for a COPPERPLATE ENGRAVING—especially such an image composed of a series of ENGRAVED lines.

TAILPIECE (endpiece). A printer's ornament at the end of a chapter or part of a chapter, usually used to fill the blank space at the foot of the page. The ornament could be a FLEURON or a picture of some kind, not necessarily relating in any way to the text.

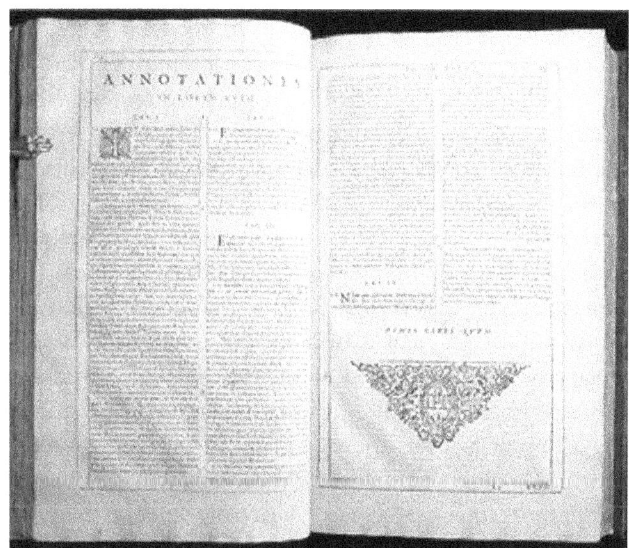

Page with a tailpiece. From Van Est, Willem Hessels (i.e., Estius), *Annotationes in praecipua ac difficiliora sacrae scripturae loca* (Duaci [Douai]: Apud Gerardum Patté, sub signo missalis aurei, 1628).

Courtesy of David Szewczyk and Cynthia Davis Buffington, Philadelphia Rare Books & Manuscripts Company.

TALL COPY. "A copy of an impression with HEAD and foot margins little trimmed in binding. Not to be confused with LARGE-PAPER COPY" (Levine-Clark and Carter, eds., *ALA Glossary of Library and Information Science*, p. 251).

TAMSCHRIFT. *See* Camouflaged books.

TANNED. Having been turned into leather. Roberts and Etherington have two entries: "chrome tanning" and "vegetable tanning." For chrome tanning, they say, "A method of tannage stemming back to the discovery, in 1858, that leather could be produced by treating skins with basic chromium sulfate (Cr[OH]SO 4). The two basic methods employed today are the one bath and two bath methods, the former being most often used. The most widely used chemical in chrome tanning is sodium dichromate (sodium bichromate) ($Na_2 Cr_7 O_7 . H_2O$), from which chromium sulfate is produced. / As in vegetable tanned leather, the degree of control exercised in the tanning process has great influence on the nature of the leather produced. If, for example, the final pH of a chrome-tanned leather is too low, the leather will be flat, hard, and wet, and may show grease spots on the surface; if it is too high, the leather will probably be plump, loose, dry, and may have a drawn GRAIN or be too soft in the blue sort. (*See below.*) It is, therefore, imperative in chrome tanning to obtain the optimum pH, i.e., 3.4 to 3.5 in the one bath method, or 3.2 to 3.4 in the combination single and double bath method, and to maintain it. / The two bath method has almost been completely superseded by the one bath tannage, except in certain cases where the older two bath process is thought to give a particularly uniform tannage and a deposit of colloidal sulfur in the leather" (p. 54). They explain that the "blue sort" means "hides and skins that have been chrome tanned but not finished" (cool.culturalheritage.org/don/dt/dt0379.html).

For vegetable tanning, they give the following: "The process of converting the protein (collagen and its related proteins) of a raw hide or skin into leather by means of vegetable materials. Vegetable tanning produces a relatively dense leather, one that is firm and solid and yields a high weight of leather per unit of raw stock. It also produces a leather that is pale brown in color, and which tends to darken upon exposure to natural light. Depending upon the finishing treatment employed, the tanning material washes out of the leather very slowly. / Vegetable tannages are used to produce bookbinding leather not only because of tradition, but because they produce leathers having a soft drape and handle (in addition to their firmness), which retain applied grain patterns particularly well. Unless specifically treated, however, vegetable tanned leathers have but little water resistance" (p. 275).

Tanned leather can be pliable, soft, textured or smooth, strong and durable, and receptive of decoration. Since acids are used in much tanning, if the acids are not properly rinsed from the skin, they can remain as an INHERENT VICE in the leather. Untold numbers of volumes with acidic leathers have flaked or fallen apart. Bummer! (the standard bibliographer's response to the situation).

TANSELLE, G. THOMAS (1934–). One of the premier American bibliographers and book historians in the United States. His work on textual criticism (*see* Bibliography, especially the section "Textual Editing") has been exemplary; he has published more—and more significant—articles on this and other topics than nearly any other scholar. His pronouncements about textual editing have been insightful and circumspect, and his approach to all bibliographical topics has always been expansive and brilliant. Tanselle's long list of publications is studded with "must read" books and articles on many aspects of textual and descriptive bibliography (see Groden, "Contemporary Textual and Literary Theory," and "G. Thomas Tanselle," https://en.wikipedia.org/wiki/G._Thomas_Tanselle [accessed 17 June 2021]). An abbreviated listing of his publications appears in the bibliography.

TAO BOX. *See* Boxes for books.

TAPA CLOTH. A PROTO-PAPER often made from the same fibers used to make Japanese paper: *Broussonetia papyrifera*—the paper mulberry plant. Breadfruit, ficus, and banyan and other fibers were also used. (*See* Kozo.) Note that the fibers are stripped, soaked, and pounded into a flat surface; they are not macerated (as in paper—thus, tapa cloth is not paper), nor are they woven (thus, tapa cloth is not strictly cloth). It is used as a covering material in bindings, and many books have tapa cloth samples tipped in.

Because the Hawaiian language does not have a *T*, the material is called "kapa" in Hawaii. It is called "siapo" in Samoa (see Neich and Pendergrast, *Traditional Tapa Textiles of the Pacific*; this information is on p. 19), "ngatu" in Tonga

Tapa cloth. Photograph by Jeff Dykes.
Collection of the author.

(p. 41), "ngatu" in Uvea (Wallis Island; p. 60), "aute" in New Zealand (p. 88), "masi" in Fiji (p. 97), "lepau" in the Santa Cruz Islands (p. 125), "ahu" in Tahiti (see Simon Kooijman, *Polynesian Barkcloth*, p. 15), and by other names in other South Pacific islands. (See also Brigham, *Ka Hana Kapa*, and Wright, *Barkcloth*.)

TAPERED RULE. A RULE that is wide in the center and tapers off at its edges. Also called a "swelled rule" or a "bulged rule," depending on where you begin your description. (If you begin with the wider part in the middle, then the rule tapers; if you begin at the fine extremities, then it bulges in the middle.) The rule could be decorative in many ways, not merely smooth lines. (For an image, *see* figure at the entry for Rule.)

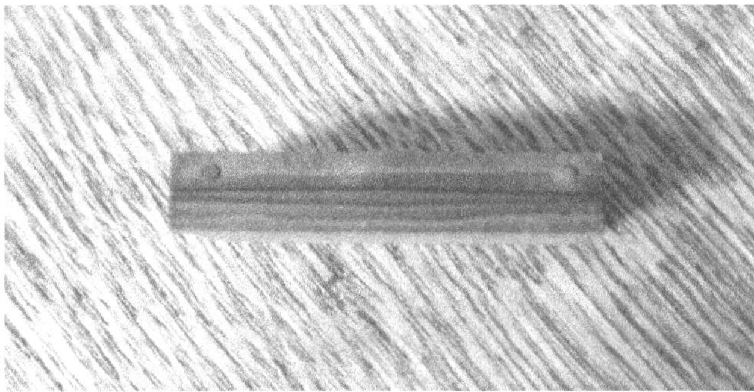

Printer's block with a tapered rule.
Collection of the author.

TAPE RESIDUE. The offensive stain one finds on any part of a VOLUME (on the binding, on LEAVES of the TEXT BLOCK) or DUST JACKET left by any of the commercial mending tapes available for nearly 100 years. "Scotch tape" and "Mystic tape" were just two of the many brand names of such tapes. They eventually dried out, leaving brownish or other stains on the SUBSTRATES to which they were attached. The phrase is self-explanatory, and probably did not need to be included here. But they are so common—on PAPERBACKS for the acetate tapes, and HARDBOUND volumes for the cloth tapes—that there needs to be a codified term to use in the book world for these nasty stains (and maybe an equivalent one for those who use the tapes—though I cannot think of one at the moment).

TAPES (in binding). "The strips of cloth (usually linen), VELLUM, nylon, etc., to which the sections of a book are sewn, and whose free ends, or SLIPS, are attached to the BOARDS, or are glued between SPLIT BOARDS to impart additional strength to the binding structure" (Roberts and Etherington, p. 260). In LACED-IN or CASED-IN bindings, these tapes could just as easily have been cords or thongs; the tapes are wider, of course, and their ends can be frayed out to make them lie flat under the pastedowns. (*See* Endleaves.) They will still be visible (and tactile) under the endleaves, evidenced by the raised paper on top of them. If they have any acid in them, or if they were glued down to the boards with an acidic adhesive, they may have discolored the endsheet, in which case a bookseller's catalog may say, "discolored at the tapes."

TARNISHED. Said of any metallic foil stamping (usually on a cover of a book) that has lost its brightness or shine. This kind of deterioration is often seen on cloth-bound volumes of the 19th century.

TATTLE-TAPE. A magnetized strip that can be embedded inside the binding of a book (usually) at the SPINE (or attached to the LEAVES for books that do not have a spine that opens, as with PERFECT-BOUND volumes). The strip, positioned between sensors, will set off an alarm, alerting library personnel that a volume is being removed from the collection without having been properly checked out. Proper checkout entails desensitizing the magnetic strip. When the book is returned, the strip will be resensitized to reactivate its security properties. The adhesive on the tape is archival, so it will not damage library materials. The product is proprietary (it is made by 3M), so the term is a brand name, but its widespread use has made it almost a generic term for such security devices.

TAUCHNITZ. A publishing firm run by a family of publishers in Leipzig, Germany, producing thousands of titles of works by American and English authors. Christian Bernhard von Tauchnitz (1816–1895) was the mastermind who began the serious operation. All of the volumes were covered in paper (not in BOARDS) and were thus quite inexpensively produced. The company scrupulously honored the COPYRIGHTS of the authors or original publishers, and they got many of their texts as PROOF sheets from the original publishers. If that was the case and if the Tauchnitz version hit the stands before those from the British or American publisher did, then the German versions are the true first editions. (*See* Follow the flag.) (The books that Tauchnitz published were primarily in English but were for distribution on the Continent. And since copyright protections were not in place to the extent that they are today, Tauchnitz could probably have gotten away with publishing without giving any royalties to the authors. But Tauchnitz paid most of them and also did not distribute the volumes in English-speaking countries, so they would not conflict with sales of the books in their countries of origin.) "Many Tauchnitz editions are of potential textual significance, having been set from proofs, ADVANCE SHEETS, or corrected editions, or variously adapted to suit the series format" (see the British Library website below).

The bibliography of Tauchnitz editions compiled by William B. Todd and Ann Bowden (*Tauchnitz International Editions in English, 1841–1955*) is a miracle of concision, listing thousands of volumes with masses of information in a minimum of space, achieved by a series of nearly impenetrable abbreviations and charts and shortcuts. The Tauchnitz volumes themselves are easily identifiable from a distance, with their spare designs and inexpensive paper WRAPPERS. They were extremely cheaply produced, with the idea of maximum profits and minimum costs to the publisher and the customers, and it would seem remarkable that so many of them have survived today if we forget that so many of them were produced. Scholars wanting to research the Tauchnitz volumes should begin at the British Museum, with its Todd-Bowden Collection of Tauchnitz Editions, amassed by the compilers and editors of the reference volume mentioned above. That collection has about 6,700 volumes, along with sale catalogs, leaflets, and other advertising material. "In the summer of 1843 Tauchnitz put a proposal to a small number of authors to pay them a fee in return for authorisation to publish their works and his proposal was accepted initially by three authors in July 1843—G. P. R. James, Bulwer Lytton and Lady Blessington. Five others—Dickens, Disraeli, Ainsworth, Samuel Warren and Captain Marryat accepted shortly after and works by all these authors and a small number of others appeared in the Tauchnitz series as editions 'sanctioned by the author' over the next three years. / This pioneering move helped to drive forward moves toward international copyright protection and in 1846 an Anglo-German treaty established an international copyright. From that point on Tauchnitz editions were published under international copyright, giving them some protection against PIRACY by other publishers. Under the terms of the copyright they could be sold throughout Continental Europe and elsewhere, but could not be imported into the British Empire, or in the case of American authors, into the USA" ("Tauchnitz Editions"; https://tauchnitzeditions.webs.com/index.htm#627152365 [accessed 5 July 2021]).

TAWING. "An ancient process of treating prepared hide or skin (usually pigskin or GOATSKIN) with aluminum salts and (usually) other materials, such as egg yolk, flour, salt, etc. A skin may actually be tawed simply by immersing it in an aqueous solution of potash alum at a temperature between 20 and 30° C; however, salt is usually included in the alum solution because it improves the substance (thickness) of the final product. After treatment the skin is dried in air (crusted) and held in this condition for several weeks to allow the development of stabilization or 'aging' effects. Tawed skins also undergo staking to impart of [*sic*] soft, flexible handle. Apart from this soft, warm handle, the tawed skins have a high degree of stretch. Handle and stretch may also be improved by the addition of egg yolk and flour to the basic alum and salt solution. A tawed skin is usually white in color but may yellow slightly with age. / Tawing does not actually produce a skin that is stable in the wet condition, i.e., imputrescible in the wet state, and therefore cannot accurately be described as having been tanned; consequently, in a strict sense, a tawed skin is not leather" (Roberts and Etherington, pp. 260–61). Alum tawing does not introduce any acids into the skins, so there is no INHERENT VICE in the final product.

TEG. *See* Gilt; Top edge gilt.

TEMPORARY BINDING. Any cover placed on (or wrapped around) or attached to a TEXT BLOCK as protection until a permanent cover can be employed. Such temporary covers can be paper, VELLUM, CLOTH, or other material. Sometimes these covers had LABELS or writing to identify the volume within. Sometimes the covers were decorated, and it may be difficult to prove that such a cover was indeed intended to be temporary, as Michèle Cloonan explains: "Although previously book collectors, dealers and librarians have generally assumed that such covers were intended to be temporary, the survival of paper-covered books proves that they were on the contrary often remarkably sturdy and enduring. Their survival also suggests that some collectors recognized their durability. So the notion that all paper covers were intended to be temporary must be examined more closely" (Cloonan, *Early Bindings in Paper*, p. 4).

TERMINUS A QUO; TERMINUS AD QUEM. *See* Dating.

TERNION. "A gathering consisting of three sheets folded once and insetted" (i.e., nested into one another; Roberts and Etherington, p. 262). This is equivalent to a FOLIO in 6s.

TÊTE-BÊCHE. Literally "head to tail." A book structure in which two volumes are bound as one but with the first bound upside down with the other. That is, a volume is bound with the first text in its covers properly. One reads halfway (or so) through the book to the end of that text. Then the book is inverted, with the SPINE still at the left, and a new cover appears (the rear cover of the book is actually the front cover of the other text). And the second text is read through until it ends and the reader encounters the first text, upside down in the TEXT BLOCK. A structure different from but similar to a DOS-À-DOS BINDING. The magnificent 17th-century volume on Oxford and Cambridge (Loggan, *Cantabrigia illustrata, sive Omnium celeberrimae istius universitatis collegiorum, aularum, bibliothecae academicae, scholarum publicarum, sacelli coll. regalis*) is a fine example of a tête-bêche book. The form was revived in the 20th century with the publication of a great number of ACE DOUBLES, and the LIMITED

EDITIONS CLUB even used the form for at least one of its publications. The term, of course, is French, but interestingly enough, the French do not use it for this kind of binding. The great French antiquarian bookseller Rodolphe Chamonal says, "The term tète-bêche simply means head-to-foot: with two people, one would have his or her head at the level of the other's feet. In binding, that could often mean that the text is inserted into the binding upside down, which was a common enough binders' mistake. So the exterior binding is normal, it has just been bound to the text upside down" (personal communication, 10 February 2021).

A tête-bêche volume of verse. Roy Blount Jr., *Webster's Ark / Soupsongs* (Boston: A Peter Davidson Book, Houghton Mifflin, 1987).

Photo by the author.

The central two-page spread of the volume shown in the figure above.

Photo by the author.

TEXT BLOCK. The space on a printed page inside of which all the page's printing is contained. Also, all of the LEAVES of a book, taken as a unit, but not counting the END SHEETS. So a bookseller may say, "Binding severely damaged, but text block in fine condition." In this latter sense, the text block comes from the printer. All other parts (cover, ENDLEAVES, and some of the FLYLEAVES) come from the binder and are not to be considered part of the text block, and they do not belong in a COLLATIONAL FORMULA. This is yet another instance in the book world in which a single locution has two or more meanings. (*See* Mold; Signature.)

TEXTBOOK. *See* Revised edition.

TEXTILE BINDING. *See* Embroidered binding.

THE TEXTILE CONSERVATION WORKSHOP. *See* Regional Alliance for Preservation.

TEXTUAL EDITING (textual bibliography). *See* Bibliography.

THEFT. *See* Book theft.

THERMOGRAPHY. Literally, "heat printing." (Sometimes called "fried printing"; see Carlsen, *Graphic Arts*, p. 51.) In the standard thermographic printing method, ink is printed onto a SUBSTRATE and then coated with a powder and heated; the heat fuses the powder onto the top of the ink, producing raised lettering above the printed surface, giving it the feel of ENGRAVING. Because of the final three-dimensionality of the printing, thermography is sometimes called "artificial (or imitation) engraving." Where engraving, with its artistry, metal plates, and special press, is expensive, thermography is only a fraction of the cost.

A thermographed text will have no signs of the engraving process: the trace of the PLATE around the printed image (*see* Plate marks) and the trace on the underside of the sheet or card of the pressure produced in the ROLLING PRESS.

THESAURUS. There are two kinds of thesauri: a book of synonyms and a listing of terms or concepts in a specialized field—the list showing the jargon of that field. The second kind of thesaurus, in modern practice, consists of two parts: an alphabetical listing of the terms and a hierarchical list showing the relationships among the words. The hierarchical list, in "layers," will show terms from the more general (at the top of the hierarchy) to the more specific (lower down on the hierarchy). For example, at the top, we may have "paper"; a layer down, we might have "decorated paper"; and beneath this, we might find "paper decorated in the pulp" or "paper decorated on its surface." The next layer down for the latter might be "marbled paper"/"paste paper"/"block-printed paper." Under marbling, another layer may be "random decoration"/"combed decoration" and so on.

Sometimes the terminology of a thesaurus is so technical that some of the terms may have "scope notes" explaining what the terms mean. And each term will have a designation of "broader terms" (i.e., the term above it in the hierarchy) and "narrower term(s)" (those beneath it in the hierarchy, if there are any). There may also be "related terms," similar but not above or below in the hierarchy.

THICKNESS COPY. *See* Dummy.

THINS (brasses, coppers, and steels; in printing) (also called "hair spaces"). Thin pieces of metal used in setting type to add space to a line—between words or letters (*see* Justification; Letterspacing). Thins, usually placed between words, are also used to tighten up a line of type in the COMPOSING STICK. They are used by the COMPOSITOR to letterspace text set in all caps. There are three kinds of thins: brasses (equal to one point in width), coppers (equal to a half point), and steels (equal to a quarter point). (*See* Points.)

THIRTY (OR 30). An indication, at the end of a MANUSCRIPT or other text, to indicate "the end." It tells the COMPOSITOR that there is no more text to set. If PROOFS or original manuscripts survive, this number might appear at the end.

THIRTY-TWO-MO (trigesimo-secundo). A book FORMAT (or the format of a single SIGNATURE) in which the original sheet is folded in half five times to produce a QUIRE of 32 leaves/64 pages. If the sheet is made of LAID PAPER, the CHAIN LINES in the volume are vertical. With this many folds of the original sheet, the resulting volume is likely to be fairly small, so the format was not uncommon for books of prayer and other religious texts and for small almanacs.

THONGS (in binding). "1. Narrow strips of leather, alum-tawed skin, etc., used to attach VELLUM covers in LIMP BINDINGS, as well as to hold the covers of books closed. Thongs were used before the invention of CLASPS and were, in fact, used on COPTIC BINDINGS. 2. The narrow strips of vellum, leather, or alum-tawed skin used in the early days of FLEXIBLE SEWING. Thongs had begun to be replaced by cords in this use by the latter part of the 16th century" (Roberts and Etherington, p. 263). (*See* Cords; Tapes.) The thongs, drawn around the SPINE of the volume, when covered with leather or vellum, create RAISED BANDS. In a LACED-IN BINDING, the thongs can be drawn through holes in the covers and then extended beyond the horizontal measure of the boards to create TIES.

THOUSAND. Carter says that many publishers, in REPRINTING texts, will show the sequence of these printings or editions by saying somewhere in the book (e.g., on the TITLE PAGE or the COPYRIGHT page) how many thousands of copies were printed, up to the most recent printing. One might find on the title page "twenty-seven thousandth," but this does not indicate if the printing is of the first or a later impression or even the first or a later edition. (*See* Edition, Impression [Printing], Issue, and State; Points.) No matter what edition or impression/printing the volume is, it is not a "first edition, first impression," and it will thus not command the price that the first/first would. (See Carter, p. 243.) By emphasizing the thousands, a psychological ploy is being exercised: making the potential buyer know that thousands of others have purchased the text and that they are out of the mainstream if they, too, do not own a copy. Also, the ploy can be untrue; to make one think that dozens of thousands of people now have this book implies that a potential buyer is not current in his reading if he did not, himself, own a copy. It's a matter of keeping up with the Rosenbachs.

THREE-DECKER. *See* Triple-decker.

THREE-PLANE WATERMARK. A WATERMARK made from a screen with three layers of depth, producing a sheet (that shows all three thicknesses of fibers) produced on that screen. In a three-plane watermark, the screen will be stamped between the faces of a male and female die, the die pushing the screen down (or "in") in some places and up (or "out") in other places while leaving the rest of the screen at the same level it was before the stamping. In the papermak-

Woven screen with three-plane watermark: "REPUBLICA DEL PARAGUAY / PAPEL SELLADO." Photograph by Jeff Dykes.
Collection of the author.

Piece of paper showing the three-plane watermark, made by the author. Photograph by Jeff Dykes.
Collection of the author.

ing process, fibers will fall onto the screen at the screen level, at the level where the screen is impressed (DEBOSSED), and where it is raised (EMBOSSED). The three thicknesses in the screen yield a sheet that itself has three thicknesses.

THREE-QUARTER BOUND. Roberts and Etherington say, "A binding having one type of material, e.g., VELLUM or CLOTH, covering the SPINE and part of the sides, as well as enlarged corners, and a different material, e.g., paper, covering the remainder of the sides. The material extends almost to the corners on the sides, i.e., much more than in the case of a HALF BINDING. Since it is difficult to imagine that the three-quarter binding was originated to economize on the more expensive covering material (cloth, or even vellum or leather), the three-quarter binding may have been developed simply as a new style. In the eyes of many, it is a style that appears badly proportioned on the sides" (p. 264). (*See* Full binding; Half-bound; Half cloth; Quarter-bound.) It should be added that the corners and spine may be covered by the same kind of *material* as the rest of the boards, just a different kind of that material. For example, the BOARDS could be covered with blue paper and the corners and spine by cream-colored paper. It is the excessive size of the corner materials (not the difference in materials) that distinguishes this as a three-quarter binding.

THREE-VOLUME NOVEL. *See* Triple-decker.

THUMB BIBLES. MINIATURE volumes on religious themes, usually containing abridgments or summaries of biblical passages, in prose or verse, usually aimed at an audience of children. They generally contained illustrations. These books have been collected partly for their text, but mostly for their size. They first appeared at the beginning of the 17th century, the first purportedly being that of John Weever (1576–1632), *An Agnus Dei* of 1606. "Weever published a thumb-book (1½ inch in height) giving a poetical history of Christ beginning with the birth of the Virgin. The title-page ran 'An Agnus Dei. Printed by V. S. for Nicholas Lyng, 1606'" (*Dictionary of National Biography, 1885–1900*, "John Weever").

In the 19th century, thanks to advances in printing technology, these tiny books were produced in great numbers. As Alyssa J. Currie says, "In the nineteenth century, miniature books and curiosities proliferated; in particular, thumb Bibles, miniature synopses of the Bible, experienced widespread popularity. Intended to provide children with a simplified introduction to Biblical narratives and religious instruction, thumb Bibles illustrate the mediation of religious instruction through material culture. The presence and influence of religious groups in the publishing industry, paired with publishers' new-found capacity to cater to middle-class demand for novelty children's books, created an environment in which thumb Bibles' popularity soared" (Currie, "The Victorian Thumb Bible as Material Object: Charles Tilt's *The Little Picture Testament* [1839]").

THUMB INDEX. (Also called a "cut-in index" or an "index notch.") "[A] series of rounded notches cut into the FORE EDGE of the book. Each generally has a LABEL bearing a letter or letters indicating the arrangement. The index proceeds from HEAD to TAIL and front to back of the volume. The maximum number of thumb cuts, and therefore the number of letters represented by each, depends on the height and thickness of the book. The thumb index is used principally for Bibles and dictionaries" (Roberts and Etherington, "thumb index"; https://cool.culturalheritage.org/don/dt/dt3508.html [accessed 24 February 2021]). According to Rob Rulon-Miller, "The patent for the thumb-index [was granted on] October 7, 1884 to C. H. Denison of New York" (Rulon-Miller, "Recent Acquisitions / March 2nd, 2021"; https://enusan.net/rulon/processwire-master/catalogs/cat210302/ [accessed 2 March 2021]). Another device used to help a reader locate a particular place in a text is the FINGER TAB.

TICKET (binder's; bookseller's). *See* Binder's ticket/Bookseller's ticket.

TIDELINE (in paper). The line made by water in a sheet of paper (or in a whole TEXT BLOCK). When paper is soaked, especially from one side (as with a volume sitting on a lower

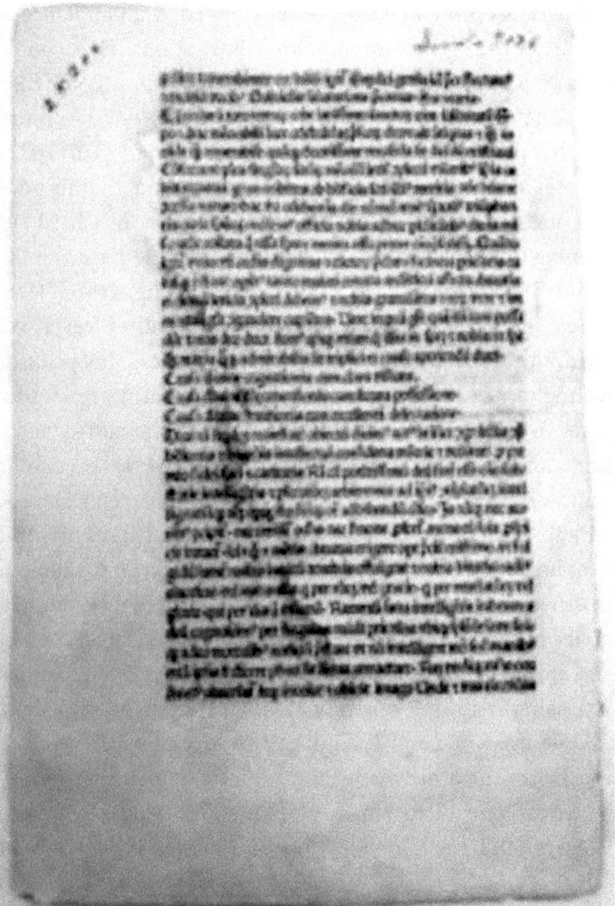

Tideline in a sheet of paper, damaged by water.

Emory University Libraries, "From the Conservation Lab: Using Gels to Remove Stains from the 'Oratio in die Omnium Sanctorum'" (1483); posted 22 January 2020; https://scholarblogs.emory.edu/woodruff/news/from-the-conservation-lab-using-gels-to-remove-stains-from-the-oratio-in-die-omnium-sanctorum-1483 (accessed 10 February 2021).

shelf onto which water has crept), the SIZING or dirt in the sheet can be "pushed" in the direction in which the water is moving, or it can sort of "migrate" in the sheet where the water soaks in. This creates a line in the sheet, usually crooked and irregularly shaped, where the sizing moves to. Such a stain is a tideline. The sheet may be permanently damaged, though CONSERVATORS can wash the LEAVES (a single leaf in a book or the whole DISBOUND and damaged text block) with the aim of removing the tideline. Such treatment is not always successful, and it is expensive since it takes a great deal of time and skill, along with special baths and other equipment and materials. The treatment removes all of the sizing of the sheet, and then the leaf or volume may need to be resized, another expense.

TIES. "TAPES or ribbons, [or cords] sometimes made of LEATHER, and usually in pairs, attached to the sides of a book close to the FORE EDGE, and occasionally at the HEAD, TAIL, and fore edge, and designed to prevent the covers from warping or gaping. They often consisted of linen, about ¾ inch wide, and were generally of a drab green color, although brown and blue were also used at times. Ties were usually threaded through a hole (not a slot) in the BOARD and, on the inside of the cover, the end was frayed out and attached to the leather TURN-IN. They were frequently used on fine bindings from about 1530 to 1640, and elaborate silk ties were used on Bibles and devotional books well into the 18th century. Their use today is largely restricted to portfolios" (Roberts and Etherington, p. 265). From a collector's perspective, if there are signs of ties but they are missing, the value of the volume goes down a bit since the collector wants the volume in its original condition and the loss of the ties can be seen as a defect. Replacement ties, as Carter notes, can usually be detected easily (p. 244).

TIGER-EYE MARBLED PAPER. One common pattern of MARBLED paper, with circular spots that look like eyes. (*See* Marbling/Marbled paper.)

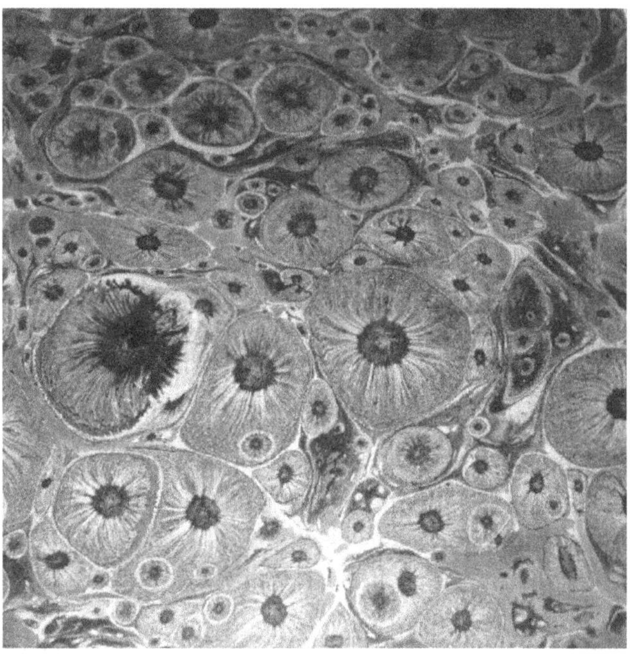

A sheet of tiger-eye-patterned marbled paper.

Collection of the author.

TIGHT. (Refers to the book, not to its owner.) One of many terms booksellers use to describe a volume in good condition. Often preceded by "nice" or "good," as in "A nice tight copy." It means that the book has seldom if ever been opened and thus is probably unused or unread. This could not be such a great selling point if one is interested in reading her books. To do so would mean to "loosen" the book and thus remove its "tightness," a selling point that almost certainly adds some value to the item. (And what does it say about a book that hasn't been read? That it is not worth reading?) Believe it or not, some collectors actually *read* their books. So perhaps seeing "tight" in a description, and knowing that that word adds cost, the potential buyer might instead look for a "nice loose copy."

TIJUANA BIBLES. These "were palm-sized, underground, explicit comic books. Produced in the United States, they were extremely popular in the 1920s and 30s. Most artists were unknown, as the publication of this explicit work was illegal at the time. . . . During the Great Depression era of the 1930s, 'Tijuana Bibles' were called eight-pagers, Tillie And Mac books, Jiggs and Maggie books, Jo-Jo books, bluesies, blue bibles, gray backs and two by fours. [Also '16-pagers.'] In the 1940s they were simply called 'Dirty Little Comics', and by the early 1950s these glorious works of dirty art would finally be known as 'Tijuana Bibles'—a term still in use today. The term 'Tijuana Bible' originated in southern California, playing on the untrue belief that these cheap little comics were manufactured and smuggled across the border from Tijuana, Mexico. This seedy backstory only added to the smutty appeal of these COMICS. They were sold under the counter for a quarter anywhere men hung out: bars, bowling alleys, auto-shops, tobacco stores, barbers, burlesque halls and tattoo parlors. If a gentlemen [*sic*] knew the right second hand bookstore or magazine stand, he could ask for the latest blue bible. The artistry of these images is simply amazing. It's clear where groundbreaking artists of the 1960s such as R. Crumb drew inspiration from: Tijuana Bibles! With pen names such as 'Mr. Prolific', 'Mr. Dyslexic' and 'Blackjack[,]' the artists . . . of Tijuana Bibles and the underground adult comics of the 1920s through the 1950s worked under great legal risk to bring their work to the public" (Book Depository International; on ABEBooks; https://www.abebooks.com/servlet/SearchResults?bi=0&bx=off&cm_sp=SearchF-_-Advtab1-_-Results&ds=30&recentlyadded=all&sortby=17&sts=t&tn=dirty%20little%20comics [accessed 13 March 2021]). These oblong comic books (about 3 × 3½ in.) were

A Tijuana bible. Anonymously published "16-pager." The only publication information on the item is shown on its cover. *Tarzan* (Hong Kong, China, n.d.).

Hake's Auctions; https://www.hakes.com/Auction/ItemDetail/57742/TARZAN-X-RATED-16-PAGER (accessed 13 March 2021).

clandestinely published through the 1950s in the United States. They were mostly printed in a single color, though occasionally one would be done in multicolor. To protect the publisher from litigation, they would seldom give the name and origin of the publisher; or they would have a fictitious publisher and place of publication. *Tarzan* was supposed to have been printed in Hong Kong, China, by Oriental Art Co., but it is almost certainly a U.S. publication. (See Wadsworth, *Stock Dirty Little Comics: A Pictorial History of Tijuana Bibles and Underground Adult Comics of the 1920s–1950s.*)

TILLIE AND MAC BOOKS. *See* Tijuana bibles.

TIMES LITERARY SUPPLEMENT. *See* TLS.

TIPPED IN/TIP-INS. Items that are tipped in are pasted into a volume, as opposed to "LAID IN." Many kinds of things are tipped into volumes: PLATES, ERRATA SLIPS, CANCELS, TICKETS, letters, other kinds of EPHEMERA, samples of various kinds, and so on. The term often means items added to a volume that were not part of the original production, such as notes or letters from authors, but in its generic sense, anything pasted in is a tip-in, as with MARBLED samples in a book about marbling, which samples are indeed part of the original production. Additionally, if a part of the original volume (like a printed LEAF) has become detached through wear or mishandling, it can sometimes be tipped in as a CONSERVATION treatment. And, of course, cancels may lead to the use of a cancellans, a replacement leaf, tipped onto a STUB, and ERRATA pages can be tipped onto full leaves, not a stub (usually at the end of a volume).

Tipped-in plate. Marie Madeleine Comtesse de Lafayette, *La Comtesse de Tende* (Lyon: Audin, 1947).

Courtesy of Rare Books and Manuscript Library at the University of Illinois, Urbana–Champaign.

Note that tip-ins like samples of marbled or PASTE PAPERS added to a volume (when it is part of the volume's original production) must be added by hand, usually adding considerably to the cost of production. HENRY MORRIS of the Bird & Bull Press once told me that his subscribers love books with tip-ins, so he catered to this clientele, though he sometimes cursed every tip-in. They took an enormous amount of time for him to prepare and mount, and he wished his customers didn't like them so much. But when he did a book with tip-ins, it sold out quickly.

TIPS. The extreme corners of the COVERS of a bound volume. Since these very corners are perhaps the most vulnerable parts of the binding, they are often BUMPED, smushed (the elegant formal term for a seriously bumped corner), or destroyed (the material covering them having been broken through, with the BOARDS [wood or cardboard] beneath them showing). Hence, they are generally mentioned in a bookseller's description only when they are damaged in some way ("Cover cloth intact, but tips smushed"). One means of protecting these exposed spots on the binding is to cover them with a material sturdier than that used to cover the boards. So one might see in a description of the volume, "Calf over boards, VELLUM tips." (*See* Corners.)

TISSUES/TISSUE GUARDS. Tissues are "fine, thin, soft, unsized papers made of strong materials such as rag and hemp fibres, beaten very finely, or of CHEMICAL WOOD PULP and a proportion of straw pulp. . . . They are usually unsized, nearly transparent, though never LAID, sometimes felt-ribbed; . . . chiefly used for wrapping and protective purposes and should as a rule be free from chemical substances which might tarnish or scratch metal or glass goods" (Labarre, *Dictionary and Encyclopaedia of Paper and Paper-Making*, p. 305). Roberts and Etherington say, "A class of papers, made in basis weights lighter than 18 pounds (24 x 36 . . .) [*see* Weight (of paper)]. These papers are made on any type of papermaking machine, from any type of pulp, including reclaimed paper stock, and may be glazed or unglazed. Some tissues are relatively transparent" (p. 265).

The term "tissue guard" is often used to denote a sheet of fine paper usually bound in (sometimes LAID IN or TIPPED-IN) that covers an illustration, the intent being to keep the ink used for the illustration from OFFSETTING onto a facing page. (*See* Offset sheets.) Often, these tissue sheets are a nuisance, making it challenging to see the illustrations, repositioning themselves when the volume is closed so that they get folded at odd angles (creating the appearance of a damaged LEAF), and being so thin that they are difficult to peel back from the image they cover. Additionally, the irony of many of them is that sometimes they were manufactured from acidic paper (Roberts and Etherington *do* say that they "are made . . . from any type of pulp"), so they may have yellowed, and the acid in them could migrate to the text pages. Also, since they are unsized (or only lightly SIZED), they can be more absorbent than are the papers used for the printing of the text (so they often are FOXED). Hence, the tissue guards introduce deleterious agents and harm the very volumes they were designed to protect. Carter says that sometimes they are used merely for "ostentation" (p. 244): the printer knows there will be no offset, but the look of the extra leaf can possibly justify the increase in price that they engender. Further, if tissue guards were in the volume when it was issued from the publisher, their absence can be anathema to a COMPLETIST collector. And if the volume, issued with these papers, still has them but they are damaging the volume, the collector must either remove them or add more guards around them as barriers—to protect the very leaves these guards were intended to protect. If the volume contains many of them, such interleaved additions could make the volume bulge and harm the binding. (We are tending toward madness here. Figure them out for yourself.)

TITLE. The so-called name of the text. The "identifying name given to a book, play, film, musical composition, or other work" (*American Heritage Dictionary of the English Language*, p. 1825). As Carter points out, the word can be used in the sense of the work itself ("This is the most popular title in the library") or to mean the TITLE PAGE (as in, "The title is torn and stained, but still attached"). (See Carter, p. 244.)

The binder sometimes stamps the title of a volume onto the cover (front or spine—the so-called BINDER'S TITLE), and may get it wrong. Likewise, a HALF TITLE may also be a shortened version of the full title, and it too may be different from that on the title page. The rule in library cataloging of books is to follow the title on the title page.

TITLE PAGE. Roberts and Etherington say, "In the usual case the RECTO of the second LEAF of a book, displaying the full title, the sub-title (if any), and usually the name of the author, the edition, the publisher and date of publication (sometimes the date is printed on the VERSO of the same leaf). The verso may also give particulars of the edition, i.e., the printer (and perhaps his address), the binder, specifications of type and paper, registration of COPYRIGHT, as well as (in the United States) the Library of Congress card number, ISBN number [*sic*], and CIP [see Cataloging in Publication] information. In cases where more than one page giving particulars of the title are present, that giving the fullest information is the title page" (p. 266). To this, we may add that the title page may also give the city or cities in which the volume was printed (or in which the publisher resides); names of translators, editors, or illustrators; a statement of whether the book is illustrated; and—in many early volumes—the name of the person or company for whom it was printed (as in "Printed by J. Johnson for R. & G. Bell and Sons at the Sign of the Scottish Tart").

While Roberts and Etherington's "usual case" may be vague since designers of books with liberal budgets may add several leaves before the title page and since the definition does not account for FLYLEAVES, "the second leaf of a book" here probably means the second *printed* leaf (the first being the HALF-TITLE). Also to be found on millions of title pages are printed and engraved decorations of various kinds (CUTS, RULES, and FLEURONS) along with epigrams and such. And where a title spans two pages, I would say that it is a "two-page title," not that the one "giving the fullest information is the title page." (See De Vinne, *A Treatise on Title-Pages*; McKerrow and Ferguson, *Title-Page Borders Used in England and Scotland, 1485–1640*; Pollard, *Last Words on the History of the Title-Page, with Notes on Some Colophons and Twenty-Seven Facsimiles of Title-Pages*; and Smith, *The Title-Page*.) Some books, especially in the 17th and 18th centuries, may have an engraved title page, a printed title page, or both.

TITLING (printing type). The term used for large type (say, 18-point or larger), used for titles. (*See* Display type.) Under "titling FONT," Richard Eckersley et al. say, "A typeface of capital letters only, occupying virtually the full depth of the BODY and thus larger than a text face of the same nominal size. More generally, one of a family of fonts that has been drawn specifically for use in larger sizes but remains in harmony with the related text font" (*Glossary of Typesetting Terms*, p. 104).

TLS (typed letter signed). *See* ALS. The abbreviation is also a common way to refer to the *Times Literary Supplement*, which publishes reviews of books, with almost every issue containing a section of books under the heading "Bibliography."

TOOLING. The use of tools (e.g., circles, PALLETS, FILLETS, ROLLS, STAMPS, and letters) in the FINISHING of a BINDING. The tools are generally metal—mostly copper or brass—with wood handles. The tooling can be in leather, VELLUM, CLOTH, paper, or other materials. The aim of tooling is usually to enhance the volume's beauty, but tools are used as well for identification: the volume can be stamped with the author's name, the title, the publisher, the place of publication, the date, or anything else the binder wishes the observer to see when the book is closed. (Of course, tooling can also take place on DOUBLURES, so some of the decoration tooled onto the volume will be inside the closed covers.) The word also means the actual decorations that the tools impart: "This binding has exquisite tooling on the front boards."

Carter points out that tooling is different from BLOCKING, which uses a press to impress BLOCKS into the surface being decorated. The tools can be impressed with no foil, creating BLIND impressions in the leather (or, later, the cloth). If gold foil is used, the tools will be heated to make the pattern adhere to the leather (though often a mordant is used in a blind-tooled pattern, followed by the impression of the foil). Dealers' catalogs will often have the phrase "blind tooled" to indicate STAMPING with no metal foil used. (*See* Blind stamped.)

TOP EDGE GILT. A self-explanatory term, though I will explain it: A description of the edge of a book at the HEAD of the TEXT BLOCK, where that edge has been decorated with gold (or a gold-colored foil). Traditionally abbreviated in dealers' catalogs as "TEG," as differentiated from "AEG" (all edges gilt). In loose parlance, a bookseller may say "this volume has gold tops," but that slangy locution flies in the face of the more staid and more commonly used "TEG." (Carter's "Gilt tops" clearly refers to a multivolume set, though it should be clear that a single volume could be TEG, the most common situation.)

TOP TEN BOOKS. *See* Big Little Books.

TORTOISE SHELL BINDING. "A 17th century technique which used tortoise shell to decorate the covers of a book. Additional decoration sometimes consisted simply of a border of silver corners and CLASPS, but more often included INLAYS of silver and mother of pearl" (Roberts and Etherington, "tortoise shell covers"; https://cool.culturalheritage.org/don/dt/dt3553.html [accessed 6 March 2021]).

TORY, GEOFFROY (c. 1480–1533). "[P]ublisher, printer, author, orthographic reformer, and prolific ENGRAVER who was mainly responsible for the French Renaissance style of book decoration and who played a leading part in popularizing in France the ROMAN letter as against the prevailing GOTHIC. His important publications include a number of 'BOOKS OF HOURS' and his famous philological work *Champfleury* (1529). In this work Tory put forward the idea of accents, the apostrophe, the cedilla, and simple punctuation marks. He was appointed *imprimeur du roi* ('printer to the king') by Francis I in about 1530" (*Encyclopaedia Britannica* online, "Geoffroy Tory"). In the 1531 *Book of Hours*, Tory used a roman typeface that did not mimic SCRIPT, opening the way, in book design, for other such FACES. Of the treatise *Champ Fleury*, the Library of Congress website Ocatvo says, "This beautifully illustrated treatise, subtitled 'The Art and Science of the Proportion of the Attic or Ancient Roman Letters, According to the Human Body and Face' is the most famous example of the Renaissance pursuit of an ideal proportion between humanity and the letters in which its achievements were recorded. Perspective, the Golden Section, classical mythology: all were called in aid by its author, Geofroy Tory, to show how letters should be made. He used a square grid that foreshadows the pixels of today's digital letterforms, a grid on which the perfect shape of a human face or body could also be set out" (Library of Congress, The Lessing J. Rosenwald Collection, "Geofroy Tory, *Champ Fleury*"; https://archive.is/20130131004008/http://www.octavo.com/editions/trychf/#selection-105.0-105.635 [accessed 20 April 2021]).

TOY BOOKS. "Books designed to stimulate play and so which function as toys have existed since the 18th century, but the term is usually applied to the large (usually 10.5 × 9 inches) colourful picture books, usually based on traditional tales and nursery rhymes, published in the 19th century in tandem with—and possibly stimulating—developments in colour printing" (*Oxford Companion to English Literature*, 7th ed., "Toy Books"). Most of these volumes had eight LEAVES with bright CHROMOLITHOGRAPHED or HAND-COLORED pictures and minimal prose text. Hence, counting books and ABCDERIA were popular, along with those with short traditional tales. (See Hunt et al., *International Companion Encyclopedia of Children's Literature*.)

TRACING PAPER. Paper so thin that, when it is laid over another surface, it will show what that other surface has on it. "It may be either a translucent, greaseproof paper, or a BOND or manifold paper treated chemically, or oiled, so as to increase transparency" (Roberts and Etherington, p. 267). Some papers have a natural translucency, not intentional (*see* Oriental binding; Show-through). But for tracing paper, it was manufactured specifically to be translucent for copying. Written about as early as the 15th century by Cennini, who gives three recipes for its manufacture (Cennini, *The Craftsman's Handbook*, pp. 13–14).

TRACING VELLUM (also called "transparent vellum"). VELLUM treated in such a way as to make it transparent when laid over another surface. Written about as early as the 15th century by Cennini, who gives a recipe for its manufacture (*The Craftsman's Handbook*, p. 13). It was used to copy images from one MANUSCRIPT for transfer to another (*see* Pounce).

TRACT. *See* Tract-volume.

TRACT-VOLUME. This term (unhyphenated—two separate words) appears in Carter's eighth edition (Oak Knoll and The British Library, 2004, hence added by Nicolas Barker), where it is defined in a way so like that of a SAMMELBAND as to be practically indistinguishable from the latter term. The term is used by Lotte Hellinga and Margaret Nickson ("A Caxton Tract-Volume from Thomas Rawlinson's Library") with no called-out definition, implying that their readers will automatically know what they are writing about. They discuss "bibliographical items . . . [that were] treated as distinct entities . . . [but had been] taken out of the original larger volumes in which they often had been bound. Thus, much evidence for what readers and owners in the fifteenth century had chosen to put together was thoroughly disturbed, practically obliterating all traces of a cultural pattern of the time when those books were printed" (p. 17). The point is, as with the sammelband, a group of printed pieces, collected and bound by someone, had taken from its binding a single piece (or several of them) to be bound separately and thus sold. In making the profit from this sale, the butcher who dismembered the volume has 1) created a new volume (since the removed piece would often be bound into its own covers); and 2) yielded a "defective" book, the defect being the loss of the original piece from its original context. Hellinga and Nickson speak of the value of trying to reconstruct the original volume, but they admit that it is usually impossible, especially when the removed item, often in its own new binding, and often having been cleaned up and having had its PROVENANCE erased, can hardly be identified as having come from such a collection of "tracts." The volume, of course, did not have to be composed of tracts; it could be PAMPHLETS of many kinds and even BROADSIDES or advertising pieces.

The term "tract," however, has a specific meaning: it is usually a short volume with a social or political—or especially a religious or moral—text, as one sees in the publications of the Religious Tract Society of London (founded in 1799; along with others in Great Britain), the New England Tract Society (founded in 1814), and the American Tract Society (founded in Boston in 1814 and its counterpart with the same name founded in New York in 1825). These societies published and distributed a tremendous number of these short texts—thousands of them—often bound in SCALEBOARD or in CARDBOARD covered in inexpensive paper; or they were merely sewn into paper covers. And most were aimed at children. For this reason, and because they were made of cheap materials and they were handled a good deal, they often survive in shabby condition. (See "A Brief History of the American Tract Society." See also M'Clintock and Strong, "Tract Societies Distinctly So-called [1894].")

TRADE BINDING. Roberts and Etherington give a traditional definition: "Plain CALFSKIN or SHEEPSKIN bindings issued by publishers in England from the 15th to the 18th centuries. They were rarely lettered" (p. 267). Carter says that from the middle of the 15th to the end of the first quarter of the 19th century, publishers sold their books to customers who could choose their bindings, with various options at various prices. Many copies have survived with no bindings or with simple paper covers that are intended as temporary covers but that have become "permanent" over the centuries. Some volumes also survive IN SHEETS. All of these say a good deal to scholars about the history and use, treatment, and reception of books. Carter warns that a bookseller may call these unbound volumes in their "original state," but that is not really accurate. And he says that collectors who want "original bindings" on their books really want *bindings*, not paper WRAPPERS. The unbound ones are really not examples of "trade bindings." He adds that true "trade bindings" of the 18th century are those in LIMP VELLUM, sheep, or calf, which he likens to the CLOTH bindings from publishers in the 19th century and later. And he says that it may be impossible to identify a true publisher's binding in vellum or calf, for example, for these materials could have been put on much later. Thus, to designate a book's cover as a "trade binding" is often suspect. (See his long discussion on this topic on pp. 246–47.)

For modern consumers (booksellers and collectors and librarians alike), this term is dying in the specialized sense that Carter delineates. What we see in a "trade binding" is a very plain, unadorned leather cover, often smooth and light brown and unremarkable, and also often in poor CONDITION and looking like any other such volume, produced in the millions, and the lack of adornment marks them as ordinary despite the possibility that these bindings could be housing an important, scarce, valuable book. In fact, many a bookseller I have spoken with used the term "trade binding" to mean a PUBLISHER'S BINDING. As with "parchment" and "vellum," the two terms seem to be blending and are now used interchangeably. This is a shame since the specificity of the terms distinguishes the two phenomena. (See Bennett, *Trade Bookbinding in the British Isles, 1660–1800*; and *see* Wholesaler's binding.)

TRADE CATALOGS. As the term indicates, these are publications listing goods from a commercial company. The contents of such a catalog can be narrowly focused (19th-century garden implements from the British Isles) or exceptionally broad, as with the Sears or Montgomery Ward catalogs, showing the massive stock these companies sold. The catalogs themselves were often seen as pieces of EPHEMERA, so many were printed on inexpensive (read "cheap") paper and poorly bound—a staple or two did the trick. Some of the merchants saw the goods they were purveying as having social or historical or other significance, and used high-quality printing, paper, and binding. These have become quite COLLECTIBLE, with certain categories of them particularly desirable on the market: jewelry, books and the book arts, children's items, and many other categories. Some of the trade catalogs had TIP-INS, as with those from textile merchants, paper mills, wallpaper manufacturers, printers showing off their skills and techniques, and the like. And the more unusual the content, and the more samples that are tipped-in, the more desirable they could be. By chance, while composing this entry, I received a catalog from a bookseller listing an "Office Equipment Salesman's sample catalogue" from about 1890; the seller had the trade catalog priced at $650—indicating that the market for these catalogs is strong, and that they can command high prices. (The catalog is from Susanne Schulz-Falster, Christmas 2020; second item on p. [3].) Perhaps the best collections of these catalogs in the United States are at the AMERICAN ANTIQUARIAN SOCIETY; The University of California, Santa Barbara; the Hagley Museum in Wilmington, DE; and the WINTERTHUR MUSEUM. The best publication about them is that by Lawrence B. Romaine (*A Guide to American Trade Catalogs, 1774–1900*), who wrote: "If a complete history of American manufacturers is ever to be compiled, American trade catalogs will unquestionably be one of the most valuable sources of material available" (cited at the UC Santa Barbara Library; https://www.library.ucsb.edu/special-collections/collections/lawrence-b-romaine-trade-catalog-collection [accessed 10 January 2021]). The UC Santa Barbara collection is fully cataloged, with about 50,000 items in hundreds of categories. (See http://www.oac.cdlib.org/view?docId=tf4w1007j8&view=dsc&style=oac4&dsc.position=1 [accessed 10 January 2021]). The Romaine text lists a great number of these items, though as everyone knows, it could only be suggestive; there was no way in the world that any text can be comprehensive in such a listing. But Romaine is so well known that many a bookseller will say, "Not in Romaine," and her readers should know what that means.

TRADE EDITION. In the FINE-PRESS world, it is not uncommon for a publisher to issue a volume in a LIMITED, DELUXE VERSION and a commercial version—the latter called the "trade edition." The limited version may be on handmade paper, printed by hand, with a special binding, and so on, and the trade edition printed offset on machine-made paper, bound much more cheaply. Naturally, the COMPLETIST collector will want both manifestations. And, of course, the term "trade edition" is slightly misleading since the text, if it is printed from the same setting of type as the "deluxe edition," will be of the same *edition*. Better terminology would be "trade version" and "deluxe version," but the term "trade edition" is so inured in the book-world vocabulary that it is unlikely that the "better" terms will ever be adopted.

TRANCHEFILES. Marks in a sheet of paper made where the pulp has been made thin, visible when backlighted, and looking like "an extra chain [line] on each side [of the sheet] without bar shadows" (Gaskell, *A New Introduction to Bibliography*, p. 61). That is, it looks like a chain line that one will see in LAID PAPER, but without the dark areas around the ribs (not the "bars") of the MOLD that one sees in antique laid paper. These marks are like WATERMARKS in that they are made where the sheet is thinner where they are than it is all around them. The word is also the French term for "HEADBAND." (For an image of Gaskell's "bar shadows," *see* Laid paper.)

TRANSCRIPT. A written, typed, or printed copy of another text. If written, it could be in the hand of the author or of another SCRIBE. As Carter points out, if a poet writes out a copy of one of his published poems, it is a transcript, not an original MANUSCRIPT. Robert Frost is known for his frequent transcriptions of his poems for autograph seekers. (In fact, he was known for signing just about anything put in front of him, leading to a tremendous number of Frost SIGNATURES in his books. In an apocryphal story, one bookseller advertised a Frost volume "in a rare unsigned copy.") With printing or typing, transcripts can exist in multiple copies. Determining how many exist can be impossible, so it is usually difficult to evaluate a transcript. Also, if no manuscript is known for a text, a transcript may look like (and actually is) a manuscript in that it is written by hand. But the transcript does not have to be done by the original author. I can transcribe a poem by Frost and what I produce would still be called a transcript.

TRANSFER CASE. *See* Type case.

TRANSFER PAPER. A kind of paper (or a plastic film) with a wax or pigment coating onto which something (a text, an image, or both—but often a decorative picture) has been printed such that it can be transferred to another surface. With water or heat, the printed image can be "printed" or pressed onto a piece of paper, cloth, or wood, for instance. (Decals that can be transferred to other surfaces—even to one's skin—are a form of transfer papers. And the term "transfer *paper*" can apply to a plastic film, even though it is not paper.) The method of transferring the image was used on MAUCHLINE BINDINGS. The papers were manufactured in Great Britain and the United States in the 19th century. (See Briggs & Co's Patent Transferring Papers, in the bibliography.) A different kind of transfer paper, manufactured by Embree Manufacturing Company, had a specially treated surface that, when pressed firmly or rubbed, would pick up texts or images from a newspaper; the sheet could then be pressed onto another piece of paper, transferring what had been picked up onto the other sheet. (See Embree Mfg. Company, *Extra Sheets: Magic Kopeefun Paper*. *See also* Copying press.)

TRANSPARENT VELLUM. *See* Tracing vellum.

TRAVELING LIBRARY (spelled with one or two L's). There are two main kinds of such libraries. The first is a collection of small volumes, packed into a mobile chest, with the idea that its owner can take his reading matter with him wherever he travels. Napoleon had such a library, as explained on the Open Culture website (Open Culture, "Napoleon's Kindle: See the Miniaturized Traveling Library He Took on Military Campaigns"; https://www.openculture.com/2017/10/napoleons-kindle-see-the-miniaturized-traveling-library-he-took-on-military-campaigns.html [accessed 8 August 2021]). The volumes were usually under 3 × 5 inches, and represented the tastes of the traveler. The Toledo Art Museum has one, with the following description: "This elaborate book box contains 30 miniature volumes of philosophy, theology, history, and poetry. The page ribbons are color-coded (philosophy and theology are blue, history is green, and poetry is pink). It is believed to have belonged to the Bacon family, probably Sir Nicolas Bacon (about 1540–1624), half-brother of philosopher Sir Francis Bacon. The set is one of only a handful of similar traveling libraries prepared for distinguished lawyers during the reign of James I (ruled 1603–1625)" (Toledo Art Museum, "Traveling Library," http://emuseum.toledomuseum.org/objects/51402 [accessed 8 August 2021]). Marissa Fessenden says, "Carrying a full collection of books on a long trip would clearly have been tiring. But in 17th-century England, four individuals or families were lucky. They had their own traveling library. / All it needed were tiny books. There were about 50 gold-tooled, vellum-bound books. They were all bundled up into a larger wooden case. It was bound in brown leather to look like a book itself. These are held in the University of Leeds' special collections. This was a true traveling library. Four were made" (Fessenden, "A Brief History of Taking Books Along for the Ride").

The term is also used to describe a 19th- and 20th-century phenomenon: collections of books that are taken to rural areas where no public library exists, or, more recently, bookmobiles. (See Passet, "Reaching the Rural Reader: Traveling Libraries in America, 1892–1920.")

TRAVELLER/TRAVELLER'S SAMPLE. *See* Book Traveller.

TRAY CASE. *See* Clamshell box.

TREASURE BINDING. *See* Jeweled binding.

TREE CALF (also called "tree marble"). "A form of cover decoration consisting of a smooth, light-colored CALFSKIN treated with chemicals in such a manner as to represent a tree trunk with branches. In the usual manner, a dual design appears on upper and lower covers" (Roberts and Etherington, p. 268, in which the method for producing the pattern is described). Roberts and Etherington add, "Late in the 19th century attempts were made to produce the tree calf effect with the use of an ENGRAVED BLOCK, which was used to print a design on the covers in black, but the results were ineffective because the block did not provide the shading which the genuine method achieved. The popularity of tree calf began to decline before the First World War, and by the late 1920s this once very popular form of decoration had virtually passed from existence. The first known tree calf decoration dates from about 1775" (p. 268). (*See* Calf; Mottled calf.) It should be noted that the use of a chemical to create this pattern sometimes left the leather with the INHERENT VICE of the acid in the cover, and the leather on many so-decorated volumes has deteriorated. Further, the same kind of acid or chemical could be used to decorate the cover in other ways, as with vertical "stripes" on the leather cover. Since such a "striped" pattern looks nothing like a tree, the decorative covers should not be said to have "tree calf" on them, though I have seen them called this by those who should know better.

The tree calf pattern was also imparted to paper, to make it look like calf. The pattern could have been done with paste, as with PASTE PAPERS, or it could have been printed on, from WOOD BLOCKS or ENGRAVED PLATES. In the 19th century, DECORATED PAPER manufacturers made such papers as a substitute for leather, and the papers could be quite sturdy and attractive—and deceptive.

TRIAL BINDING. (Sometimes called "specimen binding.") "A term descriptive of a tentative cover design for a book submitted to the publisher by the publisher's (edition) binder. Such bindings have been produced regularly since the early days of edition cloth bindings. Today, the bindings are generally DUMMIES made up of blank LEAVES. . . . In the 19th century, however, finished copies were often used, as there are examples of books with identical contents but different bindings from that of the version offered for sale. Some publishers used trial bindings to fulfill COPYRIGHT obligations or gave them as free copies to the author" (Roberts and Etherington, p. 268). In the book world, binders sometimes refer to their trial bindings as "maquettes" (the maquettes are often loose, unattached boards that show early samples of decoration that the binder presents to the publisher for approval).

Carter pretty much agrees with the Roberts and Etherington definition, and he goes further to explain that sometimes the difference between the trial bindings and those settled on by the publisher for the commercial release of the full edition is nothing more than in the color of the cloth used. But he warns that a variant binding cannot automatically be called a trial binding unless there is some evidence that the variant was done by the publisher's binder specifically for that text. There could be other reasons for variant bindings.

(I own a copy of a book published by the Bird & Bull Press [*see* Morris, Henry] that was delivered in a carton with tire tracks across it. It had gotten run over in the post office, and the binding was damaged. I contacted the original binder for the edition and asked him to REBIND my copy in full leather. Hence, the binding of my copy varies from that of all other copies in the edition. It is definitely not a trial binding, though a bookseller, not knowing the reason for the leather binding, may call it a trial binding.) Also, a binder could run out of a particular CLOTH, so he might bind some copies in a variant one. This does not produce a regular and a trial binding. Carter also mentions the situation in which a publisher asks his printer to send some copies of early sheets to the binder to be bound in whatever the binder chooses—possibly to send copies in for copyright protection or to supply the author with her copies. The binder does not have to decorate the binding of these copies in any way similar to the way the final edition will be bound and decorated. These, too, are not really trial bindings, but again, a collector, knowing why these copies differ from those of the regular edition, will certainly covet one of these early bindings. Carter adds that bindings different from those of the regular edition could exist for many reasons, none of which would point to an actual trial binding, and collectors should be wary of calling them "trials." (See Carter, p. 248; *see also* Secondary binding.)

Another possibility may arise: a copy of a book may come to light in a binding that differs from that of the regular published edition. Is this a trial binding, or has the book been REBOUND because its original cover was damaged? Sometimes the more modern materials of the binding will show it to be the latter. But if the book has been rebound in period materials, it might be impossible to determine whether the book is in a trial binding. In any case, a copy of a book in an alternate binding is usually prized by the collector—any version different from those of other collectors can be touted as UNIQUE and thus desirable. Booksellers sometimes make a virtue of such a circumstance: "The only copy we have seen in this binding." Rarity yields value.

TRIAL EDITION/TRIAL ISSUE. Carter's entry begins by discussing one practice that he and Graham Pollard expanded on in their exposure of THOMAS WISE: authors having some copies of their work set into type before a commercial version was produced. Wise claimed (and Carter seems to corroborate) that authors would want a few copies of their text to give to friends and relatives; Carter adds that an author may wish to have a copy of the text *in print* as the basis for revision before giving the final text to a commercial publisher. (See Carter, pp. 248–49.) This early copy of a text—preceding general publication—is called a "trial edition" if the text was later RESET into type for the commercial version. However, if the same setting of type was used for the early printing as was used for the commercial release, the early version is called a "trial issue." Carter points out the difficulty in distinguishing between the two. A trial edition can be created by and for the publisher to "test the waters," to see if there is some interest in the text before printing a full run, or it could be created at the request of the author for personal purposes (for PROOFREADING or, as Carter says [following Wise's explanation], as gifts to friends). Trial copies, it would seem, are rarities, primarily because they would have been produced in small numbers and also because they represent quite early versions of the texts they contain—both desiderata for collectors. But inasmuch as they are difficult to distinguish from private printings, proof copies that have been given special bindings (or ADVANCED READING COPIES sent out to reviewers), booksellers, collectors, librarians, and literary historians should be particularly wary of designating such a volume a "trial edition." (See Lewis, *Thomas James Wise and the Trial Book Fallacy*.) As Carter and Pollard broadcast to the world (see Carter and Pollard, *An Enquiry into the Nature of Certain Nineteenth Century Pamphlets*), it may well have been a practice of authors to create "prepublication" copies, often in PAMPHLET form, and such copies can just as well be faked, as Wise and HARRY BUXTON FORMAN proved.

TRICK MAGIC BOOKS. *See* Blow books.

TRIGESIMO-SECUNDO. *See* Thirty-two-mo.

TRIMMED. *See* Cropped.

TRIM SIZE. The term that shows what the final dimensions of a volume will be. Many volumes printed on massive presses are discharged from the presses in sheets much larger than the final published volume will be. The designer has designated what the trim size will be, and the volume is trimmed down to that size. The term is also used for single-leaf documents. Many a reviewer's proof copy will be created early on in the volume's production and quickly bound to be sent out for review. The cover of the book (usually on the rear panel) will have notes telling the reviewer all kinds of information, including what the trim size (the size of the book in its final release to the public) will be. I have a copy of Philip K. Dick's *Eye in the Sky*, with massive margins, and measuring 10⅜ × 6⅜ inches; but the information on the cover indicates that the trim size will be "5.50 × 8.50," and indeed, the final published version measures exactly that.

TRIPLE-DECKER (also called a "three-decker"). A work issued in three VOLUMES. The format was often DUODECIMO, the idea being that such small volumes that fit easily into one's hands would be easy to hold and comfortable to read. Also, the work could be issued over several months, so the publisher could spread out the costs of production. Further, by spreading out the sales of a text into three volumes, the publisher could guarantee the sale of three volumes, not just one, and, as suggested above, the sales of the earlier volumes could help the publisher pay for the production costs of the other volumes.

Sometimes the term "three-decker" is used for any work issued in multiple volumes—not necessarily three. Also, spreading out the publishing over several months—or more—would make it easier on the booksellers to acquire the work and could also maximize their profits. And circulating libraries that made money on the fees they charged for lending stood to increase their own profits if readers needed to rent multiple volumes—as opposed to a single one. (See Griest, *Mudie's Circulating Library and the Victorian Novel.*)

TRIPTYCH. *See* Diptych/Triptych.

TS'AI LUN(G). (Sometimes transliterated as "Cai Lun[g].") The man often (but incorrectly) cited as the inventor of paper. Some scholar decided that the eunuch Ts'ai Lun(g) (why is it that he is usually spoken of with respect to his being a eunuch?), in AD 105, decided to invent paper. That date got published and picked up by other "scholars" for more than a century, and that error has been perpetuated for so long that in some circles (and on some websites) the story has become a *truth*. We know little of this man, but we do know that he did something to further/improve papermaking in China, and we know that he is revered as the father of papermaking by those who know no better. We do know that paper was manufactured in China in the second century BC. No one, to my knowledge, has ever been able to determine exactly what it was that Ts'ai Lun did to earn his reputation (though there is much speculation about it and this speculation has reached the status of "truth," too), and I wasn't there to discuss the matter with him.

TSCHICHOLD, JAN (1902–1974). One of the premier typographers and CALLIGRAPHERS in the world. "[B]orn in Germany, but in 1933, when Nazis made a political issue of the New Typography—temporarily imprisoning him for its practice and causing him to lose his teaching position—he emigrated to Switzerland. He worked for Penguin Books as design director in the late 1940s, and established their landmark typographic style. In all his work he was guided by his own definition of a book designer—someone who is the 'loyal and faithful servant of the written word'" (blurb on the dust jacket of Tschichold, *The Form of the Book*). One blurb says his imprisonment was "being taken into 'protective custody' "; see McLean, trans., *Jan Tschichold*, blurb). (See also Bringhurst, "Introduction"; McLean, *Jan Tschichold*; and Schmoller, *Two Titans*.)

One of Tschichold's great contributions to typography was signaled in his book *The New Typography* (see the bibliography) and codified in his *Asymmetric Typography* (see the bibliography), the asymmetric arrangement of text on the page. Later, when he moved to Switzerland, he recanted some of the principles he expounded in this groundbreaking text, but it was too late: these views have been adopted by generations of book designers who, to this day, still think that asymmetry on the page is the bee's knees, even when it is not called for, when it gets between the author and the reader.

TSUNDOKU. Since there is no word in English to describe this phenomenon, we must use the term that exists in Japanese. It means to buy more and more books but not to read them, and to let them pile up. Some sufferers of this disease are true hoarders. Katherine Brooks says, "The desire to buy more books than you can physically read in one human lifetime is actually so universal, there's a specific word for it: tsundoku. Defined as the stockpiling of books that will never be consumed, the term is a Japanese portmanteau of sorts, combining the words 'tsunde' (meaning 'to stack things'), 'oku' (meaning 'to leave for a while') and 'doku' (meaning 'to read')" (Brooks, "There's a Japanese Word for People Who Buy More Books Than They Can Actually Read"). Many a non-reader, when brought into the presence of a collector's extensive library, will ask in awe, "Have you read all these books?" I would love to hear all of the responses from those suffering from tsundoku. (A more linguistic explanation of this word, which emanates from the Meiji Period in Japan [1860–1912], can be found at Open Culture, "'Tsundoku,' the Japanese Word for the New Books That Pile Up on Our Shelves, Should Enter the English Language.")

TUB SIZING. *See* Size (in paper formation).

TUMMY BAND. *See* Wraparound band.

TUNNEL BOOKS. *See* Peep shows.

TURKEY MOROCCO. Roberts and Etherington give two meanings for this term: "1. Reputedly, a strong, durable leather produced in the 18th century in Turkey from GOATSKIN, with the characteristic morocco grain [*see* Morocco (leather)]. 2. A term applied to a leather, frequently produced from CALFSKIN, EMBOSSED with a hard GRAIN or bold cross grain in imitation of a Turkey morocco" (p. 269). [The term is strange, made up of the names of two countries—like the airlines "please stow your tray tables." Is it a tray or is it a table?]

TURN-INS. "1. The extra length and width of the covering material of a book overlapping the HEAD, TAIL, and FORE EDGE of the cover, and turned over the edges of the BOARD and glued to the inside surface. In leather binding, the leather is usually pared around these edges so as to make it thinner on the inside of the boards. The extent of the turn-in varies according to the SQUARES of the book, the taste of the times, or the judgment of the binder, [not to mention the cost of the leather since the binder did not want to waste any leather, which was expensive]. 2. The extensions of a book jacket which fold over the fore edges of covers of a book and in over the inside of the covers" (Roberts and Etherington, p. 270). As the first definition says, the turn-ins can be quite narrow (say, a quarter of an inch) or quite wide (a full inch or more). When they are wide, they can be elegantly gold stamped (*see* Dentelle).

TURTLE. *See* Composing stone.

TUSCHE. The oil-based ink that makes LITHOGRAPHY possible. The black ink is also used as a resist in ETCHING and ENGRAVING.

TWELVEMO. *See* Duodecimo.

TWELVE UP. *See* Up (as in "two up," "four up," "eight up").

TWILIGHT BOOK. A term seemingly coined by JACOB BLANCK for a "publication, offered by its publishers as a book . . . made up of the sheets of the original periodical publication, or produced from the PLATES thereof, and issued in a printed WRAPPER" (Blanck, "Twilight Books"). He adds, "For a period issues of *Lippincott's Monthly Magazine* were published with a TITLE-PAGE for the full-length novel contained within a regular monthly issue. . . . [Usually] books in this classification were issued in CLOTH" (Blanck, vol. 1, p. xxi). As the entry of FIRST EDITION says, the complications of what constitutes a first are many, and a first is often considered to be the first one to appear in its own covers, as opposed to the FIRST PRINTING, which could be in serialized form (*see* Serials/Serialization). But the twilight book may be a serialized text appearing in its own covers. At least we now have a term for this. Whether or not this constitutes a first edition probably hinges on when the volume was put together into that cover, who did it, how many copies were so treated, and when it was released (if that can be proven). But it may be dependent on each such text; that is, it may not be possible to make a blanket statement that all twilight books are first editions. It's your call, dear reader.

TWINROCKER PAPER MILL/TWINROCKER HANDMADE PAPER. A paper mill in Brookston, Indiana, founded in 1971 by Kathryn and Howard Clark. "Twinrocker was pivotal to the renaissance of hand papermaking in America." They began their papermaking in San Francisco. "With encouragement from Master Printer and Director of Collector's Press, Ernest de Soto, and fine book printers and binders in the Bay Area, they decided to try to make handmade paper. Howard designed and built a HOLLANDER BEATER (the pulping machine) and other equipment, and they began to make their first sheets of handmade paper from old cotton rags in their basement" ("Twinrocker Handmade Paper," http://www.twinrocker.com [accessed 17 June 2021]). They moved to Indiana in 1972, and the mill has been producing a wide range of beautiful handmade papers for artists, printers, binders, and others since then. "Twinrocker has been technically innovative by applying modern papermaking materials to the hand craft and setting high standards for permanence and light fastness. Artistically, they began to offer papers in many sizes and shapes that had not been available before, also making larger sizes than European hand mills had made (up to three by four feet) and gradually began to influence the 'look' of some machine made papers. Now, thirty five years later, Travis Becker, who was trained at Twinrocker by Kathryn Clark and has been a master papermaker and colleague for many years[,] has become a partner and will carry Twinrocker into the future" ("Twinrocker Handmade Paper"). As of August 2021, Becker is still making paper at Twinrocker.

TWO-LINE CHARACTERS. A letter or (rarely) a number that begins a paragraph that is two lines in height and is used as the first character in the paragraph.

ONE

The seedy man who brought it to me, along with a dozen or so pieces of trash, called himself Carl Smith, and he asked me to pay him practically nothing for the other things but a great deal for this item. I had been dealing with book scouts for years, but I had never seen this one before.

His approach was typical: "I got some books to sell. Are you buying?"

However seedy he was, I took him seriously. Many of these scouts are quite expert about what they scrounge up. There are the specialists in modern fiction, who can spot true firsts with good dust jackets in a second; they never mistake them for the commoner book club editions. Some scouts can cull a choice paperback from a dozen boxes of paper trash. There are connoisseurs who deliver books on art, history, war, hunting, and cooking, knowing which will bring $25 and which $2500. But this Carl Smith brought me an incunabulum.

Things printed before 1501 are called incunabula, and little Mr. Smith had brought me a dilly.

"What have you got?"

"Some pamphlets. Some are junk, one is expensive. You interested?"

"I don't have a lot of spare cash right now [my usual stance], but let's see what's in the box."

He edged toward the table where I carried out such transactions. His torn tweed blazer smelled slightly of cigarette smoke, slightly of beer. His gray jacket and black slacks were once quite respectable, but they showed the tatters of someone who needed cash. He was nearly bald, with a fringe of gray and reddish stubble around the dome. His pudgy hands, gripping

Two-line character for the opening chapter of Sidney Berger, *The Book of Death* (Waban, MA: Doe Press, 2017), p. 1. [The reference is to a murder mystery about a rare book.] [The preceding is a plug.]

Courtesy of Sidney Berger, Doe Press.

TWO-PAGE SPREAD (also called a "double-page spread"). Two pages of a text facing each other. For most books—especially those predominantly in prose—this is the basic area for design. A designer usually does not design a single page—she designs the two pages (VERSO on the left and RECTO on the right) that face the reader when the volume is open. We hear the term in such sentences as, "Book designers usually do not lay out a text one page at a time; they work in two-page spreads."

TWO-PULL PRESS. *See* Ramage press.

TYMPAN. (1) The sheet of VELLUM or paper, tightly stretched over a frame on a HANDPRESS onto which the printer lays a sheet to be printed. The tympan gets its name from the Latin word meaning "drum" since the sheet is stretched as tightly as a drum. In fact, the tympan is more complicated than this. (2) The full apparatus consists of (a) an outer metal frame, covered on top with tympan paper (or vellum, in earlier printing), and (b) a slightly smaller inner metal frame that is attached by hinges to the back of the first frame; the second one is covered with paper as well. Between these two sheets of paper is the "PACKING," used to add or remove pressure (the pressure the PLATEN exerts on the inked type) in the printing process. Adjusting the packing inside the tympan is called "doing the MAKEREADY." (For illustrations, *see* the figure at the entry for Common press; and the figure at Frisket.)

TYPE (printer's). The "SORTS" used for printing. The sort is a rectangular piece of metal or wood (if metal, it is cast; if wood, it is cut), containing the character to be printed, standing in RELIEF from the upper tip of the sort. It is, of course, used for printing LEAVES of text, but printer's type can also be used for stamping leather in bindings, though brass type is more commonly used for bindings—especially for stamping machines. (*See* Type metal; Wood type.)

Type was invented in China, perfected in Korea, and reinvented for an alphabet with characters of varying widths by JOHANNES GUTENBERG. An extensive literature exists on type; only a few references here will suffice, but a great many sources can be found (and referred to) on the web. (Avis, *Edward Philip Prince*; Berger, pp. 104–10; Bigelow et al., eds., *Fine Print on Type*; Lawson, *Anatomy of a Typeface*; Lawson, *Printing Types*; Tracy, *Letters of Credit*; Updike, *Printing Types*, especially vol. 1, p. 15. See also Berger, "Printing Types," pp. 12–20.) (*See* figure in Appendix B.)

TYPE CABINET. The piece of furniture holding TYPE CASES. Type cabinets are usually made of wood or metal, and they contain 10, 12, 20, 24, or more cases, though there is no real predetermined number of type cases in a cabinet. The cabinets can hold FONTS of type (alphabetical and decorative) or CUTS (WOODCUTS, LINOCUTS, STEEL PLATES, and so on).

TYPE CASE. The case (like a drawer) in which type is kept, ready to be set/composed (*see* Composition). To set type is to take each SORT from the type case and put it into a COMPOSING STICK. Cases are usually laid out with the COMPOSITOR's convenience in mind. Since the typesetter will need small letters more than she will need capitals, it was common to put the capitals in a type case above a second case (which, naturally, was below) holding the small letters, hence "UPPER CASE" and "LOWER CASE." Purists cringe when they hear a neophyte call a type case a "drawer" or a "type drawer." The term is sometimes reduced to "case," as in "the type in the case was old and worn," and printers speak of the "lay of the case," meaning the way the type case compartments are distributed. It is also called a "job case," especially in commercial establishments.

These cases come in scores of configurations, depending on the language of the text being set, the typeface (e.g., some

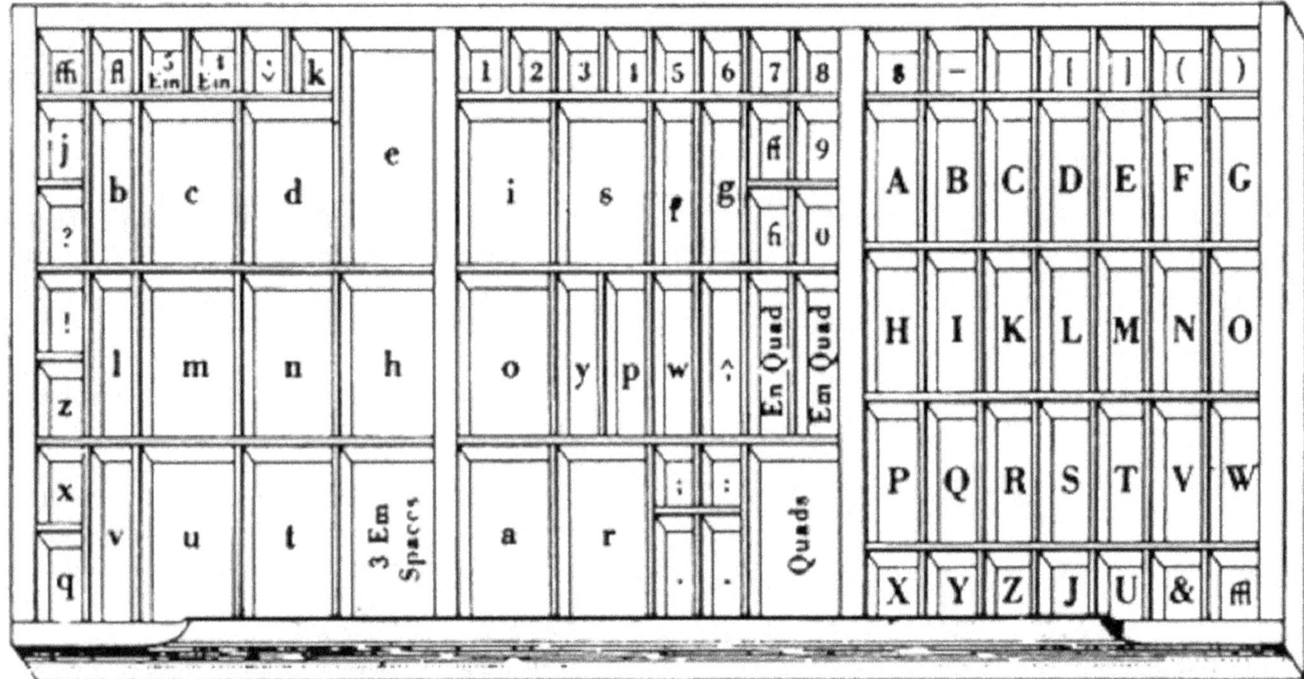

California job case. Note that on the web a host of other images of this case are depicted, with much variation in where non-alphabetical and special characters and spaces are located. The case depicted here shows the most common distribution of the spacing (quads, en quads, and em quads, along with sorts that are 3-to-em [meaning that three of them equal the width of one em], 4-to-em, and 5-to-em), along with ligatures.

http://robundo.com/salama-press-club/glossary/ka.html#ka_type-holder (accessed 10 August 2021).

SWASH faces with many KERNS and LIGATURES may need a host of extra compartments), and the number of extra, possibly decorative, pieces of type that are in use.

One particular type case is worth singling out, the California job case, the most commonly used type case design in America. It got its name from the many California type foundries that contributed to its popularity (see Pryor, ed., "The California Typecase"). The case is laid out with the ease of the compositor's efforts in mind, with lowercase letters on the left and uppercase letters on the right. Numbers are arranged at the top of the case, with various spacing and special sorts (e.g., punctuation and ligatures along with AMPERSAND and ASTERISK) distributed around the case. (*See* the figure above.) Although the lay of the case (the distribution of all the sorts) is codified as in the accompanying illustration, each printer, depending on the typeface in the case, might use the top and other compartments in his or her own way. Some ITALIC types have many kerns or ligatures, yielding many more different sorts than the case had compartments for, so it might be necessary for a printer to cut a 6-point SLUG and put it into a compartment diagonally, dividing the compartment in two, to accommodate, for example, an Æ and æ, and divide another compartment for Œ and an œ.

One occasionally sees what looks like a California job case with its compartments in reverse—that is, in a mirror arrangement from the regular case. This is a transfer case, which is placed over the regular case; the two cases are inverted, transferring all of the type in the regular case into the transfer case, then the operation is repeated such that the type is transferred into another regular case. This is used when, for whatever reason, one type case must be emptied and have its type transferred to another. Modified typecases can also hold cuts of all kinds, like linoleum blocks and other non-alphabetic items that are TYPE HIGH.

TYPE CASTING (also called "typefounding"). The creation of individual SORTS by any means. The method devised by the Chinese and perfected by the Koreans created individual sorts bearing characters that represented words. The method Gutenberg created required that each sort be a particular width, corresponding to the width of the character on each sort. He designed a FONT with all the printed characters he needed (alphabet in upper- and lowercase letters, numbers, punctuation, and other characters), created a set of PUNCHES from which he made matrices (*see* Matrix [in type making]), and cast the font in his mold (*see* Mold [typecasting]). The individual SORTS then had to be finished (e.g., with the JETS removed and slag burnished away) and then placed into a TYPE CASE, ready for COMPOSITION.

Strictly speaking, "type casting" was just this—the making of the printing type. But the term has taken on a more generic meaning of casting into metal any printing tools that will print LETTERPRESS; hence, LINOTYPE SLUGS are said to be type cast in the machine, though the printing "tool" is a slug of TYPE METAL, not individual sorts.

TYPEFACE/TYPE FAMILY. A full range of the types of a single design. The types include letters (UPPER- and LOWERCASE), figures, punctuation, and any other characters designed for that FACE. A single typeface could be part of a larger family of types. For example, the Bembo type family has regular Bembo, Bembo CONDENSED, Bembo ITALIC, Bembo Condensed Italic, Bembo TITLING, and other variations, and some of these in various sizes (6-point, 8-point, and so on). COLOPHONS of many FINE-PRESS books will list the typeface(s) used in the volume.

The word "typeface" could also refer to the part of the SORT that will receive the ink for printing: the face of the piece of type. (An enormous number of books have been published on this topic. See, e.g., Jaspert et al., *Encyclopaedia of Type Faces*; Lawson, *Anatomy of a Typeface*; Lawson, *Printing Types*; and Updike, *Printing Types*.) (See Appendix B, "Typeface Terminology.")

TYPE FACSIMILE. A printed text that is designed to look like that of an earlier edition, usually with no aim to deceive. Sometimes the FACSIMILE version merely looks like the original in its design—LAYOUT, TYPEFACE, use of RUNNING HEADS, placement of page numbers, and so on. Sometimes the facsimile is set line for line like the original. With the coming of photography and, later, scanning, it is now easy to produce a true facsimile, exactly like the original. (*See* Facsimile.) A "facsimile" that just mimics the original line for line but is the product of a new setting of type is a different edition from the original.

TYPE GAUGE (sometimes called a "line gauge" or a "PICA STICK"). A measuring device for printers. "The simplest form is . . . like a ruler, usually calibrated on one edge in POINTS and PICAS and on the other in inches. Some are printed on a transparent sheet. Some type gauges are slotted and many include calibrations in various units of points, from 5 points up to 14 points" (Eckersley et al., *Glossary of Typesetting Terms*, p. 106).

Type gauges were often long enough to accommodate a full one-foot-long ruler, but there were also smaller pocket-sized ones, and also ones long enough to accommodate the needs of those composing newspaper pages. Some have measuring scales on both sides. A printer's apron may have a deep, narrow pocket to hold a type gauge since printers would want one at hand when they were setting type or standing at the press. Some people of questionable rationality collect these gauges and have them in many sizes and shapes, on many materials, and so on, like the ones in my collection.

TYPE HIGH (height-to-paper). Anything in the CHASE, such as printing type or illustrations, that will receive ink and (usually) will print is said to be "type high." Some BEARERS, however, are in the chase and are type high but will not print. So-called height-to-paper in U.S. foundries has been .918 inch since the merger of a group of 23 foundries around 1892, when they decided to standardize their types (see De Vinne, *The Practice of Typography*, p. 105). (*See* Type [printer's].)

TYPE MEASUREMENT. Carter's entry says that type terms came from the founders and printers who made and used the type. For early books, especially those of the 15th century, the printers did not create their own terminology, so scholars had to create it. He says that they refer to type sizes by how deep 20 lines (a measurement chosen at random) measured. Thus, as Carter explains, "77R" indicates that a text was printed in ROMAN type and that 20 lines of it measure 77 millimeters deep. He says that a more accurate means of measuring is to use a 10-power loupe with a graticule (a grid with latitudinal and longitudinal lines) that measures in tenths of a millimeter and then to measure one line to the next line, using a fixed point in each line (e.g., the baseline of a character in one line to the baseline of a character in the next line). (See Carter, p. 250.) This method might be "more precise," but it yields only measurements, not any generic or specific name or principle of measurement. If the aim of the measurement is for a BIBLIOGRAPHIC DESCRIPTION, this practice would not be useful. With the technology we have today, better would be a scanned FACSIMILE of the type so described (with measurements in centimeters, inches, or both)—easy to do and also easy to attach the image to an information file (analog or digital). (*See* Point system.) (For more on type measurement and the point system, see Updike, *Printing Types*, pp. 26 ff. See also *American Dictionary of Printing and Bookmaking*, pp. 550–55.)

A related issue is the terminology we now use to designate type sizes. With a computer, we can select type sizes for printing: 8-point, 10-point, 12-point, or much smaller or larger, depending on the capabilities of the printers we have available. The point system is a useful tool for us when we print or when we, as descriptive bibliographers, want to say what the size is of a particular font of type. (*See* Points; Point system.) It may be suspect to use modern point measurements when we are describing 15th-, 16th-, 17th-, and 18th-century types, but it is an easy point (pun intended) of reference that our readers will be able to understand.

TYPE METAL. One of the miracles of the millennium is the type metal that GUTENBERG created for his printing type. The metal had to be of the right consistency to accept—and then give up—ink. It had to flow smoothly into a MOLD and set (go from liquid to solid state) in a fraction of a second. It had to cast smoothly with no striations on its surface or bubbles inside. And it had to be strong enough to withstand the force of the PLATEN pressing it against the type.

As a metallurgist (he was a goldsmith), Gutenberg knew (and had access to many) metals. As the entry on Gutenberg says, almost everything we think we know about his activities is speculation. But it is certain that he needed to experiment with many metals, individually and as amalgams, before settling on the right mixture for printing type to be made and to meet the requirements set out above. In his experiments, he quickly saw that single metals proved impracticable. He must have then gone to pairs of metals, in different proportions. Imagine the combinations and permutations. Metal A and Metal B: 5 percent and 95 percent, 10 percent and 90 percent, 15 percent and 85 percent—all the way to 95 percent and 5 percent. That didn't work. So he went to Metal A and Metal C, with the same experiments. No success. Then Metal A with Metal D, Metal B with Metal C, Metal B with Metal D, Metal C with Metal D, and on and on—perhaps with a dozen or more metals. Then he turned to three metals. Are you following this? The number of experiments had to be in the thousands. Gutenberg went into "hiding" for perhaps a decade, and I feel certain that most of this time he was perfecting the type metal. He needed money for this, and he borrowed to buy metals and to pay for his day-to-day expenses. No wonder he was invisible for most of the 1440s. And no wonder that he lost his operation to JOHANN FUST, who loaned him the money.

Since none of his type survives, we can only speculate what he settled on as an amalgam. "Modern" types, from the 15th century on, are mixtures of lead, antimony, and tin—or other metals (approximately 80 percent, 10 percent, and 10 percent, respectively, though in various proportions). (See *Type Metals.*)

TYPE MOLD. *See* Mold (typecasting).

TYPESCRIPT. A text produced on a typewriter. (*See* Manuscript.) A typescript can be produced by the author, or the author could have employed a typist (as Mark Twain did in typing the first part of his manuscript of *Those Extraordinary Twins* [see Berger, ed., *Pudd'nhead Wilson and Those Extraordinary Twins*] and other of his works). Thus, the authority of the text of a typescript may be suspect if the author employed a typist and did not PROOFREAD the typist's copy against his original manuscript.

Carbon paper was invented as early as 1801 ("The first documented use of the term 'carbonated paper' was in 1806, when an Englishman, named Ralph Wedgwood, issued a patent for his 'Stylographic Writer.' However, Pellegrino Turri had invented a typewriting machine in Italy by at least 1808, and since 'black paper' was essential for the operation of his machine, he must have perfected his form of carbon paper at virtually the same time as Wedgwood, if not before" [Laurence, "The *Exciting* History of Carbon Paper!" citing Adler, *The Writing Machine*, http://www.kevinlaurence.net/essays/cc.php (accessed 17 June 2021)]). Thus, authors who used typewriters (whose invention goes back almost as far as that of carbon paper, though they came into commercial use only in the 1860s) often used carbon paper to produce copies. Hence, a single typescript can exist in an "original" and in carbon copies. Since both were produced by a typewriter, both may be referred to as "typescripts," though one is more properly a carbon copy of a typescript.

The term has been loosely interpreted over the years, and someone creating a computer-generated text on a laser or ink-jet printer may call it a "typescript," just as a real typescript may be called a "MANUSCRIPT" by its author, as in "I have spent the last year typing this on my Underwood, and I am now ready to turn in this manuscript to the publisher."

TYPESETTER. *See* Compositor.

TYPESETTING. The composition of a text using either METAL TYPES or photomechanical or digital glyphs. Strictly speaking, creating SLUGS of text as with the Linotype machine is not typesetting since printing type (in the form of individual SORTS) is not being used, but most people referring to the composition of a text with Linotype would nonetheless call it "typesetting." (*See* Mergenthaler, Ottmar.) In the world of HANDPRESS printing, the use of sorts, gathered in proper order in a COMPOSING STICK, is a skill that takes a good deal of time to learn. It is not merely placing the sorts into the stick. One must learn how to CAST OFF COPY, design a page to achieve the proper line measure, consider LETTERSPACING and WORD SPACING, understand JUSTIFICATION of the lines, select appropriate TYPEFACES, know how to use THINS, and so on. Some of this is done automatically in digital typesetting, but even with that, with all of the power that computers give us, one can produce a truly ugly page with poor digital typesetting. ***De gustibus non est disputandum.***

(See what I mean!) (See Labuz, *Typography & Typesetting.*)

TYPE SPECIMEN BOOK. A volume that contains examples of one or more TYPEFACES, produced usually by a type foundry to display its wares, by a company selling printing types from foundries or other typecasting operations, or by a printer to show the typefaces she has in her shop. Type specimens are usually done for commercial purposes, but a private printer may do one as a record of his own type holdings. There are thousands of these volumes—a highly collected genre. Some of them are quite famous—such as the 1912 and 1923 volumes from the American Type Founders Company (with 1,148 and 1,300+ pages, respectively), showing hundreds of typefaces in many variations and sizes and sample texts set from the types. (See the entries for American Type Founders in the bibliography.) These volumes—especially for the larger companies—will also show printing equipment and supplies that they sold. (See Annenberg, *Type Foundries of America and Their Catalogs*; Dreyfus, ed., *Type Specimen Facsimiles, 1–15*; Johnston, *Alphabets to Order*; Marshall and Ellis, "Reprinting *Printing Types*"; Pankow and Dreyfus, *The Art of the Type Specimen in the Twentieth Century*; and Romaine, *A Guide to American Trade Catalogs, 1744–1900*.)

TYPESTICKER. The COMPOSITOR's jargon term for a compositor. One who uses a COMPOSING STICK. In setting type, the typesticker is said to be "sticking the type."

TYPOGRAPHICAL ERRORS (typos). Any mistake of printing in the text. There are many kinds of such mistakes: misspellings, setting of wrong words, setting with sorts inverted, incorrect page numbers, errors in RUNNING HEADS and CATCHWORDS, wrong punctuation, inverted words or lines, use of SORTS from the wrong font, repeated words of phrases (called "DITTOGRAPHY"), missing (or repeated) words, and so on. Strictly speaking, a MISIMPOSED FORME—say, with two pages reversed—is not a typographical error, though such mistakes in typography (i.e., in the IMPOSITION) could be called "typographical errors." (*See* Proofreading.)

The aim of proofreading is to remove anything from the text that is wrong, and typographical errors qualify for "anything that is wrong." They can change the meaning of a text radically (the athlete told to "resign" resigns when his manager meant "re-sign" his contract, the missing comma in "Let's eat Grandma," and the missing "not" in "Do jump off the roof"), and they should be rooted out.

TYPOGRAPHIC CODING. The use of variations in type styles to clue readers in to certain features of the text. Typographic coding, for example, is used in bibliographies to show readers where titles are, where certain data fields begin, and so on. In prose, typographic coding (as with ITALICS) can indicate stress or emphasis, the use of a foreign word, or other things. Again, for bibliographic entries, the first element in an entry (as with an author's name) can be set in all capitals or in boldface type, titles can be set in italic type, and annotations can be set in a typeface smaller than the one for the bibliographic data. These are examples of typographic coding. (*See also* Spatial coding.) (See Berger, *The Design of Bibliographies*, pp. 39–40.)

TYPOGRAPHY. In the modern sense, "typography" means "[t]he composition of printed material from MOVABLE TYPE. [and] The arrangement and appearance of printed matter" (*American Heritage Dictionary of the English Language*, p. 1878), though over the centuries the word had broader meanings, including everything one needed to do to get something into print: design and cast type, set the type, print the text, and so on. Today we might hear, "The typography of this FINE-PRESS book is exquisite," meaning that it is expertly printed and beautifully designed. Thus, there are mechanical and aesthetic dimensions to typography. The word does not refer to the accuracy of the text or the quality of the materials that the printed item is made of.

The GROLIER CLUB hosted an exhibit "100 Books Famous in Typography," for which they posted an announcement on their website. (See Jerry Kelly and Sebastian Carter, *One Hundred Books Famous in Typography*.) Here is an excerpt from that posting: "Typography a term derived from a Greek phrase that means roughly 'writing with figures cast in RELIEF'—is an essential component of book making. Encompassing the art and science of printing types, including TYPE manufacture and type design, typography has a long and distinguished history. It begins with GUTENBERG's ingenious development in the 1450s of a system for the mass-production of TEXTS, and then moves through the centuries to spotlight new technologies such as line casting, phototype, and the desktop computer composition of today" (Grolier Club, "Grolier Club Will Host Typography Exhibition"). (See Biggs, *Basic Typography*; Labuz, *Typography & Typesetting*; Legros and Grant, *Typographical Printing Surfaces*; McLean, *The Thames and Hudson Manual of Typography*; Tschichold, *Asymmetric Typography*; and *Typography and Design*.)

UDC. *See* Dewey classification.

ULRICH'S PERIODICALS DIRECTORY. Published since 1932, and founded by Carolyn F. Ulrich, chief of the periodical division of the New York Public Library, this massive reference guide lists over 300,000 serial publications, organized in more than 900 subject headings along with nearly 4,600 suspended or discontinued titles. The publisher's earlier editions are also of use to booksellers and librarians, collectors and scholars since they identify thousands of other serial publications. It is currently published by ProQuest. The company's website says, "Ulrich's Periodicals Directory is a bibliographic database providing detailed, comprehensive, and authoritative information on serials published throughout the world. It covers all subjects, and includes publications that are published regularly or irregularly and are circulated free of charge or by paid subscription. / Updated weekly, the database is searchable and browsable by title, subject, language, electronic availability and more. There is also a news section, and links to libraries and interest groups" ("Ulrich's Periodical Directory," cited at https://www.library.ucsb.edu/research/db/338 [accessed 8 August 2021]).

ULTRA-MICRO-MINIATURE. *See* Miniature.

UNABRIDGED EDITION. A version of a work that contains the full text—not one shortened in any way. Abridgment can be done for several reasons: the text might contain something deemed inappropriate for certain audiences—as with sexual or political references that might offend particular people (this kind of abridgment could be called CENSORSHIP or BOWDLERIZATION); the text could be much longer than the publisher or editor (or the original author) is happy with, so a shorter version is published that saves space and, therefore, money; some of the text is not germane to a particular audience, so the extraneous material of a long text is removed to cater to a narrower audience; or a work could be so long that the publisher wishes to offer a shortened version for its reading audience (as with a work such as *War and Peace*). The term "unabridged EDITION" is suggestive when fiction or nonfiction books are spoken of, for it implies that something that might have been objectionable to some (contents, length, or something else) has not been removed. It can be a selling point for a publisher. For a dictionary or encyclopedia, however, the word "unabridged" is practically meaningless since the kinds of things that wind up in these reference books continue to be invented/coined/created. But it offers the potential buyer a sense that she will be getting *everything* there is in a text—and who wants only a partial text! For booksellers and collectors, an unabridged text is better than an abridged one—the notion that the COMPLETIST has that he does not want anything but the full text. (*See* Abridged edition.) Scholars almost always prefer full text over abridged versions.

UNAUTHORIZED EDITION. An EDITION of a work that is issued by a publisher without the permission of the author or other COPYRIGHT holder. It could be a piracy (*see* Pirate) or a biography the writing of which was not approved of by its subject. These "unauthorized biographies" are usually done with no assistance from the party whom the text is about and without the approval of anyone who could have a say in controlling the information about the person being written about. No matter how much research the author of an unauthorized work has done, it still has the ring of inaccuracy or incompleteness, possibly an inaccurate assumption.

UNBOUND. (*See also* Disbound.) With no binding. "Disbound" implies that the item was once bound; "unbound" carries no such implication. An unbound item would have been issued "IN SHEETS." Occasionally, a bookseller calls an item "unbound" when he really means "disbound." It is possible for a TEXT BLOCK to be sewn and ready to be put into BOARDS. This is still at the "unbound" stage, though it is partly bound in that it is sewn. Booksellers would still call this "unbound."

UNCATALOGED. The bugbear of the book world. A word associated with fairly invisible items. Libraries with uncataloged books are doing their patrons a disservice in that such items are not locatable except by serendipity. One ideal of the library world is UNIVERSAL BIBLIOGRAPHIC CONTROL, and uncataloged books are in no one's control. Booksellers with uncataloged items leave their patrons at the same kind of disadvantage; and it leaves the seller at a disadvantage as well since uncataloged books in a seller's stock may not be locatable to the seller herself, and will be equally invisible to a potential buyer. (Many's the time I was told by a bookseller, "I know I have a copy of it, but I can't find it." The proper bibliographic response by the customer is, "Bummer!") And an uncataloged book in possession of a collector could cause a problem: "Do I already have this one? I better get it here in the shop so that I don't miss out on it. . . . Hmm. Now I am home and I have four copies of it!" (The message here, of course, is that collectors really need to catalog their collections. And the larger the collections, the more urgent is the cataloging of it.)

UNCIALS. "A rounded form of capital letter or MAJUSCULE first used in Latin and Greek texts about the third century and later adopted by medieval SCRIBES" (Eckersley et al., *Glossary of Typesetting Terms*, p. 109). As a kind of script, "the uncial was distinguished from the capital of the book-hands by the round character of certain letters; the chief characteristic text-letters being A, D, E, H, and M. In other words, the old informal, cursive capital hand had broken into the square capital, formal hand, and produced these uncial capitals, which, because they were very much easier to write, followed cursive rather than square capitals in shape. The uncial hand began to show itself as early as the third century, but was in its heyday in the fifth and sixth centuries. By the eighth century it greatly degenerated, although there was an attempt to revive it for certain ornamental purposes" (Updike, *Printing Types*, vol. 1, p. 44). Uncial reappears in typefaces in the 20th century, sometimes with an accompanying lowercase with figures and punctuation as well. Perhaps the most used of this family of types is that designed in 1921 by Victor Hammer, appropriately called Hammer Uncial.

A B c d e f g h i j K l
m n o p q R s t u v w x
y z 1 2 3 4 5 6 7 8 9 0 &

Victor Hammer's American Uncial.
Courtesy of Luc De Vroye.

ABCDEFGHIJKLMNOP
QRSTUVWXYZabcdefg
hijklmnopqrstuvwxyz
0123456789
.,:;'"!?@#$%&*{(/|\)}

Uncial Antiqua.
FontSpace; http://www.fontspace.com/astigmatic-one-eye-typographic-institute/uncial-antiqua (accessed 22 June 2021).

UNCORRECTED, UNREVISED. Carter's entry for these terms mentions an uncorrected TYPESCRIPT and an unrevised PROOF. But of course the terms have wider meaning than this. "Uncorrected" means that a text of one sort or another has been set into type and may have been proofread, but has not yet had errors emended. There is a huge world of publishers' REVIEW COPIES out there—copies of books sent to any publication (analog or digital) that publishes reviews of books that are about to be issued (*see* Edition, Impression [Printing], Issue, and State; Points). The aim, of course, is to get good reviews into prominent publications to spur sales. Often these review copies are early printings, sometimes even before the covers are designed, so they might have generic, merely typographic (not illustrated) covers. And they will often say something like, "Uncorrected copy," and will have a statement that the reviewer should not rely on the text as accurate enough to quote in a review; if the text is to be quoted for review purposes, the reviewer should contact the publisher for an accurate text. Uncorrected copies—as TYPESCRIPTS, in print, in photocopied form, or as any other kind of copy—usually represent early versions of the text, and they are produced in fairly short numbers (the typescript could be unique); for these reasons, they are highly sought after by the COMPLETIST collector. This obtains as well for proof copies that are unrevised—or that are revised in the hand of the author. The textual bibliographer (*see* Bibliography) is interested in these early versions of a text since they are as close to the author's original intention as it is usually possible to find (especially in the absence of a MANUSCRIPT version of the text).

UNCUT (or untrimmed). Said of a volume that still has its original DECKLES. (*See* Cropped; Deckled edge.) If the BOLTS (folds) have not been removed, as with, say, an OCTAVO or DUODECIMO, the book is properly said to be "UNOPENED." That is, the term "uncut" is sometimes incorrectly used to mean "unopened." If a book is REBOUND into a new cover, the binder can say that the volume was "uncut" if the new binding is done without her having trimmed down the TEXT BLOCK. But this is an uncommon use of the term. The term can also mean that, even if the edition had its deckles removed, the copy described as "uncut" has not been SHAVED down any further, as in a REBINDING.

Carter's long entry discusses the "desirability" of having the widest possible margins, which means that the volume has not been severely trimmed down by a careless binder. And he speaks about the uniformity of the way volumes were bound from about 1830 on, when they were issued in PUBLISHERS' BINDINGS.

UNDERBIDDER. (Sometimes hyphenated.) *See* Auctions.

UNDERGROUND PRESS. (Sometimes called a "clandestine press.") A publisher working surreptitiously, with a particularly selective clientele, issuing texts that are subversive or critical of a government, organization, religion, or some other entity that would be offended by the publications (and could pose a danger to the press if the origin of the published materials was manifest). These presses are usually formed to reach their audiences based on a particular controversial issue, and they are sometimes disbanded once the controversy has passed. Such presses also issued works that may not have been critical, but were offensive for moral reasons. (*See* Samizdat; Tijuana bibles.)

UNEXPURGATED. Said of an edition of a text that has not been CENSORED. Specifically, it is a text that is complete as the author intended it, with no parts removed by morality-conscious "editors." (*See* Bowdlerized; Expurgated.)

UNINSTITUTIONALIZED. Said of an item that is not in an institution—that is, not in a library from which the item may never be freed. The term can be found in Bradford Morrow's "In Search of America's Rarest Unknown Books by Renowned Writers," in which he mentions exceptionally rare volumes that are usually not recognized for what they are. (*See* Sleepers.) The implication is that a number of copies of a rare book could exist, but mostly in libraries, which seldom deaccession their rare holdings. Uninstitutionalized books are still in the world, before they are immured on the shelves of a rare book room, and presumably could be acquired by a bookseller or collector. The word is seldom used in the trade, but Morrow says, "'uninstitutionalized,' to use the parlance of the trade." (It is good to know that the word refers to books, not to collectors.)

UNION CATALOG. A catalog of library holdings showing the contents of more than a single institution. A town with a public library, collections at an athaneum and historical society, a junior college, a university, and several schools may have a single catalog showing the holdings of all of these otherwise unconnected institutions; or it could be a single catalog showing the holdings of a host of libraries in a single state or geographical region; these are union catalogs. The most ambitious and largest of such a database is the NATIONAL UNION CATALOG.

UNIQUE. Carter's entry points out that MANUSCRIPT materials by themselves are unique, but printed books are not necessarily unique unless they have certain features that clearly mark them as different from all other copies—features such as a person's SIGNATURE, annotations, a bookplate, or some damage. He says that we cannot describe too many volumes as unique and that when a bookseller uses the phrase "apparently unique," she should have some strong basis for saying this. (See Carter, pp. 252–53.) The collector's or bookseller's pronouncement that the volume at hand is unique proclaims its specialness and often explains its value (higher than the value of other copies because of its uniqueness)—and who does not want to own the only copy in the world thus! Certain kinds of uniqueness may add considerably to the value: the only copy signed and inscribed by the author, the only one in full leather, or the only copy with the bookplate of a famous person. But other kinds of uniqueness may detract from the volume's value: the only one in full cloth (clearly a rebinding of a damaged copy when all other copies are in the original leather), the only copy with ketchup on it, or the only one with water stains in the shape of Jimmy Durante's nose. Do not be fooled by claims of uniqueness. There may just be another copy out there with a similar water stain.

One further caution, especially for books from the HAND-PRESS PERIOD: G. Thomas TANSELLE claims that no two copies of books are alike (Tanselle, *A Rationale of Textual Criticism*, p. 51). Thus, collectors and librarians who wish to downsize to save space and want to do so by removing DUPLICATES from their collections should think twice and COLLATE their volumes with great scrutiny. If there is a COMPLETIST gene in the pool, they will want to keep copies in every manifestation, and any difference between two so-called identical copies shows each to be unique, and both should be retained in the collection. (I recently acquired a copy of a late 19th-century volume, and when it arrived, I realized I already had a copy of the same edition, with the same cover art, same cover cloth, and so on. But it was QUARTER BOUND, and one copy has a red cloth spine, the other a green cloth spine. I guess I have to keep them both.)

UNIVERSAL BIBLIOGRAPHIC CONTROL (UBC). A phrase coined in the 1960s to indicate the aim of information professionals of having all bibliographical data available to everyone (with the hardware and software to access it) from anywhere on the earth. "[T]he origins of IFLA's UBC (Universal Bibliographic Control) programme can be traced to the International Meeting of Cataloguing Experts, held in Copenhagen in 1969" (Dorothy Anderson, "IFLA's Programme of Universal Bibliographic Control: Origins and Early Years," abstract available at https://www.researchgate.net/publication/249774201_IFLA's_Programme_of_Universal_Bibliographic_Control_Origins_and_Early_Years1504404 [accessed 22 June 2021]).

UBC "is the unattainable ideal of librarianship: the ability to offer to anyone in the world (with a computer and Internet access) any piece of information from anywhere else on earth. One reason that it is unattainable is that there is too much information. Further, copyright restrictions and site licensing create inaccessible materials. Another reason traditionally given for the impossibility of achieving UBC is that there was no storage, retrieval, and delivery system around to make it possible. Today we are on the cusp of eliminating that objection: an expanding network of computers, with increasing memory capacities, linked with electronic methods of capturing information (including scanning and reformatting of analog into digital text), and supported by vastly growing numbers of computers and users combine to get us closer and closer to UBC. . . . [T]his is an asymptotic endeavor: we will never achieve 100% bibliographic control. But the amount of information being created and made accessible in digital form grows by endless gigabytes and terabytes" (Berger, p. 418).

UNIVERSAL DECIMAL CLASSIFICATION. *See* Dewey classification.

UNIVERSITY OF ILLINOIS, URBANA-CHAMPAIGN, RARE BOOK & MANUSCRIPT LIBRARY. One of the great rare book departments in the United States. "The Rare Book & Manuscript Library (RBML) of the University of Illinois at Urbana-Champaign is one of the largest publicly accessible special collections repositories in the United States. The collections—nearly 500,000 volumes and just over two linear miles of material—encompass the broad areas of literature, history, art, theology, philosophy, technology, and the natural sciences. Established in 1936, the RBML is renowned for its outstanding collections of Medieval and Renaissance manuscripts, early printed books, English literature, American wit and humor, theater history, free speech movements, Italian history, the history of economics, the history of science and technology, mathematics, geology, and natural history. The literary papers of such notable figures as Marcel Proust, Carl Sandburg, H. G. Wells, William Maxwell, Gwendolyn Brooks, Shana Alexander, and W. S. Merwin are also housed in The Rare Book & Manuscript Library" (University of Illinois Library, "Rare Book & Manuscript Library"; https://www.library.illinois.edu/rbx/about/ [accessed 5 July 2021]). The library has exceptional holdings in Elizabethan and Stuart publications, especially in Shakespeare and other Renaissance dramatists, the Bible, and schoolbooks. They hold an extensive collection of INCUNABULA, EMBLEM BOOKS, and volumes printed on the Continent.

UNJUSTIFIED (also called "ragged right"). Text that is not set with all of the characters in successive lines aligning at the right margin is said to be "unjustified." (*See* Justification [in typesetting].) One rationale for setting ragged right is that no words need to be broken by hyphens; another is that word SPACING can remain uniform since there will be no need to "tighten up" or "space out" a line to justify it. This could yield an attractive and legible page.

The term is also used to describe a MATRIX after it has been struck with a PUNCH, but before the displaced metal has been filed off. A justified matrix is ready for casting; an unjustified one is not. (*See* figure at Punch/Punchcutter.)

UNKNOWN TO _______. A phrase meaning that the volume (or PAMPHLET or photograph, among other kinds of material) is not cited by an authority who would have mentioned it if he had known about it. This implies that the item is particularly scarce and can command a special price or the awe of a collector's visitors. Carter raises three issues with regard to "unknown to" (or "NOT IN") references. The first has to do with whether the expert who did not know of whatever it was that was unknown is a true expert in the field of that subject. ("This volume on Voltaire was 'unknown to Smithers,'" when Smithers is an expert on women's fashion, means nothing.) Second, if the fact that something is unknown is revealed in a reference volume that is not strictly focused on the thing that is under discussion. ("Unknown to Blanck" might be true, but the item that is unknown focuses on Surinam Lepidoptera, whereas Blanck's bibliography focuses on American fiction.) And third, the "unknown to" is determined when the person making that claim cannot find the unknown item in a reference source when it is actually there. (See Carter, p. 253.) Also, the source that one checks that lacks the item in hand could be a shoddily compiled bibliography, done by someone new to the field; the cited source could be about topic A while the item "not in" is about topic B and does not belong in the expert's volume in the first place, or the item could actually be there and the person announcing "unknown to" has merely not been able to find it. At any rate, the locution often is accompanied by an enhanced price or a claim by a collector that his copy is particularly scarce and valuable—neither of which may be justified. (*See also* Unrecorded.)

UNLETTERED. A term not much in use these days, but Carter's entry is worth referring to. The word means that the SPINE of a volume lacks information as to the author or title of that volume; that is, it has no lettering on it. Carter points out that for about the first 150 years of printing in the West, most volumes were not identified on their spines. If they had any markings, that kind of information was more likely to appear on the FORE-EDGE of the book since that is the part that would have been exposed when the book was on a shelf. (See Carter, pp. 253–54.) The term could also mean that there is no lettering at all on the binding, including the front cover.

UNMARKED. Said of a copy of a book that has pages with no writing, underlining, stains, smudges, fingerprints, peanut butter smears, or other blemishes. In a bookseller's catalog, the phrase "an unmarked copy" may be a subtle way of suggesting that the binding is defective in some way, but the TEXT BLOCK is PRISTINE.

UNOPENED. Said of a volume with its BOLTS still intact. For example, if a volume is an octavo, the SIGNATURES are printed from sheets of paper that were folded three times, creating bolts (folds) on the top and also on the FORE-EDGE of the last four leaves of the signature. To read the book comfortably, the bolts are either slit (as with a letter opener) or trimmed away. Novice collectors will confuse this concept with "UNTRIMMED," which means that the volume still has its DECKLES. Carter adds that since these novices love books in their most PRISTINE condition—as close as they can get the volumes to the way they were issued by the publisher—having the bolts in place is greatly desired. He adds that these novice collectors prefer their books "not only unread but unreadable" (p. 251), and he says that good bibliographical information can be gleaned by uncut bolts, for one can often discern the book's FORMAT, how the type was IMPOSED, how the POINT HOLES got there, what the size of the original uncut sheet was, and so on. Hence, unopened copies often have valuable information made available by their being unopened. Carter concludes that if one is ignorant of what he can learn from an unopened state of the book but is excited to have the volume because it is unopened, the result could be what he calls "DECKLE-FETISHISM" (see Carter, p. 251; why Carter would put all this under "UNCUT" is an enigma). (*See* Cropped; Deckled edge; Opened.)

UNPAGINATED. Said of a volume with no page numbers. (*See* Foliation; Pagination.) In many early volumes (manuscript and print), each LEAF was numbered, not the pages. If a book is foliated, we generally do not (need to) say that it is unpaginated.

UNPRESSED. In the book world, this term has two meanings. First, some catalogers refer to pages that show the BITE of the TYPE when the sheet has not been pressed to remove that feature ("a sharp impression on unpressed LEAF"). Second, since most printing ink is made with oil, without dryers, the ink could stay wet for days or weeks. If a volume is bound soon after printing, the binder may put the book into a binder's press after the cover material has been glued to the BOARDS. The pressure exerted by the press could cause the ink to offset onto facing pages. So the binder may wish not to create too much pressure in the press, leaving the boards not to be pressed too strongly. The boards could splay once the volume is taken from the press. The bookseller could say, "an unpressed copy," to show this splaying.

UNPUBLISHED. As the term indicates, this describes an item that has not been released to the public. For the bookseller and collector, such a word accompanying the description of the item can indicate RARITY and can thus add considerably to the intellectual and financial value of the piece. An unpublished TYPESCRIPT, script, piece of correspondence, or anything else—especially if it is UNIQUE—gives its possessor exclusive access to its content, and bragging rights in the collecting world.

UNRECORDED. The most startling and powerful of the terms that indicate that the item in hand is valuable. Like "NOT IN" and "UNKNOWN TO," "unrecorded" means that we have here a really desirable piece. No one in history has ever recorded its existence. (Be wary of such a claim.) And this book is on such an important (read "COLLECTIBLE") topic and is so valuable in its content that it is a miracle that no one has ever taken notice of it before. But as Carter points out, unimportant books are likely to have escaped notice and are thus likely to be unrecorded. The term could be used by someone who is merely ignorant of the record—that the item so called has actually been recorded somewhere. This is a term that should be used sparingly and taken with much caution. (See Carter, p. 254.) The claim may be inaccurate. (*See* Unknown to _______.)

UNSOPHISTICATED. (*See* Sophisticated.) Said of an item that has not been augmented, repaired, or restored. This could be a virtue (in its most natural state) or a defect (damaged, but no intrusive repairs have been made). Said of a bookseller, a collector, or a librarian, for instance, the word refers to a weakness. The term can also be applied to a set of VOLUMES or FASCICLES in which all the parts are original to that set; the individual pieces have not been gathered from two or more sets. (*See* Married.)

UNTRIMMED. *See* Uncut.

UP (as in "two up," "four up," "eight up"). A number followed by "up" is an indication of how many pages of text a printer is printing in a single FORME. To print a FOLIO, the printer imposes (*see* Imposition) two pages of type in the CHASE; he is printing "two up." For a QUARTO, he prints "four up." For an OCTAVO, he is printing "eight up." And so on.

UPDIKE, DANIEL BERKELEY (1860–1941). One of the foremost book designers, scholars of typography, and printers/publishers in the United States. His work at Houghton, Mifflin & Company was so stellar that they made him the proprietor of their Riverside Press, which, under his control, produced a host of beautiful volumes. From there he founded his own Merrymount Press (in 1896), known also for its well designed and produced books. Daniel Ness says, "The Merrymount Press catered deliberately and by preference to a limited, superior public, which supported its efforts to supply a superior quality of ordinary output. This enabled it to establish a reputation for delivering only the very best obtainable TYPOGRAPHY, impression, illustrations, and binding regardless of the costs. Updike's book designs combine the functional and the beautiful; they are noteworthy for their clarity of organization, easy READABILITY, and excellent workmanship" (Ness, "Daniel Berkeley Updike," Boston Athenaeum, September 2014; https://www.bostonathenaeum.org/library/book-recommendations/athenaeum-authors/daniel-berkeley-updike [accessed 24 May 2021]). Though known in general for the excellent books he produced, perhaps his most famous production is the text he wrote, *Printing Types: Their History, Forms & Use.* (See also Updike, *Notes on the Merrymount Press.*)

UPPERCASE. The capital letters (also called "MAJUSCULES") are so called because type was kept in TYPE CASES one above the other, the lower one holding the most commonly used SORTS, the upper one holding the capitals. COMPOSITORS needed to have the small letters as close as possible since they were the most used; the capitals, less frequently used in the setting of text, were relegated to a type case above the other—the "upper case." (*See* Illuminated majuscule.)

UPPER-END BOY. "A junior member of the VAT's crew [in hand papermaking], only required when large sizes of paper (larger than 22" × 30") are being made, or double-sheet MOULDS being used. He seizes the 'upper-end' of the mould when the coucher [*see* Couch] turns it over to couch the large sheet and presses down this end on to the felt, so that the whole sheet of wet paper adheres. He also assists the coucher, in pitching or lowering the felt on to the topmost sheet of the POST, when making large sizes" (Labarre, *Dictionary and Encyclopaedia of Paper and Paper-Making*, p. 314). The upper-end boy also assists the LAYMAN, who takes the sheets from the post (removing the interleaved FELTS) and lays the sheets onto a pile of other sheets (the "WHITE POST"). If the sheets are large, the upper-end boy holds the lower corners of the still-wet sheet and guides it carefully to be placed on the previous sheet so that no sheet overlaps the edges of another; in the next pressing, if there is an overlap, the edge of one sheet will impart an impressed line into the neighboring sheet unless they are perfectly superimposed.

URL. Universal resource locator—the electronic address for a site on the Internet. (*See* Hash character.)

USE (the noun). In many booksellers' catalogs, in the description of BOOKS OF HOURS, the cataloger may say, "Use of Paris." Most such manuscripts do not give the city for which they were produced. Since the prayers given in particular cities differ from those in other cities, it is possible to determine, with a careful analysis of the prayers in these books, and using other criteria, which city that volume was created for, though as Roger S. Wieck says, "It is customary to determine where such books were written by indentifying local use for several of their standard texts: the Calendar, the Hours of the Virgin, the Litany, and the Office of the Dead. . . . The most obvious limitation of all the traditional tests is that they may indicate where a Book of

Hours was intended to be used, but not where it was made" (Wieck, *Time Sanctified*, p. 149). So the bookseller may be able to say what city the volume was created to be used in, but not where it was created.

USED BOOK. (Also called a "secondhand book"; *see* Secondhand copy.) A book that has been in the hands of at least one former owner, usually (but not necessarily) after that consumer has purchased it. The phrase, of course, is commonly encountered in "used book store" (or "used bookstore"), an establishment that sells books that are not new. The implication of the phrase "used book" is that it shows some signs of wear, though that is not always so. One bookseller told me that professionally it was unethical for him to sell books AS NEW when he had purchased them from some user—regardless of how PRISTINE the volume was.

USED COPY/USED-BOOK STORE. A copy of a book that has truly seen better days. There has always been a difficulty in describing the CONDITION of books. "Used" could mean that the volume has some fairly extensive defects and is not in "COLLECTOR'S CONDITION." The person aspiring to be an "ANTIQUARIAN bookseller" (*see* Antiquarian books) but who has a stock of mediocre volumes or cripples (the politically incorrect but often-heard term for books needing much repair) must honestly call himself a "used-book dealer." (Usually spelled as two words since people will understand that he is not a "used" party.) There are still many used-book stores, though their numbers have been declining since ONLINE BOOK SALES came to be the principal means of moving books through the world. They now exist in the ether, and the used-book dealers are selling more and more on the web. A "used-book store" may well have PRISTINE books on its shelves, along with some great treasures, but the bulk of its stock will be "used" in the sense of "pre-owned" and possibly marked by use.

UTERINE VELLUM (also called "slunk"). "The skin of an unborn or prematurely born animal. The term is applied particularly to calves, from which the very finest grade of PARCHMENT is produced. Slunks are also used in making suede LEATHER, and the smaller the fibers, the finer the nap that can be produced. The skins of unborn or prematurely born animals have skins [*sic*] with very fine fibers and a much less highly developed vascular network" (Roberts and Etherington, p. 239). There is some discussion of whether the skins come from unborn (therefore aborted) animals or from recently, naturally born ones.

"It is with reluctance that one mentions, albeit briefly, the vexed and unresolved question of uterine vellum. Old-fashioned books about medieval MANUSCRIPTS assert that the finest medieval parchment was made from the skin of aborted calves. . . . There is some medieval evidence that aborted skin was valuable and desirable, and it is true that parchment made from this rather unappealing material or from the skins of very new-born animals does [*sic*] indeed look and feel like that which antiquarians call uterine vellum. But it is very difficult to believe that thousands of cows miscarried for generations, or were deprived of their foetuses in such numbers to supply the booktrade economically. Either normal skins had been pared down so that only the tissue-thin membrane remained, or, perhaps more likely, the skins were actually split to produce two sheets out of a single thickness. Again there is some (not much) medieval evidence for this taking place. If the term uterine parchment must be used at all, it should perhaps refer to a quality of skin and not to its origin" (De Hamel, *Medieval Craftsmen*, pp. 15–16).

"The Latin word abortivum occasionally applied to fine parchment in the Middle Ages (though rarely) has given rise to another form of superstition which has become widespread, namely, that the finest medieval parchment, and particularly the very thin, flexible, opaque, small, thirteenth-century French Bible vellum was made from the skins of still-born calves. There is as nearly as possible no evidence for this belief. It may be true. I have no figures on infant mortality among livestock in the Middle Ages; but I should be inclined to think that animal husbandry must have been in a very precarious condition if enough calves were still-born in the thirteenth century to provide all the pages which pass for 'uterine vellum'" (Thompson, *The Materials and Techniques of Medieval Painting*, p. 27).

VACUUM FREEZE DRYING. *See* Freeze drying.

VADE MECUM (sometimes spelled as one word). A (usually) small volume that one can carry, as the etymology of the word says (it is Latin for "go with me"). The implication is that the text has information that a person needs, regardless of where she is. Peter Beal says that the book may be hung from a belt (as a GIRDLE BOOK would be), and he says the standard FORMAT of them is like a CONCERTINA binding. It would contain various kinds of information, like a calendar, medical information, a phrase book or dictionary for traveling to another country, or whatever the carrier might need. (See Beal, *A Dictionary of English Manuscript Terminology, 1450–2000*, p. 428.) Today we have our vade mecums: they are called smartphones.

VALENTIN HAÜY SYSTEM. *See* Printing for the blind.

VANDERCOOK PRESS. A flatbed press with a cylinder, originally designed as a PROOF PRESS but adopted by many FINE-PRESS printers as their press of choice. True HANDPRESSES require a great deal of effort in the pulling of the BAR and in the MAKEREADY. The Vandercook, in its many models, reduced the makeready to a short exercise, and the self-inking apparatus and easy hand crank streamline the operation, speeding it up and producing a fine impression from type and illustrations.

Sterne says, "Vandercook without a doubt is the most recognized name in the world for proof presses. / The company was started by Robert Vandercook in Chicago in September 1909. The first press was a 'rocker' proof press, made with a geared cylinder. Up to the development of this press all proofs were either made on a roller press that depended on gravity for impression or on a WASHINGTON HAND PRESS. / During the next 54 years they brought out 60 different press models of which nine models were made in two or more styles. In the 75 years that presses were manufactured, more than 38,000 with the name of Vandercook were produced. The name of Vandercook & Sons was used until 1968 when E. O. Vandercook sold the company to one of their suppliers, Illinois Tool Works. They only kept the company for four years and then sold it to one of their managers, Hugh Fletcher, who renamed the company Vandersons Corporation. Vandersons stopped manufacturing presses in 1976 at which time they only made models HS27, SP20, SP25 and Universal I (see Serial Number Tables). / . . . Vandercook was very prolific in producing new models. They developed 29 models before World War II and 17 of these models were still being manufactured many years after the war. The most popular of these models was #4, which was first made in 1935 and not discontinued until 1960. Many are still in use today" (Sterne, "A Short History of Vandercook," http://vandercookpress.info/articles.html [accessed 22 June 2021]).

Some purists believe that the Vandercook is not real hand printing since the press lacks the PLATEN, the bar to pull, and the TYMPAN and FRISKET of the standard handpress (e.g., the Washington or the COLUMBIAN) and also since most Vandercooks have automatic inking. But it is true LETTERPRESS in that it uses HOT METAL TYPE, and it makes an impression in the paper the same way the traditional handpress does. They are so well made that doing the makeready on them is usually quite easy and fast.

VANITY PUBLISHING/VANITY PRESS (also called "self-publishing" or "subsidy publishing"). The publishing of any text (book or pamphlet) paid for by the author. Vanity presses produced "books not at their own risk, but at the authors' risk and expense. They often sign publishing contracts with inexperienced authors by appealing to their desire to see their writings in print at whatever cost" (Peters, ed., *The Bookman's Glossary*, p. 208). This definition was published about 30 years ago, but it was written many years before this, appearing in earlier editions of *The Bookman's Glossary*. When those words were written, the phrase "vanity publishing" carried heavy derisive implications: the author's work is so bad that he cannot get a "legitimate" commercial publisher to take it, so he had to get it into print himself.

Today, the term has lost much of its original sting since, with modern technology, it is easy for anyone to publish her own work, and an increasing number of authors are turning to this kind of publishing, even those with good-quality texts. R. R. Bowker, the publishing giant that issues ISBNs, can keep a fairly accurate tally of newly published books (except for those published by authors who do not seek ISBNs). The Bowker 2018 report says, "For 2018, the numbers demonstrate that the self-publishing industry continues its steady growth, with over 1.6 million titles published—a 40% increase over the prior year. This growth trend has been ongoing since 2013, when the number of print books and ebooks with registered ISBNs stood at 461,438. This trend is likely to continue as the quality of many self-published works now rivals that of traditionally published titles. Authors now have access to a wide range of professional services, from editing to cover design, to help ensure that the highest standards are met. With these resources, coupled with the online marketing and distribution tools now available, self-publishing authors are positioned for success as never before" (Bowker, "Self-Publishing in the United States, 2013–2018"; https://www.bowker.com/siteassets/files/pdf-files/bowker-selfpublishing-report-2019.pdf [accessed 8 August 2021]). (See also PW [Publisher's Weekly], "Number of Self-Published Titles Jumped 40% in 2018.")

And the trend to increases in vanity publishing continues. The 2018 report shows that 1,677,781 ISBNs were assigned for self-publishing. (See Bowker; bowker.com/siteassets/files/pdf-files/bowker-selfpublishing-report-2019.pdf.) With so many people doing it, the stigma has pretty much worn off, though for those seriously into publishing—well-known writers, academics, and possibly a few snobs—vanity publishing still produces inferior texts. (See also Bowker, "Self-Publishing in the United States, 2008–2013"; http://media.bowker.com/documents/bowker_selfpublishing_report2013.pdf [accessed 23 June 2021].) (*See* Print on demand.) One key point to make here is that most of these self-published books come out in paper—not in digital form. Libraries have the challenges of identifying the ones worthy of collecting and being able to afford them.

Old (and even recent) predictions of the "PAPERLESS SOCIETY" are clearly wrong.

VAN KRIMPEN, JAN (1892–1958). Van Krimpen was an "outstanding modern designer of TYPEFACES for books and postage stamps. / He received a commission from the Dutch post office to draw the lettering for a special commemorative stamp to be printed by the prominent firm of Enschedé in 1923. The success of the design led Enschedé to invite him to design a new typeface for the firm. The typeface he produced, Lutetia (the Roman name for Paris), was the official lettering for an exhibition of Dutch art in Paris in 1927, and its reception led to his lifelong association with the firm. In addition to Lutetia, van Krimpen's well-known faces include Antigone Greek (1927), Romanée (1928), Romulus (1931), Cancelleresca Bastarda (1935), and Spectrum (1943). His types became well known in the United States through the LIMITED EDITIONS CLUB and in England through the Nonesuch Press" ("Jan van Krimpen," *Encyclopaedia Britannica*, http://www.britannica.com/biography/Jan-van-Krimpen [accessed 23 June 2021]). He was also a noted CALLIGRAPHER and book designer. (See Dreyfus, *The Work of Jan van Krimpen*.)

VAN VLIET, CLAIRE (1933–) (Janus Press). One of America's best-known and most accomplished fine printers. Smith College Library, with a collection of the Janus Press books, had on its website the following: "Claire Van Vliet is one of America's preeminent artists of the book, having created some of the 20th-century's most important fine editions. For decades she has made significant contributions to and innovations in the fields of fine printing, papermaking, bookbinding and printmaking. And as a teacher she has had a profound impact on several generations of aspiring book artists. / In 1955 Van Vliet printed the first book from her Janus Press, now located in the Northeast Kingdom of Vermont. She is known both for her use of traditional techniques, materials, and forms, as well as for innovation in illustration with painted paper pulp and non-adhesive and woven book structures. She also has collaborated with, and mentored, many book artists during the past 50 years, many of whom have gone on to important careers of their own. For her work as a teacher and artist Van Vliet received a 'genius grant' from the MacArthur Foundation in 1989; it was the foundation's first recognition of achievement in the book arts" (Smith College Libraries, "Paper Collaborations for the Janus Press: Books and Broadsides"; http://www.smith.edu/libraries/info/news/januspress [accessed 27 October 2015]; a dead link, but with good information). She worked at the Lanston MONOTYPE Company in the 1950s and briefly taught art at the Philadelphia Museum School of Art and the Philadelphia Museum College of Art in the 1960s and then moved to Madison, Wisconsin, to teach typography. In 1966, she moved to Newark, Vermont, where she set up her Janus Press. (See Fine, *The Janus Press, Fifty Years*, especially pp. 7–9.)

Van Vliet has one of the longest-running fine presses in history (2021 marks her 66th year of production, and as of the writing of this book, she is still producing publications). Her books exhibit clever innovation, exceptional artistry, and meticulous production, and many of them demonstrate successful collaborations with exceptional artists and writers. (See Cloonan, "Janus at 60.")

VARIANTS. The term is used for manuscripts and printed text, for the physical volume's component parts, and for bookbindings. For printed texts, scholars collate (examine and compare; *see* Collation) multiple versions of a text to see if they vary in any way. Textual variants exist in SUBSTANTIVES and ACCIDENTALS. (*See* Author's correction; Bibliography.) The variants could be scribal or could come from errors made by a COMPOSITOR, from changes made by an editor, or from the author herself. The variants within copies from the same EDITION are called "STATE VARIANTS" (*see also* Edition, Impression [Printing], Issue, and State; Points). There can also be variants between editions. Another source of variation may be seen on a title page when the printer produces a certain number of copies for one party and the rest for another. KIM MERKER printed 350 copies of the first edition of George Bernard Shaw's *Passion Play* (1971), with 250 copies for the Windhover Press in Iowa City and 100 for Bertram Rota in London—yielding two variant title pages. (See Berger, *Printing and the Mind of Merker*, p. 47.) And for Ezra Pound's *Drafts and Fragments of Cantos CX–CXVII* (1968), he printed 200 copies for New Directions in New York, 100 copies for Faber and Faber in London, and 10 copies for the Stone Wall Press in Iowa City—yielding three variant title pages. The text could vary also with changes in illustrations or TIPPED-IN items (see Berger, *Printing and the Mind of Merker*, pp. 29–30).

The component parts of a volume may vary from one copy to another. For example, one copy could be printed on one kind of paper and another on a different paper. In the FINE-PRESS world, this sometimes happens when a press, wanting to print, say, 200 copies of a book, does not have enough paper of one kind to do the whole edition, so the proprietor uses one stock of paper for some copies and another stock for the rest. Also, a volume in a single edition, but aimed at an American and a British audience, may have some of the spellings changed to be familiar to the appropriate audience. These intentional changes are variants within an edition, cognizantly made, and they constitute different states.

For bookbindings, the binding structure, material, or other features may differ from one another among what appear to be otherwise identical copies. The entire PRESSRUN may be bound in a green cloth; the variant might be bound in a blue cloth—or they might have varying decoration on them. One famous binding variant is the frog on Mark Twain's *The Celebrated Jumping Frog of Calaveras County, and Other Sketches*. The binding cloth will vary in some copies (dark green or deep reddish brown), but more startling is that in most copies the gold-stamped frog on the front cover is in the lower left, while in other copies he is higher up, in the middle of the cover, as if he had jumped. The difference is in a couple of inches and many thousands of dollars. The study of textual and binding variants can be fascinating and profitable. (*See* Bibliography.) (See also Carter, *Binding Variants in English Publishing, 1820–1900* and *More Binding Variants*.) (The bibliographer's term for such variation is, as Carter's title indicates, "binding variant.")

Carter warns not to make too much of the variants, especially when any conclusions one may draw are purely suppositions. (See Carter, p. 255.) (*See* Alteration.)

VARIORUM EDITION. (*See* Bibliography.) An EDITION of a work that shows, on the very pages of the text, TEXTUAL VARIANTS, along with commentary of scholars—the commentary usually pertaining to the textual history of the work (not evaluative or interpretive comments). For this reason, especially with texts that exist in many editions and versions, sometimes the page may contain only a few lines of the literary text, the rest of the page containing the CRITICAL APPARATUS. One of the most famous of the variorum editions is that of Shakespeare's writing. (See "The Original New Variorum Shakespeare Project, 1871–1955 [27 vols.]," https://users.pfw.edu/stapletm/NVSJC/OldNVS.html [accessed 6 July 2021]. This site gives full-text PDFs of the original 19th- and early 20th-century edition.) In one volume, for *Twelfth Night*, page 19 (act 1, scene 1) has only four lines of text; the glosses and notes extend the rest of the page, all of page 20, and part of page 21 (see https://books.google.com/books?id=th0uAAAAYAAJ&printsec=frontcover&dq=editions:0Rpp2uR9XPgXcsToBwiOLH&lr=&as_brr=1#v=onepage&q&f=false [accessed 23 June 2021]). (As an aside—this is a tour de force of typesetting and book design.)

VARIOUS DATES. A phrase used to indicate that, in a volume containing several texts, they are published in different years. This is particularly common in a SAMMELBAND. So a bookseller will indicate this either by spelling out the phrase, or with the titillating abbreviation "v.d." The term can also refer to a bookseller's or auction house's offering of a cluster of like materials, as with a collection of, say, PAPERBACKS from one publisher that are too numerous to mention individually: "A collection of 25 Dell literary paperbacks from the 1950s, v.d."; or "100 Superman comic books, various dates, sold as a lot."

VAT (in papermaking). The tub or tank, in hand papermaking, that holds the FURNISH—that is, all of the water and pulp and whatever else is in the water—at which the VATMAN stands to dip the MOLD to make sheets of paper. Handmade papers are sometimes called "vat papers."

VATMAN. The person, standing at the papermaking VAT, who makes the sheets by dipping the MOLD into the vat. Also called the "dipper." In recent years there has been a movement to remove sexism from all kinds of terminology. One person suggested that this term should be changed to "papermaker." I have no objection to this, though the original term has centuries of precedent, and today we understand that for hundreds of years women have been superb papermakers—in the West as well as in Asian countries. Also, the term "papermaker" can apply to someone working in a large commercial papermaking firm, doing any of several tasks, while "vatman" denotes a person right there at the vat, making paper by hand. We may have a challenge on our hands trying to replace the traditional word with the more generic "papermaker." ("Vatperson" just won't do. And the slangy "dipper" can be confusing.)

VATMAN'S SHAKE. The movement of the paper MOLD, left to right, front to back, by the VATMAN in the formation of the sheet. As the mold is raised from the water in the vat, all of the water and pulp are in abundance on the surface of the mold. The water has not fully drained, and the pulp needs to be distributed as evenly as possible over the mold's surface. This is accomplished with the shake. (See Thomas, ed., *Beer Will Help Your Shake*.)

Papermaking, especially with large molds that produce large sheets, is a strenuous activity. Labarre says, "It is quite common for a vatman, owing to nervous strain, to lose control of the muscles of his arms or, as it is called, 'lose his shake', sometimes temporarily, usually permanently" (Labarre, *Dictionary and Encyclopaedia of Paper and Paper-Making*, p. 315).

As the note at "Vatman" says, the effort to remove sexism from language may prompt us to create the revised term "Papermaker's shake." But this one will probably not take off since it sounds more like an ailment (or a soda-fountain offering) than does the original term. I am happy to go with it, however. As they say in the variety store: your choice.

VATMAN'S TEARS. Small round thin spots in a sheet of handmade paper caused when a drop of water hits the sheet soon after the VATMAN has taken the MOLD from the VAT—before all the water has drained off. Before all the fibers mat, a drop of water, falling on the surface of the mold, will disperse the fibers such that in the middle of the drop the fibers are left thin, but around the edge of the drop the displaced fibers "pile up," so a vatman's tear, when the sheet is held up to the light, shows as a circular spot, very light in the middle and dark around the edges. The story goes that such sheets were sometimes considered "seconds"; that is, they could not be sold as perfect, and either had to be sold for less money or be repulped since the tear was a defect in the sheet. And since the vatman was paid only for the perfect sheets that he produced, he would cry over spilled drops. Hence the term. This may be apocryphal, but it's a good story.

As the note at "Vatman" says, an effort to rid the language of sexism has prompted more than one person to ask me to promulgate the revised term: Papermaker's tears. I'm fine with this, though as with "Vatman," the older term has been around for so long that it will be difficult to get people familiar with it to change.

A sheet of wove paper with a wire watermark, and showing a vatman's tear.

Collection of the author.

VAT SIZING. *See* Size (in paper formation).

VELLUM. The skin of a calf, used for writing, printing, and binding (and for many other uses). As with so many words used imprecisely over the decades, the meaning has been diluted and is essentially lost, except to the cognoscenti; thus, "vellum" has become synonymous with the more general term "PARCHMENT." (*See also* Uterine vellum.) As Roberts and Etherington say, "Today, however, vellum is generally defined as a material made from CALFSKIN, SHEEPSKIN, or virtually any other skin obtained from a relatively small animal, e.g., antelope. Some authorities do not even distinguish between vellum and parchment, although traditionally the former was made from an unsplit calfskin, and consequently had a GRAIN pattern on one side (unless removed by scraping), while the latter was produced from the *flesh* split of a sheepskin, and consequently had no grain pattern. The important distinction between vellum (or parchment) and leather is that the former is not tanned but is prepared essentially by soaking the skin in lime and drying it under tension" (p. 277). (*See also* Flesh side; Hair side; Limp leather/Limp vellum.)

In the 19th century, papermakers came up with ingenious ways to manipulate papermaking pulp, with many kinds of additives and treatments. One kind of paper they produced was called "vellum," "a thick writing paper or CARDBOARD remotely suggestive of calf skin. In hand-made papers the term is applied to exceedingly strong imitation parchments in many ways superior to real skin parchment, being practically indestructible and not easily affected by heat, mildew and insects, as are the skins. They are chiefly used for certificates, diplomas and *èditions de luxe* and in [the] US also termed 'Art Parchment'" (Labarre, *Dictionary and Encyclopaedia of Paper and Paper-Making*, p. 316). I have seen books with imitation vellum bindings, and it is practically impossible to determine if the cover material is paper or genuine animal skin.

VERSION. One manifestation of an item or text that may vary from others of that same item or text. Of course, readers will understand what is meant by "This version written for children"; it clearly means that another version was not meant for children. The word can also designate a particular printing, as with editions of the Bible (the Douay version; the King James version). But more to the point here, the word should be used to distinguish variations in binding, edition, or illustrations when these VARIANTS signal differences in value or bibliographical information. Hence, rather than saying, "this book exists in a DELUXE EDITION, a regular edition, and a COMMERCIAL EDITION"—when they are all actually the same edition (*see* Edition, Impression [Printing], Issue, and State; Points)—the cataloger or BOOKSELLER should say that the item exists in a deluxe version, and so forth. Hence, the word "version" can denote differences in the intellectual or the physical manifestation of the item, along with differences in the monetary value and the audiences.

VERSO. The "back side" of a LEAF, that is, the reverse of the RECTO. Each leaf in a book has a recto and a verso. In books that are FOLIATED, with no page numbers, the "page" is often referred to by its FOLIO (i.e., the leaf in the VOLUME) and whether the text referred to is on the front or the back. Hence, G3^{r} means the G SIGNATURE, third leaf, recto (front); T6^{v} means the verso of the sixth leaf in the T signature. (In languages reading left to right, the verso leaves are those on the left when the volume is open.) Versos are usually even-numbered pages, though I have seen careless or ignorant designers give the versos odd numbers. I guess it is possible that a designer who is flouting tradition decides to give versos odd numbers, but then he runs the risk of being thought of as careless or ignorant.

VIALIBRI. Like ABEBOOKS, an online bookselling site that lists items from a host of dealers, and from other search services (AbeBooks is one of those), with a focus on old and rare materials. It bills itself as "The World's Largest Marketplace for Old, Rare & Out-of-Print Books" (https://www.vialibri.net [accessed 23 June 2021]), though it lists books that are not old or rare. (*See* Online book sales.) The site agglomerates many other search services, and it looks through "old and rare books offered on eighteen different web sites which aggregate the inventory of over 20,000 antiquarian booksellers world-wide" (https://www.vialibri.net/hints.php?from=index [accessed 23 June 2021]). One does not buy books from viaLibri. The site directs a user to other sites that list books from booksellers.

VIGNETTE. "A decorative design placed at the beginning or end of a book or chapter of a book or along the border of a page" (*American Heritage Dictionary of the English Language*, p. 1931). Vignettes often appear as pictures on title pages, and they usually are not printed within borders, though such a decorative element with such a border may be called a vignette. This latter use comes from the practice of providing "a photograph or an image" with indistinct or fading edges" (*American Heritage Dictionary of the English Language*, p. 1931). *See* Headpiece; Tailpiece.

VIRGULE (also called "forward slash," "slash," or "solidus"). The punctuation mark that is a forward leaning, upright, straight line: /. In a medieval MANUSCRIPT, it could indicate a pause or a separation between parts of the text, somewhat akin to a comma, though it could also indicate the end of a sentence. Occasionally, it is a straight vertical line (|), and if it is doubled (//) in a manuscript, it could indicate a new paragraph (*see* Paraph). It could be used in verse to show a break (a caesura) in the middle of a line. (*See also* Macron.) In lengthy prose passages that are quoted directly, the virgule can be used to separate paragraphs without having to move to a following line. The character has other uses, one of which is in linguistics, when it is used to indicate pronunciation: "The word 'Pay' is pronounced /pā/." The virgule is also used in web addresses.

VISITOR LOG; VISITORS' BOOK; OR VISITORS' ALBUM. *See* Guest books.

VOLUME. "A collection of written or printed sheets bound together; a book" (*American Heritage Dictionary of the English Language*, p. 1941). This simple definition ignores "BLANK BOOKS." Carter assumed his readers already knew about this word, so he did not include it in his glossary.

VOLVELLE. A paper or VELLUM (usually) circular disk, attached to a LEAF in a book or on a card in such a way as to allow the volvelle to turn. The original idea was to enable readers to make astronomical, mathematical, or geological calculations. The disk was attached to the leaf (usually in the center) by a small piece of cord or vellum. Usually, printers left the points of attachment on both sides of the leaf blank so that the cords would not interfere with the printed text on the rear of the sheet. Some volvelles had more than one moving part: a circular disk on top of which was another moving pointer, or two or more rotating disks. These were sophisticated calculator-like contraptions that allowed for sophisticated calculations. (See Gravelle et al., "Volvelles.")

Though historically volvelles were parts of calculation tools (to find stars or constellations, for instance), they were also used in children's books. The volume *In Wonderland and What Is to Be Seen There. A Book of Revolving Pictures*, created by the important children's book publisher Ernest

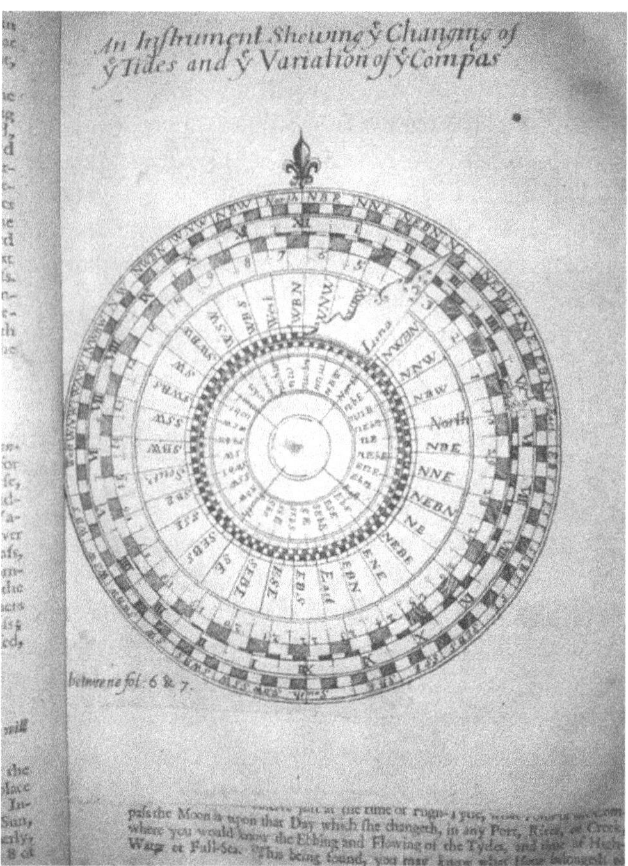

Another volvelle, this one from Samuel Sturmy, *The Mariners Magazine: or Sturmy's Mathematical and Practical Arts. Containing, The Description and Use of the Scale of Scales; It Being a Mathematical Ruler, That Resolves Most Mathematical Conclusions . . .*; 1st ed. (London: Printed by E. Cotes, 1669), showing the printed chart, the rotating disk, and the rotating "pointer." This one shows the changing of the tides and the variations of the compass. (In case you were wondering: the ellipsis in the title above saves you from having to read 295 more words from the title page! A typical 17th-century title.)

Courtesy of Phillips Library, Peabody Essex Museum.

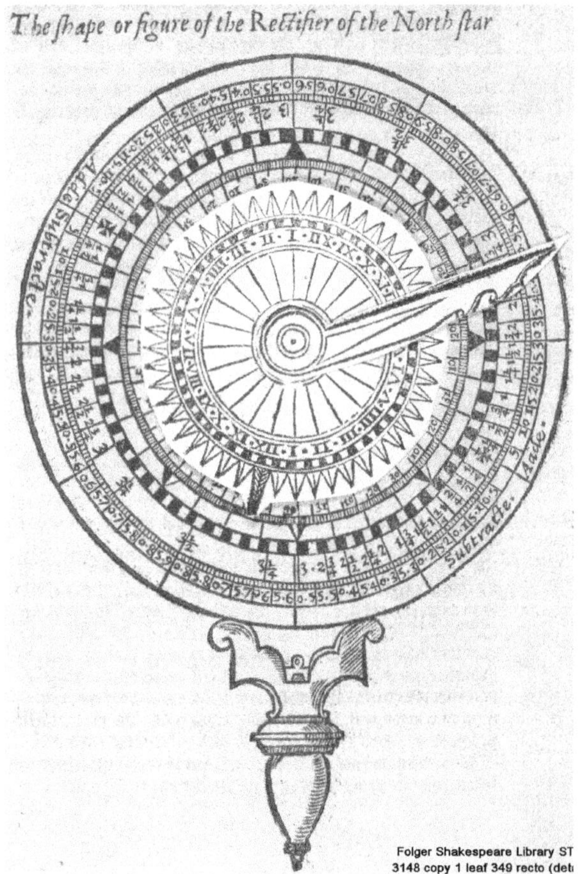

Volvelle designed to calculate the position of the North Star. Close examination will show that the page is printed with the outer circular text; the first part of the volvelle is attached (a smaller circular disk); and the "arm" or "pointer" is also attached, to rotate on its own. (Original in the Folger Shakespeare Library; http://collation.folger.edu/2012/08/folger-tooltips-digital-image-urls-part-one/ [accessed 23 June 2021].)

Courtesy of the Folger Shakespeare Library.

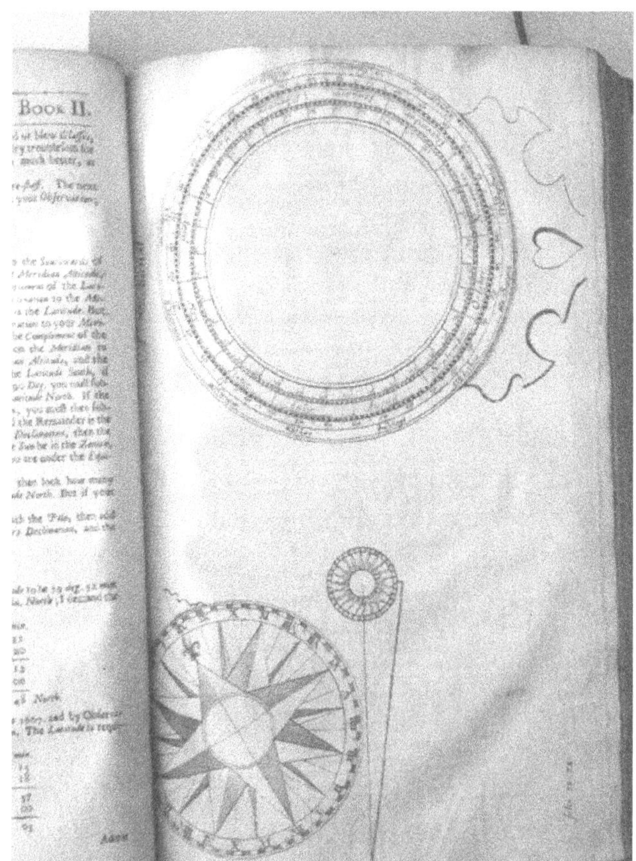

Volvelle in its state before being cut out and assembled. The publication, Samuel Sturmy, *The Mariners Magazine*, 3rd ed. (London: John Playford, 1684), printed the parts (the background circular "chart," the circular disk, and the "arm" or "pointer") and the buyer was expected to cut out the pieces and mount them onto the printed page.

Courtesy of Phillips Library, Peabody Essex Museum.

Nister (see the bibliography under the title), has eight such wheels. (*See* Movable books.)

VOYNICH MANUSCRIPT. One of the most baffling and infuriating MANUSCRIPTS to have surfaced in the last 150 years. The volume, at Yale University's Beinecke Rare Book & Manuscript Library, contains a hitherto unreadable text, and it has yet to be deciphered. The Yale website explains: "Wilfred M. Voynich, a rare-book dealer based in London, purchased a cache of medieval manuscripts from the Jesuit order in 1912. The transaction was conducted in secret. Its details remain unclear. / . . . There was one manuscript—a small volume bound in plain VELLUM—for which Voynich never found a buyer. Its 234 PARCHMENT pages are filled with an intricate and unreadable text, either a cipher or imaginary language. Strange illustrations of unidentifiable plants, mystifying astrological charts, and scenes of nude women bathing in green pools, accompany the inscrutable script on nearly every page. Several of its pages are foldouts—an unusual feature for a medieval manuscript. / While the mysterious manuscript contributed nothing to Voynich's bank account, its contents have tantalized and confounded scholars, professional code breakers, and amateur sleuths" (Cummings, "Mysterious Voynich Manuscript Reborn in Facsimile Edition"). Many volumes and articles have been published on this mysterious and thus-far undeciphered text.

Lisa Fagan Davis summarizes the situation this way: "It can be safely claimed that there is no medieval script that has been seen, analyzed, and debated more than that of the mysterious and as-yet-unread Voynich Manuscript (Beinecke MS 408). For centuries, bibliophiles, linguists, codicologists, art historians, and amateur cryptologists have pored over the manuscript, examining it from every angle, debating every wormhole, arguing over every stain and crease. Some things we know: the invented script is comprised of carefully-written glyphs without precedent or obvious model; forensic material evidence has determined that the parchment, ink, and pigments date from the early 15th century" (Davis, "How Many Glyphs and How Many Scribes? Digital Paleography and the Voynich Manuscript"). And though John Stojko has self-published *Letters to God's Eye: The Voynich Manuscript for the First Time Deciphered and Translated into English*; and Leo Levitov has published *Solution of the Voynich Manuscript: A Liturgical Manual for the Endura Rite of the Cathari Heresy, the Cult of Isis*, promising to tell us all we need to know about the manuscript's text, they can tell us nothing. A host of more reliable volumes will tell us what we do not yet know about the manuscript, which is far more than we actually know. (See, for instance, Kennedy and Churchill, *The Voynich Manuscript. The Unsolved Riddle of an Extraordinary Book Which Has Defied Interpretation for Centuries.*)

W.A.F. *See* With all faults.

WALLET EDGE. A kind of binding structure in which the material (usually LEATHER or LEATHERETTE) of the rear cover extends beyond the FORE-EDGE and around to the front cover; a protruding "tongue" or flap on the rear cover slips into a slit on the front cover to secure the volume and hold it closed. The structure is often used for pocket-sized volumes of notepads or calendars, and when these volumes are open, there are often pockets inside to hold coins or calling cards. There may also be a small loop somewhere on the volume that holds a thin pencil or pen. Often a decorated paper is used as a lining material in the little inner pockets.

WANTING. A bookseller's term for "missing," as in "rear endsheet wanting." I guess this sounds a bit more elegant than "rear endsheet missing." "Wanting" seems to minimize the sense of loss.

WANT LIST. A listing kept by a library or collector (or anyone else acquiring library materials) of items desired. (The items desired may be called "desiderata," and the list may be called that, too.) Collectors and librarians, in particular, are usually trying to fill in gaps in their collections, so the want list can be a guide for periodic searches for the elusive items. I have my own list, with some items sitting in it for decades. The longer an item has been on a want list, the more elated one feels when the item is located (and acquired). It is in the best interests of collectors to place these lists in the hands of booksellers. And many an online search service (*see* Online book sales) has a function that allows the collector to list wants. ABEBOOKS, for instance, has a link to "Save Your Search / Create a Want." Just another way to help collectors part with their resources.

WASHED. Carter has an entry (p. 258) on the CONSERVATION practice of washing LEAVES or entire volumes to remove stains and make the leaves or books "as good as new." He points out that washing removes the SIZING and that it is usually replaced, but the process leaves an odor. This odd statement does not conform to modern practices, though it may have been the case when Carter wrote. (I think his later editors should have emended this assertion.) This treatment has been used for many decades. The NEDCC leaflet 7.5, "Conservation Treatment for Works of Art and Unbound Artifacts on Paper," says, "Water washing is often beneficial to paper. Washing not only removes dirt and aids in stain reduction, but it can also wash out acidic compounds and other degradation products that have built up in the paper. Washing can also relax brittle or distorted paper and aid in flattening. For these reasons artifacts that are not visibly discolored or dirty might still benefit from washing. . . . When materials permit, objects are immersed in filtered water. On occasion, a carefully controlled amount of a chemical compound material is added to the water to raise the pH to a slightly alkaline level. This assists in the cleaning process and in the neutralization and removal of acids. Artifacts with soluble media may be locally washed, float-washed, or washed on a suction table" (NEDCC, https://www.nedcc.org/free-resources/preservation-leaflets/7.-conservation-procedures/7.5-conservation-treatment-for-works-of-art-and-unbound-artifacts-on-paper [accessed 23 June 2021]).

Although there does not seem to be a hint of sarcasm or disapproval in Carter's entry (he does point out that the French often ostentatiously wash books and PRINTS and that the English and Americans are much more subdued about their use of the treatment) and the NEDCC PAMPHLET speaks matter-of-factly about the process, the fact that an item (print, map, pamphlet, or whole book) has been washed does carry some stigma with it. It is a form of SOPHISTICATION, and such treatment should be part of the item's record. That is, a purchaser should be told that the item has undergone treatment. He should not be sold the item thinking it is in its original PRISTINE condition. And when an item in a library's collection undergoes any treatment, that should be noted in the cataloging record and in the item itself in some way. Further, the treatment usually entails pressing the washed leaves, usually flattening out whatever impression the printing type made when the piece came off the press, or the texture of the paper when it was first printed. This is a subtle but possibly important piece of information that could affect scholarly inquiry.

WASHI. The Japanese word for Japanese paper. While the word can signify merely paper, it often has the connotation of handmade paper. Many sheets are clearly not machine made or Western, and many booksellers, showing great "expertise," will use "washi" to designate the material in the items they are selling. But Asian papers of great beauty and quality can come from China, Korea, India (though those from India are often thick and rough and not of high quality), Tibet, Nepal, or other countries, and it is not possible to determine the country of origin. The word "washi" should be used only when the papers can be accurately determined to have come from Japan. (As an aside, in the Toronto company The Japanese Paper Place, with its thousands upon thousands of magnificent pieces of paper, the sign leading to their toilet says "Wash room." I suggested that they change that to "Washi room," but they declined.)

WASHINGTON PRESS. One of the standard, workhorse HANDPRESSES of the 19th and 20th centuries. These large, heavy machines were built to last, though untold numbers of them were melted down for armament in the 20th century. It was patented in 1821 by Samuel Rust, and, as James Moran tells us, the Washington press "was to become as famous as the Columbian and the ALBION" (*Printing Presses*, p. 79). The press uses a toggle (not a screw) mechanism for lowering the PLATEN. One of the problems with many presses was that, while it was easy to get the heavy platen down (gravity helped with that), it was not so easy to get it back up after the printer pulled the BAR. Rust used two heavy-duty springs on either side of the platen to raise it (by pushing it back up) after the bar was pulled, but that meant that the printer had to work against the springs to get the platen *down*. This required a strong pull of the bar. The press was a great hit, and R. Hoe and Company wanted to acquire it; through a stratagem, one of their employees was able to get Rust to sell the rights to the press, and Hoe acquired it from their employee (John Colby) in 1835 (see Moran, *Printing Presses*, pp. 79–81).

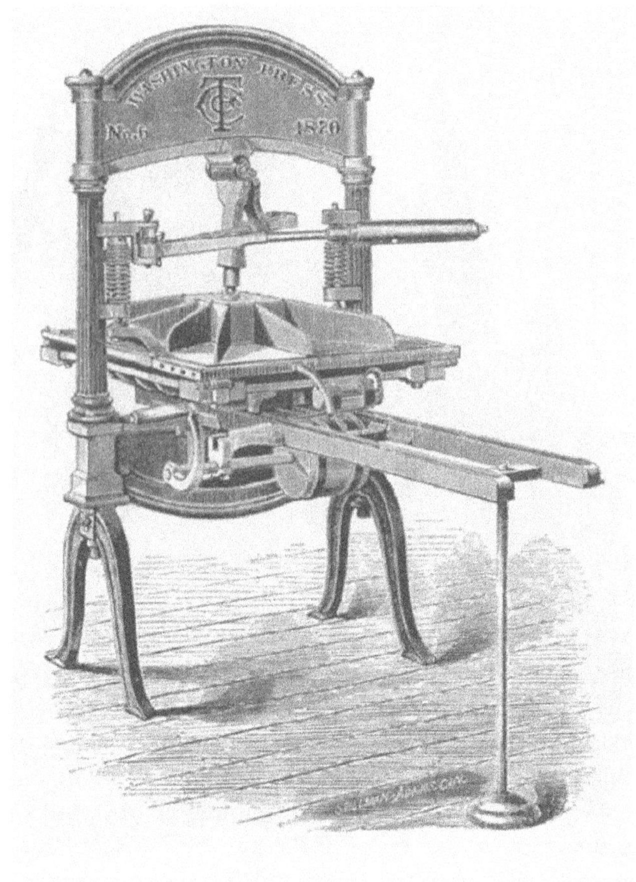

A Washington press.

While the press was made for LETTERPRESS printing, high-speed machinery and the development of newer and faster mechanical presses eventually ended the production of Washingtons. Many of these great old presses still reside in the workshops of hobby printers and FINE PRESSES, where the employment of all hand-driven tools and machines is preferred to mechanization. The Washington was used for several decades in the 20th century as a proof press—especially for illustrations. Today, a number of small fine presses use Washingtons. The MAKEREADY on them can be a challenge, but the final product on a well-maintained Washington can be beautiful. (For Columbian presses, *see* the entry for George Clymer.)

WASTE. *See* Printer's overruns.

WATCH. Writers, Artists, and Their COPYRIGHT Holders. An international database of inestimable value to help booksellers, librarians, scholars, and others determine who owns the COPYRIGHT of authors' materials. To go to press with the words or ideas of an author—especially one who has died within the last 70 years—one must often get PERMISSION. The HARRY RANSOM CENTER website says: "WATCH is a database of copyright contacts for writers, artists, and prominent people in other creative fields. It is a joint project of the Harry Ransom Center and University of Reading Library in England. Founded in 1994 as a resource principally for copyright questions about literary MANUSCRIPTS held in the U.S. and the U.K., it has now grown into one of the largest databases of copyright holders in the world. . . . All individuals and organizations listed as 'Contacts' in the WATCH File have indicated that they are the holder of an author's copyright for unpublished material or that they are the holder's representative or contact. All individuals have given written permission to have their names and addresses included in the WATCH File" (Harry Ransom Center, "About WATCH"). Note that the copyright holders guarantee that they hold the rights to *unpublished* materials; the holder of published materials may (and in many cases will) be different. Publishers often secure rights to publish materials. Also, the compilers of this information "have made no attempt to verify any individual's claim to copyright ownership or representation and cannot therefore be held responsible for any violations of copyright law which may follow use of the WATCH File. Scholars using this list are encouraged to verify such claims themselves before publishing anything on the basis of permissions received from people named in the list." This leaves the burden of proof of copyright ownership to the parties wanting to use the possibly copyrighted materials; but the database at least gives these users a place to begin research on ownership. Though a bit difficult to locate, the actual search engine is available at https://norman.hrc.utexas.edu/watch// (accessed 25 March 2021).

One problem with this database is that copyright ownership can shift from one party, institution, or other entity to another without the WATCH compilers' notice. Keeping the database up to date is a monumental task, and its compilers ask to be notified if someone learns of an inaccuracy or obsolescence in the information in the database.

WATERED SILK. *See* Silk moiré.

WATERLEAF. Paper made with macerated fiber and water, with no FILLERS. The paper is not SIZED, so it will allow ink to FEATHER. When most handmade paper is made, the fibers are matted into a sheet on the MOLD, and a sheet of waterleaf is created. Later it is sized. (*See* Bond paper; Sized/Sizing.)

WATERMARK. In the most common situation, a watermark is an area in a sheet of paper in which the pulp that forms the sheet is thinner than the pulp is around this area. The thinness of the accumulated fibers allows light to shine through the sheet more at the mark than elsewhere. Other kinds of marks are LIGHT-AND-SHADE WATERMARKS and THREE-PLANE WATERMARKS.

The simplest form of watermark is created from wires shaped to patterns or alphanumeric characters, attached by sewing or soldering to the surface of the paper MOLD. Imagine a coat-hanger type of wire shaped into the image of a bird or building, affixed to the mold. When the papermaker dips the mold into the VAT, the fibers fall over the mold's surface; the protruding wires make the fibers fall more thinly over them than they fall over the rest of the mold's surface. This thins the sheet where the wires are. The mark, then, is made by wires, not by water, despite the name of the phenomenon. Water does not make the mark. (The German word, *Wasserzeichen*, contains the same misnomer. The French *filigrane* and the Italian *filigrana* are somewhat better.) (*See below*, and also see the figure at entry for Vatman's tears.)

The areas where the paper is thinner are of two kinds: with images and with numbers or words (or both). The images can be geometric patterns or pictures of birds, houses, family crests, crowns, shields, buildings, or anything else that can be shaped in wires. Many sheets have watermarks

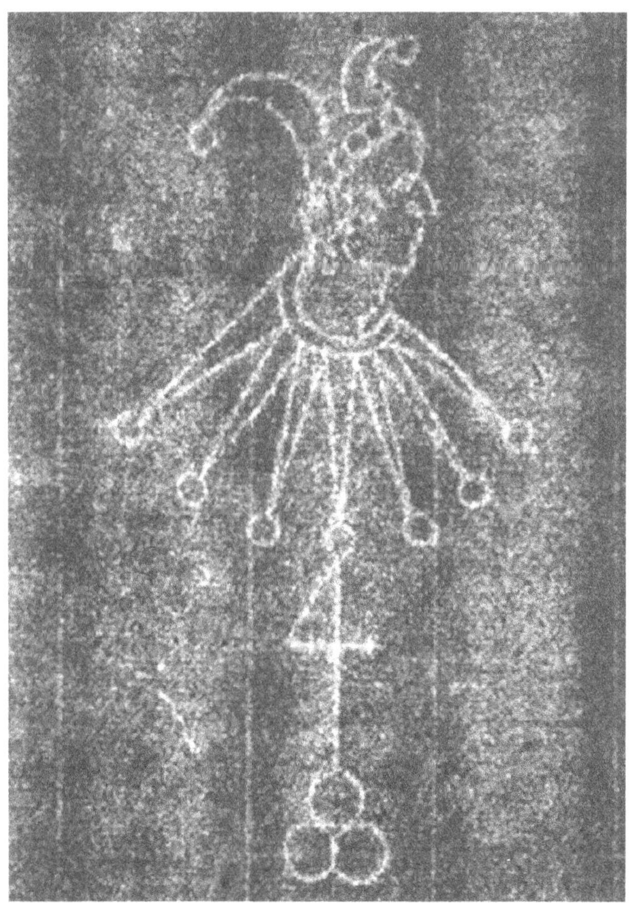

A foolscap wire watermark.
Courtesy of Delft University of Technology.

and COUNTERMARKS, the former being the main mark, usually an image of something, and the latter—on the opposite half of the sheet—usually have initials or the name of the papermaker, sometimes with a date, or other words. It is still a watermark, but when it faces a standard one, it is called the countermark.

Some watermarks, like that with a fool wearing a cap, give the sheet its name with respect to size (*see* Foolscap). A marvelous database of watermark reference tools is available at International Association of Paper Historians, "Online Watermark Databases/Catalogues."

The word "watermark" also refers to the wires that make the watermark. Thus, a craftsman can say, "I soldered the watermark to the mold."

The mold in many instances consists of two molds and one deckle. (*See* Mold [papermaking].) If the sheets to be produced with these tools are to be watermarked, then each mold has a watermark (and possibly also a countermark) on it. Allan H. Stevenson has shown this to be the case with many historical papers (see Stevenson, "Watermarks Are Twins"), and through the analysis of paper and their marks, he was able to prove that certain texts were printed later than some scholars claimed. (*See* Stevenson, Allan H.)

In machine-made paper, watermarks can be applied in two ways: (1) with the wires of the marks affixed to the wire mesh on the FOURDRINIER on which the sheets are formed or (2) with the use of a DANDY ROLL. In either case (with handmade or machine-made paper), watermarks can cover the entire sheet, as is often the case with SECURITY PAPERS. (*See* Briquet, Charles-Moïse; Tranchefiles.) (*See* figure of a watermark at the entry for Laid paper, and a light-and-shade watermark at the entry for that term.)

Watermarks are detectable with backlighting on the sheets they are in, or some watermark-detecting fluid can be used that wets the sheet but then dries, leaving no residue and not damaging the paper. (Stamp collectors use this fluid.) Some watermarks can be revealed with tracing or with the use of photosensitive papers. And low-voltage x-radiography and beta-radiography are used. (See Ash, "Recording Watermarks by Beta-Radiography and Other Means.") (See also Spector, ed., *Essays in Paper Analysis*. And Labarre's discussion is enlightening; see his *Dictionary and Encyclopaedia of Paper and Paper-Making*, pp. 328–60.)

A broad literature on watermarks exists, with many volumes showing great numbers of them. "The Paper Publications Society established in the Netherlands in 1948 published a series of books entitled *Monumenta Chartae Papyraceae Historiam Illustrantia* (National Diet Library, Japan, "The World of Watermarks"). And Thomas Gravell's "Watermark Archive" (http://www.gravell.org [accessed 23 June 2021]) and "Watermark Bibliography" (http://www.gravell.org/bibliography.php [accessed 23 June 2021]) are worth consulting.

WATERS, PETER (1930–2003). "An English bookbinder and conservator who studied bookbinding under William Matthews at the Guilford College of Art, Surrey after which he attended the Royal College of Art, London. He then worked for three years with ROGER POWELL before entering as a partner in the firm of Powell and Waters in 1956. In this same year, Waters succeeded Powell as lecturer in bookbinding at the Royal College of Art. From 1956 to 1971, he executed a number of bindings for private collectors, museums, and presentation, and worked with Powell in the repair and RESTORATION of a number of valuable books in the libraries of Trinity College, Dublin, Aberdeen and Winchester Universities, and others. In 1966 Waters served as consultant to the Biblioteca Nazionale Florence, Italy, as Technical Director for the restoration of flood-damaged collections and was principally responsible for the design and incorporation of the restoration system employed. From 1968 to 1971 he was codirector with James Lewis of a research project at the Imperial College of Science and Technology, London, relating to the conservation of library materials. In 1971 Waters was appointed Restoration Officer in the PRESERVATION Office of the Library of Congress. There he inaugurated new concepts and programs relating to the CONSERVATION of the Library's extensive collection of books, MANUSCRIPTS, maps, and other archival materials. / Waters' philosophy has been rooted in the Bauhaus tradition of 'fitness for purpose' in design, which through his extensive knowledge of book structure has found expression ranging from the binding of individual books to the planning of comprehensive conservation measures culminating in his now widely followed concept of 'phased preservation'" (Roberts and Etherington; "Peter Waters"; https://cool.culturalheritage.org/don/dt/dt3743.html [accessed 23 March 2021]).

WAX TABLET. A rectangular wooden tablet, with raised edges (forming a shallow "well" on the wooden surface), covered—in this well—with beeswax, usually on both sides. The stiff wax was the perfect surface for an author to write on. Writing surfaces like VELLUM were expensive. Authors needed a surface onto which to compose their texts, and they did not want to waste good PARCHMENT on rough drafts. The wax tablet would be incised with a STYLUS that had a sharp point at one end and a blunt or flat end for rubbing out unwanted text. The wax could be heated to "melt the whole text away" if the tablet was to be reused. Wax could cover both sides of the tablet, and two or more could be hinged or tied together to allow for a long text.

"Wax tablets of the town of Torun (Poland). Poliptych C, tablet Ia, 4v."

"Tablettes de cire" (wax tablets), hinged together to form a " book"; from Claude Mediavilla, *Histoire de la Calligraphie Française*, p. 11 (see bibliography).

WEB (World Wide Web). *See* Online book sales.

WEB PRESSES. *See* Rotary press.

WEEDING. *See* Appraisal; Deaccessioning.

WEE LITTLE BOOKS. *See* Big Little Books.

WEIGHT (of paper). "The weight of a REAM of paper of standard size; by extension the weight of a sheet of paper expressed as the weight of the standard ream of that same paper" (Lafontaine, comp., *Dictionary of Terms Used in the Paper, Printing and Allied Industries*, pages unnumbered [p. 23]). According to Labarre, "[W]eight of paper is expressed (in UK and US though the latter more frequently speaks of the 'basis weight' or the 'weight basis', etc.) in terms of weight per ream . . . of a definite number of sheets, indicating the size, usually large post . . . or demy" (Labarre, *Dictionary and Encyclopaedia of Paper and Paper-Making*, p. 297). ("Large post" and "demy" are designations of sizes of sheets, but these are not precise, as there was no standardization in the sizes of sheets until the 20th century. (*See* Appendix C, "Paper Sizes.") (See also *The Dictionary of Paper*, p. 34.) Labarre explains, "The 'substance' of the paper is the product of the density, i.e. the degree of dilution of the STUFF flowing onto the machine wire [of the FOURDRINIER], and the rapidity at which it is allowed to flow, plus the speed of the (machine) wire. The weight of a ream of a particular size and number of sheets is known as the substance number" (p. 297). So, for example, 500 sheets of 17 × 22-inch sheets weighing 20 pounds produces "20-pound paper." (*See* Rattle.)

WESTERN STATES & TERRITORIES PRESERVATION ASSISTANCE SERVICE. *See* Regional Alliance for Preservation.

WHATMAN, JAMES (1702–1759)/**WHATMAN PAPER.** "[T]he celebrated papermaker who established 'Turkey Mill,' Maidstone, Kent, England, in 1731" (Hunter, *Papermaking*, p. 16, n.). Dard Hunter says that Whatman "learned his trade from Lubertus van Gerrevink. Whatman at one time used the initials 'L V G' in his English-made paper, probably in honour of his master" (p. 16, n.). Working with JOHN BASKERVILLE, Whatman became the first papermaker to create WOVE PAPER. (For more discussion on this, *see* Baskerville, John. And see below.) Wove paper, made from a wire mesh (but see below), made possible the mechanical manufacture of paper. Until the Baskerville publication of his Virgil volume (ca. 1756–1757), all paper was made by hand and was LAID PAPER. Because the Whatmans (father and son James Whatman the Younger [1741–1798]) apparently made the first wove papers, the papers are often referred to as Whatman paper. But Baskerville is sometimes given credit for the invention of wove paper. However, A. T. Hazen casts some doubt on this and says, "If Baskerville did not manufacture, or invent, the first wove paper, however, it is of some interest to know who did. Baskerville was conscious of the effect of the paper in setting off his new types" (Hazen, "Baskerville and James Whatman," p. 187), and maybe he turned to Whatman for a new kind of paper.

Hazen says, "No paper-maker is known who would seem more likely to have invented wove paper than James Whatman, the man who lifted English paper-making from obscurity to pre-eminence. His association with Baskerville and with early wove paper seems sufficient to suggest that he (and his son) did in fact develop the first wove paper" ("Baskerville and James Whatman," p. 187). The implication is that Whatman's (or Baskerville's—or their combined efforts of the) innovation of making wove paper is suppositious.

Hazen also says, "The Vergil of 1757 is partly on a new paper perhaps made by placing woven wire or a stiff cloth screen on a conventional mould, since it is in effect an unwatermarked wove paper but shows translucent chain-lines" ("Baskerville and James Whatman," p. 188), and he immediately adds, "The second part and the CANCELS are on an excellent, unwatermarked laid paper with closely spaced CHAIN-LINES" (p. 188). This is curious, for if Baskerville wanted a smooth paper (without LAID LINES) to print his book, the *first* part would naturally be on laid paper, the second part on wove. (It is possible, however, for Baskerville to have had a batch of wove paper and use it to print the first part of the Virgil, then run out of it and supply the rest of the paper he needed from the store of laid papers he had on hand.) Provocatively, Hazen concludes that the documentary evidence "does link Whatman very firmly to Baskerville in connection with one book, and no other source of Baskerville's supply has ever been established. Furthermore, since Whatman had the same paper available for Capell's *Prolusions* in 1759, Whatman is clearly proved to be the first maker of wove paper *save for the unidentified maker of the experimental wove used for the first part of the Vergil*" (p. 188, emphasis added). Hazen concludes, "If I were seeking for the originator of wove paper for Western Europe, a quarter of a century before Johannot and Montgolfier [both in Paris] learned to make wove at Annonay, I would begin by studying the products of the Whatman mill" (p. 189). The conclusion is tentative though strong. The point is that scholars speaking of the invention of wove paper must not unequivocally give Whatman full credit. Nothing is proven, and all "proof" is circumstantial.

(That Baskerville was the inventor of this paper is part of British lore. In the 1988 novel *What Hetty Did*, we find that the book "is dedicated to the Memory of John Baskerville of Birmingham, who designed this type fount, invented wove paper and lost money cheerfully on particular books which he published" [Carr, *What Hetty Did*].)

And as for what Whatman used, there is much conversation, but seemingly the most authoritative view is that expressed by Cathleen A. Baker in her insightful and extensively researched article "The Wove Paper in John Baskerville's Virgil (1757): Made on a Cloth-Covered Laid Mould." Baker's is the latest, and perhaps the most authoritative and best-researched, view. This was what Hazen suggested.

The invention of wove paper made it possible for machines to put out sheets of whatever width the mill wanted and of immense lengths—the paper being produced on the FOURDRINIER screen and rolled onto a take-up reel. Having the paper in long rolls made it possible to mechanize printing on these long rolls. (See John Balston, *The Whatmans and Wove [Velin] Paper*; Thomas Balston, *James Whatman: Father and Son*.)

WHIP STITCHING. Roberts and Etherington describe this method of binding as follows: "The process of sewing single sheets into 'sections,' the number of sheets so sewn depending on the thickness of the paper. The 'sections' are then sewn on TAPES or CORDS in the usual manner of hand sewing" (Roberts and Etherington, "whip stitching"; https://cool.culturalheritage.org/don/dt/dt3776.html [accessed 25 May 2021]). The term has also been used to describe a binding technique in which the thread is run through STAB HOLES in the TEXT BLOCK and run over and over again around the SPINE of the item. This is often done for a single SIGNATURE, perhaps a PAMPHLET that has had its staples removed, or a QUIRE that has been removed from a larger volume. (*See* Oversewn.)

WHITE PAPER. A report written by experts concerning a particular topic—sort of a prolegomenon on the subject to inform readers about all of the practical and theoretical issues that the report covers, with informative commentary and tentative solutions. The aim is to help readers form their own opinions, solve problems, make decisions, or—at very least—have a grasp of the nature of the subject at hand. Sometimes, the white paper is used by a commercial company as a form of advertising. Also, according to TechTarget, "A white paper is an article that states an organization's position or philosophy about a social, political, or other subject, or a not-too-detailed technical explanation of an architecture, framework, or product technology. Typically, a white paper explains the results, conclusions, or construction resulting from some organized committee or research collaboration or design and development effort" ("White Paper Definition," https://whatis.techtarget.com/definition/white-paper [accessed 6 July 2021]). And Michael L. Stelzner says, "A white paper is a persuasive document that usually describes problems and how to solve them. The white paper is a crossbreed of a magazine article and a brochure. It takes the objective and educational approach of an article and weaves in persuasive corporate messages typically found in brochures" (Stelzner, "Writing White Papers"). (*See* Grey literature.) (See also Michael L. Stelzner, "How to Write a White Paper.") Depending on the subject matter of these documents, some white papers are highly COLLECTIBLE for those interested in the history of science or technology.

WHITE POST (also called the "pack"). A stack of newly made, still-wet sheets, after their first pressing, with the FELTS removed. (*See* Post. *See also* Layman.)

WHOLESALER'S BINDING. Carter gives two definitions: the term is sometimes used for "TRADE BINDING." He also says that wholesalers in the Regency (1811–1820) and early Victorian (1837–1901—so the *early* Victorian era would be from 1837 to ca. 1850, or at the death of Prince Albert in 1861) eras might buy copies of a book IN SHEETS and have them bound to their own specifications in a cover that differed from the one the original publisher used. He says that after EDITION BINDING became common (from about 1825), the practice was carried out less and less (see Carter, pp. 259–60). He then adds that a great number of wholesaler's cloth bindings were created from 1820 to 1845, using printed LABELS that were the same as the ones used by the original publisher. Sometimes, the bindings used by wholesalers and those used by the regular publisher are practically indistinguishable from one another, though a wholesaler's catalog bound into the volume will help scholars tell them apart. He also says that many collectors do not even know there is a difference in the two, and he recommends that they don't bother inasmuch as finding these volumes in their original binding is difficult enough (Carter, pp. 259–60). The practice was common for the publication of TRIPLE-DECKERS. The erudition that Carter displays here has pretty much melted away, and few booksellers or collectors today would know to make the distinction that Carter makes between publishers' and wholesalers' bindings, nor could they (as Carter says) always positively distinguish between the two.

WHOLE-STUFF. *See* Half-stuff.

WIDENER LIBRARY (Harvard University) (Harry Elkins Widener [1885–1912]). "The Harry Elkins Widener Memorial Library is Harvard University's flagship library. / Built with a gift from Eleanor Elkins Widener, it is a memorial to her son, Harry, Class of 1907. Harry was an enthusiastic young bibliophile who perished aboard the Titanic. . . . [It is] a facility of monumental proportions, with over 50 miles of shelves and the capacity to hold over three million volumes. / The library opened in 1915" ("Widener Library History," https://library.harvard.edu/libraries/widener#history [accessed 6 July 2021]).

Widener's collection contained "first editions of the authors and artists he loved best— especially Charles Dickens, Robert Louis Stevenson, and . . . and Robert Cruikshank[;] he soon branched out to include other literary notables like William Makepeace Thackeray, Charlotte Bronte, William Shakespeare, and William Blake. He also collected EXTRA-ILLUSTRATED and costume books . . . , original drawings, and MANUSCRIPTS. . . . The collection, given to Harvard by Widener's mother, Mrs. Eleanor Elkins Widener Rice, also contains a few notable items added by his family, including one of the few surviving copies of the GUTENBERG Bible, which was added to the collection in 1944 by Mr. George D. Widener on behalf of his sister, Mrs. Widener Dixon, and himself" ("Harry Elkins Widener Collection: Overview and History," https://library.harvard.edu/collections/harry-elkins-widener-collection [accessed 6 July 2021]). (See Battles, *Widener*.)

WIDOWS (in printing). Single lines at the top of a page that are the last word (or several words) of a paragraph from the previous page. This is looked upon by many book designers and typographers as anathema, and I have heard people fulminate about the careless idiots who have let such an unsightly thing occur. An ORPHAN, on the other hand—a single line at the beginning of a paragraph that is the last line on a page—is not so reviled. Microsoft Word has a feature—"Widow and Orphan Control"—that eliminates both of these stray lines, though the proscription of having orphans is not as great as is that for widows. These are particularly common in newspapers and magazines, which are often considered EPHEMERA and whose designers could not care a groat if there is a widow or an orphan.

WIKIPEDIA. One of the world's largest reference databases. (Its name is a portmanteau word coming from the Hawaiian *wiki*, meaning "fast," blended with "encyclopedia"; see the reference to "Wikimania" cited below in this entry.) It "is a free, multilingual online encyclopedia written and maintained by a community of volunteer contributors through a model of open collaboration, using a wiki-based editing system. Wikipedia is the largest and most-read reference work in history,[3] and is consistently one of the 15 most popular websites as ranked by Alexa; as of 2021, it was ranked as the 13th most popular site. The project carries no advertisements and is hosted by the Wikimedia Foundation, an American non-profit organization funded mainly through donations" (Wikipedia, "Wikipedia"; https://en.wikipedia.org/wiki/Wikipedia#cite_note-Wiki20-5 [accessed 6 July 2021]). (Note 3 cites "Wikipedia is 20, and its reputation has never been higher," *The Economist*, 9 January 2021.) Wikipedia was launched on 15 January 2001 by Jimmy Wales and Larry Sanger. "As of July 2021, Wikipedia articles have been created in 323 editions, with 312 currently active and 11 closed" (Wikipedia, "List of Wikipedias"; https://en.wikipedia.org/wiki/List_of_Wikipedias [accessed 6 July 2021]).

There are now Wikipedias in many languages. In the first edition of the present volume was the following: "The English Wikipedia is now one of more than 200 Wikipedias and is the largest with over 4.9 million articles. There is a grand total, including all Wikipedias, of nearly 35 million articles in 288 different languages" (Wikipedia), and these numbers are climbing at a fast rate. About 100,000 contributors write articles for Wikipedia ("Wikimania," CBS, *20/20* video, http://www.cbsnews.com/news/wikipedia-jimmy-wales-morley-safer-60-minutes [accessed 29 August 2015]). The preceding citation can now be brought forward: on the site "List of Wikipedias," we learn that "This page contains a list of all 321 languages for which official Wikipedias have been created under the auspices of the Wikimedia Foundation. The list includes 11 Wikipedias that were closed and moved to the Wikimedia Incubator for further development, so there is a current total of 310 active Wikipedias" (https://meta.wikimedia.org/wiki/List_of_Wikipedias [accessed 1 May 2021]). As of 1 May 2021, there was a total of 231,402,425 articles in all of these Wikipedias, with 6,289,936 of those in English ("List of Wikipedias"; https://meta.wikimedia.org/wiki/List_of_Wikipedias [accessed 1 May 2021]).

In its early days, the notion of a wiki—a site that anyone could contribute to—led to a good deal of inaccuracy in the site's articles. But with tighter controls on who contributes, who edits, and who permits articles to be added to or emended, the Wikipedia has become an increasingly accurate and all-encompassing reference tool. No article that it now contains is immutable, however, and corrections and additions (and even subtractions) can be made through formal, tightly controlled channels. (The Wikipedia entry is extensive and thorough.) The inaccuracies and intentionally embedded prank articles that the site once had (and may still have) have led many to think of the source as unreliable, a view difficult to overcome.

WILLIAMSTOWN ART CONSERVATION CENTER. *See* Regional Alliance for Preservation.

WING, DONALD G[ODDARD] (1904–1972) (*STC*). *Short-Title Catalogue of English Books, 1641–1700.* Wing was an associate librarian at Yale University from 1939 to 1970, in which position he was able to do immense amounts of bibliographical research, culminating in his behemoth work *A Short-Title Catalogue of Books Printed in England, Scotland, Ireland, Wales, and British America and of the English Books Printed in Other Countries, 1641–1700* (1945–1951), along with his complementary volume *A Gallery of Ghosts; Books Published between 1641–1700 Not Found in the Short-Title Catalogue* (1967). (*See* Ghosts.) The former of these strove to take up where POLLARD AND REDGRAVE left off, their own volume being *A Short-Title Catalogue of Books Printed in England, Scotland and Ireland and English Books Printed Abroad 1473–1640* (1926) (*see ESTC*). Wing's work was so impressive and reliable that it became the number one "go-to" reference tool for publications of the era that the text covered. In fact, scholars hardly referred to the original publications by their own titles; they would cite a Wing reference. Wing had almost 90,000 titles in his *STC*. (See also Crist, "Wing, Donald Goddard," pp. 868–69, and Cveljo, "Donald Goddard Wing.")

After the *STC* was published, Wing continued to add to the database. The second edition was published in four volumes as *Short-Title Catalogue of Books Printed in England, Scotland, Wales, and British America, and of English Books Printed in Other Countries, 1641–1700.* (*See* Pollard, Alfred William.) (See also Wing, "The Making of the 'Short-Title Catalogue, 1641–1700.' ")

WIRE LINES. Parallel, closely spaced lines visible in a sheet of LAID PAPER, running the long length of the sheet and at right angles to the CHAIN LINES. (*See* Antique laid paper; Dandy roll; Fourdrinier; Laid lines; Modern laid paper.) Carter's wording is strange, for he says that wire lines are "made by the wire mesh in the bottom of the frame." To begin with, there is no "mesh," which one sees in the production of WOVE PAPER. In a laid-paper MOLD, the wires that produce the wire lines are not part of a mesh; they are separate wires running parallel, sewn to the RIBS of the mold with a chain stitch. And Carter's incorrect "frame" should have been "mold." (One aim of the present *Dictionary* is to have people understand and use the proper vocabulary. Carter should have waited till this book came along.)

WISE, THOMAS J./WISE FORGERIES. One of England's fine bibliographers—or so he was hailed until JOHN CARTER and GRAHAM POLLARD exposed him as a forger of "PRE-FIRSTS." (But see the note at FORGERY.)

Wise was a BIBLIOPHILE who collected primarily the works of prominent 19th-century literary figures. His collection, which he called the Ashley Library, was a mecca for researchers, professional and amateur and commercial and scholarly.

As a serious collector of literary first editions, Wise became a learned bibliographer in the field, especially interested in drama and verse. As such, he had the trust of a generation of booksellers and collectors who relied on him for his bibliographical knowledge. An *Encyclopædia Britan-*

nica article says, "Thomas James Wise had the reputation of being one of the most distinguished private book collectors on either side of the Atlantic, and his Ashley Library in London became a place of pilgrimage for scholars from Europe and the United States. He constantly exposed PIRACIES and forgeries and always denied that he was a dealer. The shock was accordingly the greater in 1934 when John W. Carter and Henry Graham Pollard published *An Enquiry into the Nature of Certain Nineteenth Century Pamphlets*, proving that about 40 or 50 of these, commanding high prices, were forgeries, and that all could be traced to Wise. Subsequent research confirmed the finding of Carter and Pollard and indicted Wise for other and more serious offenses, including the SOPHISTICATION of many of his own copies of EARLY PRINTED books with leaves stolen from copies in the British Museum" (http://www.britannica.com/topic/forgery-art [accessed 23 June 2021]). (*See* Spanish forger; Trial edition.) (See Collins, *The Two Forgers*; Partington, *Forging Ahead*; and Todd, *Suppressed Commentaries on the Wiseian Forgeries*.) (*See also* Wrenn, John Henry, Library.)

WITH ALL FAULTS. Often abbreviated in dealers' or auction catalogs "w.a.f." This is a hint to the buyer or bidder that the item described is imperfect in some way (usually delineated in the item's description) and that the buyer should not expect the item to be PRISTINE. Note that the "a.f." indicates plural—there is not just one problem with the item, there are at least two, and (by implication) several. If this phrase (or abbreviation) appears in an auction catalog, the item will usually be "NOT SUBJECT TO RETURN."

WOLFENBÜTEL LIBRARY. *See* Herzog August Bibliothek.

WOODCUT/WOOD ENGRAVING/WOODBLOCK (also called "xylography"—from the Greek "xylo," meaning wood). An illustration or text (or both) carved into a block of wood—and then printable. Printing from woodblocks goes back to at least 220 BC. There are three methods of printing from blocks: stamping, rubbing, or with a press.

To demonstrate the quality of early scholarship, and to reinforce the importance of relying on such 19th-century sources as booksellers' catalogs, I quote the Barnard Quaritch paragraph on "xylography" from his *Catalogue of the Monuments of the Early Printers* (see the bibliography): "Xylography,—a term denoting that phase of wood-ENGRAVING in which certain inscriptions or portions of text were cut upon the block in addition to the pictorial design,—must have come into existence about the end of the fourteenth century. It seems to have reached its most flourishing period about the year 1450, and to have been chiefly cultivated in the Rhine-lands. It had probably a continued existence in Germany and Holland till near 1480: we find a belated specimen in 1509."

Carter makes this distinction: "Strictly speaking, a woodcut is cut with a knife along the plank, while a wood-engraving is cut with a graver or BURIN on the cross-section or end-grain, usually of a piece of box-wood. The latter makes for harder wood and therefore permits a much greater delicacy in the design." However the BLOCK is made, it is a form of RELIEF printing. Carter adds that the terms have come to be used pretty much interchangeably for any image that was printed from a wood surface (as opposed to a metal one). And he says that even images printed from an electro (*see* Electrotype), which itself was made from a wood original, may be called a woodcut. And indeed, electrotypes did produce extremely faithful reproductions of original type- or woodcut-based originals. (See Carter, pp. 260–61.)

Some people trying to be purists say that a wood engraving is just that: an engraving. Therefore, it is an INTAGLIO printing method, not a woodcut (or a woodblock), which is block printed from a relief surface. A woodblock is always a relief print. Woodblocks were usually on a TYPE-HIGH block so that they could be imposed (*see* Imposition) and printed with the type in the CHASE. A single inking operation was all that was needed if the woodblock was printed (with the same colored ink) along with the type. But there was a way to lock up the FORME so that the block could be taken out, inked in a second color or with a different kind of ink, slipped back into the chase, and printed along with the text (or other illustrations) on the page. This allowed for two color printing without the printer's having to put the text into the press for a second PRESSRUN to achieve the second color.

These three terms (and, as Carter says, along with the possibility that an illustration is printed from an electrotype) are run together in many people's minds, and they are used interchangeably without the user's being able to distinguish one kind of printing from another or knowing that there are shades of difference between one and another of the terms. In fact, with steel engravings, another wrinkle is added since it is sometimes difficult to distinguish the printing from wood from the printing done with a metal block.

In early printing, it is not uncommon for printers to reuse blocks to save time and money. Hence, in many an HERBAL, an illustration could be used to represent more than one plant. And in the *Nuremberg Chronicle*, images of cities or people might be used three or more times to represent more than one city or person.

Because "wood engraving" or "wood block" does not sound as learned or exotic as "xylographica," this latter term is often used to denote texts printed from wood.

WOOD LETTER. Thadani's odd addition to the *ABC* (9th ed., p. 261). A more proper term is WOOD TYPE. The phrase "wood letter" may exist out there, but "letter" is too narrow a word, and those in the know will know that "letter" could include numbers, punctuation, spacing matter, decorative pieces of all kinds, and images, all made from wood.

WOOD PULP. Papermaking fibers made from wood. There are two types: chemical wood pulp and mechanical wood pulp. Chemical pulp "is wood reduced to pulp by a chemical process, e.g. boiling or 'digesting.' (1) with caustic-soda solution (soda pulp/process). (2) with caustic soda and sulphate of soda (SULPHATE pulp/process). (3) with bi-sulphite of lime (sulphite pulp/process)" (Labarre, *Dictionary and Encyclopaedia of Paper and Paper-Making*, p. 46). Mechanical pulp "is a papermaking material so called from the fact that it is prepared from logs of wood by purely mechanical means (grinder) as opposed to chemical wood pulps, and used in contrast to wood free [see below]; ordinary mechanical wood pulp, though varying in tint from cream to fawn, depending on the natural color of the wood, is called white, as brown mechanical pulp undergoes treatment before grinding" (p. 160). (Labarre says that "wood free" means the paper pulp "is free from mechanical wood pulp . . . and is also a term applied to a paper manufactured from pure sulphite wood pulp" [p. 367].)

As the names of these pulps suggest, paper made from the mechanical pulp is less likely to deteriorate from the INHERENT VICE of the chemicals, but in fact, lignin in the wood is acidic. Roberts and Etherington say, "Lignin is usually determined as the residue left on hydrolysis of the plant material with strong acids after resins, waxes, tannins, and other extractives have been removed" (p. 159). And chemical pulp, if not properly washed during its manufacture, leaves a residue of the chemicals in the paper, another inherent vice.

On 12 October 1990, the United States passed the Permanent Paper Law, or P.L. 101–423, "[t]o establish a national policy on permanent papers . . . [because] it is now widely recognized and scientifically demonstrated that the acidic papers commonly used for more than a century in documents, books, and other publications are self-destructing and will continue to self-destruct; [and] Americans are facing the prospect of continuing to lose national, historical, scientific, and scholarly records, including government records, faster than salvage efforts can be mounted despite the dedicated efforts of many libraries, archives, and agencies, such as the Library of Congress and the National Archives and Records Administration. . . . [Hence,] [i]t is the policy of the United States that Federal records, books, and publications of enduring value be produced on acid free permanent papers" ("Text of the Permanent Paper Law," *Alkaline Paper Advocate*, http://cool.conservation-us.org/byorg/abbey/ap/ap03/ap03-5/ap03-504.html [accessed 23 June 2021]). With the prospect of losing government contracts if they did not have large supplies of archival paper for sale, many paper mills in the United States converted their production to archival, acid-free, lignin-free paper. Thus, it is clear that wood pulp, still the main source of fibers for paper, can be made archival. But former Vice President Al Gore pushed for recycled papers to be used for government publications, which may not be permanent/durable (the designation of "archival"). And since now most government publications are digital, the influence of P.L. 101–423 was short lived.

WOOD TYPE. Printing type made from wood. They can be alphabetical characters, numbers, punctuation, SPACING, decoration of all kinds (scrollwork, FLEURONS, MEANDERS [Greek keys], BORDERS, or even images). Metal type is heavy, especially in the larger sizes. For display FONTS (*see* Display type), printers needed a lighter material; type made from wood was the answer. Woodblock printing had been in existence since at least 220 BC. (*See* Block book.) In the West, the practicality of using wood over metal was clear, and for the larger sizes of type (larger than was used in newspapers or books), the use of wood was a desideratum. "The difficulty in their manufacture was that the process was so slow that even the most expert man could make only a few in a day" (*American Dictionary of Printing and Bookmaking*, p. 586).

"In America, with the expansion of the commercial printing industry in the first years of the 19th century, it was inevitable that someone would perfect a process for cheaply producing the large letters so in demand for BROADSIDES. Wood was the logical material because of its lightness, availability, and known printing qualities. . . . / Darius Wells of New York invented the means for mass producing letters in 1827, and published the first known wood type catalog in 1828. In the preface to his first wood type catalog, Wells outlined the advantages of wood type. Wood type was half the cost of metal type, and when prepared by machine it had smooth, even surfaces, where the possibility of unequal cooling caused large lead type to distort. / Up until that time, the usual procedure was to draw the letter on wood, or paper which was pasted to the wood, and then cut around the letter with a knife or graver, gouging out the parts to be left blank. Wells, however, introduced a basic invention, the lateral router, that allowed for greater control when cutting type and decreased the time it took to cut each letter" (Hamilton Wood Type & Printing Museum, "What Is Wood Type?"; https://woodtype.org/pages/what-is-wood-type [accessed 23 June 2021]). Eventually, a machine was invented to speed up the carving process: the PANTOGRAPH ("an instrument for copying a plane figure to a desired scale, consisting of styluses for tracing and copying mounted on four jointed rods in the form of a parallelogram with extended sides"; *American Heritage Dictionary of the English Language*, p. 1274). The pantograph had a stylus on one end and a router on the other.

In recent years, huge quantities of wood type have been showing up at flea markets and garage sales and in antiques stores, to be sold one character at a time, thus breaking up rare fonts and doing a disservice to scholarship (as has been done by BREAKERS and those compiling LEAF BOOKS). (For an image, *see* figures at Inline and at Ligature.) (*See* Hamilton Wood Type Museum.)

WOOKEY HOLE PAPER MILL. An early British handmade-paper mill. Dard Hunter says that in 1610, "[p]apermaking at Wookey Hole, Wells, Somerset, [was] recorded for the first time. The W. S. Hodgkinson and Company mill, one of the five surviving handmade-paper mills in England, is an outgrowth of this original establishment" (Hunter, *Papermaking*, p. 481). Hunter was writing in 1943. Since then, the Wookey Hole mill has ceased to be a commercial establishment—it closed down its profit-making activities in February 2008. Its owner, Gerry Cottle, disposed of the historic equipment when he determined that the mill was no longer productive enough to keep open.

This paper mill supplied beautiful, all-rag paper to innumerable FINE-PRESS PRINTERS for centuries. It was one of the last of the handmade papermakers in England. (*See* Barcham Green Paper Mill.)

WOOLF, VIRGINIA (1882–1941). Prominent author whose contributions to the book world were not merely literary. She and her husband Leonard Woolf founded the Hogarth Press in 1917. After her death, Leonard Woolf and John Lehman ran the press until 1946, when it became an associate company of Chatto & Windus. Vanessa Bell (1879–1961) created many cover designs for their publications. As Duncan Heyes explains, under the Woolfs and after, the press "published works by key modernist writers as well-important works in translation. . . . In 1921 they bought a larger printing press and increased their activities to the extent that the Press was transformed from a hobby to a largely commercial publisher. The SUBSCRIPTION system of selling books was discontinued, and they started selling books directly to booksellers. . . . Under his [John Lehman's] influence the Hogarth Press published works by an emerging new generation of poets and writers such as Stephen Spender, W H Auden, Julian Bell, Cecil Day Lewis and the novelist Christopher Isherwood. Leonard and John Lehmann ran the press for eight years but increasingly could not agree on the direction it should take. The disagreements came to a head in 1946 when Leonard decided to terminate the partnership, buying out John's share which he then sold to Chatto and Windus" (Heyes, "The Hogarth Press"). Heyes adds that "in 1924 the Hogarth Press became the publisher of the International Psycho-Analytical Library, and as such the Woolfs were the first to publish the complete works of Sigmund Freud in translation." Under the Woolfs and Lehmann, the press published 527 titles; it is now under the aegis of Penguin Random House.

WORD SPACING. The use of spaces between words in text. Uniformity of spacing between words is ideal since variations in such spacing can lead to a diminution of LEGIBILITY in challenging the reader to make small mental adjustments from one line of type to the next. In HANDSET TYPE composition, the COMPOSITOR merely puts in the same width space between words. This is not a problem in an UNJUSTIFIED (i.e., ragged-right) line since the compositor merely ends the setting of the line when the next word will not fit into the COMPOSING STICK and sets it as the first word of the next line. But if the text is JUSTIFIED (flush-right), with a character at the very right margin of every line, the line may need to be spaced out a bit to allow for such a stretched-out text, or the line may need to be tightened up to allow for the last character(s) to fit into the line. Either way, the word spacing suffers, yielding more or less space, respectively, between words so that the text is justified for each individual line and not guaranteeing that the same spacing will exist for text in successive lines. The problem was, of course, that neighboring lines (above and below) may have needed different spacing between words to achieve a justified text. This was a particular problem with machine typesetting, as with the Linotype machine. The solution for that device was to justify with SPACEBANDS, which helped the compositor get even word spacing in a single line, but, even with the Linotype's spacebands, it did not guarantee that the same amount of spacing would apply in lines above or below. Even with proportional spacing made possible with computer typesetting, achieving uniform word spacing throughout a justified text can be impossible. Witness lines of text in a newspaper today, with a single word (in a column narrowed by an accompanying illustration) having to be spaced out from margin to margin, the letters far apart, and the following line so tightly set that the words run together with seemingly no space between them. (*See* Typesetting.)

WORK-AND-TURN. *See* Half-sheet imposition.

WORKED HEADBAND. *See* Headband.

WORK FOR HIRE. *See* Ghostwriter.

WORKING COPY. *See* Reading copy.

WORKS CITED. *See* References.

WORLDCAT. *See* OCLC.

WORLD WIDE WEB. *See* Online book sales.

WORM HOLES; WORMED (sometimes spelled as one word—wormholes). Holes made in MANUSCRIPTS and printed books by the larvae of various "bookworms." Such a volume is often said to be "wormed." As Roberts and Etherington say, "There are some 160 species of beetles which can be responsible for these holes. . . . Of the types, the most notorious and destructive are: *Sitodrepa paniceum*, the drugstore beetle, the female of which is capable of producing as many as 800,000 descendants in a year; *Lyctus brunneus*, the powder-post beetle, which consumes wooden bookshelves and cases, packing the holes with a flourlike debris, so that nothing substantial remains of the shelf; *Ptinus fur*, the spider beetle, first mentioned by Linnaeus in 1766, which can cause severe damage to books, papers, and leather if left undisturbed for long periods of time; *Anobium punctatum*, the common furniture beetle, the larvae of which bore long cylindrical holes in books and bookshelves; *Catorama mexicana*, the Mexican book beetle; *Dermestes lardarius*, the larder beetle, which prefers cheese, ham, etc., but which will devour leather if nothing else is available; and *Rhizopertha dominica*, which has caused extensive damage in libraries" (p. 36). They add, "They enter libraries through windows, poorly fitting doors, etc., and seem to proliferate in libraries where dust, dirt, heat, darkness, and poor ventilation are prevalent" (p. 36). There are several ways to get rid of them. (See the Northeast Document Conservation Center preservation manual 3.10, "Integrated Pest Management," https://www.nedcc.org/free-resources/preservation-leaflets/3.-emergency-management/3.10-integrated-pest-management [accessed 23 June 2021]).

The holes these creatures make can go anywhere in the volume—even through the boards (wooden or CARDBOARD) used in the binding. Peter Beal points out that sometimes the holes made by these creatures can be helpful to scholars in revealing how a book with no FOLIATION or PAGINATION was put together. Sometimes the leaves of these volumes are pulled apart, as with a rebinding, and the worm holes can indicate the original order of the LEAVES or SIGNATURES. By realigning the worm holes, one can figure out the original sequence of the leaves. He points out how this kind of information was useful in assessing the authenticity of the Vinland Map, which claims to be created in the middle of the 15th century. If this is the case, then Columbus was not the first European to discover the New World—the Vikings did. He points out that the worm holes show that the text was once in a volume with other contemporary manuscripts, and there is no doubt of the authenticity of the others. (See Beal, *A Dictionary of English Manuscript Terminology, 1450–2000*, p. 442.) The leaves may perhaps be reassembled in the correct order by aligning the worm holes in them, or else the worm hole may show which leaf was once adjacent to or CONJUGATE with another. Also, it is possible that a BIBLIOCLAST has removed a leaf from a volume to TIP INTO and SOPHISTICATE his own copy; this would be detectable if the leaf had a worm hole in it (or if his volume had a worm hole through it and the replacement leaf did not).

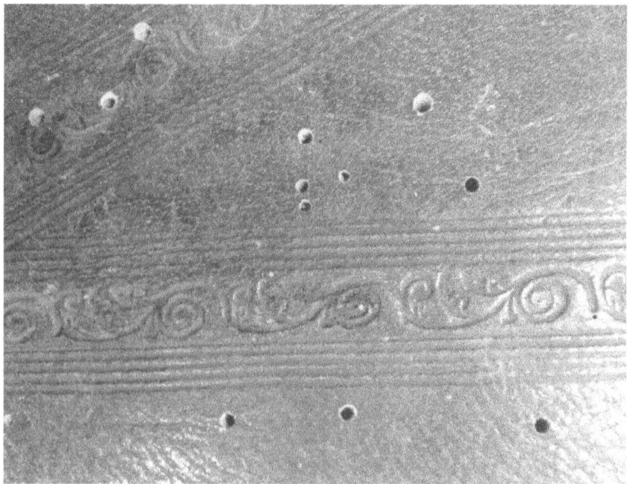

Worm holes right through the wooden boards of an unidentified medieval manuscript.
Courtesy of Phillips Library, Peabody Essex Museum.

WOVE PAPER. Paper made on a woven screen (or possibly—quite early—on a screen covered with a cloth), with no CHAIN LINES or WIRE LINES (for a discussion, *see* Whatman, James—especially the paragraph that references Cathleen A. Baker's article "The Wove Paper in John Baskerville's Virgil (1757): Made on a Cloth-Covered Laid Mould"). This paper can be machine made or handmade. (*See* Laid paper.) If the paper is made on a FOURDRINIER, it is wove paper, though it can be given the appearance of laid paper if the screen of the machine has the laid-paper pattern on it or if a DANDY ROLL imparts that pattern into the sheet. It is difficult sometimes to see if a sheet of wove paper with the LAID LINES in it is machine- or handmade. The paper, of course, can also be handmade, but whether a product of the hand or the machine, the sheet can be made with the same materials as is used in both kinds, and a scholar will be hard put to determine from the final product what the method of manufacture was. Scientific examination under a microscope will reveal the direction the fibers are sitting in (machine-made paper's fibers line up; those in handmade paper do not). The surface of the sheet of wove paper can be rough, but so can the surface of any paper that has not been CALENDERED. Hence, for Carter to say that wove paper has "an uneven, granulated texture" is simply wrong. A sheet of wove paper that has been calendered will not have a rough texture. He also asserts that this kind of paper was invented by James Whatman, though that assertion has been challenged. (See John Balston, *The Whatmans and Wove (Velin) Paper* in the bibliography. The entry in the present volume at "Whatman, James" discusses this in detail.)

WRAPAROUND BAND. (Sometimes called "belly band" or "tummy band.") A thin strip of paper (or other material) that encircles a volume, sometimes just to hold a new volume closed, sometimes carrying printed or manuscript information about the volume. For example, the band could be wrapped around a volume when it is sent out, carrying only a penciled-in number, showing what number the book is of a NUMBERED edition. Or it could be printed with an advertisement-like statement, a BLURB, or a notice that since the book was published, it has won a prize. One volume from KIM MERKER, *Kenney's* (*see* As issued), has a wraparound band with a printed notice that says, "For legal reasons, a paragraph has been excised from the introduction." (See Berger, *Printing and the Mind of Merker*, p. 40.) These bands, of course, must be removed for anyone to open the volume, and most of them fall under the rubric "EPHEMERA." Collectors, however, wanting their books the way they were issued from the publisher, will certainly want the bands, knowing that without them the volumes are incomplete and thus worth less than ones with the bands.

There are also bands that do not wrap around the entire volume, but which go around the spine and have flaps that tuck into the front and rear cover. These are still called "wraparound bands." (Such a volume is that of Alexandra Soteriou, *Gift of the Conquerors*.)

WRAPPER(S) (also called "wraps"). This term was originally used to mean the covering of a book or PAMPHLET that was made from paper—either a thin sheet or a heavy but still flexible one, but it could also have been made from VELLUM that was not over BOARDS. Also, the sheet of paper could have been mounted to cloth. Today, a modern paperback can be said to be "in wrappers" or, as we see in DEALERS' CATALOGS, "in wraps." Early wrappers were plain, with the idea that the wraps were to protect the TEXT BLOCK until the owner had the volume bound in her own covers. (See Cloonan, *Early Bindings in Paper*.) But the wrappers called out to be decorated, and they were a good place to write or print the title of the volume and whatever other information the owner or publisher decided to put onto them. Also, the standard forms of decoration (MARBLING, PASTE PAPER, or printing) can be applied to the wrappers, making them attractive enough to rival leather as a permanent binding material. Michèle Cloonan says, "The earliest known specimen [of a book in wrappers], dated 1482, is a paper woodcut wrapper from Augsburg, where at least five were made" (*Early Bindings in Paper*, p. 5, citing Sadleir, *Evolution of Publishers' Binding Styles, 1700–1900*, pp. 13–14). Now, strictly speaking, the term should be singular (wrapper) since the cover would have generally been a single piece of paper or other material. Jacob Blanck makes it clear: "The wrapper is a single piece of paper which serves as the cover of a book or pamphlet and is not an integral part of the printed sheets comprising the text, but an element added by the binder" (Blanck, *Bibliography of American Literature*, vol. 1, p. xxix). To say that a volume is "in wrappers" (or "in wraps") makes it sound as if there is more than one wrapper. But tradition has it to use the plural form, and who are we to buck tradition? (*See* Cover.)

WRENN, JOHN HENRY, LIBRARY (John Henry Wrenn, 1841–1911). "One hundred years ago today, The University of Texas acquired a collection of 6,000 first and rare editions of mostly seventeenth- and eighteenth-century English and American authors, in addition to notable MANUSCRIPTS of the Bronte sisters, Alfred Lord Tennyson, and the Brownings. This collection, known as the Wrenn Library, would plant the seed for what is today the Harry Ransom Center. / In order to help the university build its reputation as a major research institution during its formative years, university regent benefactor Major George Washington Littlefield signed a $225,000 check dated February 21, 1918, to acquire the library of the late Chicago businessman John Henry Wrenn" (Page, "University's Foundational Rare Book Collection Acquired a Century Ago"). An earlier (but now lost) link for the library explained: "He purchased many books from the English bibliographer and collector THOMAS J. WISE, later identified as a master FORGER. As a result, the Wrenn Library contains nearly one hundred examples of Wise's spurious 19th-century PAMPHLETS and many copies of 17th-century plays which Wise is known to have 'improved' with leaves torn from British Museum copies" (HARRY RANSOM CENTER, University of Texas, Austin, "John Henry Wrenn Library," http://www.hrc.utexas.edu/collections/books/holdings/wrenn [accessed 28 August 2015]).

WRITERS, ARTISTS, AND THEIR COPYRIGHT HOLDERS. *See* WATCH.

WRITING BOOKS. Books about CALLIGRAPHY—historical and practical. That is, some give the history and development of calligraphy, some exhibit the work of one or more great calligraphers, and some show the reader how to do it. (*See* How-to books.) Most of these are illustrated with COPPERPLATE ENGRAVINGS, WOODCUTS, or other images of the work of masters, and many have blank/ruled pages for readers to try their skills. Books about writing are related to, but a separate genre from, PENMANSHIP MANUALS, which aim to train practitioners in writing.

In recent years, a particular sub-genre of writing book has been recognized: the ciphering book. This consists of calligraphic texts copied from a master copy, containing alphabets, arithmetic, geometry, some drawing, and ships' logbook-like texts in which the writer "records" longitude and latitude, weather, astronomical readings, and so on. Hundreds of these volumes were produced by children—girls and boys—in schools in New England, copying from master copies, so that a group of ciphering books might have identical (or nearly identical) texts. The students were learning academic subjects along with calligraphy. (The term "ciphering books" has nothing to do with ciphers—i.e., codes.) (See Ellerton and Clements, *Rewriting the History of School Mathematics in North America, 1607–1861.*)

XEROGRAPHY. A word invented to give glossaries words to have under the letter *X*. The word actually combines the Greek *xēro* ("dry") with the Latin *graphis* ("writing"). Xerography is "a dry photographic or photocopying process in which a negative image formed by a resinous powder on an electrically charged plate is electrically transferred to and thermally fixed as positive on a paper or other copying surface" (*American Heritage Dictionary of the English Language*, p. 2003). The basic principle of xerography was invented by Pál Selényi (1884–1954). "Selényi's most important invention in industrial physics was the process of electrography. He produced pictures of good quality on waxed paper stretched on [a] manually rotated roller, and he also developed a variant of this method suitable for displaying television pictures. He also constructed an oscillograph on the basis of the same principle and its advantage was that it recorded the picture in a simpler and quicker way than photographing the picture of a conventional oscillograph. His research in electrostatic picture recording gave the basis of xerography" ("Selényi, Pál," http://www.omikk.bme.hu/archivum/angol/htm/selenyi_p.htm [accessed 27 July 2021]), but it was Chester Carlson who took out the patent for it in 1942: "In 1937, the process called Xerography was invented by American law student Chester Carlson. Carlson had invented a copying process based on electrostatic energy. Xerography became commercially available in 1950 by the Xerox Corporation" (Bellis, "The History of Xerox," http://theinventors.org/library/inventors/blxerox.htm [accessed 6 July 2021]).

Some book artists incorporate Xeroxing and color photocopying into their ARTISTS' BOOKS. Purist collectors and booksellers shy away from such mechanically produced items despite the beauty, ingenuity, and quality of some of the pieces. A similarly strong reaction to Leonard Baskin's *Mokomaki* was heard in the FINE-PRESS world when Baskin revealed that that volume was printed offset. (*See* Offset printing.) Xerography and color photocopying have opened up new avenues to book production and have brought down the cost of including color images in books and PAMPHLETS. Though the term can be construed as generic, the company called Xerox has led most people to use the capitalized form of the word as a brand name.

X-HEIGHT. The height of a character from its foot to the top of its base element, as with the LOWERCASE *x*. (*See* Ascenders; Descenders.)

X-RATED. *See* Curiosa; Erotica.

XYLOGRAPHY. *See* Wood engraving.

XYLOTECH. A collection of items—often in book form—that contains samples of various kinds of wood. The samples are often thin slices from the trees, transverse, and cut at other angles, to show the wood and its grain pattern. As book structures, and also as examples of various trees, these are COLLECTIBLE in the book world, and are also excellent reference collections to reveal the kinds of wood used in bindings (when that wood is visible). Xylotechs are often revelatory of the woods of particular areas, and they can hold hundreds or thousands of specimens. Theresia Sufa of *The Jakarta Post* newspaper notes that Indonesia has over 4,000 types of wood, and that The Netherlands has a xylotech with 125,000 specimens, but that the collection in Indonesia is larger: "On Sept. 23, [2018,] the ministry will declare Xylarium Bogoriense as the xylarium with the largest collection in the world, with 185,647 specimens" (Sufa, "Ministry to Name Bogor's Xylarium World's Largest Wood Collection." See also Lovejoy, "Xyloteks").

Y

YAPP BINDING/YAPP EDGES. "A style of binding featuring a cover (LEATHER, or other material, but customarily leather) that overlaps the three edges of both upper and lower covers continuously. The covers are always LIMP or semi-flexible, and are sometimes fitted with a zipper, which was a later refinement. Yapp books, named after the English bookseller of the second half of the 19th century, William Yapp, always have round corners, and the ENDPAPERS are frequently made from a 'surface' paper, usually black. The edges are sometimes GILT, frequently over red, or are stained or otherwise colored. The Yapp style is especially associated with books of devotion (almost exclusively today), although a half century ago books of verse were sometimes bound in somewhat similar covers" (Roberts and Etherington, p. 286). The folded edges are sometimes called "circuit cover extensions." (*See* Limp leather/Limp vellum. *See also* Circuit binding.) The edges, then, extend out from the three exposed edges of the TEXT BLOCK, and sort of "bend over" or fold down a bit.

Yapp-style binding; drawing by Margaret R. Brown; in Roberts and Etherington, p. 286.

Courtesy of Library of Congress.

YAWNING BOARDS. BOARDS of a binding that splay away from the TEXT BLOCK at the FORE-EDGE. Such poorly constructed bindings may cover a book that makes the reader yawn, too.

YELLOWBACKS. (Sometimes hyphenated.) "Yellowbacks are a distinctive category of cheap books which began to appear in the middle of the nineteenth century, at about the same time as W. H. Smith's first railway bookstalls. Described by Richard Altick as 'the most inspired publishing invention of the era', their eye-catching glazed paper covered boards, and revolutionary low price of one or two shillings, were deliberately designed to appeal to the growing reading and travelling public" (Elizabeth James, "Aspects of the Victorian Book: Yellowbacks"). Most of these books, whose name is of course derived from the color of their cover papers, were cheap fiction, REPRINTS of the work of popular contemporary writers. Elizabeth James points out that many of these writers were happy to earn some new income from these inexpensive volumes. She adds that the books "included a large number of American writers, whose work was conveniently unprotected under British law until the last decade of the century. A few publishers, such as George Routledge whose Railway Library dominated the genre, also experimented with new books and non-fiction, especially educational handbooks and a wide range of works inspired by topical events." And she adds: "In appearance, yellowbacks were startlingly different from other books of the time. They were typically small crown octavo, bound in thin STRAWBOARD cases covered with coloured paper (usually yellow) which had been BLOCK PRINTED with pictures using a technique perfected by Edmund Evans. Between 1855 and about 1870, often described as the golden age of yellowbacks, well-known artists were commissioned to provide vivid front cover and SPINE designs, while the back

Yellowback: E. Marlitt (pseudonym of Eugenie John), *The Old Maid's Secret*. Translated from the German by H. J. G. (London: Chapman & Hall [Select Library of Fiction. no. 235.], 1873).

Jarndyce, The 19th Century Booksellers; https://www.jarndyce.co.uk/stock.php?keywords=old+maid%27s+secret&stksearch=go (accessed 10 August 2021).

covers carried commercial ADVERTISEMENTS which helped to subsidise the cost." While the strawboard covers may have been a somewhat stable material, the yellowbacks were not always printed on such "archival" paper, and the TEXT BLOCK of many a yellowback today is yellowed and brittle. (Maybe we can call such volumes just Yellowbooks.) (See Sadleir, *Collecting "Yellowbacks" [Victorian Railway Fiction] Aspects of Book-Collecting*; Topp, *Victorian Yellowbacks & Paperbacks, 1849*–1905 [Vols. I, II, III, IV, V, VI, VII, VIII, IX].)

THE YELLOW BOOK. A "short-lived but influential illustrated quarterly magazine devoted to aesthetics, literature, and art. It was published in London from 1894 to 1897. / From its initial visually arresting issue, for which Aubrey Beardsley was art editor and for which Max Beerbohm wrote an essay, 'A Defence of Cosmetics,' *The Yellow Book* attained immediate notoriety. Published by John Lane and edited by Henry Harland, *The Yellow Book* attracted many outstanding writers and artists of the era, such as Arnold Bennett, Charlotte Mew, Henry James, Edmund Gosse, Richard Le Gallienne, and Walter Sickert" (*Encyclopaedia Britannica* online, "The Yellow Book"; https://www.britannica.com/topic/The-Yellow-Book [accessed 16 May 2021]). The publication was a periodical, though it was released in book form: in BOARDS. Mentioned here because I have heard scholars and booksellers mistake this for YELLOWBACKS, and also because sets of these volumes are frequently to be seen at ANTIQUARIAN BOOK FAIRS.

Z

ZAEHNSDORF, JOSEPH (1816–1886). William Younger Fletcher wrote that Joseph Zaehnsdorf, "bookbinder, son of Gottlieb Zaehnsdorf, of Pesth in Austria-Hungary, was born in that city on 27 Feb. 1816, and received his education in the gymnasium there. At the age of fifteen he was apprenticed to Herr Knipe, a bookbinder of Stuttgart, with whom he remained five years, afterwards proceeding to Vienna, where he worked in the shop of Herr Stephan, a bookbinder. . . . He left Vienna about 1836. . . . In 1837 he came to London, and obtained employment in the establishment of Messrs. Wesley & Co. . . . , for whom he worked three years. He afterwards entered the shop of Mr. Mackenzie, a binder of considerable eminence, and there he remained until 1842, when he commenced business on his own account. . . . Za ehnsdorf became a naturalised British subject in 1855, and died at 14 York Street, Covent Garden, on 7 Dec. 1886. In July 1849 he married Ann, daughter of John Mahoney, by whom he had an only child, Mr. Joseph William Zaehnsdorf, his successor in business and author of 'The Art of Bookbinding.' / Zaehnsdorf was an excellent craftsman, and his work may be ranked with that of Bedford and Riviere. The FORWARDING and FINISHING of his bindings are equally good, and much artistic taste is also displayed in their decoration. Fine examples of his workmanship are to be found in the libraries of all the great English collectors of the day. He exhibited at the London International Exhibition of 1862, where he received honourable mention. He also obtained medals at the Anglo-French Working Class Exhibition, held at the Crystal Palace in 1865, at the Dublin Exhibition of 1865, at Paris in 1867, at Vienna in 1873, and at South Kensington in 1874" (*Dictionary of National Biography*, 1885–1900, vol. 63, https://en.wikisource.org/wiki/Zaehns dorf,_Joseph_(DNB00) [accessed 23 June 2021]).

Zaehnsdorf "made innovations to the craft, not the least of which was offering bookbinding classes to women who, during the Arts & Crafts Movement, had become interested in pursuing binding as a personal means of expression. He taught Sarah Prideaux, who later established herself as a fine binder of lasting repute" (Gertz, "The Mark of Zaehnsdorf"). (*See* Sangorski, Francis, and George Sutcliffe.) (See Broomhead, *The Zaehnsdorfs [1842–1947] Craft Bookbinders.*)

ZAPF, HERMANN (1918–2015). One of the world's leading TYPEFACE designers, CALLIGRAPHERS, typographic designers, and authors on these subjects. Zapf worked over such a long career that he became adept at designing typefaces for HOT METAL, photocomposition, and digital texts. His typefaces Palatino, Optima, ITC Zapf Chancery, and Zapfino, among many others, were used often (and "borrowed" by other designers). Bruce Weber, in Zapf's *New York Times* obituary, says, "Hermann Zapf, whose calling in life—'to create beautiful letters,' as one of his students put it—found expression in lush, steady-handed calligraphy and in subtly inventive typefaces that have brought words to readers on paper, on signposts, on monuments and on computer screens for more than half a century, died on Thursday at his home in Darmstadt, Germany. He was 96. . . . Prolific and versatile, he created around 200 typefaces in numerous alphabets, including Latin, Cyrillic, Arabic and Cherokee, spanning the eras of metal typesetting, phototypesetting and digital typesetting" (Weber, *New York Times* online, "Hermann Zapf, 96, Dies; Designer Whose Letters Are Found Everywhere"). He taught at the Rochester Institute of Technology from 1977–1987. A collection of some of his writings was published in 1987: *Hermann Zapf & His Design Philosophy*.

ZIGZAG FOLD. *See* Concertina fold.

ZIGZAG GUARD. "A continuous one-piece GUARD prepared by folding a sheet of heavy paper, linen, or Japanese copying paper concertina-wise. It is used in the construction of photograph albums and similar GUARD BOOKS, as well as sewing the FOLIOS of large BLANK-BOOKS and for resewing the sections of books in CONSERVATION binding" (Roberts and Etherington, p. 287).

ZINC CUTS (zincs; zincos). Metal PLATES made from zinc that contain images for printing. Any image could be made into a zinc plate and mounted onto a TYPE-HIGH BLOCK for LETTERPRESS PRINTING. Often a photographic image is used. Since zinc has anticorrosive properties, it was a favorite metal for printers to use for images and text in books. Because it was toxic, the federal government in the United States banned its use in coins and other applications. Printing from zinc CUTS was common until then. Since the ban, printers had to resort to MAGNESIUM plates, also good to print from but subject to deterioration (the magnesium plates will eventually corrode and turn powdery and white). (*See* Block.)

ZINE. (The term a shortened version of "magazine" or, more likely, "FANZINE.") "[A]n independently or self-published booklet, often created by physically cutting and gluing text and images together onto a master flat for photocopying, but it is also common to produce the master by typing and formatting pages on a computer. The publication is usually folded and stapled. / Historically, zines have been around since 1776 when Thomas Paine self-published Common Sense and used it as an instrument in promoting the ideas that contributed to the U.S. War for Independence. Just a perfect example to demonstrate the free spirit of zine culture" (flipsnack blog, "What Is a Zine?"). As self-published pieces, these are easy to create inexpensively, and profit is not necessarily the reason they are produced. In many realms—especially with science fiction—they present the first opportunities for young writers to get into print. Seeing their names in published pieces meant more to many of these writers than did making any profit from their efforts. And the zines could be seen as a springboard to more commercial endeavors.

The University of Texas Libraries website says, "Zines can be difficult to define. The word 'zine' is a shortened form of the term fanzine, according to the Oxford English Dictionary. Fanzines emerged as early as the 1930s among fans of science fiction. Zines also have roots in the informal, underground publications that focused on social and political activism in the '60s. By the '70s, zines were popular on the punk rock circuit. In the '90s, the feminist punk scene propelled the medium and included such artists as Kathleen Hanna, who produced riot grrrl out of Olympia, Washington. / A zine is most commonly a small circulation publication of original or appropriated texts and images. More broadly, the term encompasses any self-published unique work of minority interest, usually reproduced via photocopier. A popular definition includes that circulation must be 5,000 or less, although in practice the significant majority are produced in editions of less than 1,000. Profit is not the primary intent of publication. There are so many types of zines: art and photography zines, literary zines, social and political zines, music zines, perzines (personal zines), travel zines, health zines, food zines. And the list goes on and on" (University of Texas Libraries, "What Is a Zine?"). Zines can be seen in abundance at BOOK FAIRS and EPHEMERA fairs, often touted as containing the work of writers who went on to fame. (*See* Underground press.) The Thomas Rivera Library, in its J. Lloyd Eaton Collection at the University of California, Riverside, has probably the world's largest collection of zines. "The Eaton Collection holds the largest collection of fanzines at any public institution. . . . The collection now contains more than 75,000 distinct fanzine titles, more than 100,000 issues" (University of California, Riverside, "Fanzines Collection").

ZOGRASCOPE. A device designed to take images from a flat surface and make them look three-dimensional. As Michael Quinion explains, "The zograscope, consisting of a lens and mirror on a wooden stand, was a device of the eighteenth century for viewing what were called perspective PRINTS—pseudo-stereoscopic images—sometimes also known as *vues d'optique*. It was named the Zograscope for

A Zograscope.
Courtesy of Tom Burgess, Collinge Antiques Ltd.

reasons that are now lost to us, though it was also more variously and prosaically called a *diagonal mirror,* an *optical pillar machine* or an *optical diagonal machine.* / The picture to be viewed was placed on a table and observed through a slanting mirror by means of a lens large enough to allow both eyes to see the picture at once. Its curved edges distorted the image to give a surprisingly good sensation of depth" (Michael Quinion, World Wide Words, "Zograscope.") This device generated a genre of prints showing scenes of travel, people in their fancy homes, gardens and bridges, modern and ancient cities, and so forth. Quinion cites a catalog of 1784 in which such images are available for purchase, and these wind up in ANTIQUARIAN BOOK FAIRS, often not recognized as being created for the tool through which they were to be observed. And he concludes: "These pictures were available at a price of a shilling plain or two shillings coloured, a substantial sum for the period."

ZOOMORPHIC BORDERS, ZOO-ANTHROPOMORPHIC BORDERS. *See* Borders.

APPENDIX A

Paper and Paper-Related Terminology in the Present Volume

Throughout the dictionary are terms having to do in some way with paper and PROTO-PAPERS. The listing in this appendix is all of the key words on this subject. It does not list alternative words. (For example, "Amate" is listed but not "Amatl.")

Acetate
A4 paper
Amate
Annonay paper
Antique laid paper
Ass
Barcham Green Paper Mill
Baskerville, John
Batchelor, John
Bleed through
Block-printed papers
Boards
Bond paper
Briquet, Charles Moïse
Bristol; Bristol board
British Association of Paper Historians
Brittle
Bulk
Burnished
Calendering
Carta rustica
Cartonnage
Chain Lines
Chemical wood pulp
China paper
Chipboard
Chiyogami
Closed tear
Coated papers
Cockled
C1S/C2S
Couch
Countermark
Crepe paper
Crepe paper book
Crisp
Cropped
Damp; Damping
Dandy roll
Deacidification
Deckle
Deckle(d) edge
Decorated paper
Delamination
Dutch gilt papers
Ebru
Embossing
Embrittled; Embrittlement
Enameled
Encapsulation
Ephemera
Esparto (grass)
Faux
Feathering
Felts
Filigranologist/Filigranology
Filler
Fine paper copy
Flock paper; Flocked
Flong
Foolscap
Fourdrinier
Foxing
Furnish
Gampi
Grain (in paper)
Graining
Gum tragacanth
Hog
Hollander beater
Hunter, Dard
Imperial paper copy
Inherent vice
International Association of Paper Historians
Itajime
Japanese paper
Japan paper
Japan Paper Company
Japan vellum
Joss papers
Katazome
Kinkarakami
Kozo
Kraft paper
Lace paper
Laid lines
Laid paper
Lamination
Large paper copy
Layman
Leaf
Leafcasting
Leatherette
Ledgit
Letterlocking
Light-and-shade watermark
Linen paper
Linson
Marbling; Marbled paper
Mechanical pulp
Mending tape; Mending tissue
Mitsumata
Modern laid paper
Moiré

Mold (papermaking)
Mold-made paper
Morris, Henry
Mylar
Naginata beater
Newsprint
Nonpareil
105 AD
Opacity
Open tear
Overmarbled papers
Papercuts
Paperless society
Paper splitting
Papier mâché
Papier porcelaine
Papyrus
Parchment
Paste papers
Pith paper
Porcelain cards
Post
Post and pack
Pressure-sensitive adhesives;
 Pressure-sensitive labels;
 Pressure-sensitive tapes
Proto-paper
Pyroxylin
Quilling
Rag paper
Ream
Repp
Rice paper
Rittenhouse, William
Scratting
Sheet (of paper)
Show-through
Size (in marbling)
Size (in paper formation)
Sized; sizing
Spanish marble
Split boards
Stamping mill
Stephenson Blake
Strawboard
Stuff
Substrate
Sulphate and Sulphite
Suminagashi
Tapa cloth
Three-plane watermark
Tideline
Transfer paper
Ts'ai Lun(g)
Twinrocker Paper Mill
Uncut
Unopened
Unpressed
Upper end boy
Uterine vellum
Vatman
Vatman's shake
Vatman's tear
Vellum
Washi
Waterleaf
Watermark
Weight (of paper)
Whatman, James
White post
Wire Lines
Wood pulp
Wookey Hole Paper Mill
Wove paper

APPENDIX B
Typeface Terminology

The following terminology is taken from several sources, with many terms coming from Alexander Lawson, *Printing Types: An Introduction* (Boston: Beacon Press, 1971), pp. 22–29. (The material in this appendix comes from Berger, pp. 107–10, reprint courtesy American Library Association.)

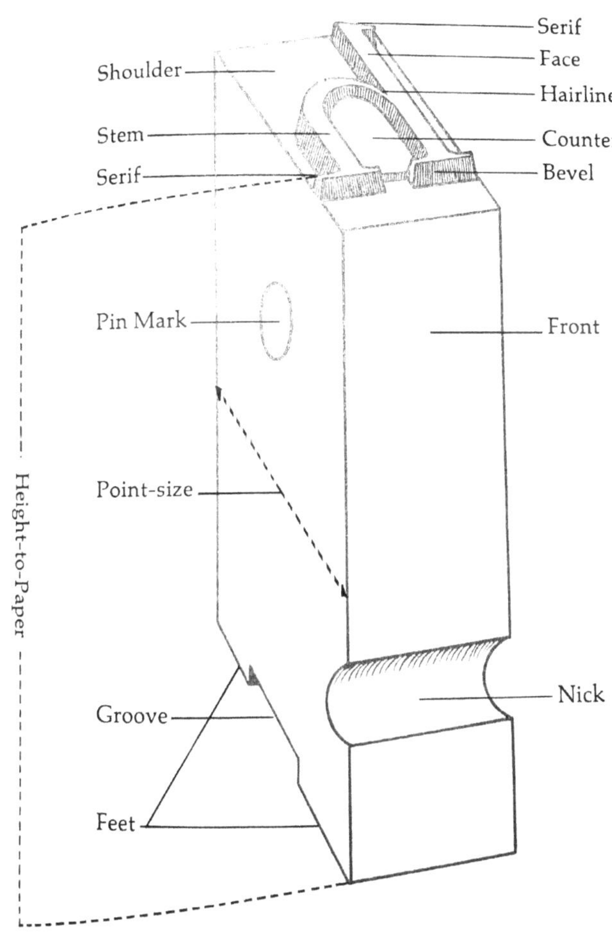

A piece of printing type. From Alexander Lawson, *Printing Types*. Copyright ©1971, Alexander Lawson.
Courtesy of Beacon Press.

A. THE TERMINOLOGY DESCRIBING THE CHARACTERS AND THEIR COMPONENT PARTS

Apex. The point in a character at which two straight lines join, as at the top of the capital A, the bottom of the capital V, and at the points of juncture of the capital M and W.

Arm. The short horizontal stroke of letters, such as the horizontal strokes in the capital E or F, or the angled strokes of letters, as in the capital Y and the upper- and lowercase K.

Ascender. A stroke of a lowercase piece of type that projects above the x-height of the sort, as with the letters b, d, f, and h.

Base line. The invisible line delineating the bottom of serifs for all letters that have serifs on their bottom; the base line would run beneath the serifs of such letters as A, E, F, f, H, h, I, i, K, k, and so on.

Beard. *See* Bevel.

Bevel. "The space in the physical type [i.e., on the actual sort] between the face, or printing surface, of the letter and the shoulder. This is often referred to in the United States as the beard" (Lawson, p. 24).

Bowl. The round, closed part of a letter, as in the closed part of the letters B, b, D, d, O, o, Q, q, and others. (*See* Counter.)

Bracket. Same as fillet.

Counter. The part of a letter that is fully or partly enclosed, as in the letters A, a, B, b, C, c, P, p, R, and others. A punchcutter, creating a punch with a counter, can remove the metal where the counter is more easily by "punching" it out than by removing the metal with tools; for this purpose, he makes a counter punch; *see* typecasting. (*See* Bowl.)

Crossbar. Sometimes called a "cross-stroke." A horizontal line connecting two lines in a piece of type, like the stroke on the A and H, or a stroke like that in the lowercase f and t.

Descender. A stroke of a lowercase piece of type that projects below the base line of the sort, as with the letters g, p, and q in many typefaces.

Ear. In some fonts, the small projection from the bottom bowl of the lowercase G.

Face. The surface of the sort that receives ink and prints onto the surface that is placed over it.

Feet. The two small areas at the bottom of the sort, formed with the removal and filing down of the jet in typecasting; the sort sits on the two small feet thus formed; if for any reason a sort is off its feet, it will not print properly.

Front. The bottom side of the sort.

Groove. The small filed-down part at the base of the sort where the jet was attached; when the jet is removed and its point of attachment is filed down, feet are formed on either side of the groove.

Hairline. An extremely fine line on a piece of type—for example, the thin "crossbar" on the lowercase E.

Jet. The extra type metal that is poured into the type mold when sorts are being cast in their matrices; *see also* Groove. The jet will be removed in the dressing (finishing) of the type.

Link. The small connecting stroke between the upper and lower bowls of the lowercase G.

Loop. The lower bowl of the lowercase G.

Nick. The indentation at the part of the sort that coincides with the bottom of the letters and numbers and other characters; when type is being set into the composing stick, the nick for each sort should be visible, indicating that the bottoms of all the sorts are where they should be—that is, that each sort is being placed into the composing stick in the right direction, with the bottoms of each letter facing out in the stick.[1]

Pin mark. In machine typecasting, the machine ejects the sort from the mold by means of a pin; this pin makes a mark on the side of the sort—a little circular depression—that indicates that the type is not hand-cast.

Point. In the United States and England, a quite thin measurement in printing, approximately 1⁄72 of an inch.

Point system. The system of designating the size of the printed characters in a font of type, as in 12-point type, 18-point caps, and so on.

Serif. The little projections that stick out of the basic shape of a character, like the horizontal lines at the top and bottom of a capital I; serifs are beaked, bracketed, hairline, hooked, slab, spur, or wedge.

Shank. "The section of a body of type [i.e., the section of the sort] between the shoulder and the foot" (*American Heritage*, p. 1610).

Shoulder. "The non-printing area on the [sort] between the base-line [*sic*][2] and the front of the [sort]. In certain styles capitals may be shorter than ascending lowercase letters, creating a shoulder between the face of the letter and the back of the [sort]."[3]

Sort. A single piece of printing type.

Stem. The vertical strokes of a letter and angled strokes that run the full height of a letter, as in the upright strokes of B, D, F, H, T, V, and W.

Tail. On the capital K and capital R and also at the bottom of the capital Q, the short downward stroke, the one on the Q usually being curved.

x-height. The height of the lowercase letters that have no ascenders or descenders—a, c, e, i, m, and so on—so called because of the height of the lowercase x.

B. OTHER TERMINOLOGY DESCRIBING TYPEFACES

Antique. "In the United States, a boldface, rather monotone letter with solid serifs, exemplified by Bookman. In Europe antique is the term applied to roman type, in its secondary meaning as an Italian-derived letter, not as simply an upright letter" (Lawson, p. 27).

Bastard (Bastarda). "A blackletter script used in France, the Burgundian Netherlands and Germany during the 14th and 15th centuries. The Burgundian variant of script can be seen as the court script of the Dukes of Burgundy and was used to produce some of the most magnificent manuscripts of the 15th century" (Wikipedia, "Bastarda"; https://en.wikipedia.org/wiki/Bastarda [accessed 28 July 2021]).

Blackletter. A term used to denote type designs that are modeled after medieval manuscript scripts, with broad counters and thick ornamental serifs; also called "gothic" or "Old English Text."

Boldface. As the name indicates, a **typeface that is heavy**, with strokes much thicker than those in the face's regular lightface manifestation.

Brasses. One of the Thins; small thin pieces of spacing material, made from brass, that are used to fill out a line of handset type; equal to 1 point in thickness.

Civilité type. "In 1557, at Lyons, Robert Granjon published a small book, *Dialogue de la vie et de la mort* by Innocenzio Ringhieri . . . and in his dedicatory address . . . prefacing the text Granjon explains the use of a new script type which he had cut."[4] Since the Civilité types were modeled after handwriting, fonts are filled with many swash characters with elaborate strokes and often with variant designs for single characters.

Coppers. One of the Thins; small thin pieces of spacing material, made from copper, that are used to fill out a line of handset type; equal to ½ point in thickness; hence, two coppers make up the thickness of one brass.

Display type. Type in large sizes, perhaps 18 point and larger, used for headlines, posters, and titles in broadsides.

Egyptian. Also called "slab serif" type, or typefaces with squared-off serifs.

Ems (or "em quads" [from "quadrats"]). A square sort cast with no part of the sort that is type high; hence, when ink is spread or dabbed over the forme, this quad, being much shorter than the sorts receiving the ink, gets none; it is a space that is the same width as it is deep.

Ens (or "en quads"). Similar to ems, only half the thickness.

Family of types. All of the typefaces based on a single design; for example, there is Bembo Roman, Bembo Italic, Bembo Condensed, Bembo Condensed Italic, Bembo Bold, Bembo Semi-Bold, Bembo Heavy, and Bembo Titling. And the family includes such variations in different type sizes (6-point, 8-point, and so on).

Fat face. "Display types having letters with vertical strokes nearly half as thick as the letters are high, vertical shading and unbracketed or only slightly bracketed serifs. Fat-faced types as fully developed date from 1805 and were probably the design of Robert Thorne. . . . Modern versions are many and include Falstaff and Ultra Bodoni."[5]

Fraktur type. A font of blackletter type used in German printing, mirroring the hand of early German scribes; millions of books were printed in Fraktur type in Germany.

Gothic. "Traditionally a term describing the lettering style of northern Europe during the period when Johann Gutenberg developed movable type, adapted as the first type. In the United States, since the 1830s, the term applied to sans serif types issued by European typefounders after 1820."[6]

Grooves. As described above, a groove is a little filed- or planed-down area on the base of a sort where the jet was once attached; once the jet is broken off, the sort is filed down where it was attached, creating the feet on which the sort stands.

Grotesque. "A style of sans-serif typeface from the 19th century."[7]

Height-to-paper. The height of a sort from its feet to its face; in the United States and England, this is .918 inches, though at least one English foundry (Riscatype) cast its type a hairline taller.

Inferior. A piece of type where the printing surface is cast low on its body so that it prints beneath the line; also called a "subscript."

Italic type. Typefaces with slanted or sloped characters.[8]

Kern. A part of the printing surface of a sort that protrudes beyond the body of the sort, as with the upper and lower swash strokes of an italic lowercase F.

Leaders. As John Ryder says, "A row of dots to lead the eye from one point to another on the page; a poor practice."[9] One might see such dots in a table of contents, between the name of the item at the gutter and the page number on the fore-edge of the page.

Ligature. An instance in which two or more characters are cast on a single sort and are joined, as with the most common ones: ff, fi, ffi, fl, and ffl; some typefaces, especially italic or cursive fonts with steeply leaning upright strokes, have many ligatures, such as ft, st, ct, gg, gy, and zy.

Lightface. The regular showing of a font of type, with no heavy strokes, as opposed to boldface or italic.

Logotype. An instance in which two or more characters are cast onto a single sort, but they are not joined, as they are with ligatures.[10]

Long S. The letter S that looks like a lowercase F but without a full crossbar as the F has; the crossbar on the S, if it has one, goes up only to the upright stroke but not through it and not out onto the right side of the upright stroke. Sometimes called a "swash S."

Oldstyle type. Early printing types that mimicked the handwriting of the manuscript scribes.

Pica. A measurement, in printing, of 12 points; there are 12 points to a pica and 6 picas to an inch.

Roman type. "The alphabets of capitals and lower-case letters usually designed upright, as against italic alphabets which are usually sloped" (Ryder, p. 128).

Sans-serif types. Fonts with no serifs.

Script types. Typefaces that mimic handwriting.

Serif types. Fonts that have small strokes protruding off the main stems of the characters; on the capital T, for instance, the two downward strokes at the ends of the crossbar at the top of the letter and the horizontal stroke at the bottom of the upright stem of the T are serifs.

Slab serif type. *See* Egyptian.

Steels. One of the thins; extremely thin pieces of spacing material, made from steel, that are used to fill out a line of handset type; equal to ¼ point in thickness; it is difficult to squeeze a thin piece of spacing material into an almost perfectly tightened-up line; the thinnest of the "thins" needs to be made from a sturdy metal that will not easily bend when it is being inserted between other sorts; two steels are the thickness of one copper.

Superior. A piece of type where the printing surface is cast high on its body so that it prints above the line; sometimes called a "superscript."

Swash types (or swash characters). Italic types with fancy, extended strokes to add to the character's elegance.

Thins. Also called hair spacing. *See* Brasses, Coppers, and Steels.

Transitional type. Fonts from the late 17th century that were modeled on earlier faces but that had elements of later design; they came before "Modern types."[11]

The following list shows the old and new names for the various sizes. (Source: L. Boyd Benton, "The Making of Type," in Frederick H. Hitchcock, *The Building of a Book*; see bibliography.)

3½ Point	Brilliant.
4½ Point	Diamond.
5 Point	Pearl.
5½ Point	Agate.
6 Point	Nonpareil.
7 Point	Minion.
8 Point	Brevier.
9 Point	Bourgeois.
10 Point	Long Primer.
11 Point	Small Pica.
12 Point	Pica.
14 Point	2-line Minion or English.
16 Point	2-line Brevier.
18 Point	Great Primer.
20 Point	2-line Long Primer or Paragon.
22 Point	2-line Small Pica.
24 Point	2-line Pica.
28 Point	2-line English.
30 Point	5-line Nonpareil.
32 Point	4-line Brevier.
36 Point	2-line Great Primer.
40 Point	Double Paragon.
42 Point	7-line Nonpareil.
44 Point	4-line Small Pica or Canon.
48 Point	4-line Pica.
54 Point	9-line Nonpareil.
60 Point	5-line Pica.
72 Point	6-line Pica.

NOTES

1. The nick on the bottom of the sort serves at least two functions. (1) It tells the compositor that the sort is being put into the composing stick in the right direction; if a line of type is set, the compositor can glance over it and see that all of the nicks are visible. If a sort does not show its nick, the sort is probably in the stick upside down. (2) The nick is not necessarily in the exact same place on sorts from different fonts. So if a sort is set into the composing stick and its nick is higher or lower than that of a neighboring sort, there are at least two typefaces represented by the two differently positioned nicks. Some fonts are cast in molds that create two or even three nicks on the edge of the sort. Types cast in the last few decades, however, will rarely show this difference if they are cast in the same molds since it is the mold, not the matrix, that imparts the nick into the sorts, and many matrices from various faces can be used to cast fonts in a single mold, thus giving many fonts of varying designs nicks in identical positions.

2. Elsewhere, the word is spelled without a hyphen.

3. Lawson, *Printing Types*, p. 25.

4. Harry G. Carter and Hendrik Vervliet, *Civilité Types* (Oxford: Oxford University Press, 1966), p. 11.

5. Geoffrey Ashall Glaister, *Glaister's Glossary of the Book: Terms Used in Papermaking, Printing, Bookbinding and Publishing with Notes on Illuminated Manuscripts and Private Presses*, 2nd ed. (London: George Allen & Unwin, 1979), p. 169.

6. Lawson, *Printing Types*, p. 27.

7. Wikipedia, "grotesque"; https://en.wikipedia.org/w/index.php?search=Grotesque+%28typeface+classification&title=Special%3ASearch&fulltext=1&ns0=1 (accessed 28 July 2021).

8. This definition, while serviceable, is an oversimplification, of course. Lawson says of italic, "A sloped or cursive variation of roman. In many cases this represents a complementary style of the upright letter, although some of the lowercase letters may change form slightly, and the serif construction is different" (*Printing Types*, p. 27). Early computer roman typefaces could be automatically slanted to produce an italic, but many of them were quite ugly and not terribly legible. More recently, designers of digital faces understand this problem and they create roman faces with perfectly complementary, legible italics.

9. John Ryder, *Printing for Pleasure* (Chicago: Henry Regnery Co., 1977), p. 126.

10. About logotypes, Lawson says, "The linecasting machine firms have developed many standard logotypes such as Ta, Te, Va, Vo [in which the vowels are positioned underneath the right-hand stroke of the top of the T rather than beyond the sort of a normal capital T], to eliminate what might be an unsightly gap of space under the overhang of an arm. In advertising terminology, logotype is simply the name or trademark of a business firm" (*Printing Types*, p. 29). And the firm's trademark image will be called its "logo."

11. Perhaps the best, most succinct text on type is Lawson's *Printing Type*. This is the text to consult for concise definitions of the various stages in type design: Blackletter, Oldstyle, Transitional, Modern, Square Serif, Sans Serif, Script-Cursive, and Display-Decorative (pp. 47–119).

APPENDIX C
Paper Sizes

A challenge for anyone working with books is grasping the vocabulary for paper, which has a lexicon of thousands of words, as the E. J. Labarre volume shows (see the bibliography). One of the difficult areas of such delineation is the terminology for paper sizes.

There are at least two reasons that the vocabulary for paper sizes is difficult to grasp. First, handmade paper is made on molds, the sizes of which were never standardized. That is, papermakers (and paper-mold makers) made this tool to whatever size they needed, possibly for a particular printer who wanted a particular size or possibly measured purely at random. Second, over the centuries, paper was made in so many places that the terminology was never fixed—sheets of various sizes were given various names. The volume by E. J. Labarre (*Dictionary and Encyclopaedia of Paper and Paper-making, with Equivalents of the Technical Terms in French, German, Dutch, Italian, Spanish & Swedish*[1]) says under the entry for "Sizes":

> A critical examination of the names of English paper sizes and their measurements in the following table reveals the entire nomenclature contains only 15 different names and not more than half-a-dozen basic sizes. These names are: Antiquarian, Atlas, Colombier, CROWN, DEMY, Eagle, Elephant, Emperor, FOOLSCAP, IMPERIAL, Hand, MEDIUM, POST, Pott, and ROYAL, of which only the seven sizes printed in capitals, and their derivatives, are in regular use. It may be said that only three of these, viz. Crown, Demy and Royal, and possibly Foolscap, are indispensable; all the other sizes vary from the one or the other of these that they could probably be abolished without causing inconvenience to the trade or the public.
>
> These fifteen names and barely a half-a-dozen different sets of measurements represent the framework on which the trade and custom have built up a bewildering number of combinations with the help of adjectives such as: Half and Single, Double and Quadruple, Large and Small, Broad and Long, Extra and Super, Reduced and Pinched, Whole and Middle, or duplications of these such as: Double Quadruple, Extra Large, Small Double or Double Small, and even fractional additions like sheet-and-a-half or sheet-and-a-third. (p. 246)

Labarre adds that with all of the combinations, there are at least 100 names for paper sizes in English, and a single denotation of one size could represent "anything from 2 to 15 slight variations" in size (p. 247). He says, "The total number of different *names* of sizes in the table, including stationery and cards, exceeds 290" (p. 247), and that some papers, judged by their measurement, do not fall under any of the names, so a "printer would speak of a 'cut size'" (p. 247). His discussion goes on to explain the lack of uniformity of nomenclature, partly occasioned by manufacturers who give papers their own size designation, and partly because many papers are named for their uses: "Bag, Cap (Foolscap), Medium and Royal Copying, Chemists', Music and Writing Demy, Index-, Pasting-, Wedding- and Writing Royal, or even a combination of two sizes such as Imperial Cap, Medium Post and Royal Hand and, finally, a size-name preceded by a fancy name, e.g. Havon Cap and Kent Cap" (pp. 247–48).

Labarre's discussion goes on for pages. The points are: 1) there is no standard terminology that is universally applicable to papers; and 2) there are no standard sizes that are fixed for any word that describes a size. This is a fascinating discussion, worth reading (the section is on pp. 246–52). And while his table titled "Ratio of Paper Sizes" is overwhelming (running from pp. 251–67), and is supplemented by the useful "Table of Dimensions of Paper Sizes and Their Names" (pp. 268–72), which is even more useful, the overall effect is stultifying. The latter table, for instance, designates all the names of paper sizes to represent nine categories: Writing, Printing, Drawing, Wrapping, Boards, Cards, Envelopes, Notes, and Miscellaneous (with some papers used for as many as six of these categories[2]). The table lists papers as small as 3" × 1½" and as large as 72" × 48", and it designates papers that are over 300 sizes.[3]

LABARRE'S TABLE

Writings	Inches	Printings	Inches
Foolscap	13½ × 16½	Large Foolscap	13½ × 17
Small Post	14½ × 18½	Crown	15 × 20
Sheet and ⅓ Cap	13½ × 22	Large Post	16½ × 21
Sheet and ½ Cap	13¼ × 24¾	Demy	17½ × 22½
Small Demy	15½ × 20	Medium	18 × 23
Large Post	16½ × 21	Royal	20 × 25
Small Medium	17½ × 22	Large Royal	20 × 27
Medium	18 × 23	Imperial	22 × 30
Small Royal	19 × 24		
Super Royal	19 × 27		
Imperial	22 × 30		

To simplify the matter, as Labarre shows, a "Standardization Agreement" was reached in England in 1925 "between the Federation of Master Printers and the National Association of Paper Merchants (then the National Association of Wholesale Stationers)" (p. 285), and they came up with "standard names and sizes for paper and boards" (p. 285). Papers were divided into "Writings" and "Printings." Labarre's table can be seen above.[4]

Another frequently consulted guide to paper terminology, *The Dictionary of Paper*,[5] has a section on "Sizes of Paper" (pp. 400–402) that lists "some of the common sheet sizes" (p. 400), not all of them. And in general, these are listed by their use (and common sizes in the United States), not by arbitrary names. So there are Bible paper, Blotting paper, Bogus bristol, Book paper (coated and uncoated), Cover paper, Ledger paper, Railroad manila, and so on to Wrapping tissues and Writing paper. For each of these, several sizes are given, indicating that the lack of standardization in the U.S. matches that in Great Britain.

Almost all of this discussion has focused on the modern paper industry. It was much more chaotic and totally unstandardized in the handpress period, so designating papers by their size for sheets made from, say, 1800 and backward is difficult. For those working with rare books, it is essential to know the kinds of things revealed in Berger (*Rare Books and Special Collections*), chapter 4, in the section on Paper. If a measurement of a full sheet of paper that is bound into the printed leaves of a book is needed, the scholar must determine the volume's format, and try to "unfold" the leaf theoretically to try to reconstitute the full sheet. But unless the volume has deckles in two directions (vertically and horizontally), there is no way to know how much paper has been trimmed from the original sheet. And even horizontal and vertical deckles may not tell the whole picture since a sheet could be trimmed from two sides and still have deckles showing on two sides of the volume. A folio or a quarto, with all four deckles intact, will show the original full sheet. It gets more difficult to "see" the full sheet with smaller formats.

If the sheets were watermarked (or even if not), it might be possible to reconstruct the original sheet, especially if the book is disbound and the signatures can be unfolded and the original leaves reconstituted.

One other term that has been the subject of conversation and confusion over the years is "ream." *The Dictionary of Paper* (3rd ed.) merely says that a ream contains "either 480 or 500 [sheets] according to grade" (p. 363). Labarre is more expansive, explaining the antiquity of the word, and says that

> the actual quantity of paper in a ream gradually became fixed through the centuries . . . probably in some relation to the amount of paper a vatman could make in a day, and has been in the neighborhood of 500 sheets for the last 3 or 4 centuries, though it may still contain, according to the class of paper, 472, 480, 504, or 516 sheets (also other quantities in various countries. (Labarre, p. 222)

He points out that the "Standard Ream," the U.S. term, has 500 sheets, a "Printer's Ream" contains 516 (made up of 2½ quires [a quire is 20 sheets] of 24 good sheets), an "Inside Ream" has 480 sheets (or 20 inside quires), and so forth.

For the most part, those in the rare books world should keep 480 and 500 in mind as the most common numbers of sheets in reams, and in the U.S, it is almost always 500.

(Source of this appendix: Berger [*Rare Books and Special Collections*], pp. 505–10. Courtesy American Library Association.)

NOTES

1. Second edition, revised and enlarged (Amsterdam: Swets & Zeitlinger, 1952). This is one of the most comprehensive and referred-to guides to paper terminology.

2. The paper called "Double Foolscap" (also called "Chancery") measures 26½ × 16½ in a full sheet; it is used for all the categories except Cards (p. 270).

3. The smallest, 3" × 1½", is called "Gents' Card" or "Third or third Large"; the largest sheet, 72" × 48", is called "Emperor" (pp. 262, 272). The 300+ names show a good deal of imagination: "Prince of Wales," "Boudoir," "Intimation," "Albert," "Billet," "Czarina," "Viscount," "Copy" or "Tea Copy," "Small Half Royall," "Large Double Loaf," "Medium Lumber Hand," "Typewriter Double Cap," "Double Hambro," "Single Lump" and "Double Lump," "Plutarch," "Double Elephant" and "Long Double Elephant," and on and on.

4. This table is in Labarre, p. 285.

5. *The Dictionary of Paper: A Compendium of Terms* Commonly *Used in the U.S. Pulp, Paper and Allied Industries,* 4th ed. (New York: American Paper Institute, 1980). The 3rd edition is abundantly available on the web, and it is the basis of the information for the present volume: *The Dictionary of Paper: Including Pulp, Paperboard, Paper Properties and Related Papermaking Terms* (New York: American Paper and Pulp Association, 1965). To hint at the complexity of the subject of "Paper Sizes," look at the Wikipedia article, under this heading, at http://en.wikipedia.org/wiki/Paper_size (accessed 23 October 2022).

APPENDIX D

Binding Terminology in the Present Volume

Album
Aldine bindings
All along (binding)
All edges gilt
Anthropomorphic bibliopegy
Applied covers
Armorial bindings
Arsenic
Author's binding
Back (in binding)
Basil
Bespoke binding
Bevelled edges
Binder's cloth
Binder's dummy
Binder's sample
Binder's ticket
Binder's title
Binding
Binding copy
Blanched/Blanching
Blank books
Blanks
Blind stamped
Block
Blocking
Bloom
Boarding
Boards
Board shear
Bolts
Book label
Bookmarks
Book shoe
Book stamp
Bosses
Bound
Bowed
Bradel binding
Brightbacks
Bristol; Bristol board
Brochure
Buckram
Bulk
Bumped
Calf
Cambridge calf
Cambridge-style binding
Cameo binding
Canvas
Cardboard
Carousel book
Carta rustica
Cartonnage
Cartouche
Case
Case bound
Cathedral binding
Chained libraries
Champleve bindings
Chemise
Chipboard
Chitsu
Circuit binding
Clasps
Cloth
Comb binding
Compensation guard
Concertina fold
Consolidant
Contemporary
Coptic binding
Copying presses
Cordoba leather
Cordovan leather
Cornerpiece
Corners
Cords
Cosway binding
Cottage binding
Cover
Cropped
Crown
Crushed
Cuir-bouilli
Cuir-ciselé
Decorator books
Delamination
Dentelle
Derome style
Designer bindings
Designer bookbinders
Diapered
Die-cut
Diploma
Disbound
Divinity calf
Dos-à-dos binding
Doublures
Drawer-handle tool
Dummy
Dust jacket
Edges of books
Edition binding
Edwards of Halifax
Embossing
Embroidered binding
Endbands; Raised bands
Etruscan calf
Extended
Extra binding
Extremities
False bands
Fanfare binding

Fan style; Fan binding
Fascicle
Fillet
Fine binding
Finger tab
Finishing
Flesh side
Flexible sewing
Folded and gathered
Forel
Forwarding
Frame
French flaps
French fold
French sewing
Full binding
Gatefold
Gatherings
Gauffered edges
Gift book
Gilt
Gilt edges
Girdle book
Glair
Glassine
Gloss
Goatskin
Gold stamping
Graining
Great Omar
Greek style
Grooves
Guard book
Guards
Guild of book workers
Gutta-percha binding
Hair side
Half-bound
Half-cloth
Hardbacks
Hard-grained goat (Hard-grained morocco)
Harleian style
Head
Headband
Headcap
Hide
Hinges
Hollow spine
Horn book
In boards
Inlaid (binding)
In sheets
Interleaved
Jansenist style
Jeweled binding
Joints
Juvenile picture-book binding
Kettle stitch
Labels
Laced-in
Lacquered bindings
Lamination
Law calf
Leaflet
Leather (in binding)
Leatherette
Lettered direct
Lettering
Levant
Library binding
Ligatus
Limp leather; Limp vellum
Linings
Longitudinal labels
Loose
Loose leaf bindings
Lyonnaise style
Mauchline binding
Mearne, Samuel
Mending tape; Mending tissue
Middleton, Bernard
Mitered
Mock-up
Moiré
Morocco (leather)
Mosaic binding
Mottled calf
Mull
Mutton thumper
Name strips
Neat
Niger
Oasis goat
Offset sheets
Onlaid (in binding)
Ooze calf; Ooze leather
Opened
Oriental binding
Orihon
Overcasting
Oversewn
Oxford corners
Padded boards
Painted binding
Pallet
Palm-leaf book
Pamphlet
Panel; Panel binding
Paperback
Parchment
Parts; In parts
Pasteboards
Payne, Roger
Peasant binding
Pebbled leather
Perfect binding
Phase box
Pigskin
Plow
Pointillé
Polished calf
Pop-up book
Post binding
Powell, Roger
Presentation binding
Primary binding
Prize binding
Publisher's binding
Publisher's cloth
Quarter-bound
Rag book
Raised bands
Re-backed
Rebound
Recased
Recessed-cord sewing
Red edges
Red rot
Red-under-gold edge
Rejointed
Remainder binding
Remboîtage
Repousé
Resewing
Restoration
Reverse; Reverse calf
Ring binder
Rivière, Robert
Roan
Roll (Scroll)
Romanesque binding
Rough gilt

Roundel
Rounding and backing
Roxburghe style
Royal bindings
Rubbed
Russia; Russia calf
Saddle stitching
Salesman's dummy
Sammelband
Sangorski, Francis, and George Sutcliffe
Scaleboard
Scored calf
Scrapbook
Scratting
Scuffed
Secondary binding
Self-wrapper
Semé
Sewing stations
Shagreen
Shaken
Shaved
Sheepskin
Shell gold
Sides
Side stitching
Signed binding
Silk moiré
Sixties books
Skiver
Sleeve
Slipcase
Slips
Smith, Philip
Solander box
Spine lining
Spinescaping
Spiral binding
Split boards
Spotted calf
Spring-back binding
Sprung
Squared
Squares
Stab holes
Stamp
Stamped
Stapled
Started
Stationery binding
Stilted
Stippling
Stitched
Straight-grain morocco
Strapwork
Strawboard
Suede
Sunned
Supralibros
Tacketing
Tanned
Tapes (in binding)
Tawing
TEG
Temporary binding
Tête-bêche
Thongs (in binding)
Three-quarter binding
Thumb index
Ticketing
Ties
Tight
Tips
Tissues; Tissue guards
Tooling
Top edge gilt
Tortoise shell binding
Trade binding
Tree calf
Trial binding
Trim size
Turkey Morocco
Turn-ins
Unbound
Uncut (or Untrimmed)
Unlettered
Unopened
Unpressed
Uterine vellum
Wallet edge
Waters, Peter
Whip stitching
Wholesaler's binding
Wrapper(s)
Yapp binding
Yawning boards
Zaehnsdorf, Joseph
Zig-zag guard

APPENDIX E

Book Collectors' Clubs and Societies

In the first edition of this dictionary, Appendix E listed a host of clubs and societies. For the present edition, this listing is brought up to date (as of 28 August 2022). This specific date is mentioned because the Fellowship of American Bibliophilic Societies has undergone some changes, the results of which may be the loss of some members. (*See below.*) Of course, membership is necessarily fluid. By the time this edition of *The Dictionary* is published, there may be additional membership changes. For instance, the Russian clubs listed below may no longer be members.

As the entry at "Fellowship of American Bibliophilic Societies (FABS)" explains, there are book collectors' clubs and societies all over the world. These groups are composed of people who love, buy and sell, make, collect, care for, and catalog books. Since the publication of the first edition of this dictionary, there has been a shake-up in the membership of FABS, partly occasioned by the fact that FABS, emanating from a meeting of their trustees on 11 March 2021, has decided to recognize only clubs with full inclusivity. Hence, the all-male Rowfant Club in Cleveland resigned from membership. For the same reason, the Club of Odd Volumes in Boston is not a FABS member.

Many of the FABS member clubs were founded in the 19th century as gentlemen's book-collecting clubs. Most of them went co-ed in the 1970s. But there is a broader issue, too. What denotes "exclusivity"? Several of the clubs have high membership fees and dues that are too expensive for many people. Their meetings are often dinners, which, also, are expensive. Some of the clubs, recognizing this, have kept their dues low, with the aim of attracting younger and more diverse members.

The movement in FABS is typical of the shift in the organization's goals and its members' predilections. This can be seen in the issue of the organization's serial publication *Fellowship of American Bibliophilic Societies*, vol. 25, no. 1 (Spring 2021), that has a "Letter From the Chair" (William E. Butler). Butler explains that FABS adheres to a strong policy of inclusivity, though it was not codified in their Articles of Association. He says, "Meeting in annual plenary session on 11 March 2021, the trustees of FABS addressed an issue that has been lying 'out there' since the founding of FABS: gender discrimination practices by one of the founding member societies, the Rowfant Club in Cleveland. In March 2020 the trustees voted to take some action with the assistance of a 'task force.' . . . The task force proposed a set of 'Canons' to set out FABS policy on this question with a view to laying the groundwork for amending the Articles of Association of FABS to this end." The amendment was "adopted as an interim measure and statement of FABS policy by an overwhelming majority." A second measure emanating from a meeting that was held during the first half of June 2021 was proposed "with a full view of amending the Articles of Association to incorporate the provision on inclusivity." Probably seeing the handwriting on the wall, and not wishing to change its policy of excluding women from their club, one of its founding members, the Rowfant Club, "resigned from FABS on 4 March 2021; all other member clubs of FABS and international affiliates are compliant with inclusivity requirements" (Butler, "Letter from the Chair," p. 4).

One of the aims of the present dictionary is to inculcate its readers into the world of the book, to make them knowledgeable about the things going on in that realm. Here is living history of a large part of the book world, evolving before our eyes.

And as this evolution is revealed in real time for me as I was writing on 28 August 2022, an email explained that the FABS board voted on the new Articles of Association on 10 June 2021 and passed these articles by a vote of 22 in favor, 1 opposed (and 1 absent; an absent vote = a yes vote). The following paragraphs, printed in boldface in the articles, showed the central issue of the organization's revamping of its articles: "Its expressed policies do not discriminate on the basis of race, color, religion (creed), gender, gender expression, age, national origin (ancestry), disability, marital status, sexual orientation, or military status, in any of its activities or operations. A member society may, however, set a minimum age for membership in compliance with state and local laws regarding the serving of alcohol. / International and foreign bibliophilic societies may apply or be invited to join the Fellowship as international affiliates, so long as any such society meets and agrees to the standards set out above. The rights and responsibilities appertaining to such international affiliates shall be determined by the Trustees of the Fellowship. / Election of the proposed member society or international affiliate, or suspension, dismissal, or expulsion of a member society or international affiliate, for not meeting or adhering to the standards shall require a majority vote of the Trustees" (file:///C:/Users/Sid/Downloads/AMENDMENT_Section%202%20(1).pdf; as this was the content of an email, the link disappeared fairly quickly, but the sentiment was taken up by the FABS constituency and the vote passed, as noted above.

The FABS clubs are as follows:

The Aldus Society, Columbus, OH
The Ampersand Club, St. Paul, MN
The Baltimore Bibliophiles, Baltimore, MD
The John Russell Bartlett Society, Providence, RI
The Baxter Society, Portland, ME
The Bixby Club, St. Louis, MO
The Book Club of California, San Francisco, CA
The Book Hunters Club of Houston, Houston, TX
The Caxton Club, Chicago, IL
The Delaware Bibliophiles, Wilmington, DE
The Book Club of Detroit, Detroit, MI
Florida Bibliophile Society, St. Petersburg, FL
The Grolier Club, New York, NY
Himes & Duniway Society, Portland, OR
The Manuscript Society, Overland Park, KS
Miniature Book Society
Northern Ohio Bibliophilic Society, Northern OH
The Philobiblon Club, Philadelphia, PA
The Roxburghe Club of San Francisco, San Francisco, CA
The Book Club of Texas, Austin, TX
The Ticknor Society, Boston, MA
Washington Rare Book Group, Washington, DC
Book Club of Washington, Seattle, WA
The William Morris Society in the U.S., Washington, DC
The Zamorano Club, Los Angeles, CA

Information about each of these can be found on the web, either at the FABS website (http://www.fabsocieties.org/members.html [accessed 2 May, 2021]) or at their own sites.

Additionally, this society has International Affiliates:

Aberystwyth Bibliographical Group, Aberystwyth, Wales
Nederlands Genootschap van Bibliofielen (Dutch Organization of Bibliophiles), Amsterdam, Netherlands
Associació de Bibliòfiles de Barcelona, Barcelona, Spain
Berliner Bibliophilen Abend E. V., Berlin, Germany
Biron Stables Bibliophile Club, St. Petersburg, Russia
Société Royale des Bibliophiles et Iconophiles de Belgique, Brussels, Belgium
Fédération Internationale des Sociétés d'Amateurs d'Ex-Libris (FISAE) / International Federation of Ex-libris Societies, Helsinki, Finland
Moscow Club of Bibliophiles, Moscow, Russia
National Union of Bibliophiles, Moscow, Russia (formerly Organization of Russian Bibliophiles)
The Society of Bibliophiles in Capetown (now calling itself merely The Bibliophile Society), Capetown, South Africa
The St. Petersburg Society of Bibliophiles, Russia
Les Amis Du Livre Contemporain, Paris, France
The Private Libraries Association, Pinner, Middlesex, England
Maxmilian-Gesellschaft e.V. für alte und neue Buchkunst, Stuttgart, Germany
Book and Graphics Section (Russian Academy of Sciences), St. Petersburg, Russia
Saint Petersburg Society of Bibliophiles, St. Petersburg, Russia
Academy of Sciences, St. Petersburg, Russia
The Dublin Odde Volume Sette, Dublin, Ireland
Pirckheimer-Gesellschaft e.V., Berlin, Germany
Jerusalem Club of Bibliophiles, Israel
International Union of Bibliophilic Societies, Moscow, Russia
University of London Bibliophiles, London, England

(This information gleaned from the FABS publication *FABS: Fellowship of American Bibliophilic Societies* 25, no. 1 [Spring 2021]: 3.)

Many of these clubs have their own newsletters and other publications, and they hold meetings—sometimes regularly, sometimes irregularly—every year.

An old text on the AbeBooks.com website said, "Book collectors tend to hunt on their own, but there are few things finer than meeting other bibliophiles. Book collecting clubs and bibliographic societies can offer meetings, lectures or seminars, libraries, and even publish books. / When deciding which club to approach remember the scope, and seriousness, of each club differs and some are aimed at general lovers of books while others are aimed at high-end collectors. It is best to conduct research and find the club that is right for you. / Most of the bibliographic clubs . . . are regional but some are national or global organizations aimed at promoting the collection of specific type such as miniature books or manuscripts" (http://www.abebooks.com/books/RareBooks/collecting-guide/buying-valuing/book-collecting-clubs.shtml [last accessed 23 October 2015]; the link is now dead). This site then lists the clubs mentioned above, along with the following:

AMERICAN CLUBS AND ASSOCIATIONS

The clubs listed here are those noted by the old AbeBooks website. They are not necessarily members of FABS, as can be seen by the fact that The Club of Odd Volumes and The Rowfant Club, in not allowing women to be members, are excluded from FABS.

The Alcuin Society
American Book Collectors of Children's Literature
American Printing History Association (APHA)
Bibliographical Society of America
Bibliographical Society of Canada
Bibliographical Society of the University of Virginia
The Bixby Club
Book Arts Guild
Book Club of Washington
British Cartographic Society
The Caxton Club
Cincinnati Book Arts Society
The Club of Odd Volumes
The Codex Foundation
The Colophon Club
Ephemera Society of America
Fine Press Book Association
Long Island Book Collectors
Movable Book Society
The No. 44 Society
Ottawa Book Collectors
[RBMS = Rare Books and Manuscript Section; see in the dictionary; printed here in brackets because this is not formally a "club," but it performs many of the functions of a club in helping its members collect, holding meetings, offering information about books and collecting, and so forth. The same applies to the Society for the History of Authorship, Reading, and Publishing.]
Rochester Bibliophile Society
The Rowfant Club
Sacramento Book Collectors Club
[Society for the History of Authorship, Reading and Publishing (SHARP); see note at RBMS above.]
William Morris Society (London)
William Morris Society of Canada

EUROPEAN CLUBS

The Bibliographical Society, UK
Edinburgh Bibliographical Society
The Finnish Comics Society
Freundeskreis Miniaturbuch Berlin
International Map Collectors' Society
The Malone Society
Penguin Collectors Society
The Printing Historical Society
The Private Libraries Association
The Roxburghe Club [Great Britain]

AUSTRALIAN AND NEW ZEALAND CLUBS

The Bibliographical Society of Australia and New Zealand
The Book Collectors Society of Australia

* * *

Since this dictionary is aimed at book collectors, booksellers, librarians, and anyone else interested in books, a knowledge of (and membership in) these clubs is useful for many reasons (no need to spell them out here). All of these clubs have a presence on the web, with their own sites and with contact information.

The Private Library website (at https://privatelibrary.typepad.com/the_private_library/2011/02/ex-library-books-and-the-private-library.html [accessed 2 May 2021]) lists additional organizations, in the United States and abroad. Those not listed above are given below. In some cases, the links given at The Private Library site are defunct, possibly indicating that the organizations listed there are no longer in operation; if the organization cannot be located on the web, they are marked "(defunct?)." A dead link could also be possible because the link that The Private Library site used had URLs that have changed. When this is the case, and I have located the organization on a web search, I have left the group in the list below. Hence, readers using The Private Library site should not rely on its links. Some organizations listed as "defunct" are left in because the institutions have a history of bookish activities, and it is possible that these groups will be revived, and also that the archives of those groups could be available. Some of the libraries and museums that they list are not included here, nor are organizations listed above. In a few instances, academic research centers are listed below because they could be valuable resources for booksellers and collectors who need information about the items they hold. For the most part, booksellers' associations are omitted, with the exception of a few that could be of use to collectors, booksellers, and librarians. A few other organizations' names have been added to this list.

Academy of American Poets
American Academy of Bookbinding
American Book Collectors of Children's Literature (apparently defunct?)
American Historical Print Collectors Society
American Society for Indexing
American Society of Bookplate Collectors & Designers
American Typecasting Fellowship
Asociación Española de Bibliografía
Asociación para el Fomento de la Encuadernación de Arte (defunct?)
Association Française pour l'Histoire et l'Étude du Papier et des Papeteries
Association Typographique Internationale
Associazione Librai Antiquari d'Italia
Bibliophile Society of Rochester (NY)
Bibliophiles of Oklahoma ("This group has become officially dormant.")
Bolton Society: An Organization of Chemical Bibliophiles
Book History Research Network (UK)
Bookplate Society (UK)
British Association of Paper Historians
British Printing Society
Bund Deutscher Buchbinder-Innungen
Cambridge Bibliographical Society
Canadian Association for the Study of Book Culture (defunct?)
Canadian Bookbinders and Book Artists Guild
Canberra Craft Bookbinders' Guild
Center for Bibliographical Studies and Research (University of California at Riverside)
Center for Book Arts (NY)
Center for the History of Print Culture in Modern America (now called the Center for Print and Digital Culture)
Centre for Manuscript and Print Studies (University of London)
Centre for the History of the Book (University of Edinburgh)
Chambre Professionelle Belge de la Librairie Ancienne et Moderne / Belgische Beroepskamer van Antiquaren
College Book Art Association
Columbia College Center for Book and Paper Arts (defunct?)
Den Danske Antikvarboghandlerforening (Danish Antique Book Dealers' Association)
Designer Bookbinders (UK)
Designer Bookbinders of America
Dictionary Society of North America
Early Book Society
Edward Johnston Foundation
Eric Carle Museum of Picture Book Art
Fine Press Book Association (referred to as FPBA) (U.S. and UK)
Folio Society
Guild of Book Workers
Hand Bookbinders of California
Hand Papermaking
HoBo (UK) (defunct? This link takes one to the University of Oxford; no HoBo is listed there.)
Horatio Alger Society
Institut d'Histoire du Livre
International Association of Master Penmen, Engrossers and Teachers of Handwriting
International Association of Paper Historians
International Bond & Share Society
International Federation of Ex-libris Societies
International Society of Typographic Designers
The Iowa Bibliophiles
Jaffe Center for Book Arts
John Jarrold Printing Museum (Norwich, UK)
Kalamazoo Book Arts Center
Les Amis de la Reilure d'Art (Quebec)
London Rare Books School
Midwest Book & Manuscript Studies (defunct)
Minnesota Center for Book Arts
Morgan Art of Papermaking Conservatory & Educational Foundation
Movable Book Society
Museum Meermanno (Dutch Museum of the Book)
Nebraska Book Arts Center (defunct)
Nederlandse Vereeniging van Antiquaren (booksellers' association)
New Australian Bookplate Society
New England Book Artists
Nordic-Baltic-Russian Network on the History of Books, Libraries and Reading

Norsk Antikvarbokhandlerforening (booksellers)
North American Hand Papermakers (formerly Friends of Dard Hunter)
NSW Guild of Craft Bookbinders (Australia)
Numismatic Bibliomania Society
Ottawa Book Collectors
Oxford Bibliographical Society
Oxford Scribes
Paper & Book Intensive
Papermakers of Victoria (Australia)
Philadelphia Center for the Book
Printing Historical Society (UK)
The Printing Museum (Houston)
Pyramid Atlantic Art Center
Queensland Bookbinders Guild (Australia)
Sacramento (CA) Book Collectors Club
Samuel Beckett Society
Scottish Printing Archival Trust
Society of Bookbinders (UK)
Society of Marbling (now the International Marbling Network)
Society of Printers (Boston, MA)
Society of Scribes
Society of Scribes and Illuminators (UK)
Society of Typographic Aficionados
Society of Wood Engravers (UK)
Société royale des bibliophiles et iconophiles de Belgique
Stichting Handboek Binden
Suomen Antikvariaattiyhdistys ry Finska Antikvariatföreningen rf (Finnish Antiquarian Booksellers)
Svenska Antikvariatföreningen
Syndicat National de la Librairie Ancienne et Moderne
Thomas Wolfe Society
Toronto Centre for the Book
Type Directors Club
Type Museum (London)
Typophiles
Verband der Antiquare Österreichs
Verband Deutscher Antiquare e.V.
Vereinigung der Buchantiquare und Kupferstichhändler in der Schweiz
Victorian Bookbinders Guild (Australia)
Virginia Arts of the Book Center (defunct?)
Washington Area Group for Print Culture Studies
Wood Engraver's Network
Worshipful Company of Stationers and Newspaper Makers (UK)
Wynkyn de Worde Society
York Bibliographical Society (UK)
日本古書籍商協会 (Japanese Old Bookstore Association)

Bibliography

ABHB: Annual Bibliography of the History of the Printed Book and Libraries (A Springer publication that was an "international bibliography in the field of book and library history. It records all publications of scholarly value, written from an historical point of view. This may include monographs, articles and reviews, dealing with the history of the printed book, its arts, crafts, techniques and equipment, its economic, social and cultural environment involved in its production, distribution preservation and description"; http://www.springer.com/series/5559; accessed 7 July 2021; now no longer being published.).

Adamowicz, Elza. "The livre d'artiste in Twentieth-Century France." *French Studies* 63.2 (April 2009): 189–98; https://academic.oup.com/fs/article/63/2/189/524221; accessed 27 April 2021.

Adams, H. M. *Catalogue of Books Printed on the Continent of Europe, 1501–1600, in Cambridge Libraries.* London: Cambridge University Press, 1967. 2 vols.

Adler, Michael H. *The Writing Machine.* London: George Allen & Unwin, 1973.

Agner, Mary Alexandra. "Using Chemistry to Learn the Provenance of Clay Tablets." *Humanities* 41.1 (Winter 2020). National Endowment for the Humanities; https://www.neh.gov/article/using-chemistry-learn-provenance-clay-tablets; accessed 1 April 2021.

Ahearn, Allen, and Patricia Ahearn. *Book Collecting: A Comprehensive Guide, 1995 Edition.* New York: G. P. Putnam's Sons, 1995.

———. *Collected Books: The Guide to Identification and Values.* 4th ed. Comus, MD: Quill & Brush, 2011.

———. *Collected Books: The Guide to Values.* New York: G. P. Putnam's Sons, 1991 (and other editions).

Aki, Ishigami. "The Reception of Shunga in the Modern Era: From Meiji to the Pre-WWII Years." *Japan Review*, Special Issue Shunga, 2013, 37–55; https://www.jstor.org/stable/41959816; accessed 28 August 2022.

Alden, John, and Dennis Landis, eds. *European Americana: A Chronological Guide to Works Printed in Europe Relating to the Americas, 1493–1776.* 6 vols. New York: Readex; Providence, RI: John Carter Brown Library, 1980–1997.

Alibris. *The Alibris Story*; https://www.alibris.com/about/story; accessed 3 January 2021.

———."Glossary of Book Terms"; https://www.alibris.com/glossary/glossary-books#raisedband; accessed 26 May 2021.

Allen, Charles Dexter. *American Book-Plates: A Guide to Their Study with Examples.* New York: Macmillan, 1894; New York: Benjamin Blom, 1968.

Allen, Sue. *The Book Cover Art of Sarah Wyman Whitman.* Boston: Society of Printers, 2002.

Allen, Sue, and Charles Gullans. *Decorated Cloth in America: Publishers' Bindings, 1840–1910.* Los Angeles: UCLA, William Andrews Clark Memorial Library, 1994.

Alston, Robin. "The Eighteenth Century Short Title Catalogue: A Personal History to 1989"; http://web.archive.org/web/20080908103158/http://www.r-alston.co.uk/estc.htm; accessed 6 July 2021.

Altar Book for Gorecki. Middletown, CT: Robin Price, Publisher, 1996 (one of 60 copies).

Alvarez, Pablo. University of Michigan, Online Exhibits. "Marks in Books"; https://apps.lib.umich.edu/online-exhibits/exhibits/show/marks-in-books; accessed 16 February 2021.

American Antiquarian Society. "Almanacs"; https://www.americanantiquarian.org/almanacs; accessed 5 January 2021.

———. "Clipper Ship Cards." American Antiquarian Society; https://www.americanantiquarian.org/clippershipcards.htm; accessed 13 March 2021.

———. "McLoughlin Bros. Collection"; https://www.americanantiquarian.org/mcloughlin-bros; accessed 16 May 2021.

———. "Rewards of Merit"; https://www.americanantiquarian.org/rewardsom.htm; accessed 21 March 2021.

American Dictionary of Printing and Bookmaking: Containing a History of These Arts in Europe and America, with Definitions of Technical Terms. New York: Howard Lockwood, 1894; reprint, New York: Burt Franklin, 1970.

American Heritage Dictionary of the English Language. 5th ed. Boston: Houghton Mifflin, 2011.

American Library Association. "1917"; https://www.ala.org/aboutala/1917; accessed 30 July 2021.

American Psychological Association. *Publication Manual of the American Psychological Association.* 7th Edition. Washington, DC: American Psychological Association, 2020.

American Tract Society. "A Brief History of the American Tract Society, Instituted at Boston, 1814: And Its Relations to the American Tract Society at New York, Instituted 1825." Boston: American Tract Society; Press of T. R. Marvin, 1857; https://

archive.lib.msu.edu/AFS/dmc/ssb/public/all/briefhistory/brie.html; accessed 6 March 2021.

American Type Founders Company. *American Specimen Book of Type Styles: Complete Catalogue of Printing Machinery and Printing Supplies*. Jersey City, NJ: American Type Founders, 1912.

———. *Specimen Book and Catalogue: Dedicated to the Typographic Art*. Jersey City, NJ: American Type Founders, 1923.

Amith, Jonathan D. *La Tradición del Amate: Innovación y Protesta en el Arte Mexicano/The Amate Tradition: Innovation and Dissent in Mexican Art*. Mexico City: La Casa de las Imágenes; Chicago: Mexican Fine Arts Center Museum, 1995.

Anderson, Charles B. *Bookselling in America and the World: Some Observations & Recollections in Celebration of the 75th Anniversary of the American Booksellers Association*. New York: Quadrangle/New York Times Book Co., 1975.

Andrews, William Loring. *Sextodecimos Et Infra* of 1899. New York: Charles Scribner's Sons, 1899.

Anglo-American Cataloguing Rules (AACR, AACR2, AACR2R). See under Librarianship Studies & Information Technology.

Annenberg, Maurice. *Type Foundries of America and Their Catalogs*. Baltimore: Maran Printing Services, 1975; 2nd ed., "With additions and an introduction by Stephen O. Saxe and an index by Elizabeth K. Lieberman." New Castle, DE: Oak Knoll, 1994. (The 1994 ed. contains 73 specimen books and one new type founder not listed by Annenberg.)

"Anthony [Tony] Cains: Book Binder and Pioneering Conservator"; obituary in *The Irish Times*, 9 January 2021; https://www.irishtimes.com/life-and-style/people/anthony-tony-cains-obituary-book-binder-and-pioneering-conservator-1.4452296; accessed 25 March 2021.

The Anthropodermic Book Project; https://anthropodermicbooks.org/; accessed 5 April 2021.

Appleton, Tony. *Writings of Stanley Morison: A Handlist*. Brighton: Tony Appleton, 1976.

Arber, Edward, ed. *Transcript of the Registers of the Company of Stationers of London,1554–1708*. Privately printed, 1875–1914; reprint, Gloucester: Smith, 1967.

Arbour, Keith. *Canvassing Books, Sample Books, and Subscription Publishers' Ephemera 1833–1951 in the Collection of Michael Zinman*. Ardsley, NY: Haydn Foundation for the Cultural Arts, 1996.

Arnold, William Harris. *Ventures in Book Collecting*. New York: Charles Scribner's Sons, 1923.

Aronsky, Eugene. Qullingcard, "The Mighty Quill: The Art of Quilling"; December 16, 2019; https://quillingcard.com/blogs/quilling-blog/the-history-of-quilling; accessed 25 February 2021.

Ascher, James P. "Progressing Toward Bibliography; or: Organic Growth in the Bibliographic Record," *RBM: A Journal of Rare Books, Manuscripts, and Cultural Heritage* 10.2 (Fall 2009), p. 98; available at http://citeseerx.ist.psu.edu/viewdoc/download?doi=10.1.1.168.5254&rep=rep1&type=pdf; accessed 6 June 2021.

Ash, Nancy E. "Recording Watermarks by Beta-Radiography and Other Means." *Book and Paper Group Annual* 1 (1982); http://cool.conservation-us.org/coolaic/sg/bpg/annual/v01/bp01-02.html; accessed 6 July 2021.

Asimov, Isaac. "Literature / Rejection Slips." *Isaac Asimov's Science Fiction Magazine* [December 1979 issue]; cited by TV tropes; https://tvtropes.org/pmwiki/pmwiki.php/Literature/RejectionSlips; accessed 23 April 2021.

Avis, F. C. *The Bookman's Concise Dictionary*. London: F. C. Avis, 1956.

———. *Edward Philip Prince: Type Punchcutter*. London: F. C. Avis, 1967.

———. *Type Face Terminology*. London: F. C. Avis, 1965.

Bachaus, Theodore [Nom de plume for Henry Morris]. *The World's Worst Marbled Paper*. North Hills, PA: Bird & Bull Press, 1978.

Baender, Paul. "The Meaning of Copy-Text." *Studies in Bibliography* 22 (1969): 311–18.

Bain, Peter, and Paul Shaw. *Blackletter: Type and National Identity*. New York: Princeton Architectural Press, Cooper Union for the Advancement of Science and Art, 1998.

Baines, Paul, and Pat Rogers. *Edmund Curll, Bookseller*. Oxford: Clarendon Press, 2007.

Baker, Cathleen A. *By His Own Labor: The Biography of Dard Hunter*. Northport, AL: Red Hydra Press, 2000; reprint, New Castle, DE: Oak Knoll, 2000.

———. *From the Hand to the Machine: Nineteenth-century American Paper and Mediums: Technologies, Materials, and Conservation*. Ann Arbor, MI: Legacy Press, 2010.

———. "The Wove Paper in John Baskerville's Virgil (1757): Made on a Cloth-Covered Laid Mould." In Tatiana Ginsberg, ed. *Papermaker's Tears: Essays on the Art and Craft of Paper*, Vol. 1. Ann Arbor, MI: Legacy, 2019.

Baker, Nicholson. *Double Fold: Libraries and the Assault on Paper*. New York: Random House, 2001.

Baker, William, and Kenneth Womack, comps. *Twentieth-Century Bibliography and Textual Criticism: An Annotated Bibliography*. Westport, CT: Greenwood, 2000.

Ball, Douglas. *Victorian Publishers' Bindings*. London: Library Association, 1985.

Balston, John. *The Whatmans and Wove (Velin) Paper: Its Invention and Development in the West: Research into the Origins of Wove Paper and of genuine* [*sic*, lower case] *Loom-Woven Wire-cloth*. West Farleigh, Kent, England: Published by J. N. Balston, 1998.

Balston, Thomas. *James Whatman: Father and Son*. London: Methuen, 1957.

Balzer, Richard. *Peepshows: A Visual History*. New York: Harry N. Abrams, 1998.

Barker, Nicolas. *Aldus Manutius and the Development of Greek Script and Type in the Fifteenth Century*. Sandy Hook, CT: Chiswick Book Shop, 1985; Ithaca, NY: Fordham University Press, 1992.

———. *Aldus Manutius: Mercantile Empire of the Intellect*. UCLA University Research Library Occasional Paper 3. Los Angeles: UCLA, 1989.

———. *The Butterfly Books: An Enquiry into the Nature of Certain Twentieth Century Pamphlets*. London: Bertram Rota, 1987.

———. *The Oxford University Press and the Spread of Learning, 1468–1978: An Illustrated History*. Oxford: Clarendon, 1978.

———. *Stanley Morison*. London: Macmillan; Cambridge, MA: Harvard University Press, 1972.

———, ed. *Two East Anglian Picture Books. A Facsimile of the Helmingham Herbal and Bestiary and Bodleian MS. Ashmole 1504*. London: Roxburghe Club, 1988.

Barnes, Paul. "James Mosley: A Life in Objects." *Eye 100* (Summer 2015); http://www.eyemagazine.com/feature/article/james-mosley-a-life-in-objects; accessed 1 April 2021.

Barr, John. *The Officina Bodoni, Montagnola, Verona: Books Printed by Giovanni Mardersteig on the Hand-press, 1923–1977*. Exhibition catalog. London: British Library, 1978.

———. *Stanley Morison: A Portrait*. London: Trustees of the British Museum, 1971.

Barrett, Grant. *Hatchet Jobs and Hardball: The Oxford Dictionary of American Political Slang*. Oxford: Oxford University Press, 2004.

Barrett, Timothy D. *European Hand Papermaking: Traditions, Tools, and Techniques*. Ann Arbor, MI: Legacy Press, 2018.

———. *Japanese Papermaking: Traditions, Tools, and Techniques*. New York: Weatherhill, 1983.

Barton, Carol. *The Pocket Paper Engineer*. Vol. 1, Glen Echo, MD: Popular Kinetics, 2005; and Vol. 2, Glen Echo, MD: Popular Kinetics Press, 2008.

Bartram, Alan. *Five Hundred Years of Book Design*. New Haven: Yale University Press, 2001.

Basic Requirements for Better Electrotypes: A Manual of Suggestions on Proper Procedures for Obtaining the Best Quality and Performance of Electrotypes. Cleveland, OH: International Association of Electrotypers & Stereotypers, 1960.

Baskin, Lisa, et al. *The Gehenna Press: The Work of Fifty Years, 1942–1992*. Dallas: Bridwell Library; [Leeds, MA]: Gehenna, 1992.

Bastian, Andreas. "Laser Etched Paper for Folding Complex Forms." Instructables Workshop; instructables.com/Laser-Etched-Paper-for-Folding-Complex-Forms/; accessed 17 August 2022.

Batista, Nino. "Why You May Not Be a Boudoir Photographer Even Though You Think You Are"; Fstoppers, August 13, 2015; https://fstoppers.com/business/why-you-may-not-be-boudoir-photographer-even-though-you-think-you-are-77741; accessed 21 February 2021.

Battles, Matthew. *Widener: Biography of a Library*. Cambridge, MA: Harvard College Library, 2004.

Baxley, George C. "Takejiro Hasegawa/Kobunsha Publications: 'Chirimen-bon' (Crepe Paper Books) and Plain Paper Books"; http://www.baxleystamps.com/litho/hasegawa.shtml; accessed 18 February 2021.

BDKR.com. "Baedeker Checklist"; http://bdkr.com/chklist.php; accessed 7 April 2021.

Beal, Peter. *A Dictionary of English Manuscript Terminology, 1450–2000*. Oxford: Oxford University Press, 2008.

Beattie, Simon. See under Simon Beattie.

Beguin, André. *A Treatise on Aquatint*. Paris: André Beguin, 1999.

Beilinson, Peter. *The Story of Frederic Goudy*. Mount Vernon, NY: Peter Pauper, 1965.

Bellis, Mary. "The History of Xerox"; http://theinventors.org/library/inventors/blxerox.htm; accessed 6 July 2021.

Bennett, Paul A., ed. *Goudy's Type Designs: His Story and Specimens*. Published in 1946 for The Typophiles; with a "Virtual Facsimile of The Typophiles Chap Books XIII and XIV, A Half-Century of Type Design and Typography by Frederic W. Goudy." 2nd ed. New Rochelle, NY: Myriade, 1978.

Bennett, Stuart. *Trade Bookbinding in the British Isles, 1660–1800*. New Castle, DE: Oak Knoll; London: British Library, 2004.

Bennett, William. *John Baskerville the Birmingham Printer, His Press, Relations and Friends*. Birmingham: City of Birmingham School of Printing, Central School of Arts and Crafts, 1939.

Benton, Josiah Henry. *John Baskerville: Type-Founder and Printer, 1706–1775*. Boston: Merrymount, 1914.

Berger, Sidney E. "The A^{8}B^{8}C^{8}s of Bibliographical Description." *Biblio* 2.11 (November 1997): 58–59.

———. *The Anatomy of a Literary Hoax*. New Castle, DE: Oak Knoll, 1994.

———. "Another Copy of Ezra Pound's 'A Lume Spento.'" *Papers of the Bibliographical Society of America* 88.1 (March 1994): 93–100.

———. "Book Format, Part One: Broadsides, Folios, Quartos." *Biblio* 2.5 (May 1997): 44–49.

———. "Book Format, Part Two: Octavos, Duodecimos, Sextodecimos." *Biblio* 2.6 (June 1997): 50–53.

———. *The Book of Death*. Waban, MA: Doe, 2017.

———. "Chester Beatty." In *Twentieth-Century British Book Collectors and Bibliographers*, Vol. 201 of *Dictionary of Literary Biography*, 12–19. Detroit: Gale Research, 1999.

———. *Chiyogami Papers*. North Hills, PA: Bird & Bull, 2011.

———. *The Design of Bibliographies: Observations, References, and Examples*. Westport, CT: Greenwood; London: Mansell, 1991.

———. "Dutch Gilt Papers as Substitutes for Leather." *Hand Papermaking* 24.2 (Winter 2009): 14–16.

———. "Editorial Intrusion in *Pudd'nhead Wilson*." *Papers of the Bibliographical Society of America* 70 (1976): 272–76.

———. "Else Fine and Other Features of the Dealer's Catalog: Part One." *Biblio* 1.2 (September–October 1996): 42–46.

———. "Else Fine and Other Features of the Dealer's Catalog: Part II." *Biblio* 1.3 (November–December 1996): 42–46.

———. "Endleaves." In Dennis Duncan and Adam Smyth, eds. *Book Parts*. Oxford: Oxford University Press, 2019, pp. 275–85; plates 8–12.

———. *Fleuronologia*. Northampton, MA: Gehenna Press, 1996.

———. "Harry Buxton Forman." In *Nineteenth-Century British Book-Collectors and Bibliographers*, Vol. 184 of *Dictionary of Literary Biography*, 95–103. Detroit: Gale Research, 1997.

———. "History of Three Basic Printing Processes." In *Encyclopedia of Library and Information Science*. 3rd ed. Taylor & Francis, online (elis@taylorandfrancis.com), 2010.

———. "Leonard Baskin and the Art of Printing (The Ego and the Ecstasy)." *Parenthesis* 17 (Autumn 2009): 13–19.

———. *Printing and the Mind of Merker: A Bibliographical Study*. New York: Grolier Club, 1997.

———. "Printing Types: Calligraphy and Letterforms." Part of chapter 1, "Books about Books." In *The Reader's Adviser*, 14th ed., edited by David Scott Kastan et al., 1–57. New Providence, NJ: Bowker, 1994.

———, ed. *Pudd'nhead Wilson and Those Extraordinary Twins*: A Norton Critical Edition. New York: W. W. Norton, 1980; 2nd ed. New York: W. W. Norton, 2004.

———. "Sir Frederic Madden." In *Nineteenth-Century British Book-Collectors and Bibliographers*, Vol. 184 of *Dictionary of Literary Biography*, 271–78. Detroit: Gale Research, 1997.

———, ed. "Textual Introduction." In *Pudd'nhead Wilson and Those Extraordinary Twins*. A Norton Critical Edition. 2nd ed., 189–98. New York: W. W. Norton, 2005.

———. *Rare Books and Special Collections*. Chicago: Neal-Schuman/American Library Association, 2014. This volume receives many citations in the present volume. It is referred to only as "Berger." Other works by this author are cited by name and key words in the title.

———. "Reconsidering Gutenberg." *Biblio* 3.2 (February 1998): 14–15.

———. "Stop the Presses! A Primer on Cancels." *Biblio* 2.9 (September 1997): 56–57.

———, comp. *Three Fine-Press Printers: Harry Duncan, Kim Merker, Doyle Moore*. Champaign: Department of Special Collections, University of Illinois, Urbana–Champaign, 1986.

Berkowitz, David Sandler. *Bibliotheca bibliographica incunabula: A Manual of Bibliographical Guides to Inventories of Printing, of Holdings, and of Reference Aids; with an Appendix of Useful Information on Place-Names and Dating, Collected and Classified for the Use of Researchers in Incunabulistics*. Waltham, MA: David Sandler Berkowitz, 1967.

Bernard, Philippa, comp. and ed., with Leo Bernard and Angus O'Neill. *Antiquarian Books: A Companion for Booksellers, Librarians and Collectors*. Philadelphia: University of Pennsylvania Press and Scolar Press, 1994.

Bernard Quaritch. See under Quaritch, Bernard.

Beros, Matthew. "Bibliomania: Thomas Frognall Dibden and Early 19th Century Book Collecting." In *TXT: Exploring the Boundaries of the Book*. Leiden University, Scholarly Publications. Den Haag: Boom Uitgevers, 2014, pp. 141–45; https://pasningverli1988.files.wordpress.com/2018/07/bibliomania-thomas-frognall-dibdin-and-early-19th-century-book.pdf; accessed 21 January 2021.

Berry, W. Turner, and H. Edmund Poole. *Annals of Printing: A Chronological Encyclopaedia from the Earliest Times to 1950*. London: Blandford, 1966.

Besterman, Theodore. *A World Bibliography of Bibliographies and of Bibliographical Catalogues, Calendars, Abstracts, Digests, Indexes, and the Like*. 4th ed. 5 vols. Lausanne: Societas Bibliographica, 1965–1966.

Bickham, George. *The Universal Penman. Engraved by George Bickham, London, 1743*; Facsimile Edition. New York: Paul A. Struck, 1941.

Bidwell, John. *American Paper Mills 1690–1832: A Directory of the Paper Trade with Notes on Products, Watermarks, Distribution Methods, and Manufacturing Techniques*. Hanover, NH: Dartmouth College Press; Worcester, MA: American Antiquarian Society, 2013.

Bigelow, Charles, Paul Hayden Duensing, and Linnea Gentry, eds. *Fine Print on Type: The Best of Fine Print Magazine on Type and Typography, 1977–1988*. San Francisco: Fine Print, 1989 (and other editions).

Biggs, John R. *Basic Typography*. New York: Watson-Guptill, 1968.

Bigmore, F. C., and C. W. H. Wyman. *A Bibliography of Printing*. London: Bernard Quaritch, 1880; reprint, London: Holland; New Castle, DE: Oak Knoll, 1978.

Billman, Carol. *The Secret of the Stratemeyer Syndicate: Nancy Drew, the Hardy Boys, and the Million Dollar Fiction Factory*. New York: Ungar, 1986.

Bishop, Philip R. "Thomas Bird Mosher: Publishing Prince . . . or Pirate?" *Biblio* 2.7 (July 1997): 38–45; http://www.thomasbirdmosher.net/biography/BIBLIO_article.html; accessed 25 October 2015. This article no longer accessible on the web; but see by the same author: "Thomas Bird Mosher, 1852–1923, Passionate Pirate and Prince of Publishers"; https://thomasbirdmosher.net/biographical-information/a-biography-of-mosher/; accessed 6 July 2021.

Blades, William. *Enemies of Books*. London: Trübner & Co., 1880 (and many other editions and printings).

———. *Life and Typography of William Caxton, England's First Printer: With Evidence of His Typographical Connection with Colard Mansion the Printer at Bruges*. London: Lilly, 1861 (and many later editions and reprintings).

Blagden, Cyprian. *The Stationers' Company: A History, 1403–1959*. London: Allen & Unwin, 1960 (and other editions).

Blanck, Jacob. *Bibliography of American Literature*. (Completed by Michael Winship.) New Haven, CT: Yale University Press, 1955–1991.

———. "Twilight Books." In his *Bibliography of American Literature* [see preceding entry], Vol. 1, p. xxi.

Blayney, Peter W. M. *The Stationers' Company and the Printers of London, 1501–1557*. 2 vols. Cambridge: Cambridge University Press, 2013.

Bliven, Bruce, Jr. *Book Traveller*. New York: Dodd, Mead & Co., 1975.

Bloom, J. Harvey. *English Tracts, Pamphlets and Printed Sheets: A Bibliography*. 2 vols. London: Wallace Gandy, 1923.

Bloy, Colin. *A History of Printing Ink, Balls and Rollers, 1440–1850*. London: Wynken de Worde Society; New York: Sandstone, 1967.

Blumenthal, Joseph. *Art of the Printed Book 1455–1955: Masterpieces of Typography through Five Centuries from the Collections of the Pierpont Morgan Library*. New York: Pierpont Morgan Library; Boston: David Godine, 1973.

Bodian, Nat G. *Bodian's Publishing Desk Reference: A Comprehensive Dictionary of Practices and Techniques for Book and Journal Marketing and Bookselling*. Phoenix, AZ; Oryx, 1988.

Bodleian Libraries. "Visit"; https://visit.bodleian.ox.ac.uk/plan-your-visit/history-bodleian; accessed 23 April 2021.

———. "Bodleian Libraries, University of Oxford"; https://www.bodleian.ox.ac.uk/home#/; accessed 23 April 2021.

Bonner, Gerald. "Forgery: Art." *Encyclopædia Britannica*; http://www.britannica.com/topic/forgery-art; accessed 6 July 2021.

Borden, Bill. *Big Book of Big Little Books*. San Francisco: Chronicle Books, 1997.

Borgman, Christine L. *Scholarship in the Digital Age: Information, Infrastructure, and the Internet*. Cambridge, MA: MIT Press, 2007.

Boston Public Library, "Sarah Wyman Whitman Bindings"; https://www.flickr.com/photos/24029425@N06/albums/72157604192955355/; accessed 2 August 2021.

Bowers, Fredson. *Bibliography and Textual Criticism*. Oxford: Clarendon, 1964.

———. "Current Theories of Copy-Text, with an Illustration from Dryden." In *Bibliography and Textual Criticism: English and American Literature, 1700 to the Present*, edited by O. M. Brack and Warner Barnes, 59–72. Chicago: University of Chicago Press, 1969.

———. *Principles of Bibliographical Description*. Princeton, NJ: Princeton University Press, 1949 (and later editions).

Bowker. "Self-Publishing in the United States, 2013–2018"; https://www.bowker.com/siteassets/files/pdf-files/bowker-selfpublishing-report-2019.pdf; accessed 8 August 2021.

"BPG Cloth Bookbinding." Book and Paper Group, 11 March 2021; https://www.conservation-wiki.com/wiki/BPG_Cloth_Bookbinding#Cloth_in_Bookbinding; accessed 20 October 2022.

Brack, O M, and Warner Barnes, eds. *Bibliography and Textual Criticism: English and American Literature, 1700 to the Present*. Chicago: University of Chicago Press, 1969.

Bragin, Charles. *Dime Novels, Bibliography, 1860–1928*. Brooklyn, NY: Bragin, 1938.

Brake, Laurel, and Marysa Demoor. *Dictionary of Nineteenth-Century Journalism in Great Britain and Ireland*. Gent: Academia Press; London: British Library, 2009.

Bregman, Alvan. *Emblemata: The Emblem Books of Andrea Alciato*. Newtown, PA: Bird & Bull, 2007.

Brenni, Vito. *Bookbinding: A Guide to the Literature*. Westport, CT: Greenwood, 1982.

Breslauer, B. H. *The Uses of Bookbinding Literature*. New York: School of Library Service, Columbia University, Book Arts Press, 1986.

Briggs & Co's Patent Transferring Papers. Manchester: Briggs & Co., n.d. (1890s?).

Brigham, William T. *Ka Hana Kapa: The Making of Bark-Cloth in Hawaii*. Honolulu: Bishop Museum, 1911; reprint, Millwood, NY: Kraus Reprint Co., 1976. Vol. III of Memoirs of the Bernice Pauahi Bishop Museum of Polynesian Ethnology and Natural History.

Bright, Betty. *No Longer Innocent: Book Art in America, 1960–1980*. New York: Granary, 2005.

Brightly, Charles. *The Method of Founding Stereotype*. Bungay: Printed by C. Brightly, 1809; reprint, New York: Garland, 1982.

Bringhurst, Robert. *The Elements of Typographic Style*. Point Roberts, WA: Hartley & Marks, 1992.

———. "Introduction." In *The Form of the Book: Essays on the Morality of Good Design*, by Jan Tschichold, translated by Hajo Hadeler, ix–xviii. Point Roberts, WA: Hartley & Marks, 1991.

Briquet Online. https://briquet-online.at/; accessed 9 June 2021.

Bristol, Roger. *Supplement to Charles Evans' American Bibliography*. Charlottesville: University of Virginia Press, 1970.

Britannica. "Areopagitica"; https://www.britannica.com/topic/Areopagitica; accessed February 12, 2021.

———. "Imprimitur"; https://www.britannica.com/topic/imprimatur; accessed February 20, 2021.

British Library. "Cotton Manuscripts"; http://www.bl.uk/reshelp/findhelprestype/manuscripts/cottonmss/cottonmss.html; accessed 6 July 2021.

———. "Database of Bookbindings"; https://www.bl.uk/catalogues/bookbindings/About.aspx; accessed 5 April 2021.

———. "New Minster *Liber vitae*"; https://www.bl.uk/collection-items/liber-vitae; accessed 26 February 2021.

British Library, Medieval Manuscript Blog. "Frying Pans, Forks and Fever: Medieval Book Curses"; 23 May 2017; https://blogs.bl.uk/digitisedmanuscripts/2017/05/frying-pans-forks-and-fever-medieval-book-curses.html; accesed 31 March 2021.

Brook, G. L. *Books and Book-Collecting*. London: André Deutsch, 1980.

Brooker, T. Kimball. See *Gazette of the Grolier Club*.

Brooks, Katherine. "There's a Japanese Word for People Who Buy More Books Than They Can Actually Read." *Culture & Arts* (23 April 2017); https://www.huffpost.com/entry/theres-a-japanese-word-for-people-who-buy-more-books-than-they-can-actually-read_n_58f79b7ae4b029063d364226; accessed 27 May 2021.

Broomhead, Frank. *The Zaehnsdorfs (1842–1947) Craft Bookbinders*. Pinner: Private Libraries Association, 1986.

Brown, Meaghan J. "Addresses to the Reader." In Dennis Duncan and Adam Smyth. *Book Parts*, pp. 81–93. Oxford: Oxford University Press, 2019.

Brown, Meg. "Flip, Flap and Crack: The Conservation and Exhibition of 400+ Years of Flap Anatomies." *The Book and Paper Group Annual* 32 (2013): 6–14.

Brown, Michelle P. *Understanding Illuminated Manuscripts: A Guide to Technical Terms*. Los Angeles: J. Paul Getty Museum, in association with the British Library, 1994.

Brown, Michelle P., and Patricia Lovett. *The Historical Source Book for Scribes*. London: British Library; Toronto: University of Toronto Press, 1999.

Brown University Library Center for Digital Initiatives. "Carriers' Addresses"; https://library.brown.edu/cds/carriers/about.html; accessed 15 February 2021.

Bruccoli, Matthew J. "What Bowers Wrought: An Assessment of the Center for Editions of American Authors," pp. 237–44. In *The Culture of Collected Editions*, edited by by Andrew Nash. New York: Palgrave Macmillan, 2003.

Bruckner, D. J. H. *Frederic Goudy*. New York: Abrams, 1990.

Brunet, Jacques-Charles. *Manuel du libraire et de l'amateur de livres*. Paris: 1810 (first edtion, in 3 vols.); Paris: Librairie de Firmin Didot Freres, 1860–64 (in 5 vols.; described by one bookseller as "fifth, final, and best edition").

Bullen, Henry Lewis. *Nicolas Jenson, Printer of Venice: His Famous Type Designs and Some Comment upon the Printing Types of Earlier Printers*. San Francisco: John Henry Nash, 1926.

Burlingham, Albert S. "The Printer's Roller," pp. 144–53. In *The Building of a Book*, edited by Frederick H. Hitchcock. New York: Grafton, 1906.

Burnet, Gilbert Thomas. *The Floral Keepsake: A Selection of Forty-eight Accurately Coloured Figures of Tender and Hardy Useful and Ornamental Plants*. London: George Willis 1858.

Burns, Ken. See under Ward, Geoffrey C.

Butler, William E. "Letter from the Chair." *FABS* [this inside the new organization logo] *of American Bibliophilic Societies* 25.1 (Spring 2021): 4–5.

Byrne, Alexander. "Chirimon-bon or Crêpe Paper Books." In *Daruma: Japanese Art & Antiques Magazine* 12.3, Issue 47 (Summer 2005): 12–27.

Cahill, Thomas, Bruce H. Kusko, and Richard N. Schwab. "Analyses of Inks and Papers in Historical Documents through External Beam PIXE Techniques." *Nuclear Instruments and Methods* 181 (1981): 205–08.

Cain, Abigail. "Before Envelopes, People Protected Messages With Letterlocking: For Centuries, Senders Used Folds, Slits, and Wax Seals to Guard Correspondence from Prying Eyes." Atlas Obscura, 9 November 2018; https://www.atlasobscura.com/articles/what-did-people-do-before-envelopes-letterlocking; accessed 22 May 2021.

Cains, Anthony (Tony). See under "Anthony [Tony] Cains: Book Binder and Pioneering Conservator."

Cains, Anthony G., and Maria Fredericks. "The Bindings of the Ellesmere Chaucer." *Huntington Library Quarterly* 58.1 (1995): 127–57.

Calè, Luisa. "Frontispieces." In Dennis Duncan and Adam Smyth. *Book Parts*, pp. 25–37. Oxford: Oxford University Press, 2019.

Cambridge University. See University of Cambridge.

Camille, Michael. *Image on the Edge: The Margins of Medieval Art*. Cambridge, MA: Harvard University Press, 1992.

Cappelli, Adriano. *Lexicon Abbreviaturarum: Dizionario di Abbreviature latine ed italiane*. Milano: Ulrico Hoepli, 1973.

Carlsen, Darvey E. *Graphic Arts*. Peoria, IL: Chas. A. Bennett Co., 1965.

Carr, J[oseph] L[loyd]. *What Hetty Did, or, Life and Letters*. Kettering, Northamptonshire, UK: Quince Tree, 1988.

Carter, David A., and James Diaz. *The Elements of Pop-Up: A Pop-Up Book for Aspiring Paper Engineers*. New York: Little Simon, an imprint of Simon & Schustter, 1999.

Carter, Harry G., and Hendrik Vervliet. *Civilité Types*. Oxford: Oxford University Press, 1966.

Carter, John. *ABC for Book Collectors*. 8th ed., with Nicolas Barker. New Castle, DE: Oak Knoll; London: British Library, 2004. This version, with Nicolas Barker's updates and additions, does indeed constitute a new edition. But since more than 95 percent of the work was Carter's, I have listed it under his name. This is one of the classic volumes in the world of books, and no bibliophile's library is complete without a copy of this standard reference tool. The present volume, as its introduction indicates, was inspired by this book and is an updating and expansion of it, correcting some of Carter's entries. The full text of the 8th edition of this book is available free online at https://ilab.org/assets/documents/articles/documentation_center_files_29_2_20abc_20forbookcollectors_20bob_20fleck.pdf; accessed 3 August 2021. Citations to the first edition are to London: Rupert Hart-Davis, 1952. A 9th edition, edited by Simran Thadani (New Castle, DE: Oak Knoll, 2016), does not correct Carter's or Barker's problems, and it introduces a host of new ones.

———. *Binding Variants in English Publishing, 1820–1900*. London: Constable, 1932.

———. *Books and Book Collectors*. London: Rupert Hart-Davis, 1956 (and other editions).

———. *A Descriptive Catalogue Illustrating the Impact of Print on the Evolution of Western Civilization during Five Centuries*, edited by Percy H. Muir, et al. London: Cassell; New York: Holt, Rinehart, Winston, 1967.

———. "Earliest Dust-Wrapper." *Publishers' Weekly* 126 (September 22, 1934): 1121.

———. *More Binding Variants: Aspects of Book Collecting*. London: Constable, 1938. (This and Carter's earlier *Binding Variants* were reprinted in a single volume: New Castle, DE: Oak Knoll, 1989.)

———. *Taste and Technique in Book Collecting*. New York: Bowker, 1948. Also (in a different edition) Cambridge: Cambridge University Press, 1948.

———. *Printing and the Mind of Man*. 2nd ed. revised and enlarged with a new introduction by Percy H. Muir, additional bibliographies by Peter Amelung, and a revised index. Munich: Karl Pressler, 1983.

———, and Graham Pollard. *An Enquiry into the Nature of Certain Nineteenth Century Pamphlets*. London: Constable, 1934 (and later reprints and editions).

Castiglione, Baldesar. *The Book of the Courtier*. Translated by Charles S. Singleton. New York: Anchor, 1959; New York: W. W. Norton, 2002.

Castle, Egerton. *English Book-Plates: Ancient and Modern*. London: George Bell & Sons, 1894.

Catich, Edward M. *The Origin of the Serif: Brush Writing & Roman Letters*. Davenport, IA: Catfish Press, St. Ambrose University, 1968 (and later editions).

Cave, Roderick. *Chinese Ceremonial Papers*. Leominster, Herefordshire, England: Whittington Press, 2002.

———. *Chinese Paper Offerings*. Hong Kong; Oxford; New York: Oxford University Press, 1998.

———. *Fine Printing and Private Presses: Selected Papers*. London: British Library, 2001.

———. *Impressions of Nature: A History of Nature Printing*. London: British Library, 2009. See also "Impressions of Nature: A History of Nature Printing," *Guardian*, 19 August 2010; https://www.theguardian.com/environment/gallery/2010/aug/19/impressions-of-nature; accessed 14 May 2021.

———. *The Private Press*. New York: Watson-Guptill, 1971; 2nd ed., New York: Bowker, 1983.

"Celestial Cartography—Maps of the Heaven." http://www.berksastronomy.org/starcharts.htm#:~:text=The%20first%20celestial%20atlas/%with,cloudy%objects%20in%%20the%sky; accessed 13 August 2022.

Cennini, Cennino d'Andrea. *The Craftsman's Handbook: The Italian "Il Libro dell'Arte."* Translated by Daniel V. Thompson Jr. New York: Dover, 1954 (and later impressions).

Chambers, Anne. *Suminagashi: The Japanese Art of Marbling: A Practical Guide*. London: Thames and Hudson, 1991.

Champney, Freeman. *Art and Glory: The Story of Elbert Hubbard*. New York: Crown, 1968 (and later editions).

Chapman, R. W. *Cancels: With Eleven Facsimiles in Collotype*. London: Constable & Co.; New York: Richard R. Smith, Inc., 1930.

Chappell, Warren. *A Short History of the Printed Word*. New York: Knopf; New York: Dorset Press, 1970.

"Cheap and Easy Room, The." See under *The Newberry.*

Chicago Manual of Style. 17th ed. Chicago: University of Chicago Press, 2017. Available as *Chicago Manual of Style Online*; https://www.chicagomanualofstyle.org/home.html; accessed 1 February 2021.

Choldin, Marianna Tax. "Access to Foreign Publications in Soviet Libraries." *Libraries & Culture* 26.1, *Reading & Libraries I* (Winter, 1991): 135–50.

Christensen, Bodil, and Samuel Marti. *Brujerías y Papel Precolombino/Witchcraft and Pre-columbian Paper.* Apartado: Ediciones Euroamericanas, 1971; 2nd printing, 1972.

"Christopher Clarkson, Book Conservator"; http://www.clarksonconservation.com/; accessed 23 March 2021.

Clair, Colin. *Christopher Plantin.* London: Cassell, 1960.

———. *A Chronology of Printing.* New York: Frederick A. Praeger, 1969.

Clapperton, R. H. *The Paper-Making Machine: Its Invention, Evolution and Development.* Oxford: Pergamon, 1967.

Clark, Robert L. A., and Kathleen Ashley. *Medieval Conduct.* Minneapolis: University of Minnesota Press, 2000.

Clark, Timothy, and C. Andrew Gerstle. *Shunga: Sex and Pleasure in Japanese Art.* London: British Museum Press, 2013.

Clarke, Matt. "Just Our Type." In *The Newberry*, 10 June 2019; https://www.newberry.org/just-our-type; accessed 2 August 2021.

Clarkson, Christopher. *Limp Vellum Binding and Its Potential as a Conservation Type Structure for the Rebuilding of Early Printed Books: A Break with 19th and 20th Century Attitudes and Practices.* Hitchin: Red Gull Press, 1982 (and later editions).

ClearlyExplained.com. "Old and New Style Dates"; http://clearly-explained.com/old-and-new-style-dates/index.html; accessed 16 May 2021.

Clemons, G. Scott. See *Gazette of the Grolier Club.*

———, and H. George Fletcher. See *Gazette of the Grolier Club.*

Clerk, Honor. "The Genius of Reynolds Stone: A Private Man in a Public World." *Guardian,* 21 December 2019; https://www.spectator.co.uk/article/the-genius-of-reynolds-stone-a-private-man-in-a-public-world; accessed 15 May 2021.

Clinton, Alan. *Printed Ephemera: Collection, Organisation and Access.* London: Clive Bingley, 1981.

Cloonan, Michèle Valerie. *Early Bindings in Paper: A Brief History of European Hand-Made Paper-Covered Books with a Multilingual Glossary.* London: Mansell; Boston: G. K. Hall, 1991.

———. "Janus at 60: Performance & Participation." *Parenthesis* 29 (Autumn 2015): 4–11.

Code of Best Practices in Fair Use for Academic and Research Libraries. N.p.: Association of Research Libraries; Center for Social Media, School of Communication, American University; and Program on Information Justice and Intellectual Property, Washington College of Law, American University, January 2012.

Codex Foundation. "Codex"; https://www.codexfoundation.org/about; accessed 4 May 2021.

Cole, John Y., ed. *In Celebration: The National Union Catalog, Pre-1956 Imprints.* Washington, DC: Library of Congress, 1981; http://files.eric.ed.gov/fulltext/ED261681.pdf.

Collins, John. *The Two Forgers: A Biography of Harry Buxton Forman & Thomas James Wise.* New Castle, DE: Oak Knoll, 1992.

Colossal. "Phénakistiscope"; 17 October 2013; https://www.thisiscolossal.com/2013/10/the-first-animated-gifs/; accessed 1 May 2021.

Columbia College, Columbia University in the City of New York. "Machiavelli False Imprint, RBML 2011"; https://www.college.columbia.edu/core/content/machiavelli-false-imprint-rbml-2011; accessed 23 February 2021.

"Condition." The statement on condition was probably written by Jake Chernofsky, the longtime editor of *AB/Bookman's Weekly.* The statement, quoted in the dictionary under the entry "Condition," was in nearly every issue of that publication. See http://www.cattermole.com/page5.htm; accessed 6 July 2021.

Conjuring Credits: The Origins of Wonder. "Blow Book"; https://www.conjuringcredits.com/doku.php?id=paper:blow_book; accessed 4 April 2021.

Cook, A. D. "Art Provenance"; https://adcook.com/provenance/; accessed 3 July 2021.

Cook, Captain James. *The Explorations of Captain James Cook in the Pacific as Told by Selections of His Own Journals, 1768–1779.* New York: Limited Editions Club, 1957.

Cooke, Simon. "Book Bindings of the 1860s: The Christmas Gift Book." *The Victorian Web: Literature, History, & Culture in the Age of Victoria*; http://www.victorianweb.org/art/design/books/cooke1.html; accessed 5 January 2021.

———. "An Introduction to the Guild of Women Binders." Victorian Web; http://www.victorianweb.org/art/design/books/wbg.html; accessed 17 March 2021.

Copinger, W. A. *Supplement to Hain's Repertorium Bibliographicum.* . . . 2 vols. in 3. London: Sotheran, 1895–1902.

Coppens, C[hristian]. "The Prize Is the Proof: Four Centuries of Prize Books." In Mirjam M. Foot, ed., *Eloquent Witnesses: Bookbindings and Their History*, pp. 53–105. London: Bibliographical Society of The British Library; New Castle, DE: Oak Knoll, 2004.

Coron, Sabine, ed. *Livres en Broderie: Reliures Françaises du Moyen Age à Nos Jours.* [Exposition à la Bibliothèque de l'Arsenal du 30 Novembre 1995 au 25 Février 1996.] Paris: Bibliothèque Nationale de France, 1995.

Cox, J. Randolph, ed. *Dashing Diamond Dick and Other Classic Dime Novels.* New York: Penguin, 2007.

———. *The Dime Novel Companion: A Source Book.* Westport, CT: Greenwood, 2000.

Crist, T. J. "Wing, Donald Goddard." In *ALA World Encyclopedia of Library and Information Services*, 3rd ed., edited by Robert Wedgeworth, pp. 868–69. Chicago: American Library Association, 1993.

Croft, Justin. See under Justin Croft.

Cummings, Mike. "Mysterious Voynich Manuscript Reborn in Facsimile Edition." *Yale News*, 31 October 2016; https://news.yale.edu/2016/10/31/mysterious-voynich-manuscript-reborn-facsimile-edition; accessed 10 May 2021.

Cunningham-Kruppa, Ellen. *Mooring a Field: Paul N. Banks and the Education of Library and Archives Conservators.* Ann Arbor, MI: Legacy, 2019.

Currie, Alyssa J. "The Victorian Thumb Bible as Material Object: Charles Tilt's *The Little Picture Testament* (1839)"; https://journals.openedition.org/cve/2910?lang=en; https://doi.org/10.4000/cve.2910; accessed 15 February 2021.

Cveljo, Katherine. "Donald Goddard Wing." In *Dictionary of American Library Biography*, edited by Bodhan S. Wynar, pp. 564–66. Littleton, CO: Libraries Unlimited, 1978.

Dambrogio, Jana, Amanda Ghassaei, et al. "Unlocking History through Automated Virtual Unfolding of Sealed Documents Imaged by X-ray Microtomography." *Nature Communications*; https://www.nature.com/articles/s41467-021-21326-w.epdf?sharing_token=I5Z_yEC69ASTP-njmQODe9RgN0jAjWel9jnR3ZoTv0Op_bI5hX6tfA3U3dzPIJkF-9efyNro2449DA3Ipgj2j7Jsj1aknDfzHwQMrG1oLT7G6R0k2A7kMMUJWa9uoKCzGQt23KZ0VPKMNx6f19iLNz9BZWuQxEJe_VOYXCScU0M%3D; accessed 22 May 2021.

Dambrogio, Jana, Daniel Starza Smith, and Massachusetts Institute of Technology [M.I.T], "Letterlocking: Unlocking History"; http://letterlocking.org/about; accessed 22 May 2021.

Dana, Robert, ed. "Harry Duncan." In *Against the Grain: Interviews with Maverick American Publishers*, pp. 43–86. Iowa City: University of Iowa Press, 1986.

Dave & Adam's Card World, dacardworld.com; "The 20 Most Expensive Comic Books Ever Sold"; https://www.dacardworld.com/comic-books/twenty-most-expensive-comics; accessed 28 May 2021.

Davies, Hugh William. *Devices of the Early Printers, 1457–1560: Their History and Development, with a Chapter on Portrait Figures of Printers*. London: Grafton & Co., 1935.

Davis, Lisa Fagan. "How Many Glyphs and How Many Scribes? Digital Paleography and the Voynich Manuscript." Abstract of article in *Manuscript Studies: A Journal of the Schoenberg Institute of Manuscript Studies* 5.1, article 6; https://repository.upenn.edu/mss_sims/vol5/iss1/6/; accessed 9 August 2021.

———. "Manuscript Road Trip: The Spanish Forger." https://manuscriptroadtrip.wordpress.com/2014/01/18/manuscript-road-trip-the-spanish-forger; accessed 6 July 2021.

Dean's New Book of Dissolving Views. London: Dean and Son, 1861.

Dearing, Vinton A. "The Poor Man's Mark IV or Ersatz Hinman Collator." *Papers of the Bibliographical Society of America* 60 (1966): 149–58.

Debachere, M. C. "Problems in Obtaining Grey Literature." *IFLA Journal* 21.2 (1995): 94–98.

Decorated Paper. "Annonay Paper"; August 24, 2013; http://decoratedpaper.blogspot.com/2013/08/annonay-paper-papier-d-annonay.html; accessed 12 February 2021.

Defintions.net. "Benedictional"; https://www.definitions.net/definition/benedictional; accessed 20 February 2021.

De Hamel, Christopher. *A History of Illuminated Manuscripts*. Oxford: Phaidon, 1986 (and other editions).

———. *Medieval Craftsmen: Scribes and Illuminators*. Toronto: University of Toronto Press, 1992.

De Hamel, Christopher, and Joel Silver. *Disbound and Dispersed: The Leaf Book Considered*. Chicago: Caxton Club, 2005.

Della Contrada, John. "UB's Hamady Collection to be Exhibited at Grolier Club in NYC." University of Buffalo; http://www.buffalo.edu/imsd/about-imsd/the-buffalo-niagara-region.host.html/content/shared/university/news/news-center-releases/2003/02/6083.detail.html; accessed 30 June 2021.

Demme, Christoph Hermann Gottfried, ed. *Altenburgisches Gesangbuch: Nebst Gebeten: Zum Gebrauch bey der öffentlichen Gottesverehrung und häuslichen Andacht*. Altenburg, Germany: Herzogl. Sächs. Hofbuchdruckeren, 1825.

Denison Library, Denison University. "Otto F. Ege Collection"; http://ege.denison.edu/; accessed 12 February 2021.

de Ricci, Seymour. *A Census of Caxtons*. Oxford: Oxford University Press, 1909.

———. *English Collectors of Books & Manuscripts (1530–1930) and Their Marks of Ownership*. Cambridge: Cambridge University Press, 1930; London: Holland; Bloomington: Indiana University Press, 1960

———. *English Collectors of Books & Manuscripts, 1530–1930: And Their Marks of Ownership*. Cambridge: Cambridge University Press, 2011.

Designer Bookbinders. "About DB"; http://www.designerbookbinders.org.uk/; and "History"; http://www.designerbookbinders.org.uk/about_db/history.html; accessed 2 April 2021.

De Vinne, Theodore Low. *Christopher Plantin and the Plantin-Moretus Museum at Antwerp*. New York: Grolier Club, 1888.

———. *The Practice of Typography*. New York: Century, 1922.

———. *A Treatise on Title-Pages. The Practice of Typography. With Numerous Illustrations in Facsimile and Some Observations on the Early and Recent Printing of Books*. New York: Century, 1902.

Dibdin, Thomas Frognall. *The Bibliomania, Or, Book-Madness; Containing Some Account Of The History, Symptoms, And Cure Of This Fatal Disease. In An Epistle Addressed To Richard Heber, Esq.* Printed for Longman, Hurst, Rees, and Orme by W. Savage, 1809 (available at https://books.google.com/books?id=fEIwAAAAYAAJ&printsec=frontcover&source=gbs_ge_summary_r&cad=0#v=onepage&q&f=false; accessed 21 January 2021); London: Henry G. Bohn, 1811 (and other editions).

———. *An Introduction to the Knowledge of Rare and Valuable Editions of the Greek and Latin Classics: Being, in Part, A Tabulated Arrangement from Dr. Harwood's View, &c. With Notes from Maittaire, De Bure, Dictionnaire Bibliographique and References to Ancient and Modern Catalogues*. Glocester: Printed by H. Ruff, for Payne, Faulder, Egerton, Evans, Robinsons, Mawman, et al., 1802. The 2nd ed. of 1804 available at https://books.google.com/books?id=TlQPAAAAYAAJ&printsec=frontcover&source=gbs_ge_summary_r&cad=0#v=onepage&q&f=false; accessed 21 January 2021.

———. *The Bibliographical Decameron; Or, Ten Days Pleasant Discourse upon Illuminated Manuscripts, And Subjects Connected with Early Engraving, Typography, and Bibliography*. London: Printed for the author, by W. Bulmer and Co., Shakespeare Press, 1817. Full text of the 3 volumes accessible at https://catalog.hathitrust.org/Record/008591150; accessed 21 January 2021.

Dickinson, Donald C. *John Carter: The Taste & Technique of a Bookman*. New Castle, DE: Oak Knoll, 2004.

Dictionary.com. "Autonym"; https://www.dictionary.com/browse/autonym; accessed 30 May 2021.

———. "Nihil obstat"; https://www.dictionary.com/browse/nihil-obstat; accessed 20 February 2021.

Dictionary of Literary Biography, Volume 187, *American Book Collectors and Bibliographers*, Second Series. "Charles Evans." Detroit, MI: Gale, 1997, pp. 92–102.

Dictionary of National Biography, 1885–1900. "John Weever"; https://en.wikisource.org/wiki/Dictionary_of_National_Biography,_1885-1900/Weever,_John; accessed 15 February 2021.

Dictionary of Paper, The: A Compendium of Terms Commonly Used in the U.S. Pulp, Paper and Allied Industries. 4th ed. New York: American Paper Institute, 1980.

Dictionnaire Poucet: Français—Allemand. Paris: Garnier Frères, n.d. [1943?].

Diringer, David. *The Book before Printing*. New York: Dover, 1982. (Originally published as *The Hand-Produced Book*. London: Hutchinson's Scientific and Technical Publications, 1953.)

Docter, Catherine. "Bradley Hutchinson—A Letterpress Fusion." *Matrix* 33 (2015): 74–82.

Donnelly, Nicole. "Douglass Morse Howell: Breaking the Mould. Part I." In Tatiana Ginsberg, ed. *Papermaker's Tears: Essays on the Art and Craft of Paper*, Vol. 1, pp. 46–85. Ann Arbor, MI: Legacy, 2019.

Dooley, Ian. "The Truth Within: A Harlequinade About Inner Virtue." Princeton University, Cotsen Children's Library, 2021; https://blogs.princeton.edu/cotsen/tag/metamorphic-books/; accessed 13 February 2021.

Dreyfus, John. *Giovanni Mardersteig: An Account of His Work*. Verona: Officina Bodoni, 1966.

———, ed., with Stanley Morison et al. *Type Specimen Facsimiles, 1–15: Reproductions of Fifteen Type Specimen Sheets Issued between the Sixteenth and Eighteenth Centuries*. London: Bowes & Bowes; London: Putnam, 1963. (A second volume was also issued with additional specimens in 1972.)

———. *The Work of Jan Van Krimpen, A Record in Honour of His Sixtieth Birthday*. Haarlem: Joh. Enschede en Zonen; London: Sylvan Press, 1952.

Duff, E. Gordon. *A Century of the English Book Trade: Short Notices of All Printers*. London: Bibliographical Society, 1905.

Dunbar, Edward E. "American Pioneering: An Address before the Travelers' Club"; listed on Amazon at https://www.amazon.com/American-pioneering-address-before-Travellers/dp/127563625X; accessed 4 July 2021.

Duncan, Dennis, and Adam Smyth. *Book Parts*. Oxford: Oxford University Press, 2019.

Duncan, Harry. "Bookworms and Type Lice." *Books at Iowa* 2 (April 1965): 17–26; http://www.lib.uiowa.edu/scua/bai/duncan.htm and http://ir.uiowa.edu/cgi/viewcontent.cgi?article=1012&context=bai (for the PDF); accessed 6 July 2021.

———. *Doors of Perception*. Austin, TX: W. Thomas Taylor, 1983.

Eckersley, Richard, Richard Angstadt, Charles M. Ellertson, Richard Hendel, Naomi B. Pascal, and Anita Walker Scott. *Glossary of Typesetting Terms*. Chicago: University of Chicago Press, 1994.

Edson, Julian I., and Anne C. Bromer. *Miniature Books: 4,000 Years of Tiny Treasures*. New York: Harry N. Abrams, 2007.

Educational Research and Applications. "Learning About Big Little Books: What Are Big Little Books?" 2012; https://www.google.com/search?q=Educational+Research+and+Applications.+Learning+About+Big+Little+Books%3A+What+Are+Big+Little+Books; accessed 26 February 2021.

Ellerton, Nerida, and M. A. [Ken] Clements. *Rewriting the History of School Mathematics in North America, 1607–1861: The Central Role of Cyphering Books*. New York: Springer, 2012.

Ellis, Doug, John Locke, and John Gunnison, eds. *The Adventure House Guide to the Pulps*. Silver Spring, MD: Adventure House, 2000.

Ellis, (Rev.) William. *The Christian Keepsake and Missionary Annual*. London, Paris, and America: Fisher, Son & Co, 1837.

Elsevier. "Permissions"; https://www.elsevier.com/about/policies/copyright/permissions#:~:text=As%20a%20general%20rule%2C%20permission,published%20by%20Elsevier%20is%20simple; accessed 20 February 2021.

Embree Mfg. Company. *Extra Sheets: Magic Kopeefun Paper*. Elizabeth, NJ: Embree, 1938.

Emory University Libraries. "From the Conservation Lab: Using Gels to Remove Stains from the 'Oratio in die Omnium Sanctorum (1483)'"; posted January 22, 2020; https://scholarblogs.emory.edu/woodruff/news/from-the-conservation-lab-using-gels-to-remove-stains-from-the-oratio-in-die-omnium-sanctorum-1483; accessed 10 February 2021.

enacademic.com. "Brittle Books Program"; https://enacademic.com/dic.nsf/enwiki/5811707; accessed 21 February 2021.

Encyclopaedia Britannica online. "Acanthus"; https://www.britannica.com/art/acanthus-ornamental-motif; accessed 24 May 2021.

———. "Geoffroy Tory"; https://www.britannica.com/biography/Geoffroy-Tory; accessed 20 April 2021.

———. "Little Magazine"; https://www.britannica.com/topic/little-magazine; accessed 17 February 2021.

———. "Mimeograph"; https://www.britannica.com/technology/mimeograph; accessed 19 April 2021.

———. "Replevin"; https://www.britannica.com/topic/replevin; accessed 20 March 2021.

———. "Stanley Morison"; https://www.britannica.com/biography/Stanley-Morison; accessed 2 July 2021.

———. "Writing Manuals and Copybooks (16th to 18th Century)"; https://www.britannica.com/art/calligraphy/Writing-manuals-and-copybooks-16th-to-18th-century; accessed 23 March 2021.

———. "The Yellow Book"; https://www.britannica.com/topic/The-Yellow-Book; accessed 16 May 2021.

The Encyclopedia of Science Fiction. "Fanzine"; http://sf-encyclopedia.com/entry/fanzine; accessed 23 February 2021.

The English Project. "The Woman's Page," 2018; http://www.englishproject.org/december-womans-page; accessed 2 March 2021.

The Ephemera Society of America. "Cartes de visite (CDV)"; https://www.ephemerasociety.org/definition/; accessed 22 February 2021.

Eric Gill: His Life and Art. Catalog of an exhibition in the Thomas Fisher Rare Book Library, University of Toronto. Toronto: Thomas Fisher Rare Book Library, 1991.

Eriş, Muin Nursen. *Mustafa Esat Düzgünman ve Ebrû / Mustafa Esat Düzgünman and Ebrû*. Istanbul: IBB Kultur A.S., 2007.

Erway, Ricky L. "Digital Initiatives of the Research Libraries Group." *D-Lib Magazine*, December 1996; http://mirror.dlib.org/dlib/december96/rlg/12erway.html; accessed 6 July 2021.

Esparto Paper. London: Newman Neame, 1956.

Espinoza, Robert, and Pamela Barrios. "Joint Tacketing: A Method of Board Reattachment." *The Book and Paper Group Annual* 10 (1991); http://cool.conservation-us.org/coolaic/sg/bpg/annual/v10/bp10-08.html; accessed 6 July 2021.

Evans, Charles. *American Bibliography: A Chronological Dictionary of All Books, Pamphlets, and Periodical Publications Printed in the United States of America from the Genesis of Printing in 1639 down to and Including the Year 1820, with Bibliographical and Biographical Notes*. 14 vols. Chicago, 1903–1959; reprint, New York: Peter Smith, 1941.

Evans, Henry Herman. *First Duet*. San Francisco: Peregrine, 1950.

"Exquisite Corpse." The Reader View of Wikipedia; https://thereaderwiki.com/en/Exquisite_corpse; accessed 15 February 2021.

Extra Binding at the Lakeside Press. Chicago: R. R. Donnelley, 1925.

Fahey, Herbert, and Peter Fahey. *Finishing in Hand Bookbinding*. San Francisco: Herbert and Peter Fahey, 1951.

Fenn, Patricia, and Alfred P. Malpa. *Rewards of Merit: Tokens of a Child's Progress and a Teacher's Esteem as an Enduring Aspect of American Religious and Secular Education*. Charlottesville, VA: Howell Press; Ephemera Society of America, 1994.

Fessenden, Marissa. "A Brief History of Taking Books Along for the Ride." *Smithsonian TweenTribune*, 5 September 2018; https://www.tweentribune.com/article/tween56/brief-history-taking-books-along-ride/; accessed 8 August 2021.

Findlay, James A. *Big Little Books: The Whitman Publishing Company's Golden Age, 1932–1938*. Ft. Lauderdale, FL: Bienes Center for the Literary Arts, 2002.

Fine, Ruth. *The Janus Press, Fifty Years: Catalogue Raisonné for 1991–2005*, with indexes for 1955–2005. Burlington: University of Vermont Libraries, 2006.

Finlay, Michael. *Western Writing Implements: In the Age of the Quill Pen*. Wetheral: Plains Books, 1990.

Fisher, Tim. "What Is a PDF File?" *Lifewire*, 4 September 2021; https://www.lifewire.com/pdf-file-2622916; accessed 26 January 2022.

Fletcher, H. George. See *Gazette of the Grolier Club*.

———. *In Praise of Aldus Manutius: A Quincentenary Exhibition*. New York: Pierpont Morgan Library; Los Angeles: University Research Library, Department of Special Collections, UCLA, 1995.

Fletcher, Keith, and Adrian Harrington. "History of the Book Fair"; Firsts: London's Rare Book Fair; https://www.firstslondon.com/about/history; accessed 28 January 2021.

flipsnack blog. "What Is a Zine?"; https://blog.flipsnack.com/what-is-a-zine/; accessed 7 March 2021.

Fontenelle, Julia de, and P. Poisson. *Nouveau Manuel Complet du Marchand Papetier et du Régleur*. Paris, 1854.

Fox, Margalit. "Mary Ann Malkin, Journal Editor and Rare-Book Collector, Dies at 92." *New York Times*, 14 August 2005.

Fraas, Mitch. "Don't Believe That Imprint," Mapping Books blog, June 14, 2013; http://mappingbooks.blogspot.com/2013/06/dont-believe-that-imprint.html; accessed 23 February 2021.

FRAD (Functional Requirements for Authority Data). *FRAD and Cataloguing*. ANSS (The Anthropology and Sociology Section of the Association of College and Research Libraries); https://anssacrl.wordpress.com/publications/cataloging-qa/frad-and-cataloging2013-apr/; accessed 30 December 2020.

Fragmentarium: A Journal for the Study of Medieval Manuscript Fragments; https://fragmentology.ms/; accessed 17 February 2021.

Franklin, Colin. *Book Collecting as One of the Fine Arts and Other Essays*. Aldershot: Scolar Press, 1996.

———. *The Private Presses*. London: Studio Vista, 1969; 2nd ed., Aldershot: Scolar, 1991.

———, Hosie Baskin, and Lisa Baskin. *The Gehenna Press: The Work of Fifty Years, 1942–1992*. Dallas, TX: Bridwell Library; N.p. [Leeds, MA]: Gehenna, 1992.

Frazer, Simon. "Kinkarakami: The Art of Japanese Leather Paper." *Crafts* 207 (July–August 2007): 68 ff.

FRBR (Functional Requirements for Bibliographic Records). OCLC. *OCLC Research Activities and IFLA's Functional Requirements for Bibliographic Records*. https://www.oclc.org/research/activities/frbr.html; accessed 30 December 2020.

Freeman, Arthur. "Conners of the Connoisseurs." *Times Literary Supplement*, June 12, 1992, 24.

———, and Janet Ing Freeman. *Anatomy of an Auction: Rare Books at Ruxley Lodge, 1919*. London: Book Collector, 1990.

French, Hannah D. *Bookbinding in Early America: Seven Essays on Masters and Methods*. Worcester, MA: American Antiquarian Society, 1986.

Futernick, Robert. "Leaf Casting on the Suction Table." *The Book and Paper Group Annual* 1 (1982): 82–91; https://cool.culturalheritage.org/coolaic/sg/bpg/annual/v01/bp01-14.html; accessed 1 February 2021.

Gallagher, James P. "Scraping away the 'Caviar.'" *Chicago Tribune*, 5 July 1993; https://www.chicagotribune.com/news/ct-xpm-1993-07-05-9307050042-story.html; accessed 7 January 2021.

Gantz, David. *The Mix or Match Storybook*. New York: Random House, 1973.

Garland For Harry Duncan: Minister Erato Ministrorum, A. Austin, TX: W. Thomas Taylor, 1989.

Gaskell, Philip. *John Baskerville: A Bibliography*. Chicheley: Paul P. B. Minet, 1973.

———. *A New Introduction to Bibliography*. New York: Oxford University Press, 1972 (and later editions).

———. "Terms of the Trade"; cited by Ken Spelman; https://www.kenspelman.com/glossary.htm; accessed 25 May 2021.

Gazette of the Grolier Club, New Series, Number 70 (2020). This volume contains 5 essays on Aldus Manutius: G.Scott Clemons, "How Aldus Manutius Saved Western Civilization" (pp. 7–23); T. Kimball Brooker, "Aldine Editions Were Seen as Very Special Throughout Five Centuries" (pp. 24–48); H. George Fletcher,

"Cardinal Pole and the Council of Trent: An Inquiry" (pp. 49–53); Robin Raybould, "Erasmus, Grolier, and Aldus" (pp. 55–68); and G. Scott Clemons and H. George Fletcher, "Aldus Manutius: A Legacy More Lasting Than Bronze: Exhibition Label Text" (pp. 69–121).

George, Albert J. *The Didot Family and the Progress of Printing*. Syracuse, NY: Syracuse University Press, 1961.

Gerry, Vance. *Flowers on a Table: A Study of an Imprudent Wood Engraving*. Pasadena, CA: Weather Bird Press, 1973.

———. Pochoir: *Practical Stencilling for the Modern Craftsman as Applied to Illustrations and Designs for Books &c*. [Pasadena, CA]: Weather Bird, 1991.

Gertz, Stephen J. "The Mark of Zaehnsdorf." *Booktryst: A Nest for Book Lovers*, 2 November 2011; http://www.booktryst.com/2011/10/mark-of-zaehnsdorf.html; accessed 6 July 2021.

Gesamtkatalog der Wiegendrucke (Union Catalogue of Incunabula). Berlin: Staatsbibliothek zu Berlin, ongoing; http://www.gesamtkatalogderwiegendrucke.de/GWEN.xhtml; accessed 6 July 2021.

Getty, J. Paul, Museum. See under J. Paul Getty Museum.

Getty Research Institute. *Art and Architecture Thesaurus*. Getty Research Institute, https://www.getty.edu/research/tools/vocabularies/aat/about.html; accessed 22 June 2021.

Gifford, Henry. *The Novel in Russia from Pushkin to Pasternak*. New York: Harper Colophon Books, Harper & Row, 1964.

Gill, Eric. *An Essay on Typography*. London: Dent, 1939; Boston: Godine, 1988.

Gill, Evan R. *Bibliography of Eric Gill*. London: Cassell, 1953.

Gilmour, Pat. *Artists at Curwen: A Celebration of the Gift of Artists' Prints from the Curwen Studio*. London: Tate Publications, 1977.

Gilreath, James, ed. *The Judgment of Experts: Essays and Documents about the Investigation of the Forging of the* Oath of a Freeman. Worcester, MA: American Antiquarian Society, 1991.

Ginsberg, Tatiana, ed. *Papermaker's Tears: Essays on the Art and Craft of Paper*, Vol. 1. Ann Arbor, MI: Legacy, 2019.

Glaister, Geoffrey Ashall. *Glaister's Glossary of the Book: Terms Used in Papermaking, Printing, Bookbinding and Publishing with Notes on Illuminated Manuscripts and Private Presses*. 2nd ed. London: George Allen & Unwin, 1979.

Goff, Frederick R[ichmond], comp. *Incunabula in American Libraries. A Third Census of Fifteenth-Century Books Recorded in North American Collections*. New York: Bibliographical Society of America, 1964; supplement, 1972.

———. *Incunabula in American Libraries: A Third Census of Fifteenth-Century Books Recorded in North American Collections Reproduced from the Annotated Copy Maintained by Frederick R. Goff, Compiler and Editor*. Millwood: Kraus Reprint, 1973.

Goldman, Paul. *Victorian Illustrated Books 1850–1870*. London: British Museum, 1994.

GoodReads. "Don Etherington"; https://www.goodreads.com/author/show/621020.Don_Etherington; accessed 29 March 2021.

Goodrich, Amanda. *Debating England's Aristocracy in the 1790s: Pamphlets, Polemics and Political Ideas*. Woodbridge: Boydell & Brewer, 2005.

Goodstone, Tony. *The Pulps: 50 Years of American Pop Culture*. New York: Chelsey House, 1970.

Gorecki, Henryk. See *Altar Book for Gorecki*.

Gottlieb, Eli. *Best Boy*. New York: Liveright, 2015.

Goudy, Frederic W. *Goudy's Type Designs: His Story and Specimens*. 2nd ed. New Rochelle, NY: Myriade, 1978. (See more information on this volume at Paul A. Bennett, *Goudy's Type Designs*, above.)

———. *Typologia: Studies in Type Design & Type Making*. Berkeley: University of California Press, 1940 (and later editions).

Goulart, Ron. *Cheap Thrills: An Informal History of the Pulp Magazine*. New Rochelle, NY: Arlington House, 1972.

Gould, Karen. "Terms for Book Production in a Fifteenth-Century Latin-English Nominale (Harvard Law School Library MS. 43)." *Papers of the Bibliographcial Society of America* 79.1 (First Quarter, 1985): 75–100.

Grabhorn, Edwin. "Recollections of the Grabhorn Press: Oral History Transcript/and Related Material, 1967–1968." University of California Bancroft Library/Berkeley Regional Oral History Office, 1968; https://archive.org/stream/grabhornrecollect00grabrich/grabhornrecollect00grabrich_djvu.txt; accessed 6 July 2021.

Grabhorn, Edwin, and Robert Grabhorn. *Leaves of Grass: Comprising all the Poems Written by Walt Whitman Following the Arrangement of the Edition of 1891–92*. New York: Random House, 1930.

Grafix. "What is Mylar Plastic Film?"; https://www.grafixplastics.com/grafix-plastics/plastic-film-plastic-sheet-faq/mylar_what/; accessed 10 February 2021.

Grafton, Anthony. *The Footnote: A Curious History*. Cambridge, MA: Harvard University Press, 1997.

Gramuglia, Anthony. "Why Manga & Comics for Kids Outsell Superheroes." CBR.com; 19 October 2019; https://www.cbr.com/manga-comics-kids-outsell-superheroes/; accessed 28 May 2021.

Graphic Design Degree Hub, "What is AIGA?"; https://www.graphicdesigndegreehub.com/faq/what-is-aiga/; accessed 24 May 2021.

Gravelle, Michelle, Anah Mustapha, and Coralee Leroux. "Volvelles." In *ArchBook: Architectures of the Book*; http://drc.usask.ca/projects/archbook/volvelles.php; accessed 6 July 2021.

"Great Omar, The: The Jewel of Sangorski & Sutcliffe," Biblio blog, https://www.biblio.com/blog/2014/12/great-omar-jewel-sangorski-sutcliffe; accessed 6 July 2021.

Green, James. *The Rittenhouse Mill and the Beginnings of Papermaking in America*. Philadelphia: Library Company of Philadelphia and Friends of Historic Rittenhouse Town, 1990.

Green, Maureen. *Papermaking at Hayle Mill 1808–1987*. Newark, VT: Janus Press, 2008.

Greenfield, Jane. *ABC of Bookbinding: A Unique Glossary with Over 700 Illustrations for Collectors & Librarians*. New Castle, DE: Oak Knoll; New York: Lyons, 1998.

Greenland, Maureen, and Russ Day. *Bryan Donkin: The Very Civil Engineer, 1768–1855*. [West Sussex, England]: Phillimore Book Publishing, 2016.

Greenwald, Marilyn S. *The Secret of the Hardy Boys: Leslie McFarlane and the Stratemeyer Syndicate*. Athens: Ohio University Press, 2004.

Greg, W. W. *Bibliography of the English Printed Drama to the Restoration*. 4 vols. London: Bibliographical Society, 1939–1959.

———. *The Editorial Problem in Shakespeare: A Survey of the Foundations of the Text*. Oxford: Clarendon, 1951 (and later editions).

———. "The Rationale of Copy-Text." In *Bibliography and Textual Criticism: English and American Literature, 1700 to the Present*, edited by O. M. Brack and Warner Barnes, pp. 41–58. Chicago: University of Chicago Press, 1969.

———. *The Shakespeare First Folio: Its Bibliographical and Textual History*. Oxford: Oxford University Press, 1955.

———. *Some Aspects and Problems of London Publishing, 1550–1650*. Oxford: Clarendon, 1954.

Grendler, Paul F. "Printing and Censorship." In *The Cambridge History of Renaissance Philosophy*, edited by by Charles B. Schmitt, pp. 25–53. Cambridge: Cambridge University Press, 1988.

Griest, Guinevere L. *Mudie's Circulating Library and the Victorian Novel*. Bloomington: Indiana University Press, 1970.

Griffiths, Antony. *Prints and Printmaking*. 2nd ed. London: British Museum Press, 1996.

Groden, Michael. "Contemporary Textual and Literary Theory." In *Representing Modernist Texts: Editing as Interpretation*, edited by George Bornstein, pp. 259–86. Ann Arbor: University of Michigan Press, 1991.

Grolier Club, The. "Grolier Club Will Host Typography Exhibition"; 12 April 2021; https://www.finebooksmagazine.com/news/grolier-club-will-host-typography-exhibition; accessed 22 May 2021.

———. *One Hundred Books Famous in English Literature*. New York: Grolier Club, 1902.

Gullans, Charles, and John Espey. *Margaret Armstrong and American Trade Bindings*. Los Angeles: Department of Special Collections, University Research Library, UCLA, 1991.

Guyot, Don. *Suminagashi: An Introduction to Japanese Marbling*. Seattle: Brass Galley Press, 1990.

Haemmerle, Albert. *Buntpapiere*. Munich: Callwey, 1961; 2nd ed. with same title and publisher, 1977. In German.

Hain, Ludwig (Ludovici) Friedrich Theodor. *Reportorium bibliographicum, in quo libri omnes ab arte typographica inventa usque ad annum md: Typis expressi ordine alphabetico vel simpliciter enumerantur vel adcuratius recensentur*. 4 vols. Stuttgart: Cotta, 1826–1838.

Haining, Peter. *Movable Books: An Illustrated History: Pages & Pictures of Folding, Revolving, Dissolving, Mechanical, Scenic, Panoramic, Dimensional, Changing, Pop-Up and other Novelty Books from the Collection of David and Briar Philips*. London: New English Library, 1979.

Haldeman-Julius, Emanuel. "Haldeman-Julius Publications: Little Blue Books." Kent State University Library, https://www.library.kent.edu/special-collections-and-archives/haldeman-julius-publications-little-blue-books; accessed 24 January 2022.

Halkett, Samuel, and John Laing. *Dictionary of Anonymous and Pseudonymous English Literature of Great Britain, Including the Works of Foreigners Written in, or Translated into the English Language*. 4 vols. Edinburgh: William Paterson, 1882–1888 (and later editions).

———. *Dictionary of Anonymous and Pseudonymous English Literature of Great Britain, Including the Works of Foreigners Written in, or Translated into the English Language*. 9 vols. London: Oliver & Boyd, 1928–1956.

Haller, Margaret. *The Book Collector's Fact Book*. New York: Arco, 1976.

Hallissy, Margaret. *Clean Maids, True Wives, Steadfast Widows: Chaucer's Women and Medieval Codes of Conduct* (Contributions in Women's Studies). Westport, CT: Greenwood, 1993.

Hamady, Walter. *In Sight of Blue Mounds*. Mount Horeb, WI: Perishable, 1972.

Hamilton, Charles Franklin. *As Bees in Honey Drown: Elbert Hubbard and the Roycrofters*. South Brunswick, NJ: A. S. Barnes, 1973.

Hamilton, Milton W. *Adam Ramage and His Presses*. Portland, ME: Southworth-Anthoensen Press, 1942.

Hamilton Wood Type Museum. "About"; https://woodtype.org/pages/about; accessed 3 May 2021.

Hand Papermaking and *Hand Papermaking Newsletter*. Periodical published by Hand Papermaking, 1986–.

Hargrave, Catherine Perry. *History of Playing Cards and a Bibliography of Cards and Gaming*. New York: Dover, 1960.

Harmon, Robert B. *Elements of Bibliography: A Simplified Approach*. Metuchen, NJ: Scarecrow, 1998.

Harris, Elizabeth. *Personal Impressions: The Small Printing Press in Nineteenth-Century America*. Boston: Godine; London: Merrion, 2004.

Harris, Elizabeth, and Clint Sisson. *The Common Press: Being a Record, Description & Delineation of the Early Eighteenth-Century Handpress in the Smithsonian Institution*. Boston: Godine, 1978.

Harry Ransom Center. "About WATCH"; https://norman.hrc.utexas.edu/watch/about.cfm; accessed 25 March 2021.

Harthan, John. *An Introduction to Illuminated Manuscripts*. London: Victoria & Albert Museum, 1983.

Harvard Gazette, The. "The History at Houghton." https://news.harvard.edu/gazette/story/2011/11/the-history-at-houghton/#:~:text=Harvard's%20neo%2DGeorgian%20Houghton%20Library,%2C%20and%20air%2Dfiltration%20systems; accessed 30 June 2021.

Hatch, Benton L. *A Checklist of the Publications of Thomas Bird Mosher of Portland Maine: MDCCCXCI–MDCCCCXXIII*. Amherst, MA: Gehenna Press and University of Massachusetts Press, 1966.

Havens, Earl. *Commonplace Books: A History of Manuscripts and Printed Books from Antiquity to the Twentieth Century*. New Haven, CT: Yale University Press, 2001.

Hayward, John. *English Poetry. A Catalogue of First & Early Editions of Works of the English Poets from Chaucer to the Present Day, Exhibited by the National Book League at 7 Albemarle Street, London*. London: National Book League and Cambridge University Press, 1947.

Hazen, A. T. "Baskerville and James Whatman." *Studies in Bibliography* 5 (1952–1953): 187–89.

Hazlitt, W. Carew. *The Book-Collector: A General Survey of the Pursuit and of Those Who Have Engaged in It at Home and Abroad from the Earliest Period to the Present Time*. London: John Grant, 1904.

Heatley, Michael. *Guitar Trivia*. New York: Metro, 2010.

Helft, Miguel. "Some Raise Alarms as Google Resurrects Out-of-Print Books." *New York Times*, 4 April 2009, pp. A1, A9.

Heller, Marvin J. *Studies in the Making of the Early Hebrew Book*. Leiden, The Netherlands: Brill, 2007.

Hellinga, Lotte. "Das Mainzer Catholicon und Gutenbergs Nachlaß: Neudatierung und Auswirkungen." *Archiv für Geschichte des Buchwesens* 40 (1993): 395–416.

———, and Margaret Nickson. "A Caxton Tract-Volume from Thomas Rawlinson's Library." *Yale University Library Gazette* 72.1/2 (October 1997): 17–26; https://www-jstor-org.ezproxy.simmons.edu/stable/40859179?seq=1#metadata_info_tab_contents; accessed 4 February 2021.

Henricus de Nova Villa (Henry of Newtown = Henry Morris). *So Long, Hot-Metal Men: The Comprehensive Bird & Bull Type Specimen Book*. Newtown, PA: Bird & Bull, 2007.

Henry, Avril. *Biblia Pauperum: A Facsimile*. Aldershot: Scolar; New York: Cornell University Press, 1987.

Herring, Ann. *Chiyogami: Hand-printed Patterned Papers of Japan*. Tokyo, New York, and London: Kodansha International, 1987.

Hertzberger, Menno, ed. *Dictionary for the Antiquarian Booktrade, in French, English, German, Swedish, Danish, Italian, Spanish and Dutch/Dictionnaire à l'usage de la libraire ancienne*. Paris: International League of Antiquarian Booksellers, 1956.

Herzog August Bibliothek. "History of the Library"; http://www.hab.de/en/home/museum-cultural-programme/history-of-the-library.html; accessed 24 October 2015; this is a lost link; but see https://www.ogn.ox.ac.uk/research-libraries#:~:text=Founded%20in%201572%2C%20the%20Herzog,to%20the%20late%20eighteenth%20century; accessed 6 July 2021.

———. "In Between Future and Past." https://www.anschlaege.de/casestudy/herzog-august-bibliothek-corporate-design/#prettyPhoto; accessed 30 June 2021.

Hewes, Lauren B., and Laura E. Wasowicz. *Radiant with Color & Art: McLoughlin Brothers and the Business of Picture Books, 1858–1920*. Worcester, MA: American Antiquarian Society, 2017 (published to accompany an exhibition at the Grolier Club, 6 December 2017 to 3 February 2018).

Heyes, Duncan. "The Hogarth Press." British Library, "Discovering Literature: 20th Century"; 25 May 2016; https://www.bl.uk/20th-century-literature/articles/the-hogarth-press; accessed 9 August 2021.

Hiebert, Helen. *Playing with Paper: Illuminating, Engineering, and Reimagining Paper Art*. Beverly, MA: Quarry, 2013.

Hilton, James. *Chronograms. 5000 and More in Number Excerpted out of Various Authors and Collected at Many Places*. London: Elliot Stock, 1882; https://archive.org/stream/chronograms5000m00hilt/chronograms5000m00hilt_djvu.txt; accessed 7 May 2021.

Hind, Arthur Mayger. *A History of Engraving and Etching from the Fifteenth Century to the Year 1914*. 3rd rev. ed. London: Constable; Boston: Houghton Mifflin, 1923; New York: Dover, 1963.

———. *An Introduction to the History of the Woodcut with a Detailed Survey of Work Done in the Fifteenth Century*. 2 vols. London: Constable, 1935.

Hitchcock, Frederick H. *The Building of a Book*. New York: Grafton, 1906; http://www.gutenberg.org/files/23754/23754-h/23754-h.htm; accessed 6 July 2021.

Hodgson, Thomas. *An Essay on the Origin and Progress of Stereotype Printing: Including a Description of the Various Processes*. Newcastle: Printed by and for S. Hodgson; reprint, New York: Garland, 1982.

Holley, Edward G. *Charles Evans: American Bibliographer*. Urbana: University of Illinois Press, 1963.

Holstun, James, ed. *Pamphlet Wars: Prose in the English Revolution*. London: Frank Cass & Co.; Portland, OR: International Specialized Book Services, 1992. (A whole volume of essays about pamphlet wars.)

Holzenberg, Eric. "Second-Hand and Antiquarian Books on the Internet." *RBM* 2.1 (March 2001): 35–44.

Hook, Philip. *Breakfast at Sotheby's: An A–Z of the Art World*. New York: Overlook, 2013.

Hopkins, Richard L., gen. ed. *The Private Typecasters Preserving the Craft of Hot-Metal Type into the Twenty-First Century*. Newtown, PA: Bird & Bull, 2008.

Houfe, Simon. *The Dictionary of British Book Illustrators and Caricaturists, 1800–1914, with Introductory Chapters on the Rise and Progress of the Art*. Detroit: Gale, 1982.

Howells, John M., and Marion V. Dearman. *Tramp Printers: Adventures and Forgotten Paths Once Traced by Wandering Artisans of Newspapering and Typography*. Pacific Grove, CA: Discovery, 2003.

HT Labels."Flexographic Applications"; https://htlabels.co.za/flexographic-printing/; accessed 30 June 2021.

Humphreys, Henry Noel, ed. *Parables of Our Lord*. London: Longman; New York: D. Appleton, 1847.

Hunt, Peter, ed. *International Companion Encyclopedia of Children's Literature*. 2nd ed. London and New York: Routledge, 2004.

Hunter, Dard. *Chinese Ceremonial Paper: A Monograph Relating to the Fabrication of Paper and Tin Foil and the Use of Paper in Chinese Rites*. Chillicothe, OH: Mountain House, 1937.

———. *My Life with Paper: An Autobiography*. New York: Knopf, 1958.

———. *Old Papermaking in China and Japan*. Chillicothe, OH: Mountain House, 1932.

———. *Papermaking by Hand in America*. Chillicothe, OH: Mountain House, 1950.

———. *Papermaking by Hand in India*. New York: Pynson, 1939.

———. *Papermaking: The History and Technique of an Ancient Craft*. New York: Knopf, 1947; reprint of the 2nd ed., New York: Dover, 1978.

———. *A Papermaking Pilgrimage to Japan, Korea and China*. New York: Pynson, 1936.

———. *Papermaking through Eighteen Centuries*. New York: William Edwin Rudge, 1930.

———. *Primitive Papermaking: An Account of a Mexican Sojourn and of a Voyage to the Pacific Islands in Search of Information,*

Implements, and Specimens Relating to the Making & Decorating of Bark-Paper. Chillicothe, OH: Mountain House, 1927.

Hunter, Dard, II. *The Life Work of Dard Hunter: A Progressive Illustrated Assemblage of His Works as Artist, Craftsman, Author, Papermaker, and Printer*, 2 vols. Chillicothe, OH: Mountain House, 1981, 1983.

Hunter, Dard, II, Dard Hunter III, and Henry Morris. *Dard Hunter & Son*. Newtown, PA: Bird & Bull, 1998.

Huss, Richard. *The Development of Printers' Mechanical Typesetting Methods, 1822–1925*. Charlottesville: University of Virginia Press, 1973.

Iacone, Salvatore J. *The Pleasures of Collecting*. New York: Harper & Row, 1976.

Ibe, Kyoko. "On Gampi." In Tatiana Ginsberg, ed., *Papermaker's Tears: Essays on the Art and Craft of Paper*, pp. 136–207. Ann Arbor, MI: Legacy Press, 2019.

Illing, Richard. *Japanese Erotic Art and the Life of the Courtesan*. London: Thames and Hudson, 1978; New York: St. Martin's, 1979.

Imhof, Dirk. *Jan Moretus and the Continuation of the Plantin Press: A Bibliography of the Works Published and Printed by Jan Moretus I in Antwerp (1589–1610)*. 2 vols. Leiden: Koninklijke Brill/Hes de Graaf, 2014.

Infelise, Mario, and Paola Marini. *Remondini: Un Editore del Settocento*. Milan: Electa, 1990. (A massive volume showing many of the decorated papers from this printing and paper establishment.)

Ing, Janet. *Johann Gutenberg and His Bible: A Historical Study*. New York: Typophiles, 1988.

International Association of Paper Historians. "Online Watermark Databases/Catalogues"; http://www.paperhistory.org/Links/; accessed 21 June 2021.

International Organisation of Book Towns. http://www.booktown.net/; accessed 24 January 2022.

In Wonderland and What Is to Be Seen There: A Book of Revolving Pictures. London: Ernest Nister; New York: E. P. Dutton, 1896.

IOBA (Independent Online Booksellers Association). *Setting the Standard . . . for Booksellers and Book Buyers*. N.p.: IOBA, 2013.

Isaac, Francis S. *An Index to the Early Printed Books in the British Museum*. See under Procter, Robert.

Ives, Samuel A., and Hellmut Lehmann-Haupt. *An English 13th Century Bestiary—A New Discovery in the Technique of Medieval Illumination*. New York: H. P. Kraus, 1942.

Jackson, H. J. *Marginalia: Readers Writing in Books*. New Haven, CT: Yale University Press, 2001.

Jackson, Holbrook. *The Anatomy of Bibliomania*. London: Soncino, 1930; reprint, New York: Avenel, 1950 (and other editions).

[Jackson, Ian.] *The Price-Codes of the Book-Trade: A Preliminary Guide*. Berkeley, CA: Ian Jackson, 2010.

Jackson, William A. "English Title-Labels to the End of the Seventeenth Century." *Harvard Library Bulletin* 2.2 (Spring 1948): 222–39; https://dash.harvard.edu/bitstream/handle/1/37363371/English%20title-labels%20to%20the%20end%20of%20the%20seventeenth%20century.pdf?sequence=1&isAllowed=y; accessed 16 February 2021.

Jacoby, Charles T. *Some Notes on Books and Printing: A Guide for Authors, Publishers & Others*. London: Charles Wittingham, Chiswick, 1903; https://books.google.com/books?id=KZBBAQAAMAAJ&pg=PA86&lpg=PA86&dq=%22thickness+copy%22+book&source=bl&ots=xTW4oAWjsr&sig=ACfU3U2wh04I6MHTJhBY-bB9WstFsKsD1w&hl=en&sa=X&ved=2ahUKEwju-8TQks3wAhXQuZ4KHQDuBR4Q6AEwEnoECAkQAw#v=onepage&q=%22thickness%20copy%22%20book&f=false; accessed 15 May 2021.

James, Elizabeth. "Aspects of the Victorian Book: Yellowbacks." British Library, n.d.; https://www.bl.uk/collections/early/victorian/pu_yello.html; accessed 6 February 2021.

James, George. "Arthur Houghton Jr., 83, Dies; Led Steuben Glass." Obituary. *New York Times*; https://www.nytimes.com/1990/04/04/obituaries/arthur-houghton-jr-83-dies-led-steuben-glass.html; accessed 30 June 2021.

James, Louis. *Fiction for the Working Man, 1830–50*: A *Study of the Literature Produced for the Working Classes in Early Victorian Urban England 1830–1850*. London: Oxford University Press, 1963; reprint, Harmondsworth: Penguin, 1974.

Jaspert, W. Pincus, William Turner Berry, and Alfred Forbes Johnson. *Encyclopaedia of Type Faces*. 4th ed. London: Blandford; New York: Barnes & Noble, 1970.

Jedin, Hubert, John Dolan, and Gabriel Adriányi. *The Church in the Modern Age*, Vol. 10. New York: Crossroads, 1981.

Jeffers, Robinson. *Granite & Cypress*. Santa Cruz, CA: Lime Kiln Press, University of California at Santa Cruz, 1975.

Jeremy Norman's *HistoryofInformation*; https://historyofinformation.com/detail.php?entryid=2915; accessed 30 June 2021.

Jeremy Norman's Historyofinformation.com, "Nicolas [*sic*] Pickwood's Tentative Observations on Dating Carta Rustica Bindings"; https://www.historyofinformation.com/detailphp?id=3757; accessed 2 March 2021.

Johanssen, Albert. *The House of Beadle & Adams*. 3 vols. Norman: University of Oklahoma Press, 1950 (vols. 1 and 2); 1962 (vol. 3).

"John M. Manly (1865–1940) & Edith Rickert (1871–1938)." In The University of Chicago Centennial Catalogues; lib.uchicago.edu/collex/exhibits/university-chicago-centennial-catalogues/university-chicago-faculty-centennial-view/john-m-manly-1865-1940-edith-rickert-1871-1938-english/; accessed 11 October 2022.

Johnson, Deirdre. *Edward Stratemeyer and the Stratemeyer Syndicate*. New York: Twayne, 1993.

Johnson, Eric J. "Students as Curators: Manuscripts in the Classroom at Ohio State University." Textmanuscripts, blog of Les Enluminures, February 17, 2021; https://www.textmanuscripts.com/blog/entry/02-21-ohio-state-univeristy-manuscripts-in-the-curriculum; accessed 17 February 2021.

Johnston, Alistair M. *Alphabets to Order: The Literature of Nineteenth-Century Typefounders' Specimens*. New Castle, DE: Oak Knoll, 2000.

jojoal. "Collins Sixpenny Paperbacks from the Pre-Penguin Era." Paperbackrevolution; https://paperbackrevolution.wordpress.com/tag/hutchinsons-famous-copyright-novels/; accessed 6 May 2021.

———. "Hutchinson's Famous Copyright Novels"; https://paperbackrevolution.wordpress.com/2018/10/12/hutchinsons-famous-copyright-novels/; accessed 6 May 2021.

Jones, Herbert. *Stanley Morison Displayed: An Examination of His Early Typographic Work*. London: Frederick Muller, 1976.

Joudrey, Daniel N., and Arlene G. Taylor. *The Organization of Information*, 4th ed. Santa Barbara, CA: Libraries Unlimited, 2017.

J. Paul Getty Museum. "Three Leaves from an Antiphonal"; http://www.getty.edu/art/collection/objects/225494/circle-of-the-master-of-the-golden-bull-three-leaves-from-an-antiphonal-bohemian-about-1405/; accessed 23 April 2021.

Justice, Donald. *Banjo Dog*. Riverside, CA: Printed by Doe Press for Thaumatrope Press, University of California, Riverside, 1995.

Justin Croft. *CTRL + P* (booksellers' catalog; issued with Heather O'Donnell, Ben Kinmont, and Simon Beattie); 2020; Item 6, "Dressed Print"; https://www.justincroft.com/wp-content/uploads/2020/09/CTRLP.pdf; accessed 19 April 2021.

Justin Croft. *CTRL + P* (booksellers' catalog; issued with Heather O'Donnell, Ben Kinmont, and Simon Beattie); 2020; Item 9, "Papier Porcelaine"; https://www.justincroft.com/wp-content/uploads/2020/09/CTRLP.pdf; accessed 19 April 2021.

Juxtapoz. "A Short History of the Phenakistoscope," 28 June 2014; https://www.juxtapoz.com/illustration/short-history-of-the-phenakistoscope/; accessed 1 May 2021.

Kafka, Francis J. *Linoelum Block Printing*. New York: Dover, 1955.

Kahan, Basil Charles. *Ottmar Mergenthaler: The Man and His Machine*. New Castle, DE: Oak Knoll, 1999.

Kainen, Jacob. *George Clymer and the Columbian Press*. New York: Typophiles; San Francisco: Book Club of California, 1950.

Kanigel, Robert. *Faux Real: Genuine Leather and 200 Years of Inspired Fakes*. Washington, DC: Joseph Henry [2007].

Kapr, Albert. *The Art of Lettering: The History, Anatomy, and Aesthetics of the Roman Letter Forms*. Munich, New York, London, and Paris: K. G. Saur, 1983.

———. *Johann Gutenberg: The Man and His Invention*. Translated by Douglas Martin. Aldershot: Scolar, 1996.

Karr, Suzanne. "Constructions Both Sacred and Profane: Serpents, Angels, and Pointing Fingers in Renaissance Books with Moving Parts." *Yale University Library Gazette* 78.3–4 (April 2004): 101–27, esp. 124–27.

Katz, Bill. *Cuneiform to Computer: A History of Reference Sources*. Lanham, MD: Scarecrow, 1998.

KCP International, Japanese Language School. "Gyotaku: The Traditional Japanese Art of Fish Printing"; December 16, 2019; https://www.kcpinternational.com/2019/12/gyotaku-traditional-japanese-art-fish-printing/; accessed 2 March 2021.

Keeline, James D. "Edward Stratemeyer & the Stratemeyer Syndicate"; http://stratemeyer.org; accessed 6 July 2021.

Keese, John. *The Floral Keepsake: With Forty-six Beautiful Colored Engravings*. New York: Leavitt, 1850.

Keller, William B. *A Catalogue of The Cary Collection of Playing Cards in the Yale University Library*. 4 vols. New Haven: Yale University Library, 1981.

Kelly, Jerry, Hermann Zapf, Martino Mardersteig, and Kevin Perryman. *Giovanni and Martino Mardersteig: Book Designers, Typographers, and Printers in Verona. Catalogue of the Exhibition Celebrating Sixty Years since the Founding of the Press Stamperia Valdonega 1948–2008*. New York: Grolier Club, 2008.

Kelly, Jerry, and Sebastian Carter. *One Hundred Books Famous in Typography*. New York: Grolier Club, 2021.

Kennedy, Gerry, and Rob Churchill. *The Voynich Manuscript. The Unsolved Riddle of an Extraordinary Book Which Has Defied Interpretation for Centuries*. London: Orion, 2004.

Ker, Neil Ripley. *Catalogue of Manuscripts Containing Anglo-Saxon*. Oxford: Clarendon, 1957.

———. *Medieval Libraries of Great Britain: A List of Surviving Books*. London: Offices of the Royal Historical Society, 1964.

———. *Medieval Manuscripts in British Libraries*. 5 vols. Oxford: Clarendon, 1969–1992.

———. *The Owl and the Nightingale: Reproduced in Facsimile from the Surviving Manuscripts, Jesus College Oxford 29 and British Museum Cotton Caligula A. ix*. London: Early English Text Society, Oxford University Press, 1963.

Keynes, Geoffrey. *William Pickering Publisher: A Memoir and a Check-List of His Publications*. Rev. ed. London: Galahad; New York: Burt Franklin, 1969.

King, Edmund M. B. *Victorian Decorated Trade Bindings, 1830–1880: A Descriptive Bibliography*. London: British Library; New Castle, DE: Oak Knoll, 2003.

Kite, Marion, and Roy Thomson, eds. *Conservation of Leather and Related Materials*. Oxford: Elsevier, 2006.

Klima, Stefan. *Artists Books: A Critical Survey of the Literature*. New York: Granary, 1998.

Kniffel, Leonard, Peggy Sullivan, and Edith McCormick. "100 of the Most Important Leaders We Had in the 20th Century." *American Libraries* 30.11 (December 1999): 38.

Knuth, Rebecca. *Libricide: The Regime-Sponsored Destruction of Books and Libraries in the Twentieth Century*. Westport, CT: Praeger, 2003.

Koch, Rudolf. *The Book of Signs: 493 Symbols Used from Earliest Times to the Middle Ages by Primitive Peoples and Early Christians*. New York: Dover, 1930, and later printings.

Kooijman, Simon. *Polynesian Barkcloth*. Aylesbury: Shire, 1988.

Kotobee, "The Comprehensive List of International Book Fairs in 2020," December 25, 2019; https://blog.kotobee.com/international-book-fairs-2020/; accessed 28 January 2021.

Krummel, Donald W. "Early American Imprint Bibliography and Its Stories: An Introductory Course in Bibliographical Civics." *Libraries & Culture* 40.3 (Summer 2005): 239–50.

Krupp, Andrea. *Bookcloth in England and America, 1823–50*. London: British Library; New Castle, DE: Oak Knoll, 2008.

Kwakkel, Erik. "Decoration, Medieval Scribes: Medieval Super Models," 12 September, 2014; http://medievalbooks.nl/2014/09/12/medieval-super-models; accessed 6 July 2021.

L-W Publishing. *Price Guide to Big Little Books & Better Little, Jumbo, Tiny Tales, A Fast-Action Story, Etc.* Gas City, IN: L-W Book Sales, 1995.

Labarre, E[mile] J[oseph]. *Dictionary and Encyclopaedia of Paper and Paper-Making: With Equivalents of the Technical Terms in French, German, Dutch, Italian, Spanish & Swedish*. 2nd ed. Amsterdam: Swets & Zeitlinger, 1952.

Labuz, Ronald. *Typography & Typesetting: Type Design and Manipulation Using Today's Technology*. New York: Van Nostrand, 1988.

Lafontaine, Gerard H., comp. *Dictionary of Terms Used in the Paper, Printing and Allied Industries*. Toronto: Howard Smith Paper Mills, 1949.

LaMontagne, Leo E. *American Library Classification: With Special Reference to the Library of Congress*. Hamden, CT: Shoe String, 1961.

Lankhorst, Otto S. "Elzevier Family." In *The Oxford Companion to the Book*, vol. 2, edited by Michael F. Suarez and H. R. Woudhuysen, p. 695. Oxford: Oxford University Press, 2010.

Larson, Mike. "Before There Were Paper Jams: A Brief History of a Little-Known Office Machine." Minneapolis, MN: Hennepin County Museum, 2017; https://hennepinhistory.org/before-there-were-paper-jams-a-brief-history-of-a-little-known-office-machine/; accessed 4 February 2021.

Law, Graham. "Reviewing in Relation to Consumption." In *The Oxford Companion to the Book*, vol. 2, edited by Michael F. Suarez and H. R. Woudhuysen, pp. 1091–92. Oxford: Oxford University Press.

———. *Serializing Fiction in the Victorian Press*. Basingstoke: Palgrave, 2000.

———. "Serials and the Nineteenth-Century Publishing Industry." In *Dictionary of Nineteenth-Century Journalism*, edited by Laurel Brake and Marysa Demoor, p. 567. London: Academic, 2009.

Lawson, Alexander. *Anatomy of a Typeface*. Boston: Godine, 1990.

———. *Printing Types: An Introduction*. Boston: Beacon, 1971.

Leavitt, David. *While England Sleeps*. New York: Viking, 1993.

Lee, Aimee. "A New Naginata Beater, in Cleveland!" *Paper Slurry: A Mixture of Hand Papermaking*; http://paperslurry.com/2014/09/09/a-new-naginata-beater-in-cleveland; accessed 6 July 2021.

Lee, Brian North. *British Bookplates: A Pictorial History*. Newton Abbot, UK: David & Charles, 1979.

———. *British Royal Bookplates: And Ex-Libris of Related Families*. Aldershot: Scolar, 1992.

———. *Early Printed Book Labels: A Catalogue of Dated Personal Labels and Gift Labels Printed in Britain to the Year 1760*. Pinner, Middlesex, UK: Private Libraries Association, 1976.

Lee, Maria. "Walter Hamady—'Irascible Curmudgeon,'" http://ua-letterpress.blogspot.com/2010/06/walter-hamady-irrasible-curmuddgeon.html; accessed 6 July 2021.

Legros, Lucien Alphonse, and John Cameron Grant. *Typographical Printing Surfaces: The Technology and Mechanism of Their Production*. London: Longmans, Green, 1916; reprint, New York: Garland, 1980.

Le Guin, Ursula. *Direction of the Road*. Santa Cruz, CA: Foolscap Press, 2007.

Lehmann-Haupt, Hellmut. *The Göttingen Model Book*. Columbia: University of Missouri Press, 1972.

Leigh, Samuel. *Panorama of the Thames from London, to Richmond: Exhibiting Every Object on Both Banks of the River; With a Concise Description of the Most Remarkable Places and a General View of London*. London: Samuel Leigh, 182(?)–.

Lemprière, John. *Bibliotheca Classica, Or a Classical Dictionary*. Reading: Printed for T. Cadell, London, 1788.

Lent, John A. *Illustrating Asia: Comics, Humor Magazines, and Picture Books*. Honolulu: University of Hawaii Press, 2001.

Lenz, Hans. *Mexican Indian Paper: Its History and Survival*. Translated by H. Murray Campbell. Mexico City: Rafael Loera y Chavez, Editorial Libros de Mexico, 1961.

Lester, Valerie. *Giambattista Bodoni: His Life and His World*. Boston: Godine, 2015.

Levine, Israel E. *Miracle Man of Printing: Ottmar Mergenthaler*. New York: J. Messner, 1963.

Levine-Clark, Michael, and Toni M. Carter, eds. *ALA Glossary of Library and Information Science*. 4th ed. Chicago: ALA Editions, 2013.

Levis, Larry. *The Afterlife*. Iowa City: Windhover, 1977.

Levitov, Leo. *Solution of the Voynich Manuscript: A Liturgical Manual for the Endura Rite of the Cathari Heresy, the Cult of Isis*. Laguna Hills, CA: Aegean Park, 1987.

Lewis, John. *Collecting Printed Ephemera: A Background to Social Habits and Social History, to Eating and Drinking, to Travel and Heritage, and Just for Fun*. London: Studio Vista, 1976.

———. *Printed Ephemera: The Changing Use of Type and Letterforms in English and American Printing*. London: Faber & Faber, 1969.

Lewis, Roger C. *Thomas James Wise and the Trial Book Fallacy*. Aldershot: Scolar, 1995.

Lewis, Roy Harley. *Antiquarian Books: An Insider's Account*. Newton Abbot, UK: David & Charles; New York: Arco, 1978.

Lexico: Oxford English and Spanish Dictionary, Synonyms, and Spanish to English Translator, "Procter Order"; https://www.lexico.com/en/definition/proctor_order; accessed 2 March 2021.

Librarianship Studies & Information Technology. *AACR, AACR2, AACR2R*; https://www.librarianshipstudies.com/2018/12/anglo-american-cataloguing-rules-aacr.html; accessed 29 December 2020.

"Library Machines: The McLeod Collator." In *The Conveyer: Research in Special Collections at the Bodleian Library*; https://theconveyor.wordpress.com/2010/09/03/library-machines-the-mcleod-collator/; accessed 6 July 2021.

Library of Congress. "A Brief History of Panoramic Photography"; https://www.loc.gov/collections/panoramic-photographs/articles-and-essays/a-brief-history-of-panoramic-photography/; accessed 23 May 2021.

———. *Fiscal 2021 Budget Justification Submitted for Use of the Committees on Appropriations*; https://www.loc.gov/static/portals/about/reports-and-budgets/documents/budgets/fy2021.pdf; accessed 16 July 2021.

———. The Lessing J. Rosenwald Collection, "Geofroy Tory, *Champ Fleury*"; https://archive.is/20130131004008/http://www.octavo.com/editions/trychf/#selection-105.0-105.635; accessed 20 April 2021.

———. "What Is MARC Record, and Why Is It Important?" https://www.loc.gov/marc/umb/um01to06.html; accessed 6 July 2021.

Ligatus. *Language of Bindings*. Ligatus Thesaurus, "Inserted endleaves"; https://www.ligatus.org.uk/lob/concept/2931; accessed 25 March 2021.

Linda Lear Center, Digital Collections and Exhibitions. "Takejiro Hasegawa and the Production of Crepe Paper Books"; https://

lc-digital.conncoll.edu/exhibits/show/hasegawa/hasegawa; accessed 18 February 2021.

Lindsey, Robert. *A Gathering of Saints: A True Story of Money, Murder and Deceit*. New York: Simon and Schuster, 1988.

Lindstrand, Gordon. "Mechanized Textual Collation and Recent Designs." *Studies in Bibliography* 24 (1971): 204–14.

"List of Literary Awards." See under Wikipedia.

Listopia. "Best Bibliomystery Books"; https://www.goodreads.com/list/show/10242.Best_Bibliomystery_Books; accessed 20 February 2021.

Little Blue Books. See under Haldeman-Julius, Emanuel.

Loeber, E[duard] G. *Paper Mould and Mouldmaker*. Amsterdam: Paper Publications Society, 1982.

Loggan, David. *Cantabrigia illustrata, sive Omnium celeberrimae istius universitatis collegiorum, aularum, bibliothecae academicae, scholarum publicarum, sacelli coll. regalis: Nec non totius oppidi ichnographia*. Canterbury: n.p., 1690(?).

López, Analú, The Newberry Library. "Satirical Calaveras and the Day of the Dead." 31 October 2017; https://www.newberry.org/satirical-calaveras-and-day-dead; accessed 15 March 2021.

Lorimer, Pamela. "A Critical Evaluation of the Historical Development of the Tactile Modes of Reading and an Analysis and Evaluation of Researches Carried Out in Endeavours to Make the Braille Code Easier to Read and to Write." Ph.D. thesis, University of Birmingham, School of Education, Education and Continuing Studies, December 1996.

lotsearch.net. "L'optique"; https://www.lotsearch.net/lot/loptique-br-loptique-g-f-cazenave-coloured-engraving-after-louis-24911124?orderBy=lot-title&order=ASC&page=5; accessed 7 April 2021.

Lovejoy, Bess. "Xylotheks: Wondrous Wooden Books That Hold Wooden Collections." *Atlas Obscura*, May 22, 2014.

Lowndes, William Thomas. *The Bibliographer's Manual of English Literature: Containing an Account of Rare, Curious and Useful Books, Published in or Relating to Great Britain and Ireland, from the Invention of Printing; with Bibliographical and Critical Notices, Collations of the Rarer Articles, and the Prices at Which They Have Been Sold in the Present Century*. London: Pickering, 1834 (and later editions).

Lowry, Martin. *Nicholas Jenson and the Rise of Venetian Publishing in Renaissance Europe*. Oxford: Blackwell, 1991.

Loy, William E., Alistair M. Johnston, and Stephen O. Saxe. *Nineteenth Century American Designers and Engravers of Type*. New Castle, DE: Oak Knoll, 2009.

Luckiesh, Matthew, and Frank K. Moss. *The Science of Seeing*. New York: D. Van Nostrand, 1937.

Luers, Helmfried. "The Postcard Album: Postcard Printer & Publisher Research"; http://www.tpa-project.info/html/body_hold-to-light.html; accessed 17 March 2021.

Maas, Paul. *Textual Criticism*. Translated by Barbara Flower. Oxford: Oxford University Press, 1958.

MacCarthy, Fiona. *Eric Gill: A Lover's Quest for Art and God*. London: Faber and Faber, 1989.

———. *William Morris: A Life for Our Time*. London: Faber, 1994.

———. "Written in Stone"; http://www.theguardian.com/artanddesign/2006/jul/22/art.art; accessed 6 July 2021.

Mackail, J. W. *The Life of William Morris*. Vol. 1 (new ed.). London: Longmans, Green, 1901.

———. *The Life of William Morris*. Vol. 2. London: Longmans, Green, 1899.

Madan, Falconer. "Degressive Bibliograhy." *Transactions of the Bibliographical Society* 9 (October 1906–March 1908): 53–65.

———. "Standard Descriptions of Printed Books." *Proceedings and Papers*, Oxford Bibliographical Society 1 (1923): 55–64.

Madan, Falconer, E. G. Duff, and S. Gibson. "Standard Descriptions of Printed Books." *Proceedings and Papers of the Oxford Bibliographical Society*, pt. 1 (1922–1923): 55–64.

Magee, David. *A Course in Correct Cataloguing, or Notes to the Neophyte*. San Francisco: David Magee, 1958.

———. *Infinite Riches: The Adventures of a Rare Book Dealer*. New York: Paul S. Eriksson, 1973.

———. *The 2nd Course in Correct Cataloguing, or Further Notes to The Neophyte*. San Francisco: David Magee, 1962. (See also David Magee, *A Course in Correct Cataloguing*, above. These two volumes were combined into *A Course in Correct Cataloguing, or Notes to the Neophyte, The Two Parts now First Collected & Reissued in the Author's Honor by His Colleagues in the NCC/ABAA*, with a preface by James D. Hart. San Francisco: n.p., 1977.)

Maggs Bros. *First Editions of the Works of Esteemed Authors and Book Illustrators of the XIXth Century / Association Books and Mss. / Sports and Pastimes*. Catalogue No. 338. London: Maggs Bros., 1915.

Magic Lantern Society, The. "About Magic Lanterns"; https://www.magiclanternsociety.org/about-magic-lanterns/; accessed 30 May 2021.

———. "Before Motion Pictures"; https://www.magiclanternsociety.org/; accessed 30 May 2021.

Majure, Bill R. "A Brief History of the Limited Editions Club"; http://www.majure.net/lechistory.htm; accessed 6 July 2021.

Mandeville's Used Book Price Guide: An Aid in Ascertaining Current Prices of Rare, Scarce, Used and Out-of-Print Books. Kenmore, WA: Price Guide Publishers, several dates.

Manning, Molly Guptill, and Brian Anderson. *The Best-Read Army in the World*. New York: Grolier Club, 2020.

Manly, John M., and Edith Rickert, eds. *The Text of the* Canterbury Tales, *Studied on the Basis of All Known Manuscripts*. 8 vols. Chicago: University of Chicago Press, 1940.

Mansour, David. "Slam Book." In Mansour, *From Abba to Zoom: A Pop Culture Encyclopedia of the Late 20th Century*, p. 436. Kansas City, MO: Andrews McMeel, 2005.

MARC Code List for Organizations; https://www.loc.gov/marc/organizations/org-search.php; accessed 4 May 2021.

Marshall, David, and Elizabeth Ellis. "Reprinting *Printing Types*: A Wander through the Design of Stephenson Blake's Type Specimens." *Matrix* 33 (2015): 96–102.

Martin, Emily, and Alice Austin. "Book Theater: The History of the Tunnel Book." In Julia Miller, ed., *Suave Mechanicals: Essays on the History of Bookbinding*, Vol. 4, pp. 214–54. Ann Arbor, MI: Legacy, 2017.

Martin, R. Orion. "Lianhuanhua: Chinese Pulp Comics." *Comics Journal*, October 17, 2014; http://www.tcj.com/lianhuanhua-chinas-pulp-comics/; accessed 26 February 2021.

Marzi, Claudia, Gabriella Pardelli, and Manuela Sassi. "A Terminology-Based Re-Definition of Grey Literature"; http://www.greynet.org/images/GL12_S1P,_Marzi_et_al.pdf; accessed 6 July 2021.

Mason, Moya K. "Grey Literature: History, Definition, Acquisition, and Cataloguing: The History and Definition of Grey Literature"; http://www.moyak.com/papers/grey-technical-literature.html; accessed 6 July 2021.

Maurer, Diane Vogel, with Paul Maurer. *Marbling: A Complete Guide to Creating Beautiful Patterned Papers and Fabrics*. New York: Crescent, 1991.

Maurer-Mathison, Diane. *The Ultimate Marbling Handbook: A Guide to Basic and Advanced Techniques for Marbling Paper and Fabric*. New York: Watson-Guptill, 1999.

McCloud, Scott. *Understanding Comics: The Invisible Art*. Northampton, MA: Kitchen Sink, 1993.

McCorison, Marcus. "Fanny Hill and Thomas's Broadside Ballads"; https://www.americanantiquarian.org/thomasballads/fanny-hill-mccorison ; accessed 6 July 2021.

McCrady, Ellen. "In Memoriam: Paul N. Banks, 1934–2000." *Abbey Newsletter* 24.1 (2000); https://cool.culturalheritage.org/byorg/abbey/an/an24/an24-1/an24-102.html; accessed 23 May 2021.

McGrane, Sally. "Diary of the Hitler Diary Hoax." *New Yorker*, April 25, 2013; https://www.newyorker.com/books/page-turner/diary-of-the-hitler-diary-hoax; accessed 30 May 2021.

McGrath, Daniel F., ed. *Bookman's Price Index: A Guide to the Values of Rare and Other Out-of-Print Books*. Detroit: Gale Research, several dates, beginning 1964.

McKay, Barry, et al. *An Introduction to Chapbooks*. Oldham: Incline, 2003.

McKay, George L. *American Book Auction Catalogues, 1713–1934: A Union List*. New York: New York Public Library, 1937.

McKerrow, Ronald B. *A Dictionary of Printers and Booksellers in England, Scotland and Ireland, and of Foreign Printers of English Books 1557–1640*. London: Printed by Blades, East & Blades for the Bibliographical Society, 1910.

———. *An Introduction to Bibliography for Literary Students*. Oxford: Clarendon, 1927 (second impression with corrections, 1928); reprint, New Castle, DE: Oak Knoll, 1995. (This 1928 text is cited in the present volume.)

———. *Printers' & Publishers' Devices in England & Scotland 1485–1640*. London: Printed for the Bibliographical Society, 1913.

———. *Prolegomena for the Oxford Shakespeare: A Study in Editorial Method*. Oxford: Clarendon, 1939 (and reprints).

McKerrow, Ronald B., and F. S. Ferguson. *Title-Page Borders Used in England and Scotland, 1485–1640*. London: Printed for the Bibliographical Society at the Oxford University Press, 1932.

McKitterick, David. *A New Specimen Book of Curwen Pattern Papers*. Gloucestershire: Whittington, 1987.

———. "Obituary: Professor Donald McKenzie"; *Independent*, 23 November 2011; https://www.independent.co.uk/arts-entertainment/obituary-professor-donald-mckenzie-1082824.html; accessed 23 April 2021.

McLaverty, James. "David Foxon, Humanist Bibliographer." *Studies in Bibliography* 54 (2001): 81–113; http://xtf.lib.virginia.edu/xtf/view?docId=StudiesInBiblio/uvaBook/tei/sibv054.xml;chunk.id=vol054.02;toc.depth=1;toc.id=vol054.02;brand=default; accessed 26 January 2021.

McLean, Ruari. *Jan Tschichold: Typographer*. Boston: David R. Godine, 1975.

———, trans. *Jan Tschichold: The New Typography*. Berkeley: University of California Press, 1988.

———. *The Thames and Hudson Manual of Typography*. London: Thames and Hudson, 1980 (and later editions).

———. *Victorian Publishers' Book-Bindings in Cloth and Leather*. Berkeley: University of California Press, 1973.

———. *Victorian Publishers' Book-Bindings in Paper*. Berkeley: University of California Press, 1983.

McLeod, Randall. "McLeod Portable Collator." *Newsletter, Humanities Association of Canada* 16 (December 1988): 33–41.

———. "A New Technique of Headline Analysis with Application to Shakespeare's Sonnets, 1609." *Studies in Bibliography* 32: 197–210.

M'Clintock, John, and James Strong. "Tract Societies Distinctly So-called (1894)"; http://www.victorianweb.org/religion/tracts/societies.html; accessed 6 March 2021. Excerpted from John M'Clintock and James Strong, *Cyclopædia of Biblical, Theological, and Ecclesiastical Literature*, Vol. 10, pp. 513–14. New York: Harper & Brothers, 1894.

McMurtrie, Douglas C. *Stereotyping in Bavaria in the Sixteenth Century: A Note on the History of Map Printing Processes and of Printer's Platemaking*. New York: Privately Printed, 1935.

Mediavilla, Claude. *Histoire de la Calligraphie Française*. Paris: Albin Michel, 2006.

Mehegan, David. "Harvard Author's Apology Not Accepted." *Boston Globe*, 26 April 2006, pp. F1, F8.

Merker, Kim, printer. *Kenney's: Twenty Poems for a Lost Tavern*. Iowa City: Windhover, 1970.

———, printer. *Völuspá*. Trans. by Paul B. Taylor and W. H. Auden. Iowa City: Windhover, 1968.

Merriam-Webster online dictionary. "Battledore"; https://www.merriam-webster.com/dictionary/battledore; accessed 20 February 2021.

———. "Proof before letter"; https://www.merriam-webster.com/dictionary/proof%20before%20letter; accessed 15 March 2021.

Merritt, Percival. "The Club of Odd Volumes." *Papers of the Bibliographic Society of America* 9 (1915): 21–44; https://www.journals.uchicago.edu/doi/pdf/10.1086/pbsa.9.1_2.24292213; accessed 7 July 2021.

Meynell, Francis, and Stanley Morison. "Printers' Flowers and Arabesques." In *The Fleuron: A Journal of Typography* 1: 1–43. London: At the Office of The Fleuron, 1923; https://archive.org/stream/fleuronjournalof00lond/fleuronjournalof00lond_djvu.txt; accessed 7 July 2021.

Middleton, Bernard C. *A History of English Craft Bookbinding Technique*. New York: Hafner, 1963 (and later editions).

———. *The Restoration of Leather Bindings*. Chicago: American Library Association, 1972 (and later editions).

Mihm, Stephen. "No Ordinary Counterfeit." *New York Times Magazine*, 23 July 2006; http://www.nytimes.com/2006/07/23/magazine/23counterfeit.html?pagewanted=all&_r=0; accessed 6 July 2021.

Miller, Edward. *Prince of Librarians: The Life & Times of Antonio Panizzi of the British Museum*. Athens: Ohio University Press, 1967.

Miller, Julia. *Books Will Speak Plain: A Handbook for Identifying and Describing Historical Bindings*. Ann Arbor, MI: Legacy, 2010.

Miller, Liam. *A Brief Account of the Cuala Press Formerly the Dun Emer Press, Founded by Elizabeth Corbett Yeats in 1903*. Dublin: Cuala, 1971.

Milton, John. *Areopagitica: A Speech of Mr John Milton for the Liberty of Unlicenc'd Printing, to the Parliament of England*. London: 1644. See the full text, with a commentary by Richard C. Jebb (Cambridge: University Press, 1918); https://oll-resources.s3.us-east-2.amazonaws.com/oll3/store/titles/103/1224_Bk.pdf; accessed 12 February 2021.

Miner, Dorothy. *The History of Bookbinding 525–1950 A.D.: An Exhibition Held at the Baltimore Museum of Art November 12, 1957 to January 12, 1958*. Baltimore: Trustees of the Walters Art Gallery, 1957.

Mitchell, William Smith. "Bookbinders' Tickets." *The Durham University Journal* 46.1 (New Series 15.1) (December 1953): 1–4; https://sevenroads.org/Articles/Mitchell1953/BookbindersTickets.html; accessed 19 April 2021.

Miura, Einen. *The Art of Marbled Paper: Marbled Patterns and How to Make Them*. London: Zaehnsdorf, 1990.

Monotype MyFonts. "Stephenson Blake"; https://www.myfonts.com/foundry/Stephenson_Blake/; accessed 15 May 2021.

Moorman, Charles. *Editing the Middle English Manuscript*. Jackson: University Press of Mississippi, 1975.

Moran, James. *Heraldic Influence on Early Printers' Devices*. Leeds: Elmete, 1978.

———. *Printing Presses: History and Development from the Fifteenth Century to Modern Times*. Berkeley: University of California Press, 1973.

———. *Stanley Morison: His Typographic Achievement*. London: Lund Humphries; New York: Hastings House, 1971.

Mordell, Albert. *The World of Haldeman-Julius*. New York: Twayne [1960].

Morris, Ellen K., and Edward S. Levin. *The Art of Publishers' Bookbindings, 1815–1915*. Los Angeles: William Dailey Rare Books, 2000.

Morris, Henry. *Omnibus: Instructions for Amateur Papermakers with Notes and Observations on Private Presses, Book Printing and Some People Who Are Involved in These Activities*. North Hills, PA: Bird & Bull, 1967.

[———.] See under Bachaus, Theodore, *The World's Worst Marbled Paper*.

Morris, William. *The Works of Geoffrey Chaucer Now Newly Imprinted*. Hammersmith, UK: Kelmscott, 1896.

Morrison, R[obert] S[tewart], ed. *Digest of the Law of Mines and Minerals and of All Controversies Incident to the Subject-matter of Mining: Comprising the Cases in the English and American Reports, from the Year Books to the Present Time* (San Francisco: A. L. Bancroft, 1878.

———, and Emilio D. De Soto, eds. *The Mining Reports: A Series Containing the Cases on the Law of Mines Found in the American and English Reports, Arranged Alphabetically by Subjects, with Notes and References*. 22 volumes. Chicago: Callaghan, 1883–1906.

Morrow, B. F. *The Art of Aquatint*. New York: G. P. Putnam's Sons, 1935.

Morrow, Bradford. "In Search of America's Rarest Unknown Books by Renowned Writers: Browsing Bookshop Shelves You May Come Across Hidden Treasures." *Crime Reads*, 9 September 2020; https://crimereads.com/in-search-of-americas-rarest-unknown-books-by-renowned-writers/; accessed 4 May 2021.

Mortimer, Edward. *Mortimer's Ready Reckoner: Paper Calculations and Printing Tables*. Halifax: Edward Mortimer, 1971.

Mosley, James. "Fallen and Threaded Types." Blog; http://typefoundry.blogspot.com/2007/06/fallen-and-threaded-types.html; accessed 7 July 2021.

———. "The Materials of Typefounding." *Typefoundry: Documents for the History of Type and Letterforms*, 6 Janaury 2006; http://typefoundry.blogspot.com/2006/01/materials-of-typefounding.html; accessed 1 April 2021.

Moxon, Joseph. *Mechanick Exercises on the Whole Art of Printing*. London, 1683–1684; reprint ed. by Herbert Davis and Harry Carter. London: Oxford University Press, 1958; 2nd corrected ed., 1962; Davis/Carter ed. reprint, New York: Dover, 1978.

Mulder, Megan. "A Token of My Affection: 19th Century Christmas Annuals." Winston-Salem, NC: ZSR [Z. Smith Reynolds] Library, Wake Forest University, December 9, 2014; https://zsr.wfu.edu/2014/a-token-of-my-affection-19th-century-christmas-annuals/; accessed 5 January 2021.

Muller, Monika E. *The Use of Models in Medieval Painting*. Cambridge: Cambridge Scholars, 2014.

Munby, A. N. L. *Portrait of an Obsession: The Life of Sir Thomas Phillipps, the World's Greatest Book Collector*. Adapted by Nicolas Barker from the five volumes of *Phillipps Studies*. New York: G. P. Putnam's Sons, 1967.

Munby, A. N. L., and Lenore Coral. *British Book Sale Catalogues, 1676–1800: A Union List*. London: Mansell, 1977.

Mustain, John. *Monuments of Printing: Gutenberg through the Book Arts Revival*. Palo Alto, CA: Stanford University Libraries, 2013.

MyFonts. "William Caslon"; https://www.myfonts.com/person/William_Caslon_I/; accessed 22 April 2021.

Mystery Readers International. "Bibliomysteries." *Mystery Readers International* 21.3 (Fall 2005); https://mysteryreaders.org/journal-index/bibliomysteries-2/; accessed 20 February 2021.

Naifeh, Steven, and Gregory White Smith. *The Mormon Murders: A True Story of Greed, Forgery, Deceit, and Death*. New York: Weidenfeld & Nicolson, 1988 (and later editions).

National Diet Library of Japan. "Glossary: Incunabula"; https://www.ndl.go.jp/incunabula/e/glossary/index.html; accessed 14 August 2022.

———. "The World of Watermarks"; https://www.ndl.go.jp/incunabula/e/chapter3/chapter3_02.html; accessed 6 July 2021.

National Endowment for the Humanities. "The New Schoenberg Database of Manuscripts: A Research Tool for Tracking the Current and Historic Locations of Manuscripts." See under Ransom, Carol.

National Library of Medicine. "Historical Anatomies on the Web"; https://www.nlm.nih.gov/exhibition/historicalanatomies/more.html; accessed 15 February 2021.

Neal, Marie. *In Gardens of Hawaii*. Special Publication 50. Honolulu: Bernice P. Bishop Museum, Bishop Museum Press, 1965.

Needham, Paul. "Allan H. Stevenson and the Bibliographical Uses of Paper." *Studies in Bibliography* 47 (1994): 23–64.

———. "Johann Gutenberg and the Catholicon Press." *Papers of the Bibliographical Society of America* 76: 395–456.

———. "Late-medieval Mysteries." *Times Literary Supplement* (31 March–6 April 1989): 346.

———. *Twelve Centuries of Bookbindings, 400–1600*. New York: Pierpont Morgan Library; London: Oxford University Press, 1979.

Neich, Roger, and Mick Pendergrast. *Traditional Tapa Textiles of the Pacific*. New York: Thames and Hudson, 1997. (Also issued as *Pacific Tapa*. Aukland: David Bateman Ltd., 1997.)

Nesbitt, Alexander. *The History and Technique of Lettering*. New York: Dover, 1957.

Ness, Daniel. "Daniel Berkeley Updike." Boston Athenaeum, September 2014; https://www.bostonathenaeum.org/library/book-recommendations/athenaeum-authors/daniel-berkeley-updike; accessed 24 May 2021.

Netz, Reviel, and William Noel. *The Archimedes Codex: Revealing the Secrets of The World's Greatest Palimpsest*. London: Weidenfeld and Nicolson, 2007.

Newberry, The. "The Cheap and Easy Room," 22 February 2012; https://www.newberry.org/cheap-and-easy-room for a shorter paragraph about these publications; accessed 29 June 2021.

Newell, L. F. *Stereotyping and Electrotyping*. London: Isaac Pitman & Sons, 1952.

New York State Library, *Guide to Almanac Collection*; http://www.nysl.nysed.gov/msscfa/almanacs.htm; accessed 5 January 2021.

De Nieuwe Toverlantaarn. Amsterdam: c. 1770. (See under Blow book.)

Nishimura, Margot McIlwain. *Images in the Margins*. Los Angeles: J. Paul Getty Museum; London: British Museum, 2009.

Nixon, Howard M. *Five Centuries of English Bookbinding*. London: Scolar, 1978.

———. *Royal English Bookbindings in the British Museum*. London: Trustees of the British Museum, 1957.

———. *Sixteenth-century Gold-tooled Bookbindings in the Pierpont Morgan Library*. New York: Pierpont Morgan Library, 1971.

———, and Mirjam M. Foot. *The History of Decorated Bookbinding in England*. Oxford: Clarendon; New York: Oxford University Press, 1992.

Non Solus Blog. "Julia Miller: Scaleboard Bindings and a Visit to RBML"; June 6, 2011; https://publish.illinois.edu/nonsolusblog/?p=118; accessed 2 February 2021.

Norman, Jeremy. "Joseph Moxon Issues the First Comprehensive Printing Manual (1683 to 1684)"; http://www.historyofinformation.com/expanded.php?id=456; accessed 7 July 2021.

———. "Nicolas [*sic*] Pickwood's Tentative Observations on Dating Carta Rustica Bindings." Jeremy Norman's HistoryofInformation.com; accessed 14 August 2022.

Northeast Document Conservation Center. "Freezing and Drying Wet Books and Records." NEDCC, Leaflet 3.12; https://www.nedcc.org/free-resources/preservation-leaflets/3.-emergency-management/3.12-freezing-and-drying-wet-books-and-records; accessed 1 August 2021.

———. *Preservation of Library & Archival Materials: A Manual*. Edited by Sherelyn Ogden. Andover, MA: Northeast Document Conservation Center, 1999 (3rd ed., rev. and expanded, and other editions). Now available as *Preservation Leaflets*. (Formerly published in a bound volume and then in a three-ring binder, now available free at https://www.nedcc.org/free-resources/preservation-leaflets/overview; accessed 7 July 2021. Now that they are in digital form, they can be updated quickly, so online searches will pull up the most recent iterations of these publications.)

Nussdorfer, Laurie. *Civic Politics in the Rome of Urban VIII*. Princeton, NJ: Princeton University Press, 1992.

O'Brian, Dave. "The Daffy Demand for Cels." *Washington Post*, January 1, 1990; https://www.washingtonpost.com/archive/lifestyle/1990/01/01/the-daffy-demand-for-cels/12f01668-0872-4301-8f0f-749676732bef/; accessed 26 January 2021.

O'Casey, Ian, and A. S. Maney. *The Nature and Making of Papyrus*. Barkston Ash, UK: Elmete, 1973.

OCLC. "Organize Your Materials with the World's Most Widely Used Library Classification System"; oclc.org/en.dewey.html; accessed 14 August 2022.

O'Connell, Bonnie, "The Quality of Response: Kim Merker and the Literary Fine Press." *Books at Iowa* 64 (April 1996); http://www.lib.uiowa.edu/spec-coll/bai/oconnell.htm; accessed 18 May 2021.

O'Connell, Brian. "History of eBay: Facts and Timeline." *The Street*, 18 December 2019; thestreet.com/markets/history-of-ebay; accessed 18 May 2021.

O'English, Lorena, J. Gregory Matthews, and Elizabeth Blakesley Lindsay. "Graphic Novels in Academic Libraries: From Maus to Manga and Beyond." *Journal of Academic Librarianship* 32.2 (March 2006): 173–82.

Oglesby, Sam. "Before Facebook Bullying, There Was the Dreaded Slam Book"; washingtonpost.com, 11 December 2010; https://www.washingtonpost.com/wp-dyn/content/article/2010/12/10/AR2010121005373.html; accessed 4 April 2021.

Oldham, J. B[asil]. *Blind Panels of English Binders*. Cambridge: Cambridge University Press, 1958.

———. *Early Stamped Bookbindings in the British Museum: Descriptions of 385 Blind-Stamped Bindings of the XIIth-XVth Centuries in the Departments of Manuscripts and Printed Books / Mainly by the Late W. H. James Weale. With 490 Illustrations of the Stamps Used on Them*. Completed by Lawrence Taylor. London: Trustees of the British Museum, 1922.

———. *English Blind-Stamped Bindings*. Cambridge: Cambridge University Press, 1952.

Oldham, Robert. "The Columbian Press at 200: A Preliminary Report on a World-Wide Census." *Journal of the Printing Historical Society*, n.s. 21 (2014): 51–66.

Open Culture. "Napoleon's Kindle: See the Miniaturized Traveling Library He Took on Military Campaigns"; https://www.openculture.com/2017/10/napoleons-kindle-see-the-miniaturized-traveling-library-he-took-on-military-campaigns.html; accessed 8 August 2021.

———. "'Tsundoku,' the Japanese Word for the New Books That Pile Up on Our Shelves, Should Enter the English Language"; 24 July 2014; https://www.openculture.com/2014/07/tsundoku-should-enter-the-english-language.html; accessed 27 May 2021.

Open Knowledge Foundation. "Open Definition: Defining Open in Open Data, Open Content and Open Knowledge"; http://opendefinition.org/od/2.1/en/; accessed 7 July 2021.

"The Original New Variorum Shakespeare Project, 1871–1955 [27 vols.]," https://us ers.pfw.edu/stapletm/NVSJC/OldNVS.html; accessed 6 July 2021.

"Orphan Works in the United States," Wikipedia; https://en.wikipedia.org/wiki/Orphan_works_in_the_United_States#:~:text=An%20orphan%20work%20is%20a,when%20fair%20use%20exceptions%20apply.States; accessed 11 June 2021.

Other People's Books: Association Copies and the Stories They Tell. Chicago: Caxton Club, 2011.

Oxford Companion to English Literature, 7th ed. "Toy Books." [Oxford]: Oxford University Press, 2009; https://www.oxfordreference.com/view/10.1093/acref/9780192806871.001.0001/acref-9780192806871-e-9465; accessed 14 March 2021.

Paekakariki Press. "Printers' Vocabulary: A Collection of some 2500 technical terms, phrases, abbreviations and other expressions mostly relating to Letterpress Printing"; https://paekakarikipress.com/?content=jacobi.php; accessed 15 May 2021.

Page, Elizabeth. "University's Foundational Rare Book Collection Acquired a Century Ago"; Ransom Center Magazine, 21 February 2018; https://sites.utexas.edu/ransomcentermagazine/2018/02/21/universitys-foundational-rare-book-collection-acquired-a-century-ago/; accessed 6 July 2021.

Panizzi, Anthony. *Rules for the Compilation of the Catalogue.* London: Nichols and Son, 1841.

Pankow, David. "The Printer's Manual—An Illustrated History: Classic and Unusual Texts on Printing from the Seventeenth, Eighteenth, and Nineteenth Centuries"; Online exhibition; https://books.google.com/books?id=NVUo5OCJGYcC&printsec=copyright#v=onepage&q&f=false; accessed 7 July 2021.

———. "The Rise and Fall of ATF." *Printing History: The Journal of the American Printing History Association* 43–44 (22.1–2): 314.

Pankow, David, and John Dreyfus. *The Art of the Type Specimen in the Twentieth Century.* New York: Typophiles and International Typeface Corporation, 1993.

Pardoe, F. E. *John Baskerville of Birmingham: Letter-Founder and Printer.* London: Frederick Muller, 1975.

Parks, Stephen, ed. *The Beinecke Library of Yale University.* New Haven, CT: Yale University Press, 2007.

Partington, Wilfred. *Forging Ahead: The True Story of the Upward Progress of Thomas James Wise, Prince of Book Collectors, Bibliographer Extraordinary and Otherwise.* New York: G. P. Putnam's Sons, 1939.

Passet, Joanne E. "Reaching the Rural Reader: Traveling Libraries in America, 1892–1920." *Libraries & Culture* 26.1, "Reading & Libraries I" (Winter, 1991), 100–18.

Pazo Espinosa, José, and Julio Baquero Cruz, comps. *Cuentos del Japón Viejo.* Spain: Langre, 2009.

Pearson, David. *English Bookbinding Styles, 1450–1800: A Handbook.* London: British Library; New Castle, DE: Oak Knoll, 2005.

———. *Provenance Research in Book History: A Handbook.* London: British Library, 1994; reprint, London: British Library; New Castle, DE: Oak Knoll, 1998; new and revised ed., Oxford: Bodleian Library, University of Oxford, 2019.

Pearson, Edmund. *Dime Novels: Or, Following an Old Trail in Popular Literature.* Boston: Little, Brown, 1929.

Pennell, Elizabeth Robbins, and Joseph Pennell. *Lithography and Lithographers: Some Chapters in the History of the Art.* New York: Macmillan, 1915.

Pentland, Gordon. *Edinburgh History of the Book in Scotland.* Vol. 2, *Enlightenment and Expansion 1707–1800.* Edinburgh: Edinburgh University Press, 2011.

Perry, Timothy P. J. "Early Depictions of the Printing Press: A Model Source." *Printing History: The Journal of the American Printing History Association*, n.s. 18 (July 2015): 27–53.

Peters, G. S. (publisher). *Metamorphosis; or, a Transformation of Pictures, with Poetical Explanations, for the Amusement of Young Persons.* Harrisburg, PA: G. S. Peters, 1831.

Peters, Jean, ed. *Book Collecting: A Modern Guide.* New York and London: Bowker, 1977. (Twelve essays by various authors.)

———, ed. *The Bookman's Glossary.* 6th ed. New York: Bowker, 1983.

———, ed. *Collectible Books: Some New Paths.* New York: Bowker, 1979. (Nine essays by various authors.)

Peterson, Roger Tory, and Virginia Marie Peterson, eds. *Audubon's Birds of America.* New York: Harrison House, 1985; New York: Abbeville, 1990.

Peterson, William S. *A Bibliography of the Kelmscott Press.* Oxford: Clarendon, 1984.

———. *The Kelmscott Press: A History of William Morris's Typographical Adventure.* Oxford: Oxford University Press; Berkeley: University of California Press, 1991.

Petherbridge, Guy. "The Compleat Binder: The Arts and Crafts Legacy of Roger Powell." *Bibliologia: Elementa Ad Librorum Studia Pertinentia* 14 (1996): 35–56. Turnhout: Brepols, 1996.

PhilipSmithBookArt blog. "Announcement"; http://www.philipsmithbookart.com/; accessed 23 April 2021.

Pickwoad, Nicholas. "Clarkson Festschrift"; 3 September 2020; https://www.tandfonline.com/doi/full/10.1080/18680860.2019.1748418#:~:text=He%20was%20born%20on%2022,school%20when%20he%20was%207; accessed 23 March 2021.

Pierce, J. Kingston. "Dell Mapbacks: A History: The Art of the Back Cover Murder Mystery." CrimeReads, 2 August 2018; https://crimereads.com/dell-mapbacks-a-history/; accessed 20 April 2021.

Pinto, Edward, and Eva Pinto. *Tunbridge and Scottish Souvenir Woodware: With Chapters on Bois Durci and Pyrography.* London: G. Bell & Sons, 1970.

Pistner, Patricia J., and Jan Storm van Leeuwen. *A Matter of Size: Miniature Bindings and Texts from the Collection of Patricia J. Pistner.* New York: Grolier Club, 2019.

Poetry Foundation. "William Blake"; https://www.poetryfoundation.org/poets/william-blake; accessed 30 July 2021.

Pogcar, Charlie. "Arsenic and Old Books." *Fine Books & Collections* 19.1 (Winter 2021): 13–14.

Poison Book Project. See under Tedone, Melissa.

Pollard, Alfred W. *Last Words on the History of the Title-Page, with Notes on Some Colophons and Twenty-Seven Facsimiles of Title-Pages.* London: John C. Nimmo, 1891.

———. *Shakespeare's Fight with the Pirates and the Problems of the Transmission of His Text.* Cambridge: At the University Press, 1937.

———, and G. R. Redgrave, comps. *A Short-Title Catalogue of Books Printed in England, Scotland, and Ireland and of English Books Printed Abroad 1475–1640.* London: Bibliographical Society, 1926 (and later editions).

———, and W. W. Greg. "Some Points in Bibliographical Description." *Transactions of the Bibliographical Society* 9 (1908): 31–52; reprint in Fred W. Roper, comp., *Alfred William Pollard: A Selection of His Essays*, pp. 116–29. Metuchen, NJ: Scarecrow, 1976.

Post, Emily. *Etiquette in Society, in Business, in Politics, and at Home.* New York and London: Funk & Wagnalls, 1922; https://www.gutenberg.org/files/14314/14314-h/14314-h.htm; accessed 21 January 2021.

Powell, J. Marsh. "The Bestseller Book That Didn't Exist: How the Author of a Beloved Christmas Classic Pulled Off the Hoax of the Century"; http://www.jmarkpowell.com/the-bestseller-book-that-didnt-exist-how-the-author-of-a-beloved-christmas-classic-pulled-off-the-hoax-of-the-century; accessed 7 July 2021.

Powers, Alan. *Art & Print: The Curwen Story.* London: Tate, 2008.

Prescott, Andrew. "'Their Present Miserable State of Cremation': The Restoration of the Cotton Library." (First published in C. J. Wright, ed., *Sir Robert Cotton as Collector: Essays on an Early Stuart Courtier and His Legacy*, pp. 391–454. London: British Library Publications, 1997.)

Price, Gary. "The Library of Congress Awards $5.5 Million Contract for 'Mass Deacidification' of Library Collection." *Library Journal*, Info Docket (5 November 2021); infodocket.com/2021/11/5/library-of-congress-awards-5-5-million-contract-for-mass-deacidification-of-library-collection/; accessed 14 August 2021.

Printing and the Mind of Man: Assembled at the British Museum and at Earls Court London, 16–27 July 1963. London: Messrs. F. W. Bridges & Sons and the Association of British Manufacturers of Printers' Machinery, 1963.

The Private Library. "In Search of Supralibros at The Private Library"; 11 October 2010; https://privatelibrary.typepad.com/the_private_library/2010/10/in-search-of-supralibros-at-the-private-library.html; accessed 6 March 2021.

Procter, Robert. *An Index to the Early Printed Books in the British Museum: From the Invention of Printing to the Year MD*, with Notes of Those in the Bodleian Library. London: Kegan Paul Trench Trübner and Comp., 1898. With a supplement published in 1899; along with a companion volume done by Francis S. Isaac, *An Index to the Early Printed Books in the British Museum*, Part II. MDI-MDXX. Section II. Italy, Section III. Switzerland and Eastern Europe. London: Bernard Quaritch, LTD, 1938.

Pryor, Lewis A., ed. "The California Typecase." *Campane, Monthly Bundle Sample, Campane* 194 (n.d.) [National Amateur Press Association]: 1–12.

Publishers Weekly. "About Publishers Weekly"; https://subs.publishersweekly.com/about-us; accessed 4 April 2021.

PW [Publishers Weekly]. "Number of Self-Published Titles Jumped 40% in 2018"; https://www.publishersweekly.com/pw/by-topic/industry-news/publisher-news/article/81473-number-of-self-published-titles-jumped-40-in-2018.html; accessed 5 July 2021.

Quaritch, Bernard. *Catalogue of the Monuments of the Early Printers in All Countries . . . Offered for Cash at the Affixed Net Prices.* London: Bernard Quaritch, 1888; https://books.google.com/books?id=k2E7AQAAMAAJ&pg=PA3592&lpg=PA3592&dq=%22sina+nota%22&source=bl&ots=YUiFkS9Ly2&sig=ACfU3U2ugynX3-ho-AEzVCD2SBiMZjuAPA&hl=en&sa=X&ved=2ahUKEwjDicybnszwAhWDrJ4KHUCVA5oQ6AEwEnoECAwQAw#v=onepage&q=%22sina%20nota%22&f=false; accessed 15 May 2021.

Quayle, Eric. *A Collector's Book of Books.* New York: Clarkson N. Potter; London: Studio Vista, 1971.

Quinion, Michael. World Wide Words. "Zograscope"; http://www.worldwidewords.org/weirdwords/ww-zog1.htm; accessed 7 April 2021.

RA: The Royal Academy. "The Curwen Press"; https://www.royalacademy.org.uk/art-artists/organisation/the-curwen-press; accessed 29 June 2021.

Raabe, Tom. *Biblioholism: The Literary Addiction.* Golden, CO: Fulcrum, 1991. Rev. ed., 2001.

Ragab, Hassan. "Papyrus and the Manufacture of Paper by the Ancient Egyptians." Ph.D. diss., Institute Polytechnique de Grenoble, 1979.

———. "Resurrection of Papyrus as a National Heritage & The Harvest of 35 Years Experience with Papyrus." *Bulletin of the Center of Papyrological Studies, Cairo* 10 (1994): 151–67.

Randall, David A. *Dukedom Large Enough: Reminiscences of a Rare Book Dealer 1929–1956.* New York: Random House, 1969.

Ransom, Carol. "The New Schoenberg Database of Manuscripts: A Research Tool for Tracking the Current and Historic Locations of Manuscripts"; https://securegrants.neh.gov/publicquery/products.aspx?gn=PW-51580-14; accessed 2 February 2021.

Ransom, Will. *Private Presses and Their Books.* New York: James Cummins, 1992.

———. *Selective Check Lists of Press Books: A Compilation of All Important & Significant Private Presses, or Press Books Which Are Collected.* New York: James Cummins, 1992.

Raybould, Robin. See *Gazette of the Grolier Club.*

[———.] *Emblemata: Symbolic Literature of the Renaissance, from the Collection of Robin Raybould.* New York: Grolier Club, 2009.

Recovering and Preserving the Author's Intention. Columbia: Center for Editions of American Authors, University of South Carolina, 1972.

Reed, Ronald. *Ancient Skins, Parchments and Leathers*. London: Seminar, 1972.

———. *The Nature and Making of Parchment*. Leeds, UK: Elmete, 1975.

Reese, William S. "The First Hundred Years of Printing in British North America: Printers and Collectors"; http://www.reeseco.com/papers/first100.htm; accessed 7 July 2021.

———. *Winnowers of the Past: The Americanist Tradition in the Nineteenth Century*. Scholar of the House Program, Yale University, April 12, 1977. "Twenty-five copies of the essay reproduced by photocopy, April, 1977."

Rees-Mogg, William. *How to Buy Rare Books: A Practical Guide to the Antiquarian Book Market*. Oxford: Phaidon/Christie's, 1988.

Rehmeyer, Julie. "The Mystery of Extraordinarily Accurate Medieval Maps: Beautifully Detailed Portolan Charts Present Historians with a Puzzle: How Were They Made? A Mathematical Analysis Offers Some Clues." *Discover*, May 27, 2014; https://www.discovermagazine.com/the-sciences/the-mystery-of-extraordinarily-accurate-medieval-maps; accessed 7 July 2021.

Reichling, Dietrich. *Appendices ad Hainii-Copingeri Repertorium Bibliographicum: Fasciculi I II, III IV, V und Indices fasciculorum I–VI*. 7 vols. Munich: Rosenthal, 1905–1911.

Reithmayr, Andrea. Library as Incubator Project. "Owen Jones: Relievo and Papier-mâché Bindings" (Part 2); 5 March 2013; http://www.libraryasincubatorproject.org/?p=9177; accessed 12 March 2021.

Reitz, Joan M. *Online Dictionary for Library and Information Science*; https://products.abc-clio.com/ODLIS/odlis_m.aspx; accessed 20 February 2021.

Rennicks, Rich. "Collecting Dell Mapbacks." The New Antiquarian blog, 9 July 2020; https://www.abaa.org/blog/post/dell-mapbacks; accessed 20 April 2021.

Revolution Performance Fabrics. "The Origins of the Greek Key Pattern"; https://revolutionfabrics.com/blogs/gotcha-covered/the-origins-of-the-greek-key-pattern; accessed 3 January 2021.

Reynolds Stone, 1909–1979. Dorchester: Dorset Natural History and Archaeological Society, Dorset County Museum, 1981.

Rhodes, Barbara, and William Wells Streeter. *Before Photocopying: The Art & History of Mechanical Copying, 1780–1938: A Book in Two Parts*. New Castle, DE: Oak Knoll; Northampton, MA: Heraldry, 1999.

Riccardo, Franci. *Takejiro Hasegawa e le fiabe giapponesi del Museo Stibbert* (Takejiro Hasegawa and the Japanese Fairy Tales Collection of the Stibbert Museum). Livorno, Italy: Sillabe, October 2008.

Rickards, Maurice. *The Encyclopedia of Ephemera: A Guide to the Fragmentary Documents of Everyday Life for the Collector, Curator, and Historian*. New York: Routledge, 2000.

Ritter, R. M. *The Oxford Guide to Style*. Oxford: Oxford University Press, 2002; https://goetheindia.files.wordpress.com/2010/01/new-harts-rules.pdf; accessed 23 January 2021.

Riviere, Michael. "The Huguenot Family of Riviere in England." *Proceedings of the Huguenot Society of London* 21 (1970).

Roberts, Matt T., and Don Etherington. *Bookbinding and the Conservation of Books: A Dictionary of Descriptive Terminology*. Washington, DC: Library of Congress, 1982. Available online at https://cool.culturalheritage.org/don/toc/toc1.html; accessed 27 August 2022.

Robinson, Duncan. *William Morris, Edward Burne-Jones and the Kelmscott Chaucer*. London: Gordon Fraser, 1982; Kingston, RI: Moyer Bell, 1986.

Roden, Robert F. *The Cambridge Press 1638–1692: A History of the First Printing Press Established in English America Together with a Bibliographical List of the Issues of the Press*. New York: Dodd, Mead, 1905.

Roethke, Theodore. *Sequence, Sometimes Metaphysical*. Iowa City: Stone Wall, 1963.

Romaine, Lawrence B. *A Guide to American Trade Catalogs, 1744–1900*. New York: Bowker, 1960.

———. "Printers' Specimens, Presses & Equipment." In Romaine, *A Guide to American Trade Catalogs, 1744–1900*, pp. 271–88. New York: Bowker, 1960.

Romalov, Nancy Tillman, and Carolyn Stewart Dyer, eds. "Children's Series Books and the Rhetoric of Guidance: A Historical Overview." In Tillman and Dyer, *Rediscovering Nancy Drew*, pp. 113–20. Iowa City: University of Iowa Press, 1995.

Romano, Frank. *History of the Linotype Company*. Rochester, NY: RIT, 2014.

Roper, Fred W., comp. *Alfred William Pollard: A Selection of His Essays*. Metuchen, NJ: Scarecrow, 1976.

Rose, David. "North Korea's Dollar Store." *Vanity Fair, VF Style*, September 2009; https://www.vanityfair.com/style/2009/09/office-39-200909; accessed 7 July 2021.

Rosenbach, A. S. W. *Books and Bidders. The Adventures of a Bibliophile*. Boston: Little, Brown, 1927 (and other editions).

Rosenbloom, Megan. *Dark Archives: A Librarian's Investigation into the Science and History of Books Bound in Human Skin*. New York: Farrar, Straus and Giroux, 2020.

Rosin, Nancy. "Valentine's Day and the Romance of Cobwebs," 10 February 2017. The Metropolitan Museum of Art; https://www.metmuseum.org/blogs/now-at-the-met/2017/valentines-day-romance-of-cobwebs; accessed 27 April 2021.

Rostenberg, Leona, and Madeleine Sterne. *New Worlds in Old Books*. New Castle, DE: Oak Knoll, 1999. (This is just one of several volumes these two authors collaborated on.)

Rubin, Ellen G. K. *Ideas in Motion: The History of Pop-up and Movable Books: Books & Ephemera from the Collection of Ellen G.K. Rubin*. New Paltz: State University of New York, New Paltz, 2005.

———. "Pop-up and Movable Books In the Context of History." From the catalog of Ideas in Motion exhibit at SUNY–New Paltz, NY, April, 2005; https://popuplady.com/about-pop-ups/pop-up-and-movable-books-in-the-context-of-history/; accessed 27 April 2021.

Rulon-Miller, Rob. "A Note on OCLC." "Recent Acquisitions / Sept. 22 2020"; https://rulon.enusan.net/cat200922.html; accessed 27 April 2021.

———. "Recent Acquisitions / March 2nd, 2021"; https://enusan.net/rulon/processwire-master/catalogs/cat210302/; accessed 2 March 2021.

Ruston, Jessica. "The Ingredients for a Blockbuster Novel." *Guardian*, https://www.theguardian.com/books/booksblog/2009/dec/09/ingredients-blockbuster-novel; accessed 18 March 2021.

Rychkov, Cheryl A. "Medieval Manuscript Production," April 15, 2003; http://library.randolphcollege.edu/hours/production.html; accessed 4 July 2021.

Saad El Din, Mursi, et al. *Sinai: The Site & the History: Essays*. New York: New York University Press, 1998.

Sabin, Joseph. *Bibliotheca Americana: A Dictionary of Books Relating to America, from Its Discovery to the Present Time*. 29 vols. New York: Joseph Sabin, 1868–1936. (Sabin began this work; it was completed by Wilberforce Eames and R. W. G. Vail.)

Sadleir, Michael. *Collecting "Yellowbacks" (Victorian Railway Fiction) Aspects of Book-Collecting*. London: Constable, n.d. [1938].

Sadleir, Michael. *Evolution of Publishers' Binding Styles, 1700–1900*. London: Constable, 1930.

Sagmeister, Stefan, and Peter Hall. *Made You Look: Another Self-indulgent Design Monograph (Practically Everything We Have Ever Designed Including the Bad Stuff)*. London: Booth Clibborn Editions, 2001; New York: Harry N. Abrams, 2009.

Sandstrom, Alan R., and Pamela Effrein Sandstrom. *Traditional Papermaking and Paper Cult Figures of Mexico*. Norman: University of Oklahoma Press, 1986.

Santa Clara University, University Library. "Grabhorn Press: Home"; https://libguides.scu.edu/grabhorn; accessed 18 July 2021.

Saxe, Stephen O. "Ramage Proof Press." *Printing History: The Journal of the American Printing History Association* 22 (11.2): 26–27.

Schatt, Carol. *House of Cods*. Phoenix, AZ: Linda Smith, Picnic Press, 1996.

Scheller, R. W. *A Survey of Medieval Model Books*. Haarlem, The Netherlands: De Erven F. Bohn, 1963.

Schleicher, Patty, and Mimi Schleicher. *Marbled Designs: A Complete Guide to Fifty-Five Elegant Patterns*. Asheville, NC: Lark Books, Altamont Press, 1993.

Schlesinger, Carl. *The Biography of Ottmar Mergenthaler*. New Castle, DE: Oak Knoll, 1993.

Schlieder, Wolfgang. *Riesaufdrucke: Volkstümliche Grafik im alten Papiermachergewerbe*. Leipzig: VEB Fachbuchverlag, 1988. (Well-illustrated book on ream wrappers [q.v.].)

Schlosser, Leonard, ed. *Paper in Printing History*. New York: Lindenmeyr Paper Corporation, 1979.

Schmoller, Hans. *Two Titans: Mardersteig and Tschichold: A Study in Contrasts*. New York: Typophiles, 1990.

Schmoller, Tanya. *Remondini and Rizzi: A Chapter in Italian Decorated Paper History*. New Castle, DE: Oak Knoll, 1990.

Schrope, Mark. "Medicine's Hidden Roots in an Ancient Manuscript." *New York Times*, June 1, 2015, 4.

Schudel, Matt. "Henriette Avram, 'Mother of MARC,' Dies"; http://www.loc.gov/loc/lcib/0605/avram.html; accessed 7 July 2021.

Schuessler, Jennifer. "'Blooks: The Art of Books That Aren't' Explores the World of Fake Books." *New York Times*, January 28, 2016; https://www.nytimes.com/2016/01/29/books/a-secret-in-every-tome-no-text-required.html; accessed 12 February 2021.

Schuyt, Michael, and Joost Elffers. *Anamorphoses: Games of Perception and Illusion in Art*. New York: Harry N. Abrams, 1976.

Schwab, Richard N., Thomas A. Cahill, Bruce H. Kusko, and Daniel L. Wick. "Cyclotron Analysis of the Ink in the 42-Line Bible." *The Papers of the Bibliographical Society of America* 77 (1983): 285–315. (The information in this article and in the one headed by Cahill et al. [above] was published under a number of titles in the journals of several disciplines.)

"Searching CiNii for Japanese Periodical Articles"; https://www.sciping.com/wp-content/uploads/2018/08/Searching-CiNii-for-Japanese-Periodical-Articles.pdf; accessed 16 February 2021.

Selvin, Claire. "A Passionate Collector's Pre-Cinema Objects Will Go to Academy Museum, Illuminating Early Film History." *ARTnews*, 29 September 2020; https://www.artnews.com/art-news/news/academy-museum-richard-balzer-donation-pre-cinema-objects-1234571932/; accessed 1 May 2021.

Sharf, Frederic A. *Takejiro Hasegawa: Meiji Japan's Preeminent Publisher of Wood-block-illustrated Crepe-paper Books*. [Salem, MA:] *Peabody Essex Museum Collections*, 130.4 (October 1994).

Shaw, Paul. "An Appreciation of Frederic W. Goudy as a Type Designer," March 13, 2014; http://www.paulshawletterdesign.com/2014/03/an-appreciation-of-frederic-w-goudy-as-a-type-designer; accessed 7 July 2021.

Shepherds / Sangorski & Sutcliffe. "The Bindery"; http://www.bookbinding.co.uk/The%20Bindery.htm; accessed 4 July 2021.

Sherman, William H. "Toward a History of the Manicule"; http://www.livesandletters.ac.uk/papers/FOR_2005_04_001.pdf; accessed 7 July 2021.

Shipton, Clifford K., and James E. Mooney. *National Index of American Imprints through 1800: The Short-Title Evans*. 2 vols. Worcester, MA: American Antiquarian Society, 1969.

Short, Matthew. *Blood and Thunder; or, A Very Brief History of the Dime Novel. Caxtonian: Journal of the Caxton Club* 27.11 (November 2019): 1–3.

Shucun, Wang. *Paper Joss: Deity Worship through Folk Prints*. Beijing: New World, 1992.

Shumaker, David. "Special Libraries." In *Encyclopedia of Library and Information Sciences*, 3rd ed., edited by Marcia Bates and Mary Niles Maack, Vol. 7, pp. 4966–74. Boca Raton, FL: CRC, 2010.

Shurtleff, Jane E., Robert D. Hale, Allan Marshall, and Ginger Curwen, eds. *A Manual on Bookselling: How to Open and Run a Bookstore*. 4th ed. New York: Harmony/Crown, 1987.

Silcox, David P. *Painting Place: The Life and Work of David B. Milne*. Toronto: University of Toronto Press, 1996.

Sillitoe, Linda, and Allen Roberts. *Salamander: The Story of the Mormon Forgery Murders*. Salt Lake City, UT: Signature, 1988.

Silver, Joel. "Bibliographies, Checklists, and Catalogs: The Core of a Collector's Reference Shelf." *Fine Books & Collections*, January/February 2008.

———. *Dr. Rosenbach and Mr. Lilly: Book Collecting in a Golden Age*. Newtown, PA: Bird & Bull, 2010; New Castle, DE: Oak Knoll, 2011.

———. *J. K. Lilly, Jr.: Bibliophile*. Bloomington: Indiana University Press, 1993.

Simon Beattie, Antiquarian Books and Music. "Never Judge a Book by Its Cover." Short List 1 (n.d. [2020]), entry #6, pp. 10, 25. See the volume referenced at *Dictionnaire Poucet*.

Simpson, Percy. *Proof-Reading in the Sixteenth, Seventeenth and Eighteenth Centuries*. London: Oxford University Press; New York: Humphrey Milford, 1935.

Sixpenny Wonderfuls: 6d Gems from the Past. London: Chatto and Windus, Hogarth, 1985.

Slinn, Judy, Sebastian Carter, and Richard Southall. *History of the Monotype Corporation*. Edited by Andrew Boag and Christopher Burke. London: Printing Historical Society and Vanbrugh Press, 2014.

Smith, Ernie. "How Mimeographs Transformed Information Sharing in Schools." EdTech; https://edtechmagazine.com/k12/article/2020/09/how-mimeographs-transformed-information-sharing-schools; accessed 19 April 2021.

Smith, Gerald A. "A Collating Machine: Poor Man's Mark VII." *PBSA* 61 (1967): 10–13.

Smith, Julian Pearce. See under Updike, Daniel Berkeley, *Notes on the Merrymount Press*.

Smith, Linda. See under Schatt, Carol, *House of Cods*.

Smith, Margaret M. *The Title-Page: Its Early Development, 1460–1510*. London: British Library; New Castle, DE: Oak Knoll, 2000.

Smith, Margit J. "The Medieval Girdle Book Project: Collecting the Information." Amigos Library Services, May 2007; amigos.org/sites/default/files/2005_smith.pdf; accessed 7 July 2021.

———, and Jim Bloxam. "The Medieval Girdle Book Project." *The International Journal of the Book* 3.4 (2005/2006): 15–24; https://www.academia.edu/358553/The_Medieval_Girdle_Book_Project; accessed 7 July 2021.

Smith, Philip. See PhilipSmithBookArt blog.

Smith, Roberta. "Douglas [*sic*] Morse Howell, 87, Artist and Papermaker" (obituary), *New York Times*, 12 February 1995, p. 9.

Smith, Stephen Escar. "'Armadillos of Invention': A Census of Mechanical Collators." *Studies in Bibliography* 55 (2002): 133–70.

———. "'The Eternal Verities Verified': Charlton Hinman and the Roots of Mechanical Collation." *Studies in Bibliography* 53 (2000): 129–62.

Soltész, Elizabeth. *Biblia Pauperum*. [Budapest & Gyoma], Hungary: Corvina, 1967.

Somers, Jeanne. *Index to* The Dolphin *and* The Fleuron. Westport, CT: Greenwood, 1986.

Sönmez, Nedim. *Ebru—The Turkish Art of Marbling*. Hückelhoven, Germany: Verlag Anadolu, 1996.

———. *From Ebru to Marbled Paper / vom Ebru zum Marmorpapier*. Tübingen, Germany: Jäckle- Sönmez, Marmorier Werkstatt und Verlag, 1995.

Sotheby and Son. *Bibliotheca Heberiana: Catalogue of the Library of the Late Richard Heber, Esq*. Vols. 1–13, [London]: Sotheby and Son, 1834; Vols. 14–15, Paris: Silvestre (Vols. 14–15, Paris & Ghent: Ch. Citerne, 1834–1837).

Sotheby, Wilkinson & Hodge. *Catalogue of the Towneley Library, Removed from Towneley Hall, Lancashire*. London: Sotheby, Wilkinson & Hodge, 1883; http://www.atoz.myzen.co.uk/towneley/downloads/books_1883sale.pdf; accessed 15 May 2021.

Sotheby's. "Update Regarding Sotheby's Buyer's Premium"; February 15, 2019; https://www.sothebys.com/en/articles/sothebys-buyers-premium-update; accessed 29 January, 2021.

———. *TheValue.com*; "Sotheby's to Charge a New 'Overhead Premium' Fee Amidst Pandemic, Effective 1 August," August 1, 2020; https://en.thevalue.com/articles/sothebys-global-auctions-new-fee-one-percent-2020#:~:text=Starting%201%20August%202020%2C%20Sotheby's,fees%20between%202015%20and%202020; accessed 29 January 2021.

Sowerby, E. Millicent. *Rare People & Rare Books*. Williamsburg, VA: Bookpress, 1987.

Speaight, Robert. *The Life of Eric Gill*. London: Methuen; New York: P. J. Kenedy & Sons, 1966.

Speckter, Martin K. *Disquisition on the Composing Stick*. New York: Typophiles, 1971.

Spector, Steven, ed. *Essays in Paper Analysis*. Washington, DC: Folger Books, Folger Shakespeare Library, 1987.

Spender, Stephen. "My Life Is Mine: It Is Not David Leavitt's." *Books: The New York Times on the Web*; 4 September 1994; https://archive.nytimes.com/www.nytimes.com/books/98/04/26/specials/leavitt-spender.html; accessed 14 April 2021.

———. *World within World*. London: Hamish Hamilton, 1951.

Spolsky, Ellen. *Iconotropism: Turning toward Pictures*. Lewisburg, PA: Bucknell University Press, 2004.

Standard Citation Forms for Published Bibliographies and Catalogs Used in Rare Book Cataloging. Prepared by Peter Van Wingen and Belinda D. Urquiza. Washington, DC: Library of Congress, 1996

Steale Not Thys Book: A Compendium of Warnings & Invectives Against Those Who Would Purloin, Desecrate, or Injure Books. [Dundas, Ontario, Canada]: Aliquando, April 2020.

Steinbeck, John. *The Grapes of Wrath*. New York: Viking, 1939.

Steinberg, S. H. *Five Hundred Years of Printing*. Harmondsworth: Penguin; Baltimore: Penguin, 1955 (and many later printings and editions).

Stelzner, Michael A. "Writing White Papers." Learn All about White Papers. Whitepaper Source Publishing, 2008. See also "How to Write a White paper: A White Paper on White Papers." Stelzner Consulting, 2007; http://eng249.pbworks.com/f/A+White+Paper+on+White+Papers.pdf; accessed 7 July 2021.

Sterne, Harold E. *A Catalogue of Nineteenth Century Printing Presses*. New Castle, DE: Oak Knoll; London: British Library, 2001.

Stevenson, Allan H. *The Problem of the Missale Speciale*. London: Bibliographical Society, 1967.

———. "Watermarks Are Twins." *Studies in Bibliography* 4 (1951–1952): 58–93.

Stevenson, Robert Louis. *Island Nights' Entertainments: Consisting of: The Beach of Falesa, The Bottle Imp, The Isle of Voices*. With Illustrations By Gordon Browne And W. Hatherell. London: Cassell & Company Limited, 1893; at Biblio.com; https://www

.biblio.com/book/island-nights-entertainments-stevenson-robert-louis/d/1359157265; accessed 30 May 2021.

Stijnman, Ad. "Terms in Print Addresses: Abbreviations and Phrases on Printed Images 1500–1900"; "an updated version of Appendix 3 in [his book] *Engraving and Etching 1400–2000: A History of the Development of Manual Intaglio Printmaking Processes*"; London and Houten, 2012, pp. 413–18; https://www.delineavit.nl/wp-content/uploads/Terms-in-print-addresses.pdf; accessed 31 July 2021.

Stillman, Michael. "117 Years in the Dismantling: The End of Perhaps the Greatest Collection Ever." *Rare Book Monthly* (December 2003); https://www.rarebookhub.com/articles/112?id=112; accessed 1 August 2021.

Stillwell, Margaret Bingham. *Incunabula and Americana 1450–1800: A Key to Bibliographical Study*. New York: Columbia University Press, 1930; reprint, New York: Cooper Square, 1961.

———. *Incunabula in American Libraries. A Second Census of Fifteenth-Century Books Owned in the United States, Mexico and Canada*. New York: Bibliographical Society of America, 1940.

Stoddard, Roger. *Marks in Books*. Cambridge, MA: Houghton Library, Harvard University, 1985.

Stojko, John. *Letters to God's Eye: The Voynich Manuscript for the First Time Deciphered and Translated into English*. New York: Vantage, 1978.

Stokes, Roy. *A Bibliographical Companion*. Metuchen, NJ: Scarecrow, 1989.

Stone, Humphrey. *Reynolds Stone: A Memoir*. Stanbridge, Dorset: Dovecote, 2019.

Stone, Reynolds. See under *Reynolds Stone, 1909–1979*.

———. *Reynolds Stone: Engravings*. Brattleboro, VT: Stephen Greene, 1977.

Stower, C[aleb]. *The Printer's Grammar; Or, Introduction to the Art of Printing: Containing a Concise History of the Art, With the Improvements in the Practice of Printing, for the Last Fifty Years*. London: Printed by the Editor for B. Crosby and Co., 1808.

Straus, Ralph. *The Unspeakable Curll: Being Some Account of Edmund Curll, Bookseller*. New York: Augustus M. Kelley, 1970.

Streeter, Thomas Winthrop, collector. *The Celebrated Collection of Americana Formed by the Late Thomas Winthrop Streeter*. 8 vols. New York: Parke Bernet Galleries, 1966–1969.

Strickland, Debra Higgs. *The Mark of the Beast: The Medieval Bestiary in Art, Life, and Literature*. New York: Garland, 1999.

Strouse, Jean. *Introduction to the Morgan Library: An American Masterpiece*. New York: Pierpont Morgan Library, 2000.

Suarez, Michael F., and H. R. Woudhuysen, eds. *The Oxford Companion to the Book*. 2 vols. Oxford: Oxford University Press, 2010.

Subramaniam, Ramanathan, and R. Venkatesh. "Optimal Bundling Strategies in Multiobject Auctions of Complements or Substitutes." *Marketing Science* 28.2 (March–April 2009): 264–73; abstract at https://www.jstor.org/stable/23884262?seq=1; accessed 17 January 2021.

Sufa, Theresia. "Ministry to Name Bogor's Xylarium World's Largest Wood Collection." *Jakarta Post*, 22 September, 2018; https://www.thejakartapost.com/life/2018/09/22/ministry-to-name-bogors-xylarium-worlds-largest-wood-collection.html; accessed 24 January 2022.

Sullivan, Kate. "Complete Guide to Small Press Publishing: The Good, The Bad, and The Ugly of Small Presses for Writers"; https://www.tckpublishing.com/complete-guide-to-small-press-publishing-for-writers/; accessed 22 April 2021.

Surina, Echo. "Boudoir Photographs Turn the Girl Next Door into a Sexy, Confident Pin Up." *Exquisite Weddings*, by *San Diego Magazine* 3.1 (Spring/Summer 2009): 54–56.

Symonds, Matthew, and Earle Havens. "The Archaeology of Reading"; https://archaeologyofreading.org/historiography/; accessed 29 July 2021.

Szirmai, J. A. *The Archaeology of Medieval Bookbinding*. Aldershot: Ashgate, 2000.

Tanselle, G. Thomas. "The Bibliographical Description of Paper." *Studies in Bibliography* 24 (1971): 27–67.

———. "The Bibliographical Description of Patterns." *Studies in Bibliography* 23 (1970): 71–102.

———. *Book-Jackets: Their History, Forms, and Use*. Charlottesville: Bibliographical Society of the University of Virginia, 2011.

———. "The Editing of Historical Documents." *Studies in Bibliography* 1 (1978): 1–56.

———. "Editing without a Copy-Text." *Studies in Bibliography* 47 (1994): 1–22.

———. *Essays in Bibliographical History*. Charlottesville: Bibliographical Society of the University of Virginia; New Castle, DE: Oak Knoll, 2013.

———. *Introduction to Bibliography: Seminar Syllabus*. 19th revision. Charlottesville, VA: Rare Book School, 2002; http://rarebookschool.org/2014/tanselle/syl-B-complete.090302.pdf; accessed 7 July 2021.

———. *The Life and Work of Fredson Bowers*. Charlottesville: Bibliographical Society of the University of Virginia, 1993.

———. "The Literature of Book Collecting." In *Book Collecting: A Modern Guide*, edited by Jean Peters, pp. 209–71. New York: Bowker, 1977.

———. "A Rationale of Collecting." *Studies in Bibliography* 51 (1998): 1–26; http://xtf.lib.virginia.edu/xtf/view?docId=StudiesInBiblio/uvaBook/tei/sibv051.xml&chunk.id=vol051.01&toc.id=vol051.01&brand=default; accessed 7 July 2021.

———. *A Rationale of Textual Criticism*. Philadelphia: University of Pennsylvania Press, 1989.

———. "Reproductions and Scholarship." *Studies in Bibliography* 42 (1989): 25–54.

———. "Review of *The Problem of the Missale Speciale*." *Library Quarterly* 39.2 (April 1969): 201–02.

———. "A System of Color Identification for Bibliographical Description." *Studies in Bibliography* 20 (1967): 203–34.

———. *Textual Criticism since Greg: A Chronicle, 1950–1985*. Charlottesville: University of Virginia Press, 1988.

———. "William H. Scheide (1994)" (delivered in part at the dinner of the Friends of the Princeton University Library honoring Scheide on his eightieth birthday, January 29, 1994). In *Portraits and Reviews*, pp. 74–79. Charlottesville: Bibliographical Society of the University of Virginia, 2015.

Taylor, Merrily E. *The Yale University Library 1701–1978: Its History, Collections, and Present Organization*. New Haven, CT: Yale University Library, 1978.

Taylor, Thomas O., "Tuck." "Not All Mylar Is Archival." *Abbey Newsletter* 13.5 (September 1989); https://cool.culturalheritage.org/byorg/abbey/an/an13/an13-5/an13-507.html; accessed 10 February 2021.

"Teaching of Ptahhotep," https://www.ucl.ac.uk/museums-static/digitalegypt/literature/ptahhotep.html; accessed 21 January 2021.

Tedone, Melissa. "Poison Book Project." Winterthur Museum, Garden & Library; http://wiki.winterthur.org/wiki/Poison_Book_Project; accessed 13 January 2021.

Thackrah, C. Turner. *The Effects of the Principal Arts, Trades and Professions, and of Civic States and Habits of Living, on Health and Longevity: With a Particular Reference to the Trades and Manufactures of Leeds: And Suggestions for the Removal of Many of the Agents, which Produce Disease, and Shorten the Duration of Life*. Philadelphia: Literary Rooms . . . Office the Journal of Health, the Journal of Law, and Family Library of Health, 1831.

Thomas, James Stuart. *The Big Little Book Price Guide*. Des Moines, IA: Wallace-Homestead Book Co., 1983.

Thomas, Peter, ed. *Beer Will Help Your Shake: Recollections of a Ninety-Two Year Old Papermaker*. Oxford: Alembic; Santa Cruz, CA: Good Book, 1990.

———. *Beater Time Tests*. Santa Cruz: Peter and Donna Thomas, 1987.

Thomas, Simon. "Ars moriendi—The Art of Dying"; Bodleian Library, http://bav.bodleian.ox.ac.uk/news/ars-moriendi-the-art-of-dying; accessed 24 May 2021.

Thompson, Daniel V. *The Materials and Techniques of Medieval Painting*. New York: Dover, 1956.

Thoreau, Henry David. *Huckleberries*. Iowa City, IA: Windhover Press; New York: New York Public Library, 1970.

Thorn, Matt. *Animerica: Anime & Manga Monthly* 4.2,4,6 (2005); http://matt.thorn.com/mangagaku/history.html; accessed 25 October 2015; this seems to be a dead link. For more information on the history of manga, see "A Short History of Manga: Art History, Design"; Widewalls; https://www.widewalls.ch/magazine/japanese-manga-comics-history; accessed 7 July 2021.

Throckmorton, George J., R. C. Christensen, and Richard H. Casper. *Motive for Murder: The Bombs, the Mormons and the Salamander*. Sandy, UT: Omega, 2005.

Thürkôw, Guus. *William Morris Wallpapers*. Zuilichem, The Netherlands: Catharijne, 1997.

Tibbetts, Robert A., comp. and ed. *The Compleat Bookman: A Centennial Exhibition of the Work of Dard Hunter as Author, Papermaker, Artist, Typemaker, Printer*. Columbus, OH: Ohio State University Libraries, 1983.

Tidcombe, Marianne. *The Bookbindings of T. J. Cobden-Sanderson: A Study of His Work 1884–1893 Based on His Time Book*. London: British Library; New Castle, DE: Oak Knoll,1984.

———. *The Doves Bindery*. London: British Library; New Castle, DE: Oak Knoll, 1991.

———. *The Doves Press*. London: British Library; New Castle, DE: Oak Knoll, 2002.

———. *Women Bookbinders, 1880–1920*. New Castle, DE: Oak Knoll; London: British Library, 1996.

Tilley, Roger. *History of Playing Cards*. New York: C. N. Potter; distributed by Crown, 1973.

Tinker, Miles A. *Bases for Effective Reading*. Minneapolis: University of Minnesota Press, 1965.

———. *Legibility of Print*. Ames: Iowa State University Press, 1963.

Todd, William B. *Suppressed Commentaries on the Wiseian Forgeries: Addendum to an Enquiry*. Austin: Humanities Research Center, University of Texas, Austin, 1969.

Todd, William B., and Ann Bowden. *Tauchnitz International Editions in English, 1841–1955: A Bibliographical History*. New York: Bibliographical Society of America, 1989; reprint, New Castle, DE: Oak Knoll; London: British Library, 2003.

Toledo Art Museum. "Traveling Library"; http://emuseum.toledomuseum.org/objects/51402; accessed 8 August 2021.

Tomlinson, William, and Richard Masters. *Bookcloth, 1823–1980: A Study of Early Use and the Rise of Manufacture, Winterbottom's Dominance of the Trade in Britain and America, Production Methods and Costs, and the Identification of Qualities and Designs*. This edition copyright 1995: N.p. [Stockport, Cheshire?]: n.p. [William Tomlinson and Richard Masters], 1996.

Tonelli, Lucia. "The 50+ Best Coffee Table Books to Gift in 2020: Terrific Tomes and Perfect Presents." *Elle Decor*, December 10, 2019; https://www.elledecor.com/shopping/g23085527/best-coffee-table-books/; accessed 28 February 2021.

Topp, Chester W. *Victorian Yellowbacks & Paperbacks, 1849*–1905 [Vols. I, II, III, IV, V, VI, VII, VIII, IX]. Denver: Hermitage Antiquarian Book Shop, 1993–2006.

Trachtenberg, Jeffrey A. [Print version title:] "What's an Author To Do With No Blurb On the Book Jacket?: Newcomers Are Accustomed To Plugs, but Old-Timers Just Don't Have the Time." [Online title:] "Authors Struggle to Get Blurbed: Newcomers Are Accustomed to Plugs But Old-Timers Just Don't Have the Time." *Wall Street Journal*, July 30, 2003; https://www.wsj.com/articles/SB105951785239555OO; accessed 11 April 2021.

Tracy, Walter. *Letters of Credit: A View of Type Design*. Boston: David R. Godine, 1986.

Tanselle, G. Thomas. "Editing without a Copy-Text." *Studies in Bibliography* 47 (1994): 1–22.

Tredwell, Daniel M. *A Monograph on Privately Illustrated Books: A Plea for Bibliomania*. 2nd ed. Flatbush, NY: Privately printed, 1892.

Trujillo, Robert G. "Dime Novels Full Text"; https://library.stanford.edu/collections/dime-novels-full-text#:~:text=Unlike%20the%20dime%20novels%2C%20which,form%20of%20wood%20engravings)%20throughout; accessed 29 June 2021.

Tschichold, Jan. *Asymmetric Typography*. Translated by Ruary McLean from the German *Typographische Gestaltung*. New York: Reinhold; Toronto: Cooper & Beatty, 1967.

———. *The Form of the Book: Essays on the Morality of Good Design*. Translated by Hajo Hadeler. Point Roberts, WA: Hartley & Marks, 1991.

———. *The New Typography: A Handbook for Modern Designers*. Berkeley: University of California Press, 1988. (*Die neue*

Typographie: Ein Handbuch für Zeitgemäss Schaffende [Berlin: Brinkmann & Bose, 1987—though first published in German in 1928].)

Tullet, Hervé. *The Game of Mix-up Art*. London and New York: Phaidon, 2011.

Tuohy, Steven, comp. *James Mosley: Librarian, St Bride Printing Library, London: A Checklist of the Published Writings 1958–95*, with two essays by James Mosley. Cambridge, UK: Rampant Lions [1995].

[Turnbull, Richard H.] "Encaustic Books from Furious Day Press (www.furiousdaypress.com)." N.p.: Furious Day, n.d. (Flyer for the press.)

Twain, Mark. *The Celebrated Jumping Frog of Calaveras County, and Other Sketches*. New York: C. H. Webb, 1867.

———. *The Innocents Abroad: Or The New Pilgrims' Progress: Being Some Account of the Steamship Quaker City's Pleasure Excursion to Europe and the Holy Land; with Descriptions of Countries, Nations, Incidents and Adventures, as They Appeared to the Author*. Hartford, CT: American, 1869.

Twyman, Michael. *A History of Chromolithography: Printed Colour for All*. London: British Library; New Castle, DE: Oak Knoll, 2013.

———. *Printing 1770–1970: An Illustrated History of Its Development and Uses in England*. London: British Library; New Castle, DE: Oak Knoll, 1998.

Type Metals: Their Characteristics and Their Performance. Philadelphia: Imperial Type Metal Company, 1950.

Typography and Design. Washington, DC: U.S. Government Printing Office, 1951; rev. ed., 1963.

UCLA Library Special Collections. "The Michael Sadleir Collection of 19th Century Fiction"; https://sites.google.com/view/ucla-library-sadleir/introduction; accesssed 2 February 2021.

UDC Consortium. "Universal Decimal Classification"; http://www.udcc.org/; accessed 31 July 2021.

Uden, Grant. *Understanding Book-Collecting*. Woodbridge: Antique Collectors' Club, 1988.

"Ulrich's Periodical Directory," cited at https://www.library.ucsb.edu/research/db/338; accessed 8 August 2021.

Underhill, Wanda, ed. *Henry S. Boutell's First Editions of Today and How to Tell Them*. 4th ed. Berkeley, CA: Peacock, 1965.

University of California, Riverside. Thomas Rivera Library. "Fanzines Collection"; https://library.ucr.edu/collections/fanzines-collection; accessed 23 October 2022.

University of Cambridge, ArchiveSearch. "Curwen Press"; https://archivesearch.lib.cam.ac.uk/agents/corporate_entities/2004; accessed 29 June 2021.

University of Chicago Press. *The Chicago Manual of Style: The Essential Guide for Writers, Editors, and Publishers*. 17th ed. Chicago: University of Chicago Press, 2017. See also *The Chicago Manual of Style* Online at https://www.chicagomanualofstyle.org/home.html; accessed 27 April 2021.

University of Texas Libraries. "What Is a Zine?"; https://guides.lib.utexas.edu/c.php?g=576544&p=3977232; accessed 7 March 2021.

University of Wisconsin–Madison. "Little Magazine Collection." Little Magazine Collection Blog, n.d.; https://www.library.wisc.edu/specialcollections/collections/little-magazine-collection/; accessed 17 February 2021.

Updike, Daniel Berkeley. *Notes on the Merrymount Press & Its Work*. With a Bibliographic List of Books Printed at the Press, 1893–1933 by Julian Pearce Smith. San Francisco: A. Wofsy Fine Arts, 1975.

———. *Printing Types: Their History, Forms, and Use: A Study in Survivals*. 2nd ed. 2 vols. Cambridge, MA: Harvard University Press, 1951 (and later editions).

U.S. Copyright Office. "International Issues"; https://www.copyright.gov/international-issues/; accessed 16 July 2021.

van Breda, Jacobus. "Rembrandt Etchings on Oriental Papers: Papers in the Collection of the National Gallery of Victoria." *Art Journal* 38 (4 June 2014); https://www.ngv.vic.gov.au/essay/rembrandt-etchings-on-oriental-papers-papers-in-the-collection-of-the-national-gallery-of-victoria/; accessed 1 August 2021.

van Elferen, Anita; Knuf Rare Books. E-Catalogue, May 2021, item 2, Trade card for D. & J. Bevernaege, lithographic printers in Oudenaarde. No place, no date [but Oudenaarde, c. 1850]; http://www.fritsknuf.com/Ecat12_hd.pdf; accessed 25 May 2021.

Van Wingen, Peter. *Your Old Books*. Washington, DC: Library of Congress, 1994 (now available from Rare Books and Manuscripts Section, Association of College and Research Libraries); http://rbms.info/yob; accessed 7 July 2021.

Vervliet, Hendrik D. L. *The Palaeotypography of the French Renaissance*. Leiden: Brill, 2008.

Verweij, Sebastian. "Through a Glass Darkly: Collating Donne's Sermons." Centre for Material Texts: A New Forum for the Study of the Word in the World, Cambridge University Library; http://www.english.cam.ac.uk/cmt/?p=991; accessed 7 July 2021.

Via, Maria, with Elbert Hubbard and Marjorie Searl, eds. *Head, Heart and Hand: Elbert Hubbard and the Roycrofters*. Rochester, NY: University of Rochester Press, 1994.

Victoria and Albert Museum. *Early Printers' Marks*. London: Her Majesty's Stationery Office, 1962.

Victoria and Albert Museum. "Paper Peepshows"; https://www.vam.ac.uk/articles/paper-peepshows; accessed 15 February 2021.

———. *Reynolds Stone 1909–1979, An Exhibition Held in the Library of the Victoria and Albert Museum from 21 July to 31 October 1982*. London: Victoria and Albert Museum, 1982.

Vilain, Jean-François, and Philip R. Bishop. *Thomas Bird Mosher and the Art of the Book*. Philadelphia: F. A. Davis, 1992.

Villanova University, Falvey Memorial Library. "Jack Butler Yeats"; https://exhibits.library.villanova.edu/jack-butler-yeats/cuala-press; accessed 31 July 2021.

Vingerhoets, Karin. Europeana, "Catchpenny Prints in The Netherlands"; https://www.europeana.eu/en/blog/catchpenny-prints-in-the-netherlands; accessed 15 March 2021.

Vinson, Michael. *Bluffing Texas Style: The Arsons, Forgeries, and High-Stakes Poker Capers of Rare Book Dealer Johnny Jenkins*. Norman: University of Oklahoma Press, 2020.

Viswanathan, Kaavya. *How Opal Mehta Got Kissed, Got Wild, and Got a Life*. New York: Little, Brown, 2006.

Vitello, Paul. "Kim Merker, Hand-Press Printer of Poets, Is Dead at 81." *New York Times*, 27 May 2013; https://www.nytimes.com

/2013/05/28/books/kim-merker-hand-press-printer-of-poets-is-dead-at-81.html; accessed 7 July 2021.

Voelkle, William, assisted by Roger S. Wieck. *The Spanish Forger*. New York: Pierpont Morgan Library, 1978.

Voet, Leon. *The Golden Compass: A History and Evaluation of the Printing and Publishing Activities of the Officina Plantiniana at Antwerp*. Vol. 1, *Christopher Plantin and the Moretuses: Their Lives and Their World*. Amsterdam: Vangendt & Co.; London: Routledge & Kegan Paul, 1969.

Voet, Leon, and Raymond H. Kaye. *The Golden Compass: A History and Evaluation of the Printing and Publishing Activities of the Officina Plantiniana at Antwerp*. Vol. 2, *The Management of a Printing and Publishing House in Renaissance and Baroque*. Amsterdam: Vangendt & Co.; London: Routledge & Kegan Paul, 1972.

Von Hagen, Victor Wolfgang. *The Aztec and Maya Papermakers*. New York: J. J. Augustin Publisher, 1944.

Voorn, Henk. *Old Ream Wrappers: An Essay on Early Ream Wrappers of Antiquarian Interest*. North Hills, PA: Bird & Bull, 1969.

Wadsworth, Dick. *Dirty Little Comics: A Pictorial History of Tijuana Bibles and Underground Adult Comics of the 1920s–1950s*. Independently Published, 2019.

Wagner, Bettina. "Johann Gutenberg." In *The Oxford Companion to the Book*, vol. 2, edited by Michael F. Suarez and H. R. Woudhuysen, pp. 771–72. Oxford: Oxford University Press, 2010.

Walker, C. B. F. *Cuneiform*. Berkeley: University of California Press and the British Museum, 1987.

Walker, Gay. *Eccentric Books: Arts of the Book*. Yale University Library, January–March 1988, An Exhibit: Eccentric Books from the Yale University Library Collections. New Haven, CT: Yale University Library, 1988.

Wallen, Burr, and Stephen Neil Greengard. *Pochoir: Flowering of the Hand-Color Process in Prints and Illustrated Books, 1910–1935: An Exhibition, January 4 to February 12, 1978*. Santa Barbara: University of California Press, 1978.

Wallis, L. W. *A Concise Chronology of Typesetting Developments, 1886–1986*. London: Wynken de Worde Society in association with Lund Humphries, 1988.

Walsdorf, John J. *William Morris in Private Press and Limited Editions: A Descriptive Bibliography of Books by and about William Morris 1891–1981*. Phoenix, AZ: Oryx, 1983.

Walsh, Judith. "The Japan Paper Company." *Hand Papermaking* 16.1 (Summer 2001): 20–23.

Warburton, Frederick W. "Composition by the Linotype Machine." In *The Building of a Book: A Series of Practical Articles Written by Experts in the Various Departments of Book Making and Distributing*, edited by Frederick H. Hitchcock. New York: Grafton, 1906; http://www.gutenberg.org/files/23754/23754-h/23754-h.htm#page053; accessed 7 July 2021.

Ward, Geofffrey C., and Ken Burns. *Baseball: An Illustrated History*. New York: Alfred A. Knopf, 1994.

Ward, Sydney. "William Morris and His Papermaker Joseph Batchelor." *Philobiblon, Eine Zeitschrift für Bücherliebhaber* 7 (1934): 177–80. Wien: Herbert Reichner, 1934.

Warkentin, Shahrzad. "Flipback Books Make It Easy to Read with Just One Hand & Lit-Loving Moms Can So Relate." tinybeans; https://redtri.com/what-are-flipback-books-they-will-change-the-way-you-read/; accessed 28 July 2021.

Watson, George, ed. *New Cambridge Bibliography of English Literature*. 5 vols. Cambridge: Cambridge University Press, 1969, 1971, 1972, 1974, 1977.

Watson, Peter. *Sotheby's: Inside Story*. London: Bloomsbury, 1997.

———. *Sotheby's: The Inside Story*. New York: Random House, 1997.

Watson, William, with John Leo Mish, trans. *Chinese Jade Books in the Chester Beatty Library: Discribed, and the Chinese Texts Translated*. Dublin: Figgis, 1963.

Wax, Carol. *The Mezzotint: History and Technique*. London: Thames and Hudson, 1990.

Webb, Brian, and Peyton Skipwith. *Design: Harold Curwen & Oliver Simon: Curwen Press*. Woodbridge: Antique Collectors Club, 2009.

Weber, Bruce. "Hermann Zapf, 96, Dies; Designer Whose Letters Are Found Everywhere." *New York Times* online, 9 June 2015; https://www.nytimes.com/2015/06/10/arts/design/hermann-zapf-96-dies-designer-whose-letters-are-found-everywhere.html; accessed 17 May 2021.

Weber, Carl J. *Fore-Edge Painting: A Historical Survey of a Curious Art in Book Decoration*. Irving-on-Hudson, NY: Harvey House, 1966.

Weber, Jeff. *Annotated Dictionary of Fore-Edge Painting Artists & Binders (Mostly English & American). The Fore-Edge Paintings of Miss C. B. Currie; with a Catalogue Raisonné*. Los Angeles: Weber Rare Books, 2010.

Weber, Wilhelm. *A History of Lithography*. New York: McGraw-Hill; London: Thames and Hudson, 1966.

Weisenburg, Michael. "'Books are weapons in the war of ideas': Armed Services Editions, the Council on Books in Wartime, and Popular Reading among Soldiers." The Irvin Department of Rare Books & Special Collections Blog, University Libraries, University of South Carolina; https://digital.library.sc.edu/blogs/rbsc/2020/09/; accessed 8 January 2021.

Weitenkampf, Frank. "What Is a Facsimile?" *Papers of the Bibliographical Society of America* 37 (2nd quarter, 1943): 114–30.

Wells, Gabriel. *A Noble Fragment: Being a Leaf of the Gutenberg Bible, with a Bibliographical Essay by A. Edward Newton*. New York: Gabriel Wells, 1921.

West, Clarence J. *Classifications and Definitions of Paper*. New York: Lockwood, 1924.

"What Is a Portolan Chart?"; University of Minnesota, Twin Cities. University Libraries; https://apps.lib.umn.edu/bell/map/PORTO/INTRO/intro2.html; accessed 22 July 2021.

"What Is Gravure?: The Process of Producing Fine, Detailed Images." GAA: Gravure AIMCAL Alliance; http://www.gaa.org/what-is-gravure; accessed 7 July 2021.

White, Alex W. "Nicolas Jenson's Typographic Contributions"; https://www.tdc.org/articles/nicolas-jensons-typographic-contributions; accessed 25 October 2015. This is a dead link as is Alex W. "Nicolas Jenson's Typographic Contributions | Type Directors Club." Type Directors Club | Promoting excellence in typography for over 65 years; http://www.tdc.org/archives/2227/ (searched 7 July 2021).

White, Eric M. *"Heresy and Error": The Ecclesiastical Censorship of Books, 1400–1800*. Dallas: Bridwell Library, Perkins School of Theology, Southern Methodist University, 2010; http://www.smu.edu/Bridwell/SpecialCollectionsandArchives/Exhibitions/HeresyandError/IndexofExpurgations; accessed 7 July 2021.

White, Gleeson. *English Illustration, "The Sixties"; 1855–1870*. Westminster: Archibald Constable, 1903; reprint, Bath: Kingmead, 1970.

Widewalls. "A Short History of Manga: Art History, Design"; widewalls.ch/magazine/japanese-manga-comics-history; accessed 28 August 2022.

Wieck, Roger S. *Time Sanctified: The Book of Hours in Medieval Art and Life*. New York: George Braziller, 1988.

Wijnekus, F. J. M., and E. F. P. H. Wijnekus. *Elsevier's Dictionary of the Printing and Allied Industries*. 2nd ed. Amsterdam: Elsevier, 1983.

Wikipedia. "List of Literary Awards"; https://en.wikipedia.org/wiki/List_of_literary_awards; accessed 1 June 2021.

———. "Steel Engraving"; https://en.wikipedia.org/wiki/Steel_engraving; accessed 5 July 2021.

Wikiwand. "Robert Riviere"; https://www.wikiwand.com/en/Robert_Riviere; accessed 4 July 2021.

Wiles, Roy McKeen. *Serial Publication in England before 1750*. London: Cambridge University Press, 1957.

Williams, Iolo A. *The Elements of Book-Collecting*. New York: Frederick A. Stokes; London: Elkin Mathews, 1927.

Williams, Roger. "Scaleboard Wood and Potential Loss Replacement." In Julia Miller, ed., *Suave Mechanicals: Essays on the History of Bookbinding*. Vol. 4, pp. 256–323. Ann Arbor, MI: Legacy, 2017.

Wilson, Robert A. *Modern Book Collecting*. New York: Knopf, 1980.

Wing, Donald G. *A Gallery of Ghosts: Books Published between 1641–1700 Not Found in the Short-Title Catalogue*. New York: Index Committee of the Modern Language Association of America, 1967.

———. "The Making of the 'Short-Title Catalogue, 1641–1700.'" *Papers of the Bibliographical Society of America* 45 (First Quarter, 1951): 59–69.

———. *A Short-Title Catalogue of Books Printed in England, Scotland, Ireland, Wales, and British America and of the English Books Printed in Other Countries, 1641–1700*. 3 vols. New York: Columbia University Press, 1945–1951.

———, comp. *Short-Title Catalogue of Books Printed in England, Scotland, Wales, and British America, and of English Books Printed in Other Countries, 1641–1700*. 2nd ed. 4 vols. Newly revised and enlarged. Revised and edited by John J. Morrison and Carolyn W. Nelson, eds., and Matthew Seccombe, assistant ed. New York: Modern Language Association of America, 1972, 1982, 1988, 1998.

Winger, Howard W. *Printers' Marks and Devices*. Chicago: Caxton Club, 1976.

Winship, Michael. See under Blanck, Jacob.

Winterich, John T., and David A. Randall. *A Primer of Book Collecting*. 3rd rev. ed. New York: Crown, 1966 (and other editions).

Witmore, Michael. "Pre-Digital Iteration: The Lindstrand Comparator"; http://winedarksea.org/?p=481; accessed 3 July 2021.

Wolf, Edwin, II, with John W. Fleming. *Rosenbach: A Biography*. Cleveland, OH: World Publishing, 1960.

Wolfe, Richard. *Marbled Paper: Its History, Techniques, and Patterns*. Philadelphia: University of Pennsylvania Press, 1990.

Wood, Frances, and Mark Barnard. *The Diamond Sutra: The Story of the World's Earliest Dated Printed Book*. London: British Library, 2010.

Wood, Kelli. "On the Edge: Medieval Margins and the Margins of Academic Life." Exhibition of illustrations in the margins of medieval manuscripts. University of Chicago, May 19–August 10, 2012; https://www.lib.uchicago.edu/e/webexhibits/ontheedge (and its subsequent links).

Word Finder. "What Is CINII" [*sic*, no question mark]; https://findwords.info/term/cinii; accessed 16 February 2021.

Wordnik. "Ledgit"; https://www.wordnik.com/words/ledgit; accessed 26 May 2021.

———. "Press-mark"; https://www.wordnik.com/words/press-mark; accessed 11 April 2021.

WordReference.com. "Grangerize"; https://www.wordreference.com/definition/grangerize; accessed 30 June 2021.

World Book Encyclopedia. "World Book Readers Choose Design for Next Encyclopedia"; 23 March 2009; https://www.prweb.com/releases/worldbook/spinescape/prweb2254404.htm; accessed 23 April 2021.

Worms, Laurence. "Provincial Booksellers Fairs Association (PBFA)." In *The Oxford Companion to the Book*, vol. 2, edited by Michael F. Suarez and H. R. Woudhuysen, p. 1063. Oxford: Oxford University Press, 2010.

Wright, Margot M. *Barkcloth: Aspects of Preparation, Use, Deterioration, Conservation and Display*. London: Archetype, 2001.

Wright, Thomas. *The Poetical Works of Geoffrey Chaucer: A New Text, with Illustrative Notes*. New York: John W. Lovell, n.d. (ca. 1890).

Wroth, Lawrence C. "The Chief End of Book Madness." *Library of Congress Quarterly Journal of Current Acquisitions* 3.1 (October 1945): 69–77.

Wu, Diyon. "The Memory of Lianhuanhua." Norman Rockwell Museum; https://www.nrm.org/2013/03/new-perspectives-on-illustration-the-memory-of-lianhuanhua-by-diyou-wu/; accessed 26 February 2021.

Yagi, Tokutaro, Rik Olsen, and Robin Heyeck. *Suminagashi-Zome*. Woodside, CA: Heyeck, 1991.

Yang, Gene Luen. "Comic Heroes." *The New York Times Book Review*, 6 November 2020: p. 20.

Young, Arthur P. *Books for Sammies: The American Library Association and World War I*. Pittsburgh, PA: Beta Phi Mu, 1981.

Zapf, Hermann. *Hermann Zapf & His Design Philosophy: Selected Articles and Lectures on Calligraphy and Contemporary Developments in Type Design* (With illustrations and bibliographical notes, and a complete list of his typefaces). Chicago: Society of Typographic Arts, 1987.

Zempel, Edward N., and Linda A. Verkler, eds. *First Editions: A Guide to Identification*. 4th ed. Peoria, IL: Spoon River, 2001 (and other editions).

About the Author

Sidney E. Berger was the Ann C. Pingree Director of the Phillips Library at the Peabody Essex Museum of Salem; he is now the library's director emeritus. For the last 20 years he has been on the faculty of Simmons University and the University of Illinois, Urbana-Champaign, teaching rare book courses in both institutions' library schools. He was Curator of Printed Books and then Curator of Manuscripts at the American Antiquarian Society in Worcester, Massachusetts, and headed the Special Collections Department at the University of California, Riverside. He is widely published in several fields—and his book *Rare Books and Special Collections* won the 2015 ABC-CLIO/American Library Association Award for the Best Book in Library Literature. He makes paper and casts type by hand, and, with his wife Michèle Cloonan, is the proprietor of Doe Press, publishing short texts from handset type, printed on a handpress.

CPSIA information can be obtained
at www.ICGtesting.com
Printed in the USA
BVHW020503130423
662186BV00003B/4